America's National Wildlife Refuges

America's National Wildlife Refuges

A Complete Guide

RUSSELL D. BUTCHER

With contributions by
Stephen E. Adair,
Lynn A. Greenwalt, and Mike Boylan

Photographs by
JOHN AND KAREN HOLLINGSWORTH
(except as otherwise credited)

Foreword by
DAN ASHE
Chief, National Wildlife Refuge System
U.S. Fish and Wildlife Service

Roberts Rinehart Publishers

In Cooperation with Ducks Unlimited

DUCKS UNLIMITED

Published by Roberts Rinehart Publishers
A Member of the Rowman & Littlefield Publishing Group
4501 Forbes Boulevard, Ste 200
Lanham, MD 20706

Published in Cooperation with
Ducks Unlimited, Inc.
One Waterfowl Way
Memphis, TN 38120

Distributed by National Book Network

Library of Congress Card Number: 2002114660
ISBN 1-57098-379-8 (cloth : alk. paper)

∞™ The paper used in this publication meets the minimum requirements of
American National Standard for Information Sciences—Permanence of
Paper for Printed Library Materials, ANSI/NISO Z39.48–1992.
Manufactured in the United States of America.

TO

All of the employees, researchers, interns, volunteers, and donors

who are helping to make the

National Wildlife Refuge System

a priceless American treasure.

contents

Author's Note

Writing this book on all of the more than 530 units of the National Wildlife Refuge System, totaling more than 93 million acres, has been an awesome but totally inspiring and fascinating endeavor. One of the special pleasures of the task has been my conversations with literally hundreds of refuge system personnel. From all across America, I have not only been given insight into the refuges and their varied management activities; I have also sensed a tremendous depth of caring and commitment that these men and women bring to their tasks as they strive to protect and enhance refuge habitats and wildlife populations. I have glimpsed how much they cherish a feeling of family with their dedicated colleagues throughout the refuge system. And I have heard again and again how much they value the generous assistance and hard work of numerous volunteers, interns, and partners, with whom so much is accomplished on the refuges that would otherwise be unattainable.

The National Wildlife Refuge System contains an almost mind-boggling diversity of wildlife and habitats. Each refuge, no matter how large or small, has an important role to play within America's overall program of wildlife conservation. Many refuges offer interpretive and educational programs, from which visitors can learn about and better appreciate the wildlife, habitats, ecological processes, and refuge management activities.

Each refuge, including the few that are closed to public visitation, is described in this volume. In most of the refuge descriptions, I have tried to provide at least some insight into what types of habitat management activities are occurring and why. To save a bit of space at the start of each description, only the refuge name is given, without its National Wildlife Refuge designation—unless the designation differs from the norm. Many refuges provide species checklists of fauna and flora. Finally, the U.S. Fish and Wildlife Service's website—www.fws.gov—offers much helpful information on the refuges.

In August 2002, Red River National Wildlife Refuge in northwestern Louisiana, containing 1,377 acres toward a goal of 50,000 acres, became the 539th refuge. Restoring bottomland hardwood forest on nonproductive farmland is the primary objective in this historic migratory bird corridor between Shreveport and Natchitoches. Refuge partners are The Conservation Fund, Entergy Corporation, Friends of the Red River, and Environmental Synergy, Inc. Information: North Louisiana Refuges Complex: telephone (318) 726-4222.

The National Wildlife Refuge System offers us valuable insight into what Native Americans have known for thousands of years: how critically important it is not to lose sight of the *interconnectedness* of all life on Earth. It is especially important for us humans, as the world's most powerful and influential species, to view ourselves as not separate from, but an integral part of, the natural environment and its long-evolved, life-supporting ecological processes. We are responsible for maintaining the health and wholeness of the life-sustaining environment around us. How well we are managing and protecting the heritage of America's National Wildlife Refuges is ultimately an indication of how well we are protecting ourselves.

—*Russell D. Butcher*
Tucson, Arizona

Acknowledgments

There is no way to adequately express my gratitude to all of the hundreds of national wildlife refuge personnel who provided research materials and who then reviewed each refuge description for accuracy. Without their enthusiastic assistance, I would not have even presumed to undertake the writing of this book. I am especially grateful to all those who provided quotable statements about some particular aspect of their refuges and to those who wrote the entire text for a refuge or management district. My thanks as well to those who so generously contributed other parts of the book: Dan Ashe for his Foreword; Lynn Greenwalt for his chapter on the history of the National Wildlife Refuge System; Mike Boylan for his "vision" chapter on the refuge system; and Steve Adair for his chapter on America's vanishing wetlands. I am hugely grateful to Karen Hollingsworth for all of the many magnificent photographs that she and her late husband, John Hollingsworth, have taken over a period of many years, and to a number of USFWS (U.S. Fish and Wildlife Service) staff and others who provided photographs (these are credited to them throughout the book). I am extremely grateful for the cooperation of Ducks Unlimited, Inc. in the publication of this book. My thanks to Rick Rinehart of Roberts Rinehart Publishers for publishing this book as well as two earlier volumes on the National Park System, and to Toni Knapp and Raven Amerman for their outstanding editing assistance. I would also like to thank Stephen Driver, Piper Furbush, Rebecca Olson, Dolly Eversole, Ollie Harmon-Gibbons, and Jeremy Hite for their contributions.

These Acknowledgments would not be complete without expressing gratitude to my parents, Mary and Devereux Butcher, for encouraging me to see and value the wonders and beauty of nature and for sharing with me some of their travels to and enthusiasm for the National Wildlife Refuge System many years ago as they were writing their book, *Exploring Our National Wildlife Refuges.* And I am lovingly grateful to my wife, Karen, for her supportive encouragement and help in this challenging book-writing endeavor.

—*Russ Butcher*

Foreword

We all like to be in on something secret. It's a privilege. Something special, held between people with a common interest or bond. In Russ Butcher's new book—*America's National Wildlife Refuges*—he shares some very special secrets with those of us who savor precious days afield in wild places and among wild things. As Chief of the National Wildlife Refuge System, I know the system is a treasure chest full of opportunity to get outdoors and experience the wonder, diversity, and beauty of our nation's wildlife heritage. But it remains one of the best-kept secrets among our nation's legacy of public lands. This book is your key to unlocking that treasure chest, and your gateway to some of the greatest spectacles that our nation has to offer.

Anyone who knows the secret of experiencing wildlife in wild places knows that timing is everything. Visiting one of our refuges at the wrong time of year might elicit a remark like "Nice house, but nobody was home." Being in the right place at the right time is an essential part of the secret shared in Russ Butcher's book. Take this book, mix with a pinch of that precious commodity that we call "time," and add some well-chosen and hopefully familiar gear like binoculars, good boots or waders, and perhaps a fishing rod or shotgun, and get outdoors! To really spice up the experience, add some family members or a good friend or two. This is a recipe guaranteed to reduce stress, strengthen families and friendships, and make great memories.

As I read through the entries in his book, my mind's eye focused on some of my most memorable days afield in the refuge system. Days in places like Blackbeard Island, Bosque del Apache, Kodiak, Tamarac, Monomoy, Klamath, and Bear River. I remember the solitude of an empty beach, the noise of thousands of geese and cranes, the grandeur of a bald eagle in flight, and the explosion of color from wild lupines blooming in the high desert. I remember days with my father, mother, and brothers; days with my wife and children; mornings and evenings with hunting buddies and a yellow Labrador retriever named Bo. This book holds promise and provides the information that we all can use to take advantage of the opportunity within our National Wildlife Refuge System.

Thanks to Russ Butcher and America's National Wildlife Refuges, you are now in on one of our nation's best-kept secrets. Use it to discover a refuge near you. With more than 530 "franchises," there is always one close by. If you like what you see, let other people know. Come back again and again, and consider becoming a refuge volunteer or joining a refuge Friends organization. There's lots more to discover.

—Dan Ashe, Chief
National Wildlife Refuge System

Prelude

President Theodore Roosevelt created our first National Wildlife Refuge in 1903. That was a time when thousands of herons, egrets, and other birds were being killed by market hunters who wanted their feathers to sell for women's hat decorations. Many kinds of birds were threatened with extinction because of a fashion trend. . . .

Today, Refuges are home to more than 700 species of birds and 800 species of mammals, reptiles, amphibians, and fish, including over 170 threatened or endangered species. More than 55 Refuges have been set aside specifically to protect species that are faced with extinction. Each Refuge is beautiful and vital in its own right. Each is a place where wildlife is protected. And many Refuges welcome people to enjoy the wonders and mysteries of nature. All it takes is one visit to understand why a Refuge is a place that matters—where wild things and their habitats are protected and preserved as part of our natural heritage.

People who work on Refuges are dedicated professionals who often work long hours in all kinds of weather performing a wide variety of tasks. A primary goal of Refuges is to provide the best possible habitat in order to fulfill the requirements of wildlife that live there. Employees actively manage Refuge lands, by changing water levels to improve wetland habitat, setting controlled fires or grazing livestock to improve pasture, farming with crops used by wildlife, and removing pest plants that out-compete desirable plants. Employees maintain facilities for the public, such as roads and historic structures, trail and observation facilities, and provide educational and interpretive information. Many employees have specialized education, training, and experience from many Refuges throughout the country, a background that is crucial when making improvements to the way Refuge lands are managed in order to increase wildlife populations. Life is not just out counting birds!

—Rich Guadagno
(Sept. 26, 1962–Sept. 11, 2001)

1

America's Vanishing Wetlands

STEPHEN E. ADAIR, PH.D., DIRECTOR OF CONSERVATION PROGRAMS, GREAT PLAINS REGIONAL OFFICE, DUCKS UNLIMITED, INC.

Today, wetlands are widely recognized as some of the most productive and valuable ecosystems on Earth. But that has not always been the case. Up until the 1960s, most Americans viewed wetlands as wastelands that were in the way of progress. The map on page 2, produced in 1919 and entitled "Wet Lands in Need of Drainage," is a vivid reminder of this historic perception.

When Europeans first arrived on America's shorelines, they found an abundance of wild lands and wildlife never before imagined in their homeland. Even discounting the astounding claims of early settlers—who perhaps embellished the abundance to encourage more immigration—ducks, geese, deer, turkeys, rabbits, pigeons, fish, and shellfish teemed in the wetlands and forests and were there for the taking.

As Captain John Smith wrote of Virginia:

The rivers became so covered with swans, geese, ducks, and cranes that we daily feasted with good bread, Virginia pease, pumpkins and putchamins [persimmons], fish, fowle and diverse sors of wild beasts, so fat as we could eate them (from *Eating in America: A History*, by W. L. and R. de Rochemont Root; New York: Ecco Press, 1976).

Although these abundant fish and wildlife populations provided important sustenance, most early settlers viewed these resources as unlimited and set out to change the landscape to support agriculture and accommodate a growing human population. Conquering the frontier also meant taming the land. The vast forests of New England and the Great Lakes region were cut down, and the lands converted for agriculture. Prairie grasslands were plowed under. Wetlands were drained and converted to farming lands. This wave of change marched westward, transforming the landscape into what were believed to be more beneficial uses.

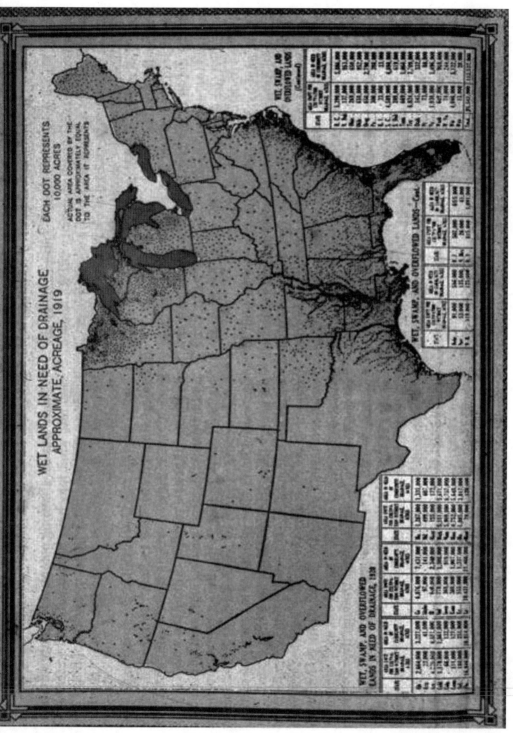

U.S. Department of Agriculture, 1919.

While many early Americans were busy draining wetlands on their own initiative, the U.S. Department of Agriculture offered financial incentives to farmers to "reclaim" wetlands and convert them to productive farmland. Millions of acres of prairie potholes were tiled (a type of underground pipe that has small gaps in it) and drained to increase crop production. The U.S. Army Corps of Engineers drained and isolated many floodplains wetlands in their efforts to improve navigation, flood control, water supplies, and hydroelectric power on most of the nation's rivers. Coastal wetlands were dredged and filled for navigation, land development, and to control diseases carried by mosquitoes.

In 1849, Congress passed the Swamp Land Act, which granted the states control over swamplands to control flooding, thereby encouraging wetland elimination. Most Americans had little understanding of or concern for the inherent values that wetlands offered them. A small but significant conservation voice began to emerge from the woods of New England in Henry David Thoreau. But still, in the eyes of most, a good wetland was a drained wetland. These prevailing attitudes and programs led to the loss and degradation of nearly 50 percent of the original wetlands in the lower 48 states by the mid-1900s. The majority of these early wetland losses were for conversion to agricultural production, but urbanization in the form of industry, housing, and roads was also taking its toll.

The end of the Civil War began the transformation of America from a rural to an industrial nation, essentially marking the end of the American frontier. America's population was now clustered in the large urban areas of the Northeast and Midwest, far removed from the source of their food, water, and fiber, and largely employed in industry instead of agriculture. Growing markets for food and fiber accelerated the loss of America's wetlands, forests, and grasslands and of the fish and wildlife that depended on them for survival. Within states, drainage districts began to form, accelerating wetland drainage even further.

However, in the 1920s, public agencies and private organizations began to elevate the awareness of wetland loss and to take positive steps to slow it. The Migratory Bird Conservation Act of 1929 authorized the federal government to acquire wetlands and associated uplands and to preserve them as waterfowl habitat. The law also established a commission of federal and state officials to evaluate land for possible acquisition, and in so doing it established the National Wildlife Refuge System.

Although the Migratory Bird Conservation Act was an important step for wetland conservation, it provided no permanent source of funding to purchase wetlands. Largely due to the lobbying efforts of Jay N. Darling, a nationally known political cartoonist and the chief of the Bureau of Biological Survey, President Franklin Delano Roosevelt signed the Migratory Bird Hunting Stamp Act in 1934. All waterfowl hunters 16 years of age and older were required under the Act to buy a Migratory Bird Hunting Stamp. Funds from stamps would be used to pay for acquisition and protection of wetlands and other important waterfowl habitats. Some 635 thousand hunters paid $1.00 each for the first stamps, which went on sale August 22, 1934. Since then, the price has gradually risen to the current $15.00. Today, approximately 1.5 million stamps are sold each year. Federal Duck Stamps have generated close to $600 million, which has been used to preserve nearly 5 million acres of wetlands and associated uplands in the United States. Many of the more than 530 National Wildlife Refuges have been paid for either entirely or in part with federal Duck Stamp revenues.

Within the private sector, a small group of sportsmen, concerned with the decline of waterfowl populations along the Atlantic Coast, formed the More Game Birds in America Foundation in 1930. One of the most ambitious early efforts of the Foundation was the inaugural International Wild Duck Census in 1935 that covered most of Canada and the northern United States. Results of surveys such as this led the Foundation to conclude that, unless prompt action was taken to preserve breeding ground wetlands, the future of waterfowl and waterfowl hunting in the United States was in jeopardy. In light of these results, members of More Game Birds and its counterpart, American Wild Fowlers, rallied together to form Ducks Unlimited (DU), which was incorporated in Washington, D.C. on January 29, 1937. DU founders formed committees in each state to begin raising funds in the United States and send them to Canada to protect and restore large, permanent wetlands, nicknamed duck factories.

Despite the positive strides of these early conservation efforts, the magnitude of change that had been forced on the landscape was fully revealed during the Great Depression or "Dust Bowl" of the 1930s. For decades, homesteaders, farmers, ranchers, and entrepreneurs in the West and Midwest had unwittingly caused the erosion and instability of much of the nation's topsoil. Clear-cutting of forests, overgrazing of grasslands, draining and filling of wetlands, and poor cropping practices had exposed the soil to the powerful forces of wind and water. The drought that savaged the country in the 1930s forced the recognition that even with the conservation progress to date, America's lands and the wildlife that depended on them were threatened with destruction.

After a difficult legislative battle, the Federal Aid in Wildlife Restoration Act (Pittman–Robertson Act) was passed in 1937. The Act created an 11 percent excise tax on rifles, shotguns, and ammunition and a 10 percent tax on handguns. Revenues from the tax were collected in federal coffers and then passed through the U.S. Fish and Wildlife Service to state fish and wildlife agencies. Over the life of the program, 62 percent of federal aid grants have been used to protect and enhance nearly 20 million acres of state wildlife management areas, many of them wetlands. These state-owned lands add a critical component of biodiversity to America's landscape. In addition to acquisition of public lands, federal aid funds were also used to secure management agreements and leases to protect and enhance important wildlife habitats. There are now nearly 60 million acres, many of them wetlands, across the country that are managed for wildlife under agreements with private and corporate landowners.

The establishment of dedicated federal conservation funding and the advocacy and implementation of private organizations undoubtedly slowed wetland loss rates. But other programs, such as the U.S. Department of Agriculture's Agricultural Conservation Program and the Great Depression-era Works Progress Administration, continued to promote and fund wetland drainage. The first rigorous scientific studies of wetland losses conducted by the U.S. Fish and Wildlife Service revealed an alarming annual wetland loss rate of 458 thousand acres per year from the mid-1950s to the mid-1970s.

During the 1950s and 1960s, American concern for the environment was elevated to new levels. Aldo Leopold's *A Sand County Almanac* and Rachel Carson's *Silent Spring* urged Americans to think in terms of living with nature instead of conquering it. In the early 1970s, wetland scientists began to identify and quantify the many ecological values of wetland ecosystems. Evidence began to accumulate suggesting that wetlands were not only important as habitats for fish and wildlife populations, but they also stored and slowed floodwaters, thereby reducing property damage. In addition, evidence began to reveal that many wetlands discharge water into subsurface aquifers that support municipalities and agricultural operations; that wetlands stabilize shorelines and protect them from storm erosion; that wetlands purify water by removing sediments and nutrients; that many wetlands store large volumes of carbon and consequently help mitigate atmospheric concentrations of carbon dioxide; that wetlands provide economically important products like timber and commercial finfish and shellfish; and that wetlands are important venues for recreation and tourism, helping to generate millions of dollars in annual revenue. Increased understanding of these functions and values translated into more federal laws and policies to protect wetlands.

In 1972, the Federal Water Pollution Control Act (Clean Water Act) was passed by Congress, giving the U.S. Army Corps of Engineers, under Section 404 of the Act, the authority to establish a permitting process to regulate the dredging and filling of materials into waters of the United States. At first, the Corps applied this authority narrowly to include only navigable waters, but later court rulings extended this authority to almost all wetlands. Although the majority of wetland permits applied for have been approved by the Corps, perhaps the greatest value of Section 404 of the Clean Water Act has been as a deterrent to developers to avoid wetlands and the required mitigation process.

The Coastal Zone Management Act of 1972 provided funding to the states to develop coastal management plans that included wetland protection. President Jimmy Carter issued two executive orders in May 1977 that made the protection of wetlands, riparian areas, and floodplains a priority of each agency of the federal government. These orders were a landmark, because they established a review of wetland and floodplain policies by all federal agencies. Subsequent to federal wetland protection legislation, some states, primarily those with coastlines, enacted their own wetland protection laws. The USFWS found evidence of progress in reducing wetland loss in its updated wetland status report, which found an annual loss rate of 290 thousand acres from the mid-1970s to the mid-1980s—a decline of 37 percent from previous decades.

Conservationists increased their lobbying efforts for governmental programs that provided new funding to protect and restore large areas of wetlands and associated uplands. The Food Security Act of 1985 (Farm Bill) authorized 45 million acres of marginal cropland to be converted to grasslands and forests in order to slow soil erosion through the Conservation Reserve Program (CRP), but the impacts were much more far-reaching. Restored grasslands began to capture the sediments that were filling wetland basins and to reduce the runoff of nutrients, herbicides, and pesticides into wetlands. Populations of many wetland species, such as waterfowl, shorebirds, and some songbirds that nest in uplands adjacent to wetlands, began to improve.

The Swampbuster Provision of the 1985 Farm Bill provided increased federal protection of small wetlands in the predominantly agricultural Midwest, Northern Great Plains, and Southern High Plains. Although often incorrectly viewed as a regulatory program, Swampbuster actually offers a disincentive for wetland drainage by withholding USDA payments from farmers who destroy wetlands in order to grow a commodity crop. Farmers still have the option either to drain wetlands for commodity crops and forgo USDA payments or to drain wetlands for other uses. However, given the reliance of most farming operations on USDA subsidies, Swampbuster has been a very effective deterrent to wetland drainage.

During the 1980s, drought returned to the northern prairies, causing wetland numbers and waterfowl populations to plummet. As concern over depressed waterfowl populations grew, a consortium of public and private organizations, including the USFWS, state game and fish agencies, Ducks Unlimited, and university scientists, joined together in 1986 to formulate the

North American Waterfowl Management Plan (NAWMP), a blueprint for recovery of water-fowl populations to 1970s levels. The 1986 Plan was signed by Canada and the United States and contained a Strategy for Cooperation, emphasizing the importance of a partnership approach to conserve habitats, improve scientific understanding, and periodically evaluate and update the Plan. Given the complex problems facing waterfowl and wetlands across the North American continent, the NAWMP partners concluded that the most effective means of securing the future of waterfowl populations was to improve land use practices on a landscape level. To achieve this objective, broad partnerships were formed between conservation organizations, private landowners, and state and federal wildlife agencies.

As public interest and funding grew for wetlands conservation, scientists began focusing more of their efforts on understanding the structure and function of habitats important to wildlife. Early works found that a diverse array of wetland types were necessary to meet water-fowl habitat requirements, both in breeding and wintering areas. Some of the most productive wetlands for wildlife were the shallowest basins, which went dry periodically and which supported rich plant communities. Unfortunately, these were the same sites that were the easiest to drain and were being lost disproportionately from the landscape.

Waterfowl biologists were becoming increasingly aware that waterfowl populations could not be maintained solely on public land, but that entire landscapes need to be preserved to meet all of the birds' habitat requirements. National Wildlife Refuges and State Wildlife Management Areas began to be viewed as core areas around which to secure wetlands and uplands, creating larger sustainable landscapes.

Wetland ecologists also began to gather evidence suggesting that wetlands could not be preserved just by protecting their boundaries. Adjacent lands must also be set aside to prevent sediments, human activity, pollutants, and nutrient-laden runoff from destroying important wetland functions. The source of water to many wetlands was found to exist beyond the wetland boundaries in shallow streams or aquifers that were recharged at upper reaches of watersheds. This understanding led to increased cooperation with farmers and ranchers to make their agricultural operations more environmentally friendly through practices such as no-till cropping, rotational grazing systems, watershed protection practices, and winter flooding of harvested agricultural fields. Long-term protection of the natural resources of private lands also began to increase through the use of conservation easements, leases, and management agreements.

In 1989, President George Bush introduced a policy of "no net loss," instructing federal agencies to achieve a zero wetland balance sheet. In that same year, the Congress and the Bush administration provided an incentive for NAWMP partners in the United States, Canada, and Mexico to accelerate efforts for conserving waterfowl and other migratory birds through passage of the North American Wetlands Conservation Act (NAWCA). NAWCA's grant program provided a funding mechanism for conservation partners throughout North America. Since 1989, NAWCA has provided $269 million in federal funds, which has been more than matched by $966 million from non-federal partners, to conserve 2.8 million acres of wetlands and associated uplands.

The 1990 Farm Bill established the Wetlands Reserve Program (WRP), which authorized that nearly 1 million acres of marginal cropland be restored to wetlands. Farmers frustrated with chronic failures to grow crops on flood-prone land for low-priced commodities quickly filled this program. Wetlands across America have been restored under this program, many protected with permanent easements. The Farm Service Agency (FSA) and the Natural Resources

Conservation Service (formerly the Soil Conservation Service), which had spent many years promoting wetland drainage and plowing of grasslands, suddenly became two of the strongest forces in the country for wetland and grassland conservation.

NAWMP partners also expanded from their traditional focus on public lands to outreach and incentives to private landowners. Rice growers across California, the Gulf Coast, and the Mississippi alluvial valley began flooding their harvested fields in winter and restoring wetlands in marginal cropland areas, to improve their farming operations and to enhance habitat for waterfowl and other wetland birds. Dedicated conservationists across the country began to voluntarily restrict the development rights on their private property in perpetuity, under the terms of donated conservation easements. According to the Land Trust Alliance, this movement has led to the voluntary protection of 6.2 million acres of land through the year 2000, with 2.6 million of these acres in permanent conservation easements. Wetlands were listed as the primary focus of the 1,263 land trusts currently in existence.

Expanding research and landscape modeling efforts through such tools as Geographic Information Systems (GIS) also began facilitating strategic placement of conservation projects in areas most limiting to wildlife populations and most threatened by habitat destruction. Beginning in 1994, wet weather finally returned to the drought-stricken Northern prairies, and the efforts of NAWMP partners to restore wetland basins and provide expansive upland nesting cover, through programs such as the Conservation Reserve Program, allowed waterfowl populations to rebound to new, record levels.

Also during that year, NAWMP was updated and became a truly continental effort when Mexico joined Canada and the United States as a signatory. In 1998, NAWMP was again updated under the theme of "Expanding the Vision." The revised plan recognized that waterfowl conservation was becoming more linked with and affected by a broad range of social and economic policies, as well as by a growing interest in conservation of other wildlife—all requiring international strategies. During the first 14 years of NAWMP, thousands of partners representing diverse interests invested more than $1.5 billion to conserve more than 5 million acres of wetlands and associated uplands, to improve habitats not only for waterfowl but also for other birds, mammals, fish, amphibians, and plants. These efforts have helped sustain this continent's rich biological diversity and have contributed to flood control, water purification, and atmospheric gas regulation.

Interest in wetland conservation has remained strong among sportsmen and sportswomen as well as among a growing number of wildlife watchers, which has boosted Ducks Unlimited's membership to more than 750 thousand, helped raise annual revenue to more than $150 million, and provided for the annual conservation of more than 500 thousand acres of wildlife habitat. Since its inception in 1937, DU has raised more than $1.2 billion, which has helped DU and its partners protect, restore, or enhance more than 10 million acres of wetlands and associated uplands across North America.

Many other public and private organizations now have some level of wetland conservation programs. The USDA Forest Service has increased its efforts in wetland conservation through its Taking Wings and Large Watershed initiatives. The Environmental Protection Agency has vigilantly guarded against wetland destruction and degradation through its authority to control water pollution. The Nature Conservancy has been especially successful in protecting many unique wetland types across the country, through its Last Great Places campaign. Many other nonprofit organizations, too numerous to list, have expended significant resources lobbying for legislation and entering into litigation to protect wetlands.

Because most of the early conservationists were sportsmen, waterfowl naturally served as the banner under which the majority of historic wetland conservation was accomplished. However, numerous other wildlife species have benefited both directly and indirectly from sportsmen-generated funding. Wildlife management areas purchased with federal aid funds and wetlands acquired through federal Duck Stamp funds support myriad fish and wildlife species. An estimated one-third of the nation's endangered and threatened species, for example, find food or shelter in National Wildlife Refuges acquired with Duck Stamp revenues. Swallow-tailed kites and Louisiana black bears, both endangered species, require large blocks of bottomland hardwood wetlands—exactly the kind of habitat that public and private conservation partners have been protecting and restoring in the Mississippi alluvial valley. Sharp-tailed and seaside sparrows nesting along the northeastern Atlantic coast require coastal marshes to successfully reproduce—exactly the same kind of habitat that NAWMP partners have been working to restore. Pacific salmon require floodplain wetlands as nursery grounds for juvenile fish to survive—exactly the same kind of habitats being restored for waterfowl in the Pacific Northwest. Increased recognition that wetland habitat is the common denominator for healthy populations of numerous fish and wildlife species has the potential to elevate conservation efforts by bringing new funds and expertise to on-the-ground efforts historically carried out by sportsmen and the public fish and wildlife agencies.

During the 1990s, multidisciplinary research teams began looking at wetlands not only for their ecological value, but also for their economic value. These efforts have led to increased documentation of the monetary significance of the functions provided by wetlands. A 9,000-acre wetland complex along the main stem of the Charles River in Massachusetts has been valued at $17 million per year, which is the estimated cost of flood damage that would occur if the wetlands were drained. A 550-thousand-acre freshwater wetland in Florida has been valued at $25 million per year for the water it recharges to an aquifer providing for municipal and agricultural needs. Wetland drainage and cultivation has released large quantities of carbon dioxide into the atmosphere, compounding the emissions from the burning of fossil fuels, and remedial actions to reduce carbon dioxide emissions could potentially cost the United States economy $10–$100 billion. New York City recently avoided spending $3–$8 billion on new water treatment plants by investing $1.5 billion to acquire and protect wetlands and associated uplands in their upstream watershed that naturally purify water sources.

Coastal wetlands provide critical nursery grounds for juvenile crabs, shrimp, and salmon, whose harvest value when they reach adulthood has been estimated at $15 million per year in the United States alone. Waterfowl hunters, wildlife watchers, and recreational fishers spend $60 billion annually in the United States pursuing their passions, often focusing their efforts on wetlands or associated habitats. Clearly, wetlands are vital not only to our recreational interests, but also to our economy and to the sustainability of America's resources.

Today, increased scientific understanding of wetlands, increased public and private conservation funding, and improved cooperation among diverse landowners and land use interests have resulted in the annual wetland loss rate slowing to 58,500 acres between 1986 and 1997. This is a reduction of 87 percent from losses during the 1950s to 1970s and 80 percent from losses during the 1970s and 1980s. However, this lower rate is a little misleading, as the vegetated wetlands that are the most important to fish and wildlife, water quality, and other valuable functions continue to be lost at a rate of 109 thousand acres per year. Open-water wetlands associated with agriculture, surface mining, and urban developments are increasing, but these fail to provide the full suite of ecological functions provided by large, diverse complexes of vegetated wetlands.

Despite progress in significantly slowing wetland loss in the United States over the past 50 years, our country has lost 115 million acres of the original 221 million acres that existed in the conterminous United States at the time of the country's settlement. Large-scale environmental problems, caused in part by historic wetland losses, persist and threaten the sustainability of our economy and our quality of life. Deterioration of water quality continues in many rivers and estuaries, affecting human drinking sources, recreational activities, and valuable commercial fisheries. In 2001, the hypoxic or low-oxygen zone in the Gulf of Mexico reached record size—8,006 square miles, which is the size of Massachusetts. (A hypoxic zone is an area of depleted oxygen in which organisms cannot survive.) Scientists have recommended that part of the solution to this nutrient loading (an overenrichment of nutrients that causes a large population explosion of plankton, which in turn results in the depletion of oxygen in the water) of nearshore Gulf waters is the restoration of 24 million acres of wetlands and riparian areas along the Mississippi River watershed, to filter nitrogen and phosphorus from agricultural and industrial runoff.

Although the arid West has been plagued with chronic water shortages, during the past several years, such normally wetter states as Illinois, Florida, Georgia, Texas, Kansas, and several New England states are confronted with projections of serious water shortages during the next decade. In many cases, wetland restorations to recharge groundwater aquifers will be an important part of the solution. Loss of wetlands, which function as sponges to absorb floodwaters, has caused increased flooding of valuable cropland and residential areas, causing billions of dollars in damage and affecting the lives of thousands of people. The 1993 floods along the Mississippi River, which have been linked to wetland loss, caused $12–16 billion in property damages. Conservationists continue to be faced with declines in populations of wetland-dependent species, such as northern pintails, lesser scaup, clapper rails, swallow-tailed kites, piping plovers, cerulean warblers, sharp-tailed sparrows, blue crabs, and Pacific salmon, just to name a few.

In addition to these issues of chronic water quality, catastrophic flooding, and declining biodiversity caused by past wetland losses, new threats have emerged. Recent studies by the US-FWS show that, for the first time since surveys began, the majority of wetland loss is now due to urban and rural development. Given that the human population in the United States is expected to increase from 285 million to 413 million by the year 2050, pressures to convert wetlands to infrastructure to support this growing human population will certainly increase. There is growing international consensus suggesting that increased levels of greenhouse gases in the atmosphere caused by the burning of fossil fuels, clearing of forests, and draining of wetlands are contributing to global warming and rising of the sea level. Climate change models consistently predict accelerated sea level rise and increased frequency of midcontinent drought, which pose new threats to an already declining wetland base.

On January 9, 2001, the U.S. Supreme Court issued a decision in the case *Solid Waste Agency of Northern Cook County v. United States Army Corps of Engineers.* The Supreme Court ruled that the jurisdiction of the Corps included only "navigable waters, their tributaries, and wetlands that are adjacent to these navigable waterways and tributaries." From the Court's perspective, the

Corps could not assert jurisdiction over isolated wetlands based on commerce related to migratory birds. This decision will likely increase the loss and degradation of isolated wetlands across the country. Lobbying efforts by many special interest groups continue to eliminate wetland regulations and policies, in order to streamline housing and industrial development. Obviously our work in wetland conservation is far from over. We must remain mindful that history has a way of repeating itself, with future generations sometimes having to relearn the lessons of the past. Aldo Leopold's guidance remains timeless:

Civilization is a state of mutual and interdependent cooperation between human animals, other animals, plants, and soils, which may be disrupted at any moment by the failure of any of them.

If we are going to make progress resolving these complex issues facing America during the new millennium, we must move into an era of not just slowing or eliminating net wetland loss, but of actually achieving a net gain. Achieving this progress requires us to think bigger and broader. Our National Wildlife Refuges have given us a critical foundation on which to build. These lands serve as cornerstones for conservation efforts, but by themselves they are not sufficient to sustain wildlife populations, water quality, and other valuable wetland functions at the levels expected by the majority of the American people. Without increased habitat conservation, especially on private lands, which contain 75 percent of our nation's remaining wetlands, the populations of fish and wildlife—and even humans—face a very uncertain future.

We must not only continue to provide funding for federal wetland acquisition and legislation, but must also seek new incentives for the private sector to contribute to larger conservation efforts. The most visionary and significant advances in wetland conservation will likely be achieved through legislation and private programs that provide landowners with increased options for voluntary, incentive-based conservation and allow them to stay on the land and work the land for both their benefit and that of society. Broader partnerships are needed with the growing number of wildlife watchers and nature-based tourists, to provide opportunities for increased financial contributions and political support for on-the-ground wetland conservation. Conservation efforts must continue to be based on the most recent scientific findings, so that efforts are strategically directed to the most critical habitats, to achieve population and biodiversity goals.

Finally, the National Wildlife Refuge System and many State Wildlife Management Areas have faced chronic shortages in funding for operations and maintenance. On a per-acre basis, National Wildlife Refuge System funding is far below that for the National Park System and other federal lands. Most refuges cannot provide for the complete suite of ecological functions for which they were purchased, because the hydrology, sediment process, exotic species abundance, and predator–prey relationships of surrounding landscapes have been so altered that natural processes do not occur without land management intervention. We as a nation have made a conscious decision that these wetlands and adjacent uplands are valuable enough to preserve; we must also provide the financial resources necessary for managing them to their full potential.

As you read Russ Butcher's marvelous accounts of our National Wildlife Refuges, notice how people, opportunity, and resources have come together in many unique ways to preserve and maintain some of America's richest treasures. Let us celebrate these accomplishments and the enduring legacy that the National Wildlife Refuge System has provided for ourselves and future generations. Let us honor the thousands of men and women who have dedicated their lives to these vital wild places—not by viewing the refuges as tokens of historic landscapes, but as foundations on which to rebuild larger ecological communities. Wetlands are critical to our nation's future, and we must protect and rebuild them. I am confident we can and will find common conservation ground among diverse landowners and organizational interests to accelerate wetlands conservation in this new millennium.

Stephen E. Adair is the Director of Conservation Programs for Ducks Unlimited, Inc., a private, nonprofit, international conservation organization. Dr. Adair began his tenure with Ducks Unlimited, Inc. in 1997. Previously, he was employed as an ecologist for several private landowners in Georgetown, South Carolina, from 1994–1997.

Dr. Adair received his Ph.D. in wildlife ecology from Utah State University, his M.S. in wildlife management from Texas A&M University, and his B.S. in biology from the University of Texas. He has extensive experience in wetland protection, restoration, management, and research including program development, supervision, and evaluation. He has served on the National Riparian Roads Team, on the Society of Wetland Scientists Awards Committee, and as a member of the Citizens Ambassador Wetland Delegation to Australia and New Zealand. In 1996, Dr. Adair received the Outstanding Achievement for Stewardship Development Award from the South Carolina Department of Natural Resources. He helped to develop Ducks Unlimited's carbon sequestration, land protection, and Latin American conservation programs. Current responsibilities include supervision of Ducks Unlimited's biological, engineering, agronomy, and contract compliance programs across the northern Great Plains.

The views expressed herein are Dr. Adair's personal views and are not necessarily official positions of Ducks Unlimited, Inc.

2

A Brief History of the National Wildlife Refuge System

LYNN A. GREENWALT, FORMER REFUGE MANAGER; FORMER DIRECTOR OF THE U.S. FISH AND WILDLIFE SERVICE, 1973–1981

Readers of this book will learn about National Wildlife Refuges as they are today; this brief and simplified review of how they came to be cannot detail the effort expended to make these places attractive to wildlife and to keep them that way. The success of each refuge is a reflection of the people of the National Wildlife Refuge System, a dimension of refuge history that should not be overlooked. The rock-solid commitment of men and women, beginning almost a century ago, has made what the visitor sees today. These people and those who came before them guarantee that all of us are heirs to a priceless treasure.

I am fortunate to have been the beneficiary of life on a National Wildlife Refuge and, much later, to have been given responsibilities that included the Refuge System and later the entire U.S. Fish and Wildlife Service, the federal agency that has always been key to the study, understanding, protection, and management of wildlife and wild places in this country. I have had a rare opportunity to learn firsthand how important the people who have been a part of the evolution of the National Wildlife Refuge System are to what the refuge visitor enjoys today.

The men and women who manage these places are given responsibility to make sure this bit of America will serve the well-being of our fellow creatures, plant and animal, forever. This produces a sense of purpose that is unusual, and along with it a sense of personal accomplishment that I believe is rare in today's work world.

This pride in place and purpose is present in those who work in the National Park Service, in the U.S. Forest Service, and in the ranks of the Bureau of Land Management; it is in those managers of the wild lands of other landholding agencies; and it is prominent among state and local organizations with similar roles to play. I have heard it said that "It goes with the territory," especially when the territory is a place set aside for the purpose of providing a lasting benefit for future generations and for our fellow passengers on this small, vulnerable, and precious planet.

Of course, I know the people of the Fish and Wildlife Service and the Refuge System best, for I have been close to them all my life, 70 years. When I speak of the men and women involved, I do not refer only to the women who have lately—far too lately, in my view—come to be professional participants of the Refuge System. I include the wives who came with their husbands to assignments that even today may entail hardships and inconveniences few people would accept voluntarily. I know of husbands, too, who have made radical accommodations to their own lives so their wives can pursue opportunities in refuge work.

I think of my mother, who was the daughter of a university vice president, and who in 1928 left city life with her soon-to-be refuge manager husband to live in an 1890s rough-rock and lumber cabin in the wilds of northwestern Nevada, where there were no neighbors and where visitors were limited to the occasional cowboy and sheepherder. The land had been the "Last Chance Ranch," so named by an old rancher making his final try for success in this arid sagebrush country. The nearest town was about 40 miles away, and the trip down the face of an intervening lava bluff (and especially back up again) was an adventure in early-day automobiling.

My mother might go for a month or more without seeing another woman, and there was nothing in her home remotely resembling luxury. Winters were harsh, and her journal reveals that "Last Chance" was a name that fit the situation more often than not. She prevailed, of course, and she and my father went on to live on two other National Wildlife Refuges during his long career. Both of the other assignments were closer to towns and people and the ordinary things of life, but my mother was happiest, I am quite sure, when she and my father proved themselves in a distant wilderness, where life was difficult but full of adventure.

My own life has a parallel experience, though it took place a quarter century after the "Last Chance." My wife, Judy, and I were in our twenties when I was given an opportunity to take on my first job as a refuge manager. We two and our small child (and another on the way, about whom I did not tell my boss until we got relocated, lest he cancel the whole idea) moved to a wild and isolated place in western Utah, where our "Last Chance" was a small camping trailer and a front yard 15 miles deep and 40 miles wide—the distances we could see from our tiny residence. My wife learned to subdue the recalcitrant electric generator so she could have electricity briefly each day, and she endured the snakes (harmless), the distances (not harmless), and the fact that our nearest neighbor was 30 miles away. We lived in this place, albeit in steadily improving circumstances, for three years. As my mother did, my wife makes clear that those years in the faraway desert, where the view was always changing and the dust devils danced across the distant flats, are among her most cherished. These two women in my life revealed an inner toughness and strong self-confidence that must have been common among the women who were immigrant pioneers a century before.

They are by no means the only examples of women who have supported their husbands in ways most wives are never called upon to do. A wife at Cold Harbor, in the Aleutian Islands of southwestern Alaska, for example, faced immense problems of transport in case someone had a medical emergency. The weather there was calculated to test the will of even the most tenacious person, man or woman. Transportation is a little more convenient now, but the climate has not improved.

Winter in northern Michigan is a time during which the lowering clouds produce snow almost every day, and the gray envelopment can be devastating to the good humor of someone who may have been brought up in, say, Texas. Yet, Texans do accept—even seek—assignments in Michigan or Alaska or in urban San Francisco. It is because they care for the resources entrusted to them and because they know theirs is one of those rare callings that focus primarily on the future. What they do now will have a profound impact upon what the world may be like for their children and grandchildren—and yours.

As you read about or visit National Wildlife Refuges, recall that what you see got that way because of the people involved, then and now. As an old hand at the trade, I know they have had hard times—sometimes dangerous, usually a little uncomfortable, sometimes in the line of political fire, and occasionally subjected to the outright hatred of individuals or groups who do not agree with the idea that there is a place in the world for wildlife or who object to the occasional need to subordinate their own needs to those of wildlife and wild places. Yet, I know that if pressed, every refuge person—and the spouses who share their lives with them—will say they have the very best jobs in the world. And they mean it. They are what has made the National Wildlife Refuge System a success, a model for other nations to follow, and a source of great pride for all who have ever served in it.

The modern National Wildlife Refuge System, composed of more than 530 refuges, encompassing more than 93 million acres, and represented in every state in the nation, began on the east coast of Florida in 1903. A three-acre island, one of several in the Indian River south of Sebastian, was a famous pelican and heron rookery and had become the focus of feather hunters, who sold the plumes of herons and egrets to the makers of women's hats. A local concern was raised to the attention of President Theodore Roosevelt, who declared the tiny island a federal bird sanctuary in March 1903.

National Wildlife Refuges embrace islands smaller than an acre in size and Alaska's Arctic National Wildlife Refuge, larger than the state of Connecticut. The entire Refuge System is the size of Montana and is growing. It represents every kind of wildlife habitat found in the United States and its Territories. It is a remarkable assemblage of lands and waters and is managed to ensure the perpetuation of habitats necessary to the support of the Nation's wildlife resources.

In 1903, there were about 80.6 million people in the United States. It was a time when space for living and growing was abundant. It is remarkable that what was happening on three acres of truly isolated land in a remote part of Florida could be made to attract the attention of a president and inspire him to exercise the authority he used many times over the next few years to create National Parks and National Forests—and more National Wildlife Refuges. In hindsight, it seems almost miraculous that such action would be taken in a time when the popular view was that the nation's resources were limitless and would always be available.

The confident nation was poised to make the most of these natural resources. The continent had been explored and inventoried, and what were then termed "Indian problems" had been resolved, after a fashion. Plans were developing to "reclaim" the desert lands of the West with irrigation schemes taking advantage of water flowing out of the western mountains. Transportation was abundant, and resources from the West could be brought to the manufacturing centers of the East to develop an economy of immense potential. There was no question that a virtually unlimited opportunity for growth and economic progress was at hand.

A considerable, but not entirely obvious, price had already been paid for this opportunity, however. Millions of bison had been all but eliminated, and only a few specimens remained in zoos. Passenger pigeons, estimated to have existed in the billions in the woodlands of the eastern half of the country, were utterly extinguished by the end of the nineteenth century as a result of profligate overharvesting and habitat destruction. Wetlands and grasslands in the East and Midwest had given way to agriculture, and cattle grazing was to be a key economic activity of the West, along with timber harvesting and mining. Taken together, these were having a serious impact on wild habitats and the creatures depending on those places.

Grasslands and the variety of wildlife living in them were disappearing as cattle herds changed the nature of the vegetation in the West; large mammals were giving way to human activity; and predator populations were beginning to be a thorn in the side of those who grazed sheep and cattle, both easy prey for coyotes and wolves. Immediate control, if not outright elimination of pest species such as prairie dogs, rabbits, and bobcats, was demanded and undertaken.

Subtle changes were occurring in the biological processes that had supported a stunning variety of wild things, both plant and animal. Those changes were causing potentially serious problems for natural systems. A few people began to recognize that living natural resources were vulnerable to habitat destruction or overuse.

Not long after the creation of Pelican Island National Wildlife Refuge in 1903, the pace of refuge establishment increased and included seven more refuge areas in Florida by 1908, and eight in the Territory of Alaska by 1913. In 1909, elements of the Leeward Islands and the surrounding oceanic territory, far to the west of the main Hawaiian Islands, were added to the system. Each action was taken to prevent continuing harm to wildlife species or habitats suffering the effects of human activity.

It is ironic that some of the first refuges established were in parts of the nation that were then far from centers of human activity and where one would least expect wildlife to encounter problems. The creation of these refuges reflected an increasing understanding of how fragile the relationship between wildlife and habitat could be and how quickly permanent loss could occur.

A growing interest in the well-being of waterfowl inhabiting North America spurred an international agreement resulting in the Migratory Bird Treaty with Great Britain (representing Canada), which was signed in 1916. This measure set the stage for rapid progress in the development of means to protect migrating birds, largely waterfowl, the hunting of which was generally unregulated. In the absence of regulation, waterfowl hunting became a commercial activity in which hundreds of thousands of birds were killed each year for sale as food. The treaty, and the legislation passed by Congress in 1918 to carry out the treaty provisions, also protected migratory songbirds, but initially the most active concern was for waterfowl.

Ducks and geese nest in Canada or the northern United States, rest during their migrations on rivers and lakes and other wetland areas in the central United States, and winter in the southern states, or in Mexico and beyond. A similar treaty with Mexico was therefore executed in 1937, extending the provisions of the Canadian treaty to apply to the Republic of Mexico and helping ensure the protection of birds and their habitats throughout the birds' range.

Much of the early work done in identifying areas of potential value as refuges was accomplished by local citizens familiar with the needs of wildlife and the problems facing the resource. Hunters and anglers, who often noted changes in the presence of wildlife or the decline in habitat quality, reported what they saw and encouraged government action to protect localities critical for wildlife.

In the early decades of the twentieth century, most refuge lands were simply set aside from the large inventory of public lands, located primarily in the western United States. This required no money for buying land, but did require funding to provide personnel to look after the new areas.

Not all of the areas were carved from free land, however. Some, like the important pronghorn and sage-grouse habitat in northwestern Nevada (now the Sheldon National Wildlife Refuge), involved private land, and national sportsperson's groups solicited private subscriptions to buy a ranch in the center of the area. The refuge was not created immediately; like many others, it required constant pressure to move it from planning to completion. Leaders of the National Audubon Society took an interest in the area, and in 1931, President Herbert Hoover made the refuge official. (This is the place of "Last Chance," which revealed my mother's indomitability.)

A powerful stimulus to refuge creation was a long and widespread drought that hovered over the central and western United States in the 1930s. This "Dust Bowl" created real problems for wildlife. There was little water for ducks and geese. Large areas of land were damaged by windstorms that sent dust clouds high into the skies, visible even in the East. Duck marshes were as vulnerable as wheat fields, and times were bleak for man and beast alike.

Once again, hunters and anglers agreed to help. In the early 1930s, a law was passed requiring waterfowl hunters to purchase a federal Duck Stamp in order to hunt waterfowl. The revenue from these stamps went into a fund to be used for the purchase of waterfowl habitat, with an emphasis on breeding grounds for ducks and geese. By 1940, 130 new refuges were bought, adding nearly 11 million acres to the system. Although most were relatively small units, some, such as the Okefenokee Swamp in Georgia, were extensive natural areas.

Even during the period of national preoccupation with the defense effort in World War II, 25 new refuges were added, including two large refuges for brown bears and other wildlife in Alaska, and several waterfowl areas in the upper Midwest. Wartime demands for military personnel and war industry support forced cutbacks in the staffs of almost every refuge in the system, and many managers found themselves assigned custodial responsibility for other areas in addition to their home stations.

In 1960, Interior Secretary Fred Seaton followed the example of Theodore Roosevelt more than a half century before: he established what is now the Arctic National Wildlife Refuge and some others in Alaska by employing at the last minute a secretarial authority that was about to expire. These refuges added nearly 12 million acres to the system. Refuges in Alaska were consolidated and expanded as a result of the far-reaching Alaska National Interest Lands Conservation Act (ANILCA), of 1980, which dealt with the future management of the public lands that make up virtually all of that resource-rich state. The Alaska refuges now embrace a total of about 77 million acres, from well above the Arctic Circle to the Aleutian Islands in far southwestern Alaska, and large tracts of interior wetlands, which are havens for an abundance of water birds as well as resident wildlife of many kinds.

The acquisition of land has been accomplished in a variety of ways over the years. Much of it has come from the public domain, land already owned by the federal government. Duck Stamp receipts have paid for more than 4.5 million acres of land, including small wetlands in the "Prairie Pothole" region of the upper Midwest, on which large numbers of waterfowl breed and raise their young each year.

On the Canadian side of the border, similar waterfowl habitat preservation has taken place, most notably by a private organization called Ducks Unlimited, Inc. (see chapter 1 for more on this organization). Using public or leased lands, DU raises money in the United States from hunters and others interested in the perpetuation of the North American waterfowl resource to create and manage hundreds of thousands of acres of wetland habitat in Canada. This is done in cooperation with the provinces and the national government. DU has been engaged in a somewhat similar program in Mexico for some years as well.

As a result of the Fish and Wildlife Coordination Act, passed shortly after World War II, federal agencies constructing major irrigation or flood control works have been required to assess the impacts those projects may have on fish and wildlife resources and to take action to diminish that impact. As a result, many National Wildlife Refuges have been created under this Act to offset losses to habitat for waterfowl and other migratory birds, and many state-managed refuges were created as replacement habitat for resident wildlife. About 2.7 million acres of National Wildlife Refuge lands have been acquired in this way. Included in this list is the very popular and decidedly atypical John Heinz National Wildlife Refuge at the southwestern edge of Philadelphia, which harbors large numbers of waterfowl during migration and is heavily used by school groups from the area. It originated as mitigation for habitat loss created by a major highway project in the vicinity. Habitat was created in a place that includes a closed landfill, hardly the sort of feature usually associated with a natural area. The refuge is now a riverside marsh between the Delaware River and Philadelphia's international airport. It is but one of several refuges successfully established within an urban setting, in which wildlife thrives close by the habitat of humans.

Some refuges have simply been gifts to the United States—often, but not always, stimulated by provisions of the tax laws that permit tax deductions for gifts. Among these is the nearly 250-thousand-acre Sevilleta National Wildlife Refuge in south-central New Mexico. This block of land was originally a Spanish land grant. The refuge is divided by the Rio Grande, and on either side is a remarkable example of desert grassland extending to the hills beyond. The entire grant was owned by one family, which conveyed it to the United States as a National Wildlife Refuge with the support of The Nature Conservancy, a national nonprofit organization that encouraged the donation and helped defray some of the legal and other costs.

Another gift stimulated by tax advantages was the Great Dismal Swamp National Wildlife Refuge in southern Virginia. Once owned by the Union Camp Paper Company, it was given to the United States, once again with the support and assistance of The Nature Conservancy. The refuge protects a rare eastern hardwood swamp rich in wildlife and history.

Wealthy individuals, small organizations, and local groups have worked to make land available to the refuge system at no cost or at sharply reduced prices. These generous actions have resulted in the addition of more than 664 thousand acres of often-unique habitat to the system.

Congress passed one of the most famous and powerful wildlife laws in the nation's history in 1973: the Endangered Species Act. This law pledged the country not to let any species of plant or animal pass into extinction if that can possibly be avoided. The legislation contained provisions that are often newsmakers, as when a species of butterfly or frog brings a major development program to a halt because the species may be put at risk by the project. These confrontations are inevitable when human activities come into conflict with the well-being of a species so vulnerable that its very existence may be in question if the activity is allowed to continue. These often-controversial dilemmas are a direct result of the fact that human population in this country has burgeoned, from the 80 million or so when Pelican Island Refuge was established, to now well over three times that number. More people demand more places to live, work, and recreate. Additional people require a steadily increasing support structure of highways, parking lots, port improvements, and flood protection. And there is a steady increase in the number of these things as our economy grows and our aspirations expand.

Humans displace wild living things by altering or destroying their habitats. Hunting may have depleted the bison and passenger pigeons a century or more ago, but now the steady removal or alteration of habitats exerts constant pressure on wildlife species, often to the point at which the most vulnerable and least numerous populations are in danger of disappearing.

The Endangered Species Act of 1973 and several subsequent amendments provided powerful legal protection, including additional authority to purchase habitats critical to the protection of endangered species in cases when land protection is key to the preservation of the species. This is not a new concept. The pronghorn refuges in Nevada and Oregon; the bison refuges in Montana and Oklahoma; and the extensive desert bighorn sheep ranges established in Arizona, New Mexico, and Nevada—all put in place in the first half of the twentieth century—were intended to ensure the preservation of these and other species requiring specialized habitat.

The majestic whooping crane, never abundant, breeds in northern Manitoba and winters along the Gulf Coast of Texas, making the long trip twice each year. Pressure on its wintering habitat reduced the population to little more than a dozen birds in the late 1930s, when the Aransas National Wildlife Refuge in Texas was established to protect its winter range. These birds have since increased to a population of more than 150 migratory individuals and another 170 or so being bred in captivity—a minor miracle, given their original situation. The tiny Key deer, found only in the Florida Keys, had habitat set aside for them when a refuge was purchased shortly after World War II. Even so, the press of human activity in the realm of the Key deer is a serious problem, requiring constant attention to finding ways that humans and the deer can live together.

The Endangered Species Act made possible the use of money from the existing Land and Water Conservation Fund, as well as other sources, to purchase refuge lands for endangered species. As a result, refuges were created for the rare Attwater's prairie chicken in Texas, and for the masked bobwhite quail found only in limited numbers along the Mexico–Arizona border. Several refuges were established in Hawai'i, a state noted for having the greatest number of species on the endangered species list. This latter situation has been brought about by decades of intensive development, as well as a long history of introducing exotic species of plants and animals that have altered the habitat of the islands' native plants and animals.

The refuge system has developed in parallel with the problems faced by wildlife in this country. Initially, lands were set aside to deal with special situations, such as the overharvesting of birds in the rookeries of Pelican Island; or the pelicans on Anaho Island, Nevada; or the herd of bison reestablished in the Wichita Mountains of Oklahoma and at the National Bison Range in Montana after these animals were hunted almost to extinction in the nineteenth century.

These refuges were put in place because of an obvious need that occurred in the first years of the twentieth century. Later on, the drought and steadily declining habitats focused special effort on the establishment of refuges for migratory birds, especially waterfowl. That emphasis continues, especially through agreements with private landowners.

National Wildlife Refuges are not necessarily restricted to the wild and remote areas once associated with special places for wild animals. Some, such as the complex of refuges in the San Francisco area, lie within highly developed urban regions. A number of wetland tracts are preserved along the East Coast, from the tip of Florida to Maine, and many lie adjacent to heavily developed residential areas.

Cape Canaveral on the east coast of Florida, a site for rocket launches and space travel departures for many years, is located within a vast complex of coastal marshland. The Merritt Island National Wildlife Refuge was established to operate in association with the space program, to take advantage of the vast expanse of coastal marsh embraced by the space center. Regular launches of the space shuttle are made from there, with all the noise and light and dramatic activities we see on television. The many wildlife species using the area during these events seem to be unconcerned, and return to the coastal marshlands as they have for millennia.

A number of refuges have been created from military bases abandoned after World War II or identified as surplus during recent rounds of military base closure reviews. The Rocky Mountain Arsenal near Denver, once heavily contaminated with chemicals, has been designated as a refuge. Full control of the 17-thousand-acre area will be given to the Fish and Wildlife Service once contamination cleanup is completed under the direction of the U.S. Army. Eagles, other birds of all kinds, deer, and other wildlife typical of the Colorado high plains thrive there, within a few miles of metropolitan Denver.

Refuges are places where benefiting wildlife is the guiding purpose; however, these are not places where nature is left to its own devices. Habitats can be manipulated to improve conditions for wildlife; in many cases habitat is created and maintained where none existed before. Within National Wildlife Refuges, managers have the flexibility to make the areas as productive as possible for wildlife.

In the Florida panhandle, land that was farmed to exhaustion and abandoned as worthless in the 1930s was acquired as part of a government plan to recover and restore abandoned lands. Fish and Wildlife Service biologists believed that good wildlife habitat could be created on these worn and degraded lands. The construction of dikes and water controls helped re-create coastal marsh habitat, and forests were restored. This is now the St. Marks National Wildlife Refuge, a place rich in wildlife. It is just one example of active human intervention succeeding in re-creating a resource once thought to be beyond saving.

Many of the refuges established during the drought of the 1930s and early 1940s are the product of habitat improvement, often done by the Civilian Conservation Corps or the Work Projects Administration (federal programs established to help employ those hard-hit by the Great Depression). Refuges such as Bosque del Apache in New Mexico, Piedmont in Georgia, and Back Bay in Virginia are products of construction and management that have resulted in renewed wildlife use and fundamental environmental improvement.

Human intervention in the process of creating a successful wildlife refuge can be dramatic, as when a dike system is built and re-creates tens of thousands of acres of marsh at Bear River on the north side of Great Salt Lake in Utah, or when ditches and pumps provide water to a former great wetland, as at Stillwater in Nevada or Benton Lake in Montana. The intervention can be modest, as when planned and controlled fires improve range habitat for pronghorn at Sheldon in Nevada or Hart Mountain in Oregon, or when water levels are changed with the season to provide waterfowl nesting habitat, as at J. Clark Salyer in North Dakota and Fish Springs in Utah. Assisting natural processes through management is a never-ending requirement, if many of these remarkable places are to continue to make their contribution to the well-being of fish and wildlife resources for the nation and for the future.

It has been 20 years since I was director of the Fish and Wildlife Service. Since then, I have had the opportunity to work in a private conservation organization having an interest in the National Wildlife Refuge System; so, I know about its remarkable advances and improvements. Even so, when I contemplate the roster of National Wildlife Refuges as set forth in this book, I am pleased to find that there are a good many about which I know very little. This demonstrates the rapid progress made in the creation of new, valuable, and important refuges in the unending effort to make sure our wildlife heritage will thrive.

When I scan the descriptions of the new areas and review the material about the refuges I knew intimately from my childhood until I left the Service, I am struck by the contrasts between those times and the present day. I feel like a parent who reviews the progress of his own children and takes pride and pleasure in the fact that their lives are better in significant ways than his may have been.

Refuges today have larger staffs than was generally the case in my time. They do not have enough yet to realize the full potential of these places, to be sure, but specialists of many kinds have been made available. Biologists, key to the success of refuge management, are present in greater numbers and provide a wide range of skills. Range management specialists are assisted by men and women trained in the use of planned burning to improve habitat; there are foresters and wetland biologists and scientists who are expert in improving habitats vital to endangered species. Public-use specialists develop and carry out programs to make visitors' trips to the refuges more informative and safer and to ensure that public use does not interfere with the well-being of the creatures for whom the refuges were established.

When I visit a refuge today, I am drawn, invariably, to mundane things of the kind that were important to refuge managers 30 or 40 years ago. I am delighted to find equipment that is new: a bulldozer or road grader that is not secondhand; a dump truck actually designed to do the work the refuge needs; stockpiles of fresh materials and supplies.

These things stir me, because in the days when I was learning the refuge management trade, it was unlikely that we would ever see many items that were new. Much of what was available to us was gleaned from among items no longer needed by the military. From the end of World War II, the military has made available to qualifying federal and state agencies all manner of items—some new, some barely used, some barely functioning—from its changing inventory of construction equipment and supplies; motor vehicles; automotive repair items; countless kinds of pipe, lumber, and steel; and lesser items such as tools, tires, and assortments of nuts and bolts and nails. It was a kind of year-round Christmas for refuge folk, who were desperately short of these things.

It was quite possible for a refuge to be equipped with a bulldozer almost as old as the person who operated it. It might have only a few hundred hours of use on its clock, but may have been displaced by a more modern one, and a sharp-eyed refuge staff person, making the rounds of the military surplus depots, had put a tag on it. Refuges across the nation were maintained and construction work was undertaken with equipment that was still painted Army olive drab, Navy gray, or Air Force blue.

Some of us learned things the hard way during those times. One manager I knew failed to look carefully at the description of some steel chain he found on a surplus list, available at no cost except for the shipping. He was not as familiar with the nomenclature of chain as he should have been and was stunned to discover that he had become the proprietor of a few hundred feet of anchor chain, each link of which weighed a hundred pounds or more. One tries not to think about how he explained the freight charges to his supervisor.

Another manager found a gross or two of new and unused Quartermaster Corps padlocks, sturdy bronze things that would be ideal for the many gates and buildings on his place. Not until he got them home did he discover that no two were keyed alike: he would have needed a coaster wagon to carry all the keys he would need to make his rounds.

Word of these misadventures got around among refuge managers; so, people learned quickly to be very careful when getting something sight unseen, or at least to check locks and keys for variety. Some of us learned to cultivate friendships among the military managers of the surplus offices so we might get a little advance information about a near-pristine dump truck that might be coming up for disposal or a batch of lumber that was in the offing. These things could be shared with nearby refuges, and over the years, a lot of work got done at minimum cost, and managers learned things never taught in wildlife biology courses. The military is still a source of surplus items of value to refuge managers, though not on the scale that prevailed in the days when such things were rare delights.

Perhaps I can be forgiven for rhapsodizing over a two-year-old bulldozer or backhoe, yellow and gleaming, when I see one in a refuge maintenance yard. You can only imagine how I feel about seeing a communications network that really works in every corner of a 200-thousand-acre refuge, or the highly trained and well-equipped firefighting teams developed through cooperative ventures with neighboring landowners and other state and federal agencies.

I am pleased and proud that visitors to larger refuges today will find a visitor center, containing always-changing and improving information about the refuge, presided over by trained information and public-use specialists, themselves often assisted by a group of volunteers, prepared to make a visitor's stay a pleasant and rewarding one.

For many years, a "visitor center" usually consisted of a little shelf of brochures and a glass-topped display case in the outermost of a two-office headquarters. Visitors were welcome, to be sure, but sometimes tentatively so, simply because there was not enough money to prepare more than the most fundamental facilities for visitors.

Now visitor centers and facilities on many refuges are as modern and inclusive as on any public lands in the country. They are designed by architects who are guided by the specific needs of, and opportunities presented by, the refuge, and they are attractive structures of which refuge personnel and visitors alike can be proud.

As heartening as it may be to note how much the budgets for National Wildlife Refuges have improved over the decades since my last days in the Fish and Wildlife Service, there is still a need for increased funding. Over the years, routine maintenance has been given short shrift, and there is a growing urgency to provide funds so that facilities are kept fully functional. Only then will there be assurance that available water is used efficiently, roads and fences are kept up, and the routine of looking after the public's investment in these remarkable areas is provided.

There is another characteristic of the National Wildlife Refuge System that has emerged in recent times and that I find as encouraging as anything I have watched unfold. That is the powerful effort made by the Fish and Wildlife Service to engage private landowners in a variety of cooperative efforts that multiply and expand the effectiveness of the system of National Wildlife Refuges and other natural areas, upon which the perpetuation of the nation's wildlife resources will depend.

Wildlife refuges alone cannot guarantee that there will be fish and wildlife resources available for the enjoyment of future generations, even if one includes all similar public landholdings, such as forests, parks, and state areas, in the calculation. Most wildlife habitat in this country is on private land. Recognizing this, in recent years, the Service has set out to work with private landowners to engage them in the process of developing, enhancing, and maintaining wildlife habitat as a part of their own land management. This becomes a kind of extension of the National Wildlife Refuge System in that habitat otherwise vulnerable to conversion to another use is recognized as being valuable in and of itself.

Regardless of the process, there is an increasing involvement of the general public in wildlife protection and preservation. The National Wildlife Refuge System and the Fish and Wildlife Service are in the forefront of developing this new ethic, based on the fundamental idea that the living natural resources of the country are valuable assets. These wild creatures and the places they inhabit add to the quality of life and enjoyment of people here and in other countries, and, through tourism and wildlife-related outdoor recreation activities, they contribute significantly to the overall economy.

A few years ago, legislation was passed permitting the National Wildlife Refuge System to use volunteers to help with the day-to-day activities of refuge operation. Hundreds have joined the ranks of the volunteers and bring remarkable talents to bear on refuge problems. Volunteers help with public use and educational work, staffing visitor centers and tour routes. Others possess skills uniquely suited to meeting particular challenges. At a refuge in New Mexico, for example, a volunteer revealed that he was trained as an electrical engineer. With his help and the cooperation of the local electric power company, miles of overhead lines providing power to pumps, with which marsh areas were maintained, were expertly buried, removing an unsightly reminder of human presence—and a hazard to thousands of birds using the area in the winter. Volunteers help make the expanding system work, freeing full-time employees for other, less routine chores.

One of the greatest contributions volunteers make, however, is that they keep no secrets: They tell their friends—and anyone else who will listen—about the importance of wildlife and wild lands and create a general understanding that is vital if the Refuge System is to fulfill its promise in the long run. When enough people care in this way, we can be sure of having wildlife and their habitats recognized and protected, because we humans will have come to recognize and accommodate the value these treasures contribute to our lives.

As director of the Fish and Wildlife Service, working with the Congress to ensure funding for the Refuge System and other parts of the Service, I was often asked—as every director before and since has been—just how large the Refuge System should be. "How many more refuges do we need?" was a recurring question, sometimes asked out of curiosity and sometimes with an angry edge to the query. My response was, and is, that the system will always grow, though it may not expand at the rate it has in the past 30 years. As long as there are conflicts between the demands of increasing human population and the needs of wildlife and the places they inhabit, one solution will be to set aside land and water to ensure the continuation of other species in addition to our own.

I am honored to have been a part of the development, growth, and management of the National Wildlife Refuge System. I am doubly proud because my own father was one of the first refuge managers, beginning his long tour almost 75 years ago. I am fortunate because I married a woman whose father was also a refuge manager, one who in his time fought valiantly against long odds to make sure at least some water from the fast-draining Florida Everglades was devoted to wildlife. His daughter, therefore, understood the kind of life she was facing in my company and accepted it without reservation.

Those who use this volume as a guide to seeing the wildlife heritage of the United States will find it rewarding. Through its use, you will come to know the system of lands and waters identified by the Blue Goose signs, which symbolize National Wildlife Refuges across the country and give notice that something remarkable is at hand. The Blue Goose marks places intended for the continuing benefit of our fellow creatures, a place where human beings are welcome but on terms that are determined by the needs of those creatures.

You may come to know certain National Wildlife Refuges intimately and in detail; if so, you will always return. You will be drawn to these places because they are special; because they are places of re-creation; and because they constantly change and so are utterly unique. You will understand something of the feeling that all of us who ever worked on National Wildlife Refuges have for these treasures. A nation that for a hundred years has recognized and supported an obligation to the other beings on this planet is a nation that is truly enlightened—because its people understand.

3

Second Nature No More: The National Wildlife Refuge System Comes of Age

MIKE BOYLAN, REFUGE SUPERVISOR FOR SOUTHERN ALASKA

"An unfertilized flower on a melon vine waiting for a passing bumble bee. . . "
—J. N. "Ding" Darling, first Director, Bureau of Biological Survey, describing the fledgling National Wildlife Refuge System

On the eve of its Centennial in 2003, the National Wildlife Refuge System is at a crossroads. The next few years will determine whether this country's third largest system of public lands has the human and financial capital it needs to fulfill President Theodore Roosevelt's vision or remains an afterthought in American conservation. But the zeal with which the Refuge System's Centennial has been embraced by advocates, ranging from the administration to conservation groups to Capitol Hill, suggests that the true importance of this event may be to recognize the emergence of a new prototype for land stewardship rather than as merely a celebration of past achievements.

Approaching 550 units and 100 million acres of land, including parcels in every state and five Territories, the Refuge System is the only federal land system managed primarily for wildlife. Its wildlife-first mission neatly reflects the growing environmental conscience of the public; yet, relatively few Americans know about the Refuge System. Of four major federal land management agencies, it has the smallest staff and budget, both of which are dwarfed by those of the U.S. Forest Service, National Park Service (NPS), and Bureau of Land Management (BLM). Even within its parent agency, the U.S. Fish and Wildlife Service, the Refuge System often gets second billing to the often-controversial endangered species program. The Rodney Dangerfield of public lands, the Refuge System has had to struggle for the recognition and stature it deserves. But that's changing.

A Split Personality

Although only Congress can oversee the birth of a national park, refuges employ multiple midwives. Refuges are established through public land withdrawals; statutory withdrawals (e.g., Alaska National Interest Lands Conservation Act or ANILCA); land transfers from other agencies; and by donation, exchange, or purchase with funds from the sale of Migratory Bird Hunting and Conservation Stamps (Duck Stamps) or funds from other sources including the Wetlands Loan Act, Land and Water Conservation Fund, and Natural Resources Damage Assessment. This flexibility has enabled the Refuge System to acquire key wildlife habitats with minimum bureaucracy and maximum opportunism. Since the 1970s, new refuges have moved beyond their traditional role of conserving migratory bird habitat to reflect federal interests in conserving threatened and endangered species, Alaskan wilderness, and unique ecosystems.

But while Refuge System acreage has grown, operations and maintenance funds have not kept pace. Conservation organizations like the National Audubon Society have observed that the complexity of the Refuge System may have outpaced the ability of the Fish and Wildlife Service to manage these lands, given the agency's other duties. The Refuge System faces internal obstacles due to the multiple mandates of the Fish and Wildlife Service. By contrast, the Forest Service, BLM, and National Park Service each has land management as its primary, if not sole, responsibility. Land issues dominate each agency's agenda, budget, and leadership. But the Fish and Wildlife Service has a hybrid mission, responsible for numerous regulatory programs as well as the Refuge System. Internal competition, bred by this shotgun marriage of a regulatory agency and a land management function (or is it a land management agency and a regulatory function?), creates unique challenges for the Refuge System, not unlike what would occur if the Environmental Protection Agency and National Park Service were merged.

Until the 1970s, the National Wildlife Refuge System was the centerpiece of the Fish and Wildlife Service. But the Refuge System's stature within the agency began to erode as a cascade of new environmental laws expanded the Service's mission. Laws such as the Endangered Species Act, National Environmental Policy Act, Marine Mammal Protection Act, Fish and Wildlife Coordination Act, Clean Air Act, Comprehensive Environmental Response Compensation and Liability Act (CERCLA), and Emergency Wetlands Resources Act required the Service to create new bureaucracies to address them. Although these new laws pushed the agency into the forefront of environmental protection, they had the unintended consequence of relegating Refuge System issues to a back seat on the Service's agenda.

First Lands of the Last Frontier

Some people think National Wildlife Refuges first came to Alaska with ANILCA in 1980. But our northernmost refuges have a storied history that predates Alaska's 1959 statehood. In fact, some contend that the first federal refuge was Afognak Island, designated in 1892 and transferred to Kodiak Refuge in 1980. But if there's debate about the first refuge, everyone agrees that ANILCA effectively put the Refuge System on steroids, adding 54 million acres by establishing nine new refuges and expanding seven existing ones. In so doing, ANILCA more than doubled the Refuge System acreage to 90 million acres, making it the third largest federal land system behind the BLM and Forest Service, and larger than the National Park System.

ANILCA increased congressionally designated wilderness tenfold, to 20 million acres. It also gave consistent purposes to Alaskan refuges, in an effort to avoid the conflicts that refuges outside Alaska had experienced due to mixed mandates. ANILCA's purposes include conserving fish, wildlife, and habitats in their natural diversity; ensuring water quality and quantity; and the most controversial purpose: providing opportunities for continued subsistence uses by local residents. The law also required development or revision of Comprehensive Conservation Plans (CCPs) to provide long-term management direction for all refuges by the end of the 1980s. This prescient planning direction in ANILCA was adopted 17 years later in the landmark Refuge System Improvement Act of 1997 and now applies to the entire Refuge System.

ANILCA not only added acreage to the Refuge System, but significantly revised the job of the refuge manager. Many Alaska refuge managers, who learned their trade manipulating water levels to provide habitat for migrating ducks in the lower 48, had to become versed in the ways of minimum-tool wilderness management and thorny questions of access. As caretakers of vast acreages that often surrounded entire villages (Yukon Delta refuge alone has 40 villages within its boundaries), Alaskan refuge managers had to learn to wear many hats. Each serves at times as an employment agency, housing official, social worker, realtor, grocer, wildlife biologist, game warden, and ombudsman. They deal with issues of unemployment, subsistence hunting and fishing, transportation, recreation, economic development, real estate, military relations, contaminant cleanups, construction management, and much more.

The Refuge System's Niche

The National Wildlife Refuge System fills a unique niche among public lands. In business terms, it has a special "market share." One way to understand this is to think in terms of television networks. Although the three major networks (ABC, CBS, NBC) each does an occasional documentary, such programs are the exception to sitcoms and dramas. By contrast, the Public Broadcasting System (PBS) specializes in documentaries. PBS airs shows of greater depth because it is not hostage to ratings and advertising dollars. So, PBS enjoys a more specialized audience than the major networks (e.g., its audience tends to be viewed as more mature, better educated, and of higher average income).

Like ABC, NBC, and CBS, the Bureau of Land Management (BLM), Forest Service, and National Park Service are the dominant Federal land management agencies by size or visitation. With nearly 300 million acres, BLM owns much of the western United States. But BLM's wide holdings demand laws, policies, and regulations that ensure liberal access and uses. So, BLM's multiple-use mission accommodates hunting, fishing, and off-road vehicle use, as well as mining and livestock grazing—for which BLM is labeled by critics as the Bureau of Livestock and Mining.

The Forest Service presides over some 200 million acres. Like BLM, the Forest Service allows a wide range of activities, in keeping with Gifford Pinchot's multiple-use mantra of "the greatest happiness for the greatest number over the longest period of time" (Pinchot is considered the father of the U.S. Forest Service). So, National Forests are home to uses from hunting and fishing to ski resorts and off-road vehicles, as well as mining, livestock grazing, and timber harvests. In recent years, however, the Forest Service's sustained-yield forestry practices have been questioned. Contemporary environmental interests favor wildlife, wilderness, and outdoor recreation over mechanical manipulation of landscapes for profit. As America's workforce has become more educated and sophisticated, Americans' regard for their public lands has moved away from their *extractive* values for mining, grazing, and timber toward an appreciation of their *attractive* values for recreation and tourism.

The third "network" of public lands is managed by the venerable National Park Service (NPS). Recognized as one of America's best ideas, National Park System units range from the "crown jewels" of Yellowstone and Grand Canyon to lesser gems like the Delaware Water Gap National Recreation Area. In fact, the National Park System has some two dozen kinds of lands, including National Historical Parks and Historic Sites, National Seashores, National Lakeshores, and National Battlefields. Even the White House is an NPS unit!

Hosting 300 million visitors annually has burdened the NPS with a de facto multiple-use mandate, albeit one that is not extraction-oriented. Although most National Park visitors pursue sightseeing, hiking, and photography, the variety among NPS lands accommodates activities as diverse as rafting, water skiing, mountain climbing, swimming, scuba diving, fishing, and even hunting (in national preserves).

Some contend that the Refuge System's lack of identity is a public relations problem. As most Americans enjoy wildlife, they say, if more people only *knew* about refuges, their public support would grow to rival that of the National Parks and would bring increased funding. But this would be a Faustian pact and is an inappropriate model for the Refuge System. Although similar to the parks, refuges have a more restrictive mission. Inherent differences in resources, seasons, and clientele ensure that refuges will never approach the popularity of the National Parks. Nor should they.

Parks and Refuges: Siblings? Yes; Twins? No

Most units of the National Wildlife Refuge System were established to protect migratory birds, especially waterfowl, which cross state lines and international borders and are a federal trust responsibility. Although Americans like wild birds, most aren't passionately dedicated to watching or hunting them, and fewer yet plan vacations around doing so. This helps explain why National Parks aren't an appropriate Refuge System model.

Units of the National Park System preserve examples of exceptional scenery and of natural and cultural history. They appeal to an audience of some 300 million people annually, a number roughly equal to the entire U.S. population visiting each year! National Parks are tourist-oriented: their dramatic scenery and history speak for themselves. No special knowledge or equipment is needed to enjoy a visit. NPS programs and facilities ensure that no visitors leave without understanding what they've seen. Groaning under its popularity, NPS's challenge is to preserve the resources while providing the personal services and facilities visitors have come to expect.

Another difference between National Wildlife Refuges and National Parks is the availability of resources. One can enjoy the Statue of Liberty or Grand Canyon all year, but a visit to a refuge should fit into the *wildlife's* schedule. Of course, people can visit any time they choose, but the visit will not be as satisfactory if key wildlife species aren't there. And migratory birds, as the name suggests, come and go. Visit a Midwest waterfowl refuge in midsummer and there's little to see. Marshes are dry as vegetation renews before autumn, when it will be flooded to welcome migrating ducks, geese, and swans en route from northern nesting grounds. The migration cycle is reversed each spring. The cycles of wild things make it essential that all refuges have an active public information/education effort so that no hapless visitor is left to wonder: "Where are the animals?" The challenge is even greater for those who wish to see endangered species, whose attraction for visitors, as with looking for diamonds, lies in their scarcity.

Just as ABC, NBC, and CBS appeal to large, diverse audiences, BLM, Forest Service, and National Park Service lands attract millions of people pursuing a wide range of activities. But as PBS caters to a smaller, more specialized audience, so does the Refuge System. Focusing on this narrow clientele, coupled with a strict compatibility standard that precludes economic and recreational activities more appropriate for multiple-use lands, promotes efficient Refuge System administration. As a veteran manager puts it: "If we can encourage people to *appreciate* refuges for what they are, we don't have to waste our time fighting those who want to *depreciate* them trying to make them what they're not."

Reflecting their unique "Wildlife First" mission, refuges find efficiencies in what they *don't* offer visitors. By providing limited services and facilities, refuges invest in priority wildlife and habitat projects, including critical surveys and data collection, wetlands restoration, strategic use of prescribed fire, reintroduction of endangered species, control of invasive exotic plants and animals, contaminant cleanup, law enforcement, and other work that ensures that the needs of wildlife come first.

Even Alaskan refuges require costly cleanups of contaminants dating back to World War II. Although it isn't necessary to manipulate lands and waters on Alaskan refuges to improve wildlife habitat, as is done on refuges outside Alaska, the costs of working in roadless Alaska, where boats and airplanes do the work of pickup trucks on the refuges in the lower 48, adds extraordinary costs to even routine tasks.

In order to dedicate more funds for priority wildlife work, most refuges don't offer the amenities people have come to expect in National Parks. Refuges seldom provide government guides to explain what you're seeing. You won't find a restaurant, snack bar, or souvenir shop (at best a small bookstore). You'll find few roads; at most a brief auto tour route that allows you to approach wildlife, using your vehicle as a place of concealment. And you'll seldom find a separate visitor center; more often a corner of the headquarters decked with photos or displays. (A very few do have park-like visitor centers, but they are the exception. And most of these are in urban refuges, such as in Philadelphia and the San Francisco Bay Area.) Few refuges have auditoriums or wide-screen films; usually an all-purpose room sufficient for a slide show or video. Because refuges cater primarily to birders, photographers, hunters, and anglers, there's less need for the expensive technology and creature comforts sought by tourists. Rather, the Refuge System's goal should be to enable visitors to physically interact with their environment rather than to embrace "interactive" technology that can become a firewall between people and the natural world.

Refuges at the Crossroads

If some potential refuge supporters are dissuaded by the lack of amenities, others are confused by the apparent contradiction of calling a place that allows hunting a "refuge." Hunting occurs on more than half the Refuge System units, according to state seasons and regulations. (Refuge hunting seasons can be shorter, not longer, than state seasons, and they may have other restrictions.) Most refuge hunts are for waterfowl, with careful attention to the number of birds harvested. Some refuges allow hunts for big game such as deer, elk, and moose—notably in Alaska, where subsistence hunting and fishing are a way of life. Outside Alaska, if hunting pressure threatens to exceed a refuge's ability to accommodate it or poses conflicts with other refuge users, a lottery or other allocation method is used to limit participation. So, although the idea of hunting on an area called a "refuge" may irritate nonhunters, regulated sport hunting or subsistence hunting has never been a threat to the health of wildlife populations within the Refuge System, and never will be.

The Refuge System Improvement Act recognized the unique nature of the Refuge System when it codified priority "wildlife dependent" recreational uses of refuges as hunting, fishing, wildlife viewing, and photography, in addition to environmental education and interpretation. These recreational activities are similar in that each requires special equipment and a basic knowledge of how to use it. So, whether hunting, fishing, watching birds, or photographing wildflowers, the Refuge System's recreational users share common ground. It's a special audience but hardly an elite one; more than 40 million visitors per year, united in their singular pursuit of experiencing and learning about wildlife in its natural habitats.

This focused support base differs considerably from that of National Parks. National Parks are beloved by an international constituency, given voice by the more than 400 thousand members of the National Parks Conservation Association. NPCA serves as both a watchdog over the National Park System and an advocate for National Parks, to keep the latter safe from inappropriate political manipulation. NPCA's educational and advocacy efforts for the National Parks contribute to their status as America's most recognized public lands.

But all politics is local and, in the absence of a strong national constituency, individual refuges have cultivated dedicated cadres of local supporters. Back to our television analogy: Much as PBS gains community support through its pledge drives, the Refuge System has developed the equivalent of local franchises through various "Friends" and other support groups. In the past decade, the Refuge System's small advocacy organization, the National Wildlife Refuge Association, has helped establish or expand more than 200 such groups. Whether known as the "Friends of Kenai Refuge," a local Audubon chapter, or as another conservation organization, these support groups are the lifeblood of local refuges, providing volunteers, issue advocacy, and fund-raising expertise.

As these lands, whose priority is providing wildlife habitat, lack the tourism appeal of National Parks, it's not surprising that threats to *individual* refuges have failed to mobilize widespread support for *all* refuges. So, although potential oil drilling in the Arctic Refuge created a Maginot Line of defenders for that issue, it has not produced a groundswell of advocacy on behalf of the Refuge *System*. Like wolves whose success requires separating one animal from the others of its group, economic interests attack one refuge at a time. Whether the issue is mineral development near Okefenokee Refuge in Georgia or building a road through the designated wilderness of Izembek Refuge in Alaska, the Refuge System's lack of stature is an asset for those who would exploit public lands for private gain.

A Little Help from Our "Friends" (And Others Who CARE)

The Refuge System Improvement Act of 1997 paved the way for a new model of land management by codifying the Refuge System's priority users. This renewed focus was energized by the 1998 Volunteer and Community Partnership Act, which empowered the Refuge System to aggressively create an extended family of local support groups.

Instead of relying on one national conservation organization as an advocate in the role NPCA has served for National Parks, since 1996 the Refuge System has enjoyed the benefits of an extraordinary collaboration of 20 national conservation and recreation organizations united as the Cooperative Alliance for Refuge Enhancement (CARE). CARE's member organizations represent millions of American outdoor enthusiasts whose views cover the spectrum of wildlife interests, from Defenders of Wildlife to Safari Club International; from the American Birding Association to the National Rifle Association. CARE members check their philosophical differences at the door in order to pool their resources in a common mission: increased funding for the Refuge System.

CARE's 2001 report, *Shortchanging America's Wildlife*, revealed that the Refuge System has a per-acre budget that is one-fifth that of the National Park System. CARE has urged Congress and the administration to more than double the Refuge System's annual budget from $300 million to $700 million for conservation and visitor services needs and to reduce an $800 million maintenance backlog.

Past Imperfect

Prior to the Refuge System Improvement Act of 1997, arguably the biggest threat to the National Wildlife Refuge System was its vague legal status and protections. The lack of an "organic act" or legal backbone left the Refuge System vulnerable to political machinations that periodically tried to push it toward a more multiple-use mission like that of BLM or the Forest Service. During the Reagan Administration, for example, Secretary of the Interior James Watt unsuccessfully sought to convince Americans that a wide range of economic uses could be compatible with conservation of wildlife habitat.

In "You Call This a Refuge?" (*Wildlife Conservation, 1991*), John G. Mitchell, a prominent environmental writer–editor, characterized refuges as lands victimized by loggers, farmers, ranchers, and the military:

If you're like most Americans, you imagine our wildlife refuges as pristine, protected habitats, but this is hardly the case. Short of testing hydrogen bombs, there is almost nothing you can't do in a national wildlife refuge.

Alas, even Mitchell was too sanguine. Amchitka Island, in the Aleutian Islands archipelago, has been part of what is now known as the Alaska Maritime National Wildlife Refuge since 1913. The Atomic Energy Commission, predecessor to the Department of Energy, held three nuclear tests on Amchitka from 1965 to 1971. One of these, "Project Cannikin," remains the largest underground nuclear test ever conducted by the United States.

What's in a Name?

Another symptom of the Refuge System's lack of stature among public lands is seen in how easily and often the natural features for which refuges were named have been displaced to honor political figures. So Iowa's Walnut Creek Refuge is renamed for Neal Smith; New Jersey's Brigantine and Barnegat Bay Refuges were combined to honor Edwin B. Forsythe; Connecticut's former Salt Meadow Refuge was renamed for Stewart B. McKinney; Philadelphia's Tinicum Refuge was rededicated to John Heinz; the Connecticut River Refuge now memorializes Silvio O. Conte; and the name of San Francisco Bay Refuge was revised to honor former representative Don Edwards.

Naming refuges for natural features reflects and respects local history and a sense of place. Sacrificing a refuge name for political trading stock enhances neither the refuge nor its community. Public lands depend upon public support. Replacing an evocative, memorable name with that of a political figure—no matter how worthy—virtually ensures that it will be forgotten. It's disturbing to contemplate that, without conviction, evocative refuge names like Blackwater, Chincoteague, Buenos Aires, and Moosehorn could be revised into tongue twisters like "Sonny Bono Salton Sea National Wildlife Refuge Complex." Refusing to honor and zealously guard the birthright and symbolism of every refuge's natural name has contributed to the erosion of the stature of the National Wildlife Refuge System.

To the Centennial—and Beyond!

For nearly a century, National Wildlife Refuges have been little more than an interesting footnote in America's conservation history. To citizens and political leaders alike, the Refuge System's challenge is to show that it protects something of value. Wildlife doesn't choose where to live based on scenery; so, refuges lack the charisma of National Parks. If nature were a movie, refuges would be character actors. Not only must the Refuge System compete for funds at the Department of the Interior's budget table with ever-popular National Parks, but with other worthy Fish and Wildlife Service programs as well, including endangered species, migratory birds, law enforcement, and fisheries.

As the Refuge System's 2003 Centennial has approached, an unprecedented alliance of refuge support groups, CARE, and others has urged the administration and Congress to fulfill the promise of the National Wildlife Refuge System envisioned by Theodore Roosevelt, J. N. "Ding" Darling, Rachel Carson, and others. Congress has responded by passing the National Wildlife Refuge System Centennial Act of 2000. This law called for the creation of a Centennial Commission made up of distinguished citizens and members of Congress to work with partners on activities and events to promote the Refuge System's Centennial.

In its early years, the Refuge System reflected the values and beliefs of an agrarian nation whose outdoor interests, by necessity, focused on hunting. In the decades following the Dust Bowl era, this value system saved precious acreage as National Wildlife Refuges and waterfowl production areas. But the history of the Refuge System's origins does not necessarily provide a vision for the future.

As expected from anyone approaching his or her 100th birthday, the National Wildlife Refuge System is experiencing physical problems. These include insufficient water supplies, invasive species, deteriorating infrastructure, insufficient staff, and inadequate visitor facilities. But in addition to its physical challenges, the Refuge System faces a quiet crisis: namely, the challenge of *relevance* (i.e., it may be producing a product few care about). It's possible that future generations raised on television and computers may gain their appreciation for wildlife vicariously via the Nature Company, the Discovery Store, National Geographic, Animal Planet, computer programs, and CDs more than from physically being in nature.

There's no doubt that National Parks will inspire awe as long as people take vacations. But a nation long on single-parent families and dual-career couples and short on leisure time may find it difficult to relate to areas whose enjoyment depends on skills such as hunting and fishing, which are traditionally passed down from fathers who now may be absent or who may lack the time. In our high-speed society, where lack of time is a constraint but virtual reality only a click away, the future well-being of the Refuge System may depend upon remembering pioneering conservationist Aldo Leopold's maxim that

Recreational development is a job not of building roads into lovely country, but of building receptivity into the still unlovely human mind.

In the Department of the Interior's 2002 budget, the House of Representatives recognized this challenge and specifically directed the Refuge System to

focus on providing on-the-ground refuge experiences for visitors and modest visitor/education centers and visitor contact stations.

By so doing, the Refuge System will fulfill its promise to new generations of Americans through investments in nature trails, boardwalks, observation decks, interpretive signs, blinds for wildlife viewing and photography, boat ramps, outdoor classrooms, and other low-tech means of access. Strategic improvements to increase opportunities for hunting, fishing, wildlife viewing and photography, and environmental interpretation and education will enable the Refuge System to reach an extended family of wildlife enthusiasts by making people feel a part of their lands, and to help them resist the siren song of technology that would keep them apart from these experiences.

Taken together, the 1997 Refuge System Improvement Act and Refuge System Centennial Act of 2000 are like a new set of glasses for the National Wildlife Refuge System, providing a clearer vision for where these lands should go and improving the focus of those who will take them there.

A century after Pelican Island became the first of 53 national wildlife refuges designated by President Theodore Roosevelt, the National Wildlife Refuge System has matured from a gangly system of exceptions following different purposes, policies, and procedures to the exceptional System envisioned by its creator. Today, National Wildlife Refuges safeguard hundreds of endangered species, teem with millions of migrating birds, give safe passage to major fisheries, protect Alaska's great wilderness areas, and welcome more than 40 million wildlife enthusiasts annually. On the Centennial of the National Wildlife Refuge System, we have recognized that the nation that set the world's standard for protecting its scenic and cultural treasures must set a similar standard for conserving its wildlife heritage. Americans can ask no more; America's wildlife deserves no less.

Mike Boylan is Refuge Supervisor for Southern Alaska, with responsibility for oversight of eight national wildlife refuges encompassing 40 million acres of lands. He has worked for 25 years for the U.S. Fish and Wildlife Service, all on behalf of the National Wildlife Refuge System in Alaska, California, Michigan, Ohio, and Washington, D.C. He has a B.A. in journalism, M.S. in natural resources and MPA in public administration. Views expressed in this chapter are personal and do not reflect those of the U.S. Fish and Wildlife Service.

4

The National Wildlife Refuge System

(Descriptions Arranged Alphabetically by State)

RUSSELL D. BUTCHER

Alabama

Bon Secour, containing more than 6,900 acres in five units, was established in 1980 to protect ecologically and scenically diverse parts of coastal barrier-island-type habitats on Fort Morgan Peninsula, between the Gulf of Mexico and Mobile Bay in southwestern Alabama. This refuge includes magnificent white sandy beaches; cypress swamps; salt marshes; gently rolling pine-and-oak woodlands; and coastal sand dunes, on and around which grow a beautiful variety of grass known as sea oats and some picturesque clumps of Spanish moss-draped, wind-sculpted live oaks. More than 370 bird species have been recorded here.

Among the rich diversity of wildlife at Bon Secour (a French name meaning "safe harbor") are alligators; sea turtles that lay their eggs in the refuge's beaches; the threatened gopher tortoise; the rare and endangered Alabama beach mouse that inhabits the coastal dunes; birds such as brown pelicans, herons, and egrets; gulls and terns; black skimmers; ospreys; and a wealth of songbirds. This is one of the Gulf Coast refuges where the remarkable neotropical migratory songbird "fallout" phenomenon can occur in April (see the Aransas, Texas text).

From east to west, Bon Secour Refuge consists of the Sand Bayou Unit, bordering Oyster Bay, a segment of the Intracoastal Waterway, and Bon Secour Bay; the Perdue Unit, bordering Little Lagoon and the Gulf of Mexico and providing the refuge's visitor center and two trails; the Little Point Clear Unit; and the Fort Morgan Unit, near the tip of the peninsula. Little

Dauphin Island, containing 280 acres, is located on the opposite side of the mouth of Mobile Bay.

Establishment of this gem of a refuge has been made possible partly with the financial assistance of The Nature Conservancy. Federal funding for acquisition has been derived from the Land and Water Conservation Fund. In 1999, the refuge was designated as an "Alabama Natural Wonder" by the Alabama Environmental Council. Friends of Bon Secour National Wildlife Refuge is a nonprofit support group that is assisting the refuge in many ways.

Bon Secour is open daily during daylight hours. The visitor center is open on weekdays, except national holidays. There is no entrance fee.

Visitor activities include birdwatching, photography, hiking (on two trails, along the beaches, and elsewhere), swimming, canoeing and boating (small boats with electric trolling motors), and fishing (freshwater fishing at 40-acre Gator Lake, saltwater fishing at Little Lagoon, and surf fishing along the beaches). Hunting and camping are not permitted on the refuge. Campground facilities are available at nearby Gulf State Park. September through November and March and April are the best months for viewing migratory birds. Monarch butterflies migrate through the refuge in October.

Although alligators are generally afraid of people, visitors are cautioned to stay a safe distance from these sluggish-looking but potentially fast-moving reptiles and to be alert for venomous snakes, fire ants, ticks, and chiggers. Insect repellent and sunscreen are advised.

Hiking opportunities include Jeff Friend Trail, a 1-mile loop (wheelchair-accessible) that provides an excellent opportunity to see Little Lagoon, and Pine Beach Trail, a 4-mile round-trip route (1 mile of which is an interpretive trail) affording views of Gator Lake and leading to a strand of beach along the Gulf of Mexico.

Lodgings and meals are available in such communities as Gulf Shores and Mobile.

Access to the refuge is from I-10 at Loxley, south on State Route 59 to Gulf Shores, and west just over 8 miles on State Route 180 to the refuge headquarters.

Further information: Bon Secour National Wildlife Refuge, 12295 State Highway 180, Gulf Shores, AL 36542; telephone: (334) 540-7720.plex, 66-590

Choctaw, consisting of 4,218 acres, was established in 1964. This refuge manages and protects southern bottomland hardwood forest, pine ridges, bald cypress sloughs, creeks and ponds, moist-soil impoundments, and croplands for the benefit of wintering waterfowl, wading birds, nesting wood ducks, and other wildlife in southwestern Alabama.

The refuge is bordered on the east by 7 miles of the Tombigbee River and is divided into three parts by Okatuppa and Turkey creeks. It overlays land acquired by the U.S. Army Corps of Engineers for its Coffeeville Lock and Dam. When this project was completed in the 1960s, the river level was raised about a dozen feet, flooding 2,000 acres of the refuge and creating important waterfowl habitat.

The U.S. Fish and Wildlife Service carries out a variety of habitat management programs here. One such program is regulating the water level of seven small moist-soil impoundments. In the spring or summer, these areas are drained of water to promote the growth of waterfowl food plants. In the autumn, the impoundments are reflooded to make this food source easily available to the large concentrations of wintering waterfowl. Additional food is grown on refuge fields that are planted with millet, winter wheat, and other crops. A program of selective thinning in the refuge's 2,000 acres of bottomland forest improves wildlife habitat diversity by opening parts of the forest canopy and allowing sunshine to stimulate the growth of plants on the forest floor. To enhance the population of wood ducks, the agency provides more than 400 nesting boxes, from which as many as 2,500 young are hatched annually.

The refuge is open daily during daylight hours. There is no entrance fee. An information kiosk is provided at the Womack Hill Work Center, near the north end of the refuge. Access within the refuge is limited. During high water, the refuge headquarters at Womack Hill can be reached only by boat. From December 1 through February, parts of Choctaw are closed to visitation to avoid disturbing waterfowl.

Visitor activities include birdwatching; photography; driving on 5 miles of refuge roads and hiking on unpaved roads and in wooded areas (during dry periods); canoeing and boating (a refuge boat ramp is available just south of the Womack Hill Work Center, and other ramps are outside the refuge); sport fishing (pole-and-line or rod-and-reel only); and hunting (including archery hunts for deer and hogs) during designated seasons. Camping is not permitted on the refuge, but nearby Corps of Engineers campground facilities are available. Because of alligators and hazardous currents, swimming is not allowed. November through April are the best months for birdwatching, with December and January the peak months for viewing waterfowl.

Although alligators are generally afraid of people, visitors are cautioned to stay a safe distance from these sluggish-looking but potentially fast-moving reptiles and to be alert for fire ants, ticks, chiggers, and venomous snakes. Insect repellent is advised.

Lodgings and meals are available in such communities as Butler and Jackson, Alabama and Meridian, Mississippi.

Access to the refuge (from refuge headquarters at 1310 College Avenue, Jackson) is north on State Route 69 from Jackson, left (west) at Coffeeville onto U.S. Route 84 for about 8 miles, right (north) onto County Road 21 for about 4 miles to Barrytown, right (east) onto County Road 14 to Womack Hill, and right (south) to the refuge entrance.

Further information: Choctaw National Wildlife Refuge, P.O. Box 808, Jackson, AL 36545; telephone: (334) 246-3583.

Eufaula, comprising 11,184 acres, was established in 1964 to enhance and manage wetland habitat of the impounded waters of Lake Eufaula and several tributary creeks along the Chattahoochee River in southeastern Alabama and southwestern Georgia. The refuge, which overlays the U.S. Army Corps of Engineers' Walter F. George Reservoir (Lake Eufaula), attracts concentrations of wintering waterfowl as well as wading birds, shorebirds, neotropical migratory songbirds, alligators, and other wildlife. In addition to 7,000 acres of open water and marsh, the refuge also includes 2,000 acres of woodland and 1,000 acres each of oak savannah-grassland and cropland. Nearly 300 species of birds have been recorded on the Eufaula refuge.

The U.S. Fish and Wildlife Service carries out a variety of habitat management programs here. For example, water control structures regulate the level of several moist-soil impoundments. During the spring and summer, these areas are drained of water to promote the growth of waterfowl food plants, such as millet, smartweed, sprangletop, and rushes. In the autumn and winter, they are reflooded to make this food source easily available for concentrations of wintering waterfowl.

To benefit waterfowl and other wildlife, other lands are managed under cooperative agricultural crop production agreements, whereby farmers leave unharvested a portion of their crops, such as corn, small grains, and peanuts. Woodlands are managed for the benefit of a diversity of neotropical migratory songbirds and other wildlife. Grasslands and former fields are maintained, with the aid of periodic prescribed burns. Nesting boxes are provided for wood ducks. And the agency is constantly striving to control undesirable non-native plants.

Ducks Unlimited, Inc. has contributed funds for the repair of dikes and for the purchase of new intake pumps, enabling the restoration of impoundment habitats.

The refuge is open daily during daylight hours. There is no entrance fee. The refuge's office/visitor station is open on weekdays, except on national holidays.

Visitor activities include birdwatching; photography; prearranged environmental education programs; driving the 7-mile tour route; hiking on dikes and a 0.3-mile trail; bicycling on the unpaved refuge roads; canoeing and boating (boat launching ramps are provided where Gammage Road crosses Cowikee Creek, in Alabama's adjacent Lakepoint State Park, in Georgia's Florence Marina State Park, and in the Corps of Engineers' Rood Creek Landing Recreational Area); fishing; and hunting (deer, waterfowl, dove, squirrel, and rabbit) during the designated seasons. Swimming is not permitted within the refuge. Areas of the refuge are seasonally closed to visitation to avoid disturbing waterfowl. Camping is not allowed on the refuge, but campground facilities are available in adjacent Lake Point State Park. The best months for birdwatching are October through April. Two viewing platforms are provided.

Although alligators are generally afraid of people, visitors are cautioned to stay a safe distance from these sluggish-looking but potentially fast-moving reptiles and to be alert for venomous snakes, fire ants, chiggers, and ticks. Insect repellent is advised.

Lodgings and meals are available in such communities as Eufaula.

Access to the refuge is north 5 miles on U.S. Route 431 from Eufaula to Lakepoint State Park, and right onto State Route 285 (Old Highway 165) for 2.5 miles to the refuge's visitor station.

Further information: Eufaula National Wildlife Refuge, 509 Old Highway 165, Eufaula, AL 36027; telephone: (334) 687-4065 (voice).

Fern Cave, containing 199 acres, was established in 1981 to protect a large limestone cave in northern Alabama containing many rooms with stalactites, stalagmites, and other formations. This refuge provides important habitat for three federally listed threatened or endangered species: the gray and Indiana bats and the American hart's-tongue fern. More than 1 million gray bats and several hundred Indiana bats hibernate in Fern Cave.

Above the cave, the refuge consists of upland hardwoods and outcroppings of limestone. The U.S. Fish and Wildlife Service is working to propagate the hart's-tongue fern and reestablish it in natural limestone sites.

The refuge is open daily during daylight hours. There is no entrance fee.

Although there are no visitor use facilities, visitor activities include birdwatching, photography, and hiking. Entry into the cave is limited to research by permit.

The refuge is located 20 miles west of Scottsboro and 2 miles north of Paint Rock.

Further information: Fern Cave National Wildlife Refuge, c/o Wheeler National Wildlife Refuge, 2700 Refuge Headquarters Road, Decatur, AL 35603; telephone: (256) 350-6639.

Grand Bay (see the text under the Mississippi listings)

Key Cave, consisting of 1,060 acres in northern Alabama, was established in 1997 to protect Key and Collier caves, which provide important habitat for two federally listed endangered species: the gray bat and the Alabama cavefish. In addition to the caves, the refuge also contains hardwood forest and cropland that are being enhanced and managed for the benefit of a wide variety of wildlife. The two caves are situated on the shore of a 38-acre sinkhole lake, which is part of a geologically important limestone karst area containing a number of sinkholes and cave systems.

Much of the formerly degraded farmland has been planted with native grasses, and other areas are being reforested with a mixture of native hardwood trees—partly to enhance and protect the ecological cave recharge processes and partly to improve wildlife habitat. Other cropland is being devoted to the production of corn and soybeans, a portion of which is left unharvested, for the benefit of wildlife.

The refuge is open daily during daylight hours. There is no entrance fee.

Although there are no visitor use facilities, visitor activities include birdwatching, photography, hiking, and hunting during the designated season. Entry into the caves is limited to research by permit.

The refuge is located about 5 miles southwest of Florence.

Further information: Key Cave National Wildlife Refuge, c/o Wheeler National Wildlife Refuge, 2700 Refuge Headquarters Road, Decatur, AL 35603; telephone: (256) 350-6639.

Sauta Cave, comprising 264 acres, was established in 1978 to protect a cave that was historically a significant maternity cave for the federally listed endangered gray bat in northern Alabama. The cave is presently a hibernation cave for both the Indiana and gray bats, with as many as 400,000 of the latter emerging from the cave at dusk during the summer, to feed on insects. During the Civil War, Sauta Cave served as a saltpeter mine. This refuge also contains an area of hardwood forest that provides habitat for many species of fauna and flora.

The refuge is open daily during daylight hours. There is no entrance fee.

Although there are no visitor use facilities, visitor activities include watching the bat flights on summer evenings, birdwatching, photography, and hiking. Entry into the cave is limited to research by permit.

The refuge is located 7 miles west of Scottsboro, just above Sautay Creek embayment of the Tennessee Valley Authority's Guntersville Reservoir.

Further information: Sauta Cave National Wildlife Refuge, c/o Wheeler National Wildlife Refuge, 2700 Refuge Headquarters Road, Decatur, AL 35603; telephone: (256) 350-6639.

Watercress Darter, containing 7 acres, was established in 1980 to protect Thomas Spring—a vitally important quarter-acre spring-fed pond that is essential habitat for a federally listed endangered species of fish, the watercress darter, in northern Alabama. In 1983, the U.S. Fish and Wildlife Service created a second pond to expand potential habitat for the darter. The rest of this small refuge consists of brushy habitat for a variety of birds and other wildlife.

The refuge is open daily during daylight hours. There is no entrance fee.

Although there are no visitor use facilities, possible activities include birdwatching, photography, and hiking.

The refuge is located near Bessemer.

Further information: Watercress Darter National Wildlife Refuge, c/o Wheeler National Wildlife Refuge, 2700 Refuge Headquarters Road, Decatur, AL 35603; telephone: (256) 350-6639.

Wheeler, consisting of 34,500 acres, was established in 1938 to manage and protect a variety of habitats for large concentrations of wintering waterfowl and a great variety of other wildlife along the middle third of the Tennessee Valley Authority's Wheeler Reservoir, on the Tennessee River in northern Alabama. This was the first national wildlife refuge to be designated on and around a multipurpose reservoir. Wheeler's ecological diversity includes upland pine plantations, southern bottomland hardwood and riparian woodlands, backwater embayments, expanses of open water, and cropland. In addition to tens of thousands of ducks, the refuge supports the southernmost significant concentration of wintering Canada geese. More than 280 species of birds have been recorded here.

The U.S. Fish and Wildlife Service carries out a variety of habitat management programs here. Water control structures regulate the level of moist-soil impoundments, thereby promoting the growth of native plants that provide food for waterfowl. Prescription burns are used periodically to enhance habitat quality. To benefit waterfowl and other wildlife, approximately 10 percent of the refuge is managed under cooperative agricultural crop production agreements, whereby local farmers leave unharvested a portion of crops of millet, corn, grain sorghum, and soybeans. In the autumn, the refuge produces wheat that provides green browse for wintering geese. Wood duck nesting boxes are provided, from which as many as 2,000 young are hatched annually. And woodlands are managed to enhance the quality of food and cover for many other species of wildlife.

Ducks Unlimited, Inc. has provided financial assistance for important wetlands enhancement projects on this refuge. The Wheeler Wildlife Refuge Association is a nonprofit support group that is assisting the refuge in many ways.

The refuge is open daily during daylight hours. There is no entrance fee. The refuge's visitor center, presenting an orientation video and interpretive exhibits, is open daily from October 1 through February (except on Thanksgiving and Christmas) and on Tuesdays through Saturdays from March 1 through September.

Visitor activities include birdwatching, photography, viewing of wildlife from an observation building; environmental education programs; driving and bicycling on unpaved refuge roads; hiking; horseback and mule riding on some of the roads; prearranged interpretive tours; canoeing and boating (six improved boat-launching ramps are available); fishing (a wheelchair-accessible fishing pier is provided); and hunting (deer [flintlock and archery], raccoon, opossum, squirrel, rabbit, and quail) on parts of the refuge during the designated seasons. Camping is not permitted on the refuge, but campground facilities are available at adjacent Point Mallard Park. September through May are the best birdwatching months.

Wheeler Refuge's unusual wildlife observation building, located near the visitor center, overlooks a waterfowl display pond. From November through February, it is not uncommon to see as many as 10,000 waterfowl resting and feeding here. The building features a large viewing room with one-way glass. Spotting scopes are provided. A sound system connected to a sensitive microphone in the middle of the pond allows visitors to hear the many sounds of ducks on the pond, geese flying overhead, frogs, and other animals. The opposite side of the building overlooks the Backyard Wildlife Habitat Area, where songbirds, hummingbirds, and butterflies are attracted. During the summer, when numerous flowers are blooming, visitors can often see as many as 200 butterflies of 15 species.

Hiking opportunities include five self-guiding, interpretive trails: the 200-yard Wildlife Observation Building Trail, the 0.5-mile Atkeson Trail, 0.75-mile Beaverdam Boardwalk, the 1.5-mile Environmental Trail, and the 4-mile Dancy Bottoms Trail.

Although alligators (uncommon in the refuge) are generally afraid of people, visitors are cautioned to stay a safe distance from these sluggish-looking but potentially fast-moving reptiles and to be alert for venomous snakes, fire ants, ticks, and chiggers. Insect repellent is advised.

Lodgings and meals are available in such communities as Decatur and Huntsville.

Access to the refuge's visitor center is east 1 mile from Decatur on State Route 67, or west 2 miles from I-65 on Route 67.

Further information: Wheeler National Wildlife Refuge, 2700 Refuge Headquarters Road, Decatur, AL 35603; telephone: (256) 350-6639.

Alaska

Alaska Maritime, encompassing 4.5 million acres, was established in 1980 to protect more than 2,400 islands, islets, sea stacks, rocks, reefs, and headlands along the coastal waters of Alaska.

All but 460,000 acres of Alaska Maritime were previously within eleven separate national wildlife refuges, beginning with St. Lazaria and Bering Sea Refuges in 1909 and the 2.72-million-acre Aleutian Islands Refuge in 1913. The Alaska National Interest Lands Conservation Act of 1980 consolidated these refuges.

The refuge's isolated habitats support enormous colonies of nesting seabirds and rookeries of sea lions and other marine mammals. Of the estimated 50 million seabirds that breed in Alaska, fully 80 percent nest in this five-unit refuge.

The GULF OF ALASKA UNIT includes Forrester Island, Hazy Islands, and St. Lazaria Island in southeastern Alaska; the Chiswell Islands, Pye Islands, and Barren Islands along the southern shore of the Kenai Peninsula; Chisik and Duck islands in Cook Inlet; and scattered small islands around Kodiak and Afognak islands. Spectacular "bird cities" of colonial nesting seabirds and rookeries of sea lions are the major attractions of these wild, rugged places.

The 65-acre St. Lazaria Island is located 15 miles by boat from Sitka, in southeastern Alaska. It protects significant seabird nesting habitat, supporting roughly 500,000 birds of 15 species. Tufted puffins, rhinoceros auklets, ancient murrelets, and fork-tailed and Leach's storm petrels create nests by burrowing into the soil, and common and thick-billed murres, and pigeon guillemots lay their eggs on ledges and crevices along the sheer cliffs. The island's vegetation includes stands of Sitka spruce and thickets of salmonberry and elderberry.

The Chiswell Islands are scattered at the mouth of Kenai Fjords National Park's Aialik and Harris bays. More than a dozen islands and sea stacks support great numbers of breeding kittiwakes, murres, guillemots, and puffins.

Visitor activities include wildlife observation and photography, boat cruises, and boat charters.

Lodgings and meals are available in Sitka, Seward, and Homer.

The ALASKA PENINSULA UNIT, with more than 700 islands, islets, sea stacks, and rocks, includes Sutwik Island, the Semidi Islands, Shumagin Islands, and Sandman Islands along the southern shore of the Alaska Peninsula. Many of these small bits of land support tremendous concentrations of colonial nesting seabirds and sea lion rookeries. Many of this unit's species of birds and mammals are also found in the Gulf of Alaska Unit (see above).

Visitor access to this unit is very difficult, and some parts are closed to public visitation to avoid disturbing the sea lions.

The ALEUTIAN ISLANDS UNIT, with more than 2.7 million acres, takes in the 1,200-mile-long chain of approximately 200 treeless tundra islands. These mostly barren habitats support enormous concentrations of colonial nesting seabirds such as fulmars, storm petrels, kittiwakes, murres, murrelets, auklets, and puffins. Tiny Buldir Island, in the western Aleutians, supports more than 3.5 million birds in one colony! Sea lions, sea otters, and other marine mammals are also abundant in the Aleutian Islands Unit.

The archipelago actually consists of 57 spectacularly scenic, emergent volcanic summits of the Aleutian Ridge. Among several active volcanoes is the highest, Mt. Shishaldin, the steaming, snow-covered cone of which rises to 9,387 feet above sea level, on Unimak Island. Two other volcanoes rise above 6,500 feet in elevation—one also on Unimak and the other on Unalaska Island. Two that are above 5,000 feet dominate Atka and Tanaga islands, and three others reach over 4,000 feet. Many of the islands rise dramatically from the ocean, with sheer, 2,000-foot-high cliffs and waterfalls that plunge into the sea. Island ponds attract many kinds of ducks and other waterbirds, such as loons. More than 250 bird species have been seen here.

The primary reason for initially establishing a National Wildlife Refuge in the Aleutian Islands was to protect the sea otter, a species that was then on the brink of extinction. In the mid-1700s, Russian explorers discovered an abundance of this marine furbearer. By the end of that century, their merchants were demanding large quantities of the high-quality pelts from the Tlingit Indians of southeastern Alaska. This exploitation, which ran counter to the native people's ancient, conservative hunting traditions and practices, led to a sharp decline in the population of the sea otter. When Russia's economic incentive for controlling Alaska diminished, the United States acquired Russia's interests under the terms of the Treaty of Cession of 1867.

For several more decades, unregulated commercial exploitation continued to push the sea otter inexorably toward extinction. Finally, the killing was banned in 1911, and in 1913, the Aleutian Islands National Wildlife Refuge was established to protect a major part of the animal's habitat, in the hope that just maybe it wasn't too late to save the species. That hope has become a dream fulfilled. Today, there are roughly 150,000 sea otters, and their numbers are continuing to rebound. They are especially abundant between Adak and Kiska islands.

The Aleutians extend from the largest, Unimak Island, off the end of the Alaska Peninsula, westward to Attu Island. The latter is a special destination for birdwatchers eager to add a number of rare Asiatic species to their life list.

Seabirds are everywhere on the Aleutians. Their numbers are mind-boggling. Former director of the U.S. Fish and Wildlife Service Dr. Ira N. Gabrielson described an awesome flight of auklets on Kasatochi Island ("America's Greatest Bird Concentrations," *Audubon*, January-February 1941):

As the sun sank toward the horizon these birds began to leave their nests in increasing numbers and to fly out over the water in front of the great slides that harbored the colony. There were flocks of thousands, each a swiftly moving ribbon or patch against the sky, twisting and turning in their evolutions like sandpipers. The flocks played around and over each other until the air seemed awhirl with birds. Sometimes one long ribbon would cross another, both undulating as they went and alternately showing white and dark in the sun. As it became a little darker, one after another of these great flocks came sweeping with a roar like a waterfall over the rock where I was sitting. The flocks passed overhead, but hundreds of individuals dropped like falling leaves to land all around me on the rocks. Some took off again to join one of the flocks but most of them stood quiet for some time, looked around, and finally disappeared into their burrows.

Of the fishes, Dolly Varden, arctic char, and several species of Pacific salmon spawn in the islands' streams.

Visitor activities include wildlife observation, photography, hiking, cross-country skiing, wilderness camping in some places, fishing, and hunting. A visitor center with interpretive displays and programs is located on Adak Island.

Most of the islands are extremely difficult to reach. Fog, wind, and storms occur much of the year. When weather permits, scheduled flights go to Cold Bay, near the end of the Alaska Peninsula, and to Adak and Attu islands. Beyond Cold Bay, there are no lodgings. Some of the islands of the Aleutians have restricted entry to avoid disturbing the wildlife. Parts of several islands are owned by Native corporations, and permission to use these private properties is required. The refuge office can provide information on land status. The Fish and Wildlife Service advises, "military clearance is required to visit Adak, Shemya, Amchitka, and Attu islands."

Further information: Aleutian Islands Unit, Alaska Maritime NWR, PSC 486, Box 5251, FPO-AP 96506; telephone: (907) 592-2406.

The BERING SEA UNIT includes the Pribilof Islands, Hagemeister Island, the wilderness of St. Matthew Island, and small capes and headlands along Norton Sound. The Pribilof Islands support one of North America's largest seabird colonies, totaling about 3 million birds—notably red-legged and black-legged kittiwakes; murres; auklets; and puffins. The Pribilofs also contain large rookeries of the northern fur seal. In the spring, approximately a million of these mammals migrate to these islands' rocky beaches to breed. Adult males arrive in May and adult females in June. In the summer, 2-year-olds and some yearlings arrive. Arctic foxes and the introduced reindeer also inhabit the Pribilofs.

Visitor activities include wildlife observation and photography. Package tours can be arranged for guided visits to the Pribilof Islands.

The CHUKCHI SEA UNIT protects Chamisso and other islands in Kotzebue Sound; Little Diomede Island, just east of the International Date Line in Bering Strait; a number of sandy barrier islands along the Chukchi Sea; and Cape Thompson and Cape Lisburne on the mainland. The high coastal escarpments of Cape Lisburne support Alaska's northern coast's largest seabird nesting colony, including hundreds of thousands of murres and kittiwakes. Hundreds of walruses winter on the Bering Sea pack ice, summer at the ice's northward receding edge, and return southward ahead of the advancing ice to come ashore at this prominent cape. The highest point in the Cape Lisburne area is 2,034-foot Mt. Hamlet. The stunning, white Dall sheep and intriguing muskox inhabit this western end of the Brooks Range.

Although access is very difficult, visitor activities include wildlife observation and photography and wilderness camping.

The best months for wildlife observation on Alaska Maritime National Wildlife Refuge are June through mid-August, when seabirds are nesting and marine mammals are giving birth to and raising their pups. The Fish and Wildlife Service advises visitors to "Expect cold, wet, windy weather at any time and dress appropriately with rain gear and layers of warm clothing."

As for visiting the bird colonies and marine mammal rookeries of the Alaska Maritime refuge, all refuge communities are served by scheduled flights; state ferries regularly serve Sitka, Seward, Homer, and Kodiak during the summer and stop once a month at Unalaska, in the Aleutians. Scheduled boat tours and charter boat excursions operate out of Sitka, Seward, and Homer. In addition, charter boat trips are offered from such other coastal communities as Kodiak, Sand Point, Unalaska, and Nome.

Lodgings and meals are available in all towns near the refuge; most also provide campgrounds. There are no camping facilities or trails on the refuge.

Visitor centers are located at the main refuge headquarters in Homer and at the Aleutian Islands Unit headquarters in Adak.

Further information: Alaska Maritime National Wildlife Refuge, 2355 Kachemak Bay Drive, Suite 101, Homer, AK 99603; telephone: (907) 235-6546.

Alaska Peninsula, comprising 3.5 million acres in two units, was established in 1980 by the Alaska National Interest Lands Conservation Act. This refuge protects spectacularly scenic wildlife habitats along much of the Alaska Peninsula's chain of volcanoes, glaciers, tundra, and rugged southern coast in southwestern Alaska.

The refuge's towering peaks include 8,225-foot Mt. Veniaminof—one of the world's largest volcanic cones. This smoldering giant has a base almost 30 miles wide, which is greater than any active volcano on record. The summit crater is more than 20 miles in circumference, and with a 25-square-mile ice field, it is the most extensive crater glacier in North America.

Other scenic and ecological highlights of Alaska Peninsula Refuge include two long stretches of magnificent Pacific coastline containing sheer cliffs, rocky points and capes, strands of beach, and deep bays and fjords. There are numerous streams; glacial-fed Chignik and Black lakes, which support large salmon spawning runs; and the large Upper and Lower Ugashik lakes, known for salmon, grayling, and brown bears. In July and August, literally hundreds of these huge bears, which range extensively across the refuge's tundra lowlands, gather along the lakeshores to feast and fatten themselves on the abundance of fish.

Many thousands of caribou, comprising the northern Alaska Peninsula herd, annually migrate between King Salmon, near the refuge's northern boundary, and Port Moller, roughly 250 miles to the southwest. Other prominent species of terrestrial wildlife include moose, gray wolves, red foxes, and beavers. Inhabiting coastal waters are such marine mammals as Steller sea lions, harbor seals, sea otters, Dall and harbor porpoises, orcas (killer whales) of the family *Delphinidae*, and migratory humpback whales. Great numbers of seabirds, such as tufted and horned puffins, pigeon guillemots, and common murres, nest in colonies along the refuge's coastal cliffs. Migratory waterfowl and shorebirds pass through the refuge during their spring and autumn migrations. Widely scattered stands of cottonwoods, which are at the westernmost extent of this tree's range in North America, offer resting and nesting habitat for many kinds of songbirds.

Alaska Peninsula also serves as an invaluable salmon nursery. All five species of Pacific salmon—pink (humpy), king (chinook), sockeye (red), chum (dog), and coho (silver)—spawn in the streams and lakes of this refuge and the adjacent Becharof National Wildlife Refuge (see the text for that refuge, below). These massive fish runs, from June into August and September, provide the majority of the world's most pristine and valuable salmon fishery, located in the Bering Sea's Bristol Bay, to the north of the Alaska Peninsula.

Visitor activities include wildlife observation, photography, hiking, boating, wilderness camping, flightseeing, fishing, and hunting. The best months for wildlife observation in Alaska Peninsula Refuge are May to October. Information on hunting and fishing can be obtained from the refuge headquarters, the King Salmon Interagency Visitor Center, or the Alaska Department of Fish and Game, P.O. Box 37, King Salmon, AK 99613; telephone: (907) 246-3340. Extensive lands within the refuge are owned by Native corporations or individuals, and visitors are required to obtain permission to use these private properties. Information on land status can be supplied by refuge personnel.

The U.S. Fish and Wildlife Service advises prospective visitors to plan far ahead. As Alaska Peninsula refuge is remote and difficult to visit, arrangements need to be carefully planned. The refuge's terrain is extremely rough, and the weather is often foggy, rainy, and windy. Severe storms with rain, snow, and cold wind can occur at any time of the year. Rainfall varies greatly, from as much as 160 inches of precipitation on the Pacific side of the peninsula to around 20 inches on the Bristol Bay side. Visitors are advised to be well prepared with warm clothing, reliable rain gear, and extra food supplies in the event that inclement weather or other circumstances force an extended stay. A travel plan should be given to a relative or friend or to the refuge headquarters.

Visitors are cautioned to avoid unwanted encounters with bears by making noise (talking, singing, whistling) while hiking; camping away from streams, wildlife trails, berry patches, and freshly killed game; maintaining a clean camp; cooking and storing food away from the campsite and where it is not accessible to wildlife; and packing out all garbage. Further information is provided in the helpful pamphlet, *Bear Facts: The Essentials for Traveling in Bear Country*, available at the refuge office.

As mosquitoes, gnats, and other pesky insects can be prolific during the warmer months, insect repellent and headnets are a must. As a precaution against *giardiasis*, a common infectious waterborne intestinal parasite in Alaska, water should be microfiltered, boiled, or chemically treated before drinking.

Lodgings and meals are available in the small community of King Salmon. Guides and air-taxi services are also available there.

Access to the refuge is by small aircraft; there are no roads to or within the area.

Further information: Alaska Peninsula National Wildlife Refuge, P.O. Box 277, King Salmon, AK 99613; telephone: (907) 246-3339; and the King Salmon Interagency Visitor Center, P.O. Box 298, King Salmon, AK 99613; telephone: (907) 246-4250.

Arctic, containing 19.65 million acres, was initially established in 1960 as the Arctic National Wildlife Range, and was renamed as a refuge and enlarged to more than twice its prior size in 1980 by the Alaska National Interest Lands Conservation Act (ANILCA). This magnificent and vast national wildlife refuge in the northeastern corner of Alaska protects one of America's most awesome wildlife and wilderness areas, reaching from the heights of the massive Brooks Range, down to the Beaufort Sea coast.

The Arctic Refuge's scenic landscapes and fragile ecosystems are virtually unaltered by human impact, functioning naturally as they have for untold centuries. The arctic and subarctic habitats of this pristine wilderness include spectacularly massive mountains rising to 9,000 feet above sea level and glaciers slowly carving mountain valleys. To the north lies a vast expanse of treeless, tundra-covered foothills and flat coastal plain that is patterned by numerous braided rivers flowing northward to the Beaufort Sea, where lagoons and barrier islands extend along the coast. To the south of the Brooks Range, many rivers and streams wind through wide valleys of spruce-dominated boreal forest and a mosaic of lakes, ponds, sloughs, and marshy wetlands.

This pristine region supports a tremendous diversity and density of wildlife. From April to early June, an estimated 130,000 barren ground caribou (*Rangifer arcticus*) of the Porcupine herd annually migrate more than 900 miles, between wintering habitat south of the Brooks Range and their traditional summer calving grounds on the refuge's coastal plain. As explained by the U.S. Fish and Wildlife Service:

For centuries, animals from the Porcupine caribou herd have used the coastal tundra to obtain nourishment, calve, avoid insects, and escape predators. . . .

The Refuge coastal plain is very important to calving success and calf survival. . . . There are two main reasons for this. First, fewer wolves, brown bears, and golden eagles live on the coastal plain than in the adjacent foothills and mountains. As a result, the newborn calves have a better chance to survive their first week, until they become strong enough to outrun their pursuers.

In addition, polar, grizzly, and black bears, wolves, wolverines, arctic foxes, lemmings, resident herds of the reintroduced muskox, and other mammals inhabit the area. Each summer, more than 65 species of birds nest and breed here, including many thousands of ducks, geese, swans, loons, and shorebirds. More than 175 species of birds from four continents, along with a hundred additional species of wildlife, make use of this vital habitat. The U.S. Department of the Interior has stated that the coastal plain is ". . .the most biologically productive part of the Arctic Refuge for wildlife." It is no wonder that this remarkable place has been referred to as the "Serengeti of North America."

Visitor activities include wildlife observation, photography, hiking, wilderness camping, river rafting, kayaking, fishing, and hunting. A number of trek operators in Fairbanks provide guided tours and/or airdrops to certain places for unguided visits. The best months for wildlife observation on the Arctic refuge are June through August. Information on hunting and fishing can be obtained by contacting the refuge personnel or the Alaska Department of Fish and Game, 1300 College Road, Fairbanks, AK 99701; telephone: (907) 459-7200.

The Fish and Wildlife Service advises that prospective visitors plan far ahead. As the Arctic refuge is remote and very challenging to visit, arrangements need to be carefully planned. Weather can suddenly change, producing storms and strong winds. Strong, damp, cold winds and foggy or cloudy conditions often prevail along the coast. Freezing temperatures can occur even during the summer months, especially from the Brooks Range northward. Greater summer rainfall can typically be expected within and south of the mountains.

Consequently, visitors should be well prepared, with sufficient warm clothing; reliable rain gear; life jackets for floating or crossing rivers, lakes, or lagoons; and extra food supplies, in the event that inclement weather or other circumstances force an extended stay. A travel plan should be given to a relative or friend.

Visitors are urged to take precautions against unwanted encounters with bears and other potentially harmful wildlife by making noise (talking, singing, whistling) while hiking; camping away from streams, wildlife trails, berry patches, and freshly killed game; maintaining a clean camp; cooking and storing food away from the campsite and where it is not accessible to wildlife; and packing out all garbage. Further information is provided in the helpful pamphlet, *Bear Facts: The Essentials for Traveling in Bear Country*, available at the refuge office.

As mosquitoes, gnats, and other pesky insects can be prolific, especially during June and July, insect repellent and headnets are a must. As a precaution against *giardiasis*, a common infectious waterborne intestinal parasite in Alaska, water should be microfiltered, boiled, or chemically treated before drinking.

Access to the refuge is mostly by scheduled flights from Fairbanks to Fort Yukon, Kaktovik, or Deadhorse. Charter flights are available from there to sites within the refuge, although weather not infrequently delays flights into and out of the refuge.

Further information: Arctic National Wildlife Refuge, 101 Twelfth Avenue, Room 236, Fairbanks, AK 99701; telephone (907) 456-0250 or (800) 362-4546.

Becharof, consisting of 1.2 million acres, was established in 1980 by the Alaska National Interest Lands Conservation Act. The refuge protects a ruggedly scenic area of tundra wetlands, rolling hills, glaciers, and volcanic peaks in the upper Alaska Peninsula of southwestern Alaska.

One-quarter of this refuge is covered by vast Becharof Lake. This second largest lake in Alaska, measuring 35 miles by 15 miles, is the nursery for the world's second largest run of salmon. The refuge's spawning streams and Becharof Lake annually produce more than 10 million adult salmon for Bristol Bay, to the north of the Alaska Peninsula. In turn, this enormous fishery supports one of Alaska's largest concentrations of the huge brown bears.

Mt. Peulik, a 4,835-foot volcanic cone, is the refuge's most prominent peak. Ukinrek Maars is a geologically active group of volcanic craters, exhibiting evidence of a violent eruption of volcanic ash in 1977 (*maar* means the releasing of pressure through cracks in the earth).

The Gas Rocks, located on a conspicuous point of Becharof Lake's south shore, is a feature of special interest. As described by the U.S. Fish and Wildlife Service: "At this outcrop of fractured rock, carbon dioxide gases continuously seep through cracks in the rock. A hot spring at the base of Gas Rocks discharges water in excess of 120°F. This release of gases and the hot water spring are both related to the heating and upward movement of groundwater by subsurface volcanic heat."

The southern edge of the refuge consists of a magnificent stretch of rugged Pacific coastline, with sheer cliffs, rocky capes, deep bays, and tidal estuaries. Thousands of seabirds, including tufted and horned puffins, pigeon guillemots, and common murres, nest on the coastal cliffs. Freshwater and saltwater wetlands attract great numbers of waterfowl and shorebirds, as well as nesting bald eagles.

Becharof refuge is bounded by Alaska Peninsula National Wildlife Refuge to the southwest and Katmai National Park to the northeast. It provides habitats for virtually the same species of wildlife as the Alaska Peninsula refuge, with which Becharof is jointly managed. More than 470,000 acres are designated as the Becharof Wilderness, a unit of the National Wilderness Preservation System.

Visitor activities, best months for wildlife observation, precautions, weather, nearby lodging, meals, guide and air-taxi services, and required permission to use Native-owned lands within the refuge are all virtually the same as those that apply to Alaska Peninsula (see text for that refuge, above).

The fauna and flora species that have been recorded on Becharof Refuge are virtually the same as on Alaska Peninsula Refuge.

Lodgings and meals are available in the small community of King Salmon.

Access to the refuge is by small aircraft; there are no roads to or within the area.

Further information: Becharof National Wildlife Refuge, P.O. Box 277, King Salmon, AK 99613; telephone: (907) 246-3339; and at the King Salmon Interagency Visitor Center, P.O. Box 298, King Salmon, AK 99613; telephone: (907) 246-4250.

Innoko, encompassing 4.6 million acres in two separate units, was established in 1980 by the Alaska National Interest Lands Conservation Act. The refuge protects significant waterfowl breeding habitat in the central Yukon River Valley of west-central Alaska.

The Innoko River basin lies within the 3.85-million-acre southern unit, and the Kaiyuh Flats are within the 750,000-acre northern unit (the latter is administered jointly with the Koyukuk/Nowitna refuges). More than half of the refuge consists of vast wetlands (river flood plain, muskeg, and bogs) that attract as many as 100,000 ducks, geese, and other waterbirds; river corridors and wetlands provide essential habitat for influxes of neotropical migratory songbirds. Innoko also supports thousands of beavers, as well as numerous moose, grizzly and black bears, gray wolves, and the wintering Beaver Mountain herd of barren ground caribou.

The refuge's habitats include extensive black-spruce bogs, marshes, wetland meadows; rivers, streams, and sloughs; thousands of lakes and ponds; and many large islands in the Yukon River. The refuge's hilly terrain is covered with expanses of black spruce and paper birch.

Visitor activities include wildlife observation, photography, hiking (no trails), wilderness camping, float trips (notably on the Innoko River), fishing, hunting, and panning for gold along some of the upper tributaries of the Innoko River. The historic Iditarod Trail also goes through the refuge. Information regarding fishing and hunting can be obtained by contacting the refuge headquarters or the Alaska Department of Fish and Game, McGrath, AK 99627; telephone: (907) 524-3323.

The Fish and Wildlife Service advises that prospective visitors plan far ahead. As Innoko Refuge is remote and difficult to visit, arrangements need to be carefully planned. Visitors should bring sufficient warm clothing; reliable rain gear, including hip boots, for much of the refuge; and extra food supplies, in the event that inclement weather or other circumstances force an extended stay. A travel plan should be given to a relative or friend or to the refuge headquarters.

Precautions should be taken to avoid unwanted encounters with bears by camping away from streams, wildlife trails, berry patches, and freshly killed game; maintaining a clean camp; cooking and storing food away from the campsite and where it is not accessible to wildlife; packing out all garbage; and making noise (talking, singing, whistling) while hiking. According to the Fish and Wildlife Service, "Another recommendation for anyone traveling on the refuge would be to carry a firearm (if they are qualified to do so). Because our bears are not used to seeing/hearing people, making noise may actually encourage them to come in to investigate what is making all that noise. On the whole, our bears are curious and not afraid of people." Further information is provided in the helpful pamphlet, *Bear Facts: The Essentials for Traveling in Bear Country*, which is available at the refuge office.

As mosquitoes, gnats, and other pesky insects can be prolific during the warmer months, insect repellent and headnets are a must. As a precaution against *giardiasis*, a common infectious waterborne intestinal parasite in Alaska, water should be microfiltered, boiled, or chemically treated before drinking.

Access to Innoko Refuge is by floatplane and boat. There are no roads to or within the area.

Further information: Innoko National Wildlife Refuge (southern unit), P.O. Box 69, McGrath, AK 99627; telephone: (907) 524-3251. Innoko NWR (northern unit), c/o Koyukuk/Nowitna Refuge Complex, P.O. Box 287, Galena, AK 99741; telephone: (907) 656-1231 or (800) 656-1231 (within Alaska).

Izembek, comprising 417,533 acres, was established in 1960 to protect an "international cross-roads" for enormous numbers of migratory waterfowl and shorebirds at the tip of the Alaska Peninsula in southwestern Alaska. Autumn is especially awesome, when a quarter million migratory birds pour through Bristol Bay and across the peninsula from their arctic and subarctic Alaskan and Siberian breeding grounds.

The major ecological highlight of this refuge is the 30-mile-long by 5-mile-wide Izembek Lagoon, which is also a state game refuge and a designated Wetland of International Importance, along the Bering Sea coast. In May and again in September and October, virtually the entire world's population of Pacific black brant gathers here to rest and feed on one of the world's most extensive beds of eelgrass—a flowering plant of the pondweed family with grasslike leaves.

This lagoon and other estuaries and bays also attract tens of thousands of Taverner's Canada geese and large concentrations of numerous other migratory waterfowl, such as green-winged teal, mallards, and pintails. Many thousands of emperor geese, most of this species' world population, stop here on their spring and autumn migrations, several thousand of which winter on the refuge. Although a population of tundra swans inhabits the refuge most of the year, in winter these birds usually fly to nearby Unimak Island, where thermal springs keep the water ice-free. This small-scale movement of 70 miles or so contrasts with that of other populations of this species that migrate thousands of miles from their breeding grounds to wintering habitat in the lower 48 states.

The largest of Izembek refuge's prominent terrestrial mammals are the brown bears. As many as six of these huge carnivores per square mile often hunt for fish and other food along the river corridors. Moose are occasionally seen. In the autumn and winter, barren ground caribou of the southern Alaska Peninsula herd migrate through the refuge.

Beginning in midsummer, hundreds of thousands of three species of Pacific salmon—pink (humpy), sockeye (red), and chum (dog)—swim from the sea to river and lake spawning grounds in the refuge. From June into October, a few king (chinook) salmon also make their runs to the refuge's streams and lakes. And in early autumn, coho (silver) salmon return to spawn.

In addition to Izembek's lagoons and bays, there are lots of lakes, ponds, marshes, sedge and grass meadows, upland heaths, streams, glaciated U-shaped valleys, glaciers, snowfields, and simmering volcanic peaks. The most prominent mountain summits, located along the boundary with the Pavlov Unit of Alaska Peninsula refuge, are Frosty Peak, Mt. Dutton, and the spectacular Aghileen Pinnacles. Most of the refuge is designated as a 300,000-acre unit of the National Wilderness Preservation System.

Visitor activities include wildlife observation, photography, hiking (no trails), wilderness camping, berry picking, fishing, and hunting. Izembek refuge is renowned for waterfowl and brown bear observation and hunting. The best months for wildlife observation on Izembek refuge are September and October. Information on hunting and fishing is available by contacting the refuge headquarters or the Alaska Department of Fish and Game, P.O. Box 25526, Juneau, AK 99802; telephone: (907) 267-2137. Guiding services are available; a current list of permitted guides is available by contacting the refuge headquarters. Several thousand acres within of the refuge consist of Native-owned inholdings, and visitors are urged to respect these private properties. Information on land status can be obtained from refuge personnel.

The U.S. Fish and Wildlife Service warns that rainy, foggy, and windy weather is a common occurrence. "Fog, drizzle, and overcast skies are often succeeded by violent storms and bitter cold snaps that slow down all activity. It is not unusual for an entire year to go by with only a few days of mostly clear skies." The average of 35 inches of precipitation falls on more than 200 days annually, with spring normally the driest season and autumn the wettest. Consequently, visitors should bring warm clothing, reliable rain gear, and extra food supplies, in the event that inclement weather or other circumstances force an extended stay. A travel plan should be given to a relative or friend or to refuge headquarters.

Visitors are advised to take precautions to avoid unwanted encounters with bears by making noise (talking, singing, whistling) while hiking; camping away from streams, wildlife trails, berry patches, and freshly killed game; maintaining a clean camp; cooking and storing food away from the campsite and where it is not accessible to wildlife; and packing out all garbage. Further information is provided in the helpful pamphlet, *Bear Facts: The Essentials for Traveling in Bear Country*, available at the refuge office.

As mosquitoes, gnats, and other pesky insects can be prolific during the warmer months, insect repellent and headnets are a must. As a precaution against *giardiasis*, a common infectious waterborne intestinal parasite in Alaska, water should be microfiltered, boiled, or chemically treated before drinking.

Lodgings, meals, and vehicle rentals are available in the small community of Cold Bay, which is located less than a mile from the refuge boundary.

Access to the refuge is by scheduled airline flights from Anchorage to Cold Bay.

Further information: Izembek National Wildlife Refuge, P.O. Box 127, Cold Bay, AK 99571; telephone: (907) 532-2445.

Kanuti, encompassing 1.6 million acres, was established in 1980 by the Alaska National Interest Lands Conservation Act. The refuge straddles the Arctic Circle and protects a vast river basin, Kanuti Flats, which is drained by the Kanuti and Koyukuk rivers as they flow westward across central Alaska. There are numerous meandering streams, marshes, black-spruce bogs, and meadows; hundreds of lakes and ponds; and extensive areas of white-spruce-dominated boreal forest (*taiga*). Throughout the refuge, the forest merges into taiga, where tall, slender spruces are widely scattered across low-lying uplands.

The refuge's wetlands provide important breeding habitat for large numbers of migratory waterfowl, such as trumpeter and tundra swans; greater white-fronted geese and many species of ducks; other waterbirds, such as loons and grebes; and lots of shorebirds. More than 100 species of birds have been recorded here. Some of the more prominent mammals are moose, part of the wintering Western Arctic herd of barren ground caribou, grizzly and black bears, gray wolves, and beavers. Among the more than 15 fish species are king (chinook), coho (silver), and chum (dog) salmon that spawn in the refuge's rivers and streams; and northern pike, sheefish, whitefish, arctic grayling, Dolly Varden, and arctic char.

Visitor activities include wildlife observation, photography, hiking (no trails), boating, float trips, wilderness camping, fishing, and hunting. The best months for wildlife observation on Kanuti refuge are June through August and March/April. Guiding services are available in Bettles/Evansville, near the refuge's northern boundary, and in Fairbanks and Anchorage. A refuge field office and a joint Kanuti NWR–Gates of the Arctic National Park and Preserve visitor center are located in the village of Bettles, near the refuge's northern boundary. Information about hunting and fishing can be obtained by contacting the refuge personnel or the Alaska Department of Fish and Game, Galena, AK; telephone: (907) 656-1345. Roughly one-quarter of the Kanuti refuge consists of Native-owned inholdings, and permission is required to use these private properties. Information on land status can be obtained from refuge offices.

The U.S. Fish and Wildlife Service advises that prospective visitors plan far ahead. As Kanuti refuge is remote and difficult to visit, arrangements need to be carefully planned. Visitors should bring sufficient warm clothing; reliable rain gear, including hip boots; and extra food supplies, in the event that inclement weather or other circumstances force an extended stay. A travel plan should be given to a relative or friend or to the refuge headquarters.

Precautions should be taken to avoid unwanted encounters with bears by making noise (talking, singing, whistling) while hiking; camping away from streams, wildlife trails, berry patches, and freshly killed game; maintaining a clean camp; storing food away from the campsite and where it is not accessible to wildlife; and packing out all garbage. Further information is provided in the helpful pamphlet, *Bear Facts: The Essentials for Traveling in Bear Country*, available at the refuge office.

As mosquitoes, gnats, and other pesky insects can be prolific during the warmer months, insect repellent and headnets are a must. As a precaution against *giardiasis*, a common infectious waterborne intestinal parasite in Alaska, water should be microfiltered, boiled, or chemically treated before drinking.

Lodgings, meals, and camping supplies are available in the village of Bettles, near the refuge's northern boundary.

Access to Kanuti refuge is by daily flights from Fairbanks to Evansville/Bettles, near the refuge's northern boundary; and to Allakaket/Alatna, near the western boundary. There are no roads or other developments within the refuge. Charter flights are available from Bettles to certain lakes and river gravel bars in the refuge.

Further information: Kanuti National Wildlife Refuge, 101 Twelfth Avenue, Room 262, Fairbanks, AK 99701; telephone: (907) 456-0329.

Kenai, containing 1.97 million acres, was established in 1941 as the Kenai National Moose Range, to protect the population of Kenai moose—the largest population of its species. In 1980, this vast area, encompassing much of the northern and western parts of the Kenai Peninsula in south-central Alaska, was expanded and redesignated by the Alaska National Interest Lands Conservation Act as the Kenai National Wildlife Refuge.

The spectacular Kenai Mountains, along the boundary with Kenai Fjords National Park, consist of jagged, snowy peaks that rise to more than 6,600 feet above sea level, the huge expanse of the Harding Icefield, and a multitude of glaciers. Lower elevations of the refuge consist of rolling foothills; vast lowland forests of spruces, birches, and aspens; numerous rivers and streams; more than 1,200 lakes and ponds; and extensive wetland habitat. Kenai is one of only two refuges in Alaska that is accessible by road (Tetlin is the other).

The refuge's diverse habitats support a wealth of wildlife. The white Dall sheep and mountain goats live high in the rugged mountains. Moose are often seen in willow thickets and other marshy and swampy places. Kenai brown bears and the smaller black bears gather along salmon-spawning rivers and streams during the summer and early autumn months. Barren ground caribou have been successfully reestablished in two parts of the refuge, after the original Kenai population of this species was wiped out by enormous, habitat-altering fires in 1890 and after subsequent hunting of the last few animals by 1912.

Major Pacific salmon runs occur in the refuge's Kenai and Russian rivers. King (chinook) and sockeye (red) salmon runs are from late June through July, pink salmon (humpy) in August, and coho (silver) in August and September. Other Kenai fish include steelhead, rainbow trout, arctic grayling, lake trout, Dolly Varden, and arctic char.

Friends of the Kenai National Wildlife Refuge is a nonprofit support group that is assisting the refuge in many ways.

The refuge is open daily. There is no entrance fee. The visitor center, which is open daily except some national holidays, is located just south of Soldotna (following directional signs, turn east immediately south of the Kenai River bridge). A visitor information station, open daily in summer, is located at the junction of State Route 1 (the Sterling Highway) and the Skilak Lake Loop Road.

Visitor activities include wildlife observation, photography, seasonal interpretive programs, hiking (more than 200 miles of established trails and other routes), driving (more than 100 miles of paved and unpaved roads—notably the nearly 20-mile unpaved Skilak Lake Loop Road), camping at a half dozen campgrounds (campsite fee charged at Kenai–Russian River, Hidden Lake, and Upper Skilak), backcountry camping (numerous small, rustic overnight campsites are provided), canoeing (brochure/map is available), boating, whitewater rafting, horse pack excursions, cross-country skiing, snowshoeing, snowmobiling, fishing, and hunting on most of the refuge.

The best months for wildlife observation on Kenai Refuge are May to October. Information on hunting and fishing is available at the visitor center or by contacting the Alaska Department of Fish and Game, 333 Raspberry Avenue, Anchorage, AK 99512; telephone: (907) 344-0541. Snowmobiling is permitted only in specifically designated areas outside the Kenai Wilderness from December through April, and then only when snow depth is sufficient to avoid damaging underlying vegetation.

One of this refuge's wilderness recreation highlights is the extensive network of canoeing routes through many of the beautiful lakes. The U.S. Fish and Wildlife Service requires that canoeists register at the trailhead and recommends giving a travel plan to family or friends. As these routes are within a unit of the refuge's Kenai Wilderness, no motorized watercraft are allowed on the canoe system, nor are wheeled vehicles permitted on any of the canoe system's portages. Canoe rentals are available near the refuge.

Hiking trails in the Skilak Lake vicinity include the easy 1.4-mile Hidden Creek Trail and 4.5-mile Seven Lakes Trail; the moderately difficult 1-mile Bear Mountain Trail, providing a great view at the end of the 500-foot climb; the 2.6-mile Skilak Lookout Trail, providing a view of Skilak and other lakes at the end of a 750-foot climb; the strenuous 4-mile Fuller Lakes Trail, climbing 1,700 feet; and the 1.5-mile Skyline Trail, climbing 3,100 feet. Trails elsewhere include three minimally maintained routes that begin at trailheads along the northern shore of

24-mile-long Tustumena Lake: moderately difficult 16.5-mile Bear Creek Trail, climbing 3,100 feet; 7.7-mile Moose Creek Trail, climbing 3,100 feet; and the strenuous 4.6-mile Lake Emma Trail, climbing 2,400 feet.

Visitors should take precautions against unwanted encounters with bears by making noise (talking, singing, whistling) while hiking; camping away from streams, wildlife trails, berry patches, and freshly killed game; maintaining a clean camp; cooking and storing food away from the campsite and where it is not accessible to wildlife; and packing out all garbage where trash receptacles are not provided. Further information is provided in the helpful pamphlet, *Bear Facts: The Essentials for Traveling in Bear Country*, available at the refuge office.

Campers are urged to be very careful with fire. During periods of extreme fire danger, fires are prohibited. Boaters and canoeists are warned to be extremely alert for sudden strong winds and the danger of capsizing into the cold water. As mosquitoes, gnats, and other pesky insects can be prolific during the warmer months, insect repellent and headnets are a must. As a precaution against *giardiasis*, a common infectious waterborne intestinal parasite in Alaska, water should be microfiltered, boiled, or chemically treated before drinking.

Lodgings, meals, camping supplies, rental equipment, and outfitters are available at Cooper Landing, Soldotna, Kenai, and Homer.

Access to the Kenai Refuge from Anchorage is approximately 110 scenic miles on State Route 1. There are flights from Anchorage to airports at Kenai and Homer.

Further information: Kenai National Wildlife Refuge, P.O. Box 2139, Soldotna, AK 99669; telephone: (907) 262-7021.

Kodiak, encompassing 1.865 million acres, was established in 1941. The refuge protects roughly the southern two-thirds of ruggedly scenic Kodiak Island, adjacent Uganik Island, a small part of Afognak Island, and adjacent Ban Island, in the Kodiak Archipelago across Shelikof Strait from the Alaska Peninsula, in southwestern Alaska. This refuge provides ecologically important habitat for a tremendous diversity of wildlife, notably the approximately 2,500 huge Kodiak brown bears—the world's largest carnivore.

Kodiak's stunning landscapes include rugged mountains, some of which rise 4,000 feet from the sea; hundreds of miles of coastline, including many fjordlike inlets and bays; hundreds of miles of salmon streams; 11 large lakes; abundant bogs, marshes, and sedge and grass meadows; extensive thickets of alders and willows; and wooded areas of Sitka spruces and black cottonwoods.

More than 235 species of birds have been recorded on the refuge. Coastal cliffs, islets, and rocks support large colonies of seabirds, such as tufted and horned puffins, pigeon guillemots, three kinds of cormorants, glaucous-winged gulls, and black-legged kittiwakes. Common murres and marbled murrelets also nest here. Bays, fjordlike inlets, and tidal marshlands are a mecca for large concentrations of seabirds and waterfowl. In winter and spring, a few emperor geese and great numbers of another goose, the Pacific black brant, pause here on their migration north to breeding grounds along the coast of Alaska and Siberia.

Numerous ducks that nest on Kodiak Refuge include green-winged teal, mallards, northern pintails, American wigeons, harlequin ducks, goldeneyes, and common and red-breasted mergansers.

Large concentrations of wintering ducks include greater scaup, king and Steller's eiders, long-tailed ducks (oldsquaws), buffleheads, and black scoters; and there is also a resident population of harlequin ducks. Bald eagles, willow and rock ptarmigans, American dippers, and boreal owls are also among the common residents.

From late May into September, five species of Pacific salmon—pink (humpy), king (chinook), sockeye (red), chum (dog), and coho (silver)—leave the ocean to spawn by the hundreds of thousands in Kodiak's streams. The refuge's spawning streams supply well over half of the salmon commercially harvested in the vicinity of the Kodiak Archipelago. Other common Kodiak fishes include steelhead, rainbow trout, Dolly Varden, and arctic char.

The refuge is open daily. There is no entrance fee. A visitor center with interpretive exhibits and trip-planning information is located 1 mile north of the state airport on Buskin River Road. It is open on weekdays except national holidays, and seasonally on Saturday and Sunday afternoons.

Visitor activities include wildlife observation, photography, hiking (no maintained trails, and hiking in most areas is extremely difficult), interpretive programs, bear-viewing charter flights, sea kayaking, rafting, canoeing, wilderness camping, fishing, and hunting. The best months for observing bears on Kodiak refuge are July through September. Information on hunting and fishing is available at the visitor center or by contacting the Alaska Department of Fish and Game, 211 Mission Road, Kodiak, AK 99615; telephone: (907) 486-1880. Outside the refuge on Kodiak Island, campgrounds are provided at Fort Abercrombie State Historical Park, Buskin River State Recreation Site, and Pasagshak River State Recreation Site. Guide services and charter flights and boats are available in the town of Kodiak. A variety of interpretive tours are provided by a number of commercial tour operators (it is recommended that prospective visitors contact the refuge office to make certain an operator has a current special-use permit). The Kodiak Island Convention and Visitors Bureau, 100 Marine Way, Kodiak, AK 99615; telephone: (907) 486-4782, and the Kodiak Chamber of Commerce (at the same address); telephone: (907) 486-5557, can also provide helpful information regarding ecotourism services.

The U.S. Fish and Wildlife Service recommends checking with refuge personnel while planning a visit, to be aware of what activities are permitted, what precautions to take, and what regulations are applicable. Some lands within the refuge are Native-owned; as permission to use these private properties is required, the refuge staff should be contacted for information on land status.

Visitors are advised to take precautions to avoid unwanted encounters with bears by making noise (talking, singing, whistling) while hiking; camping away from streams, wildlife trails, berry patches, and freshly killed game; maintaining a clean camp; cooking and storing food away from the campsite and where it is not accessible to wildlife; and packing out all garbage. Further information is provided in the helpful pamphlet, *Bear Facts: The Essentials for Traveling in Bear Country*, available at the refuge office.

As mosquitoes, gnats, and other pesky insects can be prolific during the warmer months, insect repellent and headnets are a must. As a precaution against *giardiasis*, a common infectious waterborne intestinal parasite in Alaska, water should be microfiltered, boiled, or chemically treated before drinking.

The weather on Kodiak Island is generally rainy or drizzly and cool, often with wind and sudden storms. Consequently, visitors should bring warm clothing, reliable rain gear, and extra food supplies in the event that inclement weather or other circumstances force an extended stay. Stormy weather can unexpectedly delay flights off the island for days at a time.

Native terrestrial mammals of Kodiak Refuge include Kodiak brown bear, red fox, river otter, short-tailed weasel, and little brown bat; and introduced species include mountain goat, Sitka black-tailed deer, red and arctic foxes, beaver, and snowshoe hare. Among the marine mammals in the waters around the refuge are sea otter, Steller sea lion, harbor seal, Dall and harbor porpoises, orca (killer whale) of the family *Delphinidae*, and minke and humpback whales.

Lodgings and meals are available in the town of Kodiak. Within the refuge, seven cabins are available by reservation, for which a lottery is held four times annually.

Access to Kodiak Island is by scheduled daily flights from Anchorage, and by state ferry three times weekly from either Seward or Homer. Access to the refuge from the town of Kodiak is by charter flights and by charter or tour boats. There are no roads to or within the refuge.

Further information: Kodiak National Wildlife Refuge, 1390 Buskin River Road, Kodiak, AK 99615; telephone: (907) 487-2600.

Koyukuk, comprising 3.55 million acres, was established in 1980 by the Alaska National Interest Lands Conservation Act, primarily to protect the vast lower Koyukuk River wetlands floodplain, north of this river's junction with the Yukon River, in west-central Alaska. The refuge's central feature is the meandering course of the broad Koyukuk, Alaska's third largest river, which twists and turns through 400 miles of the refuge.

Beyond the riverbanks sprawls an intricate maze of rivers, streams, sloughs, and hundreds of lakes and ponds. The refuge's diverse habitats consist of shrubby alder and willow thickets; dense forests of white spruce, Alaska paper birch, and quaking aspen; extensive black-spruce bogs; and white-spruce-dotted taiga that merges into the treeless tundra extending across gently rolling hills and mountains.

These habitats support a great variety of wildlife that primarily includes many thousands of nesting ducks and geese, hundreds of tundra and trumpeter swans, and numerous sandhill cranes and shorebirds. Moose and black bears are abundant; beavers and gray wolves are common; and the half-million-head Western Arctic herd of barren ground caribou often winters in the northern part of the refuge. Fish species include king (chinook), chum (dog), and coho (silver) salmon that make their spawning runs up the rivers and streams in summer and early autumn, and the arctic grayling and northern pike.

A scenic highlight of the refuge is the 10,000-acre active dune field, known as the Nogabahara Sand Dunes. These desert-like, large, wind-sculpted dunes were created more than 10,000 years ago when large quantities of sand from melting glaciers were blown into a nearly circular, 6-mile-wide expanse. The dunes and a significant waterfowl production area, Three Day Slough, are located within the refuge's 4,000-acre Koyukuk Wilderness.

Visitor activities include wildlife observation, photography, hiking (no trails), boating, rafting, kayaking, canoeing, wilderness camping, dogsledding, snowmobiling (except in Koyukuk Wilderness), fishing, and hunting. The upper stretch of the Koyukuk River, from Hughes down to Huslia, is the best for float trips. Information on available guiding and transporting services (by boat or air-taxi) is available by contacting the refuge headquarters.

The best months for wildlife observation on Koyukuk Refuge are June to September. Information on fishing and hunting can be obtained by contacting the refuge headquarters or the Alaska Department of Fish and Game, P.O. Box 209, Galena, AK; telephone: (907) 656-1345.

As there are some Native Athabaskan land inholdings within the refuge, visitors are urged to respect these private properties. Information on land status can be obtained from refuge personnel.

The U.S. Fish and Wildlife Service advises that prospective visitors should plan far ahead. As Koyukuk Refuge is remote and difficult to visit, arrangements need to be carefully planned. Visitors should bring sufficient warm clothing; reliable rain gear; and extra food supplies in the event that inclement weather or other circumstances force an extended stay. A travel plan should be given to a relative or friend or to the refuge headquarters.

Precautions should be taken to avoid unwanted encounters with bears by making noise (talking, singing, whistling) while hiking; camping away from streams, wildlife trails, berry patches, and freshly killed game; maintaining a clean camp; cooking and storing food away from the campsite and where it is not accessible to wildlife; and packing out all garbage. Further information is provided in the helpful pamphlet, *Bear Facts: The Essentials for Traveling in Bear Country*, available at the refuge office.

As mosquitoes, gnats, and other pesky insects can be prolific during the warmer months, insect repellent and headnets are a must. As a precaution against *giardiasis*, a common infectious waterborne intestinal parasite in Alaska, water should be microfiltered, boiled, or chemically treated before drinking.

Birds, mammals, trees, and other plants of Koyukuk Refuge are virtually the same as on Innoko.

Lodgings and meals are available in Galena.

Access to Koyukuk Refuge is by scheduled commercial or charter flights from Anchorage and Fairbanks to Galena, or charter flights to nearby villages. There are no roads or other developments within the refuge.

Further information: Koyukuk National Wildlife Refuge, c/o Koyukuk/Nowitna Refuge Complex, P.O. Box 287, Galena, AK 99741; telephone: (907) 656-1231 or (800) 656-1231 (within Alaska).

Nowitna, consisting of 1.56 million acres, was established in 1980 by the Alaska National Interest Lands Conservation Act. The refuge protects the lower two-thirds of the 300-mile Nowitna River and its extensive wetlands basin in central Alaska. This river rises in the Kuskokwim Mountains, flows through 15-mile Nowitna Canyon, and meanders northward across a broad floodplain to the Yukon River, which forms the refuge's northern boundary.

Numerous rivers and streams, hundreds of lowland lakes and ponds, and associated wetlands provide important breeding habitat for large numbers of ducks, geese, swans, sandhill cranes, loons, and other waterbirds. Moose, grizzly and black bears, gray wolves, pine marten, and wintering caribou are among the more prominent of the refuge's mammals. Fish species include king (chinook) and chum salmon that spawn in the rivers and streams; and northern pike, sheefish, and arctic grayling.

Much of Nowitna Refuge consists of a boreal forest that is dominated by white and black spruces and a mixture of balsam poplars and Alaska paper birches. Many of the white spruces tower more than 80 feet along the banks of the nationally designated Nowitna Wild River as it flows through Nowitna Canyon. Where the extensive lowland forests extend onto higher ground, a transition habitat known as taiga, consisting of widely scattered tall, slender spruces amid low-growing shrubby vegetation, merges with the still higher treeless tundra.

Visitor activities include wildlife observation, photography, hiking (no trails), wilderness camping, boating, float trips on the Nowitna River (a Class I river), dogsledding, snowmobiling, fishing, and hunting. The best months for wildlife observation on Nowitna refuge are June to September. Information on fishing and hunting can be obtained by contacting the refuge headquarters or the Alaska Department of Fish and Game in Galena, AK; telephone: (907) 656-1345.

The U.S. Fish and Wildlife Service advises that prospective visitors should plan far ahead. As Nowitna Refuge is remote and difficult to visit, arrangements need to be carefully planned. Visitors should bring sufficient warm clothing, reliable rain gear, and extra food supplies, in the event that inclement weather or other circumstances force an extended stay. A travel plan should be given to a relative or friend or to the refuge headquarters.

Precautions should be taken to avoid unwanted encounters with bears by making noise while hiking (talking, singing, whistling); camping away from streams, wildlife trails, berry patches, and freshly killed game; maintaining a clean camp; cooking and storing food away from the campsite and where it is not accessible to wildlife; and packing out all garbage. Further information is provided in the helpful pamphlet, *Bear Facts: The Essentials for Traveling in Bear Country,* available at the refuge office.

As mosquitoes, gnats, and other pesky insects can be prolific during the warmer months, insect repellent and headnets are a must. As a precaution against *giardiasis,* a common infectious waterborne intestinal parasite in Alaska, water should be microfiltered, boiled, or chemically treated before drinking.

Lodgings and groceries are available in the village of Ruby, just outside the western end of the refuge.

Access to Nowitna Refuge is by charter floatplane to the refuge's larger lakes or rivers, or by boat by way of the Yukon River and Nowitna rivers. There are no roads or other developments within the refuge.

Further information: Nowitna National Wildlife Refuge, c/o Koyukuk/Nowitna Refuge Complex, P.O. Box 287, Galena, AK 99741; telephone: (907) 656-1231.

Selawik, containing 2.15 million acres, was established in 1980 by the Alaska National Interest Lands Conservation Act. The refuge protects a vast mosaic of habitats in northwestern Alaska. These include treeless tundra hills, spruce-dotted taiga, wooded boreal areas of white spruce and paper birch, and extensive wetlands, including 24,000 lakes and ponds, bogs, sedge and grass meadows, willow thickets, numerous rivers and streams, the Kobuk River delta, and coastal estuaries.

The name *Selawik* is an Inupial Eskimo word that means "place of sheefish." In addition to the anadromous sheefish that spawn in the refuge's rivers and streams, there are northern pike, whitefish, and arctic grayling that live in the refuge's rivers, streams, lakes, and ponds.

The Waring Mountains, extending along the northeastern part of the refuge where it adjoins the Kobuk Valley National Park, are within the 240,000-acre Selawik Wilderness. The upper stretch of the Selawik River has been nationally designated as the roadless Selawik Wild River. The Continental Divide runs along the southeastern edge of the refuge, where Grizzly Peak rises to 2,398 feet above sea level.

The refuge's extensive wetlands provide significant breeding and nesting habitat for many thousands of migratory ducks and geese; tundra swans; loons and other waterbirds; shorebirds; and sandhill cranes. More than 180 species of birds have been recorded on Selawik. Prominent mammals include moose, grizzly and black bears, gray wolves, and several hundred thousand barren ground caribou that migrate across the refuge in spring and autumn.

Assistant refuge manager Jimmy Fox (2001) described his observations of moose:

Last March, I had the good fortune to be an observer for a moose survey on Selawik National Wildlife Refuge. . . . One of the state's greatest winter concentrations of these huge deer occurs in the Tagagawik River valley, in the southern portion of the . . . refuge. Our survey found that more than one thousand moose spend much of the winter along this small, meandering river and the adjacent uplands. Abundant willow shrubs attract the ungulates to the valley. Some stay year-round, while others move up the drainages to spend summer at higher elevations in the Selawik Hills and Purcell Mountains. Wind and lack of forage force most of these animals back down into the river valley by November.

Late March and early April can be a good time of year to see moose, as they congregate in certain areas before calving (travel is only by small, ski-equipped airplane or by snowmobile, and then by snowshoe for walking around). Late April and early May is the best time to witness the northward migration of the Western Arctic caribou herd (flightseeing may be the only option).

As for observing migratory birds, the Fish and Wildlife Service says, "Late May is good. . . . but don't expect to get to the refuge unless you have made arrangements to stay out in a camp until breakup is complete and you can be retrieved by boat (in early June!). June has the advantage of few bugs, but rivers can be high and treacherous with floating logs and newly undercut banks. One ought to see a fair number of migratory and breeding birds, especially waterfowl. July is serious bug season, with not many critters moving around. Sheefish start moving up Selawik River. August can be rainy (actually, any month of summer can be rainy despite a typical annual precipitation of just 12 inches), but caribou start moving north around the middle of the month. September is sport-hunting season (moose and caribou are the main species sought), so expect little solitude on the major rivers. Plan to be out of the field by September 20; freeze up can happen this early or sometimes even earlier."

Visitor activities include wildlife observation, photography, river float trips, hiking, wilderness camping, cross-country skiing, dogsledding, snowmobiling, fishing, and hunting. Information about hunting and fishing can be obtained by contacting the refuge personnel or the Alaska Department of Fish and Game in Kotzebue; telephone: (907) 442-3420. Large parts of the

Selawik along the coast, around two villages, and in scattered allotments, are owned by Native corporations and individuals. Visitors are urged to respect these private properties. Information on land status can be obtained from the refuge office.

The U.S. Fish and Wildlife Service urges that prospective visitors plan far ahead. As Selawik refuge is remote and difficult to visit, arrangements need to be carefully planned. Sudden changes in the weather commonly occur. Visitors should bring sufficient warm clothing; reliable rain gear, including hip boots; and extra food supplies, in the event that inclement weather or other circumstances force an extended stay. A travel plan should be given to a relative or friend or to the refuge headquarters.

As former refuge manager Leslie Kerr explains:

It is often difficult to get an impression of scale from reading a guidebook, so let's put things in perspective. A round trip from refuge headquarters in Kotzebue to Selawik Hot Springs, at the opposite end of the refuge, is about 550 miles via staked trails. In terms of distance, this would be equivalent to making a one-way snowmobile trip from Washington, D.C., to Detroit, or a round trip from Washington, D.C., to New York City. Of course, only the distance would be equivalent. On Selawik Refuge you would not pass any gas stations, travel on any roads or improved trails, or have a wireless network over which to summon help.

Instead, you would have the satisfaction of knowing you were 600 miles from the nearest part of the highway system. You would be surrounded by 2.15 million acres of refuge wildlands. You would likely see other people only as you passed through small Inupiat Eskimo villages. You would experience the power and solitude of the Arctic landscape the minute you stepped away from the snowgo [snowmobile] that allowed you to get there.

While one may hike in summer and cross-country ski in winter, visitors should be aware that the tundra environment can make both activities impractical. The tussock tundra characteristic of much of the refuge is extremely difficult to walk across, and may be hazardous to one's ankles and knees. Windy winter conditions, temperature extremes, and scant snowfall can make it difficult to ski, as well.

Visitors are also advised to take precautions against unwanted encounters with bears by making noise (talking, singing, whistling) while hiking; camping away from streams, wildlife trails, berry patches, and freshly killed game; maintaining a clean camp; cooking and storing food away from the campsite and where it is not accessible to wildlife; and packing out all garbage. Further information is provided in the helpful pamphlet, *Bear Facts: The Essentials for Traveling in Bear Country*, available at the refuge office.

As mosquitoes, gnats, and other pesky insects can be prolific during the warmer months, insect repellent and headnets are a must. As a precaution against *giardiasis*, a common waterborne intestinal parasite in Alaska, water should be microfiltered, boiled, or chemically treated before drinking.

Lodgings and meals are available in Kotzebue.

Access to Selawik is by scheduled commercial flights from Anchorage to Kotzebue. Charter air-taxi flights are provided from there, or from Ambler and Kiana, to numerous landing places within the refuge. The refuge is also accessible by boat and on foot; and in winter, by dogsled, cross-country skis, and snowmobile.

Further information: Selawik National Wildlife Refuge, P.O. Box 270, Kotzebue, AK 99752; telephone: (907) 442-3799.

Tetlin, encompassing 730,000 acres, was established in 1980 by the Alaska National Interest Lands Conservation Act. The refuge protects an extensive wetland mosaic of marshes, hundreds of lakes, and mixed hardwood–spruce forest in the broad, level basins of the glacier-fed Chisana and Nabesna rivers; gently rolling hills that bisect these watersheds; and foothills of the Nutzotin and Mentasta mountains in east-central Alaska. This ecologically outstanding area adjoins Canada's Yukon Territory to the east; Wrangell-St. Elias National Park to the south; the Tetlin Indian Reservation to the west; and the Alaska Highway (State Route 2) to the north. Tetlin is one of only two refuges in Alaska that is accessible by road (Kenai is the other).

The refuge is located within a major corridor for numerous species of birds that migrate to and from nesting habitat in northern and western Alaska. The most prominent among these are large flocks of lesser sandhill cranes, whose impressive autumn migration peaks in September. Many tundra and trumpeter swans pause to rest and feed on the refuge, and increasing numbers of the latter nest here. Tetlin's wetlands provide important nesting habitat for exceptionally large concentrations of ducks, such as green-winged teal, mallards, wigeons, ring-necked ducks, lesser scaups, white-winged scoters, and buffleheads. Most of the refuge's breeding waterbirds nest in May and June and have their young by July. More than 180 species of birds have been recorded on the refuge. Arctic grayling, lake trout, northern pike, burbot, and whitefish are among the fish species that inhabit Tetlin's waters.

The refuge is open daily. There is no entrance fee. The sod-covered log cabin visitor center, providing interpretive exhibits and talks at the large viewing deck, is located at Milepost 1229 of the Alaska (Alcan) Highway and is open daily from Memorial Day to Labor Day. During the same period, evening programs are given at Deadman Campground, Monday through Friday at 7:30 p.m. Seven interpretive scenic-vista pullouts are located along the west side of the Alaska Highway.

Visitor activities include wildlife observation and photography; limited hiking; camping at Alaska (Alcan) Highway Milepost 1249.3—Deadman Lake Campground and at Milepost 1256.7—Lakeview Campground; wilderness camping; rafting; canoeing; boating; fishing; and hunting. Boat-launching ramps are provided at Deadman Lake Campground and at Chisana River, 0.25 mile south of Northway Junction (Milepost 1264), and canoe/small boat access is provided at Lakeview Campground.

Hiking opportunities include the 0.25-mile, self-guided Taiga Trail at Deadman Lake Campground. An observation platform at the end of the trail offers a view of the lake, where waterfowl may often be seen.

The best months for wildlife observation on Tetlin Refuge are April to October. Information about hunting and fishing can be obtained from the refuge headquarters or by contacting the Alaska Department of Fish and Game, P.O. Box 355, Tok, AK 99780; telephone: (907) 883-2971. No designated motorized-vehicle roads or trails exist on the refuge. Large parcels of the land within the refuge are owned by Native corporations and individuals. Permission is required to access these private properties. The refuge personnel can provide information on land status.

Visitors who trek into the refuge's backcountry are advised to take precautions against unwanted encounters with bears by making noise (talking, singing, whistling) while hiking; camping away from streams, wildlife trails, berry patches, and freshly killed game; maintaining a clean camp; cooking and storing food away from the campsite and where it is not accessible to wildlife; and packing out all garbage. Further information is provided in the helpful pamphlet, *Bear Facts: The Essentials for Traveling in Bear Country*, available at the refuge office.

As mosquitoes, gnats, and other pesky insects can be prolific during the warmer months, insect repellent and headnets are a must. Insects are less of a problem along river sand/gravel bars and up on ridges. As a precaution against *giardiasis,* a common infectious waterborne intestinal parasite in Alaska, water should be microfiltered, boiled, or chemically treated before drinking. Visitors in the backcountry should also be prepared for sudden weather changes and should bring sufficient warm clothing, reliable rain gear, and extra food supplies. A backcountry travel plan should be given to a relative or friend or to the refuge headquarters.

Lodgings, campgrounds, meals, and camping supplies are available in Tok and Northway, AK; and in Beaver Creek, Yukon Territory, Canada.

Access to Tetlin Refuge is by way of the Alaska Highway and charter flights from Tok.

Further information: Tetlin National Wildlife Refuge, P.O. Box 779, Tok, AK 99780; telephone: (907) 883-5312.

Togiak, comprising 4.3 million acres, was established in 1980 by the Alaska National Interest Lands Conservation Act, greatly expanding the previously existing Cape Newenham National Wildlife Refuge and protecting a vast expanse of wilderness between Bristol and Kuskokwim bays, in southwestern Alaska. The refuge includes coastal cliffs and sandy beaches, estuaries and lagoons, inland wetlands and meadows, forests and tundra, lakes and ponds, rivers and streams, hanging valleys and cirques, and the Ahklun and Wood River mountains that comprise 80 percent of the refuge. Togiak Valley consists of an unusual geologic landform that was created when lava erupted beneath a glacier. The northern part of Togiak Refuge has been designated as the 2.3 million-acre Togiak Wilderness.

This refuge supports a tremendous diversity and quantity of wildlife. Pacific walruses and Steller sea lions haul out on ocean beaches, brown bears feed on the enormous spawning runs of salmon, moose are abundant, and barren ground caribou are thriving. More than half the world's Pacific black brant feed upon extensive beds of eelgrass around Chagvan and Nanvak bays. Sandhill cranes nest on Nushagak Peninsula. Millions of seabirds, including horned puffins, common murres, and black-legged kittiwakes, nest on the spectacular coastal headlands of Cape Newenham and Cape Peirce. Large concentrations of waterfowl and shorebirds nest, rest, and feed on the refuge, and great numbers of raptors and land birds also occur here.

The refuge's fisheries are incredible. Over a million of five species of Pacific salmon—king (chinook), sockeye (red), coho (silver), pink (humpy), and chum (dog)—spawn annually in the more than 1,500 miles of rivers and streams. In addition, there are northern pike, lake trout, Dolly Varden, arctic char, rainbow trout, and arctic grayling.

Visitor activities include wildlife observation, photography, flightseeing, hiking (no trails), wilderness camping, river rafting (both guided float trips with associated guide camps and unguided float trips), kayaking, sport fishing, and hunting during the designated seasons. The best months for wildlife observation on Togiak Refuge are mid-June through late September. Information on hunting and fishing is available at the refuge office and at the Alaska Department of Fish and Game, P.O. Box 1030, Dillingham, AK 99576. Substantial areas within the boundaries of Togiak Refuge, such as around villages, along rivers, and along the shores of and inland from Togiak, Goodnews, and Nushagak bays, are owned by Native corporations and individuals. The U.S. Fish and Wildlife Service urges that visitors respect these private properties.

The refuge's unpredictable weather, which is mostly damp and rainy during the summer, can turn from warm and sunny to windy, cold, and wet in just a matter of hours. Visitors are advised to be alert for weather changes and to bring sufficient warm clothing, reliable rain gear, and extra food supplies in the event that inclement weather or other circumstances force an extended stay. A travel plan should be given to a relative, friend, or transporter.

Precautions should be taken to avoid unwanted encounters with bears by making noise (talking, singing, whistling) while hiking; camping away from streams, wildlife trails, berry patches, and freshly killed game; maintaining a clean camp; cooking and storing food away from the campsite and where it is not accessible to wildlife; and packing out all garbage. Further information is provided in the helpful pamphlet, *Bear Facts: The Essentials for Traveling in Bear Country*, available at the refuge office.

As mosquitoes and other pesky insects can be prolific during the warmer months, insect repellent and headnets are a must. As a precaution against *giardiasis*, a common infectious waterborne intestinal parasite in Alaska, water should be microfiltered, boiled, or chemically treated before drinking.

Lodgings, meals, camping supplies, and raft and kayak rentals are available in Dillingham.

Access to the refuge is mostly by flights from Anchorage to Dillingham. There are no roads or other developments within the refuge. Numerous air-taxis provide transportation to remote areas of the refuge. A list of guide and charter aircraft services can be obtained from the refuge or from Alaska Department of Fish and Game.

Further information: Togiak National Wildlife Refuge, P.O. Box 270, Dillingham, AK 99576; telephone: (907) 842-1063.

Yukon Delta, containing 19.624 million acres of federal lands, including a million acres on Nunivak Island in the Bering Sea, was established in 1980 by the Alaska National Interest Lands Conservation Act. The refuge protects the sprawling, treeless wetland plain of the Yukon and Kuskokwim rivers in western Alaska, consolidating three previously existing, smaller national wildlife refuges: Clarence Rhode, Hazen Bay, and Nunivak. This ecologically outstanding and vitally important expanse of rivers, streams, sloughs, lakes, and ponds supports the single most productive nesting habitat in North America for waterfowl, other waterbirds, and shorebirds. Their concentrations are mind-boggling.

Roughly 750,000 geese and swans, as many as 2 million ducks, and more than 5 million shorebirds annually migrate to this refuge from all continents that border the Pacific Ocean and beyond. Among waterfowl, the refuge supports more than three-quarters of the world's population of the emperor goose, as well as major proportions of North America's populations of the tundra swan, greater white-fronted goose, and the small "cackling" subspecies of Canada goose. Among the shorebirds, the refuge supports the entire world's population of adult and juvenile bristle-thighed curlews during migration each autumn, more than 80 percent of the world's breeding black turnstones, more than 60,000 bar-tailed godwits, and the majority of the Pacific Flyway populations of western sandpipers, dunlins, and rock sandpipers.

Although seabird rookeries dot the refuge coastline, the vast majority of colonies occur on Nunivak Island. Several hundred thousand seabirds nest on Nunivak's cliffs and offshore islets, including cormorants, kittiwakes, guillemots, murres, auklets, and puffins.

The more prominent species of terrestrial mammals are muskox, barren ground caribou, moose, and grizzly and black bears. Marine mammals of the coastal waters include the walrus and four other species of seals, and beluga (belukha) whale.

Of the many fishes, five kinds of Pacific salmon—king (chinook), sockeye (red), coho (silver), pink (humpy), and chum (dog)—totaling about a million individuals, make their summer runs from the sea to spawning habitat on the refuge; rainbow trout, Dolly Varden, and arctic grayling live in mountain streams; and northern pike, whitefish, sheefish, and burbot are found in lowland areas.

The refuge's visitor center, located in the town of Bethel, provides interpretive exhibits and information. It is open on weekdays, except national holidays.

Visitor activities include wildlife observation, photography, hiking, fishing, and hunting. The best months for wildlife observation on Yukon Delta refuge are June through September. Information on hunting and fishing can be obtained by contacting the refuge headquarters or the Alaska Department of Fish and Game, P.O. Box 1467, Bethel, AK 99559; telephone: (907) 543-2979.

The U.S. Fish and Wildlife Service advises that prospective visitors plan far ahead. As Yukon Delta Refuge is remote and difficult to visit, arrangements need to be carefully planned. The weather is often windy and rainy, and sudden changes commonly occur. Visitors should bring sufficient warm clothing; reliable rain gear, including hip boots for many parts of the refuge; and extra food supplies in the event that inclement weather or other circumstances force an extended stay. A travel plan should be given to a relative or friend or to the refuge headquarters.

In addition to the nearly 20 million acres of public land, the refuge boundaries encompass another 7 million acres of private Native corporation lands. Access to these lands is by permission only, and should be secured in writing well before visiting the refuge.

Visitors are advised to take precautions against unwanted encounters with bears by making noise (talking, singing, whistling) while hiking; camping away from streams, wildlife trails, berry patches, and freshly killed game; maintaining a clean camp; cooking and storing food away from the campsite and where it is not accessible to wildlife; and packing out all garbage. Further information is provided in the helpful pamphlet, *Bear Facts: The Essentials for Traveling in Bear Country*, available at the refuge office.

As mosquitoes, gnats, and other pesky insects can be prolific during the warmer months, insect repellent and headnets are a must. As a precaution against *giardiasis*, a common infectious waterborne intestinal parasite in Alaska, water should be microfiltered, boiled, or chemically treated before drinking.

Lodgings, meals, camping supplies, guide services, and charter flights are available in Bethel.

Access to Yukon Delta Refuge is by scheduled flights from Anchorage to Bethel. From Bethel, regularly scheduled flights go to many of the more remote villages. There are no roads to the refuge, and only two intervillage roads on the entire Delta (neither connects with Bethel). Charter flights, however, provide access to and from additional sites on the refuge.

Further information: Yukon Delta National Wildlife Refuge, P.O. Box 346, Bethel, AK 99559; telephone: (907) 543-3151.

Yukon Flats, containing 8.6 million acres, was established in 1980 by the Alaska National Interest Lands Conservation Act. This refuge surrounds and protects a vast wetland basin, encompassing 300 miles of the Yukon River in east-central Alaska. Periodic flooding of the Yukon and frequent lightning-ignited fires have created a diverse mosaic of vegetation, which maintains some of the most productive wildlife habitats in Alaska. An estimated 40,000 lakes, ponds, and other wetlands within the refuge provide some of North America's preeminent duck-breeding areas.

From 1 to 2 million ducks nest annually on the Yukon Flats refuge. Canvasbacks, mallards, pintails, scaup, scoters, shovelers, and wigeon are especially abundant. In addition, there are roughly 10,000 to 15,000 geese, 20,000 loons, 100,000 grebes, 11,000 sandhill cranes, and countless songbirds. Waterfowl banded by the U.S. Fish and Wildlife Service have been recovered in 45 of the 50 states, most of Canada's provinces, Mexico, Central and South America, the West Indies, and Russia. Over 120 bird species have been seen here.

Although close to half the refuge consists of Yukon Flats wetlands, the refuge also contains rolling hills of white spruce/paper birch/quaking aspen boreal forest; merging into taiga of widely scattered tall, slender spruces; and merging still higher into the treeless tundra of surrounding mountains. Prominent among the larger mammals of these higher habitats is the barren ground caribou. The Porcupine herd sometimes winters on the northeastern part of the refuge, and the Fortymile herd winters in the White Mountains that rise along the southern edge of the refuge.

Visitor activities include wildlife observation, photography, hiking, rafting, canoeing, kayaking, boating, wilderness camping, fishing, and hunting. Information on hunting and fishing can be obtained by contacting refuge personnel or the Alaska Department of Fish and Game, 1300 College Road, Fairbanks, AK 99701; telephone: (907) 459-7200. Close to 2 million acres of the refuge consists of lands owned by Native regional and village corporations and by individuals of the five Native villages within the refuge. Visitors are urged to respect these and other private properties. Cabins and tent camps should not be used, except in the event of a real emergency. Refuge personnel can provide information on land status.

The Fish and Wildlife Service advises that prospective visitors plan far ahead. As Yukon Flats Refuge is remote and weather can change suddenly, it is important to bring sufficient warm clothing, reliable rain gear, and extra food supplies in the event that inclement weather forces an extended stay. A travel plan should be given to a relative or friend or to the refuge headquarters.

Visitors are advised to take precautions against unwanted encounters with bears by making noise (talking, singing, whistling) while hiking; camping away from streams, wildlife trails, berry patches, and freshly killed game; maintaining a clean camp; cooking and storing food away from the campsite and where it is not accessible to wildlife; and packing out all garbage. Further information is provided in the helpful pamphlet, *Bear Facts: The Essentials for Traveling in Bear Country*, available at the refuge office.

As mosquitoes, gnats, and other pesky insects can be prolific during the warmer months, insect repellent and headnets are a must. As a precaution against *giardiasis*, a common infectious waterborne intestinal parasite in Alaska, water should be microfiltered, boiled, or chemically treated before drinking.

Lodgings, meals, and supplies are available in the town of Central, located south of the refuge on the Steese Highway (State Route 6), and limited lodgings and other services in the town of Fort Yukon, within the refuge.

Access to Yukon Flats Refuge is mainly by scheduled flights from Fairbanks to five villages within the refuge and by charter flights from Fairbanks, Fort Yukon, and Circle to a number of remote lakes and rivers. Guide services are available. Road access from Fox (5 miles north of Fairbanks) is 145 miles by way of the Steese Highway (State Route 6) to the town of Circle, located at the Yukon River, just upstream from the refuge.

Further information: Yukon Flats National Wildlife Refuge, 101 Twelfth Avenue, Room 264, Fairbanks, AK 99701; telephone: (907) 456-0440.

Arizona

Bill Williams River, containing 6,105 acres, began in 1941 as a small part of the former 45,400-acre Havasu Lake National Wildlife Refuge. When some of that area was deauthorized in 1964, the Bill Williams River and Havasu refuges were established to continue the protection of especially important ecological values along the lower Colorado River. The Bill Williams River Refuge encompasses an area of cattail marsh and one of the last remaining natural riparian stands of Fremont cottonwood/Goodding willow woodland along the lower Colorado River. Surrounded by the rugged Sonoran Desert, the refuge is located along the lowest stretch of the Bill Williams River, a tributary of the Colorado River in west-central Arizona.

The refuge's narrow strip of water-dependent habitat is an oasis for a large diversity of wildlife. More than 330 species of birds have been recorded here. A small population of the secretive, endangered Yuma clapper rail breeds in the river delta's dense cattail marsh, along with the Arizona state-listed endangered California black rail and several species of grebes. Great and snowy egrets inhabit the refuge. Wintering waterfowl, such as Canada geese, mallards, three species of teal, pintails, shovelers, gadwalls, and wigeons come to the Bill Williams River Delta's marsh and adjacent open water. The endangered southwestern willow flycatcher nests in the refuge's willow thickets; and numerous other species of neotropical songbirds, such as the yellow-billed cuckoo, vermilion flycatcher, Bell's vireo, many warblers, summer and western tanagers, black-headed and blue grosbeaks, and hooded and Bullock's orioles, are attracted to this lush riparian habitat.

Among the refuge's more than 50 species of mammals are desert bighorn sheep, mule deer, mountain lion, bobcat, coyote, gray fox, collared peccary (javelina), beaver, muskrat, raccoon, striped skunk, black-tailed jackrabbit, desert cottontail, and kangaroo rat.

The river and refuge are named for Bill Williams, who came west from St. Louis, Missouri, and traveled extensively throughout Arizona during the early nineteenth century. He initially served as a missionary to Native Americans and then became a trapper.

One of the refuge's important management activities is the reintroduction of two endangered species of native fish in a cove impoundment adjacent to Lake Havasu, near the mouth of the Bill Williams River. As the Fish and Wildlife Service explains, "biologists from the . . . Service's Arizona Fishery Resources Office receive young razorback suckers and bonytail chubs from Dexter National Fish Hatchery, a New Mexico facility that produces endangered fish. The fish are introduced into the cove, where they'll grow to around 10 inches—a size that offers them a chance against predators. At that point they're released into Lake Havasu and other areas, where they'll be monitored to determine their survival. In the future, these fish will also be released into stretches of free-flowing river."

Major habitat management programs include the control of the nonnative, aggressively invasive tamarisk, which crowds out native vegetation; the planting of young cottonwood and willow trees; and working with the U.S. Army Corps of Engineers, which regulates upstream water releases from the Alamo Dam, to restore the flow of water in the lower Bill Williams River to more natural levels and thereby help restore the ecologically rich riparian habitat.

Establishment of the Bill Williams River Refuge was made possible partly with revenues from the sale of Migratory Bird Hunting and Conservation Stamps (Duck Stamps).

The refuge is open daily during daylight hours. There is no entrance fee. The refuge headquarters/visitor center is open on weekdays, except national holidays.

Visitor activities include birdwatching; photography; viewing interpretive displays at the visitor center; observing wildlife from the visitor center's observation deck; driving on the unpaved Planet Ranch Road about 3 miles east from State Route 95 (and on another road several miles to the east by four-wheel-drive vehicle); hiking on the latter road, including another couple of miles that are impassable by vehicle to the east of Mineral Wash Road; walking the 0.25-mile self-guiding trail (an interpretive leaflet is available) near the refuge office; canoeing and boating; fishing; and hunting (bighorn, by Arizona state permit issued through computer drawing; cottontail; quail; and dove) on certain parts of the refuge during the designated seasons.

Hand-carried boats and canoes can be launched adjacent to the refuge headquarters; and other boats can be launched from the end of Parker Dam Road, a mile south of headquarters. Although camping is not permitted on the refuge, campground facilities are provided in the vicinity of Lake Havasu City to the north and Parker to the south.

Sunscreen and lots of water are advised, especially during the warmer months. Visitors are cautioned to be alert for the western diamondback and Mojave rattlesnake. The best time to visit the Bill Williams River Refuge is from mid-autumn through mid-spring. Late spring through early autumn is extremely hot.

The refuge's species of flora and fauna are essentially the same as those recorded on Havasu Refuge.

Lodgings and meals are available in Lake Havasu City and Parker.

Access to the Bill Williams River Refuge from I-10 at Quartzsite, is north about 50 miles (through Parker) on Arizona State Route 95. Or, from Exit 9 on I-40, it is south about 40 miles (through Lake Havasu City) on State Route 95. This highway crosses the refuge's delta marsh on the Bill Williams Bridge, and pulloffs are provided to the north and south of the bridge from which to view this part of the refuge. Planet Ranch Road branches east from Route 95, just north of the refuge headquarters and 0.3 miles south of the bridge.

Further information: Bill Williams River National Wildlife Refuge, 60911 Highway 95, Parker, AZ 85344; telephone: (928) 667-4144.

Buenos Aires, comprising more than 117,000 acres, was established in 1985 to protect and restore an ecologically significant expanse of Sonoran Desert grassland for the masked bobwhite quail and a number of other threatened and endangered species, as well as a tremendous diversity of fauna and flora. The refuge is located in the Altar Valley, near the base of the rugged Baboquivari Mountains, about 45 miles by highway southwest of Tucson in southern Arizona. The refuge's Spanish name, *Buenos Aires,* meaning "good winds," was derived from Buenos Ayres Ranch, founded by Pedro Aguirre, Jr., in 1864.

One of the refuge's primary objectives is to reestablish a self-sustaining breeding population of the federally listed endangered masked bobwhite (*Colinus virginianus ridgwayi*). This subspecies, the male of which has a distinctive black facial mask and throat and rufous underparts, formerly ranged from the high desert grasslands of southeastern Arizona southward to central Sonora, Mexico. The last wild masked bobwhite populations occur on Mexican ranchlands. The U.S. Fish and Wildlife Service explains:

As settlements sprang up in the Altar Valley in the 1860s, the delicate balance of the ecosystem was changed. Overgrazing left the ground bare, exposing it to torrential summer rains that quickly eroded the soil. With the grass gone and natural fires suppressed, mesquite gained a foothold. The grassland could no longer support masked bobwhite quail. . . .

Lehmann's lovegrass, an African grass, was introduced in the 1970s to help stop erosion. While the grass did hold the soil down and was drought resistant, it was a poor substitute for the diverse native grasses [gramas, three-awns, windmill, and tanglehead] it replaced. An ecosystem without diversity is a bleak landscape for many wild creatures.

Staff at Buenos Aires National Wildlife Refuge are working to piece the ecosystem together, by restoring habitat, replacing key species, and protecting others still imperiled.

In early 2002, refuge biologist Sally Gall explained:

The masked bobwhite captive-rearing program is continuing at Buenos Aires with new innovations devised by refuge personnel. Quail eggs are produced by the breeding stock at the Masked Bobwhite Captive Rearing Facility in Arivaca. Once hatched, day-old quail chicks destined for release are brought to refuge headquarters, where they are raised in a controlled environment. They are indoors, with temperature and light conditions monitored daily. Foster quail parents are provided to each group of 15 chicks in order to provide role models for the chicks to imprint upon. The foster parents brood and protect the chicks. At approximately 3 to 3 1/2 weeks, the chicks are banded and placed in elevated runs inside flight pens, for acclimation to the outdoors. After several days the birds are released from the runs and allowed to roam the flight pens, where they live in a semi-natural yet enclosed environment until the covey season in the fall.

In late September or early October, groups of chicks, plus their foster parents, are transferred to release pens located in excellent habitat. During this "soft release" procedure, the birds become accustomed to their new surroundings and are better able to survive, once they are released after 5 to 7 days at the release site. Typically, more than 500 quail are released annually onto the refuge. At any one time, it is estimated that approximately 1,000 birds inhabit the refuge.

Quail populations are monitored by counting calling males during the summer breeding season and by conducting live trapping of bobwhite during the winter months (trapping helps give some insight into the survival and movements of the birds). In 1999, for the first time in the refuge's history, wild masked bobwhite were trapped at various trap sites. Twenty-two birds were caught. These monitoring activities help answer one of the most common questions asked by refuge visitors: "Are they reproducing in the wild?" YES!

Since 1985, the refuge has been expanded to give protection to ecologically significant wetland and riparian habitats along Arivaca Creek and Arivaca Cienega, and in Brown Canyon. As the Service says, "This combination of grasslands, wetlands, cottonwood-lined streambeds, and sycamore and live oak mountain canyons preserves some of the Southwest's rarest habitats for seven endangered species, ten species of concern, and many other native plants and wildlife." In addition to the masked bobwhite, the endangered species are the cactus ferruginous pygmy-owl (*Glaucidium brasiliarium cactorum*); peregrine falcon; southwestern willow flycatcher (*Empidonax traillii extimus*); razorback sucker (*Xyrauchen texanus*); Kearney bluestar (*Amsonia kearneyana*), a member of the dogbane family that is endemic to the Baboquivari Mountains; and Pima pineapple cactus (*Coryphantha sherri robustispina*). Over 320 bird species have been seen here.

The Friends of Buenos Aires National Wildlife Refuge is a nonprofit organization that helps support the refuge's environmental education and other programs.

The refuge is open daily during daylight hours. There is no entrance fee, except in Brown Canyon, which is presently open by guided tour only. For information on the Brown Canyon tour schedule, group tours, and fees: (520) 823-4251, ext. 116. The refuge visitor center is open daily, and the headquarters is open on weekdays, except national holidays.

Visitor activities include wildlife and butterfly observation; photography; driving the unpaved, 10-mile Antelope Drive (motor vehicles are restricted to refuge roads); hiking; docent-led interpretive walks; environmental education programs; horseback riding on refuge roads to the north of Arivaca Road; camping at a number of primitive campsites along back roads (14-day limit); and hunting (deer, javelina, cottontail, waterfowl, coot, and white-winged and mourning dove) on most of the refuge during the designated seasons. Near the visitor center, there are pens that afford an opportunity to see the secretive masked bobwhite, bird feeders that attract numerous species of birds, a butterfly garden, and a grassland exhibit where more than 20 species of grasses can be identified.

Hiking opportunities include the 0.5-mile Arivaca Cienega boardwalk to Willow Pond or the entire 2-mile loop trail; a 1-mile trail at Arivaca Creek beneath giant cottonwood trees and other lush vegetation that contrasts with the surrounding high desert environment; and the more challenging 5-mile round-trip Mustang Trail. A 0.5-mile walk leads around Aguirre Lake, which was created by Pedro Aguirre in the 1880s to provide water for his fields and livestock. Today, migrating waterfowl, wading birds, and shorebirds are seasonally attracted to the lake.

Visitors are cautioned to be alert for rattlesnakes, stay away from active swarms of bees (Africanized "killer bees" aggressively defend their nests from perceived threats), stay out of flooded washes that can change rapidly from dry washes to fast-moving rivers, be aware that the refuge's dirt roads become impassable during and after rainfall, and be prepared for afternoon summer 'monsoon' thunderstorm rains.

Lodgings and meals are limited in the vicinity of the refuge, but (with advance reservations) are provided at Rancho de la Osa, telephone: (800) 872-6240, just north of Sasabe; Elkhorn Ranch, telephone: (520) 822-1040, in the Baboquivari Mountains' Sabino Canyon; and Casa Bella Bed and Breakfast, toll-free telephone: (877) 604-3385, just outside Arivaca. Lodgings and meals are also available in Tucson.

Access to the refuge visitor center from I-10 in Tucson is west 22 miles on State Route 86 to Three Points, and south about 38 miles on State Route 286.

Further information: Buenos Aires National Wildlife Refuge, P.O. Box 109, Sasabe, AZ 85633; telephone: (520) 823-4251.

Cabeza Prieta, consisting of 860,010 acres, was established in 1939 to protect desert bighorn sheep in a vast expanse of the Sonoran Desert. Eight serrated mountain ranges—Childs, Growler, Granite, Bryan, Agua Dulce, Sierra Pinta, Cabeza Prieta, and Tule—rise from broad desert valleys. A lava-capped granite peak in one of the remote ranges gave rise to the Spanish name *Cabeza Prieta*, meaning "dark head." In 1990, more than 90 percent of the refuge was designated as the Cabeza Prieta Wilderness, a unit of the National Wilderness Preservation System. The refuge is located along 56 miles of the U.S.–Mexico border in southwestern Arizona.

As described by the U.S. Fish and Wildlife Service:

Imagine the state of Rhode Island without any people and only one wagon track of a road. Cabeza Prieta NWR is that big, that wild and also incredibly hostile to those who need lots of water to live. Yet, within a landscape at once magnificent and harsh, life does persist, even thrives.

From June through October, the daytime high temperature typically exceeds 100 degrees for roughly 100 consecutive days. Soaking winter rains and local midsummer 'monsoon' thunderstorm showers annually average as much as 9 inches of precipitation across the eastern end of the refuge, dropping to only about 3 inches on the western end. As desert enthusiast Bill

Broyles explains, "The greater rainfall toward the east produces denser and more lush vegetation than occurs in the drier western end. Some plants, such as beavertail cactus, many-headed barrel cactus, and Bigelow nolina, prefer drier soil and are found mainly in the west. Large cacti, such as saguaro and organ pipe, require more precipitation, and are found mainly in the east."

Shrubby trees include honey and velvet mesquites, blue and foothill palo verdes, ironwood, desert-willow, smoke tree, and elephant tree. Other common plants include catclaw acacia; crucifixion thorn; creosotebush; brittlebush; bursages; saltbushes; indigo-bush; fairy duster; ephedra; ocotillo; chuparosa; desert marigold; desert dandelion; desert sunflower; Arizona lupine; desert lily; desert globemallow; sand verbena; primroses; prickly poppy; desert gold poppy; gilias; desert trumpet; Mojave desert star; white tackstem; nolina; desert agave; and many species of cacti, such as saguaro, organ pipe, senita, chollas, barrels, hedgehogs, fishhooks, prickly pears, and night-blooming cereus.

The largest mammal on the Cabeza Prieta refuge is the desert bighorn sheep (*Ovis canadensis mexicana*). As the U.S. Fish and Wildlife Service says:

To many of our visitors the bighorn sheep is the epitome of Cabeza's desert wilderness. Bighorns are a true sheep distantly related to domestic sheep. The name 'desert bighorn sheep' applies to those bighorn inhabiting hot and dry desert mountain ranges with sparse vegetation and water. . . .

The desert bighorn has become well adapted to living in the desert heat and cold and, unlike most mammals, their body temperature can safely fluctuate several degrees. During the heat of the day, bighorn often rest in the shade of trees and caves.

Cabeza's bighorn . . . are typically found in small scattered bands adapted to a desert mountain environment with little or no permanent water. Some of Cabeza's bighorn may go without visiting one of the refuge's water developments for weeks or months, sustaining their body moisture from food and from rainwater collected in temporary rock pools [*tinajas*]. They may have the ability to lose up to 30% of their body weight and still survive. After drinking water, they quickly recover from their dehydrated condition.

Another Cabeza Prieta Refuge ungulate is the fleet-footed, federally listed endangered Sonoran pronghorn (*Antilocapra americana sonoriensis*). The refuge provides protection and habitat for several endangered species, but the Sonoran pronghorn receives primary attention because the refuge is located in the heart of its range. Past management has included the protection of habitat, removal of grazing from the refuge, placement of experimental waters, fencing parts of the boundary to prevent trespass of cattle, and study of the pronghorn's movements and habitat use. Recently, additional experimental waters and forage plots have been proposed.

A surprising recorded history of human activities has occurred in this remote part of Arizona. As described in a refuge brochure on the historic El Camino del Diablo ("the road of the devil" or "Devil's Highway"):

When the first Europeans, the Spanish, came to the region, they employed Indian guides, who led them to concealed waterholes through the maze of trails. In 1540, Captain Melchior Díaz led a detachment of the Coronado Expedition through this vicinity in route to California. From 1698–1702, Jesuit Padre Eusebio Kino probed the region in search of souls and a route to the Pacific. Traveling horseback and afoot, this premier geographer explored and mapped both sides of the trail, and put the major waterholes on his map for later visitors.

El Camino del Diablo earned its name from the large numbers of crosses and human bones that were found along the way by nineteenth-century travelers heading for the Gold Rush in California. Although this route lacked the abundance of water found along the Gila River to the north, it also lacked the risk of attacks by the Apache Indians.

The refuge is open daily. Visitors are required to obtain a free entry permit, which is available at the refuge office or from the office by mail. The refuge office and visitor center are open on weekdays, except national holidays. From November to March, the Cabeza Prieta Natural History Association presents biweekly programs on the natural history of the refuge. The refuge office can provide a schedule of free evening talks. Other special programs, events, and tours are scheduled throughout the year.

Visitor activities include wildlife observation; photography; viewing interpretive displays in the visitor center; walking a short, self-guiding path near the visitor center and hiking anywhere on the refuge; driving on nonwilderness unpaved refuge roads; primitive camping; and a limited desert bighorn sheep hunt (the state issues from one to eight permits annually). Recommended campsites are located at Papago Well, Tule Well, and Christmas Pass. Because of the scarcity of wood, only charcoal campfires are permitted.

Driving the refuge's roads, including Christmas Pass Road and the historic El Camino del Diablo, generally requires a four-wheel-drive vehicle, except on the *Charlie Bell Trail*, west from Ajo, on which a high-clearance, two-wheel-drive vehicle can generally be driven. Vehicles are required to remain within 50 feet of refuge roadways; off-roading is strictly prohibited. Sections of the refuge may be closed after rains; the Fish and Wildlife Service urges visitors not to attempt driving through or around where water is standing in ruts of the road. Sections of the refuge may also be closed during the endangered pronghorn fawning season (March 15 to July 15). Update: As of this writing, El Camino del Diablo is temporarily closed because of its impassable condition. Visitors are urged to contact the refuge office prior to arrival to obtain the latest information on road conditions.

Visitors are warned that driving and hiking excursions on Cabeza Prieta Refuge are very challenging. Consequently, adequate preparations and provisions are essential (contact the refuge headquarters for suggestions). Sunscreen and lots of water (no less than 2 gallons of water per person, per day) are recommended, especially during the warmer months. Summertime temperatures soar to 120 degrees F. Visitors are cautioned to be alert for the venomous Gila monster and rattlesnakes.

Lodgings and meals are available in Ajo.

Access to the refuge's visitor center from Exit 115 on I-8 at Gila Bend is south 42 miles on State Route 85 to Ajo; or from Exit 99 on I-19 in Tucson, it is west 115 miles on State Route 86 to Why and northwest (right) 10 miles on State Route 85 to Ajo.

Further information: Cabeza Prieta National Wildlife Refuge, 1611 North Second Avenue, Ajo, AZ 85321; telephone: (520) 387-6483.

Cibola, encompassing 17,267 acres, was established in 1964 as mitigation for the loss of habitat and other environmental impacts of dams and flood-control facilities that were built on the Colorado River from the 1930s through the 1960s. The refuge protects important floodplain wetland habitat, including historic channels, backwaters, lakes, and ponds along a 12-mile stretch of the river. This oasis in the Sonoran Desert includes more than 16,000 acres of riparian habitat and attracts the largest concentrations of wintering Canada geese and greater sandhill cranes on the lower Colorado. The refuge is located in southeastern California and southwestern Arizona. Over 280 bird species have been seen here.

Common species of ducks that winter here include mallard, northern pintail, green-winged teal, gadwall, and American wigeon. The secretive Yuma clapper rail, a subspecies that is federally listed as endangered, nests in the refuge's cattail-and-bulrush marsh habitat, along with the Arizona state-listed California black rail. Both great and snowy egrets are common. The federally listed endangered southwestern willow flycatcher and the California state-listed endangered Bell's vireo are attracted to the refuge's riparian habitat.

Establishment of Cibola refuge was made possible partly with revenues from the sale of Migratory Bird Hunting and Conservation Stamps (Duck Stamps). The U.S. Fish and Wildlife Service's habitat management activities include the restoration and flooding of former river backwaters and meanders; control of the non-native, aggressively invasive tamarisk (salt cedar); and planting of native species such as Fremont cottonwood, willows, and mesquite. In addition, under cooperative agreements with local farmers, approximately 1,600 acres of the refuge are planted with crops such as alfalfa, corn, milo, and millet that provide nutrient-rich food for wintering waterfowl and other wildlife.

As refuge manager Michael Hawkes explains:

Cibola National Wildlife Refuge is one of four national wildlife refuges on the lower Colorado River within Arizona and California. The Colorado River has historically been a key corridor for wildlife, especially neotropical migratory birds; and although the landscape, primarily vegetation and water flow, has been drastically altered over the last century, it remains a significant migration route. It is important for all of us to help preserve and restore the habitat components that numerous species of wildlife depend upon in this riparian system that lies within a harsh desert environment.

The refuge is open daily during daylight hours. There is no entrance fee. The refuge headquarters/visitor center is open on weekdays, except national holidays.

Visitor activities include birdwatching; photography; viewing displays at the visitor center; driving the Canada Goose Drive—a 3-mile loop that offers views of flooded impoundments and farm fields, where large numbers of ducks, geese, and cranes can be seen during the winter (an interpretive leaflet is available); hiking; observing wildlife on 600-acre Cibola Lake from a blufftop observation platform (on the eastern levee road); canoeing, kayaking, and boating; fishing (Cibola Lake is open from March 15 through Labor Day; old and new river channels are open all year); and hunting (deer, cottontail, waterfowl, coot, gallinule, quail, and dove) on parts of the refuge during the designated seasons. Camping is not permitted on the refuge.

Canoeing and kayaking are permitted on the Old River Channel, Three Finger Lake, and the main channel of the Colorado River all year, and, with restrictions, on Cibola Lake and Hart Mine Marsh. Cibola Lake and all other backwater areas are designated as "no wake" zones. General boating and powered personal watercraft are permitted only on the river's main channel. Hiking opportunities include a 1-mile, self-guiding nature trail that leads through an area of mesquites and a "gallery" of cottonwoods and willows. This trail leads to an observation platform overlooking a 20-acre pond, where as many as 15,000 wintering ducks, geese, and cranes gather.

Sunscreen and lots of water are advised; and visitors are cautioned to be alert for rattlesnakes. The best times to visit Cibola Refuge are from mid-autumn through mid-spring. Late spring through early autumn is extremely hot.

Lodgings and meals are available in Blythe, California; and Ehrenberg and Yuma, Arizona.

> Access to Cibola Refuge from I-10 at Blythe, California, is south on Neighbor's Boulevard, crossing the Colorado River on Cibola Bridge into Arizona, and continuing 3.5 miles (following directional signs) to the headquarters/visitor center.

> Further information: Cibola National Wildlife Refuge, Route 2, Box 138, Cibola, AZ 85328; telephone: (928) 857-3253.

Havasu, containing 37,515 acres, began in 1941 as a small part of the former, 45,400-acre Havasu Lake National Wildlife Refuge. When much of that refuge was deauthorized, the Havasu and Bill Williams River national wildlife refuges were designated in 1991 for migratory birds and other wildlife. Highlighted by the Topock Marsh and the ruggedly scenic Topock Gorge, Havasu Refuge is located on 85-mile-long Lake Havasu, a reservoir formed by Parker Dam on the Colorado River in west-central Arizona and southeastern California.

Topock Marsh, encompassing 4,000 acres in the northern end of the refuge, consists of large areas of emergent plants, such as cattails, bulrushes, rushes, and sedges. This ecologically significant wetland provides ideal habitat for numerous species of waterbirds, including two secretive, difficult-to-spot species: the federally listed endangered Yuma clapper rail and the black rail (listed by Arizona as endangered and by California as threatened). Other waterbirds include several species of grebes, double-crested cormorant, least bittern, great blue and green herons, great and snowy egrets, wintering snow and Canada geese, and numerous species of ducks. Marsh wrens and red-winged and yellow-headed blackbirds are also common here.

Much of the central area of the refuge contains both the Colorado River's spectacular Topock Gorge and adjacent wilderness, where the Sonoran Desert, to the south, and Mojave Desert, to the north, merge. This desert expanse comprises nearly one-third of the refuge. In 1990, the Needles Wilderness was designated by the Arizona Desert Wilderness Act; and in 1994, the Havasu Wilderness was designated by the California Desert Protect Act, totaling 17,606 acres in the National Wilderness Preservation System.

As the U.S. Fish and Wildlife Service describes the geology of the Topock Gorge:

The Colorado River flows through an open floodplain north and just south of the I-40 bridge and then begins a journey through canyon country. . . . The river is slowly carving through an incredible sequence of igneous and sedimentary rocks that formed between 23 and 15 million years ago, juxtaposed next to metamorphic rocks over one billion years old. The rocks formed in response to large-scale heating and movements of the Earth's crust that resulted in volcanic eruptions and magmatic intrusions, faulting and gentle folding of rocks associated with mountain uplift, large landslides, and the formation of small basins that rapidly filled in with coarse sediment. Subsequent weathering and erosion, in large part by the Colorado River, has carved a rugged, yet beautiful landscape of high spires, sheer cliffs, and numerous weathering hollows and arches in the rocks.

The contrast between the sparkling, blue color of the lake; the green of small, scattered wetland and riparian habitats bordering the shore of sheltered coves; and the jagged and multi-hued desert peaks, rock formations, and cliffs presents one of the most awesome scenes in the National Wildlife Refuge System. Boating or rafting through the 15-mile gorge provides constantly changing perspectives and points of interest. Highlights include Pulpit Rock, a variety of arches and windows, the serrated Needles near the Devil's Elbow, Split Rock, and Mohave Rock.

Desert bighorn sheep inhabit sheer, rocky cliffs and mountains of the gorge and wilderness. Other mammals of the refuge include mule deer, mountain lion, coyote, black-tailed jackrabbit, desert cottontail, and kangaroo rat. Avian inhabitants of the desert include more than 300 species, such as the greater roadrunner, ladder-backed woodpecker, verdin, cactus wren, Crissal thrasher, phainopepla, and black-throated sparrow.

Shrubby desert trees include foothill and blue palo verdes, ironwood, and desert-willow. The smoketree grows in desert washes where little else survives. Cacti include beavertail prickly pear, several chollas, barrel, and hedgehog. Other desert-adapted plants include ocotillo, creosotebush, desert holly, saltbush, bursage, yellow-flowering brittlebush, desert lily, owl's clover, desert gold poppy, Arizona lupine, desert marigold, desert dandelion, globemallow, desert gilia, sand verbena, Mojave desert star, purple mat, white tack-stem, desert sunflower, and Mojave aster. Once every few years, an autumn and early winter of abundant rainfall occurs, triggering an awakening of desert wildflowers that briefly transform the desert landscapes with their spectacular displays of brilliant colors. This desert land is also inhabited by various lizards, including the desert collared lizard, western whiptail, and chuckwalla; and four species of rattlesnakes—the western diamondback, speckled, Mojave green, and sidewinder.

Fremont cottonwoods and coyote and Goodding willows grow in scattered places along the Colorado River and its wetlands, along with honey and screwbean mesquite trees and the non-native, aggressively invasive tamarisk. These densely vegetated areas attract numerous species of neotropical migratory songbirds, including flycatchers, vireos, warblers, grosbeaks, tanagers, and orioles.

At the northern end of the refuge, the U.S. Fish and Wildlife Service provides an area of moist-soil impoundments and croplands, in the Pintail Slough Management Unit. Wheat, millet, and various other plants provide an important source of food for wintering waterfowl.

Other refuge management activities include attempting to control the tamarisk, with which the native cottonwoods and willows cannot compete; and managing water flows for the benefit of waterfowl and shorebirds.

Establishment of the Havasu Refuge was made possible partly with revenues from the sale of Migratory Bird Hunting and Conservation Stamps (Duck Stamps).

The refuge is open daily. There is no entrance fee. The refuge headquarters, located at 317 Mesquite Avenue, Needles, CA, is open on weekdays, except national holidays.

Visitor activities include birdwatching; photography; canoeing, boating, and rafting; water skiing on designated areas of the lake; camping at RV and tent facilities located at Five Mile

Landing; camping in the wilderness by permit only (restricted to areas more than 1 mile back from the lakeshore); fishing; and hunting (bighorn, by Arizona state permit issued through computer drawing; waterfowl; quail; dove; and cottontail) in specified areas during the designated seasons.

Regarding the operation of watercraft, the Fish and Wildlife Service says:

To protect floating-nest birds, jet powered personal watercraft . . . are not allowed in backwaters off the main Colorado River channel for the 15-mile [Topock Gorge] stretch from the Island/Castle Rock location, north to the Interstate 40 bridge buoy line. . . .

Boating on refuge waters is extremely popular. Please stay out of restricted areas, which are marked by signs and buoys. . . .

. . . The backwaters off the main channel in most of Topock Gorge are No Wake Zones.

As more boaters share the river, it is crucial that all watercraft operators follow safety regulations. Please check with the refuge office for copies of state and federal safety rules.

Hiking opportunities include a 4-mile loop on Havasu Refuge's Topock Farm Unit, on impoundment dikes, and in the wilderness areas. Wilderness hikers are cautioned to be well prepared before tackling the challenging conditions in these rugged and remote areas.

Insect repellent, sunscreen, and lots of drinking water are advised, especially during warmer months. Visitors are cautioned to be alert for rattlesnakes. The most favorable times to visit the refuge are mid-autumn through mid-spring. Late spring through early autumn is extremely hot.

Lodgings and meals are available in Needles, California and Lake Havasu City, Arizona.

Access to boat-launching sites in Havasu Refuge's Topock Marsh area from Exit 1 on I-40 in Arizona is north on State Route 66 and (west) left to the Catfish Paradise Day Use Area Boat Launch; or continue north on Route 66 to the south edge of Golden Shores, bearing left onto County Route 227 and proceeding north, and west (left) to Five Mile Landing Camping Area and Boat Launch; or continue farther north on Route 227 to North Dike Fishing Area and Boat Launch. Boat slips are available (fee) at Five Mile Landing; and overnight mooring of watercraft is permitted only at Five Mile Landing. To access the refuge from the south, there is a boat launch at Crystal Beach, reached off of either London Bridge Road or U.S. Route 95, north of Lake Havasu City.

Further information: Havasu National Wildlife Refuge, P.O. Box 3009, Needles, CA 92363; telephone: (760) 326-3853.

Imperial, comprising 25,125 acres, was established in 1941 to protect freshwater wetland habitat upstream from Imperial Dam, stretching along 28 miles of the lower Colorado River including the final unchannelized stretch before the river enters Mexico. The refuge, which contains an oasis of wetland habitat and backwater lakes, is located in southwestern Arizona and southeastern California. Approximately 14,000 acres of the refuge's desert upland habitat in Arizona and California have been designated as wilderness, comprising two units of the National Wilderness Preservation System.

The Imperial Refuge attracts large concentrations of wintering ducks, geese, shorebirds, and other waterbirds to its restored wetlands, moist-soil impoundments, croplands, and back-water lakes and ponds. Marsh vegetation includes cattails, bulrushes, rushes, sedges, arrowweed, and common reed (*Phragmites*). The secretive Yuma clapper rail, a subspecies that is federally listed as endangered, nests in the refuge's dense cattail-and-bulrush marsh habitat, along with the Arizona state-listed California black rail.

Crops of alfalfa, wheat, barley, milo, millet, and corn are grown on more than 300 acres of the refuge's agricultural fields, providing a nutrient-rich food supply for waterfowl and other wildlife.

More than two-thirds of the Imperial Refuge consists of adjacent areas of barren-appearing Sonoran Desert and rugged mountains. Among species adapted to this arid environment are the desert bighorn sheep, coyote, bobcat, black-tailed jackrabbit, desert cottontail, Gambel's quail, greater roadrunner, ladder-backed woodpecker, verdin, cactus wren, phainopepla, black-throated sparrow, zebra-tailed lizard, chuckwalla, and western diamondback rattlesnake. Desert vegetation includes the shrubby palo verde, ironwood, and honey and screwbean mesquite trees, smoketree, ocotillo, creosotebush, brittlebush, chuparosa, and various cacti, including beavertail prickly pear. Once every few years, autumn and early winter rains are sufficient to trigger a massive blooming of colorful spring wildflowers that carpet vast expanses of the desert. Among these are desert marigold, desert dandelion, owl's clover, Arizona lupine, globemallow, scorpionweed, desert gilia, sand verbena purple mat, desert lily, and desert sunflower.

Concerning the history of this river valley, the U.S. Fish and Wildlife Service explains:

At one time, the banks of the Colorado River were lined with cottonwood and willow forests, sustained by the river's natural periodic flooding. Animals depended on this green forest oasis for breeding, resting, feeding, and shade. Woodcutting during the steamboat era, clearing for agriculture, wild fire, exotic plants like salt cedar, and use of dams for flood prevention have devastated cottonwood and willow stands along the lower Colorado River. . . .

Refuge staff are working with other agencies and organizations to plant cottonwood and willow trees. From the observation tower, look for patches of restored forest.

Establishment of the Imperial Refuge was made possible partly with revenues from the sale of Migratory Bird Hunting and Conservation Stamps (Duck Stamps). Ducks Unlimited, Inc., has helped enhance more than 375 acres of the refuge's wetland habitat on the Martinez Marsh Unit, with another 130 acres that will soon be restored. Habitat restoration activities include the control of the non-native invasive salt cedar and common reed (*Phragmites*), construction of dikes, installation of water control structures, and enhancement of water delivery systems. These projects are providing an important complex of seasonal and permanent wetlands and native riparian habitat for such species as wintering mallards, pintails, and green-winged and cinnamon teal and for such other birds as the Yuma clapper and black rails.

The refuge is open daily. There is no entrance fee. The visitor center is open daily from November 15 through March and on weekdays from April 1 through November 14.

Visitor activities include birdwatching, photography, viewing exhibits and a video program in the visitor center, driving on the Red Cloud Mine Road through a stretch of the Sonoran Desert and providing access to Mesquite, Ironwood, and Smoke Tree points that offer excellent views of the river valley wetlands; hiking; canoeing, kayaking, and boating;

fishing; and hunting (desert bighorn, deer, coyote, fox, cottontail, goose, duck, coot, quail, and dove) on parts of the refuge during the designated seasons. Although camping is not permitted on the refuge, campground facilities are available at California's Picacho State Recreation Area.

Hiking opportunities include the Painted Desert Trail (an interpretive leaflet is available)— a 1.3-mile self-guiding loop that is located 2.8 miles from the visitor center adjacent to the Red Cloud Mine Road and provides views of desert washes, colorful rock formations, and a panorama of the Colorado River Valley from a high point. A high-clearance vehicle is recommended for driving beyond this trail on the Red Cloud Mine Road.

Sunscreen and lots of drinking water are advised, especially during the warmer months. Visitors are cautioned to be alert for rattlesnakes. The best time to visit the refuge is from mid-autumn through mid-spring; late spring through early autumn are extremely hot.

More than 270 species of birds have been recorded on the Imperial Refuge. Fauna and flora of the refuge are essentially the same as on the adjacent Cibola Refuge.

Lodgings and meals are available in Yuma, Arizona.

Further information: Imperial National Wildlife Refuge, P.O. Box 72217, Yuma, AZ 85365; telephone: (928) 783-3371.

Kofa, consisting of 665,400 acres, was established in 1939 to protect and manage important habitat for the desert bighorn sheep in and around the canyon-gashed Kofa and Castle Dome Mountains. The name *Kofa* is derived from the former "King of Arizona" gold mining operation that began in the late nineteenth century. Elevations above sea level range from 680 feet to 4,877 feet atop Signal Peak in the Kofa Mountains. In 1990, the Arizona Desert Wilderness Act designated 546,700 acres of the refuge as the Kofa Wilderness, a unit of the National Wilderness Preservation System. The refuge is located in the Sonoran Desert of west-central Arizona.

Desert bighorn sheep (*Ovis canadensis mexicana*) inhabit mainly the refuge's two dominant, extremely rugged mountain ranges—the Kofas and Castle Domes, which rise dramatically from the surrounding desert plain. The refuge supports roughly 800 of these animals. An important sheep management activity has been the enhancement of water sources on the refuge. As the U.S. Fish and Wildlife Service explains:

Natural water sources are highly variable and may not last until seasonal changes can replenish the supply. By enlarging natural water holes, shading them to reduce evaporation, and blasting artificial basins in areas previously without a water supply, refuge managers have greatly increased the availability and reliability of water. ...desert bighorn have responded to this assistance by producing a larger, healthier herd.

According to the Service, since 1979 (with the exception of 1991 and 2000, when sheep transplants occurred elsewhere), "the refuge has participated in a transplant program of bighorn sheep in cooperation with AGFD (the Arizona Game & Fish Department). Refuge employees assist the AGFD in the capture using net guns from helicopters. The animals are then transported to various locations within the southwestern U.S. in an effort to assist in the restoration of indigenous populations." (For further information on the desert bighorn, see the Cabeza Prieta Refuge text.)

Probably the only native palm trees in Arizona grow in hidden canyons of the Kofa Refuge. The California fan palm (*Washingtonia filifera*) grows more abundantly along spring-fed streams that are located within canyons and washes around the edge of California's Coachella Valley (see further information in the Coachella Valley National Wildlife Refuge text). Here in the Kofa Mountains, there are small, scattered clusters of these picturesque palms—their lush green fronds providing a fascinating contrast to the erosion-carved cliffs.

Other trees on the refuge include palo verde, ironwood, and mesquite. Shrubs and other plants include creosotebush; Kofa Mountain barberry, which has holly-like leaves; and a yucca-like plant known as nolina. Common birds in this vicinity include the verdin, canyon wren, black-tailed gnatcatcher, curve-billed thrasher, canyon towhee, black-throated sparrow, and phainopepla. The latter species feeds on the berries of mistletoe, and its fluttering flight pattern is suggestive of a butterfly. The male is jet black, the female is gray, and both have a cardinal-like crest. Over 185 bird species have been seen here.

The refuge is open daily. There is no entrance fee.

Visitor activities include wildlife observation; photography; driving on unpaved refuge roads (most of which are unmaintained trails and many of which are passable only in a four-wheel-drive vehicle); hiking; and limited hunting (bighorn, deer, coyote, fox, cottontail, and quail) on the refuge during the designated seasons. Off-road vehicle travel is prohibited. All motorized vehicles, including ATCs, ATVs, quadratracs, and motorcycles, and all operators must be licensed and insured for highway driving.

Primitive camping on the refuge is limited to 14 days in any 12-month period, is not permitted within one-quarter mile of a wildlife water hole, and vehicles are to remain within 100 feet of designated roads. Although campfires are allowed, the Fish and Wildlife Service emphasizes that only dead, down, and detached wood may be used; and dead wood may be collected only from areas not designated as wilderness. As wood is very scarce, "please use it sparingly, or bring your own supply."

Hiking opportunities include the Palm Canyon Trail—a 0.5-mile, 300-foot climb into this awesome, sheer-walled canyon for a view of California fan palms growing in the narrow slot of a side canyon. This is also a place where desert bighorn sheep can sometimes be spotted. Other hiking options include challenging wilderness excursions, for which adequate preparations and provisions are essential (information is available at the refuge headquarters).

The Fish and Wildlife Service cautions visitors that "Past mining activity has left numerous vertical shafts, drift tunnels, and open pits throughout the refuge. These are extremely dangerous" because they can cave in or collapse. "...no attempt should be made to enter or explore them. . . . " And: "Kofa was included in the desert military training exercises conducted by General [George S.] Patton during World War II. Unexploded ordnance may be encountered during cross country hiking." Visitors are warned not to pick up anything that appears to be military hardware; but to mark the location of the object and report it to refuge headquarters.

Sunscreen and lots of drinking water are advised, especially during the warmer months. Visitors are cautioned to be alert for rattlesnakes. The most enjoyable time to visit this scenically and ecologically magnificent desert refuge is generally from late autumn through early spring. Late spring through early autumn is extremely hot.

Lodgings and meals are available in Yuma and Ehrenberg, Arizona; and Blythe, California.

Access to the Kofa Refuge is east on several unpaved roads from U.S. Route 95 between I-10 at Quartzsite and I-8 at Yuma. The 7-mile, signed road to Palm Canyon branches from Route 95 just north of mile marker 85, about 18 miles south of Quartzsite and about 63 miles north of Yuma. The unpaved, county-maintained road into King Valley between the Kofa and Castle Dome mountains branches east from Route 95 at mile marker 77; and the unpaved, county-maintained road to the Castle Dome Mountains branches northeast from Route 95 at mile marker 55.

Further information: Kofa National Wildlife Refuge, 356 West First Street, Yuma, AZ 85364; telephone: (928) 783-7861.

Leslie Canyon, encompassing 2,768 acres, was established in 1988, primarily to promote the recovery and protection of a number of federally listed rare species of indigenous fish and wildlife associated with flowing stream and riparian habitat that is surrounded by Chihuahuan Desert uplands. The refuge protects approximately a mile of perennial stream and its bordering riparian corridor of Fremont cottonwoods, willows, and Arizona ash, within the headwaters of the Río Yaqui watershed, at the southern end of the Swisshelm Mountains in southeastern Arizona.

The Nature Conservancy helped make possible the acquisition of this area, holding the initial parcel in trust until the U.S. Fish and Wildlife Service was able to purchase it under authority of the Endangered Species Act. Funding for land acquisition was derived from the federal Land and Water Conservation Fund.

Although the majority of Leslie Canyon National Wildlife Refuge is closed to public access to minimize disturbance of the fragile habitat and associated protected species, a portion of the refuge is open daily during daylight hours. In addition, the Leslie Canyon Road runs through the refuge and affords opportunities to see many of the birds and other wildlife and to enjoy this scenic route. The refuge is located on the edge of the Swisshelm Mountains, 16 miles north of Douglas on Leslie Canyon Road; or 11 miles east of McNeal on Davis Road. Leslie Canyon Road continues from the refuge to Rucker Canyon in the nearby Chiricahua Mountains. (For further information on this refuge, see the San Bernardino National Wildlife Refuge text below.)

San Bernardino, containing 2,369 acres, was established in 1982 primarily to promote the recovery and protection of a number of rare species of indigenous fish and wildlife associated with *cienega* habitat that is surrounded by Chihuahuan Desert uplands and grassland. The refuge is located in the headwaters of the Rio Yaqui watershed, adjacent to the U.S.–Mexico border in the southeastern corner of Arizona.

This refuge and nearby Leslie Canyon National Wildlife Refuge are jointly managed. As described by the U.S. Fish and Wildlife Service in the refuges' *Annual Narrative Report* for 2000:

The streams, cienegas (marshy wetlands), and springs … provided historic habitat for eight different species of indigenous fish, including the beautiful shiner (*Cyprinella formosa*), Yaqui chub (*Gila purpurea*), Yaqui catfish (*Ictalurus pricei*), Yaqui topminnow (*Poeciliopsis occidentalis sonoriensis*), long fin dace (*Agosia chrysogaster*), Mexican stoneroller (*Campostoma ornatum*), roundtail chub (*Gila robusta*), and Yaqui sucker (*Catostomus bernardini*). Four of these species, the Yaqui chub, catfish, topminnow, and sucker, were found nowhere else in the United States.

Additional rare species associated with the cienega habitats include the Huachuca water umbel (*Lilaeopsis schaffneriana*, var. *recurva*), the Mexican garter snake (*Thamnophis eques*), and the Chiricahua leopard frog (*Rana chiricahuensis*). Several invertebrate species are also restricted to these unique wetlands. . . .

Both refuges currently provide a land base for recovery of Río Yaqui species.

The San Bernardino Refuge is open daily during daylight hours. There is no entrance fee. The San Bernardino/Leslie Canyon Refuge office, located about 10 miles north of Douglas along U.S. Route 191, is open on weekdays, except national holidays.

Visitor activities include wildlife observation, photography, and hiking. A selected and posted area of the refuge is open to seasonal hunting (dove, quail, and cottontail rabbit). Refuge gates may occasionally be closed and locked, at which times foot travel is the only way to enter the refuge. Over 280 bird species have been seen on these refuges.

Visitors are cautioned to be alert for rattlesnakes.

Lodgings and meals are available in such communities as Douglas, Bisbee, Tombstone, and Willcox.

San Bernardino Refuge is located on the U.S.–Mexico border, 16 miles east of Douglas, Arizona, along the Geronimo Trail Road. From the refuge, this road runs through the Peloncillo Mountains and into New Mexico.

Further information: San Bernardino and Leslie Canyon National Wildlife Refuges, P.O. Box 3509, Douglas, AZ 85607; telephone: (520) 364-2104.

Arkansas

Bald Knob, containing approximately 15,000 acres in two units, was established in 1993 to enhance and protect important feeding and resting habitat for wintering waterfowl and other wildlife in northeastern Arkansas. The refuge consists of forested wetlands and croplands situated along the Little Red River.

The refuge's ecological diversity includes bald cypress/tupelo/swamp brakes, oxbow lakes, meandering Overflow Creek, southern bottomland hardwood forest, and agricultural fields. The wooded bottomlands and wetlands are a vital remnant of once-vast forestland that once extended along the lower Mississippi River Valley region.

The U.S. Fish and Wildlife Service is working to expand and enhance the forested habitat by carrying out a reforestation program on some of the refuge's agricultural lands that originally sustained an ecologically rich forest. The regrowth of oaks, gum, pecan, and cypress trees will increase the diversity of wildlife species and will help curtail soil erosion. Other croplands are being devoted to cooperative farming, whereby a portion of such crops as rice, milo, and millet remains unharvested, for the benefit of waterfowl and other wildlife.

The refuge is open daily during daylight hours. There is no entrance fee, and very limited visitor-use facilities are provided.

Visitor activities include birdwatching, photography, driving on some of the unimproved refuge roads on the Farm Unit, hiking ATV trails on the Mingo Creek Unit, canoeing and boating, fishing, and hunting (waterfowl, deer, raccoon, rabbit, squirrel, and quail) on parts of the refuge during the designated seasons. Camping is not permitted on the refuge. November through April are the best birdwatching months. Part of the refuge's Farm Unit that is designated as "waterfowl sanctuary" is closed to visitation from November 15 through February.

Visitors are cautioned to be alert for venomous snakes, fire ants, ticks, and chiggers. Insect repellent is advised.

Lodgings and meals are available in such communities as Brinkley, Augusta, Bald Knob, and Searcy.

Access to Bald Knob Refuge's Farm Unit and headquarters from State Route 367 is by way of Coal Chute Access Road, in the town of Bald Knob; or by way of Safely Road Access, just north of the town of Judsonia. Or, from State Route 64, access is by way of Mingo Creek Access Road, approximately 5 miles east of the town of Bald Knob.

Further information: Bald Knob National Wildlife Refuge, 26320 Highway 33 South, Augusta, AR 72006; telephone: (870) 347-2614.

Big Lake, consisting of 11,038 acres, was originally established in 1915 to protect the numerous waterfowl species wintering here in northeastern Arkansas. Since then, the refuge has been expanded to enhance and protect an area of ecologically rich southern bottomland hardwood forest and old-growth bald cypress/tupelo swamp, and meandering waterways surrounding the open expanse of Big Lake.

As part of a vast floodway system encompassing southeastern Missouri and northeastern Arkansas, the refuge is surrounded by levees with water control structures on each end, which enable the U.S. Fish and Wildlife Service to manipulate water levels for the benefit of waterbirds and other wildlife. Water levels are typically lowered during late summer and early autumn, to promote the growth of smartweed and other waterfowl plant foods. The area is then reflooded in late autumn, for the benefit of large concentrations of wintering ducks and geese.

Nesting boxes are maintained on the refuge, providing supplemental nesting cavities for wood ducks and hooded mergansers. In addition to wetland-dependent migratory birds, the refuge attracts a nesting pair of bald eagles, a variety of raptors, a multitude of neotropical songbirds, and mammals such as river otters and beavers. More than 225 species of birds have been recorded here.

Expansion of the original refuge acreage was made possible partly with revenues from the sale of Migratory Bird Hunting and Conservation Stamps (Duck Stamps).

Big Lake refuge is open daily during daylight hours. Several parts of the refuge are closed at times to avoid disturbance of wildlife, and the refuge may close at any time during the year due to flooded conditions. Visitors are urged to contact the refuge in advance, especially during the autumn, winter, and spring when flooding is likely. There is no entrance fee.

Visitor activities include birdwatching, photography, driving several miles of graveled levee roads, hiking (two trails are provided), canoeing and boating (flat-bottomed boats), fishing, and hunting (raccoon and squirrel, and archery for deer) during designated seasons. Camping, fires, and ATVs are not permitted on the refuge. Winter and spring months are the best for wildlife observation.

Visitors are cautioned that ticks, chiggers, mosquitoes, and poison ivy are abundant. Insect repellent is advised. Although venomous snakes are rarely encountered, it is a good idea to be alert for them. Poison ivy and poison oak are prolific.

Lodgings and meals are available in such communities as Blytheville, to the east of the refuge, and Jonesboro, to the west.

Access to the refuge is by way of State Route 18: either west 18 miles from I-55 at Blytheville, or east 2 miles from Manila.

Further information: Big Lake National Wildlife Refuge, P.O. Box 67, Manila, AR 72442; telephone: (870) 564-2429.

Cache River, comprising 50,000 acres, was established in 1986 to enhance, restore, and protect ecologically significant habitats of southern bottomland hardwood forest, bald cypress/tupelo swamp, oxbow lakes, and winding sloughs and channels extending along the Cache, White, and Bayou DeView rivers in northeastern Arkansas. The refuge includes remnants of once-vast bottomland-and-riparian forest in the lower Mississippi River Valley region.

Tracts of land within the refuge's authorized boundary are gradually being acquired, securing vital habitat for large concentrations of wintering mallards and other waterfowl, wading birds, bald eagles, a multitude of neotropical migratory songbirds, beavers, and many other species of wildlife. The U.S. Fish and Wildlife Service is also carrying out a program of reforestation on formerly degraded agricultural lands, planting native oaks, pecan, bald cypress, and gum trees to enhance wildlife habitat and curtail soil erosion.

Establishment of Cache River refuge is being made possible with the help of The Nature Conservancy and Ducks Unlimited, Inc.

The refuge is open daily during daylight hours, but access into the refuge is limited and few visitor facilities are provided. There is no entrance fee.

Visitor activities include birdwatching, photography, hiking, canoeing and boating, fishing, and hunting (ducks, turkey, quail, deer, raccoon, rabbit, and squirrel) during the designated seasons. Camping is not permitted on the refuge. November through April are the best months for birdwatching.

Visitors are cautioned to be alert for venomous snakes, fire ants, ticks, and chiggers. Insect repellent is advised.

Fauna and flora of Cache River refuge are virtually the same as the species recorded on Bald Knob.

Lodgings and meals are available in such communities as Brinkley, Augusta, Bald Knob, and Searcy.

Access to the Cache River Refuge is limited to county-maintained gravel roads and several boat-access ramp sites, located throughout the refuge. The boundary of the refuge frequently changes as land acquisition continues along the Cache, White, and Bayou DeView rivers. Visitors are encouraged to contact the refuge headquarters for additional information and access points.

Further information: Cache River National Wildlife Refuge, Route 2, Box 126-T, Augusta, AR 72006; telephone: (870) 347-2614.

Felsenthal, containing 65,000 acres, was established in 1975 to enhance and protect 10,000 acres of pine uplands, 40,000 acres of southern bottomland hardwood forest, and the 15,000-acre Felsenthal Pool, in southern Arkansas. This refuge is upstream from the U.S. Army Corps of Engineers' Felsenthal Dam, around the junction of the Ouachita and Saline rivers.

The U.S. Fish and Wildlife Service regulates the seasonal flooding of the refuge's bottomland forest habitat, known as green-tree reservoir management. Felsenthal Pool, the world's largest such impoundment, is flooded and expanded to more than twice its normal size for the benefit of herons, egrets, and large concentrations of wintering waterfowl, including at least twenty species of ducks.

During the summer, the water level in other impoundment areas, known as moist-soil units, is lowered to promote the growth of waterfowl plant foods. In the autumn, these areas are re-flooded to make this food source readily available to the wintering waterfowl.

The refuge provides wood duck nesting boxes, supplementing the natural supply of nesting cavities. In the uplands, where the rare and endangered red-cockaded woodpecker drills nesting cavities in the boles of mature pine trees, the refuge practices selective cutting and periodic prescribed burning, to maintain open woodland with the mature pines required by this specialized species. To promote new woodpecker breeding colonies, artificial nest inserts are provided to supplement natural cavities.

Other wildlife inhabiting Felsenthal Refuge includes migratory shorebirds, wintering bald eagles, flocks of wild turkeys, numerous species of neotropical migratory songbirds, the rare Louisiana black bear, and the alligator, which is at the northern edge of its range here.

Friends of Felsenthal National Wildlife Refuge is a nonprofit support group that is assisting the refuge in many ways.

The refuge is open daily. There is no entrance fee. The visitor center, in which exhibits and programs interpret both the natural and cultural resources of the refuge, is open Mondays through Fridays and also on Sundays, except Christmas.

Visitor activities include birdwatching; photography; environmental education programs and prearranged group tours; driving on 15 miles of unpaved refuge roads; hiking; high-flotation ATV use on designated ATV trails; canoeing and boating (a dozen boat ramps are available); camping (ten primitive campsites on the refuge, campground facilities at adjacent Moro Bay State Park, and two nearby privately run campgrounds); fishing (by boat and from a wheelchair-accessible fishing area near the visitor center); and hunting (deer, rabbit, squirrel, turkey, and quail) during the designated seasons. November through April are the best months for birdwatching. Nearly 300 bird species have been recorded here.

Hiking opportunities are available on more than 60 miles of trails and several interpretive trails, including a 0.5-mile (wheelchair-accessible) path, adjacent to the visitor center; and a 2.6-mile route that is adjacent to the Crosset Harbor Recreation Site.

Although alligators are generally afraid of people, visitors are cautioned to stay a safe distance from these sluggish-looking but potentially fast-moving reptiles and to be alert for venomous snakes, fire ants, ticks, and chiggers. Insect repellent is advised.

Lodgings and meals are available in such communities as Crosset and El Dorado.

> Access to the refuge's visitor center is west 5 miles on U.S. Route 82 from Crossett, or east 45 miles on Route 82 from El Dorado.

> Further information: Felsenthal National Wildlife Refuge, 5531 Highway 82 West, Crossett, AR 71635; telephone: (870) 364-3167.

Holla Bend, containing 7,055 acres, was established in 1957 to enhance and protect an ecologically outstanding, wildlife-rich area in the Arkansas River Valley between the Ouachita and Ozark mountains in west-central Arkansas. This refuge encompasses former river-oxbow habitat that attracts large concentrations of wintering geese and ducks, nesting wood ducks, wading birds, migratory shorebirds and raptors, wintering bald and golden eagles, and numerous species of neotropical migratory songbirds. Roadrunners and scissor-tailed flycatchers are near the eastern edge of their ranges here. Over 235 bird species have been seen here.

The refuge is open daily during daylight hours. An entrance fee is charged. The refuge office is open on weekdays, except national holidays.

Visitor activities include birdwatching, photography, driving the auto tour route, viewing the refuge and wildlife from an observation tower, hiking on trails and roads, boating and fishing (on refuge lakes and ponds from March 1 through October), and hunting (deer, turkey, and raccoon, but not waterfowl) during the designated seasons. Camping is not allowed on the refuge, but nearby U.S. Army Corps of Engineers campground facilities are available, as are facilities in Mount Nebo and Petit Jean state parks and in Ouachita and Ozark national forests. November through April are the best months for birdwatching.

Visitors are cautioned to be alert for venomous snakes, ticks, and chiggers. Insect repellent is advised.

Among the birds are great blue heron; great egret; snow and Canada geese; ducks (wood, gadwall, American wigeon, mallard, green-winged and blue-winged teal, and northern pintail); bald eagle; wild turkey; northern bobwhite; ring-billed gull; belted kingfisher; blue jay; Carolina chickadee; tufted titmouse; Carolina wren; eastern bluebird; wood thrush; northern mockingbird; brown thrasher; yellow-rumped warbler; common yellowthroat; summer tanager; northern cardinal; indigo bunting; red-winged blackbird; and orchard and Baltimore orioles.

Mammals include Louisiana black bear (occasional), white-tailed deer, bobcat, coyote, red fox, mink, river otter, beaver, raccoon, opossum, striped skunk, woodchuck, eastern cottontail, swamp rabbit, eastern gray and fox squirrels, and the nine-banded armadillo.

Trees include shortleaf pine; eastern red cedar; sassafras; American sycamore; sweetgum; American and slippery elms; black walnut; pecan; hickories (bitternut, mockernut, shagbark, and pignut); oaks (white, post, southern red, black, blackjack, water, and willow); river birch; eastern cottonwood; black willow; common persimmon; eastern redbud; black locust; flowering dogwood; black tupelo; red and silver maples; boxelder; and white and green ashes.

Lodgings and meals are available in such communities as Russellville and Dardanelle.

Access to the refuge from Dardanelle is south 1 mile on State Route 7and east (left) 4 miles on State Route 155.

Further information: Holla Bend National Wildlife Refuge, Route 1, Box 59, Dardanelle, AR 72834; telephone: (501) 229-4300.

Logan Cave, containing 123 acres, was established in 1989 to protect a cave inhabited by more than 20,000 of the rare and endangered gray bat, as well as the rare grotto salamander and blind Ozark cavefish in northwestern Arkansas. The cave is open only by special permit for research.

Lodgings and meals are available in such communities as Russellville and Dardanelle.

Further information: Logan Cave National Wildlife Refuge, c/o Holla Bend NWR, Route 1, Box 59, Dardanelle, AR 72834; telephone: (501) 229-4300.

Oakwood Unit, consisting of 2,263 acres, was established in 1999 to manage wetland impoundments and reforest former farmlands in southeastern Arkansas.

The refuge is open only by special request for birdwatching and photography. Visitors are cautioned to be alert for poisonous snakes, fire ants, ticks, and chiggers. Insect repellent is advised.

Lodgings and meals are available in such communities as McGehee and Dumas.

Further information: Oakwood Unit National Wildlife Refuge, c/o Felsenthal National Wildlife Refuge, 5531 Highway 82 West, Crossett, AR 71635; telephone (870) 364-3167.

Overflow, ultimately to comprise more than 18,000 acres with continuing land acquisition, was established in 1980 to protect an ecologically significant, seasonally flooded tract of bottomland hardwood forest along the Overflow Creek watershed within the lower Mississippi River Delta region of southeastern Arkansas. In addition, there are soil management impoundments and croplands.

This refuge's wetlands provide important habitat for large concentrations of wintering waterfowl and resident wood ducks. The woodlands attract numerous species of neotropical migratory songbirds. And under cooperative agreements with farmers, a portion of the crops is left unharvested for the benefit of waterfowl and other wildlife. Ducks Unlimited, Inc., has assisted with extensive habitat enhancement projects.

The refuge is open daily during daylight hours. There is no entrance fee.

Visitor activities include birdwatching, photography, hiking on a few trails, and hunting during the designated seasons. Camping is not permitted on the refuge. November through April are the best months for birdwatching.

Visitors are cautioned to be alert for venomous snakes, fire ants, ticks, and chiggers. Insect repellent is advised.

Fauna are essentially the same as on Felsenthal.

Among the more prominent trees are loblolly pine; bald cypress; sweetgum; sassafras; cedar elm; pecan; shagbark hickory; oaks (overcup, southern red, post, Nuttall, and willow); and black and water tupelo.

Lodgings and meals are available in Hamburg, Crosset, and Lake Village.

Access to the refuge from U.S. Route 165 at Wilmot is west 8 miles on State Route 52, or from U.S. Route 425 at Hamburg, east 6 miles on State Route 8.

Further information: Overflow National Wildlife Refuge, c/o Felsenthal National Wildlife Refuge, 5531 Highway 82 West, Crossett, AR 71635; telephone: (870) 364-3167.

Pond Creek, consisting of 27,300 acres, was established as Cossatot National Wildlife Refuge in 1994 and redesignated in 1997 to protect one of the last remaining ecologically significant tracts of once-vast southern bottomland hardwood forest in the Red River Basin, along the Oklahoma–Texas border, in southwestern Arkansas.

This refuge lies mostly in the floodplain between the Cossatot and Little rivers. It was re-named to acknowledge the area's local name, "Pond Creek Bottoms."

The U.S. Fish and Wildlife Service's management objectives on this refuge include protect-ing the mature bottomland hardwood forest, meandering sloughs, and beaver ponds. These wet-lands include prime habitat for nesting wood ducks, wintering waterfowl, bald eagles, numerous neotropical migratory songbirds, and several wading-bird rookeries.

Pond Creek Refuge's drier uplands contain some areas of mixed pine/hardwood forest and about 6,000 acres of pine plantations. The latter acreage, planted by a timber company, is ex-pected to be restored to native hardwood forest.

The refuge is open daily during daylight hours. There is no entrance fee, and there are few visitor-use facilities.

Visitor activities include birdwatching, photography, hiking, canoeing and boating, fishing, and hunting during the designated seasons. November through April are the best months for birdwatching.

Although alligators are generally afraid of people, visitors are cautioned to stay a safe dis-tance from these sluggish-looking but potentially fast-moving reptiles; and to be alert for ven-omous snakes, fire ants, ticks, and chiggers. Insect repellent is advised.

Lodgings and meals are available in such communities as Ashdown and De Queen.

Access to the refuge from Ashdown is north 15 miles on U.S. Route 71 to Falls Chapel, and west 2 miles, following refuge directional signs; or from State Route 41 at Horatio, east 7 miles on Central Road.

Further information: Pond Creek National Wildlife Refuge, 560 Polk 246, Gillham, AR 71841; telephone: (870) 386-2700.

Wapanocca, consisting of 5,624 acres, was established in 1961 to restore and protect land in northeastern Arkansas that was previously a hunt club dating back to the Civil War. The refuge contains southern bottomland hardwood forest in early stages of reforestation, seasonal water impoundments, a scenic 1,200-acre bald cypress swamp, Wapanocca Lake, grassland, and cropland. The area provides important habitat for as many as 200,000 wintering waterfowl as well as wading birds, nesting bald eagles, wild turkeys, numerous species of neotropical migratory songbirds, and beavers.

Wood ducks and hooded mergansers nest here, many of them using nesting boxes, hundreds of which were made by students and other volunteers. Under cooperative agricultural agreements, farmers leave unharvested a portion of crops for the benefit of ducks, geese, and other wildlife.

Establishment of this refuge was made possible partly with the assistance of descendants of original hunt club members and partly with revenues from the sale of Migratory Bird Hunting and Conservation Stamps (Duck Stamps). The National Tree Trust donated tree seedlings for reforesting parts of Wapanocca.

The refuge is open daily during daylight hours. There is no entrance fee.

Visitor activities include birdwatching, photography, driving the refuge's auto tour route, viewing the refuge and wildlife from a (wheelchair-accessible) boardwalk and observation platform, hiking in the forest and on refuge roads, canoeing and boating (shallow-bottom boats), fishing (a fishing pier is provided), and small-game hunting on part of the refuge during the designated seasons. Camping is not permitted on the refuge, but campground facilities are provided in nearby Lake Poinsett, Shelby Forest, and Village Creek state parks. November through May are the best months for birdwatching.

Visitors are cautioned to be alert for venomous snakes, fire ants, ticks, and chiggers. Insect repellent is advised.

Lodgings and meals are available in such communities as West Memphis and Marion.

Access to the refuge is north about 15 miles on I-55 from West Memphis, to Exit 21 and then east 1.5 miles on State Route 42.

Further information: Wapanocca National Wildlife Refuge, P.O. Box 279, Turrell, AR 72384; telephone: (870) 343-2595.

White River, containing 160,000 acres, was established in 1935 as a refuge and breeding ground for migratory birds and other wildlife along the White River in eastern Arkansas. The forest of oaks, bald cypress, and other tree species is one of the largest remaining seasonally flooded, bottomland hardwood-forested, riparian habitat in the lower Mississippi River Valley and the most extensive contiguous area of this habitat under a single ownership in the United States.

As Devereux Butcher wrote in his 1963 book, *Exploring Our National Wildlife Refuges:*

The outstanding feature of this refuge is its southern bottomland hardwood forest. Although most of it is second growth, much of it today is of huge proportions, and there remain here and there towering giants. In places the effect is almost Amazonian, with vines clambering high among the trees. The White

River winds a tortuous course through the refuge, forming oxbows, and branching with a number of equally twisting tributaries. Throughout the forest are innumerable crescent-shaped lakes, remnants of former river channels, many of them rimmed with cypress trees.

Highlighting the refuge's rich abundance and diversity of wildlife are several hundred thousand wintering ducks, earning the area's reputation as the duck capital of the United States. The mallard is by far the most abundant duck at White River—more than one-half million being on the refuge lakes in early January. Other birds and animals include nesting wood ducks, thousands of wintering Canada geese, migratory shorebirds, bald eagles, wild turkeys, huge influxes of neotropical migratory songbirds, and numerous black bears and whitetail deer.

The ivory-billed woodpecker once inhabited the primeval bottomland forests of the Mississippi River Valley, including the forest of White River Refuge. The ivory-bill was the largest woodpecker north of Mexico, exceeding in size even the pileated. Like the latter, it had a flaming red crest, the remainder of the plumage being black and white, but with much more white than the pileated. The bill was ivory white. Its range extended as far north as southern Illinois and up the Ohio River valley to southern Indiana, and it lived in the forests of the east, from North Carolina to southern Florida. As late as the 1940s, two pairs were known to inhabit the Tensas Swamp, a hundred miles south of White River Refuge in northeastern Louisiana. This area was a privately owned tract of old-growth southern bottomland hardwood forest—the only kind of habitat in which the ivory-bill could live, because its food requirements consisted of certain grubs occurring in the dead trees and snags of such a forest. In the 1940s, efforts were made to save the Tensas Swamp from being logged, as a last hope of perpetuating this species. But these attempts were at least forty years too late, and ornithologists are now virtually certain that this magnificent bird is extinct. (See further discussion of the ivory-billed woodpecker in the Tensas River Refuge text.)

Establishment of the White River Refuge was made possible mostly with revenues from the sale of Migratory Bird Hunting and Conservation Stamps (Duck Stamps).

The refuge is open daily. There is no entrance fee.

Visitor activities include birdwatching, photography, driving unpaved refuge roads and two-track trails during the drier seasons, hiking many miles of trails, camping during some of the year, canoeing and boating, fishing, and hunting on parts of the refuge during the designated seasons. During the winter and spring, parts of the refuge are often closed due to flooding, and other areas, which are designated as waterfowl sanctuaries, are closed to public access. November through June are the best months for birdwatching.

Visitors are cautioned to be alert for venomous snakes, ticks, and chiggers. Insect repellent is advised.

Lodgings and meals are available in such communities as DeWitt, Helena, Stuttgart, and Clarendon.

Access to the refuge is south and east 27 miles on State Route 30 from U.S. Route 79 at Stuttgart to DeWitt; and 16 miles on State Route 1 to St. Charles and the refuge entrance.

Further information: White River National Wildlife Refuge, P.O. Box 308, DeWitt, AR 72042; telephone: (870) 946-1468.

California

Antioch Dunes, comprising 55 acres in two separate units, was established in 1980 to restore and protect important remnants of sand dunes that provide critical habitat for a number of rare and endangered species of plants and insects. The refuge is located adjacent to commercial properties, along the south shore of the San Joaquin River and just east of the city of Antioch in central California.

These isolated patches of rolling, riverine sand dunes, rising to as much as 50 feet in height, are comprised of aeolian (windblown) sand. These dunes are remnants of what was once an extensive dune system that rose more than 100 feet and stretched at least 5 miles along the riverbank. As explained by the U.S. Fish and Wildlife Service, in the refuge's *Draft Comprehensive Conservation Plan* (*Draft CCP*), "The dunes were formed by ancient deposits of glacial sands carried downriver from the Sierra Nevada, left isolated along the river after the Mojave Desert receded in prehistoric times. Over thousands of years, ocean winds and bay tides slowly shaped these sands into high dunes. Isolation of this sand dune habitat resulted in the development of species and subspecies of plants and insects that are found nowhere else in the world."

One of the endangered species for which the refuge was established is the Lange's metalmark butterfly (*Apodemia mormo langei*). This subspecies of metalmark, which is endemic to Antioch Dunes, was discovered in 1933. In 1976, it was one of the first eight insects to be placed on the federal endangered species list. Lange's metalmark is dependent upon a single species of plant. In its caterpillar stage, it feeds exclusively on the naked-stemmed buckwheat, and the adult butterfly prefers the buckwheat's nectar. The Fish and Wildlife Service explains, "Restoration efforts in Antioch Dunes National Wildlife Refuge have included planting thousands of buckwheat seedlings, controlling non-native plants that threaten to crowd out the buckwheat, and creating new sand dunes . . . by trucking in over 7,000 cubic yards of sand." The Service says that these management activities "appear to be successful."

Regarding visitation, the Fish and Wildlife Service (in its *Draft CCP*) explains:

The Refuge . . . was closed to the public in 1986 to protect the endangered species and their habitat, a concern that arose as a result of several incidents. Visitors using the refuge prior to this time commonly built illegal fires along the waterfront. On several occasions, the fires escaped and threatened the survival of the three species by indiscriminately burning surrounding habitat. In 1986, endangered plants were trampled by hundreds of people as they flocked to the Refuge to see a whale (nicknamed Humphrey) swim up the San Joaquin River.

Although the Refuge is now closed to the public, volunteers help Refuge staff by participating in endangered species surveys, wallflower and primrose plantings, picking up trash, and weeding. Occasionally, interpretive tours are also given to various groups. . . .

Among the refuge's habitat management activities are annual surveys of the three endangered species, non-native weed control, carefully prescribed burning to control certain species of pest plants, creating firebreaks, importing sand to create new dunes from a stockpile on adjacent Pacific Gas and Electric Company (PG&E) land, and planting newly created dunes with nursery-grown endangered and native plants that are endemic to the Antioch Dunes.

As for cooperative partnerships on the refuge, the Fish and Wildlife Service (in its *Draft CCP*) says, "The City of Antioch, with assistance from California Department of Transportation (Caltrans), has worked with the Service to recontour a dune, and will propagate and plant native species, and control non-native vegetation. Caltrans continues to be an important data-sharing partner and has provided the Service with numerous aerial photographs of the Refuge, as well as labor for dune construction. Chevron Oil Company has worked with the Refuge to recontour three new dunes on the Refuge. . . . The Service and PG&E are continuing to pursue a cooperative agreement on PG&E lands. The agreement would improve habitat for endangered species, allow the Service and PG&E to cooperatively manage the Sardis Unit as 27 acres of continuous habitat, and allow the Service to conduct surveys and management activities on PG&E land."

Further information: Antioch Dunes National Wildlife Refuge, c/o San Francisco Bay NWR Complex, P.O. Box 524, Newark, CA 94560; telephone: (510) 792-0222.

Bitter Creek, containing 14,094 acres, was established in 1985 to provide protection of roosting and foraging habitat for the endangered California condor. The refuge was established in an area of arid foothills of the southern San Joaquin Valley as part of the California Condor Recovery Program, with funding from the Land and Water Conservation Act. It adjoins Los Padres National Forest within parts of Kern, Ventura, and San Luis Obispo counties in southern California. The refuge contains a condor holding facility and serves as a base of operations for U.S. Fish and Wildlife Service personnel.

Habitats include open grasslands that are excellent foraging areas for condors; it also contains California juniper shrubland, interior live oak savanna, and singleleaf pinyon/California juniper/California scrub oak woodland. Bitter Creek Canyon also supports a small area of riparian habitat. Other species of wildlife include coyote, the endangered San Joaquin kit fox, golden eagle and other raptors, and the endangered blunt-nosed leopard lizard (for information on the latter species, see the Pixley Refuge text).

For information on the condor and the California Condor Recovery Program, see the Hopper Mountain National Wildlife Refuge text.

Although Bitter Creek Refuge is closed to visitation, it is possible to view some of the refuge and possibly see a condor from State Highway 166 and Cerro Noroeste Road. The latter can be reached from Maricopa by driving south just over 4 miles on State Route 166, east (left) on Klipstein Canyon Road, and westward on Cerro Noroeste Road.

Lodgings and meals are available in Maricopa.

Further information: Bitter Creek National Wildlife Refuge, c/o Hopper Mountain NWR Complex, P.O. Box 5839, Ventura, CA 93005; telephone: (805) 644-5185.

Blue Ridge, consisting of 897 acres, was established in 1982 to protect part of a historic California condor roosting area. Three vegetation types occur on the refuge: coniferous forest with ponderosa pines and incense cedars, chaparral, and woodland savanna with scattered brush and grassland. The Blue Ridge Refuge, which is a small part of the 11,100-acre Blue Ridge Wildlife Habitat Area, is located near the southern end of the Sierra Nevada, within Tulare County in southern California.

Under the California Condor Recovery Program, captive breeding and release of this endangered species has subsequently resulted in its reintroduction into the wild at other places in southern and central California and in northern Arizona. (For further information on the condor and its recovery program, see the Hopper Mountain Refuge text.) As of early 2002, condors are not yet using the refuge but have been observed nearby, such as in the vicinity of the Tule River Indian Reservation and the town of Glennville.

Blue Ridge Refuge and the adjacent wildlife habitat area support such birds as mountain quail, blue grouse, band-tailed pigeon, great horned owl, white-headed woodpecker, Steller's jay, mountain chickadee, white-breasted and red-breasted nuthatches, and Townsend's solitaire. Mammals include mule deer, mountain lion, bobcat, coyote, red and gray foxes, striped skunk, porcupine, mountain cottontail, Douglas squirrel (chickaree), western gray squirrel, and yellow pine chipmunk.

Blue Ridge Refuge is closed to visitation.

Further information: Blue Ridge National Wildlife Refuge, c/o Hopper Mountain NWR Complex, P.O. Box 5839, Ventura, CA 93005; telephone: (805) 644-5185.

Butte Sink, comprising 733 acres, was established in 1980 to restore wetland habitat primarily for the benefit of wintering waterfowl. The refuge is one of six national wildlife refuges in the Sacramento NWR Complex. It is located within an 11,000-acre expanse of wetlands and exclusive hunt clubs, east of the Sacramento River and near the community of Colusa, in the Sacramento Valley of north-central California.

The U.S. Fish and Wildlife Service states that Butte Sink refuge "typically supports one of the greatest concentrations of waterfowl in the world on a per-acre basis, over 300,000 ducks and 100,000 geese on 733 acres of habitat. It is also important habitat for the Aleutian Canada goose and several other threatened/endangered species."

The refuge is closed to visitation.

For a discussion of the Sacramento NWR Complex's habitat management activities, wildlife, and visitor center, see the Sacramento NWR text.

Further information: Butte Sink National Wildlife Refuge, c/o Sacramento NWR Complex, 752 County Road 99W , Willows, CA 95988; telephone: (530) 934-2801.

Butte Sink Wildlife Management Area (see in the Sacramento National Wildlife Refuge text)

Castle Rock, encompassing nearly 14 acres, was established in 1979 to protect one of the most significant places along the Pacific Coast for large concentrations of colonial nesting seabirds. The surf-pounded rock, which rises 335 feet from the sea, is located less than 0.5 mile offshore from Crescent City in the northwestern corner of California.

The majority of the seabirds that are attracted to Castle Rock are an estimated 75,000 common murres—the largest breeding colony on the California coast. Other bird species include double-crested, Brandt's, and pelagic cormorants; pigeon guillemot; and tufted puffin. (For additional information on the latter species, see the Farallon Refuge text.) This is also a major night roosting place during migration for a large part of the Aleutian Canada goose population, a threatened subspecies that numbers roughly 20,000 individuals. Of marine mammals that inhabit the surrounding waters, harbor and elephant seals and California and Steller sea lions haul themselves onto Castle Rock's beach.

Although Castle Rock is closed to visitation, it can be seen from the mainland with a spotting scope or binoculars from an interpretive viewing spot on North Pebble Beach Drive, or by boat (however, approaching closer than 200 yards is not permitted to avoid disturbing the wildlife).

Lodgings and meals are available in Crescent City.

> Further information: Castle Rock National Wildlife Refuge, c/o Humboldt Bay NWR, P.O. Box 576, 1020 Ranch Road, Loleta, CA 95551; telephone: (707) 733-5406.

Cibola (see text under Arizona)

Clear Lake, comprising 46,460 acres, was established in 1911. The refuge protects and manages roughly 20,000 acres of open water, plus adjacent arid uplands that predominantly contain alkali sacaton (commonly called bunchgrass), sagebrush, and scattered western junipers. It is located within the Klamath Basin in northeastern California.

Clear Lake Reservoir offers wetland habitat for concentrations of migrant waterfowl. A number of small rocky islands in Clear Lake are used as secure sites for colonial nesting birds such as American white pelicans, double-crested cormorants, and gulls. The refuge contains one of only two pelican nesting colonies in California. The upland habitat supports such wildlife as pronghorns, mule deer, and the greater sage-grouse (for discussions of the latter species, see Seedskadee and Hart Mountain refuge texts).

As the U.S. Fish and Wildlife Service explains, "The Clear Lake Reservoir is the primary source of water for the agricultural program of the eastern half of the Klamath Basin with water levels regulated by the U.S. Bureau of Reclamation." A major goal of the refuge is to "Integrate the maintenance of productive wetland habitats and sustainable agriculture consistent with waterfowl management." Clear Lake Refuge is one of six national wildlife refuges in the Klamath Basin. The others are Tule Lake, in California; Lower Klamath, in California/Oregon; and Bear Valley, Upper Klamath, and Klamath Marsh, in Oregon (see separate texts on each of these refuges). A discussion of the history of the Klamath Basin's wetlands and its peak influxes of waterfowl and other water birds is presented in the Lower Klamath Refuge text. The Klamath Basin Wildlife Association, a nonprofit organization, assists the refuge in a variety of ways.

To avoid disturbance of wildlife and to protect fragile habitats, Clear Lake refuge is closed to visitation, except for limited waterfowl and pronghorn hunting. There are opportunities to observe wildlife from unpaved U.S. Forest Service Road 136, which runs along the refuge's southern boundary. The Klamath Basin NWR's headquarters/visitor center is located 5 miles west of the community of Tulelake, California, on Hill Road.

Species of wildlife that have been recorded on Clear Lake refuge are largely the same as those on Lower Klamath Refuge.

Lodgings and meals are available in such communities as Tule Lake, California and Klamath Falls, Oregon.

Access from the community of Tulelake, California is southeast about 20 miles on California State Route 139 and northeast (left) about 10 miles on Forest Service Road 136.

Further information: Clear Lake National Wildlife Refuge, c/o Klamath Basin NWRs, 4009 Hill Road, Tulelake, CA 96143; telephone: (530) 667-2231.

Coachella Valley, containing 3,276 acres, was established in 1985 to restore and protect the majority of the vital sand dune habitat for the federally listed threatened Coachella Valley fringe-toed lizard (*Uma inornata*). The refuge, which is part of the 20,114-acre Coachella Valley Preserve, is at the northern end of the Coachella Valley, within the Colorado Desert in southern California.

As described by the U.S. Fish and Wildlife Service, this pale-colored, 6- to 9-inch-long species of lizard "is a small, highly specialized reptile that inhabits the windblown desert regions of the Coachella Valley. . . . It derives its common name not only from its home, but also from the enlarged scales along its toes [enabling it to "swim" across loose sand]. This lizard has adapted other unique forms and structures to enable it to survive in the harsh desert habitat including a wedge-shaped nose . . . [that] enables it to burrow through loose, fine sand; elongated scales [that] cover the ears to keep out blowing sand; and specialized nostrils that allow it to breathe below the sand without inhaling sand particles."

The fringe-toed lizard historically inhabited more than 170,000 acres of Coachella Valley sand dune or "blowsand" habitat. Today, only about 12,000 acres continue receiving the naturally occurring "blowsand" that is vital to the lizard's survival. One of the largest remaining populations is encompassed by the refuge and preserve.

The Fish and Wildlife Service explains:

The Coachella Valley fringe-toed lizard is threatened by a continual loss of habitat from human development. The majority of the lizard's historic habitat has been eliminated or degraded because of direct and indirect effects of development. Structures erected on the sand transport corridor areas and the introduction of non-native, invasive plant species (including tamarisk) are stabilizing the once free moving sand deposits, preventing the continued replenishment of the "blowsand" habitat. . . .

Regarding prospects for the future, the Service says:

The continuing development of the Coachella Valley will have significant effects on the long-term sustainability of "blowsand" habitat of the Coachella Valley.

Without a concerted effort to conserve the habitat in the near future, the remaining habitat will become increasingly fragmented. Shielded and degraded, this rare ecosystem could disappear entirely as soon as 50 years from now.

Other species of this specialized habitat that are protected on the refuge include the Coachella Valley round-tailed ground squirrel, flat-tailed horned lizard, Coachella giant sand treader cricket, Coachella Valley Jerusalem cricket, and the endangered, pink-flowering Coachella Valley milk vetch. The sidewinder (rattlesnake) also inhabits the "blowsand" areas. Sparse vegetation that is typical of the desert *bajadas* (alluvial fans that slope outward from the base of the Little San Bernardino Mountains to the north) includes creosotebush and smoke tree.

The Coachella Valley Preserve, of which the refuge is a part, is cooperatively managed by The Nature Conservancy, U.S. Bureau of Land Management, California Department of Parks and Recreation, California Department of Fish and Game, the Center for Natural Lands Management, and the U.S. Fish and Wildlife Service. Further information on the Coachella Valley Preserve: P.O. Box 188, Thousand Palms, CA 92276; telephone: (760) 343-2733.

Although nearly all of the refuge is closed to visitation to avoid disturbing the fragile ecosystem upon which the lizard depends, it can be seen from Ramon Road, which runs along the refuge's northern boundary. A trail that crosses a small part of the refuge is open to horseback riders. Hiking opportunities are provided on designated trails in the Coachella Valley Preserve.

The Coachella Valley ranks among the hottest and driest areas in the United States. Annual rainfall averages only around 4 inches, with some years bringing none. Summer temperatures reach as high as 120°F.

Lodgings and meals are available in such communities as Thousand Palms, Palm Springs, and Indio.

Access to the Coachella Valley Preserve from the Ramon Road exit on I-10 is east about 4 miles on Ramon Road and north (left) about 1 mile on Thousand Palms Canyon Road to the visitor station.

Further information: Coachella Valley National Wildlife Refuge, c/o Sonny Bono Salton Sea NWR, 906 West Sinclair Road, Calipatria, CA 92233; telephone: (760) 251-4860.

Colusa, consisting of 4,507 acres, was established in 1945 to restore and manage seasonally flooded marsh, riparian, permanent pond, watergrass, and upland grass habitats, primarily for the benefit of as many as 200,000 ducks and 100,000 geese, during the autumn and winter months. The refuge, which is within a Sacramento River flood-bypass area, is one of six national wildlife refuges in the Sacramento NWR Complex. It is located within the Sacramento Valley in north-central California.

Ducks Unlimited, Inc., has helped enhance more than 2,600 acres of the refuge's wetland habitat.

The refuge is open daily during daylight hours. There is no entrance fee.

Visitor activities include birdwatching, photography, driving a 3-mile auto tour route that offers opportunities to view marshes and streams, walking a 1-mile trail, and hunting (goose, duck, coot, moorhen, snipe, and pheasant) on part of the refuge during the designated seasons. Insect repellent and sunscreen are advised during the warmer months.

Access to Colusa Refuge's auto tour route from I-5 just north of Williams is east 7 miles on State Route 20 and south (right) onto the refuge. Or from State Route 45 at Colusa, it is west 2 miles on State Route 20 and south (left) onto the refuge.

> For information on Sacramento NWR Complex's habitat management activities, wildlife, and visitor center, see the Sacramento NWR text.
>
> Further information: Colusa National Wildlife Refuge, c/o Sacramento NWR Complex, 752 County Road 99W , Willows, CA 95988; telephone: (530) 934-2801.

Delevan, containing 5,797 acres, was established in 1962 to restore and manage seasonally flooded marsh, riparian, permanent pond, watergrass, and upland grass habitats, primarily for the benefit of as many as 500,000 ducks and 200,000 geese, during the autumn and winter months. The refuge is one of six national wildlife refuges in the Sacramento NWR Complex, located within the Sacramento Valley in north-central California.

Ducks Unlimited, Inc., has helped enhance approximately 500 acres of the refuge's wetland habitat.

A wildlife viewing pullout is provided at the southern boundary of the Delevan Refuge, on the northern side of Maxwell Road. The refuge is open to hunting (goose, duck, coot, moorhen, snipe, and pheasant) on parts of the refuge during the designated seasons.

> Access to the wildlife viewing pullout from I-5 at Maxwell is east 4.5 miles on Maxwell Road. The hunter check station is located in the refuge, reached from Four Mile Road, which runs along the western boundary of the refuge.

> For information on the Sacramento NWR Complex's habitat management activities, wildlife, and visitor center, see the Sacramento NWR text.
>
> Further information: Delevan National Wildlife Refuge, c/o Sacramento NWR Complex, 752 County Road 99W , Willows, CA 95988; telephone: (530) 934-2801.

Don Edwards San Francisco Bay encompasses 25,902 acres and is working toward a goal of 43,000 acres. The refuge was established in 1974 to restore, enhance, and protect significant wetland habitat for the benefit of waterfowl and other water birds, shorebirds, a number of threatened and endangered species, and other wildlife. As America's largest urban national wildlife refuge, it offers a wide range of interpretive and environmental education programs, and many opportunities for wildlife-oriented recreation. The refuge, which is one of seven in the San Francisco Bay NWR Complex, is located around the southern end of San Francisco Bay in northern California. Over 290 bird species have been seen here.

Among the refuge's habitats are about 12,000 acres of salt ponds, more than 3,600 acres of salt marsh, 1,200 acres of uplands, more than 1,000 acres of seasonal wetlands, and 4,400 acres of tidal mudflats/open water. Especially important species include the federally listed endangered California brown pelican, California clapper rail, California least tern, salt marsh harvest mouse, Contra Costa goldfields, and vernal pool tadpole shrimp; and the threatened western snowy plover.

As described in the U.S. Fish and Wildlife Service's Autumn 2001 refuge newsletter, *Tide-line*, by editor and refuge complex outdoor recreation planner Carmen Leong, refuge complex project leader Marge Kolar, and Natalie Doerr:

The history of the refuge really begins with the history of the Bay Area itself. Hundreds of years ago, the San Francisco Bay Area was a very different place. Herds of elk, deer and antelope grazed in the meadows, while grizzly bears, wolves, and mountain lions roamed nearby. Ducks and geese by the millions darkened the sky every fall and winter. But after the Spanish explorers reached the area in 1769, the Bay Area was hit with a steady influx of people. With the discovery of gold in the Sierra Nevada in 1848, the San Francisco population skyrocketed from 400 to 25,000 people in two years.

Such rapid growth was not without its effects on the environment. Hydraulic mining for gold drastically changed the hydrology of the Bay and the demand for food and housing also began to take its toll. Wetlands were converted into crop land and pastureland, while market hunters decimated waterfowl and shorebird populations. The industrial age saw improvements to the railroads and highways, which in turn led to suburban sprawl. Up went buildings, roads, houses, and garbage dumps on drained or filled wetlands. . . . By 1980, 85 percent of the wetlands, which had historically surrounded San Francisco Bay, were destroyed.

Luckily, these changes did not go unnoticed. In the mid-1960's, a group of local citizens decided too many wetlands had been lost, so they formed a grass-roots organization in hopes of creating a national wildlife refuge in south San Francisco Bay: the South San Francisco Baylands Planning, Conservation and National Wildlife Refuge Committee. At the time, the U.S. Fish and Wildlife Service was not interested in establishing a refuge in an urban area, so the Committee headed straight to Congress. . . . After two failed attempts, legislation for the establishment of the refuge passed in 1972 with an approved boundary of 23,000 acres. On October 8, 1974, the San Francisco Bay National Wildlife Refuge became . . . the first urban refuge in the nation. In the mid 1980's, some of the same folks, involved with the earlier lobbying effort, resolved to protect all the remaining South Bay wetland areas. Through the Citizen's Committee to Complete the Refuge's efforts, Congress authorized the expansion of the refuge to 43,000 acres! Retired Congressman Don Edwards' name was added to the refuge title in 1995, as a tribute to the man who played a pivotal role in the establishment and expansion of the refuge.

In 1997, an opportunity to restore an area of salt marsh known as the "entry triangle marsh" arose when a salt company closed a rainwater-runoff culvert. Ducks Unlimited, Inc., contributed its expertise and time to design the restoration plan. A maintenance road had to be removed, elevational contouring had to be accomplished to permit inundation of the marsh, tidal channels had to be cut into the marsh, and a water control structure had to be installed. The primary objective was to be able to manage the marsh for the pickleweed-dependent salt marsh harvest mouse. Other contributors to this project were the San Francisco Bay Wildlife Society, National Fish and Wildlife Foundation, Wildlife Forever, the FWS Coastal Program, and the Oracle Corporation.

In 1999, following many decades of effort by local conservationists, the Fish and Wildlife Service acquired the largest privately owned parts of Bair Island from the Peninsula Open Space Trust (POST). This 3,200-acre island actually consists of three islands that are separated by tidal channels. As the Service explains, "Bair Island was historically tidal marsh and...mudflats. It was diked in the late 1800's and early 1900's for farming and cattle grazing....[A salt company] converted the majority of the island to salt evaporation ponds.

"Various proposals for commercial and residential development were proposed and rejected. . . . Over time, portions were acquired by the State of California and the . . . Refuge. In 1997, POST purchased the majority of the remaining 1,626 acres to turn it over to the Refuge for restoration." The refuge is currently developing a restoration and management plan for Bair Island that would restore 1,600 acres of former salt ponds, one of the largest tidal marsh restoration projects in the Bay area.

The San Francisco Bay Wildlife Society is a nonprofit cooperating organization that assists the refuge. In addition to helping with wetland restoration projects, including Bair Island, it provides funds for publishing the refuge's quarterly newsletter, *Tideline.*

The refuge is open daily during daylight hours. There is no entrance fee. The refuge visitor center, in Fremont, is open on Tuesdays through Sundays, except national holidays. The Environmental Education Center, in Alviso (San Jose), is open during weekends to refuge visitors. For information on the education center, telephone: (408) 262-5513.

Visitor activities include wildlife and butterfly observation; photography; interpretive programs; environmental education programs for teachers and school groups; hiking; bicycling; canoeing, kayaking, and boating on the refuge's tidal sloughs and open bay waters; fishing from piers and shore; and hunting (goose, duck, and coot) on parts of the refuge during the designated seasons. In late June, an annual butterfly count is held on the refuge by the North American Butterfly Association. For information, telephone: (510) 792-0222.

Hiking opportunities abound on the more than 30 miles of trails, including the 1-mile Tidelands Trail and 5-mile Newark Slough Trail, two loops near the visitor center; and the 5.5-mile Mallard Slough Trail and 9-mile Alvisio Slough Trail, two loops near the Environmental Education Center. The 0.6-mile New Chicago Marsh Trail is a self-guiding, interpretive boardwalk and trail that offers views of a 365-acre tract of wetland habitat. This trail includes an observation platform and a butterfly garden. Insect repellent and sunscreen are advised during the warmer months.

Regarding the refuge's educational programs, Marge Kolar explains:

Since its inception, the Don Edwards San Francisco Bay National Wildlife Refuge has taken advantage of its unique position in the midst of 7 million people to provide Bay area communities with opportunities for environmental education. In order to reach the leaders of tomorrow, the refuge developed a nationally recognized, educator-led wetland field-trip program, which allows teachers to tailor lessons to meet the needs of particular school groups. Classes focus on wildlife and habitats on the refuge, and on off-site impacts to water quantity and quality, since the refuge contains the ultimate receiving waters for all point and non-point activities in south bay watersheds.

By involving educators and parents in planning and teaching the field activities, the refuge's educational programs reach multiple age groups. Over 8,500 students, teachers, and parent-volunteers annually participate in these full-day field trips at either the headquarters site in Fremont or the Environmental Education Center in Alviso (San Jose). The refuge also annually provides in-classroom presentations to more than 1,000 students throughout the Bay area. In addition to formal educational programs, staff and volunteers conduct three week-long day camps each summer, focusing on under-served communities in the Bay area.

Lodgings and meals are available throughout the San Francisco Bay Area.

Access to the Don Edwards SF Bay Refuge visitor center from State Route 84 (at the east end of Dumbarton Bridge) is by way of Thornton Avenue exit, south 0.8 mile, right into the refuge on Marshlands Road, and left at the stop sign. Access to the refuge Environmental Education Center from State Route 237 exit on U.S. 101 is east on Route 237 (toward Alviso) and north (left) on Zanker Road; or from the State Route 237 exit on I-880, it is west (toward Alviso) on Route 237 and north (right) on Zanker Road.

Further information: Don Edwards San Francisco Bay National Wildlife Refuge, P.O. Box 524, Newark, CA 94560; telephone: (510) 792-0222.

Ellicott Slough, comprising 196 acres, was established in 1975 to protect vital coastal upland habitat for the endangered Santa Cruz long-toed salamander (*Ambystoma macrodactylum croceum*). The refuge is managed cooperatively with the California Department of Fish and Game's adjacent ecological reserve. The salamander breeds in both the state's Ellicott Pond and the Refuge's Calabasas Pond, both of which are seasonal ponds. Ellicott Slough refuge is located 4 miles west of Watsonville, near Monterey Bay in northern California.

The refuge protects and manages a variety of habitats, including oak woodland, coastal scrub, grassland, and seasonal ponds.

Although the refuge is closed to visitation to avoid disturbance of its sensitive habitat and species, it can be viewed from San Andreas and Spring Valley roads.

Further information: Ellicott Slough National Wildlife Refuge, c/o San Francisco Bay NWR Complex, P.O. Box 524, Newark, CA 94560; telephone: (510) 792-0222.

Farallon, containing 211 acres, was established in 1909 by President Theodore Roosevelt to protect a cluster of surf-pounded islands, including South Farallons, North Farallons, Middle Farallons, and Noonday Rock. The refuge is located in the Pacific Ocean about 30 miles west of San Francisco, California.

The Farallon Islands comprise the largest continental seabird breeding colony south of Alaska, with nearly 30 percent of California's breeding seabirds. The refuge supports 12 nesting seabird species, including the world's largest breeding colonies of ashy storm petrel, Brandt's cormorant, and western gull. Among other species that nest here are common murre, pigeon guillemot, Cassin's and rhinoceros auklets, and tufted puffin. The islands also support six species of pinnipeds. After an absence of more than a century, northern elephant seals returned in 1959 and have been breeding on the South Farallon Islands for more than 25 years. Northern fur seals were extirpated in the 1800s and just recently (1996) began breeding here again.

As explained by the U.S. Fish and Wildlife Service:

Wildlife populations were heavily exploited for meat, hides, and eggs in the late 18th and early 19th centuries. Over-fishing of sardines reduced seabird food supplies. Some species were extirpated or declined drastically. Historical estimates indicate that thousands of northern fur seals and as many as 400,000 common murres once populated the islands. An active U.S. Coast Guard station further impacted island wildlife and habitat until the full automation of the light station in 1972. While some species have re-colonized the islands, others are slowly recovering.

Farallon is the southernmost nesting colony of the tufted puffin (*Fratercula cirrhata*), which is sometimes called "sea parrot." As described by refuge researcher Elsie Jensen in the Spring 2000 *Tideline*:

Tufted puffins only come ashore to nest and raise their young. The rest of the year they live, feed, and sleep on the open Pacific waters. The puffins arrive, along with thousands of other seabirds, . . . in late

March and early April. Twelve nesting seabird species compete for nesting space, vegetative nesting material, partners, and fish to feed their offspring.

The island has a carnival atmosphere, with western gulls acting the court jesters jousting and cavorting 24 hours a day. The gulls fill the air with their constant cries. Their nests pack the marine terraces and slopes of the island. They terrorize the other birds, and all species have had to adapt in order to protect themselves, their eggs, and their young. To elude the gulls, cormorants form colonial clusters of nests that are densely packed together like a circling of the wagons. Murres huddle close to the cormorants and to each other, hoping to exclude the gulls from their colony. Auklets and petrels fly to and from their burrows only at night to avoid hungry gulls, who would gladly eat the adult birds. . . .

High on the cliffs above the raucous interplay of gulls, murres, and cormorants, tufted puffins and pigeon guillemots vie for the limited number of rocky crevices where both species lay their eggs. . . . These crevices are so deep, longer than the reach of a human arm, that they are virtually gull proof. . . . In other parts of their breeding range, such as the coastal islands of Alaska, the puffin digs earthen burrows deep into hillsides. However, this is not an option on the rock-bound Farallon islands. . . .

As a researcher, I know the egg has hatched when I see the adults flying overhead carrying fish crosswise in their beak. The adults bring fish to the nest site, usually anchovies, rockfish, and squid, to feed the new chick. They forage in the water of the continental shelf, flying about 30 miles. . . , going even farther in poor fish years. Puffins swim extremely well underwater, and can dive up to 330 feet to pursue fish. The chicks fledge at 45 days, flying out to sea at night to avoid gull predation.

In the fall, the adult birds lose their tufts and bright beaks. The horny shell of the beak is shed and replaced with a smaller gray beak tipped in orange. The crisp white eye patch becomes infiltrated with gray. The adults return to the open waters of the Pacific. . . .

In the early 1900's, there were an estimated 2,000 puffins on the Farallon islands. In 1959, it declined to 26 individuals. Since then, the population has rebounded to a relatively stable 80-100 birds. . . .

Factors affecting the puffin's survival include human disturbance to which they are very sensitive, oil pollution, and fishery depletion. All of these factors have contracted the puffin's range northward so that the large colonies, numbering in thousands of birds, are seen only in Alaska.

Although the refuge is closed to visitation to avoid disturbing the wildlife, a Farallon natural history cruise from San Francisco provides a close-up view of the islands and their wildlife inhabitants as well as opportunities to see other marine mammals such as dolphins and whales. The Oceanic Society's all-day Farallon cruises depart from San Francisco's Marina District on Fridays, Saturdays, and Sundays from June through November. For information, telephone: (415) 474-3385. Other tour operators and boat charters that offer boat trips to the Farallons are based at Emeryville, Sausalito, and Half Moon Bay.

Further information: Farallon National Wildlife Refuge, c/o San Francisco Bay NWR Complex, P.O. Box 524, Newark, CA 94560; telephone: (510) 792-0222.

Grasslands Wildlife Management Area (see the San Luis NWR text).

Guadalupe-Nipomo Dunes, encompassing 2,553 acres acquired toward a goal of approximately 8,900 acres, was established in 2000 to protect, enhance, and restore an ecologically sensitive and significant stretch of Pacific coastal habitats. The refuge extends northward from the mouth of the Santa Maria River, adjacent to the city of Guadalupe within San Luis Obispo County in southern California.

Among the diverse habitats within the refuge boundary are foredunes, active sand dunes, an extensive area of coastal dune scrub, central coast sage scrub, arroyo willow riparian woodland, ephemeral dune swale, and open and deepwater wetlands. Establishment of the refuge was begun with The Nature Conservancy's donation of a 2,553-acre tract, formerly known as the Mobil Coastal Preserve. Over 230 bird species have been seen here.

As explained by the U.S. Fish and Wildlife Service:

The . . . Refuge is located in a transition zone between Northern and Southern California plant communities, resulting in a high degree of habitat diversity, a high number of local endemics, and high susceptibility to disturbance. The . . . Refuge is located within the Dunes Complex which is a complex mosaic of terrestrial, semi-aquatic, and aquatic plant communities containing 18 species of rare, endangered, or sparsely distributed plants. . . .

Development along the entire California coast has reduced the coastal dune scrub community type to less than 10 percent of its historic distribution. Significant stands of this habitat are located within the . . . Refuge.

The foredunes along the strand of beach support sparse, low-growing plants such as crisp dune mint, beach bur, and beach saltbush. As the Fish and Wildlife Service says, "This is the habitat where the endangered least tern and threatened snowy plover nest, and management efforts will concentrate on providing an optimum nesting environment for these species. Habitat management here will focus on eradication of exotic species such as European beach grass, ice plant, and veldt grass, the spread of which threaten the success of least tern and snow plover nests."

The active sand dunes support little vegetation. "The plants that do grow here are low growing pioneer plants that can withstand blowing sand; plants such as crisp dune mint and Blochman daisy. Other plants that grow in this dynamic environment include beach evening primrose and silver dune lupine. . . . Management of the active dune areas . . . [will] focus on preventing the influx of exotic plant species, damage to the fragile pioneer plants, and human-induced activation of stabilized dunes."

The central coast dune scrub habitat, occurring farther inland, covers the majority of the stabilized sand dunes and "contains evergreen low-growing shrubs such as dune lupine, mock heather, . . . coffee berry, and the striking giant coreopsis. Stabilized dune habitats suffer from the explosive invasions of exotic plants including European beach grass, veldt grass, and ice plant. Management objectives . . . [will] focus on eradication of these species and the restoration of stable native coastal dune scrub communities."

Areas of central coast sage scrub, occurring mostly on inland back-dunes, "is vegetated with woody shrubs such as coyote bush, California sagebrush, deerweed, and pygmy coast live oak. Some herbaceous species that can be found . . . are purple sand verbena, owls clover, and Indian paintbrush. Management here . . . [will] again focus on the eradication of exotic species such as veldt grass and ice plant, and limitation of recreational impacts."

Arroyo willow riparian woodland, seasonal and permanent wetlands, and deepwater wetlands "support thickets of arroyo willow, wax myrtle, . . . rushes, and endangered populations of Gambel watercress, a rare mustard plant, and marsh sandwort. These wetlands are seriously threatened by Pampas grass, Cape ivy, and in some places, eucalyptus. Efforts will be made to eradicate these tenacious exotic plants to restore a native wetland plant community for the benefit of sensitive plant species. The . . . threatened California red-legged frog makes its home in the wetland habitats within the approved refuge boundary, and would also benefit from restoration and conservation efforts. Migrating and resident waterfowl utilize the wetlands . . . as resting, nesting, and foraging areas. Only ten percent of California's wetlands remain, making these places within the approved Refuge boundary a valuable wildlife resource and a crucial link in the migrating waterfowl's Pacific Flyway."

The Guadalupe-Nipomo Dunes Center is an important nonprofit partner that assists the refuge in many ways, such as visitor orientation at its Dunes Center (open afternoons on Fridays, Saturdays, and Sundays), interpreter-guided walks, educational outreach; coordination of ecosystem-wide vegetation restoration efforts, and research facilitation to promote the protection of the Guadalupe-Nipomo Dunes. Information: Guadalupe-Nipomo Dunes Center, P.O. Box 339, Guadalupe, CA 93434; telephone: (805) 343-2455; and website: www. dunescenter.org. Other actively supportive partners include the California State Department of Parks and Recreation, Santa Barbara County Parks, the Land Conservancy of San Luis Obispo, The People for the Nipomo Dunes, Unocal Corporation, and California Polytechnic State University-San Luis Obispo.

The refuge is open daily during daylight hours. There is no entrance fee.

Visitor activities include wildlife observation, photography, hiking along the beach, and docent-led interpretive and environmental education programs by the Dunes Center.

Sunscreen is advised during the warmer months.

Lodgings and meals are available in such communities as Santa Maria and Arroyo Grande. A number of restaurants are also located in Guadalupe.

Access to the Guadalupe-Nipomo Dunes Center is by way of State Route 1 to Guadalupe; the Dunes Center is located at 1055 Guadalupe Street (State Route 1). Access onto the refuge itself is provided through two access points. The northern access is through the Oso Flaco Natural Area, where visitors can walk along a (wheelchair-accessible) boardwalk through dune habitats and across a freshwater lake; upon reaching the beach, visitors can hike south to reach the refuge. The southern access is through the Rancho Guadalupe Dunes County Park, where visitors can drive along a scenic road to a parking area within the foredunes, to watch waves break along the shore. From here visitors can hike north along the beach to reach the refuge.

Further information: Guadalupe-Nipomo Dunes National Wildlife Refuge, P.O. Box 9, Guadalupe, CA 93434; telephone: (805) 343-9151.

Havasu (see text under Arizona)

Hopper Mountain, comprising 2,471 acres, was established in 1974 primarily to protect habitat for the endangered California condor (*Gymnogyps californianus*). The refuge contains a condor holding facility for captive-bred chicks and serves as a base of operations for U.S. Fish and Wildlife Service personnel involved with the condor recovery and reintroduction program. It is located adjacent to Los Padres National Forest, along the southern edge of the rugged Topatopa Mountains in Ventura County, California.

The majority of the refuge's habitats consist of grassland that is part of the condor's historic foraging habitat, chaparral and coastal sage scrub, and woodlands of California and canyon live oaks and California black walnut. There are also small areas of riparian habitat and freshwater marsh.

With a 9-foot wingspread, the California condor is the largest native land bird in North America. As described in the mid-1960s by the National Audubon Society (NAS):

... the California condor is an inspiring spectacle as it rides the currents of air above its wilderness home. . . . The condor's steady soaring may reach 30 to 40 miles per hour in a remarkable non-flapping flight pattern.

From a distance, the bird may be identified by a double dip, in which the wings are not flapped, but merely half folded briefly, then returned to the high, dihedral angle. The condor's wings are notably broad, with the wing tips—the great primary feathers—conspicuously outspread. . . . Adult condors have a large, triangular area of white beneath each wing which is clearly visible in flight. The young condor, under six years of age, has less white or none at all, however, and even though much larger, is often confused with the turkey vulture. The immature condor, until five years of age, has a gray neck . . . , while the fully mature bird displays a long, pink-orange colored, featherless neck and head. Except for these markings, both young and adult are black.

The condor, like the turkey vulture, is primarily a carrion eater, feeding on the carcasses of cattle and sheep, deer and other wildlife which die of accident or disease or are killed by predators.

As explained by the Fish and Wildlife Service:

California condors remain within their home range year round. They require large areas of roosting, nesting and particularly foraging habitat to survive. For roosting, condors require large old growth trees, snags or isolated rocky outcrops and cliffs. For nesting, shallow caves and rock crevices on cliffs with minimal disturbance are required. Large areas of open grasslands and oak savanna foothills that support populations of large mammals such as deer and cattle are required for foraging. Condors may forage up to 150 miles in one day in search of food.

It is estimated that there were once thousands of these expert gliders, whose range extended south along the West Coast, from British Columbia to Baja California, east to Florida, and north along the East Coast to New York. In 1602, the first recorded sighting of a condor was made at Monterey Bay, in central California. In 1805, the Lewis and Clark Expedition reported seeing a condor near the Columbia River.

By the late nineteenth century, the population was estimated at around 600 individuals. Although nearly all of those birds were restricted to southern California by the turn of the century, the last known sighting of a condor in Arizona occurred in 1924. In 1937, the U.S. Forest Service established a 1,200-acre reserve, the Sisquoc Condor Sanctuary, in southern California. In 1939, with the condor population continuing its steady, ominous decline, National Audubon researcher Carl B. Koford initiated intensive studies of the species, as the result of which he estimated that between 60 and 100 condors then remained in the wild. In 1947, the Forest Service established the 35,000-acre Sespe Wildlife Area (subsequently renamed the Sespe Condor Sanctuary), encompassing a wild, mountainous part of the Los Padres National Forest. In 1951, the sanctuary was expanded to 53,000 acres, and two years later, the first legal protection was provided when the California Department of Fish and Game stated, "It is unlawful to take any condor at any time or in any manner."

In 1965, with fewer than 60 birds remaining, the Fish and Wildlife Service began a full-time condor research program at its Patuxent Wildlife Research Center in Maryland (see the Patuxent National Wildlife Refuge text). Two years later, the California condor was included on the first federal endangered species list. In 1975, the initial 1,800 acres of the Hopper Mountain National Wildlife Refuge were acquired to provide "a protective buffer" for the Sespe sanctuary. In that same year, the California Condor Recovery Team was formed and a recovery plan was adopted.

In 1981, the California Department of Fish and Game gave permission to the San Diego Wild Animal Park (SDWAP) and Los Angeles Zoo to breed California condors in captivity and gave its approval to the Fish and Wildlife Service to trap three condors for captive breeding and conduct a 3-year research program. The first chick was captured in 1982 and delivered to SDWAP. By this time, only 21 to 24 birds remained in the wild. The following year, two chicks and four eggs were removed from the wild. The eggs were hatched under artificial incubation at the San Diego Zoo. In 1985, three more eggs were taken from the wild: one hatched at the San Diego Zoo and one of the others at SDWAP.

Plans to release captive-reared condors were suspended in 1985 as a result of the disappearance of six birds during the previous winter, the death of a bird from lead poisoning, and the presence of high lead levels in the blood of a captured condor. The Service requested permission to capture all remaining wild condors; the President's Council on Environmental Quality agreed. In 1987, the last free-flying California condor, an adult male, was brought into captivity. In 1988, the first successful captive condor breeding occurred at SDWAP. Four chicks were hatched in captivity in 1989; eight in 1990; twelve in 1991 and 1992; fifteen in 1993, 1994, and 1995; eighteen in 1996; and twenty in 1997.

Meanwhile, condor release efforts were being undertaken. In 1992, two birds were taken to the Sespe sanctuary early in the year, one of which died and the other of which was returned to captivity. Later in the year, six more birds were released into the wild. Because a number of the released young condors died as a result of colliding with power poles, a more remote release site, known as Lion Canyon, was selected; and, as explained by the Service, "young condors underwent power-pole aversion training while in captivity. Since this training, very few power-pole encounters have occurred." In 1995, six birds were released at the new site.

Also in 1995, a rearing facility, "consisting of six simulated nest caves with an outdoor pen as well as a 30' x 50' flight pen," was constructed on Hopper Mountain Refuge. Four parent-reared chicks, "the first captive-bred condors reared by their parents while in captivity," were transferred to this new rearing facility, and they were released the following year at a new site within Los Padres National Forest, known as Castle Crags.

At the same time, an additional release site was being planned for the U.S. Bureau of Land Management-administered Vermilion Cliffs Wilderness, to the northeast of the Grand Canyon in Arizona. Condors released at these spectacular cliffs were designated, under the Endangered Species Act, as an "experimental nonessential" population. This designation reduces the impact of releasing an endangered species into areas where human activities are occurring. The Peregrine Fund's World Center for Birds of Prey, in Boise, Idaho, was selected to manage the reintroduction of California condors in Arizona because of its long experience and previous successes in captive breeding of endangered birds, such as the peregrine and aplomado falcons. In late 1996, six juvenile condors were released atop the Vermilion Cliffs—the first time in 70 years that condors were again flying over this part of the United States.

Many additional releases were carried out in the late 1990s, including at the Ventana Wilderness Society's Ventana Wilderness Sanctuary near the Big Sur coast in central California. The latter site is a 240-acre inholding within Los Padres National Forest's Ventana Wilderness.

As of May 2002, there were 68 condors living in the wild (39 in central and southern California, plus 29 in northern Arizona), and 115 in captivity. Thanks to the coordinated teamwork and intense commitment of all the many partners, the California Condor Recovery Program is amazingly successful for a species that only a few years ago was sliding toward extinction.

As project leader Marc Weitzel, explains, "Because of the far-ranging nature of the bird, many condor recovery program activities occur off National Wildlife Refuge System lands. However, by serving as a base of operations for condor reintroduction efforts in southern California, the Hopper Mountain, Bitter Creek, and Blue Ridge refuges are playing a key role in helping to bring this high-profile, critically endangered species back from the brink of extinction. This is but another successful example of the Refuge System's vital contribution to the recovery of this nation's vast array of endangered natural resources."

Although Hopper Mountain and two other refuges were established to protect condor habitat (see Bitter Creek and Blue Ridge refuge texts) and are not open to visitation, there are a number places from which condors can sometimes be seen.

Further information: Hopper Mountain National Wildlife Refuge Complex, P.O. Box 5839, Ventura, CA 93005; telephone: (805) 644-5185.

Humboldt Bay, currently containing about 3,000 acres in seven units and working toward a goal of nearly 10,000 acres, was established in 1971 to restore, manage, and protect one of the most significant coastal wetland habitats for migratory birds along the Pacific Coast. The refuge's authorized boundary encompasses all of South Humboldt Bay and several parts of North Humboldt Bay, near the city of Eureka in northwestern California.

The refuge's diverse habitats include eelgrass beds and mudflats, salt marsh, brackish marsh, freshwater marsh, diked seasonal wetlands, sand spits, and uplands. Humboldt Bay ranks as one of the most important places in the United States for the black brant (*Branta bernicla*), a species of goose that thrives on eelgrass. More than 30,000 of these birds have been recorded at one time on the bay. Banding has revealed that some of those birds that are attracted to Humboldt Bay have been seen in Canada, Alaska, Siberia, and Mexico. As the U.S. Fish and Wildlife Service explains, "During the spring, prior to their return to Arctic nesting grounds, the Bay is a key staging area for black brant. It contains the largest beds of eelgrass south of Willapa Bay, Washington" (see the Willapa Refuge text). This wetland habitat also provides vital spawning, nursery, and feeding habitat for many species of fish and other marine organisms.

Refuge lands acquired since the first few acres in 1971 include the 1,100-acre Salmon Creek Unit, on which the refuge headquarters and visitor center are located; the adjacent Hookton Slough Unit; and South Spit, which lies between the South Bay and the Pacific Ocean.

Among the Service's management goals for Humboldt Bay Refuge are to expand and enhance eelgrass habitat for the black brant; increase habitat diversity, consistent with other habitat management objectives; "provide optimum wintering and migratory water bird use through habitat management of former tidal marsh which is now diked seasonal wetlands"; "maintain a tideland ecosystem in which there will be limited disturbance to habitat, wildlife, and fisheries"; "restore the lower end of Salmon Creek to a more natural state and thereby increase the opportunity for anadromous fish passage upstream"; "increase the public's understanding and appreciation of fish and wildlife, wetland ecology, and man's historic and current role in the environment"; and "provide for optimum levels of wildlife-oriented education and recreation that are compatible with refuge objectives."

Humboldt Bay Refuge also includes the 473-acre Lanphere Dunes Unit, on the upper North Spit of the bay. As described by the U.S. Fish and Wildlife Service, these sand dunes are:

the most pristine remaining dune ecosystem in the Pacific Northwest. Nearly all of the dunes on the west coast of North America have become highly fragmented due to a combination of development, off-road vehicle impacts, and the invasion of non-native plants. Longstanding protection efforts have safeguarded the Lanphere Dunes, which contain one of only two remaining areas of the globally endangered native foredune grassland community. . . .

The Lanphere Dunes were first protected in the 1940's by the efforts of two biology professors from Humboldt State University, William and Hortense Lanphere, who purchased the property. The Lanpheres encouraged research projects from the university, and were active in preventing vehicle trespass, which is extremely damaging to the dune plant community. In 1974, the Lanpheres placed a conservation easement on the property, and later donated it to The Nature Conservancy. The Lanphere Dunes Unit was established in 1998, with a donation of land from The Nature Conservancy.

Both older, forested dunes and a relatively young, active dune system are found on the refuge. The stabilized dunes support a unique coniferous forest of beach pine, Sitka spruce, and grand fir, with a rich understory of shrubs and herbs. The moist fog air typical of this coastal forest nourishes a lush flora of lichens, mosses, and fungi. This unusually productive forest supports higher than usual densities of gray fox, the largest mammal found here. Together with the adjoining deciduous swamps and streamside riparian forests, the dunes support over 250 species of birds. . . .

Partners with Humboldt Bay Refuge include Ducks Unlimited, Inc., which has helped enhance more than 700 acres of the refuge's wetland habitat; the California Waterfowl Association; the Redwood Audubon Society; The Conservation Fund and The Nature Conservancy; Humboldt State University; and the California Department of Fish and Game.

The refuge is open daily during daylight hours. There is no entrance fee. The refuge headquarters and visitor center are open on weekdays, except national holidays. The visitor center may also be open on weekends (contact the refuge for the latest updates).

Visitor activities include birdwatching; photography; viewing interpretive exhibits in the visitor center; hiking; canoeing, kayaking, and boating; fishing; and limited hunting (goose, duck, coot, and snipe) on part of the refuge during the designated seasons. Camping is not permitted on the refuge, but campground facilities are located at a number of nearby places. Visitors using canoes or other small watercraft are cautioned to be alert for tidal and weather changes. One nonmotorized boat-launching site is located on the refuge, and several other boat-launching sites are available nearby.

Hiking opportunities include two self-guiding, interpretive trails: the 1.5-mile Hookton Slough Trail that offers views of grassland, freshwater marsh, mudflats, and open water; and the 0.75-mile Salmon Creek Trail that begins at the visitor center, contains observation blinds, and is open during visitor center hours. A 3-mile seasonal loop trail along South Bay may be open, depending upon wildlife disturbance and other refuge programs. In addition, interpreter-guided walks at the Lanphere Dunes Unit are offered. For information on dune tours offered by the Friends of the Dunes, telephone: (707) 444-1397.

Lodgings and meals are available in such communities as Arcata, Eureka, Fortuna, and Ferndale.

Access to Humboldt Bay Refuge's headquarters and visitor center from the U.S. 101 freeway northbound is by way of the Hookton Road exit, left at the end of the off-ramp, across the freeway overpass, and right onto Ranch Road. From U.S. 101 freeway southbound, it is the Hookton Road exit, right at the end of the off-ramp, and immediately left onto Ranch Road.

Further information: Humboldt Bay National Wildlife Refuge, P.O. Box 576, 1020 Ranch Road, Loleta, CA 95551; telephone (707) 733-5406.

Imperial (see text for this refuge under Arizona)

Kern, comprising 10,618 acres, was established in 1960 to manage and protect important wintering habitat for large concentrations of geese and ducks, replacing a small part of the once-vast Central Valley wetlands that were nearly wiped out by their conversion to farmland by the late nineteenth century. The refuge is located near the south end of the San Joaquin Valley in southern California.

Regarding the history of this part of California, nearly all of the southern San Joaquin Valley once consisted of a vast wetland. Historically, the Tulare Basin, in which the refuge is located, held 500,000-acre Tulare Lake—the second largest freshwater body of water west of the Mississippi River. Millions of waterfowl and large numbers of tule elk, mule deer, and pronghorns were among the rich diversity and abundance of wildlife that once inhabited this area.

As explained by the U.S. Fish and Wildlife Service:

Today, refuge lands are flooded in the fall to create habitat vital to migratory species. Approximately 5,000 acres are flooded and managed as marsh from September through March when waterfowl are present. The high rate of evaporation during the summer months and the high cost of pumping water makes extensive year round ponding impractical.

Every fall, ducks and geese that have nested in Canada, Alaska, and the northern states fly south to winter in California and other spots on the Pacific Flyway. Waterfowl populations on the refuge begin to rise until a peak is reached in January and February when the northward migration begins again.

The refuge is intensively managed to produce habitat for wintering waterfowl, including creation of marsh conditions and other diverse habitat production, so that lands can provide a continuing food source for waterfowl wintering on the refuge. On the 1,200 acres managed for food plants, major varieties grown include wild millet (watergrass), alkali bulrush and swamp timothy.

In the remaining area of the refuge, 2,260 acres are managed for the benefit of native plants and three endangered species, the blunt-nosed leopard lizard, Tipton kangaroo rat and the San Joaquin kit fox.

Ducks Unlimited, Inc. is working to help create 300 acres of wetland habitat for the Kern refuge. DU's funding is derived from its Matching Aid to Restore States Habitat (MARSH) program.

The refuge is open daily during daylight hours. There is no entrance fee. The refuge head-quarters is open on weekdays, except national holidays.

Visitor activities include birdwatching, photography, driving the 6.5-mile auto tour route, walking on dikes and minor refuge roads that are not posted as closed, group environmental education tours (by advance arrangement), and waterfowl hunting on parts of the refuge during the designated season. Over 210 bird species have been seen here.

Insect repellent and sunscreen are advised during the warmer months.

Lodgings and meals are available in such communities as Delano and Bakersfield.

Access to Kern Refuge from the Delano exit on State Route 99 is west 19 miles on State Route 155 (Garces Highway) to the T-junction with Corcoran Road, following directional signs either to the refuge headquarters or the auto tour route. Or from the State Route 46 exit on I-5, it is east 5 miles on State Route 46 and north (left) just over 10 miles on Corcoran Road.

Further information: Kern National Wildlife Refuge, P.O. Box 670, Delano, CA 93216; telephone: (661) 725-2767.

Lower Klamath, comprising 46,900 acres, was established in 1908 by President Theodore Roosevelt as the first national wildlife refuge primarily for the benefit of waterfowl. It is located within the Klamath Basin in northern California and southern Oregon.

The refuge's habitats include shallow cattail-and-bulrush marsh, open water, grassy uplands, and managed croplands that provide feeding, resting, and nesting habitat for awesome concentrations of migrating and wintering ducks, geese, swans, and other water birds.

Historically, the wetlands of the arid Klamath Basin of northern California and southern Oregon totaled roughly 185,000 acres of freshwater marshes and shallow lakes. This was a mecca for the more than 5 million waterfowl—the world's largest known concentration, as well as American white pelicans and other water birds that came here to rest and feed during the spring and autumn migrations or to breed and raise their young. In 1905, the U.S. Bureau of Reclamation undertook the Klamath Reclamation Project, by which a large proportion of the basin's marsh and lake habitat in the Lower Klamath and Tule Lake area were converted to agricultural development. Less than one-quarter of the basin's historic wetlands now exist, and only in fragmented remnants.

To protect and manage much of the priceless remaining wetlands, five refuges were established: Tule Lake and Clear Lake, in California; Lower Klamath, in California/Oregon; and Upper Klamath and Klamath Marsh, in Oregon. A sixth basin refuge, Bear Valley, in Oregon, was established to provide protection for a major night-roosting area of forest for large numbers of wintering bald eagles. (See separate texts on each of these refuges.)

Agricultural, wildlife refuge, and other uses of the available water supplies are coordinated under the terms of an agreement between the Bureau of Reclamation and the U.S. Fish and Wildlife Service. During periods of severe drought, as periodically occurs in this near-desert region, it becomes extremely difficult and controversial to determine just how to fairly allocate the vital but limited water resources.

As *Ducks Unlimited* senior writer Matt Young explained in his January/February 2002 article, "Wetlands Under Siege":

Despite the tremendous importance of Klamath Basin wetlands to Pacific Flyway waterfowl populations, these habitats are currently threatened by severe water shortages. . . . In 2001, a severe drought forced federal authorities to divert water from the irrigation project to provide habitat for several endangered fish species, preventing farmers from irrigating their crops and restricting water deliveries to the refuges. This also resulted in a dramatic decrease in the habitat available to waterfowl last fall, as well as greatly diminished hunting opportunities for waterfowlers.

DU [Ducks Unlimited, Inc.] has joined the Wildlife Management Institute, National Audubon Society, Audubon Society of Portland, and National Wildlife Refuge Association in support of a series of measures to improve wetland management at both the Lower Klamath and Tule Lake national wildlife refuges. The coalition also supports changes in irrigation policy and land use that would ensure more reliable water deliveries to the refuges during times of peak waterfowl use. In addition, pending funding approval by Congress, DU and the USFWS will conduct an extensive topographic and water-delivery-system survey of both refuges in an effort to improve wetland management and water-use efficiency. This will be the largest survey effort ever undertaken by DU biologists and engineers. Lastly, DU and its partners recommend additional wetland habitat restoration work on both public and private lands.

To date, DU has helped to conserve, restore, and enhance more than 17,000 wetland acres in the Klamath Basin, with an additional 25,000 acres of wetlands to be restored in the near future. DU is also exploring opportunities to expand its conservation work in the region by helping farmers flood harvested croplands and restore habitat on lands enrolled in the Wetland Reserve Program. All of these conservation activities will not only provide critical habitat for waterfowl and other wetland wildlife, but they will also help improve water quality and quantity as well, benefiting people and fisheries.

From late February through early April, peak numbers of waterfowl, including tundra swans, pause to rest and feed on the five wetland refuges on their way to breeding grounds farther north. The influx of migrating shorebirds reaches its northbound climax between mid-April and mid-May and its southbound climax from late July through August. During October and November, between 1 and 2 million waterfowl are attracted to these refuges. At least 1,000 wintering bald eagles have been counted in mid-February. More than 430 species of birds have been recorded in the Klamath Basin.

The Klamath Basin Wildlife Association, a nonprofit organization, assists the refuge in a variety of ways.

The Lower Klamath Refuge is open daily during daylight hours. There is a tour-route fee and hunting and photo-blind fees. The Klamath Basin NWR's headquarters/visitor center, located on Hill Road 5 miles west of the community of Tulelake, California, is open on weekdays, except Christmas and New Year's Day.

Visitor activities include birdwatching, photography (a number of photo blinds are available), driving and bicycling on the 10-mile auto tour loop road, viewing interpretive exhibits at the Klamath Basin refuge's visitor center, and hunting (goose, duck, coot, moorhen, snipe, and pheasant) on parts of the refuge during the designated seasons.

Among the more than 175 species of birds that have been recorded on Lower Klamath refuge are American white pelican; great blue heron; great and snowy egrets; black-crowned night-heron;

white-faced ibis; tundra swan; geese (greater white-fronted, snow, Ross's, and Canada); ducks (mallard; green-winged, blue-winged, and cinnamon teal; northern pintail; northern shoveler; gadwall; American wigeon; canvasback; redhead; lesser scaup; common goldeneye; bufflehead; common merganser; and ruddy); bald and golden eagles; the non-native ring-necked pheasant; sandhill crane; black-necked stilt; American avocet; gulls (Franklin's, ring-billed, and California); terns (Caspian, Forster's, and black); wrens (Bewick's, house, and marsh); western bluebird; yellow warbler; lazuli bunting; spotted towhee; and red-winged and yellow-headed blackbirds.

Mammals include mule deer, bobcat, coyote, red fox, mink, river otter, beaver, muskrat, raccoon, striped skunk, badger, and black-tailed and white-tailed jackrabbits.

Reptiles include western pond turtle; snakes (rubber boa, racer, gopher, garter, and western rattlesnake); spotted frog; bullfrog; and western toad.

Lodgings and meals are available in such communities as Tule Lake, California and Klamath Falls, Oregon.

Access to Lower Klamath Refuge from U.S. Route 97 just south of the California–Oregon state line is east through the refuge on California State Route 161. To reach the Klamath Basin refuges' visitor center, it is east about 6 miles beyond the refuge's east entrance on Route 161 and south (right) about 4 miles on Hill Road.

Further information: Lower Klamath National Wildlife Refuge, c/o Klamath Basin NWRs, 4009 Hill Road, Tulelake, CA 96143; telephone: (530) 667-2231.

Marin Islands, encompassing 339 acres on two islands and adjacent tidal mudflats, was established in 1992 to provide protection for nesting and roosting water birds and other wildlife. The refuge is jointly managed with the California Department of Fish and Game's adjacent ecological reserve. It is located within the west end of San Pablo Bay, which is part of the greater San Francisco Bay, in northern California.

As described by the U.S. Fish and Wildlife Service, the vegetation of the two islands is very different. East Marin Island contains a mixture of native and non-native plant species, the natives of which include California buckeye, toyon, coast live oak, and madrone. The smaller West Marin Island is dominated by native species, the most prevalent being the California buckeye, which grows much shorter than normal due to the force of winds. As of 1995, there were approximately 65 native species of vascular plants known to grow on the islands.

West Marin's buckeyes also provide habitat for the largest nesting colony of herons and egrets in northern California. Bird species that nest on the islands include great blue heron, great and snowy egrets, black-crowned night-heron, Canada goose, common raven, and western gull. Harbor seals have historically been known to haul out on West Marin Island. Apparently, no terrestrial mammals inhabit the islands.

A grassroots citizen's group, Friends of Marin Islands, rallied the support of county, state, and federal governments as well as private organizations to help fund the purchase of these islands and tidelands.

Although the Marin Islands Refuge is closed to visitation to minimize disturbing the wildlife, boating and kayaking are popular ways to enjoy viewing the refuge at a safe distance.

Further information: Marin Islands National Wildlife Refuge, c/o San Pablo Bay NWR, P.O. Box 2012, (Azuar Drive and "I" Street, Building 505), Mare Island, Vallejo, CA 94592; telephone: (707) 562-3000.

Merced, containing 8,277 acres, was established in 1951. The refuge intensively manages seasonal and semipermanent wetlands and croplands to provide natural food, such as wild millet and swamp timothy, for large concentrations of wintering and breeding waterfowl, sandhill cranes, migrating shorebirds, and other wildlife. It is located near the northern end of the San Joaquin Valley in central California.

From November through February, there are as many as 100,000 geese of four species (Ross's, snow, greater white-fronted, and cackling Canada) and thousands of ducks—mostly mallards, green-winged teal, northern pintails, and northern shovelers. As many as 15,000 wintering lesser sandhill cranes use the refuge—the largest gathering of these stately gray birds in California's Central Valley. In addition, the refuge's wetlands attract large numbers of wading birds and migrating shorebirds.

Establishment of the refuge was made possible partly with revenues from the sale of Migratory Bird Hunting and Conservation Stamps (Duck Stamps). Ducks Unlimited, Inc. has helped enhance approximately 4,000 acres of the refuge's wetland habitat.

The refuge is open daily during daylight hours. There is no entrance fee. The headquarters for the San Luis NWR Complex, of which Merced is a part, is located at 947 West Pacheco Boulevard, Suite C, Los Banos, CA and is open on weekdays, except national holidays.

Visitor activities include birdwatching; photography; driving the 5-mile, self-guiding auto tour route; viewing the refuge and its wildlife from two observation platforms; walking the 0.6-mile Meadowlark Trail; fishing; and hunting (goose, duck, moorhen, and coot) on part of the refuge during the designated season.

The species of birds and other wildlife that have been recorded on Merced refuge are essentially the same as those on nearby San Luis Refuge.

Lodgings and meals are available in such communities as Merced and Los Banos.

Access to Merced Refuge from the city of Merced is south 8 miles on State Route 59 and west (right) 8 miles on Sandy Mush Road.

Further information: Merced National Wildlife Refuge, c/o San Luis NWR Complex, P.O. Box 2176, Los Banos, CA 93635; telephone: (209) 826-3508.

Modoc, consisting of 7,021 acres, was established in 1960 to manage and protect important wetland habitat for migratory waterfowl and other wildlife. The refuge provides an oasis at the foot of the Warner Mountains, along the western edge of the Great Basin Desert in the northeast corner of California. Over 245 bird species have been seen here.

The main part of Modoc Refuge contains an extensive area of diked ponds, bulrush-and-cattail marshes, and irrigated meadows, as well as riparian corridors and adjacent sagebrush uplands. The wetland areas are managed for the benefit of waterfowl, shorebirds, wading birds, and other wildlife. Human-made islands provide habitat for many species of nesting birds, such as American white pelicans, double-crested cormorants, gulls, and terns. Hay meadows are managed to offer feeding, resting, and nesting habitat for geese, ducks, and sandhill cranes. Shorebirds include black-necked stilt, American avocet, and willet.

Spring and autumn migrations attract the largest bird concentrations to the refuge. The most abundant waterfowl include Canada geese; greater white-fronted geese (in the spring); tundra swans; and many species of ducks, including mallard, green-winged and cinnamon teal, northern pintail, gadwall, and American wigeon.

Prominent among wintering bird species are Canada goose, common goldeneye, bufflehead, common merganser, and a small number of bald eagles.

A separate unit of the refuge encompasses Dorris Reservoir.

Ducks Unlimited, Inc. acquired more than 300 acres for addition to the refuge and has helped enhance more than 400 acres of the refuge's wetland habitat.

The refuge is open daily during daylight hours. There is no entrance fee. The refuge headquarters is open on weekdays, except national holidays.

Visitor activities on the main part of the refuge include wildlife observation; photography; driving the auto tour route that loops around Teal Pond; hiking the 0.5-mile, interpretive Wigeon Pond Trail and hiking a trail along the west end of Dorris Reservoir; bicycling on roads open to motor vehicles from April 1 through September; boating and fishing on Dorris Reservoir from April 1 through September (two boat-launching sites are available); and hunting (goose, duck, coot, and snipe) on part of the refuge (bounded by U.S. Route 395 and County Road 115) during the designated seasons. Camping is not permitted on the refuge, but campground facilities are located nearby.

On Dorris Reservoir, swimming is permitted at areas open to public access, from April 1 through September; no-wake zones in coves are designated with buoys, to avoid disturbing broods of geese and other wildlife; and water skiing is allowed from June 1 through September on part of the reservoir (but personal watercraft, such as jet skis and wave runners, are prohibited). The U.S. Fish and Wildlife Service urges visitors to respect the rights of private landowners, who own most of the lakeshore.

Insect repellent and sunscreen are advised during the warmer months.

Lodgings and meals are available in Alturas.

Nearby conservation areas include Clear Lake, Tule Lake, Lower Klamath, and Sheldon national wildlife refuges; Hart Mountain National Antelope Refuge; Modoc National Forest; and Lava Beds National Monument.

Access to the main part of Modoc Refuge is south on Main Street in Alturas on U.S. Route 395 (to just south of the North Fork Pit River), east (left) at the County Museum on County Road 56, south (right) on County Road 115, and east (left) on the refuge road to the headquarters and the auto tour road. To reach the refuge's Dorris Reservoir unit, continue farther east on County Road 56 and bear left at the fork in the road.

Further information: Modoc National Wildlife Refuge, P.O. Box 1610, Alturas, CA 96101; telephone: (530) 233-3572.

North-Central Valley Wildlife Management Area (see description in the Sacramento National Wildlife Refuge text)

Pixley, containing 6,389 acres, was established in 1959 to protect an important area of wetland habitat for migratory waterfowl and shorebirds, as well as arid habitat for the endangered San Joaquin kit fox, Tipton kangaroo rat, and blunt-nosed leopard lizard (*Gambelia silus*). The refuge is located near the south end of the San Joaquin Valley in southern California.

Pixley Refuge is situated along what was once the shoreline of the historic 500,000-acre Tulare Lake. As the U.S. Fish and Wildlife Service explains, "The lake has since disappeared because of the building of dams on the rivers and the diversions of water to agriculture and development. The average rainfall is less than 10 inches per year which classifies the area as a desert." Wildlife also once included tule elk, pronghorn, and grizzly and black bears.

Most of Pixley Refuge consists of grassland that is inhabited by such species as coyote, San Joaquin kit fox, badger, black-tailed jackrabbit, Tipton kangaroo rat, northern harrier, white-tailed kite, burrowing owl, western meadowlark, killdeer, California side-blotched lizard, and the blunt-nosed leopard lizard. Saltbush and other shrubs that are adapted to this arid environment offer cover for California quail, desert cottontail, ground squirrels, and other wildlife.

The Fish and Wildlife Service manages the refuge's 300 acres of wetland habitat with well water that is carried in ditches and pipelines and controlled by a series of gates and other water control structures. As the Service explains, "Water is not present in the wetlands all year. The timing of fall flood up and spring draw downs, as well as summer irrigations determines the types of food plants and vegetation that are produced. The water levels maintained in fall and winter help determine what species of birds may use the habitat. On average, the water depth is maintained at between 5" and 10" deep...optimum feeding depth for many duck species. Shallower depths along edges provide feeding areas for shorebirds and wading species." Open water attracts such species as mallard, green-winged and cinnamon teal, northern pintail, American wigeon, and American coot. Mudflats and other shallow habitat are frequented by such shorebirds as black-necked stilt, American avocet, western sandpiper, and long-billed dowitcher. As of early 2002, the Service was anticipating soon being able to use water from the Friant-Kern Canal, "which will allow the wetland area to be nearly doubled."

The only riparian habitat borders Deer Creek, which runs along the southern and southwestern boundaries of the refuge. This lush area supports such vegetation as Fremont cottonwoods and willows and attracts many species of birds, including red-tailed hawk and great horned owl, warblers, golden-crowned and white-crowned sparrows, blue grosbeak, and Bullock's oriole.

One of the refuge's most prominent species is the sandhill crane. As many as 4,000 of these stately, gray, 3- to 4-foot-tall birds congregate here, from late September to mid-March.

The refuge is open daily during daylight hours. There is no entrance fee.

Visitor activities include walking the 1.5-mile, self-guiding trail (an interpretive leaflet is available) and photography. An elevated wildlife viewing platform from which flocks of wintering cranes can be seen is provided at the end of the trail. The trail and platform were constructed under a cost-share project with the Tulare County Audubon Society.

Insect repellent and sunscreen are advised during the warmer months.

Bird species that have been recorded on Pixley Refuge are largely the same as those on Kern Refuge.

Barn Owl, Don Edwards San Francisco Bay NWR. Mike Boylan photo

Western sandpipers and dunlins, Gray's Harbor NWR, Washington

Cow moose and calves, Kenai NWR, Alaska. Mike Boylan photo

Gray wolf, Agassiz NWR, Minnesota

Mohawk Dunes, Cabeza Prieta NWR, Arizona. Jack Dykinga photo

Pronghorn, National Bison Range, Montana

Blacktail jackrabbit, Modoc NWR, California

Endangered Karner blue butterfly, Necedah NWR, Wisconsin

Sandhill cranes at sunrise, Bosque del Apache NWR, New Mexico

Great blue heron, Montezuma NWR, New York

A U.S. Fish and Wildlife Service outdoor class for school children, Minnesota Valley NWR

Yellow-headed blackbirds in marsh, Merced NWR, California

Wild turkey, Wichita Mountains NWR, Oklahoma

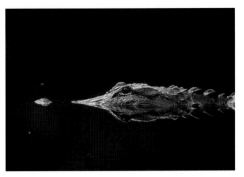

Alligator, Okefenokee NWR, Georgia

Public fishing, Choctaw NWR, Alabama

Horned Puffin, Alaska Maritime NWR

Fur seal, Alaska Maritime NWR

Tufted puffin, Alaska Maritime NWR. Mike Boylan photo

Arctic NWR, Alaska

Aerial view of the coastal plain, Arctic NWR

Arctic tern, Kenai NWR, Alaska. Mike Boylan photo

Kenai NWR

Kenai NWR

Bald Eagles, Kenai NWR, Mike Boylan photo

Kodiak NWR, Alaska

Caribou, Kenai NWR, Alaska. Mike Boylan photo

Kodiak NWR

Alaskan brown bear dining on salmon, Kodiak NWR

Dunlin in breeding plumage, Yukon Delta NWR, Alaska

Rabbit River, Selawik NWR. Leslie Kerr photo

Yukon Delta NWR, Alaska

Tundra swan nestlings, Yukon Delta NWR

Eskimo Fish Camp, Yukon Delta NWR

Storm clouds, Buenos Aires NWR

Masked bobwhite, Buenos Aires NWR, Arizona

Yucca, Buenos Aires NWR

Cabeza Prieta NWR. Jack Dykinga photo

Sunset and saguaro, Cabeza Prieta NWR

Red-tailed hawk nesting in saguaro, Cabeza Prieta NWR, Arizona

Cabeza Prieta NWR, Arizona

Greater roadrunner, Cibola NWR, Arizona

Colorado River at Topock Gorge, Havasu NWR. Russell D. Butcher photo

Kofa NWR. Russell D. Butcher photo

Desert bighorn sheep, Kofa NWR, Arizona

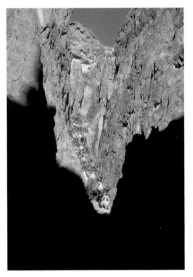

Leslie Canyon NWR, Arizona. William R. Radke photo

Palm Canyon, Kofa NWR. Russell D. Butcher photo

Blind cave crawfish, Logan Cave NWR, Arkansas

Wapanocca NWR, Arkansas

Mammals include coyote, black-tailed jackrabbit, and California ground squirrel.

Of the reptiles, there are lizards (blunt-nosed leopard, California side-blotched, and western whiptail) and snakes (Pacific gopher, California king, and western rattlesnake). Amphibians include Pacific tree-frog, bullfrog, and western toad.

Lodgings and meals are available in such communities as Tulare, Porterville, and Delano.

Access to Pixley Refuge's trailhead from the County Avenue 56 exit on State Route 99 is west about 5 miles on County Avenue 56, and north 1 mile on County Road 88.

Further information: Pixley National Wildlife Refuge, c/o Kern NWR Complex, P.O. Box 670, Delano, CA 93216; telephone: (661) 725-2767.

Sacramento, comprising 10,783 acres, was established in 1937 to restore and manage seasonally flooded marsh, riparian, permanent pond, watergrass, and upland grass habitats. The refuge, which attracts more than 500,000 ducks and 300,000 geese during the autumn and winter months, is one of six national wildlife refuges in the Sacramento NWR Complex. It is located within the Sacramento Valley in north-central California.

As the U.S. Fish and Wildlife Service describes the history of this part of California:

The Sacramento NWR Complex represents a small portion of the vast seasonal wetlands and grasslands that once existed in the Sacramento Valley. Millions of waterfowl migrated down the Pacific Flyway to winter in the valley among resident waterbirds, deer, elk, pronghorn, and grizzly bear. With the development of agriculture, in the late 1800's and early 1900's, natural habitat was replaced with rice and other crops. Waterfowl substituted these farm crops for their original wetland foods, causing serious losses for farmers.

Today, 95% of California's wetlands are gone, along with the pronghorn and grizzly bear. New wetlands cannot be created naturally, since levees have been constructed to confine the river for irrigation and flood control. However, the birds continue to fly their ancient routes along the Pacific Flyway, crowding into the remaining wintering habitat. The Refuges provide a significant amount of the wintering habitat for waterfowl in the Sacramento Valley.

The six Refuges of the Complex are almost entirely manmade. In 1937, with the establishment of Sacramento National Wildlife Refuge, managers and biologists worked to transform the Refuge's dry, alkaline lands into productive marshes. The Civilian Conservation Corps (CCC) using bulldozers and tractors, began creating marshes and ponds.

From the 1950s through the 1980s, Delevan, Colusa, Sutter, and Butte Sink refuges were established principally to create and manage additional wetlands for wintering waterfowl, and the Sacramento River Refuge was established primarily to restore and protect important stretches of the river's riparian habitat between Red Bluff and Princeton. (See separate texts on each of these refuges.)

The Fish and Wildlife Service's habitat management activities include irrigating the wetlands to mimic the Sacramento River's historic cycle of flooding. These seasonally flooded marshes are drained during the late spring and summer months to promote the growth of nutrient-rich plants and then reflooded in the autumn, making the plants and their seeds available for waterfowl and other water birds. Prescribed burning is an important management tool that is implemented to promote nutrient cycling, reduce the accumulation of organic matter, and keep ponds from becoming choked with aquatic vegetation. Fire is also used to maintain the health of upland grass habitat. The refuges' watergrass habitat is irrigated to spur the formation of seedheads that provide an additional source of food for waterfowl. More than 1,500 water control structures are used to manage the delivery of water on these refuges.

Important vegetation on the seasonal marshes includes cattail, roundstem and alkali bulrushes, swamp timothy, and smartweed. Typical plants in permanent ponds include cattail, roundstem bulrush, and sago pondweed. Areas of watergrass consist mainly of the non-native watergrass (*Paspalum dilatatum*), with lesser amounts of several other grasses and smartweed. Riparian habitat contains such species as valley (California white) oak, Fremont cottonwood, black willow, boxelder, elderberry, and wild rose.

Ducks Unlimited, Inc. has helped enhance more than 600 acres of the refuge's wetland habitat.

Sacramento Refuge is open daily during daylight hours. A modest entrance fee is charged. The Sacramento NWR Complex's visitor center is open daily (except national holidays) from October 1 through March, and only on weekdays during the rest of the year.

Visitor activities on Sacramento Refuge include birdwatching, photography (two photo blinds are available, by advance reservation and payment of a daily use fee), viewing interpretive exhibits at the visitor center, driving the 6-mile auto tour route, hiking a 2-mile, self-guiding interpretive trail, environmental education programs for school and other groups (by prior arrangement), and hunting (goose, duck, coot, moorhen, snipe, and pheasant) on parts of the refuge during the designated seasons.

Insect repellent and sunscreen are advised during the warmer months.

The Sacramento NWR Complex also includes the Butte Sink, Willow Creek-Lurline, and North-Central Valley wildlife management areas that were established in 1980. There are presently 134 private properties with a total of more than 27,500 acres, which are under easement agreements with local landowners, making possible the restoration and protection of important wildlife habitat on private properties. Although these easement parcels are not open to the public, the voluntary cooperation of many landowners is an inspiring and important partnership in the long-term conservation of environmentally significant Sacramento Valley wildlife habitat. Over 265 bird species have been seen on these refuges.

Lodgings and meals in the vicinity of Sacramento Refuge are available in such communities as Willows, Williams, and Yuba City.

Access to the Sacramento Refuge, from I-5 northbound, is by way of the Road 68 exit (20 miles north of Williams), east (right) at the end of the off-ramp, and north (left) on State Route 99W to the refuge entrance on the right. Or from I-5 southbound, it is by way of the Road 68 exit (about 7 miles south of Willows), east (left) at the end of the off-ramp, and north (left) on State Route 99W.

Further information: Sacramento National Wildlife Refuge, 752 County Road 99W, Willows, CA 95988; telephone: (530) 934-2801.

Sacramento River, consisting of 9,000 federally owned acres and an additional 6,675 easement acres within more than 23 units, is working toward a goal of approximately 18,000 acres. The refuge was established in 1989 primarily to restore and protect ecologically significant stretches of the Sacramento River's riparian habitat between Red Bluff and Princeton. It is one of six national wildlife refuges in the Sacramento NWR Complex and is located within the Sacramento Valley in north-central California.

An innovative revenue-producing arrangement is enabling the refuge to defray the high financial cost of riparian habitat restoration. As the U.S. Fish and Wildlife Service explains, "About 40 percent of the fee title acreage is under agricultural production, primarily high-value almond, walnut, and prune orchards. . . . Because of the high value and long-term nature of the crops. . . , these lands are being managed under a . . . unique cooperative agreement with The Nature Conservancy (TNC). The revenue generated from the crops is used to pay for riparian restoration, which will be phased in over approximately 20 years as the orchards decline in productivity."

Another refuge partner is the nonprofit organization Ducks Unlimited, Inc., which has helped enhance more than 1,500 acres of the refuge's wetland habitat.

The only parts of the Sacramento River refuge open to visitation during daylight hours are the Llano Seco Unit and the Packer Lake Unit. The Llano Seco Unit contains seasonally flooded marsh, permanent pond, watergrass, and upland grass habitats, primarily for the benefit of wintering waterfowl. This unit was originally part of the 18,000-acre Llano Seco Rancho. In 1991, the ranch was divided between the Parrott Investment Company, The Nature Conservancy, the California Department of Fish and Game, and the U.S. Fish and Wildlife Service.

Visitor activities on the Llano Seco Unit are wildlife observation, photography, and walking a 0.6-mile trail that connects two multilevel viewing platforms overlooking wetland habitat. Access to the unit from I-5 at Willows is east on State Route 162 to about 2 miles east of Butte City and north (left) 9 miles on Road Z, which jogs around the south end of the unit and becomes Seven Mile Road. The trail is accessed from a parking area that is located on the west (left) side of the road.

The Packer Lake Unit contains a 30-acre oxbow lake, Packer Lake, that offers opportunities for warm water angling, which is best from March to November from either the west bank or from a boat. A primitive boat-launch area (recommended only for car-top boats) is available, but no other facilities are provided in this very primitive area.

Insect repellent and sunscreen are advised during the warmer months.

Access to Packer Lake from Princeton is north 5 miles on State Route 45 and east (right) on a narrow dirt road to the lakeshore.

For information on the Sacramento NWR Complex's habitat management activities, wildlife, and visitor center, see the Sacramento National Wildlife Refuge text.

Further information: Sacramento River National Wildlife Refuge, c/o SacramentoNWR Complex, 752 County Road 99W , Willows, CA 95988; telephone: (530) 934-2801.

Salinas River, encompassing 367 acres, was established in 1991 to restore and protect a diversity of habitats, including an ecologically important coastal sand dune system, a 45-acre saline pond, salt marsh, riparian scrub, and native coastal prairie. Many species of native fauna and flora are found here, among which are a number of threatened and endangered species. The refuge is located at the mouth of the Salinas River, on the shore of Monterey Bay in northern California.

The land was acquired by the U.S. Fish and Wildlife Service through a transfer of surplus military land from the U.S. Army and the U.S. Coast Guard. The area was initially designated as a wildlife management area, under a cooperative agreement with the California Department of Fish and Game. As the Service explains in the refuge's September 2001 *Draft Comprehensive Conservation Plan* (*Draft CCP*), "By the mid-1980s, growing awareness of . . . [its] importance as habitat for sensitive species prompted a shift toward more active management and protection of its resources. In 1991, the Service began managing the area as a National Wildlife Refuge. . . ." The refuge's vision statement says, "Endangered or threatened species will receive management priority, with special emphasis placed on the conservation and recovery of the western snowy plover." In 1993, the coastal population of this shorebird, which nests on beach foredune habitat from southern Washington to Mexico's Baja California del Sur, was federally listed as a threatened species.

The *Draft CCP* explains:

Historically, the Monterey Bay area has supported one of the most productive populations of western snowy plovers on the central California coast. . . . Populations of snowy plovers in the Monterey Bay area have been dramatically reduced as a result of habitat loss and disturbance by thousands of beach visitors in summer. Since 1986, there has been a dramatic decline in plover nest success at the Refuge and on adjacent lands. . . . Nonetheless, the plover breeding colony on and near the Refuge is one of California's most important, and protection of this resource is considered essential. . . .

Other species of concern on Salinas River Refuge include the endangered Smith's blue butterfly (*Euphilotes enoptes smithi*), the black legless lizard (*Anniella pulchra nigra*), the endangered Monterey gilia (*Gilia tenuiflora arenaria*), and the threatened Monterey spineflower (*Chorizanthe pungens* var. *pungens*), all of which live on or near the coastal dune habitat. A key management activity here is the removal and control of non-native invasive plants, which, if uncontrolled, can spread rapidly, crowding out native flora and related fauna.

Additional habitat management activities and goals include the protection and enhancement of the saline pond, which attracts such shorebirds as black-necked stilts and American avocets; and the Salinas River Lagoon, which is used by threatened California brown pelicans, waterfowl, terns, ospreys, muskrats, the threatened steelhead and other fish, and numerous invertebrates. Riparian habitat along the river is to be restored to enhance its value for resident and neotropical migratory songbirds; to provide shade along the edge of the river that can enhance native fish habitat; and to stabilize the riverbank.

The refuge's native grassland habitat, a rare plant community in California, is also to be restored and managed for the benefit of many grassland-dependent birds and other wildlife. As the *Draft CCP* document explains, "Historically, native grassland was maintained naturally by recurring fires that prevented shrubs from converting the habitat to shrubland. Since the end of agricultural operations . . . in the 1960s, invasive weeds have proliferated and shrubs have been slowly invading the grassland in the absence of fire. . . ." Periodic prescribed burning is a key management tool. Not only does fire control the growth of invasive weeds and shrubs, but it promotes nutrient cycling and spurs the new growth of grasses and forbs.

The refuge is open daily during daylight hours. There is no entrance fee.

Visitor activities include birdwatching, photography, access to fishing, and hunting (goose, duck, moorhen, and coot) on a small part of the refuge during the designated seasons.

Wildlife watching opportunities are along the 0.25 River Trail that runs from the parking area through upland habitat to the south bank of the Salinas River and the 0.5-mile Ocean Beach Trail that runs from the parking area through upland habitat, along the saline pond, and through the dunes to the beach. The Fish and Wildlife Service reminds visitors that the upper beach habitat is closed (except on the designated trail) to protect the snowy plover and that the coastal dunes, salt marsh, and saline pond are closed to visitation to protect these sensitive areas from disturbance.

Lodgings and meals are available in such communities as Marina, Watsonville, Monterey, and Santa Cruz.

Access to Salinas River Refuge from State Route 1 is by way of the Del Monte/Marina Boulevard exit and left onto an unpaved road to the refuge's parking area.

Further information: Salinas River National Wildlife Refuge, c/o San Francisco Bay NWR Complex, P.O. Box 524, Newark, CA 94560; telephone: (510) 792-0222.

San Diego, containing roughly 10,000 acres in two separate units, has been designated as a Globally Important Bird Area by the American Bird Conservancy. The refuge is located within San Diego County in southwestern California.

The refuge's OTAY-SWEETWATER UNIT, consisting of 7,495 acres and working toward a goal of 44,000 acres, includes several tracts of land along and near the Sweetwater River. It was established in 1996 to protect ecologically significant areas of abundant sagebrush scrub and chaparral, coast live oak woodland, native grassland, and vernal pools. The area also includes freshwater marsh and riparian woodland. As the U.S. Fish and Wildlife Service says:

This east county refuge is part of the National Wildlife Refuge System's contribution to the Multiple Species Conservation Plan, a program designed to conserve open space and habitat for species survival while allowing compatible and appropriate development.

Otay-Sweetwater's abundant coastal sage and chaparral habitat is an important addition to the inland preserves established to conserve and restore fast diminishing habitat.

The refuge also includes an especially rare type of wetland habitat, the vernal pool, where, for only a brief time each spring, many colorfully blooming plants and unusual animals appear. As the Service explains:

Vernal pools in San Diego have survived for at least 125,000 years—perhaps as long as 400,000 years—and it was only in the 1980s that their numbers diminished drastically. Today three percent of the region's vernal pools remain.

In late summer, fall, and early winter, vernal pools appear as dry, dusty indentations mostly devoid of vegetation. Then in late winter, a spectacular transformation occurs. As these depressions fill with water, high numbers of endangered, rare and sensitive species of plants and animals appear in and around the pools, many of which can only be found in this [eco]system. San Diego fairy shrimp lie dormant in the pool's dusty crevices until rain fills the pools.

Delicately hued plants also grow during this wet phase, then change again as the water begins to evaporate in the spring. As the pools dry, blossoms of every color fill these seemingly insignificant indentations in the landscape. . . .

Vernal pools are often managed in partnership with local and regional agencies. The approved refuge boundary for the stewardship project is 8,000 acres.

The Service says, "San Diego County is now home to more federally listed threatened and endangered species than any other county in the continental United States." San Diego Refuge's Otay-Sweetwater Unit offers important protected habitat for such rare species as the federally listed threatened coastal California gnatcatcher; and the endangered least Bell's vireo, southwestern willow flycatcher, arroyo southwestern toad, and Quino checkerspot butterfly. The unit's vernal pools provide habitat for six federally listed species: San Diego and Riverside fairy shrimp, San Diego and Otay mesa mints, San Diego button celery, and California orcutt grass.

The Otay-Sweetwater Unit is open daily during daylight hours. There is no entrance fee. There is limited visitor access, and the unit provides no visitor use facilities.

Limited visitor activities include wildlife observation, photography, hiking on trails that run through some of the tracts, and interpreter-led walks.

Lodgings and meals are available in San Diego and other nearby communities.

Access to the Otay-Sweetwater Unit from I-805, I-15, or I-5 is east on State Route 94 (Martin Luther King, Jr., Freeway, which becomes Campo Road). Shortly after forking to the right at Jamacha Junction, Route 94 (Campo Road) crosses Sweetwater River and cuts through part of the refuge. To reach the refuge office (open on weekdays, except national holidays), turn left onto Lyons Valley Road and continue about 0.25 mile to a small business complex on the left: 13910 Lyons Valley Rd., Suite R.

The refuge's SOUTH SAN DIEGO BAY UNIT, consisting of 2,330 acres and working toward a goal of 3,940 acres, was established in 1999. It protects salt marsh, diked ponds, rare beds of eelgrass that are especially important to black brant, and one of southern California's largest contiguous expanses of tidal mudflat. South San Diego Bay is a site that is included in the Western Hemisphere Shorebird Network and is also designated as an Important Bird Area by the American Bird Conservancy. These wetland habitats attract hundreds of thousands of birds—notably wintering waterfowl, migrating shorebirds, and nesting seabirds.

As the Fish and Wildlife Service explains, "The largest and densest concentration of birds in San Diego Bay is found in the southern part of the bay, in and around the artificially diked ponds created by Western Salt Company. This area was purchased by the San Diego Port District and conveyed to the U.S. Fish and Wildlife Service to establish the first portion of the South San Diego Bay Unit, San Diego NWR." A proposal is pending to designate this unit as a separate national wildlife refuge.

Many of the species of water birds that have been recorded on the South San Diego Bay refuge unit are the same as those at nearby Tijuana Slough (see the listing for that refuge).

Although this unit is not open to the public, visitors can hike or bicycle on a bike path that runs along the edge of the area between Coronado and Imperial Beach. For further information on the South San Diego Bay Unit, contact the Tijuana Slough NWR, 301 Caspian Way, Imperial Beach, CA 91932; telephone: (619) 575-2704.

Further information: San Diego National Wildlife Refuge, 13910 Lyons Valley Road, Suite R, Jamul, CA 91935; telephone: (619) 669-7295.

San Joaquin River, comprising 6,713 acres and working toward an authorized goal of more than 12,000 acres, was established in 1987 primarily to manage and protect important wintering habitat for the Aleutian Canada goose. Large concentrations of other wintering waterfowl and sandhill cranes are also attracted to the refuge, which is located along the San Joaquin River, near the northern end of the San Joaquin Valley in central California.

The authorized boundary of the refuge extends from just south of the junction of the Tuolumne and San Joaquin rivers northward (downstream) to the junction of the Stanislaus and San Joaquin rivers. As the U.S. Fish and Wildlife Service says, "The landscape represents a locally and regionally significant remnant of the once broad flood plain of these three major rivers. . . ." Lands within the boundary are being acquired in both fee title (federal ownership) and under perpetual conservation easements with owners of private properties. The voluntary cooperation of landowners is an inspiring partnership in the long-term restoration and conservation of environmentally significant wildlife habitat.

San Joaquin River Refuge's initial purchase of land occurred in 1988, when the Fish and Wildlife Service acquired 777-acre Christmas Island from the National Audubon Society (NAS). This property was previously donated to the NAS by Joseph M. Long and Don Lundberg, with the understanding that it would be conveyed to the Service as a refuge.

An important aspect of this refuge is described by the Fish and Wildlife Service in the refuge's October 29, 2001 *Draft Comprehensive Conservation Plan:*

> In January 1997, a catastrophic flood event occurred on the lower San Joaquin River system. Flood control levees failed and most of the refuge . . . [was] inundated by floodwaters. . . . private lands . . . also received extensive flooding. In all, the areas surrounding the refuge suffered over $2 billion in property damages. Subsequently, several landowners in the floodplain west of the San Joaquin River approached the Service with the intent of selling their flood-prone land to the Service, for inclusion into the existing refuge. This coincided with a national mandate by Congress for the US-ACE [U.S. Army Corps of Engineers] to explore non-structural alternatives for flood protection and statewide initiatives, such as the San Joaquin River Management Plan, to restore riparian habitat and hydrologic function, and to provide alternate methods of flood control. In support of these efforts, the Service proposed a non-structural flood protection demonstration project, in which the Service would acquire those flood-prone properties, breach or remove the existing flood control levee, and allow periodic floodwaters to spread over the refuge-owned floodplain to reduce downstream flooding. This proposal grew into a multi-agency effort whose partners

included NRCS [Natural Resource Conservation Service], USACE, U.S. Bureau of Reclamation, DWR [California State Department of Water Resources], and the Service. In 1997, the Service completed an Environmental Assessment and Land Protection Plan to expand the approved refuge boundary to 12,887 acres. Following approval, in 1999 the Service acquired 2,037 acres of floodplain and riparian habitat west of the San Joaquin River. . . .

Acquisition of additional floodplain and riparian habitat is continuing, made possible partly with revenues from the sale of Migratory Bird Hunting and Conservation Stamps (Duck Stamps).

Although the refuge is not yet open to visitation pending the completion of the refuge's planning process, wildlife can be viewed from adjacent county roads.

Species of wildlife that have been recorded on San Joaquin River Refuge are essentially the same as those on San Luis Refuge.

Lodgings and meals are available in such communities as Modesto and Tracy.

Access from State Route 99 at Modesto is west 9 miles on State Route 132.

Further information: San Joaquin River National Wildlife Refuge, c/o San Luis NWR Complex, P.O. Box 2176, Los Banos, CA 93635; telephone: (209) 826-3508.

San Luis, consisting of 26,609 acres, was established in 1966. The refuge is restoring, managing, and protecting extensive wetlands and riparian habitat, with numerous tree-lined oxbows and channels, for the benefit of large concentrations of migratory waterfowl and other wildlife. It is located within the floodplain of Bear Creek, Salt Slough, and the San Joaquin River, near the northern end of the San Joaquin Valley in central California.

As explained by the U.S. Fish and Wildlife Service:

Thousands of acres of wetlands, fed by an intricate set of canals, are managed to produce natural food supplies for migratory waterfowl. San Luis also contains the most extensive network of pristine native grasslands, shrubs, and vernal pools that still remain with the Central Valley.

Hundreds of thousands of mallard, pintail, green-winged teal and ring-necked ducks flock into the managed wetlands, while colorful, yet secretive, wood ducks live throughout the tree-lined slough channels. Herons and egrets nest in majestic oaks and willows, then feed on the refuge's abundant fish, frog and crayfish populations. . . .

Few areas in California's San Joaquin Valley retain the flavor of early settlement days when wildlife was abundant, the air clear and fresh, and the landscape pleasant and pastoral.

San Luis National Wildlife Refuge is such a place, a remnant of past times contrasting with today's great cities, crowded highways, and mechanized farmlands.

The refuge's most prominent mammal is the tule elk (*Cervus nannodes*), a species (some authorities consider it a subspecies—*Cervus canadensis nannodes*) that is smaller and paler in color than either the Rocky Mountain or Roosevelt elk. During the twentieth century, the population of the tule (or dwarf) elk sharply declined through habitat loss and unregulated hunting and the species was threatened with extinction. (Conflicting accounts as to the lowest population of these elk range from a dozen animals to only a single pair.) As Devereux Butcher wrote in his 1963 book, *Exploring Our National Wildlife Refuges:*

The tule elk, smallest elk on the continent, once ranged through the valleys of California west of the Sierra Nevada, particularly the lower San Joaquin and Sacramento valleys. By the early 1920's, the total population of the species…was confined to a herd of about 400 animals on a ranch… in the San Joaquin Valley. Because there always was the danger that disease or some other cause might wipe out the elk while confined to one small area, a group of Californians interested in preserving the species had a few of the animals moved to a fenced area in Yosemite National Park. The high country here was not the natural range of the elk. By 1933, the policy of the National Park Service, with regard to wildlife, had crystallized, requiring that no animal shall be kept under fence in the national parks, and that no species not native to a park shall be introduced or retained there. The Yosemite animals were moved, therefore, from the park to Owens Valley in 1933.

A herd of 18 tule elk was brought to the San Luis Refuge in 1974. Since then, their fluctuating numbers have ranged between about 30 and 70 of these magnificent animals, living within a fenced enclosure that is encircled by one of the refuge's auto tour roads. As the population has periodically exceeded the carrying capacity of the 750-acre enclosure, some of the excess numbers have been relocated from the refuge to other suitable habitat. There are presently about 2,400 tule elk in more than two dozen locations around California.

Establishment of San Luis Refuge has been made possible partly with revenues from the sale of Migratory Bird Hunting and Conservation Stamps (Duck Stamps). Ducks Unlimited, Inc. has helped enhance more than 6,000 acres of the refuge's wetland habitat.

The refuge is open daily during daylight hours. There is no entrance fee. The San Luis NWR Complex headquarters, located at 947 West Pacheco Boulevard, Suite C, Los Banos, is open on weekdays, except national holidays.

Visitor activities include wildlife observation; viewing spring wildflower displays in vernal pool areas (during March and April); photography; driving the refuge's three unpaved, self-guiding, auto tour routes (the nearly 10-mile Waterfowl Tour Loop, the 5-mile Tule Elk Loop, and the 2.5-mile West Bear Creek Loop—the latter is accessed from State Route 165); viewing the refuge and its wildlife from several observation platforms; hiking; canoeing and boating; fishing; and hunting (goose, duck, moorhen, coot, snipe, and pheasant) on parts of the refuge during the designated seasons. Over 210 bird species have been seen on the refuge.

Hiking opportunities include the 0.75-mile Winton Marsh Loop Trail, which includes an observation platform; the 1-mile Sousa Trail, also with an observation platform; and the 1-mile Chester Marsh Trail, which is open from February 1 through September.

Insect repellent and sunscreen are advised during the warmer months.

Lodgings and meals are available in such communities as Merced and Los Banos.

The San Luis NWR Complex also includes the Grasslands Wildlife Management Area, comprising more than 70,000 acres under conservation-easement agreements that provide for the protection of vital wetland and grassland habitats on private properties, mostly private waterfowl hunting clubs. (The majority of California's remaining wetlands are privately owned.) Although these easement parcels are not open to the public, the voluntary cooperation of many landowners is an inspiring partnership in the long-term conservation of environmentally significant San Joaquin Valley wildlife habitat. As the San Luis NWR Complex's project leader, Kim Forrest, explains:

Only five percent of the four million acres of historic wetlands still exist in the Central Valley of California. The 160,000-acre Grassland Ecological Area, which includes all of the refuges of the San Luis NWR Complex (except San Joaquin River NWR), is the largest contiguous wetland area remaining in California.

Access to the San Luis Refuge from State Route 152 at Los Banos is north 8 miles on State Route 165 (Mercy Springs Road) and northeast (right) 2 miles on Wolfsen Road. The refuge's KESTERSON UNIT (the former 12,000-acre Kesterson National Wildlife Refuge) is east 4 miles from Gustine on State Route 140.

Further information: San Luis National Wildlife Refuge, P.O. Box 2176, Los Banos, CA 93635; telephone: (209) 826-3508.

San Pablo Bay, encompassing 13,189 acres, is working toward a goal of approximately 21,000 acres. The refuge was established in 1974 to restore and protect significant tidally influenced wetland habitat for the benefit of migratory waterfowl, shorebirds, endangered species, and other wildlife. It is located within the northern reach of San Pablo Bay, which is part of the greater San Francisco Bay in north-central California.

Habitats within the refuge's boundaries include open bay waters, intertidal mudflats, salt marsh, seasonal wetlands, and uplands. The bay's open water contains a mixture of fresh water flowing from the Sacramento, San Joaquin, and other rivers and salt water from the Pacific Ocean. Numerous species of fish and aquatic invertebrates inhabit these waters, including salmon, steelhead, herring, crabs, and shrimp. Twice-daily tides, which inundate and expose vast expanses of silt-and-clay mudflats, bring a huge quantity of rich nutrients that support shellfish, worms, and amphipods. Low tide enables shorebirds and other water birds to forage in the mud for these animals; and at high tide, fish feed on them.

A variety of tidal marsh habitats, including salt marsh and brackish marsh, comprise a zone of transition between the mudflats and drier, higher ground. Salt marshes provide vital feeding and nursery habitat for many species of fish and shellfish. Cordgrass, saltgrass, pickleweed, gumplant, and sea lavender are among the characteristic plants that grow here.

Regarding the history of this ecologically rich area, the U.S. Fish and Wildlife Service says:

Less than 150 years ago, the Napa-Sonoma marshes surrounding San Pablo Bay comprised one of the most extensive wetland systems along the Pacific Coast. This system provided habitat for millions of migrating waterfowl and shorebirds, as well as resident wildlife. Plants specialized to live in aquatic habitats grew bountifully, sheltering and feeding a rich diversity of species.

Rapid development in the area began with the discovery of gold in the Sierra Nevada foothills in the 1850s. Hydraulic mining operations contributed huge amounts of sediment to the San Francisco Bay Estuary. For the next one hundred years, the marshes were filled, diked or drained to support the bay's development as a major center for commerce.

By the 1950s, only 25 percent of the historical tidal marshes remained in the estuary. Today, only 15 percent of the bay's historic tidal lands remain.

Partnerships have been and continue to be vital to the success of San Pablo Bay Refuge. As the Service explains:

Since the 1960s, conservation agencies, non-profit organizations and local grassroot efforts have worked to protect the Bay for its significance to migratory birds and resident wildlife. The northern Bay's Napa-Sonoma Marshes Tolay Creek Unit are jointly managed with the California Department of Fish and Game. The Lower Tubbs Island Unit was acquired with assistance from The Nature Conservancy. . . . the Solano County Farmlands and Open Space Foundation and California State Coastal Conservancy helped acquire the Cullinan Ranch/Napa Marsh Unit.

Largely comprised of thousands of acres of tidelands leased from the California State Lands Commission, the Refuge's ultimate plans include protection and conservation of more than 20,000 acres of critical wildlife habitat in northern San Pablo Bay.

Ducks Unlimited, Inc. is another important nonprofit partner with San Pablo Bay Refuge. With financial assistance from its Matching Aid to Restore States Habitat (MARSH) program, DU is helping to create 80 acres of wetland habitat adjacent to a new visitor center.

Large concentrations of migratory waterfowl, shorebirds, wading birds, and raptors are attracted to the refuge during the autumn, winter, and spring. Peak numbers of ducks, such as canvasbacks, scaup, scoters, buffleheads, goldeneyes, and ruddy ducks; and shorebirds, such as plovers, sandpipers, willets, marbled godwits, curlews, dowitchers, and avocets, gather here from November through January. Prominent among the raptors are white-tailed kites, northern harriers, and red-tailed hawks.

San Pablo Bay Refuge's wetlands are inhabited by two federally listed endangered species, the California clapper rail (*Rallus longirostris obsoletus*) and the salt marsh harvest mouse (*Reithrodontomys raviventris*), the latter inhabiting only the San Francisco Bay salt marshes and feeding exclusively on pickleweed. The refuge protects the largest remaining pickleweed marsh in the North Bay. The survival of the salt marsh-dependent rail and mouse has been put at risk as the result of declining habitat and the introduction of non-native plants and animals. The Fish and Wildlife Service's tidal restoration projects, by providing additional habitat, are directed toward helping ensure that these species will be able to survive and flourish. As the Fish and Wildlife Service explains:

. . . the steady conversion of salt marsh habitat for urban use and salt production has had the greatest impact on the clapper rail's survival, removing over 80 percent of the tidal marshes they once called home. Almost everywhere, levees separate the remaining tidal marshes from the rail's high marsh retreats, leaving them vulnerable to predators and preventing birds from meeting and breeding.

The refuge is open daily during daylight hours. There is no entrance fee. The refuge office, located at Building 505 on Mare Island in Vallejo is open on weekdays, except national holidays. Visitor services are expected to be expanded soon, with restoration of Building 505 (the first Naval Pacific Group Communications building on the West Coast) to be used for the refuge headquarters and the North Bay Discovery Center. The best overview of the refuge is at a designated pullout off the westbound lane of I-80, three miles east of the Vallejo city limits.

Visitor activities, which presently occur mostly on the TOLAY CREEK UNIT, include birdwatching; photography; interpretive activities; environmental education programs; hiking; boating (no boat-launching on the refuge); fishing; and hunting (goose, duck, coot, and pheasant) on parts of the refuge during the designated season.

Hiking opportunities include the 8.2-mile Tolay Creek/Tubbs Island Trail.

Visitors are urged to be alert for ticks and are cautioned not to attempt walking in the marsh: "you may sink, become stuck or create trails for predators." Insect repellent and sunscreen are advised during the warmer seasons.

San Pablo Bay Refuge's fauna and flora are essentially the same as the species that have been recorded on the Don Edwards San Francisco Bay National Wildlife Refuge.

Lodgings and meals are available in Vallejo, Novato, and other communities throughout the San Francisco Bay area.

Access to San Pablo Bay Refuge's Tolay Creek Unit from U.S. Route 101 is east about 8 miles on State Route 37; or from I-80, it is west about 14 miles on State Route 37.

Further information: San Pablo Bay National Wildlife Refuge, P.O. Box 2012, (Azuar Drive and "I" Street, Building 505), Mare Island, Vallejo, CA 94592; telephone: (707) 562-3000.

Seal Beach, containing 923 acres, was established in 1972 to restore, enhance, and protect rare salt marsh habitat for the benefit of endangered species, migratory birds, and other wildlife. The refuge, which overlays part of the Seal Beach Naval Weapons Station, is located along the Pacific Coast of Orange County in southern California.

A major issue of concern on Seal Beach Refuge is the welfare of the federally listed endangered light-footed clapper rail (*Rallus longirostris levipes*). This subspecies inhabits remnant areas of salt marsh cordgrass from Ventura County southward along the Pacific Coast into Mexico, with its largest remaining U.S. population centers in Orange and San Diego counties. The refuge's other endangered subspecies include the California least tern and Belding's savannah sparrow.

As the U.S. Fish and Wildlife Service explains, "Working closely with the U.S. Navy's Natural Resources Protection staff, wildlife and habitat management programs at Seal Beach are built around the recovery of endangered species. Additionally, Seal Beach provides important habitat for a variety of migratory shorebirds, waterfowl, and seabirds." In coordination with the U.S. Navy, the Service is restoring and enhancing areas of Anaheim Bay salt marsh and converting degraded lands to wildlife habitat.

Typical salt marsh vegetation includes sea lavender, pickleweed, fleshy jaumea, alkali heath, saltwort, and salt marsh cordgrass.

The refuge is open to visitors through guided tours hosted by refuge personnel or trained volunteer interpreters. Because of the need for heightened security on this military facility, tours need to be prearranged.

Because the U.S. Navy did not acquire the subsurface mineral rights beneath its ordnance facility, limited oil development by the owner of those rights is occurring in the middle of the refuge's marsh.

Further information: Seal Beach National Wildlife Refuge, P.O. Box 815, Seal Beach, CA 90740; telephone: (562) 598-1024.

Sonny Bono Salton Sea was established in 1930 to enhance and maintain habitat for large concentrations of wintering waterfowl, migrating shorebirds, and a tremendous variety of other wildlife. The refuge's several separate parts are located on and around the south end of the Salton Sea, within the Imperial Valley in the southern end of California.

Thousands of years ago, the Gulf of California (Sea of Cortez) extended northward into what are now the Imperial and Coachella valleys. Large quantities of sediments that were deposited by the Colorado River gradually created a barrier, which cut off this extension of the sea. The resulting inland sea slowly evaporated, leaving a dry basin. According to geologists, for as many as five times during the past 2,500 years, the Colorado River has broken through its own natural levees, flowed into the basin, and created temporary Lake Cahuilla, named for the Native Americans who have lived in this area for thousands of years. The lake's most recent appearance was as late as the sixteenth century and was significantly larger than today's Salton Sea, covering much of Imperial and Coachella valleys. From then until the early twentieth century, the basin was dry. However, as described by the U.S. Fish and Wildlife Service:

In 1901, Colorado River waters were diverted from Yuma, Arizona, into Mexico and back into the . . . basin for agricultural development. In 1905, a diversion structure failed under high river levels, and the entire Colorado River flowed unchecked into the Imperial Valley between 1905-1907, creating the present-day Salton Sea. . . .

In the early 1900s when the Salton Sea was formed, it was a freshwater lake. Since then, this lake has become more and more salty due to a combination of agricultural run-off of salt and mineral laden water, evaporation, and the lack of any outflow. As the salinity increased, the freshwater fish species in the Sea gradually died out. The saltwater fish that are now present were first introduced from the ocean in the 1950s. Presently, the Salton Sea is 20-30% saltier than the Pacific Ocean, and will likely continue to increase in salinity unless preventive measures are taken. If salinity levels rise much higher, fish won't be the only organisms affected—the entire Salton Sea ecosystem could be radically altered.

Before the Salton Sea was formed, waterfowl were only found along the marshes and delta of the Colorado River (primarily in Mexico). During the 1920s, as more water was diverted from the Colorado River for agriculture, marshes were inadvertently created. These marshes, at the edge of the then smaller Salton Sea, resulted from agricultural water run-off. Waterfowl were attracted to the marshes from their former winter home in the drying Colorado River Delta.

After the originally named Salton Sea National Wildlife Refuge was established, comprising 37,600 acres, farming in the Imperial Valley greatly increased its use of Colorado River water during the 1940s. This increase has, in turn, caused larger quantities of water to flow into and expand the Salton Sea, the surface of which has risen to roughly 225 feet below sea level, covers more than 243,000 acres, and is 35 miles long and up to 15 miles wide. As the Fish and Wildlife Service says, "Now, because of flooding by the Salton Sea, only about 1,785 manageable acres remain. Dikes are expected to keep the sea from further encroachment on the refuge."

In 1999, the refuge was renamed to honor the memory of the late Congressman Sonny Bono, who led efforts in Congress to bring the plight of the Salton Sea to national attention and who supported passage of the 1998 Salton Sea Reclamation Act.

Habitat management activities on the refuge include manipulating water levels within impounded ponds to provide suitable habitat for waterfowl and shorebirds; and growing alfalfa, wheat, and sometimes barley and rye. These nutrient-rich crops, which are planted by local farmers and the Service on a cooperative basis, provide an important source of food for wintering waterfowl and other wildlife.

Another major activity on the Sonny Bono Salton Sea Refuge involves the problem of fish and wildlife diseases and contamination. The Fish and Wildlife Service explains, "the refuge routinely surveys the Salton Sea for dead or dying fish and wildlife," which "are removed from the area . . . to prevent the spread of disease and sent to the lab for investigation." Associates that assist the refuge during wildlife disease outbreaks include the Coachella Valley Wild Bird Center, in Indio; Sea World, in San Diego; Pacific Wildlife Project, in Irvine; Wetlands and Wildlife Care Center, in Huntington Beach; and International Wild Bird Rescue, in San Pedro. All of them contain wildlife rehabilitation facilities, with an emphasis on medically treating injured birds. The refuge primarily uses these facilities for the rehabilitation of American white and brown pelicans, which are stricken with avian botulism each summer.

On February 14, 2000, the Associated Press reported that "Federal officials warned . . . that the Salton Sea's rich ecosystem will die unless 9 million tons of salt . . . [are] pulled from the lake each year." David Hayes, the then-deputy secretary of the U.S. Department of the Interior, who spoke at a Salton Sea Symposium, was quoted as saying that "To let the sea die, in our view, is not an option." The goal of restoring California's largest lake, which is "one of the nation's most productive fisheries" and a major mecca for migratory birds, is to reduce its salinity to the level of the Pacific Ocean. The cost estimates of what are seen as the best alternatives for achieving this goal range from $1.6 million to $9.5 million annually.

Prominent among the refuge's species of wintering waterfowl, shorebirds, and other water birds are thousands of snow and Ross's geese; smaller numbers of Canada geese; ducks, such as northern pintail and green-winged teal; black-necked stilt; American avocet; and eared grebe. A secretive resident bird that breeds in marsh habitat around the southeastern edge of the Salton Sea (as well as along the lower Colorado River) is a federally listed endangered subspecies, the Yuma clapper rail (*Rallus longirostris yumanensis*). These small wading birds are more often heard than seen, their *chek-chek-chek-chek* call emanating from dense stands of cattails and bulrushes. Other wetland wading birds include the wood stork, great blue and green herons, and great and snowy egrets. The most abundant bird of this habitat is the red-winged blackbird, with its flashing yellow-edged crimson epaulets; and the smallest bird here is the 5-inch-long marsh wren. Many species of shorebirds also seek out mudflats along the shore of the Salton Sea.

It is especially exciting to visit the refuge during late autumn or winter and see hundreds of snow geese covering the ground like snow, then to watch and listen as they suddenly rise en masse into the air with a loud chorus of honking and fly together back and forth like a huge, undulating cloud. Over 380 bird species have been recorded here.

The Salton Sea's populations of fish attract large numbers of American white and brown pelicans, double-crested cormorants, gulls, and terns. Rows of desert trees and shrubs that grow as "coverstrips" along dikes separating farm fields include screwbean and honey mesquites, palo verde, and desert thorn. This habitat offers shelter, food, and nesting areas for such species as Gambel's quail, mourning dove, greater roadrunner, verdin, cactus wren, yellow-rumped warbler, and white-crowned sparrow. The burrowing owl lives in burrows along ditch banks.

The refuge is open daily during daylight hours. There is no entrance fee. The headquarters/ visitor center is open on weekdays, except national holidays, and on weekends during the winter.

Visitor activities include birdwatching, photography, viewing wildlife from observation platforms, walking self-guiding interpretive trails, hiking, environmental education programs for school and other groups (an Educator's Guide is available), boat fishing (no bank fishing), and waterfowl hunting on part of the refuge during the designated season. Camping is not permitted on the refuge, but campground facilities are provided to the north at the Salton Sea State Recreation Area and elsewhere.

Hiking opportunities include the 0.5-mile Michael Hardenberger Trail that loops through part of the refuge's Unit 1, and the 1-mile Rock Hill Trail from the visitor center.

Visitors are cautioned to be alert for rattlesnakes. Sunscreen is advised.

Lodgings and meals are available in such communities as Calipatria and Brawley.

Access to the Sonny Bono Salton Sea Refuge from the Forrester Road exit on I-8 is north on Forrester Road (through Westmoreland), proceeding north (from the junction with Eddins Road) on Gentry Road, and west (left) at Sinclair Road to the refuge's Union Tract and visitor center; or to the refuge's Unit 1 it is north from I-8 on Forrester Road, west (left) on Bannister Road, and north (right) on Vendel Road. From I-10, it is south from Indio on State Route 111 to 5 miles south of Niland and west (right) 6 miles to the refuge's Union Tract and visitor center.

Further information: Sonny Bono Salton Sea National Wildlife Refuge, 906 West Sinclair Road, Calipatria, CA 92233; telephone: (760) 348-5278.

Stone Lakes, consisting of more than 4,000 acres and working toward a goal of about 18,000 acres, was established in 1994 to restore and protect important wetland, riparian woodland, and grassland habitats and three permanent lakes. The refuge, which attracts thousands of migratory waterfowl during the autumn and winter months, is located near Sacramento, within the northern part of the Central Valley's delta of the Sacramento and San Joaquin rivers in central California. Over 165 bird species have been seen here.

Although a relatively small portion of the refuge is presently under public ownership, a number of privately owned tracts within the approved refuge boundary are being managed under cooperative agreements and conservation easements.

Management of the lands within the refuge boundary is a cooperative effort with a number of partners, including the Sacramento County Department of Regional Parks, Recreation and Open Space; California Department of Parks and Recreation; California Department of Water Resources; and California Department of Transportation. As the Fish and Wildlife Service says:

Restoration programs are transforming land that once lay fallow or was intensively farmed into productive grasslands, wetlands, and riparian habitat. Working together, volunteers, staff, school children and others have planted thousands of young valley oaks, cottonwoods and willows. Cattle feed on weeds and non-native grasses as part of a grazing program to bring back native vegetation and create short grass habitat that is, once again, attracting sandhill cranes, geese and shorebirds. . . .

The refuge's goals could not be accomplished alone. More than any other force, Stone Lakes was established and is being restored through partnerships. The staff has slowly built ties with other landowning agencies, conservation groups and many of its farming neighbors.

Because the refuge has limited access, the Fish and Wildlife Service recommends calling to obtain information about open trail days. There is no entrance fee.

Even though the refuge offers limited facilities, visitor activities include birdwatching, photography, walking the (wheelchair-accessible) boardwalk to a wildlife observation platform, seasonal interpreter-guided walks (such as to see a heron, egret, and cormorant rookery; spring wildflowers; and butterflies), and environmental education programs for school and other groups (by advance reservation). Opportunities are being developed for boating, fishing, and hunting "with a special emphasis on youth and barrier-free access."

Insect repellent and sunscreen are advised during the warmer months.

Lodgings and meals are available in Sacramento.

Stone Lakes Refuge is located on the west side of I-5, about 10 miles south of downtown Sacramento, in the city of Elk Grove. Access from I-5 is by way of the Elk Grove Boulevard exit. At the end of the exit ramp, turn west. The refuge entrance gate is immediately ahead, and visitors can park near the gate.

Further information: Stone Lakes National Wildlife Refuge, 1624 Hood Franklin Road, Elk Grove, CA 95758; telephone: (916) 775-4421.

Sutter, comprising 2,591 acres, was established in 1945 to restore and manage seasonally flooded marsh, permanent pond, watergrass, and upland grass habitats, primarily for the benefit of at least 160,000 ducks and 55,000 geese during the autumn and winter. The majority of the refuge is within the Sutter Bypass and was designed to withstand annual flooding events. Sutter is one of six national wildlife refuges in the Sacramento NWR Complex. It is located within the Sacramento Valley in north-central California.

Ducks Unlimited, Inc. has helped enhance more than 700 acres of the refuge's wetland habitat.

The refuge can be viewed from a public highway that cuts through the middle of the area. Hunting (goose, duck, coot, moorhen, snipe, and pheasant) is permitted on part of the refuge during the designated seasons.

Access to Sutter Refuge from State Route 45 at Colusa is east 12 miles on State Route 20, south (right) 2.5 miles on Tarke Road, east (left) 2 miles on McGrath Road, south (right) 2.5 miles on Progress Road, east (left) 3.5 miles on Oswald Road, and east through the refuge on Hughes Road. Or from State Route 99 at Yuba City, it is west 2 miles on State Route 20, south (left) 5 miles on Washington Boulevard, west (right) 3.5 miles on Oswald Road, north (right) 0.8 mile on Schlag Road, and west (left) on Hughes Road.

For information on the Sacramento NWR Complex's habitat management activities, wildlife, and visitor center, see the Sacramento NWR text.

Further information: Sutter National Wildlife Refuge, c/o Sacramento NWR Complex, 752 County Road 99W, Willows, CA 95988; telephone: (530) 934-2801.

Sweetwater Marsh, containing 316 acres, was established in 1988 to restore, enhance, and protect an important remnant area of tidal salt marsh and adjacent upland habitats and a number of endangered and threatened species. This urban refuge is located on the eastern shore of South San Diego Bay, within the city of Chula Vista in southwestern California.

More than 90 percent of San Diego Bay's wetland habitat has been filled in, drained, or diked. Sweetwater Marsh refuge came into being as the result of a mitigation tradeoff for other San Diego Bay wetlands that have been eliminated for urban development. It protects a vital remnant of habitat for many species including large concentrations of migrating and wintering waterfowl and shorebirds. More than 220 species of birds have been recorded here.

As the U.S. Fish and Wildlife Service says, "San Diego County is now home to more federally listed threatened and endangered species than any other county in the continental United States." Among these are the endangered light-footed clapper rail (see the Seal Beach Refuge text) and California least tern; the threatened western snowy plover; the state-listed endangered Belding's savannah sparrow; and two plants: the endangered 4-inch-tall salt marsh bird's beak (*Cordylanthus maritimus maritimus*), which boasts fuzzy, white tubular flowers, and the yerba reuma (*Frankenia palmeri*). The latter species is at the northern limit of its range on the refuge. Although this member of the heath family is commonly found in some coastal wetlands along Mexico's Baja Peninsula, it grows naturally nowhere else in the United States.

The educational highlight of the refuge is a nature center that is cooperatively operated by the refuge and the City of Chula Vista. As described by the Fish and Wildlife Service:

Surrounded by numerous gardens, the Chula Vista Nature Center soars like an ark above . . . Sweetwater Marsh. The Nature Center provides visitors with the opportunity to experience the marsh through interpretive and interactive exhibits, guided nature and bird walks, and a petting pool. Outdoor aviaries support burrowing owls, shorebirds, egrets, and herons. Aviary dwellers are all birds that have been injured or imprinted and cannot be released back into their native habitats. A full-time teacher leads groups of school children out on the refuge each week for outdoor classroom experiences. The Center is well known for its unique wildlife art and its architecture.

The refuge and Chula Vista Nature Center are open daily, except on Mondays. An admission fee is charged for the nature center, except for free entry on the first Tuesday of each month.

Visitor activities include birdwatching, photography, viewing interpretive exhibits at the nature center, viewing the refuge and its wildlife from the nature center's observation deck, interpreter-led walks, and walking on several short trails.

Sunscreen is advised during the warmer months.

The species of fauna and flora that have been recorded on Sweetwater Marsh Refuge are much the same as in Tijuana Slough's salt marsh and adjacent upland habitats.

Lodgings and meals are available in Chula Vista and elsewhere throughout San Diego County.

Access to Sweetwater Marsh Refuge from the E Street exit on I-5 in Chula Vista is west to a parking area at the end of E Street. A free shuttle-bus service, which operates every 20 minutes, takes visitors to the nature center.

Further information: Sweetwater Marsh National Wildlife Refuge, 1080 Gunpowder Point Drive, Chula Vista, CA 91910; telephone: (619) 691-1262.

Tijuana Slough, encompassing 1,072 acres, was established in 1980 to restore, enhance, and protect a diversity of estuarine and related habitats for the benefit of endangered species, migratory waterfowl, shorebirds, and other wildlife. The refuge, which is within the urban environment of San Diego, is located where the Tijuana River flows into the Pacific Ocean, just over 1 mile north of the U.S.–Mexico border in the southwestern corner of California.

Habitats include open water, tidal salt marsh, riparian, vernal pool, coastal sand dune, and upland. As the U.S. Fish and Wildlife Service says, "San Diego County is now home to more federally listed threatened and endangered species than any other county in the continental United States." Among these are the endangered light-footed clapper rail (see the Seal Beach refuge text), California least tern, and least Bell's vireo; the threatened western snowy plover; and an endangered plant, the 4-inch-tall salt marsh bird's beak (*Cordylanthus maritimus maritimus*), which boasts fuzzy, white tubular flowers.

As explained by the Service, "Destined at one time to become a boat marina and restaurant complex, local citizens lobbied to have the slough and its uplands protected as a National Wildlife Refuge. Later the refuge was included with other public lands in the Tijuana River National Estuarine Research Reserve, one of only 27 in the entire U.S. The refuge supports numerous research and education activities, many of which are funded by the National Oceanic and Atmospheric Administration. Education programs and the visitor center are administered by the California Department of Parks."

The refuge is open daily during daylight hours. There is no entrance fee. The research reserve's visitor center is open daily, except on Thanksgiving, Christmas, and New Year's Day.

Visitor activities include birdwatching, photography, viewing interpretive exhibits and a 5-acre native plant garden at the visitor center, interpreter-led nature walks, hiking, bicycling on a bike trail, and horseback riding on horse trails that run through the refuge.

Hiking opportunities on 4 miles of trails include the 2-mile River Mouth Trail that runs from a trailhead at the junction of Fifth Street and Iris Avenue and loops by the mouth of the Tijuana River. Over 370 bird species have been recorded here.

Sunscreen and drinking water are advised during the warmer months.

Lodgings and meals are available in Chula Vista, Coronado, and San Diego.

Access to Tijuana Slough visitor center from the Coronado Avenue exit on I-5 is west on Coronado Avenue, south (left) on Fourth Street, west (right) on Caspian Way to a traffic circle, and left into the parking area.

Further information: Tijuana Slough National Wildlife Refuge, 301 Caspian Way, Imperial Beach, CA 91932; telephone: (619) 575-2704.

Tule Lake, consisting of 39,116 acres, was established in 1928 to protect bulrush-and-cattail marsh, open water, and managed croplands, mainly for the benefit of migrating and wintering waterfowl. The refuge is located within the southern part of the Klamath Basin in northern California.

Roughly 17,000 acres of the refuge are leased by local farmers, under a U.S. Bureau of Reclamation-administered agricultural program, and another 1,900 acres of refuge grain and alfalfa cropland are farmed by refuge permit holders. As the U.S. Fish and Wildlife Service explains, "These crops, together with the waste grain and potatoes from the lease program, are a major food source for migrating and wintering waterfowl."

Tule Lake Refuge, which takes its name from the tule or hardstem bulrush (*Scirpus lacustris*), is one of six national wildlife refuges in the Klamath Basin. The others are Clear Lake in California; Lower Klamath in California/Oregon; and Bear Valley (a major wintering bald eagle night-roosting area of forest), Upper Klamath, and Klamath Marsh in Oregon (see separate texts on each of these refuges).

A discussion of the history of the Klamath Basin's wetlands, the peak influxes of waterfowl and other water birds, the problem of severe water shortages, and efforts being made to improve wetland habitat are presented in the Lower Klamath NWR text. The Klamath Basin Wildlife Association, a nonprofit organization, assists the refuge.

Tule Lake Refuge is open daily during daylight hours. There is a tour-route fee and hunting and photo-blind fees. The Klamath Basin NWRs headquarters/visitor center, which is located 5 miles west of the California community of Tulelake on Hill Road, is open daily, except on Christmas and New Year's Day.

Visitor activities on Tule Lake Refuge include birdwatching, photography, viewing interpretive exhibits at the Klamath Basin visitor center, driving a 10-mile, unpaved auto tour road, canoeing, and hunting (goose, duck, coot, moorhen, snipe, and pheasant) on parts of the refuge during the designated seasons.

A 2-mile canoe trail (usually open from July 1 through September; motorized watercraft are not permitted) offers an outstanding chance to explore the marsh and see some of its wildlife. Access from the visitor center to the canoe-launching site is north 0.5 mile on Hill Road, east (right) 3.2 miles on East-West Road (to just beyond Lost River), south (right) and then east 1.4 miles on a gravel road (to a road junction at a pump station), and south (right) 0.4 mile (the launch site is on the right).

Walking opportunities include a 0.3-mile climb from the Klamath Basin NWR's headquarters/visitor center that leads to the top of Sheepy Ridge for an excellent view across Tule Lake refuge to the east; and a 0.5-mile loop trail through Discovery Marsh.

Insect repellent and sunscreen are advised, especially on canoeing excursions.

Species of wildlife that have been recorded on Tule Lake refuge are essentially the same as those on nearby Lower Klamath Refuge.

Lodgings and meals are available in such communities as Tulelake, California and Klamath Falls, Oregon.

Access to the Klamath Basin visitor center and Tule Lake Refuge from U.S. Route 97 just south of the California-Oregon state line is east on California State Route 161 (through Lower Klamath Refuge), and south on Hill Road. The west entrance of the auto tour road is 5 miles farther south on Hill Road and east (left) onto the refuge. Or from California State Route 139 at the community of Tulelake, it is west 6 miles on East-West Road and south (left) 0.5 mile on Hill Road.

Further information: Tule Lake National Wildlife Refuge, c/o Klamath Basin NWRs, 4009 Hill Road, Tulelake, CA 96143; telephone: (530) 667-2231.

Willow Creek-Lurline Wildlife Management Area (see in the Sacramento National Wildlife Refuge text)

Caribbean Islands:
Puerto Rico

Cabo Rojo, containing 1,836 acres, was established in 1974 to restore and protect native flora and fauna—notably the endangered yellow-shouldered blackbird (*Agelaius xanthomos*), a glossy black bird with yellow epaulets, which is endemic to the island of Puerto Rico. The refuge is located on the coastal plain near the southwestern tip of Puerto Rico in the Greater Antilles of the West Indies.

Other resident birds of the refuge include the smooth-billed ani, bananaquit, black-faced and yellow-faced grassquits, Caribbean elaenia (a flycatcher), Adelaide's warbler (closely related to the yellow-throated warbler), troupial (a large orange and black oriole with a prominent white wing patch), and the Puerto Rican tody. The latter, which is endemic to Puerto Rico, is a 4.5-inch-long, plump little forest bird, with bright green head and back; bright red throat; and flat beak, white breast, and yellow flanks.

The refuge's many neotropical migratory songbirds, which winter in Puerto Rico or pause here on their flights between South or Central America and North America, include such warblers as northern parula, Cape May, black-throated green, black-throated blue, yellow-throated, prairie, black and white, and American redstart.

For nearly 200 years, the lands within Cabo Rojo refuge were used for agriculture and cattle ranching. As explained by the U.S. Fish and Wildlife Service:

The gently rolling hills of the refuge lie within the sub-tropical dry forest belt. Because of decades of overgrazing, much of the native vegetation has been replaced by plants from other regions. These exotics are undesirable because they compete with the native vegetation, reducing diversity and therefore decreasing optimal food and nesting habitat for wildlife. Grassland management, through haying, will alter composition from exotic to native grasses and provide a better home for the native species. Native trees are being planted to return the land to its original mature hardwood forest.

In 1967, the property that is now the refuge was purchased by the Foreign Broadcast Information Service for construction of a "listening post" to monitor foreign communications. This facility became obsolete with the advent of satellites. Consequently, the property was transferred to the Fish and Wildlife Service.

In 1999, the refuge was expanded with the addition of 1,249 acres in the Cabo Rojo Salt Flats. This area's hypersaline salt ponds are the best habitat for shorebirds in the eastern Caribbean. Tens of thousands of them migrate through here each year.

The refuge and visitor center are open Mondays through Fridays. There is no entrance fee.

Visitor activities include birdwatching, photography, and hiking on a 2-mile interpretive trail and roughly 12 miles of other trails. Sunscreen is advised.

Lodgings and meals are available in Ponce, Mayaguez, and Boqueron.

Access from the junction of Routes 2 and 100 (between Mayaguez and Ponce) to the visitor center and refuge office is south on Route 100, east (left) 0.8 mile on Route 101, and south (right) about 3 miles on Route 301.

Further information: Cabo Rojo National Wildlife Refuge, c/o Caribbean Islands NWRs, P.O. Box 510, Boqueron, PR 00622; telephone: (787) 851-7258.

Culebra, comprising 1,568 acres, was established by President Theodore Roosevelt in 1909 to protect important seabird colonies on and around the island of Culebra, located about 20 miles east of Puerto Rico in the Greater Antilles of the West Indies. The refuge, which includes a number of units on Culebra and on more than 20 smaller islands, cays, and rocks, also offers protection for several species of sea turtles and various communities of native tropical vegetation.

Isla de Culebra's habitats include small areas of subtropical dry forest, brush, grasslands, and bordering mangroves and seagrass. The island's Monte Resaca supports the largest remaining mountainous forested area—an unusual "boulder forest" amid boulder-strewn terrain of canyons and ravines. Culebra's Punta Flamenco, a point which was part of a former U.S. Naval bombing range, supports the refuge's largest nesting colony of seabirds, notably 60,000 sooty terns, along with brown noddies; roseate and bridled terns; and brown, masked, and red-footed boobies. The exquisitely graceful red-billed and white-tailed tropicbirds, magnificent frigatebird, white-cheeked pintail, and American oystercatcher also inhabit the refuge. The endangered leatherback and hawksbill sea turtles haul themselves onto white coral-sand beaches to lay their eggs, and the endangered green sea turtle finds food and shelter in beds of seagrass. The waters around the islands contain beautiful coral reefs that are inhabited by a myriad of colorful tropical fishes.

The Fish and Wildlife Service says, "Culebra may be the most precious jewel in the treasure chest of Caribbean refuges. More than 50,000 seabirds of 13 species find their way to this dot in the ocean every year to breed and nurture their young. . . ."

Cayo Luis Pena and Isla Culebrita are the only parts of the refuge that are open to visitation. There is no entrance fee. All other refuge lands, including Punta Flamenco, are closed because of unexploded military ordnance and/or to avoid disturbing wildlife. The refuge office, which is located in Lower Camp, a short drive from Culebra's airport, is open on weekdays, except national holidays.

Visitor activities include birdwatching, photography, and hiking. Sunscreen is advised.

Access to Culebra Refuge is either by flights from Puerto Rico or by ferry service from Fajardo, at the eastern end of Puerto Rico.

Further information: Culebra National Wildlife Refuge, P.O. Box 190, Culebra, PR 00622; telephone: (787) 742-0115.

Desecheo, consisting of 360 acres, was established in 1912 to restore and protect historic seabird colonies and natural ecosystems on Isla Desecheo. The refuge is located 14 miles from the west coast of Puerto Rico in the Greater Antilles of the West Indies.

Much of Desecheo's rocky terrain supports a native dry forest. As described by the U.S. Fish and Wildlife Service:

Large gumbo limbo trees are common in interior valleys, while a variety of cactus species, including the endangered higo chumbo, form a part of the thorny scrub vegetation covering the steep coastal slopes. The forest habitat has been degraded by introduced species such as rats, cats, goats, monkeys and guinea grass. Management goals are to eliminate these introduced species and restore Desecheo to its original condition.

The island supports two endemic lizard species and was apparently once home to vast colonies of nesting seabirds including Brown and Red-footed Boobies, Magnificent Frigatebirds, Sooty Terns and Brown Noddies. The seabird colonies have virtually disappeared, which is attributed to impacts caused by military bombing, illegal hunting, fires and the introduction of nest-predating rhesus monkeys.

The refuge is closed to visitation because of "public safety reasons, due to the presence of unexploded military ordnance."

Further information: Desecheo National Wildlife Refuge, c/o Caribbean Islands NWRs, P.O. Box 510, Boqueron, PR 00622; telephone: (787) 851-7258.

Laguna Cartagena, encompassing 1,059 acres, was established in 1989 primarily to restore and maintain habitats of this important freshwater lagoon. The refuge is located near the southwestern coast of Puerto Rico in the Greater Antilles of the West Indies.

Only about 10 percent of Laguna Cartagena consists of open water. As a result of heavy runoff containing concentrations of fertilizers, pesticides, and sediments from many years of sugarcane cultivation and intensive livestock grazing, the rest of the lagoon is choked with cattails, water hyacinths, and other aquatic plants. This dense growth, promoted by a process called eutrophication (an increase in nutrients in a body of fresh water that causes an excessive growth of aquatic plants), has greatly reduced the lagoon's value as a key resting and feeding area for migrating waterfowl and other water birds.

In 1995, the U.S. Fish and Wildlife Service began a habitat restoration program to reverse the lagoon's seriously deteriorated condition. As of 2001, the refuge's challenge-cost-share accomplishments included the installation of a water control structure, removal of some of the aquatic vegetation, and partial completion of a water diversion canal.

In addition to the lagoon, the refuge also consists of upland pastureland, abandoned sugarcane fields, and 263 acres of the Sierra Bermeja foothills. The latter hills support native forest habitat that contains numerous species of endemic plants. The upland grazing and former sugarcane lands are being converted back to forest habitat for the benefit of native wildlife.

Among the refuge's more common birds are the magnificent frigatebird, great blue and little blue herons, great egret, glossy ibis, West Indian and fulvous whistling-ducks, white-cheeked pintail, purple gallinule, black-necked stilt, smooth-billed ani, white-crowned pigeon, common ground-dove, and the endangered yellow-shouldered blackbird.

The refuge is open daily during daylight hours. There is no entrance fee.

Visitor activities include birdwatching, photography, and hiking. Sunscreen is advised.

Lodgings and meals are available in Mayaguez and Ponce.

Access to Laguna Cartagena Refuge is at pedestrian gates in Maguayo, on Highway 305 and near Hacienda Desengano, on Highway 306, south of Highway 101.

Further information: Laguna Cartegena National Wildlife Refuge, c/o Caribbean Islands NWRs, P.O. Box 510, Boqueron, PR 00622; telephone: (787) 851-7258.

Navassa Island, containing approximately 300,000 acres, was established in 1999 to protect this 1,280-acre island and an extensive area of coral reefs located to the west of Puerto Rico in the Greater Antilles of the West Indies.

The refuge is not open to visitation, because of safety concerns. Access to the island is hazardous.

Further information: Navassa Island National Wildlife Refuge, c/o Caribbean Islands NWRs, P.O. Box 510, Boqueron, PR 00622; telephone: (787) 851-7258.

Vieques, comprising 3,100 acres, was established in 2001. The refuge manages and protects the western end of the island of Vieques, which is located about 7 miles off the eastern end of the island of Puerto Rico in the Greater Antilles of the West Indies.

Several ecologically distinct habitats including beaches, coastal lagoons, wetlands, and upland forested areas lie within the Vieques Refuge. It includes approximately 250 acres of mangrove wetland and some of the best subtropical dry forest in Puerto Rico. The marine environment that surrounds the refuge contains seagrass beds and coral reefs. The surrounding waters are inhabited by at least ten federally listed endangered animals and four plants, including the brown pelican, West Indian manatee, and four species of sea turtles.

The refuge is open daily during daylight hours. There is no entrance fee.

Further information: Vieques National Wildlife Refuge, c/o Caribbean Islands NWRs, P.O. Box 510, Boqueron, PR 00622; telephone: (787) 851-7258.

Caribbean:
U.S. Virgin Islands

Buck Island, comprising 45 acres, was established in 1969 to manage this island's "value for migratory birds" and protect its rocky shores and cactus-and-grassland (thorn scrub) habitat. The refuge is located about 1 mile south of St. Thomas Island, U.S. Virgin Islands, near the western end of the Lesser Antilles of the West Indies.

As the U.S. Fish and Wildlife Service sadly explains, "birds rarely use the refuge because of an overwhelming abundance of black rats." Only a few red-billed tropicbirds and a colony of laughing gulls succeed in nesting here. The refuge's management goal is to eliminate the nonnative rats so that the island's seabird nesting colonies can be restored. Among the birds commonly seen in the vicinity of Buck Island refuge are red-billed tropicbird (a small number nest on the island), brown booby, magnificent frigatebird, American oystercatcher, and sooty and bridled terns.

Buck Island Refuge supports five species of reptiles, including the locally endangered slippery back skink and what is believed to be an endemic subspecies of the Puerto Rican racer snake.

The historic, no-longer-operational Buck Island Lighthouse stands on the island.

The refuge is open daily during daylight hours. There is no entrance fee.

Visitor activities include birdwatching, photography, and hiking. In the ocean waters beyond the refuge boundary, there are outstanding coral reefs inhabited by numerous species of colorful tropical fishes. Commercial dive excursions are offered from St. Thomas. Sunscreen is advised on boat trips to Buck Island Refuge.

Lodgings and meals are available in the town of Charlotte Amalie and elsewhere on St. Thomas.

Access to Buck Island Refuge is by boat from Charlotte Amalie, St. Thomas. Commercial dive and charter excursions are available.

Further information: Buck Island National Wildlife Refuge, Federal Building, 3013 Estate Golden Rock, Suite 167, Christiansted, VI 00820-4355; telephone: (809) 773-4554.

Green Cay, consisting of 14 acres, was established in 1977 to protect the largest remaining population of the federally listed endangered St. Croix ground lizard (*Ameiva polops*) and important colonial nesting bird habitat. The refuge is located near the north shore of St. Croix Island, U.S. Virgin Islands in the Lesser Antilles of the West Indies.

The island contains areas of dry forest (mostly of pink cedar and orange manjack trees), cactus scrub (dominated by dildo cactus), and rocky beaches. Among the birds are brown pelican, little blue heron, white-cheeked pintail, white-crowned pigeon, zenaida dove, and common ground-dove that seasonally nests in the island's vegetation. American oystercatchers and the endangered piping plover have been observed nesting on beach habitat. Fishing just offshore from Green Cay (pronounced "kee") are brown boobies, magnificent frigatebirds, and various species of terns.

The St. Croix ground lizard, which formerly inhabited St. Croix and Buck islands, was extirpated on these islands when the Indian mongoose was introduced to control an introduced population of rats. The St. Croix ground lizard currently exists only on Green Cay and other mongoose-free islands just offshore from St. Croix.

The refuge is closed to visitation, to avoid disturbing ground lizard habitat and nesting birds; but many of the island's birds can be seen from offshore. Snorkel and dive excursions from Christiansted to nearby Buck Island Reef National Monument pass by Green Cay on their way to view the coral barrier reef and its myriad of colorful tropical fishes in the monument's emerald-green lagoon (an underwater snorkel trail is provided).

> "Further information: Green Cay National Wildlife Refuge, Federal Building, 3013 Estate Golden Rock, Suite 167, Christiansted, VI 00820-4355; telephone: (809) 773-4554.

Sandy Point, encompassing 423 acres, was established in 1984. The refuge is located at the southwestern tip of St. Croix Island, U.S. Virgin Islands in the Lesser Antilles of the West Indies.

Sandy Point protects critical habitat for the largest nesting population of the federally listed endangered leatherback sea turtle (*Dermochelys coriacea*) in the United States and the northern Caribbean. This largest species of turtle in the world measures to more than 6 feet in length and weighs more than 1,000 pounds. The threatened green sea turtle (*Chelonia mydas*), measuring up to 4 feet and weighing roughly 400 pounds, and the endangered hawksbill sea turtle (*Eretmochelys imbricata*), measuring an average of 2.5 feet long and weighing 95 to 165 pounds, also haul themselves onto the refuge's 3-mile-long beach to lay their eggs.

As the U.S. Fish and Wildlife Service describes the leatherback turtles:

These giants usually reside in northern waters where they almost exclusively feed on jellyfish. Every two to three years, the turtles return to tropical waters to nest on our sandy beach from March to July. The female digs a deep egg chamber in the sand and deposits 60 to 100 eggs in this nest. She then covers the eggs with sand, disguises the nest and returns to sea. She will return to the beach in ten day intervals to nest a total of three to eight times. After about two months, the eggs hatch, the tiny turtle hatchlings crawl to the surface of the sand and hurry to the sea.

During their trek across the beach, hatchlings are subject to predators, such as hungry crabs, nightherons, feral dogs or the mongoose. They can become trapped in deep tire tracks in the sand, entangled in trash on the beach, or disoriented by artificial lights. Fish and seabirds prey on hatchlings after they reach the sea. Approximately 1 in 1,000 hatchlings survive to adulthood!

Although adult sea turtles have few natural predators, human activities have caused major declines in populations. Sea turtles often mistake trash for food they normally eat. For example, plastic debris resembling jellyfish is ingested by leatherbacks, often killing them. Death can also result from sea turtles becoming entrapped in fishing nets and hook-and-line fishing gear. Sea turtles surfacing to breathe can be killed or injured by boats. Historically, sea turtles have been heavily exploited by island residents. A strong cultural tradition encouraging the taking of eggs and turtle meat still exists in some parts of the community. Poaching continues throughout St. Croix, although infrequently at Sandy Point, due to law-enforcement presence.

The refuge's other habitats include permanent and ephemeral salt ponds, with fringing mangroves; and coastal woodland. Dry forest habitat includes pink cedar, water mampoo, and pigeon berry. Sea grape trees, with leaves that suggest the shape of a ping-pong paddle, border the beaches. St. Croix's only stand of a federally endangered species, Vahl boxwood, grows on the refuge.

More than 100 species of birds have been recorded on Sandy Point Refuge. Among them are brown pelican; brown booby; little blue heron; white-cheeked pintail; black-necked stilt; laughing gull; royal and least terns; white-crowned pigeon; zenaida and scaley-naped doves; common ground-dove; smooth-billed ani; Antillean crested hummingbird; belted kingfisher; gray kingbird; Caribbean elaenia (flycatcher); pearly-eyed thrasher; black-whiskered vireo; warblers (northern parula, yellow, and American redstart); bananaquit; and black-faced grassquit.

As evidence of early human occupation of St. Croix, the refuge contains ancient conch middens—piles of discarded, bleached conch shells—dating back thousands of years. The Aklis Site, dating from A.D. 600, was occupied for more than two centuries and is on the National Register of Historic Places. In the 1960s, sand was mined from Sandy Point's beaches; and in the early 1980s, Sandy Point was rescued from plans to turn the ecologically fragile area into a commercial development.

Especially during the sea turtle nesting period, the refuge greatly benefits from assistance generously provided by volunteers, including community groups and local students. Earthwatch volunteers help gather research data on sea turtles and relocate their nests from areas of beach erosion.

The refuge is open from 10 a.m. to 4 p.m. on weekends, unless otherwise posted. There is no entrance fee. Visitor activities include birdwatching, photography, hiking, and swimming. Major stretches of the beach are seasonally closed to visitation to protect nesting activities of the sea turtles. Sunscreen is advised.

Lodgings and meals are available at a number of resorts and elsewhere on St. Croix.

Access to Sandy Point Refuge is west of Alexander Hamilton Airport on Route 66 (Melvin Evans Highway).

Further information: Sandy Point National Wildlife Refuge, Federal Building, 3013 Estate Golden Rock, Suite 167, Christiansted, VI 00820-4355; (809) 773-4554.

Colorado

Alamosa, containing 11,169 acres, was established in 1962 to enhance and protect important river-bottom wetland habitat for migratory water birds and other wildlife in the 7,500-foot-elevation, mountain-framed San Luis Valley of south-central Colorado.

From mid-February to late March, some of the stately greater sandhill cranes pause at Alamosa on their way north from wintering areas, such as the Bosque del Apache National Wildlife Refuge in southern New Mexico, to their breeding grounds, which are mainly in Montana, Wyoming, and Idaho. A few of these birds stop by here on their way south from early September into mid-November, depending on weather and habitat conditions. Their numbers peak around mid-October. Regarding the annual springtime Monte Vista crane festival, see the text on nearby Monte Vista National Wildlife Refuge, with which Alamosa is jointly managed.

As many as 15,000 ducks of numerous species occupy Alamosa during the peak of migrations, and many Canada geese, ducks, egrets, herons, and ibises nest on the refuge's wetlands. In early spring, Alamosa is a staging area for dozens of bald eagles that congregate here. More than 200 species of birds have been recorded on Alamosa and Monte Vista refuges.

The refuge's floodplain wetlands consist of river oxbows and sloughs, wet meadows, and cottonwood-and-willow riparian corridors, mostly to the east of and along the winding course of the upper Rio Grande. In contrast to the arid valley's extensive surrounding expanses of irrigated potato, barley, wheat, and alfalfa fields, these ecologically rich habitats are a mecca for thousands of migratory and nesting geese and ducks, as well as numerous wading birds and neotropical migratory songbirds.

The Sangre de Cristo Mountains form a spectacularly scenic backdrop for the refuge. Their peaks rise more than 6,000 feet above the valley floor to more than 14,000 feet in elevation. To the west are the rugged San Juan Mountains.

Establishment of Alamosa was made possible partly with revenues from the sale of Migratory Bird Hunting and Conservation Stamps (Duck Stamps). Ducks Unlimited, Inc., and the San Luis Valley Wetlands Focus Group have assisted with important habitat enhancement projects. Friends of San Luis Valley National Wildlife Refuge is another nonprofit support group that is assisting the refuge in many ways.

The refuge is open daily during daylight hours. There is no entrance fee. The headquarters (serving both Alamosa and Monte Vista refuges) is open on weekdays, except national holidays.

Visitor activities include birdwatching; photography; driving the 3-mile self-guiding auto tour route beginning at headquarters and providing views of wetland, wet meadow, and upland habitats; hiking or bicycling a 1-mile trail from the south end of the tour road; hiking, bicycling, horseback riding, or cross-country skiing the 2-mile Rio Grande River Walk from refuge headquarters; and hunting (waterfowl and small game) on part of the refuge during the designated seasons. Although camping is not permitted on the refuge, campground facilities are available in the vicinity of Alamosa and Monte Vista, and in Rio Grande National Forest.

Visitors are urged to be prepared for a variety of weather conditions, including springtime winds. Insect repellent is advised during the warmer months.

Fauna and flora of Alamosa Refuge are essentially the same as those recorded on nearby Monte Vista Refuge.

Lodgings and meals are available in such communities as Alamosa and Monte Vista.

Access to the refuge is east 4 miles on U.S. Route 160 from the town of Alamosa, and right (south) onto El Rancho Lane for two miles.

Further information: Alamosa National Wildlife Refuge, 9383 El Rancho Lane, Alamosa, CO 81101; telephone: (719) 589-4021.

Arapaho, containing 24,804 acres, was established in 1967 to create, enhance, and protect an ecologically significant area of wetlands in north-central Colorado. The wetlands are sustained by waters diverted from the north-flowing Illinois River, a tributary of the North Platte that flows through this refuge. It is located at 8,200 feet above sea level in the mountain-framed glacial basin known as North Park. Spectacular ranges of the Rocky Mountains form an encircling backdrop, with the Medicine Bows to the east; the Rabbit Ears to the south; and the Park Range to the west.

This refuge's numerous shallow ponds and irrigated marshy meadows are managed by regulating their water levels to provide breeding and feeding habitat for migratory waterfowl, shorebirds, and wading birds. Late May is the peak of spring waterfowl migration, when at least 5,000 ducks arrive—either to merely pause in their northward flight or remain for nesting and rearing their young. Late September to early October is the peak of autumn migration, when as many as 8,000 waterfowl are concentrated here. Prominent among the water birds attracted to Arapaho are Canada goose, gadwall, lesser scaup, wigeon, mallard, shoveler, cinnamon teal, avocet, and Wilson's phalarope. Over 200 bird species have been seen here.

The sage-grouse is a special attraction in Arapaho's sagebrush habitat, with large flocks spending the winter here. In the spring, visitors can see and hear males inflating their bright orange throat sacs as they perform their remarkable courtship dances. Pronghorns also inhabit the sagebrush-covered flats and knolls.

Numerous neotropical migratory songbirds and such mammals as moose and mule deer seek out Arapaho's sheltered riparian areas. Elk are here, too, some residing year-round and others moving down from the mountains to winter on the refuge.

Establishment of this refuge was made possible partly with revenue from the sale of Migratory Bird Hunting and Conservation Stamps (Duck Stamps).

The refuge is open daily during daylight hours. There is no entrance fee. The refuge headquarters/visitor center is open on weekdays, except national holidays.

Visitor activities include birdwatching, photography, driving a 6-mile tour route (interpretive brochure is available), hiking along the Illinois River on a 0.5-mile (wheelchair-accessible) interpretive trail and elsewhere on the refuge, prearranged guided group tours, fishing (only on the Illinois River), and hunting (waterfowl, snipe, dove, sage-grouse, rabbit, and pronghorn) on parts of the refuge during the designated seasons. Although camping is not permitted on the refuge, campground facilities are available at Lake John, Delaney Butte Lakes, and Seymour Reservoir state wildlife areas; and in the Routt National Forest.

Visitors are advised to wear warm clothing, as it can be cold most of the year.

Lodgings and meals are available in Walden.

Access to the refuge headquarters is south 8 miles from Walden on State Route 125.

Further information: Arapaho National Wildlife Refuge, P.O. Box 457, Walden, CO 80480; telephone: (970) 723-8202.

Baca, authorized to ultimately contain 93,500 acres, is located in the eastern part of the San Luis Valley, near the base of the towering Sangre de Cristo Mountains in southern Colorado. At this writing, it is anticipated that the refuge will be officially established in the autumn of 2002. Although this vast, high rift valley annually receives an average of only 7 inches of precipitation, melting snows from surrounding mountains sustain a thriving agricultural economy and 230,000 acres of vital wetland habitat that supports large populations of breeding and migrating water birds. It is here in this rural western community that local citizens broke the stereotype and championed a federal land acquisition project.

In November 2000, Congress passed and President Bill Clinton signed into law the Great Sand Dunes National Park and Preserve Act of 2000. This legislation authorized the expansion and redesignation of Great Sand Dunes National Monument (established in 1932) as a national park and preserve, an addition to the Rio Grande National Forest, and the establishment of the new Baca National Wildlife Refuge.

The enabling legislation's key provision authorizes the Department of the Interior and the Department of Agriculture to purchase the Baca Ranch, which has been in private ownership since 1860. When the Mexican–American War ended in 1848, the United States government agreed to honor all Spanish land grants that were lost during the conflict. Among those grants were the 500,000-acre Vegas Grandes holdings in northern New Mexico. In 1860, the heirs of Luis Maria de Baca were permitted to select five 100,000-acre grants of land. One of these was located on the eastern side of the San Luis Valley and became known as the Luis Baca No. 4. The ranch was owned by the Baca family for only two years before being sold to William Gilpin, the first territorial governor of the Colorado territory.

Over the years, this ranch expanded its holdings but remained a site of regularly occurring speculation, starting with Gilpin and now ending after 15 years of water development proposals. Had those water developments been successful, they would have exported between 150,000 and 200,000 acre-feet of water from the valley—most likely to serve the rapidly growing Front Range cities along the eastern base of the Colorado Rockies. Although the valley is renowned for its water resources, few residents felt that the removal of such a large quantity of water from the San Luis Valley would be possible without seriously jeopardizing its agricultural economy and quality of life. Additionally, the exportation of this volume of water risked seriously damaging the ecological integrity and breeding bird habitat. Consequently, many agencies and organizations have been engaged in an almost continuous, expensive, and politically charged 15-year struggle with the water speculators, who were intent upon obtaining a behemoth water right on the Baca ranch.

During the summer of 1999, on the heels of a failed statewide ballot initiative that was meant to weaken the position of San Luis Valley's water defenders, the local community enlisted the assistance of U.S. Senators Wayne Allard and Ben Nighthorse Campbell and U.S. Representative Scott McIniss. This congressional delegation saw the environmental and economic wisdom of acquiring the Baca ranch and a small number of associated holdings in order to expand and redesignate the national monument as a national park and preserve, to acquire the mountainous holdings in the adjacent Rio Grande National Forest, and to establish the westernmost tract as the Baca National Wildlife Refuge. The Colorado governor's office and the Colorado Department of Natural Resources were also enthusiastic and supportive.

This is far from just another federal government effort toward land acquisition. The importance of the nonprofit organization The Nature Conservancy in this situation cannot be overstated. For years, TNC has been negotiating with the owners of the Baca Ranch, hoping for an opportunity to protect the property, not only for the good of San Luis Valley, but also to protect the adjoining 104,000-acre TNC-owned Medano/Zapata Ranch. The Conservancy obtained numerous loans and enlisted the financial help of the Colorado State Land Board and many others to make this $31.3 million acquisition happen expeditiously while giving the federal government the time needed to appropriate the funds to buy out TNC's interest in the property.

When completed, Baca National Wildlife Refuge will contain approximately 20,000 acres of wetland habitat, ranging from periodically flooded playas to more regularly but shallowly flooded wetlands dominated by short, emergent vegetation at the lower ends of several drainages. Currently, wetlands of this latter type are used for livestock forage and are enhanced by irrigation practices. The wetlands are of great importance to migrating birds such as the sandhill crane, white-faced ibis, and some species of ducks and shorebirds. The Colorado National Heritage Program has identified many globally significant plant and animal communities within the boundaries of the refuge and the park/preserve. One of the most exciting elements of this project is the opportunity for the U.S. Fish and Wildlife Service, National Park Service, U.S. Forest Service, and The Nature Conservancy to manage roughly 350,000 acres of a unique landscape in a coordinated manner.

The Baca and adjoining ranches presently host a year-round population of about 4,500 Rocky Mountain elk. This number has been growing for a variety of reasons, including a lack of hunting pressure and other predation, little disturbance, and ample forage. Although these animals use almost all habitats on the ranch, they are most frequently seen along some of the riparian areas. This elk population is well above the objectives set by the Colorado Division of Wildlife and will continue to be a management issue once the refuge is established.

The largest challenge facing habitat management on the Baca Refuge will be how best to manage the expansive wetlands currently used to produce hay. The initial reaction of many persons is to immediately remove livestock and the hay machine and to produce dense stands of nesting vegetation as seen on many other San Luis Valley wetlands that are managed for water birds. This may be appropriate in some places, but wholesale rest of these wetlands could easily result in a proliferation of noxious weeds, to support a goal that may not be well thought out. Some reduction and modification of haying and grazing practices may be appropriate, but only after the refuge staff has determined specific objectives of managing the habitat of this new refuge.

Opportunities for visitor access and activities, including interpretive and environmental education programs, wildlife observation, photography, hiking, and hunting, will be evaluated as part of the refuge's management planning process. The possibilities are exciting and magnified when the refuge system considers joining with the efforts of the National Park Service, U.S. Forest Service, and The Nature Conservancy. There will be opportunities for visitor access and a tremendous story to share regarding the history of this land and the interdependence of people, the land, water, and wildlife.

As of today, The Nature Conservancy, the Colorado State Land Board, the federal government, and owners of the ranch have agreed on the sale of the Baca Ranch. The transaction's closing is expected to take place following the resolution of several claims outstanding against the current owner. It will then be up to Congress to make this happen by appropriating the additional funds needed to purchase the interest held by The Nature Conservancy and the Colorado State Land Board. Supporters of those protecting "the Last Great Places" have many to thank in Colorado.

Further information: Baca National Wildlife Refuge, 9383 El Rancho Lane, Alamosa, CO 81101; telephone: (719) 589-4021.

(NOTE: Special appreciation is given to Michael Blenden, Refuge Manager of Alamosa/ Monte Vista/Baca NWR Complex, for providing this description.)

Browns Park, comprising 13,455 acres, was established in 1965. This refuge enhances and protects wet meadowland and other riparian habitat for migrating and nesting waterfowl and wintering elk and deer along the Green River in northwestern Colorado. Prior to the construction of Flaming Gorge Dam in the 1960s, these riparian wetlands were maintained by the river's annual flooding, but the dam contained the floodwaters. To make up for this loss, the U.S. Fish and Wildlife Service diverts water from the river to about 1,300 acres of the refuge's marshes and meadows.

Prominent species of breeding waterfowl are Canada geese, mallards, redheads, cinnamon teals, and ruddy ducks. Golden eagles are year-round residents, and bald eagles winter along the river. Large mammals include elk, moose, mule deer, and pronghorns.

Ducks Unlimited, Inc. has assisted with important habitat enhancement projects.

The refuge is open daily. There is no entrance fee. The refuge marshes are closed to visitors from March 1 through July.

Visitor activities include wildlife observation, photography, driving the 11-mile auto tour route, hiking, canoeing on the Green River (a boat ramp is available); camping at a primitive campground, fishing, and hunting (waterfowl, elk, and deer) on part of the refuge during the designated seasons. Over 200 birds species have been seen here.

Insect repellent is advised during the warmer months.

Lodgings and meals are available in Craig, Colorado, Vernal, Utah, and Rock Springs, Wyoming. Fuel and limited groceries are available at Browns Park Store, located about 10 miles from the refuge.

Access to the refuge headquarters is northwest 60 miles on paved State Route 318 from U.S. Route 40 at Maybell; or from U.S. Route 191 in Utah (near the Utah-Wyoming state line, north of Dutch John), southeast about 30 miles on an unpaved road, connecting with paved Route 318.

Further information: Browns Park National Wildlife Refuge, 1318 Highway 318, Maybell, CO 81640; telephone (970) 365-3613.

Monte Vista, encompassing 14,800 acres, was established in 1953 to enhance and protect wetland habitat for migratory ducks and other water birds, at an elevation of 7,500 feet in the mountain-framed San Luis Valley of south-central Colorado.

The refuge consists of wetlands and numerous ponds that are maintained with a system of wells, canals, ditches, drains, and other water control structures for the benefit of many species of waterfowl and other wildlife. In addition, the U.S. Fish and Wildlife Service raises some grain crops on fields that are feeding areas for sandhill cranes, ducks, and other wildlife.

The Sangre de Cristo Mountains form a spectacular scenic backdrop to the refuge. Their jagged peaks rise more than 6,000 feet above the valley floor to more than 14,000 feet in elevation. To the west are the rugged San Juan Mountains.

Monte Vista Refuge, which is jointly managed with nearby Alamosa National Wildlife Refuge, is especially famous for its thousands of migratory sandhill cranes. From mid-February through late March, roughly 24,000 to 32,000 of these stately, red-crowned, gray birds pause here in the San Luis Valley on their northward migration from wintering areas, such as the Bosque del Apache National Wildlife Refuge in southern New Mexico, to breeding areas mainly in Montana, Wyoming, and Idaho. Of this awesome number, 18,000 to 22,000 comprise about 95 percent of the total population of the Rocky Mountain greater sandhill subspecies, and there are from 3,000 to 5,000 each of the lesser and Canadian subspecies. Roughly 8,000 to 13,000 migrating cranes rest and feed on Monte Vista Refuge. During their southward autumn migration, somewhat smaller concentrations of these birds stop by from September into mid-November, depending on weather and habitat conditions. Their numbers generally peak around mid-October.

Since the early 1980s, the spring return of these birds has been celebrated by Monte Vista's Annual Crane Festival. This popular event is sponsored by the nonprofit Monte Vista Crane Committee and includes guided tours of Monte Vista Refuge, educational workshops, demonstrations, and lectures on a variety of environmental topics. Information and reservations: (719) 852-3552.

Monte Vista Refuge is also a mecca for migratory waterfowl. As senior writer Matt Young explained in his article "High Country Ducks," in the March–April 2001 issue of *Ducks Unlimited*:

Believe it or not, some of the continent's most productive breeding habitat for ducks lies in a mountain valley in the heart of the southern Rockies. This remarkable place is Colorado's San Luis Valley, a broad expanse of high desert surrounded by majestic 14,000-foot mountains. Managed wetlands in the valley support an average of 200 to 300 duck nests per square mile, with some areas boasting as many as 1,000 nests per square mile.

But DU's Matt Young also points out a potential threat:

As in many parts of the West, groundwater is the lifeblood of wetlands in the San Luis Valley. Beneath the valley floor lie two massive aquifers whose artesian springs, along with snowmelt from the surrounding mountains, historically supported a vast network of playa wetlands. However, people have increasingly tapped the valley's groundwater for a variety of purposes, depleting the underlying aquifer and, in effect, draining many crucial wetland systems from below. Stream runoff also has been largely diverted into ditches for human use, robbing many more wetlands of their supply.

Fortunately, state and federal agencies have established several large managed wetland complexes in the San Luis Valley that provide excellent habitat for breeding, migrating, and wintering waterbirds and a variety of other wildlife. The crown jewel of the valley's wildlife areas is . . . Monte Vista National Wildlife Refuge. Located nearby are several other highly productive managed wildlife areas, including the Alamosa National Wildlife Refuge, Blanca Waterfowl Management Area, and the Rio Grande State Wildlife Areas.

Establishment of this refuge was made possible partly with revenues from the sale of Migratory Bird Hunting and Conservation Stamps (Duck Stamps). Ducks Unlimited, Inc. (DU) and the San Luis Valley Wetlands Focus Group have assisted with extensive habitat enhancement projects. The latter group consists of a large partnership of federal and state governmental and nongovernmental agencies, organizations, and private citizens that have been working together for many years to accomplish numerous wetland restoration projects on the refuge complex and elsewhere within the San Luis Valley. A recent example of DU's assistance is the development of dikes and ditches and the installation of water control structures in the refuge's Unit 7. These improvements have created an extensive wetland impoundment, within which water levels are manipulated for the maximum benefit of waterfowl and other wildlife.

Friends of San Luis Valley National Wildlife Refuges is a local nonprofit support group that is also assisting the refuge in many ways.

The refuge is open daily during daylight hours. There is no entrance fee. A visitor contact station is open daily in March and April, and only periodically the rest of the year.

Visitor activities include birdwatching, photography, driving the 3-mile tour route (walking and bicycling on this road are not permitted) and driving several county roads, and waterfowl and small-game hunting on part of the refuge during the designated seasons. Although camping is not permitted on the refuge, campground facilities are available in the vicinity of Monte Vista and Alamosa, and in Rio Grande National Forest.

Visitors are urged to be prepared for a variety of weather conditions, including springtime winds. Insect repellent is advised during the warmer months.

Lodgings and meals are available in the towns of Monte Vista and Alamosa.

Access to this refuge is 6 miles south on State Route 15 from the town of Monte Vista.

Further information: Monte Vista National Wildlife Refuge, 9383 El Rancho Lane, Alamosa, CO 81101; telephone: (719) 589-4021.

Rocky Flats is a recent addition to the National Wildlife Refuge System, originating in December 2001 with passage of the Rocky Mountain National Wildlife Refuge Act. This former nuclear weapons production facility is a 6,500-acre piece of the transition zone between the western Great Plains and the Rocky Mountains, situated 16 miles northwest of Denver.

"The Flats" started out in 1951 as an Atomic Energy Commission site to produce plutonium "pits" or triggers for nuclear weapons and continued as a U.S. Department of Energy (DOE) nuclear weapons facility from 1977 to 1989. The abrupt end to the Cold War, with the collapse of communism in Eastern Europe in 1989, changed the mission of this DOE site from weapons production to environmental restoration. This change was accelerated when the "Flats" was declared a Superfund site for hazardous materials cleanup in 1989, with regulatory oversight from the U.S. Environmental Protection Agency and the Colorado Department of Public Health and Environment. Cleanup is currently scheduled for completion by 2006.

"Flats" is a misnomer for parts of this site, where shallow canyons with permanent or intermittent streams dissect prairie uplands, all located at the immediate boundary between mountains to the west and plains to the east. These canyons and the associated streamside (riparian) habitats, including wetlands, account for much of the reason why more than 225 species of wildlife have been documented at the site. By one estimate, more than 75 percent of Colorado's wildlife species reside on or migrate through Rocky Flats each year. This area also provides riparian habitat for a population of the federally listed threatened Prebles meadow jumping mouse. Much of the site (more than 6,100 acres) is a relatively undisturbed buffer zone surrounding a central core of industrial facilities. For Rocky Mountain elk, mule deer, black bear, mountain lion, coyote, bald eagle, and many other species, the Flats has been a refuge for decades; it's now simply official.

The transition of this site to a national wildlife refuge is just beginning and will commence with development of a Comprehensive Conservation Plan by the U.S. Fish and Wildlife Service, in close coordination with DOE and numerous local governments and stakeholders. Public access is currently restricted but will be a significant part of the future refuge.

Rocky Flats Refuge is bounded on the east by Indiana Street, on the north by State Route 128, on the west by State Route 93, and on the south by 100th Avenue.

> Further information: Rocky Flats National Wildlife Refuge, c/o Rocky Mountain Arsenal NWR, Building 111, Commerce City, CO 80022; telephone: (303) 289-0232.

Rocky Mountain Arsenal, comprising more than 16,000 acres, was established in 1992 to restore, protect, and interpret a remnant expanse of western Great Plains shortgrass prairie, scattered riparian woodland, marsh, intermittent streams and ditches, and more than a half dozen human-made lakes and ponds. It is located just 10 miles northeast of downtown Denver in Commerce City, Colorado. This is a unique paradox of a place: The area's ecologically important habitats surround a central area of former weapons and chemicals production and disposal facilities. Over 225 bird species have been seen here.

Through a gradual transformation, the arsenal is becoming one of the largest urban wildlife sanctuaries and environmental education centers in the country. The great diversity of wildlife includes many species of migrating waterfowl; wintering bald eagles and other raptors, such as burrowing owls and ferruginous and Swainson's hawks; numerous neotropical migratory songbirds; prairie dogs; and herds of both white-tailed deer and mule deer.

By the late 1930s, most of the land that is now the arsenal had been cleared of its original shortgrass prairie and was devoted to farming. The U.S. Army purchased the land in 1942 to produce weapons, such as mustard gas and napalm, during World War II, and it subsequently manufactured incendiary weapons, nerve gas, and other chemical warfare munitions at the Rocky Mountain Arsenal until the 1960s. The arsenal then became a major center for destroying these lethal materials. Also after World War II, some of the arsenal's industrial facilities were leased to Shell Oil Company for the commercial manufacture of agricultural pesticides and herbicides.

In 1953, in response to the Cold War, the arsenal was reactivated for the production of additional military weapons, primarily artillery shells and bombs containing nerve agent. In 1969, rocket fuel was produced here for the lunar landing.

Beginning in 1979, a number of interim cleanup actions on the property were undertaken. Beginning in 1993 to 1994, the incineration of certain liquid wastes and a groundwater intercept-and-treatment program were undertaken. As of the beginning of the twenty-first century, this latter process continues to treat millions of gallons of groundwater annually, resulting in steadily decreasing levels of contamination.

In 1982, all military and commercial chemical production activities were terminated, and in 1983, the U.S. Environmental Protection Agency declared the Rocky Mountain Arsenal a Superfund cleanup site.

Both the production and subsequent disposal of these highly toxic military and commercial substances were limited to the arsenal's 3,840-acre core. Surrounding the central area was a 13,440-acre buffer zone, established for security and safety reasons. This relatively undisturbed open space was essentially a de facto wildlife refuge. The discovery in 1986 of a communal roost of wintering bald eagles, a species that symbolizes this nation's pride, inspired the goal of establishing a national wildlife refuge here. Intense local public support spurred national commitment to both a refuge and appropriately high standards for a hazardous-waste cleanup program.

Although the arsenal's multifaceted environmental restoration program was initially delayed by intense distrust and contentious litigation, the enormous, $2-billion challenge of tearing down munitions and pesticide factories and cleaning up the contaminated central core was finally begun in 1996. This is a cooperative Superfund remediation program that is funded by the Department of Defense and Shell Oil Company, with regulatory participation by the U.S. Environmental Protection Agency, the Colorado Department of Public Health and Environment, and the Tri-County Health Department. The incredibly complex job of collecting contaminated materials into a state-of-the-art hazardous-waste landfill is expected to be completed by 2011. Once the Superfund cleanup program is completed, the area will officially become an integral unit of the National Wildlife Refuge System, as the Rocky Mountain Arsenal National Wildlife Refuge.

Beginning in 1987, the U.S. Fish and Wildlife Service started managing the arsenal's wildlife, and since 1992, when Congress passed the Rocky Mountain Arsenal National Wildlife Refuge Act, the Service has been engaged in a number of habitat restoration projects. These include revegetating parts of the area with native grasses and other plants and enhancing and maintaining riparian corridors, wetlands, and lakes for the benefit of wildlife. Other objectives include managing the deer population so that its genetic diversity is maintained and so that the herds do not exceed the area's carrying capacity; reintroducing such native prairie fauna as the American bison (buffalo), pronghorns, sharp-tailed grouse, and greater prairie chickens; and providing for visitor access, enjoyment, and education.

The program for visitors, which will require a few years to fully implement, is intended to include a visitor center with interpretive exhibits, an auditorium for interpretive programs, and a bookstore; an environmental education center and laboratory; a picnic area; a trail network winding through the southern part of the area to offer views of a variety of marsh, wooded riparian, and lake habitats and their wildlife; and a tram route through the northern part of the arsenal for viewing prairie habitat and its wildlife. The Rocky Mountain Arsenal Wildlife Society is a nonprofit support group that is assisting the refuge in a variety of ways.

The refuge is currently closed to visitors but is expected to open in the near future. Potential visitors should call the number below for details on access and available programs.

When the Rocky Mountain Arsenal's cleanup is completed, the refuge will be open daily. Visitor activities are expected to include wildlife observation; photography; tours by tram (fee) and nature walks led by staff and trained volunteers who will interpret the arsenal's habitats, wildlife, history, and environmental cleanup program (reservations required); school and other youth group environmental education programs (reservations required); hiking; bicycling; fishing (catch-and-release, in spring and summer); and a wide variety of programs (a calendar of events will be available). November to March are the best months to see bald eagles. Although their numbers fluctuate over the winter, about 20 to 50 of these birds spend part of the winter preying on prairie dogs and roosting at night in large cottonwoods that border the lakes. Visitors are cautioned to be alert for rattlesnakes during the warmer months.

Lodgings and meals are available throughout the Denver metropolitan area.

Access to the Rocky Mountain Arsenal National Wildlife Refuge will be north on Quebec Street from either I-70 or I-270, right at Seventy-Second Avenue, and east into the main entrance. Plans call for eventually shifting the entrance to the southwest corner of the property, to be accessed from Sixty-Fourth Avenue and Quebec Street.

Further information: Rocky Mountain Arsenal National Wildlife Refuge, Building 111, Commerce City, CO 80022; telephone: (303) 289-0232.

Two Ponds, containing 72 acres, was established in 1992 to restore, enhance, and protect an area of ecologically valuable upland prairie and wetland habitats, including three human-made ponds, within the Denver, Colorado suburban community of Arvada. The refuge also provides a hands-on environmental education opportunity for area schoolchildren and other groups. Educational programs emphasize "the inherent values of wetlands and wildlife in an urban environment." Although a relatively small area, Two Ponds refuge supports a rich diversity of wildlife including more than 100 species of nesting, wintering, and neotropical and other migratory birds that have been recorded here.

The U.S. Fish and Wildlife Service's habitat management programs include restoring the upland areas back to native prairie. Currently, these areas are dominated by non-native brome grass. When restored, these uplands will contain such native grasses as western wheatgrass, green needlegrass, needle-and-thread, blue grama, and big bluestem; such native forbs and wildflowers as prairie cone flower, purple prairie clover, Lewis blue flax, Rocky Mountain beeplant, dotted gayfeather, evening primroses, and scarlet globemallow; and such native shrubs as winterfat, fourwing saltbush, rabbitbrush, and fringed sagebrush. The refuge will also be managed to enhance and maintain the prairie cottonwoods, willows, and other trees and shrubs along the irrigation canals; cattails, rushes, bulrushes, and other wetland vegetation; and the 1.5 acres of the three ponds.

This refuge came from being a dream to a reality, principally because of the committed driving force of the Two Ponds Preservation Foundation. This small, nonprofit citizens' advocacy group was founded in 1990 in direct response to a proposed residential development on 13 acres of this land.

As the *Arvada Sentinel* reported on June 4, 1992: "Two Ponds was the scene of a bitter two-year battle between local environmentalists who wanted to preserve the site and a developer who wanted to turn it into a posh housing development. Members of the Colorado congressional delegation were drawn into the fray, and they pushed the legislation needed for the Fish and Wildlife Service to buy the land."

The refuge is open daily during daylight hours. There is no entrance fee.

Visitor activities include birdwatching, wildlife photography, hiking on established trails (wheelchair-accessible, where feasible), prearranged guided tours, and interpretive and educational programs. Flora and fauna are much the same as on the Rocky Mountain Arsenal Refuge.

Lodgings and meals are available in Arvada and elsewhere in the Denver area.

Two Ponds Refuge is bounded on the north by West Eightieth Avenue and on the west by Kipling Street in Arvada.

Further information: Two Ponds National Wildlife Refuge, c/o Rocky Mountain Arsenal National Wildlife Refuge, Building 111, Commerce City, CO 80022; telephone: (303) 289-0232.

Connecticut

Stewart B. McKinney consists of 825 acres in eight units scattered along 60 miles of the Long Island Sound coastline of southern Connecticut. The refuge was established with the Salt Meadow National Wildlife Refuge in 1971 and has developed as the Connecticut Coastal NWR. In 1987, it was renamed for the late Congressman Stewart B. McKinney, in honor of his efforts that succeeded in winning approval for the refuge's first five units. Four of the units are described below.

The 9-acre MILFORD POINT UNIT, which was one of the initial parts of the refuge, encompasses part of a narrow barrier peninsula at the mouth of the Housatonic River. The point of land contains a sandy barrier beach, where piping plovers and least terns nest during the spring and summer. Low sand dunes rise just inland from the beach, and salt marsh and mudflats are sheltered behind the peninsula. Part of the unit also contains an area of dredged sediments from the adjacent lower Housatonic River.

Although this unit is closed to visitation, the Connecticut Audubon Coastal Center, which is located almost adjacent to the refuge unit, offers interpretive exhibits, programs, walks, and wildlife viewing opportunities from an observation tower. The center is open daily, except on Mondays and national holidays. Further information: (203) 878-7440.

The 247-acre SALT MEADOW UNIT was donated to the U.S. Fish and Wildlife Service in 1971 and was initially managed as part of the Ninigret National Wildlife Refuge in Rhode Island. This property was formerly owned by Esther Lape, who was a medical advisor to President Franklin D. Roosevelt and a good friend of the president's wife, Eleanor. The fieldstone house that dates from 1929 has been converted to the Stewart B. McKinney refuge headquarters. The unit's habitats include mixed hardwood forest and an area of tidally influenced salt marsh. Ducks Unlimited, Inc. has helped enhance about 20 acres of this unit's wetland habitat.

This unit is open to visitation daily during daylight hours. There is no entrance fee. The refuge headquarters is open on weekdays, except national holidays. Hiking opportunities on the Salt Meadow Unit include 2.5 miles of trails.

The 450-acre GREAT MEADOWS UNIT protects an area of salt marsh near the Housatonic River. This unit has not been opened to visitation, except by prearrangement for school and other groups. However, a 2,000-foot-long (wheelchair-accessible) access trail is being constructed in partnership with local nonprofit organizations and volunteers.

The 67-acre SHEFFIELD ISLAND UNIT provides a 2,000-foot-long (wheelchair accessible) nature trail that was recently created with the help of volunteers and local nonprofit organizations.

Refuge land acquisition was made possible partly with revenues from the sale of Migratory Bird Hunting and Conservation Stamps (Duck Stamps).

Visitor activities include wildlife observation, photography, viewing the Milford Point Unit from an observation platform, and walking designated trails. Although camping is not permitted on the refuge, campground facilities are available at Hammonasset Beach State Park, located near the Salt Meadow Unit. Over 310 bird species have been seen on the refuge.

Visitors are cautioned to be alert for ticks, which may carry Lyme disease.

Lodgings and meals are available in such communities as Milford, Stratford, and Bridgeport (near the Milford Point Unit); and Clinton, Westbrook, and Old Saybrook (near the Salt Meadow Unit).

Access to the Milford Point Unit from Exit 34 on I-95 is right 0.5 mile, left 0.8 mile on Naugatuck Road, right 0.5 mile on Milford Point Road, and right 0.3 mile on Sea View Avenue, then go right at a fork that ends at the Hubbell Wildlife Sanctuary and the Connecticut Audubon Coastal Center.

Access to the Salt Meadow Unit from Exit 64 on I-95 is south to a stop at a blinking red light, and east (left) 1.1 mile on Old Clinton Road (the refuge's parking area is on the right).

Further information: Stewart B. McKinney National Wildlife Refuge, P.O. Box 1030, Westbrook, CT 06460; telephone: (860) 399-2513.

Delaware

Bombay Hook, comprising 15,978 acres, was established in 1937 to manage and protect a significant area of coastal wetlands for spectacular concentrations of migrating, wintering, and nesting waterfowl and shorebirds as well as other wildlife. The refuge is located along the bay shore in northeastern Delaware.

Approximately three-quarters of Bombay Hook Refuge contains extensive, tidally influenced salt marsh. More than 1,000 acres consist of impounded freshwater pools, as well as brushy and wooded swamp habitat; and more than 1,000 acres include mixed pine and deciduous woodland, grassland, and agricultural fields. The latter are managed under cooperative agreements with local farmers, who plant such crops as winter wheat, buckwheat, and millet for the benefit of waterfowl and other wildlife.

Regarding the impounded pools, water levels are seasonally raised and lowered with a system of dikes and water control structures. This manipulation promotes the growth of emergent and underwater plants for waterfowl. While pools are drawn down, their mudflats attract great numbers of shorebirds and wading birds. When water levels are raised, the impoundments provide habitat for large concentrations of waterfowl that either winter on the refuge or pause here on their flights farther south.

October and November are usually the best months for observing impressive concentrations of migrating waterfowl. More than 150,000 ducks and geese are commonly attracted to Bombay Hook during the autumn. The second annual peak of waterfowl generally comes in March. Although early migrating shorebirds from South America normally arrive in April, the peak numbers of these birds are present in May. Large influxes of neotropical migratory songbirds, including numerous species of warblers, arrive in late April and early May. The greatest numbers of herons, egrets, and glossy ibis are on the refuge during the summer.

The refuge's salt marsh habitat, with its mosaic of intersecting tidal streams and rivers, not only provides habitat for many species of birds and mammals, but also serves as an ecologically rich nursery and spawning area for finfish and shellfish and numerous other marine organisms.

As one of *Ducks Unlimited*'s senior writers, Matt Young, wrote in the September–October 2001 issue of the magazine, "Acre for acre, coastal wetlands are among the most productive ecosystems on the planet. Their bountiful waters, rich in plant and animal life, support a remarkable diversity of waterfowl. . . . Sadly, thousands of acres of coastal wetlands continue to be lost each year. Protection is clearly the best line of defense against these losses, because once these fragile habitats disappear, they are gone forever."

The U.S. Fish and Wildlife Service explains how Bombay Hook got its name:

Known to the Native Americans as Canaresse, meaning "shaggy bushes" or thicket, Bombay Hook evolved from the Dutch name "Bompies Hoeck" meaning "little-tree point." Dutch settlers cut salt hay from the marsh, trapped muskrats, and hunted waterfowl. The tidal streams that interlace the marsh were plied for fish, crabs, and oysters.

An architectural highlight of Bombay Hook Refuge is the 2-story, Queen Anne-style Allee House that dates from around 1753 and is one of the best preserved examples of an early red-brick farmhouse in the state of Delaware. The structure contains exceptional exterior brickwork and beautiful interior wood paneling, cabinetry, and other details. In 1971, after careful restoration and furnishing, the house was placed on the National Register of Historic Places. Tours of the house are provided on weekend afternoons during the spring and autumn.

Establishment of Bombay Hook Refuge was made possible partly with revenues from the sale of Migratory Bird Hunting and Conservation Stamps (Duck Stamps). Ducks Unlimited,

Inc. has helped enhance approximately 800 acres of the refuge's wetland habitat. The Friends of Bombay Hook is a local nonprofit support group that is assisting the refuge in many ways.

The refuge is open daily during daylight hours. An entrance fee is charged. The visitor center is open daily during spring and autumn and on weekdays, except national holidays, during the rest of the year.

Visitor activities include birdwatching, photography, driving the 12-mile auto tour route (an interpretive brochure and tape tour are available), hiking, viewing interpretive displays and programs at the visitor center, and hunting (deer and waterfowl) on parts of the refuge during the designated seasons. The refuge annually hosts more than 4,000 students and teachers for its environmental education programs.

Hiking opportunities include three trails (for which interpretive brochures are available): the Boardwalk Trail—a 1-mile round trip that offers views of woodland, freshwater and brackish ponds, and salt marsh habitats; Parson Point Trail—a 0.5-mile route (closed Nov.–June) on a wooded, marsh-bordered point that extends out from the northern shore of Shearness Pool; and Bear Swamp Trail—a 0.25-mile (wheelchair-accessible) route that loops through marsh and successional stages of woodland near the southern edge of Bear Swamp Pool and includes an observation tower. Over 265 bird species have been seen on the refuge.

Visitors are cautioned to be alert for ticks. Insect repellent is advised during the warmer months.

Lodgings and meals are available in such communities as Dover and Smyrna.

Access to Bombay Hook Refuge from Dover is north on U.S. Route 13 to Bishops Corner, east (right) on State Route 42 to Leipsic, north (left) 2 miles on State Route 9, and east (right) just over 2 miles on Whitehall Neck Road. Or from Smyrna, it is southeast 5 miles on Smyrna-Leipsic Road (State Route 12) to its junction with State Route 9, south (right) 0.25 mile on Route 9, and east (left) just over 2 miles on Whitehall Neck Road.

Further information: Bombay Hook National Wildlife Refuge, 2591 Whitehall Neck Road, Smyrna, DE 19977; telephone: (302) 653-9345.

Prime Hook, containing 9,722 acres, was established in 1963 to manage and protect a significant area of coastal wetlands for spectacular concentrations of migrating, wintering, and nesting waterfowl and shorebirds, as well as other wildlife. The refuge is located along the western shore of Delaware Bay in southeastern Delaware.

Roughly three-quarters of Prime Hook Refuge consists of tidally influenced salt marsh, open water, and managed freshwater impoundments, one of which covers 2,500 acres. As the U.S. Fish and Wildlife Service describes the impounded wetlands:

Water levels on more than 4,200 acres of marsh are raised or lowered at different times of the year through a system of low dikes and water control structures. This management stimulates the growth of emergent aquatic plant species for wildlife use. Management of the water level is important for restoring and maintaining suitable resting and feeding habitat for migratory waterfowl and shorebirds.

The best times to observe large numbers of waterfowl and shorebirds on the refuge are during their migrations. Concentrations of Canada and snow geese and such ducks as American black, mallard, northern pintail, and teal are especially impressive during the autumn. The Fish and Wildlife Service has provided nesting boxes for wood ducks and nesting platforms for ospreys.

In addition to the wetlands, the refuge also includes about 2,300 acres of upland habitat and areas that include mixed woodland of pines and deciduous trees, grasslands, and agricultural fields. These habitats are managed for the benefit of many species of neotropical migratory songbirds and for resident wildlife, including the Delmarva Peninsula fox squirrel (*Sciurus niger cinereus*), an endangered species that was reintroduced to Prime Hook Refuge in 1986. (A description of this squirrel is included in Maryland's Blackwater Refuge text.) As refuge manager Barron Crawford describes:

Current land acquisitions adjoining the refuge are focusing on creating a buffer between the rapid development of the local county and to protect future habitat for Delmarva Peninsula fox squirrels and other forest-dwelling species for the future. Through a cooperative effort between the U.S. Fish and Wildlife Service; the nonprofit organization, American Forests; the Delaware Department of Agriculture's Forest Service; and the Delaware Department of Natural Resources and Environmental Control, the refuge was able to reforest 100 acres with 47,000 hardwood seedlings. Refuge staff hope to continue creating and managing more forested habitat for wildlife, including the Delmarva Peninsula fox squirrel and forest-dwelling birds.

The refuge also contains about 1,300 acres of grassland and agricultural fields. The latter are managed under cooperative agreements with local farmers, who leave unharvested a portion of crops such as corn and wheat to provide an important supplemental source of food for waterfowl and other wildlife.

Establishment of Prime Hook Refuge was made possible partly with revenues from the sale of Migratory Bird Hunting and Conservation Stamps (Duck Stamps). Ducks Unlimited, Inc. and a variety of private contributions have provided major assistance for the refuge's wetland habitat enhancement efforts. The Friends of Prime Hook National Wildlife Refuge is a local nonprofit support group that is assisting the refuge in many ways.

The refuge is open daily during daylight hours. There is no entrance fee. The visitor center is open daily from April 1 to Thanksgiving and on weekdays, except national holidays, from November 1 through March.

Visitor activities include birdwatching, butterfly observation, photography, viewing interpretive displays and programs at the visitor center, driving on the entrance road and several state highways that cut through the refuge, hiking, canoeing on more than 15 miles of streams and ditches, boating on Turkle (Turtle) and Fleetwood ponds and tidal waters (several boat-launching ramps are provided), fishing, and hunting (deer, waterfowl, upland game birds, and small game) on parts of the refuge during the designated seasons. A 7-mile, self-guiding canoe trail follows Prime Hook Creek (an interpretive pamphlet is available). Although camping is not permitted on the refuge, campground facilities are available at Cape Henlopen State Park.

Hiking opportunities include the Boardwalk Trail—a 0.5-mile self-guiding (wheelchair-accessible) loop through upland and freshwater marsh habitats (an interpretive pamphlet is available); Dike Trail—a 0.5-mile route along Headquarter's Dike; Black Farm Trail—a

0.6-mile route that provides views of woodland, agricultural fields, and freshwater marsh; and Pine Grove Trail—a 0.8-mile loop through a pine and deciduous woodland near Turkle and Fleetwood ponds. A butterfly garden is located near the visitor center.

Visitors are cautioned to be alert for ticks. Insect repellent is advised during the warmer months.

The birds, mammals, reptiles, and amphibians are essentially the same as on Bombay Hook National Wildlife Refuge.

Lodgings and meals are available in such communities as Milford, Lewes, Rehoboth Beach, and Dewey Beach.

Access to Prime Hook Refuge from the junction of U.S. Route 113 and State Route 1 (near Milford) is south 15 miles on State Route 1, east (left) on Broadkill Beach Road (State Route 16) 1 mile, and north (left) 1.5 miles on the refuge entrance road to the visitor center. Or from Dewey Beach, it is north 14 miles on State Route 1, east (right) on Broadkill Beach Road (State Route 16), and north (left) on the refuge entrance road.

Further information: Prime Hook National Wildlife Refuge, 11978 Turkle Pond Road, Milton, DE 19968; telephone: (302) 684-8419.

Florida

Archie Carr was established in 1991 to protect the most important nesting habitat for the loggerhead sea turtle in the Western Hemisphere and its second most important nesting habitat in the world. It is here that 25 percent of all loggerhead sea turtle nests and 35 percent of all green sea turtle nests in the United States occur.

The refuge is located along a 20.5-mile stretch of seashore between Melbourne Beach and Wabasso Beach on the central Atlantic Coast of Florida. The core acreage being acquired comprises nearly 10 miles of this coastal strip in four separate tracts. When land acquisition is completed, it is expected that the refuge will contain approximately 900 acres.

The primary management activity at the Archie Carr refuge is "protecting critical nesting sites from human activity and development." This challenging mission is being coordinated with the state and local governments for jointly managing the beaches, conducting sea-turtle nesting surveys, offering public education programs, and providing environmentally compatible visitor use facilities.

The refuge is named in honor of naturalist Dr. Archie F. Carr (1909–1987), who, at the time of his death, was the world's foremost authority on sea turtles. As a highly esteemed research biologist, he traveled and worked extensively throughout the Gulf of Mexico, the Caribbean Sea, the Pacific Coast of Costa Rica, and such other places as Australia, the east coast of Africa, and Papua New Guinea. For many years, he taught ecology at the University of Florida, Gainesville, and was named Graduate Research Professor—the university's most distinguished academic post. For 20 years, he served as chairman of the Marine Turtle Specialist Group of the International Union for the Conservation of Nature's Survival Service Commission. And he was the founding director of the Caribbean Conservation Corporation, an international leader in the protection of sea turtles. Further information: Caribbean Conservation Corporation, 4424 NW Thirteenth Street, Suite AI, Gainesville, FL 32609; telephone: (352) 373-6441 or (800) 678-7853; email: ccc@cccturtle.org.

The refuge is open daily during daylight hours. There is no entrance fee.

Visitor activities include birdwatching, photography, hiking, and swimming.

Many of the birds of Archie Carr Refuge are the same as those recorded on Pelican Island Refuge.

Lodgings and meals are available in such communities as Melbourne, Melbourne Beach, and Sebastian.

Access to the northern units of the Archie Carr Refuge from U.S. Route I at Melbourne is east on U.S. Route 192 (across the Intracoastal Waterway) to Indialantic and south (right) on State Route AIA. Access to the southernmost unit from U.S. Route I at Wabasso is east on County Route 510 (across the Intracoastal Waterway) and north (left) on State Route AIA.

Further information: Archie Carr National Wildlife Refuge, 1339 Twentieth Street, Vero Beach, FL 32960; telephone: (772) 562-3909.

Arthur R. Marshall Loxahatchee, containing 147,392 acres, was established in 1951. The refuge protects the last remaining pristine expanse of the northernmost part of the "River of Grass," known as the Everglades, in south Florida. It consists of extensive wet prairies and sawgrass marshes; numerous tree islands; and smaller areas of sloughs, cattails, a number of managed wetland impoundments, and a 400-acre cypress swamp.

The refuge provides important nesting, roosting, and foraging habitat for great, snowy, and cattle egrets; great blue, little blue, and tricolored herons; black-crowned night heron; white ibis; anhinga; and limpkin. Other species of birds include the wood stork, Florida sandhill crane, and Everglades snail kite. Loxahatchee is the southernmost significant wintering area for ducks in the Atlantic Flyway and is also visited by many species of shorebirds and neotropical songbirds during spring and autumn migrations.

As Devereux Butcher wrote in his 1963 book, *Exploring Our National Wildlife Refuges*:

One of the most characteristic birds of Loxahatchee is the limpkin [*Aramus guarauna*], a brown wading bird...[larger than] a bittern, with long, downward-curving bill. On one of those brilliant days typical of winter in Florida, we visited Loxahatchee. At nearly every turn among the islands a limpkin flew from a thicket. The weird cries of this bird carried across the vast solitudes of the marshes. Long lines of white ibises flew across or soared against the blue sky adding a touch of indescribable beauty; while occasionally the clear, gleaming white of an American egret or a flock of little snowy egrets flew overhead to settle far beyond the irregular skyline of the island forests.

... but the bird which many hope will benefit from protection in this area is the Everglade [snail] kite [Rostrhamus sociabilis]. . . . this handsome species is now close to extinction. Formerly it inhabited most of the fresh water marshes of the Florida Peninsula, and favorite places were the headwaters of the Saint Johns River, the Loxahatchee Marshes and the Lake Okeechobee country. . . .

[Habitat loss is the main reason] . . . for the present serious plight of this bird. The fresh water [apple] snail, Pomacea caliginosa, which is the bird's . . . [primary] food, depends on permanent shallow bodies of water. Man has drained marsh after marsh, and when an area is once dried up, the snail perishes. Even though a marsh may again become covered with water, the snail remains absent (unless reintroduced artificially), so that the area no longer serves as kite habitat. . . .

Whether Loxahatchee Refuge will serve as a haven for the Everglade kite and help to restore it to safer numbers depends on whether the snail can be brought back in the area.

By the end of the twentieth century, the U.S. Fish and Wildlife Service reported that:

The Everglades snail kite has had poor nesting success on the refuge with a total of only seven nests observed from 1976 to 1997. With the change in the water regulation schedule in 1995 providing better habitat for its primary prey, the apple snail, it is hoped the nomadic Everglades snail kite will increase its nesting activities at the refuge. In 1998, 18 Everglades snail kite nests were found and approximately one-third of the nests were thought to be successful. . . . The bird is mobile, moving from one watershed (or conservation area) to another as foraging conditions change.

Regarding the history of this area, as the Fish and Wildlife Service describes in its A.R.M. Loxahatchee National Wildlife Refuge *Comprehensive Conservation Plan*:

Beginning with the Swampland Act of 1845, and later the 1907 Everglades Drainage Act, excessive drainage activities occurred in the Everglades to pave the way for agriculture and development. To meet the ever-increasing water needs of agriculture and population expansion, three water storage areas called Water Conservation Areas 1, 2, and 3 . . . , were constructed by the U.S. Army Corps of Engineers in the 1940s. Bounded by levees and connected by a series of canals, these areas were placed under the jurisdiction of what is now the South Florida Water Management District, an agency of the State of Florida.

In 1951, a license agreement . . . between the South Florida Water Management District and the [Fish and Wildlife] Service . . . enabled the establishment of the . . . Loxahatchee National Wildlife Refuge at Water Conservation Area I. This "refuge interior" land, as it is called, is owned by the State of Florida, but managed by the Service. The license agreement was later amended to include the 1,604-acre Strazzulla Marsh, which lies adjacent to Water Conservation Area I.

In addition . . . , the Fish and Wildlife Service owns 2,550 acres to the east and west of the refuge interior. This acreage is sub-divided into four management compartments . . . and the Cypress Swamp.

The refuge was originally called the Loxahatchee National Wildlife Refuge, because of the area's connection to the Loxahatchee River. That slough connection has since been cut off by dredging and filling for land development. In 1986, the refuge's name was changed to honor Arthur Raymond Marshall, a prominent local wildlife conservationist and former employee of the U.S. Fish and Wildlife Service.

Loxahatchee Refuge's main vegetative communities are:

- Sloughs, which contain the Everglades' deepest natural marsh habitat, with water that may be three feet or more in depth and that supports the growth of such plants as white water lily, spatterdock, floating heart, bladderwort, fanwort, and chara.

- Wet prairies, which cover about 50 percent of the refuge, provide important foraging habitat for wading birds and the Everglades snail kite, are characterized by shallower water than the sloughs, and support emergent plants such as beakrushes, spike rushes, and red-root.
- Sawgrass, which covers about 25 percent of the refuge and is dominated by the saw-edged sedge that grows in dense stands or is mixed with wax myrtle, dahoon holly, shrubs, and other species.
- Tree islands, which cover about 20 percent of the refuge (mostly in the northern part), with thousands of islands ranging from one acre to more than 300 acres, and which support such species as redbay, dahoon holly, wax myrtle, buttonbush, cocoplum, and ferns. Unfortunately, large numbers of these tree islands have been ecologically impaired by aggressively invasive, non-native plant species.
- The Cypress Swamp, a 400-acre area at the eastern edge of the refuge, which is the largest remaining remnant of this plant community on the east side of the Everglades and which supports such species as pond cypress; pond apple; myrsine; numerous epiphytes (air plants), such as Spanish moss and the cardinal, giant, reflexed, and twisted wild pine; and many ferns, such as giant leather, sword, shield, strap, royal, resurrection, and swamp.

Cattails grow in small amounts in the interior of the refuge. As the Fish and Wildlife Service says, "The cattail growth is dependent upon the intense pulse of nutrients deposited by the concentration of nesting birds. After a tree island is abandoned by nesting birds, cattails often die back because of the loss of nutrients."

For many decades, a number of significant resource degradation problems have been seriously impacting the integrity of the Everglades. As the refuge's *Comprehensive Conservation Plan* points out:

The defining element of the refuge and the whole of the Everglades is water, its quality, delivery timing and amount. This unique ecosystem has had a very low nutrient base for thousands of years and is comprised of species that have evolved to thrive under low nutrient conditions. Human activities adjacent to the refuge have introduced nutrients, primarily fertilizers, which enhance the growth of many non-indigenous and invasive species to the detriment of native species. [Approximately 90 percent of the water pumped into the refuge drains from agricultural lands and developed lands east of the refuge.] Increased nutrients change bacteria and algae, the most basic level of the system. This moves through the system until it is visible as the vast unnatural acreages of cattail. [Dense stands of cattails occupy roughly 6,000 acres of the refuge.] Replacing the natural Everglades marsh vegetation, these nuisance species create monotype stands that are far less productive for wildlife and lacks visual appeal of a diverse natural Everglades.

The reduction of nutrients [phosphorus loads] entering the refuge has been and will continue to be a major issue. . . .

Because the Everglades is no longer a free-flowing system that relies on temporal weather patterns to sustain it, humans must now attempt to provide water when and where the system can most benefit. Unfortunately, the water delivery system in place often exhibits its inadequacies in the form of extended droughts and floods. Technology must be developed and implemented to allow water managers to be more responsive to the natural system's needs. . . .

Landmark political events that occurred in the nation's capital in the year 2000 are holding out the hope, however, that South Florida water managers will one day actually be able to be "more responsive." A $7.8-billion, 20-year plan intended to restore the hydrology of the Everglades ecosystem—a blueprint for the most ambitious environmental restoration program in American history—was approved in a vote of 85 to 1 by the United States Senate on September 26; was passed, 312 to 2, by the U.S. House of Representatives on November 3; and was signed into law by President Bill Clinton on December 11.

The challenging task of restoring the historic and vitally important flows of freshwater to the Everglades is to be accomplished, as described by a July 13, 2000, *New York Times* editorial, ". . . by recapturing and rerouting most of the 1.7 billion gallons of water that are wastefully flushed out to sea every day in the name of flood control. The bill specifically authorizes over $1 billion for the first 10 of 68 planned projects. Much of this money would be used to construct massive reservoirs to store Florida's copious rainwater that, at least in theory, will be delivered to the natural system through a redesigned network of canals and levees."

This elaborate redesign and construction program will be carried out by the U.S. Army Corps of Engineers—the same federal agency that originally diverted water away from the Everglades. With construction of 240 miles of new canals and levees, 180,000 acres of water storage reservoirs, and recycling of more than 200 million gallons of water, it is anticipated that 1 million acre-feet of water will annually become available to help rescue and restore this unique ecosystem.

But water quantity is not the only problem facing the Everglades. According to the Fish and Wildlife Service, research has shown that widely used chemical pesticides and herbicides, which flow from agricultural lands into the refuge and other parts of the Everglades, are harmful to invertebrates, fishes, birds, and mammals. Some have been linked to hormonal disruption and reproductive impairment. And there is also extensive evidence of mercury contamination in fish and wildlife in south Florida's freshwater ecosystems. "Scientists suspect that increased mercury exposure may partially explain the 50-year decline in wading bird numbers. Fish and alligators sampled in the Everglades have high mercury levels in their tissues. . . . In 1989, after discovering the extent and severity of mercury in fish, the Florida State Health Officer advised anglers to avoid consumption of several species of fish in more than 1,000,000 acres of the Everglades."

The refuge is open daily during daylight hours. An entrance fee is charged. The visitor center is open daily from mid-October through April, except on Christmas, and is closed on Mondays and Tuesdays during the rest of the year.

Visitor activities include birdwatching, photography, viewing wildlife from an observation platform (wheelchair-accessible) and from an observation tower, viewing butterflies at the visitor center's butterfly garden, interpretive programs, interpreter-guided walks, interpreter-guided canoe excursions, hiking, bicycling (mountain bikes on the perimeter levee, from the headquarters area south to the Hillsboro Recreation Area), canoeing on the 5.5-mile Everglades Canoe Trail, boating on the 57-mile perimeter canal (three boat-launching ramps are provided), fishing (a wheelchair-accessible fishing pier is provided; bank fishing in the Hillsboro Recreation Area), and waterfowl hunting in a designated hunt area at the south end of the refuge during the designated season. Over 250 bird species have been seen on the refuge.

Although camping is not permitted on the refuge, campground facilities are available at Jonathan Dickinson State Park (about an hour away) and elsewhere in the general area. Swimming, personal motorized watercraft, airboats, and hovercraft are not permitted on the refuge.

Walking and hiking opportunities include the 0.4-mile (wheelchair-accessible) Cypress Swamp Boardwalk loop near headquarters; the 0.8-mile Marsh Trail loop; the 6-mile Compartment C perimeter route around ten wetland impoundments; the 12-mile round-trip levee route between headquarters and Strazzulla Marsh; and the 7.5-mile one-way route south from headquarters to the Hillsboro Recreation Area, with an additional 12-mile one-way stretch on to the S-6 water structure.

Even though alligators, which are abundant on the refuge, are generally afraid of people, visitors are cautioned to stay a safe distance from these sluggish-looking but potentially fast-moving reptiles and be alert for venomous snakes and fire ants. Insect repellent and sunscreen are advised.

Lodgings and meals are available in such nearby communities as West Palm Beach, Boynton Beach, Delray Beach, Boca Raton, and Fort Lauderdale.

Access to the A.R.M. Loxahatchee Refuge, from either Exit 86 on Florida's Turnpike or from Exit 44 on I-95, is west on Boynton Beach Boulevard (State Route 804), south (left) on State Route 441/U.S. Route 7, and west (right) on Lee Road into the refuge. Access to the refuge's Hillsboro Recreation Area, at the southern end of the refuge, is to continue south on State Route 441 and west on County Route 827 from Deerfield Beach.

Further information: Arthur R. Marshall Loxahatchee National Wildlife Refuge, 10216 Lee Road, Boynton Beach, FL 33437; telephone: (561) 732-3684.

Caloosahatchee comprises 40 acres of mangrove and upland habitats on a cluster of eight islands in the Caloosahatchee River adjacent to the city of Fort Myers and a few miles upriver from the southwestern Gulf Coast of Florida. As the U.S. Fish and Wildlife Service explains, when the refuge was established in 1920, "It originally consisted of several small mangrove islands. . . , but shoreline development, dredging of the Caloosahatchee River as part of the Intracoastal Waterway, and construction of the I-75 bridge have changed the physical arrangement of those islands."

Because Caloosahatchee Refuge adjoins Florida Power & Light's Orange River power-generating plant, the outflow of warm water provides favorable wintering habitat for the endangered West Indian manatee. (See further description of manatees in the Crystal River Refuge text.) Other wildlife includes herons and egrets, ospreys, and bald eagles.

Access to the refuge is only by boat. The Fish and Wildlife Service urges boaters to consult navigational charts and tide schedules before attempting to visit any of the refuge islands. Numerous oyster bars and shallow back bay/estuary waters are difficult to navigate, and damage to fragile seagrass beds is common due to boaters running aground. Boaters are discouraged from approaching the refuge islands during the nesting season. There is no entrance fee. Visitor activities include birdwatching and photography. Insect repellent and sunscreen are advised.

Further information: Caloosahatchee National Wildlife Refuge, c/o J. N. "Ding" Darling NWR, 1 Wildlife Drive, Sanibel, FL 33957; telephone: (941) 472-1100.

Cedar Keys, consisting of about 800 acres, was established in 1929 to protect 13 subtropical coastal islands in the Gulf of Mexico. The refuge is located about 14 miles south of the mouth of the Suwannee River and close to Lower Suwannee Refuge's SHELL MOUND UNIT, on the northern West Coast of Florida. Over 250 bird species use both refuges.

These small islands, which range in size from 1 to 165 acres, support one of north Florida's largest colonial nesting rookeries for such birds as the white ibis, great and snowy egrets, great and little blue herons, tricolored heron, black-crowned night-heron, brown pelican, and double-crested cormorant. As the U.S. Fish and Wildlife Service points out, "Historically, Cedar Keys Refuge was a tremendous nesting area for colonial birds, with a peak population of 200,000 birds nesting during the 1960s and 1970s. In recent years, peak populations have been in the 8,000- to 10,000-range. . . ." Ospreys also frequently nest on the refuge, bald eagles are common during the winter, wood storks sometimes occur here, and magnificent frigatebirds are seasonally common. Numerous species of neotropical songbirds briefly pause on these coastal islands during their spring and autumn migrations.

Raccoons are abundant residents on most of the refuge's islands. The federally listed endangered West Indian manatee inhabits the coastal waters from spring through autumn (see description of this species in the Crystal River text). Three species of sea turtles—the federally listed endangered Kemp's ridley, the state-listed endangered green, and the federally listed threatened loggerhead—are common in the offshore waters but are not known to nest within the refuge.

The refuge's Seahorse Key contains an especially large population of the Florida cottonmouth. If disturbed, this snake, also known as the water moccasin, is likely to challenge the intruder by standing its ground and opening its mouth wide—exposing the whitish, cotton-colored interior lining. A cottonmouth's highly venomous bite can be fatal.

Snake, Bird, North, and Seahorse islands have been designated as a unit of the National Wilderness Preservation System. Atsena Otie Key, the newest addition to the refuge, is owned by the Suwannee River Water Management District and is managed by the U.S. Fish and Wildlife Service under a cooperative agreement with the district.

The refuge's maritime hammocks contain a canopy of live oak, cabbage palmetto, southern redcedar, hackberry, redbay, pignut hickory, and Carolina laurelcherry; with an understory of yaupon (holly), beautyberry, catbrier, grape, coontie, and saw palmetto. Xeric hammocks are characterized by a canopy of sand live oak, tree lyonia (staggerbush), and occasionally slash pine, with a thick understory of saw palmetto, wax myrtle, hog (flatwood) plum, pricklypear cactus, and Spanish bayonet (yucca). Beach dunes are dominated by beach cordgrass, beach dropseed, and sandspur, along with beach sunflower, beach morning glory, and beach bean.

Intertidal salt marsh is dominated by smooth cordgrass. As the Fish and Wildlife Service explains, "Black mangroves dominated much of these [intertidal] areas prior to a freeze killing them in 1985. In recent years, the mangroves have started to reestablish and have formed thick stands in the protected coves." An invasive exotic species, the Brazilian pepper tree, proliferates mostly in the transition zone between the upland and salt marsh/mangrove habitats. A program to control, if not eradicate, this pest has been launched.

Visitor entry onto these islands is restricted. The interiors of all islands, except Atsena Otie Key (where there is a short trail), are closed to visitation, both for protection of the fragile ecosystems and for the safety of visitors. The beaches of all islands except Seahorse Key are open all year during daylight hours. All of the islands are relatively inaccessible, as they are surrounded by shallow sand and mud flats.

Visitor activities include birdwatching; photography; picnicking; sunbathing; sea kayaking (especially to Scale, Live Oak, and Atsena Otie keys); boating (boat-launching sites are available in the town of Cedar Key); fishing; and hiking (only on Atsena Otie Key's trail through that island's interior). The Fish and Wildlife Service emphasizes, "Seahorse Key, and a 300-foot buffer around the island, is closed to all public entry annually from March 1 through June 30, to protect the nesting colonial wading birds." Camping and hunting are not permitted on the refuge.

Visitors are cautioned to be alert for the venomous cottonmouth snake. Insect repellent and sunscreen are advised.

The town of Cedar Key, where lodgings and meals are available, is reached from I-75 at Gainesville, southwest 53 miles on State Route 24.

Access to the refuge is only by boat. As all of the islands are surrounded by shallow sand, mud, and grass flats, they are "relatively inaccessible," especially at low tide.

Further information: Cedar Keys National Wildlife Refuge, c/o Lower Suwannee NWR, 16450 Northwest Thirty-First Place, Chiefland, FL 32626; telephone: (352) 493-0238.

Chassahowitzka, comprising more than 31,000 acres, was established in 1943 to protect a magnificent expanse of pristine estuaries, bays, brackish marshland, and some bottomland hardwood swamps extending for 12 miles along and adjacent to the lower Chassahowitzka River on the northwest Gulf Coast of Florida. Approximately three-quarters of the refuge has been designated as a unit of the National Wilderness Preservation System.

Although this area formerly attracted great numbers of wintering ducks and coots, their numbers have declined in recent years. However, the refuge has become an increasingly important haven of bays and tidal rivers and streams for the federally listed endangered West Indian manatee (see description of this species in the Crystal River Refuge text).

There are also numerous species of birds, notably cormorants, herons, egrets, white ibis, anhinga, wood stork, brown pelican, osprey, bald eagle, swallow-tailed kite (in the spring), and wood duck. Species that nest on the refuge include double-crested cormorant, great egret, herons (great blue, little blue, tricolored, and green), and black-crowned night heron; those nesting near the refuge include bald eagle, osprey, brown pelican, and wood stork. Great numbers of warblers and other species of neotropical migratory songbirds pass through the refuge during spring and autumn migrations. Reptiles include abundant alligators and several species of sea turtles.

As the U.S. Fish and Wildlife Service describes the refuge:

Chassahowitzka is unspoiled habitat...that serves as important breeding and feeding ground for marine life. Shallow bays support an abundant growth of muskgrass which provides food for various birds and the endangered manatee.

Inland from the bays are the brackish creeks and ponds where widgeongrass, watermilfoil and other foods grow in abundance. The eastern boundary provides a few thousand acres of swamp habitat, where oaks, cypress and red cedar grow.

The outer islands consist mainly of red and black mangrove which provides habitat for colonial [nesting] birds.

An especially exciting wildlife management program at Chassahowitzka Refuge is the reintroduction of the endangered whooping crane (see the Aransas National Wildlife Refuge, Texas text for a description of this species). In the summer of 2001, chicks that were hatched in the captive breeding program at the Patuxent Wildlife Research Center in Maryland were taken to the Necedah National Wildlife Refuge in Wisconsin. There the birds underwent training with small ultralight aircraft (with crane-costumed pilots) that prepared them for an amazing migration. In October 2001, the cranes flew more than 1,200 miles with several ultralights from Necedah to Chassahowitzka, pausing more than 30 times along the route. (See further discussion of this historic event in the Necedah NWR text.)

The Friends of Chassahowitzka National Wildlife Refuge Complex is a nonprofit support group that is helping the refuge in many ways.

Although the refuge is open daily, accessible only by boat, visitation is subject to special regulations. To provide protection for the manatee, slow speed limits are posted for boats on parts of the Chassahowitzka River from April 1 through August 31. The use of airboats is restricted to the southern end of the refuge (in Hernando County) and to two posted airboat routes (in Citrus County). There is no entrance fee. The refuge headquarters, in the town of Crystal River, is open on weekdays, except national holidays.

Visitor activities include birdwatching, photography, boating, fishing, and hunting (designated hunts) on part of the refuge during the designated seasons (part of the refuge is a no-hunting zone). Camping is not permitted on the refuge, but campground facilities are available in Homosassa and Crystal River. Insect repellent and sunscreen are advised.

Lodgings and meals are available in such communities as Homosassa, Crystal River, Weeki Wachee, and Brooksville.

Access to the Chassahowitzka Refuge from U.S. Route 19/98 at Homosassa Springs is southwest about 2 miles on County Road 490 to a boat-launching ramp at Homosassa onto the Homosassa River; or, from the intersection of U.S. Routes 19 and 98 it is west just over 1 mile on County Road 480 to a boat-launching ramp onto the Chassahowitzka River.

Further information: Chassahowitzka National Wildlife Refuge, 1502 Southeast Kings Bay Drive, Crystal River, FL 34429; telephone: (352) 563-2088.

Crocodile Lake, encompassing 6,700 acres, was established in 1980 to protect critical habitat for the federally listed endangered American crocodile (*Crocodylus acutus*). The refuge is located on North Key Largo in south Florida.

Key Largo and the extreme southern tip of Florida are within the northern end of the crocodile's range, which extends southward through the coastal waters of the Caribbean islands and Central and South America. This large reptile, measuring as much as 15 feet in length, is similar to the American alligator (*Alligator mississippiensis*) but is distinguished from the alligator by its long, tapered, much more slender snout. As the U.S. Fish and Wildlife Service explains, "The southeastern United States hosts two of the world's 22 crocodile species. Many Americans are quite familiar with the American alligator. . . . Few are aware of the American crocodile . . . our crocodiles are shy, solitary creatures who would rather run and hide than have anything to do with humans." As for their habitat, "Crocodiles prefer mangrove-lined saltwater bays, creeks, and mangrove swamps; alligators primarily reside in inland freshwater glades, sloughs, bayous, cypress swamps, marshes, ponds, and canals. Both may be found in brackish water (water near the coast that has some salt content)."

The refuge's habitat, which had been threatened with real estate development, consists of mangrove wetlands and wooded hammocks of slightly higher terrain. As the Fish and Wildlife Service says, "An abandoned subdivision development on the Refuge with miles of canals and exposed canal banks provides the only known nesting area for crocodiles on Key Largo. Fringing mangrove wetlands . . . support a wide variety of wildlife including wading birds and songbirds. Mangrove wetlands also serve as important nursery areas for many fish species. . . ."

Although crocodile numbers are difficult to estimate, there may be somewhere between 600 and 800 of them in south Florida and around 100 on the refuge. The population is reportedly doing well, but the Service emphasizes, "Their future is in the hands of factors such as hurricanes, cold spells, poaching, road kills, continued habitat degradation, and disturbances by humans to them and their nests."

Crocodile Lake Refuge and the adjacent Dagny Johnson Key Largo Hammock Botanical State Park contain the largest continuous tract of tropical hardwood forest remaining in the Florida Keys. Eighty percent of the diverse plant species are of West Indian origin. These wooded hammocks contain close to 100 species of native trees and shrubs, including such species as gumbo limbo, lignumvitae, and paradise tree. This forested habitat attracts numerous species of neotropical migratory songbirds. Common breeding birds on the refuge and park include the mangrove cuckoo and black-whiskered vireo. These areas are also inhabited by tree snails, butterflies, and such federally listed endangered and threatened species as the Key Largo woodrat, Key Largo cotton mouse, eastern indigo snake, Stock Island tree snail, and Schaus' swallowtail butterfly. These latter five species dwell only in the shade within hardwood hammocks.

An interpretive butterfly garden (with a wheelchair-accessible path) has been created adjacent to the refuge headquarters, which is located at 10750 County Road 905, Key Largo. However, to avoid human disturbance of sensitive habitat and wildlife, the remainder of the refuge is presently closed to visitation, except by special use permit. The Service is assessing a proposal to build a (wheelchair-accessible) boardwalk and observation deck. The adjacent Dagny Johnson Key Largo Hammock Botanical State Park provides a self-guiding nature trail into an area that is similar to Crocodile Lake Refuge. The cooler winter months are the most comfortable season for visiting this area. Summers are typically hot and humid, with an abundance of biting insects.

One of the annual avian highlights of the Florida Keys is the spectacular autumn concentration of migrating raptors. Casey Lott, project director for the Florida Keys Raptor Migration Project, says that "the largest-known concentration of migrating peregrine falcons in the world" occurs along the Florida Keys. The biggest concentration of hawks can be seen from within Curry Hammock State Park, at mile marker 56 on Little Crawl Key (just south of Grassy Key). The Florida Keys Raptor Migration Project is sponsored and funded by the

Florida Fish and Wildlife Conservation Commission and is run by HawkWatch International and the Audubon of Florida. For information on the Project's research and environmental education programs: e-mail: caseylott@hotmail.com or telephone: (305) 852-5318 or 5092.

The Friends and Volunteers of the Refuges (FAVOR) is a nonprofit organization that is helping to support the educational and other programs of the national wildlife refuges in the Florida Keys.

Lodgings and meals are available in such communities as Key Largo, Islamorada, Long Key, Marathon, Florida City, and Homestead.

Further information: Crocodile Lake National Wildlife Refuge, P.O. Box 370, Key Largo, FL 33037; telephone: (305) 451-4223.

Crystal River, containing 46 acres, was established in 1983 to protect the ecologically significant, undeveloped parts of Kings Bay—the headwaters of Crystal River on the upper West Coast of Florida. This refuge's primary mission is to preserve the exceptional ecosystem of warm, spring-fed waters and rich aquatic vegetation that provides outstanding wintering habitat for roughly 250 of the critically endangered West Indian manatee. Crystal River attracts the largest concentration of the species at an area of natural springs. This strange-looking aquatic mammal, which weighs around 75 pounds at birth, grows to an average of 1,000 pounds and 10 feet long. Over 250 bird species use Crystal River and Chassahowitzka refuges.

As the U.S. Fish and Wildlife Service explains:

The refuge . . . aids in preserving Florida's most significant naturally occurring warm water haven for the manatee and provides critical habitat for approximately twenty percent of the nation's manatee population. Six hundred million gallons of fresh water flow daily from more than thirty natural springs. The temperature of the water flowing from the springs remains a constant 72 degrees Fahrenheit. Manatees, like people, are susceptible to cold and hypothermia and cannot survive for extended periods when water temperatures fall below 68 degrees Fahrenheit. These warm water springs are essential for manatee survival.

This gentle giant is endangered largely because of alteration and destruction of coastal habitats by man. . . .

During times of heavy manatee concentrations [from November through March], certain areas in Kings Bay are designated, "Manatee Sanctuary Areas." These sanctuaries provide places for manatees to rest and feed undisturbed in the warmth of the springs.

In an effort to reduce the number of manatees killed and injured by boats, idle and slow speed zones are in effect throughout Kings Bay. . . .

Many manatees exhibit scars where they have been struck by boats and their propellers . . .

To prevent the loss of this irreplaceable habitat, the 20 refuge islands and adjacent underwater manatee sanctuary areas were purchased by The Nature Conservancy, with local citizens leading a fund-raising campaign. The Fish and Wildlife Service subsequently acquired these land and water areas.

The Friends of Chassahowitzka National Wildlife Refuge Complex is a nonprofit support group that is assisting Crystal River Refuge in various ways.

The refuge is open daily during daylight hours and is accessible only by boat. There is no entrance fee. Visitor activities include boating, canoeing, and swimming, to observe manatees.

The refuge does not provide boats or boat access. Private boats may be launched at public boat ramps. Visitors may rent boats and obtain a guided tour through the dive shops in the community of Crystal River. A list of dive shops that hold permits from the Fish and Wildlife Service is available at the refuge office.

Entry into the designated manatee sanctuaries is prohibited for any reason from November 15 through March 31. Boats are to be operated at idle or slow speed where speed zones are posted and in effect. Visitors are urged to quietly observe and to swim slowly like manatees, at a distance from the water surface—using snorkel gear (the noise of scuba equipment can frighten the animals away). Harassing manatees is unlawful.

A volunteer program, "Manatee Watch," assists the Fish and Wildlife Service in "educating visitors about sanctuary locations and boating speeds." The Manatee Education Center, a joint project of the Fish and Wildlife Service and the Florida Park Service, is located in Homosassa Springs State Wildlife Park, south 7 miles from the town of Crystal River on U.S. Route 19/98. The center, which is open daily, provides (wheelchair-accessible) interpretive exhibits, and staff are available to help orient visitors to the refuge and answer questions.

Other visitor activities include birdwatching, photography, and fishing. Although camping is not permitted on the refuge, campground facilities are available at such nearby towns as Crystal River and Homosassa.

Even though alligators are usually afraid of people, visitors are cautioned to stay a safe distance from these sluggish-looking but potentially fast-moving reptiles and to be alert for venomous snakes. Insect repellent and sunscreen are advised.

In addition to the manatee, other wildlife and the flora of Crystal River Refuge are much the same as the species recorded on nearby Chassahowitzka Refuge.

Lodgings and meals are available in such communities as Crystal River and Homosassa.

Access to Crystal River Refuge headquarters from the town of Crystal River is south 1 mile on U.S. Route 19/98 (from State Route 44) and west (right) 0.5 mile on Southeast Paradise Point Road.

Further information: Crystal River National Wildlife Refuge, 1502 Southeast Kings Bay Drive, Crystal River, FL 34429; telephone: (352) 563-2088.

Egmont Key consists of a 350-acre barrier island located at the mouth of Tampa Bay on the Gulf Coast of Florida. The refuge was established in 1974 and protects important nesting, feeding, and resting habitat for many species of colonial nesting water birds.

Among the birds inhabiting the island's wetland habitat are the double-crested cormorant, brown pelican, great blue heron, snowy egret, yellow-crowned night-heron, and white ibis. Shorebirds include black skimmer; black-bellied plover; sanderling; willet; ruddy turnstone; short-billed dowitcher; American oystercatcher; dunlin; gulls (laughing, herring, and ring-billed); and royal and sandwich terns. The critically endangered West Indian manatee inhabits the waters around the island. Reptiles include the endangered loggerhead sea turtle, which nests on the island; Florida box turtle; gopher tortoise; and eastern diamond-back rattlesnake.

Prominent among the island's species of flora are cabbage palmetto (*Sabal palmetto*), southern redcedar, and wax myrtle.

The island is protected and managed jointly by the U.S. Fish and Wildlife Service and the Florida Park Service. The Friends of Chassahowitzka National Wildlife Refuge Complex is a nonprofit support group that is assisting Egmont Key Refuge in various ways.

The refuge is open daily during daylight hours. There is no entrance fee. It is accessible only by boat, with guided trips offered by several commercial tour companies in St. Petersburg.

Visitor activities include birdwatching, photography, hiking on several trails through the island's maritime forest, sunbathing, swimming, boating, and fishing. A wildlife sanctuary is located at the southern end of the island and another along the eastern side of the island to avoid disturbing the nesting habitat of brown pelicans and other species.

Visitors are cautioned to be alert for venomous snakes. Insect repellent and sunscreen are advised.

Lodgings and meals are available in such communities as St. Petersburg, Clearwater, and Tampa.

Further information: Egmont Key National Wildlife Refuge, c/o Chassahowitzka NWR, 1502 Southeast Kings Bay Drive, Crystal River, FL 34429; telephone: (352) 563-2088.

Florida Panther, containing nearly 30,000 acres, was established in 1989 to help promote the recovery of the federally listed endangered Florida panther. The refuge encompasses the northern part of the Fakahatchee Strand—a forested swamp that lies along the main drainage slough of the Big Cypress Swamp. This area is located about 20 miles east of Naples, bordered on the east by State Route 29 and on the south by I-75 (Alligator Alley), in southwestern Florida. The refuge adjoins the National Park Service-administered Big Cypress National Preserve/ Everglades National Park and the Fakahatchee Strand State Preserve. All these public lands total more than 1 million acres that are offering protected panther habitat.

The Florida panther (*Puma concolor coryi*), a subspecies of the cougar (mountain lion), has adapted to South Florida's subtropical environment but is ranked as one of the world's rarest and most endangered mammals. The most common morphologic characteristic that distinguishes this subspecies from other cougars is its skull, which has been described as having higher-arched nasal bones than other cougars. This gives the panther the appearance of having a prominent or "Roman" nose. Other differences are so subtle that most experts would have a difficult time distinguishing one subspecies from another. Florida panthers are large, long-tailed, tawny-colored cats. The males weigh between 100 and 150 pounds, and the females weigh between 65 and 100 pounds. A mere 60 to 70 of these secretive, mostly nocturnal cats remain in the mixed forest swampland and pineland habitat, where they stalk and ambush such prey as deer, wild hogs, raccoons, and nine-banded armadillos.

This cat needs large areas of wilderness with little human intervention or disturbance. A single male panther in South Florida maintains at least 200 square miles of territory. As refuge manager Jim Krakowski states:

Because of the panther's widespread use of undisturbed forested habitats, it truly could be labeled as a "barometer" of healthy swamps and forests of south Florida. These same forests provide habitat to a myriad of other animal and plant species, many of which are also threatened. In addition, these forests and wetlands safely soak up and store the heavy summer/fall rains. Without our natural areas, the neighboring agricultural and urban lands would flood during the wet season and thirst during the dry winter/spring seasons.

Unfortunately, a long history of hunting (a bounty was once offered) and dwindling habitat have caused the subspecies' alarming decline. Of major concern to wildlife biologists is the evidence among a high percentage of panthers of harmful impacts that are believed caused by isolation and inbreeding. As the refuge's March 2000 *Comprehensive Conservation Plan* document states:

Population viability is threatened by numerous physiological and reproductive abnormalities prevalent within the population. For the most part, these conditions are considered manifestations of isolation and inbreeding, and possible environmental contamination.

In an attempt to restore genetic diversity within the Florida panther population, a number of females of a closely related subspecies, the Texas cougar, were brought to Florida in 1995. This crossbreeding effort received the endorsement of federal and state wildlife agencies, environmental groups, and independent biologists. It has been managed by the Florida Fish and Wildlife Conservation Commission.

Jim Krakowski reports, "None of the eight female Texas cougars were released in the Florida Panther refuge, because it appeared no available female niche was open. However, since 1995, several Texas cougars have ranged into the refuge, probably seeking the abundant prey within. In March 2001, TX106 denned in the refuge and produced two kittens. As of October 2001, three of the Texas cougars remain in south Florida (five have died). The cougars have produced 17 kittens, some of which have also mated, to produce a total of 50 intercross kittens (not all have survived to adulthood)."

The refuge includes lakes and ponds that are surrounded by swamps, grassy prairies, cypress domes, hardwood hammocks, and pine forests. Rising slightly higher than the grassy prairies and swamps are island-like areas known as hammocks. They support the growth of such species as cabbage palmetto (*Sabal palmetto*), saw palmetto (*Serenoa repens*), live and laurel oaks, gumbo limbo, and holly.

The Fakahatchee Strand area also boasts North America's greatest numbers and density of native species of orchids, with more than 46 species recorded. But according to the refuge's *Comprehensive Conservation Plan*, "Many of these orchids have been pilfered by humans and are now rare. Through a combination of agency and organization partnership, . . . [the Rare Orchid Restoration] project would restore rare orchid species to suitable, historic habitats in southwest Florida. Cooperating land management entities include Florida Panther National Wildlife Refuge, Big Cypress National Preserve, Fakahatchee Strand State Preserve, Picayune Strand State Forest, CREW lands, and National Audubon Society's Corkscrew [Swamp] Sanctuary. The project is supported by state and federal agencies, Florida Native Plant Society, and Florida Orchid Society. The project would focus on the creation of a small greenhouse at the refuge where orchids would be grown for eventual transplantation."

The Friends of the Florida Panther Refuge is a nonprofit support group that is also assisting the refuge in many ways.

The refuge is presently not open to public visitation, except for limited, small-group tours, to avoid disturbance of endangered species and their habitat. Refuge staff offer environmental education programs at schools and elsewhere. A self-guiding foot trail of about 1 mile in length with interpretive exhibits is proposed for construction in the southeast corner of the refuge.

Further information: Florida Panther National Wildlife Refuge, 3860 Tollgate Boulevard, Suite 300, Naples, FL 34114; telephone: (941) 353-8442.

Great White Heron, consisting of 7,407 acres of land and 186,287 acres of water, was established in 1938 to protect great white herons, egrets, and other migratory birds from plume hunters (see description of this commercial exploitation in the Key West Refuge text). The Great White Heron Refuge encompasses many of the small keys that are located north of U.S. Route 1 (Overseas Highway) between Marathon and Key West, Florida.

The refuge's habitats consist mostly of mangrove wetlands, with small areas of wooded hammocks of slightly higher terrain, salt marshes, and beaches where the threatened loggerhead and endangered green sea turtles come ashore to deposit their eggs in summer. Great White Heron Refuge is named for the elegant white phase of the great blue heron. The refuge provides important resting, feeding, and, to some extent, nesting habitat for more than 250 species of birds. Prominent among them are numerous wading birds, as well as the magnificent frigatebird, brown pelican, ducks, shorebirds, gulls, terns, osprey, bald eagle, white-crowned pigeon, and many species of migrating raptors (see the Crocodile Lake refuge text) and neotropical migratory songbirds. Over 280 bird species have been seen here as well as at Key West, and National Key Deer Refuges.

Although the refuge islands may be accessed only with a special-use permit, the state-controlled waters are accessible at any time. There is no entrance fee. The refuge headquarters, located on Big Pine Key, is open on weekdays, except national holidays.

Visitor activities include birdwatching, photography, kayaking, sailing, boating (except where posted as closed), and fishing. Commercial guided tours and boat rentals are provided. Camping is not permitted on the refuge islands. Motorized personal watercraft, water skiing, hovercraft, airboats, and seaplane landings are not permitted within the refuge, to avoid disturbing the wildlife. Part of the refuge has been designated as a unit of the National Wilderness Preservation System.

Insect repellent and sunscreen are advised.

The Friends and Volunteers of the Refuges (FAVOR) is a nonprofit organization that is helping to support the educational and other programs of the national wildlife refuges in the Florida keys.

The birds of Great White Heron Refuge are essentially the same as those recorded on National Key Deer Refuge (see the listing for that refuge).

Lodgings and meals are available in such communities as Marathon, Little Torch Key, Summerland Key, and Key West.

Access to Great White Heron Refuge is by boat from a number of places from Marathon to Key West, reached from the mainland by way of U.S. Route 1 (Overseas Highway).

Further information: Great White Heron National Wildlife Refuge, P.O. Box 430510, Big Pine Key, FL 33043; telephone: (305) 872-0774.

Hobe Sound, consisting of 967 acres, was established in 1969 and is located about 20 miles north of West Palm Beach on the Atlantic Coast of South Florida. The refuge protects coastal barrier island beach, sand dune, and mangrove swamp habitats on its 735-acre Jupiter Island tract and a remnant of sand pine/scrub oak/saw palmetto forest on its 232-acre mainland tract. Among the birds of Hobe Sound Refuge are the brown pelican, herons, egrets, terns, shorebirds, osprey, and numerous species of neotropical songbirds during the spring and autumn migrations. Over 180 bird species have been recorded here.

One of the major purposes of Hobe Sound Refuge is to protect a 3.5-mile beach where the threatened loggerhead sea turtles and the endangered green and leatherback sea turtles deposit their eggs during the summer. Each egg-laden female hauls herself ashore, scoops out a nest with her rear flippers, lays about a hundred eggs, covers them with sand, and returns to the sea. For about 2 months, if undisturbed by predators or humans, the eggs are incubated within the sun-warmed sand. Under the cover of darkness, the hatchlings, as a group, finally burst from their eggshells, scramble out of their nest, and dash into the ocean. Public use of the beach is limited, to avoid disturbing the sea turtles.

Another goal of the refuge is to help the state protect the endangered West Indian manatee, a marine mammal that inhabits the Intracoastal Waterway in Hobe Sound. (See the description of this marine mammal in the Crystal River National Wildlife Refuge text.) Bobcat, gray fox, raccoon, and eastern gray squirrel are among the terrestrial mammals that visitors may see.

As the Fish and Wildlife Service explains, fire management, with periodic low-intensity burning, is ecologically important:

The mainland unit of sand pine-scrub forest requires fire for its regeneration. Without fire, sand pine becomes too dense and tall, over-shadowing the scrub oak and rosemary, as well as covering open sand with needles. The numerous endemic plants and animals that have adapted to the open oak-scrub, including the Florida scrub-jay, cannot survive. Although the tract is small, its value is magnified by the fact that over 90 percent of this community type in South Florida has been lost to development.

Establishment of Hobe Sound Refuge was made possible when local landowners generously donated the properties to The Nature Conservancy, which then transferred them to the U.S. Fish and Wildlife Service. In addition, a 173-acre parcel, which is listed as a National Natural Landmark, was donated by the Reed family as the Reed Wilderness Seashore Sanctuary.

The refuge is named for the Jobe (pronounced HO-bay) Indians, who were inhabiting this area when Jonathan Dickinson and his party were shipwrecked at Jupiter Inlet during a hurricane in 1696. On lands now within the refuge, settlers constructed dwellings of palmetto fronds, called chickee huts. Later, the area was settled by Euro-Americans, and the Native Americans were driven out. As the Fish and Wildlife Service says, "Today, little remains of the historical past. A chimney here, and an old dock there is all that remains of a once thriving community. In their place the sand pines, oak thickets, and palmetto plants have covered man's presence."

The Hobe Sound Nature Center, Inc. is a nonprofit educational support group that is assisting the refuge.

The refuge is open daily during daylight hours. An entrance fee is charged at the beach parking area. The refuge headquarters is open on weekdays, except national holidays. Public entry onto the refuge is permitted at only three places: the headquarters area on the mainland unit, the beach area on Jupiter Island unit, and the Peck Lake stretch of the Intracoastal Waterway.

Visitor activities include birdwatching; photography; hiking; interpreter-guided sea turtle watches; swimming; canoeing, kayaking, boating on the Intracoastal Waterway; and saltwater fishing along the beach and Intracoastal Waterway. Camping is not permitted on the refuge, but campground facilities are available across the highway at Jonathan Dickinson State Park and elsewhere in the vicinity. Hiking opportunities include the mainland unit's 0.4-mile self-guiding Sand Scrub Trail and along the beach.

A special environmental education program is provided at the refuge by the nonprofit Hobe Sound Nature Center, Inc. This organization operates the refuge's interpretive museum, which is open only on weekdays until 3 p.m., presents a lecture series during the spring and autumn, runs a summer camp for youth, and offers outreach programs for schools and other groups in the area.

Visitors are cautioned to be alert for venomous snakes. Insect repellent and sunscreen are advised.

Lodgings and meals are available in Stuart, Jensen Beach, Tequesta, and Jupiter.

Access to the Hobe Sound Refuge headquarters from Exit 60 on I-95 is east on State Route 708/Bridge Road, and south (right) 2 miles on U.S. Route I. To access the beach tract, it is east on State Route 708/Bridge Road to its end and north (left) to the end of the road at the refuge parking area.

Further information: Hobe Sound National Wildlife Refuge, P.O. Box 645, Hobe Sound, FL 33475; telephone: (561) 546-6141.

Island Bay contains 20 acres in six separate tracts, located near Cape Haze on the southwestern Gulf Coast of Florida. The refuge was established in 1908 by President Theodore Roosevelt. It protects parts of four keys at the mouth of Turtle Bay and two large oyster shell mounds (middens) that were created centuries ago by Calusa Indians who lived on the mainland adjacent to the bay. In 1970, Island Bay Refuge was designated as a unit of the National Wilderness Preservation System.

Vegetation on the higher sandy parts of the keys includes such species as cabbage palmetto (*Sabal palmetto*), buttonwood, strangler fig, gumbo limbo, and sea grape, the thick leaves of which resemble the shape of a ping-pong paddle. Lower elevations consist predominantly of thick stands of black mangrove, with scattered edges of red mangrove (see a description of mangroves in the J. N. "Ding" Darling Refuge text).

Great numbers of wading birds, waterfowl, and shorebirds feed, roost, and nest on the refuge. The endangered West Indian manatee inhabits its brackish waters.

Access to the refuge is only by boat. The Fish and Wildlife Service urges boaters to consult navigational charts and tide schedules before attempting to visit any of the refuge islands. Numerous oyster bars and shallow back bay/estuary waters are difficult to navigate, and damage to fragile seagrass beds is common due to boaters running aground. Boaters are discouraged from approaching the refuge islands during the nesting season. There is no entrance fee. Insect repellent and sunscreen are advised.

Further information: Island Bay National Wildlife Refuge, c/o J. N. "Ding" Darling NWR, I Wildlife Drive, Sanibel, FL 33957; telephone: (941) 472-1100.

J. N. "Ding" Darling, containing 6,400 acres, was established in 1945 to protect a magnificent area of important subtropical wildlife habitats on part of Sanibel Island, a barrier island on the southwestern Gulf Coast of Florida. Roughly 2,800 acres have been designated as a unit of the National Wilderness Preservation System.

The refuge consists of a variety of brackish estuarine and interior freshwater wetlands, including cordgrass marshes, dense stands of mangrove swamp, and West Indian hardwood hammocks. About half of the refuge supports mangrove estuary habitat, which is dominated by three species of mangrove. The red mangrove, growing partially or entirely in the water, is the most common, its tangle of twisted roots suggestive of the name "the tree that walks." Large seedlings, known as propagules, commonly hang from the branches of these trees. The black mangrove "breathes" through pneumatophores—specially developed roots that grow upward through the marshy soil. The white mangrove, growing the farthest from the water, excretes salt through the nodes at the base of its leaves.

As the U.S. Fish and Wildlife Service explains:

Mangroves play a vital role in the food chain of this marine environment. Microorganisms thriving on the decaying leaves of mangroves become food for animals such as shrimp, crabs, snails and worms. Rich in marine life these shallow waters attract thousands of small fish which are preyed upon by the numerous wading birds of the refuge.

The distinctive roots of the mangrove tree serve as nursery areas for many fish species such as mullet, snook, and snapper, and provide shelter for numerous marine organisms. The roots also serve to stabilize sediments and to provide coastal protection against erosion and storm damage.

The refuge's slightly higher ground consists of sand-and-shell ridges, on which grow such species as cabbage palmetto (*Sabal palmetto*), saw palmetto (*Serenoa repens*), sea grape, wild coffee, and Jamaica caper. Hardwood hammocks include gumbo limbo, strangler fig, and mastic.

J. N. "Ding" Darling Refuge, which extends along the inland, Pine Island Sound side of Sanibel Island and parts of Buck Key adjacent to Captiva Island attract large numbers of such birds as the roseate spoonbill, anhinga, brown pelican, white ibis, wood stork, great and snowy egrets, little blue and tricolored herons, mottled duck, osprey, and bald eagle. The largest of the refuge's reptiles is the abundant American alligator, the federally listed endangered American crocodile, and several species of endangered sea turtles that haul themselves onto island beaches to deposit their eggs.

The refuge was initially known as the Sanibel National Wildlife Refuge but was renamed in 1967 to honor the nationally syndicated, twice Pulitzer Prize-winning editorial cartoonist and pioneer wildlife conservationist, Jay Norwood "Ding" Darling (1876–1962).

As described by the Fish and Wildlife Service:

An avid hunter and fisherman, Mr. Darling became alarmed at the loss of wildlife habitat and the possible extinction of many species. Concerned about wildlife conservation, he worked this theme into his cartoons.

In July 1934, President Franklin D. Roosevelt appointed "Ding" Darling as the Director of the U.S. Biological Survey, the forerunner of the U.S. Fish and Wildlife Service. While Director, Darling initiated the Federal Duck Stamp Program, designed the first duck stamp, and vastly increased the acreage of the National Wildlife Refuge System. . . .

Darling also designed the Blue Goose logo, the national symbol of the refuge system.

Habitat management activities on the J. N. "Ding" Darling Refuge include periodic, low-intensity, prescribed burning to reduce fuel overloads and dense undergrowth that can cause destructive wildfires, cycle nutrients and maintain a diversity of important plant communities for the benefit of wildlife, control invasive nonnative species of plants, and approximate ecologically natural fire cycles. Hundreds of acres of the refuge are also chemically treated to control such invasive non-native plants as the Brazilian pepper and Australian pine, species that rapidly impair the quality of natural wildlife habitat.

As with all refuges, parks, and other conservation lands, J. N. "Ding" Darling National Wildlife Refuge does not exist in a vacuum but is vulnerable to environmental impacts beyond its borders. According to the Fish and Wildlife Service:

The health of . . . the Refuge and its estuarine environment is dependent on the health of the Everglades watershed, which encompasses the Kissimmee River, Lake Okeechobee, and the Caloosahatchee River. Artificially regulated freshwater releases from the Caloosahatchee directly affect the refuge and its water quality. Too much freshwater (or too little), at the wrong time, can disrupt the fragile estuarine ecosystem and its dependent wildlife.

The refuge is open daily, except Fridays, during daylight hours. There is an entrance fee to the Wildlife Drive. The Center for Education is open daily. This visitor center was constructed entirely with private donations raised by the nonprofit organization "Ding" Darling Wildlife Society, which assists the refuge in many ways.

Visitor activities include birdwatching; photography; interpretive and environmental education programs at the visitor center; driving and bicycling the 4-mile Wildlife Drive auto tour route (an interpretive leaflet is available); viewing wildlife from an observation tower; seeing alligators from several (wheelchair-accessible) observation platforms; hiking; joining guided walks and tours by refuge rangers and trained volunteer interpreters (reservations are requested for some outings: [941] 472-1100, ext. 222); canoeing and kayaking (two launch sites are provided along Wildlife Drive); boating (one launch site is provided); fishing; and crabbing (blue crabs). All refuge waters, including Tarpon Bay, are zoned slow speed/minimum wake; and the Fish and Wildlife Service urges extreme caution, to avoid disturbing or harming manatees.

Even though alligators and crocodiles are usually afraid of people, visitors are cautioned to stay a safe distance from these sluggish-looking but potentially fast-moving reptiles and to be alert for venomous snakes. Insect repellent and sunscreen are advised.

Although camping is not permitted on the refuge, campground facilities are provided on Sanibel, at Fort Myers Beach, and elsewhere in the Fort Myers vicinity. Swimming is not permitted on the refuge, but there are ample opportunities on the outer beaches of Sanibel and Captiva islands, where shelling has also long been popular.

Hiking opportunities include the 2-mile Indigo Trail that begins at the visitor center, the 0.25-mile (partially wheelchair-accessible) Cross Dike Trail; and the 0.3-mile, interpretive (wheelchair-accessible) Shell Mound Trail. The refuge's separate Bailey Tract also provides 1.75 miles of levee trails. Over 240 bird species have been seen on the refuge.

The refuge offers two canoe routes through red mangrove habitat: the 2-mile Commodore Creek Canoe Trail in the vicinity of Tarpon Bay, and the 4 miles of canoe trails on Buck Key, adjacent to Captiva Island. Canoe rentals are available near the refuge.

Tram tours of Wildlife Drive, tours of Commodore Creek Canoe Trail, and other interpretive tours and programs are offered by Tarpon Bay Recreation, Inc., 900 Tarpon Bay Road. Information and reservations: (941) 472-8900.

The Sanibel-Captiva Conservation Foundation's Nature Center and Native Plant Nursery are located just outside the refuge, at 3333 Sanibel-Captiva Road (mile marker 1). The Nature Center, which offers interpretive exhibits and programs, is open on weekdays, and the Native Plant Nursery is open on weekdays and Saturdays. Information: (941) 472-2329.

The Sanibel-Captiva Audubon Society, a chapter of the National Audubon Society, offers weekly evening educational programs at the Sanibel Community Center on Periwinkle Way, sponsors bird identification and wildlife photography classes, and conducts bird outings. Information: (941) 472-3156.

The Bailey-Matthews Shell Museum, on Sanibel-Captiva Road a mile west of Tarpon Bay Road, presents exhibits in its Great Hall of Shells and contains a library, auditorium, and museum store. The museum is open on Tuesdays through Sundays. Information: (941) 395-2233.

Lodgings and meals are available in Sanibel, Captiva, Fort Myers Beach, and Fort Myers.

Access to the J. N. "Ding" Darling Refuge from U.S. Route 41 in Fort Myers is southwest 17 miles on State Route 867 (MacGregor Boulevard, Sanibel Causeway [toll], and Periwinkle Way) to the city of Sanibel; right on Palm Ridge Road, which becomes Sanibel-Captiva Road; and just over 2 miles to the refuge entrance on the right.

Further information: J. N. "Ding" Darling National Wildlife Refuge, 1 Wildlife Drive, Sanibel, FL 33957; telephone: (941) 472-1100.

Key West, comprising 2,019 acres of land and 206,289 acres of water, was established in 1908 by President Theodore Roosevelt to protect egrets and herons from plume hunters. The refuge encompasses a cluster of small mangrove keys to the west of Key West, Florida.

The refuge's islands consist mostly of mangrove wetlands, with small areas of wooded hammocks of slightly higher terrain, salt ponds, and beaches where the threatened loggerhead and endangered green sea turtles come ashore to deposit their eggs in summer. The refuge provides important resting, feeding, and, to some extent, nesting habitat for more than 250 species of birds. Prominent among them are numerous wading birds, as well as the magnificent frigatebird, brown pelican, ducks, shorebirds, gulls, terns, osprey, bald eagle, white-crowned pigeon, and many species of neotropical migratory songbirds.

As described by the U.S. Fish and Wildlife Service, fortune hunters formerly came to the Florida Keys:

. . . in search of the wealth that could be obtained from the plumage that the snowy egret, great white heron [the white phase of the great blue heron] and other wading birds produced.

The feathers of these birds identified the socially prominent and fashionably conscious members of society during the late 1800's. During this time it was perfectly acceptable to walk around with hats as large as umbrellas adorned with stuffed bird wings and large plumes hanging haphazardly off the edges. Bird populations were severely suffering from over harvesting for their plumage and meat. To counteract this destructive trend, plume-hunting became an outlawed activity in 1891. But, to place the plume industry and continued blatant poaching in perspective, imagine a London auction in 1902 that sold 48,240 ounces of plumes at $32.00 an ounce, for a grand total of $1,543,680.

Sponging and turtling were also major industries at this time. Sponging ranked second only to cigar making as a top dollar career and led to the over exploitation and disease of the sponges. Turtling devastated adult sea turtle populations in the Keys because they were a main staple food. Turtle rookeries were further impacted by egg harvesting because eggs were a delicacy.

Marine turtles became protected with the Endangered Species Act in 1973. However, even today turtle populations have not recovered because of entanglement in nets and traps, collisions with powerboats, disease and loss of nesting habitat.

The Friends and Volunteers of Refuges (FAVOR) is a nonprofit organization that is helping support the educational and other programs of the national wildlife refuges in the Florida keys.

Parts of the Key West Refuge are open to visitation during daylight hours. Areas open to visitor use are the beach on the northwestern half of Boca Grande Key, the western half of the beach on Woman Key, and most beaches on the Marquesas Keys. There is no entrance fee. The refuge headquarters, on Big Pine Key, is open on weekdays, except national holidays.

Visitor activities include birdwatching, photography, boating, sailing, snorkeling, and fishing. Commercial guided tours and boat rentals are available. Camping is not permitted on the refuge islands. Motorized personal watercraft, water skiing, hovercraft, airboats, and seaplane landings are not permitted within the refuge, to avoid disturbing the wildlife. Part of the refuge has been designated as a unit of the National Wilderness Preservation System.

Insect repellent and sunscreen are advised.

The more than 250 species of birds of Key West Refuge are essentially the same as those recorded on the National Key Deer Refuge.

Lodgings and meals are available in such communities as Key West, Summerland Key, Little Torch Key, and Marathon.

Access to Key West Refuge is by boat from Key West, at the end of U.S. Route I (Overseas Highway).

Further information: Key West National Wildlife Refuge, P.O. Box 430510, Big Pine Key, FL 33043; telephone: (305) 872-0774.

Lake Wales Ridge is the first national wildlife refuge designated primarily to preserve flora. It is located in central (interior) Florida. When completed, it will protect 31 rare plants (19 listed and 13 candidate species), as well as four federally listed vertebrates and more than 40 rare, endemic invertebrate species. The refuge was authorized in 1993, and acquisition of the proposed 19,630-acre refuge began in 1994. As of late 2001, the U.S. Fish and Wildlife Service had purchased more than 1,840 acres.

The Lake Wales Ridge is an ancient beach and sand dune system that is 100 miles long and ranges from 4 to 10 miles wide. It was formed roughly 25 million years ago, when sea levels were much higher than they are now. Atop these ancient islands evolved species unique to this isolated habitat. Today, the Atlantic Ocean is 60 miles east of the Lake Wales Ridge, but many unique plant forms still persist. This habitat, the oldest in the southeast, has been disappearing faster than any other in the United States. It is estimated that about 80,000 acres of the Lake Wales Ridge scrub existed before the arrival of European settlers. About 85 percent of this habitat has subsequently been converted to citrus growth and to residential, and commercial development. Many of the endemic plants, found nowhere else on Earth, face extinction.

Among Lake Wales Ridge Refuge's rare and endangered species are the scrub plum, pygmy fringe tree, short-leaved rosemary, scrub blazing star, scrub lupine, and Florida ziziphus. Of the numerous species of birds, there are the Florida scrub-jay and crested caracara. Reptiles include the indigo snake, scrub lizard, blue-tailed mole skink, and sand skink.

The proposal to protect the Lake Wales Ridge scrub is a joint venture between the State of Florida's Conservation and Recreation Lands (CARL) Program, The Nature Conservancy, Southwest and South Florida Water Management Districts, Polk County, and Archbold Biological Station. The collaborative land acquisition strategy worked out among the partners calls for the U.S. Fish and Wildlife Service to acquire all or part of five parcels totaling about 3,108 acres. Acquisition of the remaining 16,522 acres of the refuge is to be accomplished by one of the other partners.

Although the refuge's four widely separated units are not open to visitation, for those persons wishing to see scrub habitat, the Fish and Wildlife Service recommends contacting The Nature Conservancy to visit the Tiger Creek Preserve, telephone: (863) 635-7506; or Lake Wales Ridge State Forest, telephone: (941) 648-3163.

Further information: Lake Wales Ridge National Wildlife Refuge, c/o Merritt Island NWR, P.O. Box 6504, Titusville, FL 32782; telephone: (321) 861-0667.

Lake Woodruff, consisting of approximately 21,750 acres, was established in 1964. The refuge protects the 2,200-acre, spring-fed Lake Woodruff and surrounding habitats of cordgrass and sawgrass marsh, hardwood swamp, a stretch of the upper St. John's River, and uplands of largely pine flatwoods. It is located adjacent to the Ocala National Forest near the town of DeLeon Springs in northeastern Florida.

This ecologically rich area provides a mecca for wildlife. Among them are several species of herons and egrets, white and glossy ibises, wood stork, limpkin (more numerous here than on any other national wildlife refuge), nesting wood ducks, wintering waterfowl, lots of nesting ospreys, and numerous neotropical songbirds that pass through the refuge in early spring and late autumn migrations. Over 240 bird species have been seen here.

In 1998, the U.S. Fish and Wildlife Service discovered that Lake Woodruff Refuge contains the second largest premigratory roosting colony of swallow-tailed kites in the United States, with about 500 individuals during recent years out of an estimated total population of between 3,000 and 5,000 birds. The endangered Everglades snail kite has also been recorded here in recent years, near the northern end of its range (see the discussion of this species in the A.R.M. Loxahatchee Refuge text).

During most of the year, the endangered West Indian manatee (see the description in the Crystal River Refuge text) inhabits many of the refuge's 50 miles of waterways, nearly half of which are designated as manatee protection zones. There are also numerous alligators.

Lake Woodruff is named for Joseph Woodruff, who acquired Ponce DeLeon Springs in 1823 to provide power to operate sugar and grist mills.

The refuge is open daily during daylight hours. There is no entrance fee. The refuge office/contact station is open on weekdays, except national holidays.

Visitor activities include birdwatching, photography, viewing the refuge and wildlife from an award-winning observation tower that was designed and built by the West Volusia Audubon Society, hiking, bicycling on refuge roads and trails, canoeing and boating (rentals and launching sites are provided in DeLeon Springs and Hontoon Island state parks), fishing, and hunting (deer and feral hog) on part of the refuge during the designated season. Camping is not permitted on the refuge, but campground facilities are available at Ocala National Forest and Blue Springs State Park.

The refuge's public use area is situated at the end of Mud Lake Road, about a mile west of the refuge headquarters. The dikes bordering three wetland impoundments offer up to 6 miles of hiking opportunities. In addition, two self-guiding, interpretive trails meander through wooded habitat.

Even though alligators are usually afraid of people, visitors are cautioned to stay a safe distance from these sluggish-looking but potentially fast-moving reptiles and be alert for ticks and venomous snakes. Insect repellent and sunscreen are advised.

Lodgings and meals are available in such communities as DeLeon Springs, DeLand, Lake Helen, and Orange City.

Access to Lake Woodruff Refuge's contact station from Exit 88 on I-95 is west 25 miles on State Route 40, south (left) on U.S. Route 17 about 6 miles to DeLeon Springs, right on Retta Street for 1 block, left for about 0.5 mile on Grand Avenue, and right for about 0.10 mile on Mud Lake Road.

Further information: Lake Woodruff National Wildlife Refuge, 2045 Mud Lake Road, DeLeon Springs, FL 32130; telephone: (386) 985-4673.

Lower Suwannee, containing 52,935 acres and working toward a goal of nearly 63,000 acres, was established in 1979 to enhance and protect an ecologically rich diversity of wildlife habitats in one of the most extensive undeveloped estuarine river deltas in the United States. The 2-unit refuge is located along the lower 20 miles of this river, made famous by Stephen Foster's song, "The Old Folks at Home," and stretches along 26 miles of the Gulf Coast of Florida.

The wetlands of the river's floodplain consist of bald cypress swamps, tidally flooded bottomland hardwood forests, and freshwater marshes. Some of the river's tributaries are freshwater creeks, and others are tidal saltwater streams. The refuge's uplands support areas of scrub oak habitat and pine plantations. Along the coast, extensive salt marshes, numerous tidal creeks, and scattered islands comprise a magnificent, pristine coastal ecosystem.

As the U.S. Fish and Wildlife Service explains:

A constant influx of nutrients from the river system coupled with numerous offshore islands and tidal creeks create excellent wildlife habitat. Marine mammals such as bottlenose dolphin and the endangered West Indian Manatee, along with several species of marine turtles, utilize the coastal waters of the Suwannee Sound. Natural salt marshes and tidal flats attract thousands of shorebirds and diving ducks while acting as a valuable nursery area for fish, shrimp and shellfish. . . .

Floodplain wetlands . . . support nesting wood ducks, black bear, otter, alligator, wading birds, raccoons and . . . wintering waterfowl. Mixed hardwood-pine forests and uplands offer cover to turkey and white-tailed deer.

The refuge's habitat management activities include seasonally managed wetlands that provide supplemental habitat for egrets, herons, ibises, wood storks, and other water birds. Nesting boxes are provided for wood ducks, and nesting platforms offer extra sites for ospreys.

Forest habitats are being enhanced and maintained by the restoring of woodland communities that were previously altered by commercial timber harvesting; by selective thinning; and with periodic, low-intensity prescribed burning. These low-burning, relatively 'cool' fires promote nutrient cycling, trigger the growth of understory vegetation that is of value to wildlife, create or maintain habitat diversity, and reduce fuel overloads of organic debris that pose the risk of high-intensity wildfires.

The refuge is open daily during daylight hours. There is no entrance fee. Refuge headquarters is open on weekdays, except national holidays.

Visitor activities include birdwatching, photography, driving 50 miles of designated road (including the Wildlife Drive and Dixie Mainline Trail), hiking on trails and roads, bicycling on refuge roads, canoeing (canoe rentals available in the town of Suwannee), boating (boat-launching ramps onto the Suwannee River are provided at Fowler's Bluff and in the town of Suwannee), fishing (piers/observation decks at Salt Creek and Shell Mound are wheelchair-accessible), and hunting (deer, feral hog, raccoon, squirrel, turkey, and waterfowl) on parts of the refuge during the designated seasons. Camping is not permitted on the refuge, but county campground facilities (and boat-launching sites) are available at the end of Dixie County Road 357 and adjacent to the refuge's SHELL MOUND UNIT, at the end of Levy County Road 326.

One of the refuge's popular drives and bicycle rides is the Dixie Mainline Trail. This self-guiding route, for which there is an interpretive brochure, runs between County Roads 349 and 357 (may be closed during wet periods). According to the Fish and Wildlife Service, "The Dixie Mainline was constructed in the 1920's as a tram road (narrow gauge railroad) to transport timber out of the swamps and forests. After logging ended around 1940, the road was not maintained until the 1960's, when another timber company refurbished the road and wooden bridges. These bridges later deteriorated and the road again became impassable. The U.S. Fish and Wildlife Service purchased the land in 1979. . . . In 1998 the bridges were replaced and the road was opened to the public."

The Dixie Mainline route provides excellent opportunities to see a diversity of habitats. There are upland plantations of slash pine, which were planted by a timber company prior to the refuge's establishment and are now being managed to restore them to more natural forest conditions. There is a variety of wetlands: bald cypress swamp, bottomland hardwood forest, and marsh, with numerous winding freshwater and brackish creeks. And there are hammocks— island-like areas of slightly higher, drier ground than surrounding wetlands, on which grow such trees as Spanish moss-festooned live oaks, cabbage palmettos (*Sabal palmetto*), sweetgums, pines, and bay trees.

Hiking and bicycling opportunities include the refuge's 40 miles of improved roads and 50 miles of unimproved roads. There are also several hiking trails. Near the refuge headquarters is the 0.5-mile (wheelchair-accessible) River Trail, which includes a 400-foot-long boardwalk and observation platform offering a view of the Suwannee River. On the refuge's Shell Mound Unit are two trails: the 0.3-mile Shell Mound Trail, an interpretive loop that offers views of the coastal estuary and Gulf of Mexico and leads to one of Florida's largest mounds (middens) of oyster shells, which were piled up by Timucuan Indians more than 1,000 years ago; and the 1-mile Dennis Creek Trail, which loops through a wooded area of pines and cabbage palms and across mudflats on a boardwalk. To the west of the Suwannee River, near the end of Dixie County Road 349, is the 0.1-mile (wheelchair-accessible) Salt Creek Observation Trail and boardwalk.

One of the most exciting ways to explore Lower Suwannee Refuge is by canoe or kayak. A popular route near the town of Suwannee consists of several interconnecting loops, ranging in length from 1.5 to 4 miles. As described by the Fish and Wildlife Service's Lower Suwannee National Wildlife Refuge Canoe/Kayak Trail brochure:

Even though alligators are usually afraid of people, visitors are cautioned to stay a safe distance from these sluggish-looking but potentially fast-moving reptiles and be alert for venomous snakes and for ticks. Insect repellent and sunscreen are advised.

Lodgings and meals are available in such communities as Cross City, Old Town, Chiefland, and Cedar Key.

Access to the Lower Suwannee Refuge headquarters from U.S. Route 19/98 at Chiefland is west and then south 6 miles on County Road 345, west (right) 12 miles on County Road 347, and west (right) into the refuge. The Shell Mound Unit is reached by continuing south on County Road 347 and west (right) on County Road 326. To the west of the Suwannee River, there are two other access routes: from U.S. Route 19/98 at Old Town, it is south 23 miles to the town of Suwannee on County Road 349 (the refuge borders much of this route to the east); and from U.S. Route 19/98 at Cross City, it is south about 17 miles to the refuge on County Road 357.

Further information: Lower Suwannee National Wildlife Refuge, 16450 Northwest 31st Place, Chiefland, FL 32626; telephone: (352) 493-0238.

Matlacha Pass contains 825 acres on 23 islands, located in Matlacha Pass estuary and San Carlos Bay near Fort Myers on the southwestern Gulf Coast of Florida. The refuge was established in 1908 by President Theodore Roosevelt. It protects important nesting and roosting habitat for large concentrations of such birds as the brown pelican, anhinga, double-crested cormorant, herons (great blue, little blue, tricolored, and green), egrets (great, reddish, snowy, and cattle), wood stork, white ibis, and magnificent frigatebird.

Access to the refuge is only by boat. The U.S. Fish and Wildlife Service urges boaters to consult navigational charts and tide schedules before attempting to visit any of the refuge islands. Numerous oyster bars and shallow back bay/estuary waters are difficult to navigate, and damage to fragile seagrass beds is common due to boaters running aground. Boaters are discouraged from approaching the refuge islands during the nesting season. There is no entrance fee. Visitor activities include birdwatching and photography. Insect repellent and sunscreen are advised.

Further information: Matlacha National Wildlife Refuge, c/o J. N. "Ding" Darling NWR, I Wildlife Drive, Sanibel, FL 33957; telephone (941) 472-1100.

Merritt Island, consisting of 140,000 acres, overlays NASA's John F. Kennedy Space Center at Cape Canaveral on the central Atlantic Coast of Florida. The refuge was established in 1963 to protect the diverse habitats of this barrier island, including extensive saltwater estuaries, brackish marshes, freshwater impoundments, coastal sand dunes, scrub oaks, cabbage palmetto-and-oak hammocks, and pine forests and flatwoods. The refuge lies between the Kennedy Space Center to the south and the National Park Service-administered Canaveral National Seashore to the north.

Merritt Island Refuge provides important habitat for numerous federally and state-listed endangered and threatened species. Among these are an aquatic mammal, the West Indian manatee (see the discussion in the Crystal River text); reptiles, including sea turtles (loggerhead, green, and leatherback), gopher tortoise, eastern indigo and Atlantic salt marsh snakes, and an estimated 5,000 alligators; and such birds as the wood stork, roseate and least terns, piping plover, southern bald eagle, and Florida scrub-jay.

Of the more than 330 species of birds that have been recorded here, more than 23 are migratory waterfowl that winter by the thousands on the refuge's areas of open water. Resident water birds include herons, egrets, double-crested cormorants, brown and white pelicans, rails, and shorebirds.

To enhance the wetland habitat, a program of marsh restoration was begun in 1993 that has reconnected many of the refuge's impoundments with either the Indian or Banana river. Ducks Unlimited, Inc. has assisted by enhancing approximately 5,000 acres of the refuge's wetlands.

The palm-and-oak hammocks are especially fascinating areas, supporting a mixture of tropical, subtropical, and temperate trees and other plants, including epiphytes (airplants). Numerous species of neotropical songbirds pass through the wooded hammocks and pine forest during their spring and autumn migrations.

The refuge's habitat management activities include the seasonal manipulation of water levels within 76 impoundments for the benefit of migratory waterfowl, wading birds, shorebirds, and other wildlife. Low-intensity prescribed burning is periodically implemented to enhance and maintain vegetative communities that are dependent upon or positively influenced by fire, for the benefit of wildlife; to promote nutrient cycling; and to reduce an unnatural buildup of fuels that can otherwise create hazardous, high-intensity wildfire. Pine woodlands are thinned to enhance nesting habitat for bald eagles. Aggressive, invasive, nonnative plant species such as the Brazilian pepper and Australian pine (*Casuarina equisetifolia*), which displace native species and impair the natural ecosystem, are controlled by mechanical and chemical means.

The Merritt Island Wildlife Association is a nonprofit support group that is assisting the refuge in various ways.

The refuge is open daily during daylight hours. From time to time, part or all of the refuge is temporarily closed during NASA's space launches or for other national security reasons. There is no entrance fee. The visitor center is open daily, except on national holidays, and on Sundays from April through October.

Visitor activities include birdwatching; photography; driving the 7-mile, self-guiding Black Point Wildlife Drive (an interpretive leaflet is available); hiking; canoeing on the estuaries and lagoon; boating (boat-launching ramps are provided; speed limits are posted in some areas to protect manatees); fishing; and hunting (ducks and coot) on parts of the refuge during the designated season. Although camping is not permitted on the refuge, campground facilities are provided at such places as Titusville, Cape Canaveral, Cocoa Beach, New Smyrna Beach, various county parks, and (on a first-come, first-served basis) Canaveral National Seashore.

Hiking opportunities include the 0.25-mile (wheelchair-accessible) boardwalk adjacent to the visitor center; the 0.5-mile interpretive Oak Hammock Trail that winds through an area of subtropical woodland; the 2-mile Palm Hammock Trail that leads through hardwood forest, cabbage-palmetto hammocks, and marsh; the 0.5-mile Scrub Ridge Trail; and the 5-mile Cruickshank Trail (beginning at stop #8 on Black Point Wildlife Drive) that loops around a shallow wetland and includes an observation tower.

Even though alligators are usually afraid of people, visitors are cautioned to stay a safe distance from these sluggish-looking but potentially fast-moving reptiles and to be alert for venomous snakes and for ticks. Insect repellent and sunscreen are advised. The best seasons for visiting Merritt Island Refuge are spring, autumn, and winter.

Lodgings and meals are available in such communities as Titusville, Cape Canaveral, Merritt Island, Cocoa Beach, Melbourne, New Smyrna Beach, and Orlando.

Access to Merritt Island Refuge from Exit 80 on I-95 is east 2 miles on State Route 406 to Titusville, continuing east 5 miles across the Intracoastal Waterway, and right onto State Route 402 to the visitor center.

Further information: Merritt Island National Wildlife Refuge, P.O. Box 6504, Titusville, FL 32782; telephone: (321) 861-0667.

National Key Deer Refuge, containing 8,381 acres, was established in 1957 to protect the critically endangered Key deer (*Odocoileus virginianus clavium*), the smallest of all the subspecies of white-tailed deer, which lives in the Lower Keys northeast of Key West, Florida. The refuge consists of scattered tracts of land on both islands, with about three-quarters of the deer population inhabiting Big Pine Key and No Name Key. At shoulder height, adult bucks measure only 24 to 32 inches tall and average 85 pounds.

As a direct result of the destruction of the natural habitat and unregulated hunting, the numbers of Key deer sharply declined for many years and were estimated at fewer than 50 individuals in the 1940s. After the refuge was established and a law enforcement program was implemented, their numbers gradually increased and now appear to have stabilized between 700 and 800 animals.

It is believed that these deer originally migrated from the mainland thousands of years ago, following a land bridge that existed when the sea level was lower during the most recent period of continental glaciation. Over the subsequent centuries, these deer, living on what became a series of small islands, gradually evolved into a diminutive form of the mainland deer.

Habitats of the National Key Deer Refuge include pine rocklands; freshwater and brackish wetlands; hardwood hammock; and dense areas of red, black, and white mangroves. Among the numerous species of birds that breed and forage on the refuge are the white-crowned pigeon, mangrove cuckoo, and black-whiskered vireo. More than 280 species of birds have been recorded here.

The Friends and Volunteers of the Refuges (FAVOR) is a nonprofit organization that is helping to support the educational and other programs of the national wildlife refuges in the Florida keys.

The refuge is open daily during daylight hours. There is no entrance fee. The refuge headquarters is open on weekdays, except national holidays.

Visitor activities include wildlife observation, photography, driving roads within and adjacent to the refuge, and hiking. Visitors are urged to drive cautiously to avoid hitting a deer. Camping is not permitted on the refuge.

Hiking opportunities consist of three short trails: the (wheelchair-accessible) Blue Hole Trail, leading to an old quarry that contains fresh water inhabited by alligators; the one-eighth-mile, self-guiding, interpretive (wheelchair-accessible) Mannillo Trail; and the 0.7-mile, self-guiding, interpretive Watson Trail that loops through pine rockland habitat of slash pines and thatch palms.

Even though alligators are usually afraid of people, visitors are cautioned to stay a safe distance from these sluggish-looking but potentially fast-moving reptiles and to be alert for venomous snakes. Insect repellent and sunscreen are advised.

Lodgings and meals are available in such communities as Key West, Summerland Key, Little Torch Key, and Marathon.

Access to National Key Deer Refuge is southwest on U.S. Route 1 (Overseas Highway) from the mainland to Big Pine Key, and right at the traffic light onto Key Deer Boulevard for 0.25. The refuge visitor center is on the right, in the Big Pine Key Plaza (across from Winn Dixie).

Further information: National Key Deer Refuge, P.O. Box 430510, Big Pine Key, FL 33043; telephone: (305) 872-0774.

Okefenokee (see the text under Georgia).

Passage Key, containing a 30-acre coastal barrier island at the mouth of Tampa Bay, Florida, was established in 1905 by President Theodore Roosevelt as one of America's first national wildlife refuges. The island originally consisted of mangrove wetlands and a freshwater lake, but a powerful hurricane in 1920 destroyed this habitat. Passage Key is now a curving barrier island that supports one of Florida's largest nesting colonies of royal and sandwich terns. Other birds that nest, rest, and feed here include the brown pelican, black skimmer, American oystercatcher, and laughing gull. The refuge is designated as a unit of the National Wilderness Preservation System.

To avoid disturbing these birds, visitor entry onto the island is not permitted.

The Friends of Chassahowitzka National Wildlife Refuge Complex is a nonprofit support group that is assisting Passage Key Refuge in various ways.

Further information: Passage Key National Wildlife Refuge, c/o Chassahowitzka NWR, 1502 Southeast Kings Bay Drive, Crystal River, FL 34429; telephone: (352) 563-2088.

Pelican Island, located in the Indian River Lagoon stretch of the Intracoastal Waterway on the central Atlantic Coast of Florida, was established on March 14, 1903, as the first national wildlife refuge in the United States. Under the terms of an Executive Order issued by President Theodore Roosevelt, 5.5-acre Pelican Island was "reserved and set aside...as a preserve and breeding ground for native birds." In 1970, Pelican Island became the smallest unit of the National Wilderness Preservation System, and in 1993, the refuge was designated as a Wetland of International Importance.

As the U.S. Fish and Wildlife Service describes the island's landmark history:

Pelican Island has long been home to many kinds of birds. In 1859, Dr. Henry Bryant reported seeing thousands of herons, egrets, pelicans, ibises, and spoonbills, all nesting in harmony among the tree tops of black and red mangroves. However, plume hunters had already arrived to begin their relentless slaughter of countless egrets, herons, spoonbills, and even pelicans. The annihilation was so complete that by 1903 only brown pelicans were left. And Pelican Island was the last breeding ground for brown pelicans along the entire east coast of Florida.

The pelicans might not be here today . . . [had it not been] for a man by the name of Paul Kroegel. . . . a German immigrant who homesteaded in Sebastian with his father and brother. They settled at Barker's Bluff in Sebastian, partly because of the proximity to Pelican Island.

Paul Kroegel took a special interest in the pelicans as he watched them from his home. In 1883, he became Game Warden for the American Ornithologist's Union, began lobbying for the birds, and initiated a campaign to protect the birds from plume hunters at Pelican Island and invited influential visitors to go with him and witness the carnage. When well known naturalists . . . [such as] Dr. Frank Chapman arrived in the area . . . Kroegel enlisted their support.

In 1900, a federal law, the Lacey Act, was passed by Congress to make the interstate transport of birds illegal. It was at the urging of both the Florida Audubon Society and the American Ornithologist's Union, that President Theodore "Teddy" Roosevelt issued the Executive Order on March 14, 1903. . . . Two weeks later, on April 1, Kroegel was appointed warden by the federal government for a salary of $1 per month. The refuge was expanded by a second executive order to include several neighboring mangrove islands on January 26, 1909.

The threat from plume hunters diminished, but a new threat was looming. In the Spring of 1918, a group of young commercial fishermen set out for Pelican Island at night and killed hundreds of defenseless pelican chicks. They claimed that the pelicans were taking too many fish. This controversy was spreading until a Florida Audubon Society study showed that the bulk of the pelican's diet consisted of commercially unimportant baitfish.

In 1918, the Migratory Bird Treaty Act, passed by Congress, made hunting of nongame birds and taking of eggs illegal. The threat of a $500 fine or six months in prison halted plume hunting.

Paul Kroegel protected and managed Pelican Island NWR until 1926 after the island became flooded and the pelicans abandoned Pelican Island for several years. . . .

In 1963, an unnatural threat arose. The bottomlands surrounding Pelican Island were proposed to be sold by the State . . . [for] private development. The Indian River Preservation League was formed by local citrus growers, commercial fishermen, and sportsmen to fight this proposal which included the dredging of a bulkhead and filling of vitally important seagrass beds. The local citizens won their fight. The State leased the 616 acres of nearby mangrove islands to Pelican Island National Wildlife Refuge. The lease with the State was renewed in 1968 to encompass about 4,760 acres of submerged bottomlands and grass beds. Since 1979, the refuge has acquired over 100 acres of buffer along the shoreline of the adjacent barrier island. The buffer will help protect the integrity of the nation's first national wildlife refuge from encroaching residential development.

After years of decimation at the hands of plume hunters and the ravishing effects of DDT, the birds have begun to make a comeback. The diversity of bird species as seen in 1859 can be seen again. However, the total number of birds that once were counted in the thousands, are now counted in the hundreds. . . . the island has diminished in size due to erosion. . . . the once ground-nesting pelicans compete with other birds for the limited space in mangroves.

Looking to the future of Pelican Island Refuge, the Fish and Wildlife Service has nearly completed the acquisition of an eastern buffer area. This buffer "will not only provide an effective buffer from approaching development, but will also establish a connection with Archie Carr National Wildlife Refuge," a section of which is located along a portion of the outer shore of the barrier island.

Increasing human population growth and land development around Indian River Lagoon and increasing recreational watercraft traffic are posing challenges to the welfare of America's first national wildlife refuge. Since 1943, the island has diminished in size by more than 50 percent. In 2000, to curtail erosion, the Fish and Wildlife Service began a shoreline restoration project, which consisted of planting smooth cordgrass and red mangroves along the eroding northern and western edges of the island and installing a natural wave break of an oyster bar that reduces and deflects wave energy from the island, provides habitat for shorebirds, and reestablishes mangroves for nesting habitat.

On other parts of the refuge, a program of habitat restoration is underway to remove aggressive, invasive, non-native vegetation such as Australian pine (*Casuarina equisetifolia*), Brazilian pepper, citrus trees, and Johnson grass; and to reestablish ecologically important areas of mangrove forest, saltwater-wetland impoundments, freshwater marsh, palm prairie, and hydric and maritime island-like hammocks of slightly higher terrain.

Pelican Island Preservation Society is a nonprofit support group that is assisting the refuge in many ways.

Although there will be no facilities open until March 2003, the refuge is open daily during daylight hours. There is no entrance fee. Facilities will include various walking trails, a "Centennial

Trail" boardwalk, and an observation tower from which to view Pelican Island. A wildlife drive is planned for the future.

Insect repellent and sunscreen are advised.

Lodgings and meals are available in such communities as Sebastian, Vero Beach, and Melbourne.

Access to Pelican Island Refuge from Exit 69 on I-95 is east on State Route 512 to Sebastian; from Exit 69 on I-95 it is east on State Route 512 and Route 510, across Wabasso Island, north (left) 3.7 miles on State Route AIA, and left onto the Jungle Trail. Or, the refuge can be accessed by boat from boat-launching sites at Sebastian, at the east end of State Route 512, or on Wabasso Island (there are three commercial boat tour operators located in Sebastian).

Further information: Pelican Island National Wildlife Refuge, 1339 Twentieth Street, Vero Beach, FL 32960; telephone: (772) 562-3909.

Pine Island comprises 548 acres on 17 islands that are clustered in Pine Island Sound estuary near Fort Meyers on the southwestern Gulf Coast of Florida. The refuge was established in 1908 by President Theodore Roosevelt. It protects important nesting and roosting habitat for large concentrations of brown pelicans, as well as anhinga; double-crested cormorant; herons (great blue, little blue, tricolored, and green); egrets (great, reddish, snowy, and cattle); black-crowned and yellow-crowned night herons; wood stork; white ibis; and magnificent frigatebird.

The largest of these islands, from north to south, are Patricio Island, Black Key, Cove Key, Anhinga Island, and Big Panther Key. Dominant vegetation on the lower elevations consists of black and red mangroves (see a description of mangroves in the J. N. "Ding" Darling Refuge text).

Access to the refuge is only by boat. The U.S. Fish and Wildlife Service urges boaters to consult navigational charts and tide schedules before attempting to visit any of the refuge islands. Numerous oyster bars and shallow back bay/estuary waters are difficult to navigate, and damage to fragile seagrass beds is common due to boaters running aground. Boaters are discouraged from approaching the refuge islands during the nesting season. There is no entrance fee. Visitor activities include birdwatching and photography. Insect repellent and sunscreen are advised.

Further information: Pine Island National Wildlife Refuge, c/o J. N. "Ding" Darling NWR, I Wildlife Drive, Sanibel, FL 33957; telephone: (941) 472-1100.

Pinellas, consisting of several islands totaling 403 acres, is located near the mouth of Tampa Bay just offshore from St. Petersburg, Florida. The refuge was established in 1951 and protects important breeding and roosting habitat for such colonial nesting birds as the brown pelican; double-crested cormorant; great and snowy egrets; herons (great blue, little blue, and tricolored); black-crowned and yellow-crowned night herons; white ibis; and roseate spoonbill. Tarpon Key supports one of Florida's largest rookeries of brown pelicans. Vegetation consists mostly of red mangroves.

To avoid disturbing these nesting habitats, visitor entry onto the islands is not permitted.

The Friends of Chassahowitzka National Wildlife Refuge Complex is a nonprofit support group that is assisting Pinellas Refuge in various ways.

Further information: Pinellas National Wildlife Refuge, c/o Chassahowitzka NWR, 1502 Southeast Kings Bay Drive, Crystal River, FL 34429; telephone: (352) 563-2088.

St. Johns, containing 6,160 acres, was established in 1971 to protect habitat for the endangered dusky seaside sparrow (*Ammodramus maritimus nigrescens*). The dusky, a race of seaside sparrow, was discovered in 1872 in brackish and salt marshes around Titusville in central (interior) Florida.

The dusky seaside sparrow had an extremely limited range and very specialized habitat requirements. When humans began altering and draining this marsh habitat, the bird's population of around 6,000 individuals began to decline. Annual surveys were begun in the mid-1960s to identify population centers. Land acquisition for the refuge soon followed. However, in 1968, before the refuge was established, wildfires burned throughout much of the dusky's range, reducing the estimated population from 373 to 143. In 1975, wildfires once again burned, impacting about 75 percent of the bird's range and slashing its numbers to only a dozen individuals. The population never recovered, and there was no evidence of reproduction since then. From 1979 to 1980, all the remaining birds (six males) were captured and taken into captivity. In 1986, the last dusky seaside sparrow died in captivity at Discovery Island, in Lake Buena Vista, Florida. The species is now considered to be extinct.

Even though the dusky seaside sparrow is gone, the salt marsh and cordgrass habitat is being managed for many other species, such as herons, egrets, wood storks, ibises, bitterns, and rails. The refuge provides particularly good habitat for the black rail, and special "rail tours" are offered several times each year.

Although St. Johns Refuge is presently open to visitation only by special-use permit, the U.S. Fish and Wildlife Service is planning for expanded visitor use opportunities.

Further information: St. Johns National Wildlife Refuge, c/o Merritt Island NWR, P.O. Box 6504, Titusville, FL 32782; telephone: (321) 861-0667.

St. Marks, comprising more than 68,000 acres in three contiguous units, was established in 1931 with acquisition of the St. Marks Unit. The Wakulla and Panacea units were added in the late 1930s. This ecologically spectacular refuge is located along the shores of Apalachee Bay in the Big Bend region of Florida's Gulf Coast.

The refuge manages and protects a wide diversity of habitats that attract tens of thousands of wintering waterfowl as well as such other birds as anhingas, brown pelicans, egrets, herons, ibises, and swallow-tailed and Mississippi kites; nesting bald eagles, ospreys, wood ducks, bluebirds, and red-cockaded woodpeckers; and numerous migrating shorebirds and neotropical songbirds. Over 300 bird species have been recorded here.

Major habitats include extensive needlerush salt marshes; freshwater marshes; meandering rivers, streams, and tidal creeks; swamps containing bald cypresses, gums, oaks, willows, and other water-tolerant trees; bogs; hardwood hammocks; picturesque cabbage palm-and-pine hammocks; forests of longleaf pine, slash pine, and loblolly/mixed hardwoods; several freshwater lakes and ponds, notably cypress-framed Otter Lake; and nearly 2,000 acres of levee-contained pools.

A number of forest communities contribute to the refuge's rich habitat diversity. These are in three main categories: sandhills, flatwoods, and hammocks. On the refuge's WAKULLA AND PANACEA UNITS, there are dry sandhills dominated by such species as longleaf pine, turkey oak, bluejack oak, and some live oaks. On these two units, there are also extensive mesic flatwoods with longleaf pines and an understory of wiregrass, saw palmettos (*Serenoa repens*), and various shrubs; on the ST. MARKS UNIT, these flatwoods are dominated by slash pine. Both types of these pine flatwoods provide important habitat for the federally listed threatened Flatwoods salamander and the endangered red-cockaded woodpecker (see a description of the latter species in the Carolina Sandhills Refuge, South Carolina text). On the PANACEA UNIT, there are flatwoods, predominately containing pines and wiregrass; on the ST. MARKS UNIT, the flatwoods mostly contain slash pine, sedge, and some pond cypress.

On the St. Marks and Wakulla units, there are wet-soil (hydric) hammocks characterized by the picturesque cabbage palmetto (*Sabal palmetto*) and such species as loblolly or slash pines, the low-growing saw palmetto (*Serenoa repens*), yaupon holly, and sawgrass; or cabbage palmetto mixed with such species as diamond-leaf oak, red maple, sweetbay, swamp ash, blackberry, and sawgrass. There are also mesic hammocks, which the Fish and Wildlife Service explains "have developed in the absence of frequent fires." These hammocks contain such species as live oak, sweetgum, water and laurel oaks, redbay, wax myrtle, persimmon, pignut hickory, yaupon holly, and/or flowering dogwood, with an understory of saw palmetto and various shrubs.

The refuge's forest management activities include periodic, low-intensity prescribed burning of the pine woodlands to promote nutrient cycling, trigger the growth of new plants of value to wildlife, and reduce dangerous fuel overloads of accumulated dead leaves, needles, and branches that risk harmful, high-intensity wildfires. Other activities include selective thinning of pine woodlands to promote the growth of understory vegetation, and the restoration of the native longleaf pine forests. Much of this woodland management is carried out for the benefit of the federally listed red-cockaded woodpecker, which requires an open-grown forest with nesting cavities in older growth pines (see further description of this species in the Carolina Sandhills Refuge text).

The refuge's ecologically rich tidal salt marshes are invaluable as vital spawning and nursery habitat for many species of marine organisms. As the U.S. Fish and Wildlife Service explains, "The food and cover available in these wetlands are used by a variety of juvenile estuarine fish and shellfish, which, in turn, are found in other habitats as adults. For this reason, salt marshes are considered to be an important nursery ground for much of the Florida Gulf Coast's commercial seafood harvest." Salt marshes such as these also act as buffers that "can absorb most of the impact associated with storm surges" such as occur during hurricanes.

Among the Fish and Wildlife Service's other management activities on St. Marks Refuge are ongoing efforts to reduce the impacts of invasive, non-native plants, notably the Southeast Asian cogongrass (considered "one of the world's ten worst weeds"), which has spread throughout the refuge's system of dikes and, growing in dense clumps, crowds out all native plants; the Chinese tallow tree, which is quickly spreading into natural and disturbed habitats in the Southeastern United States; and the Japanese climbing fern, which can climb into a tree and ultimately smother it.

The most dramatic insect event in the refuge is the southward migration of great numbers of monarch butterflies, which climaxes during October. Other colorful butterflies of St. Marks Refuge include the tiger swallowtail, zebra, viceroy, queen, sulfurs, fritillaries, and the American painted beauty.

Establishment of the refuge was made possible partly with revenues from the sale of Migratory Bird Hunting and Conservation Stamps (Duck Stamps). In the 1930s, the Civilian Conservation Corps built levees and other structures for the benefit of wintering waterfowl. In 1975, approximately 17,546 acres of St. Marks Refuge were designated as a unit of the National Wilderness Preservation System. Ducks Unlimited, Inc. has helped enhance about 350 acres of the refuge's wetland habitat. The St. Marks Refuge Association is a local nonprofit support group that is assisting the refuge in many ways.

The refuge is open daily during daylight hours. An entrance fee is charged at the St. Marks Unit of the refuge. The visitor center is open daily, except on national holidays. A fee is charged for the use of the Aucilla Boat Ramp, at the eastern end of the refuge.

Visitor activities include birdwatching; photography; driving the 6.8-mile, self-guiding Lighthouse Road Wildlife Drive (an interpretive guide booklet is available); viewing the refuge from an observation deck that overlooks an expanse of salt marsh and a managed pool; hiking; bicycling; viewing interpretive exhibits and programs at the visitor center; environmental education programs for school and other groups; guided migratory bird tours; and viewing the historic St. Marks Lighthouse, which dates from 1831 (at the south end of Lighthouse Road).

Other activities include picnicking (picnic areas are provided next to the Mounds Trail and at Otter Lake Recreation Area); canoeing (rentals are available near the refuge); boating (not more than 10 HP motors on refuge pools from March 15 to October 15; four launching ramps onto Apalachee Bay are provided); fishing (on impoundments along Lighthouse Road and on Otter Lake, along State Route 372A in the refuge's Panacea Unit); crabbing; and hunting (deer, feral hogs, raccoon, squirrel, bearded turkey) on parts of the refuge during the designated seasons. A 2-day hunt is held for mobility-challenged visitors in early December.

Although camping is not permitted on the refuge, campground facilities are available at Newport Recreation Area, Ochlockonee River State Park, and in Apalachicola National Forest.

St. Marks Refuge offers numerous hiking opportunities, including the 0.3-mile (wheelchair-accessible) Plum Orchard Pond Trail near the visitor center; the 0.25-mile Headquarters Pond Trail; the 1-mile Mounds Interpretive Trail; the 0.25-mile Lighthouse Levee Trail; two primitive trails (7 and 13 miles) on the St. Marks Unit; two primitive trails (5 and 9 miles) on the Panacea Unit; and 43 miles of the Florida National Scenic Trail that run through the refuge. The most favorable seasons for hiking or biking on the refuge trails are late autumn through early spring.

From mid-November through January are the best months to see the large concentrations of wintering waterfowl. March and early April are the best times to see and hear large numbers of warblers and other neotropical migratory songbirds. One aspect of this huge influx is referred to as "fallout," a frenzied phenomenon that occasionally occurs in the spring when unfavorable headwinds from the north slow down and make even more difficult the birds' energy-depleting nonstop flight across the Gulf of Mexico. Coming from such launching places as Mexico's Yucatan Peninsula, the exhausted birds drop into coastal wooded areas from the Florida Panhandle to Texas (see the Aransas Refuge text for a further description of this migration event).

Even though alligators are usually afraid of people, visitors are cautioned to stay a safe distance from these sluggish-looking but potentially fast-moving reptiles and to be alert for venomous snakes and for ticks. Insect repellent and sunscreen are advised.

Lodgings and meals are available in St. Marks, Wakulla Springs, and Tallahassee.

Access to the St. Marks Refuge visitor center from U.S. Route 98 at Newport is south three miles on County Route 59.

Further information: St. Marks National Wildlife Refuge, P.O. Box 68, St. Marks, FL 32355; telephone: (850) 925-6121.

St. Vincent, containing 12,358 acres, was established in 1968 to protect an undeveloped coastal barrier island located at the western end of Apalachicola Bay on the central Gulf Coast of the Florida Panhandle.

Roughly triangular in shape, St. Vincent Island measures about 9 miles long and 4 miles wide and consists of ten types of habitat. Among this subtropical diversity are Spanish "moss"-festooned live oaks and/or scrub oaks that grow on a series of east-west trending dune ridges, slash pine woodlands, magnolia-and-cabbage palmetto hammocks, lakes and streams, sloughs and salt marshes, sand dunes, and broad, sandy beaches along the south and east shores.

In addition to attracting concentrations of waterfowl, St. Vincent Refuge is a haven for a number of endangered and threatened species of wildlife. These include loggerhead sea turtles, which come ashore to lay their eggs on the beaches.

In 1990, St. Vincent became one of several coastal islands in the southeastern United States on which the endangered red wolf (*Canis rufus*) was reintroduced and is being bred. This species, which has mostly brown and buff fur with some black color along the back, is between the size of the larger gray wolf and the smaller coyote. As the U.S. Fish and Wildlife Service explains:

The red wolf is one of the most endangered animals in the world. It is a shy species that once roamed throughout the Southeast as a top predator. Aggressive predator control programs and clearing of forested habitat combined to cause impacts that brought the red wolf to the brink of extinction. By 1970, the entire population of red wolves was believed to be less than 100 animals confined to a small area of coastal Texas and Louisiana.

To save the species from extinction, the Service captured as many as possible of the few remaining animals from 1974 through 1980. Only 14 captured animals met the criteria established to define the species and stood between existence and extinction. These animals formed the nucleus of a captive-breeding program established at the Point Defiance Zoo and Aquarium in Tacoma, Washington, with the final goal of reestablishing the species in portions of its original southeastern range. Thirty-three zoos and nature centers in 21 states and the District of Columbia now cooperate in a national breeding program and are valuable partners in efforts to restore red wolves.

The red wolf is now back in the wild, hunting, rearing young, and communicating by its characteristic howl, in several locations. . . . Since 1987, red wolves have been released into northeastern North Carolina and now roam over more than 560,000 acres that includes three national wildlife refuges. . . . Other red wolves have been released on coastal islands in Florida, Mississippi, and South Carolina as a steppingstone between captivity and the wild. Although these islands are not large enough to provide for the needs of more than a few red wolves at a time, they provide the opportunity for them to breed and exist in the wild in order to produce animals for future mainland reintroductions. . . .

By 2001, the total population of red wolves in the wild was estimated at approximately 100 individuals. Of this number, two were inhabiting St. Vincent Refuge. (For a further discussion of the red wolf recovery program and the Red Wolf Coalition, see the Pocosin Lakes Refuge text.)

Among the more prominent species of birds are nesting bald eagles and ospreys, wood storks, anhingas, great and snowy egrets, wood ducks (for which the refuge provides nesting boxes), swallow-tailed kites, wild turkeys, oystercatchers that feed along the beaches, and brown pelicans.

In 1968, St. Vincent Island was acquired by The Nature Conservancy. Shortly thereafter, the Fish and Wildlife Service purchased the island with revenues from the sale of Migratory Bird Hunting and Conservation Stamps (Duck Stamps). Ducks Unlimited, Inc. has helped enhance wetland habitat on more than 100 acres of the refuge.

The refuge is open daily during daylight hours. The refuge is reached by boat. There is no access fee. The refuge's visitor center and headquarters, located in the Harbor Master Building, Market Street, Apalachicola, are open on weekdays, except national holidays.

Visitor activities include birdwatching, photography, hiking on 80 miles of sand roadways and 14 miles of beaches, boating (a public boat-launching ramp is provided in Indian Pass, at the end of State Route C30B), fishing on refuge lakes (except when seasonally closed, to protect nesting bald eagles), and hunting (annual hunts for deer and feral hogs). Camping is not permitted on the refuge (except for primitive camping associated with designated annual hunts for deer and feral hogs), but campground facilities are provided at St. George Island State Park and other nearby places.

Late November through December are the best months to see the peak concentrations of wintering waterfowl. March and early April are the best times to see and hear large numbers of warblers and other neotropical migratory songbirds. One aspect of this impressive influx is referred to as "fallout," a frenzied phenomenon that occasionally occurs in the spring, when unfavorable headwinds from the north slow down and make even more challenging the birds' energy-depleting nonstop flight across the Gulf of Mexico. From such launching places as Mexico's Yucatan Peninsula, the exhausted birds drop into coastal wooded areas from the Florida Panhandle to Texas (see the Aransas text for a further description of this migration event).

Even though alligators are usually afraid of people, visitors are cautioned to stay a safe distance from these sluggish-looking but potentially fast-moving reptiles and to be alert for venomous snakes and for ticks. Insect repellent and sunscreen are advised. As there is no drinking water available on the island, visitors should bring an adequate supply.

Migrating and resident birds of St. Vincent Refuge are essentially the same as those on St. Marks Refuge.

Lodgings and meals are available in Apalachicola.

Access to the boat ramp at Indian Pass from Apalachicola is west about 7 miles on U.S. Route 98, left 10 miles on State Route 30, and left 3 miles to the end of State Route C30B.

Further information: St. Vincent National Wildlife Refuge, P.O. Box 447, Apalachicola, FL 32329; telephone: (850) 653-8808.

Ten Thousand Islands, containing about 35,000 acres, was established in 1996, with the transfer of private lands to the U.S. Fish and Wildlife Service, under authority of the Arizona-Florida Land Exchange Act of 1988. The refuge protects a large part of the vast Ten Thousand Islands estuary on the southwestern Gulf Coast of Florida. This ecologically rich area lies down the watershed from the Florida Panther National Wildlife Refuge and Big Cypress National Preserve, between Everglades National Park and Marco Island and about 20 miles southeast of Naples.

On the northern part of the refuge is an extensive freshwater marsh system, with scattered freshwater ponds and small island-like hammocks of slightly higher terrain. The hammocks support such species as live and laurel oaks, cabbage palmetto (*Sabal palmetto*), saw palmetto (*Serenoa repens*), and gumbo limbo. Along some areas where fresh water mixes with salt water, there are expanses of salt marsh. The southern part of the refuge encompasses an estuarine ecosystem of coastal lagoons, embayments, brackish streams, and a multitude of coastal saline islands. Dense stands of mangroves are the dominant vegetation of these islands and mainland tidal edges. The most coastal of the islands have sand or shell beaches, some of which contain ancient Indian shell middens that have raised the elevation of the islands by several feet (Dismal Key has an elevation of 13 feet). Here subtropical plant species of stopper, gumbo limbo, bay trees, cabbage palm, and sea grape thrive.

As the U.S. Fish and Wildlife Service explains in the refuge's November 2000 *Comprehensive Conservation Plan*:

The refuge . . . represents a nearly pristine mangrove estuary system. [It] . . . is part of the larger Ten Thousand Islands system, one of the largest mangrove-forested regions in the New World.

Several significant threatened and endangered species of wildlife inhabit the Ten Thousand Islands Refuge, including the loggerhead, green, and Kemp's ridley sea turtles; West Indian manatee; and wood stork. Regarding the latter, the Fish and Wildlife Service says, "West Indian manatees use refuge waters throughout the year. Collier County is the third highest area of watercraft-related manatee mortality in the state. With the predicted boat traffic increase in county waters, it will be important for the refuge to monitor the impacts of this traffic and enforce manatee protection areas." (See further description of manatees in the Crystal River Refuge text.)

As described by refuge manager, Jim Krakowski:

The Ten Thousand Islands refuge is truly a unique area with tremendous opportunities to observe a wide variety of wildlife. As one quietly paddles through the backcountry maze of mangrove islands, the peace and solitude are broken by surprising views of wildlife: manatees and dolphins surface near your boat to loudly suck air; giant sea turtles bob up for a look; a huge 100-pound tarpon may roll on the water surface showing a big eye and dorsal fin; spoonbills, storks, and ibis squawk and feed on an exposed oyster bar; and bald eagles, swallow-tailed kites, and ospreys soar overhead; while raccoons and river otters scour the shoreline.

The refuge is open daily, with visitation preferably only during daylight hours in the northern marshes. There is no entrance fee.

Visitor activities include birdwatching; photography; canoeing and kayaking float trips and motorized boating during the winter months; sport fishing, and duck hunting on part of the refuge during the designated season. Camping on the refuge is limited, for the most part, to the coastal beaches of Panther, Hog, and Round keys during the winter. This activity does not conflict with loggerhead and green sea turtles, as they deposit their eggs on beaches during the summer.

Even though alligators and crocodiles are usually afraid of people, visitors are urged to stay a safe distance from these sluggish-looking but potentially fast-moving reptiles and to be alert for venomous snakes. Insect repellent is advised.

Lodgings and meals are available in such communities as Naples and Everglades City.

Ten Thousand Islands Refuge lies just east of the Collier-Seminole State Park, extending south from the Tamiami Trail (U.S. Route 41). Although there is presently no access into the refuge's northern freshwater-marsh habitat from the Tamiami Trail, the Fish and Wildlife Service is evaluating proposals to establish a 1-mile, self-guiding, interpretive hiking trail and an observation tower along an abandoned oil pad road, and a canoe and nonmotorized boat loop trail that could be used during periods of high water.

Although motorboat access into the southern part of the refuge is presently largely unrestricted, the Fish and Wildlife Service and the Rookery Bay National Estuarine Research Reserve are planning "to assess the impacts of powered watercraft operating in shallow water environments within the Ten Thousand Islands region on wildlife and submerged land resources. . . . Potential parameters for impact assessment include wildlife/bird populations, seagrass, nonvegetated substrate, and user conflict. Results of this study will assist state and federal managers in determining future site management options."

Further information: Ten Thousand Islands National Wildlife Refuge, 3860 Tollgate Boulevard, Suite 300, Naples, FL 34114; telephone: (941) 353-8442.

Georgia

Banks Lake, containing 3,559 acres, was established in 1985 to manage Banks Lake and adjacent marsh habitat. The refuge is located near Lakeland in southeastern Georgia. The refuge attracts wading birds, wood ducks, sandhill cranes, and shorebirds. Banks Lake is a popular fishing area for largemouth bass and various other species of sunfish.

The refuge is open daily during daylight hours. There is no entrance fee.

Visitor activities include birdwatching, photography, hiking on trails, canoeing and kayaking, and fishing. A fishing pier and boat-launching ramps are provided.

Lodgings and meals are available in such communities as Lakeland and Valdosta.

Access to Banks Lake Refuge from Lakeland is west 2 miles on State Route 122.

Further information: Banks Lake National Wildlife Refuge, c/o Okefenokee NWR, Route 2, Box 3330, Folkston, GA 31537; telephone: (912) 496-7836.

Blackbeard Island, encompassing 5,618 acres, was established in 1940 to protect this barrier island's ecologically rich habitats of maritime forest, salt marsh, human-made freshwater pools, and sandy beach on the central coast of Georgia. In 1975, more than half of the refuge (the southwestern part) was designated as a unit of the National Wilderness Preservation System, and within the wilderness is a 450-acre research natural area, about one-quarter of which contains an area of virgin-growth slash pines.

Brown pelican, black skimmer, osprey, clapper rail, and many species of wading birds, wintering ducks, shorebirds, gulls, terns, painted bunting, and seaside sparrow are just a few of the more common birds that use Blackbeard Island. A large wading-bird rookery is located at Flag Pond. White-tailed deer and raccoons are abundant. In summer, loggerhead sea turtles haul themselves onto the 7-mile ocean beach to lay their eggs. Alligators are numerous.

The island is named for Edward Teach, known as Blackbeard the Pirate. According to legend, he sailed up and down the coast, plundering and murdering, and making occasional stops on this island to bury his stolen fortunes. Although rumors still abound as to the whereabouts of Blackbeard's buried treasure, nothing has ever been discovered.

Blackbeard Island has actually been in federal ownership since 1800, when the U.S. Navy Department acquired it at public auction as a source of live oak lumber for shipbuilding. A limited amount of timber harvesting occurred. From 1880 to 1910, the South Atlantic yellow fever quarantine station was located here. As the U.S. Fish and Wildlife Service explains, "In addition to housing for medical personnel, a wharf with disinfecting tanks, a hospital and associated buildings were constructed on the island. As crews disembarked from ships, those that were sick were hospitalized, while the healthy were housed separately and examined daily for yellow fever symptoms. Once disinfected, the ships were allowed to continue to their destination."

In 1924, Blackbeard Island was transferred to the Bureau of Biological Survey, to be managed as a breeding ground for migratory birds and other wildlife. Under the terms of a Presidential Proclamation signed in 1940 by President Franklin D. Roosevelt, the island became a national wildlife refuge.

As described by the Fish and Wildlife Service:

The island comprises interconnecting linear dunes thickly covered by oak/palmetto vegetation. Between these ridges are numerous ponds and savannas. The savannas, as a rule, are narrow, although some are over several hundred acres. Protected from tides by dikes and dunes, these savannas are filled by seasonal rains and are utilized by waterfowl and wading birds. . . .

Approximately one-half of the island's habitat types include open freshwater or freshwater marsh (1,163 acres) and regularly flooded salt marsh (2,000 acres). Waterfowl, wading birds (including the endangered wood stork), and American alligator are common in and around these areas. Island habitat types also include approximately 340 acres of sand beach. These areas provide nesting or feeding areas for the threatened loggerhead sea turtle, endangered piping plover and numerous [other] species of shorebirds, gulls, and terns. The remainder of the habitat . . . consists of noncommercial forest (2,115 acres). The island's forests range from maritime live oak forest on the north end, mixed live oak/pine forests in the middle of the island, to predominantly slash pine on the south end. These forests are used by numerous species of resident and migrant songbirds, hawks, and owls.

The refuge is open daily. There is no entrance fee. A visitor information kiosk is located near Blackbeard Creek.

Visitor activities include birdwatching, photography, hiking and bicycling on a network of trails, boating (a dock is provided on Blackbeard Creek), saltwater fishing, and archery deer hunting during the designated season. Camping is not permitted on the refuge, except during managed deer hunts. Over 230 bird species have been seen here.

Even though alligators are generally afraid of people, visitors are cautioned to stay a safe distance from these sluggish-looking but potentially fast-moving reptiles and to be alert for venomous snakes and for ticks, chiggers, and fire ants. Insect repellent and sunscreen are advised.

Lodgings and meals are available in such communities as Darien, Brunswick, St. Simons Island, and Richmond Hill.

Access to Blackbeard Island Refuge can be by chartered boat from Shellman Bluff (reached from U.S. Route 17 on Shellman Bluff Road) or by boat from Barbour River Landing—a public boat-launching ramp on Harris Neck National Wildlife Refuge that is open all day (fishing and other activities at the landing are limited to daylight hours only).

Further information: Blackbeard Island National Wildlife Refuge, c/o Savannah Coastal Refuges, Parkway Business Center, Suite 10, 1000 Business Center Drive, Savannah, GA 31405; telephone: (912) 652-4415.

Bond Swamp, comprising more than 6,290 acres and working toward a goal of about 18,000 acres, was established in 1989 to enhance and protect a stretch of bottomland hardwood swamp and adjacent upland along the Ocmulgee River, about 7 miles south of the city of Macon in central Georgia. Meandering creeks and sloughs, oxbow lakes, and beaver swamps are scattered throughout the floodplain. Among the key species of trees of the floodplain forests are bald cypress, a number of water-loving oaks (overcup, swamp chestnut, water, and willow), American sycamore, bitternut hickory, red maple, and black tupelo.

The refuge provides important habitats for a great diversity of wildlife, including wintering waterfowl; nesting wood ducks; herons and egrets; wild turkey; bald eagle; numerous neotropical migratory songbirds such as Swainson's and prothonotary warblers; black bear;

white-tailed deer; and alligator, which are at the northern end of their range at Bond Swamp. Unfortunately, the nonnative feral hog also inhabits the refuge.

As explained by the U.S. Fish and Wildlife Service, "The Nature Conservancy helped make possible the refuge's original land acquisition. Subsequently, a partnership of the Trust for Public Land, the Ocmulgee Heritage Greenway, and the Georgia Department of Natural Resources assisted with expansion of the refuge. The Ocmulgee Heritage Greenway is an important partnership that seeks to protect the Ocmulgee River's threatened wetland ecosystem by creating an integrated system of scenic, historic and recreational resources along the river for public enjoyment." As ultimately envisioned, not only will Bond Swamp National Wildlife Refuge be expanded to roughly triple its present size, but it will become a vital link in the conservation of scenic, ecological, and historic values along the river corridor in this rapidly growing part of Georgia.

The refuge is open daily during daylight hours. There is no entrance fee.

Visitor activities include birdwatching, photography, hiking, group interpretive programs (by advance arrangement), fishing (bank fishing only, from March 15 to October 15), and hunting (deer and feral hogs) on parts of the refuge during the designated archery and gun quota hunts. Some parts of the refuge may be closed to visitation during periods of river flooding, during deer and feral hog hunts, or to avoid disturbing sensitive wildlife, such as nesting eagles.

There are plans to open some areas to canoeing in the future.

Hiking opportunities include the Beaver Swamp Trail, which contains a 0.9-mile inner loop and a 1.3-mile outer loop and leads through an area of Stone Creek bottomland hardwood forest; and Longleaf Pine Trail, a 1.9-mile route that loops through an area of upland mixed pine-and-hardwood forest.

Even though alligators are generally afraid of people, visitors are advised to stay a safe distance from these sluggish-looking but potentially fast-moving reptiles and to be alert for venomous snakes, poison ivy and sumac, ticks, and chiggers. Insect repellent is advised.

Lodgings and meals are available in Macon.

Access to Bond Swamp Refuge from Exit 6 on I-16 is south 4.2 miles on U.S. Route 23 to Stone Creek parking area, on the right side of the road.

Further information: Bond Swamp National Wildlife Refuge, c/o Piedmont NWR, 718 Juliette Road, Round Oak, GA 31038; telephone: (478) 986-5441.

Eufaula (see text under Alabama).

Harris Neck, comprising 2,824 acres, was established in 1962 to protect an extensive area of salt marsh, smaller acreages of fields and grassland, and mixed deciduous woods and scattered swamplands along the South Newport River on the north-central coast of Georgia. Six human-made impoundments are managed for the benefit of a rookery for the endangered wood stork, as well as a feeding and roosting area for wading birds and wintering habitat for waterfowl. White-tailed deer, raccoons, and American alligators are common residents.

Ducks Unlimited, Inc. has helped enhance 150 acres of Harris Neck Refuge's wetland habitat.

The refuge is open daily. There is no entrance fee. The refuge headquarters is open on week-days, except national holidays.

Visitor activities include birdwatching, photography, interpretive programs, driving an auto tour route, hiking, bicycling, and fishing in tidal creeks bordering the refuge (fishing piers are provided on Harris Neck Creek, near the refuge entrance). Camping is not permitted on the refuge. More than 15 miles of roads and trails offer easy access into many parts of the refuge. To avoid disturbing wildlife, some areas may be seasonally closed to visitation.

Even though alligators are generally afraid of people, visitors are cautioned to stay a safe distance from these sluggish-looking but potentially fast-moving reptiles and to be alert for venomous snakes and for ticks and chiggers. Insect repellent and sunscreen are advised.

Among the more than 230 species of birds that have been recorded on Harris Neck refuge are brown pelican; anhinga; herons; egrets (great, snowy, and cattle); black-crowned and yellow-crowned night-herons; white and glossy ibises; wood stork; Canada goose; ducks (wood, American black, mallard, green-winged and blue-winged teal, mottled, American wigeon, northern pintail, northern shoveler, gadwall, canvasback, ring-necked, lesser scaup, bufflehead, hooded and red-breasted mergansers, and ruddy); osprey; wild turkey; northern bobwhite; gulls; terns; black skimmer; common ground-dove; belted kingfisher; woodpeck-ers (red-headed, red-bellied, downy, hairy, and pileated); blue jay; Carolina chickadee; tufted titmouse; brown-headed nuthatch; wrens (Carolina, house, and marsh); eastern bluebird; thrushes (gray-cheeked, Swainson's, hermit, and wood); gray catbird; northern mockingbird; brown thrasher; warblers; summer tanager; rufous-sided (eastern) towhee; northern cardi-nal; indigo and painted buntings; red-winged blackbird; boat-tailed grackle; and orchard oriole.

Lodgings and meals are available in such communities as Richmond Hill and Darien.

Access by road to Harris Neck Refuge from Exit 67 on I-95 is south 1 mile on U.S. Route 17 and east (left) 7 miles on Harris Neck Road. Boat access to the refuge's tidal waters and the is-land is from a public boat-launching ramp located on the Barbour River at the end of Harris Neck Road. Barbour River Landing is open daily for boat launching, or as posted.

Further information: Harris Neck National Wildlife Refuge, c/o Savannah Coastal Refuges, Parkway Business Center, Suite 10, 1000 Business Center Drive, Savannah, GA 31405; tele-phone: (912) 652-4415.

Okefenokee, containing 395,080 acres, was established in 1937 to protect migratory birds and their habitat within one of the world's most extensive, intact freshwater ecosystems. The refuge is located mostly in the southeastern corner of Georgia, with several thousand acres in northeastern Florida. The Okefenokee, which has been designated as a Wetland of Inter-national Importance, consists of a mosaic of bog habitats that includes forested cypress swamps, open wet "prairies," natural lakes, islands, shrub-scrub thickets, and upland pine forests. More than 353,000 acres have been designated as a unit of the National Wilderness Preservation System. Over 230 bird species have been seen on the refuge.

The refuge's habitats are a haven for a rich variety of wildlife—from egrets, herons, ibises, wood storks, anhingas, wood ducks, sandhill cranes, red-cockaded and pileated woodpeckers, and numerous species of neotropical migratory songbirds; to black bears, white-tailed deer, bobcats, gopher tortoises, a multitude of snakes and turtles, and one of America's largest populations of the American alligator (*Alligator mississippiensis*).

The word Okefenokee is derived from a Choctaw Indian expression meaning "land of the trembling earth." Much of the swamp contains 10- to 15-foot-thick deposits of peat. In some places, it is possible to walk on these thick deposits and cause nearby trees and other vegetation to shake.

A description of the Okefenokee Swamp during the heat, humidity, and green of springtime is provided by Delos E. Culver, writing in the January-March 1947 issue of *National Parks*:

The swamp lay shimmering in the midday heat enveloped in a silence unbelievable in this day and age. Its appearance seemed to carry us back to the pre-dawn of man. Our tiny boat turned its prow from the deep waters of a canal into a fringe of maidencane as we obtained our first view. Before us spread the forest primeval. . . . Stretching off to the horizon lay mile upon mile of shallow open swamp—a vast plain of clear amber water, dotted with islands near and far. . . . Perhaps the magnificent beauty is due in part to the uniform uncrowded distribution of plant life over the surface of the water that reflects the towering moss-draped pine and cypress between lily pads and golden club. Rising from the water on erect stems are the lavender blossoms of bladderworts, . . . while around the shallow borders of islets grow clumps of "southern trumpet" in full bloom. The latter, a species of pitcher plant, . . . attains a maximum height of thirty inches.

An occasional egret or great blue heron and scattered pairs of soaring, screaming red-shouldered hawks could be seen. Vultures, both black and turkey, perched motionless on dead cypresses. . . . The motionless vultures staring fixedly at the glassy waters add to the effect. . . .

As regularly as day follows night, storm followed storm. There were four thunderstorms daily, accompanied by torrential rain. One minute we would be dripping; the next enveloped in steam as our clothing dried in the scorching sun. While the last faint rumble of a passing storm would die away in the northeast, there would be heard the first rumble of another approaching from the southwest. . . .

Nights, and particularly the dim hours following dawn, were sonorous with amphibian thunder [of chorusing frogs]. Rolling across the miles of swamp land it was interspersed occasionally with the growl of an old bull alligator exhibiting his vocal powers in mighty tones that echoed and re-echoed.

Somewhere from out of the distant past, as one gazes upon this primitive grandeur, there comes an indescribable feeling. Somehow it seemed that the civilization we knew but yesterday had passed, and here before our eyes the world had resumed its steady march of evolution through time.

In 1891, the Suwannee Canal Company acquired 234,000 acres of the Okefenokee from the state of Georgia, with the intention of draining it, logging its cypress forests, and planting crops. After spending 3 years and $1 million digging the Suwannee Canal 11.5 miles through the swamp's prairies, the company went bankrupt. In 1899, the land was sold to the Hebard Cypress Company. A log-hauling railroad, which was constructed on pilings through 35 miles of the swamp's western edge, connected with a sawmill near Waycross. Between 1910 and 1927, more than 400 million board-feet of timber—three-quarters of which was cypress—was harvested from the Okefenokee Swamp.

Cornell University biologists, who had been researching the swamp since 1909, initiated a proposal to protect the Okefenokee. With the backing of a number of conservation organizations, the Georgia state legislature passed a resolution in 1919 that asked the federal government to purchase the swamp. Federal acquisition finally began in 1936, followed the following year by an Executive Order by President Franklin D. Roosevelt that officially established the Okefenokee National Wildlife Refuge. The first refuge manager was John Hopkins, who had previously been the surveyor and timber cruiser for the Hebard Cypress Company and had been the railroad's general superintendent.

The Okefenokee Wildlife League is a nonprofit support group that is assisting the refuge in many ways.

The refuge is open daily, except on Christmas. Entry fees are charged at each of the three manned entrances: the East Entrance at Suwannee Canal Recreation Area, near Folkston; the West Entrance (known as the Stephen C. Foster State Park, which is under a concession contract with the Fish and Wildlife Service) near Fargo; and the North Entrance (known as Okefenokee Swamp Park, which is also under a concession contract with the Service) near Waycross. There are also two unmanned entrances: Kingfisher Landing, 15 miles north of Folkston; and Suwannee River Recreation Area, 6 miles west of Stephen C. Foster State Park.

The refuge's Richard S. Bolt Visitor Center, which is located just west of State Route 121/23 at the East Entrance, is open daily, except on Christmas. A camping permit (fee is charged), which is required to overnight on the refuge, can be reserved by telephone only: (912) 496-3331, within 2 months prior to the start of the visit.

Visitor activities include birdwatching, photography, visitor center interpretive programs, driving the Swamp Island Drive, walking (wheelchair-accessible) boardwalks, hiking on trails, viewing the refuge and wildlife from observation towers, bicycling on Swamp Island Drive and the refuge's entrance roads, canoeing on a network of canoe trails, motorboating on boat trails, guided boat tours, camping (at a number of overnight camping sites; permit required), and fishing.

At the East Entrance, interpretive exhibits and programs are provided at the visitor center. The Swamp Island Drive is a 9-mile excursion (an interpretive brochure is available) that begins near the visitor center and leads to Chesser Island. Walking and hiking opportunities include Canal Digger's Trail, a 0.5-mile route (an interpretive brochure is available) that leads around the historic Suwannee Canal, built in 1891 in an attempt to drain the swamp; Upland Discovery Trail, which loops through an area of open pine forest inhabited by the endangered red-cockaded woodpecker (see a description of this species in the Carolina Sandhills Refuge text); and Swamp Walk, a 0.75-mile boardwalk (an interpretive brochure is available) that winds from the end of the Swamp Island Drive through cypress trees and the open grassy marsh of Chesser Prairie and ends at 50-foot Owl's Roost Tower, which offers a panorama of Seagrove Lake and Chesser Prairie. The historic Chesser Island Homestead, dating from 1927, Deerstand Trail, and a second observation tower are also located near the end of the drive.

The refuge's extensive canoe trails are accessed from the East Entrance/visitor center/Suwannee Canal area; from the Kingfisher Landing Entrance toward the northeast corner of the refuge, reached from U.S. Route 1; and from the West Entrance at Stephen C. Foster State Park, reached from near the town of Fargo on State Route 177. A Wilderness Canoe Guide brochure, explaining regulations, trip options, and safety advice, is available. Canoe rentals are available at the East and West entrances.

Even though alligators are generally afraid of people, visitors are cautioned to stay a safe distance from these sluggish-looking but potentially fast-moving reptiles and to be alert for venomous snakes and for ticks, chiggers, and fire ants. Insect repellent is advised, to ward off mosquitoes and biting flies.

Lodgings and meals are available in such communities as Waycross and Folkston.

Access from Exit 3 on I-95 to Okefenokee Refuge's visitor center is west, through Kingsland, 22 miles to Folkston, southwest (left) 8 miles on State Route 121/23, and west (right) 3 miles on the refuge's East Entrance road. From U.S. Route 84 at Waycross, it is southeast 34 miles on U.S. Route 1 to Folkston, southwest (right) on State Route 121/23, and west (right) 3 miles on the refuge's East Entrance road.

Further information: Okefenokee National Wildlife Refuge, Route 2, Box 3330, Folkston, GA 31537; telephone: (912) 496-7836.

Piedmont, comprising 34,967 acres, was established in 1939 to restore an area of gently rolling hills and bottomland that had previously been denuded, and the soil severely eroded and depleted from past farming practices. The refuge, located in central Georgia, is a shining example of how an utterly devastated ecosystem can successfully be restored to fertility with a rich diversity of habitats and wildlife. More than 200 species of birds have been recorded here.

As described by the U.S. Fish and Wildlife Service:

When Franklin D. Roosevelt signed the Executive Order establishing Piedmont National Wildlife Refuge…, the land's fertility and abundant wildlife populations had been ravaged. The vast forest, which had reigned supreme for eons, had been cleared by European settlers in the early 1800's. Cotton became king and farming soon robbed the soil of its natural fertility. The loss of forest, with its soil stabilizing root system, led to massive erosion problems. The Civil War, the boll weevil, and the Great Depression [of the 1930s] combined to cause large scale land abandonment. . . .

Today, through the efforts of the U.S. Fish and Wildlife Service, the . . . refuge is once again a forest. It hosts loblolly pines on the ridges with hardwoods found along creek bottoms and in scattered upland coves. Clear streams and beaver ponds provide ideal wetlands for migrating waterfowl. Wildlife populations have been restored. . . . Piedmont National Wildlife Refuge now serves as a model of forest ecosystem management for wildlife.

The refuge consists of 34 management compartments, each containing approximately 1,000 acres. One of the primary resource management activities in this mosaic of habitats is periodic prescribed burning. Relatively "cool," low-burning fires promote nutrient cycling that spurs the growth of plants valued by many species of wildlife. To maintain open-grown stands of pine forest, these controlled fires suppress the growth of hardwood seedlings, the dense growth of which, without fire, would eventually replace the pines. And these fires reduce hazardous accumulations of dead wood, needles, leaves, and other organic debris—fuel overloading—that could otherwise contribute to uncontrolled and destructive stand-replacing wildfires.

Other key forest management activities include timber thinning to promote wildlife habitat diversity. For example, even-aged stands of loblolly pines are scattered throughout the refuge "to ensure a continuous replacement of older pine." Such older pine stands provide essential habitat for many species of wildlife—notably nesting cavities for the federally listed endangered red-cockaded woodpecker (see a description of this species in the Carolina Sandhills Refuge text).

Areas of hardwoods are managed for such birds as the wild turkey and numerous species of neotropical migratory songbirds. Openings in the forest are maintained by mowing, burning, and planting of grasses and forbs. Eleven ponds are managed for the benefit of fish and wildlife, and nesting boxes are located around the ponds for wood ducks.

Because of the rapid population and urban growth and the resulting loss of forest and agricultural lands in the state's Piedmont region, the Georgia Piedmont Natural Resources Cooperative (GPNRC) has been formed. As explained by the Fish and Wildlife Service, this partnership "provides a unique opportunity for landowners with different management objectives to voluntarily cooperate" for the benefit of wildlife management and environmental stewardship. In addition to the Fish and Wildlife Service, GPNRC's partners include the U.S. Forest Service, the Georgia Department of Natural Resources' Wildlife Resources Division, the University of Georgia's Warnell School of Forest Resources, Hitchiti Experimental Forest, Georgia Power Company, John Hancock Mutual Life Insurance Company, the Timber Company, and Weyerhaeuser Company. More than 200,000 acres are represented by the partnership. Among its goals are to "use the best available science-based information"; "respect partners' different resource management objectives to identify voluntary roles needed to meet mutually agreed upon objectives"; and "serve as a model that can be used by land managers in other geographic areas."

Piedmont Refuge is open daily during daylight hours. There is no entrance fee. The visitor center is open daily, except on national holidays.

Visitor activities include wildlife observation; photography; viewing interpretive exhibits at the visitor center; group interpretive programs and tours (by advance reservation); driving the 6-mile Little Rock Wildlife Drive (a self-guiding brochure is available); hiking numerous trails; fishing by boat (electric motors only) on Allison Lake and Pond 2A from May through September (a boat-launching site is available); bank fishing on some ponds (Pond 21A is reserved for youths 12 years of age and younger) from May through September; fishing from piers at Pond 2A and the Children's pond; and hunting (deer, raccoon, opossum, rabbit, squirrel, quail, and turkey) on part of the refuge during the designated seasons. On days when deer gun quota hunts are held, the refuge is closed to general public visitation. In mid-October, a 2-day deer hunt for mobility-challenged hunters is offered (arrangements can be made by contacting the refuge office by October 1). Camping is not permitted on the refuge, except during big game hunts, at which times Pippen Lake Campground in Compartment 19 (near the western edge of the refuge), is available for hunters with a refuge hunt special use permit.

Hiking opportunities include a 1.5-mile trail that begins at the visitor center and loops through forests of pine and bottomland hardwoods; the 1-mile, self-guiding Allison Lake Trail (an interpretive leaflet is available) that offers views of wintering waterfowl (an observation and photography blind is provided); and the 2.5-mile Red-Cockaded Woodpecker Trail that leads through a colony site of this endangered species (May and June are the best months to see the birds, during their nesting season).

Visitors are cautioned to be alert for venomous snakes and for ticks and chiggers. Insect repellent is advised during the warmer months.

Lodgings and meals are available in such communities as Macon, Forsyth, and Gray.

Access to Piedmont Refuge's visitor center is northeast 18 miles on Juliette Road, from Exit 186 on I-75 in Forsyth.

Further information: Piedmont National Wildlife Refuge, 718 Juliette Road, Round Oak, GA 31038; telephone: (478) 986-5441.

Savannah (see text under South Carolina)

Wassaw, consisting of 10,053 acres, was established in 1969 to protect Wassaw Island—a scenically beautiful barrier island near the northern end of the Georgia coast. The island includes extensive salt marshes, a 7-mile-long sandy beach, gently rolling sand dunes, and virgin-growth woodlands of slash pines and live oaks, the branches of the latter festooned with resurrection ferns.

The refuge supports heron and egret rookeries, and, in addition to the many wading birds, it attracts numerous species of wintering waterfowl, shorebirds (including the federally listed threatened piping plover), and a multitude of neotropical migratory songbirds, one of the most prominent of which is the painted bunting. Bald eagles nest here. White-tailed deer, raccoon, and the American alligator are common residents. During the summer, loggerhead sea turtles haul themselves onto the 7-mile beach at night to lay their eggs. The endangered West Indian manatee inhabits the waters in and adjacent to the refuge.

The refuge actually consists of two islands, separated by the tidal Odingsell River. Wassaw Island contains large expanses of salt marsh. Its uplands consist of a central sand-dune ridge that stretches the length of the 5.5-mile-long island and rises to about 45 feet above mean sea level at its highest point, and a number of lesser sandy ridges paralleling the main one, between which are many interdunal swales and ponds.

Little Wassaw Island, which consists of two parts—Pine Island and Flora Hammock—is virtually flat. More than 7,000 acres of the refuge is salt marsh, marsh hammocks, and meandering tidal creeks that rise and fall twice daily with the lunar tides. Salt marsh habitat provides vital breeding and nursery grounds for fish and shellfish. As *Ducks Unlimited* senior writer Matt Young wrote in the September-October 2001 issue of the magazine, "Acre for acre, coastal wetlands are among the most productive ecosystems on the planet. Their bountiful waters, rich in plant and animal life, support a remarkable diversity of waterfowl. . . . Sadly, thousands of acres of coastal wetlands continue to be lost each year. Protection is clearly the best line of defense against these losses, because once these fragile habitats disappear, they are gone forever."

The refuge's Wassaw Island and Pine Island (but not Flora Hammock) are open daily during daylight hours. There is no entrance fee.

Visitor activities include birdwatching, photography, hiking (on a network of trails and along the beach), fishing (on Odingsell River and its tributary creeks that meander through the salt marsh), and deer hunting (bow and gun) on part of the refuge during the designated seasons.

Even though alligators are generally afraid of people, visitors are cautioned to stay a safe distance from these sluggish-looking but potentially fast-moving reptiles and to be alert for venomous snakes and for ticks and chiggers. Insect repellent and sunscreen are advised.

More than 250 species of birds have been recorded on Wassaw Refuge.

Lodgings and meals are available in such communities as Savannah, Richmond Hill, and Tybee Island.

Access to Wassaw Refuge is only by boat. A boat-launching ramp is provided adjacent to Skidaway Island Bridge. Boat charter trips to the refuge can be arranged at marinas that are located on Skidaway Island and Isle of Hope.

Further information: Wassaw National Wildlife Refuge, c/o Savannah Coastal Refuges, Parkway Business Center, Suite 10, 1000 Business Center Drive, Savannah, GA 31405; telephone: (912) 652-4415.

Wolf Island, containing 5,126 acres, was established as a migratory bird sanctuary in 1930. The refuge protects three coastal barrier islands—Wolf, Egg, and Little Egg—and an extensive expanse of adjacent saltwater marsh primarily for the benefit of migratory birds on the central coast of Georgia. In 1975, the refuge was designated as a unit of the National Wilderness Preservation System.

Brown pelicans and many species of wading birds, wintering ducks, shorebirds, gulls, and terns are just a few of the more common birds using the refuge. Loggerhead sea turtles nest on the island, but the U.S. Fish and Wildlife Service says that they "rarely are successful due to tidal inundation or predation."

Approximately 300 acres of the 4,519-acre Wolf Island consist of uplands that support such vegetation as sea oats, sand spurs, and other beach-dune plants; and wax myrtle and southern redcedar that grow on the island's highest elevations, only a few feet above sea level. The remainder of the island consists of salt marsh, small wetland hammocks, and tidal creeks. The Fish and Wildlife Service explains that these creeks "flood daily with lunar tides of five to nine feet. Tidal action constantly influences the physical shape of the island. Each high tide flows across low lying portions of the northern dunes, and has resulted in a wide mud flat through the central marsh. High spring and flood tides inundate most of the refuge." The island's salt marsh is dominated by salt meadow cordgrass.

About one-third of 593-acre Egg Island consists of uplands that support a thick growth of redcedar, blackberry, and greenbrier, with a few slash pines and live oaks. Other upland habitat is dominated by wax myrtle, and a narrow stretch of ocean beach supports sea oats, sand spurs, and other beach-dune species. Nearly 400 acres of Egg Island and all of 14-acre Little Egg Island are cordgrass-dominated salt marsh.

When the refuge was established in 1930, under an Executive Order by President Herbert Hoover, its initial 538 acres were already owned by the federal government. In 1972, The Nature Conservancy made possible the addition of just over 4,000 acres.

The refuge's beach, marsh, and upland areas are closed to visitation. Only the adjacent areas of open salt water and meandering tidal creeks are open to such visitor uses as birdwatching, boating, saltwater fishing, and crabbing. Visitors have to make their own arrangements for reaching the refuge, such as from marinas in the nearby town of Darien. Insect repellent and sunscreen are advised.

More than 120 species of birds have been recorded on Wolf Island Refuge.

Lodgings and meals are available in such communities as Darien, Brunswick, and St. Simons Island.

Access to the refuge can be by chartered boat, from marinas in Darien.

Further information: Wolf Island National Wildlife Refuge, c/o Savannah Coastal Refuges, Parkway Business Center, Suite 10, 1000 Business Center Drive, Savannah, GA 31405; telephone: (912) 652-4415.

Hawai'i and Pacific Remote Islands Complex: Hawai'i

Hakalau Forest, consisting of 32,733 acres, was established in 1985 to enhance and protect an outstanding area of the often-misty, mid-elevation, montane rainforest that is vital habitat for a number of endangered species of forest birds on the windward slope of Mauna Kea, on the Big Island of Hawai'i. Of the 14 kinds of native birds inhabiting this refuge, eight are listed as endangered.

One of the most interesting of the latter species is the rare 'akiapola'au (*Hemignathus munroi*), a member of the Hawaiian Honeycreeper family. It has an unusual-shaped beak— a short, stout, lower mandible and a long, down-curving, upper bill, uniquely adapted to peck holes into and pull off tree bark in search of insect larvae and other prey. The male has a yellow head and breast and olive-green back, and the female has dull greenish plumage.

Another endangered honeycreeper is the Hawai'i 'akepa (*Loxops coccineus*), which feeds on insects with its slightly crossed bill and nests in tree cavities. The male is bright orange, and the female is greenish-gray.

The Hawai'i creeper (*Oreomystis mana*) is an endangered, small, olive-green bird with habits similar to North America's brown creeper and nuthatches—creeping up and down tree trunks and along the underside of branches in search of insects.

The endangered 'io (*Buteo solitarius*), the Hawaiian hawk, is often seen soaring over the forest. This species, whose numbers have been increasing in recent years, is revered by many Polynesian-Hawaiians as their guardian spirit, or 'aumakua. The state-listed, endangered pueo, the Hawaiian short-eared owl (*Asio flammeus sandwichensis*) is sometimes seen gliding across open habitat seeking rodents, small birds, and other prey.

The endangered nene (*Branta sandvicensis*), known as the Hawaiian goose, has recently been reintroduced to Hakalau Forest Refuge. This official state bird of Hawai'i also inhabits nearby Hawai'i Volcanoes National Park and Maui's Haleakala National Park. It has a black head and nape, buff-yellow cheek and neck, and heavily barred brownish-gray plumage on the back.

Common native birds of the Refuge include the i'iwi (*Vestiaria coccinea*), a striking bright red bird with black wings and a long, orange, down-curved bill; the 'apapane (*Himatione sanguinea*), a bright scarlet little bird that flies in flocks through the forest; the 'amakihi (*Hemignathus virens virens*), a yellowish honeycreeper; and the 'oma'o (*Myadestes obscurus*), also known as the Hawai'i thrush, which forages for fruits in understory vegetation and which is recognized by its whistled, slurred, flute-like musical trills.

In addition, a dozen of the Hakalau Forest Refuge's 29 rare plants are listed or proposed for listing as endangered. Over the decades, the diminishing of these and related fauna and flora has resulted from the destruction and impairment of this habitat.

Elevations within the refuge extend from 2,500 to over 6,600 feet above sea level, with rainfall dramatically decreasing upward. Below 4,000 feet elevation, slopes and deep gulches, which annually receive from 250 to 300 inches of rainfall, contain dense forest vegetation, areas of tree ferns, and bogs.

From around 4,500 to near 6,000 feet elevation, annual precipitation averages around 150 inches. Here grows a beautiful, closed-canopy forest that is dominated by the 'ohi'a (*Metrosideros polymorpha*), a tree bearing distinctive, brush-like flowers without petals and with clusters of long, bright-red stamens; and the majestic koa (*Acacia koa*), from the massive trunks of which the Polynesian-Hawaiians once carved their great ocean canoes (wa'a opela). Understory trees, shrubs, and ferns also grow here, such as 'olapa (*Cheirodendron trigynum*), with trifoliate-compound leaves and clusters of small, purple, berrylike fruits; kolea (*Myrsine*) of several species, with densely growing, black to purple fruits; 'ohelo (*Vaccinium dentatum*) or Hawaiian huckleberry, with red-striped, green to whitish tubular flowers; kawa'u (*Ilex anomala*) or Hawaiian holly, with dark green, oval leaves, the upper surface of which are patterned with recessed veining; and hapu'u (*Cibotium glaucum*), the graceful Hawaiian tree fern.

Where there are only 100 inches or less of rainfall, at the highest and driest elevations, non-native grasses and other small plants dominate former livestock pasture land. The U.S. Fish and Wildlife Service has been implementing a number of habitat restoration management projects at Hakalau Forest Refuge. These include the elimination of livestock grazing; fencing of some key units, from 500 to 2,000 acres, to keep out wild pigs and cattle; the removal of feral and exotic animals, such as pigs, mongooses, cats, and rats, by hunting, trapping, and drives; control of non-native plants with hand grubbing, fire, and herbicides; and the propagation in the refuge's nursery of thousands of seedlings and cuttings of ohia and other native trees, shrubs, and ferns for planting to restore native habitat that was previously impaired by cattle grazing and the invasion of exotic plants. This refuge is, in fact, an outstanding example of major ecological restoration in Hawai'i.

The Nature Conservancy of Hawai'i helped make possible the establishment of Hakalau Forest Refuge, by purchasing nearby lands to be added to the refuge.

Visitors are permitted into the refuge's Maulua Tract, but only on Saturdays, Sundays, and holidays, with prior permission from the refuge headquarters staff. There is no entrance fee. Twice-monthly refuge ecotours are offered by Hawai'i Forest and Trail; telephone: (800) 464-1993. Volunteer service trips can also be arranged for six to ten persons, these must be at least 2 days long, with lodging at cabins in the refuge.

Visitor activities include birdwatching, photography, and hiking.

Lodgings and meals are available in Hilo, Mountain View, and Hawai'i Volcanoes National Park.

Access to the refuge is west by way of Saddle Road (State Route 200) from Hilo, right (north) onto the Mauna Kea Summit Road for 2 miles, and right onto Keanakolu Road for about 14 miles—a 40-mile drive, requiring nearly 2 hours each way, only accessible by four-wheel-drive vehicle (rentals available in Hilo).

Further information: Hakalau Forest National Wildlife Refuge, 32 Kino'ole Street, Suite 101, Hilo, HI 96720; telephone: (808) 933-6915.

Hanalei, containing 917 acres, was established in 1972 to protect ecologically important habitat for a number of endangered Hawaiian water birds in scenically beautiful Hanalei Valley, near the north shore of the Island of Kaua'i, Hawai'i. Carrying on a 1,200-year tradition here, local farmers cultivate crops of taro (wetland kalo) within the refuge's wetlands.

A system of ditches diverts some of the Hanalei River water to maintain open impoundments and to irrigate the taro "patches"—pond-fields that the Polynesian-Hawaiians refer to as lo'i. For the benefit of the birds, an area of the taro plants around nest sites is left unharvested, and for a month following harvest, the patches are permitted to lie fallow so the birds can feast on invertebrates that thrive in the decaying vegetation.

The taro patches, ponds, and marshy areas provide vital feeding and nesting habitat for the koloa maoli (Hawaiian duck); 'alae ke'oke'o (Hawaiian coot) with white forehead shield and beak and dark gray body plumage; 'alae 'ula (Hawaiian moorhen) with bright red forehead shield and base of beak, yellow-tipped beak, and slate gray body plumage; and the slender, red-legged, black-and-white ae'o (Hawaiian black-necked stilt). The 'auku'u (black-crowned night-heron) also inhabits the refuge, and migratory shorebirds and waterfowl come here.

For more than 1,000 years, taro has been cultivated to provide a food staple in the traditional Polynesian-Hawaiian diet. It is still a popular carbohydrate. After being baked, the corm (stem) can be mashed to create a smooth, paste-like substance called poi, which, like rice or potato, can be eaten with fish or meat. When poi is mixed with water and batter and baked, it becomes a delicious bread. Or taro can be baked or steamed, cut into pieces, and eaten as a vegetable. The leaves, too, can be cooked and eaten.

Matching habitat restoration funding has been contributed by Ducks Unlimited, Inc., and other private sources to help enhance water bird habitat here. A local nonprofit support group, 1000 Friends of Kaua'i, is also assisting Hanalei Refuge in various ways.

Public access into the refuge ponds is prohibited. However, a viewing overlook is provided just west of (downhill from) the Princeville Shopping Center, on State Route 56. This is a magnificent panorama of the lush green valley. During the rainier times of the year, numerous long ribbons of waterfalls plunge down the surrounding steep mountainsides. Another view of the refuge and its wildlife is available from Ohiki Road, which starts after crossing the long Hanalei River bridge. Visitors may park in the small parking lot on the west side of Ohiki Road and enjoy a short hike to a heiau overlooking Hanalei Valley.

Lodgings and meals are available in such communities as Princeville, Kapa'a, Wailua, and Lihu'e.

Further information: Hanalei National Wildlife Refuge, P.O. Box 87, Kilauea, HI 96754; telephone: (808) 828-1413.

Hule'ia, comprising 241 acres, was established in 1973 to protect ecologically rich, seasonally flooded bottomlands, estuary, and wooded slopes along the Hule'ia River, near the southeastern shore of the Island of Kaua'i, Hawai'i. The bottomland along the river was formerly cultivated for taro and rice. It then became densely overgrown with non-native plants. For the benefit of a number of endangered species of water birds and other wildlife, this land is being enhanced to provide areas of open water, reestablish native vegetation, and restore some of the former taro patches.

The endangered water birds here are the same as those inhabiting Hanalei Refuge (see the description for that refuge).

Matching habitat restoration funding has been contributed by Ducks Unlimited, Inc. and other private sources to help enhance the water bird habitat here. A local nonprofit group, 1000 Friends of Kaua'i, is also assisting Hule'ia Refuge in various ways.

This refuge is not open to public entry. However, there is a view of the area from the Menehune Fishpond Overlook. Access to this view is south from Lihu'e on Rice Street-Waapa Road, in the direction of Nawiliwili Harbor (near Kalapaki); and right at the Menehune Fish Pond sign onto Hulemalu Road for 0.6 mile to the overlook (on the left).

Lodgings and meals are available in such communities as Lihu'e, Wailua, and Kapa'a.

Further information: Hule'ia National Wildlife Refuge, P.O. Box 87, Kilauea, HI 96754; telephone: (808) 828-1413.

James C. Campbell, containing 164 acres in two units, was established in 1976 to manage and protect KII UNIT'S human-made ponds and PUNANMANO POND UNIT'S spring-fed marsh on the northern shore of the Island of O'ahu, Hawai'i. These wetlands provide vital habitat for several endangered water birds: the Hawaiian moorhen, Hawaiian coot, Hawaiian stilt, and Hawaiian duck. (See the Hanalei Refuge text for a further description of these species.) Many years ago, the Kii ponds were created as waste-settling basins associated with the commercial production of sugar cane.

Other birds inhabiting this refuge include black-crowned night-heron and a number of migrant shorebirds, including Pacific golden plover, wandering tattler, and ruddy turnstone.

Matching habitat restoration funding and other assistance has been contributed by the Hawai'i Audubon Society, Ducks Unlimited, Inc., and other private organizations and volunteers to help enhance water bird habitat here.

Visitor activities are birdwatching and wildlife photography, in the context of interpretive tours. Entry onto this refuge is limited. The refuge can be viewed only by prearranged 2-hour, interpretive group tours on Thursdays and Saturdays between August 1 and February 15 (the refuge is closed during the stilt nesting season).

Lodgings and meals are available in such communities as Kahuku, Laie, and Honolulu.

Further information: James C. Campbell National Wildlife Refuge, c/o O'ahu NWR Complex, 66-590 Kamehameha Highway, Room 2C-D, Haleiwa, HI 96712; telephone: (808) 637-6330.

Kakaha'ia, comprising 44 acres, was established in 1977 to enhance and protect two ponds primarily for two endangered water birds, the Hawaiian black-necked stilt and Hawaiian coot. Pintails and a number of migratory shorebirds also visit the refuge, which is located on the south shore of the Island of Moloka'i, Hawai'i.

One of the ponds is an expanse of open water that was created in the mid-1980s, and the other is a historic Polynesian-Hawaiian fishpond (loko i'a) that contains marshy habitat. Ponds such as this were used for fish farming to supplement seasonal deep-sea fishing. Some of these were individual projects on a small scale, but others were substantial cooperative enterprises directed by ruling chiefs.

As explained by E. S. Craighill Handy and Elizabeth Green Handy in their book, *Native Planters in Old Hawaii: Their Life, Lore, and Environment* (Bishop Museum Press, 1991):

The most spectacular of these were the great walled-in sea ponds or loko i'a kuapa, many of which can be seen today still in use or in only partial or complete disrepair. Until very recent years many still flourished. Others have been silted up as forested uplands were cleared and the areas put under cultivation.

. . . Moloka'i, in proportion to its land area, had the greatest number of ponds, strung along a great part of its low south shore.

Archaeological studies have revealed that the Big Island of Hawai'i had approximately 20 of these fish ponds and Maui 16, but much smaller Moloka'i had 58 of them. The earliest fish ponds were situated at the mouths of streams and were consequently enriched by the wealth of nutrients, 'opae ula (shrimp), and other freshwater organisms that were carried down from the mountains, especially during periods of heavy rainfall. 'Anae (*Mugil cephalus*; mullet), the most preferred fish for its sweet flavor, aholehole (*Kuhlia sandwichensis*; silver fish), and awa'aua (milkfish) were the primary fishes raised in these managed impoundments. The presence of the ponds' shrimp also attracted additional ocean species, such as kahala (amberjack), uhu (parrot fish), kumu (goat fish), 'o'opu (guppy), and puhi (eel).

As described by Maui resident Kekai Kapu, who traces his ancestry back to Tahiti and neighboring Polynesian islands in the South Pacific:

A massive wall of large lava rocks was built to enclose and protect the pond. The wall contained a gated opening, through which the waters of the ocean and pond flowed back and forth with the rising and falling tides. Young mullet would swim from the open sea through narrow openings in the gate. Once inside, they would feed upon the rich nutrients that the stream brought down from the uplands. As the fish grew bigger and bigger, they became too big to swim back through the gate and were trapped in the fishpond. When the people caught some of the mullet, mainly for special occasions, they would first give thanks for their catch by making an offering to their akua (gods). The fish would then be shared by the people.

Kakaha'ia Refuge is open only by special use permit.

Lodgings and meals are available in Kaunakaka'i, which is five miles west of the refuge, on State Route 450.

Further information: Kakaha'ia National Wildlife Refuge, c/o Maui Refuge Complex, P.O. Box 1042, Kihei, HI 96753; telephone: (808) 875-1582.

Kealia Pond, containing 700 acres, was established in 1992. The refuge enhances and protects a brackish pond that provides vital wetland habitat for two endangered water birds and a number of migratory ducks and shorebirds on the south-central shore of the Island of Maui, Hawai'i.

During winter rainfall and runoff from 56 square miles in the West Maui Mountains, Kealia Pond expands to its capacity of about 400 acres. As water recedes during the dry summer months, broad expanses of mudflats and margins of crusty crystalline salt are exposed, providing foraging areas for resident and migrant birds. The name *Kealia* means "salt-encrusted place."

The pond was naturally formed and used by the Polynesian-Hawaiians, but to what extent for "fisheries" is not known. There were numerous fish ponds in the Hawaiian Islands, managed to provide an important source of food. Although adjustable sluice gates (makaha) and ditches allowed such saltwater species as mullet and milkfish to enter many of those ponds, there is no evidence that a gate and ditch were installed at this pond. (A contemporary cement culvert exists beneath the North Kihei Road bridge.) Kealia was an important source of salt.

A series of diked impoundments, located between the main pond and the refuge headquarters, also provides valuable habitat for coots, stilts, sanderlings, and other shorebirds and waterfowl. These smaller ponds were built prior to the refuge's establishment, in an unsuccessful attempt to create an aquaculture business.

A cooperative agreement with Ducks Unlimited, Inc. is making possible the restoration and enhancement of the pond habitat for the benefit of Hawai'i's endangered water birds. Other co-operators include the neighboring sugar company, Hawaiian Commercial and Sugar (Alexander & Baldwin) and the Hawai'i Department of Land and Natural Resources.

A community project called Kokua Kealia (Help Kealia) was formed by the U.S. Fish and Wildlife Service and the Kihei Canoe Club—with additional funding from the state and county—to restore the native ecology of the coastal sand dunes. A greenhouse was installed on the refuge to provide volunteers with the opportunity to propagate native plants for out-planting. Community volunteer groups assist with the project by removing the non-native vegetation and replanting with native species.

The refuge is open on weekdays during daylight hours, except national holidays. There is no entrance fee. Public access is limited during the Hawaiian stilt and Hawaiian coot nesting season, from March through August, to minimize disturbing the birds during this critical period.

Visitor activities include birdwatching, photography, and minimal walking along the old aquaculture ponds.

Lodgings and meals are available in such communities as Kihei, Wailea, Kahului, Lahaina, Ka'anapali, and Napili.

Access to the refuge headquarters is north just over 0.75 mile on State Route 311 from the junction of State Routes 31 and 311, in Kihei (look for the "Mile 6" marker), and left onto a 0.4 mile paved spur road. To the northwest of Kihei, North Kihei Road (State Route 31) runs along the southern edge of the refuge, between the pond and the ocean beach.

Further information: Kealia Pond National Wildlife Refuge, P.O. Box 1042, Kihei, HI 96753; telephone: (808) 875-1582.

Kilauea Point, consisting of 203 acres, was established in 1985 to enhance and protect an ecologically outstanding seabird nesting colony on the ruggedly scenic north coast of the Island of Kaua'i, Hawai'i. Because of predator-proof fencing and a program of trapping feral animals, this vital habitat is one of the few places on the main islands of Hawai'i where colonial seabirds, such as the Laysan albatross, red-footed booby, red-tailed and white-tailed tropicbirds, wedge-tailed shearwater, and great frigatebird are able to breed. In 1988, the refuge was expanded to provide protection for the endangered nene, the Hawaiian goose.

At the northernmost point on Kaua'i, the spectacular, surf-pounded sheer cliffs provide a breathtaking backdrop to the refuge's incredible wealth of wildlife. The albatrosses (moli, in Hawaiian), navigate annually across thousands of miles of the open Pacific Ocean. They appear to fly without effort, held aloft on their 7-foot wingspread. Returning each spring to breed and raise their young, these amazing birds perform elaborate courtship rituals of bowing, "sky-pointing," and bill-clapping, accompanied by an array of strange whistling and moaning sounds.

More than a thousand nests of the red-footed booby ('a) are crowded together across a steep hillside's windswept trees and shrubs. These predominantly white birds, with black wing tips and large, pale-bluish beaks, build crude nests of sticks and breed here from March through May.

Among the most graceful birds in the world are the red-tailed tropicbirds (koa'e 'ula), which perform elaborate, paired aerial courtship displays during their March–October breeding season. This red-billed species nests beneath sheltering rock ledges and shrubs, and the smaller white-tailed tropicbird (koa'e kea) nests along stretches of sheer, inaccessible cliffs.

The gracefully soaring, brownish-gray, wedge-tailed shearwaters ('ua'u kani) return in March, after wintering in the Gulf of Panama. As many as 1,000 nests occupy crevices and burrows, the latter scraped out with their beaks and feet. These birds' nocturnal courtship activities are accompanied by weird wailing and moaning sounds. In June, when a pair's single egg hatches, the adults fly off during the day to gather food for their chick.

The great frigatebird ('iwa) is another graceful soaring bird. Cruising effortlessly on oceanic trade winds, it has a wingspan of 7.5 feet; slender, angular-shaped wings; and a long, deeply forked tail. During courtship, the predominantly black males boast an inflated, bright red throat pouch.

The nene is the official state bird of Hawai'i. This species of goose has a distinctive black head and nape, pale yellowish-buff cheek and neck, and barred brownish-gray plumage on the upper body. It came perilously close to extinction, but thanks to successful captive propagation and reintroduction programs in recent decades, it now inhabits this refuge after vanishing from Kaua'i hundreds of years ago. It is also found in Haleakala National Park on the island of Maui, and in Hawai'i Volcanoes National Park on the Big Island.

In addition to the birds described above, there are such others as ruddy turnstone, wandering tattler, Pacific golden plover, lesser yellowlegs, and several non-native species: cattle egret, spotted and zebra doves, common myna, and northern and red-crested cardinals.

From December through April, the North Pacific humpback whale (kohola, in Polynesian-Hawaiian) can often be seen in the waters around Kilauea Point. In the autumn, this endangered species migrates 3,500 miles from Alaska to the warm tropical waters around Hawai'i, where it mates and gives birth to its young. Adults weigh more than 40 tons (80,000 to 90,000 pounds), females average 45 feet in length, and males are slightly smaller. Newborn calves weigh as much as two tons (4,000 pounds) and are 10 to 15 feet in length.

It is simply awesome to watch these powerful, acrobatic giants suddenly breaching out of the ocean with their 15-foot pectoral fins outstretched like wings, then crashing onto the water's surface in a spectacular, geyser-like splash. Other visible behavior includes head slaps, "pec" (pectoral fin) slaps, and repeated tail slaps.

In 1992, to help protect these magnificent marine mammals, the five-unit Hawaiian Islands Humpback Whale National Marine Sanctuary was established around parts of the Hawaiian Islands—including a stretch of Kaua'i's north shore waters. For further information on the sanctuary: 726 South Kihei Road, Kihei (Maui), HI 96753; telephone: (800) 831-4888, (808) 335-0941 (Kaua'i), or (808) 541-3184 (O'ahu).

Spinner dolphins can sometimes be spotted cavorting offshore. They are named for their remarkable spinning leaps out of the ocean.

The Hawaiian monk seal, an endangered marine mammal, can sometimes be seen hauled out on the rocks below the cliffs.

A prominent historical feature of this refuge is Kilauea Lighthouse. It was built in 1913 as an aid to ships sailing between Hawai'i and the Orient. In 1979, it was placed on the National Register of Historic Places.

The refuge and its visitor center are open daily from 10 a.m. to 4 p.m. Trained volunteers provide interpretive services for visitors. A visitor center bookstore, operated by the Kilauea Point Natural History Association, offers publications and other items on environmental subjects. There is a refuge entrance fee. A local nonprofit support group, 1000 Friends of Kaua'i, is assisting Kilauea Point Refuge in various ways.

Visitor activities include birdwatching (binoculars may be borrowed at the visitor center), photography, and walking the 0.2-mile path from the parking area to the point. Picnicking is not permitted, as crumbs of food attract rodents that are harmful to the ground-nesting seabirds. As part of an annual whale festival in March, the refuge hosts a Hawaiian Islands Humpback Whale National Marine Sanctuary whale count by volunteers and an ocean fair that includes interpretive displays and lectures about whales, children's activities, and musical and other cultural presentations.

Coastal plants include naupaka, a densely branching, succulent-leaved shrub with small whitish, six-petaled flowers that look as though half the flower is missing; 'ilima, a low-growing shrub related to the hibiscus with heart-shaped leaves and bright, yellowish-orange flowers; akoko, a low-growing shrub with grayish-green, oval leaves; ahea'hea, a member of the goosefoot family with cream-colored flowers; and hala (screwpine or pandanus), originally from Polynesia, with tufts of long leaves roughly resembling a palm frond, fruit that looks somewhat like a pineapple, and unusual "stilt" roots spreading from the base of the trunk.

Another plant is the extremely rare and endangered olulu or alula (*Brighamia insignis*). In cooperation with the National Tropical Botanical Garden on Kaua'i, efforts are being made to restore this species to the refuge. It is a shrub or small tree that grows on sheer coastal cliffs and looks like a cabbage on a stick, with a thick, tapered trunk, broad succulent leaves, and white to cream to yellow flowers.

Lodgings and meals are available in such communities as Princeville, Kapa'a, Wailua, and Lihu'e.

Access to the refuge is north 2 miles on a paved spur road from State Route 56 at Kilauea.

Further information: Kilauea Point National Wildlife Refuge, P.O. Box 87, Kilauea, HI 96754; telephone: (808) 828-1413.

O'ahu Forest, consisting of 4,525 acres, was established in the year 2000 to protect some of the last remaining native forest habitats in the Waipio area on the Island of O'ahu, Hawai'i. According to the U.S. Fish and Wildlife Service, the mission of this refuge is "to conserve the structure and function of the native ecosystem and the natural diversity of flora and fauna, and to assist in the recovery of native plants and animals that are federally listed as threatened or endangered in the northern Ko'olau Mountains."

The Hawai'i Chapter of The Nature Conservancy helped to conduct biological surveys of this property, obtained funding, and negotiated the acquisition with the private landowner, Castle & Cooke, Inc. The Fish and Wildlife Service anticipates "working with the U.S. Army and the State of Hawaii's Department of Land and Natural Resources to protect a larger area of the northern Koolaus through the Koolau Forest Watershed Partnership."

The O'ahu Forest Refuge contains at least nine natural habitat communities. These include the dense, 'ohi'a-dominated rainforest on leeward upper mountain slopes; wind-gnarled 'ohi'a- and 'olapa-dominated cloud forest on windward upper slopes and ridge crests; scattered groves of loulu hiwa fan palms in the upper reaches of valleys and on steep windward slopes; 'uluhe-dominated wet shrubland on lower slopes; and koa-dominated mesic (moderately moist) forest at the refuge's lowest elevations. Numerous native species of plants are found on the refuge, including 17 that are listed as endangered, 1 that is a candidate for listing, and 2 others that are species of concern.

In addition, there are four species of endangered endemic O'ahu tree snails (*Achatinella* spp.).

Among the greatest threats to O'ahu Forest Refuge's ecosystem are a number of non-native animals including feral pigs; rats; mongooses; a predatory land snail; mosquitoes that transmit deadly avian malaria and pox diseases to birds; and insect pests, such as the two-spotted leafhopper and the black twig borer, that are harmful to native plants. The Fish and Wildlife Service considers the feral pig to be "one of the most pervasive and disruptive non-native animals in Hawaiian forests." A number of invasive non-native plant species, such as strawberry guava, paperbark, lantana, haole koa, Koster's curse, New Zealand tea tree, and Christmas berry, also pose a serious ecological challenge. The Fish and Wildlife Service is planning "to implement long-term management efforts to address the most critical threats and to promote rehabilitation of the natural ecosystem."

Visitor activities, such as birdwatching, photography, and interpretive and environmental education programs, are expected to eventually be offered to small groups of visitors, consistent with the refuge's management goals. Fees may be charged to help cover costs. Research projects that relate to management goals will likely be encouraged and allowed under the terms of special use permits.

Further information: O'ahu Forest National Wildlife Refuge, c/o O'ahu NWR Complex, 66-590 Kamehameha Highway, Room 2C-D, Haleiwa, HI 96712; telephone: (808) 637-6330.

Pearl Harbor, comprising 61 acres in two units, was established in 1972 to manage and protect human-made wetlands in the Pearl Harbor U.S. Naval Reservation, about 10 miles west of Honolulu on the Island of O'ahu, Hawai'i. This habitat provides important habitat for several endangered wetland birds: the Hawaiian moorhen, Hawaiian coot, Hawaiian stilt, and Hawaiian duck. Other birds include black-crowned night heron, a number of migratory ducks and shorebirds, and an occasional pueo (short-eared owl).

Entry onto this refuge is limited. Permits are issued for environmental education classes; guided tours are offered to the public during special events; and nonguided visitor activities include birdwatching and wildlife photography. A wildlife observation platform is provided at the refuge's HONOULIULI UNIT, on Pearl Harbor's West Loch.

Lodgings and meals are available in Honolulu and a number of other communities.

Further information: Pearl Harbor National Wildlife Refuge, c/o O'ahu NWR Complex, 66-590 Kamehameha Highway, Room 2C-D, Haleiwa, HI 96712; telephone: (808) 637-6330.

Hawai'i and Pacific Remote Islands Complex: Pacific Remote Islands Complex

Baker Island, encompassing 30,909 acres, was established in 1974 to protect this uninhabited, 27-foot-high, coral-topped emergent seamount island and a narrow fringing tropical coral reef.

This refuge is located 13 miles north of the Equator, about 1,600 nautical miles southwest of Honolulu, Hawai'i, in the mid-Pacific Ocean. It mainly provides nesting, roosting, and foraging habitats for approximately 20 species of seabirds and shorebirds. It is also home to 59 species of corals, 160 varieties of reef fish, and rare giant clams.

Prominent among the seabirds is the lesser frigatebird. Although this is normally a tree-nesting species, here on 405-acre Baker Island, it is forced to nest on the ground, where hundreds of its eggs are laid barely one and one-half feet apart. Other nesting seabirds include the graceful red-tailed tropicbird; boobies (masked, brown, and red-footed); sooty tern; noddies (brown, black, and blue-gray); common fairy-tern; and wedge-tailed and Audubon's shearwaters. The U.S. Fish and Wildlife Service is attempting to encourage the restoration of nesting colonies of the Phoenix petrel and white-throated storm petrel to Baker Island.

Among the wintering shorebirds, which breed in Alaska and/or Siberia, are the Pacific golden plover, wandering tattler, bristle-thighed curlew, ruddy turnstone, and sharp-tailed sandpiper.

Because of low rainfall and intense sunshine, terrestrial plant life consists of only low growing shrubs, ground-growing vines, and grasses. Eight of the 26 recorded plant species are believed to be native. Sand and coral shingle beaches fringe all sides of the island.

The most common and conspicuous land invertebrates are numerous red hermit crabs (*Coenobita perlatus*), which take up residence in abandoned marine snail shells. The threatened green sea turtle is abundant, and pods of bottlenose dolphins inhabit the waters around Baker.

More than 135 species of tropical fish have been identified in and around the surrounding reef, where more than 30 species of coral have also been identified.

In the words of the Fish and Wildlife Service, "Baker Island is a model of both sensitivity of insular ecosystems and mechanisms by which they recover following disturbance."

From 1830 to 1870, Baker Island served whaling ships as a provisioning and mail drop station. In 1857, the commander of the U.S.S. Saint Mary's, Charles S. Davis, officially took possession of the island for the United States, and accompanying representatives of the American Guano Company claimed the island for commercial mining of guano. From 1858 to the 1890s, company miners extracted 200,000 tons of seabird manure.

In 1935, the U.S. government sent five Americans to Baker to establish a small settlement, known as Meyertown, and help reinforce America's claim to this isolated outpost. In 1942, Japanese warplanes shelled the island and forced its evacuation. Soon thereafter, U.S. military personnel constructed a number of facilities on Baker Island, including an aircraft runway that was more than 1 mile long and 150 feet wide. These installations, like those on a number of other United States-claimed Pacific islands, were an integral part of America's strategic military operations in conjunction with the U.S. Navy's Pacific Fleet to counter Japanese aggression in the Pacific Theater of World War II. The Baker Island military facilities were abandoned in 1944.

In 1987, an examination of the island's historical sites identified the remains of the settlement and its lighthouse, a guano-mining structure, runway matting, and various trenches and mounds.

In March 2000, the first comprehensive marine surveys at the reefs around Baker were accomplished by the Fish and Wildlife Service and the National Marine Fisheries Service scientists. As explained by the Fish and Wildlife Service, "These surveys revealed that the coral reefs are healthy, but have been damaged by bleaching events and storm surges. Residual iron debris at the western anchorage may also be stimulating invasive species of blue-green algae. Fish populations were diverse and plentiful, and reef sharks were usually small but numerous."

Visitation to Baker Island is only by special permit for approved scientific and research purposes.

Further information: Baker Island National Wildlife Refuge, Pacific Remote Islands NWR Complex, P.O. Box 50167, Honolulu, HI 96850; telephone: (808) 541-1201.

Guam, containing 23,228 acres, was established in 1993 to enhance and protect ecologically significant marine and terrestrial habitats for native fauna and flora on the Island of Guam, a U.S. Territory in the southwestern Pacific Ocean. The refuge's stated goals are "to manage and conserve coral reef resources, restore native forest for the reintroduction of Guam's native birds, and protect the area's rich cultural heritage."

In 1993, the U.S. Navy's 371-acre Ritidian property, at the northern tip of the island, was transferred to the U.S. Fish and Wildlife Service. In 1994, cooperative agreements were signed with the U.S. Navy and Air Force, establishing overlay units of the refuge on 22,456 acres of U.S. Department of Defense properties. The latter lands are naturally not open to visitor use.

In the 1970s, conservationists began to be aware of and become alarmed by the rapidly dwindling numbers of many native bird species. A major culprit was the non-native brown tree snake (*Boiga irregularis*), which was accidentally introduced onto Guam soon after the end of World War II.

According to the U.S. Department of Agriculture's Animal and Plant Health Inspection Service, "Brown tree snakes are excellent climbers. The fact that they can support their weight with their tail enables them to stretch both upward and sideways." Large adults can grow to as much as 10 feet in length. With no natural predators to control this nocturnal snake, its population rapidly increased over the past half century as it aggressively preyed upon vulnerable small mammals and many native birds and their eggs. In the late 1990s, estimates ran as high as 15,000 of these mildly venomous snakes per square mile on Guam.

The young of an endangered mammal, the Mariana fruit bat, are a favored prey of the snake. The last remaining colony of these bats is located on one of the refuge's overlay units, on the Andersen Air Force Base.

At least eight species of native forest birds, several of which formerly lived only on Guam, have been eliminated. The Guam rail, Mariana moorhen, Mariana crow, and Mariana gray swiftlet, which are federally listed as endangered or threatened, are presently at risk. According to the Fish and Wildlife Service, however, "multi-agency recovery efforts are underway" for the swiftlet and moorhen, "and both species' prospects for future recovery are good."

A few other birds that are believed no longer to inhabit Guam still live on islands to the north. The Fish and Wildlife Service holds out the hope that these species can eventually be reestablished—if adequate snake control is continued, if the habitat is actively managed to combat invasive alien species, and if the habitat remains protected. Among these species are the totot (Mariana fruit dove), paluman apaka (white-throated ground-dove), egigi (Micronesian honeyeater), sasangal (Micronesian megapode), chichirika (rufous fantail), and ga'kaliso (nightingale reed-warbler).

To carry the snake's ecological impacts further, some of the native trees and other plants, which depend upon the birds and fruit bats for pollination and dispersal of seeds, may no longer be able to reproduce. Research has also shown that, without the forest birds, the island's populations of insects and spiders have significantly increased. Although a partnership of federal civilian and military agencies, the territorial government, and private organizations and individuals is actively working on various strategies to reduce the numbers and impacts of the brown tree snake, it continues to be an ecologically disruptive pest.

In addition, Guam's native terrestrial fauna and flora have been seriously impacted by habitat destruction, overhunting, and the introduction of three other non-native species—the feral pig, water buffalo, and deer. These three species, in particular, are major factors in the continuing decline of Guam's native forest.

As in many places around the world, the island's magnificent but fragile coral reef ecosystems have been impaired by soil erosion, pollution, and overfishing. And the vital nesting and foraging habitat of the threatened haggan (green sea turtle) continues to be severely impacted by human activities. A small part of this habitat is being given special protection along the 3-mile beach in the RITIDIAN UNIT and elsewhere on overlay refuge lands.

In the late 1970s, prior to establishment of the Guam National Wildlife Refuge, the Fish and Wildlife Service received a petition from the government of Guam recommending the listing of certain species of wildlife as endangered under the provisions of the Endangered Species Act. In 1984, seven native birds and two bats were federally listed.

In 1987 and 1988, the Fish and Wildlife Service received petitions from the governor of Guam and a resolution passed by the legislature seeking the designation of critical habitat for five species of birds and two species of fruit bats. During the subsequent, nearly 3-year rule-making process, several options were evaluated for achieving urgently needed habitat protection. Then in 1991, Guam's delegate to the U.S. Congress urged establishment of a national wildlife refuge.

In 1992, the Fish and Wildlife Service released a draft of an environmental assessment document for public comment. The government of Guam's Division of Aquatic and Wildlife Resources responded:

A refuge . . . will be extremely valuable to Guam for a number of reasons. . . . it will preserve habitat for wildlife; will provide a federally funded budget and personnel to help in solving problems associated with depredations by introduced animals, the recovery of endangered species, and illegal hunting; and will provide opportunities for public education and recreation. Other beneficial aspects of the refuge will be to preserve populations of many native plant species, protect numerous archaeological sites and large areas of watershed, and assist in the preservation of adjoining coral reefs by prohibiting most development.

We believe that the establishment of a national wildlife refuge is truly in the best interests of the people of Guam. . . . We encourage the Service to make the refuge as large as possible, thereby giving permanent protection to the natural resources on the lands under consideration.

Two years later, 401 acres of lands submerged to a 30-meter depth were added to the adjacent RITIDIAN UNIT, to enhance protection of an ecologically significant coral reef habitat that contains more than 90 varieties of coral. As former refuge manager Roger C. Di Rosa has explained, "A tropical coral reef is often referred to as the world's largest living organism because of its constantly growing and interconnected structure." By contrast, the basic creator of these enormous structures is a tiny animal known as a coral polyp. Guam's marine environment supports more than 800 species of colorful fish; many other animals, such as sea stars, sea cucumbers, sea snails, and crabs; and well over 50 kinds of marine plants. The refuge's protected area also serves as a vital nursery (spawning habitat) for numerous marine organisms. Some of the free-floating larvae are carried by ocean currents and help replenish more heavily fished reefs that are located elsewhere around Guam.

Except on Christmas, New Year's Day, and Thanksgiving, the refuge's Ritidian Unit is open daily. The refuge is closed at night. There is no entrance fee. Refuge headquarters, located here, is open on weekdays, except national holidays.

Visitor activities include hiking (along a forest road that loops back along the beach); guided interpretive programs on the natural resources and cultural history for families, teachers, and youth groups (by prior arrangement); picnicking; fishing in certain areas (rod and reel, throw nets, spears, and Hawaiian slings are allowed, but not gill or surround nets); and swimming, snorkeling, and scuba diving. Visitors are cautioned that ocean currents can be "very strong and hazardous," there are no lifeguards on duty, and visitors swim at their own risk. Coconuts, lemai (breadfruits), and plants containing medicinal properties may be collected by obtaining a free permit from the refuge headquarters. Collecting coral is prohibited. Camping is not allowed on the refuge.

Lodgings and meals are available elsewhere on the island.

The Andersen Air Force Base's Marine Resources Preserve, established in 1993, is near the refuge and protects additional important coral reef habitat.

Access to Guam Refuge's Ritidian Unit from Agana is north 5.5 miles on Marine Drive (Route 1), north (left) 6 miles on Route 3, and north (left) 6 miles on Route 3a.

Further information: Guam National Wildlife Refuge, P.O. Box 8134, MOU-3, Dededo, GU 96912; telephone: (671) 355-5096.

Hawaiian Islands contains 1,769 acres of land and more than 3,300,000 acres of coral reefs and water in the Northwestern Hawaiian Islands. This island chain stretches across 1,000 miles of mid-Pacific Ocean to the northwest of the main islands of Hawai'i. This refuge was established by President Theodore Roosevelt in 1909 to protect a remarkable array of wildlife. For many years prior to the refuge's establishment, numerous species of nesting seabirds were slaughtered for the commercial millinery value of their beautiful feathers, to satisfy the demands of fashion.

Island landscapes within the refuge range from low strands of beach with adjacent coral reefs and coral-reef-fringed, submerged volcanoes, to sheer cliffs of volcanic summits that rise from the depths of the sea.

Among the colonial nesting seabirds that crowd onto these bits of land are the Laysan and black-footed albatrosses; bonin and Bulwer's petrels; wedge-tailed and Christmas shearwaters; the graceful red-tailed tropicbird; boobies (masked, red-footed, and brown); great and lesser frigatebirds; terns (fairy, gray-backed, and sooty); and noddies (brown, black, and blue-gray).

On Laysan Island alone, there are as many as 1 million sooty terns. Resident species that inhabit nowhere else but these islands are the Laysan teal, Laysan finch, Nihoa finch, and Nihoa millerbird. Migratory shorebirds include Pacific golden plover, wandering tattler, and bristle-thighed curlew.

Other wildlife includes the federally listed endangered Hawaiian monk seal, which lives only in the Hawaiian Archipelago, with breeding populations at just eight locations between Nihoa and Kure islands. These light gray to brown marine mammals, which reach as much as 7 feet in length and weigh up to 500 pounds, are estimated to total only 1,300 individuals.

Of the reptiles, there are three species of sea turtles: the federally listed threatened Pacific green, and the federally listed endangered leatherback and hawksbill. Ninety percent of the Pacific greens in Hawai'i breed and lay their eggs within this refuge, at French Frigate Shoals.

Unfortunately, increasing quantities of marine debris are posing a serious threat to corals, seabirds, monk seals, and sea turtles. Many animals become hopelessly entangled in fishing nets and die. Shipwrecks may also harmfully impact the marine ecology. Recent research by the U.S. Fish and Wildlife Service has revealed that iron from the rusting hulls of steel ships apparently acts as a fertilizer that promotes extensive and unnatural growth of a certain kind of seaweed—blue-green algae, including Lyngbya. This growth causes long-term harm to the coral reef ecosystem.

Fortunately, research scientists have also been coming up with some good news. In September and October 2000, a research team of 50 scientists aboard 2 vessels during 60 field days, surveyed the reefs of the Northwestern Hawaiian Islands. They discovered some previously unknown marine species, including corals and sponges. Notable among the latter are ten new varieties of sponges from a single coral reef. Of the approximately 15,000 known species of sponges around the world, 200 to 300 of them inhabit Hawaiian waters, of which about 100 are found only in Hawai'i.

These multicellular animals function as filters as they take in seawater, use the nutrients it contains, and pump out the water, purified. As described by a front-page *Honolulu Advertiser* news story, "Sponges far more colorful than those in your kitchen grasp the walls of a 60-foot-deep sinkhole in the coral reef of Pearl and Hermes Atoll. Red and pink, purple and black, some branched and tube-shaped, they are species never before seen, anywhere." These sponges are but a tiny part of the complex and largely untouched but fragile web of life within this unique national wildlife refuge.

In recent years, Laysan Island has been the focus of an encouraging native species recovery program to restore its devastated ecological balance. The island's 913 acres were previously mined for guano, its large colonies of nesting seabirds were slaughtered to furnish feathers for the millenary trade, and non-native plants and animals were introduced, further degrading the fragile ecosystem. By the year 2000, a scientific survey by the Northwestern Hawaiian Islands Expedition was able to report that non-native grasses have been eliminated and other aliens are being removed, native grasses have been planted, and Laysan's percentage of native flora has increased from less than 50 percent to more than 80 percent.

All the islands of this refuge are closed to public access, except by special permit.

In December 2000, additional protection was given to the northwestern Hawaiian Islands region when, by executive order, President Bill Clinton established the Northwestern Hawaiian Islands Coral Reef Ecosystem Reserve, which he characterized as "a special place where the sea is a living rainbow." This underwater area contains close to 70 percent of all coral reefs in the

United States, encompasses 84 million acres, and is America's largest nature preserve. As with a number of other marine reserves, the U.S. Department of Commerce has been given the authority to protectively manage the area's ecologically rich marine ecosystem (the refuge is managed by the U.S. Department of the Interior).

As reported in *The New York Times* (Dec. 5, 2000), "The order bans oil and gas exploration, the dumping of any material and any alterations of the seabed or the coral in the preserve. It also caps fishing at recent or current levels." In President Clinton's words, ". . . the world's reefs are in peril. Pollution, damage from dynamite fishing, coral poachers, unwise coastal development and global warming have already killed more than 25 percent of the world's reefs."

Referring to President Theodore Roosevelt's establishment of the national wildlife refuge, President Clinton said, "He knew then that our natural wonders on land and sea form an integral part of who we are as a people, and that every generation of Americans must do its part to sustain and strengthen this legacy. Today we do just that, incorporating the refuge he created into a new, vast and wonderful Yellowstone of the sea."

Further refuge information: Hawaiian Islands National Wildlife Refuge, c/o Pacific Remote Islands NWR Complex, P.O. Box 50167, Honolulu, HI 96850; telephone: (808) 541-1201.

Howland Island, comprising 32,074 acres, was established in 1974 to protect this uninhabited, 20-foot-high, coral-topped emergent seamount island and a fringing coral reef. This refuge is located 48 miles north of the equator, about 1,600 nautical miles southwest of Honolulu, Hawai'i in the mid-Pacific Ocean. It mainly provides nesting, roosting, and foraging habitats for about 20 species of seabirds and shorebirds.

This island's nesting seabirds include the graceful red-tailed tropicbird; boobies (masked, brown, and red-footed); sooty tern; brown and black noddies; common fairy-tern; and wedge-tailed and Audubon's shearwaters. In 1986, the U.S. Fish and Wildlife Service eliminated a number of feral cats, which were introduced onto the island in the late 1930s. The absence of these unnatural predators now makes possible the restoration of breeding populations of the smaller burrow-nesting seabirds, such as the Phoenix petrel, white-throated storm petrel, and the smallest of the world's terns, the blue-gray noddy. The island's wintering shorebirds, which breed in Alaska and/or Siberia, are the Pacific golden-plover, wandering tattler, bristle-thighed curlew, ruddy turnstone, and sharp-tailed sandpiper.

Because of low rainfall, intense sunshine, and other ecological factors, plant life on this 455-acre island consists mostly of low-growing shrubs, ground-growing vines, and grasses. Of the 14 species, nine are believed to be native. A grove of Kou trees (*Cordia subcordata*) on the island's interior provides nesting habitat for red-footed boobies and shelter for bristle-thighed curlews. Sand and coral shingle beaches fringe the island.

The most conspicuous terrestrial invertebrates are the abundant red hermit crabs (*Coenobita perlatus*), which take up residence in abandoned marine snail shells. The threatened green sea turtle and pods of Pacific bottlenose dolphins inhabit the waters around the island.

Beginning in 1822, a number of whaling ships visited this island. Commercial mining of guano was carried on here. From 1857 to 1878 and from 1886 to 1891, miners extracted 85,000 tons of seabird manure.

In 1935, the U.S. government sent a small group of Americans to Howland to establish a small community, known as Itascatown, and help reinforce America's claim to this isolated outpost. In 1942, Japanese warplanes shelled the island, killed two residents, and forced the evacuation of the others. In 1987, a survey of the island's historical sites identified a lighthouse and the remains of the settlement.

In March 2000, the Fish and Wildlife Service and National Marine Fisheries Service marine biologists conducted detailed surveys of Howland for the first time, reporting many new records of corals, fish, and invertebrates. A total of 154 fish species, 53 coral species, and 26 species of other invertebrates have now been recorded at Howland. One permanent, 100-meter coral reef monitoring transect was also established.

Visitation to Howland Island is only by special permit for approved scientific and research purposes.

Further information: Howland Island National Wildlife Refuge, c/o Pacific Remote Islands NWR Complex, P.O. Box 50167, Honolulu, HI 96850; telephone: (808) 541-1201.

Jarvis Island, containing 36,483 acres, was established in 1974 to protect this uninhabited, low-lying emergent seamount island and a surrounding tropical coral reef. This refuge is located 25 miles south of the equator, 200 nautical miles southwest of the Line Islands' Kiritimati (Christmas Island) and about 1,300 nautical miles southwest of Honolulu, Hawai'i in the mid-Pacific Ocean. It mainly provides nesting, roosting, and foraging habitats for approximately 20 species of seabirds and shorebirds.

Of the 14 kinds of seabirds, there are the graceful red-tailed tropicbird; boobies (masked, brown, and red-footed); sooty tern (one of the world's largest colonies); noddies (brown, black, and blue-gray); common fairy-tern; wedge-tailed and Audubon's shearwaters; and Phoenix and white-throated storm petrels. Many species of seabirds no longer nested on Jarvis Island following the introduction of cats to the island. Since these unnatural predators were eliminated, the numbers and diversity of nesting seabirds have been encouragingly escalating.

Migratory shorebirds, which breed in Alaska and/or Siberia, include the Pacific golden plover, wandering tattler, bristle-thighed curlew, ruddy turnstone, and sharp-tailed sandpiper. In March 2000, the first-ever marine biological surveys of Jarvis were accomplished around the shallow reefs of the island by a cooperative U.S. Fish and Wildlife Service and National Marine Fisheries Service expedition. Despite the pristine nature of this island and its reefs, only 32 species of coral and 30 species of other invertebrates were recorded here—about half the totals for Howland and Baker. However, 160 species of fish were recorded in the waters of Jarvis Island Refuge.

This 1,086-acre island provides nesting habitat for the threatened green sea turtle. Pods of bottlenose dolphins inhabit the water around the island, and numerous species of tropical fish live in and around the coral reef formations.

Because of low rainfall and intense sunshine, plant life consists of low-growing shrubs, ground-growing vines, other herbaceous plants, and grasses.

In 1821, Jarvis Island was discovered by Captain Brown of the English ship *Eliza Francis*. By 1879, the American Guano Company had mined 300,000 tons of guano from here. In 1889, Britain laid claim to Jarvis, and in 1906, a London and Melbourne company leased the island to extract additional quantities of the seabird manure.

In 1935, the U.S. government sent a small group of Americans to Jarvis to establish a settlement, known as Millerville, and help reinforce America's claim to this island. The settlers built a monument to symbolize the change from British to United States ownership. As a consequence of Britain's lack of response, Jarvis Island has remained under American ownership.

Visitation to Jarvis Island is only by special permit for approved scientific and research purposes.

Further information: Jarvis Island National Wildlife Refuge, c/o Pacific Remote Islands NWR Complex, P.O. Box 50167, Honolulu, HI 96850; telephone: (808) 541-1201.

Johnston Atoll, containing 696 acres of land, was established as a wildlife reserve in 1926 to offer protection for numerous species of nesting seabirds and the fragile coral reef ecosystem at one of the world's most isolated atolls. This refuge is located 718 nautical miles southwest of Honolulu, Hawai'i. Johnston Atoll is an unincorporated United States territory in the central Pacific Ocean.

About 70 million years ago, numerous volcanic eruptions of lava at the bottom of the sea gradually created a submarine volcano whose summit ultimately reached the ocean surface as an island. During subsequent millions of years, the mountaintop island gradually eroded and sank. As it slowly subsided, coral reef formations grew around its edges.

The resulting extensive growth of corals and coralline algae now comprises a broad, submerged, platform-like, 50-square-mile reef. Its shallow, warm tropical waters, at depths of less than 100 feet, are rich in marine life that flourishes on an abundance of sunlight and clean ocean water. A stretch of emergent reef along the northwest side of the atoll is awash at low water; four islands—Johnston, Sand, North, and East—are scattered in the lagoon across the atoll. As the only emergent land and shallow water in more than 800,000 square miles of Pacific Ocean, this atoll is a true oasis for birds and reef life.

Johnston Atoll, originally two small islands, was initially enlarged from 56 acres of land by the U.S. Navy in 1939 and continued to be increased in subsequent stages to support various U.S. military missions.

From 1958 to 1962, rockets were launched from Johnston Atoll as part of the atmospheric nuclear testing program, which was later banned by international treaty. In 1972, Agent Orange (1.37 million gallons) was brought to the island and stored here until 1977. Some of the agent leaked into the ground. The remaining agent was destroyed aboard an incinerator ship at sea. Chemical munitions were brought here from Okinawa in 1971 and from Germany in 1990. From June 1990 through November 2000, the Johnston Atoll Chemical Agent Disposal System (JACADS) destroyed about 2,000 tons of nerve agent (GB and VX) and blister agent (HD, mustard) and more than 412,000 individual munitions. All chemical weapons agents here have been destroyed.

One might presume from this history that Johnston Atoll had become seriously contaminated and was thus rendered uninhabitable by native fish and wildlife. Ecological monitoring and research programs are carried out by staff biologists of the U.S. Fish and Wildlife Service and by U.S. Department of Defense-sponsored, independent scientists from the Boston University Marine Program. Other partnerships include Woods Hole Oceanographic Institute. Although all the scientific evidence gathered over a period of 15 years has apparently confirmed that the chemical disposal operations did not adversely impact the atoll's natural terrestrial and marine ecosystems, the Fish and Wildlife Service cautions against reading too much into this conclusion. It is possible "there may be more subtle effects that we have not detected yet or even looked for."

The atoll is inhabited by 15 species of nesting seabirds, 5 species of migratory shorebirds, 33 species of corals, and more than 300 species of tropical fishes. Also found at the refuge are several federally listed threatened or endangered species: the green sea turtle, the Hawaiian monk seal (a rare visitor), and the wintering North Pacific humpback whale.

Seabirds are uniquely adapted to their marine environment. Many have bills suited to catch fish and squid, and long, slender wings designed for effortless soaring and gliding. Salt glands make it possible for them to drink seawater and excrete excess salt. Because of the seabird colonies on Sand, North, and East islands, public access is strictly regulated.

As explained by refuge manager D. Lindsey Hayes:

Most, but not all, of the seabirds breed on the three smaller islands of the atoll, where public access is restricted to prevent disturbance. Sooty terns are by far the most abundant bird; as many as 150,000 or more may breed on these islands. Also breeding on the outer islands are brown noddies; gray-backed terns; great frigatebirds; red-footed, brown, and masked boobies; red-tailed tropicbirds; wedge-tailed and Christmas shearwaters; and Bulwer's petrels.

White terns (except a few) and black noddies breed exclusively on Johnston Island, where trees are present. Most of the red-tailed tropicbird population breeds on Johnston Island, where most of the shade from vegetation is available to them. Some shearwaters breed on the older portions of Johnston Island; and an occasional white-tailed tropicbird and rarely a blue-gray noddy will breed here, as well.

A few migratory shorebirds winter at Johnston Atoll, such as the abundant Pacific golden plover; common ruddy turnstone; and less common bristle-thighed curlew, wandering tattler, and sanderling.

Some of the more abundant and colorful reef fishes at Johnston Atoll include butterflyfish, surgeonfish, squirrelfish, goat fish, parrot fish, triggerfish, and wrasses. Moray eels and gray reef sharks are common; manta and eagle rays are also frequently seen.

Further information: Johnston Atoll National Wildlife Refuge, P.O. Box 396, APO AP 96558; telephone: (808) 421-0011, extension 3182.

Kingman Reef, containing approximately 483,700 acres, was established in 2001. This refuge consists of less than 3 acres of unvegetated coral rubble, more than 25,800 acres of coral reef habitat, and surrounding waters within the 12-nautical-mile United States territorial sea. It is the northernmost of the Line Islands, about 1,000 miles south of Hawai'i in the central Pacific Ocean.

As described by regional director Anne Badgley of the U.S. Fish and Wildlife Service's Pacific Islands Ecoregion, "The refuge will protect a spectacular diversity of coral reef fishes, corals, giant clams, and other marine organisms, as well as provide habitat for migratory seabirds and shorebirds and threatened green sea turtles."

The refuge is not open to visitation.

Further information: Kingman Reef National Wildlife Refuge, 300 Ala Moana Boulevard, Room 5-231, Box 50167, Honolulu, HI 96850; telephone: (808) 541-1201.

Midway Atoll, encompassing 298,369 acres, was established in 1988 to restore and protect vital habitats for a remarkable variety of birds and marine life. This ecologically rich atoll, which consists of a coral-reef-encircled lagoon and three islands, is located about 1,250 nautical miles west-northwest of Honolulu, Hawai'i, near the west end of the Hawaiian archipelago in the mid-Pacific Ocean. Sand Island consists of about 1,200 acres, Eastern Island 334 acres, and Spit Island 6 acres. The entire atoll measures approximately 5 miles in diameter.

The refuge is an astounding mecca for nearly 2 million birds, highlighted by 15 species of colonial nesting seabirds. From late October or early November through July, Midway supports the world's largest nesting colony of the Laysan albatross ("white gooney"), totaling close to 400,000 pairs. These graceful gliders are held aloft on slender wings that span about 6.5 feet. They appear to fly without effort, annually navigating across thousands of miles of open Pacific Ocean and feeding mostly on squid. On Midway, these birds choose nesting sites that are densely scattered across grassy and other open areas. Here they perform elaborate courtship rituals of bill-clapping, bowing, head-wagging, and "sky pointing," accompanied by an array of whistling and moaning sounds. The female usually lays the pair's single egg by mid-December, and the fuzzy chick hatches in late January or early February, fledges in July, and remains at sea for several years before returning to breed on Midway.

The world's second largest nesting colony of the darker and slightly larger black-footed albatross ("black gooney"), with a 7-foot wingspan, numbers about 18,000 pairs. It is typically seen along the atoll's sandy shorelines, feeding mostly on the eggs of flying fish. A few of the rare short-tailed albatross, with a 7.5-foot wingspread, also nest on Midway.

From February to August, Midway hosts about 5,000 pairs of the ground-nesting red-tailed tropicbird. These stunningly beautiful and graceful birds have mostly pure white plumage, red bills, and long red tail streamers. There are also just a few breeding pairs of the smaller and more slender white-tailed tropicbird.

A few hundred red-footed boobies build their nesting platforms of sticks on Eastern Island's shrubby tree heliotropes (*Tournefortia argentea*) and beach naupakas (*Scaevola sericea*). A few of the ground-nesting masked boobies also breed on Eastern Island. Roughly 100 pairs of the great frigatebird nest among the red-footed boobies. Riding the air currents on their 7.5-foot wingspan and long, forked tail, they easily circle and glide long distances without flapping their wings. These "pirates" have a habit of ganging up on a tropicbird or booby that is bringing food to a hungry chick, and forcing it to disgorge its catch of squid or fish. During courtship, the male frigatebird inflates its bright-red throat pouch to attract a mate.

Five species of terns nest on Midway. From March through August, roughly 50,000 pairs of ground-nesting sooty terns breed and raise their young on Eastern and Spit islands. Researchers have discovered that the female sooties lay a single egg almost simultaneously. Gray-backed terns also nest on these two islands. About 6,000 pairs of black noddies, occupying Sand Island from November through August, build their nests in ironwood trees, and roughly 1,000 brown noddies may be seen between May and November. More than 7,000 pairs of the common fairy-tern (also known as the white tern) breed and raise their young on Midway.

These graceful birds simply lay their single egg—often precariously, with no semblance of a nest—on the branch of an ironwood tree or other handy surface.

Three species of nocturnal seabirds come to Midway. Up to 50,000 pairs of the burrow-nesting Bonin petrel return in August to breed. In March, about a thousand pairs of the wedge-tailed shearwater return to nest in shallow burrows, and a few of the smaller, ground-nesting Christmas shearwater occupy Eastern Island.

Wintering shorebirds, which nest in Alaska, include the Pacific golden plover, wandering tattler, bristle-thighed curlew, and ruddy turnstone. Two non-native species of birds reside on Midway: canaries, descendants of pets released in the early twentieth century; and the common myna, originally from India, which occasionally preys upon the eggs of white and sooty terns and black noddies.

Most endangered of Midway's marine fauna is the Hawaiian monk seal. The world's total population of this species in the wild is fewer than 1,500. Approximately 60 of them inhabit the waters around the atoll and haul themselves up on island beaches to rest. About 250 spinner dolphins regularly seek the shelter of the atoll's lagoon during the day to rest, play, or mate after feeding in the open ocean at night. Threatened green sea turtles frequent Sand Island's harbor and sometimes haul themselves onto the atoll's beaches. Spotted eagle rays are often seen swimming in the lagoon. Tiger sharks enter the lagoon when vulnerable albatross chicks offer tempting prey; and Galapagos sharks inhabit the waters outside the reef. The more than 250 kinds of tropical reef fishes include such species as convict and other surgeonfishes, angelfishes, butterflyfishes, damselfishes, regal and other parrot fishes, reef triggerfish, yellow and other tangs, Hawaiian squirrelfish, Hawaiian morwong, sunrise and other wrasses, and the dragon moray. Marlin and tuna inhabit the ocean waters outside the atoll.

In 1988, the U.S. Navy agreed to the establishment of an "overlay" national wildlife refuge at Midway, so that threatened and endangered species of seabirds and other wildlife could be given urgently needed enhanced protection. Closure of the naval air facility was announced in 1993, and the atoll was transferred to the U.S. Fish and Wildlife Service in 1996. Before departing, the U.S. Navy spent nearly $100 million in a major cleanup and restoration program. More than 100 dilapidated buildings and other structures were demolished. Many above-ground and underground fuel storage tanks were also removed, and environmentally harmful contaminants were cleaned up.

Habitat restoration programs have continued in earnest. Rats, which had preyed upon the eggs and chicks of petrels and other seabirds since being introduced to Midway, have been eradicated. With the assistance of refuge volunteers, some of the Australian ironwood trees (*Casuarina*), golden crown-beard, and other non-native plants are being removed, and grasses and native shrubs, such as beach naupaka, are being planted to reestablish and enhance habitat for the nesting seabirds and other wildlife.

Among the refuge's historic structures are the cable station buildings, the military's power plant and command post, U.S. Marine barracks, radar buildings, ammunition storage huts, gun emplacements, pillboxes, runways, and a seaplane hangar and ramps.

The Friends of Midway Atoll National Wildlife Refuge is a nonprofit support group that provides assistance to the refuge.

Midway Atoll Refuge was first opened to visitors in 1996. However, in March 2002, an agreement was terminated between the Fish and Wildlife Service and a private-sector partner that had been providing lodgings, food, and other services. By 2003, the Service hopes to obtain the services of a new partner that will maintain and manage the small community's infrastructure and provide various visitor services. Prospective visitors should contact the Fish and Wildlife Service for information on flights to Midway, package tours, lodgings, food, and other visitor services and activities.

Further information: Midway Atoll National Wildlife Refuge, P.O. Box 29460, Honolulu, HI 96820; telephone: (808) 599-3914 or (808) 541-1201.

Palmyra Atoll, containing more than 515,200 acres, was established in 2001. This refuge consists of a wet tropical atoll in the Line Islands, just over 1 thousand miles south of Hawai'i and about 300 miles north of the equator in the central Pacific Ocean.

As the U.S. Fish and Wildlife Service explains:

The islets at Palmyra Atoll are densely vegetated with native coastal strand flora and an outstanding natural Pisonia grandis rainforest community. The islets and surrounding waters of the atoll support endangered and threatened sea turtles and a large and diverse seabird community. Large areas of tidal sandflats are exposed at low tide and serve as important foraging grounds for migratory shorebirds. The lagoon, reefs, and open waters of the atoll support a diversity of coral reef and other marine species, including giant clams, pearl oysters, and reports of endangered Hawaiian monk seals.

As described by regional director Anne Badgley of the Fish and Wildlife Service's Pacific Islands Ecoregion:

Palmyra hosts the second-largest nesting colony of red-footed boobies in the world and large colonies of other seabirds, including 750,000 sooty terns. These birds rely on the surrounding waters to provide the food they and their chicks need, and it's critical that the entire atoll ecosystem be protected.

In addition to the forests of *Pisonia* trees that grow up to 80 feet tall, other native flora include several species of ferns, such as bird's-nest fern (*Asplenium nidus*) and lau'ae fern (*Phymatosorus scolopendria*), and two plants of the coastal strand, beach naupaka (*Scaevola sericea*) and tree heliotrope (*Tournefortia argentea*). Among non-native species, coconut palms are prominent. A botanical survey has identified 27 native plant species, out of a total of 117 species on the atoll.

The nearly 30 varieties of birds that have been recorded here include nesting red-footed, brown, and masked boobies; black and brown noddies; sooty and white terns; white-tailed and red-tailed tropicbirds; and great frigatebird. Wintering species include Pacific golden plover, ruddy turnstone, bristle-thighed curlew, and wandering tattler.

Land crabs are abundant—notably two kinds of land hermit crabs (*Coenobita brevimanus* and *C. perlatus*), a native land crab (*Cardisoma carnifax*), and the coconut crab (*Birgus latro*). The latter species is recognized as the largest terrestrial invertebrate in the world.

According to the Fish and Wildlife Service's Jim Maragos, a preliminary survey of coral fauna has revealed many genera:

Of particular interest at Palmyra is the spectacular development of table and staghorn Acropora species on the shallow western reefs outside the lagoon. The southern reefs and eastern pools provide an amazing display of coral diversity, abundance, and high underwater visibility. Additionally, the coral reefs on the western portion of the atoll were less affected by past Navy dredging activities. Despite major dredging impacts to the three lagoon areas, the outer reefs remain healthy and vibrant and support approximately 36 genera and 150 species of stony corals. This is more than double the coral species diversity of that in the main Hawaiian Islands or Johnston Atoll; nearly double that of Howland and Baker islands; and five times that of Jarvis Island. This unusually diverse coral community may be the result of Palmyra Atoll's proximity to the equatorial countercurrent, which brings coral larvae from the diversity-rich western Pacific, and the atoll's great variety of habitats favorable for coral development.

The endangered Hawaiian monk seal has twice been seen at Palmyra Atoll, and the pilot whale and bottlenose dolphin have been spotted in the lagoon. Both the endangered hawksbill sea turtle and the threatened green sea turtle are known to nest on the atoll.

About 200 fish species have already been identified in the waters around the reefs and in the lagoon, including bonefish, milkfish, mullet, and blacktip reef sharks. More thorough surveys in deeper water and in the lagoon would yield numerous additional species.

The atoll was named for a vessel, the *Palmyra*, which came ashore during a storm in 1802. In 1922, the Fullard-Leo family of Honolulu purchased the atoll. Starting in 1938, in spite of strong opposition from the owners, the U.S. Navy constructed an airstrip and then used the atoll as a strategic military base during World War II. Following the war, the owners successfully defeated the federal government's attempt to retain ownership, in a lawsuit that was appealed to the U. S. Supreme Court.

At the time the refuge was added to the National Wildlife Refuge System, the atoll's 680 acres of emergent lands had been acquired from the surviving Fullard-Leo family members and were owned by a private conservation organization, The Nature Conservancy (TNC). According to the Fish and Wildlife Service, the agency "is negotiating with TNC to purchase a major part of the atoll, and both entities would work together to conserve the atoll's rich biological diversity. The submerged lands and waters at Palmyra were [previously] administered by the Office of Insular Affairs and . . . were transferred to the Fish and Wildlife Service. . . ."

A few visitor activities, compatible with the needs of protecting the atoll's natural ecosystems, are anticipated by the Fish and Wildlife Service, in partnership with The Nature Conservancy. It is expected that guided and unguided activities will include birdwatching, photography, hiking on designated trails, snorkeling and scuba diving in certain areas, limited recreational fishing, and possibly kayak tours on the lagoon. "Visiting boats would be allowed to come to Palmyra on a 'prior permission required' basis." An entrance fee is likely to be charged, to cover costs of managing the visitor use program. Upon arrival, all visitors would be required to attend an orientation session on the refuge's resources and on guidelines for visitor activities. It is also expected that lodging and dining facilities will be provided.

Further information: Palmyra Atoll National Wildlife Refuge, 300 Ala Moana Boulevard, Room 5-231, Box 50167, Honolulu, HI 96850; telephone: (808) 541-1201.

Rose Atoll, consisting of 39,251 acres, was established in the 1970s to protect a 15-acre emergent island and surrounding submerged land and water. The refuge features one of the world's smallest atolls, located in the U.S. territory of American Samoa, about 2,700 nautical miles south of Hawai'i in the southwest Pacific Ocean. Rose Atoll Refuge is managed jointly with the government of American Samoa. Rose is the only protected area in the Territory of American Samoa, supporting the majority of seabirds, sea turtles, and giant sea clams found in the territory, and several rare species of fish found there.

Of the birds inhabiting Rose Island, the red-footed booby and great and lesser frigatebirds place their nests atop buka trees; the common fairy-tern and black noddy build their nests among these trees' lower branches; and the sooty tern and brown noddy lay their eggs among barren "coral rubble." The gray-backed tern nests on Sand Island, where there is no vegetation.

During the 1990s, several detailed marine biological surveys were conducted at the atoll. More than 40 species of coral, 100 species of fish, and large populations of the rare giant clam (*Tridacna maxima*) were recorded. The refuge also provides vital egg-laying habitat for two species of sea turtle—the Pacific green and the federally listed endangered hawksbill.

Because of the sensitivity of the seabird colonies and other wildlife, entry onto this refuge is strictly regulated—authorized only by permit, which is issued by the refuge manager and the government of American Samoa.

Further information: Rose Atoll National Wildlife Refuge, c/o Pacific Remote Islands NWR Complex, P.O. Box 50167, Honolulu, HI 96850; telephone: (808) 541-1201.

Idaho

Bear Lake, comprising 18,085 acres, was established in 1968 primarily to manage and protect an extensive wetland, locally known as Dingle Marsh, for the benefit of migrating and nesting waterfowl. The refuge is scenically located in mountain-framed Bear Lake Valley in the southeastern corner of Idaho. The roughly 17,000 acres of wetland habitat within the refuge consist mostly of a bulrush marsh, with areas of open water and flooded meadows of rushes, sedges, and grasses. Adjacent parts of the refuge are comprised of scattered grassland habitat and shrub-covered, lower mountain slopes.

Among the most common of the refuge's nesting waterfowl are Canada geese, mallards, cinnamon teal, northern shovelers, gadwalls, canvasbacks, and redheads. One of the most prominent birds on the refuge is the greater sandhill crane. In late September, flocks numbering from 200 to 500 of these magnificent birds are frequently attracted to the refuge's grain fields before their southward migration to wintering areas in New Mexico, Arizona, and Mexico.

As the result of water diversion for agricultural uses and of Utah Power and Light Company's system of canals and a pumping station for water storage and power generation activities, water levels in the marsh seasonally fluctuate—from high in the spring to significantly lower levels in the late summer and autumn.

Bear Lake Refuge's management activities include hay cutting to offer ibises, cranes, and waterfowl important feeding and rearing habitat in low cover that is flooded in the spring; planting several fields adjacent to the marsh in nutrient-rich crops such as barley and alfalfa to provide a supplemental food source for geese and cranes; and controlling non-native, invasive species of plants. Periodic prescribed burning is also used to create areas of open water amid dense expanses of marsh vegetation, to promote nutrient cycling, and to spur the growth of new plants of value to waterfowl and other wildlife.

The dominant plant species of the deeper area of the wetland is the hard-stemmed bulrush (*Scirpus lacustris*), or "tule," that grows to a height of about 7 feet. As described by the Fish and Wildlife Service, the "Bulrush provides life needs for a diversity of migratory birds and small mammals. It affords shelter from the elements and cover for escape from predators. It provides concealment for nest sites and it is used for nesting material. Various wildlife species eat the plant's seeds, stems and roots. The tall stems serve as perches for certain birds to sing and establish their territories. In addition, the vastness of the bulrush marsh contributes to the seclusion needed by many species for successful nesting."

Establishment of Bear Lake Refuge was made possible partly with revenues from the sale of Migratory Bird Hunting and Conservation Stamps (Duck Stamps). Ducks Unlimited, Inc., PacifiCorp, and the Idaho Department of Fish and Game were key partners in enhancing approximately 1,800 acres of the refuge's wetland habitat.

The refuge is open daily during daylight hours. There is no entrance fee. The refuge headquarters, located at 370 Webster Street, Montpelier, is open on weekdays, except national holidays.

Visitor activities include birdwatching; photography; driving the unpaved Wildlife Observation Route around the SALT MEADOW UNIT; hiking; cross-country skiing and snowshoeing (on roads open to motor vehicles, and in all areas that are not closed to all entry, from July 1 through February); canoeing and boating on parts of the refuge between September 20 and January 15 (boat-launching sites are provided on the refuge's RAINBOW UNIT and at adjacent North Beach State Park); swimming at the state park; and hunting (waterfowl, coots, snipe, gray partridge, sage-grouse, and cottontail) on parts of the refuge during the designated seasons. Although camping is not permitted on the refuge, campground facilities are provided in Bear Lake State Park's NORTH BEACH UNIT.

Hiking opportunities are available on all roads that are open to motor vehicles, and in all areas from July 1 through February, except in areas designated on the refuge map as closed to all entry.

Insect repellent is advised during the warmer months. Visitors are cautioned to be prepared for cold weather at this refuge's 5,900-foot elevation.

Lodgings and meals are available in Montpelier.

Access to Bear Lake Refuge from the junction of U.S. Routes 30 and 89 in Montpelier is west 3 miles on U.S. Route 89 and south (left) 5 miles on unpaved Bear Lake County Airport Road.

Further information: Bear Lake National Wildlife Refuge, 370 Webster, Box 9, Montpelier, ID 83254; telephone: (208) 847-1757.

Camas, containing 10,578 acres, was established in 1937 primarily to protect wetlands that attract concentrations of migrating and nesting waterfowl, shorebirds, and other wildlife. The refuge is located at the northeastern end of the arid Snake River Plains in southeastern Idaho.

Roughly 60 percent of the refuge is a mixture of wetland habitats, from subirrigated meadows and bulrush marshes to open lakes and ponds. Most of the remaining acreage consists of a variety of upland meadows and sagebrush-and-grass and other arid-environment shrub habitats. Camas Creek, which flows for 8 miles through the refuge, is the source of water for many of the lakes and ponds. About 40 acres of Camas Refuge are available for growing nutrient-rich crops of barley, wheat, and alfalfa for the benefit of waterfowl.

Among the most prominent or common nesting waterfowl are Canada geese, mallards, cinnamon teal, northern shovelers, gadwalls, and redheads, and a few trumpeter swans. Both trumpeter and tundra swans are abundant during spring and autumn migrations. The peak of waterfowl concentrations on the refuge occurs in March–April and October–November, sometimes totaling as many as 50,000 birds.

Other species that nest on Camas Refuge include the greater sandhill crane, long-billed curlew, black-necked stilt, American avocet, Wilson's phalarope, and red-winged and yellow-headed blackbirds. The refuge attracts a number of colonial nesting species, such as the great blue heron, black-crowned night-heron, snowy egret, white-faced ibis, Franklin's gull, several species of terns, and double-crested cormorant. American white pelicans summer on the refuge, and a few bald eagles usually winter here, often roosting at night in the refuge's cottonwood trees. In 1983, the refuge erected a nesting tower for the endangered peregrine falcon. Six years later, this species nested successfully in the tower and has since nested there every year. Today, peregrines may be observed in spring, summer, and fall. Over 210 bird species have been recorded on the refuge.

Mammals include moose, Rocky Mountain elk, white-tailed and mule deer, pronghorns, bobcat, coyote, red fox, beaver, muskrat, striped skunk, porcupine, badger, black-tailed jackrabbit, mountain cottontail, Richardson ground squirrel and Uinta ground squirrels, and Ord kangaroo rat.

To benefit waterfowl and other wetland wildlife, an elaborate system for water distribution and containment has been constructed, some of it by crews of the Works Progress Administration in the late 1930s. The system presently includes more than 30 miles of canals and ditches, 12 miles of dikes, and 25 water control structures.

Establishment of the refuge was made possible partly with revenues from the sale of Migratory Bird Hunting and Conservation Stamps (Duck Stamps). Ducks Unlimited, Inc. has helped enhance approximately 600 acres of the refuge's wetland habitat.

The refuge is open daily during daylight hours. There is no entrance fee. The refuge headquarters is open on weekdays, except national holidays.

Visitor activities include birdwatching, photography, driving on the Wildlife Viewing Route, hiking, bicycling on roads open to motor vehicles, cross-country skiing and snowshoeing, and hunting (waterfowl and upland game birds) on two parts of the refuge during the designated seasons. Camping is not permitted on the refuge, but facilities are provided at a privately owned campground in Roberts and at public campgrounds in the Targhee National Forest.

Hiking opportunities include a trail that winds through a riparian woodland of cottonwoods, willows, and boxelders; any of the refuge roads that are not closed to visitors; and elsewhere on the refuge, from July 16 through February.

Insect repellent is advised during the warmer months. Visitors are cautioned to be prepared for cold weather from autumn through spring at the refuge's 4,800-foot elevation.

Lodgings and meals are available in such communities as Dubois, Idaho Falls, Rexburg, and Arco.

Access to Camas Refuge is north 32 miles from Idaho Falls on I-15, exiting at Hamer and proceeding north 3 miles on the frontage road, and (at the refuge directional sign) west (left) 2 miles.

Further information: Camas National Wildlife Refuge, 2150 East 2350 North, Hamer, ID 83425; telephone: (208) 662-5423.

Deer Flat encompasses 11,427 acres in two separate sectors. The refuge's 10,587-acre LAKE LOWELL SECTOR, which was established in 1909 by President Theodore Roosevelt, is located between the Boise and Snake rivers in southwestern Idaho and eastern Oregon. It overlays a U.S. Bureau of Reclamation reservoir that receives water through a canal from the Boise River. The lake is managed to supply water for irrigation for agricultural production in the surrounding area. During normal years, water management also sustains a variety of aquatic habitats that benefit a diversity of wildlife. As explained by the U.S. Fish and Wildlife Service:

The refuge is a significant waterfowl wintering area in the Pacific Flyway. The slow summer draw-down of the lake exposes mud flats which produce bumper crops of aquatic vegetation, particularly smartweed. The refuge cooperatively farms 250 acres of land for wildlife. Crops grown include corn, wheat and alfalfa. Crops are manipulated to "set the table" for the arrival of migratory waterfowl. Historic average waterfowl populations have been 300,000 ducks and 7,500 geese. . . . Current populations are 150,000 ducks and 15,000 geese.

The refuge's SNAKE RIVER SECTOR consists of 840 acres on 94 islands that are scattered along a 113-mile stretch of the Snake River between near Melba, Idaho, and Huntington, Oregon. Acquisition of these islands began in 1937. They are particularly important for waterfowl and other migratory birds and provide a vital riparian corridor through the surrounding arid, high-desert region. As described by the Fish and Wildlife Service:

The islands range in size from less than one acre to 58 acres. Elevations range from four to ten feet above mean river level. Islands at the upstream portion . . . have grass-sagebrush middles and are ringed with thick brushy edges. Islands at the lower portion tend to be more heavily vegetated by trees such as maples, boxelders and cottonwoods.

The LAKE LOWELL SECTOR is open daily, and the SNAKE RIVER SECTOR is open daily from June 1 through January during daylight hours. There is no entrance fee. The refuge headquarters is open on weekdays, except national holidays.

Visitor activities on the LAKE LOWELL SECTOR include birdwatching, photography, driving the 29.5-mile, self-guiding Bird Watching Tour loop, hiking, mountain biking on all maintained roads and trails (within all recreation areas), horseback riding on maintained roads and trails (within the north, south, and east side recreation areas), cross-country skiing and ice skating (within all recreation areas), swimming at designated areas on the Upper and Lower Embankments (no lifeguards), boating (motor and sail, from April 15 through September), fishing from upper and lower embankments, and hunting (ducks and upland game birds within the east and south side recreation areas) during the designated seasons. Camping is not permitted, but campground facilities are available in the general vicinity.

Hiking opportunities include the 0.5-mile, self-guiding Headquarters Trail and several miles of refuge roads. Over 215 bird species have been seen on the refuge.

On the Snake River Sector, bank fishing is permitted from June 1 through January, and hunting is permitted during the designated seasons.

Lodgings and meals are available in such communities as Nampa, Meridian, Caldwell, Marsing, and Weiser, Idaho and Ontario, Oregon.

Access to the Lake Lowell Sector of Deer Flat Refuge from Twelfth Avenue in Nampa is west on Lake Lowell Road to Upper Embankment Road, and west 1 mile across the upper embankment to the end of the road and the refuge headquarters.

Further information: Deer Flat National Wildlife Refuge, 13751 Upper Embankment Road, Nampa, ID 83686; telephone: (208) 467-9278.

Grays Lake, containing approximately 19,000 acres and working toward a goal of more than 32,000 acres, was established in 1965 primarily to restore and protect important wetland habitat for migrating and nesting geese and ducks. The refuge is scenically located just west of, and 3,400 feet below, the 9,803-foot summit of Caribou Mountain in southeastern Idaho. Grays Lake itself is actually an extensive, shallow cattail and bulrush marsh—the largest wetland of hardstem bulrush in the world, the majority of which lies within the refuge.

Among the most common of the refuge's nesting waterfowl are Canada geese, mallards, cinnamon teal, canvasbacks, redheads, and lesser scaup. Grays Lake is also one of this region's most important breeding places for the trumpeter swan—a rare species that has reestablished itself here in recent years. According to the U.S. Fish and Wildlife Service, "In a typical breeding season, the refuge may produce up to 5,000 ducks, 2,000 geese, and over 20 swans." In addition, "Franklin's gulls nest in large colonies in bulrush habitat, along with a lesser number of white-faced ibis. Grebes, bitterns and elusive rails are also present."

One of the most prominent and exciting birds of Grays Lake Refuge is the sandhill crane. As the Fish and Wildlife Service describes, the refuge

hosts the largest nesting population of greater sandhill cranes in the world. Over 200 nesting pairs have been counted in some years.

Sandhills begin arriving in early April. In the fall, the refuge serves as a staging area, a place where cranes gather before migrating south to New Mexico, Arizona and Mexico for the winter.

During the staging period in late September and early October, as many as 3,000 cranes have been observed in the valley at one time.

On refuge lands surrounding the lake, vegetation is managed by hay cutting, limited livestock grazing, and prescribed burning. The controlled use of fire promotes nutrient cycling and spurs the growth of new vegetation that is of value to wildlife. The refuge also plants fields in barley and other grain crops that provide a supplemental, nutrient-rich source of food for the cranes and geese before their southward migration.

The refuge also includes several hundred acres of arid sagebrush-and-grass habitat that merge, at the base of the adjacent mountains, with shrubby areas of Rocky Mountain maple, bitterbrush, common chokecherry, and snowberry. The refuge barely extends into Douglas-fir forest, and beyond the boundaries are extensive stands of quaking aspen, mixed with lodgepole pine and other conifers.

Establishment of Grays Lake Refuge was made possible partly with revenues from the sale of Migratory Bird Hunting and Conservation Stamps (Duck Stamps).

The refuge is open daily during daylight hours. There is no entrance fee. The refuge headquarters is open daily, from April 1 to November 15.

Visitor activities include wildlife observation; photography; driving the roads that encircle the refuge; viewing the refuge and wildlife from the headquarters overlook (open from May 1 to November 15) from Beavertail Point next to State Route 34 at the southern end of Grays Lake, and from a roadside overlook adjacent to unpaved Westside Road; hiking; cross-country skiing and snowshoeing; canoeing and boating (with nonmotorized, car-top watercraft only); and hunting (only ducks, geese, and coots) on part of the refuge during the designated season. Camping is not permitted on the refuge, but campground facilities are provided in the adjacent Caribou National Forest. Although opportunities are limited, hiking is permitted on the northern half of the refuge from September 20 through March. The Fish and Wildlife Service urges visitors that "Permission should be obtained from landowners before crossing private land to enter open portions of the refuge. Please leave all gates as you find them."

Insect repellent is advised during the warmer months. Visitors are cautioned to be prepared for cold weather at this refuge's 6,400-foot elevation.

Lodgings and meals are available in such communities as Idaho Falls, Pocatello, and Soda Springs.

Access to Grays Lake Refuge from U.S. Route 30 at Soda Springs is north 33 miles on State Route 34, and turning onto the entrance road, 2 miles to the northwest of Wayan.

Further information: Grays Lake National Wildlife Refuge, 74 Grays Lake Road, Wayan, ID 83285; telephone: (208) 574-2755.

Kootenai, comprising 2,774 acres, was established in 1964 to restore and manage an important area of valley-bottom wetlands along the Kootenai River. The refuge is located in Kootenai Valley, which is bounded on the west by the spectacular Selkirk Mountains and on the east by the Purcell Range, less than 20 miles south of the border with Canada in northern Idaho.

Regarding the history of this part of the state, the U.S. Fish and Wildlife Service explains:

In the 1920s, humans began to tame the wild Kootenai River. Dikes were built to contain spring floods within the river channel. Once the river bottom lands were protected from flooding, the [riparian] cottonwood forests were removed and the wetlands were drained or leveled. The rich soils were planted with crops.

The construction of Libby Dam in Montana in 1975, to provide flood control and power generation, completed the taming of the river. Today, the Kootenai River meanders through fields of wheat and barley. The Kootenai National Wildlife Refuge was established . . . to reclaim some of the Idaho Panhandle wetlands lost to development.

The centerpiece of the refuge's diverse habitats is the more than 800 acres of impounded wetland habitat, in which water levels are regulated to maintain a series of permanent ponds and to flood moist-soil food plots for concentrations of migrating waterfowl in the autumn. Water for these wetlands is mainly derived from Myrtle Creek, which flows northward through the western part of the refuge on its way to the Kootenai River. Some additional water is pumped from Deep Creek and the river, which flow northward along the refuge's eastern boundary. Canada geese, wood ducks, mallards, cinnamon and blue-winged teal, and common goldeneyes are prominent among the waterfowl that migrate to the refuge in the spring and nest here. Other migrants that pause on the refuge's wetlands during migration include tundra swans, American wigeons, northern pintails, and redhead ducks. During the autumn, there may be as many as 3,500 geese. Other wetland inhabitants include moose, river otters, beavers, and muskrats.

Adjacent upland areas of grassland habitat provide nesting cover for geese, ducks, and other ground-nesting birds. More than 300 acres are devoted to the planting of wheat and barley by refuge personnel. These crops are left unharvested to provide a supplemental food source for waterfowl and other wildlife. Additional habitats include riparian woodlands of cottonwoods and willows, shrubby areas, and a narrow strip of Douglas fir and Engelmann spruce forest where the western edge of the valley and refuge meet the base of the Selkirk Mountains. Among the wildlife inhabiting this coniferous forest are Rocky Mountain elk, white-tailed and mule deer, moose, black bear, ruffed grouse, and pileated woodpecker.

Establishment of Kootenai Refuge was made possible with revenues from the sale of Migratory Bird Hunting and Conservation Stamps (Duck Stamps).

The refuge is open daily during daylight hours. There is no entrance fee. The refuge headquarters is open on weekdays, except national holidays.

Visitor activities include wildlife observation, photography, driving the 4.5-mile, one-way auto tour route, hiking, canoeing and boating on the Kootenai River (launching sites are available near the refuge), cross-country skiing, fishing only along Myrtle Creek, and hunting (waterfowl except swans; grouse; elk; deer; moose; black bear; and mountain lion) on parts of the refuge during the designated seasons. Although camping is not permitted on the refuge, campground facilities are available in the Panhandle National Forest. Horseback riding and swimming are among other activities not allowed.

Hiking opportunities include the 0.2-mile (wheelchair-accessible) Chickadee Trail near the refuge office; the 0.25-mile Myrtle Falls Trail to a beautiful waterfall (especially in the spring); the 1.5-mile Island Pond Trail that loops around a cattail marsh in which water levels are managed to provide a balance between open water and the growth of cattails; and the 2.2-mile Deep Creek Trail. Some refuge trails are open all year, but others are closed on waterfowl hunt days for public safety. Over 220 bird species have been seen on the refuge.

There are also two roadside overlooks: (wheelchair-accessible) Cascade Pond Overlook near the northern end of the refuge, and Island Pond Overlook in the southern part of the refuge.

And there are two observation blinds: Myrtle Pond Observation Blind in the central part of the refuge, and (reservations required and wheelchair-accessible) South Pond Observation/Hunting Blind at the southern end of the refuge. Many hunting blinds are scattered throughout the part of the refuge that is open to waterfowl hunting on certain autumn days.

Insect repellent is advised during the warmer months.

Lodgings and meals are available in Bonners Ferry.

Access to Kootenai Refuge from U.S. Route 95 at Bonners Ferry is 5 miles west on Riverside Road to the refuge office.

Further information: Kootenai National Wildlife Refuge, HCR 60, Box 283, Bonners Ferry, ID 83805; telephone: (208) 267-3888.

Minidoka, containing 20,699 acres, was established in 1909 by President Theodore Roosevelt for the protection of native birds. The refuge overlays lands that were withdrawn by the U.S. Bureau of Reclamation (BOR) for the construction from 1904 to 1906 of Minidoka Dam, on the Snake River in southeastern Idaho.

The refuge's central feature is a reservoir known as Lake Walcott, the water level of which is regulated by the BOR. Slightly more than half of the refuge consists of open water, several islands, small areas of bulrush and cattail marsh that are located in shallow coves and inlets, and a stretch of the Snake River upstream from the reservoir. Along the shorelines are willows, cottonwoods, and other trees and shrubs.

The most numerous birds attracted to Minidoka Refuge include American white pelicans, many species of migrating and nesting waterfowl, wading birds, shorebirds, gulls, and terns. The refuge contains the only consistent pelican nesting colony in Idaho, and it is a major waterfowl molting area, annually attracting as many as 100,000 ducks. Unlike most birds, waterfowl molt their wing and tail feathers at the same time and are flightless for about one month while their feathers grow back. During this month, they need good habitat that is free of human disturbance. During spring and autumn migrations, more than 500 tundra swans come here. A number of bald eagles winter on the refuge, and golden eagles can be seen from spring through autumn. Because of the nesting colonies and concentrations of waterfowl, the Minidoka Refuge has been designated by the American Bird Conservancy as an Important Bird Area of Global Importance. Over 230 species have been recorded here.

Most of the rest of the refuge contains semiarid uplands of predominantly sagebrush-and-grass and grassland, a gently rolling landscape that is frequently punctuated with outcroppings of volcanic basalt. Southern Idaho's vast expanse of the Snake River Plain is covered with lava flows and dotted with cinder cones that were formed during periods of volcanism that occurred along the Great Rift Zone from around 15,000 to 2,000 years ago. An exceptional example of this rugged expanse can be seen at the Craters of the Moon National Monument, the southern boundary of which is located about 3 miles north of the refuge.

Management of the uplands, as explained by refuge manager, Steve Bouffard, is particularly challenging:

The sagebrush on the refuge and the rest of the Snake River Plain is rapidly being lost to wildfire and invasion by exotic, invasive grasses, such as cheat grass. Not all sagebrush is created equal. The sage on the Snake River Plain is primarily the Wyoming subspecies of big sagebrush (*Artemisia tridentata*). Mountain big sage, which grows at higher elevations, and tall big sage, which grows in deeper soils, are less likely to be displaced by exotic grasses. Mountain big sage sites recover well after fires. The Wyoming sage, on the other hand, grows in the driest sites and is the most susceptible. The loss of sagebrush, especially the vulnerable Wyoming subspecies, is at the root of petitions to list the sage and sharp-tailed grouse as threatened and endangered species.

Management of sage areas on the refuge are aimed at fire prevention and suppression, to prevent the loss of additional sagebrush habitat. In the past 10 years, more than 50 percent of the refuge uplands have been burned. Chemical suppression on weeds and cheat grass, followed by seeding native plant species, is also implemented, but is expensive and often unsuccessful in this arid climate.

The refuge is open daily during daylight hours. There is no entrance fee. The refuge headquarters is open on weekdays, except national holidays.

Visitor activities include birdwatching, photography, driving on unpaved and unimproved roads, hiking, boating on the western one-third of the lake, fishing within the designated boat fishing area, and hunting (waterfowl, pheasant, gray partridge, and cottontail) on two parts of the refuge during the designated seasons. Camping is not permitted on the main part of the refuge. Campground and picnic facilities and a boat-launching ramp are available at the 30-acre Lake Walcott State Park (entrance fee is charged), which overlays part of the refuge's western end. For further information on the state park: (208) 436-1258.

Hiking opportunities include a number of the refuge's unpaved and unimproved roads, including the one along the refuge's northern boundary, and the short hike from parking area A on Bird Island Road (open from the third week in September to mid-January) to a lakeshore view of Bird Island. There is also a short paved trail in the state park that leads from the campground/picnic area to a point with an overlook and a (wheelchair-accessible) fishing pier, and another trail that leads east from the boat ramp in the park. Parts of the refuge are seasonally closed to visitors, to avoid disturbing colonial bird nesting activities.

Visitors are cautioned to be alert for rattlesnakes.

Lodgings and meals are available in such communities as Chubbuck/Pocatello Rupert, and Burley.

Access to Minidoka Refuge from Exit 211 on I-84 at Heyburn is northeast 5.9 miles on State Route 24: through Rupert (after crossing the railroad tracks, bear right and continue northeast on Route 24), and east (right) on Minidoka Dam Road. Or from Exit 216 on I-84, it is north about 3 miles on State Route 25, west (left) on Baseline Road about 2 miles to Rupert, northeast (right) on State Route 24 (after crossing the railroad tracks, bear right and continue northeast on Route 24), and east (right) on Minidoka Dam Road.

Further information: Minidoka National Wildlife Refuge, 961 E. Minidoka Dam Road, Rupert, ID 83350; telephone: (208) 436-3589.

Oxford Slough Waterfowl Production Area (WPA), comprising 1,878 acres, was established in 1985 for the management of marsh, meadow, and arid upland habitats near the southeast corner of Idaho. The area provides important nesting habitat for waterfowl, notably redhead ducks, and for a nesting colony of white-faced ibis.

Establishment of the WPA was made possible with revenues from the sale of Migratory Bird Hunting and Conservation Stamps (Duck Stamps).

The WPA is open daily during daylight hours. There is no entrance fee, and no visitor use facilities are provided. Visitor activities include birdwatching, photography, hiking, and hunting (waterfowl and limited upland game bird).

Lodgings are available in Pocatello/Chubbuck and Soda Springs.

Access to Oxford Slough WPA from the junction of I-86 and I-15 at Chubbuck is south 32 miles on I-15/U.S. Route 91 to Exit 36, south 19 miles (3 miles south of Swanlake) on U.S. Route 91, and west (right) 1 mile on the road toward Oxford.

Further information: Oxford Slough Waterfowl Production Area, c/o Southeast Idaho NWR Complex, 4425 Burley Drive, Suite A, Chubbuck, ID 83202; telephone: (208) 237-6615.

Illinois

Chautauqua, containing 4,488 acres, was established in 1936 to protect Illinois River floodplain and bordering upland habitats in west-central Illinois. The refuge's major feature is 3,200-acre Lake Chautauqua, comprising two shallow, impounded pools along a stretch of the river where water levels are seasonally regulated. In addition, Chautauqua Refuge consists of adjacent, seasonally flooded wooded bottomland, backwater lakes, a small area of upland forest, and two remnants of prairie grassland. Over 250 bird species have been seen here.

Adjacent to the impounded Illinois River that borders the refuge to the west, habitats include mixed bottomland and hardwood forests; buttonwood-willow swamps; and sedge marshes. Forty-foot-high sandy bluffs rise along the east side of the refuge, on the crests of which are oak-hickory upland hardwoods, which grade downslope to the floodplain, with cottonwood, maple, ash, and sycamore. A number of springs seeping out from below the bluffs keep stretches of the lake near the shore open during the winter.

Chautauqua Refuge attracts enormous concentrations of waterfowl and shorebirds. As many as 10,000 to 20,000 migrating shorebirds pour onto the refuge's mudflats as they stop on their southward migration in late summer and early autumn. During the autumn months, as many as 150,000 to 250,000 waterfowl pause to rest and feed before continuing to wintering grounds farther south. Anywhere from 50 to 80 bald eagles also often winter on Chautauqua Refuge, preying upon weakened waterfowl and fish. May brings the peak influx of neotropical migratory songbirds, including numerous warblers. Many wood ducks nest in tree cavities and in nest boxes that are provided by the U.S. Fish and Wildlife Service.

Trees of Chautauqua Refuge include the eastern cottonwood, willows, silver maple and green ash that dominate the floodplain forest; and the black oak, bitternut and shagbark hickories, persimmon, sassafras, red mulberry, and black cherry that grow on the uplands. Other plants include compass plant; spiderwort; goldenrods; boneset; butterfly milkweed; prairie coneflowers; prairie dock; and grasses (big and little bluestems, Indian grass, and switchgrass) that grow in two small restored prairie areas. Rice cutgrass, teal grass, Walter's millet, common arrowhead, arrowleaf, bidens, and pigweeds provide important waterfowl food during the draw down of Lake Chautauqua. In the extended flood of 1993, most of the pin oaks, pecans, and hackberries were killed. Remains of these trees can still be seen on Chautauqua Refuge. Bald eagles have nested in the dead trees with limited success, because these nest trees often fall during high winds. Seven beaver colonies moved in to take advantage of willow growth in Lake Chautauqua, as evidenced by large stashes of cut willows for winter food reserves at the base of their lodges.

The refuge is open daily during daylight hours. There is no entrance fee. The refuge office is open on weekdays, except national holidays.

Visitor activities include birdwatching; photography; driving the road along the eastern edge of the refuge; viewing the refuge and wildlife from four observation decks; hiking on the 0.5-mile, self-guiding Chautauqua Nature Trail (wheelchair-accessible) and on refuge dikes from mid-January through mid-October; fishing from the bank or by boat (a boat-launching ramp is provided at the Eagle Bluff Access Area); and waterfowl hunting on the Liverpool Lake part of the refuge during the designated seasons. Camping is not permitted on the refuge, but campground facilities are available at Sand Ridge State Forest and other nearby places.

Insect repellent is advised during the warmer months.

Chautauqua is one of three national wildlife refuges comprising the Illinois River National Wildlife and Fish Refuges complex, located along a 125-mile stretch of the river. Meredosia and Emiquon refuges and the Cameron/Billsbach units are the other Fish and Wildlife Service areas. The Friends of Illinois River is a nonprofit support group that is assisting these refuges.

The CAMERON UNIT, containing 636 acres, was established in 1958, when the area was donated to the U.S. Fish and Wildlife Service by the late Judge Glen J. Cameron, of Pekin, Illinois. The unit, located 65 miles upriver from Chautauqua Refuge along the west side of the Illinois River, contains bottomland forest, backwater habitat, and old fields along the west side of the Illinois River's Weis and Meridian lakes.

The BILLSBACH UNIT, consisting of 1,072 acres, was established in 1981. The unit, located across the river from the Cameron Unit, contains wetland habitats and part of Billsbach Lake. The Illinois Chapter of The Nature Conservancy purchased this land from the Armour Club (a private hunting club) and sold it to the Fish and Wildlife Service.

Lodgings and meals are available in such communities as Havana and Peoria.

Access to Chautauqua Refuge from U.S. Route 136 at Havana is north on Promenade Street, which turns into Manito Blacktop. Proceed northeast 8 miles on Manito Blacktop, left onto County Road 1950E, and left at the refuge headquarters entrance sign.

Further information: Chautauqua National Wildlife Refuge, c/o Illinois River National Wildlife and Fish Refuges, 19031 E. County Road 2110N, Havana, IL 62644; telephone: (309) 535-2290.

Crab Orchard, consisting of 43,890 acres, was established in 1947 to enhance, protect, and manage a variety of habitats for the benefit of migratory waterfowl and other wildlife in southern Illinois. The refuge contains 8,810 acres in three human-made lakes—Crab Orchard Lake, Devil's Kitchen Lake, and Little Grassy Lake. Roughly 21,000 acres of the refuge are densely forested, and scattered here and there are marsh and other wetland habitats and about 1,500 acres of grasslands. Over 220 bird species have been seen here.

In addition, there are about 5,000 acres of cropland, where a portion of the corn, soybeans, and other crops cultivated by local farmers, is left unharvested for the benefit of Canada geese and other wildlife. Just over 4,000 acres of Crab Orchard Refuge is designated as a unit of the National Wilderness Preservation System.

From November to March, anywhere from 67,000 to 275,000 Canada geese and 30,000 to 40,000 ducks of many species are attracted to the lakes of the refuge. During the spring, the forests are filled with great numbers of neotropical migratory songbirds, such as warblers of many species. More than 250 bluebird nesting houses have been erected.

The U.S. Fish and Wildlife Service's management activities include the regulation of water levels for the benefit of waterfowl and other wildlife, and prescribed burning, limited grazing, and haying to help maintain areas of prairie and other grasslands within the refuge.

As the Fish and Wildlife Service explains about this area's history:

Corn and cattle were the predominant crops for years.

When the depression [of the early 1930s] came, the soil was depleted in fertility and badly eroded. Farmers were destitute. . . .

In 1936 the Resettlement Administration acquired 32,000 acres of the depleted land when farming had failed. This became known as the Crab Orchard Creek Project. The original plans called for the construction of three lakes. The project was to be developed for an industrial water supply, recreation and land utilization.

Basically, three major accomplishments were made from 1938 until 1941. Approximately 3,000 acres were planted with 3,497,000 trees. . . . The Works Progress Administration (WPA) completed Crab Orchard Lake in 1939 and funds were made available to construct WPA projects for Little Grassy and Devils Kitchen Lakes.

Little Grassy was completed in 1951 by the WPA and the Soil Conservation Service. World War II halted construction of a third reservoir, Devils Kitchen Lake. Construction on this lake was resumed in 1956 by the [U.S.] Army Corps of Engineers and the U.S. Fish and Wildlife Service, and was completed in 1959.

When World War II started, the geographic location, water supply and federal ownership led to the establishment of the [U.S. Department of War's] Illinois Ordnance Plant (Ordill) on the area. Approximately 12,000 additional acres were purchased.

The plant was scattered across more than 20,000 acres and became one of the largest munitions manufacturing facilities in the United States. Initial production began in 1942. At its peak, Ordill employed 10,000 workers and each month produced 250,000 105mm shells,

175,000 155mm shells, and more than 70,000 500-pound bombs. Production at the plant was suspended in 1945.

After the war, the 21,425 acres of the Soil Conservation Service's Crab Orchard Creek Project and the 22,575 acres of the Department of War's Illinois Ordnance Plant were transferred by Act of Congress to the Fish and Wildlife Service as the Crab Orchard National Wildlife Refuge. The refuge's vision statement says, "Crab Orchard National Wildlife Refuge is recognized as an outstanding example of enlightened resource management and use. Refuge resources are managed so that agricultural, industrial, recreational and wildlife conservation purposes of the Refuge are accomplished in concert with each other and in full compliance with a long-term natural resource stewardship responsibility."

The Friends of Crab Orchard is a nonprofit support group that is assisting the refuge in many ways.

The refuge is open daily, with some parts open 24 hours. Fees are charged for motor vehicles and boats. The visitor center is open daily.

Visitor activities include birdwatching; photography; driving (more than 30 miles of public roads provide access to and through the refuge); hiking; picnicking; camping (campgrounds are provided—one on the shore of each lake); swimming (a designated swimming area is provided on Crab Orchard Lake); canoeing, kayaking, and boating (one or more boat-launching ramps are provided on each lake, and power boats and water skiing are permitted only on Crab Orchard Lake); fishing; horseback riding; bicycling; and hunting (deer, squirrel, waterfowl, turkey, and pheasant) on parts of the refuge during the designated seasons.

Designated hiking routes include the Visitor Center Trail—a paved, 0.5-mile (wheelchair-accessible) self-guiding, interpretive loop; the 1-mile, self-guiding, interpretive Chamnesstown School Trail; the 1.4-mile Rocky Bluff Trail that loops close to the northern end of Devil's Kitchen Lake; and the 3-mile Wild Turkey Trail.

Visitors are urged to be alert for the venomous copperhead snake, especially in rocky areas. Insect repellent is advised during the warmer months.

Lodgings and meals are available in such communities as Marion and Carbondale.

Access to Crab Orchard Refuge's visitor center is west 3 miles from I-57 at Marion on State Route 13; and south (left) 1.75 miles on State Route 148.

Further information: Crab Orchard National Wildlife Refuge, 8588 Route 148, Marion, IL 62959; telephone: (618) 997-3344.

Cypress Creek, containing more than 14,000 acres and working toward a goal of 35,200 acres, was established in 1990 to restore and protect an ecologically significant corridor of wetlands along the Cache River, at the southwestern tip of Illinois. The Cache River Wetlands, also referred to as the "Illinois bayou," consists of the largest remaining area of wetland habitat in the state, attracting large numbers of migratory waterfowl, wading birds, neotropical migratory songbirds, and other wildlife. The refuge includes bald cypress-and-tupelo swamps, bottomland forest, and gently rolling upland. Notable among the area's natural assets are numerous thousand-year-old cypress trees. Over 250 bird species have been seen here.

During many past decades, as the U.S. Fish and Wildlife Service explains:

. . . 230,000 acres, more than half of the former wetlands in southern Illinois, have been drastically destroyed and changed. . . . The European settlers arrived in 1803 and brought sawmills, farming and finally drainage and land clearing to the region. Although bottomland soils were rich, they were too wet for farming, eventually turning many settlers' efforts to harvesting timber.

. . . Pilings were cut from huge cypress trees to rebuild Chicago after its devastating fire in the late 1800s. In the early 1900s, the Cache River was straightened and ditched, diverting the river to separate directions. New technology and equipment of the 1920s brought extensive land clearing and conversion of the newly drained wetlands to croplands. Today, after nearly a century of intensive use, the tide of wetland destruction is being reversed.

Cypress Creek Refuge is part of the cooperative ecosystem restoration and protection effort, along 50 miles of the river, known as the Cache River Wetlands Joint Venture. In addition to the Fish and Wildlife Service, there are a number of key project partners. The Illinois Department of Natural Resources manages its 3-unit Cache River State Natural Area, located just upstream from the refuge. The Illinois Chapter of The Nature Conservancy (TNC), which has been involved with land protection along the river since 1970, made possible a 2,000-acre expansion of the refuge (formerly TNC's Limekiln Springs Preserve) and owns the nearby Grassy Slough Preserve. Ducks Unlimited, Inc. formerly owned and created shallow-water habitat on the 1,000-acre Frank Bellrose Waterfowl Reserve, which is now part of Cypress Creek NWR. The Friends of the Cache River Watershed is a local nonprofit support group that is assisting Cypress Creek Refuge in many ways.

The refuge is open daily during daylight hours. There is no entrance fee. The refuge headquarters is open on weekdays, except national holidays. A Wetlands Environmental Education Center is being planned for the refuge.

Visitor activities include birdwatching and photography from observation sites, hiking, canoeing and boating (several launching sites of available), fishing, and hunting (deer, small game, and waterfowl) during the designated seasons. The 3- and 6-mile stretches of marked Lower Cache River Canoe Trail are provided on the Cache River State Natural Area. Although camping is not permitted on the refuge and the state natural area, campground facilities are provided at nearby Ferne Clyffe State Park and Horseshoe Lake Conservation Area.

Hiking opportunities in the Cache River wetlands area include the 1.5-mile Hickory Bottom Trail that winds through an area of old-growth bottomland forest; the 2.5-mile Limekiln Slough Trail that offers views of woods, fields, cypress swamp, sloughs, ponds, limestone outcrops, and one of the refuge's springs; the 1-mile Lookout Point Trail that leads along a hillside and offers views of the river, its swamps, and floodplain forest; the popular 1.5-mile, self-guiding Heron Pond Trail that crosses the Cache River on a bridge and accesses a cypress swamp (Heron Pond) on a floating boardwalk (an interpretive leaflet is available); and the 5.5-mile Little Black Slough Trail that offers views of cypress-tupelo swamps, floodplain forests, hillside glades, and sandstone bluffs.

Visitors are urged to be alert for the several species of venomous snakes here, and for poison ivy. Insect repellent is advised during the warmer months.

Lodgings and meals are available in the communities of Ullin, Vienna, Anna, and Cairo.

Access to Cypress Creek Refuge from I-57 is by way of Exit 18 and east on Shawnee College Road. The refuge headquarters is located near the junction of Shawnee College Road and State Route 37.

Further information: Cypress Creek National Wildlife Refuge, 0137 Rustic Campus Drive, Ullin, IL 62992; telephone: (618) 634-2231.

Emiquon, a refuge-in-progress toward a goal of approximately 11,000 acres, was established in 1993 to restore and protect wetland and related habitats in the Illinois River Valley of west-central Illinois. As ultimately envisioned, Emiquon Refuge will consist primarily of backwater lakes, permanent marsh, and bottomland forest and other seasonally flooded wetlands. Smaller areas of the refuge will include upland forest and prairie grassland, as well as some land retained for planting crops for the benefit of waterfowl and other wildlife.

The refuge's waterfowl, other wildlife, and flora are much the same as those on Chautauqua National Wildlife Refuge.

Approximately 2,100 acres of this refuge have been acquired with the assistance of Ducks Unlimited, Inc., The Nature Conservancy, and the State Duck Stamp Fund.

The refuge is open daily during daylight hours. Visitor activities include wildlife observation; photography; fishing from banks or by boat (a boat-launching ramp is located east of State Highway 97 on the south side of the Spoon River); and hunting (deer, small game, and waterfowl) on parts of the refuge during the designated seasons.

Insect repellent is advised during the warmer months.

Emiquon is one of three national wildlife refuges comprising the Illinois River National Wildlife and Fish Refuges, located along a 125-mile stretch of the river. Chautauqua and Meredosia refuges and the Cameron/Billsbach units are the other U.S. Fish and Wildlife Service areas. The Friends of Illinois River is a nonprofit support group that is assisting these refuges in a variety of ways.

Lodgings and meals are available in such communities as Havana and Lewistown.

Access to Emiquon Refuge from Havana is west 1 mile on U.S. Route 136 and north (right) on State Route 78/97.

Further information: Emiquon National Wildlife Refuge, c/o Illinois River National Wildlife and Fish Refuges, 19031 E. County Road 2110N, Havana, IL 62644; telephone: (309) 535-2290.

Great River (see text under Missouri)

Meredosia consists of 3,400 acres, with plans to expand to about 5,200 acres. This refuge was established in 1973 to protect and manage floodplain and adjacent upland habitats at the upper end of the Alton Navigation Pool, along the east bank of the Illinois River in west-central Illinois.

Meredosia Refuge includes backwater lakes, seasonally flooded bottomland forest, permanent marsh, upland forest, and remnants of prairie grassland. The refuge's waterfowl, other wildlife, and flora are much the same as those on Chautauqua National Wildlife Refuge, which lies about 45 miles upriver (see the description and listings of fauna and flora for that refuge).

The Nature Conservancy helped to make possible the acquisition of a 2,100-acre part of Meredosia Refuge. More than 200 acres of the refuge's wetland habitat have been enhanced with the assistance of Ducks Unlimited, Inc. and the State Duck Stamp Fund.

The refuge is open daily during daylight hours. Visitor activities include wildlife observation; photography; hiking on a 0.25-mile, self-guiding (wheelchair-accessible) interpretive trail; viewing Meredosia Lake from a scenic overlook; and fishing from bank or by boat (a boat-launching ramp is located toward the north end of Beach Road).

Insect repellent is advised during the warmer months.

Meredosia is one of three national wildlife refuges comprising the Illinois River National Wildlife and Fish Refuges, located along a 125-mile stretch of the river. Chautauqua and Emiquon refuges and the Cameron/Billsbach units are the other U.S. Fish and Wildlife Service areas. The Friends of Illinois River is a nonprofit support group that is assisting these refuges in a variety of ways.

Lodgings and meals are available in such communities as Beardstown and Jacksonville.

Access to Meredosia Refuge from State Highway 104 in the town of Meredosia, is north on Putnam Street to the refuge entrance at the north edge of town.

Further information: Meredosia National Wildlife Refuge, c/o Illinois River National Wildlife and Fish Refuges, 19031 E. County Road 2110N, Havana, IL 62644; telephone: (309) 535-2290.

Middle Mississippi River, containing approximately 5,000 acres, began as part of the Mark Twain National Wildlife Refuge that was established in 1958. In 2000, lands along this stretch of the Mississippi, located downstream from St. Louis in southwestern Illinois and southeastern Missouri, were redesignated as a separate, multiunit refuge to manage important wetland habitat for migratory waterfowl and other wildlife.

Acquisition of this refuge's lands was made possible with funding from special congressional appropriations to address concerns arising from the "Great Flood of 1993." The goal has been to convert the most flood-prone lands along the river corridor from agriculture to riverine habitat, while providing economic relief to the affected farmers.

The refuge is open daily during daylight hours. There is no entrance fee.

Visitor activities include birdwatching, photography, hiking, fishing, and hunting.

Insect repellent is advised during the warmer months.

The fauna and flora of Middle Mississippi River Refuge are essentially the same as those recorded on Clarence Cannon Refuge in Missouri.

Lodgings and meals are available in such communities as Festus, Ste. Genevieve, and Perryville, Missouri and Chester, Illinois.

Regarding access: As a new refuge located in the floodplain, the Middle Mississippi is completely undeveloped and contains minimal signs or other facilities. The U.S. Fish and Wildlife Service urges calling ahead for visitor information.

Cottonmouth snake, White River NWR, Arkansas

Endangered Lange's metalmark butterfly on naked buckwheat, Antioch Dunes NWR, California

California condor, Hopper Mountain NWR. U.S. Fish and Wildlife Service photo

Endangered fringe-toed lizard, Coachella Valley NWR, California

American avocet, Don Edwards San Francisco Bay NWR. Mike Boylan photo

Don Edwards San Francisco Bay NWR

White pelicans, Don Edwards San Francisco Bay NWR

Long-billed dowitcher, Don Edwards San Francisco Bay NWR. Mike Boylan photo

Shorebirds in salt water marsh, Humboldt Bay NWR, California

American coot feeding young, Kern NWR, California

Lower Klamath NWR

Lower Klamath NWR, California

Male buffleheads, Lower Klamath NWR

Canada goose with brood, Modoc NWR, California

Dowitchers feeding in wetland, Sacramento NWR, California

Light-footed clapper rail, Tijuana Slough NWR, California

Alamosa NWR, Colorado

Displaying sage grouse, Arapaho NWR, Colorado

Arapaho NWR, Colorado

Greater sandhill cranes in flight, Monte Vista NWR, Colorado

Outdoor classroom, Rocky Mountain Arsenal NWR, Colorado

Brown pelican silhouette, Cedar Key NWR, Florida

Endangered Florida panther, Florida Panther NWR

Florida panther research, Florida Panther NWR

Snowy egret in breeding plumage, J.N. "Ding" Darling NWR, Florida

Roseate spoonbills, J.N. "Ding" Darling NWR

White ibis, J.N. "Ding" Darling NWR

Children exploring a wetland at Lake Woodruff NWR

Prescribed burn, Lake Woodruff NWR, Florida

White ibis, Merritt Island NWR, Florida

Courting common moorhens, Merritt Island NWR, Florida

Endangered Key deer buck, Key Deer NWR

Brown pelicans and great blue herons, Pelican Island NWR

Pelican Island NWR, Florida

St. Marks NWR, Florida

Ghost crab, St. Vincent NWR, Florida

Bond Swamp NWR, Georgia

Okefenokee NWR

Wood stork young, Harris Neck NWR, Georgia

White ibis, Okefenokee NWR, Georgia

Okefenokee NWR

Okefenokee NWR

U.S. Fish and Wildlife personnel installing a nest box for red-cockaded woodpeckers in Piedmont NWR

Red-cockaded woodpecker at nest cavity, Piedmont NWR, Georgia

Red-footed boobies courtship, Kilauea Point NWR, Kauai, Hawai'i

Endangered nene, Kilauea Point NWR

Kilauea Point NWR

Further information: Middle Mississippi River National Wildlife Refuge, c/o Crab Orchard NWR, 8588 Route 148, Marion, IL 62959; telephone: (618) 997-3344.

Port Louisa (see text under Iowa)

Two Rivers, comprising 8,501 acres, began as part of the Mark Twain National Wildlife Refuge that was established in 1958. In 2000, that refuge's Calhoun, Gilbert Lake, and Batchtown divisions, along the Illinois and Mississippi rivers in southwestern Illinois, were redesignated as a separate, multiunit refuge to manage important wetland habitat for migratory waterfowl and other wildlife.

Parts of the refuge's three units are managed as moist-soil units. The water is drained from these impoundments in early summer to promote the growth of plants such as smartweed, pigweed, millet, and nutgrass. After this vegetation has produced seeds, tubers, and other waterfowl foods, these units are reflooded in time for autumn migration, when thousands of migrating ducks and geese pause to rest and feed. Bald eagles accompany this influx of waterfowl, as they prey upon weak and dying birds. The greatest numbers of eagles usually gather here from late October through freeze-up.

Under cooperative agreements with the refuge, local farmers plant certain areas of all three units with corn, wheat, and soybeans—leaving a portion of these crops in the fields as a supplemental source of food for wildlife.

The GILBERT LAKE UNIT, within a bend of the Illinois River, and the BATCHTOWN UNIT, located a few miles upriver along the Mississippi from the refuge's other two units, offers important nesting habitat for wood ducks, mallards, and other water birds.

Establishment of this refuge was made possible partly with revenue from Migratory Bird Hunting and Conservation Stamps (Duck Stamps).

The refuge is open daily from December 16 through October. There is no entrance fee. The refuge headquarters/visitor contact station, located in the CALHOUN UNIT, is open all year on weekdays, except national holidays. The observation deck at the headquarters building and the Gilbert Lake Overlook Road are open year-round for daylight use only.

Visitor activities include birdwatching, photography, hiking, boating (several boat-launching ramps are provided in the Batchtown Unit), and fishing.

Insect repellent is advised during the warmer months.

The fauna and flora of Two Rivers Refuge are essentially the same as on Clarence Cannon Refuge in Missouri.

Lodgings and meals are available in such communities as Alton, Illinois and in and around St. Louis, Missouri.

Access to the Gilbert Lake Unit from Alton, Illinois is west about 20 miles on State Route 100 and left onto the refuge overlook road. Access to the Calhoun Unit from State Route 100 is 0.75 mile east of the latter refuge overlook road, turning south (right) onto County Route 1, crossing the Illinois River by ferry, continuing south and then west on the county road, and following signs to the refuge office near the shore of Swan Lake. Directions to the remote Batchtown Unit can be obtained from refuge headquarters.

Further information: Two Rivers National Wildlife Refuge, HCR 82, Box 107, Brussels, IL 62013; telephone: (618) 883-2524.

Upper Mississippi River (see text under Minnesota)

Indiana

Big Oaks, consisting of approximately 50,000 acres, was established in 2000 under a joint agreement with the U.S. Army and U.S. Air Force, "to preserve, conserve, and restore biodiversity and biological integrity for the benefit of present and future generations of Americans." The refuge is located on the U.S. Army's now-closed Jefferson Proving Ground, which extends across parts of Jefferson, Ripley, and Jennings counties in southeastern Indiana.

Several large blocks of habitat types that are rare in the surrounding landscape are present within the boundaries of Big Oaks Refuge. It contains the largest forested expanse in southeastern Indiana and some of the region's largest areas of grassland. The refuge provides managed habitat for at least 120 species of breeding birds and more than 40 species of fish and is also home to the federally endangered Indiana bat, white-tailed deer, wild turkey, river otter, bobcat, and coyote. More than 25 state-listed animal species and 46 state-listed plant species have so far been discovered here.

Most notable of the many species of management concern is the large population of Henslow's sparrows, of which more than 1,000 singing males have been estimated during the U.S. Fish and Wildlife Service's annual surveys in the large grasslands. Breeding bird surveys have also revealed such species as yellow-crowned night herons, sharp-shinned and red-shouldered hawks, Virginia rails, sedge wrens, and warblers (cerulean, Swainson's, worm-eating, black-and-white, and hooded).

Big Oaks Refuge has been designated as a Globally Important Bird Area because of its value to Henslow's sparrows and other migratory birds. The Indiana Department of Natural Resources states that the area ". . . is indeed a natural treasure that contains a full array of the region's natural communities and species assemblages."

Big Oaks Refuge's habitat management activities include enhancing and maintaining a variety of ecosystems—grasslands, early successional shrublands, and forest. Habitat continuity and diversity will ultimately be addressed to ensure healthy populations of wildlife, especially the declining species of grassland- and forest-dwelling birds and other wildlife. Where appropriate, a landscape mosaic of habitats, comprised of grassland, shrubland, forest, and wetlands, will serve to provide wildlife the appropriate habitats for survival and reproduction.

Grasslands within "Grassland Management Areas" are being maintained with an extensive prescribed burning program that annually encompasses approximately 5,000 acres. As these areas are being maintained by fire, species dependent upon early successional habitats benefit from these management practices. White-tailed deer, northern bobwhite, many nongame species, and rare plants thrive in these habitats that are maintained by periodic fire.

Big Oaks Refuge contains approximately 14,000 acres of contiguous blocks of forest—one of the largest in the state that provide significant habitat for declining populations of numerous neotropical migrant bird species. Additional forested areas within "Forest Management Areas" are to be managed as additional large, contiguous blocks of woodland.

Interior-forest bird species that require large blocks of forest, such as wild turkey, wood thrush, and cerulean and worm-eating warblers, will benefit from this management.

Wetlands also constitute a large proportion (more than 30 percent) of the refuge. Beavers are constantly reworking their shallow ponds throughout the refuge's drainages. New beaver impoundments are rapidly and naturally increasing the area of permanent water and the diversity of wetland habitat on the refuge.

The northeast corner of the refuge is presently open to visitors during daylight hours on Mondays and Fridays and on the second and fourth Saturdays of each month, from April through November. A small entrance fee is charged.

Visitor activities include wildlife observation, photography, walking on gravel roads, interpretive environmental education tours (by prior arrangement), fishing (excellent opportunities on Old Timbers Lake), and hunting (deer and turkey) in designated areas and seasons. As this refuge is a former U.S. Army test site, visitors are required to attend a safety briefing and sign an acknowledgment of danger agreement.

Insect repellent is advised during the warmer months.

Flora and fauna of Big Oaks Refuge are much the same as on Muscatatuck Refuge. Over 200 species have been recorded here.

Lodgings and meals are available in such communities as Madison, Versailles, and North Vernon.

The entrance to Big Oaks Refuge is located on U.S. Route 421, approximately 5 miles north of Madison. The refuge office is located in Building 125, in the cantonment area of the former Jefferson Proving Ground. From Madison, drive north on U.S. Route 421 through the Main Entrance onto the Jefferson Proving Ground, proceed west on Ordnance Drive, right onto Shun Pike, and left onto Niblo Road.

Further information: Big Oaks National Wildlife Refuge, 1661 West JPG Niblo Road, Madison, IN 47250; telephone: (812) 273-0783.

(NOTE: Special appreciation is given to Joe Robb, Refuge Operations Specialist, for providing this description.)

Muscatatuck, comprising 7,802 acres in two units, was established in 1966 to restore, enhance, and protect wetland, forest, and grassland habitats for the benefit of waterfowl, neotropical migratory songbirds, and other wildlife in southeastern Indiana. The refuge is named for the Muscatatuck River, which meanders from east to west along the southern boundary of the refuge's main unit. The name *Muscatatuck* is derived from a Native American word meaning "the land of winding waters."

As the U.S. Fish and Wildlife Service describes the refuge's water level manipulation:

Many wetland units are connected by pipes and water control structures so that water can be moved between units at different times of the year. Muscatatuck's moist soil units, low open areas surrounded by dikes, are drained of water in the spring to promote plant growth and filled with water in the fall to provide feeding and resting areas for waterfowl and shorebirds. Similarly, green tree units, diked lowland forests, are flooded with water in the fall for waterfowl and drained in the spring to keep the trees healthy. These units provide feeding and nesting areas for the wood duck, a bird that naturally nests in tree cavities in wetland areas.

One result of this water manipulation is the creation of permanent marshes—swampy areas of lush vegetation interspersed with pockets of shallow open water, which are ideal homes for ducks and geese to raise their young.

Other management activities include periodic prescribed burning in certain areas to keep the growth of woody plants in check and provide open habitat, while trees are planted in other areas to reduce forest fragmentation. In 1995, Muscatatuck Refuge became the first place in Indiana where the river otter was reintroduced. This formerly abundant species was previously extirpated from the state by overtrapping and loss of habitat.

Crops are cultivated on 724 acres of the refuge to provide supplemental food and cover for wildlife. As the Fish and Wildlife Service explains:

This acreage is maintained using examples of Integrated Pest Management and also Best Management Practices including no till, minimum till, no insecticide use, crop rotation, grass buffer areas and waterways, etc. . . . Primary crops are corn, soybeans, hay and wheat. . . . In 1995 . . . [the refuge] began a program on a 57-acre area dedicated to the "Farming for a Clean Watershed" project to promote improved water quality within the agricultural community.

The copper-bellied water snake (*Nerodia erythrogaster neglecta*), a federally listed threatened/state-listed endangered subspecies of the plain-bellied water snake, inhabits Muscatatuck Refuge. A 97-acre acid seep spring also provides conditions favorable to more than 80 species of vascular plants, including a number of orchids, such as the southern rein orchid. Refuge volunteers have restored the historic Myers' Cabin and Barn. These buildings date from around 1900 and offer visitors some insight into life in this part of the Midwest a century ago.

Land acquisition for the refuge, which was primarily to provide nesting habitat for wood ducks, was made possible with revenues from the sale of Migratory Bird Hunting and Conservation Stamps (Duck Stamps). Ducks Unlimited, Inc. has helped enhance part of the refuge's wetland habitat. Muscatatuck Wildlife Society is a local nonprofit support group that is assisting the refuge in various ways.

The refuge's main unit is open daily from sunrise to sunset. There is no entrance fee. The visitor center is open during all refuge hours.

Visitor activities include birdwatching, photography, interpretive programs, interpreter-guided walks, driving 9 miles of refuge roads including an auto tour route, hiking, horseback riding, bicycling, fishing, and hunting (deer, rabbit, and quail) on parts of the refuge during the designated seasons. Although camping is not permitted on the refuge, campground facilities are available at Muscatatuck County Park, Jackson Washington State Forest, and Hardy Lake State Recreation Area.

Hiking opportunities include eight designated trails, including the self-guiding (wheelchair-accessible) Chestnut Ridge Interpretive Trail and the Richart Lake Hiking Trail, which offers an excellent view of Richart Lake from Hackman Overlook.

The refuge's RESTLE UNIT, containing 78 acres, is located several miles northwest of Bloomington in south-central Indiana. In 1990, this tract was donated to the Fish and Wildlife

Service by Mrs. Barbara Restle. Although the unit is not open to visitors, an observation deck overlooks the unit, which adjoins two protected areas that are owned by the Sycamore Land Trust.

Lodgings and meals are available near the refuge's main unit in such communities as Seymour, Scottsburg, North Vernon, and Columbus, Indiana.

Access to Muscatatuck Refuge from Exit 50 from I-65 is east 3 miles on U.S. Route 50 and south (right) on the entrance road.

Further information: Muscatatuck National Wildlife Refuge, 12985 East U.S. Highway 50, Seymour, IN 47274; telephone: (812) 522-4352.

Patoka River National Wildlife Refuge and Management Area was established in 1994 to protect, restore, and manage 22,083 acres of bottomland hardwood forest wetlands and adjacent upland slopes in the Southern Bottomlands Natural Region of southwestern Indiana. Stretching for 20 miles (as the crow flies) in an east-west direction along the lower third reach of the 162-mile Patoka River, the acquisition area includes 30 miles of river channel, 19 miles of cut-off river oxbows, and 12,700 acres of existing wetland habitat. Primary resource management efforts are directed toward restoring more than 5,000 acres of bottomland hardwood forest on prior wetlands that were converted to farmland.

In the late 1700s, European settlers entering southwestern Indiana heard the resident Piankashaw Indians refer to one of the rivers as Pah-tah-ka-tah. This translated as either "crooked river filled with logs" or "logs on the bottom." Eventually shortened to Patoka, the name was very descriptive then, as it is today.

This area represents one of the most significant bottomland hardwood forests remaining in the Midwest. This portion of the Patoka River bottoms is often referred to as a "biodiversity factory," with a new species of mud darter and burrowing crayfish discovered in 2001 in addition to 380 recorded species of wildlife, including a pair of nesting bald eagles and the endangered Indiana bat. At least 20 plant species and 62 animal species that inhabit the river valley are considered as threatened, endangered, or of special concern by the State of Indiana. The refuge provides habitat for 21 species on Audubon's Watchlist. The refuge is the result of persistent, informed citizens' support that entailed 8 years of planning and public involvement, topped off with an Environmental Impact Statement to receive acquisition approval.

Patoka River has the distinction of being the only refuge project in the country with surface coal mines operating within the acquisition area. This apparent enigma was the result of a compromise worked out to avoid conflict with the Surface Mining Control and Reclamation Act of 1977 (SMCRA).

A provision of SMCRA states that any lands within the boundary of a national wildlife refuge are off-limits to surface coal mining. A U.S. Department of the Interior (DOI) solicitor advised that establishment of the refuge acquisition boundary could result in the prohibition of surface coal mining on both public and private lands within the defined boundary area. This could, in turn, result in "takings" claims (taking a property right without just compensation) being filed by landowners not permitted to sell or lease their coal rights for surface mining.

Consequently, Patoka River National Wildlife Refuge and Management Area was approved as a 6,800-acre national wildlife refuge adjacent to a 15,283-acre wildlife management selection area. Lands within the selection area are not off-limits to surface coal mining until owned by the U.S. Fish and Wildlife Service. The DOI solicitor advised that establishing a wildlife management selection area would be similar to establishing a waterfowl production area. Although an acreage acquisition goal is identified, there is no implicit understanding that all lands within a wildlife management selection area will be purchased, as there is when a refuge boundary is established.

It was irrelevant that it would take many years to purchase all the lands within the designated Patoka River Refuge, based on the willing-seller-only acquisition policy. To avoid potential costly "takings" claims, the refuge acquisition boundary was defined based on the absence of surface minable coal deposits. The presence or absence of minable coal was determined after 3 years of detailed coal-bed surveys by the U.S. Office of Surface Mining, under contract with the Fish and Wildlife Service.

Determining fair market value of individual tracts within the wildlife management selection area always includes a mineral appraisal, along with the surface appraisal, to determine if there is added value for coal or oil deposits. The mere presence of minerals does not necessarily mean there is added value, as many factors must be considered in determining whether it is feasible to develop a mineral right. If there is added value for coal or oil, this value is either added to the purchase offer, or the tract is rejected because of funding constraints.

By January 2002, more than 5,100 acres, including surface and mineral rights, had been purchased from 38 landowners, with no added value paid for surface minable coal. Since 1994, four mining companies have operated five surface mines within the wildlife management selection area. Most of the area being mined consists of row-crop farmland on north and south upland slopes above the Patoka River bottoms. The total amount of land likely to be mined within the wildlife management selection area will probably not exceed 2,500 acres. Much of this land has already been mined and is in various stages of reclamation. After final reclamation and bond release, efforts will be made to purchase these areas to be managed for upland wildlife habitat.

Recent refuge-funded studies by Indiana State University have shown that similar reclaimed minelands managed as grasslands in southwestern Indiana are now providing critical habitat for the reproduction of grassland-nesting birds, such as Henslow's sparrow and eastern meadowlark. These and other grassland-dependent species are actually showing positive recruitment of their declining populations as a result of the availability of grassland on reclaimed minelands. The management personnel of the Patoka River Refuge and management area view the presence of surface coal mining activity as an opportunity to provide important grassland habitat that might not otherwise be provided.

Cane Ridge Wildlife Management Area (WMA) was acquired in 1999 to be managed as a unit of the Patoka River National Wildlife Refuge and Management Area. This 464-acre property is located 16 miles west of the refuge, within Gibson County in southwestern Indiana. The name *Cane Ridge* is based on a local historical natural site known for its high concentration of swamp rabbits and wild cane.

The property is strategically located off the southwest corner of the 3,000-acre Gibson Lake, which is owned by the Cinergy Corporation. This impoundment, which is contained by an earthen levee, was constructed in the 1960s to provide cooling water for the Gibson Generating Station—one of the largest coal-fired power plants in the world. Located in the heart of what was once a vast bottomland forested wetland and historic migratory bird corridor, the Gibson Lake area has been identified as a Globally Important Bird Area, due to the presence of a nesting colony of the federally listed endangered interior least tern (*Sterna antillarum*). This is the largest and easternmost colony of interior least terns in the United States and is one of only two colonies east of the Mississippi River.

In 1986, a single pair of these terns was found nesting on the gravel-surfaced dike that bisects most of the lake. Since then, the tern nesting colony has increased, with a record number of 85 adults producing 72 fledglings in 1998. The 6,000-acre Cinergy Corporation property also attracts nearly 20 species of waterfowl, numbering as many as 45,000 ducks in midwinter and 35 species of shorebirds in spring and fall migrations. A pair of bald eagles successfully fledged young in 2001 and are year-round residents. Based on species numbers, this is one of the top birding areas in the Midwest.

When purchased, the Cane Ridge property consisted of 33 acres of bottomland forest, with the remainder converted from forested wetland to row-crop farming. Restoration efforts have led to the construction of 18,000 feet of low-level earthen dikes to encircle 193 acres encompassing four separate moist-soil management units. Cinergy Corporation has installed piping and has agreed to provide water by gravity flow from their adjacent Gibson Lake.

As of early 2002, 70 acres of the Cane Ridge WMA were planted with a diverse mix of bottomland hardwood seedlings, and by the end of 2002, forest restoration cover nearly 180 acres. The key restoration effort will involve construction of a 59-acre impoundment containing two 3-acre islands. Management efforts will focus on attracting the interior least terns to these islands, to increase their production and reduce the chances that these birds will nest in power-plant operation areas where their nests might be accidentally destroyed. The combination of moist-soil management units and least tern nesting impoundments will also provide outstanding opportunities for wildlife observation.

For those involved in the establishment of this important WMA, it still seems hard to believe that it has actually happened, considering the many obstacles that had to be overcome. To briefly describe the background of cooperation engendered by a diverse group of partners, it all started when an employee of the Zeigler-Old Ben Coal Company asked farmer–conservationist Ray McCormick of Knox County, Indiana if he might be interested in buying one of their bottomland properties, as the company was divesting itself of lands in this state. Ray brought the availability of the Cane Ridge property to the attention of other volunteer members of the Southwest Indiana Four Rivers Project Committee.

This committee is composed of private citizens, state and federal conservation agencies, nonprofit organizations, and private industry. The group functions under the auspices of the North American Waterfowl Management Plan (NAWMP), which receives federal funding from the North American Wetlands Conservation Act to promote the long-term conservation of wetland ecosystems and the wildlife that depends upon such habitat. Local committees such as this are formed to prepare grant requests, using private and state funds as a minimum one-to-one match to secure the federal funding for the acquisition, creation, and restoration of wetlands and associated habitats. The Southwest Indiana Four Rivers Committee agreed to prepare a NAWMP grant proposal for submittal in April 1997. The Cane Ridge property was the key area identified for acquisition and habitat restoration funding.

The coal company offered to sell this property for $1,700 per acre, regardless of its appraised value. As there was insufficient nonfederal match money to secure the full purchase amount as a NAWMP grant, other funding sources were required. The Natural Resource Conservation Service (NRCS) was asked if the lands qualified for a Wetland Reserve Program easement (WRP). (This voluntary program offers the landowner a federally funded opportunity under the terms of a conservation easement agreement to restore, enhance, and protect wetland habitat on the privately owned property.) NRCS said they did qualify. Zeigler-Old Ben Coal agreed to nominate the lands to receive a WRP easement, but only if the remaining fee title property rights were purchased to provide the full $1,700 per-acre asking price. NRCS agreed to pay $750 per acre for a 30-year WRP easement. The committee then applied for the rest of the funding as a NAWMP grant. This grant was approved by the Migratory Bird Commission in September 1997.

Even though sufficient funds were now available to meet the asking price, an appraisal had yet to be performed to justify the value. As the U.S. Fish and Wildlife Service had no land-acquisition funding for this project, the Service's Realty Office said they could not pay for the appraisal. Cinergy Corporation again stepped forward and paid $6,000 to secure the required appraisal within 2 weeks.

Zeigler-Old Ben Coal had previously sold the deep-mining coal rights to another company. As surface activities in support of an underground mine, such as a portal entry or air shaft, would not be compatible with the WRP easement or lands that became part of the National Wildlife Refuge System, the company (Alliance Coal) that now owned the deep-mining rights donated their surface access rights, valued at $200,000. Alliance also negotiated a reduction of $75,000 in Zeigler-Old Ben's asking price for their remaining fee-title surface rights being purchased with NAWMP grant funds.

Finally, after 2 years of negotiating and coordinating with all the above partners, the Service received title to the Cane Ridge WMA. Restoration funds totaling $100,000 were provided in the NAWMP grant; NRCS provided $80,000 for restoration, and Cinergy Corporation donated $59,192 of in-kind labor and materials to install the underground gravity-flow water delivery system from Gibson Lake and also donated $8,500 that they had previously provided as earnest money to hold the property.

NRCS and the Gibson County Soil and Water Conservation District provided a comprehensive ground elevation survey of the entire property, as well as completing the archaeological reconnaissance survey for clearance on future construction. Ducks Unlimited, Inc. provided engineering and design plans and signed a cooperative agreement with the Service to bid, let, and oversee the construction contract for the moist-soil management units.

Additional funds were required to construct the least tern nesting impoundment. The U.S. Army Corps of Engineers agreed to provide 75 percent of this cost, with 25 percent needed as nonfederal match. Cinergy Corporation/PSI Energy, Inc., donated $25,000 initially. Then early in 2000, Cinergy Corporation/PSI Energy, Inc., Wabash Valley Power Association, and Indiana Municipal Power Agency donated an additional $121,500. The entire $146,500 is being held by Ducks Unlimited, Inc. in an interest-bearing account until needed to pay for construction costs. Final restoration work involving tree planting, native grass establishment, levee construction, and water control structure installation has been scheduled for the summer of 2002.

It is noteworthy that the entire acquisition cost and most of the restoration costs associated with the Cane Ridge WMA have been provided or obtained by grants by partners. The U.S.

Fish and Wildlife Service has contributed $45,000 for restoration, staff time to coordinate the partnership effort, and the Realty Division's support for appraisal review and the mineral appraisal report. The major Service commitment is fee title ownership and long-term management. Cane Ridge is, therefore, a true partnership-driven endeavor to develop significant habitat for waterfowl, shorebirds, and endangered species, while providing a high-quality, nonconsumptive, wildlife-dependent recreational and environmental learning area.

Further information: Patoka River National Wildlife Refuge & Management Area, P.O. Box 217 (510 West Morton), Oakland City, IN 47660; telephone: (812) 749-3199.

(NOTE: Special appreciation is given to Bill McCoy, Refuge & Management Area Manager, for providing this description.)

Iowa:
National Wildlife Refuges

DeSoto, comprising 7,823 acres, was established in 1959 to enhance and protect ecologically important wetland habitat of a former Missouri River bend. The 750-acre, 7-mile-long DeSoto Lake in southwestern Iowa was created when the U.S. Army Corps of Engineers straightened and channelized the river.

More than one-half million lesser snow geese of both the white and blue morphs (color phases), numerous greater white-fronted and Canada geese, and as many as 50,000 mallards and other ducks typically pause on this refuge to rest and feed during their autumn migration from Arctic breeding grounds. Only a few snow geese stop on DeSoto Refuge during their northward spring migration. Bald eagles often accompany these concentrations of migratory waterfowl, preying upon weak individuals. Well over 100 eagles have been seen at a time.

One of the most prominent breeding waterfowl on DeSoto Refuge is the wood duck. Beavers and muskrats inhabit the lake's backwaters and other wetland habitat. Wild turkeys, northern bobwhite, the non-native ring-necked pheasant, and numerous songbirds can often be seen and heard in areas of woodland, prairie grassland, and hedgerows.

Refuge management activities include prescribed burning to help maintain areas of native-grass habitat (1,100 acres of the refuge have been restored to grassland); installing nesting boxes for wood ducks; and managing expanses of sandbar, especially for the benefit of two rare nesting species—the piping plover and least tern. In addition, roughly 1,800 acres of the refuge are cooperatively cultivated by local farmers, providing a portion of grain crops for deer, pheasants, and other wildlife. This latter area is scheduled to be reduced to around 500 acres by the year 2010.

Establishment of DeSoto Refuge was made possible partly with revenues from the sale of Migratory Bird Hunting and Conservation Stamps (Duck Stamps). Midwest Interpretive Association is a nonprofit educational support group that is assisting the DeSoto Refuge.

The refuge is open daily during daylight hours. An entrance fee is charged. The visitor center is open daily, except on New Year's Day, Thanksgiving, and Christmas.

Visitor activities include birdwatching; photography; interpretive films (on weekends); environmental education programs; driving (12 miles of paved and gravel refuge roads); hiking; bicycling (only on refuge roads); boating and fishing from April 15 to October 14 (a boat-launching ramp, no-wake speeds up to 5 mph, and wheelchair-accessible fishing piers); and hunting (waterfowl, and archery and muzzleloader deer hunting) on parts of the refuge during the designated seasons. Although camping is not permitted on the refuge, campground facilities are available at the adjacent Wilson Island State Recreation Area. The peaks of migrating waterfowl concentrations are usually from around mid-October through November, and less spectacularly from early March to mid-April.

The refuge's hiking opportunities include the Missouri Meander Trail, a twin-looped route from the visitor center, one loop of which is a 900-foot-long paved (wheelchair-accessible) path, and the other of which loops just under 1 mile through woodland and along the shore of DeSoto Lake; Bertrand Trail, a 0.4-mile route through marsh and grassland habitats of the old river channel; Cottonwood Trail, a 0.75-mile interpretive route through woodland; and Wood Duck Pond Trail, a 0.75-mile interpretive route that leads across Wood Duck Pond and winds through woodland and along the edge of grassland.

Insect repellent is advised during the warmer months.

Lodgings and meals are available in Missouri Valley and Council Bluffs, Iowa and in Blair and Omaha, Nebraska.

Access to this refuge from Interstate-80 in Council Bluffs, Iowa is north 25 miles on Interstate 29 to the Missouri Valley exit, and west about 5 miles on U.S. Route 30; or from Interstate 680 in Omaha, Nebraska, north 18 miles on U.S. Route 75 to Blair, and east (right) about 7 miles on U.S. Route 30.

Further information: DeSoto National Wildlife Refuge, 1434-316th Lane, Missouri Valley, IA 51555; telephone: (712) 642-4121.

Driftless Area, containing more than 600 acres in seven scattered units, consists of a mixture of hardwood forest and grassland habitats in northeastern Iowa. This refuge was established in 1989 to promote the recovery and protection of the federally listed endangered Iowa Pleistocene snail and a threatened wildflower, the northern monkshood.

Land acquisition is continuing, toward providing these species with protection sufficient to ultimately merit their removal from the endangered and threatened species lists. The Nature Conservancy, a nonprofit land-preservation organization, has been intimately involved with the establishment of this refuge and works with private landowners to protect rare habitats.

The name *Driftless Area* refers to parts of northeastern Iowa, southeastern Minnesota, and southwestern Wisconsin that were left partly or entirely uncovered by the most recent continental glacial advances of the Pleistocene Ice Age, which spread southward across most of the upper Midwest roughly 12,000 to 14,000 years ago.

According to the U.S. Fish and Wildlife Service:

Erosion created much of the characteristic terrain we have today. Certain slopes, usually north facing, have loose rock that allows cool air to exit from underground cracks and fissures. Upland sinkholes contribute to the air flow regime and are an important component of a unique system called an algific talus slope, meaning cold producing rocky slope. . . . This air flow [cooled by slowly melting underground ice] provides a climate similar to what was prevalent in glacial eras.

The Iowa Pleistocene snail (*Discus macclintocki*), which was known only from fossil records prior to being found alive in 1955, measures a mere one-quarter inch in diameter across its light brown or olive-colored shell. It inhabits leaf litter on cool, moist hillside slopes. This unique shady microclimate, which is found mostly in northeastern Iowa, maintains a relatively narrow ground temperature range, from not more than about 50°F in summer to not less than 15°F in winter. The snail, thriving in this naturally "air-conditioned" habitat, feeds on decaying maple and birch leaves. Paleontological research of fossilized remains has shown that this species ranged far more widely during the colder periods of the most recent Ice Age than it is known to range today.

Some areas of the algific habitat have been seriously degraded or are threatened by such activities as timber harvesting, livestock grazing, limestone quarrying, and filling in of sinkholes. To prevent the extinction of the snail, monkshood, and other rare species, a cooperative program of habitat protection has been undertaken by the Fish and Wildlife Service, state and county agencies, nonprofit environmental organizations, and private landowners under voluntary protection agreements.

The ecologically fragile parts of the refuge, which contain these microclimates that are vital to the endangered and threatened species, are closed to visitation. Some buffer lands around the algific slopes are open daily during daylight hours. There is no entrance fee.

Visitor activities include birdwatching, hiking (there are no trails), cross-country skiing, fishing, and deer hunting (muzzleloader and archery only) on certain parts of the refuge during the designated season.

Lodgings and meals are available in such communities as Waukon, Iowa and Prairie du Chien, Wisconsin.

For information regarding access points onto those units that are open to visitation, prospective visitors are urged to contact the refuge headquarters.

Further information: Driftless Area National Wildlife Refuge, P.O. Box 460, McGregor, IA 52157; telephone: (319) 873-3423.

Neal Smith, containing more than 5,000 acres and working toward a goal of 8,654 acres, was established in 1990 to restore, protect, and interpret an ecologically significant area of native tallgrass prairie in the Walnut Creek watershed, 20 miles east of Des Moines in central Iowa. A key part of this national wildlife refuge is its Prairie Learning Center, where interpretive exhibits and programs are presented and where ecologically important prairie research is being carried out.

The refuge was initially known as the Walnut Creek National Wildlife Refuge. It was renamed in honor of former U.S. Congressman Neal Smith, who was instrumental in obtaining federal funding for the refuge's biodiversity restoration and habitat restoration program and for construction of its major environmental education center.

As the U.S. Fish and Wildlife Service's Master Plan (1992) for the refuge and learning center stated, this national wildlife refuge ". . . is unlike any existing refuge in that it has been established by Congress to restore a major expanse of tallgrass prairie. The Refuge is the largest prairie reconstruction effort in the country and is symbolic of a growing national and international interest in healing the environment."

The refuge boundary initially encompassed a mixture of cropland, pasture, and remnant native plant communities. Privately owned lands have gradually been acquired from willing sellers and, as the refuge's bird checklist says, "Over the past several years, much of the Neal Smith National Wildlife Refuge landscape has been transformed from cropland to tallgrass prairie. The reconstructed and restored prairies and savannas are providing food, cover, and breeding habitat for local and migratory birds. Each year, ornithologists conduct singing bird surveys and the results have shown that more and more grassland-dependent bird species are using the refuge." Over 250 bird species have been recorded on the refuge.

A major goal of the Neal Smith Refuge is the reestablishment and protection of biological diversity. The Fish and Wildlife Service's stated management objectives include "reconstructing native tallgrass prairie, oak savanna, and riparian woodlands for the benefit of migratory and resident wildlife." To achieve this habitat diversity, native seed stock is being used to restore and maintain native grassland prairie; areas of bur oak savanna are being restored and maintained "to achieve a biologically rich transition between riparian woodlands and open prairie"; existing riparian woodlands along the floodplain of Walnut Creek and its major tributaries are being enhanced; and new wetland habitat is being created "to contribute to a national net gain of migratory bird habitat."

Although an autonomous entity, the refuge lies within the more extensive Des Moines Recreational River and Greenbelt. This regional open-space corridor extends along more than 50 miles of the Des Moines River and a number of its tributaries, including Walnut Creek. The Friends of the Prairie Learning Center is a nonprofit support group that is providing assistance to the refuge in a variety of ways.

The refuge is open daily during daylight hours. The Prairie Learning Center is open Mondays through Saturdays, and on Sunday afternoons.

Visitor activities include wildlife observation, photography, viewing interpretive exhibits and attending interpretive programs at the Prairie Learning Center, driving the auto tour route, hiking, bicycling on the refuge's entrance road, and picnicking in the Center's lunchroom and at picnic tables outside the lunchroom.

Hiking opportunities include the Overlook Trail, a 0.5-mile (wheelchair-accessible) self-guiding path; the Tallgrass Trail, a 2-mile, paved, self-guiding route that leads through tallgrass prairie; the 0.5-mile Basswood Trail; and the 0.5-mile Savanna Trail.

Lodgings and meals are available in Prairie City and Des Moines.

Access to the Neal Smith Refuge entrance is just west of Prairie City, on State Route 163, following refuge signs to the south.

Further information: Neal Smith National Wildlife Refuge, P.O. Box 399, Prairie City, IA 50228; telephone: (515) 994-3400.

Northern Tallgrass Prairie (see the text under Minnesota)

Port Louisa, comprising 8,185 acres (plus 2,606 acres in the HORSESHOE BEND UNIT), began as the Wapello District of Mark Twain National Wildlife Refuge, which was established in 1958. In 2000, the lands along this stretch of the Mississippi River floodplain in southeastern Iowa and western Illinois were redesignated as a separate, multiunit national wildlife refuge. It continues the management of important wetland, grassland, and woodland habitats for the benefit of waterfowl and other wildlife.

Tens of thousands of migrating ducks of many species and a few thousand geese pause to rest and feed on Port Louisa Refuge. Their concentrations generally peak from March through April and October through November. Bald eagles, which prey upon weak and dying waterfowl, are most numerous from late autumn to early spring.

The wooded parts of Port Louisa Refuge, especially on the Big Timber and Keithsburg units, consist of such bottomland trees as pin and white oaks, shagbark and shellbark hickories, silver maple, eastern cottonwood, green ash, and black willow. These ecologically rich hardwood and softwood forest habitats provide excellent nesting cavities for hundreds of wood ducks.

Some of the refuge's more prominent resident mammals are white-tailed deer, beavers, muskrats, raccoons, and gray and fox squirrels.

The 1,758-acre BIG TIMBER UNIT, located about 10 miles south of Muscatine, Iowa, is the northernmost part of the refuge. It is known locally as The Breaks because of numerous, flood-caused levee breaks that have occurred in this area. As the Fish and Wildlife Service explains, very little active habitat management is feasible, as it is situated entirely within a navigation pool of the Mississippi River. "Flooding from the Mississippi is a major concern due to the resulting siltation of the backwater sloughs and marshes on the refuge. The U.S. Fish and Wildlife Service, along with the Iowa Department of Natural Resources and the U.S. Army Corps of Engineers, are presently investigating methods to reclaim sloughs and marshes along the river that have been lost as a result of siltation."

The refuge's 3,338-acre LOUISA UNIT is located 6 miles east of Wapello, Iowa. Before acquisition as a wildlife refuge, major efforts were made to convert this river bottomland to farming—efforts that proved unsuccessful because of the Mississippi's frequent flooding. Parts of this unit are managed as moist-soil impoundments. The water is drained from these areas in early summer to promote the growth of plants such as smartweed, millet, foxtail, and nutgrass. After this vegetation has produced seeds, these units are reflooded in time for the autumn waterfowl migration.

Other management activities on the LOUISA UNIT include periodic prescribed burning, mowing, and discing (shallow plowing that breaks up the soil), to maintain the health and diversity of wet meadows and areas planted with native grasses. On a few areas of this unit's higher land, crops such as corn, milo, buckwheat, and winter wheat provide supplemental food for wildlife.

The 1,471-acre KEITHSBURG UNIT, located 1 mile north of Keithsburg, Illinois, manages riverine wetland habitat for the benefit of waterfowl and other wildlife. This unit also contains areas of riparian hardwood forest.

Another part of the refuge is the 2,606-acre HORSESHOE BEND UNIT. It is located in southeastern Iowa and protects waterfowl, grassland birds, resident wildlife, riparian forests, and prairie habitat.

Establishment of the refuge was made possible partly with revenues from the sale of Migratory Bird Hunting and Conservation Stamps (Duck Stamps).

The refuge is open daily during daylight hours—except as follows, to avoid disturbing the concentrations of waterfowl: the Louisa Unit is closed from mid-September through January; the Keithsburg Unit is closed to visitation from mid-September through December; and the Horseshoe Bend Unit is closed from mid-September through November. There is no entrance fee. The refuge headquarters, located on the Louisa Unit, is open on weekdays, except national holidays.

Visitor activities include birdwatching, photography, hiking (a trail on the Louisa Unit runs northward from the refuge headquarters, along the shore of Muscatine Slough), boating (boat-launching ramps are provided on the Big Timber, Louisa, and Keithsburg units), fishing, and hunting during the designated seasons (waterfowl and resident game on the Big Timber Unit and squirrels on the Keithsburg Unit, but no hunting on the Louisa Unit).

Insect repellent is advised during the warmer months.

Fauna and flora of Port Louisa Refuge are essentially the same as Clarence Cannon National Wildlife Refuge.

Lodgings and meals are available in such communities as Wapello, Muscatine, Burlington, Keithsburg, and Aledo.

Access to the Big Timber Unit from Muscatine is south approximately 10 miles on the Great River Road (County Route X-61). Access to the refuge's Louisa Unit from Wapello is 6 miles east on the Great River Road (County Route X-61). Access to the Keithsburg Unit from the town of Keithsburg is north 1 mile on Illinois Route 17. Access to the Horseshoe Bend Unit is approximately 6 miles southeast of Wapello on State Route 99.

Further information: Port Louisa National Wildlife Refuge, 10728 County Road X61, Wapello, IA 52653; telephone: (319) 523-6982.

Union Slough, comprising 2,845 acres, was established in 1937 to enhance and protect ecologically important wetland habitat for migratory waterfowl and other wildlife in north-central Iowa. The refuge extends along nearly 8 miles of Union Slough and Buffalo Creek. As the U.S. Fish and Wildlife Service explains, "Actually, the area is a connection or 'Union' slough between two watersheds; that of the Blue Earth River of Minnesota [to the north] and the East Fork of the Des Moines River [to the south]. It is so nearly level that originally the wind determined the direction of the flow."

The slough's wetlands have been enhanced with the construction of dikes, dams, and other water control structures. Six managed wetland units cover approximately half the refuge. Their water levels are seasonally regulated to promote the growth of aquatic food plants of benefit to waterfowl, and to provide habitat both for nesting ducks and other water birds and for thousands of geese and ducks that pause here to rest and feed during spring and autumn migrations. Hundreds of migrating American white pelicans also frequently stop here.

Some of the refuge also consists of prairie grassland, with native grasses that are typical of the tallgrass prairie along the eastern edge of the northern Great Plains. Periodic prescribed burning, which is used as a management tool by the refuge, mimics fire's ecologically important role in the past. It helps to maintain the health of the grassland ecosystem by recycling plant nutrients, reducing annual accumulations of litter, and curtailing the invasion of woody plants. The refuge's other habitat management activities include mowing, haying, and cultivating food crops that benefit wildlife.

Establishment of Union Slough Refuge was made possible partly with revenues from the sale of Migratory Bird Hunting and Conservation Stamps (Duck Stamps). Ducks Unlimited, Inc. has helped enhance more than 500 acres of this refuge's wetland habitat and is also is working toward the restoration and protection of other wetland areas under the Iowa Conservation Plan. Pheasants Forever has assisted with harvesting seeds of native grasses and forbs to help restore tallgrass prairie habitat. The Friends of Union Slough National Wildlife Refuge is a local nonprofit support group that is assisting the refuge in many ways.

Parts of the refuge are open only certain times of the year during daylight hours, for birdwatching, photography, hiking, and picnicking. There is no entrance fee. The deer observation area is open all year (viewing from the parking lot only, just south of County Route B-14). Deer Meadow, with the picnic area and Indian Bluff Nature Trail toward the southern end of the refuge (south of County Route B-14), is open from March 1 to November 15. Vanishing Prairie Grassland, near the northern end of the refuge (just south of County Route A-40), is open from July 15 through September. Wildlife Drive (between County Routes A-42 and B-14) is open daily from October 7-15 and on Fridays through Sundays from August 1 through September.

Other visitor activities include fishing and hunting (upland game birds, waterfowl, and deer) on parts of the refuge during the designated seasons. Although camping is not permitted on the refuge, campground facilities are available at Ambrose A. Call State Park and elsewhere. The refuge office, located just south of County Route A-42, is open on weekdays, except national holidays. Over 240 bird species have been recorded on the refuge.

Insect repellent is advised during the warmer months.

Lodgings and meals are available in such communities as Algona, Iowa, and Blue Earth, Minnesota.

Access to Union Slough Refuge from Algona is north about 14 miles on U.S. Route 169 (to the southern end of Bancroft) and east (right) 6 miles on County Route A-42; or from Interstate-90 at Blue Earth, Minnesota, south about 33 miles on U.S. Route 169 (to the southern end of Bancroft) and east (left) 6 miles on County Route A-42.

Further information: Union Slough National Wildlife Refuge, 1710-360th Street, Titonka, IA 50480; telephone: (515) 928-2523.

Upper Mississippi River (see text under Minnesota).

Iowa:
Wetland Management District

Iowa Wetland Management District, currently containing more than 16,000 acres, was established in 1979 to enhance and protect waterfowl habitat. The District encompasses 35 counties in north-central Iowa, overlying the most recently glaciated area of the state, known as the Des Moines Lobe. Rich soils and abundant rainfall support waterfowl production rivaling the best habitats in the United States. In spite of the nearly complete conversion of Iowa's native prairies and wetlands to row crops, aggressive acquisition and restoration efforts within the District are making a significant positive impact on the landscape for wildlife.

As an integral component of the tallgrass prairie ecosystem, the District has the unique opportunity to reconstruct more prairie/wetland habitat than any other under the U.S. Fish and Wildlife Service. And as part of the Union Slough NWR Complex, the District's management is unique, compared to others in the Service's Region 3. Authorized by a Memorandum of Understanding in 1988, the Iowa Department of Natural Resources (Iowa DNR) manages most of the District's waterfowl production areas (WPAs) in the state. This is one of the largest, most complex, and beneficial partnerships associated with the Fish and Wildlife Service. Together, the Iowa DNR and the Service have been able to develop large complexes of habitat for waterfowl and other wildlife. Nearly all wetlands on newly acquired tracts are restored.

As with wetlands, most WPAs require extensive restoration of upland habitats, since most lands have been used for row-crop agriculture. On the uplands, native grasses, legumes, and introduced grasses are seeded to provide nesting cover attractive to waterfowl and other wildlife. This habitat may be managed by rotational prescribed burning, haying, or grazing. Sometimes, part of the crop is left standing for winter feed and cover for resident game.

Currently, there are 60 WPAs in 16 of Iowa's counties. Most of these areas are small—from 100 to 500 acres, but several have grown considerably. Union Hills WPA, in Cerro Gordo County, is the largest, at 2,000 acres.

As authorized by enabling legislation, all waterfowl production areas are open for hunting, fishing, and trapping, in accordance with state regulations and seasons. Other visitors are permitted to observe wildlife, photograph, hike, or use the sites for educational purposes, at certain times of the year. Motorized vehicles are prohibited. No public use facilities are maintained, except for parking areas. Contact the wetland manager for current regulations.

Limited lodgings and meals are available in Titonka, and full lodgings and meals are available in Algona and Clear Lake, Iowa and Blue Earth, Minnesota.

Access to the Iowa WMD and Union Slough NWR headquarters is from U.S. Route 169 at Bancroft, east 6 miles on County Road A-42.

Further information: Iowa Wetland Management District, 1710-360th Street, Titonka, IA 50480; telephone: (515) 928-2523.

(NOTE: Special appreciation is given to Bryan Schultz, Wetland Manager, for providing this description.)

Kansas

Flint Hills, comprising 18,500 acres, was established in 1966 to enhance and protect an area of important wildlife habitats along the Neosho River and the upstream end of the U.S. Army Corps of Engineers' John Redmond Reservoir in east-central Kansas. The refuge, which is managed under an agreement with the Corps of Engineers, consists of marsh, sloughs, wooded bottomland, grassland, and gently rolling uplands. In addition, some agricultural lands on the refuge are sharecropped with local farmers, with the refuge's share of the grain crop usually left standing to provide food for migrating waterfowl.

Tens of thousands of migratory waterfowl—notably snow and Canada geese and many species of ducks—and thousands of white pelicans and numerous bald eagles pause here during the spring and autumn migration. As many as 100,000 mallards spend the winter here. In spring, greater prairie chickens visit the refuge (from the nearby Flint Hills) and perform their courtship displays. Numerous neotropical migratory songbirds also migrate through this area.

Ducks Unlimited, Inc., has provided funds for the engineering and construction of the refuge's moist-soil management units. These wetlands are mowed and disced in the summer to promote the growth of natural food plants. In the autumn, the wetlands are flooded (by pumping), which produces an extremely attractive feeding habitat for migrating waterfowl. The Wild Turkey Federation has also contributed funding to help with the planting of trees to restore the refuge's riparian habitat.

The refuge is open daily during daylight hours, although there are times when seasonal flooding inundates much of the refuge, including its roads and trails. Parts of the refuge are closed to public use from November 1 through February. There is no entrance fee. The refuge headquarters, in Hartford, is open weekdays, except on national holidays.

Visitor activities include birdwatching; photography; driving on refuge roads; hiking on three, self-guiding, interpretive trails (Headquarters Trail, Burgess Trail, and Dove Roost Trail) and elsewhere; picnicking; camping; canoeing and boating; fishing; and hunting on parts of the refuge (but not on the Neosho River) during the designated seasons. November is the best season to see the peak of the autumn waterfowl migration, and April and May are the best months to see neotropical migratory songbirds. Over 290 bird species have been seen here.

Visitors are cautioned to be alert for ticks, venomous snakes, and poison ivy. Insect repellent is advised during the warmer months.

Lodgings and meals are available in Emporia.

Access to the refuge headquarters is east of Emporia on I-35 North, south from Exit 141 on State Route 130 to Hartford, right (west) on Maple Avenue (Hartford High School is on the southeast corner) 3 blocks, and right (north) 1 block.

Further information: Flint Hills National Wildlife Refuge, P.O. Box 128, Hartford, KS 66854; telephone: (316) 392-5553.

Kirwin, containing 10,778 acres, was established in 1954 as an overlay refuge on and surrounding a U.S. Bureau of Reclamation irrigation and flood control reservoir in north-central Kansas. The refuge supports diverse wildlife habitats, including wooded riparian areas, marsh, open water, grasslands, and croplands.

The reservoir is fed by the North Fork of the Solomon River and Bow Creek. Its level fluctuates widely from year to year, depending upon runoff from rain and snow. Although the Bureau of Reclamation owns the land and controls the level of the reservoir, the U.S. Fish and Wildlife Service manages all other activities on the refuge.

Thousands of Canada and white-fronted geese, many species of ducks and shorebirds, sandhill cranes, and white pelicans pause at Kirwin Refuge during their spring and autumn migrations. As many as 20,000 Canada geese and 10,000 mallards spend the winter here. Waterfowl that nest on Kirwin include Canada geese, wood ducks, and mallards.

Kirwin Refuge is located in the transition zone between the tallgrass prairie of the eastern Great Plains and arid shortgrass plains of the west. Management practices that are used to provide optimum habitat for wildlife include controlled burning, grazing, farming, mowing, and haying. Crops such as wheat, milo, and corn are grown under a cooperative farming program. A portion of the crop is harvested for use by the farmer, and the rest is left to provide food for the thousands of ducks and geese that use the area during spring and autumn migrations. Over 200 bird species have been seen here.

The refuge is open daily. There is no entrance fee.

Visitor activities include birdwatching; photography; driving the refuge's auto tour route; hiking on two interpretive trails (at Dog Town and Crappie Point); bicycling on roads open to vehicular travel; picnicking; camping (four campsites are available); canoeing and boating (two boat ramps are provided); fishing; and hunting (waterfowl, turkey, prairie chicken, pheasant, quail, dove, rabbit, squirrel, and archery only for deer) on parts of the refuge during the designated seasons. The Solomon River Arm of the reservoir is closed to motorboating, to avoid disturbance of wildlife. Nonmotorized boating is permitted on Solomon Arm from August 1 through October.

Visitors are cautioned to be alert for ticks. Insect repellent is advised during the warmer months.

Lodgings and meals are available in Kirwin and Phillipsburg.

Access to the refuge is south 5 miles from Phillipsburg on State Route 183, east 6 miles from Glade on State Route 9, and south 1 mile on a county road, following the refuge directional signs.

Further information: Kirwin National Wildlife Refuge, R.R. 1, Box 103, Kirwin, KS 67644; telephone: (785) 543-6673.

Marais Des Cygnes, consisting of 7,500 acres, was established in 1992 to restore and protect an area of ecologically important bottomland hardwood forest along the Marais des Cygnes River, next to the Missouri border in eastern Kansas. The river and refuge's French name, meaning "Marsh of the Swans," apparently came from the historical use of the area by trumpeter swans.

In addition to the river and adjacent woodland, refuge habitats include floodplain ponds, small farm and mine ponds, upland oak-hickory forest, tracts of native tallgrass prairie, and former farm fields. Seasonal flooding occurs on about one-quarter of the refuge. Waterfowl, shorebirds, raptors, and neotropical songbirds are among the many migratory birds attracted here, and resident species include wild turkey and bobwhite quail. More than 300 bird species have been recorded on Marais des Cygnes.

The initial parcel of land for this refuge was acquired by The Nature Conservancy. The remaining acreage has been purchased with funds from the Land and Water Conservation Fund. The U.S. Fish and Wildlife Service's habitat restoration programs include the planting of native pecan and pin oak trees and some wetlands enhancement for the restoration of bottomland hardwood forest, as well as restoration of native prairie by removing trees and planting native grasses and forbs.

The refuge is open daily during daylight hours. There is no entrance fee.

Visitor activities include birdwatching; photography; hiking; canoeing and boating (visitors are cautioned that boat-launching is "generally an arduous venture"); fishing; and hunting (deer, turkey, quail, rabbit, and squirrel) on parts of the refuge during the designated seasons. Camping is not permitted. Parts of the refuge are designated as wildlife sanctuary and are closed to public entry, except on established trails.

Visitors are cautioned to be alert for ticks, venomous snakes, chiggers, and extensive areas of blackberry brambles. Insect repellent is advised during the warmer months.

Fauna of this refuge are much the same as on Flint Hills National Wildlife Refuge.

Among the trees are American sycamore; pecan; hickories (shagbark, big shellbark, and pignut); a number of oaks (bur, post, chinkapin, northern red, pin, Shumard, and blackjack); eastern cottonwood; and persimmon.

Lodgings and meals are available in such communities as Butler, Missouri and Pleasanton and Fort Scott, Kansas.

Access to the refuge is north 5 miles from Pleasanton on U.S. Route 69, and right (east) 1 mile on State Route 52.

Further information: Marais des Cygnes National Wildlife Refuge, 24141 State Highway 52, Pleasanton, KS 66075; telephone: (913) 352-8956.

Quivira, comprising 22,135 acres, was established in 1955 to enhance and protect an area of cattail marsh, salt flats, cropland, prairie grassland, gently rolling sandhills, and a bit of woodland in south-central Kansas. These ecologically significant habitats are a mecca for vast numbers of migratory waterfowl and shorebirds, white pelicans, sandhill cranes, wintering bald and golden eagles, resident turkeys and bobwhite, briefly a few of the endangered whooping cranes, yellow-headed blackbirds, and numerous other species of wildlife. Even the refuge's salt flats have special significance, as this is favored nesting habitat for the endangered interior least tern.

From mid-September through November, as many as one-half million Canada geese and ducks and nearly 200,000 sandhill cranes pause here on their way south to wintering habitats along the Gulf of Mexico. From mid-February into April, as many as 200,000 geese and ducks stop on their way north to breeding areas in the north-central United States and Canada. Tens of thousands of shorebirds of many species pause at Quivira Refuge, with the spectacular peak of their migrations occurring from late April through early May and again from mid- to late October, depending upon the weather. Some of the plovers and sandpipers that use Quivira Refuge as a resting and feeding place spend the winter as far south as Tierra del Fuego, at the southern tip of South America, and nest in the far north of Canada, Alaska, and Siberia.

The refuge is named for the Quiviran Indians, a tribe of Native Americans who were living in this area when Spanish explorer Coronado led his landmark exploration through here in 1541, searching in vain for gold.

The largest part of the refuge is its 13,000 acres of grassland. Quivira is situated within the transition zone of the vast Great Plains, where the lush tallgrass prairie to the east merges with the arid grassland of the shortgrass prairie to the west. Periodic prescription burns and short-term, prescribed livestock grazing programs are helping to enhance and maintain the ecological health of the refuge's prairie grassland habitat for wildlife. Fires and intensive, short-term grazing by huge herds of bison occurred naturally before the arrival of European settlers. The U.S. Fish and Wildlife Service's grassland management practices on refuges such as Quivira, are designed to reestablish this important ecological pattern.

The environmental centerpiece of Quivira Refuge is its wetland habitat—notably the 1,500-acre Big Salt Marsh and 900-acre Little Salt Marsh. Many years prior to the refuge's establishment, populations of geese, ducks, and shorebirds were decimated by profit-driven market hunting in the marshlands. Then more than a dozen private hunting clubs, each with exclusive membership hunting rights, acquired parts of the wetland. They improved some of the vital habitat, initially creating a channel to bring water from Rattlesnake Creek directly into Little Salt Marsh. More than 80 water control structures, 15 miles of additional canals, and flood spillways were subsequently built, ensuring a more dependable water supply for the entire 6,000-acre marshland, which is comprised of 34 managed wetland units.

The 1,300 acres of agricultural lands are another important aspect of the refuge. Under cooperative agreements with farmers, a portion of crops such as winter wheat and milo are left unharvested for the benefit of waterfowl and other wildlife.

Funding and other assistance for the establishment and expansion of Quivira Refuge have come from a variety of sources, including a number of private organizations and a relatively small proportion of revenues from the sale of Migratory Bird Hunting and Conservation Stamps (Duck Stamps). The Conservation Fund recently assisted with acquisition of an ecologically significant wet-meadow habitat containing the only known bobolink nesting colony in

Kansas. Because the Fish and Wildlife Service could not acquire the subsurface mineral rights when the refuge was established, oil development by the owner of those rights occurs at 17 producing wells on Quivira Refuge.

Friends of Quivira National Wildlife Refuge is a nonprofit support group that is assisting the refuge in various ways.

The refuge is open daily during daylight hours. There is no entrance fee. The visitor center, featuring interpretive exhibits, hands-on displays, and programs, is open weekdays, except national holidays. Over 310 bird species have been recorded here.

Visitor activities include birdwatching; photography; driving 20 miles of refuge roads, including a self-guiding interpretive tour; hiking; prearranged interpretive group tours and educational gatherings; fishing (a wheelchair-accessible fishing pier is provided, located at a children's fishing pond); and hunting (waterfowl, pheasant, quail, dove, snipe, rabbit, and squirrel) on parts of the refuge during the designated seasons. The children's fishing pond is available for youths up to 14 years of age and for accompanying adults. The refuge is closed to hunting from March 1 through August. Boating and camping are not permitted.

Hiking opportunities include Birdhouse Boulevard, a 0.2-mile paved (wheelchair-accessible) path adjacent to the visitor center; and Migrants' Mile, a 1.2-mile trail (a 0.75-mile loop of which is wheelchair-accessible) that provides views of woodland, marsh, and grassland habitats.

Visitors are cautioned to be alert for rattlesnakes and ticks. Insect repellent is advised during the warmer months. Violent thunderstorms are most likely in late spring and early summer.

Lodgings and meals are available in such communities as Stafford, Hutchinson, and Great Bend.

Access to the refuge is west from Hutchinson approximately 30 miles on Fourth Avenue; or west from Hutchinson on U.S. Route 50 to Zenith, right (north) on State Route 14 for 5 miles, and left (west) on Seventieth Street for 17 miles.

Further information: Quivira National Wildlife Refuge, Route 3, Box 48A, Stafford, KS 67578; telephone: (316) 486-2393.

Kentucky

Clarks River, currently containing more than 7,000 acres and working toward a goal of around 18,000 acres, was established in 1997. The refuge's mission is to protect and manage a diversity of floodplain habitats for migratory waterfowl, neotropical songbirds, and other wildlife along the Clarks River in western Kentucky.

As refuge manager Rick Huffines has described the history of the Clarks River Refuge:

In the 1960's, Kentucky lost the only jewel it had in the crown of the National Wildlife Refuge System, when most of the Kentucky Woodlands National Wildlife Refuge was flooded by the impoundment of

Kentucky Lake. Sometime around 1969, the Kentucky Department of Fish and Wildlife Service, and other conservation organizations, contacted the U.S. Fish and Wildlife Service and began a mission to restore Kentucky's place back in the crown of the National Wildlife Refuge System.

Together, these trailblazers, as I like to call them, identified an area on the east fork of the Clarks River as an area of high priority for protection. It was a rare complete river system that remained unchannelized and free from dams: a bottomland hardwood forest, with cherrybark oaks, towering sycamore trees, and natural ponds and sloughs; a place teeming with migratory songbirds, waterfowl and a wide array of other wildlife all dependent on this wetland; a place worthy of inclusion in the crown.

For the next 28 years, those trailblazers fought head-on to protect this place and make it part of the refuge system.

During that same time, in 1969, one day in late spring, there was a seven-year-old boy playing hooky from school. I was that boy. It was a special day for me, because, by permission from my mother, I had been given the day off from school. You see, my Grandmother, who was a Native American with very little formal education, and who I loved as much as the air I breathed, had taught my mother that a classroom didn't hold all of the knowledge of this earth. So, occasionally my mother would give me a day away from school to explore and appreciate the wild things. These days were unannounced, unplanned, and to me as precious as a birthday.

It was one of these days in late spring that a 28-year journey for me began to unfold. While exploring with my mother, I saw a beautiful bird in the top of a hackberry tree near my home. I was spellbound and had to know more about that bird. I showed it to my mother and asked her "What is that?" And she answered with what were probably the most influential words she ever spoke to me: "I don't know, but we'll find out."

Well, those words opened a path for me to a world that I never knew existed. It was a path grown thick with the answers I needed, if only I had the will to blaze the trail. For the next 28 years of my life, I devoted everything to protecting, appreciating, and learning about all of those wild things.

Three and a half years ago, those two parallel events finally crossed paths. In December 1997, I was asked to go to Benton, Kentucky, to start up a new refuge—the newly authorized 516th Refuge in the System: Clarks River National Wildlife Refuge. Well, they gave me an acquisition map, an environmental assessment, and told me there were 18,000 acres identified in the proposed boundary, and to go and get them. So, I arranged for a temporary apartment, packed a bedroll, a beanbag chair and a cardboard box of cooking utensils, dumped all of the heavy responsibility of the move on my wife and son, as it seems we always do, and I headed for Kentucky.

The next morning, I woke up in the apartment all by myself, looked around the room and thought to myself "What in the heck have I gotten myself into." Surely there was a manual lying around here somewhere on how to start a National Wildlife Refuge. But there wasn't and I began to panic. So, I sat down in my beanbag chair and pulled my cardboard box beside me to make a desk and a place to think. It was there that I thought about my responsibility to all of those dedicated individuals who had blazed the path to this very room; and a calm came over me. In that calm, I realized that I had no reason to panic, because I wasn't truly alone. I had an army of trailblazers, past and present, in that room. I knew at that very moment that, if all I had was a beanbag chair and a cardboard box, with the help of those trailblazers and the backing of my family, we would make a place called the Clarks River National Wildlife Refuge: a place of wild things; a place where a child would be guaranteed the opportunity to ask the same question I had asked 28 years earlier, "What is that?"; a trailhead to the next journey.

This ecologically rich refuge-in-the-making already consists of about a dozen tracts of land along roughly 20 miles of the Clarks River Valley, in the vicinity of Benton and Sharpe-Elva. The refuge continues to grow, through the purchase of land from willing sellers.

Two neotropical migratory birds for which Clarks River Refuge's protected bottomland forest is especially important are the cerulean and Swainson's warblers. Other species that are attracted to this habitat include the black-throated green, northern parula, prothonotary, and Kentucky warblers; vireos; thrushes; and scarlet tanager. Mammals include white-tailed deer, bobcat, mink, river otter, raccoon, and muskrat. Of the reptiles, there are eastern box turtle and ringneck snake. Trees include bald cypress, tulip tree, sassafras, American sycamore, sweetgum, American elm, hackberry, butternut, black walnut, pecan, bitternut hickory, oaks (overcup, post, swamp chestnut, pin, and cherrybark), American hornbeam, river birch, eastern cottonwood, black willow, eastern redbud, flowering dogwood, red and silver maples, boxelder, and green ash. One of the refuge's most spectacular wildflowers is the cardinal flower.

The refuge is open daily during daylight hours. There is no entrance fee. The refuge headquarters, located at 91 U.S. Highway 641N in Benton, is open on weekdays, except national holidays.

Visitor activities include birdwatching, photography, hiking, horseback riding, bicycling on the refuge's gravel roads that are open to visitors, interpretive and environmental education programs, fishing, and hunting (waterfowl, coot, turkey, dove, deer, coyote, and bobcat) on parts of the refuge during the designated seasons. Although camping is not permitted on the refuge, campground facilities are provided at Land Between the Lakes Recreation Area and Kenlake State Recreational Park.

Lodgings and meals are available in such communities as Benton and Paducah.

For information on how to reach the various parcels of refuge land, prospective visitors are urged to contact the headquarters.

Further information: Clarks River National Wildlife Refuge, P.O. Box 89, Benton, KY 42025; telephone: (270) 527-5770.

Ohio River Islands (see text under West Virginia).

Reelfoot (see text under Tennessee).

Louisiana

Atchafalaya, containing 15,000 acres, was established in 1984 to protect and enhance a portion of the nation's most extensive bottomland hardwood swamp habitat, located just north of I-10 between Baton Rouge and Lafayette in southeastern Louisiana. More than 150 species of birds have been recorded in this ecologically rich area. Public use of this refuge is managed, in conjunction with the Sherburne Wildlife Management Area, by the Louisiana State Department of Wildlife and Fisheries.

Establishment of this refuge was made possible partly with revenues from the sale of Migratory Bird Hunting and Conservation Stamps (Duck Stamps).

The refuge is open daily. There is no entrance fee.

Visitor activities include birdwatching, photography, hiking along ridges and on many unimproved paths, boating (shallow-draft boats), primitive camping, fishing, and hunting during the designated season. Because of the area's numerous waterways, public access is limited. Best months for birdwatching are March through May and August through October.

Visitors are cautioned to be alert for venomous snakes and possible sightings of black bears. Insect repellent is advised.

Birds of Atchafalaya are essentially the same as on Bogue Chitto.

Except for black bears on this refuge, the species of mammals are virtually the same as on Bogue Chitto.

Reptiles include turtles (musk, mud, red-eared slider, and yellow-bellied), snakes (rat, mud, king, and several species of water snakes), and American alligator.

Trees are the same as on Bogue Chitto. One of the more prominent wildflowers is the swamp lily.

Lodgings and meals are available in such communities as Baton Rouge, Breaux Bridge, and Lafayette.

Access to the refuge is by State Route 975 and by way of the Whiskey Bay Exit from I-10.

Further information: Atchafalaya National Wildlife Refuge, c/o Sherburne Wildlife Management Area, P.O. Box 127, Krotz Springs, LA 70750; telephone: (337) 566-2251.

Bayou Cocodrie, comprising 13,168 acres, was established in 1992 to protect and enhance critically important habitats for nesting wood ducks, wintering and resting waterfowl, wading birds, migratory songbirds, and other wildlife in the Lower Mississippi River Valley of east-central Louisiana.

About one-quarter of this refuge is wetland where seasonal rains fill basins and where beavers build dams and create ponds—all of great benefit to large concentrations of wintering ducks and other water birds. More than three-quarters of Bayou Cocodrie consists of cypress swamp and a relatively pristine remnant of bottomland hardwood forest. Part of this forest is designated by the U.S. Fish and Wildlife Service as a Natural Resource Area for special research, to determine how best to protect, manage, and restore this habitat.

Bayou Cocodrie's bottomland forest also provides an ecologically significant corridor connecting Tensas River National Wildlife Refuge and the Red River Wildlife Management Area. This contiguous area benefits many species of wildlife, including the Louisiana black bear.

Since the early 1970s, much of this region's ecologically rich forests were cut down to clear the land for rapidly expanding agricultural development. Because of the loss of so much vital wildlife habitat, a number of important reforestation efforts, of which this refuge is a part, are now under way throughout the region.

Establishment of Bayou Cocodrie was made possible partly with revenues from the sale of Migratory Bird Hunting and Conservation Stamps (Duck Stamps).

The refuge is open daily during daylight hours. There is an entrance fee.

Visitor activities include birdwatching, photography, interpretive tours and environmental education programs (by prior arrangement), driving on parish roads, hiking on a number of trails, ATVs on designated trails, fishing, and deer and small game hunting on certain areas of the refuge during the designated season. Camping is not permitted within the refuge, but there are two nearby commercial campgrounds—Bayou Cocodrie and Cross Bayou.

Visitors are cautioned to be alert for venomous snakes, as there is an abundance of copperheads, cottonmouths, and timber rattlesnakes. Insect repellent is advised.

Lodgings and meals are available in such communities as Ferriday, Louisiana and Natchez, Mississippi.

Nearby conservation areas include St. Catherine Creek, Catahoula, Lake Ophelia, Grand Cote, and Tensas River national wildlife refuges.

Access to Bayou Cocodrie visitor contact station is south from Ferriday by way of State Route 15, and right about 3.5 miles on Poole Road.

Further information: Bayou Cocodrie National Wildlife Refuge, P.O. Box 1772, Ferriday, LA 71334; telephone: (318) 336-7119.

Bayou Sauvage, consisting of 22,770 acres, was established in 1986 to protect and enhance ecologically important freshwater and brackish marshes and swamp habitats within the city of New Orleans, Louisiana. This is the largest urban wildlife refuge in the United States. It provides habitat for great concentrations of wintering waterfowl and other water birds. Over 265 bird species have been recorded here. The American alligator is abundant.

Because most of this refuge lies within the confines of huge hurricane-protection levees that block storm surges but that also disrupt natural water flows, the U.S. Fish and Wildlife Service is struggling to maintain the productive quality of these wetlands for the benefit of wildlife. The Intracoastal Waterway cuts through the southern part of the refuge.

Establishment of this refuge was made possible partly with revenues from the sale of Migratory Bird Hunting and Conservation Stamps (Duck Stamps).

The refuge is open daily during daylight hours. There is no entrance fee.

Visitor activities include birdwatching, photography, walking the (wheelchair-accessible) Ridge Trail Boardwalk (from U.S. Route 90), interpretive tours (by reservation), environmental education programs, bicycling, boating and canoeing (canoe touring), and fishing. Monthly schedules of outings are available. Hunting and camping are not permitted. The best months for birdwatching are November through May.

Even though alligators are generally afraid of people, visitors are cautioned to stay a safe distance from these sluggish-looking but potentially fast-moving reptiles and to be alert for venomous snakes. Insect repellent is advised.

Lodgings and meals are available in and around New Orleans.

Access is by way of U.S. Route 11 (south from I-10) or by way of U.S. Route 90, just northeast from downtown New Orleans.

Further information: Bayou Sauvage National Wildlife Refuge, c/o Southeast Louisiana Refuges, 1010 Gause Blvd., Building 936, Slidell, LA 70458; telephone: (504) 646-7555.

Bayou Teche, comprising 9,040 acres and working toward a goal of approximately 27,000 acres, was established in 2001 primarily for the protection of the threatened Louisiana black bear. The refuge, which is the 537th in the National Wildlife Refuge System, is located in southern Louisiana.

As explained by the U.S. Fish and Wildlife Service, "Previously owned by the Bailey family of St. Mary Parrish, the...property is a critical link" and important year-round habitat for this subspecies of black bear. Other wildlife includes wintering waterfowl, numerous species of neotropical migratory birds, white-tailed deer, bobcat, red and gray foxes, and river otter.

This new refuge will also offer interpretive and environmental education programs and wildlife-oriented recreation, such as wildlife observation, fishing, and hunting.

Further information: Bayou Teche National Wildlife Refuge, c/o Mandalay NWR, 3599 Bayou Black Drive, Houma, LA 70360; telephone: (985) 853-1078.

Big Branch Marsh, consisting of roughly 14,000 acres, was established in 1994. This refuge protects and enhances an area of ecologically important freshwater and salt marshes, bayou and cypress-slough habitats, sandy beaches, cypress-and-hardwood hammocks, and low ridges of pine woodland along the northeastern shore of Lake Pontchartrain, near New Orleans, Louisiana. Among the many species of wildlife are concentrations of wintering waterfowl, nesting wood ducks, and numerous wading birds, shorebirds, and neotropical migratory songbirds. The federally listed endangered red-cockaded woodpecker inhabits the refuge (see a description under South Carolina of this species in the Carolina Sandhills Refuge text).

The refuge's marshes are also significant spawning and nursery habitat for shrimp, crabs, and many species of finfish.

Establishment of this refuge was made possible partly with revenues from the sale of Migratory Bird Hunting and Conservation Stamps (Duck Stamps).

The refuge is open daily during daylight hours. There is no entrance fee. The visitor center, providing information, interpretive exhibits, and a sales area, is open daily, except on New Year's Day, Mardi Gras, Thanksgiving, and Christmas. It is located in Lacombe on a 110-acre unit of the refuge bordering Bayou Lacombe at 61389 State Highway 434, 2 miles south of I-12, and 0.25 mile north of U.S. Route 190.

Visitor activities include birdwatching, photography, hiking, interpretive tours (on foot and by canoe and bicycle) led by refuge staff and trained volunteers, environmental education programs, fishing, and hunting during the designated season.

Hiking opportunities include The Boardwalk, a one-eighth-mile walk through pine woodland (habitat that is being managed for the benefit of the rare and endangered red-cockaded woodpecker). There is also the Boy Scout Road Nature Trail, a 2.2-mile hike through pine woodland; across an expanse of salt marsh inhabited by waterfowl, wading birds, muskrats, and a turtle called the red-eared slider; through an area of live oaks and devil's walking stick (a low-growing tree that produces clusters of autumn-ripening black berries that are eaten by birds and small mammals); and ending with a view of Bayou Lacombe.

Visitors are cautioned to be alert for venomous snakes. Insect repellent is advised.

The birds that have been recorded Big Branch Marsh Refuge are much the same as those on Bayou Sauvage Refuge.

Lodgings and meals are available in and around Covington, Slidell, and New Orleans.

Access is from U.S. Route 190 and State Route 434.

Further information: Big Branch Marsh National Wildlife Refuge, c/o Southeast Louisiana Refuges, 1010 Gause Blvd., Building 936, Slidell, LA 70458; telephone: (504) 646-7555.

Black Bayou Lake, consisting of 4,200 acres, was established in 1997 to protect important wildlife habitats several miles north of Monroe in northeastern Louisiana. This refuge includes a scenic, 2000-acre lake with impressive bald cypress and tupelo trees, bottomland cypress-and-hardwood forest habitat, mixed pine-and-hardwood uplands, a 3-acre demonstration prairie, and an arboretum.

Although the lake is owned by the City of Monroe, the U.S. Fish and Wildlife Service, under a free 99-year management lease, is protecting and enhancing the area's important habitats for waterfowl, neotropical migratory songbirds, and other wildlife and is developing an environmental education program.

Friends of Black Bayou, Inc., is a nonprofit support group that is assisting Black Bayou Lake Refuge in a variety of ways.

The refuge is open daily during daylight hours. There is no entrance fee.

Visitor activities include birdwatching, photography, interpretive tours, environmental education programs, canoeing and boating (50-horsepower motors or less; a boat-launching ramp is available), and fishing. An interpretive (wheelchair-accessible) pier extends 400 feet onto Black Bayou Lake. Although camping is not permitted on the refuge, campground facilities are available in the Monroe vicinity.

The fauna and flora recorded on this refuge are essentially the same as at D'Arbonne.

Lodgings and meals are available in Monroe.

Access to the refuge is north approximately 4 miles from Monroe on U.S. Route 165, and right onto Richland Place.

Further information: Black Bayou Lake National Wildlife Refuge, c/o North Louisiana Refuges, 11372 Highway 143, Farmerville, LA 71241; telephone: (318) 726-4222.

Bogue Chitto, comprising 37,000 acres, was established in 1980. This refuge protects and enhances an important remnant area of the Pearl River's pristine cypress-and-mixed-hardwood bottomland forest habitat, extending along both sides of the Louisiana–Mississippi border about 40 miles northeast of New Orleans.

More than 50 miles of waterways, including oxbow lakes and sloughs, wind throughout the refuge. Water levels fluctuate widely, by a dozen feet or more, so that most of the refuge is at times under water. This ecologically rich area provides important habitat for wintering waterfowl, nesting wood ducks, and a multitude of neotropical migratory songbirds. More than 160 species of birds have been recorded at Bogue Chitto.

The ivory-billed woodpecker formerly inhabited the bottomland forests along the Pearl River. This magnificent species is now generally believed to be extinct, although an alleged sighting of two birds in 1999 has spurred an intensive search effort. For further information, see the Tensas River National Wildlife Refuge text.

The refuge is open daily. There is no entrance fee.

Visitor activities include birdwatching, photography, hiking on trails and boardwalks, boating (by canoe or shallow-draft boat), primitive camping at designated sites, fishing, and hunting during the designated season. Self-guiding canoe routes offer excellent opportunities to explore the refuge, with favorable water-level conditions being most likely from around the beginning of the year through spring. Private outfitters provide canoes and guides for one-day or multiday excursions.

Visitors are cautioned to be alert for venomous snakes. Insect repellent is advised.

The birds recorded on Bogue Chitto Refuge are much the same as those on Catahoula Refuge.

Lodgings and meals are available in such communities as Slidell, Louisiana and Picayune, Mississippi.

Access to the refuge is by way of Exit 3 from I-59, west 1 mile on U.S. Route 11, and north just over 8.5 miles on State Route 41.

Further information: Bogue Chitto National Wildlife Refuge, c/o Southeast Louisiana Refuges, 1010 Gause Blvd., Slidell, LA 70458; telephone: (504) 646-7555.

Breton, containing more than 10,000 acres, was established in 1904 by President Theodore Roosevelt, is the nation's second oldest national wildlife refuge, and lies along coastal Louisiana. It consists of a chain of storm-pounded, sandy barrier islands, curving from near Louisiana's Delta toward Mississippi's gulf coast, and protects the largest breeding colonies of brown pelicans and terns in the United States. The habitats of Breton and Chandeleur islands include beautiful white-sand beaches, as well as expanses of salt marsh sheltered behind the islands.

Protection of this wildlife-rich area stemmed from a request of the Louisiana Audubon Society.

The refuge is open daily. There is no entrance fee. Parts of the refuge are marked with "Closed Area" signs during the nesting season of bird colonies.

Visitor activities include birdwatching, photography, hiking along the beaches, boating, fishing, and primitive camping. Hunting is not permitted. Insect repellent and sunscreen are advised.

Among the birds of Breton Refuge are magnificent frigatebird; brown pelican; Wilson's plover; willet; gulls (laughing, ring-billed, and herring); terns (sandwich, royal, Caspian, least, and sooty); and black skimmer.

Access to the refuge is by seaplane or a seaworthy boat.

Further information: Breton National Wildlife Refuge, c/o Southeast Louisiana Refuges, 1010 Gause Blvd., Slidell, LA 70458; telephone: (504) 646-7555.

Cameron Prairie, comprising 24,548 acres, was established in 1988 to protect and enhance important wildlife habitats on two units in southwestern Louisiana. The 9,621-acre Gibbstown Unit contains freshwater marsh, coastal prairie, and former rice fields and provides feeding and resting areas for the tremendous concentrations of wintering waterfowl and other water birds. The EAST COVE UNIT, which was formerly part of Sabine National Wildlife Refuge until 1992, contains 14,927 acres of brackish and saltwater marsh that is an important nursery for shrimp, crabs, and many species of finfish.

At the GIBBSTOWN UNIT, more than a thousand acres of former rice-farming lands are being restored, with the help of discing, mowing, and occasional burning, to promote the growth of moist-soil plants that benefit wildlife. The unit's freshwater marshes are managed with water control structures and levees. Some of these wetlands are drained and periodically burned in the autumn to help promote a healthy ecosystem. In early winter, these areas are reflooded with water to benefit ducks and other water birds.

At the East Cove Unit, water control structures, which are located along a 19-mile levee bordering Calcasieu Lake, regulate an essential delicate balance between fresh and salt water in the marshes, to restore important wildlife habitat that was historically impaired or destroyed by the intrusion of saltwater.

Establishment of Cameron Prairie was made possible partly with revenues from the sale of Migratory Bird Hunting and Conservation Stamps (Duck Stamps). Ducks Unlimited, Inc. has assisted with important habitat enhancement projects.

The refuge's Gibbstown Unit is open daily during daylight hours. The East Cove Unit is open daily during daylight hours to general visitation, except during the Louisiana waterfowl hunting season and when the Grand Bayou Boat Bay is closed to public access. The visitor center, located on the Gibbstown Unit, is open on weekdays, except national holidays, and on Saturdays. There is no entrance fee to either unit.

Visitor activities at the Gibbstown Unit include birdwatching, photography, driving refuge roads—notably Pintail Wildlife Drive, hiking on levees and dikes, boating (non-motorized boats in the bank fishing area and motorized boats in the outfall canal from March 15 to October 15), fishing (from March 15 to October 15), and bow hunting for white-tailed deer during the designated season. Although camping is not permitted on the refuge, a campground is provided at Sam Houston Jones State Park, to the north of Lake Charles.

At the East Cove Unit, visitor activities (access by boat only) include birdwatching, photography, boating (motorized boats on canals, bayous, and lakes; only electric trolling motors in marshes), and fishing (except during the Louisiana waterfowl hunting season and when Grand Bayou Boat Bay is closed). November through February are the best months for birdwatching.

Even though alligators are generally afraid of people, visitors are cautioned to stay a safe distance from these abundant, sluggish-looking but potentially fast-moving reptiles. Visitors should also be alert for venomous snakes, including the cottonmouth, whose bite can be fatal. Insect repellent is advised.

The more than 200 species of birds that have been recorded on Cameron Prairie Refuge are essentially the same as those at nearby Lacassine.

Lodgings and meals are available in such communities as Lake Charles, Sulphur, and Jennings.

Access to Cameron Prairie's visitor center is south from Holmwood 11 miles on State Route 27.

Further information: Cameron Prairie National Wildlife Refuge, 1428 Highway 27, Bell City, LA 70630: telephone: (337) 598-2216.

Catahoula, consisting of 6,535 acres, was established in 1958 to protect and enhance an eco-logically rich, annually inundated floodplain, lying along the northeastern end of Catahoula Lake in east-central Louisiana. Habitats include marsh, bottomland hardwood forest, cypress-bordered Cowpen Bayou, and the 1,200-acre Duck Lake impoundment, which is managed to promote the growth of moist-soil plants for the benefit of wintering waterfowl. Tens of thousands of ducks spend part or all of the winter on and near the refuge, wood ducks nest here, and a nearby wading bird rookery is used by a large concentration of herons and egrets.

Many species of neotropical birds return to the refuge in the spring to nest and rear their young. Special acreage is set aside for some declining neotropical and other species, including the dickcissel in the spring and LeConte's and Henslow's sparrows in the autumn. The American alligator also inhabits the refuge.

Catahoula Refuge was acquired to preserve bottomland hardwood forest. New additions to the refuge are being restored by planting oak, bald cypress, water and black tupelos, and pecan trees on the land that was previously cleared for agriculture.

Usually in March and April, this refuge becomes flooded by backwater from the rising level of adjacent Catahoula Lake. During the summer, the lake is partially drained to promote the growth of an important source of food for waterfowl—a member of the sedge family known as chufa.

The refuge manages the water level under a cooperative agreement with the Louisiana Department of Wildlife and Fisheries and the U.S. Army Corps of Engineers, which built the structure that regulates the water level. Because of the lake's value to more than 350,000 wintering waterfowl, this 26,000-acre, State of Louisiana-owned expanse of water is designated as a Wetland of International Importance.

Establishment of the refuge was made possible partly with revenues from the sale of Migratory Bird Hunting and Conservation Stamps (Duck Stamps). Because the U.S. Fish and Wildlife Service could not acquire the subsurface mineral rights when the refuge was established, limited oil drilling by the owner of those rights occurs on Catahoula Refuge.

The refuge is open daily during daylight hours. There is no entrance fee.

Visitor activities include birdwatching; photography; environmental education programs; interpretive tours; viewing wildlife from an observation tower; driving the 9-mile Wildlife Drive around Duck Lake and along Cowpen Bayou; hiking a 1-mile interpretive nature trail and other trails; canoeing and boating (two boat-launching ramps are provided, one for Duck Lake and the other for Cowpen Bayou); fishing on both Duck Lake and Cowpen Bayou (a wheelchair-accessible fishing pier is located on the bayou); and small game and deer (firearm and archery) hunting on most of the refuge during the designated seasons. Camping is not permitted on the refuge, but campgrounds are available nearby.

Even though alligators are generally afraid of people, visitors are cautioned to stay a safe distance from these sluggish-looking but potentially fast-moving reptiles and to be alert for venomous snakes. Insect repellent is advised.

Lodgings and meals are available in such communities as Jena, Jonesville, Ferriday, and Alexandria.

Access to Catahoula is about 1.5 miles west on U.S. Route 84 from the junction of Route 84 and State Route 28; or approximately 12 miles east of Jena on U.S. Route 84.

Further information: Catahoula National Wildlife Refuge, P.O. Drawer Z, Rhinehart, LA 71363; telephone: (318) 992-5261.

Cat Island, containing 2,354 acres, was established in 2000 to restore, manage, and protect eco-logically important forested bottomland wetlands for the benefit of migratory birds, aquatic resources, and threatened and endangered fauna and flora. The refuge is located near the Mississippi River in southeastern Louisiana.

As the U.S. Fish and Wildlife Service said in late 2001, "In 2000, about 9,500 acres of forested wetlands were purchased by The Nature Conservancy of Louisiana for eventual purchase by the Fish and Wildlife Service. To date, the Land and Water Conservation Fund has provided funding to acquire about 2,350 acres. The Congressionally approved acquisition boundary is 36,500 acres."

Cat Island Refuge, which floods up to 15 feet in most years, lies along the southernmost unleveed stretch of the Mississippi River. It provides habitat for the Louisiana black bear, a federally listed endangered species. The river is also a major corridor for neotropical migratory birds, including the swallow-tailed kite. Among the many other avian species are the black-crowned night heron, wood stork, wood duck, blue-winged teal, wild turkey, greater yellowlegs, solitary sandpiper, American woodcock, pileated woodpecker, and northern parula and prothonotary warblers. In addition to the black bear, mammals include white-tailed deer, bobcat, mink, and river otter. Of the reptiles, there are red-eared slider (turtle), yellow-bellied and banded water snakes, and cottonmouth. Amphibians include the green tree frog.

Of the refuge's several types of habitat, the old-growth bald cypress-tupelo is exceptional. As the Fish and Wildlife Service explains, "Many of the bald cypress trees are estimated to be anywhere from 500 to 1,000 years old. In fact, the Grand National Champion bald cypress, which is also the largest tree of any species east of the Sierra Nevada [in California]... , is located within the acquisition boundary. Public access to the tree will be permitted beginning in mid-2002." The Cat Island bald cypress measures 83 feet tall and has a 53-foot trunk circumference. According to calculations by the nonprofit organization American Forests, considering its girth, canopy, and height, this is the largest of the species. (A bald cypress in Florida measures 118 feet tall, but only has a 35-foot trunk circumference.) Other forest habitat types on Cat Island refuge include overcup oak-bitter pecan, hackberry-elm-ash, Nuttall oak-ash-sweetgum, and shrub-scrub swamp.

One of the establishing purposes of the Cat Island Refuge was specifically "to encourage the use of volunteers and facilitate partnerships among the Service, local communities, conservation organizations, and others to promote the public awareness of the resources of the refuge and the National Wildlife Refuge System." Dozens of volunteers have worked with refuge staff to create public use opportunities, such as developing a 3-mile hiking trail along Blackfork Bayou. In addition, the Friends of Cat Island National Wildlife Refuge, Inc. was formed to "collaborate with the Refuge management to promote the historical and environmental resources of the Refuge and development and public use of the Refuge. . . ."

The refuge is open daily during daylight hours. There is no entrance fee.

Visitor activities include wildlife observation; photography; hiking a number of trails; canoeing; fishing; and hunting (deer, rabbit, squirrel, and waterfowl) on part of the refuge during the designated seasons.

Lodgings and meals are available in such communities as St. Francisville and Baton Rouge.

Access to the Cat Island Refuge headquarters from U.S. Route 61 in St. Francisville is by way of Commerce Street into town (intersection is located at a traffic light); at the 3-way intersection at the next traffic light, veer to the right and immediately turn right into the parking area for the refuge office, which is located with the St. Francisville Inn.

Further information: Cat Island National Wildlife Refuge, P.O. Box 1936, St. Franciscville, LA 70775; telephone: (225) 635-4753.

D'Arbonne, comprising 17,421 acres, was established in 1975 to protect and enhance the winding course of D'Arbonne Bayou, adjacent cypress-and-tupelo swamp, seasonally flooded bottomland hardwood forest, upland pine and hardwood forests, and numerous sloughs, creeks, and oxbow lakes and ponds on the western edge of the lower Mississippi River's alluvial valley in northeastern Louisiana.

An important part of D'Arbonne is known as the Beanfield. The U.S. Fish and Wildlife Service is using this tract of former farming land as a moist-soil management area. This area's water level, which promotes the growth of native wetland plants, is regulated seasonally for the benefit of migratory waterfowl, wading birds, and shorebirds. Visitors have the opportunity to view wildlife from the Andy Anders memorial observation platform (wheelchair-accessible) that overlooks the Beanfield.

This ecologically rich refuge provides habitat for such species as herons and egrets; nesting wood ducks; wild turkeys; the roadrunner, near the northeastern end of its range here; and eight species of woodpeckers, including the federally listed endangered red-cockaded woodpecker, which nests in specially managed, open pine woodlands (see a description of this species in the Carolina Sandhills Refuge text). A few alligators, near the northern end of their range, also inhabit the refuge.

Much of the refuge's bottomland hardwood forest habitat is flooded by shallow backwater as the rising level of the Ouachita River peaks, usually in March and April.

Because the Fish and Wildlife Service could not acquire the subsurface mineral rights when the refuge was established, extensive natural-gas drilling by the owner of those rights occurs at about 60 producing wells on D'Arbonne Refuge.

The refuge is open daily during daylight hours. There is no entrance fee.

Visitor activities include birdwatching; photography; driving a few refuge roads; hiking and bicycling on 50 miles of woods roads and pipeline rights-of-way; canoeing and boating (three boat-launching ramps are available) on 15 miles of the bayou; fishing (however, elevated levels of toxic mercury have been found in fish from the Ouachita River); and deer, small game, and waterfowl hunting on various parts of the refuge during the designated seasons. Camping is not permitted on the refuge, but campground facilities are available in Monroe and elsewhere. December and January are generally the best months for viewing concentrations of waterfowl, and songbirds are at their greatest numbers and diversity in April.

Even though alligators are generally afraid of people, visitors are cautioned to stay a safe distance from these sluggish-looking but potentially fast-moving reptiles and to be alert for venomous snakes. Insect repellent is advised.

Lodgings and meals are available in Monroe.

Access to D'Arbonne is north, from either I-20 (Mill Street exit) or U.S. Route 80 in Monroe, just over 12 miles on State Route 143 to the refuge entrance.

Further information: D'Arbonne National Wildlife Refuge, c/o North Louisiana Refuges, 11372 Highway 143, Farmerville, LA 71241; telephone: (318) 726-4222.

Delta, encompassing 49,000 acres, was established in 1935 to protect and enhance part of the ecologically significant Mississippi River Delta in southeastern Louisiana. The refuge mostly contains extensive marshes, bayous, and ponds. These habitats provide sources of food and resting places for an enormous variety of wintering waterfowl, including both the white and "blue" phases (morphs) of snow geese and more than a dozen species of ducks. Brown pelicans and wading birds, such as several species of herons and egrets, live here.

This is also one of the Gulf Coast refuges where the neotropical migratory songbird "fallout" occurs in April (see Aransas text). Great concentrations of warblers, buntings, tanagers, grosbeaks, and other birds land here after their exhausting nonstop flight across the Gulf of Mexico. Among the mammals inhabiting this refuge are river otters, mink, raccoons, and muskrats. Reptiles include turtles, snakes, and alligators.

The U.S. Fish and Wildlife Service is working to divert some of the flow of the Mississippi and its load of silt into the coastal marshes to replenish and enhance this vital habitat. Coastal wetlands are of enormous value not only to wildlife, but as nurseries for shrimp and many species of finfish. As one of *Ducks Unlimited*'s senior writers, Matt Young, wrote in the

September–October 2001 issue of the magazine, "Acre for acre, coastal wetlands are among the most productive ecosystems on the planet. Their bountiful waters, rich in plant and animal life, support a remarkable diversity of waterfowl....Sadly, thousands of acres of coastal wetlands continue to be lost each year. Protection is clearly the best line of defense against these losses, because once these fragile habitats disappear, they are gone forever."

Establishment of this refuge was made possible partly with revenues from the sale of Migratory Bird Hunting and Conservation Stamps (Duck Stamps).

Because the Fish and Wildlife Service could not acquire the subsurface mineral rights when the refuge was established, oil-and-gas development activities by the owner of those rights occur on Delta Refuge. As reported by Douglas Jehl, in *The New York Times* (February 20, 2001):

Jetta [Production Company] and Texaco operate some 78 oil and gas wells in the refuge, making the operation the largest at any wildlife refuge in the lower 48 states.

Under these companies and Jetta's predecessor, the Chevron Corporation, there have been a number of small oil and gas spills here in the last 10 years, during which a concerted effort at environmental record-keeping began. Wildlife service officials describe several as having been significant, killing vegetation and affecting 40 to 80 acres of marsh. But the agency says there was no indication of harm to wildlife.

That record is roughly comparable with those of other refuges where oil and gas activity is under way, with no major spills or widespread death of wildlife in recent memory, wildlife officials say. . . .

At the D'Arbonne refuge and others in the South, environmental problems arise when drilling brings to the surface saltwater that is not part of the natural habitat. And in the Delta refuge and others along the Gulf Coast, the dredging of canals has contributed to the loss of wetlands. . . .

At the refuge[s] in Louisiana, wildlife managers say, oil companies have been quick to report even the smallest spill and willing to shift pipelines and even drilling sites to meet environmental concerns.

In the last 10 years, said James O. Harris, supervisory biologist for the federal refuges in southeast Louisiana, the wildlife service has collected about $1 million in fees from the oil companies to mitigate damage in the Delta refuge. That, Mr. Harris said, has been enough to help the agency recover more than 1,000 acres of wetlands, or 10 times the amount lost to energy operations in the period [the last decade]. . . .

The refuge is open daily. There is no entrance fee.

Visitor activities include birdwatching, photography, boating, canoeing the refuge's waterways and bayous, primitive camping, fishing, and hunting during the designated season.

Visitors are cautioned to be alert for venomous snakes. Insect repellent and sunscreen are advised.

Lodgings and meals are available in and around New Orleans.

Access to this refuge is by way of State Route 23 and from there only by a seaworthy boat.

Further information: Delta National Wildllife Refuge, c/o Southeast Louisiana Refuges, 1010 Gause Blvd., Slidell, LA 70458; telephone: (504) 646-7555.

Grand Cote, consisting of 6,000 acres, was authorized in 1989 to enhance and protect remnants of original bottomland hardwood forest, reforested lands that were cleared for agriculture in the 1970s, cypress sloughs, open wetlands, and croplands in central Louisiana.

In Cajun-French (Acadian), *grand cote* means "big hill," in reference to a prominent bluff. In this case, the land below the Grand Cote is a natural sump, bordered on the north and east by ridges along the Red River and by terraced uplands on the south and west. Among the refuge's great variety of wildlife are concentrations of wintering waterfowl—notably pintails—as well as shorebirds, numerous neotropical migratory songbirds, and alligators.

The U.S. Fish and Wildlife Service manages ecologically important expanses of open wetland, known as moist-soil habitat, for the benefit of the wintering waterfowl. With levees and water control structures, these shallow units are drained of water to promote the growth of moist-soil plants during the warmer months and then reflooded in winter for waterfowl and other water birds.

The Nature Conservancy made possible Grand Cote's establishment, and Ducks Unlimited, Inc. has assisted with a number of important habitat enhancement projects.

The refuge is open daily during daylight hours. There is no entrance fee.

Visitor activities include birdwatching, photography, hiking, and fishing.

Even though alligators are generally afraid of people, visitors are cautioned to stay a safe distance from these sluggish-looking but potentially fast-moving reptiles and to be alert for venomous snakes. Insect repellent is advised.

Flora and fauna of this refuge are similar to those at Lake Ophelia.

Lodgings and meals are available in such communities as Marksville and Alexandria.

Access to Grand Cote is northwest 7 miles from Marksville on State Route 1, in Fifth Ward Community left (south) onto State Route 1194, and about 4 miles to the refuge.

Further information: Grand Cote National Wildlife Refuge, 401 Island Road, Marksville, LA 71351; telephone: (318) 253-4238.

Handy Brake, consisting of 466 acres, was established in 1988 to restore a small tract of land originally containing mixed hardwood bottomland forest that was cleared for agriculture in northeastern Louisiana. An observation platform (wheelchair-accessible) offers visitors a view of refuge's 300-acre shallow lake wetland habitat and an opportunity to see some of the waterfowl and wading birds. The species of fauna and flora here are essentially the same as at the other national wildlife refuges in northern Louisiana.

This refuge is open daily during daylight hours. There is no entrance fee.

Visitor activities include birdwatching and photography. Although camping is not permitted on the refuge, campground facilities are available at nearby Chemin-a-Haut State Park and in the vicinity of Monroe.

Lodgings and meals are available in communities such as Bastrop and Monroe.

Adjacent to Handy Brake Refuge is Rector's Prairie, a part of the Louisiana Wetland Management District, which is managed by the North Louisiana Refuges Complex. The district presently consists of 9 federally owned tracts, 37 easements on privately owned lands, and 6 leases, all of which total more than 26,000 acres. As the U.S. Fish and Wildlife Service explains,

"Habitat management focuses primarily on two practices—reforestation of marginal agricultural areas and the development and maintenance of moist-soil units. Over the last several years, many areas have been reforested." Visitor activities on the federally owned tracts include wildlife observation and photography. Because many of these parcels are remote, the Service urges prospective visitors to contact the Refuges Complex headquarters for information.

Access to the Handy Brake Refuge is east 1.1 miles on U.S. Route 165 from the courthouse square in Bastrom; north (left at the third stoplight) 6.4 miles on Parish Road 830-4 (Cooper Lake Road); and east (right) at the refuge sign.

Further information: Handy Brake National Wildlife Refuge, c/o North Louisiana Refuges, 11372 Highway 143, Farmerville, LA 71241; telephone: (318) 726-4222.

Lacassine, encompassing 34,878 acres, was established in 1937 partly to protect and enhance 16,000-acre Lacassine Pool—an extensive levee-contained impoundment of open water and freshwater marsh of great benefit to an enormous concentration of wintering waterfowl, including the white and "blue" phases (morphs) of lesser snow goose, numerous species of ducks, and other water birds. The refuge staff continually manages the pool's habitat to maintain beneficial ecological conditions for waterfowl. In past years, as many as 800,000 ducks and geese have been seen here, where the Central and Mississippi Flyways converge.

Approximately 1,500 acres of the refuge are managed to produce grain crops and moist-soil plants for waterfowl. An ecologically important area of sawgrass marsh borders the circuitous course of Lacassine Bayou, and 3,345 acres of Lacassine have been designated as wilderness. Outside this relatively pristine area of the refuge, oil and gas development occurs. The Intracoastal Waterway slices through the southern part of the refuge.

Virtually the only trees on the refuge are bald cypresses that grow in two groves along the edge of Mud Lake. During the breeding season, these small groves are filled with nests—a veritable bird city of herons, egrets, cormorants, and anhingas.

The refuge's 345-acre VIDRINE UNIT (Duralde Prairie), to the north of Eunice, Louisiana, was added to Lacassine in 1993. Since 1994, it has been the focus of a prairie restoration project—converting former agricultural land to coastal prairie that consists of native grasses and forbs. Few remnants remain of this natural ecosystem that once covered more than 2 million acres of southwestern Louisiana.

Establishment of Lacassine was made possible partly with revenues from the sale of Migratory Bird Hunting and Conservation Stamps (Duck Stamps).

The refuge is open daily during daylight hours, and the headquarters is open on weekdays, except for national holidays. There is no entrance fee.

Visitor activities include birdwatching; photography; driving on 4 miles of refuge roads; hiking on about 30 miles of levees and service roads; boating during most of the year on canals, bayous, and other waterways (two boat-launching sites are provided at Lacassine Pool [March 15 to October 15], and commercial [fee] launching sites provide access to other parts of the refuge); recreational fishing on both the pool and bayou; archery deer hunting; and waterfowl hunting on part of the refuge during the designated season. November through April are the best months for birdwatching. Although camping is not permitted on the refuge, campgrounds are provided at Myers and Garys Landings, along State Route 3056 near the refuge office and at Sam Houston Jones State Park to the north of Lake Charles.

Even though alligators are generally afraid of people, visitors are cautioned to stay a safe distance from these sluggish-looking but potentially fast-moving reptiles and to be alert for venomous snakes. Insect repellent is advised.

Lodgings and meals are available in such communities as Lake Charles, Sulphur, and Jennings.

Access to Lacassine's visitor contact station is south from westbound I-10 at Jennings on State Route 26 to Lake Arthur, right onto State Route 14 for 7 miles, and left onto State Route 3056 for 4.5 miles to the refuge entrance; or south from eastbound I-10 at Welsh on State Route 99, left onto Route 14 for 3 miles, and right onto Route 3056 for 4.5 miles to the refuge. Access to Lacassine Pool is west from Lake Arthur on State Route 14 for 15 miles or east from Hayes on Route 14 for 3 miles, and south 4.5 miles on Illinois Plant Road.

Further information: Lacassine National Wildlife Refuge, 209 Nature Road, Lake Arthur, LA 70549; telephone: (337) 774-5923.

Lake Ophelia, containing 15,000 acres, was authorized in 1988 to protect and manage wetlands for the benefit of waterfowl and to restore an area of bottomland hardwood forest, laced with winding waterways and a cypress-bordered oxbow lake that was formerly a bend of the Red River, in central Louisiana. Wildlife includes great concentrations of wading birds, wood ducks that nest here, and tens of thousands of wintering ducks. The American alligator also inhabits the refuge.

The Nature Conservancy made possible Lake Ophelia Refuge's establishment.

The refuge is open daily during daylight hours. Although there is no entrance fee, a fee is charged for fishing, hunting, and ATV use.

Visitor activities include birdwatching, photography, hiking, ATV riding, boating on Lake Ophelia, fishing on the lake from March through October, and hunting during the designated seasons.

Even though alligators are generally afraid of people, visitors are cautioned to stay a safe distance from these sluggish-looking but potentially fast-moving reptiles and to be alert for venomous snakes. Insect repellent is advised.

The birds recorded on Lake Ophelia Refuge are much the same as those on Catahoula Refuge.

Lodgings and meals are available in such communities as Marksville and Alexandria.

Access to the refuge is 25 miles northeast from Marksville on State Highway 452.

Further information: Lake Ophelia National Wildlife Refuge, 401 Island Road, Marksville, LA 71351; telephone: (318) 253-4238.

Mandalay, containing 4,212 acres, was established in 1996 to protect extensive freshwater marshes located within the western Terrebonne Parish wetland complex in south-central Louisiana. Habitats also include bald cypress-tupelo swamp, ponds, and many canals that are used by the petroleum industry. The refuge, which is bisected by the Gulf Coast Intracoastal Waterway, attracts large concentrations of wading birds, wintering waterfowl and other migratory birds, and many wintering bald eagles.

As described by refuge manager, Paul Yakupzack:

Ninety-five percent of Mandalay National Wildlife Refuge is freshwater marsh that is largely vegetated with maidencane—a grass that grows up to four feet tall, and arrowhead (bulltongue). Large clumps of wax myrtle and cattails are also common. Black willows line the banks of almost all the waterways and canals. Much of the refuge consists of flotant marsh (trembling earth). It is vegetated with pennywort, yellow-flowering bur marigold of the Sunflower Family, and maidencane. Common aquatic plants in ponds and waterways include wild celery, many species of pond weed, southern naiad, hydrilla, and salvinia. American lotus provides acres of beautiful yellow aromatic flowers in summer, and southern blue flag (wild iris) is also common.

With a grant of North American Wetlands Conservation Act funds and a generous contribution from Dow USA, The Nature Conservancy obtained the land from a prior owner and donated it to the U.S. Fish and Wildlife Service. Paul Yakupzack credits generous local conservationist Michael St. Martin as having been "very active in the acquisition process."

The refuge is open daily during daylight hours and is accessible only by boat. There is no entrance fee. The refuge headquarters, which is located just west of Houma on the south side of State Route 182, is open on weekdays, except national holidays.

Visitor activities include birdwatching, photography, boating, fishing, and hunting (archery hunts for deer and feral hog; lottery hunts for waterfowl). There are presently no boat rentals, but a number of swamp tours are provided in the vicinity of Houma.

Even though alligators are generally afraid of people, visitors are cautioned to stay a safe distance from these sluggish-looking but potentially fast-moving reptiles and to be alert for the venomous cottonmouth snake. Insect repellent and sunscreen are advised. The best seasons for visiting the refuge are spring, autumn, and winter.

Lodgings and meals are available in Houma.

Access onto Mandalay Refuge by boat is about 2 miles south of State Route 182 (old U.S. Route 90), which is about 5 miles west of Houma. As the Fish and Wildlife Service explains, "A visitor can reach the refuge by boat from Cannon's Landing, on Southdown-Mandalay Road, which is parallel to LA 182, but on the north side of Big Bayou Black. From Cannon's, proceed south down Minors Canal for about 2 miles to the Gulf Intracoastal Waterway (GIWW). About 75 percent of the refuge, the Hatch Unit, is south of the GIWW and features Lake Hatch, a shallow, 200-acre expanse that provides refuge for thousands of waterfowl during hunting season. We don't allow hunting on Lake Hatch. The Hanson Unit, to the north of the GIWW, is where we have the lottery waterfowl hunts."

Further information: Mandalay National Wildlife Refuge, 3599 Bayou Black Drive, Houma, LA 70360; telephone: (985) 853-1078.

Sabine, consisting of 124,511 acres, was established in 1937 to protect and enhance an extensive expanse of impounded freshwater marsh, estuarine coastal marsh, bayous, lakes, ponds, low ridges, and wooded islands in the southwestern corner of Louisiana. This largest national wildlife refuge along the Gulf Coast of the United States provides significant habitat for thousands of wintering and migratory birds—notably thousands of white pelicans and snow geese. There are also roseate spoonbills and several species of herons, egrets, and rails.

Sabine is one of the Gulf Coast refuges where the spectacular neotropical migratory songbird "fallout" phenomenon occurs in April (see Aransas text). This ecologically rich refuge also provides important nursery habitat for estuarine-dependent marine animals, such as shrimp and many kinds of finfish. More than 25,000 of the large reptile known as the American alligator (*Alligator mississippiensis*) inhabit the refuge.

The U.S. Fish and Wildlife Service manages the refuge by implementing periodic prescription burns to maintain native marsh and coastal prairie habitats, and by regulating water levels and water quality with ten main water control structures and more than 60 miles of levees. Unfortunately, natural and human environmental impacts over the past few decades have caused the impairment or loss of roughly 40,000 acres of the refuge, resulting from significant amounts of saltwater intrusion. Attempts are being made to halt or even reverse this ecological damage.

Establishment of this refuge was made possible partly with revenues from the sale of Migratory Bird Hunting and Conservation Stamps (Duck Stamps). Sabine Refuge is open daily during daylight hours. There is no entrance fee. The visitor center is open daily.

Visitor activities include birdwatching; photography; hiking on the 1.5-mile, interpretive (wheelchair-accessible) Marsh Trail and viewing wildlife from an observation tower; boating on more than 150 miles of canals, bayous, and other waterways (two boat-launching facilities are provided; boat access on canals may be seasonally restricted); recreational fresh- and saltwater fishing; crabbing (traps and pots not permitted); shrimping by castnet; and waterfowl hunting on part of the refuge during the designated season. Camping is not allowed on the refuge, but a campground is provided at Sam Houston Jones State Park, to the north of Lake Charles.

Even though alligators are generally afraid of people, visitors are cautioned to stay a safe distance from these sluggish-looking but potentially fast-moving reptiles and to be alert for venomous snakes. Insect repellent is advised.

October through May are the best months for birdwatching. And Sabine consistently runs up one of the nation's largest annual National Audubon Society-sponsored Christmas bird counts, totaling nearly 200 species. More than 250 bird species have been recorded on the refuge since it was established.

Lodgings and meals are available in such communities as Lake Charles and Sulphur, Louisiana and Beaumont and Port Arthur, Texas.

Access to Sabine is south from I-10 at Sulphur 27 miles on State Route 27 to the refuge entrance.

> Further information: Sabine National Wildlife Refuge, 3000 Holly Beach Highway, Hackberry, LA 70645; telephone: (337) 762-3816.

Shell Keys, containing 78 acres, was established in 1907 by President Theodore Roosevelt to protect several low-lying sand-and-shell islands in the Gulf of Mexico south of New Iberia, Louisiana. These nearly submerged bits of land are often overwashed during storms. Brown pelicans, gulls, and terns are among the birds that are seen here. Limited visitor activities include birdwatching, boating, and fishing.

> Further information: Shell Keys National Wildlife Refuge, c/o Southeast Louisiana Refuges, 1010 Gause Blvd., Slidell, LA 70458; telephone: (504) 646-7555.

Tensas River, containing roughly 66,000 acres (with additional tracts of land still planned for purchase), was established in 1980 to protect and enhance ecologically rich, seasonally flooded bottomland cypress-and-hardwood forest and oxbow lakes along the winding course of the Tensas River in northeastern Louisiana. This remnant of pristine forest had been targeted for timber harvesting and agricultural development, but a coalition of conservationists was instrumental in mounting a campaign that rescued the area in the nick of time.

More than 400 species of birds, mammals, reptiles, amphibians, and fish inhabit the refuge, including the American alligator, wood duck, wild turkey, pileated woodpecker, numerous songbirds, and a remnant population of the rare and threatened Louisiana black bear. Unfortunately, the ivory-billed woodpecker (*Campephilus principalis*), apparently last recorded in the 1940s on what is now the Tensas River Refuge, is generally believed to be extinct. This woodpecker measured to about 20 inches in length, compared to another red-crested species, the pileated woodpecker, which measures to around 16 inches.

The U.S. Fish and Wildlife Service is managing the Tensas River Refuge to protect, enhance, and restore its bottomland hardwood forest habitat. Other parts of the refuge are devoted to moist-soil management (seasonally raising and lowering water levels) and farming that benefit thousands of wintering waterfowl. Ducks Unlimited, Inc. has assisted with important habitat enhancement projects. The Tensas River Refuge Association is a nonprofit support group that is assisting the refuge in a variety of ways.

The refuge is open daily during daylight hours. There is no entrance fee. The visitor center is open daily, except on national holidays.

Visitor activities include birdwatching; photography; environmental education programs; driving and bicycling on refuge roads; hiking; canoeing (a primitive canoe-launching site is available); ATVs (only on ATV trails during the designated period); fishing on two refuge lakes; and hunting (waterfowl and deer) during the designated seasons.

Hiking opportunities include the Boardwalk Wildlife Trail through forested slough habitat, the 0.25-mile Hollow Cypress Wildlife Trail, and a 5-mile hiking trail.

Even though alligators are usually afraid of people, visitors are cautioned to stay a safe distance from these sluggish-looking but potentially fast-moving reptiles and to be alert for venomous snakes. Insect repellent is advised.

Lodgings and meals are available in such communities as Tallulah and Winnsboro.

Access to Tensas River Refuge from the Waverly exit on I-20 is north 1.5 miles on State Route 577, east 4 miles on U.S. Route 80, right at the refuge sign, and south 10 miles to the visitor center.

Further information: Tensas River National Wildlife Refuge, Route 2, Box 295, Tallulah, LA 71282; telephone: (318) 574-2664.

Upper Ouachita, containing more than 40,000 acres, was established in 1978 to protect and enhance ecologically rich bottomland hardwood forest habitat that borders 18 miles of the Ouachita River, extending south from the Louisiana–Arkansas border in northeastern Louisiana. There are numerous bayous, sloughs, and creeks that wind throughout this part of the refuge, and along its western edge lies an area of pine-covered uplands.

The separate 16,000-acre Mollicy Unit was subsequently added to the refuge so that this area, originally containing bottomland hardwood forest that was cleared for agriculture, can be restored.

Much of the refuge's bottomland hardwood forest habitat is flooded by shallow backwater when the rising water level of the Ouachita River peaks, generally in March and April.

Upper Ouachita Refuge was established partly with revenues from the sale of Migratory Bird Hunting and Conservation Stamps (Duck Stamps). Because the U.S. Fish and Wildlife Service could not acquire the subsurface mineral rights when the refuge was established, extensive natural gas development by the owner of those rights occurs at more than 200 wells on the Upper Ouachita Refuge.

The refuge is open daily during daylight hours. There is no entrance fee.

Visitor activities include birdwatching; wildlife photography; driving or walking on River Road; canoeing and boating (two boat-launching ramps are available); fishing (however, elevated levels of toxic mercury have been found in fish from the Ouachita River); and hunting (deer, small game, and waterfowl) during the designated seasons. During and following periods of heavy winter and spring rainfall, the river level rises and may flood River Road. Camping is not permitted in the refuge, but campground facilities are available at Finch Bayou Recreation Area, Chemin-a-Haut State Park, and in the vicinity of Monroe.

Even though alligators are generally afraid of people, visitors are cautioned to stay a safe distance from these sluggish-looking but potentially fast-moving reptiles and to be alert for venomous snakes. Insect repellent is advised.

The fauna and flora of Upper Ouachita Refuge are essentially the same as those on D'Arbonne.

Lodgings and meals are available in such communities as Bastrop and Monroe.

Access to Upper Ouachita is north from Monroe on U.S. Route 165, left onto State Route 2 to Sterlington, right onto State Route 143 to Haile, and right onto Haile Baptist Church and Hooker Hole roads for 4 miles to the refuge.

Further information: Upper Ouachita National Wildlife Refuge, c/o North Louisiana Refuges, 11372 Highway 143, Farmerville, LA 71241; telephone: (318) 726-4222.

Maine

Aroostook, containing 9,516 acres, was established in 1998 to restore and protect valuable wildlife habitats on what was formerly part of the Loring Air Force Base in northeastern Maine. The refuge includes wetlands, lakes, and ponds that attract migratory waterfowl, such as wood ducks, black ducks, and hooded mergansers. The forested uplands, which comprise the majority of the refuge lands, provide nesting habitat for numerous species of neotropical migratory songbirds, such as thrushes and warblers. Grasslands offer nesting habitat for upland sandpipers and bobolinks, and woodcocks perform their aerial courtship displays over these open areas (see a discussion of management for this species in the Moosehorn Refuge text).

As the U.S. Fish and Wildlife Service explains, Loring Air Force Base played a key role during the Cold War in ensuring this nation's safety. "The Strategic Air Command (SAC) was stationed here from 1950 to 1994, flying long-range bombers capable of delivering nuclear weapons. Caribou Air Force Station was a Top-Secret, self-contained base in the northeast corner of the site."

In describing the tremendous challenge in converting this former military installation to a wildlife refuge, refuge manager Donald Lima says that substantial progress has already been made:

. . . we acquired a lot of extraneous items, i.e., over 100 buildings and structures, miles of fence, railroad track and roads, and hazardous materials, to name a few. . . . the USAF . . . removed all known asbestos, unexploded ordnance, underground storage tanks. . . . The refuge is now charged with habitat restoration, i.e., some heavy duty building demolition.

I have been very fortunate to have formed several productive partnerships. The following partial list will provide you with some idea of the number and complexity of our partnerships:

- Maine Army National Guard removed 15-20 acres of asphalt roadway and parking lots.
- U.S. Air Force—a huge help when I first arrived and to this day has helped with acquiring equipment and supplies, as well as "putting aside" items for refuge use.
- U.S. Navy SEALS and Seabees made five trips up here to conduct building demolition. To date (September 2001), they have "knocked down" 18-20 structures, saving the Service and the Refuge nearly $1 million.
- Maine School of Science & Mathematics has provided high school students (averaging two or three per semester) who have worked in the office answering phones, filing, and cleaning; and cleared trails.
- U.S. Job Corps has cleared trails and accomplished other useful work.
- A local scrap-metal dealer has removed about 1,000 tons of steel. This includes railroad track, water towers (each 136 feet tall), a 300,000-gallon fuel-storage tank, and much, much more.

The Fish and Wildlife Service has already begun implementing a program of habitat enhancement and management. Carefully prescribed burning is reducing the fuel load of dead organic material, promoting nutrient cycling, spuring new growth, and maintaining grassland habitat. Timber harvesting on small blocks of forest is designed to create a successional matrix of diverse woodland habitats, thereby increasing the refuge's wildlife diversity. Water-control structures are used to seasonally regulate water levels in wetland impoundments, for the benefit of waterfowl.

Although Aroostook Refuge is mostly not yet open to visitation, a 1.5-mile trail was recently opened for hiking, wildlife observation, photography, and cross-country skiing. A newly renovated building contains the refuge's office/visitor contact station, which is open on weekdays, except national holidays.

The Friends of Aroostook National Wildlife Refuge is a nonprofit support group that is assisting the refuge with fund-raising, volunteer projects, and education.

Lodgings and meals are available in such communities as Caribou and Presque Isle.

Access to Aroostook Refuge from U.S. Route 1 at Caribou is east about 7 miles on State Route 89, and north (left) onto East Gate Road, following signs to the refuge entrance; or from U.S. 1A at Limestone, it is west about 3 miles on State Route 89, and north (right) onto East Gate Road.

Further information: Aroostook National Wildlife Refuge, P.O. Box 554, Limestone, ME 04750; telephone: (207) 328-4634.

Cross Island (see Petit Manan text)

Franklin Island (see Petit Manan text)

Lake Umbagog (see text under New Hampshire)

Moosehorn, comprising 27,616 acres in two divisions, was established in 1937 to protect and manage a diversity of ecologically significant wetland and forest habitats in eastern Maine. The 7,577-acre Edmunds Division borders the tidal waters of Cobscook Bay, along U.S. Route 1 between Whiting and Pembroke. The 20,039-acre Baring Division includes an extensive inland area of mixed coniferous-and-deciduous forest and freshwater wetlands, near Calais. Roughly one-quarter of the refuge has been designated as two units of the National Wilderness Preservation System. Over 225 bird species have been recorded on the refuge.

The refuge provides important feeding, resting, and nesting habitat for waterfowl, wading birds, shorebirds, upland game birds, raptors, and numerous neotropical migratory songbirds. Moosehorn's impressive habitat diversity includes northern forests, freshwater marshes and bogs, lakes and ponds, and more than 50 managed freshwater impoundments. There are numerous streams and beaver flowages. Stretches of rocky shore and salt marsh are tidally influenced by 20-foot, twice-daily fluctuations. Areas of blueberry barrens and grasslands are scattered here and there within the expanses of forest.

The U.S. Fish and Wildlife Service carries out a number of important management activities. To help create and maintain habitat diversity for the benefit of wildlife, selected areas of forest are harvested and/or enhanced with prescribed burning. As the Service explains:

Woodcock, ruffed grouse, moose, deer, and a variety of songbirds prosper in a young forest. In the past, wildfires revitalized the forest, while farming maintained open areas. However, wildfire is a rare event today, and farmland acreage has decreased dramatically. Habitat management programs, including timber harvesting and controlled burning, mimic the natural effects of wildfire, blowdowns, and insect damage by providing clearings and early growth forests.

Small clearcuts [five-acre sections] throughout the forest provide openings and young, brushy growth that serve as food and cover for many wildlife species. Each year, the Service awards timber units to local harvesters according to the refuge forest management plan. The harvesters pay for the timber based on a stumpage schedule. . . . This management has produced significant increases in woodcock, grouse, bear, and moose populations.

The refuge's fire management program consists of periodic, relatively "cool," low-burning fires. These ecologically sound burns reduce fuel loads of accumulated dead vegetative debris, thereby reducing the potential for destructive wildfires; promote nutrient cycling; and spur the growth of vigorous new vegetation that offers important food and cover for many species of wildlife. Controlled fires are used especially to burn slash, following timber harvesting activities. Areas of blueberry barrens and grassland are also periodically burned, to revitalize them and prevent the invasion of woody shrubs and trees.

The American woodcock (*Scolopax minor*) is one of Moosehorn Refuge's avian species that most benefits from woodland habitat management activities. It has steadily declined throughout much of its range because of the loss of its natural habitats. Woodcock need clearings for roosting and their aerial spring courtship displays, shrubby alder thickets for foraging with their long beaks for earthworms, and young deciduous woodlands for nesting. Here at Moosehorn, refuge staff have pioneered efforts to understand woodcock biology and develop management strategies.

As explained by the Fish and Wildlife Service:

Woodcock are best known for their spectacular courtship flights. At dusk and dawn from early April to mid-May, the males fly to their territories in open areas. Each bird begins this mating ritual with a series of nasal "peents." He then takes wing in a spiral flight that carries him several hundred feet into the air while he warbles a plaintive song to waiting females. He returns to the same spot after each flight and repeats his performance several times over the next half hour.

In describing Moosehorn, refuge manager Tim Cooper says:

The refuge is famed for its involvement in research on the American Woodcock. Intensive management for this species has been a hallmark of the refuge since the 1940's. Management practices primarily targeted for the woodcock have provided ideal habitats for other species. Coupled with the 52 impoundments and coastal frontages, this mix of habitat types results in the overall abundance of wildlife. Early successional forest management creates a rolling mosaic of habitat types. Everything from clear openings to old-growth forest can be found on the refuge. Research indicates that Moosehorn's innovative management practices have resulted in more quality habitats for a greater variety of species than in unmanaged areas. It is hoped that some of these practices can be used to address the decline that the woodcock is experiencing throughout its range.

Management of the refuge's freshwater wetlands is carried out with water control structures that enable the raising and lowering of water levels within pond and wetland impoundments. Three of these structures, which have been designed and installed by Ducks Unlimited, Inc., provide for the annual migration of the alewife (*Alosa pseudoharengus*). This silvery gray species of anadromous fish, a member of the herring family, is a living link between the sea and freshwater lakes and ponds. In May, large numbers of these 10- to 12-inch-long alewives migrate from coastal waters up the streams that lead them back to their ancestral spawning places. They swim upstream—mysteriously and relentlessly driven against great odds, fighting the current, and battering themselves against rocks and each other. Finally they reach the tranquil waters where they once again ensure the continuation of their species. Soon after spawning, the adult fish return to coastal waters, and the young spend the summer growing to a size of 3 or 4 inches before dashing down to the sea in early autumn.

As described by the Fish and Wildlife Service:

Wetland management on the refuge has greatly increased waterfowl numbers. Dabbling ducks, such as black ducks and wood ducks, require water depths of no more than 18 inches on which to feed. Water control structures on marshes and ponds allow managers to maintain optimal water levels for plant growth and feeding by waterfowl. Water level control provides necessary food and cover during the breeding season. It also allows marshes to be drained periodically for rejuvenation.

To enhance nesting opportunities for bald eagles and ospreys, the refuge has erected nesting platforms on both divisions of Moosehorn. Common loons nest on Bearce Lake and on Vose and Cranberry ponds, where their nesting activities are protected and monitored. An air quality monitoring station is located on the Baring Division.

Establishment of Moosehorn Refuge was made possible partly with revenues from the sale of Migratory Bird Hunting and Conservation Stamps (Duck Stamps). In addition to assistance provided by Ducks Unlimited, other nonprofit organizations that have helped include the Ruffed Grouse Society, The Nature Conservancy, and the Quoddy Regional Land Trust.

The refuge is open daily during daylight hours. There is no entrance fee. The refuge headquarters, located on the Baring Division, is open on weekdays, except national holidays.

Visitor activities include wildlife observation, photography, driving on public highways that run through both divisions, hiking, bicycling, cross-country skiing and snowshoeing, canoeing (especially enjoyable on Bearce Lake), fishing (a wheelchair-accessible pier is provided), and deer hunting on parts of the refuge during the designated season. The refuge offers a limited environmental education program that is focused mainly on woodcock and eagles. Although camping is not permitted on the refuge, campground facilities are available at Cobscook Bay State Park, which is located on the Edmunds Division.

Hiking opportunities include three self-guiding, interpretive walks: the Woodcock Trail, a 0.3-mile (wheelchair-accessible) route near the refuge headquarters that offers a chance to see woodcock courtship flights in late April; the Habitat Discovery Trail, a 1.2-mile route through wooded habitat; and the Bird Walk, a 0.25-mile route through forest that is filled with an abundance of neotropical songbirds from late April through early June. The refuge also contains more than 50 miles of unpaved roadways that are closed to motor vehicles and open to hiking, bicycling, cross-country skiing, and snowshoeing. A viewing platform on the west side of U.S. Route 1 in the Baring Division provides opportunities to see nesting bald eagles and ospreys.

Insect repellent is advised during the warmer months.

Lodgings and meals are available in such communities as Calais and Robbinston.

Access to the Moosehorn Refuge headquarters, on the Baring Division, is about 3 miles from Calais on U.S. Route I (to the southwest of Calais), south (left) 3 miles on the Calais-Charlotte Road, and west (right) on the headquarters entrance road; or from the junction of U.S. Route I and State Route 214 in Pembroke, it is northwest 6 miles on Route 214, north (right) 8.3 miles on the Calais-Charlotte Road, and west (left) on the refuge

Further information: Moosehorn National Wildlife Refuge, RR1, Box 202, Suite 1, Baring, ME 04694; telephone: (207) 454-7161.

Petit Manan, a complex of five national wildlife refuges encompassing roughly 7,000 acres, was established in 1972. The refuges are 5,500-acre Petit Manan, 1,355-acre Cross Island, 20-acre Franklin Island, 65-acre Seal Island, and 10-acre Pond Island. Together they comprise 40 coastal islands and three mainland units spanning more than 200 miles along the coast of Maine.

As explained by the U.S. Fish and Wildlife Service:

The Service's primary focus at Petit Manan is colonial seabird restoration and management. Refuge islands provide nesting habitat for common, Arctic, and endangered roseate terns, Atlantic puffins, razorbills, black guillemots, Leach's storm-petrels, laughing gulls, and common eiders. Over the last 25 years, the Service has worked to reverse the decline in these birds' populations. As a result, many species have returned to islands where they nested historically. . . .

Seabirds have always relied on Maine's offshore islands as havens for raising their young. Small unforested, rocky islands provide a setting free of mammalian predators such as foxes, coyotes, and raccoons.

In the seventeenth century, Euro-Americans started to settle on many coastal islands, farming and raising sheep and other livestock. Carl W. Buchheister, former president of the National Audubon Society, wrote in his Preface for the book *Maine Paradise* (Russell D. Butcher, 1973):

Not long after the European immigrants settled along America's East Coast, the rape of Maine's island seabird colonies began. The eggs of gulls and other species were gathered for food—at first, here and there, but then with increasing fervor and thoroughness. Egging was carried on as if the supply were inexhaustible; no one gave thought to the welfare of the species. Consequently, under the impact of egging and related disturbances, the bird populations began to decline.

Then a still more devastating practice descended upon the island bird colonies. Fashion, the most powerful of dictators, demanded more and more plumage for the millinery trade, and the gulls and terns of Maine were among its principal victims. Both the native Indians and white man invaded the island nurseries during the summer months, killing the parent birds and leaving their eggs and young to perish. A crueler and more lethal method of exploitation could hardly have been devised.

As great barrels filled with the bodies of dead birds were brought to the villages of the inhabited islands and mainland, scores of women were employed to prepare the skins, keeping their feathers intact. After being treated with alum, salt, and preservatives, the skins were packed in cases and shipped aboard coastal sailing vessels to New York City, the major center of the booming, multimillion-dollar millinery industry.

For many years thousands upon thousands of these birds were slaughtered. . . .

In fact, . . . following three hundred years of egging and slaughter, the summer islands of Maine that had once been so crowded with avian life had virtually become biological deserts.

Around the end of the nineteenth century and start of the twentieth century, the American Ornithologists' Union's Committee on Bird Protection engaged the services of several outer-island light-station personnel, such as those on Matinicus Rock (now a refuge island), to help protect the seabird colonies. As Buchheister said, "These early Maine wildlife wardens did much to advance a new, but at that time extremely unpopular, gospel of conservation—a gospel that germinated in the fertile soil of the humane reaction to the slaughter, the cruelty, and the greed. With it began the Audubon movement, starting with the Massachusetts Audubon Society in 1896. Within three years there were sixteen similar groups: in New Hampshire, Rhode Island, Connecticut, New York, New Jersey, and even in far-off Texas and California. The appalling destruction of the island-nesting birds of Maine did more to trigger this movement than did any other killing of birdlife elsewhere in the country."

Public concern for the welfare of birds in general resulted in the passage by Congress of the Migratory Bird Treaty Act, in 1918. This landmark legislation was enacted into law to protect migratory birds, their eggs, and their nests.

As a result of these and other wildlife conservation efforts, the populations of arctic and common terns rebounded, increasing to more than 15,000 pairs along the coast of Maine. But as described by the Fish and Wildlife Service:

The recovery was short-lived, however. During the mid-1900s, the spread of open landfills along the coast and an increase in fishery waste provided easy pickings for herring and great black-backed gulls. These birds nest earlier than terns, claiming prime habitat and relegating terns to inferior nest sites. Some gulls also prey on tern eggs and chicks. The artificial food sources led to an explosion in gull populations. By 1977, the tern population in the Gulf of Maine had declined to roughly 5,000 nesting pairs.

Between 1972 and 1980, the Petit Manan refuge complex was established mainly to provide the management necessary to restore breeding populations of terns. According to the Fish and Wildlife Service:

To restore terns to an island, it must first be made suitable for the birds again. This requires...[discouraging the] herring and great black-backed gulls. In some cases, human presence on the island during the start of the gull nesting season is enough. Small populations of gulls can be controlled through egg and nest destruction and noise-makers. . . .

If terns have recently abandoned an island, they may return rapidly once the gulls are gone. However, in many cases, it has been decades since terns nested on an island. To entice them back, the Service uses sound systems playing recordings of a tern colony and tern decoys scattered in suitable nesting habitat. This method has been highly effective on several islands. . . .

Large nesting colonies of arctic and common terns are now supported on Petit Manan, Matinicus Rock, and Seal Islands, the latter comprising the largest tern colony in the Gulf of Maine; and the federally listed endangered roseate tern is also now nesting on Petit Manan Island. Similar tern restorations have also occurred on other islands, including Ship, Metinic, and Pond islands.

Other species of colonial nesting seabirds have fortunately benefited from these successes. Among them are the Leach's storm petrel and three alcids—Atlantic puffin, black guillemot, and razorbill. The latter is at the southern extremity of its range on the Maine coast, nesting on three refuge islands: Old Man, Seal, and Matinicus Rock.

The mainland properties of the Petit Manan Refuge complex consist of the 628-acre Sawyer's Marsh Division, at the head of an expanse of salt marsh in Milbridge; the 572-acre Gouldsboro Bay Division, containing mixed upland hardwood forest; and the 2,166-acre Petit Manan Point Division in Steuben. This latter area is a scenic and ecological jewel of the National Wildlife Refuge System. It contains a remarkable diversity of habitats on a narrow peninsula that juts into the Atlantic Ocean, including the intertidal zone, cobble beaches, granite shoreline ledges with visually contrasting bands of basaltic dikes, salt marsh, tidal mudflats, cedar swamps, freshwater marsh, sphagnum-and-heath bogs, spruce forest, picturesque open stands of jack pines, blueberry barrens, and old hay pastures.

Concentrations of migrating waterfowl, wading birds, and shorebirds are attracted to the refuge's salt marsh and tidal mudflat habitats. During the autumn, Petit Manan Point's 80-acre Cranberry Flowage draws more than 4,000 ducks, many of which are black ducks, along with mallards and green-winged teal. During the winter, large numbers of common eiders; surf, black, and white-winged scoters; common goldeneyes; and long-tailed ducks (oldsquaws) are abundant offshore.

Blueberry barrens and open grassy areas, which are maintained by periodic mowing and prescribed burning, offer nesting habitat for bobolink and other grassland species. During the spring, woodcock make use of these open places to perform their aerial courtship displays (see discussion of this species in the Moosehorn Refuge text).

Management and protection of the Petit Manan Refuge complex is accomplished in partnership with a number of governmental agencies and nonprofit organizations. Among these are the State of Maine's Department of Inland Fisheries and Wildlife, the Canadian Wildlife Service, National Audubon Society, Maine Audubon Society, College of the Atlantic, and the Gulf of Maine Seabird Working Group. The latter group was established to help guide restoration efforts on Maine's offshore islands, including those within the refuge complex.

One successful partnership has been with the National Audubon Society, which has worked with the Fish and Wildlife Service since the early 1980s to restore colonial nesting seabirds to Seal Island, located about 20 miles southeast of Rockland. As described by the Service, "Through its Project Puffin, the Society successfully reintroduced Atlantic puffins to the island by transplanting chicks from Newfoundland, Canada, and hand-raising them. Puffins now nest on the island, after a 150-year absence. . . . Audubon is working with the Service to manage and restore seabirds on Matinicus Rock and Pond Island."

Some parts of the refuge complex, including Petit Manan Point, are open daily, during daylight hours. There is no entrance fee. Scotch, Cross, Halifax, and Bois Bubert islands are open all year. Seal Island is not open to visitation, because of the risk of harm from unexploded ordnance that results from previous U.S. military shelling and bombing activities. All other islands are closed, to avoid disturbing the nesting seabird activities, from April 1 through August. There are no visitor use facilities on the Gouldsboro and Sawyer's Marsh divisions.

Visitor activities include birdwatching, photography, hiking, commercial boat tours (as from Bar Harbor) that offer views of nesting seabirds on Petit Manan and Machias Seal islands, and hunting on parts of the refuge during the designated seasons.

Hiking opportunities on the Petit Manan Point Division include two trails: The Birch Point Trail is a 2-mile route from a parking area through mixed coniferous-and-deciduous forest to Birch Point, providing views of Dyer Bay salt marsh.

The self-guiding, interpretive John Hollingsworth Memorial Trail is a 1.5-mile loop that winds from the parking area and an expanse of blueberry barrens, across granite ledges where jack pines grow, through shaded stands of spruces and small cedar swamps, and emerges on the shore of cobble beaches and rocky ledges that shelve into the sea. From here on a clear day, you can see low-lying, treeless Petit Manan Island with its tall lighthouse. The Hollingsworth Trail is named to honor the memory of the late John Walker Hollingsworth, Jr. (1942–1995), who beautifully and tirelessly photographed a great many of the national wildlife refuges throughout the United States. As former Secretary of the Interior Bruce Babbitt said, in a Citation for Conservation Services (Nov. 7, 1995), "Mr. Hollingsworth was a man of patience, vision and fortitude and one of those remarkable individuals whose achievements have left a profound and indelible mark on others. . . . It is reassuring to know that his images will continue to capture the hearts, souls, and support of future generations." Most of the photographs in this book were taken by John and his wife, Karen.

Insect repellent is advised during the warmer months.

Lodgings and meals near Petit Manan Point Division are available in such communities as Milbridge, Ellsworth, and Machias.

Access to the Petit Manan Point Division is west from Milbridge 2 miles on U.S. Route 1, and south (left) 5.8 miles on Pigeon Hill Road to the Birch Point Trail parking area or 6.2 miles to the Hollingsworth Trail parking area; or from Steuben, it is east 2.5 miles on U.S. Route 1 and south (right) on Pigeon Hill Road, as above.

Further information: Petit Manan National Wildlife Refuge Complex, P.O. Box 279, Milbridge, ME 04658; telephone: (207) 546-2124.

Pond Island (see Petit Manan text)

Rachel Carson, presently containing over 5,000 acres and working toward a goal of more than 7,600 acres, was established in 1966 as the Coastal Maine National Wildlife Refuge. The refuge's ten divisions are scattered along a nearly 50-mile coastal stretch between Kittery Point and Cape Elizabeth in southwestern Maine.

In 1970, the refuge was renamed to honor the memory of the late environmental author Rachel Carson (1907–1964), who wrote the landmark book *Silent Spring*. Published in 1962, it described the post-World War II unrestricted use and widespread, harmful impacts of highly toxic chemical pesticides and herbicides upon humans and wildlife. She also wrote *The Sea Around Us* (1951) and *The Edge of the Sea* (1955) and was employed by the U.S. Fish and Wildlife Service from 1936 to 1952, serving as an aquatic biologist and editor-in-chief.

The refuge consists of strategic places along this part of the Maine coast that are important feeding, resting, and nesting areas for migratory waterfowl, colonial seabirds, wading birds, shorebirds, raptors, and songbirds. As the Fish and Wildlife Service explains, "The unique mixture of over 5,000 acres of salt marsh estuary/barrier beach habitat, rocky shore, forests, scrub/shrub and grassland supports nearly 400 species of birds, mammals, fish, reptiles and amphibians."

The refuge's marsh habitat offers vital food and cover for nesting waterfowl such as American black and wood ducks, mallards, green-winged and blue-winged teal, common eiders, and Canada geese. Of the wintering waterfowl, black ducks are the most abundant. The bald eagle, piping plover, and roseate and least terns are among the many other avian species that are attracted to the refuge.

Habitat management activities on the refuge include the restoration of tidal wetland areas that were previously drained and ditched, to reestablish the natural tidal flow for the benefit of waterfowl and shorebirds and to provide vital nursery habitat for various species of finfish and shellfish. As *Ducks Unlimited* senior writer, Matt Young, wrote in the September–October 2001 issue of the magazine, "Acre for acre, coastal wetlands are among the most productive ecosystems on the planet. Their bountiful waters, rich in plant and animal life, support a remarkable diversity of waterfowl. . . . Sadly, thousands of acres of coastal wetlands continue to be lost each year. Protection is clearly the best line of defense against these losses, because once these fragile habitats disappear, they are gone forever."

Prescribed burning and mowing are implemented to maintain existing refuge grasslands and to convert some areas of shrub-invaded habitat back to productive warm-season grasses for the benefit of nesting waterfowl and grassland songbirds. To protect the endangered piping plover, refuge beaches are protectively managed and monitored during the spring and summer nesting period. The refuge staff report that "Least tern populations have dramatically increased due to their proximity to protected plover habitat."

The Friends of Rachel Carson National Wildlife Refuge is a nonprofit support group that is assisting the refuge in many ways.

The refuge is open daily during daylight hours. There is no entrance fee. The refuge headquarters and visitor contact station, located on the Upper Wells Division near the intersection of U.S. Route 1 and State Route 9, is open on weekdays, except national holidays, and during limited weekend hours in the summer.

Visitor activities include birdwatching, photography, hiking, cross-country skiing, environmental education programs, limited fishing, and hunting on some of the refuge's divisions during the designated seasons. Although camping is not permitted on the refuge, a number of private campground facilities are provided in the vicinity.

Hiking opportunities include the Carson Trail, a 1-mile loop that begins at the refuge headquarters, winds through pine woodland, and offers views across the extensive salt marsh. An interpretive trail leaflet is available.

Insect repellent is advised during the warmer months.

The more than 245 species of birds that have been recorded on the Rachel Carson Refuge, as well as the other fauna and flora, are much the same as those on the Petit Manan Refuge complex and Moosehorn Refuge.

Lodgings and meals are available in such communities as Kittery, York, Ogunquit, Wells, Kennebunk, Kennebunkport, Biddeford, Scarborough, Cape Elizabeth, and Portland.

Access to the Rachel Carson Refuge headquarters and the Upper Wells Division from the intersection of U.S. Route 1 and State Route 9 in Wells is east 0.7 mile on State Route 9 and right into the refuge on Port Road.

Further information: Rachel Carson National Wildlife Refuge, 321 Port Road, Wells, ME 04090; telephone: (207) 646-9226.

Seal Island (see Petit Manan text)

Sunkhaze Meadows, consisting of 10,190 acres in three units, was established in 1988 to protect the second most extensive peat bog in the state of Maine, as well as adjacent forested wetland and upland habitats. The refuge's main unit is located in the town of Milford, about 15 miles north of Bangor in central Maine.

As explained by the U.S. Fish and Wildlife Service:

The bogs and stream wetlands, along with the adjacent uplands and associated transition zones, provide important habitat for many wildlife species. The wetland complex consists primarily of wet meadows, shrub thickets, cedar swamps, extensive red and silver maple floodplain forests and open freshwater stream habitats, along with those plant communities associated with peatlands such as shrub heaths and cedar and spruce bogs.

Regarding the history of the bog, in the early 1980s, the peat mining industry proposed to extract the commercial quality peat, which averages from around 10 to 15 feet in thickness, for use as a heating fuel. These plans were scuttled and, as the result of increased public support, the area was acquired by The Nature Conservancy and subsequently purchased by the federal government for the national wildlife refuge.

The two smaller Sunkhaze Meadows Refuge units are located in the towns of Unity and Benton. The American woodcock is one of the common inhabitants of the Unity unit. When the sedge wren, a state-listed endangered species, was discovered in the Benton vicinity, that refuge unit was established.

In addition, the refuge manages the 1,068-acre Carlton Pond Waterfowl Production Area (WPA), about 20 miles southwest of Bangor in the town of Troy. Purchased by the Fish and Wildlife Service in the mid-1960s and containing open water, marsh, and other wetland habitat behind a dam, the area offers important nesting habitat for Canada geese, various ducks, and the black tern. Access into the WPA is mainly by canoe. Habitat management activities on the Carlton Pond area include water level management; efforts to control the non-native, invasive purple loosestrife (see description of this pest species in the Montezuma Refuge text); and the installation, maintenance, and monitoring of nesting boxes for wood ducks, with the assistance of volunteers. Four non-federally-owned conservation easement areas are also managed by the refuge staff.

Ducks Unlimited, Inc. has helped enhance more than 1,000 acres of the refuge's wetland habitat. The Friends of Sunkhaze Meadows National Wildlife Refuge is a local nonprofit support group that is assisting the refuge in a variety of ways.

The refuge is open daily during daylight hours. There is no entrance fee. The refuge headquarters is open on weekdays, except national holidays.

Visitor activities include wildlife observation, photography, environmental education programs, hiking, bicycling (on certain roads), cross-country skiing and snowshoeing, canoeing, snowmobiling (on the Interconnected Trail System 84, where it crosses the southwestern part of the refuge), fishing, and hunting (big game, upland game, and waterfowl) during the designated seasons. Over 180 bird species have been recorded here.

Hiking opportunities include the 0.25-mile Ash Landing Trail, which begins at a parking area that is located 0.5 mile south of where Stud Mill Road crosses Sunkhaze Stream and leads through the forest to the stream; the 2.5-mile Johnson Brook Trail, a loop that begins at a parking area (on County Road, just to the southwest of Johnson Brook—8.1 miles east of U.S. Route 2 in Milford); the 1-mile Carter Meadow Road, a gated roadway (on County Road, just to the west of Little Birch Stream—6.4 miles east of U.S. Route 2 in Milford) that becomes a footpath out to the peatland; and the 1-mile Oak Point Trail (on County Road, between Little Birch and Birch streams—6.8 miles east of U.S. Route 2 in Milford) that leads to an oak grove opening onto the peatland. A network of abandoned logging roads, known as the North and South Buzzy Brook Trails, offers additional hiking opportunities in the northwestern part of the refuge.

Canoeing opportunities, which offer the best way to see the refuge, include Sunkhaze Stream (accessed by way of the 250-yard portage on Ash Landing Trail); and Baker Brook, accessed from a point on County Road (no parking area) located 4.2 miles east of U.S. Route 2.

Insect repellent is advised during the warmer months.

Species of fauna and flora that have been recorded on Sunkhaze Meadows Refuge are much the same as those of inland habitat at Moosehorn Refuge.

Lodgings and meals are available in such communities as Milford, Orono, and Bangor.

Access to Sunkhaze Meadows Refuge from Exit 51 on I-95 at Orono is northeast 4 miles on U.S. Route 2 to Old Town and across the Penobscot River bridge to Milford, east (right) (after the stoplight) just over 4 miles on County Road.

Further information: Sunkhaze Meadows National Wildlife Refuge, 1033 South Main Street, Old Town, ME 04468; telephone: (207) 827-6138.

Maryland

Blackwater, containing more than 26,000 acres, was established in 1933 and is located in Dorchester County on the Eastern Shore of Maryland. It was the first and is the largest refuge in the Chesapeake Marshlands National Wildlife Refuge Complex.

The refuge consists of extensive brackish tidal marshes; seasonally regulated, freshwater moist-soil impoundments; and a variety of croplands. This trio of habitats attracts large numbers of migrating and wintering waterfowl and is one of the major wintering places for Canada geese in the Atlantic Flyway. During the peak of the autumn concentrations in early November, the wetlands and fields of crops support as many as 35,000 Canada geese and more than 20 species of ducks, many of which winter here. The best months for observing waterfowl, including several hundred tundra swans, are from mid-October to mid-March. Waterfowl that nest on Blackwater Refuge include Canada geese, American black and wood ducks, mallards, and blue-winged teal.

This is also a haven for the majestic bald eagle. The refuge is the center of the greatest nesting density of these majestic birds on the Atlantic Coast. About a dozen pairs nest and as many as 150 spend the winter. Ospreys, which are here from March to September, build their nests on platforms that are placed throughout the wetlands by the refuge staff. During spring and autumn migrations, the refuge also hosts large influxes of neotropical migratory songbirds, including many species of warblers. Over 300 bird species use the refuge.

Prior to the refuge's establishment, the Blackwater River marshes were used as a fur farm, largely for the trapping of muskrats. Most of the area's forest had been harvested, and some of the land was drained and farmed. Today, muskrats are common residents, along with the non-native nutria. The population of the latter South American rodent has unfortunately greatly increased, causing significant impairment of the marsh habitat. As on many national wildlife refuges where this invasive, non-native species has proliferated, the U.S. Fish and Wildlife Service is attempting to control its numbers.

Other mammals include the white-tailed deer; the much smaller Asian elk, known as sika; and the Delmarva Peninsula fox squirrel (*Sciurus niger cinereus*). The latter large squirrel, with steel gray fur (lacking the yellowish, orange, tawny, or black phases of fox squirrels elsewhere), formerly ranged throughout open woodlands, primarily on the Delmarva Peninsula of Delaware and the Eastern Shore of Maryland and Virginia. As the Fish and Wildlife Service explains, "currently only four counties along Maryland's Eastern Shore support . . . populations. The loss of suitable woodland habitat (due primarily to land clearing) is the major factor in the squirrel's decline. Forest management programs at Blackwater are designed to restore and protect forest habitats that are essential for the long-term viability of this endangered species."

Establishment of Blackwater Refuge was made possible partly with revenues from the sale of Migratory Bird Hunting and Conservation Stamps (Duck Stamps). Ducks Unlimited, Inc. has helped enhance more than 350 acres of the refuge's wetland habitat. Another national nonprofit organization, the National Park Trust, is currently working with the Fish and Wildlife Service to help coordinate the purchase of private lands by conservation groups within and around the refuge. The Friends of Blackwater National Wildlife Refuge, Inc. is a local nonprofit support group that is assisting the refuge in many ways.

The refuge is open daily during daylight hours. There is an entrance fee. The visitor center is open daily, except on Thanksgiving and Christmas.

Visitor activities include birdwatching; photography; driving the paved, 3.5-mile Wildlife Drive (an interpretive brochure and a tape tour are available at the visitor center) that offers views of ponds, brackish and freshwater marshes, woodland, and fields; hiking; bicycling on 5 miles of the Wildlife Drive and bike trail; canoeing and boating (from April 1 through September); fishing and crabbing (from April 1 through September; but not shore fishing); trapping; and white-tailed deer and sika hunting during the designated season. A boat-launching site is available at Shorter's Wharf, just outside the refuge boundary, adjacent to Shorter's Wharf Road. Camping is not permitted on the refuge.

Hiking opportunities include the Marsh Edge Trail, a 0.3-mile (wheelchair-accessible) loop with a boardwalk that extends into the cattail-and-bulrush marsh; and the 0.5-mile Woods Trail that loops through an area of loblolly pine woodland that is inhabited by the Delmarva Peninsula fox squirrel. The refuge provides interpretive pamphlets for these trails.

Visitors are cautioned to be alert for ticks and chiggers. Insect repellent is advised during the warmer months.

Lodgings and meals are available in such communities as Cambridge and Salisbury.

Access to Blackwater Refuge from U.S. Route 50 at Cambridge is southwest 6 miles on State Route 16 to Church Creek, south (left) 4 miles on State Route 335, and east (left) into the refuge on Key Wallace Drive.

Further information: Blackwater National Wildlife Refuge, c/o Chesapeake Marshlands NWR Complex, 2145 Key Wallace Drive, Cambridge, MD 21613; telephone: (410) 228-2677.

Chincoteague (see text under Virginia)

Eastern Neck, encompassing 2,286-acre Eastern Neck Island, was established in 1962 to protect important habitat for wintering migratory waterfowl, the endangered Delmarva fox squirrel, and other wildlife. The refuge is located at the confluence of the Chester River and Chesapeake Bay near the Chesapeake Bay Bridge and toward the northern end of the Eastern Shore of Maryland.

Among Eastern Neck Refuge's spectacular concentrations of wintering waterfowl, the U.S. Fish and Wildlife Service has recorded more than 7,000 tundra swans, 20,000 Canada geese, and 15,000 canvasbacks, their peak numbers generally occurring in mid-November through January. The refuge is a major staging area for migrating tundra swans.

Nesting birds include wood ducks, eastern bluebirds, ospreys, and bald eagles. The eagles rebuild their nests in late December and in January and lay their eggs in February, and their eaglets start to hatch in late April and fledge in July. Woodcocks perform their unusual courtship activity in February, and their chicks are hatched in May. Neotropical migratory songbirds, including many species of warblers, reach their peak influxes from late April to early May and from late September to October. More than 240 species of birds have been recorded here.

Of the resident mammals, white-tailed deer are commonly seen, and less obvious is the federally listed endangered Delmarva Peninsula fox squirrel (*Sciurus niger cinereus*) (see discussion of this squirrel in the Blackwater Refuge text). The refuge's forest habitat is managed to benefit this species and the bald eagle. The National Tree Trust has assisted by donating hundreds of tree seedlings for an upland reforestation program on some of the refuge's former agricultural land. As explained by the Fish and Wildlife Service, "The two primary objectives of this effort are to create a forested buffer zone between . . . [Chesapeake Bay] and refuge agricultural fields and to provide future habitat and travel corridors for the endangered Delmarva Peninsula fox squirrel." Two other nonprofit organizations, American Forests and the Chesapeake Bay Trust, have similarly assisted with restoration of riparian habitat along the bay and the Chester River.

In addition to nearly 1,000 acres of brackish, tidally influenced wetlands containing salt marsh and salt meadow cordgrasses and bulrushes, the island refuge consists of 40 acres of open-water impoundments, more than 500 acres of woodland containing a mixture of loblolly pines and various deciduous trees, 50 acres of grassland, and more than 600 acres of cropland.

Under a cooperative agreement with a local farmer, a portion of crops, such as corn, winter wheat, sunflowers, soybeans, and clover, is left unharvested, to provide supplemental food and cover for waterfowl and other wildlife. The Chesapeake Wildlife Heritage, a nonprofit organization that works with public and private landowners on habitat projects within the Chesapeake Bay watershed, has given assistance to the refuge's sustainable agriculture practices, such as crop rotation, cover crop plantings, reduced tillage, and limited chemical usage.

The refuge's wetland habitats are managed for the benefit of waterfowl and other wildlife. Lowering the water levels within moist-soil impoundments promotes the growth of nutrient-rich plants such as smartweeds, panic grass, cyperus, millet, softrush, and beggarticks for the benefit of waterfowl and also provides favorable habitat for wading birds and shorebirds. Raising the water levels during the winter provides habitat for migrating and wintering waterfowl.

The refuge's five winter-flooded green-tree reservoirs, dominated mostly by swamp chestnut and willow oaks, sweetgum, black tupelo, and red maple, total 25 acres. The water levels in these areas are manipulated so that such species as wood ducks and American black ducks are able to forage for mast and invertebrates during the winter.

The southeasternmost point of Eastern Neck Island consists of brackish marsh surrounding an area of loblolly pine and American holly. In 1975, this wild area was designated as the Hail Point Research Natural Area.

In a cooperative effort with other federal and state agencies to protect the refuge's marshland and halt shoreline erosion, which historically was lost at the rate of as much as 10 feet per year, the Fish and Wildlife Service is using clean, sandy dredge material from shipping channels for shoreline protection and to restore marshland habitat lost through erosion.

Establishment of Eastern Neck Refuge was made possible partly with revenues from the sale of Migratory Bird Hunting and Conservation Stamps (Duck Stamps). Ducks Unlimited, Inc. has assisted with a wetland restoration project. The Friends of Eastern Neck, Inc., is a local nonprofit support group that is assisting the refuge in many ways.

The refuge is open daily during daylight hours. There is no entrance fee. The refuge office is open on weekdays and most weekends, except national holidays.

Visitor activities include birdwatching; butterfly observation; photography; driving and bicycling on unpaved refuge roads that are not closed to visitation and on a number of paved county roads; hiking; picnicking (at the Ingleside Recreation Area, from April 1 through September); canoeing and boating; fishing; crabbing; and deer hunting (archery, muzzleloader, shotgun, nonambulatory, and youth hunts) on parts of the refuge during the designated season. A hand-carried (car-top) boat-launching site is provided at the Kent County-managed Ingleside Recreation Area, from April 1 through September; and trailered boat-launching facilities are provided at Bogle's Wharf landing, for which a permit is required from the county.

Hiking opportunities include Tubby Cove Boardwalk, a 0.12-mile (wheelchair-accessible) route that extends across an area of marsh to a pine-wooded "island" and ends at an enclosed observation platform; Butterfly-Bay View Trail, a 0.3-mile (wheelchair-accessible) route that begins at the refuge office, offers opportunities in the summer to see many species of butterflies (where native wildflowers and other plants have been planted to attract these colorful insects), and provides a panorama of the Chesapeake Bay; Wildlife Trail, a 0.5-mile loop through forest habitat (with a spur to an observation blind overlooking a marsh); Duck Inn Trail, a 0.5-mile route that offers views of mixed pine-and-deciduous forest, marsh, a field, and the Chester River; and Boxes Point Trail, a 0.6-mile route offering views of mixed pine-and-deciduous forest, an agricultural field that attracts Canada geese in the autumn and winter, and marsh, and ending with a panorama of the Chester River, Fryingpan Cove, and Eastern Neck Narrows. In the autumn and winter months, tundra swans and other waterfowl are frequently seen from Boxes Point.

Visitors are cautioned to be alert for ticks and chiggers. Insect repellent is advised during the warmer months.

Species of flora and fauna of Eastern Neck Refuge are much the same as those on Blackwater Refuge.

Lodgings and meals are available in such communities as Rock Hall, Grasonville, Chestertown, and Annapolis.

Access to Eastern Neck Refuge from State Route 213 at Chestertown is southwest 13 miles on State Route 20 to Rock Hall, and south (left) 7 miles on State Route 445, which crosses Eastern Neck Narrows onto the island.

Further information: Eastern Neck National Wildlife Refuge, 1730 Eastern Neck Road, Rock Hall, MD 21661; telephone: (410) 639-7056.

Martin was initially established in 1954 and protects important lower Chesapeake Bay tidal marshlands along parts of a 60-mile archipelago. This island chain extends from southeastern Maryland into northeastern Virginia.

The main area of the refuge consists of 4,423 acres on Smith Island, in Maryland, located in the central part of the archipelago 11 miles west of the town of Crisfield. Also in Maryland, the refuge includes 177-acre Barren Island; 52-acre Spring Island; and a 380-acre mainland division on Bishops Head. In Virginia, the refuge consists of 125-acre Watts Island. Martin National Wildlife Refuge and its four divisions are part of the Chesapeake Marshlands NWR Complex, which also includes the Blackwater and Susquehanna refuges.

Martin refuge's islands provide ecologically valuable habitat for large concentrations of migratory waterfowl, and nesting and feeding habitat for marsh birds, wading birds, shorebirds, gulls, terns, and other wildlife.

As explained by the U.S. Fish and Wildlife Service:

The islands . . . are almost entirely salt marsh, broken here and there by a maze of tidal creeks and several freshwater potholes. A few ridges, slightly higher than the surrounding marsh, support wetland shrubs and small red cedar and loblolly pine trees. Shallow water areas offshore support submerged aquatic grasses which are a vital food source for waterfowl and other wildlife.

Wintering waterfowl at Martin Refuge frequently total more than 1,500 tundra swans, 4,000 Canada geese, and 10,000 ducks, including American black, northern pintail, long-tailed (oldsquaw), bufflehead, surf scoter, and red-breasted merganser. Prominent among the islands' nesting birds are herons (great blue, little blue, and green), egrets (great, snowy, and cattle), and glossy ibis, which nest in rookeries. According to the Fish and Wildlife Service, the Watts Island Division supports "one of the largest mixed species rookeries in Virginia, boasting almost 1200 birds on its 125 acres." Spring Island boasts "the largest colony of brown pelicans in the Maryland portion of Chesapeake Bay."

The osprey is the refuge's most common raptor. Nesting platforms that are provided by the refuge have increased the number of nesting pairs on the refuge, creating "the largest concentration of nesting ospreys in the region, producing 850 fledglings." Bald eagles also feed, nest, and roost throughout the islands. Regarding another raptor, the Fish and Wildlife Service explains that four active nesting towers (three on Smith Island and one on Spring Island) are helping the endangered peregrine falcon. "The first tower was constructed in 1984. Six young peregrines were placed at the tower to get accustomed to the surroundings. In a process known as hacking, they were cared for until they were able to fly and then released. Two years later. . . , an adult pair, most likely from other nests along the mid-Atlantic coast, nested on the tower and successfully raised three chicks. Peregrines have nested at the refuge every year since. . . . Nests are monitored and the chicks are banded annually."

These refuge islands provide significant breeding habitat for American black ducks and attract large numbers of neotropical songbirds, raptors, and monarch butterflies during spring and autumn migrations. The refuge is a focal point for numerous herons, egrets, ibises, swans, ducks, and American oystercatchers.

Refuge manager John Gill says, "Both ecologically and culturally, visiting the islands is like stepping back in time." But a serious, long-term problem that faces Martin Refuge's Chesapeake Bay islands is erosion. As the Service explains:

Particularly hard hit are the islands located off the eastern shore. . . . Many of the islands are exhibiting shoreline recession rates which exceed 3 meters [approximately 10 feet] per year. . . . Water clarity and the health of submerged aquatic vegetation beds are being impacted, and some of the most important colonial waterbird nesting areas and waterfowl wintering habitats in the region are being lost.

The issue of sea level rise and wave-generated erosion is of particular concern . . . because the Chesapeake Bay Island Unit, among others, is significantly affected. . . .

At present erosion rates, without human intervention, most Chesapeake Bay islands will disappear within the next 100 years.

Martin Refuge is not open to visitation, to avoid the disturbance of nesting and wintering wildlife. A small visitor center, providing interpretive information and displays, is located at the Middleton House in the town of Ewell, on the middle part of Smith Island.

> Further information: Martin National Wildlife Refuge, c/o Chesapeake Marshlands NWR Complex, 2145 Key Wallace Drive, Cambridge, MD 21613; telephone: (410) 228-2677.

Patuxent Research Refuge, comprising 12,750 acres, was established in 1936 specifically to support wildlife research. It is located adjacent to the Baltimore-Washington Parkway, roughly midway between Baltimore and Washington, D.C. in central Maryland. The Patuxent and Little Patuxent rivers wind through the refuge. A great diversity of resident and migratory wildlife inhabits the refuge's ecologically rich forests, meadows, and wetlands, which include 40 managed impoundments. As urban development has fragmented and destroyed large areas of forest, Patuxent Refuge has continued to protect one of the largest forested areas in the mid-Atlantic region. The name *Patuxent* is derived from an Algonquin Indian name meaning "where the water falls."

Patuxent has been at the forefront of world-renowned endangered species research, pioneering captive breeding and release technologies in support of the recovery of many species. For example, during the 1950s and 1960s, scientists at Patuxent (as well as elsewhere) documented irrefutable evidence of the harmful impacts upon bald eagles, ospreys, and other wildlife of a chlorinated hydrocarbon, DDT (dichloro-diphenyl-trichloro-ethane), and other highly toxic chemical insecticides and herbicides. Widespread publicity of these findings, notably by Rachel Carson in her landmark 1962 book, *Silent Spring*, eventually led to the banning or curtailed use of DDT and certain other of these chemical poisons in the United States. This has allowed the gradual recovery of the eagles, ospreys, and other species and to the recent delisting of the bald eagle from the federal endangered species list. Today, bald eagles are frequently observed on Patuxent, as well as numerous other national wildlife refuges and elsewhere.

Among other endangered avian species that have been the focus of Patuxent's research are the California condor, Aleutian Canada goose, masked bobwhite, Mississippi sandhill crane, and the whooping crane. (Recent reorganization at Patuxent shifted whooping crane research from the Fish and Wildlife Service to the U.S. Geological Survey's Biological Resources Division.)

The refuge's Central Tract, which is not open to visitation, contains the Patuxent Wildlife Research Center, where the offices and study sites of the many research biologists are located. The Center's mission is "To excel in wildlife and natural resource science, providing information needed by federal, state and other agencies to better manage the Nation's biological resources."

Patuxent Refuge is divided into two other parts, both of which are open to visitation. The South Tract contains the National Wildlife Visitor Center—one of the U.S. Department of the Interior's largest science and educational centers. As described by the U.S. Fish and Wildlife Service:

The National Wildlife Visitor Center features interactive exhibits which focus on global environmental issues, migratory bird studies, habitats, endangered species, and the tools and techniques used by scientists. The visitor center also offers hiking trails, tram tours, a seasonal fishing program, wildlife management demonstration areas, and an outdoor education site for school classes. A large auditorium and meeting rooms can accommodate scientific conferences, meetings, teacher workshops, lectures, and traveling displays. A bookstore, Wildlife Images, operated by the Friends of Patuxent Wildlife Research Center, Inc., a non-profit cooperating association, offers a variety of conservation books and other educational materials.

The Visitor Center is open daily, except on Thanksgiving, Christmas, and New Year's Day. There is no fee. Tram tours (fee) are operated seasonally. A variety of trails offer about 5 miles of hiking opportunities on this part of the refuge.

The 8,100-acre North Tract, which was formerly a military training facility and was transferred from the U.S. Department of Defense in 1991, is open for wildlife observation, photography, driving on the 9-mile Wildlife Loop, hiking, viewing wildlife from an observation tower, interpreter-led walks, educational programs, fishing, and hunting on parts of the tract during the designated seasons. Approximately 20 miles of trails offer opportunities for hiking and horseback riding on this part of the refuge. Although camping is not permitted on the refuge, several campground facilities are available nearby.

All visitors are required to check in at the North Tract's visitor contact station and receive an access pass. The North Tract is open daily during daylight hours, except on Thanksgiving, Christmas, and New Year's Day.

Patuxent's Internship Program is an important aspect of this refuge. Interns help provide visitor information services, assist with an extensive program of refuge volunteers, lead interpretive programs, help with teacher workshops and public events, and assist with a wide variety of biological monitoring and computer-based projects. (Further information can be obtained by contacting the refuge's Internship Program Coordinator.)

Lodgings and meals are available in such nearby communities as Laurel, Beltsville, Greenbelt, College Park, Bowie, Jessup, Baltimore, and Washington, D.C.

Access to Patuxent Refuge's South Tract and its visitor center from Washington, D.C. is north on the Baltimore-Washington Parkway to the Powder Mill Road exit, and east (right) 2 miles on Powder Mill Road. From Baltimore, it is south on the B-W Parkway to the Powder Mill Road exit, east (left) 2 miles on Powder Mill Road, and following directional signs to the visitor center.

Access to the refuge's North Tract from Washington, D.C. is north of the B-W Parkway to the State Route 198 exit, and east (right) 1.4 miles on Route 198. From Baltimore, it is south on the B-W Parkway to the State Route 198 exit, and east (left) 1.4 miles on Route 198.

Further information: Patuxent Research Refuge, 10901 Scarlet Tanager Loop, Laurel, MD 20708; telephone: (301) 497-5580.

Susquehanna was established in 1939 to protect part of the Susquehanna Flats, in what was then exceptional habitat for large concentrations of diving ducks—notably canvasbacks. The refuge is located at the mouth of the Susquehanna River in northeastern Maryland.

The refuge was subsequently expanded to provide additional habitat and waterfowl protection. But by 1978, the area's waterfowl food source had seriously deteriorated, and its use by waterfowl had sharply declined. Consequently, the two prior refuge expansions were rescinded, leaving only 3.79-acre "Shad Battery" (Battery Island) within the refuge boundaries. Erosion has subsequently reduced the island to less than one-half acre. According to the U.S. Fish and Wildlife Service, the refuge presently "possesses little or no value to wildlife." However, the Service is considering the potential for a large-scale wetland habitat restoration effort, by putting to beneficial use the clean sediments that are dredged from the nearby shipping channel.

Further information: Susquehanna National Wildlife Refuge, c/o Chesapeake Marshlands NWR Complex, 2145 Key Wallace Drive, Cambridge, MD 21613; telephone: (410) 228-2677.

Massachusetts

Assabet River, consisting of 2,230 acres in two parcels, was established in 2000 to restore and manage an area of freshwater wetlands, forested uplands, and grasslands. The refuge is located along the Assabet River on the U.S. Army's former Fort Devens' Sudbury Training Annex, near Sudbury in eastern Massachusetts.

According to the U.S. Fish and Wildlife Service, "The potential to restore large tracts of native grasslands, one of the most endangered habitats in the world, is tremendous. Once the Refuge is cleared of human safety hazards (such as old storage bunkers and deteriorating buildings), it will be opened to a variety of public uses." In addition, the refuge contains a large area of wetland and adjacent woodland that provides important feeding and nesting habitat for migratory and resident birds.

Anticipated visitor activities include birdwatching, photography, hiking, interpretive programs, fishing, and hunting. A visitor contact station is planned.

Birds that have been recorded on Assabet River Refuge are largely the same species as on Great Meadows Refuge.

Further information: Assabet River National Wildlife Refuge, c/o Eastern Massachusetts NWR Complex, 73 Weir Hill Road, Sudbury, MA 01776; telephone: (978) 443-4661.

Great Meadows, comprising more than 3,700 acres in two units, was established in 1944 "for use as an inviolate sanctuary, or for any other management purpose, for migratory birds." The refuge protects important freshwater floodplain wetlands and bordering woodlands along 12 miles of the Concord and Sudbury rivers about 20 miles west of Boston in eastern Massachusetts. The rivers have been federally designated as Wild and Scenic Rivers. In addition, the CONCORD UNIT includes a number of impoundments, the water levels of which are seasonally managed for the benefit of migrating waterfowl, wading and marsh birds, and shorebirds.

A large part of Great Meadows Refuge contains expanses of marsh that are largely dominated by cattails, along with other emergent plants such as sedges, arrowhead, pickerelweed, bladderwort, American lotus, wild iris, and the non-native purple loosestrife. One of the U.S. Fish and Wildlife Service's management goals is the control of the latter aggressive, invasive European species. Certain types of beetles and weevils, which were brought from Europe, feed only on the loosestrife and appear to be the most effective control technique (see further explanation in the Montezuma Refuge text).

Another exotic pest is the water chestnut. This small plant spreads across the surface of ponds and impoundments. As with loosestrife, this species crowds out native plants and has little or no wildlife value. The refuge utilizes water level manipulation to encourage the growth of plants beneficial to wildlife and to inhibit the growth of water chestnut.

Other refuge habitats include areas of swamp containing red maples, willows, and various species of shrubs; and woodland with such trees as white pine, hemlock, white and red oaks, and hickory species. A number of ponds and diked impoundments provide important habitat for waterfowl and other water birds. Water levels within the impoundments are seasonally regulated to promote the growth of plants that provide food and cover for fish and wildlife. Other habitat management activities include the placement of nesting boxes for such species as bluebirds and wood ducks, to supplement the limited number of natural tree cavity nest sites.

Expansion of the refuge has been made possible partly with revenues from the sale of Migratory Bird Hunting and Conservation Stamps (Duck Stamps). Friends of Great Meadows National Wildlife Refuge is a nonprofit support group that is assisting the refuge in many ways.

The refuge is open daily during daylight hours. There is no entrance fee. The refuge's headquarters and visitor center, located on the Sudbury Unit, are open daily, except on winter weekends and national holidays. More than 220 bird species have been seen here.

Visitor activities include birdwatching; photography; interpretive programs and exhibits at the visitor center; hiking; canoeing, boating, and fishing on the rivers; and cross-country skiing and snowshoeing. Environmental education and interpretive programs are provided, for which schedules are announced at the visitor center and in the refuge's newsletter. Canoe- and boat-launching sites are available adjacent to the State Route 225 bridge, onto the Concord River; and adjacent to the U.S. Route 20 bridge, onto the Sudbury River. A canoe-landing (but not launching) site is provided near the visitor center, in the SUDBURY UNIT. Although camping is not permitted on the refuge, campground facilities are provided at Harold Parker State Forest. Hunting is not permitted on Great Meadows Refuge, but hunting opportunities are available on the state's adjacent Pantry Brook Wildlife Management Area.

Hiking opportunities on the refuge's Sudbury Unit include the Weir Hill Trail, a 0.75-mile route that begins at the visitor center, loops onto Weir Hill (named for fishing weirs that Native Americans once used along the river), and provides views of marsh, woodland, field, river, stream, and pond habitats; and on the Concord Unit, 2.7 miles of trails, including Dike Trail, Timber Trail, Edge Trail, and Black Duck Creek Trail.

Visitors are cautioned to be alert for ticks, which may carry Lyme disease. Insect repellent is advised during the warmer months.

Lodgings and meals are available in such communities as Concord and Sudbury.

Access to the Great Meadows Refuge's visitor center in the Sudbury Unit from U.S. Route 20 at Wayland is northwest 1.7 miles on State Route 27, north (right) 1.2 miles on Water Row Road, east (right) 0.5 mile on Lincoln Road, and north (left) on Weir Hill Road.

Further information: Great Meadows National Wildlife Refuge, 73 Weir Hill Road, Sudbury, MA 01776; telephone: (978) 443-4661.

Mashpee, comprising 284 acres within an authorized boundary encompassing 5,871 acres, was established in 1995 to protect a variety of habitats that are associated with Waquoit Bay. The refuge, which includes pine barrens, Atlantic white cedar swamps, cranberry bogs, freshwater and salt marshes, and a vernal pool, is located within the towns of Mashpee and Falmouth in southeast coastal Massachusetts.

The U.S. Fish and Wildlife Service (FWS) explains that only 341 acres of the authorized Mashpee Refuge are owned by or are under conservation easement protection with the FWS.

"A partnership of nine landowners jointly manage this Cape Cod refuge: the Commonwealth of Massachusetts DEM [Department of Environmental Management] and DF&W [Department of Fisheries and Wildlife], Waquoit Bay National Estuarine Research Reserve, Mashpee Wampanoag Indian Tribal Council, the Towns of Mashpee and Falmouth, the Falmouth Rod and Gun Club, and Orenda Wildlife Land Trust. Each partner manages . . . [its] lands for the benefit of wildlife resources."

Many species of migratory waterfowl, shorebirds, and neotropical songbirds are attracted to the refuge's habitats. One of the most prominent species is the osprey.

The Friends of Mashpee National Wildlife Refuge is a nonprofit support group that is assisting the refuge in a variety of ways.

Although the refuge's federally owned portion is currently closed to visitation, it is expected that eventually it will be open during daylight hours. Several other refuge partners provide for visitor use activities on their portions of the refuge.

Lodgings and meals are available in such communities as Falmouth, East Falmouth, Cotuit, Sandwich, and Barnstable.

Further information: Mashpee National Wildlife Refuge, c/o Eastern Massachusetts NWR Complex, 73 Weir Hill Road, Sudbury, MA 01776; telephone: (978) 443-4661.

Massasoit, encompassing 196 acres in two parcels, was established in 1983 to protect an area of pitch pine-scrub oak habitat and a coastal pond known as Crooked Pond. The refuge is located in the town of Plymouth in southeastern Massachusetts.

The primary mission of Massasoit Refuge is to "Provide undisturbed habitat for the endangered Plymouth redbelly turtle. Support the research and head-starting of...[these] turtles. [and] Work cooperatively with partners to protect...[the] turtles through land acquisition, cooperative management, research, and education."

Massasoit Refuge is managed under the terms of a cooperative agreement with the Massachusetts Division of Fisheries and Wildlife, which in turn subcontracts research with Worcester State College. Since 1985, researchers have been gathering hatchlings from the wild, raising them in captivity for 9 months, and releasing the head-started turtles into Crooked Pond. The U.S. Fish and Wildlife Service notes, "Because Plymouth redbelly turtles do not reach sexual maturity for 15-20 years, it is unknown how successful the head-start program has been."

The refuge is presently closed to visitation, to protect the turtles and their habitat from disturbance. Unfortunately, trespassing by hikers, bikers, horseback riders, and ATVs is increasing and poses a threat to the refuge's protective management.

Further information: Massasoit National Wildlife Refuge, c/o Eastern Massachusetts NWR Complex, 73 Weir Hill Road, Sudbury, MA 01776; telephone: (978) 443-4661.

Monomoy, containing 7,604 acres, was established in 1944 to protect barrier island habitats extending about 10 miles southward from the southeastern end of Cape Cod, Massachusetts. The refuge, which lies between Nantucket Sound and the Atlantic Ocean, contains beaches, sand dunes, intertidal mudflats, salt and freshwater marshes, and freshwater ponds. It is a major stopping place for large numbers of migratory birds. In 1970, most of the refuge was designated as a unit of the National Wilderness Preservation System—the only one in southern New England. Over 300 bird species have been recorded on the refuge.

Although North and South Monomoy islands can be reached only by boat, the refuge's 40-acre parcel on Morris Island is accessed by road. As the U.S. Fish and Wildlife Service explains:

Monomoy has evolved from a series of small, sand-spit barrier islands in the 1800s to an arm of land connected to the mainland in the 20th century. In 1958, a spring storm tore the sand spit from the mainland, creating a single island separated from Morris Island, Chatham. Twenty years later, the island split in two during a turbulent blizzard. Left in its wake was the present-day 2.5-mile stretch of North Monomoy and the six mile arm of South Monomoy.

Shorebird migrations through the refuge are spectacular, and during the autumn and winter months, large concentrations of eiders, scoters, mergansers, brant, and other waterfowl gather offshore. Parts of the refuge are closed to visitation, to avoid disturbing the nesting activities of such birds as the federally listed threatened piping plover, several species of terns, and a large colony of gulls. The gull colony grew from a single nesting pair in 1961 to as many as 20,000 in the 1990s. One of the refuge's most successful management activities is occurring on a small part of the refuge. This area is being kept free of the omnivorous and aggressive great black-backed and herring gulls that typically monopolize nesting habitat. This gull-free area has provided vital habitat for nesting common and roseate terns, black skimmers, and other species.

Establishment of Monomoy Refuge was made possible partly with revenues from the sale of Migratory Bird Hunting and Conservation Stamps (Duck Stamps). Friends of Monomoy National Wildlife Refuge is a nonprofit support group that is assisting the refuge in many ways.

The refuge is open daily during daylight hours. There is no entrance fee. The refuge headquarters is open on weekdays, except national holidays, and is also open on summer weekends.

Visitor activities include birdwatching, photography, hiking, and surf fishing on Morris Island. Camping is not permitted on the refuge, but campground facilities are provided elsewhere on Cape Cod.

Hiking opportunities include the 0.75-mile Morris Island Trail, which provides views of beach, sand dune, woodland, salt marsh, and intertidal mudflat habitats.

Visitors are cautioned to be alert for poison ivy and ticks. The latter may carry Lyme disease. Insect repellent and sunscreen are advised during the warmer months.

Lodgings and meals are available in such communities as Chatham, East Harwich, Harwich Port, and Orleans.

Access to Monomoy Refuge from Exit 11 on U.S. Route 6 is south 3 miles on State Route 137, east (left) 3.5 miles on State Route 28 through Chatham to the Chatham Lighthouse and Coast Guard Station, the first left turn after the lighthouse, and then the first right onto Morris Island Road.

Further information: Monomoy National Wildlife Refuge, Wikis Way, Morris Island, Chatham, MA 02633; telephone: (508) 945-0594; or c/o Eastern Massachusetts NWR Complex, 73 Weir Hill Road, Sudbury, MA 01776; telephone: (978) 443-4661.

Nantucket, comprising 24 acres, was established in 1973 for the benefit of migratory birds. The refuge, which is presently managed by the Trustees of Reservations, owner of the adjacent Coskata-Coatue wildlife sanctuary, is located on the tip of Great Point, at the northern end of Nantucket Island in southeastern Massachusetts.

The beach at Great Point provides important habitat for numerous species of shorebirds, including the federally listed threatened piping plover. This beach is also popular with swimmers and sunbathers during the summer and early autumn. The Trustees of Reservations is a nonprofit organization that presently leads tours on the refuge, including an opportunity to see the U.S. Coast Guard Lighthouse, which is located within the refuge.

Further information: Nantucket National Wildlife Refuge, c/o Eastern Massachusetts NWR Complex, 73 Weir Hill Road, Sudbury, MA 01776; telephone: (978) 443-4661.

Nomans Land Island, consisting of 628 acres, was established in 1975 to protect wetland and early successional upland habitats. The island refuge is located about 5 miles south of Martha's Vineyard, Massachusetts.

Because the island was previously used as a U.S. Naval bombing range, there is still the possibility of unexploded, hazardous ordnance, even though a surface cleanup operation has been completed. Consequently, Nomans Land Island Refuge is closed to visitation.

Many species of migratory birds rest, feed, and/or nest on the island. According to the Fish and Wildlife Service, "The Refuge is considered the most important site in the state of Massachusetts for peregrine falcon during their fall migration." Several rare species of grasses and other plants are being protected on the refuge.

Further information: Nomans Land Island National Wildlife Refuge, c/o Eastern Massachusetts NWR Complex, 73 Weir Hill Road, Sudbury, MA 01776; telephone: (978) 443-4661.

Oxbow, encompassing 1,647 acres in several parcels, was established in 1974 to enhance and protect important areas of oxbow wetlands, floodplain woodlands, freshwater marshes, and upland habitat along the Nashua River. The refuge is named for the many crescent-shaped oxbow lakes and ponds that have been created as the river has gradually altered its meandering course. It is located about 40 miles northwest of Boston in eastern Massachusetts.

The refuge's initial land was transferred from the U.S. Army's Fort Devens Military Reservation to the U.S. Fish and Wildlife Service in 1973. A second parcel was transferred in 1999, when the military base was closed. Land acquisition is continuing, so that additional riparian and upland areas can be restored and protected.

The wetlands attract wood ducks and other waterfowl; wading birds; numerous species of neotropical migratory songbirds, such as thrushes and warblers; ruffed grouse; and American woodcock. In the spring, the woodcock's nasal "peent" call can be heard at dusk and dawn as these birds perform their courtship flight displays over the refuge's fields.

The Friends of Oxbow National Wildlife Refuge is a nonprofit support group that is assisting the refuge in a variety of ways.

The refuge is open daily during daylight hours. There is no entrance fee.

Visitor activities include wildlife and butterfly observation, photography, hiking, cross-country skiing and snowshoeing, canoeing (a canoe-launching site is available near the parking area), river fishing, and hunting (upland game birds and small game) on parts of the refuge during the designated seasons. Camping is not permitted on the refuge, but campground facilities are available at such places as Willard Brook State Forest and Pearl Hill State Park.

Hiking opportunities are provided on 7 miles of trails, include a 2-mile, self-guiding, interpretive route that runs along the riverbank and crosses two oxbow ponds.

Visitors are cautioned to be alert for poison ivy and ticks. Insect repellent is advised during the warmer months.

Birds that have been recorded on Oxbow Refuge are essentially the same as those of Great Meadows Refuge.

Lodgings and meals are available in such communities as Shirley and Leominster.

Access to Oxbow Refuge from the town of Harvard Center is southwest 1.8 miles on State Route 110 and west (right) on Still River Depot Road; or from I-495, it is west 3 miles on State Route 117, north (right) 3 miles on State Route 110, and west (left) on Still River Depot Road.

Further information: Oxbow National Wildlife Refuge, c/o Eastern Massachusetts NWR Complex, 73 Weir Hill Road, Sudbury, MA 01776; telephone (978) 443-4661.

Parker River, containing 4,662 acres, was established in 1942 to protect important feeding, resting, and nesting habitat for migratory birds and other wildlife. The refuge is located near Newburyport, much of it on Plum Island on the northeastern coast of Massachusetts. The ecologically rich diversity of habitats includes sandy ocean beaches, sand dunes, shrub thickets, woodlands, bog, swamp, freshwater and salt marshes, salt pannes (shallow tidal pools), tidal creeks and river, and estuary.

The U.S. Fish and Wildlife Service says, "Parker River Refuge is noted as one of the finest birding areas in the nation with more than 300 species recorded. While any season can produce a memorable visit, spring, summer, and fall offer the best birdwatching opportunities."

Plum Island's 6.3-mile ocean beach provides vital nesting habitat for the federally listed threatened piping plover and least tern. Although this beach is closed to visitation from April 1 through mid- or late August to avoid disturbing the birds' sensitive nesting activities, parts of the beach not being used for nesting may be reopened to visitor use on July 1.

The refuge's nesting waterfowl include Canada geese, American black ducks, mallards, gadwalls, and green-winged and blue-winged teal. American woodcocks begin their aerial courtship displays in March. The peak influxes of northbound neotropical songbird migration occurs during May, and the largest numbers of southbound shorebirds and tree swallows come through the refuge in August.

Among the Fish and Wildlife Service's habitat management activities are seasonally regulating water levels within impoundments: lowering them to provide mudflat feeding and resting areas for concentrations of migrating shorebirds and to promote the growth of nutrient-rich plants that provide food and cover for waterfowl and other water birds in the autumn and winter, when water levels are raised. Parts of the refuge are mowed to maintain open areas, providing food and cover for such species as the bobolink and woodcock. Periodic prescribed burning of freshwater marsh and other grasslands is implemented to promote nutrient cycling and spur new growth. Invasive, non-native plants such as the purple loosestrife, which crowd out native species and offer little or no value for wildlife, are controlled (see further discussion in the Montezuma Refuge text). Nesting boxes are provided for purple martins and other cavity-nesting birds; and nesting platforms are placed near open water for the benefit of ospreys.

Ducks Unlimited, Inc. has helped enhance several hundred acres of the refuge's wetland habitat. The Friends of Parker River National Wildlife Refuge is a local nonprofit support group that is assisting the refuge in many ways.

The refuge is open daily during daylight hours. The Fish and Wildlife Service alerts prospective visitors to the possibility that the Plum Island section of the refuge often fills to capacity during the warmer months. "Public entry is then restricted typically for several hours. Plan on arriving early in the morning to avoid this inconvenience." An entrance fee is charged for the Plum Island section. The headquarters, which is presently located at the northern end of Plum Island near Newburyport Harbor Lighthouse, is open on weekdays, except national holidays. A new headquarters/visitor center is being planned for construction on a mainland site, at the junction of Plum Island Turnpike and Rolfe's Lane, near Newburyport.

Visitor activities include birdwatching, butterfly observation, photography, driving the 6.5-mile road on Plum Island, viewing the refuge and wildlife from a number of observation places along the road, hiking, bicycling on the road, periodic interpretive programs, swimming, surf fishing, shellfishing, and hunting (waterfowl in certain salt marsh areas, and a controlled deer hunt may be held) on part of the refuge during the designated times. Camping is not permitted on the refuge, but campground facilities are available at Salisbury Beach State Reservation.

Hiking opportunities include the 1.4-mile, two-part Hellcat Interpretive Trail (an interpretive brochure is available). One part is the Dunes Trail, which offers a chance to view sand dunes that rise as much as 50 feet, sheltered areas of trees and shrubs, and a small red maple swamp—an interdunal habitat that is typical of Atlantic coastal barrier islands. One of the more dominant plants of the dunes is the false heather or beach heath (*Hudsonia tomentosa*). Because of its ability to grow in nutritionally poor sand or sandy soil, this species enriches the soil with nitrogen. This little evergreen plant is covered with tiny, grayish, fuzzy, scalelike leaves and forms a dense carpet over the sand, thereby helping to stabilize the dunes.

Plum Island gets its name from another native plant, the beach plum (*Prunus maritima*). Within sheltered places among the sand dunes, it forms shrubby thickets along with northern bayberry, shadbush, poison ivy, and other shrubs and vines. Growing on the dunes closest to the beach and most exposed to wind and salt spray are beach pea and American beach grass. The latter, which grows to more than 3 feet tall, is an important sand-binding grass that is found on coastal sand dunes from North Carolina to Newfoundland.

The other part of the Hellcat Trail is the Marsh Trail. It offers opportunities to see the evidence of beaver activities and wetland areas where water levels are seasonally regulated. Less than 1 mile south of the Hellcat Trail area is the 0.3-mile (wheelchair-accessible) Pines Trail.

Visitors are cautioned to be alert for poison ivy and ticks. The latter may carry Lyme disease. Insect repellent and sunscreen are advised during the warmer months.

Lodgings and meals are available in Newburyport.

Access to Parker River Refuge's Plum Island section from Exit 57 on I-95 is east 3.5 miles on State Route 113 and U.S. Route IA South, northeast (left, at a stoplight) 0.5 mile on Rolfe's Lane, east (right) 2 miles on Plum Island Turnpike (across the bridge), and south 0.5 mile on Sunset Drive.

Further information: Parker River National Wildlife Refuge, 261 Northern Boulevard, Plum Island, Newburyport, MA 01950; telephone: (978) 465-5753.

Silvio O. Conte was established in 1991. The refuge's partnership mission is to help restore, enhance, and protect the diversity and abundance of native fish and wildlife species and the health of the ecosystems on which they depend, within the 7.2-million-acre Connecticut River watershed in eastern Vermont, western New Hampshire, and central Massachusetts and Connecticut. The refuge is named in honor of the late Congressman Silvio O. Conte, from Massachusetts, who had ". . . a dream that includes a Connecticut River, cleaned, fishable, swimmable, and with salmon restored to abundant numbers. And a dream that someday my children and grandchildren will continue to enjoy the outdoors as I have. . . ."

The main emphasis of this watershed-oriented refuge is achieving and maintaining a constructive and positive working partnership among many stakeholders. These partners include private landowners, land trusts, nonprofit environmental organizations, water supply districts, municipalities, state agencies, and the U.S. Fish and Wildlife Service and other federal agencies. The refuge acts through these partnerships in three main areas: environmental education; performing research, inventories, and habitat management assistance; and land acquisition.

As a summary of the refuge's activities explains:

The Refuge provides financial and technical support to improve stewardship and habitat management on lands throughout the watershed. Research, inventory and management projects assist a variety of landowners . . . and help accomplish Refuge purposes. Notable projects have included the songbird stopover habitat survey, the invasive plant control initiative, cooperating with the U.S. Department of Agriculture to target their Wildlife Habitat Incentives Program to important habitats within the watershed, and providing fish passage facilities at small mill dams on tributaries in Connecticut. . . . [Many] local projects are also supported.

Among examples of these partnership projects are the following:

- A cooperative study that produced data showing that migrating songbirds, especially early spring migrants, favor riverside habitat.
- The Nature Conservancy's identification of 28 important areas of nesting habitat for neotropical migratory songbirds within the watershed, including Vermont's Nulhegan Basin, New Hampshire's Mount Wantastiquet, Massachusetts' Mount Toby, and Connecticut's Meshomasic area.
- Cooperative efforts by the Fish and Wildlife Service (FWS), the Connecticut Department of Environmental Protection, and The Nature Conservancy to prepare and implement plans for the restoration, enhancement, and protection of tidal wetlands around the

mouth of the Connecticut River and to control the aggressively invasive common reed (Phragmites).

- A cooperative inventory and management of grassland habitat at several sites by the FWS and the Audubon Society of Massachusetts.
- A regional plan for managing invasive plants and to support many individual control projects against the invasive water chestnut and hydrilla, made possible by grants from the National Fish and Wildlife Foundation.

Environmental education is another key component of the Silvio O. Conte Refuge's mission. The refuge's Great Falls Discovery Center in Turners Falls, Massachusetts provides educational information and programs on the refuge, and the Colebrook Interpretive Center on U.S. Route 3 in Colebrook, New Hampshire provides exhibits and information on the refuge. Further information on these centers: (413) 863-0209.

The Montshire Museum of Science in Norwich, Vermont has recently been expanded with nearly $3 million in funding from the Fish and Wildlife Service. It provides educational exhibits and programs on habitats and species of the Connecticut River watershed. This museum is accessed from Exit 13 on I-91 in Vermont; follow directional signs. Further information: (802) 649-2200.

The Springfield Science Museum's River Education and Awareness Program (REAP) in Springfield, Massachusetts is partially supported with a Conte Refuge Challenge Cost-Share Grant. As described by the Fish and Wildlife Service, "REAP has involved thousands of middle school students, their teachers, and some parents in an interdisciplinary watershed-based science program. . . . In the classroom and in the field, the classes involved . . . have been monitoring the health of the Mill River and learning about the Connecticut River watershed. The refuge also supports a number of other educational programs throughout the watershed.

Another important part of the Silvio O. Conte Refuge's partnership program is the protection of specific areas of land. Most of these land protection projects are accomplished in partnership with nonprofit conservation organizations or state agencies that end up owning adjacent parcels. As of 2001, the Fish and Wildlife Service owned the following lands:

- a 3.8-acre Connecticut River island in Deerfield, Massachusetts
- an 18-acre wetland and upland parcel in Westfield, Massachusetts
- a 278-acre area that supports a federally listed endangered plant species in Putney, Vermont
- the 670-acre Pondicherry parcel, which includes a stretch of northwestern New Hampshire's John's River and bordering riparian forest, and which abuts two ponds in Jefferson, owned by the Audubon Society of New Hampshire
- a 26,000-acre tract within the 71,000-acre Nulhegan Basin in northeastern Vermont

The refuge's Nulhegan Basin Division encompasses part of an ecologically outstanding area in which the Nulhegan Basin's cold microclimate and acidic, nutrient-poor peat soils combine to produce an environment that is typical of areas at least 200 miles farther north. Nearly 7,000 acres of the refuge's division consist of black spruce swamp, black spruce-balsam fir-tamarack swamp, black spruce woodland bog, dwarf shrub bog, sedge meadow, shallow emergent marsh, northern white cedar swamp, beaver meadow, alder swamp, and riparian wetlands.

One of Vermont's most outstanding areas of black spruce woodland bog habitat is located at the refuge's 76-acre Mollie Beattie Bog. A boardwalk and viewing platform extends into the bog, offering visitors an easy (wheelchair-accessible) opportunity to see this scenic area without damaging the fragile habitat. For information on access, call (802) 723-4398.

The largest body of water in the Nulhegan Basin Division is far more difficult to reach. The 69-acre Lewis Pond, which is poor in plant-nutrient minerals and organisms (oligotrophic), is situated in a small basin that is separated by low hills from Nulhegan Basin, near the northwestern corner of the division. Surrounding the pond, where common loons are known to nest, habitats include extensive northern white cedar swamp, where some of the cedars are nearly 20 inches in diameter at breast height (dbh); spruce-fir-tamarack swamp; sweetgale shoreline swamp, beaver meadow, and alder swamp. The Fish and Wildlife Service requests that visitors avoid disturbing the owners of camps on this pond.

Nulhegan Basin was long owned by the Champion International Corporation, as part of extensive timber holdings in New York State and northern New England. In 1999, negotiations between Champion and The Conservation Fund resulted in a landmark transaction by which the timber company sold nearly 330,000 acres of its land in New York, Vermont, and New Hampshire to The Conservation Fund. The Fund, in turn, transferred some acreage to public ownership and sold other lands to timber companies after placing conservation easement restrictions on them. The transaction has been described as the most extensive land conservation project ever implemented east of the Mississippi.

In Vermont, the former Champion lands, totaling 133,000 acres, were divided three ways: 22,000 acres were donated to the State of Vermont as the West Mountain Wildlife Management Area; 85,000 acres, with state-acquired conservation and public access easements, were sold to Essex Timber; and 26,000 acres were acquired by the Fish and Wildlife Service as the Nulhegan Basin Division of the Silvio O. Conte National Wildlife Refuge.

Lodgings and meals are available in Turners Falls, Greenfield, and many other communities throughout the Connecticut River watershed.

> Access to the refuge headquarters and Great Falls Discovery Center from Exit 27 on I-91 in Massachusetts is east a few miles on State Route 2 and right at the second traffic light.

> Further refuge information: Silvio O. Conte National Wildlife Refuge, 52 Avenue A, Turners Falls, MA 01376. Telephone: (413) 863-0209.

Thacher Island, consisting of 22 acres, was established in 1972 to protect colonial nesting water birds on the northern end of this island, located just off Cape Ann in northeastern Massachusetts. The refuge includes shrub, grass, and rocky shoreline habitats that attract mainly large concentrations of herring and great black-backed gulls. A U.S. Fish and Wildlife Service survey in 1995 recorded more than 500 herring gulls and more than 1,300 great black-backed gulls, along with a few glossy ibises and evidence of Canada goose nests. The ocean waters around the refuge are used by such species as double-crested cormorants, common eiders, and scoters.

A 100-foot light tower, which is listed on the National Register of Historic Places, is situated within the refuge. All of the land within the refuge was transferred from the U.S. Coast Guard to the Fish and Wildlife Service in 1972.

Under a memorandum of agreement, the town of Rockport provides oversight, protection, and periodic interpretive tours as conditions allow.

Further information: Thacher Island National Wildlife Refuge, c/o Parker River NWR, 261 Northern Boulevard, Plum Island, Newburyport, MA 01950; telephone: (978) 465-5753.

Michigan

Detroit River International Wildlife Refuge was established in December 2001 as the first international refuge in North America. Its boundaries include the former 322-acre Wyandotte National Wildlife Refuge and encompass more than 5,000 acres along the Lower Detroit River in southeastern Michigan and adjacent Ontario, Canada.

The Lower Detroit River is located at the intersection of the Atlantic and Mississippi migratory bird flyways. According to the U.S. Fish and Wildlife Service, "an estimated three million ducks, geese, swans, and coots migrate annually through the region. More than 300,000 diving ducks stop each year to feed on wild celery beds in the river. The Canada-United States North American Waterfowl Management Plan has identified the Detroit River as part of one of 34 waterfowl habitat areas of major concern in the U.S. and Canada (Lower Great Lakes-St. Lawrence Basin)."

The refuge's authorized boundaries include islands, coastal marshes and other wetlands, shoals, and riverfront lands along 18 miles of the river and northwestern shore of Lake Erie, stretching from Zug Island south to the southern boundary of Sterling State Park. When Antoine de la Mothe Cadillac founded Detroit in 1701, the river contained extensive marshes and other wetlands and adjacent uplands that were inhabited by a great diversity of wildlife. It is estimated that more than 95 percent of the river's coastal wetlands that once existed have been eliminated by development. The U.S. and Canadian governments have designated the river as a Waterfowl Habitat Area of Concern. The goal of this refuge is, therefore, to protect, manage, and restore the most important remaining habitat for the benefit of 65 species of fish and more than 300 species of birds, including approximately 30 species of waterfowl.

As the Fish and Wildlife Service further explains:

The refuge is a result of an unprecedented partnership of government agencies, business, conservation groups, landowners and private citizens on both sides of the border who came together to improve the quality of life on the Lower Detroit River. The refuge is also a key component of the Downriver Linked Greenways Initiative, a community-based program that seeks to build "green" infrastructure and create outdoor recreational opportunities in Wayne County, Mich. The public-private partnership gained momentum over the past year through a series of intricate cooperative agreements, land exchanges and acquisitions involving governments, private businesses, citizens and conservation groups.

The former Wyandotte Refuge was established in 1961 to restore and protect Grassy and Mamajuda islands, "as a refuge and breeding place for migratory birds and other wildlife." In 2001, 18-acre Mud Island, located northeast of Grassy Island, was added to the refuge through a donation from the National Steel Corporation. These islands are now part of the international refuge.

Canada's Canard River Marsh Complex, located across the river from Grassy Island, is a major waterfowl staging area. Its wetland habitat is an especially significant resting and feeding area for canvasbacks, as they migrate from their nesting grounds in the Canadian prairie provinces to wetlands along the East Coast. As of this writing (early 2002), members of the Canadian parliament are working toward enactment of Canada's component of the international refuge, including the Canard River Marsh area.

The Detroit River Refuge's U.S. refuge manager, Doug Spencer, explains, "As managers of the refuge, one of our first initiatives will be to reach out and engage partners and citizens and involve them in the planning process, to help us plot conservation and recreation decisions for the future of the refuge. ...it is our policy to make areas of this refuge open to hunting, fishing, wildlife observation, wildlife photography, environmental education and environmental interpretation."

Further information: Detroit River International Wildlife Refuge, c/o Shiawassee NWR, 6975 Mower Road, Saginaw, MI 48601; telephone: (989) 777-5930.

Harbor Island was established in 1983 to protect this wild, U-shaped, 695-acre island located in Lake Huron's Potaganissing Bay, 1 mile north of Drummond Island in northeastern Michigan. Higher ground supports northern red oak, American beech, red and sugar maples, and some scattered paper birch and aspen. Balsam fir and eastern white cedar are among the island's lowland trees. Marshy habitat fringes the island's sheltered bay.

Among the birds of Harbor Island Refuge are pied-billed grebe, mallard, American black duck, common goldeneye, red-breasted merganser, white-winged and surf scoters, black tern, great blue heron, a variety of migrating shorebirds, bald eagle, osprey, ruffed grouse, blue jay, black-capped chickadee, winter and marsh wrens, white-throated sparrows, red-winged blackbirds, and numerous neotropical migratory songbirds, including thrushes and more than a dozen species of warblers. Mammals include black bear, white-tailed deer, coyote, red fox, beaver, snowshoe hare, red squirrel, and eastern chipmunk.

Visitor activities in the island's sheltered bay include birdwatching, photography, boating, fishing, and swimming at a sandy beach. There are no visitor facilities on the island. Access to Harbor Island, during daylight hours only, is by private boat.

Further information: Harbor Island National Wildlife Refuge, c/o Seney NWR, HCR #2, Box 1, Seney, MI 49883; telephone: (906) 586-9851.

Huron Islands was established in 1905 by President Theodore Roosevelt to protect a cluster of eight small islands that total 147 acres. The refuge is located in Lake Superior, 3 miles north of the northern shore of Michigan's Upper Peninsula and about 18 miles east of the Keewenaw Peninsula. The islands are designated as a unit of the National Wilderness Preservation System.

Sparse vegetation includes red and white pines and paper birch, low-growing plants, such as yew and common juniper, and scattered areas of lichens on expanses of exposed granite. Among the refuge's wildlife are bald eagle and nesting colonies of gulls on Cattle and Rock islands. A lighthouse dating from 1868 stands on West Huron Island. It is listed in the National Register of Historic Places.

Access to West Huron Island, the refuge's only island open to visitation, is during daylight hours and is by private boat. Overnight camping is not permitted.

Further information: Huron Islands National Wildlife Refuge, c/o Seney NWR, HCR #2, Box 1, Seney, MI 49883; telephone: (906) 586-9851.

Kirtland's Warbler Wildlife Management Area, containing more than 6,600 acres in 118 units, was established in 1980 to protect nesting habitat that is vital to one of North America's rarest birds, the Kirtland's warbler (*Dendroica kirtlandii*). The management area's units are located within eight counties in the northern part of Michigan's Lower Peninsula. Breeding "colonies" of this federally listed endangered species are scattered primarily throughout the Au Sable River watershed, especially within Crawford, Oscoda, and Ogemaw counties.

As the U.S. Fish and Wildlife Service explains:

The Kirtland warbler nests primarily in young jack pine forest growing on Grayling sand. This soil type is found only in a few counties in northern lower Michigan. The warblers prefer to nest in forests that are about 80 acres or larger with numerous small, grassy openings. Kirtland's warblers prefer to nest in groups. They build their nests only on the ground among grass or other plants like blueberries. Jack pine trees . . . must be about 5 to 16 feet tall and spaced to let sunlight reach the ground. The sunlight keeps the lower branches alive and bushy, hiding the . . . nest beneath them. When the trees grow larger, their upper branches block the sun and the lower branches die. Grasses and other plants become less dense. The warblers then cease use of the area.

Prior to 1973, the U.S. Forest Service and Michigan Conservation Department (now the Michigan Department of Natural Resources) had set aside certain areas of public forest specifically for management as warbler habitat. To meet the warbler's exacting environmental needs for successful breeding, there would always have to be sufficient stands of jack pines containing trees of the appropriate age and size.

In 1973, Congress passed the Endangered Species Act. Under its provisions, the Kirtland's warbler was among the first species to be listed as endangered. A recovery plan, which was completed in 1976 and revised 9 years later, provided for intensive habitat management activities on state and federal forestlands to maintain a self-sustaining population of 1,000 pairs. As described by the Fish and Wildlife Service, "Management consists of commercial logging of 50 year old jack pine stands followed by planting or seeding to regenerate the stand. . . . The objective is to manage a minimum of 127,600 acres of habitat for the Kirtland's warbler."

Annual population censuses of Kirtland's warblers have shown that there were about 200 singing males recorded during the 1970s and 1980s, dropping to a low of only 167 in 1974 and 1987. Beginning in 1990, however, their numbers began a generally steady climb, rising to 766 singing males in 1995, 805 in 1998, and 905 in 1999.

The warbler's breeding areas are posted, and visitors are not permitted onto these lands during the nesting season, except on guided tours that are provided by the U.S. Fish and Wildlife Service (USFWS) and U.S. Forest Service (USFS). The best period for hearing and perhaps seeing these birds is from late May through June. Tour reservations are required for groups of five or more. For information on daily USFWS-escorted tours (free, as of this writing) from mid-May to early July, departing at 7 a.m. and 11 a.m. from the Holiday Inn in Grayling, Michigan: U.S. Fish and Wildlife Service, 2651 Coolidge Road, East Lansing, MI 48823; telephone: (517) 351-2555. For information on daily USFS-conducted tours (a fee is charged) from mid-May to early July (except Memorial Day), departing at 7 a.m. from the USFS district ranger office in Mio, Michigan: District Ranger, Huron National Forest, Mio, MI 48647; telephone: (517) 826-3252.

> Further information: Kirtland's Warbler Wildlife Management Area, c/o Seney National Wildlife Refuge, HCR #2, Box 1, Seney, MI 49883; telephone: (906) 586-9851.

Michigan Islands, containing 623 acres, was established in 1943 and protects eight islands that provide habitat for migratory birds and other wildlife. The refuge's goals include the restoration and protection of the islands' endangered and threatened fauna and flora. Gull, Pismire, Shoe, and Hat islands, in the Beaver Island group, are located in northern Lake Michigan, about 15 miles south of the southern shore of Michigan's Upper Peninsula. Scarecrow and Thunder Bay islands are in Lake Huron, about 2.5 miles east of North Point, in northeastern Michigan's Lower Peninsula. Big Charity and Little Charity islands are situated in Lake Huron's Saginaw Bay, approximately 10 miles east of Michigan's Lower Peninsula community of Au Gres.

The first islands to be acquired for the refuge were 1-acre Shoe, 3-acre Pismire, and 7-acre Scarecrow. They have since been designated as units of the National Wilderness Preservation System. In 1965, under a revocable permit agreement with the U.S. Coast Guard, 121 acres of Thunder Bay Island were added to the refuge. Although this island is presently managed under a cooperative agreement with the U.S. Coast Guard, the Fish and Wildlife Service hopes eventually to acquire it. In 1969, ownership of one of the refuge's largest islands, 230-acre Gull, was transferred from the Coast Guard to the refuge. In 1995, The Nature Conservancy assisted with the addition of 10-acre Hat Island. In 2000, the 250-acre Big Charity Island and 5.4-acre Little Charity Island were transferred to the refuge.

Gull Island supports such vegetation as balsam fir, northern white cedar, and red maple on the island's interior and a variety of forbs and grasses near the shore. Among the refuge's wildlife are nesting colonies of double-crested cormorants, Caspian terns, and ring-billed and herring gulls. Big Charity Island supports habitat for bald eagles and the threatened pitcher's thistle. Scarecrow and Little Charity islands are used entirely by colonial nesting birds during the breeding season.

Thunder Bay Island supports such trees as eastern white cedar, white spruce, balsam fir, and paper birch. The shore is fringed with cobble beaches, expanses of bedrock limestone, and some marshy habitat. Ring-billed and herring gulls nest here.

The islands in Lake Michigan are closed to visitation, to avoid disturbing the sensitive nesting activities of the colonial water birds.

Further information regarding Michigan Islands National Wildlife Refuge's islands in Lake Michigan: c/o Seney NWR, HCR #2, Box 1, Seney, MI 49883; telephone: (906) 586-9851. Further information regarding the refuge's islands in Lake Huron: c/o Shiawassee NWR, 6975 Mower Road, Saginaw, MI 48601; telephone: (989) 777-5930.

Seney, encompassing 95,212 acres, was established in 1935 to enhance and protect an extensive mosaic of marsh, bog, and swamp wetland habitats interspersed with scattered areas of northern woodlands, for the benefit of migratory birds and other wildlife. The refuge is located in the central Upper Peninsula of Michigan.

As described by refuge manager Tracy Casselman:

Within its boundaries is a 25,000-acre designated wilderness area and tens of thousands of acres of roadless areas. Vast expanses are dominated by knee-high sedge grass, with scattered red and jack pine islands. One can almost see and feel the power of the glaciers that created the sedge meadow complexes. In the drier uplands, beautiful stands of red, white, and jack pine are dominant, with aspen and paper birch scattered throughout. Pockets of northern hardwoods of sugar maple, beech, yellow birch, and northern hemlock add diversity. Black spruce, tamarack, and other lowland trees occupy habitats between the open sedge meadows and the uplands. Three rivers and several streams wind their way through the refuge.

Water levels of the impounded pools are seasonally manipulated to regulate the growth of aquatic vegetation. High water helps protect nesting water birds from predation and protect populations of fish during the winter months. Low water exposes mudflats that offer feeding habitat for cranes, shorebirds, and waterfowl and makes feeding on fish easier for bald eagles and ospreys.

Other activities that are designed to maintain healthy and diverse habitats include periodic prescribed burning to promote nutrient cycling, wetland and river restoration, mowing, and forest management.

A particularly exciting Seney success story is the reintroduction of the trumpeter swan, the largest species of North American waterfowl. In the early 1990s, the Fish and Wildlife Service released 42 captive-reared swans as part of a program to increase North America's interior population, which had been extirpated during the late nineteenth century. Seney Refuge was selected because of its extensive, ideal swan habitat of actively managed, open, shallow water; the abundance of submergent vegetation that is an important source of food; and the absence of power lines and toxic lead shot. Over 200 bird species use the refuge.

As shown by the refuge's monitoring, "In 2001, the refuge contained an adult flock of 151 swans, with 76 hatched and 29 fledged." "The flock continues to expand off the refuge. The reintroduction has been the most successful in Michigan, and prospects appear favorable for continued growth of the Seney flock."

The Seney Natural History Association is a nonprofit educational support group that is assisting the refuge in various ways. The association's activities include providing binoculars and field guides for visitors to borrow; providing funds for observation decks, scopes, brochures, and visitor center displays; purchasing supplies for school group field trips; and cosponsoring special events such as the Children's Fishing Contest, Scout Activity Days, Backyard Wildlife Day, Endangered Species Day, and Snowfest.

The refuge is open daily during daylight hours. There is no entrance fee. The visitor center is open daily from May 15 to October 15.

Visitor activities include wildlife observation; photography; driving the 7-mile, self-guiding Marshland Wildlife Drive, along which are three wildlife observation decks; hiking; bicycling the refuge roads, except where posted; canoeing on a stretch of the Manistique River (but not on refuge pools or in the marshes); interpretive programs at the visitor center and interpreter-led field pro-grams; cross-country skiing on 9 miles of groomed trails; snowshoeing anywhere except the groomed ski trails; fishing along a 3-mile Fishing Loop or at the (wheelchair-accessible) fishing pier; and hunting (deer, bear, snowshoe hare, ruffed grouse, and woodcock) on parts of the refuge dur-ing the designated seasons. Boats and other flotation devices are not permitted on refuge pools. Camping is not permitted on the refuge, but campground facilities are available at Germfask, Seney, Newberry, and in the adjacent Lake Superior State Forest.

Hiking opportunities include the Pine Ridge Nature Trail, a 1.4-mile loop that starts at the visitor center; and the many miles of backcountry gravel roads. Canoe rentals are available at outfitters in the nearby town of Germfask.

The best months to see migratory birds are late March through early April, when Canada geese usually arrive, soon followed by sandhill cranes; late May through early June, for the in-flux of neotropical songbirds, such as warblers and thrushes; and late September through Oc-tober, for the peak of the autumn waterfowl migration. The height of the autumn foliage color of aspens, birches, and maples is around the first week in October.

Insect repellent is advised during the warmer months, and visitors should be alert for the possibility of ticks.

Lodgings and meals are available in such communities as Manistique and Newberry.

Access to Seney Refuge from U.S. Route 2 near the town of Blaney Park is north 12 miles on State Route 77; or from State Route 28 at the town of Seney, south 5 miles on State Route 77.

Further information: Seney National Wildlife Refuge, HCR #2, Box 1, Seney, MI 49883; telephone: (906) 586-9851.

Shiawassee, containing of more than 9,700 acres with plans to expand to about 16,000 acres, was established in 1953. The refuge protects part of the extensive Shiawassee Flats, within the Saginaw River floodplain in the central Lower Peninsula of Michigan.

The Shiawassee, Flint, Cass, and Tittabawassee rivers converge here, forming the Saginaw River near the refuge's northern boundary. Roughly three-quarters of the refuge consists of marsh and seasonally flooded bottomland hardwood forest. Much of the remaining land is devoted to im-pounded moist-soil units, within which water levels are seasonally manipulated for many species of waterfowl and shorebirds. Part of the refuge contains cultivated croplands, where cooperative agree-ments with local farmers provide for a portion of such crops as corn, barley, soybeans, and winter wheat to be left unharvested for the benefit of migrating waterfowl and other wildlife.

During the most recent period of continental glaciation, between 5,000 and 15,000 B.C., much of what is now east-central Michigan lay beneath the waters of vast Glacial Lake Saginaw. The former lakebed formed the basis of today's level landscape, known as "The Flats."

Beginning in the late nineteenth century, human impacts upon the area and its resources sharply increased. Lumber companies logged off the swampland's virgin-growth trees. In the early twentieth century, farmers started draining the wetlands, and by mid-century, extensive agricultural production was made possible with elaborate networks of dikes, ditches, and other water control facilities. Coal mining also occurred in part of the area during the early twentieth century.

The primary goal of the refuge is to restore, enhance, and manage part of these historically significant wetlands for the benefit of migrating waterfowl and other wildlife. As the U.S. Fish and Wildlife Service explains:

Shallow marshes and forested areas are drained and flooded periodically to provide optimal and productive feeding sites for migrating birds. Natural foods, such as the seeds of smartweed, millet and other wetland plants, are readily eaten, along with invertebrates generated by the flooded conditions. Permanent water areas or pools are maintained and managed at depths which are suitable for nesting and brood cover.

During the peak of spring and autumn migrations, more than 20,000 Canada geese are attracted to the refuge, and during autumn migration as many as 35,000 ducks of many species, including up to 4,000 black ducks, are attracted to the refuge. The best months for viewing these concentrations of waterfowl are March-April and September-November. The refuge supports a large nesting colony of great blue herons. Other commonly seen birds include tundra swans, bald eagles, wading birds, shorebirds, and songbirds. May is the best month to see influxes of warblers and other neotropical migratory songbirds.

Establishment of Shiawassee Refuge was made possible partly with revenues from the sale of Migratory Bird Hunting and Conservation Stamps (Duck Stamps).

Regarding partners that provide generous assistance to Shiawassee Refuge, the assistant refuge manager, Edward P. DeVries, explains:

Our partnerships include the Saginaw Bay Watershed Initiative Network, which is a group of local, state, and federal agencies and private organizations teamed up with funding sources to improve the quality of life in this part of Michigan. This group has funded a wheelchair-accessible wildlife watching platform at our Curtis Road parking lot. The Shiawassee Flats Citizens and Hunters Association has provided funding and manpower to improve some of our dikes, and the Shiawassee Flats Advisory Council (SFAC) has funded some of our special public events. The SFAC is a council of area recreationists who mostly represent local hunting, fishing, and trapping organizations; but the Council includes local farming interests, as well. The Friends of the Shiawassee NWR was started in 1998 for the purpose of providing the Refuge with additional support through funding, grant-writing, and volunteerism. Their main focus has been on generating public support and funding for the construction of a state-of-the-art refuge visitor center at Exit 144 on I-75. This visitor center will be called the Great Lakes Discovery Center. The Nature Conservancy helped us purchase the 113-acre tract of land, on which this building will be constructed. Ducks Unlimited, Inc., continues to be an active partner with the Refuge through funding sources such as the North American Wetlands Conservation Act. Through NAWCA, the Refuge acquired a 33-acre wooded/agricultural tract of land along the Cass River in 1988. This partnership continues as land-acquisition negotiations continue to this day.

Ducks Unlimited has also helped enhance several hundred acres of the refuge's wetland habitat. The Friends of Shiawassee National Wildlife Refuge is a local nonprofit support group that is assisting the refuge in many ways.

The refuge is open daily during daylight hours. There is no entrance fee. The refuge headquarters is open on weekdays, except national holidays.

Visitor activities include birdwatching; photography; hiking; bicycling; cross-country skiing (ungroomed trails); and hunting (controlled, permit-only deer and goose hunts) on parts of the refuge during the designated seasons. Camping is not permitted on the refuge.

The refuge provides two self-guiding, interpretive hiking opportunities. The Ferguson Bayou National Recreation Trail is just over 4.5 miles long, plus an extra 1.5-mile loop. It follows dikes in the southern part of the refuge, includes two wildlife observation decks, and offers views of pools, sloughs, moist-soil impoundments, forested wetlands, and croplands. It is accessed from the west end of Curtis Road. The Woodland Trail is just over 3.5 miles long, plus an extra 1-mile loop. It winds mostly through bottomland hardwood forest in the northern end of the refuge, between the Tittabawassee River and Bullhead Creek. It is accessed from the east end of Stroebel Road. Over 265 bird species use the refuge.

Interpretive and educational exhibits and programs for youth groups, families, and other visitors are provided at the Green Point Environmental Learning Center, operated by the Fish and Wildlife Service; it is located near the northern end of the refuge at 3010 Maple Street, Saginaw, MI 48602; telephone: (517) 759-1669. The center consists of the interpretive building and 76 acres of bottomland habitats, with 2.5 miles of self-guiding interpretive trails.

Insect repellent is advised during the warmer months.

The refuge lies within the extensive Shiawassee NWR Wetland Management District. Established in 1988, the district encompasses 45 counties in central and southern Michigan. It includes more than 4,600 acres in 113 easements with private landowners in 34 counties; and the district also manages a 22-county program of wetland habitat restoration.

Lodgings and meals are available in Saginaw.

Adjacent to Shiawassee Refuge is the 10,000-acre Shiawassee River State Game Area.

Access to the refuge headquarters from Saginaw is south about 5 miles on State Route 13 and west (right) about 0.5 mile on Curtis Road.

Further information: Shiawassee National Wildlife Refuge, 6975 Mower Road, Saginaw, MI 48601; telephone: (989) 777-5930.

Whitefish Point, containing 30 acres, was established in 1998 to protect a strategic point of land that is used by major concentrations of migrating birds during the spring and autumn. The point juts into Lake Superior at the northeastern tip of Michigan's Upper Peninsula.

Adjacent to the refuge is the Whitefish Point Bird Observatory (WPBO). This nonprofit membership organization was founded in 1978 and is affiliated with the Michigan Audubon Society. It is "dedicated to the study and conservation of migrating birds in the Great Lakes region." As characterized by WPBO, "Whitefish Point is a phenomenal concentration spot for

migrating raptors, waterbirds, and song birds." To contact this organization: 169 North Whitefish Point Road, Paradise, MI 49768; telephone: (906) 492-3596. Also adjacent to the refuge
is the Great Lakes Shipwreck Historical Society, which is dedicated to interpreting the maritime
history of Lake Superior. A maritime museum and other restored historic buildings are open to
the public.

Access to Whitefish Point Refuge from Paradise is north 11 miles on Whitefish Point Road.

Further information: Whitefish Point National Wildlife Refuge, c/o Seney NWR, HCR #2,
Box 1, Seney, MI 49883; telephone: (906) 586-9851.

Minnesota: National Wildlife Refuges

Agassiz, comprising 61,500 acres, was established in 1937 to restore and manage a diversity of
ecologically important wildlife habitats in northwestern Minnesota. This refuge lies within the
aspen-parkland transition zone between the coniferous forest, tallgrass prairie, and prairie pothole regions of the Red River watershed. The refuge was originally named the Mud Lake Migratory Waterfowl Refuge and was changed to Agassiz National Wildlife Refuge in 1961.

There are 40,100 acres of open water and marshes that attract large concentrations of
breeding and migrating waterfowl; about 10,000 acres of willow and alder thickets and other
shrubby habitat; 7,000 acres of scattered stands of woodland, predominantly aspen; 4,250 acres
of grassland; and 150 acres of cropland that is for the benefit of wildlife. The refuge protects
two black-spruce-and tamarack bogs and related bog lakes, Kuriko and Whiskey, which are located within a 4,000-acre unit of the National Wilderness Preservation System.

During an average year, Agassiz Refuge attracts roughly 250 nesting pairs of Canada
geese, and 7,500 nesting pairs of ducks (especially blue-winged teal, mallard, gadwall, and ring-
necked ducks) that produce an average of 12,000 ducklings. The largest nesting colony of
Franklin's gulls in North America—20,000 to 40,000 pairs—is found on the refuge. Other
colonial nesting birds include 300 to 900 pairs of black-crowned night herons, 1,000 black
terns, eared and western grebes, Forster's terns, and double-crested cormorants. There are also
four pairs of nesting bald eagles. Over 285 bird species use the refuge.

The refuge supports a long-term average of approximately 1,700 white-tailed deer.
Moose also use the refuge's habitats. Populations have varied from a high of 450 animals during the 1980s to a low of 50 during the late 1990s. Other noteworthy mammalian species include black bear, eastern gray wolf, fisher, and river otter.

Agassiz Refuge occupies a small part of an enormous glacial lake that was created some 10,000 years ago, by the melting and receding continental glacier. The lake covered an area larger than the present five Great Lakes combined. The refuge is named in honor of the Swiss-American glacial geologist and Harvard professor, John Louis Rodolphe Agassiz.

Prior to Euro-American settlement of this part of Minnesota, extensive lakes and marshes attracted enormous concentrations of waterfowl, shorebirds, and other wildlife. As described by the U.S. Fish and Wildlife Service:

In 1909, the first drainage district was organized in the area to convert the marshes to arable land. The drainage system earned the distinction of being the largest single public drainage project in the United States.

By 1933, approximately one million dollars had been expended on the drainage system without success. High tax assessments on drainage costs seriously affected landowners, and ultimately the financial conditions of Marshall County. To save the County from bankruptcy, the State legislature passed an act absorbing the drainage taxes and authorized the lands to be purchased for the development of Mud Lake Migratory Waterfowl Refuge. Mud Lake (later renamed Agassiz) . . . was purchased by the federal government at a cost of $6.14 an acre.

The Fish and Wildlife Service's primary habitat management activity on Agassiz Refuge is the regulation of water levels to create a diversity of emergent and submergent wetland plant communities. Twenty pools, ranging from 100 to 10,000 acres, the largest of which is Agassiz Pool, are manipulated with a system of dikes and water control structures. Although cattails are the dominant emergent variety of plant, wetland management also promotes the growth of bulrushes, spike rushes, and sedges. Submergent species include sago pondweed, water milfoil, and muskgrass. In addition, there are free-floating aquatic plants, such as bladderwort and duckweed.

Other management activities include prescribed burning and brush mowing, to maintain grass and shrub habitats for the benefit of deer, moose, nesting waterfowl, and other wildlife. Crops of barley, oats, and winter wheat are planted to provide supplemental food for waterfowl during autumn migration.

Establishment of Agassiz Refuge was made possible partly with revenues from the sale of Migratory Bird Hunting and Conservation Stamps (Duck Stamps). Ducks Unlimited, Inc. helped enhance 2,400 acres of wetland habitat at Farmes Pool, constructing 7 miles of dike and a water control structure and revamping Ditch 200.

The refuge is open daily during daylight hours. There is no entrance fee. The refuge office, which includes wildlife displays and a bookshop, is open on weekdays (except national holidays) and on Sunday afternoons in June, July, and August.

Visitor activities include wildlife observation; photography; observing the refuge from a 14-foot observation platform; driving the 4-mile, self-guiding Lost Bay Habitat Drive—open May through October; hiking on designated trails; group tours (by prior arrangement); and deer hunting on most of the refuge during the designated regular-firearm season. Although camping is not permitted on the refuge, campground facilities are available at such places as Old Mill State Park; and primitive camping areas are available on the state's nearby Elm Lake and Eckvoll wildlife management areas.

Hiking opportunities are offered on two designated trails. The Maakstad Hiking Trail, a 0.25-mile route along the auto drive, is open from May through October. The Headquarters Hiking Trail, a 0.5-mile, interpretive (wheelchair-accessible) path in the vicinity of the refuge headquarters, is open during the snow-free period.

The best months for observing concentrations of migratory waterfowl are May to mid-June and late September through October. In the autumn, as many as 25,000 Canada geese, 500 snow geese, 100,000 ducks (especially mallard and gadwall), and up to 6,000 sandhill cranes can be seen on the refuge. The peak of the spring warbler migration through the refuge occurs from about May 15–25. September and October are the best months to see moose.

Lodgings and meals are available in such communities as Thief River Falls, Roseau, and Grygla; meals are also available in Middle River and Newfolden.

In 1989, with the addition of the 1985 Food Security Farm Bill and Consolidated Farm Service Agency (CFSA) responsibilities, the scope of the Agassiz NWR was expanded to include the Agassiz Refuge Management District. This district includes Minnesota's northwestern counties of Red Lake, Pennington, Marshall, Kittson, Roseau, Lake of the Woods, and part of Beltrami County. The duties and responsibilities of the staff now include working with the Natural Resources Conservation Service and CFSA on wetland determinations, the Swamp-buster responsibility, and the Conservation Reserve Program. (See Stephen E. Adair's chapter, "America's Vanishing Wetlands," for a discussion of these latter programs.) The district staff is also involved with wetland restoration on private lands under agreements with landowners.

Access to Agassiz Refuge headquarters from State Route 32 at Holt is east 11 miles on Marshall County Route 7.

Further information: Agassiz National Wildlife Refuge, 22996-290th Street, NE, Middle River, MN 56737; telephone: (218) 449-4115.

Big Stone, encompassing 11,520 acres, was established in 1971 to protect an ecologically important area of tallgrass prairie, marsh, swamp, and woodland habitats along more than 11 miles of the upper Minnesota River valley in west-central Minnesota. The refuge also includes a 100-acre area of scenic reddish granite rock-outcrop formations of a canyon that was carved thousands of years ago by a river flowing from Lake Agassiz. This enormous body of water, which covered an expanse of this region that was larger than all five of today's Great Lakes combined, was created as the last Ice Age's continental glacier was melting and retreating northward some 10,000 years ago.

In the early 1970s, the U.S. Army Corps of Engineers constructed a dam that created a reservoir. Although the Corps retained control of the dam's water control facilities, lands and wetlands upriver from the dam were transferred in 1975 to the U.S. Fish and Wildlife Service. As a result of the reservoir, more than 4,200 acres of new wetlands came into being. These marshy areas are of great value to migrating waterfowl, wading birds, and other wildlife. Ducks Unlimited, Inc. has helped enhance several hundred acres of the refuge's wetland habitat.

Big Stone Refuge also contains about 850 acres of low-lying, seasonally flooded woodlands of silver maple, green ash, and black willow. Wood ducks and hooded mergansers utilize nesting cavities in old-growth tree trunks. Influxes of neotropical migratory songbirds, such as warblers, arrive in the spring to nest here or pass through these wooded bottomlands on their way to breeding territory farther north.

About 1,700 acres of the refuge consist of native tallgrass prairie, with scattered bur oaks. Periodic prescribed burning and limited livestock grazing help to enhance and maintain the health of this grassland ecosystem. Fire and grazing release and recycle vital plant nutrients needed to promote vigorous new growth of native grasses and forbs. These ecologically sound management activities also help to curtail the unnatural invasion of woody plants that would otherwise compete with and eventually take over the prairie.

Roughly 4,000 acres of the refuge are either planted with such crops as corn and soybeans for the benefit of wildlife or are restored to grasslands. Some of the latter areas have been seeded with native grasses.

The Big Stone Natural History Association is a nonprofit support group that assists the refuge in a variety of ways.

The refuge is open daily during daylight hours. There is no entrance fee. The refuge headquarters is open on weekdays, except national holidays.

Visitor activities include birdwatching; photography; hiking; cross-country skiing and snowshoeing; canoeing (from mid-April through September on the refuge's stretch of the state's official canoe route on the Minnesota River); fishing (along the banks of the reservoir and the Minnesota and Yellowbank rivers); and hunting (deer, rabbit, squirrel, partridge, and pheasant) on parts of the refuge during the designated seasons.

The 0.75-mile, self-guiding Outcrop Prairie Interpretive Trail, beginning near the interpretive shelter, offers opportunities to see prairie flora, granite outcroppings, river meanders, and wildlife. The best months for birdwatching on the refuge are late April through early June and September through October. Big Stone Refuge has been named as a Globally Important Bird Area. More than 235 species of birds have been recorded here.

Insect repellent is advised during the warmer months.

Lodgings and meals are available in such communities as Ortonville, Minnesota and Milbank, South Dakota.

Access to Big Stone Refuge from U.S. Route 12 at Ortonville is southeast 2 miles on U.S. Route 75 and west (right) onto the refuge's tour road.

Further information: Big Stone National Wildlife Refuge, 25 N.W. Second Street, Ortonville, MN 56278; telephone: (320) 273-2191.

Crane Meadows was established in 1992 to restore and protect ecologically important wetland habitat and its associated uplands for the benefit of migratory birds, including waterfowl, and other wildlife in central Minnesota. The refuge has an authorized boundary of 13,540 acres that will be acquired from landowners, as they are willing to sell their property, over the course of many years. Federal ownership at Crane Meadows presently consists of several parcels totaling more than 1,600 acres. Consequently, only limited visitor use facilities are available.

The refuge includes large expanses of sedge-meadow wetland and two shallow lacustrine wetlands—Rice and Skunk lakes. The latter produce an abundance of wild rice in the autumn and are located at the confluence of the Platte and Skunk rivers and Rice and Buckman creeks. Upland habitats surrounding these wetlands include scattered remnant stands of two rare upland plant communities—tallgrass prairie and the globally endangered oak savanna. In addition to these remnants, active restoration of these rare habitat types is under way on former agricultural lands that have been acquired.

The area attracts large numbers of migrating and breeding waterfowl. During spring and autumn migrations, up to 10,000 ducks may be present. In addition, the refuge is used as a staging area for more than 400 greater sandhill cranes on their autumn migration, and it is also one of the most important crane breeding areas in central Minnesota, supporting more than 30 nesting pairs. The bald eagle nests here, as well. Crane Meadows also supports breeding populations of a number of other bird species that are uncommon or are identified as particularly important in central Minnesota. The latter species include American bittern; upland sandpiper; short-eared owl; sparrows (LeConte's, clay-colored, and grasshopper); and bobolink.

The refuge is open daily during daylight hours. There is no entrance fee.

Visitor activities include birdwatching, photography, hiking, cross-country skiing, and snowshoeing. The refuge is not open to hunting. Camping is not permitted on the refuge, but campground facilities are located in the vicinity of Little Falls.

There is presently one hiking trail: Platte River Hiking Trail, a 3-mile loop (bicycling and horseback riding are not permitted) that follows the banks of the Platte River and circles around by the shore of Rice Lake. This route is groomed for cross-country skiing in winter.

Insect repellent is advised during the warmer months.

Although only a preliminary bird list has been compiled for Crane Meadows Refuge, many of the species are the same as those recorded on Sherburne Refuge.

Lodgings and meals are available in such communities as Little Falls and St. Cloud.

Access to the refuge's Platte River trailhead from Little Falls is south about 3 miles on U.S. Route 10 and east (left) 4.5 miles on County Road 35. After crossing the Platte River bridge, turn left onto the second road to the north, into the parking area

---

Further information: Crane Meadows National Wildlife Refuge, 19502 Iris Road, Little Falls, MN 56345; telephone: (320) 632-1575.

Hamden Slough, containing approximately 3,150 acres, was established in 1989 to restore and manage prairie wetland habitat and to increase the production of waterfowl in northwestern Minnesota. Land acquisition is continuing toward a goal of nearly 6,000 acres.

This refuge consists of gently rolling hills, small wetlands, and grassland. It lies within the transition zone between two major ecosystems: the eastern Great Plains tallgrass prairie, extending westward from here, and the eastern hardwood forest, the western edge of which is just a couple of miles to the east of Hamden Slough.

As the U.S. Fish and Wildlife Service explains, "On the tall grass prairie, the upland and almost all of the prairie wetlands have been converted to cropland. During the last 30 years, almost 100 percent of the small protein-producing wetlands have been drained in Becker County." To complete the development and enhancement of Hamden Slough Refuge, which includes the installation of water control structures to create water impoundments for the reestablishment of ecologically valuable waterfowl habitat, is expected to require 15 to 20 years from the date of its founding.

By the year 2000, approximately 3,000 acres of the refuge's wetland habitat had been restored or enhanced for waterfowl and other wildlife, more than 2,000 acres of upland habitat had been restored for the benefit of nesting species, and about 500 acres of cropland had been cultivated to provide a supplemental food source for wildlife. The Fish and Wildlife Service's management activities include the use of prescribed burning to help restore and maintain the health of grassland and other habitats.

Hamden Slough is the first refuge in the National Wildlife Refuge System to be designed by computer—using the Mallard Management Model to predict waterfowl production. As explained by Refuge Manager Mike Murphy, "Seven different models were entered into the computer to analyze the costs and effectiveness of various sizes, acreages, and habitat selections. The final design was a combination of the best values of each of the seven models." This design also included a lease zone around the refuge. Hamden Slough is the first and only refuge with an adjacent designated zone of lands leased by the Fish and Wildlife Service. Approximately 400 acres of these privately owned properties will be protected or restored to wetland habitat, and more than 2,000 acres of cropland will be cultivated partly for the benefit of wildlife.

Establishment of the refuge has been made possible partly with revenues from the sale of Migratory Bird Hunting and Conservation Stamps (Duck Stamps). Ducks Unlimited, Inc. has helped enhance several hundred acres of Hamden Slough's wetland habitat.

The refuge is open daily during daylight hours. There is no entrance fee. The refuge headquarters is open on weekdays, except national holidays.

Visitor activities include birdwatching, photography, and hiking. Hunting is not permitted on this refuge. The best months for birdwatching are May through October.

Insect repellent is advised during the warmer months.

Lodgings and meals are available in the town of Detroit Lakes.

Access to the Hamden Slough headquarters from U.S. Route 10 at Audubon is 1 mile north on County Route 13 and east (right) 1.5 miles on a township road, following refuge directional signs.

Further information: Hamden Slough National Wildlife Refuge, 21212-210th Street, Audubon, MN 56511; telephone: (218) 439-6319.

Mille Lacs, at one-half acre, has the distinction of being the smallest refuge in the National Wildlife Refuge System. The unit consists of two small rock islands, Hennepin and Spirit, which lie isolated in the southern portion of Mille Lacs Lake in east-central Minnesota. Spirit Island was set aside in 1915 as a bird sanctuary. With the addition of Hennepin Island in 1920,

Mille Lacs National Wildlife Refuge was officially designated by executive order as a refuge for colonial nesting water birds. As the largest refuge—Arctic, in northern Alaska—is often considered the "crown jewel" of the refuge system, Mille Lacs could be deemed the "baby jewel" of the system.

This treeless bird sanctuary provides prime nesting habitat for common terns, ring-billed and herring gulls, and, as of recently, double-crested cormorants. The refuge is one of only five common tern breeding colonies in Minnesota, which lists the species as threatened. Two major threats to this species are competition with ring-billed gulls for nesting sites and wave action due to weather and high lake levels. The U.S. Fish and Wildlife Service's active management to increase the productivity of the terns on Hennepin Island began in 1993 with construction of a gull-deterrent string grid system and the addition of gravel substrate to provide optimal nesting habitat. Since these two enhancement projects were undertaken, the terns' nesting population has increased dramatically.

Other species that utilize the tiny refuge during migration include Caspian and black terns; mallard; common merganser; common loon; American white pelican; ruddy turnstone; sanderling; and several sandpipers (least, semipalmated, and Baird's).

No visitor use facilities are available, and opportunities for public use are limited to birdwatching and photography from a distance. The islands, which lie several miles off the south shore of Mille Lacs Lake, can be accessed from numerous boat landings along the south shore. In addition, several motor launches are available for charter. Brochures about the nesting colony are provided at information kiosks at Isle and Cove Bay boat accesses. When observing the islands during the nesting season, visitors are asked to stay at least 200 feet away from the islands to minimize disturbing the birds. The refuge is jointly administered with Rice Lake National Wildlife Refuge.

Lodgings and meals are available in such communities as Isle and Onamia.

Access to Mille Lacs Refuge is from boat landings located along State Route 27, between that route's junction with U.S. Route 169 and the town of Isle.

Further information: Mille Lacs National Wildlife Refuge, c/o Rice Lake NWR, 36289 State Highway 65, McGregor, MN 55760; telephone: (218) 768-2402.

(NOTE: Special appreciation is given to Wayne Brininger, Refuge Biologist, for providing this description.)

Minnesota Valley presently encompasses 11,500 acres in eight separate units, within and upriver from Minneapolis, along 34 miles of the Lower Minnesota River Valley in southeastern Minnesota. The refuge was established in 1976 to restore and protect riverine wetlands, floodplain and hillside forest, oak savanna, and remnant prairie habitats. The valley's bluffs rise about 150 feet above the floodplain. Over 225 bird species have been seen here.

As refuge interpreter Ed Moyer explains:

This Refuge is an urban green belt consisting mostly of marsh areas, bordered by grain terminals, highways, residential areas, office buildings, and in some places farmland. It is probably the largest natural corridor within an urban setting in America today. Bald eagles soar over rush-hour traffic and nest in cottonwood trees below office towers. Foxes and mink snatch prey outside the visitor center door; and wild turkeys and an occasional coyote visit the courtyard.

The wetland habitat includes fens, seeps, and marshy lakes along the cottonwood-lined Minnesota River. The wetlands contain sedge meadow, cattail, and river bulrush. Water lilies, duckweed, and pondweeds thrive in areas of open water.

Floodplain forest is dominated by silver maple, black willow, eastern cottonwood, and elm. Small willows, dogwoods, and alders line the forest edges. Within the woods, there is a carpet of nettles with occasional river-bank grape. Hillside forest includes an overstory of ash, elm, oak, and other trees, with dogwood, chokecherry, and other shrubs beneath.

Sumac, hazel, and prickly ash are among the shrubs that encroach on the dry grasslands. Remnant prairies and savannas provide nesting habitat for dabbling ducks, wild turkeys, and a variety of songbirds. Native grasses include big and little bluestem, switchgrass, and Indian grass. . . .

The Visitor Center is a focal point of the Refuge. It features an 8,000 square-foot exhibit space, a 125-seat auditorium, two multi-purpose classrooms, a bookstore, an observation deck, and an adjacent, half-mile, loop hiking trail. Environmental education and interpretive programs are conducted in and from this facility.

The refuge's nine separate parts, in upriver sequence, are as follows:

- LONG MEADOW LAKE UNIT is a 2,400-acre area of lakes, ponds, marshes, spring-fed streams, floodplain woodlands, and historic sites. The Minnesota Valley Refuge Visitor Center is located here, providing interpretive exhibits and programs. Visitor activities on this unit include birdwatching, photography, hiking, cross-country skiing, and fishing. Bicycling is limited to the Minnesota Valley State Trail or designated areas.
- Hiking and birdwatching opportunities are available at the Bass Ponds and Old Cedar Avenue trailheads. An interpretive leaflet on the Bass Ponds loop around these historic ponds is available.
- BLACK DOG PRESERVE is a 1,400-acre area containing tallgrass prairie and a variety of wetland habitats. Visitor activities on this unit include birdwatching, photography, hiking, cross-country skiing, and fishing. Two miles of trail pass a variety of wetland habitats and remnants of tallgrass prairie. Bicycling is limited to the Minnesota Valley State Trail or designated areas.
- BLOOMINGTON FERRY UNIT is a 400-acre area containing riparian hardwood forest and a historic site where barge-type ferries transported passengers and livestock across the Minnesota River. Visitor activities on this unit include birdwatching, photography, hiking, and fishing. Bicycling and horseback riding are limited to the Minnesota Valley State Trail or designated areas.
- WILKIE UNIT is a 2,100-acre area of marshes and bottomland hardwood forest. Visitor activities on this unit include birdwatching; photography; hiking; cross-country skiing; fishing; and hunting (bow-and-arrow deer hunting on most of the unit; and waterfowl hunting on Rice Lake) during the designated seasons.

    Five miles of former farm roads and dirt trails offer opportunities for hiking and cross-country skiing to wetland and floodplain forest habitats. A major wildlife attraction of this unit is the large colony of great blue herons, containing more than 600 nests in the tops of cottonwoods, maples, and other trees (this area is closed to visitation from

March I through August, to avoid disturbing the nesting birds). Bicycling and horseback riding are limited to the Minnesota Valley State Trail or designated areas.

- Louisville Swamp Unit is a 2,600-acre area containing remnants of tallgrass prairie, old fields, oak savanna, riparian forest, and historic stone farmsteads. Prominent among the wildlife of this unit are busy beavers that build dams that alter habitat by flooding parts of the refuge and creating new wetlands. Visitor activities include birdwatching; photography; hiking; cross-country skiing; fishing; and hunting (bow-and-arrow deer hunting, and small game, waterfowl, and turkey on part of the unit) during the designated seasons.

  Four established trails offer opportunities for hiking and cross-country skiing: Mazomani Trail, a 4.5-mile route that loops around Louisville Swamp and passes the historic Ehmiller homestead; Little Prairie Loop, a 2-mile route (including part of the Mazomani Trail) that climbs a bluff into upland forest; Johnson Slough Trail, a 1.5-mile route on the state's adjoining Carver Rapids Unit; and Minnesota Valley State Trail, which passes through this unit and offers opportunities for hiking, bicycling, horseback riding, and snowmobiling.

- Rapids Lake Unit is a 1,480-acre area acquired in cooperation with the Minnesota Department of Natural Resources, containing areas of restored tallgrass prairie, oak savanna, "goat prairies" along steep bluffs, former upland farm fields, bottomland hardwood forest, and one of the largest private wetland restorations in Minnesota.

  As the U.S. Fish and Wildlife Service explains, "This unit was a century farm—in the same family for 100 years! More than sixty years ago, the Gehl family raised thousands of turkeys on this area. When Wild Turkeys were first stocked on the farm in 1986, wildlife managers made sure that all domestic birds had disappeared in the vicinity. This was to prevent interbreeding of wild and domestic turkeys, because this genetically weakens the birds and reduces their ability to survive in the wild."

  Visitor activities on this unit include birdwatching, photography, hiking 3 miles of dirt trail, fishing, and hunting during the designated seasons.

- Chaska Unit is a 600-acre area that contains Chaska Lake and surrounding farmland that is prone to river flooding. A few Canada geese of the once-nearly-extinct giant subspecies Branta canadensis maxima nest and raise their young around the shore of this lake. Visitor activities on this unit include birdwatching, photography, hiking on 2 miles of abandoned farm roads, and fishing.

- Upgrala Unit is a 2,450-acre area of wetlands and farmland. Great egrets and great blue herons nest in the tops of cottonwoods and other floodplain forest trees. As much of this unit is still privately owned, no visitor use facilities have yet been provided.

The Fish and Wildlife Service's habitat management activities include prescribed burning to maintain areas of grassland, and water level manipulation to promote productive wetland habitats. Friends of the Minnesota Valley is a nonprofit support group that is assisting the refuge in many ways.

The refuge is open daily during daylight hours. There is no entrance fee. The Visitor Center, located on the Long Meadow Lake Unit, is open daily, except on Mondays and national holidays. Many environmental education programs are provided for school and other youth groups. A calendar of interpretive and educational events and programs is available. Among these are birdwatching treks and tours, including an "accessibility birding trip" for visitors with disabilities (reservations are required for the latter excursion).

Insect repellent is advised during the warmer seasons, and visitors are cautioned to be alert for ticks.

Lodgings and meals are available throughout the Minneapolis–St. Paul area.

The refuge Visitor Center is located at the northern end of the Long Meadow Lake Unit. Exit from Interstate 494 onto Thirty-Fourth Avenue southbound, left onto East Eightieth Street for 0.25 mile, and right, opposite the Airport Hilton Hotel. Directions to other units can be obtained by contacting the Visitor Center, or they may be found in the refuge brochure.

Further information: Minnesota Valley National Wildlife Refuge, 3815 East Eightieth Street, Bloomington, MN 55425; telephone: (952) 854-5900.

Northern Tallgrass Prairie presently contains more than 2,000 acres and is working toward a multiunit goal of 77,000 acres within 48 counties in western Minnesota and within 37 counties in northwestern Iowa. The refuge was established in 1998 to protect, restore, enhance, and manage areas of the fragmented northern tallgrass prairie and aspen parkland ecosystems.

A significant refuge objective is to encourage and develop partnerships with landowners, communities, educational institutions, local and state governments, and nonprofit organizations that will assist in permanently protecting the biological and cultural prairie heritage. An integral part of this objective, as explained by the U.S. Fish and Wildlife Service, is "To foster an awareness of the tallgrass prairie ecosystem as a unique and important part of the American landscape, and to publicize the . . . Service's efforts to preserve and restore the few remaining parcels." Acquisition of native prairie lands from willing sellers is being accomplished by purchasing either permanent easements or fee-title interests. Habitat management activities will include prescribed burning, prescribed grazing, native prairie reconstruction, and wetland restoration.

At the August 9, 2001, dedication of the first prairie tract purchased in fee title for the refuge, Don Hultman, the Service's Region 3 refuge supervisor, said:

I have been thinking of this thing called prairie and wondering why it has caught the imagination and the caring of so many. What is it about the tallgrass prairie that draws us like a moth to light?

Perhaps it is its rarity. We seem drawn to the underdog, whether it is in sports, politics, or everyday life. We value those things that are uncommon, unusual, and unique.

Perhaps it is the landscape itself, the Big Sky as they say in Montana, which allows the eye and the spirit to travel unimpeded, and to dream dreams as small, as large, and as diverse as the clouds that race across the prairie sky.

Perhaps it is the plants. The names of prairie plants ring out with excitement and possibility. They seem more verb than noun: big bluestem, Indian grass, prairie cord grass, switch grass, sideoats grama, needle and thread, porcupine grass, blazing star, purple coneflower, black-eyed Susan, prairie smoke, and hundreds more.

Perhaps it is the wildlife. Badgers, coyotes, red fox, jumping mice, meadow voles, deer mice, snakes and skinks, a bunch of sparrows hard to identify, bobolinks and meadowlarks that perch and sing with pure optimism, and butterflies and bugs that bite. Yet with wildlife, it is the possibilities and "what was" that is the biggest draw. Wolves, bison, elk, and grizzlies may never come back to these fragments we save, but it is here we can look and dream and remember.

But perhaps what really draws us to the tallgrass prairie is us. A brochure we did to help kick off the prairie initiative years ago said in the beginning that prairies are "places where men and women can seek to understand the hardships, challenges, and triumphs of the native and immigrant people who came before them."

We are forever part of those who came before. Prairie helps keep that link alive and, perhaps as much as any of our conservation efforts, is a shining example of our love for ourselves and for those who will follow.

The poet, Carl Sandburg, wrote, "The prairie sings to me in the forenoon and I know in the night I rest easy in the prairie arms, on the prairie heart."

And in the end, perhaps prairie is all about heart. Thanks to all of you for this gift we give ourselves: the Tallgrass Prairie National Wildlife Refuge. . . . We in the Refuge System promise to take care of it for you, and for those who follow.

The former Northern Tallgrass Prairie NWR project leader, Ron Cole, says that much of his job in that capacity entailed talking one-on-one with landowners and their families. As he explains:

One such family is the Ericksons. They own about 400 acres in Lac Qui Parle County where they farm corn and beans and raise hogs, and they also have some 190 acres of unbroken native prairie. Nearly all of the unbroken prairie remaining in Minnesota and Iowa escaped the plow, because it was too rocky or too steep—not much use to a corn farmer, but a critical lifeline to a grassland nesting bird.

I visited the Ericksons in September. Cottonwoods and elms, standing like old soldiers, protected the north and west sides of their house, which was old and worn down . . . but not out. Charles, the seventy-something patriarch, his son Wayne, Wayne's wife Karen, and I sat at the table. Coffee was poured. We talked about the prairie in general and how Charles had been haying his own native prairie for the last 57 years, and about how much he and his family have enjoyed it.

I learned that Michaila, Charles' two-year-old granddaughter, is especially fond of "her" prairie and loves to collect bugs and hold snakes she finds there. Michaila also loves to walk barefoot in her prairie and feel the flowers under her toes. Blond-haired and blue-eyed, Michaila rushed in to hug Charles as he left for an appointment that day.

After coffee, I took a walk. The Ericksons' prairie is some of the best remaining in this part of Minnesota. Surrounded by a sea of corn and soybeans, it creates an illusion of being suspended in time. It was a great feeling to walk around a piece of prairie that I know will be protected forever (unlike Michaila, I kept my boots on).

I kicked up a brood of pheasants, walked right on top of a small buck bedded down in a patch of cordgrass, and watched an adult bald eagle fly out of a nearby tree. Not exactly marbled godwits, prairie chickens, and bison, but their company was appreciated nonetheless.

Walking in native prairie reminds me of the feeling I got when I stood on the grass at Candlestick Park as a little boy at a Giants game. It's hallowed ground, to be sure. There is not much prairie left—less than one percent remains of what once existed. What once was the largest ecosystem in North America is now our most endangered and fragmented. Many experts believe it is almost functionally extinct.

At the 1998 National Wildlife Refuge System Conference, Lynn Greenwalt exhorted us to "save dirt." That means different things to different people. To some, it may mean saving a wetland, a salt marsh, an old-growth forest, or an endangered or threatened species. To a few, it means more votes or expanding one's power base. To others, saving dirt may mean saving a farm, a ranch, or a chance to hunt and fish.

On my way home that day, it occurred to me that I had met another reason to save dirt. Her name is Michaila, she likes snakes, and she likes to feel the wildflowers between her toes. That's reason enough for me.

In addition to the private landowners, two of the key partners in the Northern Tallgrass Prairie Refuge are the Brandenburg Prairie Foundation and the Friends of the Prairie.

Visitor use activities on federally owned parts of the refuge will include wildlife observation, photography, environmental education and interpretation, fishing, and hunting.

Further information: Northern Tallgrass Prairie National Wildlife Refuge, Rural Route 1, Box 25, Odessa, MN 56276; telephone: (320) 273-2191.

Rice Lake, containing 18,281 acres, was established in 1935 to enhance and protect ecologically important habitat for many thousands of migratory waterfowl—notably ring-necked ducks—and for an abundance of other wildlife in east-central Minnesota. The refuge consists of the shallow, 4,500-acre, wild-rice-producing Rice Lake; smaller Mandy Lake and Twin Lakes; surrounding areas of freshwater marsh; white cedar swamp; muskeg-like tamarack-and-black-spruce bogs; a stretch of the meandering Rice River that includes a managed impoundment; and some grasslands remaining from prior farming. This area straddles a transition zone between the coniferous forest to the north and deciduous forest to the south. Over 270 bird species have been seen there.

Roughly 10,000 years ago, as this region's vast continental glacier gradually melted and retreated northward, huge chunks of melting ice created shallow basins with poorly drained soils. Gravel and other glacial debris that were deposited around the edge of the glacier created scattered islands and meandering ridges known as moraines, behind which snowmelt and rainwater are contained. This water-saturated landscape of wetlands and adjacent moraines has long attracted both wildlife and humans.

According to the U.S. Fish and Wildlife Service:

Refuge history centers around Rice Lake and its large beds of wild rice—a staple food for early Indians and wildlife. Woodland Indians lived in this area from 1000 B.C. to A.D. 1700. Recording their presence are various artifacts and earthen burial mounds. Those people were probably ancestors of the Sioux, who later occupied this area.

Indian village sites and seasonal encampments were in repeated use on the shore of Rice Lake. Each fall, Indians would gather here to harvest and prepare wild rice for storage, which would last until the next season's ricing season.

In the mid-1700s, Chippewa Indians moved into this region from the east. This led to sporadic warfare with the Sioux, who were expelled from Minnesota by the U.S. Government in 1862. The Chippewas then occupied the old Sioux villages and burial sites and continued the intensive wild rice harvesting from the lake.

Wild rice (*Zizania aquatica*), not related to the white rice that is cultivated in warmer regions, is a tall variety of native grass that thrives in the mucky soils of shallow lakes and marshes. In September, local Ojibwe Indians continue their traditional methods and harvest part of Rice Lake's crop of wild rice. As the Fish and Wildlife Service explains, "Ricing boats or canoes are propelled by hand with long poles. A standing boatman, or poler, maneuvers the ricing craft. A ricer sits in the front, middle or rear and alternately works each side of the boat. Rice stalks are bent over the boat with a 30-inch ricing stick and gently stroked or tapped with another stick to discharge ripe grains." No machines are used in this harvesting process, to ensure that sufficient grains will remain for wildlife and to naturally reseed the lake.

In addition to regulating the water level of Rice Lake to promote the production of wild rice, the Fish and Wildlife Service manages the refuge's lowland forest habitat to protect trees offering nesting cavities for wood ducks and to provide crops of green browse. In addition, a small proportion of grains is left unharvested for the benefit of such species as Canada geese, sandhill cranes, sharp-tailed grouse, and white-tailed deer.

Establishment of Rice Lake Refuge was made possible partly with revenues from the sale of Migratory Bird Hunting and Conservation Stamps (Duck Stamps). Much early development of the refuge was performed in the late 1930s by the Civilian Conservation Corps.

The refuge is open daily during daylight hours. There is no entrance fee. The refuge office is open on weekdays, except national holidays.

Visitor activities include birdwatching; photography; observing the refuge and its wildlife from an observation tower; driving the 9.5-mile, self-guiding auto tour route (an interpretive brochure is available); hiking; picnicking (two picnic areas are provided); bicycling (on roads, but not trails); boating (only boats without motors or with electric motors, on Mandy Lake and Twin Lakes); fishing, especially for northern pike (from the Rice River bridge and in Mandy Lake and Twin Lakes, but not in Rice Lake); and hunting (deer, hare, rabbit, squirrel, grouse, woodcock, and snipe) on parts of the refuge during the designated seasons. In winter, cross-country skiing is popular on several groomed loop trails. Ice fishing opportunities are available on Mandy Lake. Although camping is not permitted on the refuge, campground facilities are available at Savanna Portage State Park, Big Sandy Lake Dam, and at a number of nearby communities, such as Aitkin and Palisade.

Hiking trails, most of which begin at Mandy Lake, lead through a mixture of upland and lowland hardwood forest, marsh, and small areas of grassland habitats. They include Twin Lakes Trail, a 0.75-mile loop; CCC Camp Trail, a 1-mile loop; North Bog Trail, a 1.25-mile loop; Mandy Lake Trail, a 1.5-mile loop; and Rice Lake Pool Trail, a 2.5-mile loop. All of these trails are either level or gently sloping.

Insect repellent is advised during the warmer months. Visitors are cautioned to be alert for ticks, which are abundant from late May through early July. If hikers should happen to encounter a bear on a trail, they are urged to "remain calm, for these are black bears, the least aggressive of the bear species. . . . If you see a bear which does not leave, make some noise and give it an easy escape route."

September and October are especially good months for visiting Rice Lake Refuge, to observe large concentrations of waterfowl, and mid-May is the best time to observe a large diversity of forest songbirds, including many warblers.

Rice Lake Refuge also manages the separate, 2,045-acre SANDSTONE UNIT, located about 40 miles southeast of the main RICE LAKE UNIT. In 1932, the U.S. Government acquired land for a federal prison. In 1969, the Justice Department declared part of the prison property as surplus, and in 1970, this area was transferred to the Fish and Wildlife Service "for use in carrying out the national migratory bird management program." This unit contains a mixture of habitats: mostly forested upland, but also some shallow marshes, bogs, and riverine wetlands, grassland, and lowland forested wetland along a stretch of the winding Kettle River and several tributary streams.

Among the wildlife inhabiting the Sandstone Unit are wood ducks, mallards, ruffed grouse, woodcock, numerous species of songbirds, white-tailed deer, and beaver.

Part of the unit is open to visitation during daylight hours. Visitor activities include wildlife observation and photography, hiking on old logging trails and roads, cross-country skiing and snowshoeing, and hunting (small game and archery deer) on part of the refuge unit during the designated seasons. Although camping is not permitted on the refuge, campground facilities are available at nearby Banning State Park.

Access to the Sandstone Unit from Exit 191 on I-35 is east 2.25 miles on County Route 123, south (right) 1 mile on County Route 29, and then east (left) 1 mile and south 1 mile on County Route 20, to a parking area just west of the road.

Lodgings and meals are available in Sandstone, or near the main refuge unit in such communities as McGregor, Aitkin, Croquet, Carlton, and Duluth.

Access to the main unit of Rice Lake Refuge from McGregor is east approximately 2 miles on State Route 210 and then south (right) 5 miles on State Route 65.

Further information: Rice Lake National Wildlife Refuge, 36289 State Highway 65, Mc Gregor, MN 55760; telephone: (218) 768-2402.

Rydell, consisting of 2,120 acres, was established in 1992 to protect marshes, deciduous woodlands, and grassland for the benefit of wood ducks, migratory waterfowl, neotropical migratory songbirds, and other wildlife. The refuge is located within Polk County in northwestern Minnesota. The Mellon Foundation acquired the land from the Leonard Rydell family and then donated it to the federal government as a national wildlife refuge. Among the more prominent species of wildlife are trumpeter swans, Canada geese, wood ducks, white-tailed deer, and beavers. Nearly 200 bird species have been recorded here.

As the U.S. Fish and Wildlife Service explains:

Prior to settlement, the land which now lies within the boundaries of the Refuge was a mosaic of wetlands, bog, Maple/basswood forest and scattered grasslands—a transition zone between the tallgrass prairie zone to the west and the forest to our east. As the land was cleared and plowed for agriculture, wetlands were drained. Today, in addition to ten natural large wetlands, the Refuge has restored 5 small wetlands with 8 additional restorations planned. Plans also call for the restoration of several hundred acres of hardwood forest habitats for neotropical bird habitat.

The Friends of Rydell Refuge Association is a nonprofit support group that is assisting the refuge with management, public use, and fund-raising activities. The Friends organization has four electric golf carts available to transport persons with disabilities around the trail system on

Sunday afternoons (by prior arrangement). In 2000, the Friends of Rydell Refuge was awarded the Friends Association of the Year Award by the National Fish and Wildlife Foundation and the National Wildlife Refuge Association.

In 1994 and 1995, a team of biologists from the University of Minnesota-Crookston conducted a baseline inventory of plants, with emphasis on native remnant communities. The biologists concluded, ". . . the Refuge is in a uniquely positioned ecotonal setting on the borders of major North American biomes." The biologists further identified Sundew Bog as the most unusual remnant community on Rydell Refuge. Numerous species of bog plants may be observed from the 400-foot elevated bog walk.

The refuge is open daily during daylight hours. There is no entrance fee. The visitor center is open on Sunday afternoons only.

Visitor activities include birdwatching, photography, hiking 9 miles of trails (4 miles are paved and wheelchair-accessible), and hunting on part of the refuge during the designated season (including a 2-day wheelchair deer hunt). The best months for observing wildlife are May through June and August through October. In the winter, the trails are groomed for cross-country skiing.

Insect repellent is advised during the warmer months.

Lodgings and meals are available in such communities as Fosston, Crookston, Mahnomen, and Thief River Falls.

Access to Rydell Refuge's visitor center from U.S. Route 2 (about 3 miles east of Mentor or 3 miles west of Erskine) is south about 2.5 miles on Polk County Road 210. If arriving from the south, turn north from Polk County Road 41 onto Polk County Road 210, and proceed north about 3.5 miles.

Further information: Rydell National Wildlife Refuge, Route 3, Box 105, Erskine, MN 56535; telephone: (218) 687-2229.

Sherburne, consisting of 30,665 acres, was established in 1965 to restore and protect a stretch of the ecologically rich St. Francis River Valley in east-central Minnesota. The refuge is located within the biologically diverse transition zone between tallgrass prairie and eastern deciduous forest. Its wetland, oak savanna, and woodland are being restored and managed for the benefit of a great diversity of wildlife. Over 230 bird species have been seen here.

Regarding the history of this area, the U.S. Fish and Wildlife Service explains:

Historically, the St. Francis River Basin was known as one of the finest wildlife areas in the state. Tremendous numbers of ducks, muskrats, beaver and mink were supported on small lakes and marshes near the river, which were abundant with wild rice and other wetland plants. The surrounding upland was primarily oak savanna, which provided habitat for elk, bison, and timber wolves.

By the early 1940s, several developments had severely reduced the value of wildlife habitat in the basin. A ditch system, built in the 1920s, enhanced drainage to increase agricultural acreage. This resulted in fewer wetlands holding water throughout the year. In the early 1940s, carp invaded the lakes and streams in the basin. The feeding activities of these fish resulted in the uprooting of submerged vegetation important to aquatic life. In addition, the native oak savanna upland habitat was converted to agriculture or home sites, through logging and/or plowing. In other areas, protection from fire converted the oak savanna to dense woodlands.

At the urging of local conservationists, the State of Minnesota undertook studies to determine how the river basin's once-rich wildlife habitat could be restored. But by the 1960s, it became clear that the task of acquiring and enhancing more than 30,000 acres, stretching across several hundred private properties, far exceeded the state's financial capability. Consequently, the state requested that the federal government take over the project as a national wildlife refuge.

All of Sherburne Refuge's lands were acquired with revenues from the sale of Migratory Bird Hunting and Conservation Stamps (Duck Stamps). Since then, the refuge's management has included a variety of activities to restore, enhance, and maintain its three basic habitat types: wetlands, oak savanna, and deciduous-forested "big woods."

Approximately one-third of Sherburne Refuge consists of wetlands. Twenty-three of these low-lying areas are managed impoundments, which are regulated at various fluctuating levels, to promote a diversity of habitats for waterfowl and other wildlife.

The oak-savanna plant community consists of scattered individual oaks or clumps of oaks, growing amid openings and expanses of understory native prairie forbs (wildflowers) and tall grasses, such as big and little bluestems, Indiangrass, and switchgrass. The Fish and Wildlife Service carries out periodic prescribed burns as an ecologically natural and essential method of helping to restore and maintain this fire-dependent plant ecosystem.

Prescribed burning releases essential plant nutrients from dead plant matter, thereby promoting vigorous growth of the native forbs and warm-season grasses, which provide food and cover for nesting waterfowl and upland wildlife. Carefully managed fire is used to curtail an invasion of competitive species of trees, shrubs, and nonnative grasses that otherwise take over and ultimately convert the oak savanna community to forest. And fire is also used to create openings in the canopy of heavily wooded habitat, thereby helping to reestablish oak savanna.

Some of the refuge's more prominent nesting birds are common loon, Canada goose, wood duck, hooded merganser, sandhill crane, bald eagle, and black tern.

Friends of Sherburne National Wildlife Refuge is a nonprofit support group that is assisting the refuge in a variety of ways.

The refuge is open daily during daylight hours. There is no entrance fee. The refuge headquarters is open on weekdays, except national holidays.

Visitor activities include birdwatching and photography (four observation decks are provided); driving the 7.3-mile loop road, Prairie's Edge Wildlife Drive (open from late April through late October); hiking; cross-country skiing and snowshoeing; canoeing (four canoe-launching sites are available); fishing (limited to four access sites along the St. Francis River); and hunting (deer, small game, and waterfowl) on parts of the refuge during the designated seasons. Although camping is not permitted on the refuge, campground facilities and a picnic area are available on adjacent Sand Dunes State Forest.

The refuge's hiking/cross-country skiing trails include a 0.25-mile (wheelchair-accessible) loop path and wildlife observation deck, located just north of the entrance road to the wildlife drive; two 0.5-mile loops, Prairie Trail and Woodland Trail, both located along the wildlife drive; Mahnomen Trail, up to nearly 2.7 miles on its three interconnected loops; and Blue Hill

Trail, up to nearly 4 miles on its three interconnected loops. In addition, refuge service roads are open to hiking and bicycling from September 1 through February.

Insect repellent is advised during the warmer months.

Lodgings and meals are available in such communities as Princeton, Elk River, Becker, and St. Cloud.

Access to the refuge headquarters and to Mahnomen and Blue Hill trails is north 4 miles from Zimmerman on U.S. Route 169; then, at a refuge directional sign, west (left) 4 miles on County Route 9, which runs east-west through the refuge. An informational kiosk is located at the refuge entrance. From Princeton, it is south 5 miles on U.S. Highway 169 and west (right) 4 miles on County Route 9. Access to the refuge's Prairie's Edge Wildlife Drive from U.S. Route 10 at Big Lake is north about 8 miles on County Route 5 to Orrock (where a refuge informational kiosk is located at the junction of County Routes 5 and 4), continuing north 1.2 miles from Orrock on County Route 5, and east (right) onto the entrance road.

Further information: Sherburne National Wildlife Refuge, 17076-293rd Avenue, Zimmerman, MN 55398; telephone: (763) 389-3323.

Tamarac, containing 42,724 acres, was established in 1938 to protect ecologically important wetlands for large concentrations of migratory waterfowl and other wildlife within an area of glacial lakes in northwestern Minnesota. This refuge lies within a transition zone of the boreal forest to the north, northern deciduous forest to the south, and tallgrass prairie to the west. Tamarac's diverse habitats include forest-covered, gently rolling hills; marshes, bogs, and shrubby swamps; rivers and streams; and 21 lakes.

For many centuries, Native Americans treasured this area for hunting, fishing, maple-sugaring, and harvesting the nutrient-rich wild rice (*Zizania aquatica*) that grows extensively in marshes and along the edges of lakes and rivers. The Dakota Sioux Indians formerly occupied the area, followed by the Chippewa. The northern half of Tamarac Refuge is located within the White Earth Indian Reservation, which was established in 1867.

In the late 1930s and 1940s, initial development of the refuge was carried out by the Civilian Conservation Corps. In the 1960s, assistance was provided by a Job Corps Conservation Center, and in the 1970s and 1980s, further help was provided by the Young Adult Conservation Corps.

The U.S. Fish and Wildlife Service carries out a number of important habitat management activities. Prominent among these is the regulation of water levels on seven of the refuge's lakes, to promote the growth of wild rice for the benefit of migratory waterfowl and the Chippewas (see the Rice Lake Refuge text for description of traditional Native American ricing, which occurs on Tamarac Refuge for about a month beginning in mid-August).

Other management activities include prescribed burning of forested habitat to reduce unnatural and hazardous fuel overloads, and selective cutting and follow-up prescribed burning to maintain woodland diversity. Efforts are also being made to increase age diversity of aspen stands. Refuge grassland habitat is also managed with the aid of prescribed burns, as well as haying in some circumstances; and efforts are being made to reseed areas with native grass species.

Among Tamarac's great diversity of wildlife are large concentrations of ducks during the autumn migration; a nesting population of the trumpeter swan, a species that was successfully reintroduced in 1987; many pairs of nesting bald eagles; spectacular numbers of warblers and other neotropical migratory songbirds that reach peak concentrations around the middle of May; and a resident pack of the eastern gray wolf, which has annually produced young in recent years.

Establishment of the refuge was made possible with revenues from the sale of Migratory Bird Hunting and Conservation Stamps (Duck Stamps). Several private organizations have assisted in the refuge's efforts to enhance habitats, including the Ruffed Grouse Society, Minnesota Deer Hunters Association, Ducks Unlimited, Inc., and the Minnesota Waterfowlers Association. The Tamarac Interpretive Association is a nonprofit educational support group that is providing assistance to the refuge.

Refuge manager Jay Johnson says, "I believe Tamarac to be one of the National Wildlife Refuge System's 'crown jewels' and as ecologically diverse as any areas in the Upper Midwest. It contains an unusual mix of woodland/prairie flora and fauna, and remains as near pristine as any refuge in the lower 48 states." Over 250 bird species have been seen here.

The refuge is open daily during daylight hours. There is no entrance fee. The visitor center, which features interpretive exhibits, interpretive programs in its auditorium, a bookshop, and an observation deck, is open on weekdays, except national holidays and on Saturday and Sunday afternoons during the summer months.

Visitor activities include birdwatching; photography; interpretive programs; driving the 5-mile, self-guiding Blackbird Auto Tour Route (open from May through October, as road conditions allow), hiking; snowshoeing and cross-country skiing; picnicking (Chippewa picnic area is provided, by the banks of Otter Tail River); boating (boat-launching sites are provided at lakes open to summer fishing); fishing (for northern pike and other species, under state and/or tribal regulations); and hunting (deer, hare, rabbit, squirrel, goose, duck, grouse, woodcock, and snipe) on parts of the refuge during the designated seasons.

Bicycling and horseback riding are permitted only on the Blackbird Auto Tour Route, the Refuge Service Road, and on county and township roads. ATVs, snowmobiles, personal watercraft, water-skiing, and swimming are not permitted on the refuge. In 1992, a Challenge Grant project with the White Earth Indian Reservation brought about the installation of a 64-foot-long fishing pier (wheelchair-accessible) on the shore of Many Point Lake, at the northeast corner of the refuge. Although camping is not permitted on the refuge, campground facilities are available at many nearby locations, including at Island and Shell lakes; and in the vicinity of the towns of Detroit Lakes, Park Rapids, and Mahnomen.

Hiking opportunities include the 0.25-mile Visitor Center Interpretive Trail, which provides views of woodland and marsh habitats; and Old Indian Hiking Trail, a 1.5-mile route through maple-basswood and other forest habitat. Pine Lake Ski Trail is open seasonally, offering two ungroomed loops, one of which is about 1.5 miles and the other about 6 miles. Many miles of service roads are also available for hiking and snowshoeing, including those within the refuge's Sanctuary Area (to the north of County Route 26), which is open to visitation from September 1 through February. The height of the usually-spectacular autumn foliage color display occurs during the latter part of September.

Insect repellent is advised during the warmer months.

Lodgings and meals are available in such communities as Detroit Lakes, Park Rapids, and Mahnomen.

Access to Tamarac NWR visitor center from Detroit Lakes on U.S. Route 10 is east 8 miles on State Route 34, and north (left) 10 miles on County Route 29.

Further information: Tamarac National Wildlife Refuge, 35704 County Highway 26, Rochert, MN 56578; telephone: (218) 847-2641.

Upper Mississippi River National Wildlife and Fish Refuge comprises roughly 230,000 acres in four districts along more than 260 miles of the Mississippi River, from just upriver of Wabasha, Minnesota southward to just upriver of Rock Island, Illinois. This refuge was established in 1924 for the benefit of migratory birds, game animals, furbearers, wildflowers, aquatic plants, fish, and other aquatic life. It manages ecologically vital components of the river floodplain, including wooded islands, open water, river channels, meandering sloughs, marshes and other wetlands, bottomland forest, and remnants of sand prairie.

In 1930, the U.S. Army Corps of Engineers was directed by U.S. Congress to construct a series of 26 locks and dams between Minneapolis, Minnesota, and St. Louis, Missouri. The reservoir-like 'pools' that were formed behind these structures provided a 9-foot-deep navigation channel to accommodate commercial barge traffic. These pools also greatly altered much of the refuge's habitats, creating three basic ecological zones. Immediately upriver from each lock and dam, the open water zone consists of open and deep expanses of water, attracting large concentrations of diving ducks. The central zone of each pool consists of shallow water with extensive marsh habitat that attracts large concentrations of dabbling ducks. The upper stretch of each pool consists of the braided-stream zone, in which river channels, narrow cuts, and meandering sloughs wind between bottomland forested islands—resembling conditions prior to the construction of the locks and dams.

The refuge's districts, in downriver sequence, are the WINONA DISTRICT, including pools 4, 5, 5A, and 6, extending along the river in southeastern Minnesota and western Wisconsin; LACROSSE DISTRICT, including pools 7 and 8, also along the river in southeastern Minnesota and western Wisconsin; McGREGOR DISTRICT, including pools 9, 10, and 11, along the river in the southeastern tip of Minnesota, western Wisconsin, and northeastern Iowa; and SAVANNA DISTRICT, including pools 12, 13, and 14, along the river in the southwestern tip of Wisconsin, northwestern Illinois, and eastern Iowa. A series of ten detailed pool maps is available at the refuge headquarters.

Since creation of the locks, dams, and pools, the quality of many wildlife habitats has been gradually declining. As the Fish and Wildlife Service explains, "Sediment is filling valuable backwaters, islands are eroding, and vegetation is disappearing from the river." In an effort to restore these degraded habitats, Congress funded the Corps of Engineers' Environmental Management Program in 1986, to be jointly implemented by the Fish and Wildlife Service and the natural resources agencies of the four adjoining states. Dikes and other water control structures have been constructed, by which water levels are regulated for the benefit of waterfowl and other wildlife; islands have been restored and protected from erosion; and water flows have been enhanced. As a result, thousands of acres of habitat have been restored.

Why is the word *fish* included in the name of this refuge? According to the Fish and Wildlife Service:

... this refuge was established ... as the result of a victorious battle to save critical Mississippi River bass spawning areas from destruction, so the name makes sense.

The richness and diversity of the refuge's water areas are unequaled in the Midwest. The main channel, with its navigation dams and wing dams, side channels, sloughs, chutes, backwater lakes and ponds, marsh areas, flooded bottomland forest and tributaries make this a complex and magnificent home for at least 118 species of fish.

The Upper Mississippi River Interpretive Association is a nonprofit educational support group that is providing assistance to the refuge.

The refuge is accessed primarily by water and is open daily. There is no entrance fee. There are two visitor centers located on the refuge, in McGregor, Iowa and Thompson, Illinois, complete with interpretive exhibits. The LaCrosse District office, located in Onalaska, Wisconsin, includes exhibits in the Resource Center. Refuge headquarters and Winona District office are located in downtown Winona, Minnesota.

Visitor activities include birdwatching; photography; interpretive and environmental education programs; driving an interconnected series of bordering highways known as the Great River Road, with numerous overlooks; hiking trails that are located at various places along the river; picnicking; primitive camping; canoeing, kayaking, and boating (numerous boat-launch ramps are provided); cross-country skiing and snowshoeing; fishing and ice fishing; trapping; and hunting (deer, small game, waterfowl) on parts of the refuge during the designated seasons.

More than 300 species of birds have been recorded on the refuge, which has been designated as a Globally Important Bird Area. Prominent among them are tundra swans, as many as 25,000 of which pause on the refuge to rest and feed during their spring and autumn migrations—notably in an area about 15 miles north of Winona, Minnesota; numerous species of ducks, including up to 400,000 canvasbacks; hundreds of bald eagles; 16 rookeries of nesting great blue herons and great egrets; and multitudes of warblers and other neotropical migratory songbirds that funnel through the river corridor's bottomland forests during April and May.

Insect repellent is advised during the warmer months. Visitors are urged to be alert for ticks.

Lodgings and meals are available in numerous communities along the river corridor, such as Winona, Minnesota; Fountain City, LaCrosse, Genoa, and Prairie du Chien, Wisconsin; Marquette, Dubuque, and Clinton, Iowa; and Galena and Savanna, Illinois.

Access into the refuge is from numerous boat-launching sites, and there are many roadside turnouts from which to view the refuge and its wildlife.

Further information: Upper Mississippi River National Wildlife and Fish Refuge, 51 East Fourth Street, Room 101, Winona, MN 55987; telephone: (507) 452-4232.

Minnesota:
Wetland Management Districts

Big Stone Wetland Management District was established in 1996 to restore, enhance, and manage scattered areas of ecologically important wetlands and associated grasslands within Lincoln and Lyon counties in southwestern Minnesota. The district includes more than 2,300 acres in 11 federally owned waterfowl production areas (WPAs) and more than 1,200 acres that are being managed under the terms of perpetual wetland, grassland, and conservation easements with landowners.

Black Rush Lake WPA, containing nearly 1,000 acres, was acquired and developed in a partnership that has enabled the U.S. Fish and Wildlife Service to restore more than 400 acres of previously drained prairie wetlands. The most notable part of this effort was the restoration of 350-acre Black Rush Lake.

The WPAs are generally open to visitation during daylight hours. There are no entrance fees. No visitor use facilities are provided. Visitor activities include wildlife observation, photography, hiking, cross-country skiing, and trapping and hunting during the designated seasons.

Further information: Big Stone Wetland Management District, c/o Big Stone NWR, 25 N.W. Second Street, Ortonville, MN 56278; telephone: (320) 273-2191.

Detroit Lakes Wetland Management District was established in 1968 to restore, enhance, and protectively manage scattered areas of ecologically important wetlands and associated rolling tallgrass prairie habitat in the counties of Becker, Clay, Mahnomen, Norman, and Polk of northwestern Minnesota.

This extensive district includes more than 40,000 acres in 162 federally owned waterfowl production areas (WPAs) and more than 11,000 acres that are being protectively managed under the terms of perpetual wetland easement agreements with local landowners. Within the district are some of the largest remaining native prairies in Minnesota. Hellikson Waterfowl Production Area in Becker County is the showpiece of the district's collection of these "prairie jewels." Because of the sizable prairie remnants and the district's restorations, a sizable population of the greater prairie chicken still persists in the region.

The district is bordered on the west by the flat Red River Valley floodplain and on the east by the gently rolling hardwood forest and lake region. Most of the prairie wetlands and much of the forested lands within the district's boundaries have been converted to agricultural crop production. The primary mission of the district is to increase quality waterfowl production habitat through the Small Wetlands Acquisition Program and subsequent restoration of wetlands and native grasslands.

The district's extensive fee-acquisition and easement program is funded with revenues from the sale of Migratory Bird Hunting and Conservation Stamps (Duck Stamps). Habitat restoration and management efforts are often funded through partnerships with organizations such as Ducks Unlimited, Inc. and local sportsman's clubs. The district has earned a reputation as a regional leader in the restoration of prairie habitats through alternative seeding methods that maximize species diversity.

WPAs are generally open to visitation during daylight hours. There are no entrance fees. No visitor use facilities are provided. Visitor activities include birdwatching, photography, hiking, cross-country skiing, and hunting and trapping during the designated seasons.

Lodgings and meals are available in such communities as Detroit Lakes, Moorhead, Mahnomen, Fosston, and Crookston.

Further information: Detroit Lakes Wetland Management District, 26624 North Tower Road, Detroit Lakes, MN 56501; telephone: (218) 847-4431.

Fergus Falls Wetland Management District was established in 1962 with the advent of the Accelerated Small Wetlands Acquisition Program. The district includes Douglas, Grant, Otter Tail, Wadena, and Wilkin counties in west-central Minnesota.

This district's mission is to emphasize waterfowl production and ensure the preservation of habitat for migratory birds, threatened/endangered native species, and resident wildlife while providing compatible opportunities for public use. For these purposes, the district currently manages more than 42,000 acres in 217 waterfowl production areas (WPAs) and also administers more than 22,000 wetland acres and 3000 upland acres under the terms of perpetual wetland easement agreements with local landowners. An active acquisition program is continually adding new lands to the district.

WPAs are managed for optimum waterfowl production by reestablishing native grasses and forbs on the uplands, which are primarily managed through controlled burning. Wetlands on WPAs are restored and generally allowed to fluctuate with the natural prairie wet-dry cycles. Water level manipulation is used on more than 40 larger wetlands to enhance wildlife habitat. The district's perpetual easements are located near WPAs and preserve many supplementary acres of privately owned wetland and upland habitats.

The Fergus Falls district lies on the eastern edge of the prairie pothole region of North America. Wetlands range in size from tiny, ephemeral wetlands to large, deep lakes. Wetland fringes are dominated by cattail, river bulrush, sedges, and smartweed, and open water areas contain pondweeds, duckweed, and other typical freshwater aquatic vegetation.

Remnant areas of the northern tallgrass prairie are represented by such species of native grasses as big bluestem, porcupine, Indian, and sideoats grama; and many forbs. The district transitions from prairie on the west to forested terrain to the east. Forested areas contain a mixture of bur oak, green ash, basswood, aspen, and maple, with an understory of chokecherry, prickly ash, hazel, and gooseberry. Shrubs and trees often encroach on the grasslands when not controlled by fire.

More than 285 species of birds frequent the district, of which approximately 165 nest here. Among those that can be found using several large prairie remnants and adjacent grasslands in the western part of the district are greater prairie chicken, upland plover, and LeConte's and grasshopper sparrows. The most common species of breeding ducks include mallard, blue-winged teal, gadwall, shoveler, and ruddy duck. Other common breeding birds include pied-billed grebe, Canada goose, red-tailed hawk, eastern phoebe, marsh wren, and bobolink. Approximately 35 pairs of bald eagles nest on the district's public and private lands.

This avian diversity is complemented by at least 40 species of mammals and 25 species of reptiles and amphibians. Mammals include muskrat, white-tailed deer, beaver, red fox, mink, raccoon, longtail weasel, and meadow vole. Common reptiles consist of the plains garter snake, painted turtle, and prairie skink. Amphibians include periodic population explosions of leopard frogs on certain WPA wetlands.

Acquisition of this district's WPAs was and continues to be made possible with revenues from the sale of Migratory Bird Hunting and Conservation Stamps (Duck Stamps).

Fergus Falls district's WPAs are generally open to visitation during daylight hours. There are no entrance fees. Visitor activities include birdwatching, wildlife photography, hiking, cross-country skiing, and hunting during the designated seasons.

Fergus Falls district also manages the Prairie Wetlands Learning Center—the first major environmental education center in the United States that is focused upon prairie wetlands and grasslands. Operated by the U.S. Fish and Wildlife Service in cooperation with the City of Fergus Falls and the State of Minnesota, it is dedicated to advancing public and private stewardship responsibility for the prairie pothole ecosystem and to promoting public understanding and appreciation of the multiple values of prairie wetlands and grasslands.

The learning center, which is located south of the city of Fergus Falls and less than one-half mile from Exit 57 on Interstate 94, includes a large area of interpretive exhibits, classrooms, a field laboratory, dormitory rooms, a kitchen, a large viewing deck, and an adjacent trailhead. The surrounding 325-acre WPA contains an amphitheater, prairie wildflower conservatory, 4 miles of trails through native prairie grassland, and more than 30 different prairie wetlands. The center offers scheduled environmental education and interpretive programs. To contact the Prairie Wetlands Learning Center for further information: (218) 736-0938. The Friends of the Prairie Wetlands Learning Center is providing assistance to the center.

Lodgings and meals are available throughout the 5-county district, with the larger communities of Fergus Falls and Alexandria being close to large numbers of the district's WPAs.

Fergus Falls WMD headquarters is located 0.75 mile east of Fergus Falls along State Route 210.

Further information: Fergus Falls Wetland Management District, 21932 State Highway 210, Fergus Falls, MN 56537; telephone: (218) 739-2291.

(NOTE: Special appreciation is given to Kevin Brennan, Wetland Manager, for providing this description.)

Litchfield Wetland Management District was established in 1978 to manage tracts of land purchased under the Small Wetlands Acquisition Program that contain ecologically important wetland and grassland habitats. These lands are located within the counties of Kandiyohi, McLeod, Meeker, Renville, Stearns, Todd, and Wright in south-central Minnesota.

The district manages more than 145 federally owned waterfowl production areas (WPAs) covering approximately 32,000 acres, and also manages more than 420 perpetual wetland and grassland easements purchased from local landowners. The main purpose of the district is waterfowl production and management. In addition, major emphasis is placed on managing these tracts for the preservation and enhancement of the biodiversity of native tallgrass prairie and prairie pothole ecosystems, including all wildlife that utilizes these communities.

The Litchfield district is also part of the Northern Tallgrass Prairie National Wildlife Refuge project. The goal of this ecologically significant endeavor in Minnesota and Iowa is to protect and manage remaining tracts of tallgrass-prairie habitat, either by federal acquisition or under the terms of perpetual grassland easement agreements with landowners.

Establishment of the Litchfield district's WPAs and other units is made possible partly with revenues from the sale of Migratory Bird Hunting and Conservation Stamps (Duck Stamps). In addition, the Minnesota Department of Natural Resources, Minnesota Waterfowlers Association, Ducks Unlimited, Inc., The Nature Conservancy, Pheasants Forever, and many other partners contribute in a variety of ways, such as funding, volunteer staffing, and technical expertise, to help make possible the enhancement and protection of these vital areas.

Potential land acquisitions, offered by willing sellers, are carefully screened. A mix of fee title and easement purchases is selected in an effort to protect wetland complexes and associated uplands. Once a new tract of land is purchased, drained wetlands are restored. In an agricultural area such as Minnesota, wetland restorations usually involve drainage issues: ditches must be plugged, drainage tile removed, etc. The restored wetlands revegetate naturally upon the return of water. Associated wetland wildlife is soon attracted. Permanent cover on the upland portions of the tract must also be established, which frequently requires the conversion of cropland by seeding a diverse mix of native warm-season and cool-season grasses, and native forbs. If native vegetation is already present on part of a tract, management may only necessitate enhancement activities, such as weed control or prescribed burning.

Once established, WPAs are managed to maintain these ecologically important wetland and grassland habitats. A major management tool is prescribed burning, which is conducted to replicate fires that historically occurred across the vast expanses of tallgrass prairie. Fire maintains the integrity of the tallgrass prairie ecosystem by releasing nutrients into the soil, slowing the invasion of woody plant species, and reducing competition from nonnative invasive species.

Most wetlands in Minnesota are located on private lands. Thus, private landowners play a key role in the preservation of these valuable habitats. Through the Partners for Wildlife Program, the district provides technical and financial assistance to landowners and other partners who wish to improve habitat by restoring drained wetlands on their own land. Since 1987, the district has restored more than 3,500 wetlands on private property through this program. In addition, district staff participate in and provide assistance on many projects, issues, and events concerning wildlife and the management of land and water.

WPAs are generally open to visitation during daylight hours. There are no entrance fees, and no visitor use services are provided. Visitor activities include wildlife observation, photography, hiking, and hunting during the designated seasons.

Further information: Litchfield Wetland Management District, 22274-615th Avenue, Litchfield, MN 55355; telephone: (320) 693-2849.

(NOTE: Special appreciation is given to Barry Christenson, Wetland Manager, and Mary Soler, Staff Biologist, for providing this description.)

Minnesota Valley Wetland Management District was established to restore, enhance, and protectively manage scattered areas of ecologically important prairie wetland and grassland habitats in a 13-county region of southern Minnesota. Within this district, there are more than 3,600 acres of federally owned waterfowl production areas (WPAs) and 1,830 acres being managed under the terms of wetland and grassland easement agreements with private landowners. In addition, there are a number of conservation easements with the U.S. Department of Agriculture's Farmers Home Administration. Remnant habitats found throughout the district include prairie potholes, tallgrass prairie, floodplain and upland forest, and oak savanna.

Further information: Minnesota Valley Wetland Management District, c/o Minnesota Valley National Wildlife Refuge, 3815 East Eightieth Street, Bloomington, MN 55425; telephone: (952) 854-5900.

Morris Wetland Management District was established in 1964 to restore, enhance, and protectively manage scattered areas of ecologically important prairie wetland and grassland habitats in Traverse, Big Stone, Stevens, Pope, Swift, Lac Qui Parle, Chippewa, and Yellow Medicine counties in west-central Minnesota.

This extensive district includes more than 50,000 acres in nearly 250 federally owned waterfowl production areas (WPAs) and more than 20,000 acres that are being protectively managed under the terms of perpetual wetland easement agreements with local landowners.

Some of the WPA wetland areas are managed by seasonally manipulating water levels to provide high-quality waterfowl habitat and promote the growth of plants that offer food and cover. Grassland habitat is maintained by periodic prescription burning, an ecologically important process to help recycle plant nutrients that enhance the growth of native grasses and forbs, and to control the growth of invasive woody vegetation.

Acquisition of WPA lands was and continues to be made possible with revenues from the sale of Migratory Bird Hunting and Conservation Stamps (Duck Stamps).

The WPAs are generally open to visitation during daylight hours. There are no entrance fees. No visitor use facilities are provided. Visitor activities include birdwatching, photography, hiking, cross-country skiing, and hunting during the designated seasons.

The highest nesting density of waterfowl in Minnesota occurs within this district. A few of the more common water birds that breed in the Morris Wetland District include pied-billed and western grebes, American white pelican, double-crested cormorant, great blue and green herons, great egret, black-crowned night-heron, more than a dozen species of ducks (especially wood, mallard, gadwall, pintail, blue-winged teal, and redhead), Virginia and sora rails, and American coot. Others, such as tundra swan, white-fronted and snow geese, common goldeneye, and bufflehead pause here on their migrations to and from breeding grounds far to the north.

Lodgings and meals are available in such communities as Granite Falls, Montevideo, Willmar, Benson, Ortonville, and Morris.

Further information: Morris Wetland Management District, Route 1, Box 877, Morris, MN 56267; telephone: (320) 589-1001.

Windom Wetland Management District was established in 1990 to restore, enhance, and protectively manage scattered areas of ecologically important wetland and grassland habitats in the southeastern edge of the prairie pothole region of southwestern and southern Minnesota. The district encompasses Pipestone, Rock, Murray, Nobles, Redwood, Brown, Cottonwood, Jackson, Watonwan, Martin, Faribault, and Freeborn counties. The majority of habitats are wetland/riverine and grassland/farmland, but there are smaller areas of native tallgrass prairie and woodland.

This extensive district includes approximately 11,500 acres in 59 federally owned waterfowl production areas (WPAs) and more than 1,800 acres that are being protectively managed under the terms of perpetual wetland/flowage, habitat, and other conservation easement agreements with local landowners.

Establishment of the district's WPAs and other units was made possible partly with revenues from the sale of Migratory Bird Hunting and Conservation Stamps (Duck Stamps).

The WPAs are generally open to visitation during daylight hours. There are no entrance fees. Visitor activities include birdwatching, photography, hiking, cross-country skiing, and hunting during the designated seasons. The Windom Wetland Management District's headquarters and visitor center, located on the Wolf Lake WPA, is open on weekdays, except national holidays.

As emphasized by the district manager, Steven W. Kallin:

The Wolf Lake WPA site provides access to an outstanding variety of habitats, which can be viewed by the public and used to convey wildlife-management concepts, ecosystem functions, and the benefits provided by prairie/wetland habitats. These habitats include: restored wetlands with water-level management capabilities; a 120-acre, shallow prairie lake with water-level capabilities; remnant oak savanna; unbroken native prairie; former cropland restored to native prairie grasses; and tree/shrub plantings for wildlife. It is also home for a variety of resident and migratory species.

As the U.S. Fish and Wildlife Service says:

The District also contains the renowned Heron Lake, which is located in Jackson County. The 8,251 acre body of water was once nationally recognized as one of the premiere waterfowl lakes in North America. At the turn of the century [1900], an estimated 700,000 canvasbacks used the lake as a migratory stopover, feeding on the abundant wild celery and sago pondweed. Thus, the lake was often referred to as the "Chesapeake Bay of the Midwest." Eventually several factors led to the severe degradation of the lake. Among these were intensive agricultural practices in the drainage of approximately 90% of the watershed's wetlands. This dramatically increased the volume and velocity as well as the sediment, fertilizer and chemical content of the water reaching the lake. Other factors contributing to the lake's degradation included the infusion of municipal waste water and the introduction of rough [bottom-feeding] fish. These factors have had, and continue to have, a negative effect on emergent and submergent plant growth.

The U.S. Fish and Wildlife Service is currently a partner involved in a Prairie Pothole Joint Venture project to stop and reverse the degradation of this once magnificent waterfowl area.

The Heron Lake Watershed Restoration Project was initiated in 1989. Its goals have included enhancement of water quality, application of soil and water conservation practices on public and private lands, the reduction of flooding, the restoration and management of vital wildlife and fish habitat, and environmental education.

Among the many waterfowl and other birds attracted to this district's protected habitats are Canada goose, numerous species of ducks, and American white pelican.

Lodgings and meals are available in such communities as Windom, Jackson, Worthington, and Marshall.

Access to the Windom Wetland Management District's headquarters and visitor center, located on the Wolf Lake WPA, is 1 mile east from the town of Windom on County Route 17 and following the directional sign onto the WPA.

Further information: Windom Wetland Management District, Route 1, Box 273A, Windom, MN 56101; telephone: (507) 831-2220.

Mississippi

Bogue Chitto (see text under Louisiana)

Coldwater River was initially a unit of Tallahatchie and was changed to a separate 2,069-acre refuge in 1999. It was established to enhance and protect an area of abandoned farmland in northwestern Mississippi. Some of this annually flooded land is being restored to native bottomland hardwood forest and bald cypress-tupelo swamp habitats.

This refuge also includes 24 former catfish ponds, covering nearly 500 acres. The water level of these ponds is being regulated with water control structures, such as pumps, ditch plugs, and earthen levees, for the benefit of many species of shorebirds, waterfowl, marsh birds, and other wildlife.

Thirty-four species of shorebirds have been recorded here, including American golden plover; killdeer; greater and lesser yellowlegs; long-billed dowitcher; and semipalmated, least, and pectoral sandpipers. Large concentrations of wintering waterfowl, such as greater white-fronted geese, mallards, and green-winged teal, are attracted to Coldwater River. The U.S. Fish and Wildlife Service provides nesting boxes for wood ducks. Numerous species of neotropical migratory songbirds pass through this refuge.

Visitor access is limited to wildlife viewing from the Panola-Quitman Floodway Levee Road. There is no entrance fee.

Visitor activities include birdwatching and photography. Although camping is not permitted on the refuge, campground facilities are available at George Payne Cossar State Park and Holly Springs National Forest. Winter is the best time to see concentrations of waterfowl, and spring is the best season to see and hear neotropical migratory songbirds.

Visitors are cautioned to be alert for venomous snakes, fire ants, chiggers, and ticks. Insect repellent is advised.

Fauna and flora are essentially the same as on Dahomey Refuge.

Lodgings and meals are available in such communities as Grenada, Batesville, and Clarksdale.

Access to the refuge is north 2 miles from Charleston on State Route 35, left onto Puducah Wells Road, and right onto the Panola-Quitman Floodway Levee Road. The refuge extends west from this levee road.

Further information: Coldwater River National Wildlife Refuge, c/o North Mississippi Refuges Complex, P.O. Box 1070, Grenada, MS 38902; telephone: (662) 226-8286.

Dahomey, consisting of 9,691 acres, was established in 1990 to enhance and protect an area of ecologically important bottomland hardwood forest and meandering bayous near the Mississippi River in northwestern Mississippi. Approximately 1,600 acres of the refuge consists of abandoned, annually flooded farmland that is being restored to forest with the planting of such species as bald cypress and Nuttall, water, and willow oaks. A small population of the endangered Louisiana black bear has been reestablished on this refuge.

Every other year, the U.S. Fish and Wildlife Service floods areas of the refuge's bottomland forest, creating what is known as a green-tree reservoir. This wetland habitat, which is regulated by water control structures, provides feeding and roosting areas for wintering waterfowl and is beneficial to many other species of wildlife. Nesting boxes are provided for wood ducks. A moist-soil unit is managed for migratory shorebirds (see Tallahatchie text). Ducks Unlimited, Inc. has assisted with important habitat enhancement projects. The Friends of Dahomey National Wildlife Refuge, Inc. is a nonprofit support group that is assisting the refuge in various ways.

Visitor use of Dahomey is limited, and there is no entrance fee.

Visitor activities include birdwatching and photography from state and county roads in the refuge, and hunting (deer, small game, waterfowl, and turkey) during the designated seasons. Although camping is not permitted on the refuge, campground facilities are available at Great River Road State Park. Winter is the best time to see waterfowl, and spring is the best season to see and hear neotropical migratory songbirds.

Visitors are cautioned to be alert for venomous snakes, fire ants, chiggers, and ticks. Insect repellent is advised.

Lodgings and meals are available in such communities as Cleveland, Greenville, and Clarksdale.

Access to the refuge is south on State Route 61 from Cleveland, and right at Boyle onto State Route 446 for 6 miles west. The refuge extends to the north and south along this highway.

Further information: Dahomey National Wildlife Refuge, c/o North Mississippi Refuges Complex, P.O. Box 1070, Grenada, MS 38901; (662) 226-8286.

Grand Bay, comprising 9,510 acres, was established in 1989 to protect and enhance an ecologically important area for a wide variety of wildlife in southeastern Mississippi and southwestern Alabama. The refuge's major habitats are significant remnants of wet pine savanna and pine woodlands, intermingled with evergreen bays and stands of the pond cypress (a variant of the bald cypress), and freshwater and brackish marshes. The estuarine salt marshes are essential nursery habitat for more than 80 species of finfish and shellfish, such as shrimp, blue crab, flounder, spotted sea trout, and red drum.

Among the primary objectives of this refuge are to enhance and protect wet pine savanna habitat for the benefit of fish, wildlife, and plant populations and to provide suitable habitat for the establishment of a second breeding flock of the endangered Mississippi sandhill crane. (See the Mississippi Sandhill Crane Refuge text.)

The refuge is open daily during daylight hours, although the station is frequently un-manned. There is no entrance fee. The refuge shares a building, at 6005 Bayou Heron Road, with the Grand Bay National Estuarine Research Reserve, which focuses on water-related habi-tats, education, and research.

Visitor activities include birdwatching, photography, environmental education programs, boat-ing, and fishing. Camping is not permitted on the refuge, but campground facilities are available at such places as Gulf Islands National Seashore and Shepard State Park. Hunting is not permitted.

Even though alligators are generally afraid of people, visitors are cautioned to stay a safe distance from these sluggish-looking but potentially fast-moving reptiles and to be alert for ven-omous snakes, fire ants, chiggers, and ticks. Insect repellent is advised.

The species of fauna and flora on this refuge include those of the savanna, similar to the ones in the Mississippi Sandhill Crane National Wildlife Refuge and of the estuarine ecosys-tem. The rich diversity of estuarine species include salt marsh vegetation such as sawgrass, cord-grass, and black needlerush; wintering waterfowl, such as lesser scaup, ring-necked ducks, mal-lards, and red-breasted mergansers; marsh furbearers, such as mink and the nonnative nutria; alligators; and fishery resources, totaling more than 80 fish species, along the northeastern Gulf Coast.

Lodgings and meals are available in such communities as Gautier, Pascagoula, and Moss Point.

Access to this rural refuge from Interstate 10's Exit 75 is south for 0.25 mile on Franklin Creek Road, cross U.S. Route 90 and continue straight onto Pecan Road (unmarked at this writing), and left (east) onto the first paved road (which crosses a railroad track). Where this road divides, bear right onto Bayou Heron Road, and continue for about 1 mile to the refuge building (on the right).

Further information: Grand Bay National Wildlife Refuge, P.O. Box 1062, Grand Bay, AL 36541; telephone: (228) 475-0765.

Hillside, encompassing 15,572 acres, is located in west-central Mississippi. The refuge was es-tablished in 1975 to restore, enhance, and protect an ecologically important area of bottom-land hardwood forest, bald cypress-tupelo brakes, buttonbush and swamp privet thickets, and agricultural areas providing crop residues for the benefit of wildlife. These habitats attract large concentrations of wintering waterfowl, nesting wood ducks, wild turkeys, numerous species of neotropical migratory songbirds, white-tailed deer, bobcats, river otters, beavers, raccoons, alli-gators, and other wildlife.

Habitat management goals for Hillside are similar to those of Yazoo National Wildlife Refuge (see the text for that refuge), with which it is jointly managed along with Mathews Brake, Morgan Brake, and Panther Swamp.

Establishment of Hillside Refuge was made possible partly with revenues from the sale of Migratory Bird Hunting and Conservation Stamps (Duck Stamps). Ducks Unlimited, Inc. has helped enhance more than 400 acres of the refuge's wetland habitat.

Matt Young, Senior Writer for *Ducks Unlimited*, cherishes his memories of many visits to this refuge:

My father and I hunted ducks several times a year at Hillside throughout the 1980s. Two things stand out in my recollection of this watery wilderness. First was its unique location nestled against the loess bluffs on the very edge of the Mississippi Delta. From parts of the refuge, you can gaze up into the forested hills rising to the east—quite a view for Mississippi. The other thing I remember was the vastness of its flooded bottomlands. We would launch our canoe from the levee and then paddle seemingly for miles through expanses of flooded cypress, tupelo, buttonbush, and cane to inaccessible areas that were rarely hunted. I have especially fond memories of gliding silently through the flooded woods just before dawn and listening to hundreds of mallards, gadwalls, wigeons, green-winged teal, and wood ducks calling all around us in the darkness. When Hillside is flooded and full of ducks, it is truly a magical place.

The refuge is open daily during daylight hours. There is no entrance fee.

Visitor activities include birdwatching; photography; hiking, fishing; and hunting (deer, small game, and waterfowl) during the designated seasons. An annual hunting and fishing permit is required that applies to all five refuges in the Yazoo National Wildlife Refuges Complex. Camping is not permitted on the refuge, but campground facilities are available in Leroy Percy State Park and Delta National Forest. November through April are the best months for birdwatching.

Hiking opportunities include the 0.6-mile Alligator Slough Nature Trail, which leads through a bald cypress-tupelo swamp and along levees and refuge roads.

Even though alligators are generally afraid of people, visitors are cautioned to stay a safe distance from these sluggish-looking but potentially fast-moving reptiles and to be alert for venomous snakes, fire ants, chiggers, and ticks. Insect repellent is advised.

Fauna and flora that have been recorded on Hillside Refuge are essentially the same as on Yazoo National Wildlife Refuge.

Lodgings and meals are available in such communities as Yazoo City and Greenwood.

Access to the refuge is north 13 miles from Yazoo City on U.S. Route 49E, turning east (right) at Thornton, and continuing 5 miles.

Further information: Hillside National Wildlife Refuge, c/o Yazoo National Wildlife Refuges Complex, 728 Yazoo Refuge Road, Hollandale, MS 38748; telephone: (662) 235-4989.

Mathews Brake, comprising 2,418 acres, was established in 1980 to restore and protect an ecologically important 600-acre area of bottomland hardwood forest and an 1,800-acre oxbow lake adjacent to the Yazoo River in west-central Mississippi. These habitats benefit concentrations of wintering waterfowl, nesting wood ducks, wild turkeys, numerous species of neotropical migratory songbirds, white-tailed deer, bobcats, river otters, beavers, raccoons, and alligators.

Habitat management goals for Mathews Brake are similar to those on Yazoo National Wildlife Refuge (see the text for that refuge), with which it is jointly managed along with Hillside, Morgan Brake, and Panther Swamp refuges.

Establishment of this refuge was made possible partly with revenues from the sale of Migratory Bird Hunting and Conservation Stamps (Duck Stamps).

Mathews Brake is open daily during daylight hours.

Visitor activities include birdwatching; photography; limited hiking; boating (a wheelchair-accessible boat-launching ramp is provided onto the oxbow lake); fishing; and hunting (deer, small game, and waterfowl) during the designated seasons. An annual hunting and fishing permit is required that applies to all five refuges in the Yazoo National Wildlife Refuges Complex. Camping is not permitted on the refuge, but campground facilities are available at Leroy Percy State Park. November through April are the best months for birdwatching.

Even though alligators are generally afraid of people, visitors are cautioned to stay a safe distance from these sluggish-looking but potentially fast-moving reptiles and to be alert for venomous snakes, fire ants, chiggers, and ticks. Insect repellent is advised.

Fauna and flora that have been recorded on Matthews Brake Refuge are essentially the same as on Yazoo National Wildlife Refuge.

Lodgings and meals are available in such communities as Yazoo City, Greenwood, and Winona.

Access to the refuge is south 9 miles from Greenwood on U.S. Route 49E, turning right at Sidon, continuing southwest for 3 miles, and then left onto the refuge entrance road.

Further information: Mathews Brake National Wildlife Refuge, c/o Yazoo National Wildlife Refuges Complex, 728 Yazoo Refuge Road, Hollandale, MS 38748; telephone: (662) 235-4989.

Mississippi Sandhill Crane, containing more than 19,000 acres in four units, was established in 1975. The refuge provides protection for the critically endangered Mississippi sandhill crane and for vital remnants of the bird's wet pine savanna habitat in southeastern Mississippi. This bird is a nonmigratory subspecies (*Grus canadensis pulla*) whose original range extended along the Gulf Coast plain, from the western Florida panhandle westward through Alabama and Mississippi to Louisiana. As the wet pine savanna was degraded or destroyed during the past half century, the crane's numbers dwindled to 30 or 40 birds by the 1970s. Today's population of about 100 to 120 individuals is limited to a relatively small area on and adjacent to this refuge.

Research has revealed that this sandhill, although similar to the two other nonmigratory and three migratory subspecies, has certain physiological, morphological, and behavioral differences from the others. For instance, they have noticeably darker gray plumage that gives greater emphasis to their white cheek patch. These red-crowned birds stand 3 to 4 feet tall and have a wingspread of roughly 6 feet. Their call is a rolling, trumpeting sound that can be heard for at least a mile.

Mississippi Sandhill Crane Refuge's savanna habitat consists of extensive wet prairies with many grasses and sedges, and a tremendously rich variety of low-growing herbaceous species, including native orchids and an array of carnivorous plants. Scattered across these open expanses are occasional longleaf pines and pond cypresses (a variant of the bald cypress). One of the major management programs of this refuge is the restoration and maintenance of its savanna habitat, with periodic prescription burns, timber sales, and other tree removal strategies. To restore the savanna ecosystem, which has been unnaturally invaded by dense growths of trees and shrubs as the result of fire suppression, planting, and ditching for pulpwood, some ecologists are urging that as much as 90 percent of the slash pines be removed.

The refuge includes several other habitat types: forested swamp; pine scrub, much of which is former pine savanna that has become overgrown with slash pine; and tidal marshes, in which there are extensive expanses of sawgrass and (in the higher-salinity wetland of the refuge's Fontainebleau unit) salt meadow cordgrass and needlegrass rush.

In addition to the cranes, many other kinds of wildlife inhabit this area. The bird list of the savannas may not be long, but it is definitely distinctive, including several species that are declining throughout their ranges, such as Bachman's sparrow, red-headed woodpecker, loggerhead shrike, brown-headed nuthatch, American kestrel, and many wintering sparrows, including Henslow's and LeConte's. Because of the cranes and more, Mississippi Sandhill Crane Refuge has been designated as a Globally Important Bird Area by the American Bird Conservancy.

A significant aspect of this refuge is that its establishment was the direct result of environmental lobbying and the first legal use of Section 7 of the Endangered Species Act of 1973. This section provides for "taking such action necessary to insure that actions authorized, funded, or carried out . . . [by the federal government] . . . not jeopardize the continued existence of such endangered species and threatened species or result in the destruction or modification of habitat of such species. . . ."

In 1975, the National Wildlife Federation filed a lawsuit that succeeded in blocking construction of federally funded Interstate 10 through critical Mississippi sandhill crane habitat, until steps were taken to provide for the continued existence of the cranes. The Nature Conservancy assisted by acquiring much of the initial acreage for the refuge, and the organization continues to provide its active support.

The refuge is open on weekdays during daylight hours, except national holidays. There is no entrance fee.

Visitor activities include viewing a short video about the refuge; birdwatching; photography; environmental education programs (including a video) at the visitor center; hiking (a 0.75-mile level loop trail from the visitor center and a 1-mile trail that starts from Ocean Springs Middle School); and picnicking next to the visitor center. During the annual Crane Festival (call the refuge for the date), visitors may participate in prescribed fire and other management demonstrations.

To avoid disturbing the cranes, most of the refuge is not open to visitation. However, with reservations, refuge staff and trained volunteers will take groups onto the refuge for tours that may include a visit to an elevated viewing blind. Picnicking is allowed at the visitor center. Camping is not permitted on the refuge, but campground facilities are available at a number of nearby locations, including Gulf Islands National Seashore and Shepard State Park. Fishing, hunting, and trapping are not permitted on the refuge.

Visitors are cautioned to be alert for venomous snakes, fire ants, chiggers, and ticks.

Lodgings and meals are available in such communities as Ocean Springs, Biloxi, Moss Point, Pascagoula, and Gautier.

Access to the refuge is 0.5 mile north on the Gautier-Vancleave Road from Exit 61 on I-10, and right to the entrance and the visitor center.

Further information: Mississippi Sandhill Crane National Wildlife Refuge, 7200 Crane Lane, Gautier, MS 39553; telephone (228) 497-6322.

Morgan Brake, consisting of 7,381 acres, was established in 1977 to enhance and protect ecologically important bottomland hardwood forest, sloughs, cypress-tupelo brakes and sloughs, ponds, and agricultural fields in west-central Mississippi. These habitats benefit concentrations of wintering waterfowl, nesting wood ducks, wild turkeys, numerous species of neotropical migratory songbirds, white-tailed deer, bobcats, river otters, beavers, raccoons, alligators, and other wildlife.

Habitat management goals for this refuge are similar to those on Yazoo National Wildlife Refuge (see the text for that refuge), with which it is jointly managed along with Hillside, Mathews Brake, and Panther Swamp refuges.

Establishment of this refuge was made possible partly with revenues from the sale of Migratory Bird Hunting and Conservation Stamps (Duck Stamps). Ducks Unlimited, Inc. has assisted with important habitat enhancement projects.

Morgan Brake Refuge is open daily during daylight hours.

Visitor activities include birdwatching; photography; driving on roads in and adjacent to the refuge; hiking; fishing; and hunting (deer, small game, and waterfowl) on parts of the refuge during the designated seasons. An annual hunting and fishing permit is required that applies to all five refuges in the Yazoo National Wildlife Refuges Complex. Camping is not permitted on the refuge, but campground facilities are available at Leroy Percy State Park. November through April are the best birdwatching months.

Even though alligators are generally afraid of people, visitors are cautioned to stay a safe distance from these sluggish-looking but potentially fast-moving reptiles and to be alert for venomous snakes, fire ants, chiggers, and ticks. Insect repellent is advised.

Fauna and flora that have been recorded Morgan Brake Refuge are essentially the same as on Yazoo National Wildlife Refuge.

Lodgings and meals are available in such communities as Yazoo City, Greenwood, and Winona.

Access to the refuge is north 3 miles from Tchula on U.S. Route 49E.

Further information: Morgan Brake National Wildlife Refuge, c/o Yazoo National Wildlife Refuges Complex, 728 Yazoo Refuge Road, Hollandale, MS 38748.

Noxubee, encompassing 48,026 acres, was established in 1940 to restore and protect an area that had previously been seriously degraded by overgrazing, intensive agricultural development, and soil erosion along the Noxubee River (pronounced NOX-u-bee) in east-central Mississippi. Following decades of conservation enhancement, this refuge has become a model of forest and wildlife habitat restoration.

More than three-quarters of the refuge consists of upland pine woodland, bottomland hardwood forest, and seasonally flooded bald cypress swamp. Among the numerous species of wildlife inhabiting these forested lands are wild turkey, northern bobwhite, and the federally listed endangered red-cockaded woodpecker (*Picoides borealis*). In its program to enhance populations of this habitat-specific woodpecker, the U.S. Fish and Wildlife Service manages areas of pine woodland, using prescription burning and selective thinning, to maintain open stands with mature trees, in which the bird creates nesting cavities. Some human-made cavities are also provided. (See further description of this species in the Carolina Sandhills Refuge text).

Noxubee Refuge contains 1,200-acre Bluff Lake and 600-acre Loakfoma Lake, plus 16 smaller impoundments, beaver ponds, and streams. These wetlands provide important resting and feeding habitat for wintering waterfowl, bald eagles, resident and migratory Canada geese, and wading birds including the wood stork, hundreds of which visit the refuge in late summer. More than 250 species of birds have been recorded on Noxubee. Alligators are near the northern edge of their range here.

As part of the refuge's waterfowl habitat management, several low levees have been built, allowing for periodic winter flooding of some bottomland hardwood forest—a practice known as "green-timber reservoir management." Noxubee contains four of these water management areas.

The refuge is also taking steps to restore part of the vanishing "Alabama Black Belt Prairie." Morgan Hill Overlook Trail offers visitors an opportunity to hike through this ecologically important habitat.

Establishment of the refuge was made possible partly with revenues from the sale of Migratory Bird Hunting and Conservation Stamps (Duck Stamps). Ducks Unlimited, Inc. has assisted with important habitat enhancement projects.

The refuge is open daily during daylight hours. Its office, overlooking Bluff Lake, is open on weekdays, except for national holidays. There is no entrance fee.

Visitor activities include birdwatching; photography; environmental education programs (by prearrangement); driving some of the refuge roads; hiking on a number of trails; watching wildlife from (wheelchair accessible) viewing platforms; canoeing and boating; fishing; and hunting (deer, turkey, and small game) during the designated seasons. Although camping is not permitted on the refuge, campground facilities are available in nearby the Tombigbee National Forest and Legion State Park.

Walks and trails include: less-than-0.25-mile (wheelchair-accessible) Canada Goose Overlook Trail (near the refuge office), 0.25-mile (wheelchair-accessible) Bluff Lake Boardwalk, 0.25-mile Morgan Hill Overlook Trail, 0.25-mile Woodpecker Trail, 1.75-mile Scattertown Trail, 2-mile Beaver Dam Trail, 3.4-mile Wilderness Trail, and 4-mile Trail of the Big Trees.

Even though alligators are generally afraid of people, visitors are cautioned to stay a safe distance from these sluggish-looking but potentially fast-moving reptiles and to be alert for venomous snakes, fire ants, chiggers, and ticks. Insect repellent is advised.

Lodgings and meals are available in Starkville.

Access to the refuge from Starkville is south 12 miles from State Routes 12/25 (at Hampton Inn) on Oktoc Road and west (right) about 6 miles on the dirt road to the refuge office; or south 15 miles on State Route 25 and east (left) 10 miles on a dirt road.

Further information: Noxubee National Wildlife Refuge, Route 1, Box 142, Brooksville, MS 39739; telephone: (662) 323-5548.

Panther Swamp, comprising 38,601 acres, was established in 1978 to restore and protect ecologically important bottomland hardwood forest, cypress-tupelo brakes, bayous, and sloughs along the Yazoo River in west-central Mississippi. These habitats benefit concentrations of wintering waterfowl, nesting wood ducks, wild turkeys, numerous neotropical migratory songbirds, white-tailed deer, bobcat, river otters, beavers, raccoons, alligators, and other wildlife.

Habitat management goals for this refuge are similar to those on Yazoo National Wildlife Refuge (see the text for that refuge), with which it is jointly managed along with Hillside, Mathews Brake, and Morgan Brake refuges.

Establishment of the refuge was made possible partly with revenues from the sale of Migratory Bird Hunting and Conservation Stamps (Duck Stamps). Ducks Unlimited, Inc. has assisted with important habitat enhancement projects.

Panther Swamp is open daily during daylight hours. There is no entrance fee.

Visitor activities include birdwatching; photography; driving on designated roads; hiking (on levees, refuge roads, and ATV trails); canoeing and boating (two boat-launching ramps are provided onto Lake George and Deep Bayou); fishing; and hunting (deer, small game, and waterfowl) during the designated seasons. An annual hunting and fishing permit is required that applies to all 5 refuges in the Yazoo National Wildlife Refuges Complex. Camping is not permitted on the refuge, but campground facilities are available in Delta National Forest and Leroy Percy State Park. November through April are the best months for birdwatching.

Although alligators are generally afraid of people, visitors are cautioned to stay a safe distance from these sluggish-looking but potentially fast-moving reptiles and to be alert for venomous snakes, fire ants, chiggers, and ticks. Insect repellent is advised.

Fauna and flora that have been recorded on Panther Swamp Refuge are essentially the same as on Yazoo Refuge.

Lodgings and meals are available in such communities as Yazoo City and Jackson.

Access to the refuge is north 2 miles from Yazoo City on U.S. Route 49W, left onto River Road for about 6 miles, and right at Gumbo Acres to the refuge headquarters.

Further information: Panther Swamp National Wildlife Refuge, c/o Yazoo National Wildlife Refuges Complex, 728 Yazoo Refuge Road, Hollandale, MS 38748; telephone: (662) 746-5060.

St. Catherine Creek, consisting of 24,442 acres, was established in 1990 to restore and protect seasonally flooded bottomland hardwood forest, cypress swamp, sloughs, and other open-water areas. The refuge is located along old St. Catherine Creek and the Mississippi River near Natchez in southwestern Mississippi. Large concentrations of wintering waterfowl, nesting wood ducks, many wading and shorebirds, wild turkeys, and great numbers of neotropical migratory songbirds are among the refuge's diverse wildlife.

To benefit wildlife, the U.S. Fish and Wildlife Service is working to reforest significant parts of this refuge. Bald cypresses and several species of oaks are being planted on lands that were originally forested but were logged off for agricultural development.

Management plans also include construction of water control structures, culverts, and enhanced levees. Seasonal backwater flooding from the creek and river can thereby be regulated, retaining areas of water during dry periods and releasing water during spring flooding to provide some needed feeding and resting habitat for such species as migratory shorebirds. For wintering waterfowl, several areas are managed to produce moist-soil plants, such as millet, smartweed, sprangletop, and rushes. Under cooperative agreements, other lands are devoted to the production of agricultural crops, whereby farmers leave a portion of their crops unharvested to benefit waterfowl.

Establishment of the refuge was made possible partly with revenues from the sale of Migratory Bird Hunting and Conservation Stamps (Duck Stamps). Ducks Unlimited, Inc. has assisted with important habitat enhancement projects. St. Catherine Creek Refuge Association, Inc. is a local nonprofit support group that is assisting the refuge in a variety of ways.

The refuge is open daily during daylight hours. There is an entrance fee (either a daily use permit or an annual use permit).

Visitor activities include birdwatching, photography, hiking (an interpretive trail is located near the refuge headquarters), canoeing and boating, fishing, and hunting during the designated seasons. Camping is not permitted in the refuge, but campground facilities are available in Natchez State Park and Homochitto National Forest.

Even though alligators are generally afraid of people, visitors are cautioned to stay a safe distance from these sluggish-looking but potentially fast-moving reptiles and to be alert for venomous snakes, fire ants, chiggers, and ticks. Insect repellent is advised.

Lodgings and meals are available in Natchez.

Access to the refuge is 10 miles south from Natchez on U.S. Route 61, right onto York Road for 2 miles, and left onto Pintail Lane and the refuge entrance.

Further information: St. Catherine Creek National Wildlife Refuge, P.O. Box 117, Sibley, MS 39165; telephone: (601) 442-6696.

Tallahatchie, containing more than 4,200 acres, was established in 1990 to enhance and protect an area of abandoned farmland, meandering bald cypress-bordered bayous, and scattered small parcels of forest in northwestern Mississippi. To benefit a rich diversity of wildlife, some of this annually flooded land, which was previously cleared for agricultural development, is being restored to native bottomland hardwood forest with the planting of such species as Nuttall oak, sweetgum, pecan, and bald cypress.

With levees and other water control structures, the U.S. Fish and Wildlife Service is regulating water levels of moist-soil habitat impoundments to benefit migratory shorebirds and wintering waterfowl. For example, a water management unit is drained for a year, so that vegetation can grow. In midsummer, the unit is flooded with roughly one-half foot of water for about 2 weeks. From late July through September, the water level is then lowered for the benefit of migrating shorebirds. Higher water levels provide habitat for wading birds, such as herons and egrets.

Ducks Unlimited, Inc. has acquired some of the land for Tallahatchie and has assisted with important habitat enhancement projects.

The refuge is open daily and is located on public roads that run through or are adjacent to the refuge. There is no entrance fee.

Visitor activities include birdwatching; photography; boating and fishing (on Tippo Bayou, south of State Route 8); and hunting (deer, small game, and waterfowl) during the designated seasons. Although camping is not permitted on the refuge, campground facilities are available at Hugh White and George Payne Cossar state parks and Holly Springs National Forest. Autumn is the best time to see migratory shorebirds, winter is the best season to see concentrations of waterfowl, and spring is the best time to see and hear neotropical migratory songbirds.

Visitors are cautioned to be alert for venomous snakes, fire ants, chiggers, and ticks. Insect repellent is advised.

The fauna and flora that have been recorded on Tallahatchie Refuge are essentially the same as on Dahomey Refuge.

Lodgings and meals are available in such communities as Grenada, Greenwood, and Batesville.

Access to the refuge is west on State Route 8 from Grenada and through Holcomb. Just west of the junction with State Route 35, Route 8 borders and then cuts through the refuge.

Further information: Tallahatchie National Wildlife Refuge, c/o North Mississippi Refuges Complex, P.O. Box 1070, Grenada, MS 38901; telephone: (662) 226-8286.

Yazoo, consisting of 12,941 acres, was established in 1936 to restore and protect ecologically important bottomland hardwood forest, swampy bald cypress-tupelo brakes (thickets), bayous, sloughs, marsh, ponds, lakes, and impoundments. The refuge is located in the Lower Mississippi River Valley of west-central Mississippi.

The refuge's diversity of wildlife includes as many as 50,000 wintering geese, 100,000 wintering ducks, numerous neotropical migratory songbirds, the endangered Louisiana black bear, and alligators. More than 250 species of birds have been recorded here.

The U.S. Fish and Wildlife Service is working to reforest parts of this refuge that were previously cleared for agricultural development. Among the tree species being planted are a number of oak species, pecan, green ash, persimmon, and bald cypress. Some of the refuge's impoundment wetlands are regulated seasonally for the production of moist-soil plants that provide food for waterfowl and shorebirds. Other managed impoundments, known as green-tree reservoirs, are flooded in the autumn and winter for the benefit of wintering waterfowl. Many nesting boxes are provided for wood ducks. Under cooperative agreements, farmers leave a portion of their crops, such as corn, wheat, rice, milo, and soybeans, unharvested for the benefit of waterfowl.

Establishment of this refuge was made possible with revenues from the sale of Migratory Bird Hunting and Conservation Stamps (Duck Stamps). Ducks Unlimited, Inc. has helped enhance more than 400 acres of the refuge's wetland habitat.

Yazoo is open daily during daylight hours. There is no entrance fee.

Visitor activities include wildlife observation, photography, driving on designated refuge roads, hiking on dikes and levees, and hunting (deer and small game) on part of the refuge during the designated seasons. An annual hunting and fishing permit is required that also applies to four jointly managed national wildlife refuges—Hillside, Mathews Brake, Morgan Brake, and Panther Swamp (see separate texts). Although camping is not permitted on the refuge, campground facilities are available at nearby LeRoy Percy State Park. Because refuge waters are polluted with runoff from agricultural pesticides, Yazoo is closed to fishing. November through April are the best months for birdwatching.

Although alligators are generally afraid of people, visitors are cautioned to stay a safe distance from these sluggish-looking but potentially fast-moving reptiles and to be alert for venomous snakes, fire ants, chiggers, and ticks. Insect repellent is advised.

Lodgings and meals are available in Greenville and at Leroy Percy State Park.

Access to the refuge is 22 miles south from Greenville on State Route I, left into the refuge on Yazoo Refuge Road, and 3 miles to the refuge headquarters.

Further information: Yazoo National Wildlife Refuge, 728 Yazoo Refuge Road, Hollandale, MS 38748; telephone: (662) 839-2638.

Missouri

Big Muddy National Fish and Wildlife Refuge, containing more than 8,200 acres in six locations along the Missouri River, was established in 1994 "for the development, advancement, management, conservation, and protection of fish and wildlife resources." The Big Muddy Refuge has a land acquisition target of 60,000 acres of floodplain habitat along 367 miles of the river, from its confluence with the Kansas River near Kansas City to its junction with the Mississippi near St. Louis, Missouri. The vision for this refuge is not the creation of a single large block of habitat, but the inclusion of numerous separate units all linked by the Missouri River. Perhaps former refuge manager J.C. Bryant said it best, when he described his vision of the completed refuge as "habitat pearls on a string."

For many years, the refuge's staff will continue to focus on acquiring floodplain areas that have the potential for being reconnected with the Missouri, thereby allowing for the restoration of ecologically natural riverine processes. Initially, the refuge staff are managing six sites, the largest of which are the 2,050-acre OVERTON BOTTOMS UNIT in Cooper County; the 1,870-acre JAMESON ISLAND UNIT in Saline County; and the 2,014-acre LISBON BOTTOM UNIT in Howard County. Land acquisition will continue to be an integral and active part of Big Muddy Refuge's management program. Providing vital support and assistance are numerous individuals and a number of nonprofit organizations, such as the National Audubon Society, American Rivers, and Ducks Unlimited, Inc., as well as those urging protection of the historic route traversed by the Lewis and Clark Expedition from 1804 to 1806.

The Lisbon Bottom and Jameson Island units became part of the refuge following the Great Flood of 1993, which devastated much of this area's floodplain farmlands and agricultural levees. These units occupy an S-shaped loop, with the Lisbon area located immediately upstream and on the opposite riverbank from the Jameson area. Subsequent flooding in 1994 and 1995 created a new side channel on the Lisbon tract. Working with the U.S. Army Corps of Engineers, the refuge staff and other U.S. Fish and Wildlife Service biologists have been able to help the river expand rare habitat types including sandbars with shallow, slow-flowing water. The result has been a short stretch of the Missouri that functions at least somewhat in the way the entire free-flowing river once did, prior to the implementation of navigation and flood control projects in the late nineteenth and twentieth centuries. The recreation of some of these natural functions has led to a number of diverse interdisciplinary studies that have been undertaken by federal, state, and university researchers. The information being gathered and the lessons learned should prove enormously helpful in crafting restoration strategies for the Big Muddy Refuge, as well as elsewhere on this and other rivers.

The Friends of Big Muddy is a nonprofit support group that is assisting the refuge in a variety of ways.

Some of the refuge lands have been purchased with visitor access available from adjacent public roads, but others are accessible only by boat or by obtaining permission from adjoining landowners. The Fish and Wildlife Service cautions visitors that trespassing across private land to reach the refuge is illegal and could lead to prosecution. There is no refuge entrance fee.

Visitor activities include wildlife observation, photography, hiking, boating, fishing, and hunting during the designated seasons. Camping and horseback riding are not permitted on the refuge. Motorized vehicles are restricted to established public roads and parking areas.

Insect repellent is advised during the warmer months.

Lodgings and meals in the vicinity of the refuge are available in such communities as Columbia, Booneville, Glasgow, Arrow Rock, Rocheport, and Jefferson City.

Access to the Lisbon Bottom Unit is west from State Route 87, between Booneville and Glasgow.

Further information: Big Muddy National Fish and Wildlife Refuge, 4200 New Haven Road, Columbia, MO 65201; telephone: (573) 876-1826.

NOTE: Special appreciation is given to Thomas G. Bell, Refuge Manager, for providing this description.

Clarence Cannon, comprising 3,751 acres, was established in 1964. The refuge manages eco-logically important wetland impoundments, bottomland forest, grassland, and cultivated fields for the benefit of migratory birds, primarily waterfowl, wading birds, and shorebirds. It is lo-cated in the Mississippi River floodplain of eastern Missouri.

The refuge's most significant habitat management activity is the regulation of water levels in the impoundment units. As explained by the U.S. Fish and Wildlife Service:

Water is drained from impoundments in early summer to allow the natural regrowth of plants such as foxtail, millet, smartweed, and nutgrass. These impoundments (or moist soil units) are then flooded in the fall after the plants have produced seed. Migrating waterfowl find this combination of water and nat-ural seed source an irresistible invitation to feed and rest before continuing on their tiring journey.

Green-tree reservoirs (bottomland forests with large, cavity-ridden trees) are seasonally flooded and drained like the moist soil units. The abundant food supply and available nesting cavities make attractive feeding and spring nesting areas for wood ducks and other wildlife.

Other habitat management practices include mowing, discing, and periodic prescribed burning to maintain the health of grassland. In addition, a small amount of acreage is devoted to the cultivation of corn and wheat, to provide a supplemental source of food for waterfowl and other wildlife.

Prominent among the more than 230 kinds of birds that have been recorded on Clarence Cannon Refuge are the thousands of ducks of numerous species and the Canada and snow geese that pause here on their spring and autumn migrations. These impressive concentrations peak from March through April and from October through November. Bald eagles accompany the waterfowl to prey upon weak and dying birds. The largest numbers of migrating warblers and shorebirds normally come through the refuge during the end of April and early May.

Clarence Cannon Refuge is one of the few areas in Missouri where the state-endangered king rail is known to nest. This normally secretive marsh bird may be glimpsed along refuge roads in July or August, when it comes into the open to capture prey for its young.

Establishment of the refuge was made possible partly with revenues from the sale of Mi-gratory Bird Hunting and Conservation Stamps (Duck Stamps).

The refuge is open daily during daylight hours. There is no entrance fee. The refuge head-quarters is open on weekdays, except national holidays.

Visitor activities include birdwatching, photography, driving the refuge roads, and hiking. Fishing and hunting are not permitted on this refuge.

Insect repellent is advised during the warmer months.

Lodgings and meals are available in such communities as Louisiana, St. Peters, St. Charles, O'Fallon, Clarksville, Elsberry, Troy, and Bowling Green.

Access to Clarence Cannon Refuge from I-70 at St. Peters is north 35 miles on State Route 79 to Annada and east (right) 1 mile on County Road 206.

Further information: Clarence Cannon National Wildlife Refuge, c/o Great River NWR, P.O. Box 88, Annada, MO 63330; telephone (573) 847-2333.

Great River, containing 9,800 acres, was established in 1958 as the Annada District of Mark Twain National Wildlife Refuge. In 2000, these lands along the Mississippi River floodplain in northeastern Missouri and western Illinois were redesignated as the Great River National Wildlife Refuge. It continues the management of important wetland habitat for the benefit of migratory waterfowl and other wildlife. From north to south, the refuge consists of the 1,800-acre Fox Island Division in Clark County, Missouri (formerly called Gregory Landing); the 6,300-acre Long Island Division in Adams County, Illinois (formerly called the Gardner); and the 1,700-acre Delair Division in Pike County, Illinois.

Establishment of these refuge lands was made possible partly with revenues from the sale of Migratory Bird Hunting and Conservation Stamps (Duck Stamps).

The Fox Island and Long Island divisions of Great River Refuge are open daily during daylight hours. There is no entrance fee.

Visitor activities include birdwatching, photography, hiking, boating, fishing, and hunting during the designated seasons. Camping is permitted only at the U.S. Army Corps of Engineers' Bear Creek campground near the Long Island Division.

Insect repellent is advised during the warmer months.

Fauna and flora of these areas are essentially the same as those recorded on the Clarence Cannon National Wildlife Refuge.

Lodgings and meals are available in such communities as Louisiana and Hannibal, Missouri; Quincy, Illinois; and Keokuk, Iowa.

Access to these refuge lands is very difficult. Currently, no improved roads provide access to the flood-prone Fox Island Division. The Long Island Division is comprised primarily of a series of 22 large and small islands. There are no public use facilities maintained on the islands, but a primitive experience can be enjoyed by reaching the islands by boat. Nearby launch facilities are located at the Bear Creek and Canton Chute recreation areas and in the city of Canton. Poison ivy is abundant on the islands.

The Delair Division is closed year-round to public use, except for a limited deer hunt in January and scheduled environmental education activities.

Further information: Great River National Wildlife Refuge, P.O. Box 88, Annada, MO 63330; telephone: (573) 847-2333.

Middle Mississippi River (see text under Illinois)

Mingo, comprising 21,676 acres, was established in 1945 to restore and protect Mingo Swamp in southeastern Missouri. More than 7,700 acres of the refuge have been designated as the Mingo Wilderness, a unit of the National Wilderness Preservation System. In the early part of the twentieth century, largely unsuccessful efforts were made to drain this ecologically rich swamp, log off the timber, and convert the land to agricultural production.

However, as the U.S. Fish and Wildlife Service has described the swamp at the time it was acquired for the refuge:

The condition of the land was deplorable. In the previous 50 years, man had reduced a beautiful swamp, lush with the growth of plants and alive with animals, into a burnt and eroded wasteland.

Through careful management, most of the natural plants and animals were restored. Native trees have replaced much of the brush and briers, and a canoe trip down the Mingo River will now reveal little to the casual observer of the abuses to this land in years past. Deer, wild turkey, bobcat, and beaver have returned and are plentiful. The . . . refuge is now able to accomplish its primary objective; providing food and shelter for migratory waterfowl.

Mingo Refuge encompasses the only remaining large tract of the linear basin that was formed when the Mississippi River abandoned its former channel, roughly 18,000 years ago. In addition to its swamp and bottomland-forest habitat, the refuge also contains upland forests and fields, and rocky bluffs.

Establishment of the refuge was made possible partly with revenues from the sale of Migratory Bird Hunting and Conservation Stamps (Duck Stamps). The Midwest Interpretive Association is a nonprofit educational support group that is providing assistance to Mingo Refuge.

The refuge is open daily during daylight hours. An entrance fee is charged. The visitor center is open on weekdays, except national holidays; and weekends from March 1 through June 15 and from September 1 through November.

Visitor activities include birdwatching, photography, driving a seasonal auto tour route, hiking, canoeing, fishing, and hunting.

Hiking opportunities include the Boardwalk Nature Trail—a 1-mile (wheelchair-accessible) loop through bottomland hardwood forest; Bluff Trail—a 0.25-mile loop from the visitor center that provides views of steep former Mississippi River bluffs that border the swamp; and Hartz Pond Trail—a short path from the visitor center parking lot to a small lake and picnic area. Another 50 miles of refuge roads, dikes, and levees that are closed to motor vehicles are available for hiking from March 15 through September.

Visitors are cautioned to be alert for venomous snakes. Insect repellent is advised during the warmer months.

Lodgings and meals are available in such communities as Puxico, Wappapello, Poplar Bluff, and Dexter.

Access to Mingo Refuge from Poplar Bluff is east 14 miles on U.S. Route 60 and north (left) 11 miles on State Route 51; or from Dexter it is west 13 miles on U.S. Route 60 and north (right) 11 miles on State Route 51.

Further information: Mingo National Wildlife Refuge, Route 1, Box 103, Puxico, MO 63960; telephone (573) 222-3589.

Ozark Cavefish, containing 40 acres, was established in 1991 to protect Turnback Creek cave spring, which is the outlet of an underground stream that contains a population of endangered blind cavefish in southwestern Missouri. The refuge is not open to visitation.

Further information: Ozark Cavefish National Wildlife Refuge, c/o Mingo NWR, 24279 State Highway 51, Puxico, MO 63960; telephone: (573) 222-3589.

Pilot Knob, consisting of 90 acres, was acquired in 1987 by donation from the Pilot Knob Ore Company. The refuge is located on top of Pilot Knob Mountain in southeastern Missouri. Some abandoned iron ore mine shafts, dating from the mid-1800s, have created critical roosting habitat for the endangered Indiana bat as well as the little brown and long-eared bats. The refuge is not open to visitation.

Further information: Pilot Knob National Wildlife Refuge, c/o Mingo NWR, 24279 State Highway 51, Puxico, MO 63960; telephone: (573) 222-3589.

Squaw Creek, encompassing 7,350 acres, was established in 1935 to restore, enhance, and protect more than 3,000 acres of ecologically important wetland habitat for the benefit of migratory waterfowl and other wildlife. Initially called a "migratory waterfowl refuge," it is located along the bluffs-bordered eastern edge of the Missouri River floodplain, in the northwest corner of Missouri. Other habitats include 350 acres of moist-soil units; more than 1,500 acres of woodland; 2,000 acres of upland grassland, including small remnants of native tallgrass prairie; and more than 500 acres of cultivated cropland. More than 300 bird species have been recorded on the refuge.

The refuge attracts large concentrations of lesser snow geese—sometimes as many as 300,000 of them stopping to rest and feed during the autumn migration. Both the white and blue morphs (phases) make up this spectacular show, which peaks in November. Up to 100,000 migrating ducks of numerous species also pause at Squaw Creek Refuge, along with 1,000 or more American white pelicans. From mid-November into January, approximately 200 to 250 bald eagles commonly gather here, preying upon weak and dying waterfowl and roosting in the large cottonwood trees. This is one of the largest wintering eagle concentrations in the lower 48 states.

Management of Squaw Creek Refuge's wetlands is accomplished by a system of dikes, dams, and other water control structures—a few of which were built by the Civilian Conservation Corps in the mid-1930s. A dozen separately regulated areas of marsh habitat contain ten designated pools. Two of the refuge's impoundments are permanent pools, with such marsh vegetation as bulrushes, cattails, arrowhead, and American lotus (water lily), which provide important habitat for waterfowl, marsh and water birds, and muskrats. There are also two areas dedicated as habitat for the spring and autumn shorebird migrations.

Three other managed wetlands consist of moist-soil units. These areas are drawn down during the summer to promote the growth of plants that are an important source of food for ducks, and are then reflooded during the autumn waterfowl migration. Another impoundment consists of a moist-soil green-tree reservoir, an area of woodland that is seasonally flooded, for the benefit of such species as wood ducks.

In addition to the water regulation program for the maintenance of wetlands, the refuge's other habitat management activities include periodic prescribed burning, mowing, and haying, to maintain the health of grasslands and control the growth of invasive woody plants.

Under cooperative agreements with local farmers, corn and soybeans are cultivated in rotation, with wheat sown in the bean fields. Portions of these crops are left unharvested in the fields for the benefit of wildlife.

Establishment of the Squaw Creek Refuge was made possible partly with revenues from the sale of Migratory Bird Hunting and Conservation Stamps (Duck Stamps). The Friends of Squaw Creek National Wildlife Refuge is a nonprofit support group that is assisting the refuge in a variety of ways.

The refuge is open daily during daylight hours. There is no entrance fee. The refuge headquarters/visitor contact station is open on weekdays, except national holidays. Open house weekends for public visitation are held during spring and autumn migration periods. Volunteers, who staff the visitor contact station, provide information and conduct sales of educational materials.

Visitor activities include birdwatching, photography, viewing interpretive exhibits in the visitor contact station, environmental education programs for teachers and student groups, driving the 10-mile Wild Goose Interpretive Auto Tour Loop (but periods of rain can make refuge roads impassable), hiking, fishing, and hunting (a managed deer hunt to reduce an overpopulation) on part of the refuge during the designated seasons. Although camping is not permitted on the refuge, campground facilities are available at nearby Big Lake State Park.

An observation tower (wheelchair-accessible) overlooking 900-acre Eagle Pool provides an excellent opportunity for wildlife watching and photography. Hiking opportunities include the 0.25-mile (wheelchair-accessible) Mike Callow Memorial Trail, from refuge headquarters to the base of the loess bluff grasslands; the 0.5-mile Loess Bluff Interpretive Trail, near headquarters; and the 1.5-mile Eagle Pool Trail, between Eagle and Pelican pools. In early December, the refuge and the Missouri Department of Conservation cosponsor "Squaw Creek Eagle Days." This weekend event features special educational programs, displays, and eagle viewing opportunities.

Insect repellent is advised during the warmer months. Visitors are cautioned to be alert for rattlesnakes. The Fish and Wildlife Service also asks that special care be taken while driving on refuge roads, to avoid running over the state-listed endangered eastern massasauga. This species is described as "a small, timid rattlesnake that lives in the big river floodplains of northern Missouri. . . . Massasaugas are primarily encountered by visitors during the spring and fall."

Lodgings and meals are available in such communities as Mound City and St. Joseph.

Access to Squaw Creek Refuge from Exit 79 on Interstate 29 is west 2.5 miles on U.S. Route 159.

Further information: Squaw Creek National Wildlife Refuge, P.O. Box 158, Mound City, MO 64470; telephone: (660) 442-3187.

Swan Lake, containing 10,795 acres, was established in 1937 to restore, enhance, and protect ecologically important wetland and grassland habitats for the benefit of migratory waterfowl in north-central Missouri. According to the U.S. Fish and Wildlife Service, "this refuge has one of the largest concentrations of Canada geese in North America and is now the primary wintering area for the Eastern Prairie Population." There may be between 100,000 and 200,000 Canada geese here at one time, and perhaps as many as 75,000 wintering over.

Swan Lake also attracts at least 100,000 ducks of numerous species during autumn migration, with peak concentrations in November. As many as 150,000 snow geese and 1,000 to 2,000 American white pelicans also pause on the refuge. Up to 125 bald eagles normally accompany the influx of migrating waterfowl, to prey upon the weak and dying birds.

Restoration of wetland habitat and other improvements on the refuge were begun in the late 1930s by the Civilian Conservation Corps. Today, the refuge includes a great diversity of wildlife habitats. There are more than 3,800 acres of managed wetlands and moist-soil units, approximately 3,000 acres of open water, 600 acres of grassland, and nearly 1,500 acres of farmland, in which such crops as corn, sorghum, wheat, and clover provide a supplemental source of food for wildlife. The refuge also includes a 1,000-acre research natural area of riparian woodlands. As one of the very few remaining areas of old-growth bottomland hardwoods in this part of the state, it is being given special protection within the Yellow Creek watershed.

The refuge's staff works in close cooperation with the Missouri Department of Conservation. In addition, a number of nonprofit organizations, such as Quail Unlimited, National Audubon Society, and Ducks Unlimited, Inc. assist the refuge with volunteer staffing or technical support.

The refuge is open daily during daylight hours. There is no entrance fee. The visitor center is open on weekdays, except national holidays.

Visitor activities include birdwatching, photography, driving refuge roads, hiking (a short nature trail loops near the south shore of Swan Lake), and fishing. An observation tower, located just east of the visitor center, offers a panoramic view of Swan Lake.

To avoid disturbing the significant numbers of wintering geese, visitor access to the interior of the refuge, including the auto tour road, is permitted only from March 1 to October 15. Hunting is allowed on the refuge for a special primitive-weapons deer hunt and a public goose-hunting program. Camping is not permitted on the refuge, but campground facilities are available at Pershing State Park.

Insect repellent is advised during the warmer months.

More than 230 species of birds have been recorded on Swan Lake Refuge.

Lodgings and meals are available in such communities as Macon and Chillicothe.

Access to Swan Lake Refuge from Macon is west 40 miles on U.S. Route 36, south 7 miles on State Route 139 to Sumner, and south 1 mile on Swan Lake Drive to the refuge entrance.

Further information: Swan Lake National Wildlife Refuge, Route 1, Box 29A, Sumner, MO 64681; telephone: (660) 856-3323.

Two Rivers (see text under Illinois)

Montana:
National Wildlife Refuges

Benton Lake, comprising 12,383 acres, was established in 1929 to enhance and protect a 5,000-acre, closed-basin, cattail-and-bulrush marsh that is surrounded by a mountain-framed expanse of gently rolling, shortgrass prairie, just north of Great Falls, in north-central Montana. The refuge is a mecca for large concentrations of migratory and nesting waterfowl, shorebirds, and other water birds. Over 200 bird species have been seen here.

During the spring and autumn migrations, as many as 5,000 tundra swans, 100,000 snow and Ross's geese, 20,000 Canada geese, 100,000 ducks, 50,000 shorebirds, and some bald eagles and peregrine falcons pause at Benton Lake's marsh. As early as mid-March, large concentrations of tundra swans, pintails, and mallards arrive as the lake's ice is melting. During the summer months, an average of 20,000 ducklings of a dozen species are hatched—twice that number in especially favorable years. Species that nest in colonies, such as Franklin's gulls and eared grebes, raise their young here.

The star attraction of the grassland habitat is the sharp-tailed grouse. Males perform their incredible courtship displays in the spring (described in the Medicine Lake text). Observation blinds are available in April and May for viewing and photographing the grouse (reservations required). Other common grassland wildlife includes pronghorn, badgers, burrowing owls, horned larks, and chestnut-collared longspurs.

During the first 28 years of the refuge's existence, this priceless wetland habitat was unfortunately dry more often than it contained water. In 1957, thanks largely to the urging of the Cascade County Wildlife Association, congressional funding was obtained, by which the marsh became a more consistently wet habitat. A pump and pipeline were constructed that brought Muddy Creek water to the refuge, and dikes were built, dividing the marsh into sections for easier water level management.

Subsequently, the U.S. Fish and Wildlife Service has divided the marsh still further, into eight diked units, and has installed an interior pumping system. These improvements have resulted in enhanced water management that promotes the growth of submergent and emergent aquatic plants for the benefit of water birds and other wildlife. This enhanced water management flexibility also enables the refuge to control outbreaks of botulism—an often fatal poisoning of water birds caused by a toxin that is produced by the bacterium *Clostridium botulinum.*

Areas of former farmlands have been restored to a mixture of grasses and forbs, providing nesting habitat for waterfowl and other species. Roughly once every decade, these areas are revitalized by such management tools as haying, prescription burning, grazing, and reseeding.

Four mountain ranges provide a distant scenic backdrop for this refuge. To the west are the Rocky Mountains, to the east the Highwoods, to the southeast the Little Belts, and to the south the Big Belts.

Establishment of Benton Lake Refuge was made possible partly with revenues from the sale of Migratory Bird Hunting and Conservation Stamps (Duck Stamps). Ducks Unlimited, Inc., has helped with a number of important habitat enhancement projects, including the construction of several water control structures.

The refuge is open daily during daylight hours. There is no entrance fee.

Visitor activities include wildlife observation, photography, driving the refuge's 9-mile Prairie Marsh Wildlife Drive and Lower Marsh Road (the latter rough road is open from July 15 through September), hiking on a short trail and elsewhere, and limited hunting (waterfowl and upland game birds) on part of the refuge during the designated seasons. In winter, refuge roads are not plowed beyond the headquarters. Although camping is not permitted on the refuge, campground facilities are available in Great Falls and in the Lewis and Clark National Forest.

Visitors are cautioned to be alert for prairie rattlesnakes, and for the possibility of sudden weather changes and extremely strong Chinook winds that frequently blow across from the Rocky Mountains in spring and autumn. Insect repellent is advised during the warmer months.

Lodgings and meals are available in Great Falls.

Access to Benton Lake Refuge from Great Falls is north about 1 mile on U.S. Route 87, and left onto Bootlegger Trail (at the refuge directional sign).

Further information: Benton Lake National Wildlife Refuge, 922 Bootlegger Trail, Great Falls, MT 59404; telephone: (406) 727-7400.

Black Coulee, containing 1,494 acres, was established in 1938 to enhance and protect a small area of predominantly upland grassland habitat and a small reservoir for migratory birds, about 38 miles to the northwest of Bowdoin National Wildlife Refuge in northeastern Montana. Wildlife species and visitor activities are much the same as on Bowdoin (see the text for that refuge), with which it is jointly administered.

Lodgings and meals are available in Malta and Harlem.

Access to Black Coulee Refuge (located to the north of U.S. Route 2 and the Fort Belknap Indian Reservation) is north and northeast about 24 miles from Harlem on a paved road, and then south (right) 5 miles on a gravel road to the refuge entrance.

Further information: Black Coulee National Wildlife Refuge, c/o Bowdoin NWR Complex, HC 65, Box 5700, Malta, MT 59538; telephone: (406) 654-2863.

Bowdoin, consisting of 15,552 acres, was established in 1936 to enhance and protect an ecologically significant area of lakes, ponds, marshes, shelterbelts, and prairie grassland for migratory birds in northeastern Montana. The refuge's open water and wetland habitats attract large concentrations of migratory waterfowl and shorebirds, with as many as 1,000 tundra swans and 30,000 ducks and geese pausing here in the autumn to rest and feed.

Numerous species nest and raise their young here. White pelicans, Caspian terns, ring-billed and California gulls, great blue herons, and cormorants nest on islands in 5,459-acre Lake Bowdoin. Fifteen species of ducks, including mallards, green-winged and blue-winged teal, shovelers, and gadwalls nest and raise their young here. In good years, up to 100 broods of Canada geese are hatched at nest sites placed on muskrat houses or on human-made islands and structures. Nesting in the cattail and bulrush marshes are grebes, bitterns, coots, rails, and colonies of black-crowned night herons, white-faced ibises, and Franklin's gulls.

The sharp-tailed grouse is an important inhabitant of Bowdoin Refuge's grasslands. In early spring, they perform elaborate courtship displays on their dancing grounds, known as leks. They begin at the first light of day and increase in tempo with sunrise. The cocks fan their tails, vibrate their outstretched wings, rattle the quills of their wing feathers, and rapidly shuffle and stamp their feet. As if possessed, these pale, brown-speckled birds rush about, leaping wildly over each other and fighting. They make cackling sounds and repeatedly inflate a pair of lavender air sacs on their necks. Lowering their heads and forcing the air out of the sacs, they create a low coo-oo-ing sound that can be heard across the prairie.

Prior to establishment of Bowdoin Refuge, the lakes and ponds that were replenished by flood waters from Beaver Creek, which has headwaters in the Little Rocky Mountains, would shrink to shallow, disease-infested, stagnant pools of hot water during this arid region's long, dry summers. Thousands of waterfowl and other birds were consequently poisoned and killed in epidemics of botulism caused by a toxin that is produced by the bacterium, *Clostridium botulinum*.

Responding to this serious botulism problem, the U.S. Fish and Wildlife Service constructed a system of dikes, ditches, and other water control structures with which to manage water levels with greater flexibility. And in exchange for agency funds to help build the U.S. Bureau of Reclamation's Fresno Dam (nearly 100 miles upstream), the refuge received rights to 3,500 acre-feet of water annually to supplement the spring runoff.

Establishment of this refuge complex was made possible partly with revenues from the sale of Migratory Bird Hunting and Conservation Stamps (Duck Stamps). Ducks Unlimited, Inc. has provided funds and staff efforts toward habitat enhancement.

The refuge is open daily during daylight hours. There is no entrance fee. The headquarters is open on weekdays, except national holidays.

Visitor activities include birdwatching; photography; driving the 15-mile self-guiding tour road that loops around Lake Bowdoin (an auto tour guide is available); hiking; boating and canoeing during the waterfowl hunting season (motors greater than 10 hp are not permitted; a boat-launching ramp is provided near headquarters); and hunting (waterfowl and upland game birds) on parts of the refuge during the designated seasons. Camping is not permitted on the refuge, but campground facilities are available in the community of Malta and at Nelson Reservoir State Recreation Area.

Visitors are cautioned to be alert for prairie rattlesnakes, and for the possibility of sudden weather changes and strong Chinook winds in the spring and autumn. Insect repellent is advised during warmer months. Over 260 bird species have been seen here.

Lodgings and meals are available in Malta, Saco, and Glasgow.

Access to Bowdoin Refuge is 1 mile east of Malta on U.S. Route 2, and right (at the refuge directional sign) onto County Route 2 for 6 miles to the headquarters.

Further information: Bowdoin National Wildlife Refuge, HC 65, Box 5700, Malta, MT 59538; telephone: (406) 654-2863.

Charles M. Russell, containing 1.1 million acres, was established in 1936 as the Fort Peck National Game Range and redesignated in 1976 as the Charles M. Russell (CMR) National Wildlife Refuge. It encompasses a 125-mile stretch of Fort Peck Lake and the Missouri River, upstream from Fort Peck Dam in north-central Montana. From 1933 to 1939, this earth-filled dam was constructed by the U.S. Army Corps of Engineers and the Public Works Administration to serve as a flood control and navigation enhancement project. Its waters inundated about 245,000 acres of river, riparian habitat, and lower tributary valleys.

The refuge is named for the cowboy artist Charles Russell (1864-1926), who arrived in Montana at the age of 16, was employed as a range rider and herder, and lived with and deeply respected the Native Americans. In numerous watercolor and oil paintings, as well as bronze sculptures, he dramatically portrayed the wildlife, Indians, cowboys, and magnificent landscapes of this region.

The refuge overlays the huge Fort Peck reservoir and protects a variety of adjacent ecologically significant habitats: prairie grassland, wooded coulees, river bottom (riparian) woodlands, and colorful and scenically spectacular eroded breaks, mesas, and badlands. The steep-sided Missouri River Breaks were created over a long period of geologic time by the river as it cut a deep, winding channel into a relatively flat plain and by side drainages dropping down to meet the river and eroding steep ravines and gullies, known as coulees.

Upstream from the reservoir, the western end of the refuge contains an inspiringly beautiful, 35-mile, free-flowing stretch of the Missouri. The upper dozen miles of this part of the river (upstream from the U.S. Route 191 bridge) are within the lower end of the specially designated, 149-mile Upper Missouri National Wild and Scenic River. This area provides outstanding opportunities for float trips by canoe and raft. For information on the latter, visitors are urged to contact the U.S. Bureau of Land Management, P.O. Box 1160, Lewistown, MT 59457; telephone: (406) 538-7461.

From 1804 to 1806, the 29-man Corps of Discovery, under the leadership of Meriwether Lewis and George Rogers Clark, carried out the instructions of President Thomas Jefferson, "to explore the Missouri river, & such principal stream of it, as, by its course & communication with the waters of the Pacific Ocean, may offer the most direct & practicable water communication across this continent, for the purposes of commerce." The Lewis and Clark Expedition journeyed up the Missouri on a 55-foot-long keelboat with a large square sail and 22 oars, and on two smaller, canoe-like pirogues, with sails and seven oars. In the stretch of river that is within today's CMR Refuge, the explorers camped at 16 sites on the nights of May 9 through 24, 1805.

Today, except for the reservoir, the refuge contains much the same landscapes as seen and described by the Lewis and Clark Expedition. The area is dominated by four main vegetative types. Nearly two-thirds of the refuge land consists of sagebrush-greasewood-grassland. About one-third is the ponderosa pine-juniper. Less than a mere 2 percent is grassland-deciduous shrub. And less than 1 percent of the land consists of the ecologically rich, riparian-deciduous habitat of cottonwoods and willows, along the river bottom and in the coulees.

Although grizzly bears and bison (buffalo) no longer inhabit this part of Montana, visitors can still see elk (reintroduced from Yellowstone National Park in the early 1950s), deer, pronghorn, Rocky Mountain bighorn sheep (introduced in 1980; the original Audubon bighorn became extinct), beavers, and prairie dogs. Large numbers of sharp-tailed grouse and greater sage-grouse perform their incredible courtship rituals in the spring (see expanded description of sharp-tail grouse courtship in the Bowdoin text and of sage-grouse in the Seedskadee, Wyoming, text).

The CMR Refuge is open daily. There is no entrance fee. Refuge headquarters, located on Airport Road in Lewistown, is open on weekdays, except national holidays. Some of the land along the north shore of the reservoir, including the peninsula within the lake's large U-turn, lies within the UL Bend National Wildlife Refuge. Much of this area has been established as the UL Bend Wilderness, a unit of the National Wilderness Preservation System. This area is often one of the best places to see sage-grouse.

Visitor activities include wildlife observation; photography; driving the 20-mile, gravel, self-guiding tour drive (an interpretive pamphlet is available) and numerous dirt roads (many of the latter require a high-clearance four-wheel-drive vehicle); hiking (no established trails); horseback riding; camping (throughout the refuge, at James Kipp Recreation Area, and at a number of Corps of Engineers recreation area campgrounds); boating (boat ramps are provided); river rafting and canoeing; fishing; and hunting (elk, white-tailed deer, mule deer, pronghorn, bighorn sheep, coyote, waterfowl, dove, and upland game birds) on parts of the refuge during the designated seasons. Over 235 bird species use the refuge.

Visitors are cautioned to be alert for western (prairie) rattlesnakes and for the possibility of rapid weather changes and very strong Chinook winds in the spring and autumn, and are encouraged to carry sufficient water, especially when backpacking in the remote backcountry.

Lodgings and meals are available in such communities as Lewistown, Malta, Glasgow, and Jordan.

Access to the entrance of CMR Refuge's 20-mile graveled auto tour road from Lewistown is north 67 miles on U.S. Route 191; or from Malta it is south 66 miles on route 191. To reach Fort Peck Dam, it is south 15 miles on paved State Route 24 from U.S. Route 2 at Glasgow; or from State Route 200, it is north 60 miles on route 24. A paved road leads to Flat Lake Recreation Area, and a number of unpaved, backcountry routes lead to Hell Creek and Devils Creek recreation areas on the south shore of the reservoir from State Route 200 in the vicinity of Jordan; to Crooked Creek Recreation Area on the south shore from state routes 200 and 19; to Fort Peck, The Pines, and Bone Trail recreation areas on the north shore from near the dam; and to Fourchette Creek Recreation Area on a number of roads from U.S. Route 2.

Further information: Charles M. Russell National Wildlife Refuge, P.O. Box 110, Lewistown, MT 59457; telephone: (406) 538-8706.

Creedman Coulee, comprising 2,728 acres, was established in 1941 to enhance and protect a small area of open water, marsh, sagebrush coulee, and grassland habitats for migratory birds close to the United States–Canada border crossing at Port of Willow Creek, in north-central Montana. This refuge is about 15 miles to the northwest of Lake Thibadeau National Wildlife Refuge, both of which are administered jointly with Bowdoin NWR.

The wildlife species and visitor uses are much the same as those on Bowdoin (see the text for that refuge), except that most of this refuge's acreage is privately owned and managed by the U.S. Fish and Wildlife Service under the terms of perpetual conservation easement agreements. Permission is required from the local landowners for visitor access onto these private lands.

Lodgings and meals are available in Havre and Chinook.

Access to Creedman Coulee is north about 30 miles on State Route 233 from U.S. Route 2 at Havre.

Further information: Creedman Coulee National Wildlife Refuge, c/o Bowdoin NWR Complex, HC 65, Box 5700, Malta, MT 59538; telephone: (406) 654-2863.

Hailstone, encompassing 1,988 acres, was established in 1942 to enhance and protect important wetland and surrounding shortgrass prairie located about 28 miles northwest of Billings in south-central Montana. Most of the refuge's acreage is managed under the terms of perpetual conservation easement agreements with a local landowner. The refuge is adjacent to a 1,828-acre U.S. Fish and Wildlife Service-owned waterfowl production area.

Hailstone Lake, which occupies a shallow basin, was enlarged to about 300 acres when an earthen dike was constructed by the Work Projects Administration in the 1930s. Because saline-rich mudflats around the lakeshore create alkaline water conditions, the lake attracts water birds that are relatively salt-tolerant, such as wigeons, shovelers, eared grebes, avocets, and Wilson's phalaropes. In late July and early August, flocks of Franklin's gulls also come to the lake.

Some of the refuge's surrounding uplands were previously farmed, and these lands have been restored to prairie grasses. Inhabiting the uplands are such species as pronghorn, coyote, black-tailed prairie dog, burrowing owl, lark bunting, and prairie rattlesnake. A prairie dog town is located along the eastern side of the lake.

Rock outcroppings of a ridge rising prominently along the southern edge of the refuge are a scenic highlight of the area.

Hailstone Refuge is open daily during daylight hours. There is no entrance fee. No visitor use facilities are provided.

Visitor activities include birdwatching; photography; hiking; and hunting (pronghorn, waterfowl, and upland game birds) during the designated seasons.

Visitors are cautioned to be alert for rattlesnakes, especially on and around the rocky ridge and for the possibility of rapid weather changes and very strong Chinook winds in the spring and autumn.

Lodgings and meals are available in such communities as Columbus, Billings, Big Timber, and Roundup.

Access to Hailstone Refuge from I-90 at Columbus is north nearly 25 miles on County Road 306 to Rapelje; east (right) 4 miles on the Rapelje-Molt road; and north (left) 1.5 miles on Hailstone Basin Road.

White terns, Hawaiian Islands NWR. Robert Shallenberger photo

Spinner dolphin, Midway Atoll NWR. Robert Shallenberger photo

Kayaking, Midway Atoll NWR. Robert Shallenberger photo

Albatross display, Midway Atoll NWR. Robert Shallenberger photo

Eastern monk seal, Midway Atoll NWR. Robert Shallenberger photo

Great frigatebird, Midway Atoll NWR. Robert Shallenberger photo

Albatross, Midway Atoll NWR. Robert Shallenberger photo

Palmyra Atoll NWR. Robert Shallenberger photo

Palmyra Atoll NWR. Robert Shallenberger photo

Rose Atoll NWR. Robert Shallenberger photo

Canada goose in nest basket, Kootenai NWR, Idaho

Cypress trees and "knees," Cypress Creek NWR, Illinios

Wood ducks, Muscatatuck NWR, Indiana

Snow geese at sunset, DeSoto NWR, Iowa

Ring-necked pheasant, Quivara NWR, Kansas

American bittern swallowing a snake, Rachel Carson NWR, Maine

Bayou Sauvage NWR, Louisiana

Lacassine NWR, Louisiana

Vose Pond beaver lodge, Moosehorn NWR, Maine.
Tim Cooper photo

Water control structure at Moosehorn NWR, Maine.
U.S. Fish and Wildlife Service photo

Petit Manan NWR, Maine

Observation Deck, Rachel Carson NWR, Maine

Rachel Carson NWR

Sunkhaze Meadows NWR, Maine

Bald eagles at sunset, Blackwater NWR, Maryland

Delmarva Fox Squirrel, Eastern Neck NWR, Maryland

National Wildlife Visitor Center, Patuxent NWR, Maryland

Gray Seals, Monomoy NWR, Massachusetts

Seney NWR, Michigan

Common Loon, Seney NWR

Spruce Grouse, Seney NWR, Michigan

Red fox pups, Agassiz NWR, Minnesota

Agassiz NWR, Minnesota

Rice Lake NWR, Minnesota

Beaver activity, Rice Lake NWR

Mingo NWR, Missouri

Mingo NWR

Bald eagle, Squaw Creek NWR

Bald eagle viewing, Squaw Creek NWR, Missouri

Charles M. Russell NWR, Montana

Lee Metcalf NWR, Montana

Elk in silhouette, National Bison Range, Montana

National Bison Range

Red Rock Lakes NWR

Yellow-headed blackbirds, Red Rock Lakes NWR, Montana

Further information: Hailstone National Wildlife Refuge, c/o Charles M. Russell NWR, P.O. Box 110, Lewistown, MT 59457; telephone: (406) 538-8706.

Halfbreed Lake, consisting of 4,318 acres, was established in 1942 to enhance and protect important habitat for concentrations of migratory waterbirds and other wildlife located within Stillwater County in south-central Montana. The refuge was in private ownership until 1987, when the land was acquired by the U.S. Fish and Wildlife Service. A proposal to obtain funding for wildlife observation facilities has been prepared but is not yet approved.

Three extensive areas of wetland habitat are joined by Cedar Creek: semi-permanent, 248-acre Halfbreed Lake, with a mixture of open water and emergent wetland vegetation; and the less permanent 375-acre Grass Lake and 220-acre Goose Lake, both with expanses of submergent vegetation. These wetlands are a mecca—when there is sufficient water—for great numbers of waterfowl and shorebirds. Some of them pause to rest and feed during spring and autumn migrations, and others nest and raise their young here. The greatest influx of waterfowl is generally during April and October—a few hundred Canada geese typically gather on the refuge in July and August, and shorebird concentrations usually peak in May and August.

Upland shortgrass prairie, which surrounds these lakes, consists of such species as western wheatgrass, prairie junegrass, and greasewood and provides habitat for a variety of wildlife, including pronghorns, coyotes, black-tailed prairie dogs, greater sage-grouse, burrowing owls, and prairie rattlesnakes.

Establishment of Halfbreed Refuge was accomplished with the assistance of Ducks Unlimited, Inc. and The Nature Conservancy.

The refuge is open daily during daylight hours. There is no entrance fee. No visitor use facilities are provided. Visitor use of Halfbreed Refuge is limited to birdwatching and hiking.

Access to the refuge from I-90 at Columbus is north nearly 25 miles on County Road 306 to Rapelje, east (right) 7 miles on the Rapelje-Molt Road, and then south (right) 1 mile.

Further information: Halfbreed National Wildlife Refuge, c/o Charles M. Russell NWR, P.O. Box 110, Lewistown, MT 59457; telephone: (406) 538-8706.

Hewitt Lake, containing 1,680 acres, was established in 1938 to enhance and protect a small area of former river oxbow ponds, marsh, and grassland for migratory birds in northeastern Montana. It is located about 7 miles north of Bowdoin National Wildlife Refuge, with which it is jointly administered. Wildlife species and visitor uses are much the same as on Bowdoin (see the text for that refuge), although permission is required from the local landowners to access the private lands within the refuge.

Lodgings and meals are available in Malta and Saco.

Access to Hewitt Lake Refuge from U.S. Route 2 at Saco is north 5 miles on Route 243, and then west (left) 3 miles on a gravel road to the entrance.

Further information: Hewitt Lake National Wildlife Refuge, c/o Bowdoin NWR, HC 65, Box 5700, Malta, MT 59538; telephone: (406) 654-2863.

Lake Mason, comprising 11,204 acres in three contiguous units, was established in 1941 to enhance and protect a lake and areas of shortgrass prairie, and contains the "premier migratory bird area in central Montana." It is located about 60 miles south of the western end of the Charles M. Russell National Wildlife Refuge, with which it is jointly managed. The refuge is open daily during daylight hours. There is no entrance fee.

The 3,721-acre LAKE UNIT contains 1,288-acre Lake Mason, which, in wet years, attracts large concentrations of migratory Canada geese, ducks and shorebirds. The best months for seeing migratory waterfowl are usually April and October, and the best for migratory shorebirds are usually May and August. This lake, occupying a natural shallow basin, was enlarged in 1937 in a federal Work Projects Administration project, by diverting water from Willow Creek. During dry years, the lake contains little or no water.

Most of the lands surrounding the lake are shortgrass prairie. This habitat, containing such grasses as needle-and-thread, western wheatgrass, blue grama, and prairie junegrass, is inhabited by such species as pronghorns, coyotes, badgers, and black-tailed prairie dogs. In addition, several former agricultural fields have been seeded to provide dense wildlife nesting cover.

Visitor activities on the LAKE MASON UNIT include birdwatching, wildlife photography, hiking on an access trail, nonmotorized boating and canoeing (a primitive boat-launching site is provided), and hunting during the designated seasons. The northern part of the Lake Mason Unit is closed to public use.

Visitors are cautioned to be alert for western (prairie) rattlesnakes and for the possibility of rapid weather changes and very strong Chinook winds in the spring and autumn.

Access from the north side of Roundup to the Lake Mason Unit is south 1 block on Fourth Street West from U.S. Route 87; west (right) 6.5 miles on Golf Course Road; and north (right) 3 miles.

The 2,160-acre WILLOW CREEK UNIT contains shortgrass prairie habitat. A majority of this unit's acreage was homesteaded and devoted to raising livestock and growing grain crops during the early twentieth century. As a result of the hardships during the Depression of the 1930s, the land was abandoned, and ownership reverted to the federal government. Today, the U.S. Fish and Wildlife Service manages the grassland with livestock grazing for the benefit of such species as the endangered mountain plover, black tailed prairie dogs, and burrowing owls.

Visitor activities in the Willow Creek Unit include wildlife observation, photography, hiking, and hunting (pronghorn, deer, waterfowl, and upland game birds) during the designated seasons. No visitor facilities are provided on this unit. Visitors are cautioned to be alert for prairie rattlesnakes.

Access from Roundup to the Willow Creek Unit is north 11.8 miles on U.S. Route 87, and west (left) 13.8 miles on Snowy Mountain Road.

The 5,323-acre NORTH UNIT contains areas of shortgrass prairie-covered ridgetops and flats, and alluvial draws with a mixture of sagebrush and grassland. Early twentieth-century homesteaders plowed the ridgetops to grow small-grain crops. As a result of the hardships during the Depression of the 1930s, these lands were abandoned, and ownership reverted to the federal government. The former farm fields have grown back to prairie grassland. Today, this unit's habitats support such species as pronghorns, sage-grouse, upland sandpipers, long-billed curlews, golden eagles, and chestnut-collared longspurs.

Visitor activities include wildlife observation, photography, hiking an access trail, and hunting during the designated seasons. Visitors are cautioned to be alert for prairie rattlesnakes (a subspecies of the western rattlesnake).

Lodgings and meals are available in Roundup, Lewiston, and Billings.

Access from Roundup to the North Unit is north 11.8 miles on U.S. Route 87, west (left) 6.9 miles on Snowy Mountain Road, north (right) 7.2 miles on Graves Road, and west (left) 2.2 miles on the road to the entrance.

Further information: Lake Mason National Wildlife Refuge, c/o Charles M. Russell NWR, P.O. Box 110, Lewistown, MT 59457; telephone: (406) 538-8706.

Lake Thibadeau, encompassing 4,040 acres, was established in 1937 to enhance and protect an area containing ponds, marsh, and grassland habitats for migratory birds in north-central Montana. This refuge is about 15 miles to the southeast of Creedman Coulee National Wildlife Refuge and about 87 miles to the west-northwest of Bowdoin National Wildlife Refuge, with which they are both jointly administered. Wildlife species and visitor uses are much the same as on Bowdoin (see the text for that refuge).

Nearly all of this refuge's acreage is privately owned and managed by the U.S. Fish and Wildlife Service under the terms of perpetual conservation easement agreements with local landowners. There is no public access onto this refuge.

Further information: Lake Thibadeau National Wildlife Refuge, c/o Bowdoin NWR, HC 65, Box 5700, Malta, MT 59538; telephone: (406) 654-2863.

Lamesteer, consisting of 800 acres, was established in 1942 to protect important wetland habitat in northeastern Montana. The U.S. Fish and Wildlife Service has acquired only the water rights with which to manage the impounded waters of a 110-acre marsh for the benefit of waterfowl and other wildlife. This refuge's acreage is managed under the terms of perpetual conservation easement agreements with local landowners. There is no public access.

Further information: Lamesteer National Wildlife Refuge, c/o Medicine Lake NWR, 223 North Shore Road, Medicine Lake, MT 59247; telephone: (406) 789-2305.

Lee Metcalf, containing 2,800 acres, was established in 1963 to enhance and protect an ecologically important area of Bitterroot River bottomland, nestled within the spectacularly scenic, mountain-framed Bitterroot Valley of western Montana. This refuge includes ponds, sloughs, meadows, marsh, and woodlands of pine and riparian cottonwoods. These habitats attract a great diversity of wildlife, including numerous migratory birds and a nesting pair of bald eagles. To the west, the rugged, snow-capped Bitterroot Mountains rise dramatically from this long, narrow valley, and along the east are the Sapphire Mountains.

The refuge is named for former United States congressman and senator Lee Metcalf, who for many years was an outstanding congressional leader in promoting wildlife conservation legislation. In the words of author James B. Trefethen in his book, *An American Crusade for Wildlife*, published in 1975 by the Boone and Crockett Club, Missoula, MT:

The [Eisenhower Administration's] Republican choice for Secretary of the Interior was Douglas McKay, a wealthy automobile dealer . . . whose sole qualification for office was a substantial contribution to the Republican war chest. One of McKay's first steps was to introduce the spoils system to the U.S. Fish and Wildlife Service. . . .

As a result of the Administration's threats to dedicated wildlife lands, Congressman Lee Metcalf of Montana introduced a bill early in 1956 to exempt the national wildlife refuges from oil and gas exploration. Metcalf was joined by Congressman Henry S. Reuss of Wisconsin and Senator Hubert Humphrey of Minnesota, who introduced identical bills to stay McKay's open-handed generosity. These three congressional leaders became the nucleus of a conservation bloc that thwarted the virtual dismantling of the American conservation system under McKay's leadership.

Seven years later, the then United States senator was instrumental in the establishment of the Ravalli National Wildlife Refuge. In 1978, this refuge was renamed to honor the late senator for his many years of conservation accomplishments.

Among the more prominent wildlife of the Lee Metcalf Refuge are waterfowl such as Canada geese and twenty species of ducks. Ospreys, wintering bald eagles, magpies, white-tailed deer, and moose also inhabit the refuge. Ospreys and Canada geese may be seen nesting atop dead pine and cottonwood trees. Over 230 birds species use the refuge.

Managing the refuge's fishery resources is another priority for the benefit of many fish-eating birds, such as the osprey, bald eagle, and great blue heron. Other management programs include controlling a number of non-native, noxious plant species such as hound's tongue (*Cynoglossum officinale*), with periodic prescription burns, mowing, reseeding, and grazing.

One of the refuge's native wildflowers is the attractive but rarely seen bitterroot (*Lewisia rediviva*). This neat little low-growing plant, with bright rose, pink, or white blossoms, is the official Montana state flower. Its generic Latin name honors the Lewis and Clark Expedition's Captain Meriwether Lewis, who collected samples of the plant as he journeyed down the Bitterroot Valley on September 9–11, 1805. Its species Latin name means "revived" or "brought to life." This plant was once gathered for its edible, starchy root by the Salish-speaking Native Americans who formerly lived in this valley.

Of historical interest is the Whaley Homestead, a white clapboard house built here by early settlers in 1885. This unusual house is a hand-hewn log structure that is sided over to give the appearance of a more expensive frame home.

Establishment of this refuge was made possible partly with revenues from the sale of Migratory Bird Hunting and Conservation Stamps (Duck Stamps). Ducks Unlimited, Inc. has assisted with important habitat enhancement projects.

The refuge is open daily during daylight hours. There is no entrance fee.

Visitor activities include wildlife observation, photography, driving the refuge road to the Whaley Homestead historic site and to the 160-acre Bitterroot River Recreation Area, hiking, educational programs at a teaching pavilion, picnicking at a (wheelchair-accessible) picnic area by the river, fishing along the river and within the sloughs (a wheelchair-accessible wildlife viewing and fishing deck overlooks one of the sloughs), and hunting of deer (bow-and-arrow) and waterfowl on parts of the refuge during the designated seasons (two wheelchair-accessible blinds are available). Although camping is not permitted on the refuge, campground facilities are available in the nearby Bitterroot National Forest.

Hiking opportunities include more than 2 miles of nature trails in the recreation area that wind through riparian woodland and meadows and along sloughs, and the 0.5-mile (wheelchair-accessible) trail that runs between the parking area and the picnic area.

Visitors are cautioned to stay an especially safe distance from the high, fast-moving floodwaters of the river during springtime.

Lodgings and meals are available in such communities as Stevensville, Hamilton, Darby, and Missoula.

Access to the Lee Metcalf Refuge is south about 25 miles on U.S. Route 93 from Missoula, left (east) onto the road across the river to Stevensville, left (north) onto East Side Highway (State Route 203), and left (west) onto Wildfowl Lane (at the refuge sign); or north 114 miles on U.S. Route 93, over 6,995-foot Lost Trail Pass, from Salmon, Idaho to the Stevensville turnoff. Refuge headquarters is located at 115 West Third Street, Stevensville.

Further information: Lee Metcalf National Wildlife Refuge, P.O. Box 247, Stevensville, MT 59870; telephone: (406) 777-5552.

Lost Trail, comprising 9,325 acres, was established in 1999 to enhance and protect ecologically important migratory bird habitats on a former cattle and horse ranch within Pleasant Valley in northwestern Montana. This scenically beautiful, montane-valley refuge includes 160-acre Dahl Lake, subirrigated wet meadows of largely reed canary grass (*Phalaris arundinacea*), a mosaic of upland prairie grasslands of native and non-native grasses, and surrounding forested lower mountain slopes. Elevations range from 3,488 to 4,600 feet above sea level.

Cattle ranching on the former Lost Trail Ranch dated back to the late 1800s. In 1996, the property was acquired by the Montana Power Company to partially satisfy a "mitigative settlement order." This order was issued by the Federal Energy Regulatory Commission to mitigate environmental impacts and wildlife losses on the Flathead Waterfowl Production Area that are attributable to past and future operations of the Kerr Dam. In 1999, MPC conveyed approximately 3,100 acres of the ranch to the Fish and Wildlife Service, which then acquired the remaining ranch acreage with funding from the Migratory Bird Conservation Fund and the Land and Water Conservation Fund.

The refuge is open daily during daylight hours. There is no entrance fee. The refuge headquarters is open on weekdays, except national holidays.

Visitor activities include wildlife observation, photography, hiking, environmental interpretation, fishing, and hunting.

Lodgings and meals are available in Kalispell.

Access to the Lost Trail Refuge from Kalispell is west 21 miles on U.S. Route 2, right (northwest) at Marion onto Pleasant Valley Road, and bearing right at the road fork at 1.3 miles. At the northern end of Bitterroot Lake, Pleasant Valley Road becomes a dirt road that soon crosses Haskill Pass at 5 miles from Marion; continue about 8 miles from the pass to the refuge boundary, and another 7 miles to refuge headquarters.

Further information: Lost Trail National Wildlife Refuge, 6295A Pleasant Valley Road, Marion, MT 59925; telephone: (406) 858-2216.

Medicine Lake, encompassing 31,660 acres in two units, was established in 1935 to enhance and protect an ecologically important prairie pothole area of lakes and ponds, impoundments, marshes, brush-covered coulees (ravines), cultivated lands, and gently rolling prairie grasslands in the northeastern corner of Montana. The refuge provides vital resting and nesting habitats for a great diversity of waterfowl and other wildlife.

The northern unit consists of 8,200-acre Medicine Lake, a number of smaller lakes and ponds, and numerous potholes. In 1976, the 11,360-acre Medicine Lake Wilderness was established, providing additional protection for the lake, its islands, and an adjacent 2,320-acre area of sandhills. The latter gently rolling hills support a diversity of prairie flora: native grasses, cacti, chokecherry, buffaloberry, snowberry, and various wildflowers. The southern unit contains a 1,280-acre impoundment known as Homestead Lake, and surrounding upland prairie.

Medicine Lake Refuge's marsh and open-water habitats are a mecca for thousands of waterfowl during spring and autumn migrations. Mallards, blue-winged teal, gadwalls, shovelers, lesser scaup, and ruddy ducks are generally in the greatest abundance. Some of the ducks nest on the refuge, annually raising as many as 30,000 ducklings. More than 1,000 Canada geese reside on the refuge, raising around 900 goslings each year. Medicine Lake's Big Island supports one of the nation's largest American white pelican rookeries, with more than 10,000 birds. More than 2,000 young are raised here annually. Refuge islands offer nesting habitat for other species, including herons, gulls, shorebirds, and cormorants. As many as 30 pairs of the endangered piping plover breeds on the refuge. And in October, thousands of sandhill cranes pause in the refuge vicinity on their southward migration.

Prominent among the prairie grasslands wildlife is the sharp-tailed grouse. In early spring, they perform elaborate courtship displays on the refuge's numerous dance grounds, known as leks. They begin at the first light of day and increase in tempo with sunrise. The cocks fan their tails, vibrate their outstretched wings, rattle the quills of their wing feathers, and rapidly shuffle and stamp their feet. As if possessed, these pale, brown-speckled birds rush about, leaping wildly over each other and fighting. They make cackling sounds and repeatedly inflate a pair of lavender air sacs on their necks. Lowering their heads and forcing the air out of the sacs, they create a low coo-oo-ing sound that can be heard across the prairie. The refuge provides a viewing blind (reservations advised) so that visitors can see and photograph these birds' incredible ritual.

From 1937 to 1941, the Civilian Conservation Corps (CCC) completed a number of refuge enhancement projects such as dams, dikes, roads, buildings, fences, and shelterbelts. Today, the U.S. Fish and Wildlife Service manages a series of impoundments, canals, and other water control structures that help maintain and enhance water quality and water bird habitat. The refuge has created wildlife nesting cover on nearly 3000 acres of former agricultural lands. And under cooperative agreements, a portion of grain crops, planted on certain refuge lands by nearby farmers, is left unharvested for the benefit of waterfowl and other wildlife.

During periods of drought, the refuge waters and concentrations of water birds are greatly diminished. In the words of the Fish and Wildlife Service:

Though large-scale drought can be devastating to waterfowl populations, this drying of wetland basins [potholes] is very important to maintain the productivity of the wetlands. Nutrients that are accumulated in dead plant matter decompose in the presence of oxygen and return to the soil. With the return of the wet cycle comes an increased growth of aquatic vegetation and invertebrates, both a prime food source for waterfowl.

Establishment of Medicine Lake Refuge was made possible partly with revenues from the sale of Migratory Bird Hunting and Conservation Stamps (Duck Stamps). Ducks Unlimited, Inc. has contributed funds and staff efforts toward the restoration and enhancement of the refuge's wildlife habitats. Because the Fish and Wildlife Service could not acquire the subsurface mineral rights when the refuge was established, oil and gas development by the owner of those rights occurs on Medicine Lake Refuge.

The refuge is open daily during daylight hours. There is no entrance fee. The headquarters is open on weekdays, except national holidays.

Visitor activities include birdwatching; photography; driving a self-guiding auto tour route; viewing the refuge and wildlife from an observation platform; hiking; picnicking (a picnic area is available); boating (motors not permitted on Medicine Lake, and landing on the lake's islands is prohibited) and canoeing; fishing; trapping; and hunting (deer, waterfowl, and upland game birds, but not tundra swans or sandhill cranes) on parts of the refuge during the designated seasons. Camping is not permitted on the refuge. May to October are usually the best months for seeing wildlife. Over 225 bird species have been recorded here.

Visitors are cautioned to be alert for the possibility of rapid weather changes and strong Chinook winds in the spring and autumn. Insect repellent is advised during the warmer months.

Lodgings and meals are available in Culbertson and Plentywood, and meals are available in the town of Medicine Lake.

Access to Medicine Lake Refuge is north from U.S. Route 2 at Culbertson 25 miles on State Route 16, right at a refuge directional sign, and east 2 miles to headquarters.

Further information: Medicine Lake National Wildlife Refuge, 223 North Shore Road, Medicine Lake, MT 59247; telephone: (406) 789-2305.

National Bison Range, consisting of 18,560 acres, was established in 1908 to help save the American bison (buffalo) from extinction. Located in northwestern Montana, this refuge consists of steeply rolling hills that are predominantly covered with prairie grasslands, scattered areas of ponderosa pines and Douglas-firs on some of the higher slopes, occasional groves of quaking aspens, several ponds, and a number of streams. Some of the latter flow intermittently, but others—notably Mission Creek—are permanent and are bordered by lush riparian wetlands, thickets, and woodlands. These habitats support a great diversity of wildlife, including more than 210 species of birds that have been recorded here. Elevations on the Range extend from 2,582 to 4,885 feet above sea level.

The bison was once one of the world's most abundant large mammals. Population "guesstimates" range from 30 to 60 or 70 million, or even as many as 100 million, of them inhabiting the vast prairie grasslands of the Great Plains and ranging far to the east of the Mississippi River and west of the Rocky Mountains. As Euro-American civilization pushed westward across the continent, the vast, seemingly endless herds were slaughtered.

As Victor H. Cahalane wrote in his book, *Mammals of North America*:

By 1820 not a bison was left east of the Mississippi River. Through the fifties and sixties the slaughter went on. With the Civil War out of the way, the nation turned to the West. Like slender steel tentacles, the transcontinental railroads stretched toward the Rockies and out through the buffalo range. They brought men to slaughter buffalo. . . .

Buffalo Bill Cody contracted to supply the Kansas Pacific construction crews. . . . In eighteen months Cody killed four thousand two hundred and eighty animals and earned the nickname which became world famous. Railroads advertised special excursions, "with refreshments," and practically guaranteed a kill from the [railroad] car windows. . . . By 1889 [William T.] Hornaday was able to account for only five hundred and forty-one buffaloes remaining alive in the United States.

The greater number of these millions of slaughtered buffaloes were wasted. Many were killed merely for their hides, or for their tongues alone. Thousands were shot for sport and never touched. Buffaloes in the northern plains region killed for the express purpose of destroying the principal food supply of the Sioux, the Crows, and other tribes, in order to starve them off the warpath. Soon the grasslands were empty. The hordes of big game had vanished, and only their bones lay bleaching in the sunshine.

Responding to this dramatic decline in the latter half of the nineteenth century, Congress passed legislation in 1893 that banned the hunting of a remnant wild band of bison still surviving in Yellowstone National Park. Toward the end of the century, a number of fenced, zoo-like wildlife parks were created in the eastern United States for captive herds—notably one in New Hampshire that grew to hold nearly 100 animals.

During the first several years of the twentieth century, concerned individuals and groups began advocating a bison protection program. Prominent among the organizations were the New York Zoological Society and the Boone and Crockett Club, which joined to advocate setting aside a bison reserve in the Wichita Mountains of Oklahoma. In 1905, President Theodore Roosevelt signed into law a measure authorizing this area within the Wichita National Forest Reserve "for the protection of game animals and birds and be recognized as a breeding place thereof." Later that year, the president signed an executive order redesignating the area as the Wichita National Game Reserve (see the Wichita Mountains Wildlife Refuge text). After the area was fenced, the New York Zoological Society donated 15 purebred Great Plains bison as the nucleus of the reserve's breeding stock.

Still later that same year, the American Bison Society was founded to help promote the bison restoration program. Its president was Dr. William T. Hornaday, who was also the director of the New York Zoological Society and who, back in 1887, had tallied only 541 free-roaming bison remaining in the United States.

Three years later, only about 20 free-roaming bison and a few hundred others in captivity remained in the United States. At that time, the American Bison Society succeeded in obtaining congressional authorization, signed by President Theodore Roosevelt, to purchase land from the "Confederated Tribes of the Flathead, Kootenai and Pend d'Oreille" (Flathead Indian Reservation) in Montana to establish a national refuge specifically for the bison—"a permanent national bison range."

The American Bison Society then sponsored a fund-raising campaign, which raised $10,000, including nickels and dimes from schoolchildren, for the purchase of a nucleus breeding herd. In 1909, after the refuge lands were fenced, 34 bison were purchased from the privately owned Conrad herd near Kalispell, Montana. Six more animals were donated to the federal government—two from the Conrad herd, one from the Goodnight herd in Texas, and three from the Blue Mountain Forest Association's Austin Corbin herd in New Hampshire.

The following year, Dr. Hornaday enthusiastically wrote in a report for the American Bison Society:

The American people have thus become owners in perpetuity of what we believe to be the richest and the most beautiful grazing grounds ever trodden by bison hoofs. We have seen the best portions of the American great buffalo plains all the way from Texas panhandle to the sweet grass hills of northern Montana, and for abundance of rich grass, pure water, winter shelter, picturesque interior and picturesque surroundings, the Montana National [Bison] Range is absolutely beyond compare.

Today, there are more than 250,000 bison in North America. Of that population, between 350 and 500 of these great mammals range across the hills of the National Bison Range. The U.S. Fish and Wildlife Service carries out a program of rotational grazing, so that no part of the range becomes overgrazed. To keep the population from exceeding the habitat's carrying capacity, surplus animals are rounded up annually and sold or donated, to provide breeding stock for other public and private herds. In addition, animals are donated to the Inter-Tribal Bison Cooperative, to help promote the restoration of bison herds on Native American lands.

Other ungulates inhabiting this refuge are about 130 elk (this species was introduced here from Wyoming and Idaho between 1911 and 1916); from 40 to 50 bighorn sheep (introduced here from the Canadian Rockies in 1922); from 150 to 200 white-tailed deer (first introduced here in 1910); from 200 to 300 mule deer (introduced here from Yellowstone National Park in 1918); about 100 pronghorns (introduced here beginning in 1951); and from 14 to 18 mountain goats (introduced here from the Sun River area of Montana, in 1964). Like the bison, the numbers of these species are managed to maintain an ecologically sound balance between all these grazers and the forage of native bunchgrasses and forbs. Excess animals are transplanted to other places.

The National Bison Range's management programs also include testing to control diseases in the bison herd, and controlling non-native noxious plants to help maintain a healthy grassland ecosystem. Where feasible, insects are used that feed only on specific weed species.

The National Bison Range is open daily during daylight hours. There is an entrance fee during the summer season. The visitor center is open daily from mid-May through September and on weekdays during the rest of the year, except for national holidays.

Visitor activities include wildlife observation; photography; viewing interpretive exhibits in the visitor center; student environmental educational programs; driving the range's roads; hiking (only on several short designated trails); picnicking (a day use area is provided a short distance from the visitor center); and fishing (along certain stretches of Mission Creek and Jocko River, with a joint State of Montana-Flathead Reservation Use and Conservation Permit and joint Fishing Stamp, under the State-Tribal Cooperative Agreement). Camping is not permitted on the range, but campground facilities are available near St. Ignatius, Ravalli, and Ronan; at five state recreation areas around Flathead Lake; and in Lolo National Forest. Hunting is not permitted on the range.

The range's gravel tour roads are the 5-mile West Loop and Prairie Drive, which are open all year (winter weather permitting); and the 19-mile, one-way Red Sleep Mountain Drive, which is open from mid-May to late October. As the latter road contains numerous switchbacks and steep grades, vehicles more than 32 feet in length and trailers are not permitted. From late October to mid-May, a 10-mile stretch of Prairie Drive and Red Sleep Mountain Drive is open, weather permitting.

The designated hiking trails are the 0.25-mile Grassland Trail at the visitor center; a paved (wheelchair-accessible) loop around a pond near Mission Creek and a slightly longer loop that branches from the latter paved path and follows a short stretch of Mission Creek near the visitor center; and the 0.5-mile Bitterroot Trail and 1-mile High Point Trail at two interpretive stops along Red Sleep Mountain Drive.

Visitors are warned: "Bison can be very dangerous. Keep your distance." Consequently, among the regulations: "Remain at your car and on the road. If you are near bison, do not get out of your vehicle. Hiking is permitted only on designated footpaths." Visitors are also cautioned to be alert for western (prairie) rattlesnakes.

Lodgings and meals are available in such communities as St. Ignatius, Polson, Missoula, and Kalispell.

Access to the National Bison Range is 8 miles west on I-90 from Missoula to Exit 96, north 27 miles on U.S. Route 93 to Ravalli, west (left) 6 miles on State Route 200 to Dixon, north (right) 4 miles on Route 212 to Moiese, and east (right) at the refuge sign.

Further information: National Bison Range, 132 Bison Range Road, Moiese, MT 59824; telephone: (406) 644-2211.

Ninepipe, containing 2,062 acres, was established in 1921 to enhance and protect open water and marsh habitats of an irrigation reservoir and a surrounding narrow area of grassland in the Flathead Valley of northwestern Montana. The reservoir's wetland provides important nesting, feeding, and resting areas for an abundance of waterfowl, especially Canada geese, mallards, teal, pintails, shovelers, gadwalls, wigeons, redheads, and ruddy ducks, and some tundra swans.

This refuge is situated on Tribal Trust Lands of the Confederated Salish and Kootenai Tribes, in the Flathead Indian Reservation. In 1910, the acreage now within the refuge was withdrawn to create an agricultural irrigation water storage project. As the U.S. Fish and Wildlife Service has acquired the rights relating only to the management of wildlife and its habitat,

Ninepipe is an "easement" refuge, operated under an agreement with the Bureau of Indian Affairs-Flathead Irrigation Project and the Confederated Salish and Kootenai Tribes. Consequently, water levels greatly fluctuate with seasonal needs for irrigation water. At full pool, Ninepipe Reservoir covers more than 1,600 acres.

The refuge's habitat enhancement programs, for which Ducks Unlimited, Inc. has provided assistance, include the construction and maintenance of islands for nesting water birds, planting of cover crops and food crops for the benefit of grasslands birds, and periodic prescribed burns to revitalize vegetation that provides brooding habitat and browse for geese.

The road over the main dam is open daily to visitors, during daylight hours. Other parts of the refuge are closed during the nesting season (March 1 to July 15) and during the waterfowl hunting season. There is no entrance fee.

Visitor activities include birdwatching; photography; driving (a short unpaved road from U.S. Route 93 ends at the refuge boundary, where there is a wildlife viewing area that was jointly created by the Fish and Wildlife Service, the Montana Department of Fish, Wildlife and Parks, and the Confederated Salish and Kootenai Tribes); hiking (a short interpretive trail leads along the east shore of the reservoir); and fishing (the refuge is open to shoreline fishing from mid-July until the waterfowl hunting season; fishing from the main reservoir dam is allowed to continue during the hunting season; part of the refuge is closed during the nesting season, from March 1 to mid-July; the refuge is closed to fishing, as posted, when the reservoir's level is drawn below a certain point; and a joint State of Montana-Flathead Reservation Use and Conservation Permit and joint Fishing Stamp, under the state Tribal Cooperative Agreement, is required).

Boats and flotation devices are not permitted on the reservoir. Although camping is not allowed on the refuge, campground facilities are available close by and at a number of state recreation areas around Flathead Lake. And although hunting is not permitted on this refuge, opportunities are available on adjacent state wildlife management lands. The best months for seeing large concentrations of waterfowl at Ninepipe are from late March to early May and from early October through November. Waterfowl nesting runs from April to July.

Lodgings and meals are available in such communities as St. Ignatius, Polson, and Missoula.

Access to this refuge from Missoula is west 8 miles on I-90 to Exit 96, and north about 40 miles on U.S. Route 93; or from Polson south about 20 miles on U.S. Route 93.

Further information: Ninepipe National Wildlife Refuge, c/o National Bison Range, 132 Bison Range Road, Moiese, MT 59824; telephone: (406) 644-2211.

Pablo, comprising 2,541 acres, was established in 1921 to enhance and protect open water and marsh habitats of an irrigation reservoir and a surrounding narrow area of grassland in the Flathead Valley of northwestern Montana. The reservoir's wetland provides important nesting, feeding, and resting areas for an abundance of waterfowl, especially Canada geese, mallards, teal, pintails, shovelers, gadwalls, wigeons, redheads, and ruddy ducks, and some whistling swans. More than 180 species of birds have been recorded here and on nearby Ninepipe Refuge.

This refuge is situated on Tribal Trust Lands of the Confederated Salish and Kootenai Tribes, in the Flathead Indian Reservation. In 1910, the acreage now within the refuge was withdrawn to create an agricultural irrigation and flood control water storage project. As the U.S. Fish and Wildlife Service has acquired the rights relating only to the management of wildlife and its habitat, Pablo is an "easement" refuge, operated under an agreement with the Bureau of Indian Affairs-Flathead Irrigation Project and the Confederated Salish and Kootenai Tribes. Consequently, water levels greatly fluctuate with seasonal needs for irrigation water. At full pool, Pablo Reservoir covers more than 1,800 acres.

The refuge's habitat enhancement programs, for which Ducks Unlimited, Inc. has provided assistance, include the construction and maintenance of islands for nesting water birds, planting of cover crops and food crops for the benefit of grasslands birds, and periodic prescribed burns to revitalize vegetation that provides brooding habitat and browse for geese. A small grove of cottonwood trees at the north end of the refuge and willow thickets around some of the shoreline offer habitat for a variety of migratory songbirds and other wildlife.

The refuge is open daily during daylight hours, except during the waterfowl hunting season. There is no entrance fee.

Visitor activities include birdwatching, photography, driving and hiking (on roads across the dam and along the northern end of the refuge), and fishing (a joint State of Montana-Flathead Reservation Use and Conservation Permit and joint Fishing Stamp, under the state Tribal Cooperative Agreement, is required). Part of the refuge, as posted, is open to shoreline fishing except during the waterfowl hunting season, and is closed to fishing when the reservoir's level is drawn below a certain elevation.

Boats and flotation devices are not permitted on the reservoir. Although camping is not allowed on the refuge, campground facilities are provided close by and at a number of state recreation areas around Flathead Lake. And although hunting is not permitted on the refuge, opportunities are available on adjacent state wildlife management lands. The best months for seeing large concentrations of waterfowl at Pablo are from late March to early May and from early October through November. Waterfowl nesting runs from April to July.

Birds and mammals of Pablo Refuge are virtually the same as at nearby Ninepipe Refuge. Over 185 bird species have been recorded on the two refuges.

Lodgings and meals are available at such communities as Polson, St. Ignatius, Missoula, and Kalispell.

Access to this refuge from Missoula is west 8 miles on I-90 to Exit 96, and north about 65 miles on U.S. Route 93; or from Polson south about 3 miles on U.S. Route 93.

Further information: Pablo National Wildlife Refuge, c/o National Bison Range, 132 Bison Range Road, Moiese, MT 59824; telephone: (406) 644-2211.

Red Rock Lakes contains 45,597 acres in the upper Centennial Valley of southwestern Montana. The refuge was established in 1935 to help rescue from extinction the then-vanishing and nearly extinct trumpeter swan (*Cygnus buccinator*)—America's largest waterfowl. With white plumage and a black bill, it measures as much as 5 feet long and has an 8-foot wingspread. The bird is named for its clear, resonant, French horn-like trumpeting note that carries great distances.

This remote, mountain-framed refuge enhances and protects a great diversity of ecologically significant marsh-prairie-alpine habitats near the headwaters of the Missouri River and below the Continental Divide. Upper and Lower Red Rock lakes, marshy Swan Lake, and a number of smaller ponds provide major waterfowl habitats on the refuge. There are also many dashing streams, riparian and willow-bog wetlands, and subirrigated meadows (fens), as well as sagebrush- and grassland-covered foothills, numerous stands of quaking aspens, and conifer forests on the lower mountain slopes of the rugged Centennial Mountains. With elevations ranging from 6,600 to just under 10,000 feet, the area also extends well up the north slope of the mountains, where wind-sculpted clumps of firs are scattered across the open expanses of alpine meadows. In addition, trumpeter swans are attracted to two impounded warm-water springs that remain partially open during the winter, at which time visitor access to these ponds is not permitted to avoid disturbing the swans.

During the nineteenth century, commercial harvesting, subsistence hunting, and loss of habitat devastated the swan populations in the United States and Canada. Wildlife experts warned that this species was on the brink of extinction and would likely soon disappear. Small flocks of Rocky Mountain trumpeters remained only in remote places of the northern Rockies region, notably in the vicinity of Yellowstone National Park, including Red Rock Lakes. (Subsequently, an Alaskan swan population was discovered, most of which were inhabiting wilderness lakes in what is now the Kenai National Wildlife Refuge.) The Rocky Mountain birds, some of which breed in Canada, dwindled to around 200 swans. In 1932, a survey of breeding trumpeters within the Greater Yellowstone Ecosystem in Montana, Wyoming, and Idaho, tallied only 69. When the refuge was established, there were fewer than 50 swans inhabiting the Red Rock Lakes.

As the result of successful conservation efforts spanning many subsequent decades, trumpeter swans breeding in the Greater Yellowstone region now total nearly 500 birds, with an average of 100 on and in the vicinity of Red Rock Lakes Refuge. Nesting begins in May, with muskrat houses frequently used as nest sites. About a month after incubation begins, the eggs hatch, and the cygnets soon leave the nest to swim. Four months later, they are able to fly. In the autumn, around 2,000 swans migrate south from Canadian breeding grounds, joining the resident birds in and around Yellowstone for the winter.

Wildlife experts believe, however, that expanding the swans' wintering range from the relatively small, high-elevation Yellowstone region is essential to the long-term survival of this species. Consequently, in recent years, a joint federal-state-private Rocky Mountain Trumpeter Swan Expansion Program relocated more than 1,000 trumpeters from Red Rock Lakes Refuge and elsewhere in the hope that these efforts will restore the swans' historic, expanded migration patterns to warmer wintering habitat. Their range formerly reached from interior Canada to the Mississippi Delta, and from the northwestern United States to the Gulf Coast of Texas and Mexico.

Rocky Mountain trumpeter swans now nest and winter on such other national wildlife refuges as the National Elk Refuge and Seedskadee, in Wyoming; Lacreek, in South Dakota; Grays Lake and Camas, in Idaho; Ruby Lake, in Nevada; and Malheur, in Oregon; as well as in Yellowstone and Grand Teton national parks, Idaho's Harriman State Park, and elsewhere.

Other prominent wildlife on Red Rock Lakes Refuge includes moose, pronghorns, white-tailed and mule deer, white pelicans, numerous species of ducks, and sandhill cranes. The male cranes perform their remarkable, high-stepping courtship rituals in the spring.

A wide variety of habitat management programs are carried out on Red Rock Lakes Refuge. The U.S. Fish and Wildlife Service carefully manages the refuge's water, to ensure favorable nesting habitat for the trumpeter swans and other waterfowl. Periodic prescribed burns help maintain the health of forage for the elk, mule deer, and other grazers and to provide favorable habitat of mixed shrubs and grasses for numerous nesting birds and other wildlife. Extensive, dense willow thickets are maintained to provide moose forage and habitat for many other species.

Ducks Unlimited, Inc. has assisted with important habitat enhancement projects on more than 1,500 acres of the refuge. Another nonprofit organization, the National Park Trust, saved from residential development an ecologically important 40-acre area of wetland along the Red Rock River and near Shambow Lake. This parcel, which has been added to the refuge, is rated as one of the most significant natural landscapes in Montana because of its intact ecosystems, expansive wetlands, and diversity of native fauna and flora, including a concentration of rare species.

Red Rock Lakes is open on weekdays, except national holidays. There is no entrance fee. Much of the refuge has been established as a unit of the National Wilderness Preservation System—one of the system's very few marshland wilderness areas.

Visitor activities include wildlife observation; photography; driving refuge roads; hiking (two former roads are designated for short hikes; but no trails within the wilderness area); bicycling; nonmotorized boating in designated areas (canoeing, kayaking, and rowboating; launching sites on Upper and Lower Red Rock lakes); picnicking; camping (two primitive campgrounds are available on a first-come, first-served basis, with wheelchair-accessible facilities at Upper Lake Campground); fishing; and hunting (waterfowl hunting on Lower Red Rock Lake) during the designated season. The best months to view swans and other wildlife are June through September. Over 230 bird species have been seen here.

Visitors are urged to be prepared for cold and wet weather at this high altitude; boaters are cautioned to be alert for sudden storms and strong winds; and hikers are advised to stay clear of sinkholes and other potentially hazardous boggy areas. Insect repellent is recommended during the warmer months.

Lodgings and meals are available in such communities as West Yellowstone, Dillon, and Ennis, Montana and St. Anthony, Idaho.

Access to Red Rock Lakes Refuge is east 28 miles on a partially graveled dirt road from I-15 at Monida, Montana; or west for about 12 miles on U.S. Route 20 from West Yellowstone, northwest (right) for about 5 miles on Idaho Route 87, south (left at the Sawtell historical marker) on a paved road (passing Henry's Lake State Park) for about 5 miles, and west (right) on the Red Rock Pass Road (an improved dirt road that crosses over this 7000-foot-elevation pass into Montana) for about 25 miles to the refuge entrance.

Access to Red Rock Lakes is seasonal, and roads are open as weather allows. Summer rains sometimes make access difficult or impassable, and snow frequently blocks the access route in winter (except for snowmobiles). The road from Monida to the refuge is usually open from around mid-April (although difficult for passenger cars until around mid-May) until sometime in November. The road across Red Rock Pass is generally open from around mid-May to November. Visitors are advised to check on road conditions and to fill up the fuel tank before heading for the refuge.

> Further information: Red Rock Lakes National Wildlife Refuge, 27820 Southside Centennial Road, Lima, MT 59739; telephone: (406) 276-3536.

Swan River, encompassing 1,568 acres, was established in 1973 to enhance and protect an area of marsh, riparian woodland, and grassland along the Swan River and around the south (upper) end of Swan Lake in northwestern Montana. This refuge is located in mountain-framed Swan Valley, with the Mission Range to the west and the Swan Range to the east. It provides important habitats for a diversity of wildlife including elk, moose, deer, black and grizzly bears, beavers, and numerous waterfowl. In autumn, tundra swans are commonly on the refuge.

Swan River formerly meandered through its floodplain. Silt deposits, however, have since forced it to flow along the west side of the refuge, creating a series of oxbow sloughs within the refuge. Most of the floodplain consists of reed canary grass habitat, with cottonwood trees along the riverbanks. Over 170 bird species have been recorded here.

Establishment of this refuge was made possible partly with revenues from the sale of Migratory Bird Hunting and Conservation Stamps (Duck Stamps). This area was added to the National Wildlife Refuge System at the request of United States Senator Lee Metcalf of Montana (see the Lee Metcalf National Wildlife Refuge text for further information on this distinguished senator who was deeply committed to wildlife conservation).

The refuge is open daily during daylight hours. There is no entrance fee.

Visitor activities include birdwatching, photography, hiking on and wildlife viewing from Bog Road (a route not recommended or maintained for vehicles), boating and canoeing through the refuge on the river, fishing (on the river year-round and on Spring Creek except from March 1 to mid-July), and hunting (waterfowl only) on part of the refuge during the designated season. Although camping is not permitted on the refuge, campground facilities are available at a number of state recreation areas around Flathead Lake and elsewhere.

Lodgings and meals are available in such communities as Bigfork and Kalispell.

> Access to this refuge from Kalispell is south 8 miles on U.S. Route 93 from Kalispell, left (east) for about 5 miles on State Route 82, right (south) about 2 miles on State Route 35, and left (east and then south) 23 miles on State Route 83 to the refuge; or from Missoula east 6 miles on I-90 to Exit 109, east 32 miles on State Route 200, and left (north) 72 miles on State Route 83 to the refuge.

> Further information: Swan River National Wildlife Refuge, c/o National Bison Range, 132 Bison Range Road, Moiese, MT 59824; telephone: (406) 644-2211.

UL Bend, consisting of 58,400 acres, was established in 1969 to protect part of the central part of the north shore of Fort Peck Lake on the Missouri River, in central Montana. The refuge is bounded by the U-turn of the reservoir on the south, and by the Charles M. Russell (CMR) National Wildlife Refuge on the east and west.

This refuge is for the most part less accessible than the CMR lands. About 20,000 acres of the refuge has been established as the UL Bend Wilderness, a unit of the National Wilderness

Preservation System. Many of the species of fauna and flora, and the refuge regulations, are the same as on the CMR. It is often one of the best places to see sage-grouse, and large herds of pronghorns winter here.

Further information: UL Bend National Wildlife Refuge, c/o Charles M. Russell NWR, P.O. Box 110, Lewistown, MT 59457; telephone: (406) 538-8706.

War Horse, comprising 3,192 acres in three tracts, was established in 1958 to protect ecologically important habitats for migratory birds and other wildlife in central Montana. It is located about 30 miles south of the western end of the Charles M. Russell National Wildlife Refuge, with which it is jointly administered. The refuge lands were formerly homestead properties that were abandoned during the hardships of the Depression in the 1930s, with ownership reverting back to the federal government.

The WILD HORSE LAKE UNIT consists of a natural shallow basin that is frequently dry. When it is filled with water, which is usually during the spring, it attracts great numbers of migratory waterfowl and shorebirds. The surrounding arid upland is predominantly covered with sagebrush and is inhabited by such species as sage-grouse and pronghorns.

Access to the Wild Horse Unit is east 11 miles on State Route 200 from Grass Range to the old community of Teigen; north (left) 10 miles on Blakeslee Road to a four-way junction; and east 1.5 miles.

The WAR HORSE LAKE UNIT contains a natural shallow basin that is frequently dry. When it is filled with water from sufficient watershed runoff, this lake produces submergent vegetation and attracts concentrations of waterfowl and shorebirds. The surrounding arid upland is predominantly covered with sagebrush and is inhabited by sage-grouse and pronghorns.

This unit also boasts an area of stunted, slow-growing ponderosa pines along the southern shore of War Horse Lake. This is an unusual acid shale-pine forest association that has been found at only a few scattered places in central and eastern Montana.

Access to the War Horse Unit is east 11 miles on State Route 200 from Grass Range to the old community of Teigen; north (left) about 6.5 miles on Blakeslee Road (the lake is then visible, to the east); and at a cement bridge, east on a dirt trail to the lake.

The YELLOW WATER RESERVOIR UNIT consists of a state-owned reservoir constructed for agricultural irrigation. Shallow mudflats around the western end of the reservoir that produce some emergent vegetation, as well as shallow-water and deep-water habitats, attract concentrations of waterfowl and shorebirds. The reservoir is stocked annually with trout. Two separate refuge tracts consist of small areas of upland habitat.

Access to the Yellow Water Reservoir Unit is south just over 7 miles on State Route 244 from State Route 200 near Winnett, and west (right) 6 miles on Yellow Water Road (a gravel road) to the reservoir.

The refuge is open daily during daylight hours. There is no entrance fee. No visitor use facilities are provided.

Visitor activities include wildlife observation, photography, hiking, and hunting during the designated seasons. Boating and canoeing are also permitted on the Yellow Water Reservoir Unit, where a small boat-launch site is available. Visitors are cautioned to be alert for prairie rattlesnakes.

Lodgings and meals are available in Lewiston and Roundup.

Further information: War Horse National Wildlife Refuge, c/o Charles M. Russell NWR, P.O. Box 110, Lewistown, MT 59457; telephone: (406) 538-8707.

Montana:
Wetland Management Districts

Benton Lake Wetland Management District was established in 1975 to initiate the Small Wetlands Acquisition Program in north-central Montana. Stretching across 10 counties, the district is spread over 25,000 square miles, an area roughly the size of West Virginia. The district's mission has evolved since its inception, from focusing on only waterfowl and associated wetland and grassland ecosystems to a broader focus that includes protecting habitat important to all federal trust species.

The district includes 22 federally owned waterfowl production areas (WPAs), totaling approximately 15,000 acres. More than 56,000 additional acres are protected under the terms of perpetual conservation easements purchased from willing sellers.

Several of Benton Lake district's WPAs contain unique characteristics. Jarina WPA is located only 4 miles off the east front of the Rocky Mountains. Winds here frequently exceed 90 MPH. Large numbers of trumpeter and tundra swans use the wetlands to rest on their spring and fall migrations. Elk use the area as wintering and calving grounds. Grizzly bears have been documented here, as well as on the Blackfoot Valley, Kleinschmidt Lake, and H2-O WPAs. Several pairs of burrowing owls nest on the Kingsbury Lake WPA, and sandhill cranes nest on several of these areas. The wetlands of Blackfoot Valley are magnificently framed by the high peaks along the Continental Divide of the Rocky Mountains to the northeast and the Garnett Range to the southwest.

The WPAs are open daily during daylight hours. There are no entrance fees or visitor use facilities. Visitor activities include birdwatching, photography, and hiking. Hunting is allowed during the designated seasons on all WPAs, except H2-O and Sands. Camping and motorized vehicle use off established trails is prohibited.

Conservation easements are located throughout the district. Conservation easements are voluntary agreements with private landowners, whereby the U.S. Fish and Wildlife Service purchases certain rights to protect habitat while the land remains in private ownership. As these easement areas are privately owned, public access is controlled by each individual landowner.

Further information: Benton Lake Wetland Management District, 922 Bootlegger Trail, Great Falls, MT 59404; telephone: (406) 727-7400.

Bowdoin Wetland Management District was established in 1958. It currently consists of seven federally owned waterfowl production areas (WPAs), totaling 8,862 acres, and more than 113 grassland and/or wetland easement tracts, totaling more than 34,000 acres, on private properties. The District is spread over a four-county area in northern Montana, but most of the easements and all of the WPAs are located in Blaine and Phillips counties. Easement acreage is frequently changing, as the result of accelerated grassland easement acquisition since March 1997.

Most of the easements and WPAs were purchased in the 1970s. The first, the Holm WPA, was acquired in 1973, when three brothers decided to have their farm north of Chinook preserved as a nesting area for Canada geese. The brothers intended to donate the land to the U.S. Fish and Wildlife Service. But when the gift was legally challenged by a relative, the court ruled in favor of the plaintiff, and the Service was required to pay $135,000 to retain ownership of the property.

The most recent WPA acquisition occurred in 2000. This 965-acre tract, which enlarged the Beaver Creek WPA, is located along Beaver Creek and is adjacent to the eastern boundary of Bowdoin National Wildlife Refuge. It was purchased in partnership with the Gallatin Valley Chapter of Pheasants Forever.

Other WPAs provide a variety of natural and introduced nesting habitats. Pearce WPA, located along the northern boundary of Bowdoin Refuge, is the only WPA that can receive water from an irrigation canal. Many waterfowl traffic back and forth between the WPA and the refuge. The area is popular for pheasant and white-tailed deer hunting; and it also offers a handicapped-accessible hunting and observation blind that was built in cooperation with a Malta Boy Scout troop and the Montana Department of Fish, Wildlife and Parks.

Dyrdahl and Webb WPAs, in northwestern Phillips County, lie on the edge of an end moraine and are covered with natural wetlands. Some potholes are large and deep, and consequently can carry water over to a second nesting season. Korsbeck WPA in west-central Phillips County was acquired in 1989 and contains a large natural wetland, many small potholes, and a large retention reservoir. McNeil Slough and Beaver Creek WPAs, located in east-central Phillips County, were purchased in 1991. Both came with extensive water rights from perennial streams, and they have tremendous wildlife diversity and potential recreational use.

WPAs and easement areas are typical of prairie pothole wetlands that go through wet and dry climatic cycles. When conditions are favorable, nesting production can be quite high, but dry periods, in which production declines, may last for several consecutive years.

Many of these areas are adjacent to large blocks of native grassland that are managed as grazing allotments by the U.S. Bureau of Land Management. Other adjoining lands are owned by the State of Montana or are grasslands owned by a grazing association. One-half or more of the land in the four counties will never be cultivated due to land ownership, topography, or soil type. This results in an abundance of native wildlife species, including sharp-tailed and greater sage-grouse, white-tailed and mule deer, coyote, white-tailed jackrabbit, and many grassland songbirds, such as Baird's sparrow, Sprague's pipit, and chestnut-collared longspur.

> Further information: Bowdoin Wetland Management District, HC 65 Box 5700, Malta, MT 59538; telephone: (406) 654-2863.
>
> NOTE: Special appreciation is given to Dwain M. "Fritz" Prellwitz, Wildlife Biologist, Bowdoin NWR Complex, for providing this description.

Charles M. Russell Wetland Management District (WMD) presently consists of three federally owned waterfowl production areas (WPAs) that total more than 2,000 acres, and more than 8,300 acres of wetland and grassland easements. These important conservation lands are located in south-central Montana.

Spidel WPA, in Golden Valley and Yellowstone counties, contains 1,250 acres, just over half of which are wetland habitat that was drained years ago by previous owners to increase crop production. The U.S. Fish and Wildlife Service is planning to restore the habitat for the benefit of nesting waterfowl and other water-dependent wildlife. As the Service explains, "Despite the fact that it is drained, the wetland and surrounding uplands produce and harbor large numbers of waterfowl and shorebirds. However, it does not impound enough water to assure over summer broods survival, as the basin is often dry by mid- to late summer." Access to this WPA, from State Route 3 at Broadview, is east 1 mile and then north 2 miles.

Tew WPA, containing 538 acres in Musselshell County, consists of several depressional wetland basins surrounded by uplands that are seeded to dense nesting cover. When the basins are wet, they provide valuable nesting and brood-rearing habitat for waterfowl and other water-dependent wildlife. Access to this WPA, from State Route 3 at Broadview, is east about 12.5 miles and then north 4 miles.

Clark's Fork WPA, containing 271 acres in Carbon County, consists of a 66-acre wetland surrounded by dense nesting cover. This area attracts such wildlife as waterfowl, sharp-tailed grouse, ring-necked pheasant, and white-tailed deer. After the tract was acquired through the Farmer's Home Administration, the Fish and Wildlife Service coordinated a wetland creation project with Ducks Unlimited, Inc. and Montana Fish, Wildlife and Parks. Access to this WPA from Bridger is north about 0.5 mile on U.S. Route 310, east 0.5 mile, and north 0.5 mile to a designated parking area.

All three WPAs are open daily during daylight hours. Visitor activities are birdwatching, photography, hiking, and hunting during the designated seasons. Fishing is also permitted on the Clark's Fork WPA. There is no entrance fee, and no facilities are provided other than parking areas. The privately owned easement areas are not open to visitation.

> Further information: Charles M. Russell Wetland Management District, P.O. Box 110, Lewis-

Northeast Montana Wetland Management District (WMD) was established in 1968 to conserve and manage scattered tracts of ecologically significant wetland and grassland habitats for nesting waterfowl and other migratory birds in Daniels, Sheridan, and Roosevelt counties. The WMD is located on the western edge of the glaciated prairie pothole region, within the transition zone between the tallgrass prairie to the east and the shortgrass prairie of central Montana. Native vegetation is of the mixed-grass prairie type. Cool-season grasses predominate, with scattered shrub communities also present. Trees are scarce.

The WMD includes 44 waterfowl production areas (WPAs) totaling more than 12,500 managed acres. These WPAs vary in size from 4 acres to more than 2,000 acres. Under the terms of perpetual wetland easements, more than 8,500 acres of privately owned wetland are protected from drainage, burning, leveling, and filling. Perpetual grassland easements encompass more than 10,900 acres that are protected from cultivation. Acquisition of the WPA and easement tracts is largely funded with revenues from the sale of Migratory Bird Hunting and Conservation Stamps (Duck Stamps).

The WPAs are open daily during daylight hours. There are no entrance fees. No visitor use facilities are provided. Visitor activities include birdwatching, photography, hiking, and hunting and trapping during the designated seasons. Wildlife species on these areas are generally the same as those recorded on the Medicine Lake National Wildlife Refuge (see listings for that refuge). Easement tracts are privately owned, and no public access is authorized without permission from the landowner.

The U.S. Fish and Wildlife Service has worked with more than 300 landowners in the WMD to improve wildlife habitat on private property through its Partners for Wildlife Program. Other conservation partners in this effort include Montana Fish, Wildlife and Parks; The Nature Conservancy; and Ducks Unlimited, Inc. Most wetlands and native grasslands in Montana are in private ownership; thus, working with individual landowners is key to conserving these valuable wildlife habitats.

Further information: Northeast Montana Wetland Management District, Medicine Lake NWR Complex, 223 North Shore Road, Medicine Lake, MT 59247; telephone (406) 789-2305.

NOTE: Special appreciation is given to Mike Rabenberg, District Manager, for providing this description.

Northwest Montana Wetland Management District was established in 1970 to conserve and manage scattered parcels of important wetland and grassland habitats for nesting waterfowl and other birds located in Lake and Flathead counties, in northwestern Montana.

The district includes 14 federally owned waterfowl production areas (WPAs) totaling approximately 8,500 acres. More than 6,300 additional acres are protected under the terms of perpetual conservation easements from willing landowners. These areas consist of intermountain grasslands interspersed with wetlands in high densities, on the valley floors of Flathead and Mission valleys.

Flathead WPA encompasses 7 miles of shoreline and adjacent upland along the northern end of Flathead Lake, including remnants of delta islands (alluvial deposits) at the mouth of the Flathead River.

The wetlands support an abundance of waterfowl, including such species as Canada goose, mallard, redhead, pintail, American wigeon, northern shoveler, and blue-winged and green-winged teal. The upland habitat supports the non-native ring-necked pheasant and gray partridge and provides nesting habitat for such birds as western meadowlarks and savannah and song sparrows. These areas also support large nesting concentrations of the short-eared owl and northern harrier, plus significant wintering areas for northern goshawk and rough-legged and red-tailed hawks. Shorebirds are attracted to the WPAs during migration and for nesting. Among these are killdeer, American avocet, black-necked stilt, Wilson's phalarope, and yellowlegs. One of the WPAs supports a peregrine falcon hacking tower, which has had a pair of nesting birds for the past decade. Young falcons are regularly fledged from this nest. Mammals include muskrat, badger, porcupine, and striped skunk.

Establishment of all the WPAs has been made possible with revenues from the sale of Migratory Bird Hunting and Conservation Stamps (Duck Stamps).

Further information: Northwest Montana Wetland Management District, c/o National Bison Range, 132 Bison Range Road, Moiese, MT 59824; telephone: (406) 644-2211.

Nebraska: National Wildlife Refuges

Boyer Chute comprises more than 2,500 acres of the 9,000 acres projected for acquisition. This refuge was established in 1996 to restore and protect a 2.5-mile stretch of bottomland riparian habitat along a chute (river channel) that parallels the main course of the Missouri River on the eastern edge of Nebraska.

The refuge is named for the Boyer River, which in turn was named for an early settler who hunted and trapped in that area of western Iowa. This river deposited at its mouth most of the sand and other sediments that originally created an island in the Missouri River. Through this island, the Missouri cut channels such as Boyer Chute.

In the late 1930s, Boyer Chute was one of numerous braided channels that were cut off from the Missouri. The U.S. Army Corps of Engineers, as part of its program to enhance the navigability of the Missouri, constructed a wall and dikes across the upstream end of this channel. Even though culverts were installed that permitted some river water to enter the chute, accumulating sediments eventually blocked most of that flow. Responding to the radically changed ecosystem, a forest of trees began to grow within and bordering the chute. Also, some of the bottomland was planted with fields of corn and soybeans.

In 1994, the Boyer Chute Restoration Project was initiated. As part of the region-wide Missouri River Streambank Stabilization and Navigation program by the Corps of Engineers and the Papio-Missouri Natural Resources District, it was designed primarily to restore ecologically significant wildlife habitats that were previously impaired or destroyed by the navigation enhancement program. The chute's historic channel was excavated, structures were installed to maintain its appropriate gradient, former croplands were restored to areas of native prairie grasses and forbs, and more than 40 species of trees, shrubs, and vines have been planted along the channel to re-create a floodplain woodland. As the U.S. Fish and Wildlife Service says, "The chute is once again a functioning part of the Missouri River. . . . Boyer Chute provides fish and wildlife habitat that will enrich the entire river ecosystem." This is also an inspiring place, where visitors may come and see firsthand how a formerly altered and degraded environment can be successfully restored.

The nonprofit organization National Park Trust provided a grant that helped raise funds for the addition of an ecologically important 40-acre parcel to Boyer Chute Refuge. This area of wetland provides important habitat for such species as the peregrine falcon, interior least tern, piping plover, and pallid sturgeon. The parcel is part of an important migration corridor for numerous species including the bald eagle.

The refuge is open daily during daylight hours, except on Thanksgiving, Christmas, and New Year's Day. There is no entrance fee. Some parts of the refuge are closed to public visitation.

Visitor activities include birdwatching, photography, driving 2 miles of paved roads, hiking (on two interpretive loop trails), bicycling, picnicking (two picnic shelters are available), fishing (two wheelchair-accessible fishing piers are provided), and hunting on part of the refuge during designated seasons. Camping is not permitted on the refuge, but campground facilities are available elsewhere in the area. Because of strong currents and other hazards, swimming is not permitted.

Visitors are cautioned to be alert for poison ivy. Insect repellent is advised during the warmer months.

Lodgings and meals are available in such communities as Blair and Omaha, Nebraska.

Access to Boyer Chute is north 8 miles from Omaha on U.S. Route 75, and east 3 miles from Calhoun.

Further information: Boyer Chute National Wildlife Refuge, c/o DeSoto NWR, 1434 - 316th Lane, Missouri Valley, IA 51555; telephone: (712) 642-4121.

Crescent Lake, encompassing 45,995 acres, was established in 1931 to enhance and protect a scenically beautiful and ecologically rich area of scattered lakes, ponds, and marshes set amid a vast expanse of grass-covered, gently rolling sandhills in the Nebraska panhandle. The refuge's 21 lakes, numerous ponds, cattail and bulrush marshes, lushly vegetated meadows, and arid shortgrass prairie attract a great diversity of wildlife.

Large concentrations of migrating and nesting Canada geese and ducks, such as blue-winged teal, mallards, gadwalls, shovelers, and pintails, are drawn to the lakes and wetlands. Many species of migratory shorebirds, such as avocets, phalaropes, and curlews, stop here in the spring and autumn or nest and raise their young. Various raptors and neotropical migratory songbirds also come through this area. Over 275 bird species use the refuge.

The prairie grasslands are inhabited by deer, pronghorn, prairie dogs, and sharp-tailed grouse. In April, the sharp-tails perform their elaborate courtship displays on as many as 45 dancing grounds, known as leks. They begin at the first light of day and increase in tempo with sunrise. The cocks fan their tails, vibrate their outstretched wings, rattle the quills of their wing feathers, and rapidly shuffle and stamp their feet. As if possessed, these pale, brown-speckled birds rush about, leaping wildly over each other and fighting. They make cackling sounds and repeatedly inflate a pair of lavender air sacs on their necks. Lowering their heads and forcing the air out of the sacs, they create a low coo-oo-ing sound that can be heard across the prairie. The refuge provides viewing blinds (reservations advised), so that visitors can see and photograph these birds' incredible ritual.

The U.S. Fish and Wildlife Service carries out a number of habitat enhancement programs, including the operation of water management systems to regulate water levels from Martin Lake through Lower Harrison Lake. Water levels are periodically lowered to permit prescribed burns that reduce some of the vegetation and slow down plant succession. To enhance breeding opportunities, the refuge provides nesting boxes for wood ducks and more than 100 hay-filled tubs or baskets for Canada geese.

Establishment of Crescent Lake refuge was made possible partly with revenues from the sale of Migratory Bird Hunting and Conservation Stamps (Duck Stamps).

The refuge is open daily during daylight hours. There is no entrance fee.

Visitor activities include birdwatching, photography, driving the interpretive tour route, hiking (on two established trails and elsewhere), fishing, and hunting (deer, prairie grouse, and pheasant) on parts of the refuge during the designated seasons. Although camping is not permitted on the refuge, campground facilities are available at Oshkosh and Alliance, and in Smith Lake State Recreation Area.

Lodgings and meals are available in such communities as Oshkosh and Alliance.

Access to the refuge is north on West Second Street from Oshkosh for 28 miles, following refuge directional signs. Visitors are advised that this route and some refuge roads become muddy and difficult to drive.

Further information: Crescent Lake National Wildlife Refuge, 115 Railway Street, Scottsbluff, NE 69361; telephone: (308) 762-4893.

DeSoto (see text under Iowa)

Fort Niobrara encompasses 19,131 acres of gently rolling sandhills and wooded breaks along the Niobrara River in north-central Nebraska. Six important natural ecosystems converge here—sandhills prairie, mixed prairie, tallgrass prairie, eastern deciduous forest, Rocky Mountain coniferous forest, and northern boreal forest, as they occur in few other parts of North America. Although this refuge consequently supports a great diversity of wildlife, it was established in 1912 initially as a sanctuary to manage breeding habitat for native birds.

Later that same year, the refuge's wildlife management mission was expanded to protect remnant herds of the then-dwindling bison, elk, and deer that formerly inhabited the Great Plains in great numbers. J. W. Gilbert, of the community of Friend, Nebraska, offered to give the federal government six bison, seventeen elk, and a few deer if a suitable area of land could be found for these animals. The U.S. Government's Fort Niobrara had helped maintain the peace, from 1879 to 1906, between the Sioux Indians and the influx of Euro-American settlers.

Soldiers stationed here never fought any battles, and the facility was abandoned soon after the turn of the century. Property associated with this old fort was chosen to become the Fort Niobrara National Wildlife Refuge.

Today, Fort Niobrara Refuge's grasslands habitat supports approximately 350 bison and between 70 and 100 elk. In the spring, the refuge's staff, riding on horseback, drive the bison herd south across the Niobrara River to summering grasslands, where the calves are born. From time to time during the summer, the animals are moved to fresh pastures. In July and August, the 2,000-pound bulls battle furiously with each other as they compete for females during the rutting season. In the autumn, most of the herd is driven back north across the river, where the animals spend the winter on the grasslands and timbered breaks. In September, the bull elk begin their rutting, and refuge visitors can hear the piercing, musical whistles that carry far across the prairie. As with bison, the elk calves are born in the spring.

Maintaining an appropriate carrying capacity of bison and elk is a guiding management priority here. So that their numbers are in balance with an ecologically healthy habitat, the U.S. Fish and Wildlife Service donates or auctions off excess animals.

Many other species of native wildlife inhabit Fort Niobrara Refuge. Wild turkeys and many species of songbirds live among the river-bordering oaks and pines; and mule deer, prairie dogs, burrowing owls, greater prairie chickens, and sharp-tailed grouse favor the open sandhill prairie.

In April, the prairie chickens and sharp-tails congregate on their dancing grounds, known as leks. The cocks perform elaborate, frenzied courtship rituals. The prairie chickens repeatedly inflate and deflate their golden neck sacs, emitting eerie, hollow, oo-loo-woo moaning sounds that sound like air being blown across the top of an empty bottle. The sharp-tails' foot-stomping, shuffling, and wing-vibrating are accompanied by coo-oo-ing and cackling sounds as they deflate their purplish neck sacs. More than 230 species of birds have been recorded here.

All that remains of Fort Niobrara, which was dismantled by 1912, are some foundations, earthworks, and one building—a red barn.

Fort Niobrara Natural History Association is a nonprofit, educational support group that is providing assistance to the refuge.

The refuge is open daily during daylight hours. There is no entrance fee. The visitor center is open daily from Memorial Day to Labor Day, and on weekdays, except national holidays, during the remainder of the year.

Visitor activities include wildlife observation; photography; driving the self-guiding, 3.5-mile Wildlife Drive (an interpretive brochure is available); hiking the self-guiding, 0.6-mile Fort Falls Nature Trail (an interpretive brochure is available) and trails into the 4,635-acre Fort Niobrara Wilderness; canoeing, kayaking, and float-tubing downstream from Cornell Bridge on the refuge's stretch of the 76-mile Niobrara National Scenic River (a small user fee to float the river through the refuge is charged, a canoe-launching site is located near Cornell Bridge, and canoe rentals are available in Valentine); fishing; picnicking (picnicking facilities are provided at the Bur Oak Wildlife Viewing Area, near Cornell Bridge); and viewing the bison roundup and auction in the autumn. Although camping is not permitted on the refuge, campground facilities are available at Ballards Marsh Wildlife Management Area, Merritt Reservoir, Smith Falls State Park, and several in and near the town of Valentine.

Visitors are cautioned to stay in their vehicles on the Wildlife Drive, as bison and elk are potentially dangerous, and to be alert for rattlesnakes while hiking.

Access to Fort Niobrara Refuge is east 4 miles from the town of Valentine on State Route 12.

Further information: Fort Niobrara National Wildlife Refuge, HC 14, Box 67, Valentine, NE 69201; telephone: (402) 376-3789.

John W. and Louise Seier was established in 1999 and is located in the Sandhills of north-central Nebraska. This state's sandhills region is the largest remaining tract of mid and tall-grass prairie in North America, encompassing 19,000 square miles. It is also the most extensive sand dune area in the Western Hemisphere. This 2,400-acre refuge was donated to the U.S. Fish and Wildlife Service by John W. and Louise Seier to be managed as part of the National Wildlife Refuge System. As the refuge is still in the planning stage, it is presently closed to visitation.

The purpose of the refuge is to preserve, restore, and enhance the ecological diversity and abundance of migratory and resident wildlife. Management of the refuge will provide the opportunity for wildlife observation, photography, and hunting. Environmental education and interpretation will be developed for the visiting public to learn about the valuable refuge resources and the National Wildlife Refuge System. In 2001, the American Bird Conservancy designated this refuge as a Globally Important Bird Area in recognition of its value to the conservation of birds and their habitats.

The mid-continental position of the John W. and Louise Seier Refuge, the large groundwater reservoir beneath the Sandhills (known as the Ogallala Aquifer) and the highly varied topography of the Sandhills are partly responsible for the unique mix of the refuge's plant and animal species. The refuge grassland is composed of plants from the tallgrass prairie, shortgrass prairie, and plants unique to sandy soils. Plants such as big bluestem, switchgrass, blue and hairy grama, sandy muhly, and sand lovegrass grow in association with each other to create an abundance of diversity. A few trees and shrubs add to this diversity, including eastern cottonwood, peachleaf willow, American plum, snowberry, and Arkansas rose. Bloody Creek and Skull Creek and the rich wetland communities adjacent to these areas cut across the refuge.

The Seier Ranch was originally homesteaded by John and Louise Seier's grandparents in the mid-1800s and has been owned by the family since then. Because they had no immediate family but did have a love of wildlife and an interest in preserving wildlife, John and Louise Seier donated their property to the Service.

The refuge is located 26 miles south of Bassett and is managed through the Fort Niobrara-Valentine National Wildlife Refuge Complex.

Further information: John W. and Louise Seier National Wildlife Refuge, c/o Fort Niobrara-Valentine NWR Complex, HC 14, Box 67, Valentine, NE 69201; telephone: (402) 376-3789.

NOTE: Special appreciation is given to Royce Huber, Refuge Manager, for providing this description.

North Platte, consisting of 2,909 acres in four separate units, was established in 1916 to enhance and protect Lake Minatare, Winter's Creek Lake, and Lake Alice, which provide important habitat for large concentrations of geese and ducks just north of the town of Scottsbluff, in the western end of the Nebraska panhandle. This refuge also protects Stateline Island, in the North Platte River, near the town of Henry.

As many as 200,000 waterfowl, along with sandhill cranes, bald eagles (a pair nests on the refuge), and numerous shorebirds, pause here to rest and feed during their migrations.

A variety of management "tools" are used to promote an ecologically healthy grassland environment on North Platte Refuge, including periodic prescription burning, grazing, and haying. Mechanical, biological, and chemical methods are carefully used to control undesirable non-native plants.

The refuge's STATELINE ISLAND UNIT is open daily during daylight hours. THE LAKE MINATARE UNIT is open to visitation during daylight hours from January 15 through September and is closed to all public entry during the rest of the year. The southern part of WINTER'S CREEK LAKE is open to visitation from January 15 through September, but the northern end of the lake and northeastern upland areas are closed year-round. The eastern half of the LAKE ALICE UNIT is open to visitation from May 15 through September, but the western half is closed year-round. There is no refuge entry fee.

The Nature Conservancy has assisted with land acquisition at North Platte Refuge.

Visitor activities include birdwatching, photography, hiking, and fishing. Although camping is not permitted on the refuge, campground facilities are available in Oshkosh and Alliance, and in Lake Minatare State Recreation Area.

Visitors are cautioned to be alert for rattlesnakes.

Lodgings and meals are available in Scottsbluff, Nebraska, and Torrington, Wyoming.

Access to the refuge's Stateline Island unit is 1 mile south from U.S. Route 26 at Henry; access to the Minatare and Winters Creek units is north 7 miles on Stonegate Road from Minatare; and to the Lake Alice unit it is north 10 miles on Sugar Factory Road from Scottsbluff.

Further information: North Platte National Wildlife Refuge, c/o Crescent Lake NWR Complex, 115 Railway Street, Scottsbluff, NE 69361; telephone: (308) 635-7851.

Valentine, containing 71,516 acres, was established in 1935 as a breeding ground for migratory birds and other wildlife. The refuge protects an ecologically significant area of numerous lakes, marshes, small patches of woods, tallgrass-covered meadows, and extensive, gently rolling sandhills prairie in north-central Nebraska. The lakes, pothole ponds, and wetlands attract thousands of migratory and breeding waterfowl and shorebirds. May and October are the peak months, when as many as 150,000 ducks are present on this refuge.

In April, greater prairie chickens and sharp-tailed grouse congregate on their dancing grounds—the cocks performing elaborate, frenzied courtship rituals. The prairie chickens' performance is accompanied by eerie, hollow, oo-loo-woo moaning sounds that resemble air being blown across the top of an empty bottle. The sharp-tails' foot-stamping, shuffling, and wing-vibrating are accompanied by coo-oo-ing and cackling sounds (see Crescent Lake Refuge for additional description of the latter).

Although few sandhill cranes stop, large numbers of them fly over the refuge on their spring and autumn migrations. Several thousand white pelicans summer here. Many Canada geese build their nests on top of muskrat houses. Numerous neotropical songbirds come through Valentine in the spring. Over 260 bird species have been seen here.

Although most of Valentine Refuge's lakes and marshes are natural, the U.S. Fish and Wildlife Service has created a few additional ponds, and the water levels on some of the latter are regulated for the benefit of waterfowl. Marsh and prairie grassland habitats are enhanced with springtime livestock grazing and prescribed burns. These management activities spur the release and recycling of plant nutrients, help control nonnative species of grasses, and stimulate regrowth. Large areas of the refuge that are rested from grazing and prescribed fire provide tall, thick cover that is preferred by ground-nesting birds.

Establishment of this refuge was made possible partly with revenues from the sale of Migratory Bird Hunting and Conservation Stamps (Duck Stamps). In 1976, Valentine was designated as a national natural landmark, in recognition of this ecologically outstanding part of the vast sandhills prairie region.

The refuge is open daily during daylight hours. There is no entrance fee. The headquarters is open on weekdays, except on national holidays.

Visitor activities include birdwatching, photography, driving designated roads, hiking refuge trails and roads, viewing elaborate prairie chicken and sharp-tailed grouse courtship displays in April from blinds (reservations advised), fishing, and hunting (deer, upland game, and waterfowl) on parts of the refuge during the designated seasons. Although camping is not permitted on the refuge, campground facilities are available at Ballards Marsh Wildlife Management Area and at Merritt Reservoir.

Lodgings and meals are available in the community of Valentine.

Access to Valentine Refuge is south 16 miles from the town of Valentine on State Route 83, and west 13 miles on Spur Route 16B to the refuge's Hackberry Headquarters.

Further information: Valentine National Wildlife Refuge, HC 14, Box 67, Valentine, NE 69201; telephone: (402) 376-3789.

Nebraska: Wetland Management District

Rainwater Basin Wetland Management District was established in 1963 to restore and enhance wetland habitat and adjacent uplands for the benefit of large concentrations of migratory waterfowl and other wildlife. The district consists of scattered tracts of both federally owned and private lands within a 17-county area of southern Nebraska.

Federally owned areas, many of which have been acquired with revenues from the sale of Migratory Bird Hunting and Conservation Stamps (Duck Stamps), include more than a dozen waterfowl production areas (WPAs) that range in size from just over 60 acres to nearly 2,000 acres. The WPAs are open to visitor activities such as birdwatching, photography, hiking, and hunting.

Many other tracts that are not open to the public are privately owned, with landowners volunteering to help conserve wetland habitat under the Nebraska Partners Program. Other important partnerships are with the State of Nebraska and private organizations. Ducks Unlimited, Inc. has helped acquire the district's wetlands and has assisted with many important wetland habitat enhancement projects.

Further information: Rainwater Basin Wetland Management District, P.O. Box 1686, Kearny, NE 68848; telephone: (308) 236-5015.

Nevada

Anaho Island was established in 1913 as the Anaho Island Reservation and was redesignated as a national wildlife refuge in 1940. The refuge protects important colonial nesting bird habitat, notably for a large concentration of the American white pelican (*Pelecanus erythrorhynchos*). The island is located in 25-mile-long Pyramid Lake, within the Pyramid Lake Paiute Indian Reservation in northwestern Nevada.

Under the terms of a 1992 cooperative agreement with the Tribal Council, the U.S. Fish and Wildlife Service manages the island by conducting biweekly bird monitoring during the March-to-September breeding season and by annually banding up to 400 juvenile pelicans in late July and August. The Tribe provides law enforcement patrols of the island during the breeding season. The Paiute name for Anaho Island is Pai-sa-ka-tu-do, which means "the dry island sitting out there all by itself."

As refuge manager Donna L. Withers explains:

The refuge encompasses the entire island, which has fluctuated in size from 220 acres in 1913 to 750 acres in recent history, due to fluctuating lake water levels. . . . In the 1970's, a land bridge was being exposed between Anaho Island and the eastern shore of Pyramid Lake, as a result of the rapid decline in Pyramid Lake water levels due to diversion of Truckee River Water. Since then, court mandates and public laws have provided for increasing flows to Pyramid Lake. . . .

As for the breeding activities of white pelicans on Anaho Island, Fish and Wildlife Service biologist C. Anne Janik and former Stillwater/Anaho Island refuge manager Ronald M. Anglin wrote in their article, "Nevada's Unique Wildlife Oasis" (*Nevada Public Affairs Review*, University of Nevada, Reno, 1992, No. 1):

The continental white pelican populations have declined dramatically from historic numbers. . . . Anaho Island has become one of the last, prime inland breeding areas for white pelicans in the west. The reproductive success and the continued existence of this colony . . . [are] crucially dependent on the availability of prime foraging marshes within 60 to 80 miles of the island. Unfortunately, the continuing drought is reducing foraging areas. . . . However, current efforts by federal and state agencies to acquire water will restore many of Nevada's precious yet diminishing wetlands, ensuring the survival of one of the state's most spectacular wildlife treasures—the white pelicans of Anaho Island.

The Fish and Wildlife Service reports that, since this article was written, the continental white pelican populations are now stable; the species has been removed from the listing as sensitive (except for the Great Basin population); and pelican numbers have increased on Anaho Island National Wildlife Refuge. In 2000, there were more than 16,000 adults and 4,800 young.

Because of the importance of avoiding human disturbance, the island refuge is closed to visitation year-round, and boating is not permitted within 500 feet of the island's shore. In addition to the pelicans, other species of colonial nesting birds using Anaho Island are double-crested cormorant, great blue heron, great egret, black-crowned night-heron, and California gull.

Lodgings and meals are available in Reno and Fernley.

Access to Pyramid Lake from I-80 at Sparks is northeast 33 miles on State Route 445 (which becomes State Route 446), or from I-80 at Fernley it is north 16 miles on State Route 447 and branching left at Nixon on State Route 446 (which becomes State Route 445).

Further information: Anaho Island National Wildlife Refuge, c/o Stillwater NWR Complex, 1000 Auction Road, Fallon, NV 89406; telephone: (775) 423-5128.

Ash Meadows, encompassing 23,000 acres, was established in 1984. The refuge protects and manages a desert oasis ecosystem of spring-fed wetlands, located within an area of alkaline desert uplands of the Mojave Desert in southwestern Nevada.

The refuge's habitats support at least 24 species of endemic plants and animals, including four species of endangered fish that are found nowhere else in the world. As the U.S. Fish and Wildlife Service says:

This concentration of indigenous life distinguishes Ash Meadows NWR as having a greater concentration of endemic life than any other local area in the United States. . . . Ash Meadows provides a valuable and unprecedented example of desert oases that are now extremely uncommon in the southwestern United States.

The wetlands habitat is fed by more than 30 seeps and springs. At least 10,000 gallons of water per minute are discharged year-round from an enormous subsurface aquifer system. Most of this water emerges from seven major springs. According to the Fish and Wildlife Service:

The reason for this abundance of water in an otherwise dry and desolate region is the presence of a geological fault. The movement of this particular fault acts as an "underground dam," blocking the flow of water and forcing it to the surface. The water arriving at Ash Meadows is called "fossil" water, because it is believed to have entered the ground water system thousands of years ago.

In addition to Ash Meadows' colorful spring pools, springbrook channels, and wetlands that are scattered across the refuge, there are groves of mesquite and ash trees in the vicinity of the wetlands and stream channels, and sand dunes rising as much as 50 feet in the central part of the refuge. Drier areas are dominated by four-winged saltbush, creosotebush, a number of species of cacti, and other high-desert vegetation.

Regarding the history of this area, the Fish and Wildlife Service explains:

Ash Meadows was intensively farmed prior to its establishment as a National Wildlife Refuge. During the 1960's and early 1970's in particular, irrigated row crops, grazing, and development took a heavy toll on the area's natural resources. Plants, fish, and wildlife declined as pumping and diversion of spring channels, development of roads, large scale earth moving, and introduction of over 100 non-native plants and animals occurred in a "blink" of evolutionary time. The Carson Slough, an area in the northwestern portion of the refuge, which was historically the largest wetland in southern Nevada, was drained and mined for its peat in the 1960's.

In the early 1980s, the area's fragile habitat was further impaired by speculative land developers as they began preparing for an extensive residential development. Fortunately, The Nature Conservancy acted in the nick of time by acquiring 12,654 acres in 1984 and selling it to the Fish and Wildlife Service later that year. The agency says:

The refuge is currently in the habitat restoration stage and will likely remain so for years to come. The overall goal of the refuge and its Recovery Plan for threatened and endangered species is to restore the area to its natural historic condition. This will involve re-directing spring outflows back into former natural channels, restoring wetlands, removing non-native species (particularly saltcedar, bass, tropical fish, and crayfish), restoring native riparian and upland vegetation, and removing unnecessary structures such as roads, fences, and power lines.

Four endemic, endangered species of fish of the minnow family inhabit the refuge: Devil's Hole pupfish (*Cyprinodon diabolis*), Ash Meadows pupfish (*C. nevadensis mionectes*), Warm Springs pupfish (*C. nevadensis pectoralis*), and Ash Meadows speckled dace (*Rhinichthys osculus nevadensis*). They are most easily seen at Crystal, Point of Rocks, and Jackrabbit springs.

There are also a number of endangered or threatened plant species at Ash Meadows, including the Amargosa niterwort, Ash Meadows gumplant, Ash Meadows ivesia, spring-loving centaury, Ash Meadows milk vetch, Ash Meadows sunray, and Ash Meadows blazing star.

Within the Ash Meadows Refuge's authorized boundary, the Fish and Wildlife Service manages more than 22,600 acres, the U.S. Bureau of Land Management cooperatively manages 9,460 acres, and the National Park Service cooperatively manages the 40-acre Devil's Hole Unit of Death Valley National Park. In addition, there are a few scattered private properties that total just over 700 acres. Over 210 bird species have been seen in the area.

The refuge is open daily (including holidays) during daylight hours. There is no entrance fee. A refuge leaflet can be obtained from an information box at each of the three main refuge entrances. The refuge office is often open for additional information, but hours vary depending on staffing.

Visitor activities include birdwatching, photography, driving refuge roads, walking the 0.3-mile (wheelchair-accessible) Crystal Springs Interpretive Boardwalk Trail (adjacent to the refuge office) and elsewhere on the refuge, swimming only in the Crystal Reservoir, canoeing and non-motorized boating only on Crystal and Peterson reservoirs, horseback riding in designated areas, picnicking, and hunting (waterfowl, coot, moorhen, snipe, quail, dove, and rabbit) on parts of the refuge during the designated seasons.

Swimming is prohibited in the spring pools; and although permitted in Crystal Reservoir, visitors are warned that the water may be infested with larvae that cause a dermatitis known as "swimmer's itch." Camping is not permitted on the refuge, but campground facilities are provided in the main unit of Death Valley National Park.

Sunscreen and lots of drinking water are advised. Visitors are cautioned to respect private properties within the refuge boundaries.

Lodgings and meals are available in Amargosa Valley, Pahrump, Las Vegas, and Beatty, Nevada; and Death Valley National Park, California.

Access to Ash Meadows Refuge from Exit 33 on I-15 is west/northwest 56 miles on State Route 160 (through Pahrump), west (left) about 20 miles on the Bell Vista Road-Bob Rudd Memorial Highway, and north (right) on an unpaved road into the refuge.

Further information: Ash Meadows National Wildlife Refuge, HC 70, Box 610-Z, Amargosa Valley, NV 89020; telephone: (775) 372-5435.

Desert National Wildlife Range, comprising 1.588 million acres, was established in 1936. The refuge protects a diversity of habitats for the desert bighorn sheep and other wildlife within and above the Mojave Desert of southern Nevada.

Within this largest unit of the National Wildlife Refuge System in the lower 48 states, there are six major mountain ranges, the highest of which rises from around 2,500 feet elevation in desert valleys to 9,920 feet atop the Sheep Range's Hayford Peak. The ranges and valleys, which run mostly north and south through the area, are geologically part of the vast basin-and-range province that sprawls across nearly all of Nevada and parts of several adjacent states.

As explained by refuge manager Amy Sprunger-Allworth:

The name, "Desert National Wildlife Range," does not provide an adequate overall description of the refuge. One might envision sand and cactus. However, most visitors begin their visit to the refuge by stopping at Corn Creek. They are awed by the beauty and solitude of the natural springs that have existed here for centuries, providing a desert oasis for Native Americans and European settlers. As visitors continue towards the interior of the refuge, they experience extreme elevational changes offering unexpected expansive vistas. Pinyon and juniper dominate the landscape above 6,000 feet, affording quiet respites for travelers who have bounced in their vehicles up the rugged roads.

The refuge's single most important mission is the protection of the Nelson's desert bighorn sheep (*Ovis canadensis nelsoni*) and the natural environment that supports this species. Because of the low-elevational rainfall that annually averages a mere 4.5 inches, the U.S. Fish and Wildlife

Service has developed a number of springs and rainwater catchments to ensure adequate supplies of water during periods of drought and heat. The desert bighorn belongs to the same species as the Rocky Mountain bighorn sheep, but the desert environment has brought about certain basic differences. The desert subspecies is smaller and of a lighter grayish-buff color, and has horns that are thinner and are more outward-spreading.

Bighorns occur on all six of the refuge's mountain ranges, but nowhere are they densely populated. Use of different elevations varies with season, food availability, and reproductive cycle. Sheep are generally below timberline on desert-shrub and grass-covered slopes. Because they blend extremely well with their surroundings and tend to remain widely scattered in small groups during the majority of the year, the best opportunity to observe them occurs during the summer. At this time, they tend to concentrate at or within a 2-mile radius of a water course. As of late 2001, the Fish and Wildlife Service estimates that there are between 700 and 750 desert bighorn sheep on the Desert National Wildlife Range.

More than 500 species of plants have been identified on the Desert National Wildlife Refuge. Vegetative types include the saltbush community in a number of high-salinity valley basins; the creosotebush community (roughly between 2,600 and 4,200 feet elevation), with such species as Mojave yucca, Mormon tea, bursage, and several species of cacti; the blackbrush community (between 4,200 and 6,000 feet), within which are scattered, open-grown stands of Joshua trees; the single-leaf pinyon-Utah juniper woodland (between 6,000 and 7,400 feet); the ponderosa pine-white fir forest (from 7,500 to over 9,000 feet); areas of bristlecone pine (*Pinus longaeva*), the world's oldest known living tree species (above 8,500 feet); and black sagebrush (on south- and west-facing slopes above 9,500 feet).

Many species of desert wildflowers bloom with spectacular abundance, spreading their bright colors across the landscape following periodic winters of generous rainfall. Among them are the yellow desert marigold, orange globemallow, pink penstemon and sand verbena, red paintbrush, blue desert larkspur, and lavender Mojave aster.

The refuge is open daily. There is no entrance fee. The refuge office is open on weekdays, except national holidays.

Visitor activities include wildlife observation, photography, driving, hiking, horseback riding, picnicking, camping, and hunting (bighorn ram only) on parts of the refuge during the designated seasons. Although camping is permitted, all camps, except backpack camps, are required to be within 100 feet of designated roads.

Except for the 4-mile main entrance road, the refuge's other unpaved, rough, unimproved roads are best negotiated with a four-wheel-drive, high-clearance vehicle, as these routes may be impassable for passenger cars. These routes include the 47-mile Mormon Well Road, which climbs northeast from Corn Creek Field Station to Mormon Pass and descends out the eastern refuge boundary to U.S. Route 93; 16-mile Gass Peak Road, which branches from Mormon Well Road and winds between Gass Peak and the Las Vegas Mountains in the southeastern corner of the refuge; and 70-mile Alamo Road, which runs north from the field station through the length of the refuge. Off-road driving is not permitted.

Hiking opportunities include trails in the immediate vicinity of the Corn Creek Field Station, where numerous species of birds are attracted to this oasis—especially migratory birds, during spring and autumn. Visitors are permitted to hike anywhere on the refuge, but there are no designated trails. Over 320 bird species have been recorded here.

Visitors are advised to bring an adequate supply of drinking water on backcountry excursions, especially during the intense heat of summer, when a person requires at least a gallon of water per day.

As the Fish and Wildlife Service explains, "traveling through this immense range requires preparation to ensure a safe, enjoyable trip. Plan your trip carefully or a day trip can turn to disaster if weather or equipment breakdowns catch you unprepared. . . . Protect yourself from the sun! Wear a hat, light colored clothing and use sunscreen. Protect yourself from heat exhaustion by avoiding extreme midday sun. Pace yourself carefully and avoid overexertion. . . . Make sure you start with a full fuel tank [before coming into the refuge]. All roads are primitive and rough, so be sure your vehicle is in good working condition and adequately supplied for emergencies. Don't forget to check your spare tire. . . . Don't hike or travel alone. Let someone know your travel plans, schedule, and the general area you will be in. Stick to your plan and don't forget to report your return."

The U.S. Air Force's Nevada Test and Training Range, where bombing, gunnery, and aerial warfare training activities occur, overlays the western half of the Desert National Wildlife Range (to the west of Alamo Road). All public access into this area of the range is strictly prohibited.

Lodgings and meals are available in Las Vegas.

Access to the Desert National Wildlife Range from downtown Las Vegas is northwest about 25 miles on U.S. Route 95 and right 4 miles on the gravel entrance road to the Corn Creek Field Station.

Further information: Desert National Wildlife Range, HCR 38, Box 700, Las Vegas, NV 89124; telephone: (702) 879-6110.

Fallon, consisting of 17,902 acres, was established in 1931. The refuge, which is located in the Great Basin Desert of west-central Nevada, consists of flat to gently rolling desert-shrub habitat, dominated by greasewood and saltbush, and a system of both active and stable sand dunes. A branch of the Carson River ends here in the Carson Sink, providing wetlands that attract waterfowl and other water birds.

A proposal is pending to change the status of this refuge to a unit of nearby Stillwater National Wildlife Refuge (see the text for that refuge).

Access to the Fallon Refuge is limited to open roads, and the U.S. Fish and Wildlife Service recommends the use of four-wheel-drive vehicles.

Further information: Fallon National Wildlife Refuge, c/o Stillwater NWR, 1000 Auction Road, Fallon, NV 89406; telephone: (775) 423-5128.

Moapa Valley, consisting of 104 acres, was established in 1979 to protect and enhance vital habitat for a federally listed endangered species of fish, the Moapa dace (*Moapa coriacea*). The refuge is located in the Warm Springs area of the upper Muddy River watershed within the Mojave Desert, about 60 miles northeast of Las Vegas in southern Nevada. This was the first refuge within the National Wildlife Refuge System to be established for an endangered fish.

In recent years, the population of the Moapa dace has declined as the result of habitat modification, degradation, and destruction and also as the result of competition from the non-native fish and aquatic vegetation. A survey of the dace in the year 2001 revealed fewer than 900 of this small fish species. They depend upon stream channels that are fed by six thermal springs on the refuge.

As described by the U.S. Fish and Wildlife Service:

The refuge is comprised of three distinct units. The Pedersen Unit was acquired in 1979 and is 30 acres in size. The Plummer Unit was acquired in 1997 and is 28 acres. The Apcar Unit was purchased in 2001 and contains 46 acres. . . . Each unit has a separate stream system supported by the steady and uninterrupted flow of several springs that come to the surface at various places throughout the refuge. . . . These springs are thermal in nature and have an average annual water temperature of 90 degrees Farenheit at the point of discharge. Water quality is good, although high in calcium carbonate.

. . . The Moapa dace is unique because it is the only representative of its genus and it is found nowhere else in the world. . . .

Prior to acquisition, both the Pedersen and Plummer Units had been developed and operated as resorts, with swimming pools, bath houses, snack bars, and recreational vehicle hook-ups. The primary management objectives of the refuge are to restore these units to as near a natural condition as possible and to optimize available stream habitat for recovery and de-listing of Moapa dace. Restoration efforts are underway at the Pedersen Unit, where all non-native fish and most artificial structures have been removed.

The refuge's vegetation includes non-native species, such as California fan palm, oleander, and tamarisk; native species, such as honey and screwbean mesquites, velvet ash, fourwing saltbush, and creosotebush; and aquatic plants, such as spike rushes, water nymph, watercress, and pondweed.

Although Moapa Refuge is presently not open to general visitation, plans anticipate that the refuge will welcome visitors in the foreseeable future. As habitat enhancement is completed and as funding and staffing become available, public use facilities may include a self-guiding interpretive trail, interpretive and environmental education programs, and opportunities for bird-watching and photography.

> Further information: Moapa Valley National Wildlife Refuge, c/o Desert NWR Complex, HCR 38, Box 700, Las Vegas, NV 89124; telephone: (702) 879-6110.

Pahranagat, encompassing 5,382 acres, was established in 1964. The refuge protects and manages an ecologically significant Mojave Desert oasis of lakes and marshes and associated desert uplands located along a 10-mile stretch of Pahranagat Valley, about 90 miles north of Las Vegas in southern Nevada. The name *Pahranagat* is derived from a Paiute Indian expression, meaning "valley of shining waters." Over 240 bird species use the refuge.

The water that sustains this wetland habitat for many species of waterfowl and other water-dependent wildlife comes from large thermal springs to the north of the refuge. The U.S.

Fish and Wildlife Service manages four primary water impoundments: North Marsh, Upper Pahranagat Lake, Middle Marsh, and Lower Pahranagat Lake. The spring water, flowing onto the refuge from the north, is initially stored in North Marsh and the upper lake. As the Service explains, it is then "released to create conditions . . . [that] will enhance the growth of wildlife food plants and to supplement lakes, marshes, and grasslands south of the refuge headquarters. . . . The water in some of the marsh units is occasionally drawn down to encourage the decomposition of plant residue and promote vigorous plant growth. Fire is also used periodically to remove decadent stands of marsh vegetation and make essential nutrients available for the newly sprouting marsh plants."

In addition to the marshes and lakes, Pahranagat Refuge includes areas of riparian cottonwoods and willows, open fields, and Mojave/Great Basin desert scrub.

Establishment of Pahranagat Refuge was made possible partly with revenues from the sale of Migratory Bird Hunting and Conservation Stamps (Duck Stamps). Ducks Unlimited, Inc. and a variety of other partners have recently worked to restore more than 600 acres of the refuge's converted wetlands from previously used farm fields. The project area, which lies between the Upper Lake and the Middle Marsh, now incorporates a variety of flooded wetland cells, riparian areas, and wet meadows, and it affords a much-needed and improved capacity of habitat management through water transfer from the Upper Lake to the Lower Lake units.

The refuge is open daily during daylight hours. There is no entrance fee. The refuge office is open on weekdays, except national holidays.

Visitor activities include birdwatching; photography; driving U.S. Route 93 through the length of the refuge and driving an auto tour route; bicycling on refuge roads; hiking; picnicking and camping along the eastern shore of the Upper Lake; canoeing and boating (small nonmotorized and electric-power boats) only on Upper, Middle, and Lower lakes (no boat-launching ramps); fishing; and hunting (geese and ducks, coot and moorhen, snipe, quail, dove, and cottontail) on parts of the refuge during the designated seasons. Swimming is not permitted in refuge waters.

Hiking opportunities include the 2.5-mile trail and road route around the Upper Lake, and other trails and roads.

Insect repellent and sunscreen are advised. Visitors are cautioned to be alert for rattlesnakes in the desert-scrub habitat.

Lodgings and meals are available in Las Vegas.

Access to Pahranagat Refuge from Las Vegas is northeast 22 miles on I-15 to Exit 64 and north approximately 68 miles on U.S. Route 93.

Further information: Pahranagat National Wildlife Refuge, P.O. Box 510, Alamo, NV 89001; telephone: (775) 725-3417.

Ruby Lake, comprising 37,632 acres, was established in 1938 to protect an extensive area of marshes, ponds, islands, bordering wet meadows, and sagebrush-and-grass uplands. The bulrush wetlands attract large concentrations of nesting and migrating waterfowl and other water birds, with as many as 25,000 ducks in September–October. The refuge is scenically located at the

6,000-foot elevation of Ruby Valley, nestled along the eastern base of the rugged Ruby Mountains, which rise to more than 11,000 feet on the highest peaks in northeastern Nevada.

The juxtaposition of rugged, upthrusted mountain ranges, such as the Ruby Mountains, and intervening valleys or basins, such as Ruby Valley, is typical of the vast "washboard" topography of this region's basin-and-range province, which extends throughout nearly all of Nevada and parts of several neighboring states. The oasis of the Ruby Marshes is a fascinating and wonderful contrast to the surrounding high-desert Great Basin landscape.

Water from more than 160 springs along the base of the mountains either surfaces within various marsh units or flows into the Collection Ditch and is then directed by a network of dikes into the 3,000-acre central area of marsh habitat. Water that reaches the southern end of the ditch flows into the 7,300-acre South Marsh, which is situated in a natural depression, and water that is sometimes allowed to flow from the ditch's northern end helps to maintain the shallower 6,800-acre North Marsh. In 1972, the South Marsh was designated by the National Park Service as a National Natural Landmark, because of its biological diversity and its pristine habitat condition. The North Marsh is an especially important wetland habitat for puddle ducks and shorebirds. More than 220 species of birds have been recorded on the refuge.

As the U.S. Fish and Wildlife Service explains:

Water is managed to provide optimum nesting and feeding habitat for migratory waterfowl and water-dependent birds. By careful manipulation of water levels and flows, 12,000 acres of marshlands can be maintained. Periodically, individual habitat units are rejuvenated by drying them up. As a result, the food resources and productivity of the aquatic environment are greatly enhanced. Management tries to imitate the processes of naturally occurring wetland ecosystems as much as possible to maintain the vitality and productivity of the marshes. . . .

Waterfowl are the most conspicuous and most important to the primary objectives of the refuge. Nesting canvasbacks and redhead ducks are particularly important. The South Marsh supports the largest nesting population of canvasback ducks west of the Mississippi River and holds the highest concentration of this species in North America. In good years, the refuge has produced 3,500 canvasbacks and 2,500 redheads.

The trumpeter swan, originally a transplant from the Red Rock Lakes National Wildlife Refuge in Montana, is also found on the refuge. Several pairs nest each year. [Both the trumpeter and tundra swans may winter on the refuge.] In all, 15 . . . species of waterfowl nest on the refuge, as well as a variety of other water-dependent birds, such as coots, grebes, sandhill cranes, great blue herons, black-crowned night-herons, white-faced ibis, and snowy egrets.

Although most of the marsh habitat contains dense stands of bulrush that provide nesting sites for waterfowl, marsh birds, and other birds, transition areas around the edge of the wetland support rushes, sedges, grasses, and various forbs. Wet meadows and drier grasslands are important feeding and nesting habitats for many migratory birds. Haying, limited grazing, and periodic prescribed burning are implemented to help revitalize and maintain the health of meadows and grassland areas. The refuge's upland habitat predominantly consists of sagebrush to the west of the marsh, and greasewood is the dominant shrub to the east.

Establishment of the refuge was made possible partly with revenues from the sale of Migratory Bird Hunting and Conservation Stamps (Duck Stamps). Ducks Unlimited, Inc. has helped enhance more than 2,600 acres of Ruby Lake Refuge's wetland habitat.

The refuge is open daily during daylight hours. There is no entrance fee. The refuge head-quarters/visitor center is open on weekdays, except national holidays.

Visitor activities include birdwatching; photography (two photo blinds are available on a permit basis); driving the 7.5-mile, unpaved auto tour route and the Ruby Valley Road; inter-pretive programs and environmental education; bicycling on the tour route; hiking; canoeing and boating; fishing; and hunting (dark geese, including white-fronted and Canada; ducks, includ-ing merganser; coot, moorhen, and snipe) on parts of the refuge during the designated seasons. To protect the trumpeter swans, Ruby Valley is closed to the hunting of all white waterfowl.

Canoeing and boating are permitted from June 15 through December. From June 15 through July, only canoes and boats with electric motors are allowed south of Brown Dike, and from August 1 through December, canoes and motorboats of 10 horsepower or less are allowed in the South Marsh. Canoes and other car-top boats may be launched only at the Main Boat Landing, Narciss Boat Landing, Gravel Pit Pond, and Brown Dike; boats on trailers may be launched only at the Main and Narciss boat landings. No boats are allowed on refuge waters from January 1 to June 14. These boating restrictions are in place to protect nesting waterfowl.

Although camping is not permitted on the refuge, the South Ruby Campground, located 1.5 miles south of the refuge headquarters, is available in the Humboldt-Toiyabe National For-est. For reservations, telephone: (877) 444-6777. Primitive camping is also allowed on the na-tional forest 300 feet west of County Road 767; and on U.S. Bureau of Land Management lands to the east of the refuge.

Hiking opportunities include the refuge roads and the 0.5-mile Cave Creek Trail, which starts just south of the refuge headquarters/visitor center.

Insect repellent is recommended during the warmer months. Visitors are advised to be alert for rattlesnakes, especially in the drier parts of the refuge, and to be prepared for cold weather at this high elevation. Canoeists and boaters are cautioned that it is all too easy to become dis-oriented and lost in the South Marsh's maze of waterways through the tall, dense stands of bul-rushes.

Lodgings and meals are available on a seasonal basis in Ruby Valley at the Ruby Lake Resort; telephone: (775) 779-2242. Otherwise, the nearest accommodations are in Wells, Elko, and Ely.

Access to Ruby Lake Refuge's headquarters/visitor center from Exit 352 on I-80 at Wells, is south 28 miles on U.S. Route 93, southwest (right) 15 miles on State Route 229, and south (left) 35 miles on unpaved Ruby Valley Road; or from Ely, it is west 32 miles on U.S. Route 50, north (right) 35 miles on unpaved Long Valley Road (recommended only in good weather), and con-tinuing north 32 miles on Ruby Valley Road. Prospective visitors are encouraged to call ahead to the refuge to ask about road conditions, especially from November to May.

Further information: Ruby Lake National Wildlife Refuge, HC 60, Box 860, Ruby Valley, NV 89833; telephone: (775) 779-2237.

Sheldon, containing more than 573,503 acres, was initially established in 1931. The refuge protects a vast expanse of high-desert habitat for the benefit of the pronghorn (antelope),

California bighorn sheep, mule deer, greater sage-grouse (see HART MOUNTAIN and SEED-
SKADEE Refuge texts for discussions of the latter), and many other species of wildlife. It is located mostly in northwestern Nevada, with a few hundred acres in Oregon.

In the 1870s, livestock ranching began in the Great Basin Desert of northern Nevada and
parts of neighboring states. These operations grew and prospered, soon developing into extensive empires. Where previously there had only been such native animals as the pronghorn, mule
deer, and bighorn sheep using the arid land, there were now huge numbers of cattle, sheep, and
horses. As the U.S. Fish and Wildlife Service explains:

. . . range deterioration resulted from excessive use. Soon, both wildlife and the ranching industry were in
trouble. Native wildlife had been exploited for food and was unable to compete with domestic livestock
on the deteriorating rangelands. California bighorn sheep disappeared, mule deer became rare, antelope
numbers were drastically reduced, and sage grouse, once numerous, became hard to find. Overgrazing
changed plant types and led to erosion; economic hardships caused livestock empires to sell out to small
family owned ranches. By the . . . [start of the twentieth] century, only a few small ranches remained in
existence on the Sheldon.

In the late 1800's and early 1900's, the decreasing antelope populations of northwestern Nevada began to concern both residents and conservation groups.

In 1920, E. R. Sans, a biologist with the U.S. Biological Survey, saw his first pronghorn—
an event that inspired a vision in his mind of establishing an antelope refuge and seeking the
enactment of hunting regulations including a closed season on this species. As a result of his
efforts, both Washoe and Humboldt counties set closed seasons, soon followed by a statewide
seasonal closure established by the Nevada State Fish and Game Commission. As described by
Sheldon Refuge volunteer history recorder/compiler Ralph Murphy (*Sheldon National Wildlife
Refuge: A Collection of Historical Vignettes*, 1984):

Sans, and others concerned about the pronghorn and other threatened species, had meanwhile been . . .
[urging enactment of] a law authorizing the Governor to set aside certain state controlled lands for recreation and game refuges. This was signed into law by Governor James C. Scrugham on March 5, 1923.
Washoe County Commissioners also designated 400 square miles in northern Washoe County as an antelope refuge. Later Governor Scrugham issued a Proclamation, setting aside eleven areas within the state
for the purposes of recreation and game refuges. One was the area previously set aside by Washoe County
and another covered the major portion of what would become the Charles Sheldon Range and Sheldon
Antelope Refuge.

In spite of the county and state actions, these lands remained seriously overgrazed, and
their widely scattered springs, creeks, lakes, and other aquatic habitats continued to be severely
degraded. There was no funding for habitat management or enforcement of hunting regulations.

In 1927, Sans took Gilbert Pearson, the president of the National Association of Audubon
Societies (subsequently the National Audubon Society), on a tour of the 30,000-acre Last Chance
Ranch, on which Sans envisioned the headquarters for a national antelope range. Pearson was so im-
pressed with the proposal that he returned to New York City, met with the association's board of
directors, and secured a commitment of $10,000. He then contacted the Boone and Crockett Club,
which provided an equal sum, with the suggestion that the refuge be named in memory of Charles
Sheldon, who was an avid sportsman, conservationist, and the organization's long-time member and

chairman of its Game Preservation Committee. The ranch was acquired in 1928. The following year, a 6- by 8-mile area surrounding the ranch was withdrawn from mineral entry; in 1931, the Charles Sheldon Wildlife Refuge was established by executive order; and the following year, Audubon transferred its ranch property to the federal government.

Ernest J. Greenwalt, the ranch's resident manager, remained in that capacity for the new refuge until 1933, when Sans was named refuge manager. Greenwalt continued as a refuge employee until he was transferred in 1936 to the Wichita Mountains Refuge in Oklahoma. His son, Lynn Greenwalt, spent his childhood years on both refuges, subsequently spent much of his long wildlife conservation career living on and being manager of a number of national wildlife refuges, and ultimately served as the Director of the U.S. Fish and Wildlife Service from 1973 to 1981.

In 1936, another area, encompassing more than 500,000 acres, was established as the Charles Sheldon Antelope Range. In 1976, both areas were combined and renamed the Sheldon National Wildlife Refuge.

The refuge's habitat management activities include a program of prescribed burning. Fire is mostly used to create and maintain patches of grassland within the predominant high-desert sagebrush, thereby providing habitat diversity that benefits many species of wildlife. Fire also promotes nutrient cycling that in turn spurs new growth of grasses and forbs.

Other management activities include the enhancement of stream flow. For example, in 1981, an experimental rehabilitation of severely eroded (deeply incised) Rodero Creek was carried out by installing a number of loose rock dams, to trap sediments and allow water to flow slowly. As the Fish and Wildlife Service explains, "Since then, sediment deposited behind the dams has built up the stream bottom. Plants are colonizing the sediment, creating a series of small, wet meadows."

The Service goes on to say: "Today, areas of the creek that had flowed periodically now flow year-round. Ponds behind dams are used by ducks as brood habitat. Other riparian areas are currently being rehabilitated throughout the refuge, in fulfillment of one of the prime management objectives."

As for the pronghorn, current estimates range between 1,200 and 1,500 of these fleet-footed animals that summer on the Sheldon Refuge. During hard winters, their numbers may increase to 3,000 or more as animals migrate from the Hart Mountain National Antelope Refuge in southern Oregon and other surrounding areas.

Two nonprofit organizations, Friends of Sheldon Refuge and the Order of the Antelope, assist the refuge in a variety of ways.

The refuge is open daily. There is no entrance fee. The refuge's administrative headquarters, located in the U.S. Post Office building in Lakeview, Oregon, is open on weekdays, except national holidays.

Visitor activities include wildlife observation; photography; driving paved State Route 140 and the refuge's graded roads and backcountry jeep routes; hiking; camping at more than a dozen primitive campgrounds; fishing at the Dufurrena Ponds that are near the refuge field office; and hunting (antelope, deer, bighorn sheep, chukar, and quail).

The Fish and Wildlife Service advises visitors to enquire about road conditions, especially in winter and spring, before venturing into the remote backcountry of the refuge. Visitors are cautioned to be alert for rattlesnakes.

More than 200 species of birds that have been recorded on Sheldon Refuge.

Lodgings and meals are available in such communities as Winnemucca, Nevada; Lakeview, Oregon; and Cedarville, California.

Access to the Sheldon Refuge's Dufurrena Ponds/field office from I-80 at Winnemucca, is north 31 miles on U.S. Route 95 and northwest (left) 99 miles on State Route 140; or from Lakeview, Oregon, it is north 5 miles on U.S. Route 395, and southeast (right) 73 miles on State Route 140.

Further information: Sheldon National Wildlife Refuge, P.O. Box 111, Lakeview, OR 97630; telephone: (541) 947-3315.

Stillwater, encompassing 79,600 acres in two units, was originally established in 1948. The refuge protects and manages an extensive area of the Stillwater Marsh, an oasis for large concentrations of waterfowl, shorebirds, and other wildlife at the end of the Carson River, within the Great Basin Desert of west-central Nevada.

When the first Euro-American explorers discovered this marshland, it was filled with an abundance of fish and wildlife, and the native "Cattail-Eater" Paiute people had long been deriving sustenance from the wealth of resources. As for subsequent human history of this area, the U.S. Fish and Wildlife Service explains:

In 1898, one visitor described the wetland as a "half shallow lake, half tule swamp which extends for 20 miles along the valley bottom . . . a breeding ground for great numbers of water and shore birds."

Then, in the early 1900s, the Newlands Irrigation Project was developed by the [U.S.] Bureau of Reclamation to supply Lahontan Valley farmers with an abundant and reliable water source. The Carson River was dammed, creating the Lahontan Reservoir. This reduced water flowing into the marsh to a trickle. . . . The great flights of birds that Pony Express riders saw darkening the skies in the 1860s dwindled to a remnant.

In 1948, action was taken to prevent complete loss of the Stillwater marshes. The U.S. Fish and Wildlife Service and the Nevada Fish and Game Commission entered into an agreement with the Truckee-Carson Irrigation District to develop and manage . . . lands for wildlife and grazing. These were designated as the 140,000-acre Stillwater Wildlife Management Area and 24,200-acre Stillwater National Wildlife Refuge. Although at that time Carson River flows sustained only a fraction of the original marsh, this action prevented the loss of the Pacific Flyway in western Nevada. In 1990, 55,000 acres of the management area were added to the Stillwater National Wildlife Refuge.

As *Ducks Unlimited* senior writer Matt Young explained in his January/February 2002 article, "Wetlands Under Siege":

In partnership with the USFWS and U.S. Bureau of Reclamation (BOR), DU [Ducks Unlimited, Inc.] has completed several wetland conservation projects on the refuge. DU currently is participating in a project to refurbish the refuge's water-delivery system by constructing new canals, installing water-control structures, and repairing levees. These improvements will enable managers to more efficiently use limited water supplies and provide better habitat for waterfowl and other wildlife.

The refuge's STILLWATER UNIT is today a vast stretch of diked ponds and bulrush- and cattail-dominated marshland—an oasis, surrounded by greasewood-and-saltbush desert and pickleweed-bordered salt flats. In years of adequate water (there are periodic cycles of drought, as between 1986 and 1992, when there was virtually none), several thousand ducks may pause here in March and April on their way to breeding grounds farther north. Other concentrations of ducks, such as redheads, cinnamon teal, and gadwalls, along with grebes, herons, ibises, Canada geese, plovers, sandpipers, stilts, avocets, and phalaropes, raise their young on the refuge during the summer. Flotillas of American white pelicans swim about on the ponds, grabbing fish with their large orange beaks; flocks circle overhead in V formations, flapping and gliding in sequence or unison, and fly to Anaho Island National Wildlife Refuge, where they nest and raise their young (for further information on these pelicans, see the text for Anaho Refuge).

The major migration influx occurs, however, from August to November, when as many as a one-quarter million ducks, including redheads, canvasbacks, pintails, shovelers, and green-winged teal, may gather here on their southward migration. The Stillwater wetlands also provide vital resting and feeding habitat for enormous numbers of migrating shorebirds—sometimes totaling more than 300,000 individuals. In 1988, Stillwater was recognized as a key area in the Western Hemisphere Shorebird Reserve Network. Major winter attractions are tundra swans, which may number 1,000 or more of these graceful white birds. Lahontan Valley also attracts the largest concentration of bald eagles in Nevada. More than 280 bird species have been recorded on this refuge.

A proposal is pending to change the status of the nearby 17,902-acre Fallon National Wildlife Refuge to a unit of Stillwater Refuge (see the Fallon Refuge text).

The refuge is open daily during daylight hours. There is no entrance fee. The refuge headquarters, located at 1000 Auction Road in Fallon, is open on weekdays, except national holidays.

Visitor activities include birdwatching, photography, driving the 15-mile auto tour route and other refuge roads, hiking on refuge roads, canoeing and boating (more than a dozen boat-launching sites are available), camping (8-day limit), fishing, and hunting on the refuge's public use areas during the designated seasons.

Insect repellent and sunscreen are advised during the warmer months.

Lodgings and meals are available in Fallon.

Access to Stillwater Refuge from Fallon is east 5 miles on U.S. Route 50, east/northeast about 10 miles on State Route 116, and on unpaved Stillwater Road (State Route 116) within the refuge.

Further information: Stillwater National Wildlife Refuge, P.O. Box 1236, Fallon, NV 89407; telephone: (775) 423-5128.

New Hampshire

Great Bay, containing 1,083 acres in two units, was established in 1992 to restore and manage a diversity of wildlife habitats, including wooded and shrub uplands, fields, vernal and beaver ponds, intertidal mudflat, and open bay. The main part of the refuge, containing 1,057 acres, is located along the eastern shore of Great Bay in southeastern New Hampshire.

The bay and mudflats attract concentrations of waterfowl, wading birds, shorebirds, gulls, and terns. Among the waterfowl, there are large numbers of wintering American black ducks, as well as Canada geese, wood ducks, mallards, green-winged teal, ring-necked ducks, greater scaup, common goldeneyes, buffleheads, and mergansers (hooded, common, and red-breasted). Wading birds include great blue and green herons, snowy egrets, and glossy ibis. The most common shorebirds are greater and lesser yellowlegs, spotted sandpiper, and semipalmated and least sandpipers. Nesting ospreys and wintering bald eagles are among the refuge's raptors.

Upland areas support ruffed grouse, wild turkey, and American woodcock. In May, peak influxes of neotropical migratory songbirds come here to nest or pause on their way to breeding areas farther north.

The lands in and around what is now the refuge were long used for farming and the harvesting of hay. Most of the area was grassland. Then the federal government purchased the area and established the Pease Air Force Base, which included a weapons storage area. In 1990, the base was closed, and 2 years later, Great Bay Refuge was established. The task is under way to remove buildings and other structures formerly used by the U.S. Air Force. In addition, the U.S. Fish and Wildlife Service is beginning to restore and manage the refuge to enhance the quality and diversity of its habitats. One major goal is to bring back areas of grassland for the benefit of many species of wildlife, such as the bobolink, woodcock, and upland sandpiper. Ducks Unlimited, Inc. has helped enhance about 50 acres of the refuge's wetland habitat.

The refuge's smaller unit is the 26-acre Karner Blue Butterfly Easement, located in pine-barrens habitat in Concord, New Hampshire. In 1991, the Fish and Wildlife Service acquired a conservation easement (mostly from the City of Concord), with the goal of reestablishing the federally listed endangered Karner blue butterfly (*Lycaeides melissa samuelis*) to the area. This northeastern subspecies of the orange-bordered blue butterfly is named for Karner, New York, where it was initially described more than a century ago. As described by the Fish and Wildlife Service, "The male is distinctively silvery or dark blue with narrow black margins on the back of his wings. The back of the female's wings is grayish brown with irregular, orange bands inside a narrow black border. The underside of both sexes is gray with orange bands and black spots circled with white." (Regarding this butterfly, see also the Necedah Refuge text.)

As for the butterfly's life history, "The existence of Karner blue . . . depends upon wild lupine (*Lupinus perennis*). Caterpillars feed only on the leaves of this plant. Adults consume nectar of wild lupine and other flowers and lay their eggs on or near lupine."

In the past, this butterfly's range extended across the pine barrens and oak savannas from Minnesota, Wisconsin, and Michigan to New York and New Hampshire. In 1983, researchers discovered roughly 5,000 Karner blues in the Concord Pine Barrens. But by 1998, a mere 30 individuals were found. Why the sharp decline?

According to the Fish and Wildlife Service:

Suppressed wildfires, forest succession, and urbanization are the greatest threats to the Karner blue's continued existence in New England and elsewhere. . . . The fragmentation that results from these factors, combined with the extremely small size of the remaining population, prevents movement and dispersal of butterflies, resulting in small isolated populations. The Karner blue's habitat is very specific and the butterfly is unable to adapt to the swift changes in its environment.

In an effort to enhance the easement property's habitat toward the hoped-for repopulating of the area with the butterfly, The Nature Conservancy and the Service have been planting lupine, New Jersey tea, spreading dogbane, common milkweed, and meadowsweet (all crucial sources of nectar) since 1991. Exclosure fences erected within the easement keep woodchucks and white-tailed deer from eating new plants. The Conservancy also manages a crucial Karner blue captive breeding program.

Historically, wildfires maintained Concord's Karner blue habitat by curtailing plant succession and creating a network of openings. Annual prescribed burning and mowing by the U.S. Fish and Wildlife Service, The Nature Conservancy, and New Hampshire Fish and Game attempt to duplicate the favorable effects of these natural disturbances. Active management may be the only means of protecting this species and its dwindling habitat.

The Friends of Great Bay National Wildlife Refuge is a local nonprofit support group that is assisting the refuge in a variety of ways.

The refuge units are open daily during daylight hours. There is no entrance fee.

Visitor activities include wildlife and butterfly observation, photography, hiking, and cross-country skiing and snowshoeing.

Hiking opportunities on the main unit include the Peverly Pond Trail—a 0.5-mile (wheelchair-accessible) loop that begins at the parking area, leads through a wooded area, and passes Upper Peverly Pond and several vernal (seasonally wet) pools; and Ferry Way Trail—a 2-mile walk that offers views of woods, a beaver pond, a field, and an apple orchard, on the way to the shore of Great Bay. Hiking on the Karner Blue Butterfly Easement is limited to the 0.5-mile Karner Blue Butterfly Trail.

Visitors are cautioned to be alert for ticks, which may carry Lyme disease. Insect repellent is advised during the warmer months.

Lodgings and meals are available in such communities as Newington and Portsmouth.

Access to the Great Bay Refuge from Exit 4 on I-95, is north about 5 miles to Exit 1 on U.S. Route 4, left at the stoplight at the bottom of the exit ramp, proceeding straight about 0.5 mile to a T junction in the Peas Tradeport, and right a couple of miles on Arboretum Drive, following refuge directional signs.

Further information: Great Bay National Wildlife Refuge, 100 Merrimac Drive, Newington, NH 03801; telephone: (603) 431-7511.

John Hay, consisting of 164 acres, was established in 1972 as part of the management and protection of the former 876-acre Hay Estate. The refuge contains the summer home and associated gardens, known as The Fells, of American diplomat and writer John M. Hay (1838–1905) and is located along the eastern shore of Lake Sunapee in southwestern New Hampshire.

Under the terms of a memorandum of understanding with the U.S. Fish and Wildlife Service, the nonprofit Friends of the John Hay National Wildlife Refuge manages 62 acres of the refuge and the buildings and operates the refuge's environmental education center, which provides a year-round program of guided interpretive walks, workshops and classes, exhibits, and special events. The Friends organization works in partnership with the Society for the Protection of New Hampshire Forests and the Lake Sunapee Protective Association, which cosponsor environmental education programs, and in partnership with The Garden Conservancy, which sponsors the rehabilitation of the gardens. The remaining 712-acre part of the former estate, the Hay Forest Reservation, is owned and managed by the Society for the Protection of New Hampshire Forests.

As described by the Friends organization:

The Fells is one of New England's finest examples of an early 20th century garden. Stroll the length of a 100 foot perennial border, and admire the view of Lake Sunapee from the formal Rose Terrace. In the hillside alpine garden, a brook trickles to a Japanese water lily pool, and a hidden walled garden awaits discovery.

Spectacular rhododendrons, azaleas, dogwoods, and heather complement the natural landscape of ferns and wildflowers.

The main house dates from the 1890s and is listed on the National Register of Historic Places. John Hay served as President Abraham Lincoln's private secretary, U.S. Ambassador to Great Britain in the administration of President William McKinley, and Secretary of State in the administration of President Theodore Roosevelt. President Roosevelt, who founded the National Wildlife Refuge System (beginning with establishment of Pelican Island Refuge in Florida in 1903), was a guest at the Hay Estate in 1902.

The refuge is open daily during daylight hours. The main house is open on weekends and holidays from Memorial Day to Columbus Day. A fee is charged for tours. Because of the fragile nature of The Fells, pets are not permitted on the property.

Visitor activities include touring the historic gardens and house, wildlife and butterfly observation, photography, and hiking a 5-mile network of trails on the refuge and adjacent Hay Forest Reservation. Among these routes are the Hay Forest Ecology Trail, which follows Beech Brook, and a former carriage road to the summit of Sunset Hill.

Lodgings and meals are available in such communities as Newbury, Mt. Sunapee, and Sunapee.

Access to the John Hay Refuge from State Route 103 at Newbury is north 2.2 miles on State Route 103A and west (left) on the entrance road.

Further information: Friends of John Hay National Wildlife Refuge, P.O. Box 276, Newbury, NH 03255; telephone: (603) 763-4789.

Lake Umbagog, comprising 14,640 acres, was established in 1992 to protect ecologically important lands around Lake Umbagog (pronounced um-BAY-gog) in northeastern New Hampshire and western Maine. The name *Umbagog* is derived from a Native American word, meaning "clear water." The refuge is a partnership involving the U.S. Fish and Wildlife Service, the states of New Hampshire and Maine, the Society for the Protection of New Hampshire Forests, and other landowners. Under a combination of ownerships and conservation easements, much of the lakeshore in both states and long stretches of the shoreline of the Androscoggin and Magalloway rivers is under protective management.

As the U.S. Fish and Wildlife explains:

The lake itself—more than 10 miles in length and covering more than 8,500 acres—is one of the largest lakes along the New Hampshire/Maine border. It has an average depth of only 15 feet. . . . More than 50 miles of shoreline, many islands, and extensive wetlands and marshes along the rivers all provide ideal habitat for waterfowl pairing, nesting and brood rearing during the summer. The forested swamplands and upland areas are important habitat for many species of passerines, including 24 varieties of warblers. . . .

Lake Umbagog hosts the largest nesting concentration of common loons in New Hampshire. Abundant fish populations and wetland habitat support one of the highest concentrations of nesting osprey in New Hampshire. The area's forested wetlands support good numbers of black ducks, hooded and common mergansers and mallards also nest in the area. The lake provides habitat for migrating scaup, three varieties of scoters and Canada geese.

. . . Also found around the lake are gray jay, spruce grouse, black-backed and northern three-toed woodpeckers and palm warblers, all northern species considered rare in New Hampshire.

The lake area also supports a variety of mammals, including white-tailed deer, a high density of moose, black bear, beaver, fisher, coyote and bobcat.

The Fish and Wildlife Service's habitat management activities include forest management for the benefit of wildlife diversity, through a cooperative forest management plan; monitoring common loon nesting activities (more than 20 nesting pairs) and the effects of dam-controlled water levels on nesting birds; and monitoring and protecting nesting bald eagles and their habitat.

The Friends of Umbagog is a nonprofit support group that is assisting the refuge in a variety of ways.

The refuge is open daily. There is no entrance fee. The refuge headquarters is open on weekdays, except national holidays.

Visitor activities include wildlife observation, photography, hiking, canoeing, kayaking, and boating, camping, fishing, and hunting (migratory bird, and upland game and big game) on parts of the refuge during the designated seasons. The refuge's campground facilities are managed by the State of New Hampshire's Division of Parks and Recreation. To call for camping reservations: (603) 271-3628.

Canoeing opportunities include a number of suggested half-day trips: Big Island to Thurston Cove—a 6- to 9-mile route along the southwestern shore of the lake, from a public boat-launching site next to State Route 26 in Cambridge, New Hampshire; Harpers Meadow and Sweat Meadows—into backwater habitat along the Androscoggin River from a public boat-launching site next to State Route 26, just upriver from Errol Dam in Errol, New Hampshire, "providing easy access to some of the most outstanding wildlife areas in the Refuge"; and Magalloway River to Leonard Pond—an 8- to 12-mile route that follows the Magalloway River southward from the refuge headquarters, located on State Route 16 in Wentworth Location,

New Hampshire, to Leonard Pond, where a cluster of islands occupies the confluence of the Magalloway and Androscoggin rivers and Lake Umbagog. A canoe trips leaflet is available from the refuge headquarters.

Insect repellent is advised during the warmer months.

Lodgings and meals are available in such communities as Berlin and Gorham, New Hampshire, and Bethel and Rangeley, Maine.

Access to Umbagog Refuge's headquarters from State Route 26 at Errol, New Hampshire is northeast 4.5 miles on State Route 16.

Further information: Umbagog National Wildlife Refuge, P.O. Box 240, Errol, NH 03579; telephone: (603) 482-3415.

Sylvio O. Conte (see text under Massachusetts)

Wapack, encompassing 1,672 acres, was established in 1972 to protect a scenic and ecologically important area on 2,290-foot North Pack Monadnock Mountain in south-central New Hampshire. The refuge lands were donated to the U.S. Fish and Wildlife Service by Dr. Laurence K. Marshall, with deed restrictions that prohibit consumptive wildlife uses, vehicles, and tree cutting, to preserve the land for "wilderness" and "wildlife refuge" purposes.

Regarding the area's history, the Fish and Wildlife Service explains, "Historically, this area was logged off in the late 1700s and used for grazing of sheep until the mid-1800s. Although some logging was done in the early 1960s on the lower western slope, these areas are filling in. The rest of the area has reverted back to native timber during the past 100 plus years."

Today, the refuge consists mostly of mixed coniferous and deciduous forest, with areas of open, grassy "balds" and granite outcroppings around the mountain summit. Trees include eastern white pine; red spruce; eastern hemlock; balsam fir; eastern redcedar; American beech; northern red and scarlet oaks; birches (yellow, paper, and gray); quaking and bigtooth aspens; black and pin cherries; and maples (striped, red, and sugar). Other plants include the shrubby, low-growing common juniper, mountain and sheep laurels, lowbush and highbush blueberries, goldthread, starflower, Canada mayflower, clintonia (blue bead lily), bunchberry, pink lady's-slipper, wintergreen, partridgeberry, wild sarsaparilla, and various species of ferns, clubmosses, mosses, and lichens.

The open summit of North Pack Monadnock is a good place from which to observe the migration of hawks—sharp-tailed, broad-winged, red-tailed, and others (much like at the Hawk Mountain Sanctuary in eastern Pennsylvania). Wapack Refuge provides important nesting habitat for many species of birds, such as Swainson's and hermit thrushes, magnolia and other warblers, ruffed grouse, pileated woodpecker, winter wren, red-breasted nuthatch, white-throated sparrow, and pine grosbeak. Mammals include white-tailed deer, black bear, bobcat, gray fox, fisher, mink, raccoon, striped skunk, snowshoe hare, red and eastern gray squirrels, and eastern chipmunk.

The refuge is open daily during daylight hours. There is no entrance fee.

Visitor activities include wildlife observation, photography, hiking, and cross-country skiing and snowshoeing. Camping is not permitted on the refuge, but campground facilities are available at Greenfield State Park and elsewhere in the vicinity.

Hiking opportunities include a 3-mile section of the 30-mile Wapack Trail, which runs through the refuge and offers spectacular views of the surrounding mountains. This stretch of trail is being maintained by the nonprofit organization Friends of Wapack. This trail is most easily reached from the parking area in the Miller State Park, located off State Route 101, to the southeast of Peterborough. The trail is also reached from Old Mountain Road, which borders the refuge on the northeast. The *Wapack Trail Guide* is a helpful publication about this trail. For further information and to purchase a copy of the trail guide: Friends of Wapack, P.O. Box 115, Peterborough, NH 03458; telephone: (603) 878-4251 (or e-mail: www.wapack.org).

Insect repellent is advised during the warmer months.

Lodgings and meals are available in such communities as Peterborough, Temple, Milford, and Greenfield.

Access to Wapack Refuge is by way of Wapack Trail, as mentioned above.

Further information: Wapack National Wildlife Refuge, c/o Great Bay NWR, 100 Merrimac Drive, Newington, NH 03801; telephone (603) 431-7511.

New Jersey

Cape May, containing more than 10,000 acres in three parts and working toward an anticipated goal of 21,000 acres, was established in 1989, when the U.S. Fish and Wildlife Service acquired the initial 90-acre tract from The Nature Conservancy. The refuge manages and protects vital habitat for spectacular concentrations of migrating birds on Cape May Peninsula in southeastern New Jersey. Over 315 bird species have been recorded here.

Nearly 100 species of neotropical migratory songbirds traveling between Central or South America and the northern United States or Canada, and at least 17 species of raptors, notably sharp-shinned, Cooper's, broad-winged, red-tailed, and red-shouldered hawks, northern harriers, and merlin, pause to rest and feed on the peninsula. Large numbers of the American woodcock congregate here in the autumn. The vicinity of Cape Charles, at the southern end of the Delmarva Peninsula on Virginia's Eastern Shore, is the only other major "funneling" place along the Atlantic coast where woodcock gather in such numbers (see the Eastern Shore of Virginia Refuge text for discussion of woodcock).

As the U.S. Fish and Wildlife Service explains:

Cape May Peninsula's unique configuration and location concentrate songbirds, raptors and woodcock as they funnel south to Cape May Point during their fall migration. Faced with 12 miles of water to cross at . . . [the mouth of] Delaware Bay, [many of the] migrants linger in the area to rest and feed until favorable winds allow them to cross the Bay. . . .

The Refuge's five-mile stretch along . . . Delaware Bay is a major resting and feeding area for migrating shorebirds and wading birds each spring. The Delaware Bay shoreline has gained international recognition as a major shorebird staging area in North America, second only to the Copper River Delta in [southern] Alaska. Each year, hundreds of thousands of shorebirds—nearly 80 percent of some populations—stop to rest and feed here [on Cape May Peninsula] during their spring migration from Central and South America to their Arctic breeding grounds.

The arrival at Cape May of more than twenty shorebird species—primarily red knots, ruddy turnstones, sanderlings and semipalmated sandpipers—coincides with the horseshoe crab spawning season, which occurs in May/early June. The crab eggs provide an abundant food supply which these long-distance flyers use to replenish their energy reserves before moving on. (In May, virtually the entire North American red knot population gathers along Delaware Bay beaches!)

The refuge's diverse habitats include expanses of tidally influenced salt marsh and salt meadow that are interspersed with a mosaic of meandering tidal creeks and inlets; freshwater ponds, creeks, marshes, and shrub/scrub wetlands and bogs; seasonally flooded lowland swamp; upland forest; fields; and a stretch of ocean beach. Nearly half of the refuge consists of upland habitat, dominated by such species of trees as pitch pine and oaks (white, chestnut, black, and scarlet). The other half of the refuge is wetland, with the majority of this area consisting of ecologically rich deciduous-forest swamp.

The refuge's Great Cedar Swamp Division, in Dennis and Upper townships, is named for its once-abundant Atlantic white cedar trees, which now generally occur only in small patches. Several miles to the southwest, the Delaware Bay Division stretches along 5 miles of the eastern shore of Delaware Bay. And the nearly 500-acre Two-Mile Beach Unit, containing a stretch of Atlantic Ocean beach, sand dunes, and salt marsh, is about 5 miles to the southeast of the Delaware Bay Division, near the southern tip of the peninsula. The latter unit's beach is seasonally closed (from April I through September). As of this writing, the Fish and Wildlife Service anticipates the opening of the Two-Mile Beach area to visitation in the spring of 2002. There are some interior trails, but the beach will still be seasonally closed to avoid disturbing the beach-nesting piping plovers, least terns, and black skimmers.

Following decades of ecologically unnatural fire suppression, the Fish and Wildlife Service's planned habitat management activities, as indicated in the July 2000 Revised Draft *Comprehensive Conservation Plan*, include periodic prescribed burning in upland forests to "reduce hazardous fuel, reduce overstory stand density, reduce understory density, increase heath or grass/forb density, [and] control invasive species"; in upland brush habitat to "reduce hazardous fuel, set back succession, [and] control invasive species"; and in grassland to "reduce hazardous fuel, set back succession (woody growth), [and] control invasive species."

Establishment of the refuge is being made possible partly with revenues from the sale of Migratory Bird Hunting and Conservation Stamps (Duck Stamps).

The refuge is open daily during daylight hours. There is no entrance fee. The refuge headquarters, located at 24 Kimbles Beach Road in the town of Cape May Court House, is open on weekdays, except national holidays.

Visitor activities include birdwatching, observing butterflies (including migrating monarchs), photography, hiking, fishing, crabbing, and hunting (deer and woodcock) on parts of the refuge during the designated seasons. Although camping is not permitted on the refuge, campground facilities are available at several nearby locations. Swimming, sunbathing, and surfing are not permitted on the Two-Mile Beach Unit. Hiking opportunities on trails and woodland roads include the Woodcock Trail—a 1.5-mile path, located a short distance south of the refuge headquarters, that loops from State Route 47 through a variety of habitats.

Visitors are cautioned to be alert for ticks, which may carry Lyme disease. Insect repellent is advised during the warmer months.

Lodgings and meals are available in such communities as Cape May Court House and Cape May.

Access to the Cape May Refuge headquarters from Exit 10 on the Garden State Parkway is west about 0.2 mile on Stone Harbor Boulevard (Route 657), south (left at the stoplight) about 0.5 mile on U.S. Route 9, west (right) 2.8 miles on Hand Avenue, south (left) 0.1 mile on State Route 47, and west (right) on Kimbles Beach Road to the refuge headquarters on the right.

Further information: Cape May National Wildlife Refuge, 24 Kimbles Beach Road, Cape May Court House, NJ 08210; telephone: (609) 463-0994.

Edwin B. Forsythe, comprising more than 43,000 acres, protects and manages coastal habitat for migratory water birds in southern New Jersey. The refuge's first segment was established in 1939 as the Brigantine National Wildlife Refuge. In 1984, Brigantine was combined with Barnagat National Wildlife Refuge (which had been established in 1967), and the complex was renamed in honor of the conservation achievements of the late Congressman Edwin B. Forsythe.

More than 80 percent of the refuge consists of ecologically important tidal salt marsh and salt meadow habitat, interspersed with bays and coves. Approximately 5,000 acres of the refuge contain woodlands with such trees as pitch pine, white cedar, and oaks.

Refuge wetlands have long attracted large concentrations of migratory waterfowl—notably the Atlantic brant and American black duck, the populations of which have significantly declined in recent decades. In spring, peak concentrations of migrants generally occur from late March into early April. During the spectacular autumn migration, the refuge can attract more than 100,000 ducks and geese. The greatest numbers of brant and snow geese are here from mid-November through December. The peak of the spring influx of neotropical songbirds, including many species of warblers, occurs in early May. When horseshoe crabs spawn in May and June at such places as Turtle Cove, large numbers of shorebirds gather to feast on crab eggs.

Regarding habitat management activities, the U.S. Fish and Wildlife Service explains:

At the Brigantine Division, refuge staff have used the management technique of "diking" to create 1,415 acres of impounded fresh-and brackish-water marsh habitat in the heart of naturally occurring tidal salt marsh. We created these wetlands to support a wider variety of wildlife than could native salt marsh alone. Water levels in the impoundments are managed to enhance the resources on which wildlife depend[s]. In spring, refuge staff draw the water down to maximize growth of plants beneficial to waterfowl. The drawdown also provides mud flat feeding habitat for shorebirds and wading birds. We reflood the impoundments just in time for the arrival of fall migrants.

Each spring and fall, tens of thousands of migrating ducks and geese, wading birds and shorebirds concentrate here. They linger to rest and feed on the rich resources provided by our managed impoundments. . . . Several migratory species, including the black duck, remain at the refuge through summer to nest and raise their young. Atlantic brant and black ducks also overwinter here.

The refuge also includes the HOLGATE UNIT, which protects an ecologically important area of wild barrier island beach and sand dunes at the southern end of Long Beach Island. Piping plovers, least terns, and black skimmers nest here, in one of the very few remaining places along the New Jersey coast where these and other beach-nesting species can find suitable nesting habitat. All three of these birds are state-listed endangered species, and the plover is also a federally listed endangered species. As the Fish and Wildlife Service explains:

These birds, along with other beach-nesting species, have suffered drastic population declines as human beach developments and recreational uses have eliminated the habitat they need. Forsythe Refuge is one of their last strongholds.

Consequently, during the nesting season, which runs approximately from April 1 through August, the Holgate Unit is closed to all public entry to avoid disturbing the birds' nesting activities. Another stretch of protected barrier island beach and sand dunes, which is closed all year to general visitation, is located on Little Beach Island. In 1975, both of these ecologically sensitive areas, along with about 6,000 acres of the refuge's previously unditched salt marsh, were designated as the 6,600-acre Brigantine Wilderness Area, a unit of the National Wilderness Preservation System.

Habitat management activities include the use of prescribed burning (for a discussion of the reasons for using fire in the same habitat types, see the Cape May Refuge text).

Establishment of the Edwin B. Forsythe Refuge was made possible partly with revenues from the sale of Migratory Bird Hunting and Conservation Stamps (Duck Stamps). Ducks Unlimited, Inc. has helped enhance nearly 1,000 acres of the refuge's wetland habitat. The Friends of Forsythe National Wildlife Refuge is a local nonprofit support group that is assisting the refuge in many ways.

The refuge is open daily during daylight hours. An entrance fee is charged. The refuge's headquarters is open on weekdays, except national holidays. Most of the refuge's visitor use facilities are located at the Brigantine Division headquarters area.

Visitor activities include birdwatching; photography; viewing wildlife displays at refuge headquarters; environmental education; driving the 8-mile, self-guiding Wildlife Drive that loops around freshwater pools and the brackish East Pool and offers views of wetlands and uplands; and viewing the refuge and wildlife from two observation towers along the drive. The refuge's education specialist, Linda Rubenstein, describes this drive as "one of the most famous birding sites on the East Coast. Water birds use Refuge wetlands adjacent to the Drive more than any other on the Refuge, since its most intense habitat-management occurs right there. Each spring and fall, tens of thousands of migrants stop and linger to rest and feed, and visitors from near and far come to see them."

Elsewhere on the refuge, visitor activities include nature walks, canoeing and boating, fishing, and hunting during the designated seasons. A boat-launching ramp is provided at Scotts Landing, which is reached by way of Moss Mill and Scotts Landing roads. Swimming is not permitted on the refuge, and although camping is also not allowed, campground facilities are available at the Wharton State Forest.

Hiking opportunities on the Brigantine Division include the Akers Woodland Trail—a 0.25-mile path through woodland habitat, and the Leeds Eco-Trail—a 0.5-mile footpath through woodland and on boardwalks across areas of salt marsh (the initial 700 feet of the trail are wheelchair-accessible). Nature-walk opportunities on the Barnegat Division include the deCamp Wildlife Trail—a 1-mile footpath (wheelchair-accessible for the initial 1,300 feet) through woodland habitat. It is located in Brick Township, at the junction of Mantoloking and Adamston roads. This division also provides the Barnegat Observation Platform, offering a view of wildlife on the 600-acre Barnegat impoundment. This wheelchair-accessible facility is located adjacent to Bay Shore Drive, between Ridgeway and Edison avenues, to the east of State Route 9.

Visitors are cautioned to be alert for ticks, some of which may carry Lyme disease. Insect repellent is advised during the warmer months.

The more than 290 species of birds that have been recorded on the Edwin B. Forsythe Refuge are much the same as those of Cape May Refuge (see the latter listing).

Lodgings and meals are available in such communities as Smithville, Absecon, and Atlantic City.

Access to the refuge's headquarters is east from U.S. Route 9 at Oceanville, by way of Great Creek Road.

Further information: Edwin B. Forsythe National Wildlife Refuge, P.O. Box 72, Oceanville, NJ 08231; telephone: (609) 652-1665.

Great Swamp, encompassing 7,530 acres, was established in 1960 to protect a miraculously surviving, ecologically rich area of swamp woodland, cattail marsh, grassland, and wooded upland ridges. The refuge, which lies a mere 26 miles to the west of Manhattan's skyscrapers in New York City, is surrounded by the sprawling suburban, urban, and industrial development in northern New Jersey. Over 240 bird species have been seen here.

Historically, parts of the Great Swamp were logged for its virgin-growth timber, and other parts were drained and converted to agriculture. Real estate subdivisions and other developments subsequently hemmed in the area. But then, in 1959, the Port Authority of New York and New Jersey proposed construction of a huge jetport to occupy 10,000 acres, including the Great Swamp. An outpouring of public opposition succeeded in defeating the proposed destruction of the swamp's irreplaceable ecological values. The Great Swamp Committee of the North American Wildlife Foundation, with the assistance of numerous volunteers, spearheaded a fund-raising campaign that raised more than $1 million to acquire 3,000 acres of the swamp's core. This success quickly led to saving the Great Swamp when this acreage was donated to the U.S. Fish and Wildlife Service as a unit of the National Wildlife Refuge System. In 1966, the area was honored when it was designated as a National Natural Landmark, and two years later, roughly 3,600 acres became the refuge system's first unit of the National Wilderness Preservation System.

The Great Swamp's diverse habitats are home to more than 600 documented species of trees and other plants. Among the most spectacular of these are some huge, virgin-growth beech and oak trees, the trunks of which measure as much as 10 to 12 feet in circumference at breast height. Lowland swamp habitat consists primarily of such species as eastern redcedar, American sycamore, sweetgum, swamp white and pin oaks, river birch, black willow, black tupelo, red and silver maples, and green ash. The drier forested uplands contain such species as tulip tree, sassafras, hickories, beech, white and northern red oaks, flowering dogwood, and some large stands of mountain laurel.

Areas of marsh support such aquatic plants as cattails, sedges, blue flag (wild iris), marsh marigold, white water lily, spatterdock (yellow pond lily), arrowhead, and pickerelweed.

Refuge habitat management activities include the seasonal raising and lowering of water levels within a number of shallow, diked pools, known as moist-soil impoundments. Water levels are lowered part of the year to promote the growth of submergent and emergent vegetation that later in the year provides nutrient-rich food and shelter for migratory waterfowl. Previously drained wetlands and other habitats are restored, including the controlling of non-native, invasive pest species. The refuge's several hundred acres of grassland and shrubby habitats are maintained with periodic mowing to prevent woody plants from taking over this important wildlife area. Early- to old-age growth forests are maintained to provide a diversity of habitats. Nesting boxes are placed on the refuge for wood ducks and bluebirds, to supplement the limited number of natural nesting cavities.

The Friends of Great Swamp National Wildlife Refuge is a nonprofit support group that is assisting the refuge in many ways.

The refuge is open daily during daylight hours. There is no entrance fee. The refuge headquarters is open on weekdays, except national holidays, and on Sundays. Also, the Friends of Great Swamp office and book/gift shop is open on Saturdays during the spring and autumn.

Visitor activities include wildlife observation; photography; driving Pleasant Plains Road, which leads to the refuge headquarters, and Long Hill Road, which leads to the refuge's Wildlife Observation Center; hiking; prearranged group tours; and limited deer hunting. Boating, fishing, and camping are not permitted on the refuge. Campground facilities are available on Mahlon Dickerson and Lewis Morris county parks.

Hiking opportunities include two (wheelchair-accessible) boardwalks in the vicinity of the Wildlife Observation Center, one of which extends 0.2 mile and the other 0.4 mile. There are also about 8 miles of hiking trails within the refuge's wilderness area: the 0.7-mile White Trail, accessed from the Morris County Outdoor Education Center at the eastern edge of the refuge; the Orange Trail that runs between the end of White Bridge Road and Meyersville Road; and a trail network between the end of Long Hill Road and Woodland Road. Waterproof footgear is recommended for hikes in the wilderness area.

Two environmental education centers are located near the refuge. Morris County's Great Swamp Outdoor Education Center, with a 1-mile trail and boardwalk, is adjacent to the east end of the refuge and is accessed from Southern Boulevard; information: (973) 635-6629. And Somerset County's Environmental Education Center, with 8.5 miles of hiking trails, is to the west of the refuge in Lord Stirling Park; information: (908) 766-2489.

Visitors are cautioned to be alert for poison ivy and ticks. The latter may carry Lyme disease. Insect repellent is advised during the warmer months.

Lodgings and meals are available in numerous communities, including Summit, Chatham, Madison, Basking Ridge, Morristown, Whippany, and Parsippany.

Access to the Great Swamp Refuge's Wildlife Observation Center (WOC) from Exit 30A on I-287, is south on North Maple Avenue to a stoplight; east (left) 2.7 miles on Madisonville Road, which becomes Lee's Hill Road; and south (right) 2.2 miles on Long Hill Road to the WOC on the right. To reach the refuge headquarters, continue south on Long Hill Road, west (right) on White Bridge Road, and north (right) on Pleasant Plains Road.

Further information: Great Swamp National Wildlife Refuge, 152 Pleasant Plains Road, Basking Ridge, NJ 07920; telephone: (973) 425-1222.

Supawna Meadows, consisting of 2,856 acres, was begun in 1971 as the "Goose Pond Addition" to the Killcohook Migratory Bird Refuge, located on the eastern bank of the Delaware River in southwestern New Jersey. Killcohook Refuge was established in 1934 on property managed by the U.S. Army Corps of Engineers. The Corps, however, used Killcohook land as a spoil-disposal site for sediments dredged from the Delaware River's shipping channel. By 1974, the area's value as wildlife habitat had significantly declined. Consequently, in that year, the Goose Pond Addition was renamed as the Supawna Meadows National Wildlife Refuge. In 1998, Congress revoked the 1934 Executive Order that had established Killcohook Refuge, thereby ending the U.S. Fish and Wildlife Service's management role in that area.

Supawna Meadows Refuge protects important tidally influenced wetlands for the benefit of migrating, wintering, and nesting waterfowl, wading birds, shorebirds, and other wildlife. Large concentrations of wintering waterfowl on Supawna Meadows Refuge include American black ducks, mallards, and northern pintails. The Fish and Wildlife Service provides nesting boxes for wood ducks. Ospreys nest here, and bald eagles visit the area. During spring and autumn migrations, large influxes of neotropical birds, including tree swallows and many species of warblers, pause here during their migrations or nest within the refuge's upland habitat.

Establishment of the refuge was made possible partly with revenues from the sale of Migratory Bird Hunting and Conservation Stamps (Duck Stamps). The nonprofit organization The Philadelphia Conservationists, Inc. helped with the protection of the refuge by acquiring land that was held in trust until the Fish and Wildlife Service was able to purchase the Goose Pond Addition.

Designated areas of the refuge are open daily during daylight hours. There is no entrance fee.

Visitor activities include birdwatching, photography, hiking, fishing, and hunting (deer and waterfowl) on parts of the refuge during the designated seasons.

Visitors are cautioned to be alert for ticks. Insect repellent is advised during the warmer months.

Lodgings and meals are available in such communities as Pennsville, Carney's Point, Salem, and Bridgeton, New Jersey and Wilmington, Delaware.

Access to the Supawna Meadows Refuge office from Exit 1 on I-295 (off the east end of the Delaware Memorial Bridge) is east on State Route 49, right about 1.5 miles on Fort Mott Road, and left on Lighthouse Road, following directional signs.

Further information: Supawna Meadows National Wildlife Refuge, RD 3, Box 540, Salem, NJ 08079; telephone: (856) 935-1487.

Wallkill River, containing more than 4,600 acres toward an anticipated goal of about 8,200 acres, was established in 1990. The refuge's mission is to enhance and protect a diversity of ecologically important habitats along a 9-mile stretch of the north-flowing Wallkill River and a number of its tributaries in northwestern New Jersey and southern New York. Over 220 bird species have been recorded here.

Forested wetlands and wet meadows border the Wallkill River. This rich bottomland provides outstanding habitat for migrating and nesting waterfowl, such as American black and wood ducks, mallards, green-winged teal, common mergansers, and Canada geese. Among the trees and shrubs of the swamps and other floodplain habitats are red maple, American sycamore, river birch, green ash, buttonbush, spicebush, highbush blueberry, and silky dogwood. The refuge also contains a small area of Atlantic white cedars.

Higher-elevation mixed hardwood forest contains such species as white oak, sugar maple, shagbark hickory, flowering dogwood, witch hazel, mayapple, trout lily, white trillium, columbine, and pink lady's-slipper. Scattered here and there are outcroppings of limestone, which support "islands" of hemlock trees.

Much of the refuge's upland terrain consists of grasslands. Under cooperative agreements with local farmers, former farm fields are being restored and maintained with native warm-season grasses that are harvested as hay crops late in the summer.

One of Wallkill River Refuge's biologically outstanding aspects is its large number of butterflies and dragonflies. According to the U.S. Fish and Wildlife Service, more than 50 species of butterflies and approximately 60 species of dragonflies and damselflies (of the Order *Odonata*) have been identified here. Wallkill River Refuge reportedly supports the third highest dragonfly biodiversity in the United States.

Regarding the refuge's management, the Fish and Wildlife Service explains:

Many of the historic wetland areas along the river were drained in the past. Management activities include restoring some areas to their natural wetland condition, creating "potholes" which hold spring and fall floodwaters in areas where the original hydrology cannot be restored, and managing some areas as moist soil units for waterfowl and wading birds.

Other refuge activities include the "management of early successional growth to benefit breeding woodcock and songbirds such as the golden-winged warbler"; the "protection and management of upland forests in large unfragmented blocks to benefit songbirds such as the cerulean warbler and worm-eating warbler"; and the "management of non-native invasive species, such as purple loosestrife, garlic mustard, Phragmites [common reed], Canada thistle, and Japanese buckthorn." (See further discussion of purple loosestrife and its control in the Montezuma Refuge text.)

Establishment of Wallkill River Refuge has been made possible partly with revenues from the sale of Migratory Bird Hunting and Conservation Stamps (Duck Stamps). Among the refuge's nonprofit partners are a number of chapters of the National Audubon Society, two chapters of The Nature Conservancy, Trust for Public Land, The Conservation Fund, National Fish and Wildlife Foundation, Orange County Land Trust, Wallkill River Task Force, and Ducks Unlimited, Inc.

The refuge is open daily during daylight hours. There is no entrance fee. The refuge head-quarters is open on weekdays, except national holidays.

Visitor activities include birdwatching, butterfly observation, photography, hiking, canoe-ing and kayaking, fishing, and hunting (deer, turkey, and waterfowl) on parts of the refuge dur-ing the designated seasons. Although camping is not permitted on the refuge, campground fa-cilities are available nearby. Canoeing and small boat access to the Wallkill River is provided at County Route 565 in Vernon, New Jersey; at Bassetts Bridge Road in Wantage, New Jersey; and at Oil City Road in Pine Island (Warwick), New York. The refuge is planning for a canoeing and fishing access and a Wood Duck Nature Trail parking area near the south end of the refuge, adjacent to Scenic Lakes Road, about 200 yards north of that road's junction with State Route 23 in Hardyston.

Hiking opportunities include the Dagmar-Dale Nature Trail—a double-loop path (the first 0.6 mile of which is wheelchair-accessible) in the vicinity of the refuge headquarters; Wood Duck Nature Trail—a 1.6-mile path on a former railroad bed near the south end of the refuge, offering views of a red-maple swamp, a cattail marsh, a wet meadow, and a beaver flowage (an interpretive trail brochure is available); and the Liberty Loop Trail—a 2.5-mile loop around a wetland and grassland management unit at the north end of the refuge straddling the New York-New Jersey state line. A 1-mile section of the latter trail is co-aligned with the Ap-palachian Trail that runs from Maine to Georgia.

As described by refuge manager Libby Herland:

Your impression of the refuge is greatly influenced by your mode of transportation. Driving along the edge of the refuge, one gets a sense of broad, open expanses with wonderful Appalachian Mountain views and valleys. From the trails, one experiences the intimacy of singing songbirds right above your head, bobolinks perched on the tip of a grass blade, and wood ducks flying through the trees. From the river, the quiet stillness reflected in the great blue heron, the forest canopy reaching over the river, and the moss-covered limestone provide a completely different experience.

Visitors are cautioned to be alert for poison ivy and ticks. The latter may carry Lyme dis-ease. Insect repellent is advised during the warmer months.

Lodgings and meals are available in such communities as Hamburg, Colesville, and Vernon, New Jersey and Warwick, New York.

Access to Wallkill River Refuge from State Route 23, about midway between Hamburg and Sussex, is north 1.5 miles on County Route 565.

Further information: Wallkill River National Wildlife Refuge, 1547 County Route 565, Sus-sex, NJ 07461; telephone: (973) 702-7266.

New Mexico

Bitter Lake, containing 24,551 acres in three units, was established in 1937 to enhance and protect ecologically significant habitats for a great diversity of migratory waterfowl and other wildlife in the Pecos River Valley of southeastern New Mexico. As many as 10,000 wintering lesser sandhill cranes and at least 20,000 geese (snow, Canada, and Ross's), along with several thousand ducks, congregate here. The refuge's name is derived from late-nineteenth-century ranchers, who described the taste of the lake's alkaline waters as "bitter."

The refuge includes natural wetlands, such as playa lakes, marsh, colorful gypsum sinkholes and springs, seeps, streams, a stretch of the Pecos River, and brushy riparian bottomland; managed impoundments and agricultural croplands; gently rolling desert uplands; sand dunes; and some scenic, erosion-sculpted, reddish bluffs. To the west, the Capitan Mountains provide a scenic backdrop.

Bitter Lake is at a major environmental crossroads. It is located where the northern end of the Chihuahuan Desert, extending up from Mexico, merges with the shortgrass prairie at the western edge of the southern Great Plains. It is also strategically situated where the ranges and migration routes of some eastern birds overlap with many western birds.

The refuge's fish management program is focused on the protection, maintenance, and enhancement of native species and their habitats. Springs and gypsum sinkholes provide vital habitat for such rare native fish species as the Pecos pupfish (*Cyprinodon pecosensis*), greenthroat darter (*Etheostoma lepidum*), and the endangered Pecos gambusia (*Gambusia nobilis*). Bitter Lake Refuge has designated three sinkhole areas in which environmental protection and scientific research are the top management priorities: Lake St. Francis, Inkpot, and Bitter Lake research natural areas.

Unfortunately, human uses of underground water in the Pecos River Valley have gradually drawn down the water table and pose a serious threat to these ecologically unique and fragile water-filled depressions. Groundwater contamination from septic tanks and oil and gas development are also a major concern. Visitor access to the research areas is limited to scientific and educational groups, by special permission only.

Most of the roughly 10,000-acre NORTH UNIT of the refuge has been designated as the Salt Creek Wilderness—part of the National Wilderness Preservation System. It features brushy bottomland, native grassland, and sand dunes. The MIDDLE UNIT, protecting a variety of wetland and other habitats, contains the refuge headquarters and an 8-mile loop tour road, from which some of the refuge's impoundments and other habitats may be viewed. The SOUTH UNIT, which is not open to visitation, contains a number of seasonally flooded ponds, as well as some grain croplands that are planted for the benefit of the great concentrations of wintering waterfowl and cranes.

The U.S. Fish and Wildlife Service carries out a number of important habitat enhancement programs. Water impoundments are seasonally regulated. They are lowered in the spring, providing shallow water areas where shorebirds can feed and where snowy plovers, avocets, and stilts can find suitable nesting habitat. The water levels are raised in time for the autumn arrival of wintering ducks and other water birds. An ongoing program of tamarisk eradication is helping to control this extremely aggressive, densely growing, nonnative, riparian shrub. And periodic prescription burns enhance the release of nutrients and thereby revitalize the native grasslands.

Matching habitat restoration funding has been provided for this refuge by Ducks Unlimited, Inc. for the ecologically important Hunter Marsh Wetland Restoration Project. As a result, water control structures now enable the management of water levels in this natural wetland habitat, for the benefit of many wetland birds and other wildlife and to provide protection for the threatened Pecos sunflower (*Helianthus paradoxus*).

The Friends of Bitter Lake National Wildlife Refuge is a nonprofit support group that is assisting the refuge in a variety of ways.

The refuge is open daily during daylight hours. There is no entrance fee. Refuge headquarters is open weekdays, except on national holidays.

Visitor activities include birdwatching; photography; driving the 8-mile, self-guiding, interpretive loop tour road; hiking (on two established trails, including the 1.7-mile loop Oxbow Trail, and within the wilderness area); and waterfowl hunting during the designated season. Camping is not allowed in the refuge, except backcountry camping by special use permit. Campground facilities are available in Bottomless Lakes State Park. November through February are the best months to see waterfowl, with November and December the peak for cranes and geese. April and May are the best for neotropical migratory shorebirds and songbirds.

Visitors are cautioned to be alert for rattlesnakes. Insect repellent is advised during the warmer months.

Fish and Wildlife Service research has recently revealed that more than 50 species of dragonflies and 30 species of damselflies inhabit, and nearly all breed on, the Bitter Lake Refuge. Many of them are far outside their normal range. This abundance is the result of the refuge's diversity of aquatic habitats—from the Pecos River to the freshwater springs and saline sinkholes. Consequently, Bitter Lake Refuge may well contain the greatest diversity of this order of insects, *Odonata*, for any place in the United States.

Lodgings and meals are available in Roswell.

Access to the refuge is east about 3 miles on U.S. Route 380 (Second Street) from Roswell, left onto Red Bridge Road (at a refuge sign), and follow refuge signs for about 8 miles to the headquarters; or north about 2 miles on U.S. Route 285 (Main Street) from Roswell, right onto Pine Lodge Road, and follow refuge signs for about 8 miles to the headquarters.

Further information: Bitter Lake National Wildlife Refuge, P.O. Box 7, Roswell, NM 88202; telephone: (505) 622-6755.

Bosque del Apache, comprising 57,191 acres, was established in 1939 to enhance and protect an ecologically diverse and scenically spectacular area at the northern end of the Chihuahuan Desert in the middle Rio Grande Valley of south-central New Mexico. This magnificent refuge reaches across the valley, between the Chupadera Mountains on the west and the San Pascual Mountains on the east. The 7,000-acre central core of the area consists of riparian floodplain habitat, onto which Rio Grande waters are diverted to maintain wetlands and croplands for the benefit of large concentrations of wintering geese, ducks, sandhill cranes, and other wildlife. Over 375 bird species have been recorded here.

The Spanish name *Bosque del Apache* means "woods of the Apache," derived from the time when Apache Indians occupied encampments in the sheltered riparian woodlands of willows and great cottonwood trees bordering the Rio Grande. In 1845, the land within today's refuge was designated by the Mexican government as the Bosque del Apache land grant.

From mid-November through mid-February, this is an especially magical place, where visitors may enjoy seeing huge clouds of snow geese against the distant mountains: flock after flock, wave upon wave of undulating lines and Vs, circling, gliding, and calling as they come, then landing and covering the ground like snow, to feed for a while, only to erupt en masse into the air once more amid a great chorus of their honking calls. Up to 50,000 of these Arctic-nesting geese spend the winter here.

This, too, is the time to see sandhill cranes, groups of these stately, red-crowned, gray birds stalking slowly across cornfields in search of food, their guttural, deep-rolling, honking calls heard for miles. When this refuge was established, there were fewer than 1,000 of these sandhills remaining in the Central Flyway—and a mere 17 of them wintering here. Today, thanks to the U.S. Fish and Wildlife Service's management programs, this refuge hosts roughly 18,000 of these birds.

Huge undulating flocks of red-winged and yellow-headed blackbirds fill the air above the wetlands, and wintering mallards, shovelers, pintails, and other ducks find areas of open water on ponds partially frozen over and bordered by frost-highlighted cattails. Flocks of wild turkeys strut across fields and in the bosque woodlands.

The refuge implements a number of ecologically important habitat management programs. Water control structures, including 50 miles of irrigation canals, divert and contain some of the waters of the Rio Grande to maintain marshes, rotational moist-soil units, and cropland. Grain crops are produced, some under cooperative agreements with farmers, for the benefit of the geese, cranes, and other wildlife. Marshy, moist-soil impoundments are drained, burned or disced, and refilled to promote the growth of marsh plants such as smartweed, chufa, bulrushes, sedges, and wild millet for the benefit of ducks and other water birds. Areas of tamarisk, an aggressive, non-native shrubby tree, are eradicated to allow the reestablishment of cottonwoods, willows, and other native bosque species.

Roughly 30,000 acres of the refuge's Chihuahuan Desert uplands and foothills have been designated as the Chupadera, Indian Well, and Little San Pascual Wilderness—units of the National Wilderness Preservation System.

Adjacent to the refuge's visitor center, volunteers and refuge staff have created a native plant garden that presents an extensive area of cacti, many flowering plants that attract more than sixty species of butterflies, native desert shrubs, and a tiny cienega where seeping water creates a pond that draws quail and other wildlife.

Establishment of Bosque del Apache was made possible partly with funding from the sale of Migratory Bird Hunting and Conservation Stamps (Duck Stamps). Ducks Unlimited, Inc. has assisted with important habitat enhancement projects. Friends of Bosque del Apache National Wildlife Refuge is a local nonprofit support group that is assisting the refuge.

The refuge is open daily. There is a tour-road entrance fee. The visitor center, which is open daily, presents interpretive displays and programs, information on species of wildlife presently on the refuge, and a bookstore.

Visitor activities include birdwatching; photography; driving the 12-mile tour loop road (entrance fee; open daily 1 hour before sunrise to 1 hour after dark); listening to an audio cassette that interprets the tour drive; seeing wildlife from seven (wheelchair-accessible) observation platforms along the tour road; hiking on a number of established trails; bicycling on roads open to motor vehicles and on designated bike trails; picnicking (a picnic pavillion is available adjacent to the visitor center); interpretive group tours (reservations required); primitive group camping for educational and volunteer groups only (reservations required); fishing; and limited hunting on part of the refuge during the designated season. Although there are no camping facilities provided on the refuge, campgrounds are located near the refuge and in Socorro.

Hiking opportunities include the Marsh Overlook Trail, an easy, 1.5-mile loop (closed occasionally to avoid disturbing the wildlife) with a 0.25-mile side trail to the top of a hill for a view of the bosque; Lagoon Trail, an easy, 0.75-mile route combining a path along this permanent marsh and a boardwalk across part of this wetland habitat; Rio Viejo Trail—an easy, 2-mile loop along a former river channel with young cottonwoods (spring flooding possible); River Trail, an easy, slightly more than 2-mile loop beneath an old-growth cottonwood bosque; Canyon Trail, a fairly easy, 2.5-mile loop that leads through a desert canyon and up to a lookout, providing a grand panorama of the refuge's bosque woodlands, wetlands, and fields; and Chupadera Wilderness Trail, a strenuous, 4.8-mile route, crossing desert terrain and climbing 1,700 feet to the 6,272-foot summit of Chupadera Peak for a spectacular view of this portion of the Rio Grande Valley and surrounding mountains.

Visitors are cautioned to be alert for rattlesnakes. Insect repellent is advised during the warmer months. Hikers are urged to apply sunscreen and bring along a generous supply of water, especially on the longer excursions.

In late November, the Bosque del Apache Festival of the Cranes features guided refuge tours, study groups, demonstrations, workshops, exhibits, and other environmental education programs for adults and children. This annual event, highlighting the return of the cranes to Bosque, was initiated in the late 1980s by the former, widely acclaimed refuge manager, Phil Norton, and is jointly hosted by the refuge and the Socorro Chamber of Commerce. A festival brochure may be obtained by calling (505) 835-0424.

Lodgings and meals are available in Socorro; and two B&Bs are located in San Antonio.

Access to the refuge is south 9 miles from Socorro on I-25 to San Antonio (exit #139), east 0.25 mile on State Route 380, right (south) onto Old State Route I (at the flashing signal light), and 9 miles to the visitor center. Or, go north 10 miles on I-25 from Las Cruces to San Marcial (exit #124), and north on Old State Route I.

Further information: Bosque del Apache National Wildlife Refuge, P.O. Box 1246, Socorro, NM 87801; telephone: (505) 835-1828.

Grulla, consisting of 3,236 acres, was established in 1969 to enhance and protect habitat for lesser sandhill cranes and other migratory birds near the Texas state line in eastern New Mexico. The name (pronounced GRU-ya) means "crane" in Spanish. Roughly two-thirds of this refuge is a playa, or saline lake bed, called Salt Lake, while most of the rest is western Great Plains shortgrass prairie, with predominantly buffalo grass and a number of grama grasses.

Salt Lake frequently remains dry for a year or more. But during years of sufficient precipitation, a body of water provides an important resting area for the cranes and a variety of waterfowl.

The refuge is open daily during daylight hours. There is no entrance fee.

Visitor activities include birdwatching, photography, driving on the entrance road that ends at a parking area and the trailhead, and hiking on a short trail that leads to a hilltop for a view of Salt Lake. Although camping is not permitted on the refuge, campground facilities are provided at nearby Oasis State Park.

Visitors are cautioned to be alert for rattlesnakes.

Lodgings and meals are available in such communities as Portales and Clovis.

Access to this refuge is southeast about 25 miles on State Route 88 from Portales.

Further information: Grulla National Wildlife Refuge, P.O. Box 549, Muleshoe, TX 79347; telephone: (806) 946-3341.

Las Vegas, containing 8,672 acres, was established in 1965 as a sanctuary for the conservation of migratory birds. The refuge protects a scenically beautiful, canyon-bordered plateau in the 6,000- to 6,500-foot elevation foothills of the rugged Sangre de Cristo Mountains in northern New Mexico.

Here at the merging of the western edge of the Great Plains with the southern end of the Rocky Mountains, habitats atop the plateau include broad expanses of shortgrass prairie; scattered marshes, ponds, and impoundments in which water levels are regulated for the benefit of water birds; groves of cottonwood trees; and croplands that are planted with wheat, barley, corn, and peas for the benefit of waterfowl and other wildlife. Gambel oak and pinyon pine-juniper woodlands grow on canyon slopes; tall ponderosa pines rise along canyon rims.

Raptors are prominent among the migratory and nesting birds of this refuge—bald and golden eagles, numerous hawks, and falcons. When there is sufficient water, thousands of geese and ducks, hundreds of sandhill cranes, and many shorebirds pause on their southward autumn migration or spend the winter on the refuge. Numerous neotropical songbirds also pass through here during spring and autumn. Over 270 bird species use the refuge.

Establishment of the refuge was made possible partly with revenues from the sale of Migratory Bird Hunting and Conservation Stamps (Duck Stamps).

The refuge is open daily during daylight hours. There is no entrance fee. The refuge office is open on weekdays, except national holidays.

Visitor activities include birdwatching; photography; driving the 8-mile loop tour road (also, on Sunday afternoons in November, driving a 4.5-mile autumn-wildlife route through part of the refuge that is closed to visitors during the rest of the year); hiking the scenic but fairly steep 0.5-mile Gallinas Nature Trail (by permit only and open only on weekdays) that descends into scenic Gallinas Canyon; fishing (only at Lake McAllister—a state-owned waterfowl area within the refuge, managed by the New Mexico Department of Game and Fish); and limited goose and dove hunting on part of the refuge during the designated seasons. Although camping is not permitted on the refuge, primitive camping is allowed on Lake McAllister Waterfowl Area and campground facilities are available in Storrie Lake State Park.

Visitors are cautioned to be alert for rattlesnakes.

Lodgings and meals are available in the community of Las Vegas.

Access to the refuge is east 1.5 miles on State Route 104, from I-25's exit 345 at Las Vegas, and south about 4 miles on State Route 281.

Further information: Las Vegas National Wildlife Refuge, Route 1, Box 339, Las Vegas, NM 87701; telephone: (505) 425-3581.

Maxwell, comprising 3,698 acres, was established in 1965 to enhance and protect an area of scattered lakes and grassland at the mountain-bordered western edge of the Great Plains in northeastern New Mexico. Thousands of Canada geese and ducks, along with sandhill cranes and bald eagles, spend the winter on Maxwell Refuge. Migratory white pelicans pause here on their southward, late-summer/early-autumn migration, and some shorebirds and several species of grebes nest and raise their young.

Regarding the habitat, refuge manager Dan Winkler has explained:

Because of prior agricultural uses, the refuge's landscape has been fragmented and altered. To date, there has been little habitat restoration by the U.S. Fish and Wildlife Service. However, there are a number of exotic, invasive plant species, such as hoary cress, Russian knapweed, and musk and Canada thistles, that have unfortunately been established and are proliferating. A current emphasis of refuge management is to control these undesirable species, as a first step toward restoring the native shortgrass prairie.

The refuge is open daily. There is no entrance fee. The refuge office is open on weekdays, except national holidays.

Visitor activities include birdwatching, wildlife photography, hiking on two trails, driving on 7 miles of roads (slippery when wet), prearranged guided tours for groups, primitive camping and shallow-draft boating (no boat-launching ramp) on Lake 13, and fishing at Lakes 13 and 14. Over 340 bird species have been recorded here.

Visitors are cautioned to be alert for rattlesnakes. Insect repellent is advised during the warmer months.

Lodgings and meals are available in such communities as Raton, Springer, and Cimarron.

Access to Maxwell Refuge is south on I-25 from Raton to the Maxwell exit, north 0.8 mile on State Route 445, and left (west) onto State Route 505 for 2.5 miles.

Further information: Maxwell National Wildlife Refuge, P.O. Box 276, Maxwell, NM 87728; telephone: (505) 375-2331.

San Andres, encompassing 57,215 acres, was established in 1941 to enhance and protect important habitat of the desert bighorn sheep and other wildlife inhabiting the southern part of the canyon-carved San Andres Mountains, in the Chihuahuan Desert of southern New Mexico. This refuge is located within the boundaries of the White Sands Missile Range and is closed to public entry.

In addition to a small population of bighorns, there are mule deer, mountain lions, and at least another 40 species of mammals living in this scenically spectacular desert mountain range. The more than 130 kinds of birds include golden eagle and other raptors; scaled, Gambel's, and Montezuma quail; white-winged dove; Costa's hummingbird; and hooded oriole.

Further information: San Andres National Wildlife Refuge, P.O. Box 756, Las Cruces, NM 88004; telephone: (505) 382-5047.

Sevilleta, consisting of 229,673 acres, was established in 1973 to restore and protect a vast, ecologically outstanding area of diverse wildlife habitats at the northern end of the Chihuahuan Desert in central New Mexico's middle Rio Grande Valley. The refuge extends across the valley, from the Ladrone Mountains on the west to the Los Pinos Mountains on the east. Although there are extensive expanses of semiarid and arid upland and foothills, a relatively small but significant portion of Sevilleta contains riparian wetland.

The major focus of this refuge is long-term ecological research, combined with ecologically sensitive restoration and protective management of land that was previously impaired by many years of livestock grazing, aggressive invasion of non-native vegetation, ecologically disruptive fire suppression, and other harmful human impacts.

Geese, ducks, sandhill cranes, shorebirds, and neotropical songbirds pause on Sevilleta refuge during their spring and autumn migrations. Rocky Mountain bighorn sheep, pronghorns, and mule deer are among the roughly 90 species of mammals.

Most of this refuge was formerly part of a Spanish land grant that was established in 1819 and known as the Sevilleta de la Joya ("the Jewel"). After New Mexico became a territory of the United States, the former grant was bought by a businessman, General Thomas Campbell, who grazed cattle on the land. Following prolonged drought and grazing, the Campbell Family Foundation decided to make the Sevilleta available for environmental research and protective management. In 1973, at far below market value, the foundation conveyed the land to The Nature Conservancy, which then donated it to the U.S. Fish and Wildlife Service.

Since establishment of Sevilleta Refuge, a variety of ongoing habitat restoration programs have been and continue to be implemented. Among them are the reintroduction of fire by means of periodic prescribed burning; removal and control of non-native plant species, such as tamarisk and Russian olive; replanting with native plant species, such as cottonwoods and willow; and restoration of natural wetland areas with construction of water control structures and impoundments.

The first of a number of wetland restoration projects on the refuge was at the 125-acre Cornerstone Marsh. Dense thickets of the tamarisk and Russian olive were eradicated. Water control structures were installed, and historic Rio Grande wetlands habitat was reestablished for the benefit of waterfowl, wading birds, shorebirds, and other wildlife. This Fish and

Wildlife Service project, which was completed in 1998, was jointly accomplished with financial and other assistance provided by Ducks Unlimited, Inc., Bosque Improvement Group, New Mexico State Game & Fish, Intermountain West Joint Venture, and the U.S. Bureau of Reclamation.

In 1995, Sevilleta Refuge was chosen for its remoteness and size to help implement the Mexican Gray Wolf Reintroduction Program. The Mexican wolf (*Canis lupus baileyi*) is genetically the most distinct, rarest, and southernmost subspecies of the North American gray wolf.

The refuge is open daily during daylight hours. There is no entrance fee. The visitor center is open on weekdays, except national holidays.

Visitor activities include birdwatching and photography in Unit A, Cornerstone Marsh, and Unit B; hiking in scenic San Lorenzo Canyon and on a 1-mile interpretive trail with four "biome" loops featuring Great Plains prairie grassland, Rocky Mountain pinyon-juniper woodland, Great Basin steppe-shrubland, and Chihuahuan Desert; and hunting (duck and dove) in Unit A during the designated seasons. Educational programs and interpretive tours may be scheduled with the refuge staff.

Visitors are cautioned to be alert for rattlesnakes.

More than 200 species of birds have been recorded on Sevilleta Refuge.

Lodgings and meals are available in Socorro.

Access to Sevilleta is west from I-25's exit 169.

Further information: Sevilleta National Wildlife Refuge, P.O. Box 1248, Socorro, NM 87801; telephone: (505) 864-4021.

New York: National Wildlife Refuges

Amagansett, containing 36 acres, was established in 1968 to protect a unique area of double-dune Atlantic Ocean barrier beach located in the Town of East Hampton, on the south fork of eastern Long Island, New York. The refuge, which was previously a U.S. Coast Guard property, contains one of the few remaining undeveloped coastal barrier beaches on Long Island. It is being managed to preserve the fragile beach, dunes, seabeach amaranth, and interdunal cranberry bogs and swales. These habitats provide important habitat for a large variety of migratory shorebirds, raptors, songbirds—including wintering Ipswich sparrows—and other wildlife.

The U.S. Fish and Wildlife Service is managing the beach for potential nesting by the federally listed threatened piping plover and least tern. Although the ocean beach is open to visitation, the rest of the refuge is only open by special use permit. Visitor activities include wildlife observation, photography, environmental education, hiking along the beach, and surf-fishing.

Lodgings and meals are available in such communities as East Hampton and Southampton.

Access to Amagansett Refuge from State Route 27 at the Town of Amagansett is south on Atlantic Avenue.

Further information: Amagansett National Wildlife Refuge, c/o The Long Island NWR Complex, P.O. Box 21, Shirley, NY 11967; telephone: (631) 286-0485.

Conscience Point, consisting of 60 acres, was established in 1964 to manage and protect an area of mature oak-beech forest, shrub, maritime grassland, and freshwater and salt marsh habitats. The refuge is located on the northern shore of Long Island's south fork, near North Sea, New York. Conscience Point is one of a number of important tidal wetland areas in the vicinity, which local residents refer to as the Cow Neck Complex.

The refuge's wetlands attract concentrations of waterfowl—notably wintering American black ducks—as well as wading birds and shorebirds. During the spring, numerous species of neotropical songbirds nest here or pause on their way to breeding areas farther north.

The U.S. Fish and Wildlife Service's habitat management activities include tidal wetland restoration, grassland expansion and maintenance, erection of nesting structures for ospreys and other species, control of invasive plants such as the common reed (*Phragmites*), introduction of the federally listed endangered sandplain gerardia, management for the protection of the rare Nantucket serviceberry and bush rockrose, and periodic prescribed burning to promote nutrient cycling and spur the growth of plants that offer food and cover for waterfowl and other wildlife.

Conscience Point Refuge is accessible by special use permit.

Further information: Conscience Point National Wildlife Refuge, c/o The Long Island NWR Complex, P.O. Box 21, Shirley, NY 11967; telephone: (631) 286-0485.

Elizabeth A. Morton, comprising 187 acres, was established in 1954 to protect an area of sand-and-pebble beaches, steeply eroded bluffs, upland deciduous woodlands, freshwater and brackish ponds, kettle holes, fields, salt marsh, and a lagoon. The refuge encompasses Jessups Neck, a narrow peninsula extending between Noyac and Little Peconic bays. It is located on the northern shore of Long Island's south fork, just west of Sag Harbor, New York. The refuge is named for the donor of the land to the U.S. Fish and Wildlife Service.

Morton Refuge also provides habitat to several federally and state-listed endangered and threatened species, including the piping plover; roseate, common, and least terns; osprey; peregrine falcon; and Kemp's ridley and loggerhead sea turtles. Wading and shore birds are common in the warmer months, and sea ducks and other waterfowl are common in winter.

Morton Refuge's habitat management activities include closing the peninsula to visitation during the April through August breeding season of the piping plovers and least and roseate terns, providing nesting platforms for ospreys and nesting boxes for other species, mowing the refuge's fields to maintain grassland habitat, and managing the ponds for the benefit of waterfowl and other wildlife.

The refuge is open daily during daylight hours. An entrance fee is charged.

Visitor activities include wildlife observation, photography, interpretation and environmental education, hiking, and surf-fishing. Hiking opportunities include a 1-mile interpretive trail that offers views of woodland, wetland, and grassland habitats as it leads to a bay beach; and a 3-mile trail that invites exploration of Jessups Neck peninsula.

Visitors are cautioned to be alert for ticks, which may carry Lyme disease.

Lodgings and meals are available in such communities as Sag Harbor, East Hampton, and Southampton.

Access to Morton Refuge from Exit 9 on State Route 27 is north on North Sea Road, east (right) 5 miles on Noyack Road, and north (left) on the refuge entrance road.

Further information: Morton National Wildlife Refuge, c/o The Long Island NWR Complex, P.O. Box 21, Shirley, NY 11967; telephone: (631) 286-0485.

Iroquois, consisting of 10,818 acres, was established in 1958 to manage and protect an area of hardwood swamps, woodlands, freshwater marshes, wet meadows, pastures, and croplands for the benefit of migratory waterfowl and other wildlife. The refuge is located midway between Rochester and Buffalo in northwestern New York. Initially the Oak Orchard National Wildlife Refuge, it was subsequently renamed the Iroquois National Wildlife Refuge.

A primary purpose of Iroquois Refuge is to offer migratory birds a resting and feeding area on their flights between breeding and wintering grounds. The largest influx of migrating waterfowl occurs here from mid-March through early April, with totals averaging from 40,000 to 80,000 Canada geese and more than 4,000 ducks of two dozen species. According to the U.S. Fish and Wildlife Service, only a few hundred stay to nest on the refuge each year. The less spectacular peak of autumn waterfowl migration generally runs from mid-September through early October. Migrating shorebirds reach the peak of their northbound numbers in May and southbound numbers in July and August. Large influxes of neotropical songbirds, including many species of warblers, occur from late April through mid-May. Although a few of the latter remain to nest here, most continue to nesting habitat farther to the north.

A variety of habitat management activities occur on Iroquois Refuge. Water levels are managed within each of 16 diked shallow impoundments. Draw downs for each impoundment are on a five-year cycle, so that several of these areas are drained down each year. The pools are drained to provide habitat for migrating shorebirds and to promote the growth of nutrient-rich submergent and emergent plants. These aquatic plants provide food and shelter for migratory waterfowl when water levels are subsequently raised.

Woodland areas are managed with selective cutting (i.e., mowing "woodcock strips" with a brush hog). Grassland habitat is maintained by mowing and with periodic prescribed burning to prevent the invasion of woody plants and to promote nutrient cycling. The refuge also controls certain pest plants, notably the non-native, invasive purple loosestrife (see discussion of this species in the Montezuma Refuge text). These activities offer a diversity of managed habitats for wildlife, along with areas of older-growth forest that are essentially protected.

Establishment of Iroquois Refuge was made possible partly with revenues from the sale of Migratory Bird Hunting and Conservation Stamps (Duck Stamps). Ducks Unlimited, Inc. has helped enhance more than 300 acres of the refuge's wetland habitat. Friends of Iroquois National Wildlife Refuge is a local nonprofit support group that is assisting the refuge.

The refuge is open daily during daylight hours. There is no entrance fee. The visitor center headquarters is open on weekdays, except national holidays. The visitor center is also open on weekends during the spring migration.

Visitor activities include birdwatching, photography, viewing interpretive exhibits in the visitor center, driving on a number of public highways and roads that run through or adjacent to the refuge, viewing refuge wetlands from four observation overlooks, hiking, cross-country skiing and snowshoeing, bicycling (only on Feeder Road and public roads), canoeing and nonmotorized boating only on Oak Orchard Creek (which winds through the eastern part of the refuge), fishing, trapping, and hunting (deer, turkey, waterfowl, and small game) on parts of the refuge during the designated seasons. Although camping is not permitted on the refuge, campground facilities are available at a number of places in the general vicinity, including Darien Lakes, Golden Hill, and Lakeside Beach state parks (the latter two on the shore of Lake Ontario).

Hiking opportunities include three self-guiding trails: part of the Kanyoo Trail—a 1-mile loop (or a shorter 0.6-mile loop) near the junction of Feeder and Lewiston roads that offers views of Mohawk Pool; Onondaga Trail—a 1.2-mile route from Sour Springs Road that offers views of Onondaga Pool (the latter trail is open only to hunters during the shotgun deer season); and Swallow Hollow Trail—a 1-mile loop, two-thirds of which consists of an elevated boardwalk. This trail has been temporarily closed for much-needed repairs of the boardwalk. Hiking is also permitted on 3.5-mile Feeder Road, except from March 1 to July 15, when only the refuge's three nature trails and the four overlooks are open to visitation to avoid disturbing nesting wildlife. Cross-country skiing and snowshoeing are permitted on Kanyoo and Onondaga trails, Feeder Road, and Mohawk Ski Trail (the latter closes on March 1).

Visitors are cautioned to be alert for ticks, which may carry Lyme disease. Insect repellent is advised during the warmer months.

Of the more than 265 species of birds that have been recorded on Iroquois Refuge, many are the same as those on Montezuma Refuge.

Lodgings and meals are available in such communities as Batavia, Medina, and Corfu.

Access to the Iroquois Refuge from Exit 48A on the New York State Thruway (I-90) is north and northwest 8 miles on State Route 77 and northeast (right) on Casey Road to the refuge headquarters.

Further information: Iroquois National Wildlife Refuge, 1101 Casey Road, Basom, NY 14013; telephone: (716) 948-5445.

Montezuma, comprising 7,889 acres, was established in 1938 to restore and protect part of the once-vast Montezuma Marsh for the benefit of large concentrations of migratory waterfowl and other wildlife. The refuge is located at the northern end of Cayuga Lake in the Finger Lakes Region of north-central New York. The New York State Thruway (I-90) cuts through the refuge.

For thousands of years, this marsh, which measured roughly 12 miles in length by 8 miles at its widest, was among North America's most important freshwater wetlands. Native Americans, first the Algonquin Indians and then the Cayugas of the Iroquois Nation, obtained some of their food and other needs from the marsh while leaving the habitat intact. As Euro-American settlers moved into the region in the nineteenth century, small areas around the edge of the wetlands were drained for agriculture. But the U.S. Fish and Wildlife Service explains:

There were no dramatic changes in the marsh until the development of the Erie Canal . . . [constructed from 1817 to 1825], when it became apparent that feeder canals from Seneca and Cayuga Lakes would in time link these lakes with the main line. . . . The Erie Canal did not greatly affect the marshes, as the Seneca River still flowed directly from Cayuga Lake into the marshes.

In 1910, construction of the Seneca and Cayuga extension of the New York State Barge Canal altered the marshes. A lock was built at the north end of Cayuga Lake and a dam was constructed at the outlet of the lake. This effectively lowered the level of the river by eight to ten feet . . . and the waters drained from the marshes. The meandering rivers were straightened and deepened, thereby creating additional drainage-ways.

In 1937, after the Bureau of Biological Survey (which later became the U.S. Fish and Wildlife Service) acquired 6,432 acres of the former marshland, the Civilian Conservation Corps started to create a network of low dikes within which water could be held and regulated to begin the task of marsh restoration. The following year, the Montezuma Migratory Bird Refuge (subsequently renamed as a national wildlife refuge) was established. By the early 1940s, the refuge's wetlands were gradually restored.

Today, efforts are continuing toward restoring and managing the Montezuma Marsh—not only within the refuge, but well beyond its boundaries. Under a cooperative conservation program, known as the Montezuma Wetlands Complex Initiative, other lands, totaling more than 30,000 acres, are being enhanced and managed for the benefit of the wetland-dependent wildlife and compatible public recreational uses. These lands are a mixture of marsh habitat, grasslands and farm fields, and small patches of woodland. Partnerships are essential to the success of this program.

How did it happen that a place in New York state was named "Montezuma"? The Fish and Wildlife Service explains, "The name . . . was first used in 1806 when Dr. Peter Clark named his hilltop home . . . after the palace of the Aztec Emperor Montezuma in Mexico City. Eventually the Marsh, the Village, and the Refuge all acquired the name."

Montezuma Refuge contains about 3,500 acres of diked shallow pools, also known as moist-soil impoundments, within which water levels are seasonally regulated. The largest of these are the 1,600-acre Main Pool and the 1,300-acre Tschache Pool. During part of the year, the water is lowered to provide shallow water and mudflats for shorebirds and wading birds and to promote the growth of emergent and submergent plants that will later provide food for the influx of migrating waterfowl. During the remainder of the year, water levels are raised to provide resting and feeding habitat for the large concentrations of waterfowl. Submergent plants include sago pondweed, water milfoil, waterweeds, coontail, and bladderwort. At times, mats of tiny duckweed plants float on parts of the water's surface. Emergent species consist mostly of cattails and purple loosestrife.

The refuge also includes some areas of woodland and grassland habitats that are managed to enhance and maintain a diversity of wildlife. During the late 1970s, Montezuma Refuge, in cooperation with the state's Department of Environmental Conservation, successfully implemented a bald eagle release program. According to the Fish and Wildlife Service, "Over a period of four years, 23 eagles were released through a 'hacking' program. Since the program's inception, bald eagles have returned to Montezuma and have successfully reared young." Over 320 bird species have been recorded here.

The refuge has also been a major focus of efforts to research methods for controlling and managing a wetland pest plant: the non-native, invasive purple loosestrife (*Lythrum salicaria*). Although this species is visually attractive with its tall, slender spikes of brilliant purplish-pink flowers that bloom from June to September, it aggressively competes with and overwhelms native wetland plants. As described by the Fish and Wildlife Service:

Purple loosestrife appeared along the New England seaboard in the early 1800's. A native of Eurasia, it probably arrived with the early maritime traffic. Seeds are believed to have been transported in the materials (soils, sand, and rocks) used by ships for ballast. This material was then dumped upon arrival at ports. . . . Valued as an herb in Europe, purple loosestrife was also probably brought in by many immigrants. By the late 1800's, . . . [it] had spread throughout the northeastern United States and southeastern Canada. . . .

After the turn of the century, when purple loosestrife began its westward expansion . . . , the plant became a serious threat to wetland communities throughout the northeastern and north central regions of the country. . . .

The impact of this weed on North American wetlands has been disastrous. Native wetland plants have been crowded out by purple loosestrife. The loss of these [native] plants has led to a reduction in suitable habitat for wildlife, resulting in reduced productivity for all species of wetland-dependent wildlife in aquatic ecosystems.

For example, platform nesting species cannot use the stiff stems for nest construction, nor are stems or rootstocks palatable to muskrats. Dense, closely spaced clumps do not provide brood cover or foraging areas for waterfowl. These clumps are fairly resistant to decay and over several years the ground level surrounding these clumps is raised as organic litter is trapped in the root system. As a result, native plants such as cattails, smartweed, rushes and sedges are greatly reduced, or even eliminated.

Montezuma National Wildlife Refuge has been, and will remain, a key area for research into management and control of purple loosestrife. In part, this is due to the fact that the refuge has suffered one of the nation's worst infestations of loosestrife over the past . . . [half century]. In 1951, loosestrife was found only in sparse stands; by 1980, the plant occupied 1,500 acres. . . .

Since 1985, the refuge's loosestrife research program has been carried out with the assistance of Cornell University scientists and the International Institute of Biological Control. This program has included the study of natural enemies of loosestrife in the species' native habitat in Europe. According to Cornell's Department of Natural Resources:

After years of testing, three species of weevils and two species of leaf-beetles have been identified as host-specific (they live and feed exclusively on purple loosestrife) and approved for introduction and release by the Animal and Plant Health Inspection Service and the U.S. Fish and Wildlife Service.

One of the weevils attacks the rootstock and the other two weevils feed on the flowers and seeds. The beetles feed on the leaves of the plant. Cornell scientists have set up large cages on the Refuge to study how each species and different combinations of the species influence the growth of purple loosestrife. This research will identify the "best" agent or agent-combination for release. At the same time, the experiments will study the response of native plants to the insects. . . .

A 1998 Cornell University pamphlet, *Biocontrol Insects Feast on Purple Loosestrife*, states, " . . . biological control, the use of natural enemies to control a pest, shows real promise. . . . Since 1992, a nationally coordinated program has introduced four species of European insects (one root-mining weevil, one flowering-feeding weevil and two leaf-feeding beetles) in North America." In 1993, the two species of beetles were released at a site in southern Ontario where there was a solid stand of loosestrife. By 1995, the beetles had "defoliated nearly all the loosestrife." By 1996, "the purple loosestrife biomass was reduced by over 90 percent," while native species such as cattails were flourishing. "The results observed in Ontario are expected to be repeated at many purple loosestrife infestations where insects are introduced. The level of . . . reduction will depend on individual site characteristics and the insect species introduced. However, it is anticipated that purple loosestrife will be controlled over large areas within the next decade."

Establishment of Montezuma Refuge was made possible partly with revenues from the sale of Migratory Bird Hunting and Conservation Stamps (Duck Stamps). Ducks Unlimited, Inc. has helped enhance more than 3,700 acres of the refuge's wetland habitat. Friends of Montezuma National Wildlife Refuge is a local nonprofit support group that is assisting the refuge in many ways.

The refuge is open daily during daylight hours. There is no entrance fee. The visitor center is open daily from March to November and on weekdays during the rest of the year, except Christmas and New Year's Day.

Visitor activities include birdwatching, photography, viewing interpretive exhibits and programs at the visitor center, viewing the Main Pool and Tschache Pool from observation towers, driving the 3.5-mile self-guiding Wildlife Drive (an interpretive brochure is available), hiking, guided tours in the spring and autumn, picnicking (at a wheelchair-accessible picnic area), and hunting (deer and waterfowl) on parts of the refuge during the designated seasons. Educational programs are offered to organized groups by prearrangement. Camping is not permitted on the refuge, but campground facilities are available at a number of places in the general vicinity, including nearby Cayuga Lake State Park.

Hiking opportunities include the Esker Brook Nature Trail—a 1.5-mile path (open from January through October). This trail consists of three interconnecting parts: the Brook Trail, the Orchard Trail, and the Ridge Trail. The latter segment runs along the top of a narrow ridge, known as an esker, consisting of sand and gravel that was deposited roughly 10,000 years ago by a stream flowing through a tunnel at the base of a stationary or retreating glacier. Additional trails are located on the state's Northern Montezuma Wetlands Management Area and other parts of the Montezuma Wetlands Complex.

Visitors are cautioned to be alert for ticks, which may carry Lyme disease. Insect repellent is advised during the warmer months.

Lodgings and meals are available in such communities as Seneca Falls, Waterloo, Auburn, Weedsport, Ithaca, and Syracuse.

Access to Montezuma Refuge from Exit 41 on I-90 (the New York State Thruway) is south on State Route 414, left (east) at the traffic light and proceeding about 5 miles on State Route 318 (to the end of the latter route, where it meets U.S. Route 20), left (east) 1.25 miles on U.S. Route 20, and left (north) onto the entrance road.

Further information: Montezuma National Wildlife Refuge, 3395 Route 5 & 20 East, Seneca Falls, NY 13148; telephone: (315) 568-5987.

Oyster Bay, encompassing 3,209 acres, was established in 1968 to protect salt marsh and tidal-bottom bay habitats and a small freshwater wetland. The refuge is located along Oyster Bay, about 20 miles east of New York City on the north shore of Long Island, New York. It is adjacent to Sagamore Hill National Historic Site—a National Park Service-administered area that protects the home of former U.S. President Theodore Roosevelt, who established the first National Wildlife Refuge (Pelican Island, in Florida) in 1903.

During the winter, large concentrations of waterfowl are attracted to the refuge, with peak numbers sometimes reaching as many as 24,000 birds. Generally the most common species are greater scaup, American black duck, bufflehead, canvasback, mallard, long-tailed (oldsquaw), common goldeneye, red-breasted merganser, and Canada goose. The refuge's Frost and Mill Neck creeks provide nesting habitat for black ducks, clapper rails, and ospreys. More than 125 species of birds have been recorded on Oyster Bay Refuge, many of which are the same as those on nearby Target Rock Refuge (see listings in the text for that refuge).

The bay waters and wetlands attract a number of marine fauna, including harbor and gray seals, Kemp's ridley and loggerhead sea turtles, and an exceptionally large number of the northern diamondback terrapin.

The refuge is open daily during daylight hours. There is no entrance fee.

Visitor activities include wildlife observation, photography, environmental education and interpretive programs, boating, and fishing. As the U.S. Fish and Wildlife Service explains, "The Refuge receives heavy use from recreational boaters from May through September, numbering three thousand boats on peak weekends and a thousand boats a day during the week. . . . The only remaining commercial oyster farm/aquaculture operation on Long Island operates on the Refuge. It provides 90 percent of New York State's oysters. In addition, fifty independent commercial shellfishers (mainly clammers) are active at the Refuge."

Lodgings and meals are available in such communities as Oyster Bay, East Norwich, Huntington Station, and Glen Cove.

Access to Oyster Bay Refuge is by boat, public beach, and private docks.

Further information: Oyster Bay National Wildlife Refuge, c/o The Long Island NWR Complex, P.O. Box 21, Shirley, NY 11967; telephone: (631) 286-0485.

Sayville, consisting of 126 acres, was established in 1992 to protect an area of pitch pine-oak woodland and scattered fields that provide important habitat for migrating neotropical song-birds. The refuge is located in West Sayville, about 4 miles inland from the northern shore of Great South Bay in south-central Long Island, New York.

The refuge's habitat management activities include prescribed burning to promote nutrient cycling and spur new growth, placement of supplemental nesting structures for a number of bird species, control of invasive plant species such as bittersweet, and the expansion and main-tenance of native grasslands. Sayville Refuge supports one of only 12 known populations of a federally listed endangered plant, the sandplain gerardia. The refuge contains the most prolific site of the six on Long Island and serves as a transplant site for other locations on the island.

Visitation is allowed on Sayville Refuge by special use permit.

Further information: Sayville National Wildlife Refuge, c/o The Long Island NWR Complex, P.O. Box 21, Shirley, NY 11967; telephone: (631) 286-0485.

Seatuck, containing 196 acres, was established in 1968 to protect an area that is about evenly divided among pine barren, grassland, and salt marsh habitats. The refuge is located on the northern shore of Great South Bay in south-central Long Island, New York. The name *Seatuck* is derived from a Native American word meaning the mouth of a tidal river or creek.

Except for the small slice of nature provided by the National Audubon Society's Scully Sanctuary, adjoining the refuge to the west, and the bay to the south, Seatuck is surrounded by suburban development. Its wetland habitat attracts wading birds, shorebirds, and many species of waterfowl—notably concentrations of wintering American black ducks and Atlantic brant. Ospreys nest on the refuge. To enhance this raptor's nesting opportunities, the U.S. Fish and Wildlife Service has erected supplemental nesting platforms at various sites. During the spring, numerous species of neotropical migratory songbirds, such as thrushes and warblers, nest in the refuge's wooded uplands or pause on their way to breeding areas farther north. More than 200 species of birds have been recorded here.

In 1994, the refuge was the site of a significant salt marsh restoration project to im-prove tidal flow, restore natural panne habitats, and reduce the prevalence of the invasive common reed (*Phragmites*) for the benefit of migratory birds. This project entailed the con-struction of a tidal channel in the spring of 1992 to increase the tidal exchange with Great South Bay. Thanks to funding and other assistance from the National Fish and Wildlife Foundation and Ducks Unlimited, Inc., the project was very successful. A beneficial result of this project was that the mosquito population plummeted, which the neighboring com-munity greatly appreciated and applauded.

Other habitat management activities include grassland restoration and periodic prescribed burning to promote nutrient cycling and spur the growth of plants that offer food and cover for waterfowl and other wildlife. The Seatuck Refuge also offers the potential for introducing a federally listed endangered plant, the sandplain gerardia.

Visitation is allowed by special use permit.

Further information: Seatuck National Wildlife Refuge, c/o The Long Island NWR Complex, P.O. Box 21, Shirley, NY 11967; telephone: (631) 286-0485.

Shawangunk Grasslands, containing 566 acres, was established in 1999 to manage and protect one of the most extensive, intact, and ecologically significant wet grasslands remaining in the northeastern United States. The refuge is located near the village of Wallkill, at the southern edge of Ulster County in southeastern New York. It encompasses most of the former U.S. Army's Galeville Training Site, a West Point Military Academy facility that most recently was being leased to the FBI. When neither the U.S. Army nor the FBI had any further use for the area, it was transferred to the U.S. Fish and Wildlife Service. The name *Shawangunk* is pronounced SHAWN-gum.

As the Fish and Wildlife Service explains, "The primary habitat management priority of the refuge is grassland management to increase the productivity of nesting grassland birds. This includes the management of non-native invasive species, such as purple loosestrife, *Phragmites* [common reed], and Canada thistle." While it is not possible to completely eliminate the attractive but aggressive loosestrife, it is important to keep it from competing with native species of the refuge's wet-grassland ecosystem. Biological controls are being implemented. (See further discussion of this species and its control in the Montezuma Refuge text.)

Among the many breeding species of grassland birds that are attracted to the refuge are bobolink, upland sandpiper, eastern meadowlark, and a number of sparrows including savannah, vesper, and grasshopper. Wintering raptors include short-eared owl and northern harrier.

In addition to the 400 acres of grassland, the refuge includes about 160 acres of mixed hardwood forest, predominantly of oak and beech trees, around the edges of the grasslands. There are also two very small ponds.

The Fish and Wildlife Service anticipates eventually removing most of the airport runways but leaving some narrow (wheelchair-accessible) paved routes across part of the refuge. Shawangunk Grasslands also offers an outstanding opportunity to plant and manage various grassland wildflowers that attract numerous species of butterflies.

The Trust for Public Land has assisted with land acquisition. Ducks Unlimited, Inc. has helped enhance approximately 150 acres of the refuge's wetland habitat.

The refuge is open daily during daylight hours. There is no entrance fee. The headquarters is open on weekdays, except national holidays.

Visitor activities are presently limited to wildlife and butterfly observation, photography, walking on the former aircraft runways, and hiking on the self-guiding, 2.7-mile Dagmar Dale Trail, consisting of a 1-mile south loop and a 1.7-mile north loop. Future refuge plans include offering interpretive programs, developing an environmental-education program, and providing for limited hunting. Over 150 bird species have been recorded here.

Visitors are cautioned to be alert for ticks, especially as some of them may carry Lyme disease. Insect repellent is advised during the warmer months.

Lodgings and meals are available in such communities as New Paltz, Highland, Poughkeepsie, Milton, Newburgh, and Middletown.

Access to Shawangunk Grasslands Refuge from Exit 5 on I-84 is north about 5 miles on County Route 208 into the village of Wallkill, then 1 block west, south (left) t2wo miles on Bruyn Turnpike, and west (right) 1 mile on Hoagerburg Road.

Further information: Shawangunk Grasslands National Wildlife Refuge, c/o Wallkill River NWR, 1547 County Route 565, Sussex, NJ 07461; telephone: (973) 702-7266.

Target Rock, comprising 80 acres, was established in 1967 to manage and protect an area of oak-hickory uplands, a brackish pond, several vernal pools, and one-half mile of rocky beach. The refuge is located at the eastern end of Lloyd Neck Peninsula, along Huntington Bay on the north shore of Long Island, New York.

As described by the U.S. Fish and Wildlife Service:

The chestnut oak/mountain laurel association and oak hardwood forest offer good food and cover for migrating neotropical birds. The sand ridge areas have juniper trees which provide habitat for olive-sided hairstreak butterflies. The prickly pear cactus which is a New York State protected species is found in the sand ridge areas of the beach. Excellent marine invertebrate populations in the off-shore, beach and pond habitats provide foraging areas for piping plovers, [other] shorebirds, wintering waterfowl and fish species.

The refuge's habitat management activities include tidal wetland restoration, placement of nesting structures for ospreys and other birds, grassland expansion and maintenance, invasive plant species control, and periodic prescribed burning to promote nutrient cycling and spur the growth of plants valued for food and cover by waterfowl and other wildlife.

The refuge is open daily during daylight hours. An entrance fee is charged.

Visitor activities include wildlife observation, photography, hiking, environmental education and interpretive programs, and saltwater fishing.

Hiking opportunities include three trails that invite visitors to explore mature oak-hickory forest, fields, and beach. Over 240 bird species have been seen here.

The high, eroded bluffs above the shore provide nesting habitat for a colony of bank swallows, and the beach offers nesting habitat for the federally listed threatened piping plover. To avoid disturbing the swallows and plovers, this shore area, in the vicinity of 14-foot-high Target Rock, is closed to visitation from April 1 through August.

Visitors are cautioned to be alert for poison ivy and ticks. The latter may carry Lyme disease.

Lodgings and meals are available in such communities as Huntington Station, East Norwich, and Comack.

Access to Target Rock Refuge from State Route 110 in Huntington is west 0.25 mile on State Route 25A, north (right) on West Neck Road and continuing on Lloyd Harbor Road to its end.

Further information: Target Rock National Wildlife Refuge, c/o The Long Island NWR Complex, P.O. Box 21, Shirley, NY 11967; telephone: (631) 286-0485.

Wallkill River (see text under New Jersey)

Wertheim, containing 2,550 acres, was established in 1947 and protects one of the last remaining undeveloped estuary systems and the largest contiguous wetland on Long Island, New York. The refuge is located on the island's central south shore, near the town of Shirley. The Carmans River, which flows south through the refuge and into Great South Bay, is a state-designated Wild and Scenic River.

Roughly half of the refuge's varied habitats consists of marine bay, tidal river, freshwater streams, hardwood swamp, and emergent wetlands that range from salt marsh to freshwater marsh. Forested uplands include pitch pine, mixed pine-oak, and oak woodlands. A small part of the refuge contains grassland and shrub habitats.

Wertheim refuge's initial acreage was donated to the U.S. Fish and Wildlife Service by Cecile and Maurice Wertheim, who had previously managed the area as a private waterfowl conservation and hunting reserve. Since then, the refuge has been expanded with other donated and purchased parcels of land.

During the winter, large concentrations of waterfowl, notably American black ducks, are attracted here, where the Carmans River estuary is one of the south shore's last or least likely expanses of water to freeze over. Waterfowl that breed on the refuge include Canada goose, black duck, mallard, gadwall, green-winged teal, and wood duck. The refuge's nesting population of wood ducks is the largest of any refuge or parkland on Long Island. Large influxes of neotropical migratory songbirds, such as thrushes and warblers, pass through or nest on the refuge.

The Fish and Wildlife Service's habitat management activities include restoring subtidal areas; erecting nesting platforms for ospreys and nest boxes for such species as wood ducks, bluebirds, tree swallows, house wrens, and flying squirrels; and controlling such non-native plants as the aggressive, invasive common reed (*Phragmites*) and purple loosestrife (see the discussion of loosestrife control techniques in the Montezuma Refuge text). In addition, the refuge maintains areas of grassland, manages stands of pitch pines, and periodically implements prescribed burning to promote nutrient cycling to spur the growth of nutrient-rich plants for waterfowl and other wildlife. More than 280 species of birds have been recorded here.

Land acquisition has been made possible partly with revenues from the sale of Migratory Bird Hunting and Conservation Stamps (Duck Stamps). Ducks Unlimited, Inc. has helped enhance more than 700 acres of the refuge's wetland habitat. The Friends of Wertheim is a local nonprofit support group that is assisting the refuge in various ways.

The refuge is open daily during daylight hours. There is no entrance fee. The refuge headquarters, which also serves as headquarters for all the other national wildlife refuges on Long Island, is open daily.

Visitor activities include wildlife observation, photography, interpretation and environmental education, hiking, canoeing on the Carmans River, and fishing. A parking area, a Cooperative New York State fishing-access site, and an associated canoe-portage trail, located adjacent to Sunrise Highway (State Route 27), are open daily for launching watercraft. Another launching site is provided at Squassux Landing. The refuge offers wonderful canoeing opportunities on the Carmans River.

Hiking opportunities include the White Oak Nature Trail—a 3-mile loop through a variety of woodlands offering views of marsh, grassland, shrub, and pond habitats; and Indian Landing Trail—a 1-mile loop through pine barrens habitat that is reached by canoe or boat.

Visitors are cautioned to be alert for ticks, which may carry Lyme disease. Insect repellent is advised during the warmer months.

Lodgings and meals are available in such communities as Medford and Bellport.

Access to the Wertheim Refuge headquarters from the junction, in Shirley, of County Route 46 (William Floyd Parkway) and State Route 27A is west 0.6 mile on County Route 80W and south (left) 0.25 mile on Smith Road.

Further information: Wertheim National Wildlife Refuge, P.O. Box 21, Shirley, NY 11967; telephone: (631) 286-0485.

New York:
Wildlife Management Area

Lido Beach Wildlife Management Area protects 22 acres of estuarine salt marsh and adjacent shrub-thicket habitats, for the benefit of wintering waterfowl, wading birds, shorebirds, and other wildlife. It is located on the Hempstead Bay side of Long Beach, a coastal barrier island on the south shore of Long Island. The U.S. Fish and Wildlife Service's habitat management activities include tidal wetland restoration, control of invasive non-native plants, and the placement of nesting structures for ospreys and other birds.

In 1969, the U.S. Army transferred this area to the Fish and Wildlife Service in recognition of its "particular value in carrying out the national migratory bird management program." Hempstead Bay is viewed as a "significant coastal habitat" by the Fish and Wildlife Service's Northeast Estuary Program, which has suggested that the entire bay is deserving of protection as a national wildlife refuge.

Further information: Lido Beach Wildlife Management Area, c/o The Long Island NWR Complex, P.O. Box 21, Shirley, NY 11967; telephone: (631) 286-0485.

North Carolina

Alligator River, containing 152,195 acres, was established in 1984 to enhance and protect an expanse of diverse wetland habitats in northeast coastal North Carolina. The Alligator River/Intracoastal Waterway borders the refuge to the west, Albemarle Sound lies to the north, Croatan Sound is to the east, and Pamlico Sound extends to the southeast.

The refuge contains hardwood and Atlantic white cedar swamps, freshwater and brackish marshes, bogs, and areas of pocosin. The latter, also known as "southeast scrub bog," consists of very thick growths of largely evergreen shrubs and scattered pond pines. It is characterized by poorly drained peat soils that are rich in organic matter. Pocosin is derived from a Native American word that means "swamp-on-a-hill."

Large concentrations of migratory waterfowl, wading birds, shorebirds, and neotropical songbirds are attracted to Alligator River Refuge's diverse habitats. Prominent among these are wintering tundra swans, greater snow and Canada geese, and numerous species of ducks, such as mallards, green-winged teal, northern pintails, ring-necked, and hooded mergansers. As the refuge name implies, a few of the large American alligator (*Alligator mississippiensis*) inhabit this area, near the northern end of their range.

One of the management highlights of Alligator River Refuge has been the reintroduction of the red wolf (*Canis rufus*) to this area in 1987, as part of the U.S. Fish and Wildlife Service's recovery program. This endangered species historically ranged widely throughout the southeastern United States. Its population declined nearly to extinction. Today, Alligator River, Pocosin Lakes, Cape Romain, and St. Vincent national wildlife refuges are among a few key places where this species is gradually rebuilding its numbers. (See further discussion of the red wolf recovery program and the Red Wolf Coalition in the Pocosin Lakes Refuge text, as well as in the St. Vincent and Cape Romain texts.)

Another endangered species inhabiting Alligator River Refuge is the red-cockaded woodpecker. Areas of pine woodlands are being managed to enhance its nesting success. (For further description of this species and its habitat needs, see the Carolina Sandhills National Wildlife Refuge text.)

With assistance of The Nature Conservancy, a substantial portion of Alligator River Refuge was donated by the Prudential Life Insurance Company. This area had previously been targeted for the draining of its wetlands and mining of its peat deposits. Since the refuge was established, Ducks Unlimited, Inc. has helped enhance more than 400 acres of wetland. The Coastal Wildlife Society is a local nonprofit support group that is assisting the Alligator River Refuge in a variety of ways.

The refuge is open daily during daylight hours. There is no entrance fee. The refuge office, located in Manteo, is open on weekdays, except national holidays.

Visitor activities include birdwatching; photography; driving the Wildlife Drive and other refuge roads; hiking; red wolf howling and other interpretive and environmental education programs; canoeing (including guided canoe excursions [fee charged]), kayaking, and boating (several boat-launching sites are provided); fishing (a wheelchair-accessible fishing dock is provided); and limited hunting on most of the refuge during the designated seasons. Camping is not permitted on the refuge, but campground facilities are available at Cape Hatteras National Seashore and elsewhere.

Hiking opportunities include two (wheelchair-accessible) routes: the 0.5-mile Creef Cut Wildlife Trail that includes a 250-foot boardwalk into swamp habitat; and the 0.5-mile Sandy Ridge Wildlife Trail that includes a boardwalk into another area of swamp.

Even though alligators are generally afraid of people, visitors are cautioned to stay a safe distance from these sluggish-looking but potentially fast-moving reptiles and to be alert for ticks, chiggers, and venomous snakes. Insect repellent is advised during the warmer months.

The birds of Alligator River Refuge are essentially the same as those that have been recorded on nearby Pea Island Refuge (see listings in the text for that refuge).

Lodgings and meals are available in such communities as Manteo, Wanchese, and Nags Head.

Access to Alligator River Refuge from U.S. Route 17 at Williamston is east about 75 miles on U.S. Route 64, which runs through the northern part of the refuge; or from U.S. Route 17 at Washington it is about 85 miles on U.S. Route 264, which runs through the eastern part of the refuge.

Further information: Alligator River National Wildlife Refuge, P.O. Box 1969, Manteo, NC 27954; telephone: (252) 473-1131.

Cedar Island, consisting of 14,482 acres, was established in 1964 to protect extensive expanses of largely undisturbed black needlerush and cordgrass salt marsh for the benefit of thousands of wintering waterfowl and other wildlife. The refuge is located at the confluence of Pamlico and Core Sounds on the central coast of North Carolina.

The roughly 11,000 acres of brackish wetlands attract large concentrations of waterfowl, wading birds, and shorebirds. Among the multitude of water birds are brown pelican; herons and egrets; glossy ibis; black rail; ducks (wood, American black, mallard, blue-winged and green-winged teal, gadwall, American wigeon, canvasback, redhead, ring-necked, lesser scaup, surf scoter, bufflehead, and ruddy); black-bellied plover; American oystercatcher; laughing gull; terns (gull-billed, common, and Forster's); and black skimmer.

Nearly one-quarter of the refuge consists of hardwood swamp habitat. In addition, there are areas of woodland, in which the dominant species are pines (loblolly, longleaf, and pond); live oak; wax myrtle; redbay; gallberry; yaupon (holly); and fetterbush. Influxes of neotropical songbirds come through Cedar Island Refuge during their spring and autumn migrations. Other avian species include osprey, great horned and barred owls, red-headed and red-bellied woodpeckers, marsh wren, and seaside sparrow. More than 270 species of birds have been recorded on the refuge.

Mammals include white-tailed deer, black bear, mink, river otter, raccoon, marsh rabbit, and eastern gray squirrel.

The American alligator, near the northern end of its range, inhabits the refuge's wetlands.

The U.S. Fish and Wildlife Service's habitat management activities include periodic prescribed burning in the refuge's woodlands and marshes. For the benefit of wildlife, these fires promote nutrient cycling that triggers new growth and plant diversity, maintain areas of open habitat, and reduce hazardous accumulations of organic debris that can fuel destructive wildfires.

Acquisition of the refuge's lands has proceeded in stages. In 1964, the initial 7,830 acres were purchased, followed three years later with additional acreage. In 1970, an abandoned U.S. Navy radar station was procured and converted for use as the refuge's field office. In 1990, a 1,955-acre tract of land was donated to the refuge.

The refuge is open daily during daylight hours. There is no entrance fee. The refuge office is open on weekdays, except national holidays.

Visitor activities include birdwatching; photography; hiking, bicycling, and horseback riding on undeveloped trails; kayaking, canoeing, and boating (two boat-launching ramps are provided, one of which is near the refuge's field office); saltwater fishing; crabbing; and waterfowl hunting on a 400-acre public hunting area during the designated season. Camping is not permitted on the refuge, but campground facilities are available elsewhere on Cedar Island and at Sealevel and Beaufort. The use of jet skis, wave runners, and other personal watercraft; riding all-terrain vehicles; and swimming are prohibited within the refuge.

Even though alligators are generally afraid of people, visitors are cautioned to stay a safe distance from these sluggish-looking but potentially fast-moving reptiles and to be alert for ticks, chiggers, and venomous snakes. Insect repellent is advised during the warmer months.

Lodgings and meals are available in such communities as Atlantic, Sealevel, Beaufort, Morehead City, and Ocracoke.

.5Access to Cedar Island Refuge from Beaufort is about 40 miles northeast on U.S. Route 70 and State Route 12. There is also a ferry service (toll) that runs between the town of Ocracoke, at the southern end of Cape Hatteras National Seashore, and the town of Atlantic, which is about 5 miles south of the refuge.

Further information: Cedar Island National Wildlife Refuge, 38 Mattamuskeet Road, Swan Quarter, NC 27885; telephone: (252) 926-4021.

Currituck, comprising approximately 4,100 acres in five main tracts, was established in 1984 to protect sandy beaches, grassy dunes, interdunal wetlands, maritime forest, shrubby thickets, scattered ponds, and more than 1,200 acres of freshwater and brackish marshes. The refuge is located on the Outer Banks between the Atlantic Ocean and Currituck Sound in northeastern North Carolina.

The refuge's main vegetative communities generally present a transition from east to west, from the ocean to the sound. Sand dunes, just inland from the beach, support such species as sea oats, American beach grass, panic grass, salt meadow cordgrass, and the threatened seabeach amaranth. More than 700 acres of maritime forest are dominated by loblolly pine and live oak; and another 700 acres are shrub thicket habitat, containing low-growing pine, oak, wax myrtle, and bayberry. Freshwater marshes consist mostly of cattails or a combination of rushes and sedges; brackish marshes are dominated by black needlerush and giant cordgrass.

Several important management activities occur on Currituck Refuge. Refuge staff and summer interns intensively monitor the nesting of the endangered piping plover and threatened loggerhead sea turtle, to protect nest sites where possible and to help improve survival of the young. This is an especially challenging task, given the significant volume of vehicular traffic that uses the beaches of the Outer Banks.

Interdunal wetland flats are enhanced and maintained by discing, planting, and water level management to benefit large concentrations of wintering waterfowl, wading birds, and shorebirds. Prescribed burning is periodically carried out to promote nutrient cycling and spur the growth of plant foods for waterfowl and other wildlife. Efforts to expand the refuge are continuing, so that other ecologically important areas of this stretch of the Outer Banks can be protected.

The refuge is open daily during daylight hours. There is no entrance fee. The refuge provides no developed visitor use facilities.

Visitor activities include birdwatching, photography, hiking, and waterfowl hunting from specified blind sites (by drawing) during the designated season. The use of motor vehicles off the beach is not permitted, to protect the fragile dune ecosystem. As the Fish and Wildlife Service explains, "ATV use in the dunes destroys dune vegetation. Without this vegetation, sand dunes become unstable and more susceptible to wind and wave damage. Established sand dunes provide defense against storms and protect the maritime forest and interdunal habitats from impacts."

The U.S. Fish and Wildlife Service explains, "Some portions of the flat dune area, above the high tide line, may be closed to all public use during the spring and summer for protection of nesting sites of the piping plover, . . . [a federally listed threatened] species. Watch for 'area closed' signs that outline these areas. Do not trespass beyond these signs because you may step on the camouflaged nests. Also, piping plovers do not tolerate human disturbance and may abandon their nests. Free-roaming dogs also present an extreme danger to the recovery of these tiny shorebirds; therefore, the use of a leash is mandatory. Please help us restore these birds by leaving them alone."

The birds that have been recorded on Currituck Refuge are largely the same as those on Mackay Island Refuge.

Mammals include white-tailed deer, gray fox, mink, muskrat, raccoon, and opossum. The non-native nutria, feral hogs, and feral horses are also seen on the refuge. A Wild Horse Sanctuary has been designated on the Outer Banks—from the Currituck-Dare county line northward to the Virginia state line. Under a county ordinance, it is unlawful to approach, feed, harm, or kill a wild horse. Visitors are warned that feral horses can behave aggressively.

Lodgings and meals are available in such communities as Corolla, Duck, Kitty Hawk, Currituck, Elizabeth City, and Virginia Beach.

Access to Currituck Refuge's Monkey Island and Swan Island units is by four-wheel-drive vehicle (allowable only on the beach) or on foot from Corolla, the northern end of State Route 12. The southernmost unit is 0.75-mile north of the road's end. All other refuge units are reached only on foot, and all units are also reached by small boat across Currituck Sound.

Further information: Currituck National Wildlife Refuge, P.O. Box 39, Knotts Island, NC 27950; telephone: (252) 429-3100.

Great Dismal Swamp (see the text under Virginia)

Mackay Island, containing more than 8,150 acres, was established in 1961 to protect an area of extensive coastal wetlands, known as the Great Marsh, located between Currituck Sound and Back Bay in the northeast corner of North Carolina and the southeast corner of Virginia. The refuge attracts large concentrations of waterfowl—notably the greater snow goose, as well as numerous wading birds, shorebirds, neotropical songbirds, and other migratory and resident wildlife.

Nearly three-quarters of Mackay Island Refuge consists of slightly brackish to freshwater marsh that is dominated by cattails, black needlerush, and giant cordgrass. Approximately 1,500 acres support upland forest habitat of loblolly pine and hardwoods, and there is a small acreage of cropland.

The U.S. Fish and Wildlife Service carries out a number of habitat management activities. Seasonal manipulation of water levels within a number of marsh impoundments (pools) promotes the growth of aquatic plants containing high food value for waterfowl. Nest structures are provided and maintained for breeding wood ducks and ospreys. To prevent an overpopulation of white-tailed deer, the refuge administers an annual hunt. Under cooperative agreements with local farmers, a portion of such crops as corn, wheat, and soybeans is left unharvested for the benefit of waterfowl and other wildlife.

Periodic prescribed burning helps manage habitats. As explained by the Fish and Wildlife Service:

Fire can provide many benefits to the natural ecosystem. . . . Goose browse is improved by removing old, rank vegetation and enabling the fresh green growth to be accessed by the birds. Fire helps to recycle nutrients that add to the productivity of the marsh. Fire also helps set back the successional stage and prevents the growth of woody vegetation. In addition, these fires are used to help reduce the buildup of wildfire fuels.

A major mission of Mackay Island Refuge is to provide vital wintering habitat for the greater snow goose. During the spring and summer, this subspecies nests and raises its young on the Arctic tundra of Canada's Ellesmere and northern Baffin islands. In November, thousands of these magnificent birds arrive on their wintering grounds along the Atlantic Coast—principally from Delaware and Chesapeake bays south to the coastal sounds of North Carolina. Concentrations of 10,000 or more are occasionally seen on the Great Marsh.

Other waterfowl include large numbers of Canada geese, tundra swans, wood and black ducks, mallards, green-winged and blue-winged teal, pintails, northern shovelers, wigeons, and gadwalls. Over 200 bird species have been recorded here.

The earliest recorded history of Mackay Island dates back to 1761, when John Jones called the island Orphan's Island. Around 1768, John Mackie bought the island. Its name became Mackie's Island and then, for some reason, was changed to Mackay Island.

In 1918, a printing magnate and philanthropist, Joseph Palmer Knapp, acquired the property. He built a private resort, raised waterfowl, and experimented with various pioneering wetland management strategies. In 1937, he was one of the founders of Ducks Unlimited, Inc., a nonprofit conservation organization dedicated to restoring, enhancing, and protecting wetland habitats for North America's waterfowl populations. As *Ducks Unlimited* senior writer Matt Young explained in an untitled conservation article in the March–April 1997 magazine:

Knapp is regarded as the father of Ducks Unlimited. His greatest passion in life was waterfowling at his club on North Carolina's Currituck Sound. Dismayed by the decline of waterfowl populations there, Knapp dedicated his energy and much of his vast fortune toward conservation. . . .

DU's revolutionary conservation strategy was to restore extensive permanent wetlands—nicknamed "duck factories"—using modern engineering and construction methods.

Ducks Unlimited has subsequently helped enhance wetland habitats on more than 150 national wildlife refuges across the country. Since its founding, this volunteer-based, grassroots organization has helped restore and conserve roughly 10 million acres of wetlands on both public and private lands throughout the United States and Canada. In focusing on its "singleness of purpose," DU has reached out and formed countless successful partnerships with federal, state, and county governmental agencies; corporations, foundations, and landowners; and other individuals. Further information: Ducks Unlimited, Inc., National Headquarters, One Waterfowl Way, Memphis, TN 38120; telephone: (901) 758-3825; Internet: www.ducks.org.

The refuge is open daily during daylight hours. There is no entrance fee. The refuge office is open on weekdays, except national holidays.

Visitor activities include birdwatching; photography; hiking; bicycling; canoeing, kayaking, and boating (from March 15 to October 15; an unimproved boat-launching ramp is provided at the dike gate); fishing; crabbing; and hunting (autumn deer hunts) on part of the refuge during the designated season. By prearrangement, the refuge offers opportunities for disabled hunters. Waterfowl hunting is not permitted on Mackay Island Refuge, but it is permitted on nearby Currituck Refuge. Camping is not permitted on Mackay Island Refuge.

Hiking opportunities include the 0.3-mile-loop Great Marsh Trail; Kuralt Trail, which includes an elevated observation platform offering excellent views of Great Marsh and the large concentrations of wintering waterfowl; and 1.5-mile Mackay Island Road, which is accessible all year from State Route 615 to the dike gate. From March 15 to October 15, the area beyond the dike gate is also open, offering 7 more miles of hiking and bicycling around the refuge impoundments.

Visitors are cautioned to be alert for ticks, chiggers, and venomous snakes. Insect repellent is advised.

The more than 200 species of birds that have been recorded on Mackay Island Refuge are much the same as those of Mattamuskeet Refuge.

Lodgings and meals are available in such communities as Currituck and Elizabeth City, North Carolina; and Virginia City, Virginia.

Access to the Mackay Island Refuge office from the town of Currituck, North Carolina, is on the Currituck Sound Ferry and then north just over 8 miles on North Carolina Route 615. From the Virginia–North Carolina state line, at the southern edge of Virginia Beach, Virginia, it is south 1 mile on North Carolina Route 615.

Further information: Mackay Island National Wildlife Refuge, P.O. Box 39, Knotts Island, NC 27950; telephone: (252) 429-3100.

Mattamuskeet, consisting of 50,180 acres, was established in 1934 to protect outstanding wintering waterfowl habitat on Lake Mattamuskeet—North Carolina's largest natural lake—and related wetland habitats. The refuge is located just inland from Pamlico Sound on the central coast of North Carolina.

From November to March, from 20,000 to 35,000 tundra swans, which breed and raise their young in the Arctic habitat of Canada and Alaska, are drawn to this migratory bird mecca. Also during the winter, thousands of snow and Canada geese and tens of thousands of ducks, along with shorebirds and bald eagles, are also attracted to this shallow body of water.

The U.S. Fish and Wildlife Service provides nesting boxes for wood ducks, to help increase successful breeding. Bald cypress trees around the edge of the lake offer nest sites for ospreys. Influxes of neotropical songbirds come through the refuge during their spring and autumn migrations. Over 240 bird species have been seen here. The American alligator, close to the northern end of its range, occasionally inhabits the refuge's wetlands.

In addition to the lake's 40,000 acres of open water, adjacent wetland habitats comprise just over 3,100 acres of freshwater marsh, 3,500 acres of hardwood swamp, and 2,600 acres of moist-soil impoundments. The water levels within these managed wetlands are drawn down in the spring, providing habitat for egrets, herons, and other wildlife while at the same time promoting the growth of nutrient-rich plants for waterfowl. Water levels are raised later in the year, offering habitat where wintering waterfowl can rest and feed.

The refuge includes a few hundred acres of croplands on which local farmers, under cooperative agreements with the Fish and Wildlife Service, leave unharvested a portion of crops such as corn, winter wheat, and soybeans to provide supplemental food for waterfowl and other wildlife. Mattamuskeet Refuge also contains a small area of mature loblolly woodland.

Of historic interest is the Mattamuskeet Lodge, near the lakeshore at New Holland. This structure initially housed pumps that drained the lake, and it was subsequently used as a hunting lodge. It is now open for touring, offers space for educational programs, meetings, and other functions, and contains a gift shop. The lodge is open during certain hours on Tuesdays through Saturdays. Further information: (252) 926-1422.

Establishment of Mattamuskeet Refuge was made possible partly with revenues from the sale of Migratory Bird Hunting and Conservation Stamps (Duck Stamps). Ducks Unlimited, Inc. has helped enhance 1,900 acres of the refuge's wetland habitat. Partnership for the Sounds is a local nonprofit support group that is assisting Mattamuskeet Refuge in various ways. Regarding the red wolf recovery program and the Red Wolf Coalition, see discussion in the Pocosin Lakes Refuge text, as well as in the St. Vincent (Florida) and Cape Romain (South Carolina) texts.

The refuge is open daily during daylight hours. There is no entrance fee. The refuge headquarters is open on weekdays, except national holidays.

Visitor activities include birdwatching; photography; driving the 3-mile refuge entrance road and the 5-mile Wildlife Drive—a gravel road that borders the lake's southern shore; hiking (on a short interpretive trail near the refuge headquarters and on miles of grass-covered dikes); viewing the refuge and wildlife from two observation decks; canoeing, kayaking, and boating (from March I to November I; three boat-launching ramps into the lake are provided); fishing; crabbing; and hunting (deer and waterfowl, including special youth hunts) on part of the refuge during the designated seasons. Camping is not permitted on the refuge, but campground facilities are available close by.

Visitors are cautioned to be alert for ticks, chiggers, and venomous snakes. Insect repellent is advised during the warmer months.

Lodgings and meals are available in such communities as Belhaven, Fairfield, Engelhard, Swan Quarter, and Washington.

Access to Mattamuskeet Refuge from U.S. Route I7 at Washington is east 63 miles on U.S. Route 264, and north (left) I.5 miles on State Route 94 to the refuge entrance road. State Route 94 continues on north, cutting across the middle of the lake.

Further information: Mattamuskeet National Wildlife Refuge, 38 Mattamuskeet Road, Swan Quarter, NC 27885; telephone: (252) 926-4021.

Pea Island, consisting of 5,834 acres, was established in 1938 to protect a stretch of Outer Banks coastal barrier island habitat along the northern end of Hatteras Island in northeastern North Carolina. The refuge is about 13 miles long from north to south. It varies from one-quarter mile to I mile in width between the Atlantic Ocean on the east and Pamlico Sound on the west. An adjacent 25,700 acres of Pamlico Sound are also federally protected, under the terms of a Presidential Proclamation. Over 300 bird species use the refuge.

The refuge's habitats include sandy ocean beaches, coastal sand dunes, freshwater and brackish ponds and managed impoundments, saltwater marsh, and salt flats.

A major mission of Pea Island Refuge and the adjacent proclamation waters is to provide vital wintering habitat for migratory waterfowl, including the greater snow goose. During the spring and summer, this subspecies nests and raises its young on the Arctic tundra of Canada's Ellesmere and northern Baffin islands. In November, thousands of these magnificent birds arrive on their wintering grounds along the Atlantic Coast—principally from Delaware and Chesapeake bays south to the coastal sounds of North Carolina.

In addition to the geese, the refuge provides wintering, nesting, and resting habitat for other migratory waterfowl, wading birds, shorebirds, raptors, and neotropical songbirds. Several wading bird rookeries and shorebird nesting areas are located here. The U.S. Fish and Wildlife Service manages the water levels in 1,000 acres of impoundments to promote the growth of plant foods for the benefit of waterfowl and other wildlife. The federally listed threatened piping plover and loggerhead sea turtle nest on the refuge's strand of beach.

The Coastal Wildlife Society is a nonprofit support group that is assisting Pea Island Refuge in a variety of ways.

The refuge is open daily during daylight hours. There is no entrance fee. The visitor center is open daily from April I through November, and at least on weekends from December I through March.

Visitor activities include birdwatching, photography, interpretive programs, hiking, bicycling (on the beach and refuge roads), canoeing, kayaking, and boating (a Pamlico Sound boat-launching site is provided), beachcombing, and surf and sound fishing. Camping is not permitted on the refuge, but campgrounds are available on the adjacent Cape Hatteras National Seashore and elsewhere.

Hiking opportunities include the 0.5-mile North Pond Wildlife Trail, which begins near the visitor center and includes four wildlife observation platforms; a 4-mile refuge service road on which hikers may continue around North Pond; and the 12-mile ocean beach, accessed at a number of parking areas along State Route 12.

Visitors are cautioned to be alert for ticks and chiggers. Insect repellent during the warmer months and sunscreen are advised.

Lodgings and meals are available in such communities as Manteo, Wanchese, Kitty Hawk, Kill Devil Hills, Nags Head, Buxton, and Hatteras.

Access to Pea Island Refuge is on State Route 12, which runs through the refuge at the northern end of Hatteras Island, 10 miles south of Nags Head.

Further information: Pea Island National Wildlife Refuge, P.O. Box 1969, Manteo, NC 27954; telephone: (252) 473-1131.

Pee Dee, containing 8,443 acres, was established in 1963 to manage river bottomland and gently rolling hills in the Piedmont area of south-central North Carolina. The refuge's diverse habitats include hardwood and mixed pine-and-hardwood forests, pine plantations, fallow and cultivated fields, lakes and pools, seasonally flooded moist-soil impoundments, numerous creeks, and the Pee Dee River. Over 200 bird species have been seen here.

During the 1960s, concentrations of ducks and Canada geese started to decline in this part of North Carolina. As explained by the U.S. Fish and Wildlife Service:

Fortunately, lands adjacent to the Pee Dee River and Brown Creek offered excellent potential for waterfowl habitat development. With local and state support, Pee Dee National Wildlife Refuge was established . . . to provide wintering habitat for migratory waterfowl. . . .

. . . The refuge contains 3,000 acres of contiguous bottomland hardwood forest along Brown Creek. This area forms the core of the largest bottomland hardwood tract left in the piedmont of North Carolina, and has been placed on the registry of State Natural Heritage Areas.

Peak numbers of wintering waterfowl on Pee Dee Refuge can exceed 10,000 ducks, the largest proportion of which are mallards and wood ducks. "Due to an array of reasons, gone are the large migrating flocks of Canada geese, but the refuge is still used by several hundred migrating Canadas as well as a growing flock of about 200 year-round resident Canada Geese."

The Fish and Wildlife Service carries out a number of habitat management activities on the refuge:

Moist soil impoundments are managed by lowering and raising water levels, and discing, mowing, or burning every few years to maintain plants in an early successional stage. These shallowly flooded areas are drained over a period of weeks beginning in late March. This regime creates the proper germination conditions for many favorable moist soil plants, such as smartweed, and produces mudflats needed by migrating shorebirds moving through in April.

Selected impoundments are drained, disked, and shallowly flooded to create mudflats again for shorebirds during their critical August migration. All impoundments, whether they be moist soil plant areas, mudflats, or crops left in the fields by refuge farmers, are flooded in early fall to "set the table" for arriving waterfowl.

In the refuge's upland pine woodlands, prescribed burning helps to curtail dense growths of oaks and other hardwoods that would otherwise eventually become the dominant trees of the forest. Relatively low-burning fires promote nutrient cycling and maintain an open pine woodland ecosystem that is preferred by many species of flora and fauna, including the federally listed endangered red-cockaded woodpecker (see a description of this species in the Carolina Sandhills Refuge, South Carolina, text). And these fires reduce hazardous accumulations of dead wood, needles, leaves, and other organic debris—fuel overloading—that can contribute to uncontrolled and destructive stand-replacing wildfires. Upland pine stands are selectively thinned "to achieve the tree density required by the red-cockaded woodpecker." Some parts of the refuge are being reforested, particularly along stream corridors and on open land containing no value to waterfowl.

Ducks Unlimited, Inc. has helped enhance several hundred acres of the refuge's wetland habitat. The Friends of Pee Dee National Wildlife Refuge is a local nonprofit support group that is assisting the refuge in a variety of ways.

The refuge is open daily during daylight hours. There is no entrance fee. The refuge headquarters is open on weekdays, except national holidays. A refuge environmental education and visitor center is in the planning stages, with assistance from the Friends of the Pee Dee National Wildlife Refuge, a nonprofit cooperating association.

Visitor activities include birdwatching; photography; driving the refuge's 2.5-mile self-guiding, interpretive wildlife drive and other roads and several state roads that run through or border the refuge; hiking, bicycling, canoeing and kayaking; boating on Ross Pond, Andrews Pond, Beaver Ponds, and Arrowhead Lake (electric motors only); fishing (on six ponds, Brown Creek, and the Pee Dee River); and hunting (archery and gun deer hunts, and quail, dove, squirrel, raccoon, and opossum) on parts of the refuge during the designated seasons. A youth hunt is held in mid-October. Camping is not permitted on the refuge, but campground facilities are available on the Uwharrie National Forest.

Hiking opportunities include a 0.25-mile, self-guided (wheelchair-accessible) nature trail that leads to a wildlife observation blind; the 3-mile interpretive Prothonotary Warbler Trail; the approximately 0.5-mile Covered Bridge Trail; and a number of woods roads.

Visitors are cautioned to be alert for ticks and chiggers, which are prevalent from April to September.

Canoeing and kayaking opportunities on the refuge include Brown Creek and the Pee Dee River. The refuge's stretch of the river is part of the Yadkin/Pee Dee River canoe trail, the most popular segment of which runs from Tillery Dam (at State Highway 731) down to the State Highway 109 bridge.

The best months for seeing the wintering concentrations of waterfowl are from November through February. The spring influx of neotropical migratory songbirds reaches its peak during April.

Lodgings and meals are available in Wadesboro, Mount Gilead, and Albemarle.

Access to Pee Dee Refuge from Wadesboro is north 7 miles on U.S. Route 52.

Further information: Pee Dee National Wildlife Refuge, Route 1, Box 92, Wadesboro, NC 28170; telephone: (704) 694-4424.

Pocosin Lakes, encompassing 113,674 acres, was established in 1990 to enhance and protect a variety of wetlands located between Pamlico and Albemarle Sounds in northeastern North Carolina. The refuge includes the 12,000-acre PUNGO LAKE UNIT, which was formerly the Pungo National Wildlife Refuge, established in 1963.

Prominent among the refuge's habitats are the more than 50,000 acres of pocosin wetlands, also known as "southeastern shrub bog." The name *pocosin* is derived from a Native American word meaning "swamp-on-a-hill." This ecologically rich ecosystem contains very thick growths of largely broadleaf-evergreen shrubs, such as sweetbay, loblolly bay, and blueberry, along with scattered pond pines. It is characterized by poorly drained, organically rich, usually waterlogged peat soils that range from 4 to 8 or more feet in depth. As the U.S. Fish and Wildlife Service explains:

A significant percentage of the soil volume consists of buried roots, stumps, and logs that persisted as the organic soil accumulated. Most of these organic soils have been subjected to some degree of drainage and will burn when dry.

Due to the volatility of the natural vegetation, the organic soils, the drained condition of the land, and the limited accessibility, the area is one of the most hazardous areas for destructive wildfires in the eastern United States. The most recent large wildfires occurred in 1981 and 1985. Surface elevations were reduced by as much as three feet in parts of the area due to combustion of the peat.

Other refuge habitats include lakes and ponds, managed moist-soil impoundments, riverine swamp, bottomland hardwood forest, farm fields, and agricultural lands. Under cooperative agreements, local farmers who plant crops such as corn and soybeans leave a portion unharvested, providing supplemental food for waterfowl and other wildlife.

The refuge attracts large concentrations of wintering tundra swans, greater snow and Canada geese, numerous species of ducks, and a multitude of neotropical songbirds during the spring and autumn migrations. Resident wildlife includes the black bear, red wolf, and the American alligator (*Alligator mississippiensis*), the latter being near the northern end of its range.

The red wolf (*Canis rufus*) is a federally listed endangered species that historically ranged widely throughout the southeastern United States. Its population declined nearly to extinction. Today, Alligator River, Cape Romain, and St. Vincent national wildlife refuges are among a few key places where this species is gradually rebuilding its numbers, under the U.S. Fish and Wildlife Service's red wolf recovery program. In 1987, a number of these animals were introduced onto Alligator River Refuge. Since then, a few of them have been brought to Pocosin Lakes, and others have arrived on their own. (See further discussion of the red wolf recovery program in the St. Vincent, Cape Romain, and Alligator River texts.)

Since 1997, an important partner in the red wolf recovery program has been a nonprofit organization known as the Red Wolf Coalition. As the Fish and Wildlife Service explains, "The founding concepts of the Coalition were to serve as the hub of private support for the red wolf, giving the public the first real opportunity to become involved in the Fish and Wildlife Service's Red Wolf Recovery program." Pocosin Lakes Refuge is presently working with the coalition toward the goal of developing a Red Wolf Lookout and Education Center. The coalition has been receiving the support of such organizations as Defenders of Wildlife, the Turner Foundation, the Rhode Island Zoological Society, and the Roger Williams Park Zoo. Further information about the coalition and its efforts: Red Wolf Coalition, P.O. Box 2318, Kill Devil Hills, NC 27948; telephone: (252) 441-3946.

Habitat management activities include extensive restoration of wetlands on 19,000 acres of the refuge, with installation of water control structures. In the 1990s, a cooperative reforestation project with North Carolina State University was undertaken in an attempt to restore a severely impaired, 640-acre pocosin tract. Thousands of Atlantic white cedars and smaller numbers of bald cypress, pond pine, tupelo, ash, and several species of oaks were planted. Prescribed burning within the Pungo Unit's moist-soil impoundments promotes nutrient cycling, enhances habitat and spurs the growth of plant foods for the benefit of waterfowl. In addition, nesting boxes have been provided for wood ducks.

In 1989, The Conservation Fund, with the assistance of the Richard King Mellon Foundation, acquired more than 104,000 acres of wetlands. Donation of these lands the following year to the U.S. Fish and Wildlife Service made possible the establishment of Pocosin Lakes refuge. Since then, Ducks Unlimited, Inc. has helped enhance several hundred acres of the refuge's wetlands habitat. Partnership for the Sounds is a local nonprofit support group that is assisting Pocosin Lakes Refuge in various ways.

The refuge is open daily during daylight hours. There is no entrance fee. The refuge's headquarters/visitor center—the Walter B. Jones, Sr., Center for the Sounds, located next to the Scuppernong River, in the town of Columbia—is open on weekdays, except national holidays. The center is named in honor of the former congressman, who was an ardent supporter of protecting the wetlands and water resources of northeastern North Carolina during his more than one-quarter century in the U.S. Congress.

Visitor activities include birdwatching; photography; interpretive exhibits and environmental education programs at the visitor center; walking the 2,300-foot (wheelchair-accessible) Scuppernong Boardwalk near the visitor center; hiking the refuge's dikes and lakeshore roads; bicycling on dikes and roads; driving on unpaved roads (muddy in wet weather); canoeing and kayaking on creeks and canals; canoeing on Phelps, New, and Frying Pan lakes, but not on Pungo Lake, to avoid disturbing waterfowl; fishing; and hunting (deer, fox, raccoon, rabbit, opossum, squirrel, waterfowl, woodcock, snipe, rail, quail, and dove) on parts of the refuge during the designated seasons. Camping is not permitted on the refuge, but campground facilities are available on nearby Pettigrew State Park.

Even though alligators are generally afraid of people, visitors are cautioned to stay a safe distance from these sluggish-looking but potentially fast-moving reptiles and to be alert for ticks, chiggers, and venomous snakes. Insect repellent is advised during the warmer months.

The more than 200 species of birds that have been recorded on Pocosin Lakes Refuge are much the same as those on Pee Dee Refuge.

Lodgings and meals are available in such communities as Williamston, Plymouth, Columbia, Manteo, Belhaven, and Washington.

Access to the Pocosin Lakes Refuge visitor center from U.S. Route 17 at Washington is east 57 miles on U.S. Route 64 (on the right, immediately east of the highway bridge across the Scuppernong River); or from State Route 12 at Whalebone, it is west 42 miles (on the left, just before the bridge).

Further information: Pocosin Lakes National Wildlife Refuge, P.O. Box 329, Columbia, NC 27925; telephone: (252) 796-3004.

Roanoke River, containing more than 20,000 acres toward a goal of 33,000 acres, was established in 1989 to enhance and protect ecologically significant areas of forested floodplain wetlands along the lower reaches of the Roanoke River in northeastern North Carolina. The five units of the refuge along the north bank of the river encompass part of what is viewed as "the largest intact, and least disturbed, bottomland forest ecosystem remaining in the Mid-Atlantic Region." The North Carolina Wildlife Resources Commission and The Nature Conservancy manage other parts of this vital wildlife habitat, bringing the total area presently under protection to nearly 50,000 acres.

The refuge's 8,000 acres of bald cypress/tupelo swamps and 9,500 acres of bottomland hardwood forests support a tremendous diversity of wildlife. Biologists believe that the Roanoke River's wooded floodplain supports the greatest density of nesting birds—notably neotropical songbirds—of any place in North Carolina. The peak months for exceptional birdwatching are March through June. Several heron rookeries are located on the refuge, one of which is located on Conine Island and is the largest inland rookery in the state. Wood ducks, green-winged and blue-winged teal, mallards, black ducks, wigeon, and hooded mergansers are prominent among the concentrations of waterfowl that are attracted to the river and its wetlands. Wild turkeys feed and nest on the floodplain's terraces and ridges. Bald eagles winter and nest along the river.

In addition to such mammals as white-tailed deer, mink, and river otter, the lower Roanoke River bottomlands offer one of the very few remaining areas in the state for a remnant black bear population. And the refuge supports a large diversity of turtles, snakes, and frogs.

Fishes are also an important part of the ecosystem here. The U.S. Fish and Wildlife Service points out that "The Roanoke River and the associated refuge floodplain wetlands are especially important to anadromous fish, marine species that ascend rivers to spawn." Among these are hickory shad, striped bass, blueback herring, and alewife. By contrast, the American eel, a catadromous species, descends the river when it reaches reproductive readiness in 10 to 12 years, and migrates to the Sargasso Sea to spawn. In addition, there are resident species such as catfish, crappie, longnose gar, carp, largemouth bass, bluegill, darters, and white perch.

As described by the Fish and Wildlife Service:

Water is the driving force of bottomland hardwood communities. Annual floods over the centuries have overtopped the riverbanks, dropping the coarser, heavier sediments from upriver to form the levees and ridges of the floodplain, resulting in forested communities characterized by sugar berry, sycamore, green ash, beech, cottonwood, elm, sweetgum, loblolly pine, and mesic oak and hickory species. The finer, light sediments (silts and clays) gradually settle in the slack water areas ponded behind the levees supporting stands of bald cypress and tupelo gum.

This natural pattern of river floods and deposition of sediments, however, has been substantially altered by man. As Refuge Biologist Jean Richter explains, the lower stretch of the Roanoke River, where the refuge is situated, is downriver from a series of hydroelectric dams and their reservoirs (John H. Kerr Reservoir, Lake Gaston, and Roanoke Rapids Lake) and a large U.S. Army Corps of Engineers flood control project. To satisfy power generation, flood control, and recreational goals, these facilities control the river's flow of water. "As a result, the flows for the past 50-plus years are, for the most part, not ecologically compatible. Sometimes there isn't enough water coming our way because they hold it in the reservoirs for recreational needs; while at other times, they will flood the bottomland forests for weeks on end during the growing season. This is an extremely unnatural situation. The bottomland forests didn't evolve under this type of managed flow regime and we are beginning to see significant shifts in the types of forest communities. We are in the long and tedious process of documenting changes in the Roanoke River's wildlife populations and floodplain geomorphology."

Adding to the problems caused by the regulation of the river's flow is the loss of a substantial proportion of the sediment load that was formerly carried by the river. With those nutrient- and mineral-rich materials now largely trapped behind the dams, the bottomland ecosystem is consequently deprived of this source of enrichment and renewal.

In addition, Roanoke River Refuge is located in an economically depressed area, and as a consequence, heavy industry that could cause water- and air-quality degradation is being aggressively courted by representatives of a county that is eager for economic development. Refuge manager Jerry Holloman points out, "Society at large isn't fully aware of what 'biting the bullet' would entail, when it comes to protecting the environment or river ecosystem. People here haven't fully bought into the concept of preserving an ecosystem for future generations, if it means a thwarted or conservative approach to development. We're trying to deal with problems from the past 50 years, while advocating a reasonable approach to economic development, which, in many instances, runs counter to the public's perception of economic need."

In light of this frustrating reality, the refuge finds itself confronted with four basic management challenges: (1) Striving to close the broad gap between public perception and reality, as they relate to many years of river mismanagement, (2) Developing science-based background data to document the ecologically serious deterioration of the river's resources, (3) In what is characterized as a "tight-rope walk," seeking essential remedies to undo harmful impacts already created, and (4) Maintaining the integrity of being a resource protection advocate in the face of mounting pressures for industrial development designed to cure economic ills. The enormity of these challenges seems overwhelming. Yet, the long-term benefits of achieving success in the enhancement and protection of this irreplaceable riverine bottomland ecosystem are tremendous for both wildlife and people.

A key to success lies in achieving effective partnerships. For example, as the Fish and Wildlife Service explains, river flows are managed by the U.S. Army Corps of Engineers (USACOE) and Virginia/North Carolina Power. The two VA/NC Power-operated dams came up for relicensing in 2001. "Asynchronous, or aseasonal flows in downriver habitats, . . . is an issue being addressed in this relicensing process. However, the real issue of 'controlled flooding' downriver can only be addressed through partnerships with USACOE and all other stakeholders. The question of how the system can be better managed is not one of the upper (above dam) and lower (below dam) interests being in direct opposition, but rather what is good for the lower interests of the system is also good for the upper. The entire river is one system. Its health is of critical importance to all interests."

Acquisition of Roanoke River Refuge lands was made possible partly with revenues from the sale of Migratory Bird Hunting and Conservation Stamps (Duck Stamps). Establishment of the refuge occurred with the cooperative efforts of the North Carolina Wildlife Resources Commission, Bertie and Halifax counties, and such private organizations as The Nature Conservancy, the North Carolina Wildlife Federation, and Sierra Club.

The refuge is open daily during daylight hours. There is no entrance fee. The refuge headquarters, at 114 W. Water St., Windsor, is open on weekdays, except national holidays.

Visitor activities include wildlife observation, photography, hiking, canoeing and boating, fishing, and hunting during the designated seasons. Camping is not permitted on the refuge, except primitive camping in conjunction with hunts. Campgrounds facilities are provided in the vicinity of Williamston and Edenton, and at Pettigrew State Park.

Visitors are cautioned to be alert for ticks, chiggers, and venomous snakes. Insect repellent is advised during the warmer months.

The more than 200 species of birds that have been recorded on Roanoke River Refuge are much the same as those on Pee Dee Refuge.

Mammals, reptiles, and amphibians are also much the same as those on Pee Dee Refuge.

Lodgings and meals are available in such communities as Williamston, Windsor, Edenton, and Scotland Neck.

Access to Roanoke Island Refuge by canoe or boat is from public boat-launching ramps at the town of Hamilton; from U.S. Route 13/17, adjacent to the refuge's Conine Island tract; and at Plymouth, near the Great and Goodman Islands tract. U.S. Route 13/17 runs through the Conine Island tract, and State Route 45 cuts across the Great and Goodman Islands tract.

Further information: Roanoke River National Wildlife Refuge, P.O. Box 430, Windsor, NC 27983; telephone: (252) 794-3808.

Swanquarter, comprising 16,411 acres, was established in 1932 to protect an extensive expanse of salt marsh that is dominated by black needlerush, sawgrass, and giant cordgrass. The refuge is located along the shore of Pamlico Sound on the central coast of North Carolina. About half of the refuge is designated as a unit of the National Wilderness Preservation System.

The roughly 13,000 acres of brackish wetlands attract large concentrations of waterfowl, wading birds, and shorebirds. Prominent among the numerous water birds are common loon, herons and egrets, black rail, and such ducks as wood, American black, mallard, green-winged teal, northern pintail, northern shoveler, gadwall, American wigeon, canvasback, redhead, lesser scaup, surf scoter, bufflehead, and ruddy.

About one-fifth of the refuge consists of hardwood swamp habitat and small stands of loblolly pines. Ospreys and pileated woodpeckers also nest on the refuge. Influxes of neotropical songbirds come through Swanquarter Refuge during their spring and autumn migrations. The American alligator is near the northern end of its range here, with numbers annually varying from around five down to none.

Establishment of Swanquarter Refuge was made possible partly with revenues from the sale of Migratory Bird Hunting and Conservation Stamps (Duck Stamps).

The refuge is open daily during daylight hours. There is no entrance fee.

Visitor activities include birdwatching; photography; hiking on two trails; kayaking, canoeing, and boating; saltwater fishing (a fishing pier is provided); crabbing; and hunting (duck and coot) on part of the refuge during the designated season. Camping is not permitted on the refuge, but campground facilities are available at Belhaven.

Visitors are cautioned to be alert for venomous ticks, chiggers, and venomous snakes. Insect repellent is advised during the warmer months.

The fauna and flora of Swanquarter are essentially the same as those recorded on Mattamuskeet Refuge.

Lodgings and meals are available in such communities as Swan Quarter, Engelhard, Fairfield, and Belhaven.

Access to Swanquarter Refuge from the town of Swan Quarter is west 4 miles on U.S. Route 264, and south (left) 2 miles; or by boat.

Further information: Swanquarter National Wildlife Refuge, 38 Mattamuskeet Road, Swan Quarter, NC 27885; telephone: (252) 926-4021.

North Dakota: National Wildlife Refuges

Appert Lake, consisting of approximately 640 acres, was established in 1939 to enhance and protect habitat for migratory waterfowl and other wildlife in Emmons County of south-central North Dakota. Appert Lake is a 118-acre impoundment of marsh and open water that attracts concentrations of such migrating ducks as mallards, wigeons, pintails, and gadwalls. The lake's earthen dam has recently been in need of repair, and plans are being implemented by the U.S. Bureau of Reclamation to restore the structure.

Adjacent to the lake is a wooded wetland of cottonwoods and willows. The refuge's mixed-grass uplands are inhabited by such birds as sharp-tailed grouse, and the non-native gray partridge and ring-necked pheasant. White-tailed deer are the most prominent mammals.

This refuge's acreage is being managed under the terms of a conservation easement purchased from a local landowner. Two federally owned waterfowl production areas (WPAs), totaling about 250 acres, adjoin and are managed jointly with this easement refuge. The WPA acreage was acquired with revenues from the sale of Migratory Bird Hunting and Conservation Stamps (Duck Stamps).

Although the easement refuge is not open to visitor use, the adjacent WPAs are open daily during daylight hours. There are no entrance fees. No visitor use facilities are provided. Visitor activities on the WPAs include birdwatching, photography, hiking, and hunting during the designated seasons. Appert Lake's birds and mammals are much the same as those recorded on Long Lake National Wildlife Refuge.

Lodgings and meals are available in such communities as Bismarck and Steele.

Access from Interstate 94 at Sterling is south 26 miles on U.S. Route 83 and then east (left) 1 mile.

Further information: Appert Lake National Wildlife Refuge, c/o Long Lake NWR Complex, 12000-353rd Street SE, Moffit, ND 58560; telephone: (701) 387-4397.

Ardoch, containing 2,696 acres, was established in 1939 to manage a significant area of wetland that is a mecca for migratory waterfowl and other wildlife, within the largely agricultural Red River Valley in Walsh County of northeastern North Dakota. Impounded, 1,000-acre Lake Ardoch, which is located on the Forest River, is bordered mostly by marshy habitat of cattails, bulrushes, and other emergent vegetation.

During spring and autumn migrations, hundreds of tundra swans and thousands of geese and ducks pause here to rest and feed. Nesting waterfowl include such ducks as mallard, blue-winged teal, pintail, and gadwall, and the giant Canada goose (*Branta canadensis maxima*). The latter is a subspecies that was once brought to the brink of extinction by habitat loss and over-hunting. But thanks to a successful reintroduction program, it has been restored to this and many other refuges in the northern Great Plains. Ardoch Refuge also attracts several kinds of grebes, American bittern, black-crowned night-heron, American avocet, Wilson's and red-necked phalaropes, and coot.

The majority of the refuge's acreage is being managed under the terms of conservation easements with local landowners. Visitor entry onto this easement refuge is not permitted without landowner permission. Ardoch's birds and mammals are much the same as those recorded on Lake Alice National Wildlife Refuge.

Further information: Ardoch National Wildlife Refuge, c/o Devils Lake Wetland Management District, P.O. Box 908, Devils Lake, ND 58301; (701) 662-8611.

Arrowwood, containing 15,934 acres, was established in 1935 to enhance and protect more than 3,500 acres in three impounded riverine lakes and an area of marsh that attract large concentrations of migratory waterfowl. This refuge is located along a 14-mile stretch of the James River in Foster and Stutsman counties of east-central North Dakota. During spring and autumn migrations, tundra swans, Canada and snow geese, and numerous kinds of ducks pause at Arrowwood Refuge to rest and feed. American white pelicans sometimes fly the 30 miles from their summer breeding colony on Chase Lake National Wildlife Refuge to feed at Arrowwood. Over 260 bird species have been seen here.

Nesting water birds include such ducks as mallard, blue-winged teal, gadwall, wood duck, and hooded merganser, and the giant Canada goose (*Branta canadensis maxima*). The latter subspecies was brought to the brink of extinction by habitat loss and overhunting, but has been successfully restored to the northern Great Plains. Artificial nesting structures have been placed in the refuge's wetlands to provide secure sites for Canada geese and other waterfowl. In addition, because of the scarcity of natural nesting cavities in wooded habitat, the refuge has installed roughly 250 artificial cavities to enhance the nesting productivity of wood ducks and hooded mergansers.

Water levels of the refuge's wetlands vary seasonally, to provide a mix of habitats for nesting and migrating waterfowl. Runoff from winter snow and spring rainfall fills the impounded lakes. In late spring, open-water stands of sago pondweed provide favorable habitat for a variety of aquatic invertebrates that are an important source of food for duck broods. As carefully managed water levels gradually recede during late spring and summer, seasonally flooded mudflats are exposed around the edges of the impoundments, attracting shorebirds and promoting the growth of emergent marsh vegetation. Once this vegetation is well developed, the impoundments can be reflooded, so that this vital vegetative cover is available for the broods of ducks and other water birds. The refuge's moist-soil areas, which are managed during the summer to promote the growth of seed-producing plants, are reflooded in the autumn in time to be used by migrating waterfowl. At least, that's the way these wetlands are supposed to work.

However, water management in Arrowwood Refuge has been significantly compromised since Jamestown Dam was built by the U.S. Army Corps of Engineers, downstream from the refuge, in the mid-1960s. As the U.S. Fish and Wildlife Service explains, "During flood years, water from Jamestown reservoir backs into the Refuge and eliminates or severely reduces water management capability. After water in the reservoir recedes, excess water often remains in the refuge because of poor pool drainage and channel obstructions between the lowermost Refuge pool (DePuy Marsh) and the reservoir. During normal years, the difference in elevation between Jamestown Reservoir and the Refuge pools is too small to allow the Refuge to draw down pools in a timely manner."

By the late 1990s, an environmental plan was chosen for mitigating the harmful impacts of the reservoir upon the refuge. It calls for lowering the Jamestown Reservoir's joint-use pool, constructing bypass channels around Mud and Jim lakes, thereby permitting independent management of these two major impoundments, and making several other impoundment and channel improvements. As of this writing, the outcome of implementing these mitigation measures to help resolve the challenging environmental impacts is still uncertain.

This refuge's other habitats include more than 100 acres of wooded riparian habitat in coulees (narrow ravines), more than 8,200 acres of native prairie grasslands, more than 3,200 acres of seeded grasslands, and 780 acres in cultivated crops for the benefit of wildlife. Prominent among the nesting grassland birds are upland sandpiper, marbled godwit, bobolink, LeConte's and grasshopper sparrows, the non-native gray partridge and ring-necked pheasant, the reintroduced greater prairie chicken, and sharp-tailed grouse.

To view and photograph the grouse's impressive courtship displays, an observation blind is available (by reservation) during April and May. The male spreads his wings, raises his pointed tail, lowers his head, and rapidly stomps his feet. At the same time, he inflates and deflates purplish neck sacs, and makes a *coo-oo* sound that is accompanied by the rattling of wing quills.

Both the sharp-tailed grouse and prairie chicken are birds of the prairie. The sharp-tails have thrived in areas where the ecologically unnatural exclusion of periodic fire has allowed an invasion of brush and other woody vegetation. But, as the Fish and Wildlife Service explains:

Prairie-chickens failed to adapt to the changes in the prairie. Fire exclusion and intensive use of the prairie for agricultural purposes probably led to its demise in this area. No prairie-chickens were seen in the refuge after the late 1960s. Today, prescribed burns are used as a management tool by the refuge and have created conditions where prairie-chickens might again exist. A reintroduction program is underway to return the prairie-chicken to Arrowwood.

Establishment of Arrowwood Refuge was made possible partly with revenues from the sale of Migratory Bird Hunting and Conservation Stamps (Duck Stamps). Nearly one-sixth of this refuge's acreage is being protectively managed under the terms of perpetual conservation easement agreements with local landowners.

In cooperation with farmers, roughly 1,000 acres of Arrowwood's uplands are devoted to a crop-rotation program that offers cover and food for wildlife. During some years, alfalfa is produced, providing important nesting cover and soil-enhancing nitrogen. In other years, crops such as wheat, millet, barley, oats, and sunflowers are cultivated, with part of the crop left in the fields to provide important supplemental food for many species of wildlife.

Generally poor duck breeding results occur on the refuge's prairie habitat. Consequently, a 38-acre fenced exclosure of grassland has been created, with the assistance of Ducks Unlimited, Inc., to provide a predator-free nesting area for waterfowl and upland birds.

This refuge is open daily during daylight hours. There is no entrance fee. The refuge headquarters is open on weekdays, except national holidays.

Visitor activities include birdwatching; photography; driving the 5.5-mile, self-guiding, interpretive auto tour route that leads through marsh and grassland habitats, for which an interpretive brochure and audiocassette tape are available; hiking (a short loop trail is provided near the picnic area); canoeing (a canoe trail is available on a stretch of river between Arrowwood and Mud lakes); picnicking (a picnic area is provided near the southeastern shore of Arrowwood Lake); cross-country skiing and snowshoeing; and hunting (deer, fox, and upland game birds) on parts of the refuge during the designated seasons. The best months for seeing waterfowl and other water birds are from April through October, with the latter offering the best opportunities to view tundra swans and geese.

Insect repellent is advised during the warmer months.

Lodgings and meals are available in such communities as Jamestown and Carrington.

Access to Arrowwood Refuge from Interstate 94 at Jamestown is north 35 miles on U.S. Routes 281/52 and east (right) 7.5 miles on State Route 9; or from Carrington, south 9 miles on U.S. Routes 281/52 and east (left) 7.5 miles on State Route 9.

Further information: Arrowwood National Wildlife Refuge, 7745 Eleventh Street, SE, Pingree, ND 58476; telephone: (701) 285-3341.

Audubon, consisting of 14,739 acres, is located 65 miles north of Bismarck, in west-central North Dakota. The refuge was established in 1955 as the Snake Creek National Wildlife Refuge. It was renamed in 1967, in honor of the famous nineteenth-century wildlife artist and naturalist John James Audubon, who traveled up the Missouri River in 1843. The mission of this refuge is to manage habitat that replaces extensive Missouri River bottomland that was inundated when the U.S. Army Corps of Engineers built the Garrison Dam.

More than 10,000 acres of the refuge consist of the southern and eastern part of Lake Audubon, the shoreline wetlands, and roughly 100 islands, which are a mecca for large concentrations of nesting and migrating waterfowl, gulls, terns, and cormorants.

Prominent among the refuge's waterfowl is the giant Canada goose (*Branta canadensis maxima*). As many as 500 pairs nest on Lake Audubon's islands. This subspecies, which formerly inhabited the Great Plains in abundance, was reduced to the brink of extinction by the mid-1930s, as the result of extensive market hunting and egg collecting. Audubon Refuge is one of several places in North Dakota where a successful program of reintroducing, captive rearing, releasing, and transplanting the giant Canadas to numerous parts of this state has been carried out. Many private organizations and individuals have assisted the federal and state agencies in bringing this species back to the northern Great Plains.

The refuge's wetlands also support many species of nesting ducks—notably blue-winged teal, mallards, pintails, gadwalls, canvasbacks, redheads, lesser scaups, and ruddy ducks. Other nesting water birds include pied-billed and eared grebes, white pelican, gulls and terns, and double-crested cormorants. Of the nesting shorebirds, there are American avocets, willets, piping plovers, spotted sandpipers, and Wilson's phalaropes. During the spring and autumn, large numbers of snow geese, Canada geese, ducks, and shorebirds, as well as many tundra swans and sandhill cranes, migrate through the refuge. Whooping cranes pause here each autumn, on the refuge or nearby private lands. Other birds associated with the wetlands include yellow-headed blackbirds, sora and Virginia rails, and bald eagles, which are common during the winter and spring.

Another 3,000 acres of Audubon Refuge consist of grassland habitat (both native prairie and introduced tame grasses) that supports many species of upland grassland birds. Among these are sharp-tailed grouse, short-eared owls, northern harriers, upland sandpipers, marbled godwits, the non-native ring-necked pheasants and gray partridges, bobolinks, meadowlarks, lark buntings, clay-colored and Baird's sparrows, and chestnut-collared longspurs.

Several hundred acres of refuge land are also planted annually with grains. Under sharecrop agreements with local farmers, part of the crop is left standing for the benefit of wildlife—especially for waterfowl, and secondarily for pheasants and deer.

Establishment of Audubon Refuge was by perpetual, but revocable, agreement with the U.S. Army Corps of Engineers, which owns Lake Audubon. Water level management is by long-term agreement with the U.S. Bureau of Reclamation, which pumps Lake Audubon full each spring and lowers it two feet each autumn. Ducks Unlimited, Inc. has helped enhance some of the refuge's wetland habitat.

The refuge is open daily during daylight hours. There is no entrance fee. The refuge headquarters is open on weekdays, except national holidays.

Visitor activities include birdwatching; photography; driving the 7.5-mile, self-guiding, interpretive auto tour road along the south shore of Lake Audubon; riding a barge (pontoon) to a Lake Audubon bird nesting island; walking the 1-mile prairie trail; bird identification classes in May for beginners; group field trips (prior scheduling required); ice fishing; and hunting (only sharp-tailed grouse, partridge, pheasant, and deer) on part of the refuge during the designated seasons. Although camping is not permitted on the refuge, campground facilities are available at such places as Lake Sakakawea and Fort Stevenson state parks. Over 235 bird species have been seen on the refuge.

Lodgings and meals are available in such communities as Garrison, Underwood, and Minot.

Access to Audubon Refuge from Minot is south 46 miles on U.S. Route 83, and east (left) at the refuge sign for just under 1 mile to the refuge headquarters; or from Coleharbor, north 2 miles on U.S. Route 83, and east (right) to the refuge headquarters.

Further information: Audubon National Wildlife Refuge, 3275 Eleventh Street NW, Coleharbor, ND 58531; telephone: (701) 442-5474.

Bone Hill, consisting of 640 acres, was established in 1939 as a refuge and breeding ground for migratory birds and other wildlife. The refuge, which is located in LaMoure County, North Dakota, includes a natural marsh and reservoir, which are used as waterfowl brood rearing and migration rest areas. Most of the refuge consists of pasture or agricultural lands.

The refuge's land and water habitat is not owned by the U.S. Fish and Wildlife Service, but is protected under the terms of perpetual easement agreements with private landowners. Bone Hill Refuge is, therefore, generally not open to visitation and has no visitor-use facilities.

Further information: Bone Hill National Wildlife Refuge, c/o Kulm Wetland Management District, P.O. Box E (1 First Street SW), Kulm, ND 58456; telephone: (701) 647-2866.

Brumba, containing 1,977 acres, was established in 1939 to manage an important wetland habitat for the benefit of migratory waterfowl and other wildlife in Towner County of northeastern North Dakota.

The refuge's acreage is being managed under the terms of conservation easements purchased from local landowners. Visitor entry onto this easement refuge is not permitted without landowner permission, although the refuge can be viewed from public roads. The refuge's birds and mammals are much the same as those recorded on Lake Alice National Wildlife Refuge.

Access to Brumba Refuge from State Route 5 at Rocklake, is 5 miles south on U.S. Route 281.

Further information: Brumba National Wildlife Refuge, c/o Devils Lake Wetland Management District, P.O. Box 908, Devils Lake, ND 58301; telephone: (701) 662-8611.

Buffalo Lake, comprising 1,563 acres, was established in 1939 to maintain a 660-acre lake that is held behind Buffalo Lake Dam. The refuge is located on Buffalo Coulee, within the headwaters of the Sheyenne River, in southern Pierce County of north-central North Dakota.

Only 23 acres of this mostly easement refuge are federally owned public domain, and the rest consists of privately owned uplands and flowage easements purchased from private landowners. To help maintain the lake level for the benefit of migratory waterfowl and other wildlife, a water diversion ditch carries flows, as needed, from the nearby North Fork of the Sheyenne River.

There are no visitor-use facilities. Visitor activities include birdwatching, wildlife photography, hiking (with landowners' permission), and limited fishing. Buffalo Lake's birds and mammals are much the same as those recorded on J. Clark Salyer National Wildlife Refuge.

Lodgings and meals are available in such communities as Harvey and Rugby.

North Dakota Game and Fish Department's Buffalo Lake Wildlife Management Area adjoins the refuge.

Access to the refuge from U.S. Route 2 at Rugby is south 23 miles on State Route 3, east (left) about 5 miles on State Route 19, and south (right) 1 mile; or from U.S. Route 52 at Harvey, it is north 21 miles on State Route 3, east (right) about 5 miles on State 19, and south (right) 1 mile.

Further information: Buffalo Lake National Wildlife Refuge, c/o J. Clark Salyer NWR Complex, P.O. Box 66, Upham, ND 58789; telephone: (701) 768-2548.

Camp Lake, consisting of 755 acres, was established in 1939 to manage two lakes that attract a few waterfowl, especially during the spring and autumn migrations, near Butte in north-central North Dakota.

As the U.S. Fish and Wildlife Service explains:

Officially named Camp Lake NWR, this refuge was split into two units in 1974 when the State Land Department withdrew 640 acres . . . from refuge status. The Camp Lake Unit is now 185 acres of unremarkable cropland, hay land and about 90 acres of lake—all with negligible wildlife values. . . .

The Strawberry Lake unit consists of 160 acres of heavily grazed native prairie and 320 acres of lake and recreational cabins, store, park and resort. Water skiing, swimming, boating, fishing and other recreational uses developed over the last 60 or more years, starting before the refuge and continuing without refuge control.

Habitat values are very low. . . .

Both units should be dropped from refuge status permanently.

Visitor entry onto this easement refuge is not permitted.

Further information: Camp Lake National Wildlife Refuge, c/o Audubon Wildlife Refuge Complex, 3275 Eleventh Street NW , Coleharbor, ND 58531; (701) 442-5474.

Canfield Lake, containing 313 acres, was established in 1939 to protect ecologically important wetland habitat primarily for migrating waterfowl in northern Burleigh County of central North Dakota.

Most of this refuge's acreage is being managed under the terms of a conservation easement purchased from a local landowner. Visitor entry onto this refuge is not permitted. During the autumn migration, snow and Canada geese are prominent among the birds that pause here to rest and feed. Resident birds include sharp-tailed grouse and the non-native ring-necked pheasant.

The federally owned, 780-acre Basaraba Waterfowl Production Area (WPA) adjoins and is jointly managed with this refuge. This area is open daily, during daylight hours. There is no entrance fee. No visitor use facilities are provided. Visitor activities on the WPA include birdwatching, wildlife photography, and hunting during the designated seasons. Acquisition of the WPA was made possible partly with revenues from the sale of Migratory Bird Hunting and Conservation Stamps (Duck Stamps).

Canfield Lake/Basaraba's birds and mammals are much the same as those recorded on Long Lake National Wildlife Refuge.

Lodgings and meals are available in such communities as Bismarck, Washburn, and Steele.

Access to the Basaraba WPA from Interstate 94 at Sterling is north 21 miles to Wing, west (left) 7 miles on State Route 36, and north 3 miles on a gravel township road; or from Bismarck, north 22 miles on U.S. Route 83, east (right) 17 miles on State Route 36, and north 3 miles on a gravel township road.

Further information: Canfield Lake National Wildlife Refuge/Basaraba Waterfowl Production Area, c/o Long Lake NWR Complex, 12000-353rd Street SE, Moffit, ND 58560; telephone: (701) 387-4397.

Chase Lake, comprising 4,385 acres, was established in 1908 by President Theodore Roosevelt. This refuge protects the vast expanse of wetland habitat that is a major breeding, resting, and feeding area for waterfowl and other water birds. Its 2,057-acre, highly alkaline lake and surrounding grassland lies within the gently rolling, lake-dotted Missouri Coteau region in western Stutsman County of central North Dakota.

Prominent among Chase Lake's wildlife diversity is North America's largest breeding colony of the American white pelican. At the time the refuge was established, this spectacular species was threatened with extinction by overhunting and habitat loss. Less than 50 of these birds inhabited the area. In recent years, between 17,000 and 20,000 pelicans have been congregating on the lake's two nesting islands (if not inundated by high water) and a shoreline peninsula. The peak of the breeding season runs from mid-April through July. Today, Chase Lake Refuge produces an estimated one-third to one-half of the entire population of this species. To learn more about the migratory movements, breeding colonies, and nonbreeding distribution of these birds, the refuge is carrying out a pelican research program with the aid of banding and radio transmitters.

Other wetland breeding birds include double-crested cormorant, ducks (mallard, pintail, blue-winged teal, and gadwall), American avocet, ring-billed and California gulls, common tern, the endangered piping plover, and the giant Canada goose (*Branta canadensis maxima*). The latter subspecies was brought to the brink of extinction during the earlier decades of the twentieth century. Thanks to a successful propagation program, they are now a common breeding bird at this refuge and elsewhere throughout the northern Great Plains region.

The refuge's native grassland prairie provides nesting habitat for numerous species of wildlife, including upland plover, bobolink, Sprague's pipit, sharp-tailed grouse, and sparrows (Baird's, clay-colored, LeConte's, and grasshopper).

Sandhill cranes and tundra swans are among many migrating species that pause here to rest and feed. As a majority of this refuge's bird species have also been recorded on nearby Arrowwood National Wildlife Refuge, see the more extensive listing in the text for the latter.

Among Chase Lake Refuge's mammals are white-tailed deer, coyote, red fox, badger, long-tailed weasel, and striped skunk.

Marsh vegetation includes such plants as cattails, bulrushes, aquatic sedge grass, and reedgrass. Native grasses on the surrounding prairie uplands include little bluestem, green needlegrass, and needle-and-thread, and other parts of the refuge support non-native smooth brome, sweet clover, and alfalfa for the benefit of wildlife.

In 1975, more than 4,000 acres of Chase Lake Refuge was designated as the Chase Lake Wilderness—a unit of the National Wilderness Preservation System.

Establishment of Chase Lake Refuge was made possible partly with revenues from the sale of Migratory Bird Hunting and Conservation Stamps (Duck Stamps). The Chase Lake Foundation is also providing assistance to the refuge.

The refuge is open daily during daylight hours. There is no entrance fee. No visitor use facilities are provided.

Visitor activities include birdwatching, photography, driving refuge roads, hiking, and deer hunting during the designated season. A scenic panorama of Chase Lake and surrounding prairie grassland can be enjoyed from Chase Lake Pass overlook. Chase Lake's birds and mammals are much the same as those recorded on Arrowwood National Wildlife Refuge.

Insect repellent is advised during the warmer months.

Lodgings and meals are available in such communities as Jamestown and Steele.

Access to Chase Lake Refuge from Interstate 94 at Medina (Exit #230) is north 10 miles on State Route 30/County Route 68, west (left) 7 miles, and south (left) about 1 mile to Chase Lake Pass, for the best overview of the refuge; or from State Route 36 at Woodworth (where the refuge headquarters is located) south 8 miles, west (right) 7 miles, and south (left) about 1 mile.

Further information: Chase Lake National Wildlife Refuge, 5924 Nineteenth Street SE, Woodworth, ND 58496; telephone: (701) 752-4218.

Cottonwood Lake, containing 1,013 acres, was established in 1939 to maintain Cottonwood Lake as a resting and staging area for the benefit of migrating waterfowl, shorebirds, and other wildlife within southern McHenry County in north-central North Dakota. Several thousand mallards commonly pause to rest and feed at the lake during spring and autumn migrations.

This easement refuge consists of privately owned uplands and a water right that allows the U.S. Fish and Wildlife Service to maintain the lake's water levels. Although hunting is permitted on the refuge, other visitor activities, such as birdwatching and hiking, are at the discretion of the private landowners.

Further information: Cottonwood Lake National Wildlife Refuge, c/o J. Clark Salyer NWR Complex, P.O. Box 66, Upham ND 58789; telephone: (701) 768-2548.

Dakota Lake, containing 2,799 acres, was established in 1939 as a refuge and breeding ground for migratory birds and other wildlife. The refuge is located in Dickey County, North Dakota along the James River, which is an important migration corridor for waterfowl, shorebirds, and a wide variety of other migratory birds.

Refuge boundaries include the river channel with small acreage of adjacent riparian river fringe and agricultural fields. Dakota Lake Dam, managed by the U.S. Fish and Wildlife Service, and its reservoir provide habitat for over-water nesting and brood rearing. The areas of land and water within the refuge are protected under the terms of a system of perpetual easement agreements with adjacent private landowners and the State of North Dakota. Refuge lands are not owned by the Service and are, therefore, generally not open to visitor entry. There are no public use facilities on the refuge.

The southern boundary of Dakota Lake Refuge is a scant 4 miles north of Sand Lake National Wildlife Refuge in South Dakota. As project leader Bob Vanden Berge explains, "Proximity to this much larger refuge adds to Dakota Lake's richness of marsh and water birds. Spring and fall waterfowl migrations can be observed from roadways adjacent to the lake. Canada geese, snow geese, and a variety of ducks are highly visible during migrations, but the abundance and diversity of shorebirds using the James River for a migration corridor may outnumber the waterfowl." The refuge's birds and mammals are much the same as those recorded on Sand Lake Refuge.

Further information: Dakota Lake National Wildlife Refuge, c/o Kulm Wetland Management District, P.O. Box E (1 First Street SW), Kulm, ND 58456; telephone: (701) 647-2866.

Dakota Tallgrass Prairie Wildlife Management Area (see the text under South Dakota).

Des Lacs, consisting of 19,547 acres, was established in 1935 to enhance and protect an ecologically rich stretch of the Des Lacs River (River of the Lakes), extending 26 miles southward from the Canadian border, in northwestern North Dakota. The refuge contains three natural lakes and eight areas of managed marsh habitat totaling 5,000 acres. The marshland between the lakes is a mecca for vast numbers of migrating and nesting waterfowl and other water birds.

During spring and autumn migrations, many thousands of ducks and geese pause here to rest and feed. The peak months are typically April through May and September through October, with as many as one-half million snow geese in the fall. Nesting ducks, such as mallards, pintails, blue-winged teal, gadwalls, canvasbacks, redheads, and ruddy ducks, annually raise as many as 7,000 ducklings! Five species of grebes are among other water birds that nest on the refuge. Horned, eared, and western grebes are especially numerous. The latter are entertaining as they perform their elaborate and spectacular spring courtship displays. During these displays, a male and female rise to a vertical position and dash side-by-side with their feet splashing the surface of the water, before diving underwater.

Initially called the Des Lacs Migratory Waterfowl Refuge, the Des Lacs NWR is one of many refuges in this part of the country. These refuges were specifically set aside in response to the devastating impact of the severe drought of the 1930s' Dust Bowl on migratory waterfowl. To enhance the refuge's lake and marsh habitats, the 797th company of the Civilian Conservation Corps (CCC) built facilities such as a series of eight low dikes and other water-control structures.

As described by the U.S. Fish and Wildlife Service:

The purpose was to allow the manipulation of water levels, which is important in maintaining optimum nesting conditions and food production for waterfowl. The marshes and lakes are managed to provide emergent vegetation such as cattail and bulrush for nesting habitat and the submergent plant, sago pondweed, that is critically important to provide food and habitat to raise ducklings and other waterbirds.

The Des Lacs River is not a permanent flowing stream and therefore the water cycle fluctuates wildly with boom and bust years. The majority of water runoff comes in the spring during snowmelt and then sporadically during summer from thunderstorms. As recently as the early 1990s a prolonged drought dried up the middle Des Lacs Lake at Kenmare, but the refuge was completely flooded again in 3-4 days from a heavy July thunderstorm. The past few years have seen abundant water similar to the flood years of 1969, 1970, and 1979. The drought cycle will no doubt return and we'll again see low water levels in the area lakes.

Adjacent to the lakes and marshes is a mixture of other habitats. There are wooded coulees and draws, where white-tailed deer and other wildlife find shelter. Remnants of once-extensive native prairie grassland cover the steep, 50- to 125-foot-high hillsides and the gently rolling Drift Plain above. Areas of native prairie provide critical habitat for such species as Sprague's pipit, chestnut-collared longspur, Baird's and LeConte's sparrows, short-eared owl, and sharp-tailed grouse. Some of the refuge's grasslands were previously farmed and are now maintained as a mixture of cultivated grasses and alfalfa, to provide protective habitat for upland nesting ducks.

An observation blind is available (by reservation) for viewing and photographing the grouse's spring courtship displays from April through June. The male spreads his wings, raises his pointed tail, lowers his head, and rapidly stomps his feet. At the same time, he inflates and deflates purplish neck sacs, and makes a *coo-oo* sound that is accompanied by the rattling of wing quills.

Management of these grasslands is accomplished by short periods of carefully managed grazing and the haying of grasses on lands previously cultivated with crops. Periodic prescribed burning helps to curtail the spread of woody plants that results from unnatural fire suppression.

Establishment of Des Lacs Refuge was made possible partly with revenues from the sale of Migratory Bird Hunting and Conservation Stamps (Duck Stamps).

Des Lacs Refuge is open daily during daylight hours. There is no entrance fee. The refuge headquarters/visitor center is open on weekdays, except national holidays.

Visitor activities include birdwatching; photography; viewing interpretive exhibits in the visitor center; driving (an 11-mile, self-guiding, interpretive auto tour route runs along the shores of Lower, Middle, and the southern end of Upper Des Lacs lakes and the wetlands between them); hiking several trails that lead through woodland and grassland habitats; picnicking (two picnic areas—notably at Tasker's Coulee); canoeing on Upper Des Lacs Lake (a launching site is provided); cross-country skiing and snowshoeing; and hunting (deer, turkey, and upland game, but not waterfowl). Fishing is not permitted. Although camping is not permitted on the refuge, campground facilities are available in the adjacent town of Kenmare. The best months for birdwatching are from May through July and from late September through October.

Insect repellent is advised during the warmer months.

Lodgings and meals are available in such communities as Kenmare, Minot, and Stanley.

Access to the Des Lacs Refuge from Minot is northwest 52 miles on U.S. Route 52 to Kenmare, west 0.5 mile on County Route 1A, and following the refuge's directional sign.

Further information: Des Lacs National Wildlife Refuge, P.O. Box 578, Kenmare, ND 58746; telephone: (701) 385-4046.

Florence Lake, consisting of more than 1,888 acres, was established in 1939 primarily to manage important habitats for migratory waterfowl and other wildlife in northern Burleigh County of central North Dakota. The refuge's wetlands comprise just over 160 acres, and nearly 1,000 acres contain native grassland. Other areas of the refuge support non-native grasses, dense nesting cover, woodland, and grain crops that are grown for the benefit of wildlife.

Establishment of Florence Lake Refuge was made possible partly with revenues from the sale of Migratory Bird Hunting and Conservation Stamps (Duck Stamps). Approximately 400 acres of this refuge's cropland and wetland are being managed under the terms of a conservation easement purchased from a local landowner.

This refuge is open daily during daylight hours. There is no entrance fee. No visitor use facilities are provided. Visitor activities include birdwatching, photography, and hiking. Florence Lake's birds and mammals are much the same as those recorded on Long Lake National Wildlife Refuge.

Lodgings and meals are available in such communities as Bismarck and Washburn.

Access to Florence Lake Refuge from Interstate 94 at Sterling is north 30 miles on State Route 14 and west (left), following refuge signs.

Further information: Florence Lake National Wildlife Refuge, c/o Long Lake NWR Complex, 12000-353rd Street SE, Moffit, ND 58560; telephone: (701) 387-4397.

Halfway Lake, consisting of 160 acres, was established in 1939 to protect important breeding habitat for migratory waterfowl and other wildlife in southeastern North Dakota. The refuge contains about 60 acres of wetland and about 100 acres of mixed-grass prairie upland habitat.

In establishing this refuge, the U.S. Fish and Wildlife Service purchased only the hunting and trapping rights from the private landowner under the terms of an easement agreement. Halfway Lake's birds and mammals are much the same as those recorded on Arrowwood National Wildlife Refuge.

Lodgings and meals are available in such communities as Jamestown and Dawson.

> Access to Halfway Lake Refuge from Interstate 94 at Exit 230 is south about 2 miles on State Route 30. The refuge is on the east side of Route 30.

> Further information: Halfway Lake National Wildlife Refuge, c/o Arrowwood NWR Complex, 7745 Eleventh Street SE, Pingree, ND 58476; telephone: (701) 285-3341.

Hiddenwood, comprising 675 acres, was established in 1939 to protect a farmland-surrounded lake, located a few miles north of Lake Sakakawea, within the Fort Berthold Indian Reservation in west-central North Dakota. Although the lake has been popular for boating and fishing for many decades, it does attract some migrating waterfowl that pause here to rest and feed during spring and autumn migrations. As the U.S. Fish and Wildlife Service explains, "Habitat and wildlife values are quite low with the exception of an excellent strip of shrub and tree riparian habitat around the lake."

The refuge's 580 acres of cropland acreage are being managed under the terms of a conservation easement purchased from a local landowner.

> Further information: Hiddenwood National Wildlife Refuge, c/o Audubon Wildlife Refuge Complex, 3275 Eleventh Street NW, Coleharbor, ND 58531; telephone: (701) 442-5474.

Hobart Lake, comprising 2,077 acres, was established in 1939 to protect important wetland habitat for concentrations of large diving ducks and Canada geese, along with a few tundra swans and puddle ducks, in southeastern North Dakota.

Establishment of a small part of Hobart Lake Refuge was made possible partly with revenues from the sale of Migratory Bird Hunting and Conservation Stamps (Duck Stamps). For most of this refuge, the U.S. Fish and Wildlife Service purchased only the hunting and trapping rights from the private landowner under the terms of an easement agreement. Hobart Lake's birds and mammals are much the same as those recorded on Arrowwood National Wildlife Refuge.

Lodgings and meals are available in Valley City and Jamestown.

> Access is at several easy-to-find places from I-94, which cuts through the refuge between Exits 288 and 283.

> Further information: Hobart Lake National Wildlife Refuge, c/o Arrowwood NWR Complex, 7745 Eleventh Street SE, Pingree, ND 58476; telephone: (701) 285-3341.

Hutchinson Lake, consisting of 479 acres, was established in 1939 to enhance and protect an important wetland area on part of Hutchinson Lake, in Kidder County of central North Dakota. Especially during the autumn, migrating waterfowl pause here to rest and feed.

The refuge's acreage is being managed under the terms of a conservation easement purchased from a local landowner. Visitor entry onto this easement refuge is not permitted without landowner permission. Hutchinson Lake's birds and mammals are much the same as those recorded on Long Lake National Wildlife Refuge.

Further information: Hutchinson Lake National Wildlife Refuge, c/o Long Lake NWR Complex, 12000-353rd Street SE, Moffit, ND 58560; telephone (701) 387-4397.

J. Clark Salyer, containing 59,383 acres, was established in 1935, extending southward from the U.S.–Canada border in north-central North Dakota. The refuge manages a diversity of habitats, including riparian woodland, aspen parkland, various wetland types, mixed-grass prairie, and sandhills, which occur along the lower stretch of the Souris (Mouse) River. Initially the Lower Souris National Wildlife Refuge, it was renamed in 1967 to honor J. Clark Salyer, the chief of the Fish and Wildlife Service's Division of Wildlife Refuges from 1934 to 1961. Over 260 bird species have been seen on Salyer, Des Lacs, and Upper Souris refuges.

During the early decades of the twentieth century, riparian wetlands of the Dakotas were drained for the production of cash crops, resulting in the extensive destruction of waterfowl habitat. Because at that time many of these former wetlands proved unsuitable for agriculture, numerous crop failures resulted. Then in the 1930s, a severe drought greatly reduced the productivity of wetlands that were available for waterfowl populations. At this time, the federal government began establishing many national wildlife refuges in this region, launching a major program to restore these vital marshes.

The construction of five levees within J. Clark Salyer Refuge created a series of pools, to increase the availability of water bird habitat along 75 miles of meandering river. The pools' fluctuating water levels, regulated by water control structures, enhance nutrient cycling and promote the production of aquatic plants used by breeding water birds.

During spring and autumn migrations, water bird concentrations on J. Clark Salyer Refuge are spectacular—now numbering as many as 400,000 to 500,000 birds of numerous species. Approximately 50 human-made and natural islands, which are relatively secure from predators, offer summer nesting areas, especially for mallard, blue-winged teal, gadwall, and the giant Canada goose (*Branta canadensis maxima*). The Canada geese, which had previously been eliminated by habitat loss and overhunting, were successfully reintroduced when a small captive flock was brought onto the refuge in 1937. Several hundred goslings are now hatched annually.

The refuge provides nesting boxes for wood ducks and hooded mergansers. Other birds are attracted to the wetlands, including summering white pelicans, five species of grebes, sandhill cranes, herons, cormorants, terns, and large numbers of shorebirds.

The upland habitats, specifically the prairie grasslands, are managed for the benefit of nesting waterfowl, sharp-tailed and ruffed grouse, wild turkeys, the non-native gray partridges and ring-necked pheasants, upland sandpipers, chestnut-collared longspurs, bobolinks, and Baird's and LeConte's sparrows.

In the spring, the sharp-tailed grouse perform their impressive courtship displays on a number of dancing grounds, known as leks. The male spreads his wings, raises his pointed tail, lowers his head, and rapidly stomps his feet. At the same time, he inflates and deflates purplish neck sacs, and makes a hollow *coo-oo* sound that is accompanied by the rattling of vibrating wing quills.

To enhance and maintain the quality of native prairie grasses and forbs, the refuge implements rest rotation, short-term livestock grazing and periodic prescribed burning. These management activities promote nutrient cycling and help curtail woody plant expansion.

Establishment of this refuge was made possible partly with revenues from the sale of Migratory Bird Hunting and Conservation Stamps (Duck Stamps). Ducks Unlimited, Inc. has helped enhance some of the refuge's wetland habitat.

The refuge is open daily during daylight hours. There is no entrance fee. The refuge headquarters is open on weekdays, except national holidays.

Visitor activities include birdwatching, photography, hiking, driving the refuge's auto tour routes, canoeing and boating, picnicking (three picnic areas are provided), fishing (at 13 sites on the refuge), and hunting (waterfowl, big game, and upland game) on parts of the refuge during the designated seasons. Although camping is not permitted on the refuge, campground facilities are available in a municipal park in Upham, a county park near Bottineau, Lake Metigoshe State Park (adjoining the U.S.–Canada border), and in the town of Towner. The best months for birdwatching are from May through July and from late September through October.

There are two self-guiding auto tour routes (interpretive brochures are available): Scenic Trail—a 22-mile road that begins at headquarters and provides views of marsh, riparian woodland, and sandhill habitats as it winds through the southern end of the refuge; and Grassland Trail—a 5-mile route that passes by a stretch of river marsh and through prairie grassland in the central part of the refuge.

A scenic stretch of the river bottom woodland and marsh is accessible by way of the J. Clark Salyer NWR Canoe Trail—on either the entire 13-mile meandering route or a 5.5-mile segment. An interpretive brochure is available for this national recreation trail.

Insect repellent is advised during the warmer months.

The more than 300 species of birds on J. Clark Salyer Refuge are much the same as Des Lacs Refuge.

Lodgings and meals are available in such communities as Bottineau, Westhope, and Minot.

Access to J. Clark Salyer Refuge from U.S. Route 2 at Towner is north 26 miles on State Route 14. The refuge headquarters is located 3 miles north of Upham, just east of State Route 14, on Salyer Road.

Further information: J. Clark Salyer National Wildlife Refuge, P.O. Box 66, Upham, ND 58789; telephone: (701) 768-2548.

Johnson Lake, comprising 2,008 acres, was established in 1934 to manage an important wetland habitat for the benefit of migratory waterfowl and other wildlife in Eddy and Nelson counties of east-central North Dakota.

In establishing this refuge, the U.S. Fish and Wildlife Service purchased only the hunting and trapping rights from the private landowner under the terms of an easement agreement. Birds and mammals of Johnson Lake Refuge are much the same as on Arrowwood National Wildlife Refuge.

Further information: Johnson Lake National Wildlife Refuge, c/o Arrowwood NWR Complex, 7745 Eleventh Street SE, Pingree, ND 58476; telephone: (701) 285-3341.

Kelly's Slough, consisting of 1,269 acres, was established in 1936 to enhance and protect important wetland and upland habitats for the benefit of migratory waterfowl and other wildlife 8 miles west of Grand Forks, in northeastern North Dakota. During spring and autumn migrations, thousands of ducks, geese, and shorebirds pause here to rest and feed.

Nesting waterfowl include such ducks as mallard, blue-winged teal, pintail, and gadwall, and the giant Canada goose (*Branta canadensis maxima*). The latter subspecies was once brought to the brink of extinction by habitat loss and overhunting. But thanks to a successful reintroduction program, it has been restored to this and many other refuges in the northern Great Plains.

Establishment of this refuge was made possible partly with revenues from the sale of Migratory Bird Hunting and Conservation Stamps (Duck Stamps). A portion of this refuge's acreage is being managed under the terms of a perpetual conservation easement purchased from a local landowner.

The refuge is open daily during daylight hours. There is no entrance fee. A visitor information kiosk is provided.

Visitor activities include birdwatching, photography, hiking on three trails, viewing the refuge and wildlife from two observation platforms, and hunting during the designated seasons. Birds and mammals of Kelly's Slough Refuge are much the same as those recorded on Lake Alice National Wildlife Refuge.

Federally owned waterfowl production area lands, which adjoin the refuge to the north, offer additional wildlife observation and hiking opportunities (see the Devils Lake Wetland Management District [WMD] text for regulations on waterfowl production areas).

Lodgings and meals are available in Grand Forks.

Access to Kelly's Slough Refuge from Interstate 29 in Grand Forks is west 7.5 miles on U.S. Route 2 and north (right) just over 3 miles on an unpaved road, to a parking area and overlook that provides a view of the refuge.

Further information: Kelly's Slough National Wildlife Refuge, c/o Devils Lake Wetland Management District, P.O. Box 908, Devils Lake, ND 58301; telephone: (701) 662-8611.

Lake Alice, comprising 12,156 acres, was established in 1935 to enhance and protect important wetland habitat, primarily for nesting and migrating waterfowl, in Ramsey and Towner counties of north-central North Dakota. More than 7,500 acres of this refuge consist of managed wetlands, and nearly 3,500 acres are grasslands.

In 1972, the U.S. Fish and Wildlife Service acquired 8,600 acres of the refuge's original easement lands, partly with revenues from the sale of Migratory Bird Hunting and Conservation Stamps (Duck Stamps). Ducks Unlimited, Inc. has subsequently helped enhance some of the refuge's wetland habitat.

Large concentrations of snow geese pause on Lake Alice Refuge to rest and feed in April and into May, and especially from mid-September into October. An important nesting species here is the giant Canada goose (*Branta canadensis maxima*). The latter is a subspecies that was once brought to the brink of extinction by extensive habitat loss and overhunting. Fortunately, a successful propagation program has enabled its restoration to this and numerous other refuges in the northern Great Plains. Artificial nesting sites have been created for the giant Canadas. The white-tailed deer is the most prominent mammal.

The refuge is open daily during daylight hours. There is no entrance fee. The refuge headquarters, located at the Devils Lake Wetland Management Complex office, is open on weekdays, except national holidays.

Visitor activities include birdwatching, photography, driving an auto tour route, hiking, and hunting during the designated seasons. Two overlooks along the tour route offer a good view of Lake Alice.

Lodgings and meals are available in such communities as Devils Lake and Rugby.

Access to Lake Alice Refuge from U.S. Route 2 at Penn is north about 6 miles on maintained gravel roads.

Further information: Lake Alice National Wildlife Refuge, c/o Devils Lake Wetland Management District, P.O. Box 908, Devils Lake, ND 58301; telephone: (701) 662-8611.

Lake George, encompassing two units totaling 3,119 acres, was established in 1939 to enhance and protect two lakes in Kidder County of south-central North Dakota. During autumn migration, several thousand Canada geese, along with several hundred snow geese and ducks, pause here to rest and feed. A few pairs of nesting ducks also use the lakes. Adjacent uplands of grasses and forbs support such species of wildlife as sharp-tailed grouse, deer, and numerous grassland songbirds.

Most of the refuge's acreage is being managed under the terms of conservation easements purchased from local landowners. Ducks Unlimited, Inc. recently funded long-needed repairs for a small dam on the refuge's northern unit that was constructed by the Civilian Conservation Corps (CCC) during the late 1930s or early 1940s.

Visitor access onto this easement refuge is not permitted.

Further information: Lake George National Wildlife Refuge, c/o Long Lake NWR Complex, 12000-353rd Street SE, Moffit, ND 58560; telephone: (701) 387-4397.

Lake Ilo, containing 4,033 acres, was established in 1937 to protect important wetland and open-water habitat of this prairie-encircled lake, the adjacent, 145-acre, marshy Lee Paul

Slough, and a score of scattered, smaller wetlands in west-central North Dakota. Especially during spring and autumn migrations, large concentrations of waterfowl (as many as 100,000 in the fall) and shorebirds are attracted to the 990-acre reservoir created by Lake Ilo Dam. This 1,525-foot-long structure was completed in 1937 by the federal Works Progress Administration and rebuilt in the mid-1990s.

Just over half the refuge acreage consists of gently rolling uplands of native grassland, areas of introduced grasses, some plantings of non-native trees, and about 50 acres of cropland. Some of the cultivated grains are planted under cooperative agreements with local farmers, whereby part of the crop is left for the benefit of waterfowl and secondarily for deer, pheasants, and other wildlife.

About one-fifth of Lake Ilo's acreage is being managed under the terms of conservation easements purchased from local landowners. Establishment of the refuge was made possible partly with revenues from the sale of Migratory Bird Hunting and Conservation Stamps (Duck Stamps). Among the management techniques used to enhance and maintain habitat diversity are prescribed burns, grazing, and haying. To restore areas of grassland, native forbs and grasses have been planted on former croplands.

Lake Ilo Refuge also contains numerous archaeological sites. These important cultural resources, including many thousands of stone artifacts, have been carefully studied by an interdisciplinary team of Fish and Wildlife Service and university researchers and students. As the U.S. Fish and Wildlife Service explains:

The variety of spear, dart, and arrow points found along Murphy and Spring Creeks suggests that Native Americans visited this area for more than 10,000 years. Glaciers were only 500 miles to the northwest when the first humans visited this area. . . . Most of the stone artifacts from surface collections and excavations on the Refuge were produced from locally available Knife River flint . . . [that] . . . fractures like glass and can be made into very durable, sharp-edged tools. . . . Archeological remains reflect the continuous use of the area for 11,000 years. It's amazing to have an unbroken record of occupation in a single location like this.

The refuge is open daily during daylight hours. There is no entrance fee. The refuge headquarters, located on the southeast shore of the lake, is open on weekdays, except national holidays.

Visitor activities include birdwatching, photography, driving unpaved refuge roads, hiking, fishing, and boating. Idle-speed boating only is permitted for fishing and wildlife viewing from May 1 through September. A boat ramp is provided on the lake's north shore, and part of the lake and Lee Paul Slough are closed to boats and fishing. A fishing pier and picnic facilities (wheelchair-accessible) are provided in Lake Ilo Park (which is managed by Dunn County), on the north shore of the lake, and within the refuge. A 1-mile, self-guiding, interpretive trail (part of which is wheelchair-accessible) begins in the park, and other trails are provided.

Although camping is not permitted on either the refuge or park, campground facilities are provided at such places as Little Missouri State Park and Theodore Roosevelt National Park. Swimming and hunting are not allowed on either the refuge or park, and the western and most of the southern part of the refuge are closed to visitation. The best months for birdwatching are March through April and late September through October.

Insect repellent is advised during the warmer months.

More than 225 bird species have been recorded on Lake Ilo Refuge.

Lodgings and meals are available in such communities as Dickinson and Beulah.

Access from I-94 at Richardton is north 34 miles on State Route 8, and west (left) on State Route 200 to 1 mile west of Dunn Center; or from I-94 at Dickinson north 32 miles on State Route 22, and east (right) 5.5 miles on State Route 200 to the refuge.

Further information: Lake Ilo National Wildlife Refuge, 489-102nd Avenue SW, Dunn Center, ND 58626; telephone: (701) 548-8110.

Lake Nettie, containing 3,325 acres, was established in 1935 to protect a large semisaline lake, a freshwater marsh, a stretch of Turtle Creek, and adjacent uplands located 5 miles east of Lake Audubon in west-central North Dakota. The refuge attracts concentrations of waterfowl, sandhill cranes, and shorebirds, especially during spring and autumn migrations.

Roughly one-fifth of Lake Nettie's acreage is being managed under the terms of conservation easements purchased from local landowners. Establishment of the refuge was made possible partly with revenues from the sale of Migratory Bird Hunting and Conservation Stamps (Duck Stamps). Ducks Unlimited, Inc. has helped enhance some of Lake Nettie's wetlands habitat by building nesting islands.

The refuge is open daily during daylight hours for walk-in access only. There is no entrance fee. No visitor use facilities are provided. There are several public roads along the edges of the refuge.

Visitor activities include birdwatching, photography, hiking, and hunting during the designated seasons.

Access to Lake Nettie Refuge from the town of Turtle Lake is north 8 miles on paved State Highway 41 and west (left) 4 miles on paved State Highway 8.

Further information: Lake Nettie National Wildlife Refuge, c/o Audubon Wildlife Refuge Complex, 3275 Eleventh Street NW, Coleharbor, ND 58531; telephone: (701) 442-5474.

Lake Otis, containing 320 acres, was established in 1935 to protect a prairie-surrounded cluster of small wetlands a few miles to the northeast of Lake Audubon in central North Dakota. The marshy habitat attracts concentrations of waterfowl and other water birds, especially during the spring and autumn migrations. The native prairie that surrounds these wetlands is grazed by livestock under a managed rotational system. As the U.S. Fish and Wildlife Service says, "This refuge, with its long history of severe overgrazing by the landowner's tenant, continues to look the best it ever has."

The refuge's acreage is being managed under the terms of a conservation easement agreement with the North Dakota State Land Department. Visitor entry onto this easement refuge is not permitted.

Further information: Lake Otis National Wildlife Refuge, c/o Audubon Wildlife Refuge Complex, 3275 Eleventh Street NW, Coleharbor, ND 58531; (701) 442-5474.

Lake Patricia, consisting of 800 acres, was established in 1939 to manage an important area of impounded wetland habitat and some adjacent grassland for the benefit of migratory waterfowl and other wildlife. The refuge is located in Morton County, in central North Dakota.

The majority of this easement refuge is being cooperatively managed by the North Dakota Game and Fish Department, under the terms of a conservation easement.

The state-managed area is open to visitation during daylight hours (two parking areas are provided). Visitor activities include wildlife observation, photography, hiking on trails, and hunting during the designated seasons. The refuge can also be viewed from three sides—from adjacent State Route 21 and two unpaved county roads.

The U.S. Fish and Wildlife Service says that "The refuge is important particularly during dry years when wildlife is attracted to the water and surrounding habitat. A nice wildlife area off the beaten path."

Lodgings and meals are available in such communities as Mandan and Bismarck.

Access to Lake Patricia Refuge from Flasher is east 1.5 miles on State Route 21.

Further information: Lake Patricia National Wildlife Refuge, c/o Lake Ilo NWR, 489-102nd Avenue SW, Dunn Center, ND 58626; telephone: (701) 548-8110.

Lake Zahl, encompassing 3,739 acres, was established in 1939 to enhance and protect vital wetland and upland prairie habitats for migratory waterfowl and other wildlife in the northwestern corner of North Dakota. The refuge's 1,500 acres of wetlands are managed to maintain staging and resting areas for as many as 10,000 snow geese and 40,000 ducks of numerous species. The giant Canada goose (*Branta canadensis maxima*) and many ducks also nest here.

Other migratory birds that are drawn to Lake Zahl are whooping cranes, bald eagles, peregrine falcons, and a variety of shorebirds. The refuge's 1,700 acres of native upland prairie are maintained for the benefit of many species, including a number of breeding pairs of burrowing owls.

More than one-sixth of Lake Zahl's acreage is being managed under the terms of conservation easements purchased from local landowners. Establishment of the refuge was made possible partly with revenues from the sale of Migratory Bird Hunting and Conservation Stamps (Duck Stamps). Ducks Unlimited, Inc. has helped enhance some of its wetland habitat.

Lake Zahl is open daily, during daylight hours. There is no entrance fee. No visitor use facilities are provided. Visitor activities include birdwatching, photography, hiking, and hunting (deer and upland game only) during the designated seasons. Much of the wildlife on this refuge is the same as has been recorded on Des Lacs National Wildlife Refuge.

This refuge lies within the extensive Crosby Wetland Management District (see text on the latter). Information on this district: P.O. Box 148, Crosby, ND 58730; telephone: (701) 965-6488.

Lodgings and meals are available in Williston.

Access to Lake Zahl Refuge from Williston is north 12 miles on U.S. Routes 85/2, north 16 miles on U.S. Route 85, and west (left) on State Route 50 to the refuge.

Further information: Lake Zahl National Wildlife Refuge, c/o Des Lacs National Wildlife Refuge Complex, P.O. Box 578, Kenmare, ND 58746; telephone: (701) 385-3214.

Lambs Lake, consisting of 1,206 acres, was established in 1939 to manage an important wetland habitat for the benefit of migratory waterfowl and other wildlife in Nelson County of east-central North Dakota.

The refuge's acreage is being managed under the terms of conservation easements purchased from local landowners. Visitor entry onto this easement refuge is only with landowner permission, or the refuge can be viewed from a public road. Birds and mammals of Lambs Lake refuge are much the same as those recorded for Lake Alice National Wildlife Refuge.

Access to Lambs Lake Refuge from U.S. Route 2 at Michigan, North Dakota is south 6 miles on State Route 35 and east 1 mile on an unpaved county road.

Further information: Lambs Lake National Wildlife Refuge, c/o Devils Lake Wetland Management District, P.O. Box 908, Devils Lake, ND 58301; telephone: (701) 662-8611.

Little Goose, comprising 288 acres, was established in 1939 to manage an important wetland habitat for the benefit of migratory waterfowl and other wildlife in western Grand Forks County of east-central North Dakota.

The majority of the refuge's acreage is being managed under the terms of a conservation easement purchased from a local landowner. Birds and mammals of Little Goose Refuge are much the same as those recorded for Lake Alice National Wildlife Refuge.

Although visitor entry onto this easement refuge is not permitted, the refuge can be viewed from an unpaved county road, 5 miles south of U.S. Route 2 at Niagara.

Further information: Little Goose National Wildlife Refuge, c/o Devils Lake Wetland Management District, P.O. Box 908, Devils Lake, ND 58301; telephone: (701) 662-8611.

Long Lake, containing 22,498 acres, was established in 1932 to enhance and protect ecologically significant habitats, including open water and marsh of this 16,000-acre shallow lake and its surrounding prairie grassland, ravines, small areas of trees and shrubs, and cultivated fields. The refuge is located in Burleigh and Kidder counties of south-central North Dakota. Most of the lake's water is derived from Long Lake Creek and depends upon annual precipitation and runoff. Over 200 bird species have been recorded here.

This refuge was established in response to Long Lake's history of botulism epidemics that were causing massive waterfowl mortality. This bacterial toxin targets the nervous system and leads to paralysis of the respiratory system and death. In the mid-1930s, the Civilian Conservation Corps constructed a variety of facilities on the refuge. These conservation measures included two dikes to divide the lake into three parts, and spillways to regulate water levels and hold them at higher levels during periods of water shortage; a number of check dams in adjacent ravines; and nearly a score of islands for the benefit of nesting ducks.

Long Lake's most abundant nesting ducks include mallards, pintails, blue-winged teal, and gadwalls. Prominent among the birds that pause to rest and feed here during autumn migration are thousands of sandhill cranes that visit the refuge from mid-September to late October. If the lake contains sufficient water, as many as 25,000 ducks and 20,000 Canada, snow, and greater white-fronted geese stop on their way south.

The refuge's grassland provides important nesting habitat for such species as puddle ducks, marbled godwits, upland sandpipers, Baird's and sharp-tailed sparrows, and sharp-tailed grouse. With the assistance of local ranchers and farmers, short-term livestock grazing and haying help to enhance and maintain the health of these grasslands. Periodic prescribed burning helps to enhance the productivity of grassland and marsh habitats. For the benefit of wildlife, roughly 500 acres of the refuge are cultivated with corn, wheat, millet, and sunflowers.

More than 8,000 acres of this refuge are being protectively managed under the terms of perpetual conservation easement agreements with local landowners. Establishment of Long Lake Refuge was made possible partly with revenues from the sale of Migratory Bird Hunting and Conservation Stamps (Duck Stamps). Ducks Unlimited, Inc. has helped enhance some of the refuge's wetland habitat.

The refuge is open daily during daylight hours. There is no entrance fee. The refuge headquarters is open on weekdays, except national holidays.

Visitor activities include birdwatching; photography; hiking; picnicking (a picnic area is provided near the northern shore of the lake, 1 mile east of U.S. Route 83); boating (25 hp motors or less); fishing; and hunting (deer and upland game birds) during the designated seasons. The best months for birdwatching are April and May, and especially September and October.

Insect repellent is advised during the warmer months.

Lodgings and meals are available in such communities as Steele and Bismarck.

Access to Long Lake Refuge from Interstate 94 at Sterling is south 9 miles on U.S. 83, east (left) 3 miles on 102nd Avenue SE, and south (right) 1 mile on 353rd Street SE; or from U.S. Route 12 at Selby, it is north 83 miles on U.S. Route 83, and east (right) just over a mile on 128th Avenue SE.

Further information: Long Lake National Wildlife Refuge, 12000-353rd Street SE, Moffit, ND 58560; telephone: (701) 387-4397.

Lords Lake, comprising 1,915 acres, was established in 1939 to maintain a shallow, drift-plain wetland adjacent to the Turtle Mountains in Bottineau and Rolette counties of north-central North Dakota. This refuge provides important resting and feeding habitat for thousands of lesser snow geese, as well as tundra swans and various species of ducks, especially during autumn migration in September and October. Beavers and muskrats are among other species of wildlife inhabiting the wetlands. The lake level fluctuates widely and can even dry up, depending upon annual precipitation and runoff.

The refuge's acreage is being managed under the terms of conservation easements purchased from local landowners. Although hunting is permitted, other visitor activities, such as birdwatching and hiking, are at the discretion of the landowners. Opportunities for wildlife observation and photography are possible from the adjacent county road. Lords Lake's birds and mammals are much the same as those recorded on Des Lacs National Wildlife Refuge.

Access to Lords Lake Refuge from Bottineau is east about 12 miles on State Route 5 and south (right) about 1 mile on the township road; or from State Route 3 at Dunseith, it is west about 6 miles on State Route 5 and south (left) about 1 mile on the township road.

Further information: Lords Lake National Wildlife Refuge, c/o J. Clark Salyer NWR Complex, P.O. Box 66, Upham, ND 58789; telephone: (701) 768-2548.

Lost Lake, containing 960 acres, was established in 1939 to protect a 200-acre alkali lake a few miles southeast of Lake Sakakawea in central North Dakota. The open water attracts concentrations of Canada geese and other waterfowl and wildlife, especially during spring and autumn migrations. Encircling the lake is gently rolling prairie grassland, through which flows Painted Woods Creek.

The refuge's acreage is being managed under the terms of a conservation easement purchased from a local landowner. Ducks Unlimited, Inc. has assisted with enhancement of Lost Lake Refuge's wetlands habitat.

Visitor entry onto this easement refuge is allowed only with permission from the private landowner and the refuge.

Further information: Lost Lake National Wildlife Refuge, c/o Audubon Wildlife Refuge Complex, 3275 Eleventh Street NW, Coleharbor, ND 58531; telephone: (701) 442-5474.

Lostwood, consisting of 26,904 acres, was established in 1935 to manage and protect an outstanding part of the northern Missouri Coteau. The refuge contains a mixed-grass landscape of gently rolling hills with scattered copses of quaking aspens, and more than 4,000 shallow lakes, ponds, sloughs, and marshes in the prairie pothole region of northwestern North Dakota.

The refuge's topography is actually a small part of an extensive line of hills made up of gravel and rocks that were deposited as a vast moraine along the edge of the slowly melting continental glacier toward the end of North America's most recent ice age. This band of hills, ranging from 12 to nearly 20 miles in width, extends from northwestern Iowa northwestward across the Dakotas and into Alberta, Canada. The refuge contains the largest contiguous, federally owned tract of this northern Great Plains "knob-and-kettle" (hill-and-pothole) physiographic region.

In 1975, Congress designated 5,577 acres in the northwestern part of the refuge as the Lostwood Wilderness—a unit of the National Wilderness Preservation System. The enabling legislation declared that this area is ". . . a unique example of the Coteau du Missouri of the Northern Great Plains . . . that constitutes the last sizeable tract of this interesting formation," which extends from northwestern Iowa through South and North Dakota and into Alberta, Canada, and which varies from 12 to nearly 20 miles in width.

Lostwood Refuge provides valuable habitat for large concentrations of nesting waterfowl, such as mallards, blue-winged teal, wigeons, gadwalls, and lesser scaup. The giant Canada goose (*Branta canadensis maxima*) also nests here. This subspecies, which formerly inhabited the Great Plains in great abundance, was reduced to the brink of extinction in the mid-1930s by extensive market hunting and egg collecting. Giant Canadas were successfully reintroduced on Lostwood Refuge in 1964. Other nesting species attracted in substantial numbers to these pothole wetlands include eared grebes, Virginia rails, Wilson's phalaropes, American avocets, willets, and marbled godwits. Prominent among the birds that pause on the refuge during spring and autumn migrations are tundra swans, greater white-fronted and lesser snow geese, and sandhill cranes.

Prairie grassland birds of Lostwood Refuge include upland sandpipers, chestnut-collared longspurs, Sprague's pipits, bobolinks, Baird's and LeConte's sparrows, and an extraordinary concentration of the sharp-tailed grouse. From April through June, a blind is available (by reservation) for viewing and photographing the grouse's elaborate courtship displays. An average of 600 males perform on the refuge's many dancing grounds, known as leks. The male spreads his wings, raises his pointed tail, lowers his head, and rapidly stomps his feet. At the same time, he inflates and deflates purplish neck sacs, and makes a hollow *coo-oo* sound that is accompanied by the rattling of vibrating wing quills. More than 225 species of birds have been recorded on Lostwood Refuge.

Historically, profound changes were caused by the elimination of short-duration grazing of the once-vast herds of American bison (buffalo) prior to the mid-1880s, and by the subsequent introduction of long-duration domestic livestock grazing. In addition, ecologically unnatural suppression of fire from the early twentieth century to the mid-1980s and the invasion of non-native plants, such as the aggressive smooth brome grass and leafy spurge, further contributed to the decline in the quality of the prairie grasslands. As the U.S. Fish and Wildlife Service explains, "Native uplands, once dominated with waving seas of grass, were replaced in many areas with dense shrub stands. Where no trees existed prior to settlement, aspen tree clumps increased. . . , adversely affecting over 400 wetlands."

To restore and maintain the health of this grassland habitat, the refuge carries out periodic prescribed burning and carefully managed, short-duration livestock grazing. These management practices help to control an unnatural invasion of woody plants, to release vital plant nutrients, and to promote new growth of native grasses and forbs. These management activities are designed to benefit numerous species of wildlife that are dependent upon the mixed-grass prairie habitat—so much of which has previously been seriously impaired or destroyed throughout the northern Great Plains.

Establishment of Lostwood Refuge was made possible partly with revenues from the sale of Migratory Bird Hunting and Conservation Stamps (Duck Stamps).

The refuge is open daily during daylight hours. There is no entrance fee. The refuge headquarters is open on weekdays, except national holidays.

Visitor activities include birdwatching; photography; driving the 7-mile, self-guiding, interpretive auto tour route (a brochure is available); hiking a 7-mile loop trail and a trail from headquarters that offers views of Thompson Lake and Iverson Slough; cross-country skiing and snowshoeing; and hunting (deer, sharp-tailed grouse, and gray partridge) on parts of the refuge during the designated seasons. The best months for birdwatching are May to July and late September through October.

Insect repellent is advised during the warmer months.

Lodgings and meals are available in such communities as Kenmare, Stanley, and Minot.

Access to the refuge from U.S. Route 52 at Kenmare and from Des Lacs NWR is west 12 miles on County Route 2 and south 4 miles on State Highway 8; or from U.S. Route 2 at Stanley, it is north 21 miles on State Highway 8.

Further information: Lostwood National Wildlife Refuge, P.O. Box 578, Kenmare, ND 58746; telephone: (701) 848-2722.

Maple River, encompassing 1,120 acres, was established in 1939 as a refuge and breeding ground for migratory birds and other wildlife. The refuge is located along Maple River in Dickey County, North Dakota. Refuge boundaries include the main river channel with a small diversion dam, a second dam on an 82-acre marsh unit, riparian fringes of the river, and agricultural fields. Protection of land and water within the refuge is accomplished both under the terms of conservation easement agreements with private landowners (712 acres) and acquisition by the U.S. Fish and Wildlife Service (408 acres).

The portion of the refuge that is owned by the Service is open to visitors for birdwatching, photography, and fishing and hunting during the designated seasons. The remainder of the refuge is closed to visitation. No public use facilities are provided on the refuge, and there is no entrance fee.

During spring and fall migrations, a wide variety of waterfowl, shorebirds, and other marsh-related species utilize the refuge. The marsh unit is attractive as a nesting and brood-rearing area for many species of marsh and water birds.

Further information: Maple River National Wildlife Refuge, c/o Kulm Wetland Management District, P.O. Box E (1 First Street SW), Kulm, ND 58456; telephone: (701) 647-2866.

McLean, containing 824 acres, was established in 1959 to protect important wetland habitat of a small marshy reservoir known as Lake Susie, within the Fort Berthold Indian Reservation in west-central North Dakota. The refuge's marsh habitat attracts concentrations of waterfowl, especially during spring and autumn migrations.

Roughly half of this refuge's acreage is being managed under the terms of a conservation easement agreement with the North Dakota State Land Department. Establishment of McLean refuge was made possible partly with revenues from the sale of Migratory Bird Hunting and Conservation Stamps (Duck Stamps). Ducks Unlimited, Inc. and the North Dakota Wetlands

Trust have provided funding and other needs, to help enhance some of the refuge's wetland habitat. Canada geese are now well established here, after being reintroduced in 1989 and 1990.

No visitor use facilities are provided. Visitor activities include birdwatching, photography, and hiking.

Lodgings and meals are available in such communities as New Town, Minot, and Washburn.

Access to McLean Refuge from the town of Roseglen is west 4.5 miles on State Route 37, north (right) 4 miles, and west (left) 0.5 mile.

Further information: McLean National Wildlife Refuge, c/o Audubon Wildlife Refuge Complex, 3275 Eleventh Street NW , Coleharbor, ND 58531; telephone: (701) 442-5474.

Pleasant Lake consisting of 897 acres, was established in 1939 to manage important wetland habitat for the benefit of migratory waterfowl and other wildlife in northern Benson County of north-central North Dakota.

The refuge's acreage is being managed under the terms of a conservation easement purchased from a local landowner. Visitor entry onto this easement refuge is only with landowner permission, or the refuge can be viewed from U.S. Route 2 between Knox and Rugby. Pleasant Lake's birds and mammals are much the same as those recorded for Lake Alice National Wildlife Refuge.

Further information: Pleasant Lake National Wildlife Refuge, c/o Devils Lake Wetland Management District, P.O. Box 908, Devils Lake, ND 58301; telephone: (701) 662-8611.

Pretty Rock, containing 800 acres, was established in 1941 to protect important marsh wetlands habitat around the shore of a lake that attracts migratory and breeding waterfowl and other wildlife, near New Leipzig in southwestern North Dakota.

The refuge's acreage is being managed under the terms of a conservation easement purchased from a local landowner. Visitor entry is not permitted onto this easement refuge. Pretty Rock Refuge's birds, mammals, reptiles, and amphibians are much the same as those recorded on Lake Alice National Wildlife Refuge.

Further information: Pretty Rock National Wildlife Refuge, c/o Lake Ilo NWR, 489-102nd Avenue SW , Dunn Center, ND 58626; telephone: (701) 548-8110.

Rabb Lake, comprising 260 acres, was established in 1948 to maintain a remote 102-acre lake and surrounding densely wooded upland. The refuge is located on the U.S.–Canada border, within Rolette County in north-central North Dakota. Easements for this non-federally owned refuge were purchased from a private landowner (151 acres) and the state (109 acres).

The refuge and North Dakota Game and Fish Department's adjacent wildlife management area provide important resting and feeding habitat mainly for migratory diving ducks—notably canvasbacks. Ruffed grouse and white-tailed deer are among many species of wildlife inhabiting upland areas of quaking aspen and green ash. Rabb Lake Refuge's birds and mammals are much the same as those recorded on Des Lacs National Wildlife Refuge.

Although hunting is permitted on the refuge, other visitor activities, such as birdwatching and hiking, are at the discretion of the landowners.

Further information: Rabb Lake National Wildlife Refuge, c/o J. Clark Salyer NWR Complex, P.O. Box 66, Upham, ND 58789; telephone: (701) 768-2548.

Rock Lake, encompassing 5,506 acres, was established in 1939 to manage important wetland habitat for the benefit of migratory waterfowl and other wildlife, in northern Towner County of north-central North Dakota. The major feature of the refuge is the southern part of Rock Lake.

The refuge's acreage is being managed under the terms of conservation easements purchased from local landowners. Visitor entry onto this easement refuge is only with landowner permission, or the refuge can be viewed from State Route 5 at Rocklake, and from an unpaved county road to the north of Rocklake. Birds and mammals on Rock Lake Refuge are much the same as those recorded for Lake Alice National Wildlife Refuge.

Access to Rock Lake Refuge is just north of State Route 5 at Rocklake.

Further information: Rock Lake National Wildlife Refuge, c/o Devils Lake Wetland Management District, P.O. Box 908, Devils Lake, ND 58301; telephone: (701) 662-8611.

Rose Lake, containing 836 acres, was established in 1948 to manage an important wetland habitat for the benefit of migratory waterfowl and other wildlife in western Nelson County of east-central North Dakota.

The refuge's acreage is being managed under the terms of a conservation easement purchased from a local landowner. Visitor entry onto this easement refuge is only with landowner permission, or the refuge can be viewed from an unpaved county road about 3.5 miles north of the western arm of Stump Lake. Rose Lake's birds and mammals are much the same as Lake Alice National Wildlife Refuge.

Access to Rose Lake Refuge from U.S. Route 2 at Lakota is 2 miles south on State Route 1, 5 miles west on a gravel road, 1 mile south, and 1 mile west.

Further information: Rose Lake National Wildlife Refuge, c/o Devils Lake Wetland Management District, P.O. Box 908, Devils Lake, ND 58301; telephone: (701) 662-8611.

School Section Lake, consisting of 297 acres, was established in 1948 to maintain the 305-acre School Section Lake, within Rolette County in north-central North Dakota. The lake, created by a dam, is in the headwaters of Indian Creek, a tributary of Souris River, and provides habitat mainly for migratory diving ducks. Ruffed grouse and white-tailed deer are among many species that inhabit the surrounding wooded uplands of quaking aspen and green ash.

School Section Lake's birds and mammals are much the same as those recorded on Des Lacs National Wildlife Refuge.

Easements on this non-federally owned refuge were purchased from a private landowner and the state. The refuge is not open to hunting. Other visitor activities, such as birdwatching and hiking, are at the discretion of the landowners.

Further information: School Section Lake National Wildlife Refuge, c/o J. Clark Salyer NWR Complex, P.O. Box 66, Upham, ND 58789; telephone: (701) 768-2548.

Shell Lake, comprising 1,835 acres, was established in 1939 to enhance and protect vital wetland and upland prairie habitats for the benefit of migratory birds and other wildlife in northwestern North Dakota. The refuge's wetlands are managed to maintain staging and resting areas for as many as 5,000 migrating sandhill cranes, 1,000 snow geese, and 5,000 ducks of numerous species. Some ducks also nest on the refuge.

Other migratory birds that are attracted to Shell Lake are whooping cranes, bald eagles, peregrine falcons, and a variety of shorebirds. The refuge's 784 acres of upland prairie are maintained for the benefit of many species, including the burrowing owl.

More than 600 acres of the refuge are being managed under the terms of conservation easements, purchased from local landowners. Establishment of Shell Lake was made possible partly with revenues from the sale of Migratory Bird Hunting and Conservation Stamps (Duck Stamps).

Because of the refuge's combination of federally and privately owned lands, public entry onto the refuge is not permitted. However, whooping crane roosting areas can be seen from the refuge boundary. This viewing area is accessed from a prairie trail on the Moen Waterfowl Production Area (WPA). Information on the latter: Lostwood Wetland Management District, 8315 Highway 8, Kenmare, ND 58746; telephone: (701) 848-2722.

Lodgings and meals are available in such communities as New Town and Minot.

Access to Shell Lake Refuge from U.S. Route 2 at Blaisdell is south 12 miles on an unpaved road, and 0.5 mile west (right) and north.

Further information: Shell Lake National Wildlife Refuge, c/o Des Lacs National Wildlife Refuge Complex, P.O. Box 578, Kenmare, ND 58746; telephone: (701) 385-4046.

Sheyenne Lake, containing 797 acres, was established in 1935 to protect important wetland and open-water habitats of Sheyenne Lake in central North Dakota. Concentrations of waterfowl are drawn to the lake, especially during the spring and autumn migrations.

The refuge's acreage is being managed under an agreement with the U.S. Bureau of Reclamation (BOR), which acquired the area in anticipation of constructing the Garrison Diversion Project's Lonetree Reservoir. Because of concerns about the reservoir's environmental impacts, the proposal has unofficially been abandoned in favor of a canal or pipeline. The reservoir would inundate the refuge.

Visitor activities include birdwatching, photography, hiking, and fishing.

Sheyenne Lake Refuge is surrounded by 36,000 acres of additional BOR-owned land that is managed as a wildlife management area by the North Dakota Game and Fish Department.

Further information: Sheyenne Lake National Wildlife Refuge, c/o Audubon Wildlife Refuge Complex, 3275 Eleventh Street NW , Coleharbor, ND 58531; (701) 442-5474.

Sibley Lake, encompassing 1,077 acres, was established in 1939 to manage an important wetland habitat for the benefit of migratory waterfowl in Griggs County of east-central North Dakota.

This refuge's acreage is being managed under the terms of conservation easements purchased from local landowners. Visitor access onto this refuge is only with landowner permission. Sibley Lake's birds and mammals are much the same as those recorded on Arrowwood National Wildlife Refuge.

Further information: Sibley Lake National Wildlife Refuge, c/o Arrowwood NWR Complex, 7745 Eleventh Street SE, Pingree, ND 58476; telephone: (701) 285-3341.

Silver Lake, containing 3,347 acres, was established in 1948 to enhance and protect important wetland habitat for the benefit of migratory waterfowl and other wildlife in Benson County of northeastern North Dakota.

The refuge's acreage is being managed under the terms of conservation easements purchased from local landowners. Visitor entry onto this easement refuge is only with landowner permission, or the refuge can be viewed from the west side of U.S. Route 281. Silver Lake's birds and mammals are much the same as those recorded for nearby Lake Alice National Wildlife Refuge.

Access to Silver Lake Refuge is 1 mile west of Churchs Ferry on U.S. Route 2 and south 2 to 3 miles on U.S. Route 281.

Further information: Silver Lake National Wildlife Refuge, c/o Devils Lake Wetland Management District, P.O. Box 908, Devils Lake, ND 58301; telephone: (701) 662-8611.

Slade, consisting of 3,000 acres, was established in 1940 mainly to enhance and protect 900 acres of ecologically valuable wetlands in Kidder County of south-central North Dakota. The refuge's five lakes, many marshes, and fifteen pothole wetland areas provide important habitat for nesting and migrating waterfowl. In the autumn, large numbers of migrating Canada and snow geese pause here.

Beginning in 1924, a wildlife conservationist and former Northern Pacific Railroad executive, George T. Slade, committed himself to the task of purchasing, enhancing, and maintaining this area's wetlands as a private hunting reserve. During the severe drought of the Dust Bowl era of the 1930s, he provided for the digging of a large well that pumped up to 16,000 gallons of water per hour for a year and a half into Harker and Upper Harker lakes—maintaining this vital habitat for large concentrations of ducks and other water birds. He also purchased large shipments of grain to provide supplemental food during the drought. In 1940, Mr. Slade donated the reserve to the U.S. Fish and Wildlife Service.

For many years, the Fish and Wildlife Service's habitat enhancement practices on the gently rolling lands surrounding the wetlands have included short-term livestock grazing, haying, the growing of grain crops for the benefit of wildlife, and periodic prescribed burning.

In 1968, Slade Refuge, the Northern Prairie Wildlife Research Center, and the North Dakota Game and Fish Department jointly undertook a propagation project to reestablish a breeding population of the giant Canada goose (*Branta canadensis maxima*). This subspecies had been brought to the brink of extinction all across the northern Great Plains as the result of extensive habitat loss and overhunting. The program has proved successful on Slade and other refuges in the northern Great Plains. Many pairs of the giant Canadas now nest here.

The refuge is open daily during daylight hours. There is no entrance fee. No visitor use facilities are provided. Visitor activities include birdwatching, photography, hiking, and deer hunting during the designated season.

Birds that are attracted to Slade Refuge are much the same as those recorded on nearby Long Lake Refuge. In addition to ducks and geese, some of the more common species include American white pelicans, double-crested cormorants, black-crowned night herons, avocets, marbled godwits, long-billed dowitchers, willets, and Wilson's phalaropes. The best months for birdwatching are April and May, and especially September and October.

Lodgings and meals are available in such communities as Steele, Bismarck, and Jamestown.

Further information: Slade National Wildlife Refuge, c/o Long Lake NWR Complex, 12000-353rd Street SE, Moffit, ND 58560; telephone: (701) 387-4397.

Snyder Lake, comprising 1,550 acres, was established in 1941 to manage important wetland habitat for the benefit of migratory waterfowl and other wildlife in northern Towner County of northeastern North Dakota.

The refuge's acreage is being managed under the terms of conservation easements purchased from local landowners. Visitor entry onto this easement refuge is only with landowner permission, or the refuge can be viewed from the east side of U.S. Route 281. Snyder Lake is part of a chain of three refuges, with Brumba and Rock Lake to the north. The refuge's birds and mammals are much the same as those recorded for nearby Lake Alice National Wildlife Refuge.

Access to Snyder Lake Refuge from State Route 5 at Rocklake is south 7 miles on U.S. Route 281.

Further information: Snyder Lake National Wildlife Refuge, c/o Devils Lake Wetland Management District, P.O. Box 908, Devils Lake, ND 58301; telephone: (701) 662-8611.

Springwater, containing 640 acres, was established in 1941, primarily to manage an 8-acre impoundment created by an earthen/rubble dam on Clear Creek in Emmons County of south-central North Dakota. After a severe storm breached the dam in the late 1980s, the structure was finally repaired in 2001.

Although most of the refuge's wetland no longer exists, the refuge contains a mixture of important grassland, coulee (ravine), and riparian habitats. Springwater's acreage is being managed under the terms of a conservation easement purchased from a local landowner. Visitor access onto this easement refuge is only with landowner permission.

Further information: Springwater National Wildlife Refuge, c/o Long Lake NWR Complex, 12000-353rd Street SE, Moffit, ND 58560; telephone: (701) 387-4397.

Stewart Lake, consisting of 2,230 acres, was established in 1941 to protect important marsh wetlands habitat around the shores of a lake that attracts migrating and breeding waterfowl and other wildlife, in the southwest corner of North Dakota.

More than two-thirds of the refuge's acreage is being managed under the terms of conservation easements purchased from local landowners. Establishment of Stewart Lake was made possible partly with revenues from the sale of Migratory Bird Hunting and Conservation Stamps (Duck Stamps).

The refuge is open daily during daylight hours. There is no entrance fee. The refuge is remote and provides no visitor use facilities. Visitor activities include birdwatching, photography, hiking, and fishing. Hunting and trapping are not permitted. Stewart Lake Refuge's birds, mammals, reptiles, and amphibians are much the same as recorded on Lake Alice National Wildlife Refuge.

Lodgings and meals are available in such communities as Belfield, Dickinson, and Bowman.

Access to Stewart Lake is south 8 miles on U.S. Route 85 from the town of Amidon.

Further information: Stewart Lake National Wildlife Refuge, c/o Lake Ilo NWR, 489-102nd Avenue SW, Dunn Center, ND 58626; telephone: (701) 548-8110.

Stoney Slough, containing 2,000 acres, was established in 1941 to protect important wetland habitat for the benefit of waterfowl and shorebirds in east-central North Dakota. Among the more prominent species are migrating snow geese, tundra swans, and a variety of dabbling ducks that pause here to rest and feed during migrations. The refuge also includes some native upland prairie grassland.

Establishment of Stoney Slough Refuge was made possible with revenues from the sale of Migratory Bird Hunting and Conservation Stamps (Duck Stamps). Ducks Unlimited, Inc. has helped enhance some of the refuge's wetland habitat. Much of Stoney Slough's acreage is being managed under the terms of conservation easements purchased from local landowners.

The refuge is open daily during daylight hours. There is no entrance fee. No visitor use facilities are provided.

Visitor activities include birdwatching, photography, hiking, and hunting during the designated seasons. Stoney Slough's birds and mammals are much the same as those recorded on Arrowwood National Wildlife Refuge.

Lodgings and meals are available in Valley City.

> Access to Stoney Slough Refuge from Exit 276 on I-94 is south 12 miles and east (left) 3 miles.

> Further information: Stoney Slough National Wildlife Refuge, c/o Arrowwood NWR Complex, 7745 Eleventh Street SE, Pingree, ND 58476; telephone: (701) 285-3341.

Storm Lake, comprising 686 acres, was established in 1934, with a perpetual right to flood with water and manage an artificial lake for water conservation, drought relief, and migratory bird and wildlife conservation purposes. The refuge, which is especially important for western and pied-billed grebes and diving ducks, is located next to the town of Milnor in southeastern North Dakota.

Because of the limited nature of the easement agreement with the landowner, visitor entry onto this refuge is by permission of the landowner only. Storm Lake is managed as a waterfowl resting area. Hunting is not permitted. Storm Lake's birds and mammals are much the same as those recorded on Tewaukon National Wildlife Refuge.

> Further information: Storm Lake National Wildlife Refuge, c/o Tewaukon NWR Complex, 9754–143? Avenue SE, Cayuga, ND 58013; telephone: (701) 724-3598.

Stump Lake, consisting of 27 acres, was established in 1905 to manage important wetland habitat on two islands and two shoreline peninsulas at Stump Lake's western arm in western Nelson County of east-central North Dakota. It is this state's oldest national wildlife refuge and is primarily for the benefit of nesting and migrating waterfowl.

The area around Stump Lake is characterized by rolling terrain with woodland habitat in sheltered places that did not have the fire frequency of the surrounding grasslands. Stump Lake is actually a semipermanent brackish wetland, with large beds of sago pondweed that are alleged to be the single most extensive such habitat in the state. During periods of drying, the level of Stump Lake declines, creating East and West Stump lakes, and during wetter conditions, the two lakes are joined as one. In addition, East Stump is a saline lake with very different water chemistry from that of West Stump, thereby altering the wetland plant composition and the species of birds that utilize the lake.

Historically, the Stump Lake area was a favorite destination for egg collectors and waterfowl hunters, because of the abundance and diversity of bird species that were attracted to the area. As late as 1920, this was the only known breeding site in the United States for the white-winged scoter. However, since the 1920s, no nesting of either the scoter or of the common goldeneye has been recorded. Other colonial nesting water birds presently using the area include ring-billed gulls, double-crested cormorants, white pelicans, and American avocets. The refuge is an important staging area for canvasbacks, with their numbers sometimes exceeding 25,000 individuals. Concentrations of the many species of waterfowl attracted to Stump Lake sometimes consist of as many as 70,000 birds. These include the tundra swan (sometimes totaling more than 5,000); snow and Canada geese; numerous ducks (mallard, American black, greenwinged and blue-winged teal, northern pintail, northern shoveler, gadwall, American wigeon, canvasback, redhead, ring-necked, lesser scaup, bufflehead, and ruddy); and American coot.

Visitor entry onto Stump Lake Refuge is not permitted.

Further information: Stump Lake National Wildlife Refuge, c/o Devils Lake Wetland Management District, P.O. Box 908, Devils Lake, ND 58301; telephone: (701) 662-8611.

Sullys Hill National Game Preserve, containing 1,674 acres, was initially set aside in 1904 by President Theodore Roosevelt as "Sullys Hill Park." Located on the south shore of Devils Lake in east-central North Dakota, it manages herds of American bison (buffalo), Rocky Mountain elk, and white-tailed deer.

The park's mission was part of an early twentieth-century national effort to help save from extinction the remnant population of once-vast numbers of bison and elk. In North Dakota, the bison had been wiped out by 1884, and elk were gone by the end of the century. In 1914, Congress appropriated funds to provide for the construction of game preserve facilities (corrals, sheds, etc.), within a fenced enclosure. In 1917, fifteen elk were brought to Sullys Hill from Yellowstone National Park, and in 1918, six bison arrived from Oregon.

In 1931, the park's name was changed to Sullys Hill National Game Preserve, and the responsibility for administering the area was transferred from the National Park Service to the U.S. Fish and Wildlife Service. The preserve is part of a complex of refuges and waterfowl production areas that are managed by the Devils Lake Wetland Management District (see separate text on the latter).

Sullys Hill is named for a nineteenth-century U.S. general, Alfred Sully, who had been expected to join a cavalry unit from Illinois. When he failed to arrive, the troops named the highest hill in this vicinity after him. Nearby resident Dakota Sioux refer to the hill by its traditional name, Paha Tanka, which means Big Hill. Most of the preserve consists of woodland- and grassland-covered glacial moraine hills. Wetland habitats border the preserve's 12-acre Sweetwater Lake and the shore of Devils Lake.

The preserve's bison herd is maintained at between 20 and 30 animals, the elk number at between 25 and 40, and the white-tailed deer at between 20 and 30. In addition to the three large mammal species, there are red and gray foxes, mink, beaver, woodchuck, raccoon, striped skunk, eastern cottontail, eastern fox squirrel, and a colony of the introduced black-tailed prairie dog.

Prominent among the more than 260 species of birds that have been recorded on the preserve are wild turkey; white pelican; snow (both white and blue morphs) and Canada geese; ducks (mallard, green-winged and blue-winged teal, pintail, shoveler, wigeon, gadwall, wood duck, and hooded merganser); several species of grebes; great blue heron; plovers; sandpipers; other shorebirds; and numerous neotropical migratory songbirds, including flycatchers, vireos, and warblers.

Sullys Hill Wildlife Refuge Society is a nonprofit support group that is assisting the preserve in a variety of ways.

The refuge is open daily during daylight hours. A fee is charged to drive the 4-mile tour road, which is normally open from May through October. The visitor center is open daily during the summer months.

Visitor activities include wildlife observation; photography; viewing interpretive displays in the visitor center; watching summer interpretive programs in the amphitheater; guided interpretive walks; driving the 4-mile tour road (excellent wildlife viewing and photography opportunities and two scenic overlooks), hiking a 1-mile, self-guiding, interpretive trail (part of which is wheelchair-accessible) along a stream and through a wooded area; and cross-country skiing (a 1.5-mile trail is available). The preserve also provides conservation education programs in its two classroom facilities for school and other groups. The best months for peak bird influxes are from late April to early June and from late August to mid-October.

Lodgings and meals are available at such communities as New Rockford and Devils Lake.

Access to Sullys Hill Preserve from U.S. Route 2 at the town of Devils Lake is south 13 miles on State Route 57, and south (left) on BIA Route 6, following signs to the preserve.

Further information: Sullys Hill National Game Preserve, c/o Devils Lake Wetland Management District, P.O. Box 908, Devils Lake, ND 58301; telephone: (701) 662-8611.

Sunburst Lake, encompassing 328 acres, was established in 1941 to manage a 27-acre impoundment that provides habitat for a few nesting and migrating waterfowl in Emmons County of south-central North Dakota.

This refuge's acreage is being managed under the terms of a conservation easement purchased from a local landowner. In the mid-1990s, Ducks Unlimited, Inc. funded repairs to the impoundment's earthen dam. Visitor access onto this easement refuge is not permitted without landowner permission.

The adjacent, federally owned, 580-acre Schiermeister Waterfowl Production Area (WPA) provides important habitat for upland birds, such as the non-native ring-necked pheasant, and for white-tailed deer. This area is open daily during daylight hours. There is no entrance fee. No visitor use facilities are provided. Visitor activities on the WPA include birdwatching, hiking, and hunting (pheasant and deer) during the designated seasons. Acquisition of the WPA was made possible partly with revenues from the sale of Migratory Bird Hunting and Conservation Stamps (Duck Stamps).

Lodgings and meals are available in such communities as Bismarck and Steele.

Access to Schiermeister WPA from Interstate 94 at Sterling is south 32 miles on U.S. Route 83 to Temvik and west (right) 12 miles on an unpaved road.

Further information: Sunburst National Wildlife Refuge and Schiermeister Waterfowl Production Area, c/o Long Lake NWR Complex, 12000-353rd Street SE, Moffit, ND 58560; telephone (701) 387-4397.

Tewaukon, comprising 8,363 acres in two units, restores, enhances, and protects important wetland and prairie grassland habitats for the benefit of migratory birds and other wildlife. In 1934, a non-federally owned easement refuge was initially established, with authority to acquire perpetual easements from landowners for flowage and refuge purposes. Refuge easements reserved the right to impound water and maintain it during periods of drought.

In 1945, Tewaukon National Wildlife Refuge was established, and federal land acquisition began the following year, with the purchase of 512 acres around Lake Tewaukon. Named for an ancient legendary Native American leader, Te Wau Kon, meaning "Son of Heaven," this refuge is located along Wild Rice River in southeastern North Dakota.

The Tewaukon area is located within what was once a vast expanse of nearly 200 million acres of tallgrass prairie extending along the eastern part of the Great Plains, from Manitoba, Canada, southward to Texas. As briefly described by the U.S. Fish and Wildlife Service in its September 2000 *Comprehensive Conservation Plan* for the refuge:

Prior to settlement by Europeans, this area was inhabited by several plains nomadic tribes that were primarily hunter-gatherers. They utilized the area around Lake Tewaukon including the lake's peninsula extensively. . . .

. . . They consumed large ungulates (bison and elk), birds, and plants. Very little farming took place, and the majority of the grassland remained intact. As European settlers moved into southeastern North Dakota, farming was introduced and the highly productive cropping potential of the soils was discovered. . . . Currently, the majority of the land . . . capable of producing a crop is farmed. . . . A few areas of native prairie still remain primarily due to poorer soil quality and cattle or buffalo are raised on these sites.

The refuge's many prairie pothole wetlands and marshes, which are scattered across a gently rolling glacial till plain, are a mecca for as many as tens of thousands of geese and ducks during the spring and autumn migrations. Especially from mid-October to mid-November, large concentrations of snow, greater white-fronted, and Canada geese pause here to rest and feed. Bald eagles also pass through here during migrations.

In the 1960s, four large concrete dams were built on the river, creating hundreds of acres of lakes and wetlands, the largest of which is 1,057-acre Lake Tewaukon. On the refuge's dozen primary impoundments and nearly 40 other ponds, water levels are carefully regulated to promote high-quality water bird nesting and feeding habitat. In addition, numerous natural prairie potholes, scattered across the refuge's uplands, provide more than 100 acres of additional wetland habitat.

Shelterbelt trees and shrubs have been planted on Tewaukon Refuge, offering valuable cover and food for many species of wildlife, including white-tailed deer and numerous songbirds. More than 4,000 acres of the refuge consist of grasslands, of which only 616 acres of native prairie remain. Some tallgrass habitat has been restored from former cropland. Grassland birds include the upland sandpiper, chestnut-collared longspur, grasshopper sparrow, and bobolink. Over 240 bird species have been seen here.

The health of the refuge's grassland ecosystems is maintained with the help of grazing, mowing, haying, and periodic prescribed burning. The Tewaukon Refuge carries out prescription burning to mimic historic fire occurrence and promote nutrient cycling. As the refuge's *Comprehensive Conservation Plan* further explains:

Since the 1960s, . . . managers have used prescribed fire to restore, change, and maintain the diversity in plant communities. Prescribed fire is also used to reduce hazardous fuels. . . . A large amount of litter can cause additional control problems for fire suppression efforts. Reducing these high amounts of litter can reduce fire intensity and make wildfires easier and more cost effective to control.

Approximately 500 acres of the refuge are devoted to a cooperative program of sharecropping, by which local farmers leave unharvested a portion of cultivated grain crops of corn, millet, winter rye, and winter wheat to provide a supplemental food source for migrating waterfowl, wintering deer, and other wildlife.

More than one-sixth of the refuge's acreage is being protectively managed under the terms of perpetual conservation easement agreements with local landowners. Such organizations as Ducks Unlimited, Inc., the North Dakota Wetlands Trust, and the Delta Waterfowl Foundation, have helped enhance some of Tewaukon's wetland habitat.

The refuge is open daily during daylight hours. There is no entrance fee. The refuge's headquarters/visitor center is open on weekdays, except national holidays.

Visitor activities include birdwatching; photography; viewing interpretive exhibits in the headquarters/visitor center; driving the unpaved, 8.5-mile, self-guiding Prairie Lake Auto Tour route (open from May 1 through September; interpretive brochure is available); walking a short self-guiding, interpretive (wheelchair-accessible) trail through a section of native prairie near the refuge headquarters; hiking (east of County Road 12 only) in the vicinity of Lake Tewaukon; picnicking (two picnic areas are provided on the shore of Lake Tewaukon); boating on Lake Tewaukon and Sprague Lake (May 1 through September—boat ramps are available, no power boating, jet skiing, or water skiing); fishing (year-round, from the banks of Tewaukon and Sprague lakes); and hunting (pheasant and deer, but not waterfowl) on parts of the refuge during the designated seasons. Waterfowl hunting is permitted on the adjacent North Dakota State Game Management Area. Although camping is not permitted on the refuge, campground facilities are available at nearby Silver Lake County Park.

Lodgings and meals are available in such communities as Lidgerwood, Milner, Forman, Lisbon, Wahpeton, and Fargo.

Access to Tewaukon Refuge from Interstate 29 at Exit 8 is west 28 miles on State Route 11 to Cayuga, and south (left) 5 miles on County Road 12.

Further information: Tewaukon National Wildlife Refuge, Cayuga, ND 58013; telephone: (701) 724-3598.

Tomahawk, consisting of 440 acres, was established in 1941 to protect important wetland habitat for migratory waterfowl and other wildlife in east-central North Dakota. The refuge attracts a large population of Canada geese and concentrations of diving ducks during spring and autumn migrations.

This refuge's acreage is being managed under the terms of a conservation easement purchased from a local landowner. Visitor access onto this easement refuge is only with landowner permission. Tomahawk's birds and mammals are much the same as those recorded on Arrowwood National Wildlife Refuge.

Further information: Tomahawk National Wildlife Refuge, c/o Arrowwood NWR Complex, 7745 Eleventh Street SE, Pingree, ND 58476; telephone: (701) 285-3341.

Upper Souris, containing 32,311 acres, was established in 1935 to restore and manage ecologically important wetland and grassland habitats for migrating and nesting waterfowl and other wildlife in northwestern North Dakota. The refuge extends for more than 35 miles along the Souris River Valley, with lakes and ponds, marshes, meandering river, and shrubby habitat of coulees and draws.

As refuge manager Dean F. Knauer describes the Upper Souris Refuge:

The backbone of this unique refuge, one of the most scenically beautiful in North Dakota, is the Souris River and its striking, deeply incised drainages called coulees that flow into it. These narrow, shortgrass-prairie-covered ridges quickly transition to steep sides covered with tallgrass-prairie species where snowdrifts have been the heaviest. The coulee bottoms are intermittently wet, with nearly impenetrable patches of thorny wild plum, hawthorn, chokecherry, and Juneberry, the latter laden with blueberry-like fruit in July. Solitary green ash trees and/or stands of American elms are interspersed here and there. The river bottoms are covered with mature elms, boxelders, and ashes. The large variety of habitats within a short distance help give the refuge a surprising and fascinating diversity of plant and animal species. While much of the area is not easily accessible from public roads, thus making it a challenge for visitors, the remoteness also leaves many ecologically rich places undisturbed throughout the year.

The primary focus of the Upper Souris Refuge is 9,900-acre Lake Darling. This impoundment, occupying about one-third of the refuge, was created in 1936 by a dam on the Souris River. As explained by the U.S. Fish and Wildlife Service:

Lake Darling was named in honor of Jay N. "Ding" Darling, a flamboyant political cartoonist from Iowa, who became the director of the newly formed Bureau of Biological Survey in 1934, the precursor of the U.S. Fish and Wildlife Service. The primary purpose of the lake is to furnish a regulated supply of water to marshes downstream on Upper Souris and J. Clark Salyer Refuges.

The refuge attracts roughly 350,000 waterfowl during the spring and autumn migrations, including as many as 300,000 lesser snow geese, 50,000 ducks of many species, and 5,000 Canada geese. Tundra swans; ducks such as mallards, pintails, blue-winged teal, shovelers, gadwalls, canvasbacks, redheads, and ruddies; and five species of grebes are among the nesting water birds. In 1940, the Canada goose was reintroduced, and as the result of a successful management program, the refuge's resident flock now numbers roughly 250 birds. Canada geese, white pelicans, and white-tailed deer are among the wildlife frequently seen in the vicinity of the spillway from "A" Pool.

The refuge's prairie habitat is managed for the benefit of many species, such as Sprague's pipit, Baird's and LeConte's sparrows, upland sandpiper, the non-native gray partridge, and sharp-tailed grouse. During April and May, blinds are available (by reservation) for observing and photographing the grouse's fascinating spring courtship displays. The male spreads his wings, raises his pointed tail, lowers his head, and rapidly stomps his feet. At the same time, he inflates and deflates purplish neck sacs and makes a *coo-oo* sound that is accompanied by the rattling of wing quills.

In addition to mixed-grass native prairie, some areas of the refuge are planted with a mixture of grasses, alfalfa, and clover to provide important protective habitat for upland nesting ducks such as mallards, pintails, and shovelers.

Upper Souris is one of many refuges in this part of the country that was established in response to the devastating impact of the severe drought of the Dust Bowl era of the 1930s upon migratory waterfowl. To enhance the wetland habitats of this and other nearby refuges, more than 250 men were hired under the Civilian Conservation Corps (CCC) and the Works Project Administration to build such habitat improvement facilities as dikes, water control structures, and nesting islands. Water levels are regulated to prevent flooding of nest sites and to promote the growth of emergent and other aquatic plants. Mudflats can also be "produced" to benefit shorebirds.

Establishment of Upper Souris Refuge was made possible partly with revenues from the sale of Migratory Bird Hunting and Conservation Stamps (Duck Stamps). "Ding" Darling was instrumental in advocating congressional enactment of the Duck Stamp Act in 1934, which required waterfowl hunters 16 years of age and older to purchase an annual Duck Stamp. Funds from the sale of these stamps are earmarked for the federal acquisition of waterfowl habitat.

The refuge is open daily during daylight hours. There is no entrance fee. The refuge office and visitor center are open on weekdays, except national holidays.

Visitor activities include birdwatching; photography; viewing interpretive exhibits at the visitor center; educational programs; driving the 3.5-mile, self-guiding, interpretive auto tour route (Prairie-Marsh Scenic Drive); walking five trails (one of which is wheelchair-accessible); cross-country skiing; picnicking (picnic facilities are provided at four sites); canoeing (two canoe trails, from May 1 through September); boating (for fishing or wildlife observation only; five boat-launching sites are provided); fishing (the Outlet Fishing Area pier is wheelchair-accessible); and hunting (on parts of the refuge). Although camping is not permitted on the refuge, campground facilities are available at Mouse River Park and in Carpio and Grano. The best months for birdwatching are April to June and late September through October.

Insect repellent is advised during the warmer months.

The more than 300 species of birds that have been recorded on Upper Souris Refuge are much the same as those recorded on Des Lacs Refuge.

Lodgings and meals are available in Minot and Mohall.

Access to Upper Souris Refuge's visitor center from Minot is northwest about 19 miles on U.S. Route 52 to Foxholm, and north (right) 7 miles on County Route 11; or from Minot north 18 miles on U.S. Route 83, and west (left) 12 miles on County Route 6 to the refuge headquarters/visitor center.

Further information: Upper Souris National Wildlife Refuge, 17705-212th Avenue NW, Berthold, ND 58718; telephone: (701) 468-5467.

Trumpeter swan family, Red Rock Lakes NWR, Montana

Mule deer buck, Crescent Lake NWR, Nebraska

American bison, Fort Niobara NWR, Nebraska

Bison herd, Fort Niobara NWR

Spring-fed pool, Ash Meadows NWR

Endangered Amargosa pupfish, Ash Meadows NWR, Nevada

Ash Meadows NWR

Amargosa pupfish research, Ash Meadows NWR, Nevada

Sheep Range Desert, NWR, Nevada. Russell D. Butcher photo

Ruby Lake NWR, Nevada

Ruby Lake NWR. Russell D. Butcher photo

Stillwater NWR, Nevada. Russell D. Butcher photo

Desert NWR, Nevada

Great Bay NWR, New Hampshire

Great egret, Edwin B. Forsythe NWR, New Jersey

Eastern cottontail, Edwin B. Forsythe NWR

Great Swamp NWR, New Jersey

Great Swamp NWR

Snow geese, Bosque del Apache NWR. Russell D. Butcher photo

Bosque del Apache NWR

Blackbird flock, Bosque del Apache NWR, New Mexico

Snow geese and marsh at sunrise, Bosque del Apache NWR

Wild turkey flock, Bosque del Apache NWR, New Mexico

Greater sandhill cranes in flight, Bosque del Apache NWR

Sevilletta NWR, New Mexico

Cardinal, Elizabeth A. Morton NWR, New York

Raccoon in marsh, Montezuma NWR, New York

Great blue heron catching fish, Montezuma NWR

Wertheim NWR, New York

Royal tern nest colony, Cedar Island NWR

Brown pelican rookery, Cedar Island NWR, North Carolina

Mattamuskeet NWR, North Carolina

Nesting osprey, Pea Island NWR, North Carolina

Northern shoveler pair, J. Clark Salyer NWR, North Dakota

J. Clark Salyer NWR

J. Clark Salyer NWR

"Prairie pothole" country, Lostwood NWR

Savannah sparrow, Lostwood NWR,
North Dakota

Lostwood NWR

Little River NWR, Oklahoma

Scissor-tailed flycatcher, Sequoyah NWR, Oklahoma

River of boulders, Wichita Mountains NWR

"Kissing" blacktail prairie dogs, Wichita Mountains NWR, Oklahoma

Old growth forest, west central Oregon

Cape Meares NWR, Oregon

White Lake, containing 1,040 acres, was established in 1941 to protect important marsh wetlands habitat around the shores of a lake that attracts migrating and breeding waterfowl and other wildlife, just east of Amidon in the southwest corner of North Dakota.

Visitor use is allowed only by special permit, which can be obtained at Lake Ilo Refuge headquarters. No visitor use facilities are provided. White Lake Refuge's birds, mammals, reptiles, and amphibians are much the same as those recorded on Lake Alice National Wildlife Refuge.

Lodgings and meals are available in such communities as Amidon and Bowman.

Further information: White Lake National Wildlife Refuge, c/o Lake Ilo NWR, Dunn Center, ND 58626; telephone (701) 548-8110.

Wild Rice Lake, containing 778 acres, was established in 1934 to provide habitat for migratory waterfowl and other wildlife in southeastern North Dakota. According to the U.S. Fish and Wildlife Service, this non-federally owned easement refuge "is no longer providing waterfowl values due to a lack of permanent water with the loss of water control structures." Consequently, it is the agency's "desire to eventually divest" this refuge from the National Wildlife Refuge System.

Further information: Wild Rice Lake National Wildlife Refuge, c/o Tewaukon National Wildlife Refuge Complex, 9754 143? Avenue SE, Cayuga, ND 58013; telephone: (701) 724-3598.

Willow Lake, comprising 2,621 acres, was established in 1935 to maintain this 1,200-acre lake, located in the Turtle Mountains 3 miles south of the U.S.–Canada border in northwestern Rolette County of north-central North Dakota. In 1969, a waterfowl production area was purchased within this easement refuge. As the lake depends upon annual precipitation and runoff, its level fluctuates widely. The refuge lies in the headwaters of Willow Creek, a tributary of the Souris River. Many species of ducks and other waterfowl are attracted to Willow Lake, especially during autumn migration in September and October.

Easements for this non-federally owned refuge were purchased from private landowners and the state. Although hunting is permitted, other visitor activities, such as birdwatching and hiking, are at the discretion of the landowners.

Lodgings and meals are available in such communities as Bottineau, Rugby, and Minot.

Access to Willow Lake Refuge from Dunseith is west 3 miles on State Route 5 and north (right) 7 miles on an improved gravel township road.

Further information: Willow Lake National Wildlife Refuge, c/o J. Clark Salyer NWR Complex, P.O. Box 66, Upham, ND 58789; telephone: (701) 768-2548.

Wintering River, containing 239 acres, was established in 1935 to enhance and protect a shallow, 86-acre marsh created by a dike and other water control structures in southern McHenry

County of north-central North Dakota. The wetland habitat is dominated (even choked) by dense growths of cattails, along with bog rush and bulrushes.

Several thousand mallards and lesser concentrations of other migratory waterfowl pause here to rest and feed, especially during autumn migration in September and October. Because the refuge's wetland depends upon annual precipitation and runoff, the water level fluctuates widely. White-tailed deer and the non-native ring-necked pheasant are among other species of wildlife that inhabit this area. Wintering River's birds and mammals are much the same as those recorded on Des Lacs National Wildlife Refuge.

Easements for this non-federally owned refuge were purchased from private landowners. Although hunting is permitted, other visitor activities are at the discretion of the landowners.

Further information: Wintering River National Wildlife Refuge, c/o J. Clark Salyer NWR Complex, P.O. Box 66, Upham, ND 58789; telephone: (701) 768-2548.

Wood Lake, consisting of 280 acres, was established in 1948 to manage important marsh habitat for the benefit of migratory waterfowl and other wildlife on the Devils Lake Sioux Indian Reservation, in Benson County of northeastern North Dakota.

The refuge's acreage is being managed under the terms of a conservation easement purchased from a local landowner. Visitor entry onto this easement refuge is only with landowner permission. Wood Lake's birds and mammals are much the same as those recorded on Lake Alice National Wildlife Refuge.

Access to Wood Lake Refuge is 1.5 miles west of Tokio.

Further information: Wood Lake National Wildlife Refuge, c/o Devils Lake Wetland Management District, P.O. Box 908, Devils Lake, ND 58301; telephone: (701) 662-8611.

North Dakota: Wetland Management Districts

Regarding the non-federally owned parts of the wetland management districts in this state, the U.S. Fish and Wildlife Service explains: "Most wetlands in North Dakota are on private lands, thus private landowners are key to preservation of these valuable wildlife habitats. Landowners who are interested in improving habitat on their land can receive assistance through the Partners for Wildlife Program. By working together, landowners, conservation groups, and the U.S. Fish and Wildlife Service can improve more habitat. Ultimately, people and wildlife will benefit."

Arrowwood Wetland Management District was established in 1935 to restore, enhance, and protectively manage scattered areas of ecologically important wetland and grassland habitats within the prairie pothole region in Eddy and Foster counties of southeastern North Dakota.

This extensive district includes more than 6,138 acres in 28 federally owned waterfowl production areas (WPAs); Arrowwood and Johnson Lake national wildlife refuges (see separate texts); and more than 19,000 acres that are being managed under the terms of perpetual wetland easements purchased from local landowners.

The WPAs are generally open to visitation during daylight hours. There are no entrance fees. No visitor use facilities are provided. Visitor activities include birdwatching, photography, hiking, and hunting during the designated seasons.

Further information: Arrowwood Wetland Management District, 7745 Eleventh Street, SE, Pingree, ND 58476; telephone: (701) 285-3341.

Audubon Wetland Management District was established in 1962 to restore, enhance, and protectively manage scattered areas of ecologically important wetland and grassland habitats within McLean, Sheridan, and Ward counties in central North Dakota.

This extensive district includes more than 18,500 acres in a number of federally owned waterfowl production areas (WPAs); Audubon, Camp Lake, Hiddenwood, Lake Ilo, Lake Nettie, Lake Otis, Lost Lake, McLean, Pretty Rock, Sheyenne Lake, Stewart Lake, and White Lake national wildlife refuges (see separate texts); and more than 110,000 acres that are being managed under the terms of perpetual wetland and grassland easements purchased from local landowners.

The WPAs are generally open to visitation during daylight hours. There are no entrance fees. No visitor use facilities are provided. Visitor activities include birdwatching, photography, hiking, and hunting during the designated seasons.

Further information: Audubon Wetland Management District, 3275 Eleventh Street NW, Coleharbor, ND 58531; telephone: (701) 442-5474.

Chase Lake Wetland Management District was established in 1993 to restore, enhance, and protectively manage scattered areas of ecologically important wetland and grassland habitats within the prairie pothole region in Stutsman and Wells counties of central North Dakota.

This extensive district includes more than 35,000 acres in 128 federally owned waterfowl production areas (WPAs); Chase Lake and Halfway Lake national wildlife refuges (see separate texts); and more than 55,000 acres that are being managed under the terms of perpetual wetland and grassland easements purchased from local landowners.

The WPAs are generally open daily to visitation during daylight hours. There are no entrance fees. No visitor use facilities are provided. Visitor activities include birdwatching, photography, hiking, and hunting during the designated seasons.

Further information: Chase Lake Wetland Management District, 5924 Nineteenth Street, SE, Woodworth, ND 58496; telephone: (701) 752-4218.

Crosby Wetland Management District was established in 1962 to restore, enhance, and protectively manage scattered areas of ecologically significant wetland and grassland habitats within the prairie pothole region in Divide, Burke, and Williams counties of northwestern North Dakota.

This extensive district includes more than 17,800 acres in 96 federally owned waterfowl production areas (WPAs); Lake Zahl National Wildlife Refuge (see the separate text); and more than 70,000 acres that are being managed under the terms of perpetual wetland, grassland, and other conservation easements purchased from local landowners.

Among waterfowl production areas are Appam Lake, supporting one of the highest-density northern Great Plains nesting habitats of the threatened piping plover (public access is restricted); Beaver Lake, containing a nesting colony of Franklin's gulls; and Big Meadow, encompassing more than 2,000 acres of vital wetlands.

The WPAs are open daily during daylight hours. There are no entrance fees. No visitor use facilities are provided. Visitor activities include birdwatching, photography, hiking, and hunting during the designated seasons. Wildlife species on these areas are generally the same as those recorded on the Lostwood National Wildlife Refuge.

Further information: Crosby Wetland Management District, P.O. Box 148, Crosby, ND 58730; telephone: (701) 965-6488.

Devils Lake Wetland Management District was established in 1962 to restore, enhance, and manage ecologically important wetland and grassland habitats within the heart of the prairie pothole region in Towner, Calier, Pembina, Benson, Ramsey, Walsh, Nelson, and Grand Forks counties of northeastern North Dakota.

This extensive district includes more than 47,000 acres in 207 federally owned waterfowl production areas (WPAs); Brumba, Kelly's Slough, Lake Alice, Lake Ardoch, Lambs Lake, Little Goose, Pleasant Lake, Rock Lake, Rose Lake, Silver Lake, Snyder Lake, Stump Lake, and Wood Lake national wildlife refuges (see separate texts); Sullys Hill National Game Preserve (see separate text); and more than 154,000 acres being managed under the terms of perpetual wetland easement agreements purchased from local landowners.

The WPAs are generally open daily during daylight hours. There are no entrance fees. No visitor use facilities are provided. Visitor activities include birdwatching, photography, hiking, and hunting during the designated seasons. Wildlife species are generally the same as those recorded on Lake Alice National Wildlife Refuge.

Further information: Devils Lake Wetland Management District, P.O. Box 908, Devils Lake, ND 58301; (701) 662-8611.

J. Clark Salyer Wetland Management District was established in 1958 in Pierce, McHenry, Rolette, Bottineau, and Renville counties of north-central North Dakota. This extensive district includes more than 27,000 acres in 130 federally owned waterfowl production areas (WPAs); Buffalo Lake, Cottonwood Lake, Lords Lake, Rabb Lake, School Section Lake, Willow Lake, and Wintering River national wildlife easement refuges (see separate texts); and more than

140,000 acres that are being protected under the terms of perpetual wetland and grassland easements purchased from local landowners.

The WPAs are generally open daily during daylight hours. There are no entrance fees. No visitor use facilities are provided. Visitor activities include birdwatching, photography, hiking, and hunting during the designated seasons. Wildlife species are generally the same as those recorded on J. Clark Salyer National Wildlife Refuge.

Further information: J. Clark Salyer Wetland Management District, P.O. Box 66, Upham, ND 58789; telephone (701) 768-2548.

Kulm Wetland Management District was established in 1971 to manage wetland and grassland habitats within LaMoure, Logan, McIntosh, and Dickey counties in south-central North Dakota. This district comprises more than 45,400 acres in 200 federally owned waterfowl production areas (WPAs) and 120,000 acres that are protectively managed under perpetual wetland and grassland easement agreements with private landowners.

As explained by Project Leader Bob Vanden Berge, "Most WPAs in the Kulm Wetland Management District are in the glacial end-moraine hills, known as the Missouri Coteau. Large blocks of grasslands and a high-density of wetlands (potholes) in the Coteau provide a wealth of habitat for ground-nesting and over-water-nesting birds. The migratory bird contribution from the prairie pothole region forms the core of the United States' waterfowl population. Opportunities to see large groups of migrating birds abound during the spring and fall months. Many species of waterfowl, shorebirds, and other marsh birds nest in the area and are readily visible from the available system of township, county, and state roads."

WPAs are generally open to visitation. Prospective visitors should contact the district headquarters for regulations. No visitor use facilities, hiking trails, or motorized vehicle routes are provided. There is no entrance fee. Primary visitor activities are birdwatching, photography, hiking, and fishing and hunting during the designated seasons.

Further information: Kulm Wetland Management District, P.O. Box E (1 First Street SW), Kulm, ND 58456; telephone: (701) 647-2866.

Long Lake Wetland Management District was established in 1961 to restore, enhance, and manage scattered wetland and prairie habitats within Burleigh, Kidder, and Emmons counties in central North Dakota.

This extensive district includes more than 21,700 acres in 77 federally owned waterfowl production areas (WPAs); Appert Lake, Canfield Lake, Florence Lake, Hutchinson Lake, Lake George, Long Lake, Slade, Springwater, and Sunburst Lake national wildlife refuges (see separate texts); and more than 101,400 acres that are being managed under the terms of perpetual wetland and grassland easements purchased from local landowners.

The WPAs are generally open to visitation during daylight hours. There are no entrance fees. No visitor use facilities are provided. Visitor activities include birdwatching, photography, hiking, and hunting during the designated seasons.

Further information: Long Lake Wetland Management District, 12000-353rd Street SE, Moffit, ND 58560; telephone: (701) 387-4397.

Lostwood Wetland Management District was established in 1962 to restore, enhance, and manage scattered areas of ecologically significant wetland and prairie grassland habitats within the prairie pothole region in Montrail and Ward counties of northwestern North Dakota.

This district includes more than 12,000 acres in 55 federally owned waterfowl production areas (WPAs); Lostwood and Shell Lake national wildlife refuges (see the separate texts); and more than 37,000 acres that are being managed under the terms of perpetual wetland, grassland, and other conservation easements purchased from local landowners.

Among the WPAs (from north to south) are: Coteau Prairie, containing more than 2,700 acres of wetlands and native mixed-grass prairie; North Dakota #2, protecting an expanse of shallow wetland, within which is a large island that provides ideal nesting habitat for mallards; Halvorson, containing wetlands that attract concentrations of geese and ducks during autumn migration, and areas of deeper water that are a mecca for diving ducks such as canvasbacks and redheads; Piping Plover, protecting alkaline beaches that provide important nesting habitat for the threatened piping plover (public access to this area is restricted); Sikes Dam, attracting large numbers of waterfowl and other wildlife to the 340-acre marsh that was created by the dam; and Moen, protecting a riparian corridor along Shell Creek— a rare habitat in this prairie region.

The WPAs are generally open to public access for such visitor activities as birdwatching, photography, hiking, and hunting during the designated seasons. Wildlife species on these areas are generally the same as those recorded on Lostwood National Wildlife Refuge.

Further information: Lostwood Wetland Management District, 8315 Highway 8, Kenmare, ND 58746; telephone: (701) 848-2466.

Tewaukon Wetland Management District was established in 1960 to restore, enhance, and manage scattered ecologically important wetland and grassland habitats within Sargent, Ransom, and Richland counties in southeastern North Dakota.

This district includes more than 14,000 acres in more than 100 federally owned waterfowl production areas (WPAs) and more than 45,000 acres being managed under the terms of perpetual wetland and grassland easements purchased from local landowners. It is managed by the Tewaukon National Wildlife Refuge Complex staff (see separate text on the refuge).

The WPAs are open to hunting, trapping, and fishing during the designated seasons. A self-guiding prairie trail (grass trail) is available on the Stacks Slough WPA Complex near Hankinson in Richland County, for the observation of wildlife and native plants during the summer months.

Further information: Tewaukon Wetland Management District, 9756–143? Avenue, SE, Cayuga, ND 58013; telephone: (701) 724-3598.

Valley City Wetland Management District was established in 1971 to restore, enhance, and manage scattered ecologically important wetland and prairie habitats within Barnes, Griggs, Steele, Cass, and Traill counties in east-central North Dakota.

This district includes more than 17,000 acres in 82 federally owned wetland production areas (WPAs); Hobart Lake, Sibley Lake, Stoney Slough, and Tomahawk national wildlife refuges; and more than 40,000 acres that are being managed under the terms of perpetual wetland easements purchased from local landowners.

The WPAs are generally open to visitation during daylight hours. There are no entrance fees. No visitor use facilities are provided. Visitor activities include birdwatching, photography, hiking, and hunting during the designated seasons.

Further information: Valley City Wetland Management District, 11515 River Road, Valley City, ND 58072; telephone: (701) 845-3466.

Ohio

Cedar Point, consisting of 2,445 acres, was established in 1964 to protect important marsh habitat. The refuge is located where the southwestern end of Lake Erie meets Maumee Bay, near Toledo in northwestern Ohio. The area, which had been owned since 1882 by the Cedar Point Club, was threatened with development in the early 1960s. This private hunt club donated the marsh to the North American Wildlife Foundation, which then transferred it to the U.S. Fish and Wildlife Service with the stipulation that it not be used as a public park, campground, or picnic area.

The refuge manages the water level of three extensive, impounded pools that support the growth of cattails, bulrushes, and other emergent vegetation. This wetland habitat attracts herons, egrets, bald eagles, and large concentrations of migrating ducks of many species. In recent years, a small colony of black terns has been nesting here. Cedar Point Refuge also protects an area of remnant beach that supports hardwoods.

Except for seasonal bank fishing along the shore of a pond accessed off Yondota Road, visitor entry onto this refuge is allowed only by special permit.

Further information: Cedar Point National Wildlife Refuge, c/o Ottawa NWR, 14000 West State Route 2, Oak Harbor, OH 43449; telephone: (419) 898-0014.

Ottawa, containing more than 5,500 acres in three units, was established in 1961 to restore, enhance, and manage a diversity of habitats along the southwestern shore of Lake Erie in northwestern Ohio. The refuge includes part of the once-extensive, heavily wooded Great Black Swamp, expanses of coastal marshland, and small areas of hardwood forest, scrub/shrub habitat, grassland, and cultivated cropland.

The refuge, which lies within a major migration corridor at the crossroads of the Mississippi and Atlantic flyways, attracts large concentrations of migrating waterfowl, shorebirds, raptors, and neotropical songbirds. Its wetland and other habitats provide significant resting and feeding staging areas before these migrants cross Lake Erie in the spring and after crossing the lake in the autumn. Concentrations of at least 15,000 geese and 30,000 ducks are attracted to the refuge. During autumn migration, roughly 70 percent of the Mississippi Flyway's black ducks use the Lake Erie marshes. Canada geese, wood ducks, mallards, and blue-winged teal are the most common nesting waterfowl. Bald eagles are frequently observed during migrations, and a number of active nests are located on the refuge.

As the U.S. Fish and Wildlife Service explains the history of this area:

In the 1794 *Battle of Fallen Timbers*, the Ottawa Indians were defeated and forced out. . . . Their departure opened up the area to white settlers. Soon, "progress" prevailed: the formidable Black Swamp was drained; farmers and farm fields replaced Indians and forests; eagles and panthers were supplanted by the blackbird. The Great Black Swamp was reduced from 300,000 to 15,000 acres.

The refuge's 591-acre NAVARRE MARSH UNIT is located on the Lake Erie shore about 6 miles to the southeast of the main unit, and the 520-acre DARBY MARSH UNIT is on the lakeshore about 12 miles to the southeast. The Darby Marsh Unit was added to the refuge in 1966, when the Fish and Wildlife Service gave up ownership of Navarre Marsh in exchange for Darby Marsh. The Navarre Marsh property is jointly owned by two power companies for their Davis Besse Nuclear Power Station, but the wildlife habitat continues to be managed as part of the refuge. Visitor entry onto these two units is allowed only by special permit.

Ottawa Refuge's habitat management activities include the manipulation of water levels within moist-soil and marsh impoundments with dikes, ditches, and water control structures. These wetland units are drained in the late spring or early summer to promote the growth of plants, and are reflooded in the autumn to provide food and habitat for migrating waterfowl and other wildlife. As the Fish and Wildlife Service states in the refuge's *Comprehensive Conservation Plan* (*CCP*) document (2000):

Managing the marshes for wildlife is essentially based on controlling plant succession to meet seasonal needs. Intensive management is best achieved by controlling water levels, since fluctuating water levels has a marked influence on *aquatic plant succession*. Current marsh management practices for waterfowl and other wetland wildlife include the use of pumps and/or dikes to provide a variety of wetland types in marsh units throughout the year. These generally include combinations of *moist soil units* and *hemi-marshes*.

Moist soil units are typically dewatered in the spring to provide shallow water conditions for waterfowl and shorebirds and [to stimulate plant germination and promote] plant growth. They are reflooded in the fall to attract and provide food for fall migrants. Hemi-marshes are shallow water areas that contain water throughout the year. . . .

Seasonal manipulation of water levels simulates the natural fluctuations that occur in wetlands connected to Lake Erie. The majority of the wetlands at Ottawa National Wildlife Refuge are diked wetlands with no direct connection to the lake. Diking . . . is done in an effort to protect wetlands from the rapid water level changes and wave action associated with Lake Erie. However, the dikes prohibit the entry of fish into the marshes for spawning and reduce the exchange of nutrients between a marsh and the lake, two important functions of coastal wetlands.

The *CCP* document goes on to describe a wetland management case study in which one dike-protected marsh is now being managed with a connection to the lake:

Metzger Marsh is a 650-acre Lake Erie coastal wetland jointly managed by Ottawa National Wildlife Refuge and the Ohio Division of Wildlife (ODOW). Until the 1970s, the marsh was protected from Lake Erie by a naturally occurring barrier beach that deflected waves due to storm events and reduced the effects [of] lake level fluctuations on the marsh, but allowed water and nutrient exchange and fish access for spawning. High Lake Erie water levels in the 1970s eroded the barrier beach and exposed Metzger Marsh to the full impact of Lake Erie.

Over the following years, waves and rapid water level changes reduced wetland vegetation . . . to scattered clumps of cattails. In the 1990s, a decision was made by the U.S. Fish and Wildlife Service and ODOW to build a dike to protect Metzger Marsh and reestablish vegetation and management capabilities. With the help of many partners, and a permit from the [U.S.] Army Corps of Engineers, a 7,700-foot dike was constructed across the mouth of Metzger Marsh. This dike was different from others in the area because it was built with a connection to Lake Erie.

Conditions of the Corps . . . permit required a fish passage structure to be installed in the dike to allow Lake Erie fish to enter and exit the marsh for feeding, spawning and protection. . . . Regrowth of vegetation was extremely successful and an emergent wetland community returned to Metzger Marsh. In March 1999, the gates were opened to Lake Erie and will be left open for four years. . . . Water levels will rise and fall with Lake Erie . . . as they did when the barrier beach was present. Fish passage and nutrient flow will resume.

Under cooperative agreements, farmers cultivate crops of corn, sorghum, and buckwheat on a number of fields within the refuge. A portion of these crops is left unharvested for the benefit of waterfowl and other wildlife.

Establishment of Ottawa Refuge was made possible with revenues from the sale of Migratory Bird Hunting and Conservation Stamps (Duck Stamps). Ducks Unlimited, Inc. has helped enhance several hundred acres of the refuge's wetland habitat. The Ottawa National Wildlife Refuge Association is a local nonprofit support group that is assisting the refuge in a variety of ways.

The refuge's main unit is open daily during daylight hours. There is no entrance fee. The refuge headquarters is open on weekdays, except national holidays.

Visitor activities on the refuge's main unit include birdwatching, photography, hiking 7 miles of self-guiding, interpretive trails, cross-country skiing, interpretive and environmental education programs, fishing, and hunting (deer and waterfowl) on parts of the refuge during the designated seasons. Although camping is not permitted on the refuge, campground facilities are available at Maumee State Park and elsewhere in the surrounding area.

The refuge's self-guiding, interpretive (wheelchair-accessible) hiking loops (mostly on dikes) are the 0.25-mile Red Trail that offers a view of marsh habitat, the 2-mile Yellow Trail that provides an observation platform overlooking a marsh impoundment, the 3.1-mile Green Trail that offers views of marsh habitat, and the 4.5-mile Blue Trail that offers views of Crane Creek, marsh impoundments, and an impressive remaining portion of the Black Swamp. There are also two short, interpretive Wood Lot Tree Trails, where a few of the common tree species are identified. Over 300 bird species have been seen on the refuge.

The best months for concentrations of birds are March–April for migrating waterfowl; April for migrating shorebirds; May for the peak of warblers and other migrating songbirds;

July–August for herons, egrets, geese, and shorebirds; September for bald eagles; and October for the peak of migrating waterfowl. Mammals include white-tailed deer, coyote, red and gray foxes, mink, muskrat, raccoon, and striped skunk.

Lodgings and meals are available in such communities as Oregon, Port Clinton, and Toledo.

Access to Ottawa Refuge is east approximately 15 miles from Toledo on State Route 2; or about 90 miles west from Cleveland on State Route 2.

Further information: Ottawa National Wildlife Refuge, 14000 West State Route 2, Oak Harbor, OH 43449; telephone: (419) 898-0014.

West Sister Island, comprising 77 acres, was established in 1937 to protect the largest rookery of great blue herons and great egrets in the Great Lakes region. This refuge, near the western end of Lake Erie in northwestern Ohio, is located 9 miles offshore from, and is managed by, Ottawa National Wildlife Refuge. Other nesting species include double-crested cormorants and black-crowned night herons. Vegetation consists largely of tall hackberry trees, 7- to 9-foot-tall great Solomon's seal, many species of ferns, and abundant poison ivy—much of the latter reaching 12 feet in height.

In 1975, the refuge was designated as a unit of the National Wilderness Preservation System. The U.S. Coast Guard manages 5 acres of the 82-acre island and a lighthouse that dates from 1847.

Visitor entry onto West Sister Island is allowed only by special permit to avoid disturbing the rookeries.

Further information: West Sister Island National Wildlife Refuge, c/o Ottawa NWR, 14000 West State Route 2, Oak Harbor, OH 43449; telephone: (419) 898-0014.

Oklahoma

Deep Fork, containing more than 9,000 acres, was established in 1993 to restore and protect important bottomland hardwood forest habitat along the Deep Fork River, and adjacent native upland tallgrass prairie, in eastern Oklahoma. The refuge is currently in an acquisition phase, with a goal of about 18,000 acres, and is working with organizations such as Trust for Public Land to purchase properties from willing sellers. Among the rich variety of wildlife are wintering waterfowl, nesting wood ducks, many neotropical migratory songbirds, and mammals such as deer and beavers.

Habitat restoration on Deep Fork Refuge is a major focus of the U.S. Fish and Wildlife Service. Bottomland areas that were previously cleared of forest for grazing or pecan orchards are being replanted with native hardwoods. Over 250 bird species use the refuge.

The refuge is open daily during daylight hours. There is no entrance fee.

Visitor activities include birdwatching, photography, viewing wildlife from observation sites, hiking on designated trails, canoeing and boating, fishing, and hunting (deer, rabbit, squirrel, and duck). October through May are the best months for birdwatching.

Visitors are cautioned to be alert for ticks, chiggers, and venomous snakes. Insect repellent is advised. Mammals include white-tailed deer, bobcat, coyote, gray and red foxes, beaver, raccoon, and opossum.

Lodgings and meals are available in such communities as Okmulgee, Henryetta, and Tulsa.

Access to the refuge from Tulsa is south about 35 miles on U.S. Route 75 to Okmulgee; or from I-40 it is north 14 miles on Route 75 to Okmulgee. Refuge lands are situated to the west and south of Okmulgee, along the Deep Fork River. A refuge map can be used to locate the properties.

Further information: Deep Fork National Wildlife Refuge, P.O. Box 816, Okmulgee, OK 74447; telephone: (918) 756-0815.

Little River, consisting of more than 13,000 acres, was established in 1987. This refuge protects an ecologically important area of oak-hickory bottomland hardwood forest and bald cypress swamp with meandering creeks, sloughs, and former river oxbows, along the northern side of Little River in the southeastern corner of Oklahoma. It is the largest remaining area of this habitat in Oklahoma. Among the many species of wildlife are wintering mallards and nesting wood ducks, as well as herons and egrets, wild turkeys, Mississippi kites, neotropical migratory songbirds, beavers, and alligators. Over 225 bird species use the refuge.

Establishment of this refuge was made possible with revenues derived from the sale of Migratory Bird Hunting and Conservation Stamps (Duck Stamps).

The refuge is open daily during daylight hours. There is no entrance fee.

Visitor activities include birdwatching, photography, interpretive programs, primitive driving on 10 miles of refuge roads (some of which are flooded during high water), hiking on trails, canoeing and boating, fishing, and hunting during the designated seasons. Camping is not permitted on the refuge, but campground facilities are available in Beavers Bend State Park. November through April are the best months for birdwatching.

Little River Refuge serves as a destination in the state for viewing alligators. Although they are generally afraid of people, visitors are cautioned to stay a safe distance from these sluggish-looking but potentially fast-moving reptiles and to be alert for ticks, chiggers, fire ants, and venomous snakes. Insect repellent is advised.

Lodgings and meals are available in such communities as Broken Bow and Idabel.

For detailed directions to Little River Refuge, visitors are urged to stop at the headquarters, located at 635 South Park Drive in Broken Bow.

Further information: Little River National Wildlife Refuge, P.O. Box 340, Broken Bow, OK 74728; telephone: (580) 584-6211.

Optima, comprising 4,333 acres in the Oklahoma Panhandle, was established in 1975 to provide habitat for migratory waterfowl and other birds on the U.S. Army Corps of Engineers' Optima Lake. Changes in the area's hydrology occurred, however, between the time the reservoir project was authorized and when it was completed, and the lake's conservation pool has never reached its expected elevation. The much smaller than anticipated Optima Lake lies approximately one-half mile from the refuge boundary.

Consequently, the primary objectives of this refuge shifted to the enhancement and protection of prairie grassland, migratory birds, and resident wildlife. Roughly half of the grassland habitat consists of a tallgrass vegetative type known as sandsage-bluestem prairie, and much of the rest is shortgrass prairie, dominated by blue grama and buffalograss.

Optima is an important refuge for a variety of neotropical migratory songbirds including scissor-tailed flycatcher and Bullock's oriole, and it provides nesting habitat for raptors such as Mississippi kite and red-tailed hawk. Common resident birds include bobwhite and scaled quail, Rio Grande turkey, and the non-native ring-necked pheasant.

The refuge is open daily during daylight hours. There is no entrance fee.

Visitor activities include birdwatching, photography, and hunting during the designated seasons. Although camping is not permitted on the refuge, campground facilities are provided at adjacent Corps of Engineers' sites below the dam.

More than 250 bird species have been recorded here.

Lodgings and meals are available in such nearby communities as Hardesty, Hooker, and Guymon, Oklahoma; and Liberal, Kansas.

Directions to three access points (with parking areas) for wildlife observation and hunting are: about 1.2 miles northwest of Hardesty on State Route 3 and 0.6 mile west on Z Road (gravel); about 2.4 miles due west of Hardesty on a paved county road that becomes gravel; or about 2 miles north from State Route 3, just east of Hardesty.

Further information: Optima National Wildlife Refuge, c/o Washita NWR, Route 1, Box 68, Butler, OK 73625; telephone: (580) 664-2205.

Ozark Plateau consists of about 3,000 acres within a complex of nine small, forested tracts of land in northeastern Oklahoma that contain numerous caves. The refuge was established in 1985 (initially as the Oklahoma Caves National Wildlife Refuge) to protect several species of federally listed endangered bats; the federally listed threatened blind Ozark cavefish; and other species of concern that are endemic to the Ozarks, including a cave crayfish found only from one cave. This protection is being accomplished through an ecosystem approach to managing caves and surrounding Ozark forest habitat.

The refuge's caves offer hibernation and maternity habitat for the Ozark big-eared bat, one of Oklahoma's most endangered species and one that has very restricted roosting preferences. The endangered gray bat raises its young by the thousands in certain refuge maternity caves during the summer. The endangered Indiana bat, which is at the western edge of its range, could be found here. Several other bats, considered "species of concern," also inhabit the refuge. In addition, numerous neotropical migratory songbirds are attracted to the refuge's areas of Ozark forest.

Establishment and enhancement of the Ozark Plateau Refuge has been made possible with the assistance of The Nature Conservancy; caving organizations, including the Tulsa Regional Oklahoma Grotto and Central Oklahoma Grotto; several private landowners; the Oklahoma Department of Wildlife Conservation; the Cherokee Nation; and the City of Tulsa.

Because of the sensitive nature of the resources, there is only limited public use of the refuge at this time. The caves are open only to scientific research and educational purposes by permit.

Much of Ozark Plateau Refuge's woodland fauna and flora are similar to the species found on Sequoyah Refuge, but this refuge is dominated by the more upland Ozark species.

Lodgings and meals are available in such communities as Stilwell, Tahlequah, and Jay.

Access to the refuge is limited at this time because of the susceptibility of the sensitive cave resources to human disturbance and because the refuge boundaries have not yet been marked.

Further information: Ozark Plateau National Wildlife Refuge, Route 1, Box 18A, Vian, OK 74962; telephone: (918) 773-5251 or (918) 581-7458, ext. 227.

Salt Plains, containing 32,000 acres, was established in 1930 to enhance and protect important resting and feeding habitats for migratory waterfowl and other wildlife on the Salt Fork of the Arkansas River in north-central Oklahoma. This refuge features 12,000 acres of salt flats that are famous for their unique, hourglass-shaped selenite gypsum crystal formations; 10,000 acres of the Great Salt Plains Reservoir behind the U.S. Army Corps of Engineers' Great Salt Plains Dam; and a network of freshwater ponds and marshes.

The water level of the ponds and marshes fluctuates seasonally—either from rainfall, or regulated as necessary with the use of water control structures. This provides for the growth of waterfowl plant foods, such as millet and grasses, during the dry summer months, and reflooding of these areas to accommodate the autumn and winter influx of ducks. The U.S. Fish and Wildlife Service also provides wood duck nesting boxes.

The refuge includes roughly 10,000 acres of gently rolling upland, of which most is native grassland with some areas of brush and woodland habitats; prescription fires help to maintain the ecological health of certain habitats, such as the grasslands. For the benefit of waterfowl and other wildlife, more than 1,000 acres of cropland are planted in wheat, milo, and cowpeas.

Acquisition of lands for the Salt Plains Refuge was made possible with revenues from the sale of Migratory Bird Hunting and Conservation Stamps (Duck Stamps). The Great Salt Plains Association is a nonprofit support group that is assisting the refuge in various ways.

The refuge is open daily. There is no entrance fee. The visitor center is open daily from April 1 to October 15 and on weekdays the rest of the year, except national holidays.

Visitor activities include birdwatching; photography; interpretive programs and tours; driving the 2.5-mile Harold F. Miller Auto Tour Route, affording views of the refuge's diverse habitats of woods, ponds, marsh, and fields; hiking; viewing the refuge and wildlife from Casey Marsh Tower, from another tower at the entrance to the Selenite Crystal Area, and from several overlooks; picnicking; swimming; canoeing and boating on some parts of the refuge from April to mid-October; fishing; and hunting on parts of the refuge during the designated seasons. Camping is permitted on the refuge at the Jet Recreation Area from April I to October 15 and all year on the adjacent Great Salt Plains State Park.

Hiking opportunities include a number of trails, such as the Eagle Roost Nature Trail. This 1.25-mile loop seasonally affords opportunities to see migratory and wintering ducks and geese, nesting wood ducks, herons and egrets, many kinds of migratory shorebirds, white pelicans, sandhill cranes, and even a few whooping cranes. Some of the latter pause here in the autumn on their 2,400-mile flight from breeding grounds in northern Canada's Wood Buffalo National Park to their wintering habitat on Aransas National Wildlife Refuge, on the Texas Gulf coast (see the Aransas text). Among the birds that inhabit, and nest on, the salt flats are the endangered least tern, the threatened snowy plover, and avocet. November through May are the best months for birdwatching. Over 300 bird species have been seen here.

Between April I and October 15, visitors are allowed to collect selenite gypsum crystals within a number of digging areas, which are annually rotated to allow sufficient time for crystal growth replacement. A refuge brochure on the crystals explains: "Only in certain places on the Salt Plains, gypsum and saline solutions in the soil are sufficiently concentrated to promote crystal growth. When temperature and brine conditions are ideal, the crystals may form very rapidly." The brochure tells how to carefully collect them to observe the beauty of their fascinating shapes, which vary from single crystals to twins and clusters.

Visitors are cautioned to be alert for rattlesnakes (western massasauga), ticks, chiggers, and poison ivy. Insect repellent and sunscreen are advised, the latter especially on the glary salt flats of the Selenite Crystals Area. During the spring, there is the potential for violent thunderstorms and tornadoes.

Lodgings and meals are available in such communities as Cherokee, Alva, and Enid.

Access to this refuge from U.S. Route 64 at Jet is north 14 miles on State Route 38 and left at the refuge sign, continuing I mile to headquarters. The entrance to the Selenite Crystal Area is 6 miles west of Jet on U.S. Route 64, right onto an unpaved road for 3 miles, and right onto a paved road for I mile. From Cherokee, the crystal area entrance is south approximately 3 miles on U.S. Route 64, and left 5 miles on a paved road.

Further information: Salt Plains National Wildlife Refuge, Route I, Box 76, Jet, OK 73749; telephone: (580) 626-4794.

Sequoyah, comprising 20,800 acres, was established in 1970 upon completion of the U.S. Army Corps of Engineers' Robert S. Kerr Reservoir. This refuge enhances and protects a variety of habitats including woodlands, wetlands and flooded fields, and cropland of winter wheat and soybeans at the junction of the Arkansas and Canadian rivers in eastern Oklahoma. Cradled in a river valley in the gently rolling Ozark Mountain foothills, Sequoyah attracts large concentrations of wintering mallards, many thousands of snow geese, nesting wood ducks, herons and egrets, white pelicans, migratory shorebirds, nesting bald eagles, scissor-tailed flycatchers, and numerous species of neotropical migratory songbirds. More than 250 species of birds have been recorded here.

An oxbow lake restoration project was recently completed with the assistance of the Oklahoma Department of Wildlife Conservation, the U.S. Army Corps of Engineers, Ducks Unlimited, and Tulsa-based Natureworks. The project now enables the Fish and Wildlife Service to manage approximately 700 acres of previously unmanageable wetlands in a manner that is hydrologically similar to the lake's natural conditions. Other ongoing habitat improvement actions include the restoration of bottomland hardwoods, native grassland savannah, and other plant communities. Periodic prescription burns are used to enhance the health of certain native plant ecosystems.

This refuge is named in honor of Sequoyah, the Cherokee Indian who created his tribe's alphabet, which was instrumental in preserving his Native American people's customs and history in writing. By the nineteenth century, the Cherokees lived to the north of the Arkansas and Canadian rivers, and the Chickasaw and Choctaws lived to the south. Several sites of the much earlier pre-Columbian Caddoan Indian culture's encampments, dating from A.D. 1100 to 1400, are protected within the refuge.

The refuge is open daily during daylight hours. There is no entrance fee.

Visitor activities include birdwatching; photography; driving and bicycling on unpaved refuge tour roads (especially the 6-mile loop in the Sandtown Bottoms area and the 2-mile route to Dirty Creek in the Webbers Bottom area); hiking on trails and in other areas such as Girty Bottom; viewing wildlife from observation platforms; prearranged interpretive programs and tours for groups; canoeing and boating (five boat-launching ramps are available); fishing; and hunting (waterfowl and upland game) on parts of the refuge during the designated seasons. Camping is not permitted, but campground facilities are available at three nearby state parks—Brushy Lake, Greenleaf, and Tenkiller. November through April are the best months for birdwatching. Part of the refuge is closed to entry from September 1 through the end of the waterfowl season, except on designated trails.

Hiking opportunities include the Horton Slough Trail—a 1-mile loop walk, providing opportunities to see wading birds and wood ducks, that begins at the headquarters information kiosk, follows the north shore of this slough, crosses a swinging bridge, returns along the south shore, and provides opportunities to see turtles, songbirds, wading birds and wood ducks; and Sandtown Woods Trail—a 1-mile route from which bald eagles are often seen along the river.

Visitors are cautioned to be alert for ticks, chiggers, wasps, venomous snakes, and poison ivy. Insect repellent is advised.

Lodgings and meals are available in such communities as Vian, Gore, Sallisaw, and Webbers Falls.

Access to the refuge is south 3 miles on a county road from I-40 (Exit 297) at Vian.

Further information: Sequoyah National Wildlife Refuge, Route 1, Box 18A, Vian, OK 74962; telephone: (918) 773-5251.

Tishomingo, containing 16,464 acres, was established in 1946 to enhance and protect a diversity of wildlife habitats in south-central Oklahoma. The refuge includes areas of hardwood forest; wild-plum thickets; riparian woodland; a number of ponds; the meandering course of the Washita River; the broad expanse of Cumberland Pool—the northern arm of Lake Texoma, created by the U.S. Army Corps of Engineers' Denison Dam—and crops of corn, milo, and winter wheat that are planted for the benefit of wintering waterfowl.

Wildlife includes tens of thousands of wintering ducks and geese, nesting wood ducks, migratory white pelicans, thousands of migratory gulls, herons and egrets, wintering bald eagles, many migratory shorebirds, and numerous neotropical migratory songbirds. More than 250 species of birds have been recorded here.

Tishomingo Refuge is named for a former Chickasaw Indian chief.

Friends of Tishomingo Refuge is a nonprofit support group that is assisting the refuge in various ways.

The refuge is open daily. There is no entrance fee.

Visitor activities include birdwatching; photography; guided interpretive walks and tours led by trained volunteers; driving the 15 miles of refuge roads; walking the 1-mile loop Craven Nature Trail offering views of Dick's Pond; hiking throughout most of the refuge (from March 1 through September, with limited access from October 1 through February; spring flooding can inundate trails); viewing wildlife from an observation platform; limited camping; picnicking; canoeing and boating (from March 1 through September); fishing; and hunting (waterfowl, deer, upland game, turkey, and dove) on parts of the refuge during the designated seasons.

Campground facilities are provided at nearby Blue River State Recreation Area and Murray State Park. November through February are the best months to see wintering waterfowl and eagles, and March and April are the best months for observing the influx of migratory songbirds.

Visitors are cautioned to be alert for venomous snakes, as well as ticks and chiggers. Insect repellent is advised. During the spring, there is the potential for violent thunderstorms and tornadoes.

Lodgings and meals are available in such communities as Tishomingo and Ardmore.

Access to this refuge is east from I-35 at Ardmore on State Route 199 to Tishomingo, east on State Route 78 to the eastern end of town, right onto Refuge Road, and south 3 miles to the refuge headquarters.

Further information: Tishomingo National Wildlife Refuge, 12000 S. Refuge Road, Tishomingo, OK 73460; telephone: (580) 371-2402.

Washita, containing 8,200 acres, was established in 1961 to enhance and protect an ecologically important area around and upstream from Foss Reservoir in west-central Oklahoma. The refuge includes gently rolling prairie grassland hills, brushy ravines, and bottomlands. There are scattered areas of riparian woodland and marsh along the tributary creeks and meandering course of the Washita River, which merges with the upper end of the U.S. Bureau of Reclamation reservoir. Under cooperative agreements with farmers, 2,100 acres of cropland are planted with wheat and milo, part of which is left unharvested for the waterfowl.

The refuge's habitats attract a large diversity of wildlife, including tens of thousands of wintering geese and ducks; migratory white pelicans, shorebirds, Mississippi kites, bald eagles, Swainson's hawks, and sandhill cranes (as many as several thousand of the latter stately gray birds sometimes pause here in early November); neotropical migratory songbirds; nesting scissor-tailed flycatchers and roadrunners; and such mammals as prairie dogs, deer, and beavers.

Ducks Unlimited, Inc. has helped (cost-sharing) with development of a moist-soil unit.

The refuge is open daily during daylight hours. There is no entrance fee. The refuge office is open on weekdays, except national holidays.

Visitor activities include birdwatching; photography; driving to such places as Owl Cove, Pitts Creek, and Lakeview from county roads adjacent to the refuge; hiking (limited trails); viewing wildlife from an observation platform; canoeing and boating (a boat-launching ramp is provided at the mouth of Panther Creek in Foss Lake State Park, near the southern end of the refuge); fishing; and limited hunting (quail, rabbit, goose, and crane) on certain parts of the refuge during the designated seasons. Camping is not permitted on the refuge, but campground facilities are available in adjacent Foss Lake State Park. November through May are the best months for birdwatching.

Visitors are cautioned to be alert for venomous snakes, ticks, and poison ivy. Insect repellent is advised. There is the potential for violent spring and summer thunderstorms and tornadoes.

The more than 240 species of birds that have been recorded on Washita Refuge are much the same as those of Optima Refuge.

Lodgings and meals are available in such communities as Clinton and Elk City.

Access to this refuge's headquarters is west 5 miles on State Route 33 from Butler, right (north) 1 mile, and left (west) 0.5 mile.

Further information: Washita National Wildlife Refuge, Route 1, Box 68, Butler, OK 73625; telephone: (580) 664-2205.

Wichita Mountains, containing 59,020 acres in southwestern Oklahoma, is one of the magnificent showplaces of the National Wildlife Refuge System, and is the oldest managed wildlife preserve in the United States. This ecologically rich and scenically beautiful area was initially set aside in 1901 as a forest reserve. It was redesignated as a game preserve by President Theodore Roosevelt in 1905, partly to help rescue from extinction the American bison (buffalo), and was established as the Wichita Mountains Wildlife Refuge in 1935. The mountains and refuge are named for the tribe of Native Americans who were living here when seventeenth-century Spanish explorers traveled through this region.

The refuge's rugged, uplifted range of geologically ancient granite peaks, hills, and ridges is adorned with weather-sculpted rocky outcrops and rises from surrounding gently undulating grassy valleys, meadows, and plains. Some of the narrower mountain valleys are densely wooded, with groves of trees extending up their slopes. The endlessly fascinating, lichen-covered rock formations are fractured and eroded into extensive jumbles of huge, rounded boulders. Exposed rocky slopes, ridges, peaks, gorges, crevices, and ledges are picturesquely interspersed with groves and clumps of oaks, cedars, and other trees and shrubs.

More than 20 lakes and ponds scattered throughout the refuge add tremendously to the refuge's scenic charm and ecological diversity. These human-made impoundments, totaling 673 acres, were created or enlarged in the 1930s, when small dams were built by the Civilian Conservation Corps (CCC) to conserve water runoff. In some places, they are bordered by cattails, willows, and white-barked American sycamores, and here and there, water lily pads and their lotus-like white flowers float on the water.

The refuge contains an unusually rich diversity of plants and animals. Situated in the middle of the southern Great Plains region, the Wichita Mountains are an outstanding biotic crossroads of numerous species of flora and fauna that are representative of both the lush eastern and arid western United States.

An ecologically significant aspect of this refuge's east-west meeting and overlapping is its protected remnant of the once-vast, natural merging of eastern woodland and western Great Plains grassland—known as cross timbers biota. This term refers specifically to the "fingers" of oak woods that extend into the grasslands from the east.

The flora of the refuge contains a mixture of grasses representative of both the lush eastern Great Plains tallgrass prairie, such as the big and little bluestems, Indiangrass, and switch grass; and shortgrass species of the arid western plains, such as buffalograss and the sideoats and blue gramas.

Within this fascinating biotic mosaic, oak seedlings are constantly attempting to expand the groves of post and blackjack oaks into the grassland habitat. At the same time, the aggressive and fast-growing eastern redcedar continually tries to crowd out the oaks and ultimately become the dominant species. Bordering the refuge's intermittently flowing streams are such other trees as black walnut, ash, pecan, flowering dogwood, redbud, cottonwood, black willow, and American elm.

Among the Wichita Mountains' eastern and western birds are the ruby-throated and black-chinned hummingbirds, eastern and western kingbirds, yellow-shafted and red-shafted phases of northern flicker, broad-winged and Swainson's hawks, eastern and mountain bluebirds, Baltimore and Bullock's orioles, Carolina and canyon wrens, summer and western tanagers, painted and lazuli buntings, and the chuck-wills-widow and poor-will. Two of North America's most beautiful birds are the graceful scissor-tailed flycatcher and Mississippi kite, both of which breed on the refuge. A prominent resident species is the wild turkey, numbering several hundred individuals that are descendants of a male and two females that survived from a disease-plagued reintroduction program in 1912.

In 1907, two years after the area was designated as a game preserve, the New York Zoological Society and American Bison Society donated 15 bison (six bulls and nine cows) to reestablish this magnificent Great Plains mammal to the Wichitas. Today, the refuge's population totals approximately 570 animals, and visitors can usually enjoy seeing scattered herds of them on the refuge's grasslands.

Although the original native Merriam's elk that once inhabited these mountains had become extinct, a number of the Rocky Mountain elk were introduced from Jackson Hole, Wyoming, in 1912. They have subsequently become well established here, with annual autumn elk hunts to maintain the population within the carrying capacity of the refuge's habitat. In addition, the white-tailed deer, which in 1907 was estimated to total a mere 15 animals in the game preserve, now numbers more than 1,000 individuals.

Another species of ungulates inhabiting the Wichita Mountains Refuge is the non-native but historically significant Texas longhorn. This visually impressive animal was the first kind of cattle to be introduced to North America, arriving in 1521 with the Spanish explorers. During the last several decades of the nineteenth century, an estimated 10 million longhorns were raised on the southern Great Plains of Texas and the Oklahoma Territory. By the early years of the twentieth century, as short-horned cattle became more popular, the longhorn population sharply declined. In 1927, when this form of cattle was nearing extinction, Congress authorized the maintenance of a remnant herd in the Wichita Mountains game preserve. Today, the herd is maintained at about 300 individuals, with an annual autumn public auction of excess animals.

The U.S. Fish and Wildlife Service is carrying out a variety of management programs. One species of bird that is receiving special management attention on this refuge is the black-capped vireo (*Vireo atricapillus*), a rare and endangered neotropical songbird that breeds in oak-woodland habitat from central Oklahoma, southward through the Edwards Plateau in Texas, to Coahuila in northern Mexico (see under "Texas" the Balcones Canyonlands Refuge text). The predatory brown-headed cowbird lays its eggs in the vireo's nest. The vireo incubates the cowbird's egg, then raises the cowbird while neglecting its own young. To reduce this harmful impact of nest parasitism, the refuge has implemented an ongoing live-trapping program to reduce the cowbird population. The refuge's estimated vireo breeding population is presently at around 600 birds, having roughly tripled its numbers in just 3 or 4 years.

The refuge is also carrying out an ecologically important program of carefully reintroducing fire with periodic prescribed burns. These fires are vital in helping to maintain the natural health of the grasslands, control the invasion of the aggressive redcedar into grassland habitat, and encourage a diversity of wildflowers and other forbs and legumes.

In 1970, Congress added 8,570 acres of the refuge to the National Wilderness Preservation System. The 5,723-acre CHARONS GARDEN UNIT is open to hiking (a backcountry camping permit is required), and the 2,847-acre NORTH MOUNTAIN UNIT, which is managed as a Research Natural Area, is closed to public access except for approved scientific and educational purposes.

Nearly 280 species of birds, more than 50 species of mammals, 60 species of reptiles and amphibians, 35 species of fish, and more than 800 kinds of trees and other plants have been recorded on the Wichita Mountains Refuge.

The Association of the Friends of the Wichitas is a nonprofit support group that is assisting the refuge in many ways.

The refuge is open daily. There is no entrance fee. The visitor center, at the junction of State Routes 115 and 49, is open daily, except on Tuesdays and major national holidays.

Visitor activities include wildlife observation and photography; driving 35 miles of roads (State Routes 49 and 115, etc.) in the public use area, including a road to the summit of 2,464-foot Mt. Scott; interpretive programs; guided walks and tours (such as Saturday wildflower walks in May, elk-bugling tours in September/October, and weekend autumn foliage walks in November); hiking on 15 miles of trails in the refuge's 22,400-acre public use area; bicycling on some refuge roads; rock climbing; picnicking (four picnic areas); camping at Doris Campground (on a first-come, first-served basis; fee charged) and at a youth group campground (by prearrangement); canoeing and boating; fishing (a wheelchair-accessible fishing pier at 360-acre Elmer Thomas Lake); and hunting (elk and deer, only by lottery). Spring and autumn are the best months for birdwatching.

Hiking opportunities include the Environmental Education Interpretive Trail, a 0.25-mile, self-guiding (wheelchair-accessible) route from the Environmental Education Center parking area; the Dog Run Hollow Trail System, offering 1-, 2-, and 6-mile loop options (Elk Trail, Longhorn Trail, and Buffalo Trail, respectively) that begin at the French Lake trailhead parking area (also accessed from Boulder, Lost Lake, and Dog Run Hollow trailhead parking areas); the Elk Mountain Trail System, offering a 2-mile trail from the Sunset picnic area through the Charons Garden Wilderness to the Post Oak Lake parking area, and the other trail leading to the summit of Elk Mountain; and the Little Baldy Mountain Trail, a 1.5-mile route from either the visitor center or Quanah Parker Dam, along the western side of Quanah Parker Lake (a trail from Doris Campground connects with this route), with a spur trail to the summit of Little Baldy Mountain.

Visitors are cautioned to be alert for rattlesnakes and ticks and to stay a safe distance from bison and elk, which can become aggressive.

Lodgings and meals are available in Lawton.

Access to the refuge is north 6 miles on State Route 115 from Cache; or west 8 miles on State Route 49 from I-44 (just to the north of Lawton).

Further information: Wichita Mountains Wildlife Refuge, Route 1, Box 448, Indiahoma, OK 73552; telephone: (580) 429-3221 or 3222.

Oregon

Ankeny, comprising 2,796 acres, was established in 1965 to provide wintering habitat for the dusky Canada goose and other waterfowl. The refuge consists of flat to gently rolling areas of wetlands, riparian forest, native wet prairie, and farm fields. It is located near the junction of the Santiam and Willamette rivers between Salem and Albany, in the Willamette River Valley of western Oregon.

Many species of waterfowl and other wildlife are attracted to Ankeny (pronounced ANN-kennee). Notable among them are the large concentrations of Canada geese that remain here from autumn to the end of spring. The dusky Canada goose is a dark subspecies that breeds on southern Alaska's Copper River Delta and winters exclusively in the Willamette River Valley of Oregon and in southwestern Washington. Bald eagles, peregrine falcons, tundra swans, and multitudes of ducks and shorebirds can also be seen from autumn through spring. Most of the bird species that have been recorded on Ankeny Refuge are the same as those on William L. Finley Refuge.

More than half of the refuge's acreage is devoted to the planting of wildlife food crops, such as annual and perennial ryegrass, fescue, and a small amount of corn. Wetland habitat has been restored for waterfowl and other water birds, some with the help of Ducks Unlimited, Inc.

The refuge is open daily during daylight hours. Portions of the refuge are closed from October 1 through March 31, to provide a sanctuary for wintering waterfowl. There is no entrance fee. An information kiosk and an observation platform are located off Ankeny Hill Road, and a second kiosk and observation platform are located off Buena Vista Road.

Visitor activities include wildlife observation, photography, driving public roads that cross or border the refuge (viewing turnouts are provided), and hiking.

Hiking opportunities include two 0.5-mile (wheelchair-accessible) boardwalk trails with wildlife viewing blinds (parking and the trailhead are located off Wintel Road) that are open year-round. The trail on the south side of Wintel Road continues for another 1.5 miles and loops back to the parking area. This portion of the trail is open only from April to September.

Insect repellent is advised during the warmer months.

Lodgings and meals are available in such communities as Salem, Albany, and Corvallis.

Access to Ankeny Refuge from Exit 243 on I-5 is west about 0.25 mile on Ankeny Hill Road; at an intersection turn north (right) and continue on Ankeny Hill Road 1.5 miles to an information kiosk and viewing area.

Further information: Ankeny National Wildlife Refuge, c/o Willamette Valley NWR Complex, 26208 Finley Refuge Road, Corvallis, OR 97333; telephone: (541) 757-7236.

Bandon Marsh, containing more than 800 acres in two units, was established in 1983 to protect the largest remaining area of tidal salt marsh in the Coquille River estuary. The refuge is located in Bandon on the southern coast of Oregon.

The salt marsh provides important habitat for waterfowl, wading birds, and large concentrations of shorebirds during their spring and autumn migrations. Among these are plovers (black-bellied, American and Pacific golden, and semipalmated), whimbrel, marbled godwit, sanderling, western and least sandpipers, dunlin, and long-billed dowitcher.

The Coquille Estuary and River support significant runs of estuarine-dependent anadromous fish, such as steelhead and cutthroat trout and chinook and coho salmon. A major goal of the refuge is the restoration of more than 400 acres of tidal wetlands—the largest such project in the state. Refuge leader Roy W. Lowe says that "The proposed tidal marsh restoration project on the Ni-les'tun Unit of the refuge will greatly enhance the ecology of the Coquille estuary and provide essential habitat for juvenile salmonids, which spend from several weeks to months in the estuary before going to sea."

The BANDON MARSH UNIT of the refuge is open daily during daylight hours. There is no entrance fee.

Visitor activities include birdwatching, photography, canoeing and kayaking, fishing, clamming, and hunting. The refuge is known regionally for exceptional viewing of shorebirds, including the annual sighting of rare state species. A wheelchair-accessible boardwalk, viewing deck, interpretive panels, and parking area are located adjacent to Riverside Drive, just to the north of Bandon. Canoes and kayaks may be launched onto the river from boat ramps at Bullard's Beach State Park and the Port of Bandon; and rentals are available at the latter. Camping is not permitted on the refuge, but campground facilities are provided at Bullard's Beach State Park.

Lodgings and meals are available in Bandon.

Access to Bandon Marsh Refuge from U.S. Route 101 is west into Bandon and north along Riverside Drive.

Further information: Bandon Marsh National Wildlife Refuge, c/o Oregon Coast NWR Complex, 2127 SE OSU Drive, Newport, OR 97365; telephone: (541) 867-4550.

Baskett Slough, comprising 2,492 acres, was established in 1965 to provide wintering habitat for dusky Canada geese and other waterfowl. The refuge consists of rolling hills covered with Oregon white oaks, shallow wetlands, upland prairie, and farm fields. The refuge is named for early Willamette River Valley thoroughbred horse breeder George J. Baskett. It is located a few miles west of Salem, in the Willamette Valley of western Oregon.

Many species of waterfowl and other wildlife are attracted to Baskett Slough Refuge. Notable among them are concentrations of Canada geese that remain here from autumn to the end of spring. The dusky Canada goose is a dark subspecies that breeds on southern Alaska's Copper River Delta and winters exclusively in the Willamette River Valley of Oregon and in southwestern Washington. Bald eagles, peregrine falcons, tundra swans, and large numbers of ducks and shorebirds can also be seen on the refuge from autumn through spring. Most of the birds that have been recorded on Baskett Slough are the same as those on the William L. Finley Refuge.

The refuge plants a variety of grass crops to provide forage for the thousands of wintering Canada geese. More than 600 acres of wetland habitat have been restored for waterfowl and other water birds, some with the help of Ducks Unlimited, Inc. The refuge also provides habitat for endangered and threatened species, including Fender's blue butterfly, Kincaid's lupine, and Willamette daisy. Volunteers from the Salem Audubon Society and other local organizations are helping to restore native plant communities, including the declining oak savanna and upland prairie habitats.

The refuge is open daily during daylight hours. There is no entrance fee. An information kiosk is provided at a viewing area on State Route 22. Portions of the refuge are closed from October 1 through March 31 to provide a sanctuary for wintering waterfowl.

Visitor activities include wildlife observation, photography, driving a number of public roads that cross or border the refuge, and hiking the Baskett Butte Trail (open all year) through oak savanna and upland prairie habitat areas. Parking is located off Colville Road. An observation platform is located on the top of the butte that offers spectacular views of the refuge and nearby Cascade and Coast ranges.

Insect repellent is advised during the warmer months.

Lodgings and meals are available in Salem.

Access to Baskett Slough Refuge from Exit 253 on I-5 at Salem is west 10 miles on State Route 22 to the junction with State Route 99W, and continuing west about 2 miles on State Route 22 to a parking area and information kiosk on the north (right) side of the highway.

Further information: Baskett Slough National Wildlife Refuge, c/o Willamette Valley NWR Complex, 26208 Finley Refuge Road, Corvallis, OR 97333; telephone: (541) 757-7236.

Bear Valley, encompassing 4,200 acres, was established in 1978 to protect and manage an area of mature conifer forest, containing mostly ponderosa pines, white firs, Douglas firs, and incense cedars, that attracts several hundred wintering bald eagles that roost here at night. The refuge is located on the western edge of the Klamath Basin in south-central Oregon.

Although Bear Valley Refuge is not open to visitation (except walk-in deer hunting before November 1), there are outstanding opportunities to witness the eagles' early morning (dawn) fly-outs that occur from December through mid-March.

Lodgings and meals are available in Klamath Falls.

Access from Klamath Falls to the eagle-viewing place is southwest approximately 13 miles on U.S. Route 97, west (right) across the railroad tracks, immediately bear left on an unpaved road, and continue about 0.5 mile.

Further information: Bear Valley National Wildlife Refuge, c/o Klamath Basin NWRs, 4009 Hill Road, Tulelake, CA 96143; telephone: (530) 667-2231.

Cape Meares, comprising 138 acres in two separate tracts, was established in 1938 by a land transfer from the U.S. Coast Guard. The refuge protects one of the few remnants of magnificent coastal old-growth forest in Oregon. It is located just north of Oceanside, on the state's northern coast. In 1987, the refuge was designated as a Research Natural Area.

Some of the refuge's large Sitka spruces and western hemlocks tower more than 200 feet tall and are hundreds of years old. Among the many species of birds that are attracted to this ecologically rich habitat are the marbled murrelet, bald eagle, peregrine falcon, northern spotted owl, varied thrush, Steller's and gray jays, chestnut-backed chickadee, and winter wren. The sea cliffs support nesting common murres, tufted puffins, Brandt's and pelagic cormorants, pigeon guillemots, western gulls, and black oystercatchers.

The refuge is open daily during daylight hours. There is no entrance fee. Interpretive overlooks are provided at the adjacent Cape Meares State Park, where the 38-foot Cape Meares Lighthouse, dating from 1890, is located. From these scenic points, visitors can observe a variety of migrating seabirds and other waterbirds, as well as occasional bald eagles, peregrine falcons, and marine mammals. From December through May, migrating gray whales can sometimes be seen from here. As described by the Oregon Coast NWR Complex's project leader, Roy W. Lowe:

Cape Meares provides one of the most stunning coastal views along the entire U.S. West Coast, from a magnificent ancient forest to vertical sea cliffs with waterfalls. It also provides the unusual opportunity to stand in one location and view three national wildlife refuges—Cape Meares, Oregon Islands, and Three Arch Rocks.

The state park's entrance road runs through part of the refuge, and a stretch of the Oregon Coast Trail offers an excellent hiking opportunity. A cooperative interpretive project at the park includes a large kiosk, interpretive panels, viewing overlooks, and improved trails. These facilities were provided through the joint efforts of the Friends of Cape Meares Lighthouse and Wildlife Refuge, the Native Plant Society of Oregon, the Tillamook Utilities District, Oregon State Parks, the U.S. Forest Service, and the U.S. Fish and Wildlife Service. Additional improvements, including two wheelchair-accessible viewing decks, have recently been completed.

Lodgings and meals are available in Netarts, Oceanside, and Tillamook.

Access to Cape Meares Refuge and state park is west of U.S. 101 from Tillamook on the Three Capes Scenic Loop Road.

Further information: Cape Meares National Wildlife Refuge, c/o Oregon Coast NWR Complex, 2127 SE OSU Drive, Newport, OR 97365; telephone: (541) 867-4550.

Cold Springs, containing 3,116 acres, was established by President Theodore Roosevelt as the Cold Springs Reservation in 1909, as a breeding ground for birds. Renamed as a national wildlife refuge in 1940, it is located near the Columbia River in the high desert of northeastern Oregon. The refuge overlays a U.S. Bureau of Reclamation irrigation reservoir. The U.S. Fish and Wildlife Service manages the adjacent wildlife habitats, and the bureau manages the water. The level of the reservoir fluctuates seasonally, shrinking from a 1,500-acre body of water in late spring to a mere 200 to 300 acres by late summer.

Concentrations of migrating waterfowl are attracted to the refuge, with perhaps as many as 5,000 to 6,000 ducks and close to 1,000 geese. Prominent among the refuge's riparian vegetation around the reservoir are willows and cottonwood trees. Some of the latter support a nesting colony of great blue herons. Mule deer are among the resident mammals of this lush oasis, and there is occasional evidence that beavers reside here, as well. Shallow water and exposed mudflats attract large numbers of migrating shorebirds, such as greater and lesser yellowlegs, long-billed dowitchers, a few species of sandpipers, and black-necked stilts. A few American white pelicans and tundra swans winter here. By contrast, the refuge's upland, high-desert habitat consists largely of sagebrush and bitterbrush, inhabited by such wildlife as California quail, sage thrashers, sage sparrows, bobcats, coyotes, badgers, black-tailed jackrabbits, pygmy rabbits, and kangaroo rats.

The refuge is open daily during daylight hours. There is no entrance fee. The headquarters, located at 830 Sixth Street, Umatilla, is open on weekdays, except national holidays.

Visitor activities include wildlife observation, photography, hiking (south of the West Inlet Canal), canoeing and boating (nonmotorized and electric-powered), fishing, and hunting (geese, duck, pheasant, and quail) during the designated seasons. Two boat ramps are provided on the southern shore of the reservoir. Camping is not permitted on the refuge, but campground facilities are provided at nearby Hat Rock State Park, on the Columbia River.

Insect repellent and sunscreen are advised during the warmer months.

Lodgings and meals are available in Hermiston and Pendleton.

Access to Cold Springs Refuge from U.S. 395 at Hermiston is east 6 miles, first on Highland Hills Road and then Loop Road.

Further information: Cold Springs National Wildlife Refuge, c/o Mid-Columbia River NWR Complex, P.O. Box 700, Umatilla, OR 97882; telephone: (509) 545-8588.

Deer Flat (see text under Idaho)

Hart Mountain National Antelope Refuge, consisting of 268,997 acres, was established in 1936 to provide habitat and protection for remnant bands of the pronghorn (antelope) (*Antilocapra americana*). Located in the Great Basin Desert's vastness of southeastern Oregon, the refuge encompasses what was then one of the last places in North America where this fleet-footed mammal still survived. Over 260 bird species have been recorded here.

The scenic centerpiece of this refuge is 12-mile-long Hart Mountain, which rises from Warner Valley more than 3,500 feet to its crest at 8,065 feet elevation. As this writer described in his 1976 book, *The Desert:*

Hart Mountain is actually a giant fault-block range, steeply uplifted along the western escarpment and gently sloping downward for many miles to the east. In this lonely sagebrush country, one of the largest pronghorn herds in the country spends the spring, summer, and autumn. Only a few winter at this higher elevation, many of them migrating southward into the Sheldon Refuge.

Among the refuge's other wildlife are the majestic California bighorn sheep that skillfully scale the mountain's sheer cliffs. By 1915, this species was eliminated from Hart Mountain by diseases transmitted from livestock and by overhunting. As the result of a successful program of reintroduction and management that began in 1954, several hundred of these agile mammals now inhabit the refuge. Mule deer inhabit higher areas of bitterbrush, mountain mahogany, junipers, and ponderosa pines. Prominent among the refuge's many avian species is the greater sage-grouse (*Centrocercus urophasianus*), the largest grouse in North America (see descriptive text in the Seedskadee Refuge text). As the U.S. Fish and Wildlife Service describes the latter:

The drumming chest and elaborate strut of the male sage grouse is a renowned spectacle of the high desert. This early morning courtship dance occurs on numerous refuge strutting grounds (leks) in late March and April. Once bred, hens build a nest, generally under a sagebrush bush, and lay about 9 eggs. Grouse were once so plentiful that settlers gathered buckets of eggs for camp fare. Through careful research and management, it is hoped that sage grouse will recover some of their former abundance.

A major management mission at Hart Mountain Refuge is the restoration and management of natural ecological processes and conditions that were previously altered by human activities. Until the early 1990s, the mountain had long been heavily grazed by sheep and cattle. As the Fish and Wildlife Service says, "Releasing habitat from the pressures of livestock grazing is an important component of current refuge restoration." In addition, carefully prescribed burning that mimics natural ecological processes is the refuge's single most significant "management tool used to revitalize wildlife habitat." Fire promotes nutrient cycling, spurs the growth of forbs and grasses, and creates habitat diversity in a mosaic of successional stages that benefits numerous species of wildlife.

A Pacific Northwest native, the late U.S. Supreme Court Justice William O. Douglas described his special affection for Hart Mountain in his 1960 book, *My Wilderness: The Pacific West:*

The view from the top of Hart Mountain creates a feeling of greater depth and expanse than even the Great Plains. Valleys are as flat as a table top for seventy-five miles. The land is bleak and gray. Yet a shimmer of blue against the skyline says that there is water to be had. A streak of green along a distant hillside tells of springs and creeks. . . . And one has only to watch the plateau through glasses or walk through sagebrush to learn that it virtually teems with life. . . .

Across a ravine a buck antelope was standing in the open, alternately burying his nose in sagebrush and scanning the slopes for signs of danger. A mule deer crossed the field below and then, sensing danger, ran for a cover of mahogany.

. . . I looked up, and there in the sky—perhaps a mile above me—were white objects flying in wide circles. These were white pelicans that nest in the Malheur National Wild Life Refuge some miles to the east. Now they were wheeling in great circles ten thousand feet or more above Guano Plateau. They were promenading in the sky like a fleet of bombers on display.

The Order of the Antelope, a nonprofit organization, assists the refuge in a variety of ways.

The refuge is open daily. There is no entrance fee. The refuge's administrative headquarters, located in the U.S. Post Office building in Lakeview, is open on weekdays, except national holidays. The small visitor center on the refuge is open 24 hours daily but is generally not staffed.

Visitor activities include wildlife observation, photography, viewing Warner Valley from a spectacular overlook, driving refuge roads that range from graded roads to jeep trails, hiking, mountain biking on roads open to motor vehicles, horseback riding, backpacking (a free backcountry permit is required), camping, fishing at Warner Pond and on Rock and Guano creeks, and hunting (chukar; also, a very limited number of tags are offered for deer, antelope, and bighorn sheep hunts) on parts of the refuge during the designated seasons. Primitive camping is permitted year-round at Hotsprings Campground (14-day limit) and at seasonal campsites along Guano Creek, during special authorized hunts, from August 1 to November 1. Potable water is available at refuge headquarters. Campfires are permitted only during periods of low fire hazard.

The refuge offers excellent cross-country hiking opportunities, including wildlife trails in many of the mountain's canyons. Hikers are urged to "exercise caution when entering rocky and rugged terrain."

Insect repellent, sunscreen, warm clothing for cool nights, and a generous supply of drinking water are recommended during the warmer months. Visitors are cautioned to be alert for rattlesnakes, especially in rocky terrain. Since the nearest gas stations and grocery stores are many miles from the refuge, visitors should be sure to have a full fuel tank, a spare tire and emergency tools, and adequate first-aid and food supplies before venturing toward the refuge. Most of the refuge's unpaved roads are not suitable for regular passenger cars; high-clearance vehicles are definitely required when traveling roads other than those leading from Frenchglen, Blue Sky, and Hotsprings. Late autumn, winter, and early spring visitors should be particularly alert for sudden changes in the weather that can bring plunging temperatures and snow to the higher elevations.

Lodgings and meals are available in Lakeview and Burns. A gas station and small convenience store are located at Plush, about 25 miles from the refuge's visitor center.

Access to Hart Mountain Refuge from Lakeview is north 5 miles on U.S. Route 395, east (right) 16 miles on State Route 140, northeast (left) 19 miles to Plush, north (left) 1 mile, and northeast (right) to the refuge's visitor center (the road is paved only to the top of the west-facing escarpment). From U.S. Route 20 at Burns, it is south 71 miles on State Route 205 (through Malheur National Wildlife Refuge and Frenchglen) and southwest (right) 52 miles on a graded road to the visitor center.

Further information: Hart Mountain National Antelope Refuge, P.O. Box 111, Lakeview, OR 97630; telephone: (541) 947-3315.

Julia Butler Hansen (see text under Washington)

Klamath Marsh, comprising 40,646 acres, was established in 1958 to protect and manage a large cattail-and-bulrush marsh and surrounding meadows and pine forest. The refuge is located within the northern end of the Klamath Basin in south-central Oregon.

The refuge's wetland habitat attracts impressive concentrations of ducks, geese, swans, and shorebirds; the grasslands provide feeding and nesting habitat for sandhill cranes; and the forest of ponderosa and lodgepole pines is inhabited by numerous species of wildlife, including the Rocky Mountain elk and great gray owl. Over 160 bird species use the refuge.

The Klamath Marsh Refuge was initially established as the 16,400-acre Klamath Forest National Wildlife Refuge. It was purchased from the Klamath Indians with revenues from the sale of Duck Stamps. The refuge was expanded in 1990 and again 1998, to include virtually all of the historic wetland in this area, and it was subsequently renamed Klamath Marsh NWR. It is one of six national wildlife refuges in the Klamath Basin. The others are Upper Klamath and Bear Valley, in Oregon; Lower Klamath, in Oregon/California; and Tule Lake and Clear Lake, in California (see separate texts on each of these refuges). A discussion of the history of the Klamath Basin's wetlands and peak influxes of migratory waterfowl and other water birds is presented in the Lower Klamath Refuge text. The Klamath Basin Wildlife Association, a nonprofit organization, helps these refuges in a variety of ways.

Klamath Marsh Refuge is open daily during daylight hours. There is no entrance fee. The refuge headquarters is open daily, except on national holidays. The Klamath Basin NWRs headquarters/visitor center, located 5 miles west of the California community of Tulelake on Hill Road, is open daily, except on Christmas and New Year's Day.

Visitor activities on Klamath Marsh Refuge include birdwatching; photography; driving a gravel loop road; hiking and cross-country skiing on a 10-mile loop trail that offers views of marsh and forest habitats; canoeing; fishing; and hunting (goose, duck, coot, and snipe) on the area to the south of Silver Lake Highway, during the designated seasons. Only motorless boats are permitted within this hunting area. Roughly 700 acres at the southern end of the marsh are available for canoeing. The canoe trail is usually open from July 1 through September (closures may occur during this period, to avoid disturbing wildlife or because of fluctuating water levels). Motorized water-craft and fishing are not permitted within this area. Camping is not permitted on the refuge, but campground facilities are provided on the adjacent Winema National Forest.

Insect repellent and sunscreen are advised during the warmer months.

Lodgings and meals are available in Klamath Falls.

Access from Klamath Falls to Klamath Marsh Refuge's hiking trail and canoe launch is north 45 miles on U.S. Route 97, east (right) on Silver Lake Road, and south (right) 4 miles on U.S. Forest Service road 690.

Further information: Klamath Marsh National Wildlife Refuge, c/o Klamath Basin NWRs, 4009 Hill Road, Tulelake, CA 96143; telephone: (530) 667-2231.

Lewis and Clark, consisting of 41,034 acres, was established in 1972 to protect approximately 20 riverine islands that total about 8,000 acres of tidal wetlands amid a maze of sloughs and other waterways, adjacent to the wave-tossed, open water of the Columbia River estuary in northwestern Oregon. Over 160 bird species have been recorded here.

This place remains mostly as the Lewis and Clark Expedition must have seen it when they canoed toward the mouth of the Columbia River on November 7, 1805, and again as they began their eastward return trip, following the estuary's south shore, on March 23, 1806, after their challenging winter at nearby Fort Clatsop.

These estuarine islands contain mostly marsh habitat with smaller areas of upland pasture, sand flats, and tidal swamp with Sitka spruces, black cottonwoods, Pacific dogwoods, and willows. At high tide, some low islands virtually disappear under water.

Refuge wildlife includes large numbers of ducks, geese, gulls, terns, wading birds, shorebirds, raptors including bald eagles, and songbirds. The largest concentrations of waterfowl are attracted to the refuge during the winter months, when there are hundreds of tundra swans, thousands of Canada geese, and tens of thousands of ducks of many species.

The refuge is open daily during daylight hours. There is no entrance fee.

Visitor activities include birdwatching, photography, sea kayaking and canoeing, fishing, and hunting (goose, duck, coot, and snipe) during the designated seasons. Swimming is not permitted on the refuge.

A number of canoe/kayak-launching sites are available nearby, including Aldrich Point and John Day boat launches, in Oregon; and the Cathlamet Marina and Skamokawa boat launch, in Washington. Part of the Columbia River Heritage Canoe Trail runs through the refuge. Several kayaking/canoeing routes are suggested in the guidebook *Canoe and Kayak Routes of Northwest Oregon*, by Philip N. Jones (The Mountaineers, Seattle, WA, 1997). Visitors are cautioned that basic paddling skills are needed, that the maze of waterways can easily be disorienting (a compass is advised), and that it is important to be aware of the tides and weather forecasts. Less experienced paddlers are urged to remain in the back waterways that are more sheltered from winds and rough water. The Lower Columbia River Lewis and Clark Water Trail, running from Bonneville Dam to the Pacific Ocean, also passes through the Lewis and Clark Refuge.

Lodgings and meals are available in Astoria, Oregon and Cathlamet, Washington.

Boat access launch sites are reached from Oregon State Route 30 and Washington State Route 4.

Further information: Lewis and Clark National Wildlife Refuge, c/o Julia Butler Hansen Refuge, P.O. Box 566, Cathlamet, WA 98612; telephone: (360) 795-3915.

Lower Klamath (see text under California)

Malheur, containing more than 186,500 acres, was initially established in 1908 by President Theodore Roosevelt as a wetland bird refuge for herons, egrets, and ibis in the Harney Basin of southeastern Oregon. The refuge's diversity of habitats in and adjacent to the Blitzen Valley include lakes and ponds, extensive areas of marsh and lush meadows, stark expanses of playa, and bordering high-desert, sagebrush uplands and rimrock cliffs of dark basaltic lava rock. Over 320 bird species have been recorded here.

The most spectacular concentrations of birds come to Malheur Refuge during the spring. As early as February, tundra swans and pintails start arriving. Soon there are large flocks of greater and lesser sandhill cranes. Peak influxes of waterfowl occur during March. In March and April, there may be more than 200,000 and sometimes more than 300,000 snow and Ross's geese, the latter migrating toward their arctic breeding grounds in northern Canada. Migrating shorebirds are most numerous in April, and neotropical songbirds reach their peak numbers in May.

Some species of waterfowl, including trumpeter swans and many ducks, come to Malheur to nest and raise their young from May through July. And in early July, many shorebirds begin their return southward, pausing in great numbers on the refuge's mudflats and playas.

The autumn migration brings heightened activity at Malheur, as described by the U.S. Fish and Wildlife Service:

One of the refuge's greatest attractions occurs in September and October, when greater sandhill cranes "stage," or gather, in the southern Blitzen Valley before migrating to wintering grounds in California's Central Valley. Look for large flocks of ducks and Canada geese during these months. In November, tundra swans can be seen in abundance.

Winter provides the quietest season, and many of the ponds freeze over. Yet, bald and golden eagles, northern harriers, rough-legged hawks, mallards, and common goldeneyes are among the common wintering species.

The Fish and Wildlife Service carries out a number of habitat management activities on Malheur Refuge. A system of dams, levees, canals, ditches, and water control structures is used to regulate water supplies for the ponds, marshes, and meadows. For example, water levels are raised to provide favorable habitat for water birds while they raise their broods; and they are lowered to promote the growth of desirable plant foods for waterfowl. Willows, which are planted along the refuge's riparian border of the Donner und Blitzen River, provide additional shelter, food, and nest sites for many species of wildlife.

Other management activities include mowing, grazing, and prescribed burning of meadows to maintain feeding habitat for Canada geese and sandhill cranes and nesting habitat for many waterfowl. Fire is especially important in promoting nutrient cycling and triggering new growth of grasses and forbs valued by wildlife.

Fire is also carefully applied to Malheur Refuge's upland areas of sagebrush and greasewood to stimulate the growth of such native grasses as Great Basin wild-rye and to create diversity within the sagebrush-steppe habitat that benefits such species as the pronghorn, mule deer, quail, and greater sage-grouse (see discussions of the latter in the Hart Mountain and Seedskadee, Wyoming, texts).

During the first several decades of the twentieth century, increasing quantities of water were being diverted from the Donner und Blitzen River for agricultural irrigation, thereby reducing the water available for maintaining the wetlands for wildlife. A string of dry years in the early 1930s finally prompted the acquisition of 64,000 acres in 1935, so that the refuge could maintain water in Malheur Lake. In 1941, nearly 15,000 acres to the northwest of Harney Lake were added, and the refuge was officially named as a national wildlife refuge.

For the benefit of the redband trout and other native fishes, the Fish and Wildlife Service has carried out a 3.5-mile riparian and fish-habitat improvement project on the Donner und Blitzen River near P-Ranch. Three new fish ladders have been installed within existing water control structures to improve fish passage, and state-of-the-art fish screens have been constructed. Consequently, the historic trout migration has been reestablished and enhanced to more than 60 miles of headwater spawning areas in the Steens Mountain/Blitzen River watershed. Ducks Unlimited, Inc. has helped enhance more than 29,000 acres of the refuge's wetland habitat. The Malheur Refuge Association is a local, nonprofit organization that assists the refuge in a variety of ways.

The refuge is open daily during daylight hours. There is no entrance fee. The refuge headquarters, visitor center, and George Benson Memorial Museum are open on weekdays, except national holidays. The visitor center and museum are also open on most weekends during the spring and summer. Of historic interest are the P-Ranch's Long Barn, beef wheel, and willow corrals, located at the southern end of the refuge and dating from the 1880s. A walk on a nearby dike offers an opportunity to view wildlife that inhabits riparian willow habitat.

Visitor activities include wildlife observation; photography; viewing interpretive exhibits at the museum; driving the gravel auto tour route (Center Patrol Road), other refuge roads that are open to visitors, and paved State Route 205; bicycling and horseback riding on roads open to motor vehicles; hiking; canoeing and boating (electric motors only) on Krumbo Reservoir (a dock and ramp are provided) during the fishing season and on the north side of Malheur Lake during the waterfowl hunting season; fishing (a fishing platform is provided at Krumbo Reservoir); and hunting (antelope, deer, waterfowl, coot, quail, dove, and the non-native chukar, ring-necked pheasant, and gray partridge) on parts of the refuge during the designated seasons. Swimming is not permitted.

Although camping is not permitted on the refuge, Page Springs Campground and several others provided by the U.S. Bureau of Land Management (BLM) are located to the south of the refuge along the Steens Mountain loop road; information: (541) 573-4400. Other campgrounds are located to the north of the refuge in the Malheur National Forest; information: (541) 573-4300.

Hiking opportunities include two 0.25-mile foot paths that lead to overlooks at the headquarters/visitor center and at the Buena Vista Ponds; the Barnes Springs Foot Path near Frenchglen; the 13-mile public-fishing loop near P-Ranch; and the path encircling Krumbo Reservoir. Hiking is also permitted on roads open to motor vehicles. No other refuge lands are open to hiking.

Insect repellent and sunscreen are recommended during the warmer months. Visitors are cautioned to be alert for sudden weather and temperature changes and to be alert for rattlesnakes.

Lodgings and meals are available in Burns; meals and groceries are available at the Narrows; and fuel and limited groceries are available in Crane, Frenchglen, and Diamond.

Access to Malheur Refuge's headquarters/visitor center from Burns is east about 2 miles on State Route 78, south (right) 26 miles on State Route 205, and east (left) 6 miles on Sodhouse Lane (County Road 405); or from Hart Mountain Refuge's visitor center, it is northeast 36 miles on the graded road and north (left) 10 miles on State Route 205 to Frenchglen, at the southern end of the refuge.

Further information: Malheur National Wildlife Refuge, 36391 Sodhouse Lane, Princeton, OR 97721; telephone: (541) 493-2612.

McKay Creek, encompassing 1,837 acres, was established in 1927. The refuge overlays a U.S. Bureau of Reclamation irrigation reservoir in the high desert of northeastern Oregon. The U.S. Fish and Wildlife Service manages the bordering riparian habitat of cottonwoods, willows, and other vegetation, and the bureau manages the water. The level of McKay Reservoir fluctuates seasonally, shrinking from 1,300 acres of open water at full pool in late spring, to an average of a mere 250 acres at minimum pool by late summer.

Large concentrations of migrating and wintering waterfowl are attracted to McKay (pronounced Ma-KEY) Creek refuge. Peak populations during the winter total more than 30,000 ducks and geese, the majority of which are mallards and Canada geese, with lesser numbers of such species as northern pintail, American wigeon, and green-winged teal. Other birds include the pied-billed grebe, great blue heron, black-crowned night heron, western and least sandpipers, the non-native ring-necked pheasant and gray partridge, bald and golden eagles, Swainson's and red-tailed hawks, and great horned owl. Mammals include mule deer, bobcat, coyote, badger, black-tailed jackrabbit, pygmy rabbit, and Ord kangaroo rat.

The refuge is open daily during daylight hours to general visitation (except during the January–February waterfowl-hunting season). There is no entrance fee. The headquarters, located at 830 Sixth Street, Umatilla, is open on weekdays, except national holidays.

Visitor activities include wildlife observation, photography, driving the refuge's gravel entrance road along the reservoir's west shore and a county road along the east shore, hiking, boating from March 1 through September 30 (boat-launching ramps are available), fishing, and hunting (geese, duck, pheasant, gray partridge, and quail) on certain days during the designated seasons.

Insect repellent and sunscreen are advised during the warmer months.

Lodgings are available in Pendleton.

Access to McKay Creek Refuge from Pendleton is south approximately 8 miles on U.S. Route 395 and east (left) into the refuge.

Further information: McKay Creek National Wildlife Refuge, c/o Mid-Columbia River NWR Complex, P.O. Box 700, Umatilla, OR 97882; telephone: (509) 545-8588.

Nestucca Bay presently comprises 730 acres toward an authorized goal of 3,436 acres. The three separate parts of the refuge—the Nestucca River Unit, Little Nestucca River Unit, and Neskowin Marsh Unit—are located between Pacific City and Neskowin on the northern coast of Oregon.

The refuge was established in 1991 to enhance and protect important wintering habitat for the only coastal population of dusky Canada geese and the world's population of approximately 100 to 150 Semidi Islands Aleutian Canada geese. The refuge's pasture management program, providing habitat for the concentrations of geese, is being implemented under the terms of cooperative land management agreements with local dairy operators. The refuge also protects habitat for estuarine-dependent fish and wildlife.

Habitats include salt marsh, riparian wetlands, managed pastures, and forested uplands. The Neskowin Marsh Unit also protects the southernmost coastal sphagnum bog on the Pacific Coast.

Many species of ducks, wading birds, shorebirds, neotropical and resident songbirds, peregrine falcons, and bald eagles are attracted to the refuge. Nestucca Bay and its rivers support significant spawning migrations of such anadromous fish as steelhead and cutthroat trout, chinook, and coho salmon. Research has also shown that substantial numbers of juvenile cutthroat trout and coho salmon inhabit Neskowin Marsh.

The U.S. Fish and Wildlife Service hopes that an 86-acre tidal marsh restoration project, which is planned to improve habitat within the Little Nestucca River Unit, can soon be accomplished. Cooperative activities are currently being undertaken to restore the historic forest of Sitka spruce, western hemlock, and Douglas fir on the slopes of Cannery Hill and to enhance the riparian habitat along Upton Slough. Partners with the Fish and Wildlife Service include several local schools, The Nature Conservancy, the Nestucca-Neskowin Watershed Council, Tillamook Soil and Water Conservation District, Oregon Department of Corrections, U.S. Forest Service, U.S. Bureau of Land Management, and Ducks Unlimited, Inc.

Opportunities to view the Nestucca Bay Refuge, including geese and other wildlife, are from the county road that runs along the edge of the Nestucca River Unit between U.S. Route 101 and Pacific City; from U.S. Route 101 where it runs through the Little Nestucca River Unit between Cloverdale and Oretown; and from U.S. Route 101 where it runs close to the eastern boundary of the Neskowin Marsh Unit near Neskowin Beach. Opportunities for visitor use are currently being planned.

Lodgings and meals are available in Pacific City and Neskowin.

Further information: Nestucca Bay National Wildlife Refuge, c/o Oregon Coast NWR Complex, 2127 SE OSU Drive, Newport, OR 97365; telephone: (541) 867-4550.

Oregon Islands, consisting of approximately 900 acres, was initially established as the Goat Island Reservation in 1935 and was renamed as a national wildlife refuge in 1940. The refuge contains more than 1,400 offshore rocks, sea stacks, reefs, and islands scattered along virtually the entire length of the scenic coast of Oregon. There are also two mainland units: Coquille Point near Bandon, and Crook Point between Gold Beach and Brookings.

Thirteen species of nesting seabirds are attracted to the array of rocky, surf-pounded habitats that jut out of the Pacific Ocean. They include Leach's and fork-tailed storm petrels, Brandt's and pelagic cormorants, common murres, pigeon guillemots, rhinoceros auklets, and tufted puffins. (For a discussion of the latter species, see under California the Farallon Refuge text.) An estimated 1.2 million seabirds nest along the Oregon coast, which is more than nest along the Washington and California coasts combined. According to the U.S. Fish and Wildlife Service, more than 700,000 common murres, which is approximately two-thirds of the total nesting population south of Alaska, nest along the Oregon coast. The Oregon Coast NWR Complex's project leader, Roy W. Lowe, says, "Most of the nesting seabirds in Oregon use this refuge because of the abundance and diversity of nesting habitat managed as sanctuary for wildlife and the location of the refuge with a productive marine ecosystem."

Great numbers of pinnipeds use the refuge for haulout and/or pupping. These marine mammals include more than 5,000 harbor seals, 100 northern elephant seals, 4,000 California sea lions, and 4,000 Steller sea lions. The latter is a federally listed threatened species.

Many of the refuge's islands, sea stacks, rocks, and reefs can be viewed from mainland sites, such as state parks and other scenic overlooks along the coast. Among the best of these viewing locations (from north to south) are Ecola State Park, just north of Cannon Beach; Haystack Rock, in Cannon Beach; Yaquina Head Outstanding Natural Area, near Newport; Heceta Head Lighthouse/Devils Elbow State Park/Sea Lion Caves, between Yachats (pronounced YAH-hahts) and Florence; Cape Arago State Park, southwest of Coos Bay; Coquille Point, in Bandon; Cape Blanco, south of Bandon; and Boardman State Park, north of Brookings.

To avoid disturbing the extremely sensitive seabird colonies and marine mammals, all of the refuge's offshore islands, rocks, and reefs are closed to public visitation. In addition, all watercraft are requested to remain at least 500 feet away. Most of the refuge has also been designated as the Oregon Islands Wilderness, a unit of the National Wilderness Preservation System.

One of the largest sea stacks is 235-foot Haystack Rock, in Cannon Beach. Depending on the twice-daily tidal fluctuations, this huge rock is either surrounded by the ocean or is connected to the beach. To avoid disturbing the seabird colonies, climbing Haystack Rock is not permitted. According to the U.S. Fish and Wildlife Service, more than 700,000 common murres nest along the Oregon coast. This is approximately two-thirds of the total nesting population south of Alaska. To help the U.S. Fish and Wildlife Service promote the protection of the rock's sensitive ecosystem and provide educational information (an interpretive brochure is available), the Haystack Rock Awareness Program was established by the local Puffin Club. Assistance was provided by the City of Cannon Beach, Seaside School District 10, the Oregon Department of Fish and Wildlife, the Governor's Watershed Enhancement Board, and the Seaside Aquarium.

Two other nonprofit organizations are assisting by offering interpretive services and brochures on the Oregon south coast: Shoreline Education for Awareness, Inc. provides docent-led, on-site interpretative programs, campfire talks, and intertidal guided walks for visitors and school groups from Memorial Day to Labor Day, and by appointment as docents are available during the rest of the year. Information: P.O. Box 957, Bandon, OR 97411; telephone: (541) 347-3683. Friends of Shore Acres, Inc. offers interpretive services at Shore Acres State Park and other parks in the Sunset Bay State Park District. Information: P.O. Box 1172, Coos Bay, OR 97420; telephone: (541) 888-4902 or 888-3732.

In 1991–92, five parcels totaling 36 acres were acquired at Coquille Point, in Bandon, making this the first mainland addition to the Oregon Islands Refuge. A popular visitor use area, Coquille Point, is open daily to visitors. As Roy W. Lowe explains:

The purpose of this mainland addition to the refuge was to protect adjacent seabird nesting colonies from encroaching development, provide a highly visible public use area for environmental education and interpretation, and restore native habitat on the headland. I'm proud to say that we have been successful in all three areas. Fully accessible paved trails and a parking area were constructed and stairways to the beach, at the north and south ends of the headland, were added. Native grassland habitat has been restored and interpretive panels have been installed throughout the area. As a result, the headland is protected in perpetuity and educational efforts have all but eliminated trespass on the adjacent rocks.

Crook Point, the second mainland addition to Oregon Islands NWR, was acquired in May 2000. This site (located between Gold Beach and Brookings) contains numerous rare plant species, undisturbed cultural resource sites, and 1 mile of pristine beach and intertidal rocky habitat and serves to protect major seabird colonies. This area is managed as a biological reserve and is not yet open to visitors.

Unfortunately, there have occasionally been harmful oil spills along Oregon's ecologically vulnerable coast. Fish and Wildlife Service personnel are currently leading the seabird restoration planning effort resulting from an extensive oil spill caused when the 639-foot freighter *New Carissa* ran aground near Coos Bay in February 1999. More than 2,300 seabirds, including more than 260 of the threatened marbled murrelet, were estimated to have been killed by oil from the wrecked vessel. As of late 2001, cleanup costs were reported to have already exceeded $30 million. According to the Service, "Restoration activities could include land acquisition, seabird colony protection measures, environmental education and other measures."

Lodgings and meals are available in numerous communities along the Oregon coast, including Bandon at the refuge's Coquille Point unit.

Access to most of the viewing places of the Oregon Islands Refuge is along or just off of U.S. Route 101. Access to the Coquille Point unit from U.S. Route 101 in Bandon is west on Eleventh Street to the end of the road.

Further information: Oregon Islands National Wildlife Refuge, c/o Oregon Coast NWR Complex, 2127 SE OSU Drive, Newport, OR 97365; telephone (541) 867-4550.

Sheldon (see text under Nevada)

Siletz Bay, currently containing 519 acres toward a goal of 1,936 acres, was established in 1991 to protect salt marsh, brackish marsh, tidal sloughs and mudflats, and coniferous and deciduous forest. The refuge is located on Siletz Bay, just south of Lincoln City on the northern coast of Oregon.

Prominent among wintering waterfowl that use the refuge are northern pintail, American wigeon, green-winged teal, and bufflehead. In addition, brown pelicans, wading birds, shorebirds, neotropical and resident songbirds, peregrine falcons, and bald eagles are attracted here. A previously used nesting area of the western snowy plover lies within the authorized refuge boundary, offering the hope that this species will return to nest.

Mammals include Roosevelt elk, black-tailed deer, and river otters. Harbor seals use the bay daily and are often seen hauled out at the mouth of the bay. The Siletz Bay and River ecosystem supports large runs of anadromous fish, such as steelhead, cutthroat trout, chinook, and coho salmon, along with other estuarine-dependent fin- and shellfish.

The primary habitat management goal of this refuge is to restore, enhance, and protect this area's extensive tidal wetlands. One large restoration project has recently been completed with the assistance of Ducks Unlimited, Inc. The U.S. Fish and Wildlife Service hopes that it will be possible to accomplish two other projects, raising the total of restored tidal marsh to 325 acres.

Juvenile salmonids will benefit greatly from completed and planned tidal marsh restoration and enhancement. As the Fish and Wildlife Service explains, "The refuge is working with the U.S. Forest Service and the Confederated Tribes of the Siletz Indians through a Challenge Cost-Share Agreement to monitor juvenile salmonids in the Siletz Estuary and assess their response to habitat restoration and enhancement."

Siletz Bay can be viewed from U.S. Route 101, which runs through the refuge in the vicinity of Drift Creek and the Siletz River; and from State Route 229, which branches east from Route 101 along the Siletz River. Opportunities for visitor use are planned.

Lodgings and meals are available in Lincoln City, Gleneden Beach, and Depoe Bay.

Further information: Siletz Bay National Wildlife Refuge, c/o Oregon Coast NWR Complex, 2127 SE OSU Drive, Newport, OR 97365; telephone: (541) 867-4550.

Three Arch Rocks, encompassing 15 acres, was established in 1907 by President Theodore Roosevelt and became the first national wildlife refuge west of the Mississippi River. The refuge has also been designated as the Three Arch Rocks Wilderness, one of the smallest units in the National Wilderness Preservation System. It is located one-half mile offshore from the community of Oceanside, on the northern coast of Oregon.

The refuge consists of three gigantic, surf-pounded rocks (and six smaller rocks) that rise dramatically from the Pacific Ocean. All three large rocks contain a large arch, hence the name. These barren habitats support Oregon's largest colony of nesting seabirds, which is estimated at more than 230,000 individuals of 12 species. The state's largest nesting colony of tufted puffins is located on Finley Rock and is estimated at between 2,000 and 4,000 of these comical-looking alcids. (For a discussion of the latter species, see in California the Farallon Refuge text.) The refuge supports more than 200,000 nesting common murres—the largest murre colony south of Alaska. Other breeding birds include pigeon guillemot, rhinoceros auklet, three species of cormorants, and glaucous-winged and western gulls. The refuge's Seal Rock is the only breeding place for the threatened Steller sea lion on the state's northern coast. Other pinnipeds include California sea lions.

The U.S. Fish and Wildlife Service explains how Three Arch Rocks became the first refuge in the West:

By the early 1900s, many seabird colonies on the West Coast were in danger of being wiped out. During the California Gold Rush, egg hunters harvested millions of eggs annually to supply restaurants in San Francisco and the gold fields. Adult birds were slaughtered for target practice as weekend sport. Unfortunately, most people were unaware of the problem.

In the early 1900s, naturalist and photographer William Finley and his partner Herman Bohlman visited the Oregon Coast and documented the devastation. They launched open boats through heavy surf and then literally risked life and limb to haul heavy photographic equipment up and down steep, treacherous cliffs. Finley informed President Theodore Roosevelt of the national importance of this seabird nesting area, convincing him to issue an Executive Order designating Three Arch Rocks the first National Wildlife Refuge on the west coast. . . .

The refuge can be viewed from Oceanside Beach and Cape Meares.

To avoid disturbing the extremely sensitive seabirds and marine mammals, the refuge is closed to visitation. In addition, the waters within 500 feet of the rocks are closed to all watercraft from May 1 through September 15.

Lodgings and meals are available in Netarts, Oceanside, and Tillamook.

Access to Oceanside and Cape Meares is west from U.S. 101 at Tillamook on the Three Capes Scenic Loop Road.

Further information: Three Arch Rocks National Wildlife Refuge, c/o Oregon Coast NWR Complex, 2127 SE OSU Drive, Newport, OR 97365; telephone: (541) 867-4550.

Tualatin River, consisting of more than 1,200 acres toward a goal of 3,058 acres, was established in 1992 to protect several ecologically important remnants of floodplain habitats along the meandering Tualatin River. The refuge is located near Sherwood, about 15 miles south of downtown Portland, Oregon. Over 160 bird species have been seen here.

Habitats along this tributary of the Willamette River include permanent and seasonal emergent freshwater wetlands, creeks, ponds, grasslands, and riparian and upland woodlands. Among the trees are Douglas fir, Oregon white oak, black cottonwood, red alder, bigleaf and vine maples, and Oregon ash.

Some of the more prominent species of waterfowl are three subspecies of Canada geese (western, dusky, and cackling), as well as tundra swans, mallards, pintails, wigeons, wood ducks, and hooded mergansers. Raptors include bald eagles and peregrine falcons.

A major mission of the refuge is the implementation of what the U.S. Fish and Wildlife Service describes as "a dynamic wetland restoration program." As of this time, a few hundred acres of seasonal, permanent, and forested wetlands on the refuge's Steinborn Unit have been restored. Partners with the Fish and Wildlife Service in this important effort include the Friends of the Refuge, Tualatin Riverkeepers, Ducks Unlimited, Inc. (which has helped enhance more than 450 acres of wetland habitat), METRO, the Oregon Department of Fish and Wildlife, and the U.S. Bureau of Reclamation. The refuge staff are also presently implementing plans to restore 40 acres of wetland floodplain and 30 acres of upland habitats on various units of the refuge. As the Fish and Wildlife Service explains:

All of these restoration projects will provide valuable habitat for migratory waterfowl, shorebirds, marsh birds, neotropical migratory birds, amphibians, reptiles, resident and anadromous fish, and . . . resident mammal species. . . . Fishery efforts to date consist of the construction of fish ladders to restore movement of native cutthroat trout to upper spawning and rearing habitats of the Chicken Creek watershed and consultation with the National Marine Fisheries Service for enhancing backwater habitats for fish during flood events. Water flowing through wetland basins will improve water quality characteristics of the Tualatin River used by migrating winter steelhead and spring chinook salmon, both of which are listed as threatened species.

Project leader Ralph Webber explains that the Tualatin River Refuge was established "during unprecedented urban development and expansion, to preserve, protect, and restore a portion of the basin's habitats. . . . Purchase of lands . . . is well under way, with approximately ⅓ of the approved 3,058 acres for acquisition presently owned by the Fish and Wildlife Service. . . . public-use facility planning is proceeding, in an effort to provide unique close-to-home opportunities for people of all ages to learn about and enjoy fish and wildlife resources."

The Friends of the Tualatin River National Wildlife Refuge is a nonprofit organization that assists the refuge in a variety of ways.

Although the Tualatin River Refuge is presently not open to visitation, several county roads provide opportunities to view the area, and the refuge can be glimpsed from State Route 99W, between Metzger and Tigard. Refuge planning anticipates the development of some visitor use facilities, such as interpretive hiking trails, wildlife observation structures, and interpretive panels. Also envisioned for the refuge is an environmental education center that would provide interpretive exhibits, an auditorium for interpretive and environmental education programs, environmental education classrooms and laboratory, and adjoining refuge offices. The refuge also offers outreach and special events each year, to help the public learn about the refuge.

Lodgings and meals are available in such communities as Tigard, Tualatin, Sherwood, and Portland.

Further information: Tualatin River National Wildlife Refuge, 16340 SW Beef Bend Road, Sherwood, OR 97140; telephone: (503) 590-5811.

Umatilla, comprising 25,347 acres, was established in 1969 to mitigate the inundation of wetland habitat that resulted from the construction of the John Day Dam on the Columbia River. The refuge manages a 20-mile stretch of the river's islands and backwater sloughs, riparian woodlands of cottonwood trees, croplands, adjacent uplands of high-desert sagebrush and bitterbrush habitat, and an area of sand dunes in northern Oregon and southern Washington.

Large concentrations of wintering waterfowl are attracted to the refuge. They include tens of thousands of Canada geese and anywhere from just fewer than 100,000 to more than 400,000 ducks of many species. The islands offer important breeding habitat for Canada geese, terns, and colonies of great blue herons and cormorants. Tundra swans pause to rest and feed on the refuge during their spring and autumn migrations. Notable among Umatilla Refuge's shorebirds is the long-billed curlew, whose down-curved beak is nearly as long as its entire body and whose amazing aerial courtship of whirring wings and diving acrobatics can be seen in March. Several hundred pairs of curlews nest here from March to June.

Ducks Unlimited, Inc. has helped enhance more than 350 acres of the refuge's wetland habitat.

The refuge is open daily during daylight hours. There is no entrance fee. The headquarters, located at 830 Sixth Street, Umatilla, is open on weekdays, except national holidays.

Visitor activities include birdwatching; photography; driving the 5-mile auto tour route through the McCormack Unit, in Oregon; hiking, bicycling, and horseback riding on refuge roads open to motor vehicles; boating, kayaking, and canoeing (a number of boat-launching ramps are available); fishing; and hunting (deer, ducks and Canada geese, coot, snipe, pheasant, and quail) on parts of the refuge during the designated seasons. Camping is not permitted on the refuge, but campground facilities are provided at Oregon's Hat Rock State Park (east of the refuge) and Washington's Crow Butte State Park (west of the refuge).

Lodgings and meals are available in such communities as Boardman and Hermiston, Oregon and Kennewick and Goldendale, Washington.

Access to Umatilla Refuge units in Oregon: the BOARDMAN UNIT is reached from Exit 164 on I-84 at Boardman, and the McCormack Unit is from Exit 168 on I-84, east on U.S. Route 730, and north to the unit entrance. In Washington, the WHITCOMB, RIDGE, and PATERSON UNITS are reached from State Route 14.

Further information: Umatilla National Wildlife Refuge, c/o Mid-Columbia River NWR Complex, P.O. Box 700, Umatilla, OR 97882; telephone: (509) 545- 8588.

Upper Klamath, containing 14,966 acres in two units, was established in 1928 to protect and manage important marsh habitat containing such aquatic plants as cattail, bulrush, and spatterdock (yellow pond lily or wocus). In addition, there are bordering areas of black cottonwoods, willows, and quaking aspens. The main unit of the refuge is located along the northwest end of Upper Klamath Lake, and the smaller unit is at the southeast corner of the lake, within the Klamath Basin in south-central Oregon.

Upper Klamath Refuge is one of six national wildlife refuges in the Klamath Basin. The others are Klamath Marsh and Bear Valley, in Oregon; Lower Klamath, in Oregon/California; and Tule Lake and Clear Lake, in California (see separate texts on these refuges). A discussion of the history of the Klamath Basin's wetlands and peak influxes of migratory waterfowl and other water birds is presented in the Lower Klamath Refuge text. The Klamath Basin Wildlife Association, a nonprofit organization, helps these refuges.

The wetlands habitat attracts large numbers of nesting and migrating waterfowl, colonial-nesting American white pelicans and herons, and other water birds. River otters, beavers, and muskrats are common mammals. Birds that have been recorded on the Upper Klamath Refuge are virtually the same as those on Lower Klamath Refuge.

The refuge is open daily during daylight hours. There is no entrance fee. The Klamath Basin NWRs headquarters/visitor center, located 5 miles west of the California community of Tulelake, on Hill Road, is open daily, except on Christmas and New Year's Day.

Visitor activities on Upper Klamath Refuge include wildlife observation, photography, canoeing/boating, fishing, and hunting (goose, duck, coot, and snipe) on parts of the refuge during the designated seasons. Camping is not permitted on the refuge, but campground facilities are available on the adjacent Winema National Forest.

The best way to explore Upper Klamath Refuge's wetlands is by canoe (rentals are available nearby). The 9.5-mile Upper Klamath Canoe Trail, located partly on the refuge and partly on Winema National Forest, offers excellent opportunities to view the freshwater marsh, open water of Upper Klamath Lake's Pelican Bay, forest, and mountains. Two boat-launching sites are available. The canoe route can be enjoyed in a variety of shorter segments and loops (a canoe-trail leaflet is available). Canoeists are urged to remain on the designated canoe trail. Other areas of the refuge are closed to visitation, to avoid disturbing the activities of nesting birds.

Insect repellent and sunscreen are among a number of important items for a canoeing excursion on the refuge.

Lodgings and meals are available in Klamath Falls.

Access from Klamath Falls to Upper Klamath Refuge's canoe trail is northwest 26 miles on State Route 140 and north (right) on Rocky Point Road to Rocky Point Boat Launch; or continuing north on Westside Road to Malone Springs Boat Launch.

Further information: Upper Klamath National Wildlife Refuge, c/o Klamath Basin NWRs, 4009 Hill Road, Tulelake, CA 96134; telephone: (530) 667-2231.

William L. Finley, encompassing 5,325 acres, was established in 1964 as the first of three national wildlife refuges in the Willamette Valley NWR Complex. The primary purpose of the refuge is to provide wintering habitat for dusky Canada geese and other waterfowl. It is located between Corvallis and Eugene, in the Willamette Valley of west-central Oregon.

The refuge was named in honor of the early photographer–naturalist William L. Finley, who convinced President Theodore Roosevelt to designate national wildlife refuges in the West. As a result of Finley's efforts, Malheur, Klamath, and Three Arch Rocks were established as refuges (see the latter refuge text for further discussion).

The refuge's diverse habitats include areas of Oregon white oak savanna; old-growth bigleaf maples; bottomland Oregon ash, black cottonwood, and willows along meandering Muddy Creek; native wet prairie; and fields of food crops that are planted for the benefit of wildlife. The refuge contains one of the largest remaining native wet-prairie habitats in the Willamette Valley—a 450-acre remnant at the northeast entrance. Refuge staff and helpful volunteers are working to restore native plant communities, including oak savanna and wet prairie, through control of non-native species, planting of native species, and fire management.

During the fall, winter, and spring, Canada geese can be seen here in large numbers as they feed and rest on the refuge's rich farmed grasslands on their migratory journey south. Dusky Canada geese make the refuge their winter home, then return to the Copper River Delta in southern Alaska in the spring (see also the Ankeny, Baskett Slough, and Ridgefield [Washington] refuge texts). Many ducks, geese, swans, and shorebirds can also be seen here in the fall and winter.

Mallards, wood ducks, hooded mergansers, and coots nest on the refuge. A visit to Cabell Marsh and Beaver Pond in June or July may offer opportunities to see these birds with their young feeding and swimming. Over 235 bird species have been recorded here.

Many species of raptors are attracted to the refuge. They include ospreys, bald eagles, peregrine falcons, and white-tailed kites. The latter are occasionally seen flying over native prairie habitat near the refuge's northern entrance. Prominent among the mammals are the stately Roosevelt elk (*Cervus elaphus roosevelti*) and black-tailed deer (*Odocoileus hemionus columbianus*), the latter a Pacific Northwest subspecies of the mule deer. A number of endangered and threatened species can be found on the refuge, including several plants and the Oregon chub, a small freshwater fish.

Of historic interest is the Fiechter House, completed in 1857. This two-story, wood-frame structure, of the Classical Revival style of architecture, is believed to be the oldest house in Benton County. It is listed on the National Register of Historic Places and is opened periodically by the Benton County Historical Society. Several other historic buildings are situated on the refuge.

The refuge is open daily during daylight hours. Portions of the refuge are closed from November 1 through March 31, to provide a sanctuary for wintering waterfowl. There is no entrance fee. The refuge headquarters is open on weekdays, except national holidays.

Visitor activities include wildlife observation, photography, driving the auto tour route, hiking, and deer hunting on parts of the refuge during the designated seasons. A wildlife viewing kiosk is located just behind the refuge headquarters, which overlooks Cabell Marsh. A short trail leads to a wildlife viewing blind located at the south end of the refuge on McFadden Marsh, just off Bruce Road. An observation platform overlooking the wet prairie is located near the refuge's northeast entrance. Interpretive signs are placed at various turnouts along both Finley Refuge Road and Bruce Road. Although camping is not permitted on the refuge, campground facilities are available in the vicinity of Corvallis and Alsea.

Hiking opportunities include two trails that are open year-round: the 1.1-mile, self-guiding Woodpecker Loop Trail (an interpretive leaflet is available) and the 3-mile Mill Hill Trail. There are also four trails that are open from April 1 through October: the 2.5-mile Beaver Pond-Cattail Pond Trails; the 1.5-mile Pigeon Butte Trail, the 2.2-mile Cabell Marsh Trail, and the 0.5-mile Intertie Trail. Hiking is also permitted from May 1 through October, on a refuge road that runs southeast from headquarters and offers views of Cabell Marsh and Finger Ponds.

Visitors are cautioned to be alert for poison oak. Insect repellent is advised during the warmer months.

Lodgings and meals are available in such communities as Corvallis and Eugene.

Access to the William L. Finley Refuge from Exit 228 on I-5 is west 9 miles on State Route 34 to Corvallis, south (left) 10 miles on State Route 99W, and west (right) 2 miles on Finley Refuge Road to the refuge headquarters.

Further information: William L. Finley National Wildlife Refuge, c/o Willamette Valley NWR Complex, 26208 Finley Refuge Road, Corvallis, OR 97333; telephone: (541) 757-7236.

Pennsylvania

Erie, containing 8,780 acres in two divisions, was established in 1959 to enhance, manage, and protect significant wetland habitats for migratory waterfowl and other wildlife. The refuge is located a few miles south of Lake Erie in northwestern Pennsylvania.

The 5,205-acre Sugar Lake Division, near the village of Guys Mills, is an intensively managed area that lies in a long, narrow valley, running from north to south. Along north-flowing Woodcock Creek and south-flowing Lake Creek are many beaver ponds, pools, managed impoundments, and areas of marsh and swamp. The riparian wetlands are bordered by forested valley slopes with scattered agricultural lands, grassland, and wet meadows. The 3,571-acre Seneca Division, located 10 miles to the north, consists of another ecologically rich, forested valley with swamps, bogs, and other wetland habitat mostly along Muddy and Dead creeks.

As the U.S. Fish and Wildlife Service explains its management activities on the refuge:

Water control structures on refuge impoundments permit the [seasonal] manipulation of water levels to encourage the growth of waterfowl food and cover plants such as smartweeds and bulrushes. Future plans call for more than doubling the amount of manageable habitat now available.

Grasslands are being developed near wetlands to provide dense nesting cover for ground-nesting waterfowl and other birds. . . .

A cooperative farming program permits farmers to cultivate crops on refuge lands. Farmers agree to raise certain crops such as oats, grass, clover and corn. In return for using the land, farmers leave the refuge a share of the crops. These refuge shares are usually left in the field as supplemental food for wildlife.

The best months to see large concentrations of waterfowl are March and early April and September into November. As many as 4,500 Canada geese and 2,500 ducks are attracted to the refuge during the peak days of migration. Wood ducks are the most common nesting waterfowl, for which the Fish and Wildlife Service has placed nesting boxes to supplement tree cavities and enhance successful breeding. Other ducks that nest on the refuge include mallards, blue-winged teal, and hooded mergansers. Bald eagles also nest here, and great blue herons nest here in rookeries. Over 235 bird species have been recorded here.

Establishment of Erie Refuge was made possible partly with revenues from the sale of Migratory Bird Hunting and Conservation Stamps (Duck Stamps). Ducks Unlimited, Inc. has helped enhance a few acres of the refuge's wetland habitat.

The refuge is open daily during daylight hours. There is no entrance fee. The refuge's visitor center/headquarters, located on the Sugar Lake Division, is open on weekdays, except national holidays.

Visitor activities include birdwatching, photography, driving a number of township roads through the refuge, hiking, cross-country skiing, fishing (a wheelchair-accessible fishing pier is provided at Pool K), and hunting (deer, waterfowl, turkey, and some small game) on parts of the refuge during the designated seasons. By prearrangement, the refuge also provides programs and tours for school and other groups, and teacher workshops.

Hiking opportunities on the Sugar Lake Division include the Tsuga Nature Trail—a 1.2-mile or 1.6-mile two-loop path (named for the hemlock tree's Latin name, *Tsuga canadensis*) near the visitor center that includes a boardwalk across a beaver pond and that is also open to the winter pleasures of cross-country skiing and snowshoeing; Beaver Run Trail—a 1-mile loop and a spur, from Hanks Road; and Deer Run Trail—a 3-mile path from Boland Road that is also open to cross-country skiing and snowshoeing. Just south of Deer Run Trail, a short path leads from Boland Road to a wildlife observation blind overlooking Reitz's Pond. And Deer Run Overlook, off of Allen Road, offers a view of 130-acre Pool 9, where bald eagles can sometimes be seen. The Seneca Division provides the Muddy Creek Holly Trail—a 1-mile (wheelchair-accessible) boardwalk located off of Johnstown Road. The latter route is named for winterberry, a shrubby deciduous species of holly, the bright-red berries of which are prominent in winter.

Insect repellent is advised during the warmer months.

Lodgings and meals are available in such communities as Meadville, Edinboro, and Erie.

Access to Erie Refuge's visitor center from Exit 36 on I-79 is northeast 2 miles to Meadville, southeast 7 miles on State Route 27, northeast (left) 3.5 miles on State Route 3032 to Guys Mills, east about 0.75-mile on State Route 198, and south (right) onto Wood Duck Lane.

Further information: Erie National Wildlife Refuge, 11296 Wood Duck Lane, Guys Mills, PA 16327; telephone: (814) 789-3585.

John Heinz, comprising 1,200 acres, was established in 1972 to restore and protect Tinicum Marsh for the benefit of waterfowl and other wildlife. The refuge is located in the city of Philadelphia and adjacent Delaware County in southeastern Pennsylvania. The area was initially called the Tinicum National Environmental Center, but in 1991, the name was changed to the John Heinz National Wildlife Refuge at Tinicum, in honor of the United States senator who was instrumental in helping protect the marsh. Over 300 bird species use the refuge.

Tinicum was formerly a 5,700-acre, tidally influenced, freshwater marsh along Darby Creek on the west bank of the Delaware River. For many years, this ecologically rich habitat was viewed as a "wasteland" to be drained, diked, and filled with sediments dredged from the Delaware and Schuylkill rivers. By the mid-twentieth century, only about 200 acres of wetland remained undisturbed. Then in 1969, highway engineers announced their intention to obtain sand and gravel from the marsh for use in constructing Interstate 95. Conservationists mounted a legal challenge that delayed the sand and gravel extraction proposal and succeeded in having part of the freeway route shifted and obtaining congressional authorization for the restoration and protection of the area as a national wildlife refuge.

Restoring the marsh was one of the legislatively mandated goals of the refuge. As the Spring 1994 *Refuge Reporter* explained:

Little did anyone know that another major highway project would help serve that objective. Completion of Interstate 476 around the west side of Philadelphia took 18 acres of wetland that had to be replaced [as a "mitigation" project elsewhere]. Highway engineers turned again to Tinicum Marsh, but this time to create rather than destroy.

After nearly a year of dredging and planting and expending some $2 million, an 18-acre area on the refuge was transformed during 1991-92 from an old spoils deposition site into a replicated tidal marsh.

Several years later, another wetlands mitigation project occurred on the refuge. Because marsh habitat had to be filled in for construction of a new runway at nearby Philadelphia International Airport, it was agreed that a 26-acre part of the refuge that had previously been used for river-dredged silt would be restored as wetland at a cost of about $3 million.

Then in February 2000, a disaster struck the refuge. An estimated 190,000 gallons of crude oil leaked from a ruptured underground pipeline beneath the refuge. Sunoco, Inc. discovered a pool of oil beneath the ice of a 145-acre impoundment. Fortunately, the environmental impact was restricted to approximately 2 acres of aquatic/terrestrial habitat via the rapid deployment of a containment boom, after chainsawing an arc-shaped trough through the 10-inch-thick ice. As described by Bill Buchanan in the September 18, 2000, Delaware County *Daily Times,* during most of a year of intensive cleanup efforts, earth-moving equipment, tanker trucks, oil-sucking pumps, and hundreds of workers "turned sections of the John Heinz National Wildlife Refuge at Tinicum into what looked like a scene from a war movie." Much of the damage has apparently been successfully restored. Yet, one permanent change to the refuge's scenery and ecology occurred when Sunoco chose to remove a 50-foot-wide swath of trees along the pipeline right-of-way. Although clear-cutting enables inspectors to better monitor the pipeline, it has fragmented what was a limited area of woodland. Although this fragmentation may reduce its value to many migrating songbirds and other wildlife, the "edge habitat" created by the swath may prove attractive to other species, including woodcock and butterflies. Biological monitoring of this urban refuge will continue for years.

A major milestone for the John Heinz Refuge was the opening of the 14,000-square-foot Cusano Environmental Education Center in January 2001. Phase I of this long-anticipated, energy-efficient facility contains an exhibit and interactive display area, a multipurpose meeting room, classrooms, resource library, and a gift shop that is operated by the nonprofit Friends of the Heinz Refuge at Tinicum. Two outstanding exhibits are the life-sized, free-standing, 100-foot-long cross section of the Tinicum Marsh and a state-of-the-art greenhouse wastewater treatment plant.

The education center is named in memory of the late Antonio Cusano, whose generous bequest provided about half of the center's $5-million-dollar construction cost. The balance of the funding was raised by the National Fish and Wildlife Foundation and the Friends organization. Phase II of the center will be the construction of an administrative wing, and Phase III will be the construction of a 100-foot-tall, enclosed, handicapped-accessible viewing platform.

As refuge manager Dick Nugent says:

Some folks still debate the issue of having an urbanized national wildlife refuge, with its inherent "problems" of air, ground, and water pollution; expensive land acquisition; security concerns; and public apathy. I side with the many counterpoints and opportunities presented by each "problem" and redefine them as "challenges."

The National Wildlife Refuge System is a spectacular network of "dirt" and water oases for wildlife and humankind. The "human" aspect has only recently been highlighted—much of that via the landmark Refuge Improvement Act of 1997, which emphasizes that the refuge system "shine bright" for wildlife, habitat, and people.

Back in 1972, Congress had much foresight when it directed the U.S. Fish and Wildlife Service to acquire 1,200 acres of Tinicum's threatened freshwater tidal marsh. Priority was to be given to restoring its degraded watershed; promote environmental education; and offer visitors an opportunity to study and enjoy wildlife in its natural habitat.

While it's a never-ending challenge, we're making great strides on all fronts. One day we're restoring wetlands, the next day we're updating the news media, the public, and politicians on matters dealing with oil spills and the refuge being listed as a superfund site.

To the untrained eye, the refuge remains pretty much the same as it did some 30 years ago—except for new facilities. The behind-the-scene struggle to maintain an outward "status-quo" is, ironically, a measure of success in this most urbanized refuge. In the eye of this beholder, the John Heinz NWR at Tinicum continues each day to shine brighter.

The refuge and the environmental education center are open daily during daylight hours. There is no entrance fee.

Visitor activities include birdwatching; photography; viewing interpretive exhibits and programs at the education center; interpreter-led walks; hiking on more than 10 miles of trails including several loops; canoeing, kayaking, and nonmotorized boating on Darby Creek (a hand-carried boat launching site is provided near the education center); and fishing.

Insect repellent is advised during the warmer months.

Lodgings and meals are available in Philadelphia and Essington.

Access to the John Heinz Refuge from I-95 northbound is by way of the State Route 291/Philadelphia International Airport exit, left at the first light onto Bartram Avenue, left at the third light onto Eighty-Fourth Street, and left at the second light onto Lindbergh Boulevard. From I-95 southbound, it is by way of the Route 291/airport exit (taking the right fork and exiting for Route 291-Lester), right at the first light onto Bartram Ave., left at the second light onto Eighty-Fourth St., and left at the second light onto Lindbergh Blvd.

Further information: John Heinz National Wildlife Refuge at Tinicum, Eighty-Sixth Street and Lindbergh Boulevard, Philadelphia, PA 19153; telephone: (215) 365-3118.

Ohio River Islands (see text under West Virginia)

Rhode Island

Block Island, containing 102 acres in five units, was established in 1973 to manage and protect strategically important migratory bird habitat. The refuge is located on the northern end of Block Island, which is about 12 miles south of the mainland coast of Rhode Island.

As described by the U.S. Fish and Wildlife Service's 1991 report, *Northeast Coastal Areas Study,* Block Island is "one of the most important migratory bird habitats in the East Coast . . . [as it] . . . provides a critical link or stepping stone in the migration of many birds, particularly raptors and passerines, between southern New England and eastern Long Island, and points north and south."

The December 2000 Rhode Island National Wildlife Refuge Complex's Draft *Comprehensive Conservation Plan* (Draft *CCP*) explains:

Block Island is internationally famous among birders for its spectacular fall songbird migration. . . . the island provides crucial habitat for both spring and fall migratory shorebirds and songbirds. Its northern tip, in particular, consistently supports large concentrations of fall migrants. Thousands of Neotropical migrants, representing 70 species, have been documented . . . the vast majority of these fall migrants are juveniles. Studies indicate that juvenile birds are severely dehydrated by the time they reach Block Island, and that its . . . 365 small ponds and abundance of fruit-bearing shrubs provide life-saving rehydration. Many typically omnivorous migrants forage exclusively on berries while on Block Island (Parrish, 1999). Northern arrowwood, northern bayberry, and pokeweed were the predominant fruit-bearing shrubs used by birds. Shrub habitat also provides resting shelter for migrating birds. . . .

Shorebirds pass through in large numbers during midsummer and early fall. Typically, 40 different shorebird species have been observed using the mudflats and saltmarshes and wrack lines on open beach. . . .

Prominent among the refuge's nesting birds is a colony of black-crowned night-herons, nearly 40 nests of which have been documented on the Beane Point parcel. A few yellow-crowned night-herons nest nearby. Nests are built in Japanese black pines, a non-native species that is declining because of an infestation of the black turpentine beetle. Prior to the planting of pines on Block Island, the night-herons reportedly nested in areas of shadbush, a native shrubby tree. The refuge also supports the state's largest nesting colony of great black-backed and herring gulls. Piping plovers, a federally listed threatened species, have made a number of failed attempts to nest on refuge and other island beaches during the past few years. According to the Fish and Wildlife Service, "No one has yet determined why plovers are unsuccessful here, although human disturbance and gull predation are possible contributing factors." As the Draft *CCP* document states, protecting the piping plover "presently requires an intensive effort by Refuge staff who monitor plover nesting, manage public use and access on beaches, control predators at nest sites, and provide environmental education. . . . "

Block Island is reported to be the only place in Rhode Island where northern harriers nest. Although 15 nests have been documented, none of these is located on the refuge. Barn owls also nest on the island, but not on the refuge. According to the Fish and Wildlife Service, "Block Island is also one of only two places in the world where barn owls . . . nest in sea cliff cavities rather than human-made structures or inland cliff crevices. . . . "

When northerly winds occur during the autumn, a phenomenon known as "fallout" occurs on Block Island. Thousands of neotropical songbirds, such as warblers and vireos, take advantage of the tailwinds. As they fly southward from the southern New England mainland across Block Island Sound, they descend into the shrubs and trees of Block Island, where they rest and feed, before continuing their migration. This event is similar to the spring migration fallout that can occur along the Gulf Coast, after neotropical songbirds fly across the Gulf of Mexico (see the Aransas Refuge, Texas text). Over 250 bird species have been seen here.

As for mammals, harbor seals occasionally haul themselves onto the refuge's beach near Sandy Point. And, as the Fish and Wildlife Service explains, "The overabundant population of white-tailed deer has been an important issue in recent years because deer are not native to the island, and there are no natural predators to control the population. The Town of New Shoreham and the . . . [state] administer a hunt program to substantially reduce the deer herd on portions of the island."

The Friends of the National Wildlife Refuges of Rhode Island is a nonprofit support group that is assisting all of the refuges in the state in a variety of ways.

The refuge is open daily during daylight hours. There is no entrance fee. The Rhode Island NWR Complex headquarters, at U.S. Route IA, Shoreline Plaza, in Charlestown is open on weekdays, except national holidays.

Visitor activities include birdwatching, photography, hiking, and surf fishing. The town-maintained North Light, a former U.S. Coast Guard facility located adjacent to the refuge's Sand Point unit, is a popular visitor destination. To reach the lighthouse and this part of the refuge, go to the northern end of paved Corn Neck Road and then walk 0.5 mile on a four-wheel-drive vehicle trail. Another stretch of four-wheel-drive trail leads south from the lighthouse along the refuge's 0.5 mile stretch of beach. The Fish and Wildlife Service hopes that a cooperative agreement with the town can be reached by which this latter beach area can be seasonally closed, to avoid disturbing nesting shorebirds.

Visitors are cautioned to be alert for ticks, which may carry Lyme disease.

Limited lodgings and meals are available on Block Island. Lodgings and meals are available in such mainland communities as Narragansett and Charlestown, Rhode Island and New London, Connecticut.

Access to Block Island is by way of all-year service on the Point Judith-Block Island Ferry and the New London-Block Island Ferry (motor vehicles, by reservation: [401] 783-4613). Seasonal ferry service operates from Newport and Narragansett, Rhode Island and Montauk, Long Island, New York. Flights to the island are available from the state airport in Westerly. Access to the refuge headquarters in Charlestown from the Green Hill Beach exit on U.S. Route I (in South Kingston) is I mile on U.S. Route IA and right into Shoreline Plaza.

Further information: Block Island National Wildlife Refuge, c/o Rhode Island NWR Complex, P.O. Box 307, Charlestown, RI 02813; telephone: (401) 364-9124.

John H. Chafee, consisting of 727 acres, was originally established in 1988 as the Pettaquamscutt Cove National Wildlife Refuge and was renamed in 1999 in honor of U.S. Senator John H. Chafee for his contributions to natural resource conservation. The refuge is located around the shore of tidally influenced Pettaquamscutt Cove, which is part of the Narrow (Pettaquamscutt) River estuary near the mouth of Narragansett Bay in southern Rhode Island.

Refuge habitats include areas of salt marsh, containing salt marsh and salt meadow cordgrass, spikegrass, saltwort, and sea lavender. Several islands within the tidal wetlands support black oaks and an understory of poison ivy. Black oaks and red maples are the dominant trees on the gently sloping uplands around the western side of the cove; woodlands along the eastern side consist mostly of maples.

The refuge was established mainly to provide important wintering habitat for concentrations of American black ducks, along with Canada geese, mallards, canvasbacks, buffleheads, red-breasted mergansers, and the non-native mute swan (see discussion of the latter species in the Trustom Pond Refuge text).

Other birds of the John H. Chafee Refuge include great blue and green herons, snowy egret, osprey, saltmarsh sharp-tailed sparrow, and numerous neotropical migratory songbirds such as thrushes, vireos, and warblers.

Water pollution is unfortunately a cause of concern in Pettaquamscutt Cove. As the U.S. Fish and Wildlife Service says in the December 2000 Rhode Island Refuges Complex Draft *Comprehensive Conservation Plan,* "Failing septic systems have been implicated as one of the most significant contributions to water quality problems. . . . " Another harmful environmental impact is the aggressive, invasive common reed (*Phragmites*), which forms "virtually impenetrable stands" that choke out native emergent freshwater plants, such as cattails, sedges, and rushes, and offer "little suitable food or cover for wildlife."

The Friends of the National Wildlife Refuges of Rhode Island is a nonprofit support group that is assisting all of the refuges in the state in a variety of ways.

The refuge is open daily during daylight hours. There is no entrance fee. The Rhode Island NWR Complex headquarters, located at U.S. Route 1A, Shoreline Plaza, in Charlestown, is open on weekdays, except national holidays.

Visitor activities include birdwatching; photography; limited hiking on nonmaintained trails; canoeing, kayaking, and boating on state waters within the cove (a cooperative federal/state no-wake zone is needed to minimize shore erosion); and fishing. Although there are presently no visitor use facilities on the refuge and few places from which to view the cove, the Fish and Wildlife Service plans to provide (wheelchair-accessible) trail and observation platforms at Middle Bridge and Bridgeport Commons and to designate an interpretive canoe/kayak trail.

Visitors are cautioned to be alert for ticks, which may carry Lyme disease. Insect repellent is advised during the warmer months.

The more than 215 species of birds of the John H. Chafee Refuge, as well as the mammals, reptiles, and amphibians, are largely the same as those recorded on Trustom Pond Refuge.

Lodgings and meals are available in such communities as Narragansett, Wakefield, and Charlestown.

Further information: John H. Chafee National Wildlife Refuge, c/o Rhode Island NWR Complex, P.O. Box 307, Charlestown, RI 02813; telephone: (401) 364-9124.

Ninigret, comprising 409 acres in two units, was established in 1970 to restore and manage wetland, grassland, woodland, and barrier beach habitats for a diversity of migrating and breeding birds. The refuge is located near Charlestown, along the shore of 1,711-acre Ninigret Pond, about 3 miles west of Trustom Pond Refuge on the South Shore of Rhode Island.

Approximately 16 percent of Ninigret Refuge contains wetland habitats. These are salt marsh, most of which is on the refuge's small barrier beach unit; scrub-shrub and wooded wetlands; a number of human-made freshwater ponds; and areas of natural freshwater wetlands. Most of the latter are located in *kettles*, which are small basins created roughly 10,000 years ago by melting blocks of glacial ice. Such blocks were left behind by the main mass of the continental glacier, as its terminal zone was thinning and withdrawing northward from southern New England.

According to the U.S. Fish and Wildlife Service's December 2000 Rhode Island National Wildlife Refuge Complex Draft *Comprehensive Conservation Plan* (Draft *CCP*), "Unfortunately, most of the wetlands have diminished wildlife value because of the presence of Phragmites [common reed]. . . . [it indicates] a disturbed wetland, especially where the natural flushing of salt water has been altered, salinity has declined, or where sediment loading has occurred. The monotypic, virtually impenetrable stands of Phragmites choke out native plants, and provide little suitable food or cover for wildlife." Other emergent, freshwater-wetland plants include cattails, sedges, and rushes. Scattered areas of "scrub-shrub" wetland contain speckled alder, buttonbush, swamp rose, and swamp loosestrife (the latter not to be confused with the aggressive invasive, non-native purple loosestrife). An area of red maple swamp habitat extends along the western edge of the refuge.

In addition to the wetlands, Ninigret Refuge contains "remnant patches" of native coastal sandplain grasslands, much of·which is overgrown with or dominated by trees, shrubs, or forbs. As the Fish and Wildlife Service says, "The suitability of the Refuge to many grassland-dependent species has declined or has been eliminated. . . . "

A major goal of the refuge, therefore, is to restore and maintain more than 200 acres of grassland habitat, thereby attracting wildlife that is associated with it, such as the upland sandpipers, grasshopper sparrows, bobolinks, and eastern meadowlarks. These grasslands also attract numerous species of butterflies, including large concentrations of the monarch butterfly during their southward autumn migration.

Grassland management activities, such as periodic mowing, hydroaxing, and prescribed burning, are preventing the invasion of trees and other woody vegetation into these important open areas. Native grasses being used to restore the grasslands include little bluestem and switchgrass. Other plants that take root here include meadowsweet, steeplebush, blue-eyed grass, slender blue flag, St. Johns wort, common milkweed, black-eyed Susan, spotted knapweed, and many species of goldenrod. The refuge also hopes to reintroduce a number of species of concern, including the federally listed endangered sandplain gerardia and two state-listed endangered plants—the New England blazing star and bushy rockrose.

About a quarter of the refuge consists of upland shrub habitat that is typically dominated by northern arrowwood, northern bayberry, sumacs, shadbush, and highbush blueberry. And about a third of the refuge is wooded, with such native trees as red maple; white, northern red, and black oaks; black cherry; quaking aspen; gray birch; eastern redcedar; and a few eastern white and pitch pines.

The refuge's main unit, along the northern shore of the Ninigret Pond, occupies the U.S. Navy's former Charlestown Naval Auxiliary Land Facility (naval air station). Removal of the facility's aircraft runways and taxiways has been accomplished with the assistance of U.S. Army and U.S. Navy Seabee reserve units. Areas of wetland and other habitats, long buried under layers of silt and the runways, are being restored.

The open expanse of Ninigret Pond, which is outside the refuge, is a major attraction for many species of migratory waterfowl, notably Canada geese, American black ducks, mallards, greater scaup, common goldeneyes, buffleheads, and red-breasted mergansers. However, as explained by the Fish and Wildlife Service in its Draft *CCP* document, "The construction of a permanent breachway in 1962 to stabilize the pond radically changed its ecology of the formerly productive estuarine fisheries. Habitat degradation includes the loss of 40 percent of its eelgrass beds over the last 32 years due to sedimentation and nutrient loading. . . . Water quality in Ninigret Pond is poor, as evidenced by elevated levels of nitrogen and fecal coliform bacteria. . . . "

In addition to waterfowl, wildlife highlights of Ninigret Refuge include raptors, such as bald eagles and sharp-shinned and many other hawks, which migrate through the area during the autumn, and ospreys that nest around Ninigret Pond. Enormous concentrations of tree swallows pass through on their autumn migration. Large influxes of neotropical migratory songbirds, such as warblers and vireos, arrive in late April and early May. A few of these birds remain to nest here, but the majority continue on to breeding grounds farther north. Woodcocks nest on the refuge from March to June, during which they perform their courtship flight displays at dusk, accompanied by nasal "peent" calls and the vibrating sound of their fast-beating wings. The federally listed threatened piping plover nests from April to August on the refuge's barrier beach unit and/or on the state's adjacent Ninigret Conservation Area.

The Friends of the National Wildlife Refuges of Rhode Island is a nonprofit support group that is assisting all of the refuges in the state in a variety of ways.

The refuge's main unit is open daily during daylight hours. The barrier beach unit is closed to motor vehicles from April 1 through August, to avoid disturbing the nesting piping plovers. There is no entrance fee. The Rhode Island NWR Complex headquarters, at U.S. Route 1A, Shoreline Plaza, in Charlestown is open on weekdays, except national holidays.

Visitor activities include birdwatching, butterfly observation, photography, hiking, and surf fishing on the barrier beach. Although camping is not permitted on the refuge, campground facilities are available at the state's Ninigret Conservation Area and Burlingame and Charlestown management areas.

On the adjacent town of Charlestown's Ninigret Park, the Frosty Drew Nature Center, operated by a nonprofit organization, provides a variety of interpretive programs and outings (some of which are held on the refuge). The nature center is open and staffed on weekdays from July 1 through August and on Tuesdays through Fridays during the rest of the year. It may also be open on weekends, depending upon the availability of volunteers. Nature center information: (401) 364-9508.

Hiking opportunities on Ninigret Refuge include 3.8 miles of routes, the base of which is made of 8-foot-wide (wheelchair-accessible) swaths of the former aircraft runways. The refuge's trails include Grassy Point Trail—a 0.7-mile path to an observation platform on the shore of Ninigret Pond, and Foster Cove Trail—a 1.1-mile route that loops through the western edge of the refuge (reached from the refuge's western entrance road).

Visitors are cautioned to be alert for ticks, especially as the refuge is a known "hot spot" for deer ticks carrying Lyme disease. Insect repellent is advised during the warmer months.

The more than 250 species of birds that have been recorded on Ninigret Refuge are essentially the same as those of Trustom Pond Refuge (see the listing for that refuge).

Lodgings and meals are available in Charlestown.

Access to Ninigret Refuge from Charlestown is just west on U.S. Route IA and left into Ninigret Park, to the parking area adjacent to the refuge's eastern entrance. The refuge's western entrance road is a short distance farther west, just beyond where Route IA merges with U.S. Route I.

Further information: Ninigret National Wildlife Refuge, c/o Rhode Island NWR Complex, P.O. Box 307, Charlestown, RI 02813; telephone: (401) 364-9124.

Sachuest Point, encompassing 242 acres, was established in 1970 to enhance and manage upland shrub habitat on a prominent headland and an area of emergent wetlands on the neck of the headland. The refuge is located between Sachuest Bay to the west, and the Sakonnet River to the east, just east of Newport on Rhode Island—the largest island in Narragansett Bay in southeastern Rhode Island.

From the mid-seventeenth century through the early twentieth century, the headland, which was formerly an island, was devoted to sheep grazing and other farming uses. In World War II, just over 100 acres were acquired for a U.S. military coastal defense facility. Subsequently, the point served as a U.S. Navy radio receiver station.

Tidal wetland restoration is a major management goal on the refuge. As the U.S. Fish and Wildlife Service explains in its December 2000 Rhode Island Refuges Complex Draft *Comprehensive Conservation Plan* (Draft *CCP*):

Approximately 40 acres of Sachuest Point are salt marsh wetlands. Remnants of a salt marsh are found on the northeast end of the Refuge, but have been severely impacted by the landfill and a road. The southern, largely freshwater portion of the salt marsh has been overtaken by the invasive plant Phragmites [common reed]. In 1997, extensive baseline data . . . [were] collected in anticipation of salt marsh restoration. . . . The primary goal of the restoration was to restore a natural tidal flow into the salt marsh and, thus, reduce the domination of Phragmites in the plant community.

Actual restoration work began in 1998 on the south side of the road between Second and Third Beaches. Initial monitoring shows native plants returning to areas where Phragmites was mechanically scarified or exposed to a more natural tidal flow of salt water.

The Draft *CCP* document states, "Unfortunately, most of the wetlands have diminished wildlife value because of the presence of Phragmites," which indicates "a disturbed wetland, especially where the natural flushing of salt water has been altered, salinity has declined, or where sediment loading has occurred. The monotypic, virtually impenetrable stands of Phragmites choke out native plants, and provide little suitable food or cover for wildlife."

Native maritime shrubland species include northern bayberry, northern arrowwood, common winterberry, shadbush, beach plum, staghorn sumac, wild roses (Virginia, multiflora, and *rugosa*), highbush blueberry, poison ivy, and eastern redcedar. Scattered small areas of grassland support switchgrass, lance-leaved and slender fragrant goldenrods, white-topped and New England asters, Queen Anne's lace, spotted knapweed, racemed (bitter) milkwort, and the non-native butter-and-eggs.

Among the avian highlights of Sachuest Point Refuge are "typically thousands" of migrating tree swallows. Migrant raptors that pass through the refuge include such species as sharp-shinned,

Cooper's, broad-winged, and red-tailed hawks, as well as merlin and peregrine falcons. Influxes of thrushes, vireos, warblers, and other neotropical songbirds pause on the headland before continuing their migration. Among the many waterfowl on the waters around the point are American black duck, greater scaup, common eider, scoters (black, surf, and white-winged), common goldeneye, bufflehead, common and red-breasted mergansers, and ruddy duck. During the winter months, flocks of the strikingly patterned harlequin duck (*Histrionicus histrionicus*) commonly ride the waves close to the point or seek shelter on nearby rocks. As mentioned in the Draft *CCP*:

Sachuest Point boasts the second largest winter population of eastern harlequin ducks on the Atlantic coast. Only one site off the coast of Maine has a larger winter concentration. Annual surveys . . . indicate the number . . . fluctuates from 50 to a high of 107 from October through March each year. . . .

The harlequin duck is one of the least studied ducks in North America, because it breeds and winters in some of the most inaccessible and remote habitats in the northern hemisphere (Alaska Department of Fish and Game, 1994). Harlequin ducks congregate off the eastern side of Sachuest Point, feeding and roosting near the area known as Island Rocks. Since they expend considerable energy feeding in rough waters, they can often be seen perching on rocks to rest or sleep. They forage on a variety of intertidal invertebrates gathered from rocks and ocean-bottom close to shore.

The Friends of the National Wildlife Refuges of Rhode Island is a nonprofit support group that is assisting all of the refuges in the state in a variety of ways.

The refuge is open daily during daylight hours. There is no entrance fee. The visitor center is open daily, except national holidays.

Visitor activities include birdwatching, butterfly observation (notably the autumn-migrating monarch butterflies), photography, hiking, interpreter-guided walks, and saltwater fishing. Swimming, sunbathing, and hunting are not permitted on the refuge. Camping is not permitted on the refuge, but campground facilities are available in the general vicinity.

Hiking opportunities are provided on the refuge's 3-mile trail network: Flint Point Trail, Island Rocks Trail, and Sachuest Point Trail—each of which leads to an observation platform that offers great panoramas (except when periodic summer coastal fog obscures the view).

Visitors are cautioned to be alert for ticks, which may carry Lyme disease. Insect repellent and sunscreen are advised during the warmer months.

The more than 215 species of birds that have been recorded on Sachuest Point Refuge, as well as mammals, reptiles, and amphibians, are largely the same as those on Trustom Pond Refuge.

Lodgings and meals are available in such communities as Middletown and Newport.

Access to the Sachuest Point Refuge from U.S. Route 1 is east about 8.5 miles on State Route 138, which crosses the Newport Bridge (toll); east 0.6 mile on Miantonomi and continuing east 1.2 miles on Green End Avenue; south (right) 1.3 miles on Paradise Avenue; east (left) 0.3 mile on Hanging Rock Road; and south (right) 1.5 miles on Sachuest Point Road.

Further information: Sachuest Point National Wildlife Refuge, c/o Rhode Island NWR Complex, P.O. Box 307, Charlestown, RI 02813; telephone (401) 364-9124.

Trustom Pond, containing 787 acres, was established in 1974 to protect a 160-acre brackish pond and surrounding wetland, shrubland, fields, and a narrow stretch of barrier beach that provide important habitats for migratory birds and other wildlife. The refuge is located near South Kingston, about 3 miles east of Ninigret Refuge on the South Shore of Rhode Island.

Trustom Pond is the state's only shallow coastal salt pond that has no houses along its shore and that is entirely encompassed by a national wildlife refuge. The pond has no permanent breachway that would allow for the inflow and outflow of ocean water; in contrast to nearby Ninigret Pond, the U.S. Fish and Wildlife Service mechanically breaches it, usually in April, to provide foraging habitat for the federally listed threatened piping plover and other shorebirds. During times of high water, Trustom Pond's excess water flows into 43-acre, brackish Card's Pond, which lies partly within the refuge.

As at Ninigret Pond, there are serious concerns about poor water quality in Trustom and Card's ponds, caused by concentrations of nitrate, nitrogen, and bacteria. During the warmer months, this contamination triggers extensive growths of macro algae and phytoplankton. These algal blooms form a thick mat across the bottom of the ponds, thereby reducing the normal dense growth of submerged aquatic plants that provide a major food source for many aquatic and terrestrial animals. One of the contributors to this problem is the non-native, invasive, and aggressive mute swan—a species that was unfortunately introduced to North America from Europe in the nineteenth century. According to the Fish and Wildlife Service, "Adult swans produce about 2 pounds of manure per day, significantly increasing nutrient loading in the pond." In the early 1990s, the number of swans summering on the pond reached or exceeded 200 of these birds. Since then, the numbers have declined, as a result of an active control program, known as "addling" eggs on the nest (making them rotten)—a technique that is also being implemented statewide by the Rhode Island Department of Environmental Management (RI DEM).

A variety of freshwater wetlands comprise just over 10 percent of the refuge. These areas include five natural freshwater ponds and one small former farm pond. About 34 acres consists of a forested wetland that is dominated by red maples.

Maintaining the refuge's grasslands is a major habitat management priority. As described by the U.S. Fish and Wildlife Service in its December 2000 *Rhode Island Refuges Complex Draft Comprehensive Conservation Plan* (Draft *CCP*):

Following the completion of the Trustom Pond Refuge Grasslands Management Plan (1995), the Refuge has systematically converted former hayfields and crop lands (corn and potatoes) to native grasses for the benefit of grassland nesting birds. We have now restored 85 acres of a targeted 125 acres of little bluestem and big bluestem grasslands. . . .

A combination of mowing and burning has maintained the newly established grasslands. . . . Current management strategies require that restored grasslands be mowed or burned every 3 to 5 years to control woody vegetation.

Prominent among the species of grassland-nesting birds are the bobolink and eastern meadowlark. Although the upland sandpiper and grasshopper sparrow are also important species, the Fish and Wildlife Service doubts that the refuge's grassland is sufficiently large to support breeding populations of these latter species. The grasslands also attract many species of butterflies, including large concentrations of autumn-migrating monarch butterflies.

Shrubland and woodland total nearly 40 percent of the refuge. Dominant shrub species include shadbush, northern arrowwood, and northern bayberry. Primary forest trees are black oak, black cherry, and red maple. During late April and early May, large influxes of neotropical songbirds, such as warblers, vireos, and thrushes, are attracted to the refuge. A few of these migrants remain to nest here, but many others only pause before continuing to breeding areas farther north. Over 260 bird species have been recorded here.

A discouraging aspect of the Trustom Pond Refuge is the status of the ecologically fragile coastal barrier beach. As described in the Draft *CCP* document:

Coastal development and shoreline stabilization have been the major causes of sand dune loss and the rapid decline of barrier beaches along the Rhode Island coast. One of the state's few remaining undeveloped barrier beaches is Moonstone Beach, 1.3 miles long. Changes in its width have been an increasing concern since 1985, when it began steadily declining. . . . Without the natural processes of sand removal and replenishment, beach loss occurs. Since 1961, beach profile surveys at Moonstone and other beaches on the South Shore have documented widespread decline in sand volume. When dune habitat is lost, the barrier beaches cannot absorb large waves, and lack the volume of sand required by adjustments in beach profile during storms.

Intense summer recreational use of Moonstone Beach and other barrier beaches exacerbates the impacts on these fragile ecosystems. People continue to walk on the dunes at Moonstone Beach, despite Refuge signs that prohibit it. Pedestrian traffic destroys stabilizing vegetation and contributes to dune erosion.

Moonstone Beach also provides vital nesting habitat for the federally listed threatened piping plover and the state-listed threatened least tern. In an effort to avoid human disturbance of these nesting activities, the Fish and Wildlife Service closes the beach to public use above the mean high-tide line from April 1 through mid-September. As the Draft *CCP* document states:

The Friends of the National Wildlife Refuges of Rhode Island is a nonprofit support group that is assisting all of the refuges in the state in a variety of ways.

The refuge is open daily during daylight hours. There is no entrance fee. The refuge headquarters is open on weekdays, except national holidays.

Visitor activities include birdwatching, butterfly observation, photography, hiking on trails leading down to observation platforms overlooking Trustom Pond, surf and shoreline fishing (but fishing is not permitted on Trustom Pond), crabbing, and waterfowl hunting. Camping is not permitted on the refuge, but campground facilities are available at the state's Charlestown and Burlingame management areas and Wakamo Park.

Visitors are cautioned to be alert for ticks, especially as the refuge is a known "hot spot" for deer ticks that may carry Lyme disease. Insect repellent is advised during the warmer months.

Lodgings and meals are available in such communities as Charlestown, Matunuck, Wakefield, and Narragansett.

Access to Trustom Pond Refuge from the Moonstone Beach exit on U.S. Route 1 in South Kingston is south 1 mile, west (right) 0.7 mile on Matunuck Schoolhouse Road, and south (left) into the refuge.

Further information: Trustom Pond National Wildlife Refuge, c/o Rhode Island NWR Complex, P.O. Box 307, Charlestown, RI 02813; telephone: (401) 364-9124.

South Carolina

ACE Basin, comprising more than 11,000 acres in two units and working toward a goal of as much as 18,000 acres, is located along the Combahee and Edisto rivers in southern South Carolina. In 1990, the refuge's first tract of land, the 832-acre Bonny Hall Plantation and Club property that is now part of the refuge's COMBAHEE UNIT, was acquired from The Nature Conservancy.

The ACE Basin Project, of which the refuge is a part, was initiated in 1988, when Ducks Unlimited, Inc., The Nature Conservancy (TNC), the U.S. Fish and Wildlife Service (USFWS), the South Carolina Department of Natural Resources (SCDNR), and a number of private landowners came together and formed the ACE Basin Task Force. ACE stands for three major rivers in the basin—the Ashepoo, Combahee, and Edisto. The 350,000-acre ACE Basin is one of the largest undeveloped estuarine wetland ecosystems remaining along the U.S. Atlantic Coast. By the year 2001, more than 136,752 acres of the Basin had been brought under various forms of conservation management.

As stated by this landmark cooperative Task Force:

The mission of the ACE Basin Project is to maintain the natural character of the Basin by promoting wise resource management on private lands and protecting strategic tracts by conservation agencies. A major goal of the protection efforts is to ensure that traditional uses such as farming, forestry, recreational and commercial fishing, and hunting will continue in the area.

Task Force members provide each other with technical and logistical support in all phases of the Project. Ducks Unlimited and TNC worked closely with public resource agencies in acquiring many of the lands available for public access. Through the Private Lands Program, private landowners are provided technical assistance in wildlife habitat management by representatives of the Task Force members.

SCDNR manages Donnelley and Bear Island Wildlife Management Areas and the ACE Basin National Estuarine Research Reserve. The USFWS manages the ACE Basin National Wildlife Refuge. These areas provide public access to nearly 50,000 acres.

Ducks Unlimited and TNC work with private landowners in protecting their property through conservation easements and stewardship agreements. . . .

Private property owners have protected more than 53,860 acres [as of 2001] through voluntary conservation easements [more than 53,000 acres, as of 2000]. Easements are perpetual restrictions to preserve the natural values and protect wildlife habitat, while sustaining traditional land uses such as timber management, agriculture, hunting, and commercial and recreation fishing.

On the ACE Basin National Wildlife Refuge, the Fish and Wildlife Service is performing a number of habitat management activities to promote wildlife diversity. Ecologically productive expanses of brackish tidal marsh and island-like hammocks, comprising more than 40 percent of the refuge, are being protected. The refuge includes areas of upland pines and bottomland hardwoods. Forest habitat diversity is enhanced by selective thinning, creating edge-zone clearings, and annual prescribed burning. Fire management helps to prevent fuel overloading, reduce understory vegetation in some areas, promote nutrient cycling, and spur the sprouting of herbs and grasses for the benefit of such species as deer and wild turkeys. Several fallow fields are annually treated with fire, triggering the growth of forbs and grasses valued by turkeys, bobwhite, and numerous songbirds.

Water levels within former rice field impoundments are seasonally regulated for moist-soil management. This manipulation of water promotes the growth of nutrient-rich foods, such as aquatic plants, crustaceans, and small fish, for the benefit of ducks, herons, egrets, ibises, wood storks, bald eagles, and alligators. As explained by the Fish and Wildlife Service, the flow of water between a tidal creek or river and a moist-soil impoundment is regulated by means of rice field trunks that "operate on tidal surge and consist of wooden culverts with flap gates." These efficient devices were first used on the eighteenth-century rice plantations.

The historical and architectural highlight of the refuge's EDISTO UNIT is the Grove Plantation House, which dates from 1828. This three-story structure, which is on the National Register of Historic Places, is one of only three antebellum rice plantation mansions in the ACE Basin to survive the Civil War. In 1991, the Grove Plantation was acquired with the assistance of The Nature Conservancy. The house, which is surrounded by great spreading Spanish "moss"-draped live oaks, was beautifully renovated between 1995 and 1997 and now serves as the refuge headquarters and visitor center.

The Nature Conservancy and Ducks Unlimited, Inc. have also assisted with refuge land acquisition. In addition, North American Wetlands Conservation Act (NAWCA) funding has been awarded to ACE Basin Refuge for habitat restoration. The purpose of NAWCA, which was passed by Congress in 1989, is to encourage the formation of public–private partnerships "to conserve wetland ecosystems and waterfowl and other migratory birds and fish and wildlife that depend upon such habitats" on the North American continent. NAWCA authorized a grant program to assist with the activities of partnerships like the ACE Basin Project. The North American Wetlands Conservation Council, established by the legislation, meets three times annually to review and prioritize proposed project grants, and the Fish and Wildlife Service administers the grants.

As refuge manager Jane Griess looks to the future, she says, "Land within the ACE Basin continues to be preserved through acquisition and conservation easements. It's wonderful to have such a large, undeveloped area that will be enjoyed by future generations."

The refuge is open daily during daylight hours. There is no entrance fee. The refuge office, located on the Edisto Unit, is open on weekdays, except national holidays.

Visitor activities include birdwatching; photography; hiking (grass trails are available); boating, canoeing, and kayaking on the Basin's meandering tidal waterways; fishing in the tidal creeks and freshwater streams; and hunting (waterfowl; archery and primitive weapons hunts for deer) on parts of the refuge during the designated seasons.

Even though alligators are generally afraid of people, visitors are cautioned to stay a safe distance from these sluggish-looking but potentially fast-moving reptiles and to be alert for ticks, chiggers, and venomous snakes. Insect repellent and sunscreen are advised during the warmer months.

Lodgings and meals are available in such communities as Beaufort, Edisto Island, South Point, Yemassee, Walterboro, and Charleston.

Access to the ACE Basin Refuge headquarters on the Edisto Unit from U.S. Route 17 at Osborn is south just over 3 miles on State Route 174, west (right, at flashing light) about 2 miles on State Route 55 (Willtown Road), and south (left) about 2 miles on State Route 346 (Jehossee Island Road). The several tracts of the refuge's Combahee Unit are reached from U.S. Route 17 (just west of the Combahee River) by turning northwest onto State Route 33, from which trails offer hiking opportunities from a number of parking areas.

Further information: ACE Basin National Wildlife Refuge, P.O. Box 848, Hollywood, SC 29449; telephone: (843) 889-3084.

Cape Romain, containing 64,229 acres, was established in 1932 on the central coast of South Carolina. Large areas of the refuge consist of extensive, cordgrass-dominated, estuarine salt marsh habitat. Intricately meandering tidal creeks divide this wetland into numerous islands that are inundated during high tide, a 20-mile stretch of Atlantic coastal barrier islands with areas of sand dunes behind long, sandy beaches. Nearly half of the refuge is the open water of Bull's Bay, and a little less than half of Cape Romain is designated as a unit of the National Wilderness Preservation System. Over 330 bird species use the refuge.

The refuge's centerpiece is 5,496-acre Bull's Island, part of an ancient barrier reef that is one of the Cape Romain's three largest barrier islands. It contains several large brackish impoundments and ponds. The island's uplands support roughly 2,000 acres of maritime forest of such species as live oak, southern magnolia, loblolly pine, redbay, wax myrtle, sweetgum, yaupon and American holly, cabbage palmetto (*Sabal palmetto*), and the low-growing saw palmetto (*Serenoa repens*). In 1989, Hurricane Hugo slammed into the South Carolina coast and devastated the island's climax forest. As described by refuge biologist Craig Sasser:

The force of Hurricane Hugo's 100-plus-mile-per-hour winds and 30-foot storm surge can best be demonstrated by examining the devastation that was unfurled along South Carolina's coast, especially at "ground zero," which was Cape Romain. Bull's Island, which is a barrier island, was where the eye of the storm passed, exposing it to both a windward (ocean side) storm surge and a leeward (bay side) storm surge. This high energy zone denuded Bull's Island of most of its mature trees, thus removing almost all forest structure. Tree species that survived the initial assault have, to date, continued to die from massive scarring and saltwater stress. These species include mature live oaks, cabbage palmettos, and laurel oaks. Almost every mature pine on Bull's Island was destroyed upon storm impact.

For several reasons, this natural event may have forever changed the forest structure and composition on Bull's Island. Invasive species, such as Chinese tallow, exploded because of its opportunistic strategy of remaining in a semi-dormant stage until the upper canopy is removed, and then accelerating its growth and out-competing other species for available nutrients and sunlight. Once established, Chinese tallow trees are prolific seed producers and their seeds, which are readily transported by birds and other wildlife, can lie dormant for over one-hundred years. The creation of this seed bank virtually guarantees that Chinese tallow will always be a part of the future forest composition on Bull's Island.

Additionally, the tremendous fuel-loading left in the wake of Hurricane Hugo has also contributed to the direction of Bull's Island's forest succession. This fuel-loading has made forest management practices, such as prescribed fire, nearly impossible, because of the complexity of factors that must be considered before burning, including the protection of fire-sensitive areas. These extreme fuel loads can be difficult to reduce, especially with prescribed fire, because under ideal burning conditions, the fire will burn too hot, further stressing mature trees and killing younger trees. Other methods of fuel reduction, such as burning under less desirable conditions and mechanical removal, can be labor intensive. The refuge's current forest-management direction is to allow the forest to naturally recover, while suppressing wildfires where they may jeopardize the health and integrity of fire-sensitive areas.

Large concentrations of wintering waterfowl, including the tundra swan and numerous species of ducks, are attracted to the refuge's ponds and other open water, and great numbers of wintering shorebirds flock to its beaches and mudflats. Among the many birds that nest on the refuge are several thousand pairs of both brown pelicans and royal terns, and large numbers of least and sandwich terns, herons, egrets, ibises, black skimmers, and American oystercatchers. Many thousands of clapper rails inhabit the salt marshes. During the summer and autumn, large groups of the federally listed threatened wood stork come to Bull's Island. Resident wood ducks nest in trees around the ponds, and other resident wildlife includes the bald eagle, osprey, wild turkey, white-tailed deer, raccoon, and alligator. During spring and autumn, great influxes of neotropical migratory songbirds, including many species of warblers, pass through the refuge—notably during March and April.

Loggerhead sea turtles, a federally listed threatened species, haul themselves onto the refuge's barrier island beaches, especially on Cape Island, in such numbers to lay their eggs that Cape Romain ranks as the largest nesting beach in the United States for this species outside of Florida. The endangered leatherback sea turtle has also occasionally been recorded here.

As the U.S. Fish and Wildlife Service says:

Historically, two problems have severely hindered the success of the [sea turtle] nests after laying: beach erosion and predation by raccoons. In order to lessen the impact of these problems, a nest management program was initiated in 1979.

The management program consists of a hatchery operation, raccoon control program, collecting data on the number of nests and the number of false crawls, monitoring of control nests on the beach, and collecting information for the Sea Turtle Stranding and Salvage Network.

Cape Romain Refuge is one of the few places in the southeastern United States that has been targeted for the reintroduction of the federally listed endangered red wolf (*Canis niger* or *C. rufus*). In 1977, the first breeding pair was released on Bull's Island. As of 1999, the Fish and Wildlife Service reported, "The Bull's Island project began the year with 5 wolves on the Island consisting of the adult breeding pair, 2 adult males, and one two-year old male born in 1977." (See the St. Vincent [Florida] and Alligator River [North Carolina] refuge texts for further discussions of this species and the recovery program.)

According to the Fish and Wildlife Service, the refuge has a long and varied human history:

Two nineteenth-century lighthouses stand on Lighthouse Island. The one built in 1827 stands 60 feet tall, and the one dating from 1857 rises 180 feet high. Although neither is operational, they still serve as daytime landmarks for mariners and fishermen. Both structures are listed on the National Register of Historic Places, and refuge volunteers have helped with extensive restoration of these structures.

Bull's Island is named for Stephen Bull, one of the seventeenth-century settlers from England. Records are unclear about whether he ever actually owned the island or even lived there.

As for the beauty of Bull's Island, Craig Sasser recalls one of his most memorable experiences:

This particular evening, I was sitting on the edge of Lower Summerhouse Pond, waiting for the tide to change to close the water-control structures. As I gazed to the west, I watched the sun sinking slowly, beyond the mighty, darkly silhouetted 'wings' of ancient live oaks, infused with cabbage palmettos and Spanish moss. Like a huge painting, the sky was splashed with hues of pink, amber, yellow, and orange and was mirrored across the pond's surface—only to be shimmered by black skimmers, as they passed in formation in search of one last meal, their long beaks skimming the water. The pond was alive with the silhouettes of other bird life, as herons, terns, and wood storks chased unfamiliar prey that had just been thrust into unfamiliar hunting grounds with the last pulse of tidal water.

As the amber hues faded and darkened, a sense of sadness filled me, because it signaled the closing of this spectacular portrait. But then the eastern sky began suddenly to brighten, unveiling the rising of the full moon and signifying the onset of a new beginning—that of the nocturnals. In the distance, a family of wolves celebrated with a chorus of musical howls, for their time of foraging and exploring had just begun.

The refuge is open daily during daylight hours. There is no entrance fee. The joint Cape Romain NWR-Francis Marion National Forest's Sewee Visitor and Environmental Education Center, located on the mainland, is open on Tuesdays through Sundays. This center is managed by the South Eastern Wildlife and Environmental Education (SEWEE) Association, Inc., which also helps sponsor numerous events at the center.

Visitor activities include viewing an orientation program and interpretive exhibits at the Sewee center, birdwatching, photography, hiking, picnicking (a picnic area is provided on Bull's Island), shelling, boating, fishing, and limited hunting (archery hunts for deer and raccoon). Although camping is not permitted on the refuge, campground facilities are provided in the nearby Francis Marion National Forest.

Hiking opportunities on Bull's Island include the Bull's Island Nature Trail—a 2-mile loop (designated as a National Recreation Trail), 16 miles of road, and the beach. In the vicinity of the Sewee Visitor and Environmental Education Center, a 1-mile self-guiding interpretive loop trail goes by a red wolf enclosure and alligator-inhabited ponds. Other trails are provided in the national forest. Environmental education programs are offered to school and other groups at the center.

Even though alligators are generally afraid of people, visitors are cautioned to stay a safe distance from these sluggish-looking but potentially fast-moving reptiles and to be alert for ticks, chiggers, and venomous snakes. Insect repellent, especially during the warmer months, and sunscreen are advised.

Lodgings and meals are available in such communities as McClellanville, Georgetown, Mt. Pleasant, and Charleston.

Access to the Sewee visitor center is north 20 miles on U.S. Route 17 from Charleston. The refuge itself is reached only by boat. A passenger ferry service (fee; no reservations) takes visitors the 3 miles (30 minutes) from Moore's Landing to Bull's Island. The ferry operates on Tuesdays, Thursdays, Fridays, and Saturdays from March 1 through November and on Saturdays only from December 1 through February; it does not operate on Thanksgiving, Christmas Eve, and Christmas. Visitors are urged to take water, picnic snacks, insect repellent, sunscreen, and comfortable hiking shoes on Bull's Island excursions. Ferry service information, telephone: (843) 881-4582.

Further information: Cape Romain National Wildlife Refuge, 5821 Highway 17 North, Awendaw, SC 29429; refuge headquarters telephone: (843) 928-3264; visitor center telephone: (843) 928-3368.

Carolina Sandhills, containing 45,348 acres, was established in 1939 to restore and protect an area that had previously become an ecologically degraded and severely eroded land supporting little wildlife. The refuge is located between the Atlantic Coastal Plain and the Piedmont Plateau, in the Sandhills of northeastern South Carolina. The term *Sandhills* refers to the region's gently rolling hills, which are overlain with deep layers of porous sands.

As described by the U.S. Fish and Wildlife Service, after the federal government acquired the refuge:

Efforts began immediately to restore this damaged, barren land to a healthy, rich habitat for the plants and animals that once lived here.

The longleaf pine/wiregrass ecosystem, the characteristic habitat of the refuge, once covered more than 90 million acres across the southeastern United States from Virginia to Texas. This unique ecosystem, shaped by thousands of years of natural fires that burned through every two to four years, has been reduced to less than two million acres.

Today, only scattered patches remain, with most occurring on public lands. Factors contributing to the demise of this ecosystem include aggressive fire suppression efforts, clearing for agriculture and development, and conversion to other pine types. Carolina Sandhills Refuge serves as a demonstration site for land management practices which preserve and enhance the diminishing longleaf pine/wiregrass ecosystem.

The refuge contains extensive areas of open longleaf pine forest. The longleaf pine (*Pinus palustris*), which grows 75 to 120 feet tall, has three-per-bundle bright-green needles measuring 8 to 18 inches in length, and 6- to 10-inch-long cones. Beneath these pines is a scattered understory of scrub oaks and various shrubs. The dominant ground cover, with a sprinkling of forbs such as the pink-flowered meadow beauty, is the clump-forming, deeply rooted wiregrass (*Aristida stricta*), a species of three-awn grass that grows 2 to 3 feet tall. This grass, along with an accumulation of needles, dead wood, and other organic debris, easily fuels relatively "cool," low-burning fires that prevent or curtail the growth of most understory trees without damaging the pines, thereby maintaining an open, pine-dominated woodland. In the absence of periodic fire, dense growths of scrub oaks and other hardwoods ultimately take over as the dominant species, preventing the regeneration of the pines.

Of the wildlife species that thrive in this open longleaf pine habitat are the wild turkey, northern bobwhite, fox squirrel, and the federally listed endangered red-cockaded woodpecker (*Picoides borealis*). This woodpecker has a black cap and nape, a boldly striped black-and-white back, and a prominent white cheek patch, at the top of which (on adult males) is a small red swatch—the "cockade"—that is frequently difficult to see. As explained by the U.S. Fish and Wildlife Service:

The red-cockaded woodpecker makes its home in mature pine forests; more specifically, those with long-leaf pines averaging 80 to 120 years old and loblolly pines averaging 70 to 100 years old. While other woodpeckers bore out cavities in dead trees where the wood is rotten and soft, the red-cockaded wood-pecker is the only one which excavates cavities exclusively in living pine trees.

The older pines favored by the red-cockaded woodpecker often suffer from a fungus called red heart disease which attacks the center of the trunk, causing the inner wood to become soft.

The nesting season of the red-cockaded woodpeckers runs from April through June. According to the Fish and Wildlife Service, "Upon fledging, the young often remain with the parents, forming groups of up to nine members, but more typically four to five members. There is only one pair of breeding birds within each group, and they normally raise only a single brood each year. The other group members, usually males from the previous breeding season, help incubate the eggs and raise the young." Carolina Sandhills Refuge supports more than 140 groups of these territorial and unusually cooperative woodpeckers—the largest population in the National Wildlife Refuge System.

The Fish and Wildlife Service carries out a variety of management activities designed to enhance the refuge's diverse wildlife habitats. A major emphasis is upon enhancing and maintaining the woodpecker's vital foraging and nesting habitat by selective thinning, prescribed burning, and other methods of timber management to maintain high-quality forest of older pines; by installing artificial nesting cavities; and by monitoring breeding success and population trends.

In addition to the pine forests, Carolina Sandhills Refuge also contains many small creeks that flow into either Black Creek, along the eastern side of the refuge, or Lynches River, to the west. Bottomland hardwoods and shrubs border these streams. Sandhill seeps create bogs that are special habitats for such species as the pine barrens tree frog, sundew, and several kinds of pitcher-plants. Other habitats include 30 human-made lakes and ponds that attract waterfowl and other wildlife, forest clearings, and both fallow and cultivated fields.

The refuge is open daily during daylight hours. There is no entrance fee. The refuge office/visitor station is open on weekdays, except national holidays.

Visitor activities include wildlife observation; photography; driving the 9-mile, paved auto tour road as well as a number of gravel roads; hiking; viewing the refuge and wildlife from two observation towers; environmental educational and interpretive programs; canoeing and boating (electric motors only; boat-launching ramps on Martins and Mays lakes and Lake Bee); fishing (Martins Lake is closed to fishing; all other lakes and ponds are open unless posted otherwise); and limited hunting (deer, turkey, and some small game) on parts of the refuge during the designated seasons. Although camping is not permitted on the refuge, campground facilities are provided at Sandhills State Forest.

Hiking opportunities include the 1-mile Woodland Pond Trail encircling Pool A, near the visitor station; and the 3.5-mile Tate's Trail that winds along several lakes and interconnecting streams. The 0.25-mile Longleaf Pine Trail, located west of the wildlife drive near Pool A, interprets the longleaf pine ecosystem. Over 190 bird species use the refuge.

Visitors are cautioned to be alert for ticks, chiggers, and venomous snakes. Insect repellent is advised during the warmer months.

Lodgings and meals are available in such communities as Cheraw, Pageland, Camden, and Hartsville.

Access to Carolina Sandhills Refuge from McBee is 4 miles northeast on U.S. Route I; or from Cheraw it is 11 miles southwest on U.S. Route I.

Further information: Carolina Sandhills National Wildlife Refuge, Route 2, Box 100, McBee, SC 29101; telephone: (803) 335-8401.

Pinckney Island, encompassing 4,073 acres, was established in 1975. The refuge includes a cluster of low-lying islands, the largest of which is Pinckney Island, located just west of Hilton Head Island near the southern end of coastal South Carolina. Roughly two-thirds of the refuge consists of salt marsh and meandering tidal creeks. Higher ground supports areas of woodland, shrubland habitat, fallow fields and grasslands, and freshwater ponds.

The refuge attracts concentrations of wading birds, shorebirds, wintering waterfowl, and numerous neotropical migratory songbirds, including warblers and the painted bunting. Ospreys nest here and are frequently observed fishing in the tidal creeks. White-tailed deer and alligators are common residents. The federally listed endangered West Indian manatee inhabits the waters around the refuge but is rarely seen.

As described by the U.S. Fish and Wildlife Service:

Coastal areas, hammocks, and the north end of Pinckney are dominated by live oak with water oak, loblolly pine, and cabbage palm as associates; secondary species include hickory, pecan, magnolia, sweetgum, red cedar, and lesser numbers of maple, sassafras, hackberry, redbud, and winged elm. A small number of longleaf, loblolly, and slash pine plantations . . . are located throughout the refuge. . . . The salt marsh consists primarily of salt marsh cord grass. Other typical vegetation found in a narrow band around the islands and in the higher marsh hammocks includes glasswort, needlegrass, and sea oxeye.

Freshwater habitat on Pinckney Island is limited to approximately 38 acres. . . . When the refuge was acquired . . . , three major ponds existed on the main island. . . . Four additional ponds were created during the 1980s to provide wading bird nesting, feeding, and/or loafing habitat. . . . A greentree reservoir was created adjacent to Clubhouse Pond when the main road bed was raised in the early 1980's. Water supply for all ponds has been dependent on precipitation. Only Clubhouse Pond has a water control structure. In 1995, a private donation . . . with matching funds from the Fish and Wildlife Foundation allowed for the installation of three four-inch wells. . . . The wells supplement the water supply for Ibis, Clubhouse, and Wood Stork Ponds (14 acres) and help maintain adequate water levels . . . , thereby protecting wading bird rookeries from potential raccoon predation during dry periods.

Pinckney Island is open daily during daylight hours. There is no entrance fee. The refuge's smaller islands (Corn, Big and Little Harry, and Buzzard) are closed to visitation.

Visitor activities include birdwatching, photography, driving the entrance road to the parking area, hiking and bicycling 14 miles of trails (a map is available), boating (a boat-launching ramp is provided at the island's Last End Point, to the south of U.S. Route 278), saltwater fishing and shellfishing (from boats only), and deer hunting (when needed for population management) during the designated season.

Hiking and bicycling opportunities (distances given from the refuge's parking area) include the 1.5-mile route highlighted by the 0.6-mile Ibis Pond Trail, the 2.3-mile route to Shell Point, the 2.5-mile trail to Bull Point, the 3.1-mile route to Clubhouse Pond, the 3.7-mile route to Dick Point Pond, and the 3.9-mile route to White Point.

Even though alligators are generally afraid of people, visitors are cautioned to stay a safe distance from these sluggish-looking but potentially fast-moving reptiles and to be alert for venomous snakes, poison ivy, ticks, and chiggers. Insect repellent and sunscreen are advised.

The more than 255 species of birds that have been recorded on Pinckney Island Refuge are much the same as those of Cape Romain Refuge.

Lodgings and meals are available in such communities as Bluffton, Hardeeville and Hilton Head Island, South Carolina and Garden City and Savannah, Georgia.

Access to Pinckney Island Refuge from Exit 8 on I-95 (at Hardeeville) is east 18 miles on U.S. Route 278, and north (left) at the refuge sign.

Further information: Pinckney Island National Wildlife Refuge, c/o Savannah Coastal Refuges, Parkway Business Center, Suite 10, 1000 Business Center Drive, Savannah, GA 31405; telephone: (912) 652-4415.

Santee, consisting of 15,095 acres in four units, was established in 1941. The refuge provides mitigation for the loss of wildlife habitat resulting from construction of the Santee Dam, which created Lake Marion on the Santee River in south-central South Carolina. Approximately 10,700 acres of the refuge are under lease or agreement with the South Carolina Public Service Authority (Santee Cooper), which built the dam. The name *Santee* is derived from a Native American word meaning "river people."

The refuge's diverse habitats along the northern shore of the lake include mixed hardwood and mixed pine-hardwood forest, pine plantations, old fields and croplands, marsh, ponds and impoundments, and some open expanses of the reservoir.

The refuge attracts concentrations of wintering ducks, geese, swans, and bald eagles; influxes of neotropical migratory songbirds that pass through during the spring and autumn; as well as many resident species of wildlife, including wild turkeys, white-tailed deer, and alligators.

The U.S. Fish and Wildlife Service carries out a number of habitat management activities. Nesting boxes are provided for wood ducks in areas in which tree cavities are lacking. For the benefit of waterfowl and other wildlife, water levels in impoundments and marshes are seasonally regulated to enhance habitat, promote the growth of important plant foods, and curtail the growth of certain undesirable pest plants. Bottomland woodlands, containing hardwoods that produce nutrient-rich acorns and other nuts valued by wildlife, are periodically flooded. To supplement food for many species of wildlife, croplands are cultivated under agreements with local farmers, so that a portion of such crops as corn, wheat, millet, and soybeans is left unharvested.

The refuge is open daily during daylight hours. There is no entrance fee. The visitor center, located on the BLUFF UNIT, is open on Tuesdays through Sundays, except national holidays. To avoid disturbing waterfowl, portions of the refuge—Cantey Bay, Black Bottom, Savannah Branch, and part of the Bluff Unit—are closed to visitation from November 1 through February. The CUDDO UNIT's auto tour drive is closed for 13 days beginning the second Monday in October, and on Saturdays from November through January.

Visitor activities include birdwatching, photography, viewing interpretive displays in the visitor center, driving the Cuddo Unit's auto tour route, hiking, canoeing and boating (a boat-launching ramp is provided on the Pine Island Unit), fishing (much of the refuge is closed to fishing from November 1 through February), and hunting on parts of the refuge during the designated seasons (archery and primitive weapons hunts for deer; and if the designated period is within the state season: gray squirrel, raccoon, opossum, and dove). Camping is not permitted on the refuge, but campground facilities are available on Santee State Park and elsewhere. Hiking trails include the Bluff Unit's 1-mile, self-guiding Wright's Bluff Nature Trail, which features a waterfowl observation tower; and two 1.4-mile trails along the lakeshore in the Cuddo Unit.

Even though alligators are generally afraid of people, visitors are cautioned to stay a safe distance from these sluggish-looking but potentially fast-moving reptiles and to be alert for venomous snakes. Insect repellent is advised during the warmer months.

The more than 295 species of birds that have been recorded on Santee Refuge are much the same as those of Cape Romain Refuge.

Lodgings and meals are available in such communities as Santee and Summerton.

Access to the Santee Refuge headquarters and visitor center is 0.25 mile from Exit 102 on I-95, following directional signs. From Santee, it is 4 miles north on U.S. Route 15/301; from Summerton, it is 8 miles south on U.S. Route 15/301.

Further information: Santee National Wildlife Refuge, 2125 Ft. Watson Road, Summerton, SC 29148; telephone: (803) 478-2217.

Savannah, containing 28,168 acres, was established in 1927 to protect an area of bottomland hardwoods, freshwater marshes, and tidal creeks and rivers. The refuge is located along the Savannah River, just upriver from the city of Savannah in southeastern South Carolina and northeastern Georgia.

More than 3,000 acres of freshwater impounds were former plantation rice fields dating back to the mid- or late eighteenth century. Water levels in 20 impounds are managed for the benefit of migratory waterfowl. Roughly half of the refuge consists of periodically flooded bottomland forest, with such trees as Spanish "moss"-draped bald cypress, pond cypress, sweetgum, American elm, water hickory, oaks (swamp white, water, and laurel), swamp cottonwood, water tupelo, and red maple. Elsewhere on the refuge, there are live oaks with resurrection ferns growing on their branches; as well as the southern magnolia, yaupon holly, cabbage palmetto (palm), the understory saw palmetto, pink azalea, wild iris, white water lily, pickerelweed, arrowhead, cattails, sedges, and rushes.

Savannah Refuge attracts concentrations of wading birds, wintering waterfowl, nesting and wintering wood ducks, and numerous neotropical migratory songbirds. Bald eagles and ospreys nest here. White-tailed deer and alligators are common residents.

A proposal by the Georgia Ports Authority to deepen Savannah Harbor poses a serious threat to the refuge's tidal freshwater wetland habitat. In 1999, the $230-million Savannah Harbor Project was conditionally authorized by Congress. Part of the cost is for the implementation of a mitigation plan, and the project can proceed only after the U.S. Army Corps of Engineers, "in consultation with affected Federal, State of Georgia, State of South Carolina, [and] regional and local entities, reviews and approves an Environmental Impact Statement for the project." Meanwhile, a Stakeholders Evaluation Group has been formed to identify and study impacts of the harbor project.

The refuge is open daily during daylight hours. There is no entrance fee.

Visitor activities include birdwatching; photography; driving the 4-mile Laurel Hill Wildlife Drive, which offers views of freshwater impoundments and hardwood hammocks (on the South Carolina portion of the refuge); hiking; bicycling; boating on rivers and creeks (several boat-launching sites are available); fishing in freshwater pools from March 1 through November; and hunting (deer, feral hog, squirrel, turkey, and waterfowl) on part of the refuge during the designated seasons. Camping is not permitted on the refuge, but campground facilities are provided at Skidaway Island State Park.

Hiking opportunities include the 150-foot-long (wheelchair-accessible) Cistern Trail, the 1-mile Tupelo Swamp Trail, and 36 miles of dikes. To avoid disturbing wintering waterfowl, the impoundment dikes north of South Carolina State Route 170 are closed to visitation from December 1 through February. The largest concentrations of waterfowl occur from November through February.

Even though alligators are generally afraid of people, visitors are cautioned to stay a safe distance from these sluggish-looking but potentially fast-moving reptiles and to be alert for ticks, chiggers, and venomous snakes. Insect repellent and sunscreen are advised.

The more than 260 species of birds that have been recorded on Savannah Refuge are much the same as those of Cape Romain Refuge.

Mammals include white-tailed deer, bobcat, gray fox, river otter, raccoon, striped skunk, opossum, eastern cottontail, marsh rabbit, eastern gray and fox squirrels, and southern flying squirrel.

Of the reptiles, there are a number of turtles; snakes (black racer, corn, coachwhip, brown water, garter, mud, rainbow, hognose, copperhead, cottonmouth, and canebrake and diamondback rattlesnakes); and American alligator. Amphibians include frogs (pig frog, green and squirrel tree frogs, and bullfrog) and spadefoot toad.

Savannah is one of seven national wildlife refuges in the Savannah Coastal Refuges complex, which totals more than 55,000 acres. The others, from north to south, are Pinckney Island and Tybee (in South Carolina); and Wassaw, Harris Neck, Blackbeard Island, and Wolf Island (in Georgia).

Lodgings and meals are available in the cities of Savannah, Garden City, and Port Wentworth, Georgia and Hardeeville and Hilton Head Island, South Carolina.

Access in South Carolina to Savannah Refuge from Exit 5 (at Hardeeville) on I-95 (which cuts across the northern part of the refuge) is south 6 miles on U.S. 17, and west (right) into the refuge on South Carolina State Route 170. Or in Georgia, from Exit 109 on I-95 it is south on Georgia State Route 21, east on Georgia Route 30, north on Georgia Route 25 through Port Wentworth, east across the Savannah River, and into the refuge on South Carolina Route 170.

Further information: Savannah National Wildlife Refuge, c/o Savannah Coastal Refuges, Parkway Business Center, Suite 10, 1000 Business Center Drive, Savannah, GA 31405; telephone: (912) 652-4415.

Tybee, comprising 100 acres, was established in 1938 to manage habitat for many species of wintering waterfowl, wading birds, shorebirds, gulls, terns, and other migratory and resident birds. The refuge is located at the mouth of the Savannah River, directly opposite Fort Pulaski National Monument at the southern end of the South Carolina coast.

The nucleus of the refuge is Oyster Bed Island, which has been created by the accumulated spoil of sand and other sediments dredged from the river by the U.S. Army Corps of Engineers for river and harbor improvements. The spoil site began as a 1-acre oyster shoal. Eventually, the deposits joined Oyster Bed and Jones' islands, forming the northern bank of the river. The Corps of Engineers still retains authority to deposit spoil onto the refuge.

Some areas of Tybee Refuge are covered with dense vegetation of such species as southern redcedar, wax myrtle, and groundsel tree. Salt marsh and marsh hammocks lie between the refuge and the mainland to the west. More than 120 species of birds have been recorded on this refuge.

The refuge is closed to visitation.

Further information: Tybee National Wildlife Refuge, c/o Savannah Coastal Refuges, Parkway Business Center, Suite 10, 1000 Business Center Drive, Savannah, GA 31405; telephone: (912) 652-4415.

Waccamaw, consisting of 7,400 acres, was established in 1997 and is authorized to eventually encompass nearly 50,000 acres of floodplain swamplands along the Great and Little Pee Dee rivers and the Waccamaw River in northeastern South Carolina.

Habitats include black-water forested wetlands, tidal forested wetlands, and tidal marshes. These river systems are a vital part of the Winyah Bay watershed basin and ecosystem. The refuge attracts large concentrations of wading birds, wintering waterfowl, shorebirds, raptors, and neotropical migratory songbirds. This is also the northernmost nesting area of the swallow-tailed kite.

Among anticipated habitat management activities on Waccamaw Refuge are forest management, including prescribed burning; water level management; and control of non-native pest plants.

Waccamaw is presently an unstaffed refuge administered from Cape Romain NWR. The U.S. Fish and Wildlife Service is engaged in an active land acquisition mode. The refuge's 4,600-acre Bull

Island is the largest tract acquired so far. It is accessible by boat, and visitor activities include wildlife observation, photography, fishing, and hunting during the designated seasons (information and free permits are obtained from the headquarters at Cape Romain NWR). Once the refuge is staffed and as additional lands are acquired, more areas will be open to visitation.

Further information: Waccamaw National Wildlife Refuge, c/o Cape Romain NWR, 5821 Highway 17 North, Awendaw, SC 29429; (843) 928-3264.

South Dakota: National Wildlife Refuges

Bear Butte, comprising 566 acres, is an easement national wildlife refuge that is administered as a state park by the South Dakota Game, Fish, & Parks Department. It is located near the town of Sturgis in south-central South Dakota.

Further information: Bear Butte National Wildlife Refuge, HC5, Box 114, Martin, SD 57551; telephone: (605) 685-6508.

Dakota Tallgrass Prairie Wildlife Management Area (WMA), established in 2001, represents a new concept in wildlife conservation, one designed to help save an ecosystem from extinction. The goal is to eventually preserve 190,000 acres of what was once the vast ecosystem of the northern tallgrass prairie. The refuge will accomplish protection primarily through the purchase of perpetual grassland easements from willing sellers. The lands acquired are a part of the National Wildlife Refuge System and are administered locally by national wildlife refuges and wetland management districts. The entire Dakota Tallgrass Prairie WMA encompasses more than 80 percent of the remaining northern tallgrass prairie. The WMA includes parts of 28 counties in eastern South Dakota and 4 counties in southeastern North Dakota.

Conservation on the WMA began with the first easement on June 27, 2001. Since then, nearly 10,000 acres of conservation easements have been purchased from willing partners. Using perpetual easements, our partners retain ownership of their land, and the prairie is permanently protected. The WMA is presently in the early stages of development, and acquisition is the primary focus. As more acreage is added, the emphasis will shift to prairie enhancement and restoration.

As fragmentation of remaining prairie sites continues to reduce the viability of the ecosystem, the goal of this WMA is the preservation of the few remaining large blocks of this habitat in the Dakotas. Major focus areas include the Prairie Coteau, located in northeastern South Dakota, and lands adjacent to the Sheyenne National Grasslands in southeastern North Dakota.

Tallgrass prairie is the most altered and possibly the most endangered ecosystem in North America. Today, less than 4 percent of the old-growth northern tallgrass prairie remains, which means that nearly 45 million acres of northern tallgrass prairie have been wiped from the face of the Earth. Most of the losses are due to the continuous conversion of prairie to croplands since the late 1800s. The potential for species extinction in the northern tallgrass prairie is of serious concern. Grassland-dependent bird species have shown steeper and more consistent and geographically widespread declines than any other group of North American species.

Northern tallgrass prairie habitat is visually dominated by grasses, such as big bluestem, little bluestem, Indian grass, switch grass, prairie dropseed, porcupine grass, and needle-and-thread grass. However, 90 percent of the plants on the prairie are wildflowers. Some of the better-known species include blazing stars, hoary puccoon, catnip, Maximilian sunflower, gentians, and the white lady's-slipper orchid. These wildflowers add bright spots of color to the green and tan landscape. Historically, trees were a rarity on the northern tallgrass prairie, and several shrubs, such as leadplant, western snowberry, and buffalo currant, were locally abundant.

This biologically diverse system supports forty species of ground-nesting, neotropical migratory birds and a dozen species of waterfowl. Neotropicals include the bobolink, grasshopper sparrow, cedar waxwing, and common yellowthroat. Common waterfowl include blue-winged teal, mallard, gadwall, and the giant Canada goose. Greater prairie chicken and sharp-tailed grouse are two resident game birds that inhabit the WMA. Of the 435 bird species that nest within the United States, 160 breed in native tallgrass prairie habitat. Even in winter, when other birds leave this harsh northern climate, the ecosystem attracts the Lapland longspur, snow bunting, and snowy owl.

More than 24 species of true tallgrass prairie mammals have been recorded within the WMA. Among these are the western harvest and meadow jumping mice, least weasel, and eastern spotted skunk. The plains pocket gopher and Franklin's ground squirrel are among the few mammals that are restricted to the tallgrass prairie.

Reptiles and amphibians include the painted turtle, garter snake, tiger salamander, and northern leopard frog. The salamander and frog are the two most common; adults of these two species may be found in upland habitats, but they breed and overwinter in the water. Fish such as the Topeka shiner, which depend on clear prairie streams, may not survive if this habitat continues to be lost. Numerous butterflies, including the Dakota skipper and Regal fritillary, are dependent on a multitude of prairie plants to fulfill their life cycles.

The WMA is home to more than 317 state-listed rare or endangered plant and animal species. Federally listed threatened and endangered species include the western prairie fringed orchid, American burying beetle, and the Topeka shiner.

Northern tallgrass prairie supports tourism. The Dakotas' wildlife and rich native prairie heritage attract hunters, as well as birdwatchers from across the country. Native prairie protects water quality by reducing siltation and contaminants that reach rivers, streams, lakes, and wetlands. The northern tallgrass prairie is also important for a strong economy in the Dakotas, particularly the livestock industry. Grazing native grasslands is the most economical way to feed livestock. Without native grasslands, production costs for ranchers would increase, thus lowering profits and driving some ranchers out of the livestock business. Livestock dollars turn over more in the local economy than cropland dollars. Consequently, when native prairie is converted to cropland, the local economy and the natural environment both suffer.

Further information: Dakota Tallgrass Prairie Wildlife Management Area, 9754 – 143? Avenue SE, Cayuga, ND 58013; telephone: (701) 724-3598.

(NOTE: Special appreciation is given to Craig Mowry, Dakota Tallgrass Prairie Coordinator, for providing this description.)

Karl E. Mundt, containing 780 acres, was established in 1974 to enhance and protect one of the last stretches of essentially natural Missouri River bottomland. This refuge is located just downstream from the U.S. Army Corps of Engineers' Fort Randall Dam, in southeastern South Dakota. It is best known as America's first national eagle sanctuary.

Bald eagles gather here in winter, roosting in tall cottonwood trees that border the river and feeding on ducks and such fish as shad, goldeye, and white bass. Although wintering eagles are present on this refuge from late October until mid-March, peak numbers of these majestic birds occur in December and January—the largest concentration of wintering bald eagles in the lower 48 states. In 1967, more than 280 of these birds wintered here. Since 1990, two nesting pairs of bald eagles have made their home on the refuge, and eagles can be observed year-round near the refuge along the Missouri River.

To avoid disturbing the eagles, this refuge is not open to visitation. However, an eagle observation point, on adjacent Corps of Engineers land, provides outstanding close-up viewing of these birds, as they skillfully pluck fish from the rapidly moving tailwaters immediately below the dam.

The Latin name of this species, *Haliaeetus leucocephalus*, means "white-headed sea eagle." The female's wingspread measures approximately 8 feet, and the male's is about 1 foot less. The plumage of the juvenile is mostly dark brown, which makes the bird appear similar to a large hawk; the prominent white head and tail feathers of the adult develop in the fourth or fifth year.

Prior to establishment of the refuge, most of the eagles' communal roosting areas below the dam were located on privately owned lands. To help protect this ecologically significant riparian habitat, a fund-raising campaign was launched by the 7-Eleven Food Stores Division of Southland Corporation. Revenues derived from the sale of endangered species drinking cups and earmarked for the "Save a Living Thing Project," totaled $250,000. These funds were then donated to the National Wildlife Federation for the acquisition of 780 acres of river bottom habitat and the protective management of another 300 acres of riparian woodland under the terms of perpetual conservation easement agreements with local landowners. The federation transferred these properties to the U.S. Fish and Wildlife Service in December 1974. The new refuge was named in honor of the late United States Senator Karl E. Mundt of South Dakota, who had strongly supported passage of the Endangered Species Act of 1966.

In addition to the eagles, this refuge also attracts large concentrations of migratory waterfowl, as well as such species as white pelicans, Franklin's gulls, common and least terns, and double-crested cormorants, which rest and feed along the river. Wild turkeys, white-tailed and mule deer, bobcats, coyotes, mink, and raccoons are among the many other species of wildlife that inhabit the sheltered areas of cottonwoods and willows. Ring-necked pheasants and bob-white quail live around the edges of these woodlands. In spring, numerous songbirds, such as warblers, vireos, flycatchers, sparrows, grosbeaks, orioles, cardinal, brown thrasher, mockingbird, and meadowlark, nest or migrate through here.

The refuge's native mixed-grass prairie habitat is maintained with grazing, haying, and periodic prescription burning. This habitat is also important for waterfowl and other wildlife.

Lodgings and meals are available in such communities as Pickstown, Lake Andes, and Wagner. Campground facilities are provided near Fort Randall Dam by the Corps of Engineers, at several South Dakota state recreation areas, and in Nebraska's Niobrara State Park.

Access to Fort Randall Dam and the Corps of Engineers' eagle observation point is just west of Pickstown on U.S. Route 281.

Further information: Karl E. Mundt National Wildlife Refuge, c/o Lake Andes NWR Complex, 38672-291st Street, Lake Andes, SD 57356; telephone: (605) 487-7603.

Lacreek, comprising 16,500 acres, was established in 1935 to enhance and protect spring-fed wetlands—an expanse of subirrigated meadow. This refuge is located adjacent to shortgrass prairie uplands and sandhills in Lake Creek Valley at the northern edge of the Nebraska Sandhills, in southwestern South Dakota. Its name is derived from Lake Creek, which benefits large concentrations of migrating and nesting waterfowl.

Approximately 5,400 acres of ecologically significant marsh and open water encompass eleven water impoundment units, created by a network of dikes and other water control structures that were built in the 1930s by the Civilian Conservation Corps (CCC). Water levels in these impounded areas are regulated to produce optimum habitat for ducks, geese, swans, shorebirds, and other water birds.

During spring migration, the influx of migratory waterfowl totals close to 12,000 birds, and in the autumn their numbers exceed 20,000. Of the 1,000 to 2000 nesting ducks of many species, blue-winged teal, mallards, gadwalls, and shovelers are the most abundant. Up to 350 pairs of Canada geese, colonies of white pelicans and cormorants, great blue heron and cattle egret rookeries, and numerous shorebirds also nest on Lacreek Refuge.

Other habitats support thousands of the non-native ring-necked pheasants, and substantial numbers of sharp-tailed grouse winter on the refuge. More than 270 species of birds have been recorded on Lacreek, a number that is enhanced not only by the refuge's diversity of habitats but also by the overlapping ranges of many eastern and western species.

The refuge also supports white-tailed and mule deer, a few pronghorn, and two prairie dog towns.

Ducks Unlimited, Inc. has assisted with extensive habitat enhancement projects.

The refuge is open daily during daylight hours. There is no entrance fee.

Visitor activities include birdwatching, photography, driving a 4-mile interpretive tour route (a brochure is available) and other public roads, hiking, fishing (on some of the pools and ponds), and hunting on parts of the refuge during the designated seasons. The 223-acre Little White River Recreation Area, located at the northern end of the refuge and managed by South Dakota Game, Fish & Parks, offers opportunities for picnicking, camping, swimming, boating, fishing, and hunting.

Visitors are cautioned to be alert for rattlesnakes. Insect repellent is recommended during the warmer months.

Lodgings and meals are available in Martin.

> Access to Lacreek Refuge is southeastward 13 miles on State Route 73 from its junction with U.S. Route 18 at Martin, and following refuge directional signs.

> Further information: Lacreek National Wildlife Refuge, HC 5, Box 114, Martin, SD 57551; telephone: (605) 685-6508.

Lake Andes, consisting of 365 acres, was established in 1936 to manage shallow prairie lake and adjacent native grassland habitat, primarily for breeding waterfowl and other water birds, in southeastern South Dakota. Of this refuge's acreage, the U.S. Fish and Wildlife Service owns 938 acres and protectively manages another 4,700 acres under the terms of perpetual conservation easement agreements with local landowners.

As Lake Andes depends upon natural runoff, its level fluctuates with the amount of precipitation. Roughly once every two decades, the lake dries up completely. Under the terms of an easement agreement with the State of South Dakota, the Fish and Wildlife Service manages the lake with dikes that divide the body of water into three units. Water levels within these units are regulated, within the constraints of an impermanent water supply, to promote the growth of aquatic foods and provide sufficient water for broods of ducks and other water birds. Owen's Bay marsh is fed by an artesian well and consequently offers far more consistently reliable water management for the benefit of wildlife.

Other wildlife of this refuge includes bald eagles, eared grebes, black terns, Franklin's gulls, bobolinks and numerous other songbirds, ring-necked pheasants, white-tailed deer, beavers, and muskrats.

The refuge is open daily during daylight hours. There is no entrance fee.

Visitor activities include birdwatching; photography; hiking; picnicking; fishing (during wet years, on the south and central parts of Lake Andes); waterfowl hunting (on the central unit of the lake); and pheasant and deer hunting (around the wooded and shrubby border of the lake, in years of low water) during the designated seasons. A 1-mile interpretive loop trail leads visitors through a stretch of wooded shoreline and across areas of prairie-pond marsh and upland native grass uplands. A wildlife observation (wheelchair-accessible) platform is also provided. Guided group tours of the refuge are offered if arrangements are made in advance. Although camping is not permitted on the refuge, campground facilities are available at the U.S. Army Corps of Engineers' Fort Randall Dam, at several nearby South Dakota state recreation areas, and at Nebraska's Niobrara State Park.

Lodgings and meals are available in such communities as Lake Andes, Wagner, and Pickstown.

Access to Lake Andes Refuge is north 2 miles and west 1 mile from Ravinia.

Further information: Lake Andes National Wildlife Refuge, 38672-291st Street, Lake Andes, SD 57356; telephone: (605) 487-7603.

Sand Lake, comprising 21,498 acres, was established in 1935 to enhance and protect the ecologically significant prairie marsh ecosystem of shallow lakes, marsh, wooded lakeshore, shelterbelts, and grassland in the heart of the prairie pothole region along the James River in northeastern South Dakota. This refuge is a vitally important major staging and nesting area—a mecca for hundreds of thousands of migratory birds, especially waterfowl.

As many as one-quarter million snow geese have been seen during the autumn, and up to 1.2 million during the spring. Tundra swans and bald eagles pause on their migrations, with up to 100 eagles in the spring. White pelicans gather in large concentrations. Substantial numbers of white-faced ibises, cattle egrets, and black terns nest at Sand Lake. In recent years, the refuge has been supporting the world's largest nesting colony of Franklin's gulls, totaling from 86,000 to 155,000 pairs. Over 265 bird species have been recorded here.

Sand Lake Refuge has been designated as a "Wetland of International Importance" by the U.S. Department of the Interior and the Convention on Wetlands of International Importance. It is the first refuge in the prairie pothole region to be so honored.

Two low-head dams, a number of dikes and other water control structures, and nesting islands were built during the early years of the refuge to enhance waterfowl habitat. Sand Lake, behind Columbia Dam, and Mud Lake, behind Houghton Dam, provide long expanses of open water and some wetland habitat of cattails, bulrushes, and common reed (*Phragmites*). Great numbers of waterfowl, wading birds, and shorebirds congregate to rest and feed here during the spring and autumn migrations. Some stretches of lakeshore are bordered with cottonwood trees, willows, and other woodland vegetation that attract many kinds of migratory songbirds.

Soon after the refuge was established, the Civilian Conservation Corps (CCC) planted close to one-half million trees on the refuge to provide shelterbelts for wildlife against the powerful winter winds. Green ash, American elm, eastern cottonwood, and the non-native Russian olive and Siberian elm were the major species introduced onto the refuge. On some refuge lands that were previously cropland or pasture, the Fish and Wildlife Service has planted a mixture of native grasses. Areas of dense nesting cover for ducks and other wildlife have been planted with sweet clover, alfalfa, and wheatgrass.

One of this refuge's most outstanding wildlife conservation programs has been the restoration of the giant subspecies of the Canada goose (*Branta canadensis maxima*). This magnificent bird, with a wingspread up to nearly 6 feet, was on the brink of extinction as the result of overhunting and egg collecting during the early twentieth century. In 1962, the U.S. Fish and Wildlife Service and the South Dakota Department of Game, Fish, and Parks initiated a joint restoration program. Several thousands of these geese, which have been raised from a captive flock of 200 birds that is maintained by the State of South Dakota on Sand Lake Refuge, have been released into the wild and are now reestablished on suitable waterfowl habitats throughout the Dakotas.

Sand Lake Refuge's habitat maintenance and enhancement activities include managing water levels to provide optimum conditions for waterfowl and other wildlife, prescribed burning, planting shrubs and seeding native grasses, grazing, haying, and cooperative farming that allows a portion of crops such as corn to be left unharvested for the benefit of wildlife.

Establishment of Sand Lake Refuge was made possible partly with revenues from the sale of Migratory Bird Hunting and Conservation Stamps (Duck Stamps).

Ducks Unlimited, Inc. and other private organizations have assisted with important habitat enhancement projects. These projects have included the construction of water control facilities, a nesting exclosure, and nesting islands.

The refuge is open daily during daylight hours, between early April and late September. There is no entrance fee. The auto tour route is open from early April through late September, depending on weather conditions. The visitor center and refuge headquarters are open on weekdays, except national holidays. The visitor center may also be open on some spring weekends, depending upon the availability of volunteers.

Visitor activities include birdwatching; photography; viewing exhibits in the headquarters/visitor center; climbing a 100-foot tower near the visitor center for a panorama of the refuge; driving the 15-mile interpretive auto tour route; watching wildlife from an observation deck on the shore of Sand Lake; hiking (a 0.75-mile trail at the refuge's Columbia Recreation Area and elsewhere); picnicking (a wheelchair-accessible picnic area at Columbia Recreation Area); fishing (at four locations); and hunting (waterfowl, pheasant, and deer) on certain parts of the refuge during the designated seasons (a wheelchair-accessible waterfowl hunting blind is provided). A pond adjacent to the visitor center/headquarters offers an opportunity for close viewing of waterfowl. Although camping is not permitted on the refuge, campground facilities are available at Roy Lake, Fort Sisseton, Richmond Lake, and other nearby state parks.

Lodgings and meals are available in such communities as Aberdeen, Columbia, and Hecla.

Access to Sand Lake Refuge from Aberdeen is east 7 miles on U.S. Route 12 to Bath Corner, and north 20 miles on County Route 16.

Further information: Sand Lake National Wildlife Refuge, 39650 Sand Lake Drive, Columbia, SD 57433; telephone: (605) 885-6320.

Waubay, consisting of 4,650 acres, was established in 1935 to enhance and protect an ecologically diverse area of lakes and ponds, marshes, prairie, and deciduous forest in northeastern South Dakota's prairie hills-pothole region. The refuge's name is derived from the Lakota Indian word that appropriately means "a nesting place for birds."

Of the more than 240 species of birds that have been recorded at Waubay Refuge, more than 100 nest here. Prominent among these is the giant subspecies of the Canada goose. This magnificent bird, with a wingspan up to nearly 6 feet, was on the brink of extinction as the result of overhunting and egg collecting in the early twentieth century. Fortunately, it was successfully introduced on the refuge in 1937 from a donated privately owned flock.

Among other nesting birds are five species of grebes, and numerous kinds of ducks, including blue-winged teal, mallards, gadwalls, shovelers, redheads, and lesser scaups. Waubay is the farthest south in North America where the red-necked grebe is known to nest. In addition, there are large nesting colonies of cormorants, the white pelican is conspicuous and common, and the ranges of a number of eastern and western songbirds overlap here.

Establishment of this refuge was made possible partly with revenues from the sale of Migratory Bird Hunting and Conservation Stamps (Duck Stamps). Ducks Unlimited, Inc. has assisted with important habitat enhancement projects.

This refuge is open daily during daylight hours. There is no entrance fee. The headquarters and visitor center are open on weekdays, except national holidays.

Visitor activities include birdwatching, photography, viewing exhibits and displays in the headquarters/visitor center building, hiking a loop trail near the headquarters/visitor center, picnicking (a picnic area is available), fishing ("walk-in" ice fishing, from December to ice-out), and hunting (deer only) on part of the refuge during the designated season. Camping is not permitted on the refuge, but campground facilities are provided at Pickerel Lake and other nearby state parks.

Hiking opportunities include the 0.25-mile, interpretive Spring Lake Overlook Trail, which provides a view of four different wildlife habitats; and the 0.75-mile Headquarters Loop Trail (part of which is wheelchair-accessible), which winds through woodlands of oak, basswood, and ash. This latter trail also passes a small area of marsh, the 110-foot-tall observation tower that offers a spectacular panorama of the refuge, and a picnic area on the shore of Hillebrand's Lake.

In addition to this national wildlife refuge, more than 40,000 acres in 352 waterfowl production areas (WPAs) are scattered throughout the surrounding Waubay Wetland Management District (see separate text). The first such WPA in the United States was established in this district in 1959. The purchase of these ecologically significant habitats has been made possible with revenues from the sale of Duck Stamps. Another 250,000 acres of the district's wetland and upland habitats are protectively managed under the terms of perpetual conservation easement agreements with local landowners.

Bird species that have been recorded on Waubay Refuge are essentially the same as those of Sand Lake Refuge.

Lodgings and meals are available in such communities as Webster, Milbank, Watertown, and Aberdeen.

Access to Waubay Refuge is west 11 miles on U.S. Route 12 from I-29 at Summit, and north (right) 7 miles on County Route 1.

Further information: Waubay National Wildlife Refuge, RR 1, Box 39, Waubay, SD 57273; telephone (605) 947-4521.

South Dakota:
Wetland Management Districts

Huron Wetland Management District was established in 1992 to restore, enhance, and manage scattered areas of important wetland and grassland habitats within the prairie pothole region in east-central South Dakota. It lies within Beadle, Sanborn, Hand, Hyde, Hughes, Sully, Jerauld, and Buffalo counties.

This extensive district includes more than 13,500 acres in 57 federally owned waterfowl production areas (WPAs) and more than 127,000 acres that are being managed under the terms of perpetual wetland, grassland, and conservation easements purchased from local landowners.

The WPAs are generally open daily to visitation, during daylight hours. There are no entrance fees, and no visitor use facilities are provided. Visitor activities include birdwatching, photography, hiking, and hunting during the designated seasons.

Further information: Huron Wetland Management District, Federal Building, Room 309, 200 Fourth Street SW , Huron, SD 57350; telephone: (605) 352-5894.

Lake Andes Wetland Management District was established in 1961 to restore, enhance, and manage scattered areas of important wetland and grassland habitats within the prairie pothole region in southeastern South Dakota. These areas lie within Brule, Aurora, Davidson, Hanson, Charles Mix, Douglas, Hutchinson, Turner, Lincoln, Bon Homme, Yankton, Clay, and Union counties.

This extensive district includes more than 19,160 acres of federally owned waterfowl production areas (WPAs); Lake Andes and Karl E. Mundt national wildlife refuges (see separate texts); and more than 55,000 acres that are being managed under the terms of perpetual wetland, grassland, and conservation easements purchased from local landowners.

The WPAs are generally open daily to visitation, during daylight hours. There are no entrance fees; no visitor use facilities are provided. Visitor activities include birdwatching, photography, hiking, fishing, trapping, and hunting during the designated seasons.

Further information: Lake Andes Wetland Management District, 38672-291st Street, Lake Andes, SD 57356; telephone: (605) 487-7603.

Madison Wetland Management District was established in 1969 to restore, enhance, and manage scattered areas of important wetland and grassland habitats within the prairie pothole region in southeastern South Dakota. It lies within Minnehaha, McCook, Miner, Lake, Moody, Brookings, Kingsbury, Hamlin, and Deuel counties.

This extensive district includes more than 38,500 acres of federally owned waterfowl production areas (WPAs); and more than 91,000 acres of wetland, grassland, and conservation easements purchased from local landowners.

The 220 WPAs are open to visitation daily, during daylight hours. There are no entrance fees; no visitor use facilities are provided. Visitor activities include birdwatching; photography; hiking; and fishing, hunting, and trapping during the designated seasons.

Further information: Madison Wetland Management District, P.O. Box 48, Madison, SD 57042; telephone: (605) 256-2974.

Sand Lake Wetland Management District (WMD) was established in 1961 to restore, enhance, and manage important wetland and grassland habitats within the upper Great Plains prairie pothole region in northeastern South Dakota. It is located in Campbell, McPherson, Brown, Walworth, Edmunds, Potter, Faulk, and Spink counties and lies within three distinct physiographic regions—the Missouri Coteau, the James River Basin, and the Lake Dakota Plain.

This region of South Dakota was once dominated by wetlands and native prairie vegetation. Although the tallgrass prairie zone is primarily to the east of the WMD, a small portion of eastern Brown and northeastern Spink counties is within the tallgrass prairie zone, which is dominated by big and little bluestem, switchgrass, and Indiangrass.

The mixed-tallgrass transition zone of the James River Valley was once dominated by western wheatgrass, big bluestem, and porcupine grass. Although much of the zone has been farmed, some prairie still exists, particularly in areas with a high water table and numerous shallow wetlands.

The mixed-grass zone of the central and western portions of the WMD is dominated by western wheatgrass, little bluestem, blue grama, needle-and-thread, and green needlegrass. Somewhere between 30 and 50 percent of this drier prairie remains today.

Of the WMD's nearly 5.76 million acres, more than 56 percent (3 million acres) has been converted to cropland and 13 percent (more than 718,000 acres) to tame grass hayland, but the remaining 31 percent (1.756 million acres) is still native prairie.

Sand Lake WMD includes more than 44,000 acres in 162 federally owned waterfowl production areas (WPAs), ranging in size from 18 to 2,600 acres. Their habitats include more than 60 percent grassland, 35 percent wetland, and 0.3 percent woodland.

The WPAs are generally open daily to visitation during daylight hours. There are no entrance fees, and no visitor use facilities are provided. Visitor activities include birdwatching, photography, hiking, and hunting during the designated seasons.

In addition to the WPAs, the Sand Lake WMD protects more than 526,000 acres under the terms of perpetual wetland and grassland easements which are purchased from willing landowners. Under wetland easements, the U.S. Fish and Wildlife Service pays the landowner a lump sum payment not to drain, burn, level, or fill in natural wetlands. (The wetland easement does not affect normal farming practices, such as cropping, haying, grazing, or plowing wetlands when they are dry, due to natural conditions.) Under grassland easements, grazing is unrestricted, annual haying is permitted after July 15, and the production of agricultural crops is not permitted. A third kind of easement protects wetlands (and, in some cases, adjacent uplands) owned by the U.S. Department of Agriculture's Farmers Home Administration (FmHA). Once these properties are sold back into private ownership, the Fish and Wildlife Service accepts the responsibility of enforcing the terms of these conservation easements.

As of 2001, Sand Lake WMD was responsible for approximately 587,000 acres of WPAs and all three kinds of easements—making it the Fish and Wildlife Service's largest wetland management district in the United States.

Acquisition of the WPAs and easements is made possible with revenues from the sale of Migratory Bird Hunting and Conservation Stamps (Duck Stamps). In addition, the South Dakota Game, Fish, and Parks Department, county conservation districts, and nonprofit organizations including Ducks Unlimited, Inc. and various local sportsmen's groups contribute in a variety of ways, such as funding, volunteer staffing, and technical expertise, to help make possible the enhancement and protection of these vital areas.

More than 95 percent of the land within Sand Lake WMD is privately owned. In order to have a significant impact on the resources that the Fish and Wildlife Service is charged with protecting and enhancing, they must work with private landowners. The Partners for Wildlife Program is designed to accomplish this working relationship. The program provides technical expertise and funding to initiate habitat improvement projects on private land. The Sand Lake WMD Partners for Wildlife Program focuses on restoring and creating wetlands and providing incentives to protect and manage existing grassland, as well as converting cropland back to grass.

Typical projects include restoring drained wetlands, creating and repairing small dams for waterfowl and livestock water, seeding cropland back to native grasses, cross fencing to improve rangeland and pasture conditions, and providing wildlife nesting structures. The majority of the funding to implement these practices is derived from grants that bring together a variety of federal, state, and private partners. Each year in the Sand Lake WMD, the Partners for Wildlife Program contributes to the improvement or protection of thousands of acres of wildlife habitat on private lands.

Further information: Sand Lake Wetland Management District, 39650 Sand Lake Drive, Columbia, SD 57433; telephone: (605) 885-6320.

(NOTE: Special appreciation is given to Scott Glup, District Manager, for providing this description.)

Waubay Wetland Management District was established in 1959 to restore, enhance, and manage scattered areas of important wetland and grassland habitats within the prairie pothole region in northeastern South Dakota. It lies within Clark, Codington, Day, Grant, Marshall, and Roberts counties.

This extensive district contains the first waterfowl production area (WPA) in the United States and a total of more than 40,000 acres of these federally owned WPAs; Waubay National Wildlife Refuge; and over 250,000 acres that are being managed under the terms of perpetual wetland and grassland easements purchased from local landowners.

The WPAs are generally open daily to visitation during daylight hours. There are no entrance fees, and no visitor use facilities are provided. Visitor activities include birdwatching, photography, hiking, and hunting during the designated seasons.

Further information: Waubay Wetland Management District, Route 1, Box 39, Waubay, SD 57273; telephone: (605) 947-4521.

Tennessee

Chickasaw, containing 23,856 acres toward an authorized goal of just over 55,000 acres, was established in 1985. The refuge's mission is to restore, enhance, and protect an ecologically important stretch of the meandering Mississippi River floodplain and its natural water cycles at the western edge of Tennessee.

Large concentrations of wintering waterfowl commonly reach as many as 20,000 to 40,000 ducks (principally mallards) and sometimes up to 4,000 Canada geese. Herons and egrets are attracted to Chickasaw Refuge during the spring and summer, and a variety of shorebirds pause to rest and feed during spring and autumn migrations. In April, the woodlands are filled with migrating warblers and other neotropical migratory songbirds. Wintering and resident bald eagles prey upon fish and sick or injured waterfowl. Mississippi kites and migrating white pelicans are also attracted to the refuge.

More than 19,000 acres of the refuge consist of seasonally flooded bottomland hardwood forest, in which the major management emphasis is reestablishing and maintaining this ecologically significant habitat. As the U.S. Fish and Wildlife Service explains:

What was once a vast expanse of mature bottomland hardwood forests along the Mississippi River and its tributaries is now only small fragmented pockets of forestland. Since 1960 the losses of bottomland hardwood forests have been the most dramatic in the southeastern United States. . . . Conversion to agriculture and other uses . . . [has] accounted for most of the losses. . . .

The forest management program focuses on protection, enhancement, and regeneration of bottomland hardwood tree species, with emphasis on "red oaks" and other important mast producing species. Common bottomland hardwood tree species include a variety of oaks such as cherrybark, Nuttall, willow, and overcup, and eastern cottonwood, persimmon, sweetgum, sweet pecan, hackberry, hickory, and others. Although not truly a "hardwood," bald cypress frequently occurs throughout the bottomlands.

Other habitat management activities include seasonal water level manipulation relating to Mississippi River flood levels within levee-contained impoundments, to provide high water for wintering waterfowl and receding water levels in spring, summer, and autumn for shorebirds and wading birds. The Fish and Wildlife Service says: "Approximately 412 acres are in moist-soils/natural foods management. With the completion of the levee rehabilitation work on the refuge and the installation of a water pumping system, true 'moist-soils' management can be accomplished. Stands of fall grasses, sedges, wild millet, and smartweeds dominate these areas and are enhanced through water manipulation and soil disturbance. These areas of the impoundment system are heavily used by wading birds and migrating shorebirds during controlled drawdown of water levels."

An important management goal of Chickasaw Refuge is the restoration of the hydrology of the Forked Deer River, which historically flowed through this area.

Under cooperative agreements with local farmers, roughly 1,100 acres of the refuge are devoted to the cultivation of such crops as corn, milo, and millet, a portion of which is left unharvested for the benefit of waterfowl and other wildlife. The refuge also includes nearly 1,000 acres of open water and marsh, sloughs, several oxbow lakes, 300 acres of wooded upland, and 10 acres of sand bluffs.

Establishment of the Chickasaw Refuge was made possible partly with revenues from the sale of Migratory Bird Hunting and Conservation Stamps (Duck Stamps). Ducks Unlimited, Inc. has helped enhance 800 acres of the refuge's wetland habitat.

Most of the refuge is open daily. A 1,500-acre area is closed from November 15 to March 15, to avoid disturbing the concentrations of wintering waterfowl. There is no entrance fee. Access is limited during the annual winter–spring river flooding.

Visitor activities include birdwatching; photography; driving on established roads; hiking on a number of trails and former lumber-company roads; bicycling on roads and trails; canoeing and boating on oxbow lakes, sloughs, and small rivers (a number of boat ramps are provided); fishing; and hunting (deer, ducks, and small game) on part of the refuge during the designated seasons. Camping is not permitted on the refuge, except for primitive camping at the Barr Road campsite during refuge hunts.

Visitors are urged to be alert for venomous snakes. Insect repellent is advised during the warmer months.

Fauna and flora on Chickasaw Refuge are essentially the same as the species on Reelfoot Refuge, with which it is jointly managed.

Lodgings and meals are available in such communities as Ripley and Dyersburg.

Access to Chickasaw Refuge from the only stoplight on U.S. Route 51 in Ripley is north on Edith Central Road. At the 4-way stop in Central, the road name changes to Edith Nankipoo. Continue north on Edith Nankipoo Road to a refuge directional sign, at which turn left onto Hobe Webb Road. At a second refuge sign, turn right onto Sand Bluff Road. Refuge headquarters is located at the bottom of the hill on the left.

Further information: Chickasaw National Wildlife Refuge, 1505 Sand Bluff Road, Ripley, TN 38063; telephone: (731) 635-7621.

Cross Creeks, containing 8,862 acres, was established in 1962. The refuge produces waterfowl food crops; regulates and restricts hunting, trapping, and fishing; and otherwise manages habitats for the protection of wildlife and fish populations. The refuge is located on the Cumberland River at the headwaters of Barkley Lake in northern Tennessee.

When the U.S. Army Corps of Engineers built the Barkley Dam several miles upstream from the junction of the Cumberland and Ohio rivers, it created the reservoir known as Barkley Lake. The refuge is named for the meeting of two creeks on opposite sides of the river—North Cross and South Cross creeks. Refuge habitats include upland oak-hickory forest, seasonally flooded bottomland hardwood forest, agricultural fields, managed moist-soil units, 16 water-fowl impoundments, and various other wetlands.

Cross Creeks Refuge provides important winter habitat for migratory waterfowl. Ducks of many species and Canada geese typically arrive in large numbers during mid-November and depart in late February. Peak winter waterfowl concentrations normally range between 15,000 and 30,000 Canada geese and between 40,000 and 60,000 ducks. As refuge manager Walter Neasbitt explains:

Cross Creeks National Wildlife Refuge is one of three refuges in the southern United States where the southern James Bay population of Canada geese principally winters. Since the early 1990s, this population has been declining and by the mid-1990s had declined by almost half. Providing winter food and resting habitat for these birds is, therefore, a critically important function of this refuge.

For many years, the black duck population has also been in decline. As the human population increases its use of once-isolated sections of rivers and their wetlands, these waterfowl will have fewer and fewer places to spend the winter. While the majority of the ducks using Cross Creeks are mallards, the refuge provides a safe haven for the second largest wintering black duck concentration in the southeastern United States. Consequently, Cross Creeks Refuge plays an increasingly important role in the conservation of this species.

To ensure that the refuge provides this significantly productive winter waterfowl habitat, the U.S. Fish and Wildlife Service conducts several habitat management programs. Refuge staff manipulate water levels in impounded water units to produce moist-soil habitat. Moist soils produce seed-bearing grasses and herbaceous plants such as barnyard grass, rice cutgrass, sprangle-top, smartweeds, and sedges, which offer food and cover for waterfowl as well as for many other birds and resident wildlife. To supplement the wildlife food provided by wild grasses, trees, and other plants, the refuge manages 1,200 acres of agricultural land under cooperative agreements with local farmers. Each year, a portion of their annual corn crop is left unharvested for the benefit of wildlife. The Fish and Wildlife Service personnel farm another 600 acres in milo, buckwheat, and winter wheat. The latter crop serves as the main source of browse for Canada geese and provides the wide open spaces that geese prefer.

In addition to waterfowl, Cross Creeks Refuge is a temporary and/or permanent host to hundreds of bird species each year. Two pairs of bald eagles have nested on and around the refuge since the mid-1980s. One of these nests is the oldest, most productive nest in Tennessee, having fledged two to three eaglets each year since 1984. Throughout the year, bald eagles prefer to prey on fish but will eat anything they can catch, including ducks, rabbits, and even turtles. Occasionally, this top predator can be observed making a meal of carrion such as a deer carcass.

During spring, autumn, and winter migrations, shorebirds, raptors, and neotropical songbirds pause on the refuge for various lengths of time. For several weeks during the spring and autumn, the refuge woodlands provide feeding and resting habitat for a tremendous influx of songbirds, such as warblers, vireos, flycatchers, grosbeaks, tanagers, and orioles. When weather conditions and seasonal manipulation of the refuge's waterfowl impoundments yield exposed mudflats during spring and autumn, shorebirds, such as sandpipers, yellowlegs, and dowitchers, take advantage of a brief respite here before moving on to their terminal migratory destination. During the winter, Cross Creeks is graced with an influx of predatory birds. These species include the northern harrier,

American kestrel, and an occasional golden eagle following the food supply or just migrating to latitudes that are milder than the northern United States and southern Canada, where they spend the summer. Over 250 bird species have been recorded here.

The entire refuge is open daily during daylight hours from March 15 through October 31. From November 1 through March 14, the refuge's 30-mile road network is closed to visitation, to keep waterfowl disturbance to a minimum. However, groups wishing to visit the refuge during this latter time may contact the refuge office to set up a time for a staff-guided tour. There is no entrance fee. The visitor center is open year-round on weekdays, except national holidays.

Visitor activities include birdwatching; photography; viewing interpretive exhibits and programs at the visitor center; educational programs for youth groups, including the annual, award-winning, week-long children's environmental education camp; driving on about 15 miles of the refuge's improved gravel roads from March 15 to October 31; hiking the 1-mile Rattlesnake Trail from March 15 to October 31; hiking and bicycling on about 15 miles of gravel roads that are closed to public motor vehicles; canoeing and boating on refuge impoundments and reservoirs from March 15 to October 31 (improved and unimproved boat-launching ramps are provided); boating year-round on the Cumberland River and all bays having direct access to the river; fishing; and hunting (archery deer, squirrel, and turkey) on part of the refuge during the designated seasons. Although camping is not permitted on the refuge, campground facilities are available in such nearby places as the Land Between the Lakes National Recreation Area and Paris Landing State Park.

Visitors are urged to be alert for ticks and venomous snakes. Insect repellent is advised during the warmer months.

Lodgings and meals are available in such communities as Dover, Paris, and Clarksville and in Paris Landing State Park.

Access to Cross Creeks Refuge from Exit 4 on I-24 is west 37 miles on U.S. Route 79 through Clarksville to Dover, east (left) just over 2 miles on State Route 49, and (following refuge directional signs) north (left) less than 1 mile to the visitor center.

Further information: Cross Creeks National Wildlife Refuge, 643 Wildlife Road, Dover, TN 37058; telephone: (731) 232-7477.

Hatchie, encompassing 11,556 acres, was established in 1964. Most of the refuge consists of seasonally flooded, bottomland hardwood forest along a beautiful meandering stretch of the Hatchie River in southwestern Tennessee.

Other habitats include marshes, sloughs, creeks, oxbow and other lakes, and upland pine and hardwood forest. Water levels within moist-soil impoundments are seasonally manipulated—lowered for the benefit of migrating shorebirds and wading birds and reflooded for wintering waterfowl. Under cooperative agreements with local farmers, croplands are cultivated with corn, wheat, millet, and soybeans, a portion of which is left unharvested for the benefit of waterfowl and other wildlife.

Concentrations of as many as 40,000 wintering migratory ducks—notably mallards, along with black ducks, green-winged and blue-winged teal, gadwalls, wigeons, and pintails—are attracted to the refuge. A few bald eagles winter on the refuge, preying upon fish and weak or injured waterfowl. Wood ducks and hooded mergansers nest here, using tree cavities and several hundred nesting boxes that are provided by the refuge.

During spring and autumn migrations, the woodlands are filled with neotropical migratory songbirds, such as warblers, thrushes, flycatchers, grosbeaks, buntings, tanagers, and orioles. Ospreys visit and Mississippi kites nest on the refuge. Wild turkeys and barred owls are among the resident species. Mammals include white-tailed deer, bobcat, coyote, gray fox, river otter, beaver, and raccoon.

The Hatchie River, a state-designated scenic river, is the last unchannelized river of its type in the Lower Mississippi Valley. Unfortunately, it is being threatened with serious environmental degradation as one of the most erodable places in the world. Erosion rates in the Hatchie Valley are extremely high, sometimes annually exceeding 120 tons per acre. As explained by the U.S. Fish and Wildlife Service:

... government agencies, conservation groups and landowners have formed an organization called Hatchie Pride with goals of Protection, Restoration, Information and Education, Development and Evaluation of the Hatchie River's two-million acre watershed. They are working together to reduce the sedimentation rate of the Hatchie River by 50%. This will help prevent devastation of the forests located in this watershed.

Hatchie Refuge was established mostly with revenues from the sale of Migratory Bird Hunting and Conservation Stamps (Duck Stamps). Friends of Hatchie Refuge is a nonprofit support group that is assisting the refuge in many ways.

The refuge is open daily during daylight hours, except for parts of the refuge that are closed from November 15 to March 15 to avoid disturbance of wintering waterfowl. There is no entrance fee. The refuge office, located one-quarter mile south of the junction of I-40 and State Route 76, is open on weekdays, except national holidays.

Visitor activities include birdwatching; photography; driving and hiking on about 15 miles of refuge roads, including Whistling Wings Wildlife Drive at Oneal Lake; interpretive and educational programs; canoeing and boating (numerous boat-launching ramps provide access onto the river and oxbow and other lakes); fishing; and hunting (deer, raccoon, squirrel, waterfowl, and turkey) on parts of the refuge (but not the Oneal Lake area) during the designated seasons. Camping is not permitted on the refuge.

One of Hatchie Refuge's visitor use highlights is Project Fish, a model demonstration project designed to provide sport-fishing facilities for visitors with disabilities. Information: (731) 772-7841. As described by the Fish and Wildlife Service:

At Oneal Lake, Project Fish develops innovative facility designs for meeting the needs of anglers with disabilities. Once facilities are constructed, they are used and evaluated by fishermen with a variety of disabilities and then modified. The results are well designed, state of the art fishing facilities, that meet the needs of the majority of anglers with disabilities.

Fauna and flora that have been recorded on Hatchie Refuge are essentially the same as the species on Reelfoot Refuge.

Lodgings and meals are available in Brownsville.

Access to the refuge's Oneal Lake area from I-40 is at Exit 56 (one-quarter mile south of which is the refuge office), south 4 miles on State Route 76, and east (left) onto the entry road; or from I-40 at Exit 52, it is east 0.1-mile on State Route 179, north (left) on State Route 76, and east (right) onto the entry road. Access to the eastern part of the refuge from I-40 at Exit 52 is southeast 12 miles on State Route 179 and northeast 5 miles on Hillville Road, which loops through the southern edge of the refuge. I-40, between Exits 52 and 56, cuts through the western end of the refuge.

Further information: Hatchie National Wildlife Refuge, 4172 Highway 76 South, Brownsville, TN 38012; telephone: (731) 772-0501.

Lake Isom, comprising 1,850 acres, was established in 1938 in northwestern Tennessee. The refuge manages and protects important wintering and breeding habitats of open water, moist-soil impoundments, forested wetlands, and croplands for migratory birds and other wildlife. Concentrations of wintering waterfowl commonly total as many as 10,000 Canada geese and 30,000 ducks. Bald eagles frequent the refuge, with a pair nesting by the lake nearly every year. During the winter months, several eagles congregate on the refuge to prey upon the abundant waterfowl.

The U.S. Fish and Wildlife Service carries out a number of habitat management activities. Water levels within 75 acres of moist-soil impoundments are manipulated to promote the growth of wild millet, spike rush, and other native vegetation; and to provide habitat for shore-birds and wading birds. A 150-acre network of levee-contained impoundments at the northern end of 700-acre Lake Isom provides seasonal water level fluctuations—flooding to benefit wintering waterfowl, and gradually receding levels during spring to benefit shorebirds and wading birds. Under cooperative agreements with local farmers, corn, millet, milo, wheat, and soybeans are cultivated on 500 acres of cropland. A portion of these crops is left unharvested, to provide supplemental food for waterfowl and other wildlife.

The refuge is open daily from March 15 to October 15. There is no entrance fee.

Visitor activities include birdwatching, photography, hiking, canoeing and boating, fishing, and hunting (deer, raccoon, and squirrel, but not waterfowl) on part of the refuge during the designated seasons.

Visitors are urged to be alert for venomous snakes. Insect repellent is advised during the warmer months.

Fauna and flora of Lake Isom Refuge are essentially the same as the species on nearby Reelfoot Refuge, with which it is jointly managed.

Lodgings and meals are available at Reelfoot Lake State Resort Park and in such communities as Union City and Tiptonville, Tennessee, and Caruthersville, Missouri.

Access to Lake Isom Refuge from Union City is west and southwest about 23 miles on State Route 22 to Samburg, continuing southwest on Route 22 to the spillway, south (left) at the first paved road, and proceeding about 2.5 miles.

Further information: Lake Isom National Wildlife Refuge, c/o Reelfoot NWR, 4343 Highway 157, Union City, TN 38261; telephone: (731) 538-2481.

Lower Hatchie, consisting of 7,707 acres toward an authorized goal of just over 15,400 acres, was established in 1980. The mission of the refuge is to restore, enhance, and protect more than 4,000 acres of seasonally flooded bottomland hardwood forest along the lower meandering stretch of the Hatchie River, adjoining the Mississippi River in southwestern Tennessee. (See the Chickasaw Refuge text for description of forest management.) Large concentrations of wintering waterfowl, along with other migratory birds, such as bald eagles, wading birds, shorebirds, and neotropical songbirds, are attracted to the refuge.

Other refuge habitats include about 200 acres of moist-soil impoundments to promote the growth of wild millet, smartweed, and sedges; and about 1,000 acres of cropland, managed under cooperative agreements with local farmers in which a portion of cultivated crops of corn, milo, or millet is left unharvested to provide a supplemental food source for waterfowl and other wildlife.

Establishment of Lower Hatchie Refuge was made possible partly with revenues from the sale of Migratory Bird Hunting and Conservation Stamps (Duck Stamps). Ducks Unlimited, Inc. has helped enhance more than 350 acres of the refuge's wetland habitat.

Visitor activities on Lower Hatchie are virtually the same as those on Chickasaw Refuge (see the text for that refuge). Part of the refuge, near the junction of the Hatchie and Mississippi rivers, is closed from November 15 to March 15. A network of hiking trails winds through this latter area. Two canoe- and boat-launching ramps are provided—one accessing the Hatchie River and the other (with a wheelchair-accessible fishing pier) accessing Champion Lake. The refuge's species of fauna and flora are essentially the same as those on Reelfoot Refuge.

Just north of Lower Hatchie Refuge is the 1,900-acre Sunk Lake Public Use Natural Area. Established in 1986 under a lease agreement with the Tennessee Department of Environment and Conservation, this U.S. Fish and Wildlife Service-managed area consists of 1,435 acres of bottomland hardwood forest, 290 acres of bald cypress swamp, and 175 acres of open water in eight lakes. The area attracts concentrations of wintering waterfowl, as well as a few bald eagles. From March 15 through November 15, visitor activities include birdwatching, photography, canoeing, nonmotorized boating, and fishing. A boat-launching ramp and boardwalk are provided for visitor use. Access from State Route 87 at Three Points is about 1.75 miles west on Sunk Lake Road and north (right) into the area.

Lodgings and meals are available in such communities as Ripley, Covington, Millington, and Memphis.

Access to the Lower Hatchie Refuge headquarters from U.S. Route 51 at Henning is west about 19 miles on State Route 87.

Further information: Lower Hatchie National Wildlife Refuge, 1505 Sand Bluff Road, Ripley, TN 38063; telephone: (731) 635-7621.

Reelfoot, containing 10,428 acres in two units, was established in 1941. The refuge protects a significant staging and wintering area for migratory waterfowl on the northern part of Reelfoot Lake, which occupies a stretch of former Mississippi River floodplain in the northwest corner of Tennessee and southwest corner of Kentucky. The lake was named for a Chickasaw Indian chief, Kalopin (meaning Reelfoot), who was born with a deformed foot that caused him to walk with a staggering or reeling motion.

Reelfoot Lake was created in 1811–12 as the result of the most violent earthquake ever recorded in North America, which was followed by many months of jolting aftershocks. The New Madrid quakes caused phenomenal shaking and shifting of the region's topography all across the central Mississippi River Valley. Powerful ground waves triggered landslides that covered and cut off rivers and streams, heaved up domes of land, opened fissures, and created sunken areas, including the extensive depression that was subsequently filled with the 25,000-acre Reelfoot Lake.

The refuge's wetland habitats attract several species of herons and other resident water birds and large concentrations of wintering birds, commonly totaling as many as 100,000 Canada geese, 300,000 ducks (mostly mallards), and 200 bald eagles that prey upon fish and sick or injured waterfowl. As many as seven bald eagle nests are annually active on and around Reelfoot Refuge, as the result of a successful eagle "hacking" release program in the late 1980s. Hacking is a process by which eaglets are placed in artificial nests when they are about eight weeks old and are released for their initial flight when they are 12 to 14 weeks old. When the eagles are about five years old, it is likely that they will return to nest within roughly 75 miles of their initial flight. During spring migration, the refuge's bottomland woodlands are filled with neotropical migratory songbirds, such as warblers, vireos, thrushes, tanagers, and orioles.

As Devereux Butcher wrote in his 1963 book, *Exploring Our National Wildlife Refuges*:

Much of the lake inside the refuge boundaries is open water, but a great deal of it is . . . a beautiful forest of [bald] cypress. As one drifts by boat in the dim light of this forest, there is a sense of being in another world. The scene is so strange to unaccustomed eyes that one wants to exclaim over its fantastic effects. Here and there the water is paved with the big green leaves of yellow pond lily; and in spring and summer, the forest's beauty is heightened by the feathery leaves of the cypresses. Your boat drifts across open water areas where the sun is bright and warm; it winds through cypress strands of mottled sun and shade, and travels the narrow lily pad lanes.

Reelfoot Refuge was established under the terms of a 75-year lease agreement with the State of Tennessee. Subsequent land acquisitions expanded the refuge northward into Kentucky. The U.S. Fish and Wildlife Service carries out a number of important habitat management activities. The water level of Reelfoot Lake is seasonally regulated to enhance its wetland habitats for the benefit of waterfowl and other wildlife. Within 250 acres of moist-soil habitats, water level manipulations and mechanical vegetation management promote the growth of wild millet, spike rush, and other native vegetation that provide food and cover for water birds. Under cooperative agreements with local farmers, corn, winter wheat, and soybeans are cultivated on 900 acres of cropland. The refuge's 1,850 acres of bottomland hardwood forests are growing as marginal croplands are retired and reforested. Mature forests are being managed to promote woodland-habitat diversity for the benefit of wildlife.

Friends of Reelfoot National Wildlife Refuge is a nonprofit support group that is assisting this refuge, as well as Lake Isom Refuge, in a variety of ways.

The refuge is open daily during daylight hours. There is no entrance fee. The visitor center, containing a number of interpretive displays, is open daily from mid-January through mid-March and is open on weekdays, except national holidays, during the rest of the year.

From March 15 through November 15, visitor activities include birdwatching, photography, hiking, bicycling (on refuge roads), canoeing and boating (a boat-launching ramp is provided on the refuge's GRASSY ISLAND UNIT; others are in the adjacent Reelfoot Lake State Resort Park), and fishing (more than 55 species of fish, including crappie, bluegill, bream, and largemouth bass, inhabit Reelfoot Lake). Available all year on the refuge's Grassy Island Unit is a 2.5-mile, self-guided, interpretive auto-tour road, at the end of which is a (wheelchair-accessible) boardwalk and wildlife observation platform. The LONG POINT UNIT's auto-tour road is open from mid-March to mid-November, and there is also a (wheelchair-accessible) wildlife observation platform at the Long Point observation area that is open all year.

Hiking opportunities include the self-guiding, interpretive (wheelchair-accessible) main trail of the Backyard/Watchable Wildlife Habitat Showcase and the 0.5-mile Grassy Island Trail, located about midway on the Grassy Island auto tour road. Another observation platform is provided at the entrance to the refuge's Long Point Unit. Daily guided bus tours to see eagles are provided in the adjacent Reelfoot Lake State Resort Park from December 1 to mid-March. Although camping is not permitted on the refuge, campground facilities are available (reservations advised) in Reelfoot Lake State Resort Park; telephone: (731) 253-7756; and near Tiptonville. Hunting (deer, raccoon, squirrel, and turkey, but not waterfowl) is permitted on parts of the refuge during designated seasons. Over 250 bird species use the refuge.

As the Fish and Wildlife Service explains, "Boating on refuge waters is probably the best way to experience the refuge. Several public and commercial boat ramps are available on or adjacent to the refuge. Boat motors above 10 horse power are not recommended due to the shallow waters and density of stumps."

Among the best months for birdwatching on the refuge's Long Point observation area are January–February for the peak concentrations of wintering eagles; mid-November to mid-March for large concentrations of waterfowl; April for the peak of warblers and other neotropical migratory songbirds; and May–July for Mississippi kites.

Visitors are urged to be especially alert for venomous snakes; the western cottonmouth is very common throughout the refuge. Insect repellent is advised during the warmer months.

Lodgings and meals are available at adjacent Reelfoot Lake State Resort Park and in such communities as Union City and Tiptonville, Tennessee, and Caruthersville, Missouri.

Access to the Reelfoot Refuge headquarters from Union City, Tennessee, is northwest about 15 miles on TN State Route 22 and north (right) 1 mile on TN State Route 157. To access the refuge's Grassy Island Unit, proceed north 1 mile beyond the headquarters on Route 157, turn west (left) at Walnut Log, and continue for 1.5 miles to the entrance. To access the Long Point Unit, proceed farther north on Route 157, which becomes Kentucky State Route 311, turn southwest (left) onto Kentucky State Route 1282 and continue for 3 miles, following the directional sign south (left) into the refuge.

> Further information: Reelfoot National Wildlife Refuge, 4343 Highway 157, Union City, TN 38261; telephone: (731) 538-2481.

Tennessee, consisting of 51,358 acres in three units, was established in 1945 to manage forest, wetland, and other habitats for migratory birds around three parts of Kentucky Lake in northern Tennessee. This long reservoir was created in 1944 when the Tennessee Valley Authority built Kentucky Dam on the Tennessee River. Under a cooperative agreement, the U.S. Fish and Wildlife Service manages the refuge habitats, and the TVA regulates the level of the reservoir.

The refuge's seasonally flooded bottomland forests of hardwoods and bald cypress stands, as well as uplands of hardwood and pines, are managed to enhance and maintain habitat diversity for a wide variety of wildlife species—primarily migratory birds. Within a number of moist-soil impoundments, water levels are seasonally manipulated to promote the growth of plants such as wild millet, smartweed, and sedges, which provide food and cover for water birds. Receding water levels during the spring, summer, and autumn offer habitat for migratory shorebirds and wading birds; reflooding of these units attracts large concentrations of wintering waterfowl. Under cooperative agreements with local farmers, croplands are cultivated with corn, millet, wheat, and soybeans, a portion of which is left unharvested to provide a supplementary food source for waterfowl and other wildlife.

During the winter months, as many as 30,000 Canada geese and 200,000 to 300,000 ducks of many species, notably mallards, and 700 common loons come to the open waters and wetlands of the Tennessee Refuge. Over 90 bald eagles also winter here, preying upon fish and the sick or injured waterfowl. Nesting birds include several pairs each of eagles and ospreys, and a colony of at least 1,000 great blue herons.

The refuge has installed many nesting boxes for the benefit of wood ducks, hooded mergansers, and prothonotary warblers. During the spring and autumn migrations, the forests are filled with neotropical songbirds, such as warblers, thrushes, flycatchers, grosbeaks, buntings, tanagers, and orioles. Among many resident birds are wild turkey, northern bobwhite, and barred owl.

Tennessee Refuge's three separate sections, from north to south, are the Big Sandy Unit, Duck River Unit (the largest), and Busseltown Unit (the smallest).

The refuge is open daily during daylight hours. There is no entrance fee. Some parts of the refuge are seasonally closed to avoid disturbing waterfowl. The refuge headquarters, at 3006 Dinkins Lane, Paris, Tennessee, is open on weekdays, except national holidays. Each of the three refuge units provides visitor information at kiosks located at the main unit entrances.

Visitor activities include birdwatching, photography, wildlife observation from refuge roads, hiking on trails and roads, canoeing and boating (numerous boat-launching ramps onto Kentucky Lake are provided on and near the refuge units), fishing, and hunting on parts of the refuge during the designated seasons. Although camping is not permitted on the refuge, campground facilities are available at such places as Paris Landing and Mousetail Landing state parks, and Land Between the Lakes National Recreation Area.

Visitors are cautioned to be alert for venomous snakes. Insect repellent is advised during the warmer months.

Fauna and flora of Tennessee Refuge are essentially the same as the species on Cross Creeks Refuge.

Lodgings and meals are available in such communities as Camden, Hurricane Mills, Buffalo, and Paris.

Access to the refuge's Big Sandy Unit from U.S. Route 79 at Paris is southeast 14 miles on Alternate State Route 69 to Big Sandy and north (left) 12 miles on Lick Creek Road. Access to the Britton Ford area of the Big Sandy Unit, from Paris, is northeast 10 miles on U.S. Route 79, south (right) 3.5 miles on Oak Grove Road, and following the refuge directional signs about 1.5 miles.

Access to the Duck River Unit from Paris is south 18 miles on U.S. Route 641/State Route 69, east (left) 9 miles on U.S. Route 70 to New Johnsonville, south (right) 2 miles on Long Road to Hustburg, and following refuge directional signs about 1.5 miles; or from Exit 126 on I-40, it is north 13 miles on U.S. Route 641/State Route 69, east (right) 9 miles on U.S. Route 70 to New Johnsonville, south (right) 2 miles on Long Road to Hustburg, and following refuge directional signs about 1.5 miles. (I-40 cuts through the southern part of this unit.)

Access to the Busseltown Unit from Exit 126 on I-40 is south 14 miles on State Route 69 to Parsons, east 2 miles on U.S. Route 412, and north (left) 3 miles on Mousetail Road.

Further information: Tennessee National Wildlife Refuge, 3006 Dinkins Lane, Paris, TN 38242; telephone: (731) 642-2091.

Texas

Anahuac, comprising more than 34,000 acres, is located at the eastern end of Galveston Bay in southeastern Texas. It was established in 1963 to protect and enhance important coastal prairie, small groves of trees that grow on ancient Native American shell middens, coastal marsh, and meandering bayou habitats for the benefit of wintering waterfowl and shorebirds, neotropical migratory songbirds, and other wildlife. (See the Aransas Refuge text for description of the spectacular songbird "fallout" phenomenon that occasionally occurs along the Gulf Coast in April.)

Approximately 280 species of birds have been recorded at this refuge. During the winter, as many as 80,000 lesser snow geese feed on the refuge's moist-soil tracts and rice fields. More than two dozen species of ducks number in the thousands. Spoonbills, herons, egrets, and ibises are among the array of wading birds that may be viewed on ponds, moist-soil tracts, and rice fields. Six species of rails inhabit marshy and salt-prairie habitats.

To provide habitat and food for a diversity of species, the U.S. Fish and Wildlife Service regulates water levels, plants crops, grazes livestock, carries out periodic prescribed burns, and controls exotic plants to help foster natural plant diversity.

Butterflies are also attracted to Anahuac Refuge. As naturalist Roland H. Wauer says, "A butterfly garden was established at the refuge headquarters in 2002. It is the best place on the refuge to find resident species and strays that occur in this eastern portion of Texas. Three species, of special interest to butterfly enthusiasts, to be expected here include Red-banded Hairstreak, and Broad-winged and Salt Marsh Skippers."

Establishment of Anahuac was made possible partly with revenues from the sale of Migratory Bird Hunting and Conservation Stamps (Duck Stamps). Ducks Unlimited, Inc. has assisted with important habitat enhancement projects. The Friends of Anahuac Refuge is a local nonprofit support group that is assisting the refuge in various ways. The Friends recently assisted the U.S. Fish and Wildlife Service in the development of the 2-acre butterfly garden and trail system that is located adjacent to the visitor information station.

The refuge is open daily. No entrance fee is charged.

Visitor activities include birdwatching; butterfly observation; photography; driving the 12 miles of gravel roads (travel may be limited during wet weather); hiking on trails and roads; primitive camping; fishing (wade fishing along the shore of East Galveston Bay and freshwater fishing from the banks of, a bridge overlooking, or by boat on East Bay Bayou); and waterfowl hunting in certain parts of the refuge during the designated season. A visitor contact station and information kiosk are located at the refuge's main entrance. Two boat ramps are provided. November through April are the best birdwatching months.

Thousands of alligators inhabit the refuge. Even though these reptiles are generally afraid of people, visitors are cautioned to stay a safe distance from these sluggish-seeming but potentially fast-moving animals and to be alert for venomous snakes and fire ants. Insect repellent is recommended.

Lodgings and meals are available in such nearby communities as High Island, Winnie, Anahuac, Baytown, and Port Arthur.

> Access to Anahuac is south from I-10 either on State Route 61 and Farm Market Road (FM) 562, and left onto FM 1985 to the refuge entrance, or on State Route 124 and right onto FM 1985 to the entrance.

> Further information: Anahuac National Wildlife Refuge, c/o the Texas Chenier Plain NWR Complex, P.O. Box 278, Anahuac, TX 77514; telephone: (409) 267-3337.

Aransas, consisting of 58,983 acres, is located on the Blackjack Peninsula, between St. Charles and San Antonio bays on the central Gulf Coast of Texas. The refuge was established in 1937 to protect salt marshes along the outer coastal fringe and the peninsula's sandy, gently undulating higher ground that in places supports oak woodland and thickets (or mottes) of low-growing, wind-sculpted oak and red bay trees. Some parts of the refuge are maintained by the U.S. Fish and Wildlife Service for wildlife species requiring open meadow and grassland habitat. A few freshwater ponds occupy openings in the wooded areas.

Aransas is most famous as the primary wintering area of the endangered whooping crane (*Grus americana*)—the tallest North American bird. This majestic bird stands 4 to 5 feet tall and has a 7-foot wingspread. Adults have pure white plumage, black wing tips visible in flight, and a red face and crown. Juveniles have a rust-colored head and neck, and the rest of the body is patterned with rust and white plumage. The whooping crane gets its name from the high-pitched, trumpeting call—a sound that can carry for a mile or more. From late October to mid-April, Aransas is the bird's major wintering ground. Visitors can sometimes see these cranes from the refuge's observation tower and platforms. In the spring, these great birds migrate northward 2,400 miles to their nesting grounds in northern Canada's Wood Buffalo National Park, returning to Aransas again in the autumn.

It is estimated that, until around 1860, there were approximately 1,300 to 1,400 cranes. By 1941, their population had plummeted to a mere 15 individuals. By 1949, the number had increased to 34. But by 1952, it had dropped again—to 21. As Devereux Butcher wrote in his 1963 book, *Exploring Our National Wildlife Refuges*, "When a species, such as the whooping crane, has been so drastically reduced, its continued existence becomes precarious. The crane's population could be wiped out overnight, and once gone, it would be extinct forever."

However, with intensive conservation efforts over the past few decades in the United States and Canada, the population has been gradually increasing. By 1960, there were around 3 dozen cranes. By 1981, there were 78. By 2000, the number had climbed to 185. While this naturally occurring, wild whooping crane population is still at risk, progress is encouraging, and Aransas refuge has been instrumental in helping to rescue this great bird from the brink of extinction. (For additional information on whooping crane recovery efforts, see the Necedah National Wildlife Refuge text.)

As Devereux Butcher also wrote (*Exploring Our National Wildlife Refuges*):

Along the Texas coast, nature stages one of her grandest songbird shows. This occurs in April, when thrushes, buntings, tanagers, vireos, warblers, and dozens of other species are migrating. The songsters literally swarm through here. . . . At times they are so numerous that the trees and shrubs appear to be blossoming with animated flowers.

Influxes or arrival peaks of different species typically occur on different days—confirming the old saying, "birds of a feather flock together." For example, there could be great numbers of rose-breasted grosbeaks or scarlet tanagers arriving on one day, orchard or Baltimore orioles on the following day, hooded warblers on the next, and indigo or painted buntings on the day after.

One aspect of the huge influx of neotropical migratory songbirds is referred to as "fallout." This frenzied phenomenon occasionally occurs when unfavorable headwinds from the north slow down and make even more difficult the birds' energy-depleting, nonstop flight across the Gulf of Mexico. From such launching places as Mexico's Yucatan Peninsula, the exhausted birds drop into coastal wooded areas, from the Florida panhandle to Texas, including the Aransas Refuge.

As Scott Weidensaul described in his fascinating book, *Living on the Wind: Across the Hemisphere with Migratory Birds* (North Point Press, 1999):

I never actually saw the birds come down, but I could hear them, a series of low whooshes overhead and around me, like fast pitches that brushed past my ear or the thrumming sound of sticks whirled through the air. An instant later, the lifeless trees were seething with dozens of birds, which cascaded, branch by branch, toward the ground, spilling out into the understory. They started eating without preamble, without stretching or relaxing or preening—feeding with a fervor usually seen only at state fairs during pie-eating contests. Over and over again, small explosions of birds would materialize out of the sky, whirring from on high, beyond the limit of vision and into the trees like bolts, until the woods were stuffed to overflowing with them.

I watched for half an hour, until it was too dark to really see anything but silhouettes and dull shapes. Thousands of songbirds had arrived, dropping straight down from great heights to join the melee, then rolling out in waves through the forest, enveloping me for a few, frantic moments, then passing me by even as the next surge came through. . . . No wonder they call it the Gulf Express.

Butterflies are also attracted to Aransas Refuge. As naturalist Roland H. Wauer says, "This central Gulf site offers a high diversity of butterflies, including such special interest species as Palamedes Swallowtail, which can be commonplace along wooded edges; Tropical Buckeyes, which can be abundant along the Loop Drive; both Laviana and Turk's-cap White Skippers, which can be common throughout; and Salt Marsh and Obscure Skippers, which can be fairly common along the Heron Flats Trail and near the observation tower."

Establishment of Aransas was made possible partly with revenues from the sale of Migratory Bird Hunting and Conservation Stamps (Duck Stamps). Ducks Unlimited, Inc. has helped enhance wetland habitat on the refuge. Friends of Aransas and Matagorda Island National Wildlife Refuges is a local nonprofit support group that is assisting these two refuges in many ways.

The refuge is open daily during daylight hours. An entrance fee is charged. The visitor center, which is open daily except on Thanksgiving and Christmas, provides interpretive exhibits and programs and a nature store operated by the Friends group.

Visitor activities in Aransas include birdwatching, butterfly observation, photography, driving the 16-mile loop tour road, hiking, interpretive programs, picnicking (a small picnic area is provided), fishing, and firearm and archery hunting whitetail deer and feral hogs during the designated season. Camping is not permitted. November through April are the best birdwatching months. More than 400 bird species have been recorded here.

Hiking opportunities include Butterfly Walk—a 0.1-mile (wheelchair-accessible) paved path next to the Wildlife Interpretive Center through an area of oak and redbay to an alligator-viewing spot; Rail Trail—a 0.3-mile route along Thomas Slough; Heron Flats Trail—a 1.4-mile walk offering opportunities to see freshwater sloughs, tidal flats, salt marsh, ancient oyster-shell ridges, oak woodlands and providing two observation platforms that are equipped with telescopes; Bay Overlook Trail—a 0.1-mile (wheelchair-accessible) walk that provides a beautiful view of San Antonio Bay; Dagger Point Trail—a 1-mile route leading through oak and redbay woods and providing another beautiful view of the bay; Jones Lake Path—a 0.1-mile (wheelchair-accessible) paved path leading to a viewing platform overlooking the lake, where alligators and other wildlife may be seen; Big Oak Trail—a 0.7-mile route through some of the largest live oaks on the refuge (a boardwalk also leads through salt marsh to the outer loop of this trail); and Hog Lake Trail—a 0.9-mile loop with an observation platform for viewing alligators and other wildlife. Near the last trail is also an observation tower, providing a view of Mustang Lake and the possibility of seeing whooping cranes during the winter season.

Even though alligators are generally afraid of people, visitors are cautioned to stay a safe distance from these sluggish-looking but potentially fast-moving reptiles, to be alert for venomous snakes, and stay on trails to reduce the chance of encountering poison ivy, ticks, and chiggers. Insect repellent is recommended.

Lodgings and meals are available in Port Lavaca and Rockport. Camping facilities are provided in Rockport and nearby state and county parks.

Access to Aransas is north from Rockport by way of State Route 35 and then, following refuge signs, right onto Farm Market Road (FM) 774 for 9 miles, right onto FM 2040, and 6.5 miles to the refuge entrance; or south on State Route 35 through Tivoli, then left onto State Route 239 and FM 774, left onto FM 2040, and 6.5 miles to the refuge entrance.

Further information: Aransas National Wildlife Refuge, P.O. Box 100, Austwell, TX 77950; telephone: (361) 286-3559.

Attwater Prairie Chicken, consisting of more than 9,200 acres, is located in an area of southeast Texas coastal tallgrass prairie. The refuge was established in 1972, with the initial 3,500 acres acquired by the World Wildlife Fund and The Nature Conservancy to protect and enhance this habitat of the rare and endangered Attwater's prairie chicken (*Tympanuchus cupido attwateri*), a small, dark race of the greater prairie chicken.

Once numbering 1 million birds that inhabited roughly 6 million acres of Texas and Louisiana gulf coastal prairie, this species was brought to the brink of extinction by the destruction and fragmentation of its grasslands habitat and by overhunting. By 1919, no birds remained in Louisiana. By the late 1930s, fewer than 9,000 existed in Texas. In the 1990s, repeated periods of unfavorable weather caused the loss of significant numbers of eggs and chicks. By 1999, the refuge's prairie chicken population had declined to a mere 18. In the year 2000, there were 20.

The U.S. Fish and Wildlife Service's recovery plan for the Attwater's prairie chicken:

. . . outlines tasks to save this species from extinction, and ultimately, to remove it from the endangered species list. To reach a goal of 5,000 birds in three geographically separate, viable populations, recovery efforts focus on five strategies:

- Habitat management on both public and private lands (involving voluntary cooperators only);
- Public outreach to help generate support for ongoing recovery efforts;
- Population management consisting of captive breeding and reintroduction efforts;
- Coordination between government agencies and private interests; [and]
- Research to provide information necessary for taking efficient steps toward recovery.

Biologists believe that the captive breeding program offers the most likely means of saving this species. In 1992, the first chicks were hatched at the Fossil Rim Wildlife Center, near Glen Rose, Texas. Since then, Texas A&M University; the Houston, Abilene, and San Antonio zoos; and Sea World of Texas have been raising birds for release into the wild.

Although much of the Attwater Prairie Chicken Refuge contains virgin prairie that was never plowed or cultivated, the Fish and Wildlife Service is maintaining prairie chicken habitat where great herds of bison (buffalo) once grazed and lightning-ignited fires burned. This management program includes periodic prescribed burning to reinvigorate the grasses and control invasive, non-native, woody plants; grazing by bison and cattle; and recreating prairie by planting native grasses on former cultivated fields. In addition, the refuge cultivates small food plots for the benefit of these birds and other wildlife.

From February to mid-May, the male prairie chickens congregate and perform elaborate courtship rituals on an open area of short grass, known as a lek. With tails and neck feathers erect and wings drooping, the cocks inflate their golden neck sacs. With rapid foot-stamping, they then lower their heads, causing a deep, hollow, moaning sound as the sacs are deflated. During this frenzied "dancing," they leap about and charge toward other males.

Although March and April are the best months to possibly view the prairie chickens' courtship rituals, opportunities are limited by their low numbers. The nearby town of Eagle Lake and the refuge cohost an annual Attwater's Prairie Chicken Festival during the second weekend in April.

As refuge manager Terry A. Rossignol has said:

From my perspective, the Texas coastal prairie ecosystem, which is home for the imperiled Attwater's prairie-chicken, is perhaps one of the most misunderstood ecosystems, yet is probably the most impacted habitat type in North America. By working on a large landscape scale with private landowners, to enhance coastal prairie habitat through the Coastal Prairie Conservation Initiative, which provides cost-shared incentives and protection from any future liabilities under the Endangered Species Act, I feel that the Attwater's prairie-chicken does have a chance of surviving. However, this is a goal that will only be realized through much hard work and cooperation from everyone involved.

In addition to the prairie chicken, this refuge features such other birds as whistling-ducks and roseate spoonbills, which inhabit marshes; wintering flocks of geese and sandhill cranes; crested caracaras; white-tailed hawks; and scissor-tailed flycatchers.

The refuge is open daily during daylight hours. There is no entrance fee. The visitor center is open on weekdays, except national holidays.

Visitor activities include birdwatching, butterfly observation, photography, viewing interpretive exhibits and a prairie chicken video in the visitor center, driving the 5-mile tour road, hiking on two trails and along the tour road, and picnicking (picnic tables are provided near the visitor center). Not permitted on this refuge are camping, swimming, canoeing, fishing, or hunting.

The refuge's two hiking trails, leading through prairie and riparian areas, are the 1.5-mile Pipit Trail and the 2-mile Sycamore Trail. March and April are the best time to see great numbers of migrating neotropical songbirds. November through March are the best months for thousands of wintering geese and flocks of sandhill cranes.

Even though alligators are generally afraid of people, visitors are cautioned to stay a safe distance from these sluggish-looking but potentially fast-moving reptiles and to be alert for ticks, fire ants, and venomous snakes. Insect repellent is advised.

Lodgings and meals are available in such communities as Eagle Lake, Sealy, and Columbus. Camping facilities are provided at Stephen F. Austin State Park.

Access to this refuge is south from I-10 on State Route 36, right onto Farm-to-Market Road 3013, and 10 miles to the refuge entrance.

Further information: Attwater Prairie Chicken National Wildlife Refuge, P.O. Box 519, Eagle Lake, TX 77434; telephone: (979) 234-3021.

Balcones Canyonlands, thus far comprising 17,000 acres, was established in 1992 to conserve an ecologically important part of the limestone hills and spring-fed canyons along the eastern edge of the Edwards Plateau, which stretches across central Texas. The refuge protects the breeding habitat of two rare and endangered neotropical songbirds—the golden-cheeked warbler (*Dendroica chrysoparia*) and the black-capped vireo (*Vireo atricapillus*). Although this relatively new refuge has an active land acquisition program, the expansion of urban development and conversion of ranchland to housing subdivisions pose a grave threat to this as yet incomplete refuge.

The golden-cheeked warbler breeds only in the hills of central Texas, with its best habitat along or near the Balcones Escarpment to the west of Austin and San Antonio. It migrates here from its wintering habitat in the wooded highlands of Honduras and Guatemala in Central America and in the state of Chiapas in southern Mexico. The males arrive around mid-March, to declare and defend their favored nesting habitat in old-growth oaks and junipers. The females arrive a few days later, choose a mate, and build a nest. Together the adults raise their young on a diet of insects gleaned from the canopy of the woods. In July or early August, they begin their southward migration back to the tropics.

The entire population of golden-cheeks may number as few as 5,000 to 15,000 pairs. Dr. Chuck Sexton, the wildlife biologist at Balcones Canyonlands, describes a certain irony in the conservation efforts for this species: "Although long-term land use patterns have resulted in an expansion of second-growth juniper across the central Texas landscape, old-growth stands of oak-juniper woodlands continue to be lost to land clearing, ranching, and urbanization." By 1990, declines in warbler habitat and populations were serious enough to prompt the U.S. Fish and Wildlife Service to place the species on the Endangered Species List.

The black-capped vireo breeds from central Oklahoma, south through the Edwards Plateau and West Texas, to the state of Coahuila in northern Mexico. It migrates here from its wintering range along the west coast of Mexico, primarily from Sinaloa south to Michoacan. The males arrive at their breeding area from late-March to mid-April, and the females soon after. The male and female share in nest building, raising their young, and fending off the serious threat of nest parasitism by brown-headed cowbirds. In contrast to the warbler, vireos like a particular composition of low shrubby growths of oaks or sumacs, which typically come in after a disturbance such as fire. Sexton's research has shown that the vireo, a rather narrow-habitat specialist, occupies habitat that occurs only on a few specific soil and rock types in central Texas.

Balcones Canyonlands is one of the botanically most diverse refuges in the entire system, with nearly 700 species of plants identified thus far. Habitats are a mosaic of woodlands, savannas, and open grasslands. Upland woods contain a mixture of oaks (plateau live, Spanish, post, scaly-bark, and others) and Ashe juniper, the loose, stringy bark of which is used by the warbler as nesting material. Other trees and shrubs include cedar elm, Texas sugarberry, Texas ash, escarpment cherry, agarita, and Texas persimmon. Pecan, American elm, American sycamore, and black willow grow along narrow riparian corridors. Several other distinctive plant communities occur around springs in moist canyon heads and along canyon rimrocks. There are remnants of the original tallgrass-prairie grasslands, dominated by little bluestem, Indiangrass, sideoats grama, and a great diversity of other grasses and forbs. The wildflower displays in April and May and again in September and October can be spectacular. Among the refuge's wildflowers are prairie verbena, pink evening primrose, fireweeds, bitterweed, Blackfoot daisy, blazing star, bluebell gentian, and carpets of bluebonnets.

In addition to the warbler and vireo, a few of the other interesting birds of this refuge are Bell's vireo, cave swallow, canyon wren, yellow-breasted chat, rufous-crowned and black-throated sparrows, canyon towhee, and lesser goldfinch. Swainson's hawks dominate a diverse stream of migrant raptors passing overhead in October.

Other wildlife includes an abundance of white-tailed deer, along with such other species as bobcats, gray foxes, raccoons, ringtails, eastern cottontails, fox and rock squirrels, and nine-banded armadillos. Although diamondback rattlesnakes are present, a visitor is more likely to encounter one of the swift western coachwhips or catch a glimpse of a Texas spiny lizard on a tree trunk. Butterflies provide a display on autumn wildflowers, including the massive parade of southbound migrant monarchs heading toward their wintering grounds in Mexico.

The refuge is open daily during daylight hours. There is no entrance fee.

Visitor activities include birdwatching, photography, hiking, and hunting (deer, turkey, dove, and wild hog) during the designated seasons. Refuge staff and local volunteers lead various field trips and outdoor education programs throughout the year. National Wildlife Refuge Week, in October, is often filled with special events.

The Shin Oak Observation Deck is located in excellent vireo habitat, on Ranch Road 1869 in the northern part of the refuge. Because of the sensitive habitat, no hiking trails are available in the vireo observation area. However, a well-developed trailhead with miles of hiking trails (including some into good warbler habitat) is provided at the nearby Doeskin Ranch tract, on Ranch Road 1174. Other trail systems are planned for the future.

Lodgings and meals are available in such communities as Lago Vista, Liberty Hill, Marble Falls, Burnet, Leander, Cedar Park, Georgetown, and Austin.

Access to the refuge's Doeskin Ranch public use area is north about 15 miles from Austin on U.S. Route 183 to Cedar Park, west (left) 26 miles on Ranch Road 1431, and north (right) about 5 miles on Ranch Road 1174; or north about 25 miles from Austin on U.S. Route 183 to Seward Junction, west (left) 2.3 miles on State Route 29 to Liberty Hill, west (left) about 10 miles on Ranch Road 1869, and south (left) about 2 miles on Ranch Road 1174.

Further information: Balcones Canyonlands National Wildlife Refuge, 10711 Burnet Road, Suite 201, Austin, TX 78758: telephone: (512) 339-9432.

Big Boggy, consisting of 4,382 acres, is located on the upper Gulf coast, south of Bay City in southeastern Texas. It was established in 1983 to protect and enhance an important area of coastal prairie habitat for the benefit of wintering geese, ducks, and other wildlife. As of this writing, there is no general public access, although tours can be arranged by special appointment.

This refuge provides winter resting areas for roughly 20,000 geese (mostly lesser snows) and 5,000 to 10,000 ducks of various species. Establishment of Big Boggy was made possible partly with revenues from the sale of Migratory Bird Hunting and Conservation Stamps (Duck Stamps). It is managed jointly with Brazoria and San Bernard national wildlife refuges (see their texts), and the flora and fauna are essentially the same as at Brazoria and San Bernard.

Further information: Big Boggy National Wildlife Refuge, 1212 N. Velasco, Suite 200, Angleton, TX 77515; telephone: (979) 849-6062.

Brazoria, consisting of 43,388 acres, is located on the upper Gulf coast between Galveston and Freeport, in southeastern Texas. The refuge was established in 1966 to protect a significant area for wintering waterfowl, shorebirds, and other wildlife. Habitats include coastal prairie, freshwater and coastal salt marshes, salt flats, mudflats, freshwater potholes and ponds, several saltwater lakes, and two intermittent streams.

More than 300 species of birds have been recorded here, with more than 200 of these identified during the National Audubon Society's annual Freeport Christmas Bird Count in mid-December. This count usually places first or second in the United States for the total species in a Christmas count.

As at nearby San Bernard and Big Boggy refuges, great numbers of waterfowl winter at Brazoria. From 30,000 to 50,000 geese (predominantly the lesser snow) and from 20,000 to 30,000 ducks of many species, along with thousands of wading and shorebirds, are here in December and January. This is also one of the Gulf Coast refuges where the spectacular neotropical migratory songbird "fallout" phenomenon occurs in April (see Aransas text).

The U.S. Fish and Wildlife Service manages water levels for waterfowl food production and for waterfowl resting and feeding areas with a system of dikes and water control structures. On parts of the refuge, periodic prescribed burns are carried out to maintain habitat conditions beneficial to waterfowl.

Establishment of Brazoria was made possible partly with revenues from the sale of Migratory Bird Hunting and Conservation Stamps (Duck Stamps). Friends of Brazoria National Wildlife Refuge is a nonprofit support group that is assisting the refuge in a variety of ways.

The refuge hosts an "open house" on the first full weekend of each month throughout the year, and also on the third weekend of each month from November through April. Staff and trained volunteers offer orientation and information on the refuge and its wildlife viewing options. On weekdays, however, the refuge is open for visitation only if the gate is open. During winter months, the gate is usually opened by volunteers; during the rest of the year, it is open only if a staff member happens to be working on the refuge. There is no entrance fee.

Visitor activities include birdwatching; photography; driving the 6.3-mile Big Slough Auto Tour road (observation platforms, birding trails, and interpretive exhibits are located along this route); hiking; picnicking (a picnic shelter is provided); saltwater fishing (at the Bastrop Bayou Public Fishing Area, providing a handicapped-accessible pier; at Clay Banks Public Fishing Area, offering access to a mile of bank fishing; and by boat on Nicks, Salt, and Lost lakes); and public hunting. Waterfowl hunting is permitted in Middle Bayou and Christmas Bay public hunting areas, during the designated season. November through April are the best birdwatching months.

Alligators inhabit the refuge. Even though they are usually afraid of people, visitors are cautioned to stay a safe distance from these sluggish-looking but potentially fast-moving reptiles and to be alert for venomous snakes and fire ants. Insect repellent is advised.

The species of birds that have been recorded on Brazoria Refuge are much the same as those of Anahuec Refuge.

Lodgings and meals are available in such nearby communities as Angleton, Lake Jackson, Freeport, and Galveston.

Access to Brazoria is south from Houston by way of State Route 288 to Lake Jackson, left onto Farm Market Road (FM) 2004 for about 5 miles, and right onto FM 523 for 5.5 miles to the refuge entrance.

Further information: Brazoria National Wildlife Refuge, 1212 N. Velasco, Suite 200, Angleton, TX 77515; telephone: (979) 849-6062.

Buffalo Lake, consisting of 7,664 acres, was established in 1958 to protect and enhance the wildlife benefits of this reservoir and adjacent marsh and cultivated lands located to the southwest of Amarillo in the Texas Panhandle. Subsequent to the refuge's establishment, diversion of Tierra Blanca Creek for irrigation purposes has dried up refuge waters. What was once important waterfowl habitat is today primarily an area for arid-land wildlife, except when heavy rainfall suddenly refills the lakebed, attracting great numbers of ducks, geese, and shorebirds. The refuge also contains some colorful and scenically beautiful small canyons and rock formations. Over 300 bird species use the refuge.

The refuge is open daily during most daylight hours. As the refuge has seasonally changing hours and its gates are automatically opened and closed, visitors are advised to contact refuge headquarters for specific hours. A small entrance fee is charged.

Visitor activities include birdwatching, photography, driving the 4.5-mile interpretive route and other refuge roads, hiking on two trails and elsewhere, picnicking, and camping at the refuge campground. Autumn through spring is the best time for birdwatching.

Visitors are cautioned to be alert for prairie rattlesnakes.

Lodgings and meals are available in Canyon, Amarillo, and Hereford.

Access to the refuge is by U.S. Route 60 west from Canyon to Umbarger, and Farm Market Road 168 south 2 miles to the refuge entrance.

Further information: Buffalo Lake National Wildlife Refuge, P.O. Box 179, Umbarger, TX 79091; telephone: (806) 499-3382.

Caddo Lake, containing 7,172 acres, was established in 2000 to protect and manage a significant area of forested wetlands and bald cypress swamps surrounding Caddo Lake and along Harrison Bayou. The refuge, which overlays parts of the U.S. Army's Longhorn Army Ammunition Plant (LHAAP), is located within Harrison County, about 3 miles west of the Louisiana state line in northeastern Texas.

As described by a Notice in the October 19, 2000, *Federal Register*:

The refuge is designed to protect one of the highest quality old-growth bottomland hardwood forests in the southeastern United States. . . . These wetlands are listed as a "Wetland of International Significance" under the Ramsar Convention on Wetlands and are one of only 17 such designated areas in the United States.

The establishment of this refuge will ensure the conservation and protection of the migratory and resident waterfowl and neotropical migratory birds associated with these wetlands. Studies have listed up to 224 species of birds, 22 species of amphibians, 46 species of reptiles, and 93 species of fish in this area. A total of 20 animal species of concern are located or potentially located on the LHAAP and adjacent Caddo Lake. They include seven species of fish, six species of reptiles, six species of birds and four species of mammals. Two species are federally listed under the Endangered Species Act (Louisiana black bear and bald eagle).

The refuge also includes upland areas of mature loblolly and shortleaf pine forests that are inhabited by white-tailed deer, wild turkeys, and numerous other species of wildlife. Caddo Lake was historically the only naturally formed lake in Texas until it was enlarged by a dam in the early twentieth century.

The U.S. Army is in the process of cleaning up environmental contaminants on the LHAAP, which was declared excess to the Army's needs in 1997. When the cleanup task is completed to the satisfaction of the Army, the U.S. Environmental Protection Agency, and the U.S. Fish and Wildlife Service, it is expected that primary jurisdiction, custody, and control of up to 8,500 acres will be transferred to the Service. Until then, Caddo Lake Refuge remains closed to visitation.

Caddo Lake State Park and Wildlife Management Area adjoin the refuge.

Further information: Caddo Lake National Wildlife Refuge, c/o Little River NWR, P.O. Box 340, Broken Bow, OK 74728; telephone: (580) 584-6211.

Hagerman, comprising 11,320 acres, was established in 1946 to protect and enhance an area of marsh, prairie, woodland, ponds, and cultivated fields, around the Big Mineral Arm of Lake Texoma, 75 miles north of Dallas, Texas. This reservoir was created by Denison Dam on the Red River, which forms the border between Texas and Oklahoma. The refuge provides important Central Flyway habitat for wintering and migrating ducks and geese.

As many as 7,500 Canada geese occupy the refuge from October through March, and flocks of lesser snow geese spend the winter, from November to March. In September and April, thousands of migratory white pelicans pause at the refuge. Large flocks of gracefully fluttering scissor-tailed flycatchers gather here in the autumn, as they get ready for their migration to Mexico and Central America. Over 315 bird species have been recorded here.

The U.S. Fish and Wildlife Service actively manages this refuge for the benefit of many species. Farming of 600 acres provides milo, wheat, and corn. These refuge-produced grains not only offer an important source of food, but they help encourage the geese to ignore privately owned agricultural crops outside the refuge. In addition, low earthen dikes have been built to regulate water levels, creating autumn and winter marshy wetlands habitat for waterfowl and draining off the water for spring and summer growths of wild millet, smartweeds, and sedges. And the refuge is working to recreate and maintain areas of the gently rolling prairie habitat with a program of limited livestock grazing, occasionally implemented prescription burns, and replanting native prairie grasses and forbs. Ducks Unlimited, Inc. has assisted with important habitat enhancement projects.

Hagerman overlays a U.S. Army Corps of Engineers property.

The refuge is open daily during daylight hours. No entrance fee is charged. Depending on the availability of volunteers, the visitor center is usually open on weekdays, and from October through March it is usually open on weekends, from midmorning to midafternoon.

Visitor activities include birdwatching; photography; driving the 4-mile interpretive road; hiking the refuge roads and the 1-mile Crow Hill Trail, which leads through prairie habitat to an overlook; boating from April through September (three boat-launching sites are provided); fishing from April through September; and, during the designated seasons and on certain parts of the refuge, deer bow hunting (by drawing only) and limited hunting of dove, quail, rabbit, and squirrel. Swimming, water-skiing, and camping are not permitted. Camping facilities are provided at U.S. Army Corps of Engineers sites around Lake Texoma and at Eisenhower State Park near Denison, Texas, and Texoma State Park near Kingston, Oklahoma. The best time for birdwatching at this refuge is from autumn through spring.

Visitors are cautioned to be alert for ticks, chiggers, and venomous snakes.

Hagerman Refuge also includes the separate 822-acre NOCONA UNIT, which was established in 1992. Located about 70 miles west of Hagerman, it contains mixed open Great Plains prairie that is traversed by wooded bottomland habitat. In some places, there are scenic rock defiles composed of sandstone and limestone. The Rio Grande subspecies of the wild turkey is native to the unit, and the unit is also a flyover area for migratory whooping cranes. Other species of birds are essentially the same as on the main unit of Hagerman Refuge.

Lodgings and meals are available in such communities as Sherman and Gainesville, Texas and Durant and Ardmore, Oklahoma.

Access to the refuge is north from Dallas 60 miles on US Route 75 to the Sherman-Farm Market 1417 exit, north 13 miles on FM Route 1417 to the refuge sign, and left 6 miles to the entrance; or east from I-35 on U.S. Route 82 and following directional signs to the refuge.

Further information: Hagerman National Wildlife Refuge, 6465 Refuge Road, Sherman, TX 75092; telephone: (903) 786-2826.

Laguna Atascosa, presently comprising 69,500 acres, is located near the southern end of the Gulf Coast of Texas, in what was formerly the Rio Grande Delta. The refuge was established in 1946 to protect and enhance the most extensive area of the former delta's natural and restored habitats—originally for the benefit of redhead ducks. More than 406 species of birds have been recorded on Laguna Atascosa—more than any other refuge in the National Wildlife Refuge System!

The refuge attracts enormous numbers of migratory waterfowl and shorebirds and provides protection for a number of rare and endangered species. One of the latter species is the aplomado falcon (*Falco femoralis*), the encouraging recovery efforts for which are being cooperatively aided by a nonprofit organization, The Peregrine Fund, Inc. (For further information on this falcon, see the Matagorda Island NWR text.)

A unique combination of subtropical, desert, temperate, and coastal habitats lie within the boundaries of Laguna Atascosa Refuge. Some of the flora and fauna are typical of northern Mexico and are at the northern end of their range here, and many migratory species of birds that breed far to the north, such as waterfowl and the sandhill crane, spend the winter here.

The refuge contains expanses of flat coastal savanna and salt flats, ridges (known locally in Spanish as lomas) covered with dense thorny shrubs, some brushland of mesquite and other species, and places where yucca and cactus grow. To the east stretches Laguna Madre, a broad bay that is hemmed in from the open waters of the Gulf of Mexico by the long narrow barrier of Padre Island.

As agricultural land drainage and irrigation programs have greatly curtailed the quantity of water that flows into the refuge, water needed to maintain wildlife habitats is held in resacas (former Rio Grande oxbows), ponds, and the refuge's largest body of fresh water, Laguna Atascosa. Water levels are raised or lowered during the year to accommodate the needs of waterfowl and wading birds. In addition, the U.S. Fish and Wildlife Service carries out periodic prescribed burns to maintain areas of prairie grassland (savanna) habitat.

A highlight of Laguna Atascosa Refuge are two rare and endangered cats—the ocelot (*Felis pardalis*) and jaguarundi (*F. yagouaroundi*). Both species are secretive in the dense brushy habitat and are consequently seldom seen. The fur coat of the ocelot is beautifully patterned with black spots and elongated and angular bars and patches on a yellow background. Adult males measure roughly 3 to 4 feet from head to tip of their long tail and weigh 15 to 25 pounds. They prefer thick thorn-scrub habitat, in which they are well camouflaged beneath the shrubby canopy. About 30 ocelots are believed to inhabit the refuge. With U.S. estimates at fewer than 100 ocelots, Laguna Atascosa Refuge represents their last stronghold in this country.

The jaguarundi, on the other hand, has two uniform color phases: either russet-brown or gray. It looks like a cross between a miniature mountain lion and a weasel. From head to tip of its very long tail, it measures roughly 3 to 4.5 feet, with a small head, widely spaced rounded little ears, slender body, and short legs; it weighs from around 15 to 18 pounds. It is not known if jaguarundis still inhabit the refuge, as there has been no photographic or other evidence of them since 1985.

Butterflies are also attracted to Laguna Atascosa Refuge. As naturalist Roland H. Wauer says, "The new garden, behind and alongside the visitor center, attracts an abundance of butterflies. More than 150 species have been recorded at this site and along various roadsides. Among those that regularly occur are Silver-banded Hairstreak; Clytie Ministreak; Red-banded and Blue Metalmarks; Theona Checkerspot; White Peacock; Dorante's, Teleus, and Brown Longtails; and Fawn-spotted and Obscure Skippers."

Former Assistant Refuge Manager Tim Cooper, who expresses a special fondness for Laguna Atascosa Refuge, explains:

Laguna Atascosa NWR represents one of the finest areas for wildlife within the United States. Appreciating and finding wildlife in this refuge takes some practice. The vegetative cover is often very thick and the animals can be very cryptic. But patient observers will be rewarded for their efforts.

A mixture of influences from the Gulf of Mexico, the tropics, the Chihuahuan Desert, and temperate North America converge at this location. Therefore, species from these very diverse regions can often find suitable habitats here. For example, almost half of the U.S. endangered ocelot population depends on the refuge. The re-introduction effort for the extirpated Northern Aplomado Falcon started here and has been a great success, with the release of more than 150 birds to date. These releases have exceeded all expectations and have fostered nests in the wild since 1995.

The list of rare wildlife also includes three species of sea turtles, piping plover, peregrine falcon, Texas horned lizard, Texas tortoise, and possibly the jaguarundi. The varied habitat types, from impenetrable thornscrub to hyper-saline waters, provide cover and food resources for numerous animals. In many ways, this area represents an avian equivalent to the Serengeti Plains in East Africa, with huge concentrations of migrating and resident birds, a high diversity of species, and sweeping views. Laguna Atascosa is extremely important for migrating shorebirds, wintering piping plovers, waterfowl (especially redheads), staging peregrine falcons, and resident species. Migrations in April and May and throughout the fall bring different warblers, grosbeaks, other neotropicals, raptors, and waterfowl through the area. The refuge's total of 406 recorded bird species is, to date, unmatched in the refuge system.

Maintaining freshwater inflows and addressing the problem of habitat fragmentation will be among the major challenges that the refuge must address, to keep its values intact for the next millennium. Hopefully, the current acquisition efforts will help address these larger issues through expansion and the purchase of water rights.

Establishment of the refuge was made possible mostly with revenues from the sale of Migratory Bird Hunting and Conservation Stamps (Duck Stamps). Ducks Unlimited, Inc. has assisted with extensive habitat enhancement projects, including a large system for diverting river water to the resaca system. The Friends of Laguna Atascosa National Wildlife Refuge is a local nonprofit support group that is assisting the refuge in many ways.

The refuge is open daily during daylight hours. An entrance fee is charged. The visitor center, which is open daily from October through April and on weekends in May, provides interpretive exhibits and videos. Rangers and trained volunteers lead programs and wildlife watching tours on weekends from November through April.

Visitor activities at Laguna Atascosa include birdwatching, butterfly observation, photography, interpretive programs, driving the 15-mile Bayside Drive loop and the 1.5-mile Lakeside Drive, hiking, bicycling, and hunting (deer) during the designated season. Although camping and fishing are not permitted in the refuge, they are allowed in the adjacent Adolph Thomae Jr. County Park. November through April are the best birdwatching months at Laguna Atascosa.

Hiking opportunities include the Kiskadee Trail—a one-eighth -mile path that begins near the visitor center, loops around a shallow pond (holding water during wet years), and affords an opportunity to see some of the refuge's native vegetation; Mesquite Trail—a 1.5-mile path that begins near the visitor center parking area, passes through some savanna habitat, and loops around two small ponds (holding water during wet years); Paisano Trail—a 1-mile (wheelchair-accessible) paved route offering the possibility of seeing such birds as the chachalaca and road-runner; and Lakeside Trail—a 1.5-mile route that begins at Osprey Overlook on the shore of Laguna Atascosa and provides views of this lake and the surrounding thorn-forest habitat that offers opportunities for birdwatching.

Alligators inhabit the refuge. Even though they are generally afraid of people, visitors are urged to stay a safe distance from these sluggish-looking but potentially fast-moving reptiles and to stay on the trails to reduce the likelihood of encountering ticks, chiggers, and venomous snakes—notably the aggressive western diamondback rattlesnake. Insect repellent is recommended.

Lodgings and meals are available in such nearby communities as Harlingen and Brownsville.

Access to Laguna Atascosa from Harlingen is east on Farm Market Road 106 to Rio Hondo, continuing east 14 miles on FM 106 to its end, and left onto Buena Vista Road for 3 miles to the refuge's visitor center. An entrance fee is charged.

Further information: Laguna Atascosa National Wildlife Refuge, P.O. Box 450, Rio Hondo, TX 78583; telephone: (956) 748-3607.

Little Sandy, comprising 3,802 acres, was established in 1986 to protect an important area of old-growth bottomland hardwood forest habitat for wintering and breeding waterfowl and many other species of wildlife. The refuge is located along the Sabine River north of Tyler, in northeastern Texas.

Establishment of Little Sandy Refuge was made possible through the donation of a conservation easement to the U.S. Fish and Wildlife Service by the Little Sandy Hunting and Fishing Club. Under the terms of the easement, the Service acquired "development rights" from the club. As no rights to visitor access or use were purchased, the refuge is closed to visitation. However, the club does allow tours of the area by appointment, as long as they do not conflict with club activities.

Among the many species of wildlife are herons, egrets, wood ducks, wild turkeys, numerous neotropical songbirds, white-tailed deer, eastern gray and fox squirrels, and alligators. The forested bottomland is inhabited by a rich diversity of amphibians and reptiles. As described by the Fish and Wildlife Service,

The Refuge is particularly important to interior forest birds, as it provides essential breeding habitat in a relatively isolated, undisturbed setting.

The Refuge contains some of the highest quality old-growth bottomland hardwood forest remaining in the State of Texas. Biologists and researchers have rated this site as the number-one bottomland site in Texas and the number-five site in the Country. In the mid-1980's, it was identified by the Service as one of the highest priority sites for acquisition in the agency's Bottomland Hardwood Concept Plan. Records indicate that the Refuge contains five State Champion trees.

A threat hangs over the Little Sandy Refuge, however. As the Service explains,

Following establishment. . . , the Refuge and easement that created it have been challenged by the Sabine River Authority (SRA) and their supporters. The SRA contends that the Service and the Club established the Refuge to block the proposed Waters Bluff Reservoir Project.

The Waters Bluff Reservoir Project is being proposed for the Middle Sabine Basin to meet future water needs in the region and provide economic development and recreational opportunities. To date, the SRA has been unable to justify that the reservoir is needed . . . and the Texas Water Development Board has not approved its inclusion into the Texas Water Plan.

As proposed, this reservoir project would directly impact the Refuge. . . . All of the lands . . . would be flooded by the project.

Further information: Little Sandy National Wildlife Refuge, c/o Little River NWR, P.O. Box 340, Broken Bow, OK 74728; telephone: (580) 584-6211.

Lower Rio Grande Valley, currently containing 69,500 acres on 111 tracts of land and working toward a goal of 153,314 acres, was established in 1979 to protect habitat fragments and form wildlife corridors throughout the Rio Grande Delta region in south Texas. This refuge and the Santa Ana and Laguna Atascosa national wildlife refuges (see separate texts) collectively comprise the South Texas Refuge Complex, which is expected to eventually protect 287,902 acres, 10 percent of the four-county area.

The subtropical, semi-arid climate and the transitions from seacoast to palm forest to upland shrubland and savanna make this one of the most biologically diverse regions in the United States. With more than 480 species of birds, the Rio Grande Delta is truly a birding "hot spot." Some of the region's specialties include the following: least grebe; ducks (black-bellied whistling, masked, and muscovy); gray and white-tailed hawks; hook-billed kite; aplomado falcon; crested caracara; plain chachalaca; white-tipped dove; red-billed pigeon; green parakeet; red-crowned parrot; groove-billed ani; ferruginous pygmy-owl; common pauraque; buff-bellied humming-bird; green and ringed kingfishers; Couch's kingbird; great kiskadee; northern beardless tyran-nulet; rose-throated becard; green and brown jays; Mexican crow; clay-colored robin; long-billed thrasher; tropical parula warbler; olive sparrow; and altamira oriole.

The dense shrublands are also inhabited by two endangered cats, the ocelot and jaguarundi (see the discussion of these species in the Laguna Atascosa Refuge text), as well as bobcat and puma. Other representative mammals include Coues' rice rat, Mexican spiny pocket mouse, javelina (collared peccary), and southern yellow bat. Jaguar and coati were once known to be in the area but have been extirpated. Among reptiles and amphibians, noteworthy species include white-lipped frog, Mexican tree frog, Rio Grande chirping frog, Mexican burrowing toad, black-spotted newt, Rio Grande lesser siren, reticulated collared lizard, speckled racer, and Kemp's ridley sea turtle.

Approximately half of all species of North American butterflies occur in the Rio Grande delta region. Hidalgo County alone has more lepidopteran species than the entire states of Florida and California combined.

Roughly 1,200 species of plants are found here, including six endangered species: border ayenia, Walker's manioc, Zapata bladderpod, star cactus, Johnston's frankenia, and ashy dogweed. Numerous endemic plants include coastal sacaton, Texasgrass, Runyon's huaco, Runyon's cory-cactus, prostrate milkweed, and the recently described Lila de las Lomas (*Echeandia texensis*), a yellow-flowered lily.

The Rio Grande Delta is about 80 miles wide at the Gulf of Mexico and extends inland some 95 linear miles. Before flood control dams and levees were initiated in the 1930s, flood-water spread across the delta once or twice per year through an intricate network of oxbows (re-sacas) and distributary channels. Innumerable wetlands created by the seasonal ebb and flow through the resacas made ideal habitat for migratory birds. Riparian forests of Rio Grande ash, cedar elm, sugar hackberry, and soapberry thrived along these numerous watercourses, with massive Montezuma bald cypress trees spreading out from the water's edge.

Mesic river terraces supported evergreen forests of Texas ebony, anacua, brasil, coma, and Texas persimmon. The sabal palm (*Sabal mexicana*) occurred in scattered locations in the evergreen forests but predominated in the southmost area, below present-day Brownsville.

Beyond the floodwaters' reach, much of the delta was covered with exceedingly dense vegetation consisting of a great diversity of spiny shrubs, dominated by huge, often contorted honey mesquite trees. These shrublands gave way to an open coastal plain along the Gulf of Mexico, 10 to 15 miles wide and dominated by cordgrass prairies, saline meadows of sea ox-eye daisy, tidal mudflats, and shallow lagoons. Near Boca Chica, the mouth of the Rio Grande, the saline flats are interspersed with lomas, dunes of windblown clay capped with impenetrably dense, low shrubs. An open prairie occurred on the aeolian (wind-derived) sand plain that covered much of Kennedy, Brooks, and Jim Hogg counties. Here, four-flower Trichloris, little bluestem, switchgrass, panamerican balsamscale, Texasgrass, and other bunch grasses grew, interspersed with wildflowers and sub-shrubs such as Palafoxia, Mexican hat, partridge pea, golden Dalea, and blue mistflower. This region, once called the Wild Horse Desert, extended to about 35 miles north of the Rio Grande in northern Willacy, Hidalgo, and Starr counties. Subtropical shrub savanna formed the ecotone in the transition from the lush forests of the well-watered delta to the arid sand prairie.

In western Hidalgo and Starr counties, the delta is bordered by the Bordas Escarpment, where outcrops of sandstone, caliche, and volcanic tuff hem in the narrowed floodplain. The shrub savanna of these arid uplands is penetrated for many miles by arroyos (seasonal watercourses) forming corridors of dense riparian vegetation known as derramaderos. All of these vegetation types are mirrored on the Tamaulipas, Mexico side of the Rio Grande, although the Bordas Escarpment extends farther east, reaching Reynosa, before flaring to the southeast.

During the twentieth century, about 95 percent of the delta vegetation was cleared, and the land was leveled for irrigated farming. The shrub savannas and prairies that bordered the delta were converted to mesquite shrubland during the latter half of the nineteenth century, through overgrazing by vast herds of sheep and by other factors. More than 2 million people now live in the binational Rio Grande Delta region, and the human population continues to grow rapidly. From 1990 to 2000, the Hidalgo County population escalated by nearly 50 percent.

The Rio Grande wildlife corridor is a cooperative effort to conserve the rich biodiversity of this relentlessly developing region. In addition to the three national wildlife refuges, the Texas Parks and Wildlife Department manages more than 6,000 acres in state parks and wildlife management areas in the four-county area. Wildlife habitat is also protected in several county and municipal parks, as well as in numerous private tracts. The Nature Conservancy's Chihuahua Woods Preserve and Lennox Foundation Southmost Preserve, and Audubon's Sabal Palm Sanctuary and Green Island are significant components of the wildlife corridor. Mexican agencies are interested in extending the Rio Grande corridor south into the Laguna Madre in Tamaulipas and the Sierra Madre Oriental in Nuevo León.

The coalition of habitat fragments into wildlife corridors is being accomplished through the restoration of native vegetation on cropland acquired by the Lower Rio Grande Valley refuge. Each year, roughly 750 acres of refuge-owned cropland are planted with more than 200,000 seedlings of 60 species of native trees, shrubs, and cacti. Members of the public may participate in an annual event, "Rio Reforestation: Humanity for Habitat," that is held on the second Saturday in October. From 1994 to 2001, more than 5,900 volunteers have planted 90,000 seedlings on nearly 400 acres of retired farmland.

In addition to Laguna Atascosa and Santa Ana refuges, visitation is permitted on 40,000 acres of the Lower Rio Grande Valley Refuge's Boca Chica, La Sal Vieja, La Sal del Rey, Monte Cristo, Yturria Brush, La Puerta, and Salineño tracts. The refuge is open daily during daylight hours. There is no entrance fee. In addition, the World Birding Center (WBC) headquarters and satellite offices are being established by the Texas Parks and Wildlife Department, the Parks and Wildlife Foundation of Texas, Inc., and nine municipalities. Refuge tracts adjacent to the nine WBC sites will soon be open to the public, with the addition of hiking trails and other facilities.

Visitor activities include wildlife observation; photography; hiking; fishing (several access sites onto the Rio Grande, Laguna Madre, and Gulf of Mexico); and hunting (white-tailed deer and dove) on limited areas during the designated (annually revised) seasons. Camping is not permitted on the refuge, but campground facilities are provided at the Bentsen Rio Grande Valley State Park and elsewhere in the valley.

Lodgings are available in such communities as Brownsville, Harlingen, and McAllen.

Further information: Lower Rio Grande Valley National Wildlife Refuge, c/o South Texas Refuge Complex, Route 2, Box 202A, Alamo, Texas 78516; telephone: (956) 784-7500.

(NOTE: Special appreciation is given to Chris Best, Refuge Plant Ecologist, for providing this description.)

Matagorda Island, comprising 56,660 acres, was established in 1971 to protect and enhance ecologically important habitats on this 38-mile-long, actively accreting barrier island on the central Texas Gulf Coast. The refuge, which is largely dominated by waist-high coastal prairie, includes brackish bay marshlands, tidal flats, ponds, stabilized dune ridges, and beautiful sandy beaches. Since 1994, the refuge has been cooperatively managed by the U.S. Fish and Wildlife Service, the Texas Parks and Wildlife Department, and the Texas General Land Office. It is known as the Matagorda Island National Wildlife Refuge and State Park.

More than 320 species of birds have been recorded here—the majority during spring and autumn migrations. The whooping crane is among the wintering species (see Aransas text). This is also one of the Gulf Coast refuges where the spectacular neotropical migratory songbird "fallout" phenomenon occurs in April (see Aransas text).

The Fish and Wildlife Service is focusing efforts at Matagorda Island upon reintroducing the rare aplomado falcon (*Falco femoralis*). The adult male of this colorful species has slate-gray plumage on its back, the lower back of its head, and its narrow crown; whitish cheeks distinctively patterned with a black band from the eye to the lower back of the head and a black "sideburn" below the eye; a whitish throat and breast; a black upper belly hourglass-shaped band that broadens into the flanks; and dusty orange lower belly, thighs, and undertail coverts. Historically, this falcon ranged across the tropical coastal plains, arid grasslands, and savannas from southern Texas to southern Arizona, and southward through Mexico, Central America, and all the way to Patagonia and Tierra del Fuego in South America. During the past century, the aplomado falcon has become increasingly rare, particularly in the northern part of its range.

As explained in late 2001 by the refuge manager, Jennifer Sanchez:

Reintroduction of northern aplomado falcons into the northern edge of their former range began in 1996, with the release of six young falcons on Matagorda Island. In coordination with the Peregrine Fund, Inc., additional aplomado falcons were released on the Island over the next three years. The first documented nesting on Matagorda Island occurred in 1999, when a pair of falcons successfully raised and fledged three young from a former white-tailed hawk nest. In 2001, a total of nine falcons fledged from three nests on the north end of the Island. Today, Matagorda Island is home to more than 20 falcons. These magnificent birds can be seen over the coastal prairie and the Island's beach, along with wintering peregrine falcons.

The Friends of Aransas and Matagorda Island National Wildlife Refuges is a nonprofit support group that is assisting these refuges in many ways.

The refuge is open daily. There is no entrance fee.

Visitor activities include birdwatching, photography, interpretive programs, on-island shuttle service, hiking, bicycling, swimming, camping at two state park campgrounds, fishing, and hunting (state-sponsored deer, waterfowl, and game bird hunts during the designated season).

The 3-mile, self-guiding, interpretive Lighthouse Trail begins at the beach access road, crosses an earthen excavation known as the "Civil War Trenches," and reaches Matagorda Island Light. From there, the trail winds on toward a freshwater swale, crosses coastal prairie, and reaches a lookout over Pass Cavallo.

Even though alligators are generally afraid of people, visitors are cautioned to stay a safe distance from these sluggish-looking but potentially fast-moving reptiles and to be alert for several species of venomous snakes. Insect repellent and sunscreen are advised. Swimmers are warned that there are no lifeguards on the beaches, that there can be a hazardous undertow, and to be alert for sharks, stingrays, and man-o-wars.

Lodgings and meals are available at Port O'Connor.

Access to Matagorda Island is by passenger ferry service (fee) from Port O'Connor to the north dock on Thursdays, Fridays, weekends, and holidays. Charter services at Port O'Connor and other communities also offer boat rides to the island.

Further information: Matagorda Island State Park, P.O. Box 117, Port O'Connor, TX 77982; telephone: (361) 983-2215; and Matagorda Island National Wildlife Refuge, P.O. Box 100, Austwell, TX 77950; telephone: (361) 286-3533.

McFaddin, consisting of 57,000 acres, is located on the upper Gulf Coast near the southeastern corner of Texas. It was established in 1980 to protect and enhance mostly freshwater and intermediate marsh habitats. More than 270 species of birds have been recorded here and at the nearby Texas Point NWR (see that refuge's text). Both refuges are important resting and feeding areas for as many as 70,000 wintering lesser snow geese and 100,000 ducks of more than 2 dozen species.

The snow geese formerly migrated virtually nonstop from the Arctic tundra south to the coastal marshes along the Gulf of Mexico. But with the advent of extensive grain-producing agricultural areas along the Central Flyway in Saskatchewan and the Great Plains states, and the rice belt near the coast, geese are reducing their use of the traditional coastal marshlands. Prominent among the marsh birds are rails (king, clapper, Virginia, yellow, sora, and black) and American and least bitterns. McFaddin is also one of the Texas coastal refuges where the spectacular neotropical songbird "fallout" phenomenon can occur in April (see Aransas text). The refuge also supports one of the heaviest populations of the American alligator in Texas.

Establishment of McFaddin was made possible with revenues from the sale of Migratory Bird Hunting and Conservation Stamps (Duck Stamps). Ducks Unlimited, Inc. has assisted with extensive habitat enhancement projects.

The refuge is open daily during daylight hours. There is no entrance fee.

Visitor activities include birdwatching; photography; driving 8 miles of refuge roads; hiking on a short trail (behind headquarters) and along the strand of coastal beach; boating (shallow-draft boats) and canoeing (seven launch ramps are provided); fishing (only with rod-and-reel, pole-and-line, or hand-held line); crabbing; and waterfowl hunting during the designated season. As the area is tidally influenced, there are times at low tide when there is insufficient water for boating and canoeing. Clam Lake Road is open to Ten Mile Cut Bridge daily; the rest of the roads are closed on weekends and holidays. November through April are the best months for birdwatching.

Even though alligators are generally afraid of people, visitors are cautioned to stay a safe distance from these sluggish-looking but potentially fast-moving reptiles. The refuge personnel recommend that you stay in your vehicle and view them with binoculars or a scope. Visitors are also cautioned not to disturb fire ant mounds. Biting insects are prevalent, and insect repellent is advised.

Birds that have been recorded on McFaddin Refuge are virtually the same as those on Anahuac.

Lodgings and meals are available in such nearby communities as Sabine Pass, Port Arthur, and Beaumont.

Access to McFaddin is south 15 miles on State Route 87 from Port Arthur to Sabine Pass, and continuing west on that route for 12 miles to the refuge entrance. Route 87 along the coast has been washed out by coastal erosion and no longer exists.

Further information: McFaddin National Wildlife Refuge, P.O. Box 609, Sabine Pass, TX 77655; telephone (409) 971-2909.

Moody, containing 3,517 acres, was established in 1961. The U.S. Fish and Wildlife Service administers a perpetual conservation easement on a privately owned, working cattle ranch. The refuge is located along Galveston Bay, within south-central Chambers County in southeastern Texas.

Refuge habitats consist of coastal marsh and prairie, which are important for wintering and migrating waterfowl, shorebirds, wading birds, and other marsh and water birds. The 714-acre Lake Surprise is a centerpiece of the Moody Refuge. This shallow body of water annually hosts large concentrations of lesser scaup and other diving ducks. Tidally influenced marshes also support many species of marine fish and shellfish, and a thriving population of the American alligator can be found in the freshwater marshes.

Species of birds and mammals that have been recorded on Moody Refuge are essentially the same as those on Anahuac National Wildlife Refuge.

Although the refuge is not open to the public, the landowners do manage a waterfowl hunting club on the property.

Further information: Moody National Wildlife Refuge, c/o the Texas Chenier Plain NWR Complex, P.O. Box 278, Anahuac, TX 77514; telephone: (409) 267-3337.

(NOTE: Special appreciation is given to Andy Loranger, Project Leader, for providing this description.)

Muleshoe, comprising 5,809 acres, was established in 1935 to protect and enhance a number of shallow lakes that provide important wintering lesser sandhill crane and waterfowl habitat northwest of Lubbock in the South Plains of West Texas. Although spring-fed Paul's Lake almost always contains water, Goose and White lakes are frequently dry, as they are completely dependent upon runoff from sufficient rainfall in this arid region. Shortgrass and mid-grass plains habitat, with scattered mesquite trees in some places, surrounds the lakes. At least 316 species of birds have been recorded on the refuge.

The wintering lesser sandhill crane is this refuge's star attraction. The adults of this magnificent species stand 3 to 4 feet tall with a wingspread of more than 6 feet, and have gray plumage (sometimes stained with russet), a red face and crown, and a white cheek patch. Their call is a rolling, trumpeting sound that carries for at least 1 mile. The wintering population varies widely from year to year, from a low of 2,500 birds and a normal concentration of around 8,000, to the all-time high of 250,000 that occurred in February 1981.

The cranes generally start arriving at Muleshoe in late September or early October, with the largest numbers present during migration peaks, around December 1 and again around February 1. They are best observed around sunrise and sunset. Thousands fly from the refuge's lakes, where they spend the night, to grasslands and agricultural fields outside the refuge, where they feed on waste grain.

When there is sufficient water, many species of ducks arrive during the autumn, reaching their greatest concentrations by December.

The refuge is open daily, and the refuge headquarters, containing a small visitor center, is open on weekdays, except on national holidays. There is no entrance fee.

Visitor activities include birdwatching; photography; driving State Route 214 and the refuge's auto tour route; hiking (on a 1-mile interpretive trail near headquarters, a 0.25-mile trail at Paul's Lake, and on refuge fire lanes and service roads); and picnicking and primitive camping at a small picnic area/campground. Boating, swimming, fishing, and hunting are not permitted. November to March are the best months for birdwatching.

Prairie rattlesnakes (a subspecies of the western rattlesnake) are common, and visitors are cautioned to be alert. Insect repellent is advised during the warmer months.

Lodgings and meals are available at such communities as Muleshoe and Lubbock.

Access to the refuge is northwest from Lubbock on U.S. Route 84, left at Littlefield onto State Route 54 for 19 miles, and right onto State Route 214 for 5 miles to the refuge entrance; or southeast from Clovis, New Mexico, on U.S. Route 84, right at the town of Muleshoe, and south 20 miles on State Route 214.

Further information: Muleshoe National Wildlife Refuge, P.O. Box 549, Muleshoe, TX 79347; telephone (806) 946-3341.

San Bernard, consisting of 27,414 acres, is located just southwest of Lake Jackson on the upper Gulf Coast of Texas. It was established in 1968 to protect and enhance important habitat for wintering waterfowl, shorebirds, and other wildlife. Habitats include coastal prairie, wooded areas, freshwater marsh and ponds, an intermittent stream, a colonial water bird rookery, coastal salt marsh, and many saltwater lakes and ponds.

More than 300 species of birds have been recorded at this refuge. As at nearby Brazoria and Big Boggy refuges, San Bernard is a vital waterfowl wintering area, with as many as 50,000 lesser snow geese and 30,000 ducks of many species here in December and January. This is also one of the Gulf Coast refuges where the spectacular neotropical migratory songbird "fallout" phenomenon can occur in April (see Aransas text).

With a system of dikes and water control structures, the U.S. Fish and Wildlife Service manages water levels for waterfowl food production and for waterfowl resting and feeding areas. On parts of the refuge, periodic prescribed burns are carried out to maintain conditions beneficial to waterfowl.

Establishment of San Bernard Refuge was made possible partly with revenues from the sale of Migratory Bird Hunting and Conservation Stamps (Duck Stamps). Ducks Unlimited, Inc. has assisted with important habitat enhancement projects.

The refuge is open daily during daylight hours. There is no entrance fee.

Visitor activities include birdwatching; photography; driving the 3-mile Moccasin Pond Auto Tour gravel road; hiking on three trails; and fishing (saltwater fishing and crabbing are permitted on Cow Trap Lake and Cedar Lakes, and on Cedar Lake Creek where there is a boat ramp). Waterfowl hunting is permitted on the Salt Bay, Cedar Lakes, and Smith Marsh waterfowl hunting areas during the designated season. A reservation waterfowl hunt is available at the Sargent Permit Waterfowl Hunting Area. Information is available at the refuge headquarters. November through April are the best birdwatching months at San Bernard.

Even though alligators are generally afraid of people, visitors are cautioned to stay a safe distance from these sluggish-looking but potentially fast-moving reptiles and to be alert for venomous snakes, fire ants, and ticks. Insect repellent is advised.

Birds and mammals that have been recorded on San Bernard Refuge are essentially the same as those on Brazoria.

Lodgings and meals are available in such nearby communities as Lake Jackson, Angleton, and Freeport.

Access to San Bernard is south from Houston by way of State Route 288 to Lake Jackson; right onto State Route 2004; and proceeding 13 miles on State Routes 2004, 2611, and 2918 to the refuge entrance.

Further information: San Bernard National Wildlife Refuge, 1212 N. Velasco, Suite 200, Angleton, TX 77515; telephone: (979) 849-6062.

Santa Ana, consisting of 2,088 acres, is located along a bend in the Rio Grande, in the lower Rio Grande Valley of south Texas. The refuge was established in 1943 to protect what is today the largest remnant of dense, subtropical hardwood and shrub thorn forest along the river, providing habitat for an extensive variety of fauna. A number of wetlands and ponds—remnants of former river oxbow lakes (*resacas*) and impoundments—are managed for waterfowl and other water birds. This relatively small area is a priceless ecological gem—a sample of the kind of wildlife-rich ecosystem that once covered wide areas along both sides of the river valley.

The refuge is inhabited by many species of birds and mammals that are native to Mexico and that reach the northern end of their range in the lower Rio Grande. Approximately 400 species of birds have been recorded on this internationally famous birding mecca. Among the avian highlights are the green jay, altamira oriole, great kiskadee, buff-bellied hummingbird, ringed and green kingfishers, black-bellied and fulvous whistling-ducks, and plain chachalaca. The latter species is a large brown, pheasant-like bird with long, white-tipped tail. While it is sometimes difficult to see, the chachalaca lets forth with a raucous, attention-getting call that suggests its name.

Two major North American migratory bird flyways, the Mississippi and Central, converge in and funnel through south Texas. Consequently, numerous neotropical migrant species, which breed in the United States or Canada and winter in Mexico or Central or South America, pass through this ecologically rich oasis.

As described by refuge plant ecologist Chris Best,

Santa Ana, with over 450 species of vascular plants, is botanically diverse and has both subtropical and temperate affinities. Most of the uplands are covered with dense thickets of granjeno, lotebush, elbowbush, guayacan, colima, allthorn, Wright's acacia, and many other mostly spiny shrubs, dominated by emergent honey mesquite and ebony trees. Taller gallery forests of sugar hackberry, cedar elm, and Rio Grande ash border the river and resaca channels, flanked by evergreen forests of anacua, Texas ebony, soapberry, coma, brasil, and Texas persimmon. Gaps in the canopy are quickly filled by tepeguaje, one of the fastest growing trees in the world. These forests are festooned with two epiphytic bromeliads, Spanish moss and ball moss. Chile pequin bushes, the wild ancestors of cultivated chile peppers, thrive here in partial shade. Seasonal crops of the spicy red fruits are eagerly devoured by mockingbirds, green jays, and chachalacas.

Along the Jaguarundi Trail, south of Terrace Trail, there is a relatively open savanna known as the Shrub Garden. This dry upland becomes a florid butterfly haven after seasonal rains. Lavender-flowered cenizo, blue-flowered Eupatorium, orange-flowered Allowissadula, and yellow-flowered Viguiera shrubs intermingle with native bunch grasses, such as lovegrass Tridens, plains bristlegrass, four-flower Trichloris, purple three-awn, and red grama.

Santa Ana Refuge is a mecca for butterflies. As naturalist Roland H. Wauer says:

More butterflies (265 species) have been recorded within this refuge than at any other refuge or park in the United States. Although the garden, located at the visitor center, consistently produces the highest numbers, many of the trails, such as Jaguarundi Trail, can be superb. A few of the most-wanted species to be expected include Giant White; Yojoa Scrub-Hairstreak; Clytie Ministreak; Rounded, Red-bordered, and Blue Metalmarks; Julia and Zebra Heliconians; White Peacock; Malachite; Mexican Bluewing; Pale-banded Crescent; Guava, Mimosa, and White-patched Skippers; and White-striped, Dorante's, Teleus, and Brown Longtails.

The Valley Nature Center is a nonprofit, educational support organization that is assisting the refuge in various ways.

The refuge is open daily during daylight hours. An entrance fee is charged except on the first Sunday of each month. The visitor center is open daily, except on Thanksgiving and Christmas.

Visitor activities at Santa Ana include birdwatching, butterfly observation, photography, driving the 7-mile loop Wildlife Drive, hiking, interpreter-led tram tours (fee), and interpretive programs. November through April are the best birding months at Santa Ana. Pets must be kept on a leash. Picnicking, camping, fishing, and hunting are not permitted on the refuge. Campground facilities are available at Bentsen Rio Grande State Park; information: (956) 585-1107.

Hiking opportunities are provided on more than 12 miles of hiking trails and other routes that wind through the refuge, including Santa Ana Trail—a 0.5-mile (wheelchair-accessible) path from the visitor center to Willow Lake; Santa Ana Communities Trail—a 1.6-mile route around Willow Lake; Wildlife Management Trail—a 2-mile route through the Pintail Lake area and along a short stretch of the Rio Grande; Terrace Trail—a 0.8-mile trail between Willow and Cattail lakes; Cattail Trail—a 1.5-mile path around Cattail Lake; Jaguarundi Trail—a 1.4-mile path from the Terrace Trail to the Rio Grande; and Vireo Trail—a 0.9-mile route from the loop road to the Rio Grande.

Visitors are cautioned to be extremely careful along the Rio Grande and stay safely back from the unstable riverbank, as it is often undercut and can slump into the river. Visitors also should be alert for chiggers, scorpions, and Africanized bees that inhabit the refuge. Insect repellent is advised during the warmer months.

Lodgings and meals are available in such nearby communities as Alamo, McAllen, Weslaco, Harlingen, and Brownsville.

Access to Santa Ana is south from Expressway 83 at Alamo by way of Farm Road 907 and left 0.3 mile on U.S. Military Highway 281 to the refuge entrance.

Further information: Santa Ana National Wildlife Refuge, Route 2, Box 202A, Alamo, TX 78516; telephone: (956) 784-7500.

Texas Point, consisting of 8,900 acres, is located along the upper Gulf coast at the southeast corner of Texas. It was established in 1979 to protect and enhance estuarine and coastal salt and intermediate marsh habitats and some wooded upland. More than 270 species of birds have been recorded here and at the nearby McFaddin NWR.

Texas Point is an important resting and feeding area for as many as 100,000 ducks of more than two dozen species. It was formerly also a mecca for tens of thousands of snow geese. But because of the proliferation of helicopter activity at nearby Sabine Pass, with dozens of take-offs and landings daily that service offshore oil-drilling operations, the skittish geese no longer come here. Texas Point is also one of the Texas coastal refuges where the spectacular neotropical songbird "fallout" phenomenon can occur in April (see Aransas text).

Establishment of Texas Point was made possible with revenues from the sale of Migratory Bird Hunting and Conservation Stamps (Duck Stamps).

The refuge is open daily during daylight hours. There is no entrance fee.

Visitor activities include birdwatching; photography; hiking; boating (shallow boats can be launched, for a fee, at a private dock on Texas Bayou near the eastern end of the refuge); fishing (only with rod-and-reel, pole-and-line, or hand-held line); crabbing; and waterfowl hunting during the designated season. November through April are the best months for birdwatching. A primitive trail and a cattle walk provide access from the parking area into wooded and marsh habitats.

Alligators are abundant on this refuge. Even though they are generally afraid of people, visitors are cautioned to stay a safe distance from these sluggish-looking but potentially fast-moving reptiles. Refuge staff recommend that you stay in your vehicle and view them with binoculars or a scope. Visitors are also cautioned to avoid disturbing fire ant mounds. Biting insects are prevalent, and insect repellent is advised.

Bird species that have been recorded on Texas Point are virtually the same as those on Anahuac.

Lodgings and meals are available in such nearby communities as Sabine Pass, Port Arthur, and Beaumont.

Access to Texas Point is south 15 miles on State Route 87 from Port Arthur to Sabine Pass, adjacent to which is the refuge entrance. The headquarters for Texas Point is located at nearby McFaddin National Wildlife Refuge.

Further information: Texas Point National Wildlife Refuge, P.O. Box 609, Sabine Pass, TX 77655; telephone: (409) 971-2909.

Trinity River, containing more than 18,000 acres, was established in 1994 to protect and enhance an ecologically significant area of mixed hardwood forest, bottomland hardwood forest, and cypress swamp, with many bayous and oxbow lakes, along the Trinity River floodplain in southeastern Texas. The refuge provides important habitat for a wide variety of wildlife, including concentrations of wintering waterfowl, colonial water birds in rookeries, nesting wood ducks, and numerous species of neotropical migratory songbirds, such as warblers and vireos. Over 200 bird species have been recorded here.

Establishment of Trinity River was made possible partly with revenues from the sale of Migratory Bird Hunting and Conservation Stamps (Duck Stamps) and partly with money from the Land and Water Conservation Fund. Friends of Trinity River Refuge is a nonprofit support group that is assisting the refuge in various ways.

The refuge is open daily during daylight hours, but some units are inaccessible. There is no entrance fee.

Visitor activities include birdwatching, photography, environmental education programs, hiking, canoeing and boating, fishing, and hunting during the designated season.

Even though alligators are generally afraid of people, visitors are cautioned to stay a safe distance from these sluggish-looking but potentially fast-moving reptiles and to be alert for venomous snakes. Insect repellent is advised.

Lodgings and meals are available in such communities as Liberty and Dayton.

Access to the refuge headquarters is at 1351 N. Main Street, 0.9 mile north of U.S. Route 90, in Liberty.

Further information: Trinity River National Wildlife Refuge, P.O. Box 10015, Liberty, TX 77575; telephone: (936) 336-9786.

Utah

Bear River Migratory Bird Refuge, encompassing 73,645 acres, was established in 1928 to manage and protect an important oasis of marshes, mudflats, and open water in the desert. The refuge is located at the mouth of Bear River, on the northeastern shore of Great Salt Lake in northern Utah. This desert oasis is scenically framed by the rugged Wasatch Mountains to the east and the Promontory Mountains to the west.

The refuge's wetland habitats attract impressive concentrations of migratory waterfowl, shorebirds, and other birds. Thousands of white pelicans come to feed in the marshes while nesting on islands far across the vast expanse of Great Salt Lake. Many thousands of tundra swans stop to rest and feed here in October–November on their southward migration from breeding grounds on the Alaskan tundra. Bear River Refuge is a mecca for numerous species of ducks. Many thousands nest here, and others pause by the tens of thousands during their spring migration to breeding areas farther north. In the autumn, as many as one-half million waterfowl are attracted to the refuge's impoundments. Thousands of herons and egrets and more than three-quarters of North America's white-faced ibises nest on the refuge. Spectacular numbers of shorebirds, such as plovers, sandpipers, dowitchers, godwits, stilts, avocets, and phalaropes, either rest and feed here on their migrations or come to nest and raise their young. The wetlands draw huge flocks of red-winged and yellow-headed blackbirds. And in winter, the refuge hosts scores of bald eagles.

By the late nineteenth century, northern Utah settlers were diverting increasingly large quantities of Bear River water for the development of their communities and farmlands located between Great Salt Lake and the base of the Wasatch Mountains. By the early decades of the twentieth century, the river's flow had significantly diminished. The delta marshlands, which formerly covered roughly 45,000 acres, had dwindled to only 2 or 3 thousand acres. The resulting low water levels and exposed mudflats in the delta produced conditions that were favorable to a bacteria-caused disease that infects birds.

As described by Dr. Alexander Wetmore, a former Secretary of the Smithsonian Institution:

Following the reduction of water levels and the crowding of great concentrations of birds into smaller areas, losses from botulism were first noted about 1900. More and more ducks sickened as the epidemic spread over the stagnant waters of the shallow alkali flats, and in 1910, and again in 1913, upward of a million died around the mouth of Bear River.

The virulent toxin *Clostridium botulinum*, which attacks the nervous system, continued to cause catastrophic and gruesome avian mortality through the 1920s. Spurred by widespread public alarm, Congress authorized establishment of the Bear River Refuge. By the early 1930s, 50 miles of dikes and water control structures were completed, so that water levels within the impounded wetland habitat could be carefully managed. Thousands of birds were treated with an antitoxin injection and released after recovery. In 1936, a toxicology laboratory was built on the refuge to carry out botulism research.

By 1964, nearly 80,000 ducklings were annually produced on Bear River Refuge. In 1982, a visitor center was built and began offering interpretive and educational programs. But then in 1983, following several years of record precipitation in the region, the rising level of Great Salt Lake inundated the refuge. It rose above the dikes, flooded the impounded wetlands, heavily damaged the dikes and water control structures, and destroyed the research laboratory and new visitor center. As the U.S. Fish and Wildlife Service has said, "In short, the refuge was rendered inoperable."

In 1989 and 1990, the lake level gradually declined, revealing the remains of refuge buildings and miles of damaged dikes. Staff, assisted by numerous volunteers, began the difficult task of cleaning up and recreating the refuge. Nearly 50 miles of dikes have been restored; water control structures have been restored; smaller, more manageable impoundment units have been created; and a 35,000-square-foot Education Center is planned for construction. This latter facility will contain an exhibit hall, an auditorium for interpretive and educational programs, a classroom for use by school and other groups, a laboratory to enable continuing botulism and other research projects, a gift shop/bookstore, and refuge administrative offices. In 1993 and 1994, approximately 9,000 acres were added to the refuge's original 65,000 acres, in part to protect and manage grassland habitat for nesting waterfowl and in part to provide a location safely above flood levels for the Education Center and other refuge buildings.

Establishment of Bear River Refuge was made possible partly with revenues from the sale of Migratory Bird Hunting and Conservation Stamps (Duck Stamps). Ducks Unlimited, Inc. has assisted with the restoration and enhancement of more than 20,000 acres of the refuge's wetland habitat and is presently working with the Fish and Wildlife Service in the enhancement of waterfowl breeding habitat on the refuge's 17,000-acre grassland unit. As *Ducks Unlimited* senior writer Matt Young wrote in his January/February 2002 article, "Wetlands Under Siege":

While great progress has been made in conserving these critical wetlands, the Great Salt Lake marshes continue to face an uncertain future. The Wasatch Front is currently home to approximately 1.6 million people. Over the next 50 years, the population is expected to soar to more than 5 million. Such rapid growth will undoubtedly place extreme pressure on water supplies, open space, agricultural land, and wildlife habitat. Projections indicate 273,000 additional acres of land in the region will be developed by 2050.

In response to these threats, DU has stationed a biologist and an engineer in the area to coordinate conservation activities, partnership development, and funding acquisition. Ensuring adequate supplies of freshwater for high-value wetland habitats will also be critical in the years ahead. DU is presently seeking funding for research that would design geographic information system models that will help determine the likely impacts future water diversions would have on the Great Salt Lake marshes.

The Friends of the Bear River Bird Refuge is a nonprofit support group that assists with many refuge needs, including fund-raising for the new Education Center and building two observation platforms with volunteer labor and private donations. Utah State University is assisting the refuge's research and environmental education programs.

The refuge is open daily during daylight hours. There is no entrance fee. The refuge's Education Center is scheduled to be completed in the near future. The refuge's administrative offices are open on weekdays, except national holidays.

Visitor activities include birdwatching; photography; driving and bicycling on the entrance road and the 12-mile, self-guiding, auto tour route (may be closed by snow or water) that encircles impoundment Unit 2; interpretive and educational programs; viewing wildlife from a number of observation platforms; hiking a wetland trail network; limited fishing (a wheelchair-accessible fishing pier is provided); and hunting (waterfowl and upland game birds) on parts of the refuge during the designated seasons. Visitor activities are limited to the auto-tour route dike and the wetland trail network, except during the approved hunting seasons. Canoeing and shallow-draft boating are not permitted, except during the approved hunting seasons. Although camping is not permitted on the refuge, privately operated campground facilities are provided in Brigham City, Willard, and Mantua, and public campgrounds are located in the Wasatch-Cache National Forest. Over 220 bird species have been recorded on the refuge.

Insect repellent is advised during the warmer months.

Lodgings and meals are available in Brigham City.

Access to Bear River Refuge is from Exit 366 (Forest Street) on I-15 at Brigham City and west about 15 miles on Forest Street.

Further information: Bear River Bird Migratory Refuge, 58 South 950 West, Brigham City, UT 84302; telephone: (435) 723-5887.

Colorado River Wildlife Management Area (see the Ouray National Wildlife Refuge text).

Fish Springs, comprising 17,992 acres, was established in 1959 to protect a 10,000-acre marsh, the water of which comes almost entirely from a complex of warm, saline, artesian springs. The refuge is located in the midst of the arid expanse of the Great Basin Desert in west-central Utah.

The thermal spring water comes from deep within the Earth, at a temperature of between 71°F and 80°F all year, surfacing along a fault line or zone of fracturing at the eastern base of the Fish Springs Mountains. Dating research of this "fossil water" has shown that roughly 10,000 years have elapsed between its falling as precipitation and emanating from the springs. Over a long stretch of geologic time, movement of and friction between two immense blocks of the Earth's crust have occurred, creating the gradually uplifted fault-block mountain range to the west and the valley or basin to the east. These juxtaposed basin and range blocks are typical of this region's vast "washboard" topography of the basin and range province that stretches across much of Utah, virtually all of Nevada, and parts of several neighboring states.

Some of the ponds of this lush gem of an oasis support a population of the Utah chub. This species of native fish is known to measure up to 14 inches in length, but the vast majority of them on the refuge grow to 8 inches or less. The marsh habitat, which is maintained by a network of water delivery and control structures from the springs, annually attracts many thousands of migrating waterfowl and other wetland birds. Among them are tundra swans, Canada geese, numerous ducks, such as mallards, green-winged and cinnamon teal, pintails, wigeons, gadwalls, canvasbacks, redheads, buffleheads, goldeneyes, and ruddy ducks, along with eared grebes, great blue herons, snowy egrets, black-crowned night-herons, white-faced ibises, stilts, and avocets. Peak concentrations of migrating waterfowl generally occur around mid-April and late September. More than 270 species of birds have been recorded on the refuge.

The refuge is open daily during daylight hours. There is no entrance fee. The refuge headquarters is open on weekdays, except national holidays.

Visitor activities include birdwatching; photography; driving the 11-mile, self-guiding auto tour route and other refuge roads not closed; hiking on the tour route year-round and on most other parts of the refuge between mid-July and mid-May; mountain biking on gravel roads; picnicking at the (wheelchair-accessible) picnic area, group tours (by prearrangement); and canoeing, kayaking, and boating (gasoline motors not permitted) between mid-July and mid-May, except on Ibis and Gadwall ponds. Swimming is not permitted in refuge waters. Camping is not allowed on the refuge, but primitive camping is permitted at several places on nearby public lands administered by the U.S. Bureau of Land Management.

Visitors are cautioned to be alert for rattlesnakes in nonwetland habitats. Insect repellent is advised during the warmer months.

Mammals include mule deer, bobcat, coyote, kit and red foxes, muskrat, badger, striped skunk, black-tailed jackrabbit, desert cottontail, white-tailed antelope squirrel, Townsend ground squirrel, least chipmunk, and chisel-toothed and Ord kangaroo rats.

Of the reptiles, there are lizards (Great Basin sagebrush, western fence, desert side-blotched, and Great Basin whiptail) and snakes (striped whipsnake, wandering garter, Great Basin gopher, and Great Basin rattlesnake). Amphibians are northern leopard frog and bullfrog.

The refuge's marsh vegetation includes bulrushes, coontail, and wigeongrass.

The nearest lodgings and meals are available a long distance from this isolated refuge: in Tooele (104 miles) and Delta (78 miles). It is 42 miles to the closest gasoline and grocery supplies.

Access to Fish Springs Refuge from Exit 99 on I-80 is south about 42 miles on State Route 36 and southwest (right) 63 miles on the unpaved Old Pony Express and Stage Route. Or from Delta, it is northeast 16 miles on U.S. Route 6, west-northwest (left) about 41 miles on State Route 174 to the end of the pavement, continuing straight from the end of the pavement for about 15 miles to the intersection with the Pony Express Route, and west (left) for about 7 miles to the refuge headquarters. It is extremely important to have a full tank of fuel, a spare tire, and plenty of water before heading for the refuge.

Further information: Fish Springs National Wildlife Refuge, Dugway, UT 84022; telephone: (435) 831-5353.

Ouray, containing 11,987 acres, was established in 1960 to protect and manage an area of floodplain wetlands, riverine habitat, and riparian cottonwood groves that contrasts with adjacent, arid, semi-desert uplands. The refuge is located along a meandering, 12-mile stretch of the Green River in northeastern Utah.

This lush area provides a major migration corridor for numerous species of migrating waterfowl, neotropical songbirds, raptors, and other birds; attracts a diversity of resident wildlife; and contains critical habitat for four endangered species of fish: the Colorado pikeminnow, razorback sucker, and humpback and bonytail chubs.

Miles upstream from Ouray Refuge, the Green River has been harnessed by the Flaming Gorge Dam. Even though the Yampa River's undammed tributary flow fortunately continues to function naturally, the predam overbank flooding that annually provided important revitalizing nutrients and other benefits to the floodplain ecosystem is now a rare event. As the U.S. Fish and Wildlife Service says in the July 2000 Ouray National Wildlife Refuge *Comprehensive Conservation Plan* (*CCP*), since construction of the dam, "the Green River system has changed dramatically, resulting in long-term loss and degradation of riparian habitats and . . . species dependent on them. The Refuge's riparian habitat is now critically important to protect declining fish and migratory bird species using the Green River corridor."

Most of the refuge's wetlands consist of floodplain marshes in the wetland bottoms that are dominated by cattails, bulrushes, and other emergent aquatic plants. Under an earlier refuge management strategy, some of this marsh habitat was divided into levee- and dike-contained units. In 1997, the U.S. Fish and Wildlife Service began breaching some of the riverbank levees in an attempt to approximate a more natural, flood-renewed and nutrient-enriched wetland-bottom ecosystem; to enhance the chances for survival for endangered fish; and, as the *CCP* document says, to evaluate habitat and species responses to this "planned seasonal floodplain inundation. Responses by non-native and native fish, . . . wildlife, and plants are being recorded to gauge the effects of reestablishing overbank flooding."

The refuge also includes about 50 acres of moist-soil impoundments. Water levels, which are seasonally regulated within these units, are raised during the spring and then gradually lowered through the summer to encourage the growth of emergent aquatic plants of value to waterfowl and other wildlife.

Under a cooperative agreement with a local landowner, about 150 acres of the refuge are devoted to the growing of alfalfa, barley, and sorghum or milo. Part of these nutrient-rich crops is left unharvested as a supplemental food source for the benefit of waterfowl, deer, elk, and other wildlife.

Among the several thousand waterfowl that come to Ouray Refuge's wetlands to nest and raise their young are Canada geese, mallards, green-winged and cinnamon teal, pintails, shovelers, gadwalls, wigeons, redheads, and ruddy ducks. Wading birds include great blue herons, white-faced ibises, lesser yellowlegs, black-necked stilts, American avocets, and Wilson's phalaropes. Raptors include the northern harrier, golden eagle, Swainson's and rough-legged hawks, peregrine falcon, great horned owl, and a few wintering bald eagles. Of the numerous neotropical songbirds, there are yellow-billed cuckoo, black-headed grosbeak, lazuli bunting, and a number of flycatchers, vireos, and warblers. More than 200 species of birds have been recorded on the refuge.

A scenic highlight of Ouray Refuge are the Leota Bluffs. These wind- and water-sculpted formations consist of colorfully banded sandstone and shale. A beautiful panorama of the refuge from an overlook is provided atop the bluffs at Powell Point. The point is named in honor of John Wesley Powell, the Civil War veteran who lost his right hand and forearm in the Battle of Shiloh in 1862 and who, seven years later, led the first expedition down the uncharted Green and Colorado rivers.

This landmark river trip began at Green River Station, in Wyoming. Powell and his men descended through Flaming Gorge (now inundated behind Flaming Gorge Dam); the Canyon of Lodore, Echo Park at the junction of the Green and Yampa rivers, and Split Mountain Gorge (within what is now Dinosaur National Monument); the river's peaceful meanderings through what is now Ouray Refuge; and on through Desolation Canyon; Stillwater Canyon, the junction of the Green and Colorado rivers, and Cataract Canyon (within what is now Canyonlands National Park); Glen Canyon (now inundated behind Glen Canyon Dam); and the grandest canyon of them all (within what is now Grand Canyon National Park), in Arizona.

Establishment of Ouray Refuge was made possible partly with revenues from the sale of Migratory Bird Hunting and Conservation Stamps (Duck Stamps). Among groups that have provided assistance to the Refuge are local troops of the Boy Scouts of America and the Vernal Junior High Escape Club.

The refuge is open daily during daylight hours. There is no entrance fee. The refuge headquarters/visitor center is open on weekdays, except national holidays.

Visitor activities include birdwatching, photography, interpretive and environmental education programs, driving the 12-mile auto tour route, viewing the refuge from an observation tower and from Leota Overlook, hiking, bicycling and horseback riding (on designated roads), fishing (only on the river), and hunting (deer, waterfowl, and pheasant) on parts of the refuge during the designated seasons. Rafting and canoeing on the Green River are also a pleasurable way to view the refuge. Some rafting excursions begin upstream, within the spectacular, sheer-walled canyons of Dinosaur National Monument, and end in the refuge. A permit is required from the Unimtah and Ouray Indian Reservation in order to use a takeout facility at Ouray Bridge. About 2,600 acres of the southern end of the refuge are leased from the Native Americans. Although camping is not permitted on the refuge, campground facilities are available in Vernal and elsewhere in the general vicinity.

There are presently no designated hiking trails. As funding becomes available, plans call for the development of two interpretive trails, one of which is to be wheelchair-accessible.

Insect repellent is advised during the warmer months. Visitors are cautioned that the refuge's unpaved roads become extremely slippery when wet.

Colorado River Wildlife Management Area (WMA), which is managed from Ouray Refuge, was established in 1998 to protect ecologically important floodplain habitat along the Colorado, Green, and Gunnison river system in eastern Utah and western Colorado. As of late 2001, there were more than 950 acres in 13 individual properties along the Green and Colorado rivers, toward a goal of approximately 10,000 acres. As explained by the Colorado River WMA's assistant refuge manager Lance Koch,

The primary purpose of the WMA is to protect and restore backwater floodplain habitat for the endangered razorback sucker, Colorado pikeminnow, humpback chub, and bonytail chub. The type of habitat to be restored is flooded bottomland that is directly connected to the rivers during seasonal flooding. These shallow wetlands provide food, shelter, and resting areas for the fish. . . .

The areas are held as conservation easements with willing landowners, who agree to allow management and protection activities by refuge officials. Public use is not permitted, as the right to access the property is retained by the landowner. . . . Management activities are limited to manipulation or removal of dikes or levees to induce or improve flooding, biological studies or surveys, control of non-native vegetation, and easement monitoring and enforcement.

Lodgings and meals are available near Ouray Refuge in such communities as Vernal and Roosevelt.

Access to Ouray Refuge from Vernal is west 14 miles on U.S. Route 40 and south (left) 13 miles on State Route 88.

Further information: Ouray National Wildlife Refuge, HC 69, Box 232, Randlett, UT 84063; telephone: (435) 545-2522.

Vermont

Missisquoi, containing 6,592 acres, was established in 1943 to protect extensive wetlands on most of the Missisquoi River Delta. The refuge provides important feeding, resting, and breeding habitats for migratory waterfowl, neotropical songbirds, and other wildlife. It is located near the northern end of Lake Champlain and close to the U.S.–Canada border in northwestern Vermont.

The name *Missisquoi* is derived from an Abenaki Indian word meaning "place of flint." The river winds through extensive beds of wild rice and other wetland vegetation, such as bulrushes, rushes, sedges, wild celery, pickerelweed, and arrowhead. Although approximately 5,000 acres of the refuge contain natural marsh habitat, another 1,200 acres are managed wetlands within three diked impoundments. These pools provide a mixture of open water; nutrient-rich, emergent plants offering food and cover for waterfowl and other wildlife; and wooded and shrub-dominated swamp habitats. Water levels in the impoundments are seasonally regulated to promote the growth of such plants as wild rice and buttonbush.

The peak influx of migrating waterfowl occurs in the autumn, when thousands of ring-necked ducks; hundreds of American black ducks, mallards, and green-winged teal; and lesser numbers of other species are attracted here. Autumn concentrations of waterfowl frequently peak at around 20,000 birds. The largest rookery of great blue herons on the Vermont shore of Lake Champlain is located on Shad Island, at the northern end of the refuge. More than 500 heron nests have been counted in this area.

The refuge also provides important nesting habitat for the black tern. Although nesting success may vary from year to year, since 1999 the refuge's population is reported to have comprised 94 to 100 percent of all black terns that nested in Vermont.

According to refuge manager Mark Sweeny, "the importance of the refuge to birds is so significant that Vermont Audubon adopted the refuge in 1986 and designated it as an Important Bird Area . . . in 1999." Over 200 bird species use the refuge.

In addition to water management within impoundments, other habitat management activities include the placement of nesting boxes, cones, and other structures throughout the delta to supplement natural nesting sites for such species as wood and black ducks, common goldeneyes, and hooded mergansers. Haying, mowing, and periodic prescribed burning are implemented to maintain roughly 350 acres of grassland habitat for the benefit of bobolinks and other songbirds, as well as waterfowl that seek the cover of grass for nesting. The non-native purple loosestrife and common reed (*Phragmites*) are controlled to keep these aggressive, invasive plants from crowding out native species (see the discussion of loosestrife control techniques in the Montezuma Refuge [New York] text).

About 700 acres of Missisquoi Refuge consist of the ecologically outstanding Maquam Bog, which has been designated as a research natural area. It is the only pitch-pine bog community in Vermont and supports such other plant species as highbush blueberry, cranberry, rhodora, and sphagnum moss.

Establishment of Missisquoi Refuge was made possible in large part with revenues from the sale of Migratory Bird Hunting and Conservation Stamps (Duck Stamps). A number of nonprofit organizations are providing important assistance to the refuge, including Ducks Unlimited, Inc., Franklin County Sportsman's Club, Friends of Missisquoi National Wildlife Refuge, and the Green Mountain and Vermont Audubon societies.

The refuge is open daily during daylight hours. There is no entrance fee. The refuge headquarters is open on weekdays, except national holidays.

Visitor activities include birdwatching; photography; environmental education programs; hiking; cross-country skiing and snowshoeing; canoeing, kayaking, and boating (boat-launching sites are at Louie's Landing and on Mac's Bend Road—the latter available only from September 1 through the close of the waterfowl hunting season in December); fishing (from the riverbank, on the river, and on Lake Champlain); and hunting (waterfowl, deer, and small game) on parts of the refuge during the designated seasons. Some lakeshore parts of the refuge are closed to boating, to avoid disturbing wildlife. Camping is not permitted on the refuge, but campground facilities are available at a number of nearby state parks.

Hiking opportunities are provided on a 1.5-mile, self-guiding, interconnected route: Black Creek and Maquam Creek Trails, for which an interpretive brochure is available, are located at refuge headquarters. Two additional trails are located along Tabor Road: The 0.5-mile Stephen J. Young Marsh Trail leads from the parking area to the marsh; and the 1.5-mile Old Railroad Passage Trail runs from the parking area through Maquam Bog and ends at Maquam Bay. Visitors may also observe wildlife by walking along the 1-mile Mac's Bend Road, from Louie's Landing to Mac's Bend. A 2-mile jeep trail starts at Mac's Bend and follows the Missisquoi River to Missisquoi Bay.

Insect repellent is advised during the warmer months.

Lodgings and meals are available in such communities as Swanton, Alburg, and St. Albans.

Access to Missisquoi Refuge from Exit 21 on I-89 is west 1 mile on State Route 78 into Swanton and northwest 2 miles on Route 78 (which runs through the refuge); or from Exit 42 on I-87 it is east 13 miles (through Rouses Point, New York, and Alburg, Vermont), and left onto State Route 78 (which runs through the refuge).

Further information: Missisquoi National Wildlife Refuge, 371 North River Street, Swanton, VT 05488; telephone: (802) 868-4781.

Silvio O. Conte (see text under Massachusetts)

Virginia

Back Bay, containing more than 8,600 acres, was established in 1938. The refuge protects many islands in the northern part of Back Bay; part of a narrow, barrier-island-like, coastal peninsula that separates the bay from the Atlantic Ocean; and lands along the bay's western shore in the southeast corner of Virginia. Over 300 bird species have been seen here.

The refuge contains a stretch of sandy ocean beach, sand dunes, maritime woodland, freshwater impoundments, brackish marshes, and cropland. A tremendous diversity of wildlife is attracted to Back Bay Refuge, including large concentrations of wintering waterfowl. Especially in December and January, the refuge hosts as many as 10,000 greater snow geese and large concentrations of tundra swans, Canada geese, and many species of ducks. Large influxes of shorebirds and neotropical songbirds come through during their spring and autumn migrations. Wood ducks, ospreys, bald eagles, and the federally listed threatened piping plover are among the many species of birds that nest here.

White-tailed deer, mink, river otters, and raccoons are among the resident native mammals. Three non-natives unfortunately cause harmful impacts: nutrias, introduced from South America into the southeastern United States in the early twentieth century, continually burrow into and damage refuge dikes; feral hogs uproot and destroy important marsh plants; and wild horses trample native vegetation.

During the summer, loggerhead sea turtles haul themselves onto the ocean beach to lay their eggs. This species of marine reptile is listed as threatened under the Endangered Species Act.

Back Bay Refuge's woodland trees consist mostly of wind-sculpted loblolly pines and live oaks. Prominent species of shrubs include wax myrtle, bayberry, highbush blueberry, black cherry, and persimmon.

The U.S. Fish and Wildlife Service carries out a number of habitat management activities for the benefit of wildlife. Water levels within a number of impoundments (pools) are seasonally regulated with water control structures to enhance the growth of plants that provide food for waterfowl. Periodic prescribed burning triggers nutrient cycling, curtails the invasion of woody vegetation where it is not desired, and promotes the renewal of vegetation that provides food and cover for wildlife.

Regarding Back Bay's importance, refuge manager John P. Stasko has this to say:

To borrow a phrase from the booming real estate industry in Virginia Beach, Virginia: "It's all about location, location, location." Back Bay's significance is a result of where it is. Midway along the Atlantic

Coast, it serves as a resting and feeding spot for migratory birds. It is the southernmost location for many northern species and the northernmost for many southern species, like the loggerhead sea turtle. It's a barrier island system; yet, it has a freshwater bay with freshwater species. But perhaps its most important location is within the rapidly sprawling development of Virginia's most heavily populated city. Back Bay National Wildlife Refuge is the untouched preserve of the area's diminishing open space. It protects the natural and cultural heritage of this city and it protects it forever. Much of what the management team at Back Bay does is aligned with those protection efforts; and of the citizens in our area, the vast majority appreciates what the Refuge contributes to the quality of life.

Establishment of Back Bay Refuge was made possible partly with revenues from the sale of Migratory Bird Hunting and Conservation Stamps (Duck Stamps). Ducks Unlimited, Inc. has helped enhance more than 1,500 acres of the refuge's wetland habitat. The Friends of Back Bay is a local nonprofit support group that is assisting the refuge in a variety of ways.

The refuge is open daily during daylight hours. An entrance fee is charged during certain times of the year. The visitor contact station is open daily, except on Saturdays, from December 1 through March, and is open on Memorial Day, July 4, and Labor Day.

Visitor activities include birdwatching; photography; driving the entrance road to the contact station; viewing interpretive displays and a film at the contact station; hiking; bicycling on some interior dikes; canoeing, kayaking, and boating (only small, nonmotorized watercraft that can be hand-carried to the bay's edge); surf and freshwater fishing in some areas; and hunting (deer and hog) on part of the refuge during the designated seasons. Although camping is not permitted on the refuge, campground facilities are provided to the south on adjacent False Cape State Park; and to the north in Virginia Beach. Swimming, surfing, and sunbathing are not permitted on the refuge but are popular activities at Virginia Beach.

Hiking opportunities include the 0.4-mile End of Bay Trail, from the contact station to the bay; two (wheelchair accessible) boardwalk trails from the contact station to the beach: the 0.25-mile Seaside Trail and the 0.5-mile Dune Trail; and a 4-mile stretch of the beach and two (seasonally closed) dike routes southward to False Cape State Park. The latter two routes are also open to bicycling.

Visitors are cautioned to be alert for ticks, chiggers, and venomous snakes. Insect repellent during the warmer months and sunscreen are advised.

The more than 300 species of birds that have been recorded on Back Bay Refuge are much the same as those of Chincoteague Refuge.

Lodgings and meals are available in such communities as Virginia Beach, Chesapeake, and Norfolk.

Access to Back Bay Refuge from Exit 284 on I-64 in Norfolk is east 13 miles on I-264, the Virginia Beach–Norfolk Expressway, taking the last expressway exit and proceeding south on Bird Neck Road for just over 3 miles; right onto General Booth Boulevard for just over 2 miles; left onto Princess Anne Road; at the first stoplight proceeding left onto Sandbridge Road for 3 miles; and right onto Sandpiper Road for 4 miles to the refuge entrance.

Further information: Back Bay National Wildlife Refuge, 4005 Sandpiper Road, Virginia Beach, VA 23456; telephone: (757) 721-2412.

Chincoteague, comprising 14,032 acres, was established in 1943 to protect important habitat for the greater snow goose and other migratory birds. Most of the refuge is located on Virginia's portion of Assateague Island, a coastal barrier island in northeastern Virginia and southeastern Maryland. Over 320 bird species have been recorded here.

Smaller parts of the refuge include Wildcat Marsh at the northern end of Chincoteague Island, Morris Island, and all or part of three smaller barrier islands that extend southward from the main part of the refuge. These islands are Cedar, Assawoman, and Metompkin (part of the latter is owned and managed by the U.S. Fish and Wildlife Service and the rest by The Nature Conservancy). The refuge also includes a tract of just over 400 acres on the Maryland portion of Assateague Island.

Chincoteague Refuge is ranked as one of the top five migratory shorebird staging areas in the United States east of the Rocky Mountains. In 1990, the barrier islands of the eastern shore of Virginia and Maryland were designated as an International Shorebird Reserve, and this barrier island–coastal lagoon system has also been named as a World Biosphere Reserve by the United Nations' Educational, Scientific, and Cultural Organization. Shorebirds pass through the refuge by the hundreds of thousands from mid-April to mid-June and from mid-July to mid-August.

In addition to major concentrations of wintering waterfowl and migrating shorebirds, Chincoteague Refuge's habitats attract large numbers of wading birds, seabirds, neotropical migratory songbirds, and migrating and nesting raptors. Ospreys are commonly seen hunting for fish in the impoundments and marshes, and they like to nest on hunting blinds that are scattered across the open water of Chincoteague Bay and Assateague Channel. In recent years, one or two active bald eagle nests have been located on the refuge.

Another of the refuge's raptors is the peregrine falcon. As explained by the U.S. Fish and Wildlife Service:

Chincoteague NWR is one of the prime eastern U.S. focal points for observing arctic peregrine falcons during their autumn migration. The Wash Flats impoundments and the protected north beach provide resting and feeding habitat for an estimated 875–900 peregrines . . . [that] may stop over on the island for a day to several weeks. An international banding program indicates that more than half the peregrines observed at the refuge during the fall migration originate in Greenland, with others coming from Quebec, the Northwest Territories, and the Yukon. Some of these peregrines travel as far south as southern Argentina.

Chincoteague Refuge habitats include sandy ocean beaches, sand dunes that support dunegrass, a shrub community that is typical of backdunes and flats, several large stands of maritime forest, areas of brackish wetlands, and extensive areas of salt marsh. There are also 14 moist-soil units covering more than 2,600 acres, the operation of which is described by the Fish and Wildlife Service:

Water-control structures . . . allow biologists to lower water levels in the spring to create a mudflat-type environment to attract shorebirds. Biologists also reduce water levels . . . to concentrate fish for wading birds to feed upon, grow plants as a food source for waterfowl, and reduce the number of plants that are low in nutrition for wildlife.

In the fall, water-control structures are closed to catch rainwater in the moist-soil management units. The higher water levels provide habitat for waterfowl and other migratory birds.

The restoration and enhancement of the refuge's maritime forest is another important refuge management activity. To curtail the spread of the southern pine beetle, which impairs or kills loblolly pines, and to enhance the woodlands for the endangered, steel-gray Delmarva Peninsula fox squirrel (*Sciurus niger cinereus*) ('translocated' to the refuge in the late 1960s and early 1970s) and other wildlife, the refuge carries out a variety of silvicultural practices. These activities include thinning, prescribed burning, and planting of native hardwoods, such as oaks, persimmon, and flowering dogwood. (A description of the Delmarva Peninsula fox squirrel is included in the Blackwater Refuge [Maryland] text.)

To help protect the federally listed threatened, beach-nesting piping plover, refuge biologists "place protective closures around nests, control predation, and intensively monitor chicks from March through August."

As for some of Chincoteague's specific bird species, as explained by the Fish and Wildlife Service:

Black duck management is a high priority throughout their range because of declining populations and hybridization with mallards. Breeding and wintering habitat quality on the refuge is enhanced by controlling phragmites [a species of grass] and wax myrtle in favor of vegetation with higher waterfowl food value, such as three square, spikerush, and red root cyperus. Although Chincoteague NWR is south of the major black duck breeding range, an estimated 40–200 young are produced annually depending on impoundment conditions.

Snow goose populations have recovered since the 1930's and 1940's when they were in trouble, resulting in the formation of the Chincoteague Refuge. The refuge's current mid-winter snow goose population averages around 6,000 - 12,000 geese but can range as high as 50,000 for a few weeks.

. . . Species of egret, heron, and ibis frequent the impoundment borrow ditches, eating small finfish and eels. . . . A heron, egret, and ibis rookery is located on several marsh islands in Chincoteague Bay. Other rookeries are located in the outer marsh fringe between Chincoteague Island and the Mainland. The eastern brown pelican also delights visitors as they often soar just above the water and just beyond the breakers in the ocean. . . .

The refuge also provides excellent nesting habitat for colonial and other beach nesting birds. Colonial species include common, least, and gull-billed terns, and black skimmers. Wilson's and piping plovers nest on beach ridges and overwash areas (Assateague Island is the northern limit of Wilson's plovers' breeding range.) Willets and oystercatchers nest on the cove side beach and around the natural freshwater marsh in the Hook interior. Oystercatchers also nest in the dunes. . . .

Raptor migration through the area occurs in September and October; this event can be spectacular, depending on the weather conditions.

In an unusual boundary arrangement, all of Assateague Island and adjacent bays—from Ocean City, Maryland, southward to Toms Cove Hook, in Virginia—are encompassed by the 39,636-acre Assateague Island National Seashore, which was established in 1965. Most of the Fish and Wildlife Service's Chincoteague National Wildlife Refuge lies within the southern portion of the national seashore in Virginia, and most of the northern portion of the seashore, in Maryland, is administered by the National Park Service (NPS).

Two mammals are non-natives: The sika, an Asian elk, which is much smaller than the native white-tailed deer; and the Chincoteague "ponies," which are descendants of colonial domestic horses that were introduced onto Assateague Island in the seventeenth century. The latter are wild horses that have adapted to this coastal environment. Before the refuge was established, the ponies were bought by the Chincoteague Volunteer Fire Company, which continues to own the herd that inhabits two parts of the refuge. As a traditional means of fund-raising, the fire company rounds up the roughly 150 ponies for its Annual Pony Penning and Auction that is held on the last Wednesday and Thursday of July. (The Maryland herd of ponies is owned by the National Park Service.)

Establishment of the Chincoteague Refuge was made possible partly with revenues from the sale of Migratory Bird Hunting and Conservation Stamps (Duck Stamps). Ducks Unlimited, Inc. has helped enhance more than 2,200 acres of the refuge's wetland habitat. Chincoteague Natural History Association is a nonprofit educational organization that is assisting this refuge, as well as the Eastern Shore of Virginia Refuge, in various ways.

The refuge is open daily during daylight hours. There is an entrance fee. The refuge's new Herbert H. Bateman Educational and Administrative Center is open daily, except on Christmas. Near the southern end of the refuge, the National Park Service maintains the national seashore's Toms Cove Visitor Center, offers interpretive walks and programs, and manages recreational activities and facilities.

Visitor activities include birdwatching; photography; viewing interpretive exhibits and programs at the Bateman Center; driving the road to the Toms Cove area and, from 3 p.m. to dusk, the 3.25-mile Wildlife Loop (an interpretive brochure is available), which encircles Snow Goose Pool (B Pool South); hiking; bicycling; picnicking; swimming; boating (boats are permitted to land at Fishing Point, from September 1 to March 14); fishing; crabbing; shellfishing (in Toms Cove); and hunting (sika—a small Asian elk—deer, waterfowl, and rail) on parts of the refuge during the designated seasons. Archery and firearm white-tailed deer and/or sika elk hunts are held when control of the herds is needed. A sika hunt area is reserved for handicapped hunters. Although camping is not permitted on the refuge, facilities are available at private campgrounds on Chincoteague Island; on the National Park Service-administered portion of the national seashore, in Maryland; and at Maryland's Assateague State Park. Motor vehicles are prohibited outside of established roads, parking areas, and designated off-road vehicle (ORV) areas, for which special regulations and restrictions apply (as explained by an ORV brochure).

Hiking and bicycling opportunities include a number of routes: the 3.25-mile Wildlife Loop, where waterfowl and wading birds can be seen on Snow Goose Pool (B Pool South); a short (wheelchair-accessible) boardwalk that leads from the Wildlife Loop to an observation platform that overlooks Snow Goose Pool; the 0.25-mile Freshwater Marsh Trail (an interpretive brochure is available) that loops around an area of the marsh habitat of Snow Goose Pool; the 1-mile Black Duck Trail that branches from the Wildlife Loop; the 1.5-mile Woodland Trail (an interpretive brochure is available) that loops through a forest of loblolly pines and provides an overlook, from which wild ponies can sometimes be observed; and the 1.5-mile Swans Cove Trail that leads from the Wildlife Loop to the beach. Other routes are for hiking only: the 0.25-mile Lighthouse Trail that leads through a wooded area to the 142-foot-tall Assateague Lighthouse, which dates from 1867 (an interpretive brochure is available); and the 7.5-mile service road.

Visitors are cautioned to stay a safe distance from the Chincoteague ponies, as they are wild and unpredictable horses that can be dangerous; be careful when swimming in the ocean; and be alert for ticks. To reduce the chance of picking up ticks, which may transmit Lyme disease, visitors are urged to stay on the trails. Insect repellent during the warmer months and sunscreen are advised.

Lodgings and meals are available in such communities as Chincoteague Island, New Church, and Onancock, Virginia; and Pocomoke and Salisbury, Maryland.

Access to Chincoteague Refuge from Pocomoke City, MD, is south 8 miles on U.S. Route 13; east 10 miles on State Route 175 to the town of Chincoteague; left onto Main Street, right onto Maddox Boulevard; and just over 2 miles, crossing Assateague Channel to Assateague Island. From Virginia Beach, it is north 85 miles on U.S. Route 13, east (right) onto State Route 175, and proceeding as above.

Further information: Chincoteague National Wildlife Refuge, P.O. Box 62, Chincoteague, VA 23336; telephone: (757) 336-6122.

Eastern Shore of Virginia, containing 752 acres, was established in 1984 to enhance and protect an area of maritime forest, wax myrtle and bayberry thickets, grasslands, and freshwater and brackish ponds. The refuge is located at the southern tip of the Delmarva Peninsula on the Eastern Shore of Virginia. Over 300 bird species have been seen here.

From late August through early November, enormous numbers of migrating birds, notably songbirds, raptors, swallows, and waterfowl, fly southward along the peninsula, which encompasses Delaware and the Eastern Shore of Maryland and Virginia (Delmarva). The narrow southern end of the peninsula acts like a funnel, forcing the birds together in spectacular concentrations. At this strategic location, they often pause to await favorable wind and weather before crossing the broad mouth of Chesapeake Bay.

One species that migrates south to spend from late autumn to midwinter on the refuge is the American woodcock—a squat, comical-looking little bird, with a long beak and large eyes set high on the sides of the head. At times, scores, if not hundreds, of them, with twittering sounds and whirring wings, fly out of the woods at dusk to feed on worms in the refuge's fields.

Historically, the end of the peninsula was also strategically valued for military purposes. At the start of World War II, the federal government established Fort John Custis on much of the land that is now within the refuge. Bunkers containing 16-inch guns were placed there to help defend the U.S. naval bases and shipyards at Norfolk and Virginia Beach. In 1950, the fort was transferred to the U.S. Air Force and converted to the Cape Charles Air Force Station. This facility closed in 1980. Four years later, the Air Force transferred 180 acres to the U.S. Fish and Wildlife Service, securing the initial tract of land for the refuge.

A number of habitat enhancement activities are being carried out on the refuge. Most of the military buildings have been removed; vegetation has been planted that provides cover for wildlife; ponds have been created, offering freshwater wetland habitat for waterfowl, wading birds, and shorebirds; nesting platforms have been erected for ospreys; and nest boxes and other structures have been provided for wood ducks, bluebirds, and owls. Ducks Unlimited, Inc. has helped enhance some of the refuge's wetland habitat. In addition, the refuge contains habitat that is being managed for the numerous species of butterflies that inhabit or migrate through the area. Chincoteague Natural History Association is a nonprofit educational organization that is assisting this refuge, as well as Chincoteague Refuge, in a variety of ways.

The refuge is open daily during daylight hours. There is no entrance fee. The visitor center (located on the east side of U.S. Route 13, just north of the Chesapeake Bay Bridge Tunnel) is open daily from March through December and is open Fridays through Sundays in January–February.

Visitor activities include birdwatching, butterfly observation, photography, viewing interpretive exhibits and video programs at the visitor center, hiking, and limited deer hunting (archery by lottery on the first day and first-come first-served thereafter; and shotgun by lottery) in certain zones of the refuge during the designated times. Some areas of the refuge are closed to visitation. Although camping is not permitted on the refuge, campground facilities are available at Kiptopeke State Park; information: (757) 331-2267. The latter park also contains a butterfly garden.

Hiking opportunities on the refuge include the 0.5-mile Butterfly Trail, adjacent to the visitor center; and the 0.5-mile interpretive Wildlife Trail that loops from a parking area on Fitchett Road through woodland of loblolly pines and oaks and to an observation platform overlooking the salt marsh, tidal inlets, barrier islands, the Chesapeake Bay, and the Atlantic Ocean. A couple of refuge roads are also open for walking and bicycling.

The roughly 300 species of birds that have been recorded on the Eastern Shore of Virginia Refuge are much the same as those of Chincoteague Refuge.

Lodgings and meals are available in area communities such as Cape Charles and Virginia Beach.

The Coastal Virginia Wildlife Observatory, located near the Eastern Shore of Virginia Refuge, carries out many field studies on the refuge and in the surrounding area that are yielding important insights into the timing, size, and other aspects of the spring and autumn migrations of birds (plus butterflies and other insects) through coastal Virginia. This nonprofit membership organization permits public visitation to most of its activities and offers interpretive services. Further information: Coastal Virginia Wildlife Observatory, P.O. Box 111, Franktown, VA 23354.

Access to the Eastern Shore of Virginia Refuge is by way of U.S. Route 13 north on the 20-mile Chesapeake Bay Bridge Tunnel (toll) from Virginia Beach, and south 100 miles from Salisbury, Maryland. From U.S. Route 13, the refuge entrance to the visitor center is approximately 0.25 mile east on State Route 600.

Further information: Eastern Shore of Virginia National Wildlife Refuge, 5003 Hallett Circle, Cape Charles, VA 23310; telephone: (757) 331-2760.

Featherstone, consisting of 326 acres, was established in 1979 to protect an area of Potomac River bottomland hardwood forest, previously slated as the site of a garbage dump, in northern Virginia. Although the refuge is presently not open to visitation, hiking trails are being planned. Fauna and flora are similar to the species on nearby Mason Neck Refuge (see listings for that refuge).

Further information: Featherstone National Wildlife Refuge, c/o Potomac River NWR Complex, 14344 Jefferson Davis Highway, Woodbridge, VA 22191; telephone: (703) 490-4979.

Fisherman Island, comprising 1,850 acres, was established in 1969. The island refuge protects a vital stopover point for numerous migrating birds and butterflies, as well as nesting habitat for such species as brown pelican, glossy ibis, American black duck, black skimmer, osprey, American oystercatcher, and royal and sandwich terns. It is located just south of Cape Charles and the Eastern Shore of Virginia National Wildlife Refuge, at the mouth of Chesapeake Bay in southeastern Virginia. The Chesapeake Bay Bridge-Tunnel runs across the island.

This is an unusual barrier island. As the U.S. Fish and Wildlife Service explains, "The earliest documentation of the island's existence is from an 1815 navigational chart of the Chesapeake Bay that shows two small islands south of Cape Charles, referred to as the 'Bird Islands.' The first accurate map of Fisherman Island is from a Coast Survey of 1852 that shows Fisherman at about 25 acres. While all of Virginia's other barrier islands are shrinking in size, Fisherman Island continues to grow, reaching 1,850 acres at the present time."

Fisherman Island was initially under private ownership and was used by residents for hunting and fishing. In the 1890s, the island was acquired for use by a U.S. quarantine station for European immigrants traveling to Baltimore. During World War I and World War II, Fisherman Island was used for a harbor defense station to guard the mouth of Chesapeake Bay against the possibility of attack by Germany.

Access to Fisherman Island is only by prearranged tour, from October through March.

Further information: Fisherman Island National Wildlife Refuge, c/o Eastern Shore of Virginia NWR, 5003 Hallett Circle, Cape Charles, VA 23310; telephone: (757) 331-2760.

Great Dismal Swamp, encompassing 109,709 acres, was established in 1974 to restore and manage the ecological diversity of an extensive forested wetland in southeastern Virginia and northeastern North Carolina. In the middle of the refuge is 3,100-acre Lake Drummond, which was discovered in 1665 by North Carolina's colonial governor, William Drummond.

Great Dismal Swamp was long subjected to and greatly impacted by drainage and numerous timber harvesting activities. Twenty-six years before George Washington became the first president of the United States, he first visited this swamp and then formed the Dismal Swamp Land Company, which proceeded to drain and log off part of the area. Logging the swamp's bald cypress, Atlantic white cedar, and other trees was economically so lucrative that it continued until 1976. As the U.S. Fish and Wildlife Service explains:

The entire swamp has been logged at least once, and many areas have been burned by periodic wildfires. The Great Dismal Swamp has been drastically altered by humans over the past two centuries. Agricultural, commercial, and residential development destroyed much of the swamp, so that the remaining portion within and around the refuge represents less than half of the original size of the swamp [estimated to have been between 500,000 and 2 million acres]. Before the refuge was established, over 140 miles of roads were constructed to provide access to the timber. These roads severely disrupted the swamp's natural hydrology, as the ditches which were dug to provide soil for the road beds drained water from the swamp. The roads also blocked the flow of water across the swamp's surface, flooding some areas . . . with stagnant water. The logging operations removed natural stands of cypress and Atlantic white-cedar that were replaced by other forest types, particularly red maple. A drier swamp and the suppression of wild-fires, which once cleared the land for seed germination, created environmental conditions that were less favorable to the survival of cypress and cedar stands. As a result, plant and animal diversity decreased.

In 1973, the Union Camp Company donated just over 49,000 acres of its land to The Nature Conservancy, which transferred the property the following year to the Fish and Wildlife Service. The condition of the Great Dismal Swamp at that time was in sharp contrast to the Okefenokee Swamp in Georgia and Florida. According to Great Dismal Swamp's refuge manager, Lloyd A. Culp, Jr. (author of the chapter "Refuges and Ecosystem Protection" in the 2000 publication *The Natural History of the Great Dismal Swamp*):

The biological and physical features of the Okefenokee Swamp were basically intact when the refuge was established. An attempt to drain much of the swamp during the 1890s had failed. Following major wild-fires in the 1950s, a dike was installed at the headwaters of the Suwannee River to retain water during droughts. . . .However, subsequent hydrologic studies indicated that the influence of the dike was more limited than originally believed.

Human activity in the Great Dismal Swamp inflicted subtle but significant changes in its physical features. Beginning in the 1760s with Washington Ditch, the . . . 150 miles . . . of ditches created a drier swamp by draining surface water which, in conjunction with the logging and suppression of natural wild-fires, changed the composition of the forest. Thus, a Great Dismal Swamp with a diversity of forested habitats (including large cypress and Atlantic white cedar stands) gradually changed to an area dominated by red maple trees. Only remnants of cypress and cedar stands remain.

. . . As a result of more decades of exploitation and fewer decades of protection, the Great Dismal Swamp NWR faces more complex challenges in the restoration and maintenance of natural resources than does the Okefenokee NWR.

Lloyd Culp goes on to describe a number of twenty-first-century management issues for the Great Dismal Swamp. For example, to promote hydrologic restoration, the Fish and Wildlife Service will continue maintaining and monitoring more than 30 water control structures to slow the drainage of the forested wetlands. If recommended by environmental modeling, additional water control structures may be installed to enhance this process. Restoration of Atlantic white cedar and bald cypress forest will continue to be a major focus of refuge management, and the use of fire and other timber management techniques will be expanded. Additional land acquisition within the refuge's authorized boundary will be accomplished, as funding becomes available, to acquire land from willing sellers, with assistance from such organizations as The Nature Conservancy and The Conservation Fund. And the protection of vital wildlife corridors, as for the black bear, providing links between the refuge and other natural habitats, will also be encouraged.

The Great Dismal Swamp Refuge's major forest types include stands of pine, Atlantic white cedar, red maple-black tupelo, bald cypress-water tupelo, and sweetgum-oak-poplar. Non-forested plant communities include a sphagnum bog, a remnant marsh, and areas of evergreen shrubs.

Ducks Unlimited, Inc. has helped enhance more than 20,000 acres of Great Dismal Swamp refuge's wetland habitat. The Great Dismal Swamp Coalition, Inc. is a nonprofit support group that is assisting the refuge in a number of ways.

The refuge is open daily during daylight hours. There is no entrance fee. The refuge headquarters, at the western edge of the refuge, is open on weekdays, except national holidays.

Hart Mountain NWR, Oregon

Petroglyphs, Hart Mountain NWR, Oregon

Malheur NWR, Oregon

Oregon Islands NWR

William L. Finley NWR, Oregon

John Heinz NWR at Tinicum, Pennsylvania

Harlequin ducks, Sachuest Point NWR, Rhode Island

Short-eared owl, Lacreek NWR, South Dakota

Wintering trumpeter swans, Lacreek NWR

Sand Lake NWR, South Dakota

Reelfoot NWR, Tennessee

Black-bellied whistling duck, Laguna Atascosa NWR, Texas

Laguna Atascosa NWR

Ocelot with radio collar, Laguna Atascosa NWR

Black-shouldered kite feeding nestlings, Laguna Atascosa NWR

Green jay, Santa Ana NWR, Texas

Plain Chachalaca, Santa Ana NWR

Bear River NWR, Utah

Black-crowned night-heron, Fish Springs NWR, Utah

Fish Springs NWR

Fish Springs NWR

Canada geese, Fish Springs NWR, Utah

Fish Springs NWR

Missisquoi NWR, Vermont

Geese at sunset, Chincoteague NWR

Chincoteague NWR, Virginia

Mason Neck NWR, Virginia

Columbia NWR, Washington

Gray's Harbor NWR, Washington

Saddle Mountain NWR, Washington

Protection Island NWR, Washington

Umatilla NWR, Washington

Beaver dam and pond, Canaan Valley, West Virginia

Horicon NWR, Wisconsin

Horicon NWR

Necedah NWR, Wisconsin

Ultralight-led cranes, Necedah NWR. U.S. Fish and Wildlife Service Photo

Whooping cranes, Necedah NWR. U.S. Fish and Wildlife Service photo

Necedah NWR

National Elk Refuge, Wyoming

Bull elk at National Elk Refuge

Wintering trumpeter swans, National Elk Refuge

Sleigh ride for elk viewing, National Elk Refuge

Indian paintbrush, Seedskadee NWR, Wyoming

Trumpeter Swans

Visitor activities include birdwatching, photography, hiking, bicycling, boating and canoeing (a boat-launching ramp, offering access to Lake Drummond, is provided onto the Feeder Ditch, at the eastern edge of the refuge), fishing, and deer hunting on parts of the refuge during the designated season. Although camping is not permitted on the refuge, campground facilities are available in the general vicinity.

Hiking opportunities include the nearly 0.75-mile (wheelchair-accessible) Dismal Town Boardwalk Trail, located on Washington Ditch Road, which winds through part of the swamp habitat, and a number of the refuge's unpaved roads that are also open to bicycling. The peak influx of neotropical migratory songbirds, such as numerous species of warblers, is from late April to mid-May. Over 200 bird species have been recorded here?

Visitors are cautioned to be alert for ticks, chiggers, and venomous snakes. Insect repellent is advised during the warmer months.

Lodgings and meals are available in such communities as Suffolk, Chesapeake, Norfolk, and Virginia Beach.

Access to Great Dismal Swamp Refuge from Suffolk is south on U.S. Route 13 (Washington Street), left 7 miles on State Route 642 (White Marsh Road), and left (east) on the Washington Ditch entrance road to the boardwalk trail. Refuge headquarters is about 1 mile farther south on State Route 642, and left (east) about 2 miles on Desert Road. The boat-launching access, on the eastern edge of the refuge, is adjacent to U.S. Route 17.

Further information: Great Dismal Swamp National Wildlife Refuge, P.O. Box 349, Suffolk, VA 23434; telephone: (757) 986-3705.

James River, consisting of 4,200 acres, was established in 1991 to protect mostly wooded habitat along the James River, primarily for the long-term benefit of the bald eagle. The refuge is located about 30 miles southeast of Richmond in east-central Virginia.

Thousands of bald eagles from the East Coast congregate in the Chesapeake Bay region during the summer months. The area along the James River that includes the refuge is one of the largest summer roosting sites east of the Mississippi River. Powells Creek, which forms the western boundary of the refuge, is a spawning area for several anadromous fish species, which in turn are an important food source for eagles.

In addition to bald eagles, numerous other birds use James River Refuge for nesting or for resting and feeding during migration. Breeding bird surveys conducted on the refuge in May and June 2000 revealed a total of 53 species. Among them were common breeders such as tufted titmouse and northern cardinal, and some unusual species including the prothonotary warbler. The most numerous was the red-eyed vireo, followed by the pine warbler. Breeding bird surveys will continue on the refuge to establish a biological baseline and to evaluate the effects of future forest management activities. Other birds that have been recorded on the refuge and surrounding waters include double-crested cormorant, great blue and green herons, black-crowned night heron, Canada goose, many ducks, osprey, woodpeckers, flycatchers, vireos, numerous warblers, and scarlet tanager.

Mammals include white-tailed deer, red fox, beaver, raccoon, striped skunk, opossum, eastern cottontail, and eastern gray squirrel.

Pine forests dominate the James River Refuge, with smaller assemblages of tidal marsh, old fields, and mixed hardwoods. Rare plants found on and near the refuge include prairie senna, sensitive joint vetch, and Long's bittercrest. In cooperation with the Virginia Division of Natural Heritage, surveys began in 2001 searching for additional rare species and rare plant communities.

Managing the forest is the highest priority at James River. Prior to refuge establishment, the majority of the property was owned by a corporation that harvested trees and replanted with loblolly pine. Without active management, the planted pines become overcrowded and less valuable to wildlife, including bald eagles. Thick planted pines also present a wildfire hazard. Forest management here will create greater habitat and wildlife diversity and will also reduce the potential for destructive wildfires. Prescribed fire may then be used as an important management tool with which to maintain the understory and keep hazardous fuels in check.

Public use opportunities are currently limited to an annual hunting program for white-tailed deer. Future plans call for establishment of wildlife observation trails and outdoor classroom sites. Educational groups and other organized field studies, such as bird club visits, may be permitted through advance arrangement.

Lodgings and meals are available in Hopewell and Richmond.

Further information: James River National Wildlife Refuge, c/o Eastern Virginia Rivers NWR Complex, P.O. Box 1030 (336 Wilna Road), Warsaw, VA 22572; telephone: (804) 333-1470.

(NOTE: Special appreciation is given to Joe McCauley, Project Leader, for providing this description.)

Mackay Island (see text under North Carolina)

Martin (see text under Maryland)

Mason Neck, containing 2,277 acres, was established in 1969 as the first national wildlife refuge specifically for the then-federally listed endangered bald eagle (*Haliaeetus leucocephalus*). The refuge is located on the southern shore of the Potomac River, 18 miles south of Washington, D.C., in northern Virginia. Over 200 bird species have been seen here.

The refuge's habitats include close to 5 miles of river shoreline, the largest freshwater marsh in northern Virginia, and roughly 2,000 acres of mixed hardwood and pine forest. Other protectively managed lands on the 8,000-acre Mason Neck Peninsula are the adjacent Mason Neck State Park and Gunston Hall Plantation, as well as nearby Pohick Bay Regional Park. The refuge and these other areas, which are working together as the loosely allied Mason Neck Management Area, total more than 6,000 acres that are cooperatively managed for eagle protection. The U.S. Fish and Wildlife Service reports, "overall numbers of eagles in the area have increased dramatically . . . with up to 50 or more birds in the winter."

As described by the Fish and Wildlife Service, there is a lot of eagle activity on and movement on and off the refuge during the course of a year. In November and December, resident eagles begin their courtship and breeding, and in February, they reconstruct their nests and lay eggs. In April, the eaglets hatch. In August, after the young have fledged, the adults leave Mason Neck at about the same time as immature birds from the surrounding area arrive. In October, adult eagles that nested elsewhere arrive with their young for the winter. Wintering eagles are often seen feeding in the refuge's 258-acre, tidally influenced Great Marsh.

Mason Neck Refuge also contains one of the largest rookeries of the great blue heron in the mid-Atlantic states. It has grown tremendously, from 26 nests that were discovered in 1979, to more than 1,400 nests in 2000. The Fish and Wildlife Service carries out a variety of habitat management activities. Human disturbance of the rookery is avoided during the nesting season; nesting boxes are provided for wood ducks, bluebirds, and bats, to supplement the supply of natural tree cavities; and the growth of native food plants is promoted for the benefit of wintering waterfowl.

Among the most abundant of the many species of wintering waterfowl at Mason Neck are greater and lesser scaup, American black duck, mallard, ring-necked duck, common and hooded mergansers, bufflehead, ruddy duck, Canada goose, and tundra swan. During spring and autumn migrations, large influxes of neotropical songbirds come to or through the refuge's woodlands.

More than 200 species of birds have been recorded on the refuge.

Recorded human history of Mason Neck began at least as early as the 1600s, when colonial settlers began buying land along the Potomac River. Between 1755 and 1760, Gunston Hall was built on Mason Neck by plantation owner George Mason (1725–92). This Virginia statesman wrote the first draft of the Virginia Declaration of Rights, which was adopted in its final form by the Virginia convention in Williamsburg on June 12, 1776.

Mason's words ("That all men are by nature equally free and independent, and have certain inherent rights . . . namely, the enjoyment of life and liberty, with the means of acquiring and possessing property, and pursueing and obtaining Happiness and Safety") were the forerunner of Thomas Jefferson's Declaration of Independence, and his ideas also became the model for subsequent bills of rights that were included in many other state constitutions and in The Constitution of the United States of America. Mason was a key speaker at the Constitutional Convention in 1787 but refused to sign the document because it omitted a bill of rights. In 1791, with his continued support, the Bill of Rights was approved in the form of ten amendments to the Constitution. In 2002, the George Mason Memorial Garden, near the Tidal Basin in Washington, D.C., was dedicated and added to the National Park System.

Gunston Hall is a prime example of formal, mid-eighteenth-century Georgian-style architecture. This one-and-one-half-story, red brick structure was the center of a 5,500-acre tobacco and wheat plantation—one of numerous Virginia tidewater tobacco plantations that depended upon the labor of African-American slaves. The plantation included all the lands that are now within Mason Neck National Wildlife Refuge, Mason Neck State Park, and Pohick Bay Regional Park. Today, the 550-acre Gunston Hall is owned by the Commonwealth of Virginia and has been designated as a National Historic Landmark. The property is open daily for tours. An excellent publication on the subject is *Gunston Hall: Return to Splendor* (published by Gunston Hall Plantation, 1991). (Website address: www.gunstonhall.org.) For information on tours and events: Gunston Hall Plantation, 10709 Gunston Road, Mason Neck, VA 22079; telephone: (703) 550-9220.

During the nineteenth and early twentieth centuries, as described by the Fish and Wildlife Service,

. . . logging was the principle land use of what is now refuge lands. Roads were cut and much of the mature pine and hardwood timber removed. This human disturbance and the elimination of nest trees reduced the bald eagle population.

By the 1960s, timber had grown back, but residential development posed a new threat. Local residents worked with The Nature Conservancy to protect the land. In 1969, the U.S. Fish and Wildlife Service purchased 845 acres from the Conservancy and the Mason Neck National Wildlife Refuge was established.

Ducks Unlimited, Inc. has helped enhance an area of the refuge's wetland habitat.

The refuge is open daily during daylight hours. There is no entrance fee. The refuge headquarters is open on weekdays, except national holidays.

Visitor activities include wildlife observation, photography, hiking on designated trails, interpreter-led hikes and programs, bicycling on paved roads, and limited deer hunting (by lottery) during designated days. An environmental education pavilion and adjacent fields and trails are available for organized groups by advance reservation. Although camping is not permitted on the refuge, campground facilities are provided at Pohick Bay Regional Park and Prince William Forest Park.

Hiking opportunities are provided on two self-guiding trails, for which interpretive pamphlets are available. The 0.75-mile (wheelchair-accessible) Great Marsh Trail follows an old logging road onto a peninsula, affording a panorama of the marsh, where bald eagles are often seen and where beavers build their cone-shaped lodges. The 3-mile round-trip Woodmarsh Trail leads through deciduous forest and, as part of a loop, offers views from an observation platform at the edge of Great Marsh. Within the loop are two short cross-trails: 0.16-mile Fern Pass and 0.18-mile Hickory Pass.

Visitors are cautioned to be alert for ticks, chiggers, and the venomous copperhead snake. Insect repellent is advised during the warmer seasons.

Lodgings and meals are available in such communities as Lorton, Woodbridge, and Springfield.

Access to Mason Neck Refuge from Exit 163 (at Lorton) on I-95 is east on Lorton Road to U.S. Route 1 (Jefferson Davis Highway), south (right) on U.S. Route 1, east (left) just over 4.5 miles on Gunston Road, and right onto High Point Road to the refuge's Woodmarsh Trail directional sign. To the Great Marsh Trail, continue 1.5 miles on Gunston Road. A scenic alternative route from Washington, D.C., is south along the Potomac River on the George Washington Memorial Parkway to Mount Vernon, continuing west on State Route 235 to U.S. Route 1, and south (left) on Route 1 to Gunston Road.

Further information: Mason Neck National Wildlife Refuge, c/o Potomac River NWR Complex, 14344 Jefferson Davis Highway, Woodbridge, VA 22191; telephone: (703) 490-4979.

Nansemond, consisting of 423 acres, was established in 1974 to protect an area of tidal marsh and the Nansemond River estuary, a tributary of the lower James River located just west of Norfolk in southeastern Virginia. The refuge and river are named for the Nansemond Indians who formerly lived in the surrounding area.

Because the refuge is surrounded by a military facility, it is not open to visitation.

Further information: Nansemond National Wildlife Refuge, c/o Great Dismal Swamp NWR, P.O. Box 349, Suffolk, VA 23439; telephone: (757) 986-3705.

Occoquan Bay, containing 644 acres, was established in 1998 and is on a peninsula that lies at the junction of the Potomac and Occoquan rivers, about 20 miles south of Washington, D.C. in northern Virginia. The refuge, across Occoquan Bay from Mason Neck Refuge, protects a variety of habitats including freshwater wetlands, woodlands, and one of the last remaining, undeveloped areas of native grassland. The unusual mix of habitats in a relatively small area provides exceptional birding opportunities and allows visitors to traverse a variety of habitat types within a short distance.

The refuge combines lands that were acquired upon the closing of the U.S. Army's Woodbridge Research Facility, and 63 acres of the former Marumsco National Wildlife Refuge, which was established in 1973. The name *Occoquan* is derived from a Dogue Indian word, meaning "at the end of the water."

According to the U.S. Fish and Wildlife Service:

As a classified Army site, the Woodbridge Research Facility was closed to the public. Mowed and cleared for electronics testing, the site contains a diversity of grassland and wetland plant species unusual in the heavily developed Potomac region. Its diverse habitats support a correspondingly high number of wildlife species, particularly migrant land and waterbirds and grassland nesting species. Wetland habitats cover about 50 percent of the site, and include wet meadows, bottomland hardwoods, open freshwater marsh, and tidally influenced marshes and streams. About 20 percent of the unit is upland meadows, with the remaining vegetated areas consisting of shrubs and mature or second growth forest. The Refuge is managed to provide early successional habitats and appropriate wildlife-dependent recreational opportunities, to educate visitors on the results and benefits of habitat management for wildlife. . . .

The refuge's meadows contain such grasses as the eastern gamagrass (*Tripsacum dactyloides*), deer tongue (*Panicum or Dichanthelium clandestinum*), and bushy panic grass (*Panicum or Dichanthelium dichotomum*); and the non-native meadow fescue (*Festuca elatior*) and velvet grass (*Holcus lanatus*). Among other plants are raspberry, dogbane, beautyberry, Carolina pasture and multiflora roses, ox-eye daisy, thistle, common milkweed, goldenrods, and asters. Among the many birds that are attracted to the grasslands are bobolink; eastern meadowlark; northern harrier; American kestrel; eastern bluebird; indigo bunting; northern bobwhite; yellow warbler; and field, savannah, and grasshopper sparrows.

One of the significant aspects of Occoquan Bay Refuge is the abundance of butterflies. Naturalist Roland Wauer, author of books on butterflies and birds, has described the value of these colorful insects ("Wings of Change," *National Parks*, May–June 2001):

Few creatures are so charismatic and colorful as our native butterflies. But beyond their aesthetic appeal, these varied invertebrates help to maintain healthy ecosystems. Probably most important, these insects pollinate flowering plants. . . .

Most butterflies also serve as food for a wide assortment of wildlife, especially migrating birds. And being extremely sensitive to environmental change at both the plant-specific and community level, they are excellent creatures to study as bio-indicators.

More than 50 species of butterflies have been recorded on Occoquan Bay Refuge. They include the swallowtails (pipevine, eastern black, tiger, spicebush, and zebra); cabbage white; common and orange sulphurs; red-banded hairstreak; eastern tailed and spring azure blues; great spangled and variegated fritillaries; pearly crescentspot; comma; American painted lady; red admiral; buckeye; red-spotted purple; viceroy; monarch; and silver-spotted skipper.

As Occoquan Bay Refuge is still in its developmental stage as of this writing, the area is open only on weekends (closed on Christmas and in poor weather), and visitor facilities are limited. It is anticipated that the refuge will eventually be open daily, that interpretive and other visitor use facilities, including a visitor contact station and auto tour route, will be provided, and that an entrance fee will be charged. Parts of the refuge are closed to avoid disturbing wildlife during nesting, feeding, and resting periods.

Visitor activities include birdwatching, butterfly observation, photography, hiking on a number of gravel roads that were previously used as military patrol routes, and organized group field studies by advance arrangement. Fishing and hunting are expected to be permitted after the refuge's planning phase is completed.

Visitors are cautioned to be alert for ticks, chiggers, and the venomous copperhead snake. Insect repellent is advised during the warmer months.

Lodgings and meals are available in the nearby community of Woodbridge.

Access to Occoquan Bay Refuge from U.S. Route I in Woodbridge is east 0.7 miles on Dawson Beach Road.

Further information: Occoquan Bay National Wildlife Refuge, c/o Potomac River NWR Complex, 14344 Jefferson Davis Highway, Woodbridge, VA 22191; telephone: (703) 490-4979.

Plum Tree Island, encompassing 3,501 acres, was established in 1972 to protect wetland habitat for waterfowl, shorebirds, and other wildlife. The refuge is not open to visitation, because this former military bombing range contains hazardous unexploded ordnance.

Further information: Plum Tree Island National Wildlife Refuge, c/o Back Bay NWR, 4005 Sandpiper Road, Virginia Beach, VA 23456; telephone: (757) 721-2412.

Presquile, containing 1,329 acres, was established in 1953 to protect an island in the James River, a few miles downstream from the city of Richmond in east-central Virginia. More than one-half of the island consists of seasonally flooded bottomland hardwood forest and swamp habitat, about one-fifth is tidally influenced marsh, and the rest is upland field habitat. Formerly planted in crops, 300 acres of upland are being converted to native grassland to provide winter forage for Canada geese and nesting cover for songbirds and northern bobwhite.

Prominent among Presquile Refuge's birds are two species of raptors. Bald eagles use the refuge and vicinity all year. Two nests have been active on the island for the past several years, and this section of the James River is a popular foraging area for eagles in both summer and winter. Ospreys also nest on the refuge and can frequently be seen from mid-March through August.

In addition, concentrations of Canada and snow geese and a few thousand ducks of many species winter on and around the refuge. Wood ducks nest on the refuge, where nesting boxes are provided to supplement natural tree cavities. During the spring and autumn, large influxes of neotropical songbirds, including numerous species of warblers, migrate through the refuge and surrounding river valley. Researchers from Virginia Commonwealth University have erected nesting boxes for prothonotary warblers, and have banded thousands of the birds, in an attempt to understand and reverse the population decline of this beautiful species. Other species of wildlife include wild turkey, pileated woodpecker, barred owl, red-winged blackbird, white-tailed deer, red fox, mink, beaver, muskrat, raccoon, opossum, and gray squirrel.

Trees and other plants of the island include bald cypress; tulip tree; sassafras; American sycamore; sweetgum; slippery elm; black walnut; bitternut hickory; oaks (swamp chestnut, pin, southern red, and willow); river birch; black willow; flowering dogwood; black tupelo; American holly; red maple; green ash; white water lily; spatterdock (yellow pond lily); arrowhead; pickerelweed; cattail; horsetail; and wild rice.

Presquile, or popularly known as Turkey Point, was originally a peninsula within an oxbow turn of the river. The name *Presquile* was derived from the French *presque ile* (*presqu'île*), literally meaning "almost island" (peninsula). Union troops during the Civil War used the peninsula as a vantage point, and the Battle of Malvern Hill occurred just across the river from "Turkey Bend." In 1934, as an aid to river navigation, the U.S. Army Corps of Engineers dredged a channel across the neck of the peninsula, thereby creating Turkey Island.

The refuge is open on weekdays, except national holidays. There is no entrance fee. The refuge headquarters, which is located at 336 Wilna Road in Warsaw, is open on weekdays, except national holidays. For years, access to the refuge was provided through a cable-operated passenger ferry. Due to safety concerns, the ferry is no longer used to transport visitors. Alternatives to the ferry are in the planning stages. In the meantime, contact the Refuge Manager for information on access.

Visitor activities include wildlife observation, photography, environmental education, and deer hunting during the designated season. A 0.75-mile interpretive trail offers an opportunity to learn about the various habitats and history of the refuge. Facilities include a small visitor contact station and a wildlife viewing platform that was built by volunteers. Canoeing to the island is discouraged because of strong river currents. Although camping is not permitted on the refuge, campground facilities are available in the vicinity of Chesterfield and Petersburg.

Visitors are urged to be alert for venomous copperhead snakes. Insect repellent is advised during the warmer months.

Lodgings and meals are available in such communities as Hopewell, Petersburg, and Richmond.

Further information and directions: Presquile National Wildlife Refuge, c/o Eastern Virginia Rivers NWR Complex, P.O. Box 1030, Warsaw, VA 22572; telephone: (804) 333-1470.

Rappahannock River Valley, established in 1996, is nearly 25 percent of the way toward the goal of protecting 20,000 acres along the tidal portion of this major Chesapeake Bay tributary in eastern Virginia. As of January 2002, the refuge contained 4,800 acres of tidal marsh, woodland, and former agricultural fields. The refuge's personnel are actively engaged in establishing baseline biological inventories, restoring natural habitats, controlling invasive species, and establishing public use facilities and programs.

The stretch of the Rappahannock River encompassed by the refuge boundaries is important for a wide variety of fish, wildlife, and plants. In 2001, 80 active bald eagle nests that produced 109 young were recorded on the refuge. Hundreds of eagles roost and feed along the river and its tidal creeks during summer and winter.

In the fall, tens of thousands of waterfowl migrate along the river corridor, and many spend the winter feeding and resting in open waters, tidal marshes, and surrounding agricultural fields. Most numerous are Canada geese, which peak at more than 30,000. A full complement of puddle ducks and bay ducks can be found throughout the winter. Some species, such as the American black duck, mallard, hooded merganser, ring-necked duck, and ruddy duck, can be seen almost daily; others, such as greater and lesser scaup, canvasback, and long-tailed duck (oldsquaw), fluctuate in numbers, depending on the month and weather.

Winter raptors include the northern harrier, American kestrel, and short-eared owl, which fly low over fields in search of food. Eastern meadowlarks and savannah sparrows are also common in winter, especially in fields and adjacent hedgerows.

Breeding bird surveys conducted in May and June 2000 and 2001 revealed more than 70 species, including several "species of conservation concern," as listed by the U.S. Fish and Wildlife Service. These include whip-poor-will, red-headed woodpecker, wood thrush, and Kentucky and prairie warblers. In addition to the bald eagle, common nesting birds include osprey, wild turkey, eastern bluebird, northern parula and prothonotary warblers, common yellowthroat, yellow-breasted chat, and indigo bunting; and grasslands-nesting species, such as northern bobwhite, grasshopper sparrow, dickcissel, and eastern meadowlark.

According to Dr. Joseph Mitchell of the University of Richmond, approximately 80 percent of the frog species, 60 percent of the reptiles, and 25 percent of the salamanders that are native to Virginia can be seen within the refuge boundary area. Among the reptiles are eastern fence lizard, five-lined skink, red-bellied and eastern box turtles, black rat snake, the venomous copperhead, which is often associated with old buildings and woodpiles, spotted salamander, and bullfrog and spring peeper.

Several species of mammals are commonly found on the refuge, including white-tailed deer, red fox, river otter, beaver, muskrat, and striped skunk. A public hunting program on the Rappahannock River Valley Refuge is aimed at maintaining the deer population in balance with its available habitat.

Anglers are offered a variety of opportunities on the Rappahannock River. In the fresher upstream portion, largemouth bass, crappie, and catfish are common; the more saline middle and lower stretches offer catches of striped bass, croaker, spot, flounder, and weakfish. Seasonal restrictions apply to some species (current regulations are available from the Virginia Department of Game and Inland Fisheries and the Virginia Marine Resources Commission).

The freshwater tidal marshes of the Rappahannock support an impressive diversity of plants, including the federally listed threatened sensitive joint vetch. Some of the more showy summer-flowering plants include the Turk's-cap lily, cardinal flower, pickerelweed, nodding beggartick, and marsh hibiscus. Pale green stands of wild rice are not only beautiful, but provide an important source of seeds that are eaten by many birds. The marshes also serve as the basis of the intricate food web that exists in and along the river. Nutrients released by decaying plants are used by invertebrates, which in turn are a source of food for young fish and birds.

Since the refuge is still in its early stages of development, visitor use facilities are minimal. Until facilities are constructed, visitation is by reservation only. However, work has begun on creating an accessible fishing area, wildlife observation trails, and outdoor classroom sites. Three refuge tracts have been accepted into the new Virginia Birding and Wildlife Trail system, which is currently under development. "Wilna," the two-story, white-clapboard, nineteenth-century plantation house, the rehabilitation of which began in 2002, serves as the refuge headquarters.

Lodgings and meals are available in the towns of Tappahannock and Warsaw, which are located within the heart of the refuge boundary area.

Further information: Rappahannock River Valley National Wildlife Refuge, c/o Eastern Virginia Rivers NWR Complex, P.O. Box 1030 (336 Wilna Road), Warsaw, VA 22572; telephone: (804) 333-1470.

(NOTE: Special appreciation is given to Joe McCauley, Project Leader, for providing this description.)

Wallops Island, encompassing 3,737 acres, was established in 1971 under a special management agreement with the National Aeronautical and Space Administration (NASA), to enhance and protect parts of this coastal barrier island. The refuge is located in the northeast corner of the Eastern Shore of Virginia.

The refuge is not open to visitation.

Approximately half of the island contains extensive salt marsh habitat, through which numerous tidal creeks meander and two human-made channels intersect. The majority of this ecologically important wetland consists of low marsh, dominated by salt marsh cordgrass, with scattered areas of glasswort. Several hundred acres consist of a narrow band of high marsh, where the less salt-tolerant salt meadow cordgrass is the dominant plant species, along with some saltgrass, salt marsh bulrush, and cattails.

A transition zone between the salt marsh and loblolly pine woodland is dominated by marsh elder (*Iva frutescens*), groundsel tree (*Baccharis halimifolia*), and wax myrtle. Sassafras, wild cherry, sumac, and poison ivy also grow on the island's high elevations.

Wallops Island was initially known as Kegotank Island, and is named for John Wallop, who, in 1692, received a grant to the island from the English Crown. In 1933, the Wallops Island Association, Inc., was incorporated and became the owner—its members using the property for swimming, fishing, and waterfowl hunting. In 1947, the U.S. Navy started using the northern part of the island for aviation ordnance testing, and the southern part was leased by the forerunner of NASA for rocket-launching facilities. NASA purchased the property in 1950.

Sharing the island refuge with NASA are concentrations of migratory waterfowl, including wintering snow geese and such nesting ducks as American black, gadwall, and blue-winged teal. Ospreys nest here, too. Herons, egrets, shorebirds, and rails are all attracted to the island's rich wetlands. White-tailed deer, raccoons, muskrats, and eastern cottontails are among the resident species of mammals.

Further information: Wallops Island National Wildlife Refuge, c/o Chincoteague NWR, P.O. Box 62, Chincoteague, VA 23336; telephone: (757) 336-6122.

Washington

Columbia, containing 23,200 acres, was established in 1944 to protect and manage an important area of lakes, ponds, and irrigated croplands for the benefit of migrating and wintering waterfowl. The refuge, which also includes canyons, with dark cliffs of lavaflow-formed basalt, and sagebrush-grassland habitat, is located along Crab Creek, within the high desert of the Columbia Basin in east-central Washington.

The refuge attracts large concentrations of wintering mallards, along with smaller numbers of Canada geese. During the peak of autumn migration, more than 100,000 waterfowl have been recorded on the refuge. Nesting water birds include the abundant American coot and ducks, including mallards, gadwalls, cinnamon teal, redheads, and ruddy ducks. Regarding other species, as described by the U.S. Fish and Wildlife Service:

The ledges, cracks, and holes that abound in the numerous basalt cliffs provides important nesting habitat for many red-tailed hawks, American kestrels, great horned owls, barn owls, and a few ravens. The cliffs are used by large colonies of cliff swallows to hold and shelter their mud nests. Great blue herons are frequently seen standing like sentinels at the top of cliffs and rock outcrops near water. Increasing numbers of sandhill cranes visit the Refuge during spring and fall migrations. Northern harriers are common, as are magpies, pheasants, California quail, and black-crowned night-herons. Long-billed curlews and American avocets are less common but nest on the Refuge.

Columbia Refuge also lies within the Drumheller Channels National Natural Landmark, which was designated in 1986 to recognize and interpret the "Channeled Scablands." Starting around 100,000 years ago, continental glacial ice gradually extended southward from British Columbia across much of what are now the states of Washington, Idaho, and Montana. These advances dammed the flow of the Clark Fork River on numerous occasions, near the Idaho-Montana border. Geologists explain that, at its maximum around 12,000 years ago, the resulting huge lake covered roughly 2 million acres and was nearly 2,000 feet deep. When the ice dam was breached, it is estimated that the outpouring of water was perhaps 10 times the combined flow of all the rivers in the world. When this incredible flood reached the Columbia Basin, the water's immense volume, speed, and turbulence eroded deep canyons into the basaltic lava flows. In what is now the northern part of the refuge, there is a hodgepodge of canyons, cliffs, and remnants of lava flows. This portion of the Scablands is known as the Drumheller Channels. It is ranked as the most spectacular eroded area of its size in the world. As deputy project leader Rob Larranaga says, "The geology of the refuge is as intriguing as the wildlife." A short detour from State Highway 17 and 26 is necessary to view these landscapes.

The human history of this part of the Columbia Basin has also brought significant changes to the landscape. As described by the Fish and Wildlife Service:

During the 1860s, cattle were brought into the area and the land was soon overgrazed. When grass conditions became too poor for cattle, sheep were introduced. By the . . . [start of the 20th] century, sheep, plus 3,000 feral (wild) horses that ranged along Crab Creek . . . , had taken a heavy toll upon the land. Unsuccessful farming attempts by early settlers also altered the landscape, and many such examples can be seen on and around the Refuge.

Early irrigation efforts in the Refuge area encouraged some farmers, but failed when local water supplies proved inadequate. Serious planning to irrigate the Columbia Basin on a large scale began in 1918 and hinged on construction of a dam on the Columbia River at Grand Coulee. After years of study and debate, the Columbia Basin Project was approved, and construction of Grand Coulee Dam began in 1934. On August 10, 1951, the first irrigation water began flowing to Columbia Basin farmlands. Columbia National Wildlife Refuge was established in conjunction with the irrigation project . . . and has been actively managed since 1955.

With the availability of a reliable supply of abundant water, the project changed quickly and dramatically. The water table rose as predicted and lakes appeared in former canyons and low spots throughout the Refuge, and additional lakes and ponds were created by damming spring seepage flows. All current Refuge lakes and impoundments are the result, directly or indirectly, of irrigation water.

Around the Refuge, dryland wheat areas and many acres of sagebrush grasslands were soon converted to a wide variety of irrigated crops. Many of these crops, particularly corn, provided abundant food for ducks, geese, and sandhill cranes. The agricultural development, together with the numerous water areas, combined each year to provide ideal feeding and resting areas for thousands of migrating and wintering waterfowl.

Establishment of Columbia Refuge was made possible partly with revenues from the sale of Migratory Bird Hunting and Conservation Stamps (Duck Stamps). Ducks Unlimited, Inc. has helped enhance more than 1,100 acres of the refuge's wetland habitat.

The refuge is open daily. There is no entrance fee. The refuge office, located at 735 East Main Street, Othello, is open on weekdays, except national holidays.

Visitor activities include birdwatching; photography; driving the 23-mile auto tour route; hiking; bicycling on roads open to motor vehicles; canoeing; boating (gasoline-powered watercraft are not permitted on Hutchinson, Shiner, Royal, and Upper and Lower Hampton lakes); primitive camping (at Soda Lake Campground and at a number of nearby Washington State Department of Fish and Wildlife sites); fishing; and hunting (deer, goose, duck, coot, chukar, pheasant, and quail) on parts of the refuge during the designated seasons. Swimming is not permitted. Over 200 bird species have been recorded here.

Hiking opportunities include three interconnecting, self-guiding, interpretive trails that are open from March 1 through September: the Marsh Unit Trail—a 0.9-mile walk on a stretch of refuge service road; the Crab Creek Trail—a 1.4-mile loop that goes through lush riparian habitat; and the Frog Lake Trail—a 1.2-mile route through an area of wetland seeps and upland sagebrush-grass habitat (this portion is open all year), plus a 0.9-mile loop providing an excellent view across the refuge and beyond.

Visitors are cautioned to be alert for rattlesnakes. Insect repellent and sunscreen are advised during the warmer months.

Lodgings and meals are available in Othello.

Access to Columbia Refuge from Exit 179 on I-90 at Moses Lake is southeast about 10 miles on State Route 17, west (right) about 6.5 miles on the O'Sullivan Dam Road (State Route 262), and south into the refuge on the Morgan Lake Road; or from State Route 26, it is north on Broadway Avenue (State Route 24) to Othello, continuing north just under 2 miles on Broadway, bearing northwest for several miles on McManamon Road, and north (right) on Morgan Lake Road.

Further information: Columbia National Wildlife Refuge, P.O. Drawer F, Othello, WA 99344; telephone: (509) 488-2668.

Conboy Lake, comprising 6,532 acres, was established in 1964 to restore and manage Conboy Lake for the benefit of migrating and wintering waterfowl and other wildlife. The refuge is magnificently situated in a valley just east of the Cascade Range, at the southeastern foot of the imposing, snow-capped, volcanic cone of 12,276-foot Mount Adams in south-central Washington.

Prior to the refuge's establishment, farmers dug a drainage ditch in an attempt to eliminate the lake and expand their pastures. Although this effort failed, water is still removed from the lake, and its level declines substantially during the summer. Nevertheless, concentrations of tundra swans, Canada geese, and ducks of many species are attracted to the refuge from February to April as winter loses its grip, along with such raptors as bald eagles, various hawks, and great horned owls. The refuge has the distinction of being one of only three places in the state where sandhill cranes nest. Wild turkeys and blue and ruffed grouse are among the many resident bird species. More than 150 species of birds have been recorded on the refuge.

The scenic valley in which Conboy Lake is located consists of meadows and forest. Among the refuge's trees are black cottonwoods and low-growing willows, scattered Oregon white oaks, and many groves of quaking aspens; while the lower mountain slopes are forested mainly with ponderosa and lodgepole pines and Douglas firs.

Establishment of Conboy Lake Refuge was made possible partly with revenues from the sale of Migratory Bird Hunting and Conservation Stamps (Duck Stamps). Ducks Unlimited, Inc. has helped enhance a few acres of the refuge's wetland habitat.

The refuge is open daily during daylight hours. There is no entrance fee. Depending on staffing, the refuge headquarters is generally open on weekdays, except national holidays.

Visitor activities include wildlife observation; photography; driving public roads that run through the refuge; hiking the Willard Springs Trail—a 2-mile loop; fishing; and hunting (deer, goose, duck, grouse, coot, and snipe) on parts of the refuge during the designated seasons.

Lodgings and meals are available in such communities as Trout Lake, White Salmon, and Goldendale.

Access to Conboy Lake Refuge, from Washington State Route 14 at Underwood (in the Columbia River Gorge), is north 21 miles on State Route 141 and northeast (right) 9 miles. Or from State Route 14 at Maryhill, it is north 11 miles on U.S. Route 97 to Goldendale, west (left) 10 miles on State Route 142, northwest (right) 22 miles on the Glenwood-Goldendale Road to Glenwood, and southwest 5 miles on the Glenwood-Trout Lake Road to the refuge.

> Further information: Conboy Lake National Wildlife Refuge, P.O. Box 5, Glenwood, WA 98619; telephone: (509) 364-3410.

Copalis Rock, consisting of 60 acres, was established in 1907 by President Theodore Roosevelt to provide protection for nesting seabirds, off the Pacific Coast of the Olympic Peninsula in northwestern Washington. (See the Quillayute Needles Refuge text.)

Dungeness, encompassing 772 acres, was established in 1915 to protect the 5.5-mile-long, slender arc of Dungeness Spit; its sand and gravel beaches; and its adjacent sheltered tideflats, eelbeds, and bay. The spit extends from the northeast shore of the Olympic Peninsula into the Strait of Juan de Fuca, in northwestern Washington.

Formation of Dungeness Spit has been caused and is maintained by eastward-flowing currents from the Pacific Ocean carrying sediments that have eroded from adjacent glacially created bluffs—a process that is also assisted by prevailing winds from the west and northwest. The outer end of the spit is continuing to grow at the annual rate of nearly 15 feet.

The refuge is open daily during daylight hours. A per-family entry fee is charged.

Visitor activities include birdwatching; photography; hiking; boating (refuge waters are open to boating, clamming, and crabbing, from May 15 through September; no wake zone); fishing along the outer beach; swimming and other recreational activities in designated areas of the beach; and daily tours of the historic New Dungeness Lighthouse (provided by volunteers of New Dungeness Chapter of the U.S. Lighthouse Society).

Hiking opportunities include a 0.4-mile trail that climbs through a wooded area to an overlook on the bluff above Dungeness Spit, and the 4.5-mile beach hike to the lighthouse.

Lodgings and meals are available in such communities as Sequim and Port Angeles.

> Access to Dungeness Refuge from Sequim is west 5 miles on U.S. Route 101 and north (right) 3 miles on Kitchen-Dick Road through the county's recreation area to the parking area, just inside the refuge entrance. Or from Port Angeles, it is east 9 miles on U.S. Route 101 and north (left) onto Kitchen-Dick Road.

> Further information: Dungeness National Wildlife Refuge, c/o Washington Maritime NWR Complex, 33 South Barr Road, Port Angeles, WA 98362; telephone: (360) 457-8451.

Flattery Rocks, containing 125 acres, was established in 1907 by President Theodore Roosevelt to provide protection for nesting seabirds, off the Pacific Coast of the Olympic Peninsula in northwestern Washington. (See the Quillayute Needles Refuge text.)

Franz Lake, comprising 553 acres, was established in 1990 to provide an important wintering area for tundra swans and other waterfowl. The refuge is located along the north bank of the Columbia River, in the scenic Columbia River Gorge in southwestern Washington.

The big attraction that draws concentrations of wintering tundra swans to Franz Lake Refuge is an aquatic plant known as wapato or arrowhead (*Sagittaria latifolia*) that grows in tidal wetlands. The nutrient-rich, starchy tubers (bulbs) are a good source of food for the swans and other waterfowl. They were also important to the Chinook Indians and to the members of the Lewis and Clark Expedition, who ate these potato-like tubers and elk meat, which they obtained from the Native Americans along the lower Columbia River.

Establishment of Franz Lake Refuge was made possible with revenues from the Land and Water Conservation Fund.

Although the refuge is not open to visitors, it can be seen from an interpretive overlook near Milepost 32 on State Route 14, located about 30 miles east of Vancouver or about 14 miles west of Stevenson.

Lodgings and meals are available in such communities as Stevenson and Vancouver, Washington and Cascade Locks, Oregon.

Further information: Franz Lake National Wildlife Refuge, c/o Columbia River Gorge Refuges, 36062 State Route 14, Stevenson, WA 98648; telephone: (509) 427-5208.

Grays Harbor, consisting of 1,471 acres, was established in 1990 to protect one of the four primary staging areas in North America for awesome concentrations of shorebirds. The refuge is located on the central Pacific Coast of Washington.

The peak numbers of semipalmated plovers, western sandpipers, dunlin, dowitchers, and other shorebirds pause at Grays Harbor to rest and enhance their fat reserves, from late April through early May, on their way to Arctic breeding grounds. Some of these migrants fly from as far away as Argentina and travel more than 7,000 miles in each direction. Roughly 85 percent of the northbound shorebirds seen at Grays Harbor are western sandpipers, which nest and raise their young primarily along the northwestern edge of Alaska and the eastern end of Siberia. There are thousands of dunlin, as well as other species, that winter here.

The refuge's habitats include intertidal mudflats, salt marsh, freshwater wetlands, a grove of red alders, and uplands. Although the refuge encompasses only 2 percent of the Grays Harbor's intertidal zone, it draws roughly half of all the shorebirds that come to this estuary. As the U.S. Fish and Wildlife Service explains, "The Refuge mudflats are the last areas in Grays Harbor to be flooded at high tide and the first areas to be exposed as the tide recedes. This gives shorebirds extra time to feed. Shorebirds must peck and probe almost continuously to obtain a constant supply of food. The mudflats provide an abundance of invertebrates for food."

There are also many species of waterfowl, as well as gulls, terns, bald eagles and other raptors, and songbirds. Black-tailed deer is the most prominent mammal.

The refuge is open daily during daylight hours. There is no entrance fee.

Visitor activities include wildlife observation; photography; and hiking the 1-mile Sandpiper Trail, which is reached from the end of a paved road (parking is opposite a café) and winds onto the end of Bowerman Peninsula. Swimming, boating, fishing, and hunting are not permitted on the refuge. Camping is not allowed on the refuge, but campground facilities are available nearby.

Lodgings and meals are available in such communities as Hoquiam, Aberdeen, Ocean Shores, and Olympia.

Access to Grays Harbor Refuge, from the junction of U.S. Routes 101 and 12 in Aberdeen, is west 4 miles on U.S. Route 101 to Hoquiam, west (left) 1.5 miles on State Route 109, south (left) on Paulson Road, and west (right) on Airport Road.

Further information: Grays Harbor National Wildlife Refuge, c/o Nisqually NWR, 100 Brown Farm Road, Olympia, WA 98516; telephone: (360) 753-9467.

Hanford Reach National Monument/Saddle Mountain National Wildlife Refuge, comprising 195,000 acres, was established in 2000 to protect an outstanding diversity of ecological, geological, and archaeological values. The monument/refuge is located along the meandering Hanford Reach of the Columbia River, from 4 miles below Priest Rapids Dam downstream to the city of Richland, in south-central Washington. Over 200 bird species use the area.

As described by the Proclamation signed by President Bill Clinton establishing the first and so far only national monument under the management of the U.S. Fish and Wildlife Service:

The Hanford Reach National Monument is a unique and biologically diverse landscape, encompassing an array of scientific and historic objects. This magnificent area contains an irreplaceable natural and historic legacy, preserved by unusual circumstances. Maintained as a buffer area in a Federal reservation conducting nuclear weapons development and, more recently, environmental cleanup activities, with limits on development and human use for the past 50 years, the monument is now a haven for important and increasingly scarce objects of scientific and historic interest. Bisected by the stunning Hanford Reach of the Columbia River, the monument contains the largest remnant of the shrub-steppe ecosystem that once blanketed the Columbia River Basin. The monument is also one of the few remaining archaeologically rich areas in the western Columbia Plateau, containing well-preserved remnants of human history spanning more than 10,000 years. The monument is equally rich in geologic history, with dramatic landscapes that reveal the creative forces of tectonic, volcanic, and erosive power.

The monument is a biological treasure, embracing important riparian, aquatic, and upland shrub-steppe habitats that are rare or in decline in other areas. Within its mosaic of habitats, the monument supports a wealth of increasingly uncommon native plant and animal species. . . .

The monument includes the 51-mile long "Hanford Reach," the last free-flowing, nontidal stretch of the Columbia River. The Reach contains islands, riffles, gravel bars, oxbow ponds, and backwater sloughs that support some of the most productive spawning areas in the Northwest, where approximately 80 percent of the upper Columbia Basin's fall chinook salmon spawn.

The refuge contains five administrative units. The 57,000-acre WAHLUKE UNIT consists of riparian wetlands and shrub-steppe habitats along the east side of the Columbia River. Wahluke Lake, near the center of the unit, supports dense stands of cattails and bulrushes. The scenically spectacular, 20-mile-long White Bluffs of the Columbia contain significant paleontological resources, with a tremendous diversity of fossil remains, from ancient forms of bison, camel, and rhinoceros to dragonflies. This unit is open to visitation.

The 77,000-acre FITZER/EBERHARDT ARID LANDS ECOLOGY RESERVE UNIT, located to the west of the Columbia River, contains a prominent landmark known as the Rattlesnake Hills, the highest point of which is 3,600-foot Rattlesnake Mountain. As the Fish and Wildlife Service explains, "This unit was set aside in 1967 by the U.S. Atomic Energy Commission to preserve native shrub-steppe vegetation. It once served as a buffer zone for the Department of Energy's Hanford operations. Until a wildfire in 2000 devastated native plants, especially big sagebrush, this unit harbored one of the largest remnants of shrub-steppe vegetation in the state. . . .In the wake of the fire, the Service is working to restore big sagebrush. . . .The unit still is home to a large herd of Rocky Mountain elk." Public access onto this unit is limited to approved environmental education trips and research.

The 32,000-acre Saddle Mountain Unit, located along State Route 24 and the north bank of the Columbia River, encompasses the original Saddle Mountain National Wildlife Refuge that was established in 1971. Visitor access is not permitted onto this unit.

The 9,000-acre McGee Ranch/Riverlands Unit includes a former pioneer ranch that contains a number of rare plant species. It provides an important protected corridor of land between the Arid Lands Ecology Reserve Unit and the U.S. Army's Yakima Training Center and is presently closed to visitation, except for those lands north of the Midway road, which are open for day uses. Currently, there are no visitor facilities, and access routes are primitive.

The 25,000-acre River Corridor Unit, along the south and west banks of the Columbia River, includes 16 islands in the river's main channel and the Hanford Dune Field, which contains actively moving barchan sand dunes and partly stabilized, 10- to 16-foot-high transverse dunes. These sandy areas cover from 2 to several hundred acres in extent. The Fish and Wildlife Service explains that this unit is managed by the U.S. Department of Energy. "The shoreline and islands are owned by a number of government agencies and private landowners. Access is controlled by the owners. Some islands downstream of Savage Island are open seasonally to public use. Lands on the south and west side of the river and all islands upstream of Savage Island are closed to the public."

The Wahluke Unit is open daily during daylight hours. There is no entrance fee. Currently there are no visitor use facilities.

Visitor activities on the Wahluke Unit include wildlife observation; photography; driving the east-west State Route 24 to a signed gravel road that leads south onto the unit to a scenic river overlook and to the old White Bluffs ferry landing, where a boat-launching site is available; hiking; bicycling only on roads open to motorized vehicles; boating and fishing on the Columbia River and its backwaters (primitive boat-launching sites are available at White Bluffs Landing, Vernita Bridge, Ringold, and the ramp at the old Hanford Ferry crossing); and hunting on parts of the unit during the designated seasons.

Visitors are cautioned to be aware of certain hazards along the Hanford Reach, such as widely fluctuating river levels that are caused by flow releases from Priest Rapids Dam, swift currents, shallow-water areas, and rocky shores. Areas of the unit are within an "emergency planning zone for the Hanford Site. In the event of a siren, tune a radio to the Emergency Broadcast Station (KONA, 610 AM or 105.3 FM) or marine band radio channel 22." Federal personnel or county sheriffs may also warn visitors to leave the unit.

Lodgings and meals are available in such communities as Yakima, Sunnyside, Richland, Othello, Desert Aire, and Mattawa.

Access to Hanford Reach Monument/Saddle Mountain Refuge's Wahluke Unit from I-82 at Yakima is east and north 44 miles on State Route 24 to the junction of State Routes 243 and 24 just after crossing the Columbia River, continuing east (right) about 29 miles (through the Saddle Mountain Unit) on State Route 24, and south (right) onto the unit's gravel road. From I-82 at Sunnyside, it is north 17 miles on State Route 241, east and north (right) 13 miles on State Route 24 to the junction of Routes 243 and 24, and east (right), as above. From I-182 at Richland, it is northwest 34 miles on State Route 240, north 5 miles on State Route 24 to the junction of Routes 243 and 24, and east (right) on Route 24, as above.

Further information: Hanford Reach National Monument/Saddle Mountain National Wildlife Refuge, 3250 Port of Benton Boulevard, Richland, WA 99352; telephone: (509) 371-1801.

Julia Butler Hansen Refuge for the Columbian White-Tailed Deer, encompassing more than 5,453 acres, was initially established in 1972 as the Columbian White-Tailed Deer National Wildlife Refuge. It was renamed in 1988 to honor the memory of the late congresswoman Julia Butler Hansen (1907–1988), who advocated the protection of this small, endangered subspecies of white-tailed deer and was instrumental in establishing the refuge. The refuge is located along the north bank of the lower Columbia River in southwestern Washington, and also Tenasillahe Island (pronounced tenah-SIL-ahee) on the Oregon side of the river.

The Columbian white-tailed deer was first described in 1806 by Meriwether Lewis, of the Lewis and Clark Expedition. It is one of more than 30 deer subspecies in North America and formerly ranged from Washington's Puget Sound southward through Oregon's Willamette and Umpqua river valleys. By the 1930s, its population had declined to fewer than 150 individuals. Now the Julia Butler Hansen Refuge manages a mosaic of pastures, wetlands, and wooded habitat for roughly 300 deer, and perhaps another 400 to 500 live on private lands along the river.

A small herd of Roosevelt elk, a Pacific Northwest coastal subspecies, also inhabits the refuge. Other mammals include mink, river otters, beavers, muskrats, and the abundant, nonnative nutria, a large rodent introduced from South America.

The refuge's flooded pastures, marshes, and sloughs attract large concentrations of migrating and wintering waterfowl, including tundra swans, three subspecies of Canada geese (dusky, western, and lesser), and many species of ducks, such as mallard, northern pintail, American wigeon, green-winged teal, and bufflehead. Water levels within some wetland impoundments are seasonally regulated with water control structures—either to contain water during the drier summer months or to remove excess water and control flooding during the heavier precipitation of autumn and winter. As the U.S. Fish and Wildlife Service explains:

Before the 1920s, much of the mainland and Tenasillahe Island were marshes flooded by the daily rising tides of the Columbia River.

The Wahkiakum Diking District #4 was formed in the 1920s, at which time the area between Cathlamet and Skamokawa, as well as Tenasillahe Island, was diked and drained. The dikes converted permanent wetlands into agricultural lands which were farmed for nearly fifty years until the establishment of the refuge.

Although the dikes and fields remain today, management of the area is now focused towards managing deer and wintering waterfowl habitat.

The swans, in particular, are drawn to a favorite food, the wapato, an aquatic plant with a nutrient-rich tuber (see further discussion in the Franz Lake and texts). The refuge also supports a nesting colony of great blue herons. Raptors include nesting and wintering bald eagles, nesting ospreys, northern harriers, and occasional white-tailed kites. Steller's jays, varied thrushes, chestnut-backed chickadees, and winter and Bewick's wrens are among the smaller birds that inhabit the wooded areas, which contain such trees and other plants as Sitka spruce, black cottonwood, willows, red alder, Pacific dogwood, bigleaf and vine maples, salal, salmonberry, and sword fern.

Establishment of the Julia Butler Hansen Refuge was made possible partly with revenues from the sale of Migratory Bird Hunting and Conservation Stamps (Duck Stamps).

In recent years, a major management activity of the Fish and Wildlife Service has been to improve habitat conditions for the deer population and other wildlife. Infestations of the nonnative, invasive reed canary grass (*Phalaris arundinacea*) on more than 70 percent of the refuge's pastures and wetlands, along with difficulty in establishing areas of riparian woodland, have impaired suitable deer habitat. The encouraging news is that habitat management activities "have resulted in increased deer use, an increase in shorebird and waterfowl use, as well as a large increase in breeding amphibians."

The refuge is open daily during daylight hours. There is no entrance fee. The refuge headquarters is often open daily, including national holidays; but wildlife viewing and refuge information are available even when the headquarters building is closed.

Visitor activities include wildlife observation; photography; driving and bicycling on the 9-mile auto tour route; hiking; canoeing, kayaking, and boating; fishing (interior sloughs on all refuge units are closed); and hunting (goose, duck, coot, and snipe) on parts of the refuge during the designated seasons. Swimming is not permitted on the refuge. Although camping is not permitted on the refuge, campground facilities are available nearby.

Part of the Columbia River Heritage Canoe Trail goes through the refuge, several boat-launching sites are provided near the refuge, and canoe and kayak rentals are available in Skamokawa. The Fish and Wildlife Service warns that "Tidal flows, strong winds, and large wakes from ships can make boating difficult and sometimes dangerous. Deep channels separate most of the islands at high tide, but during low tides, sandbars and exposed logs may hinder boat travel or even ground your boat. Consult navigational charts and tide tables [and weather reports] before venturing out."

Hiking opportunities include the 3-mile Center Road (open from June through September); and Steamboat Slough and Brooks Slough roads (open all year). Hiking on Tenasillahe Island is permitted only on the encircling dike.

Lodgings and meals are available in such communities as Cathlamet, Skamokawa, and Longview.

Access to Julia Butler Hansen Refuge headquarters is northwest from Cathamet about 2.2 miles on Washington State Route 4 and south (left) onto Steamboat Slough Road. Or, it is just east of Skamokawa on State Route 4 and south (right) onto Steamboat Slough Road.

Further information: Julia Butler Hansen Refuge for the Columbian White-tailed Deer, P.O. Box 566, Cathlamet, WA 98612; telephone: (360) 795-3915.

Little Pend Oreille, containing 40,198 acres, was established in 1939 to restore and manage an ecologically diverse area of montane conifer forest and riparian and other wetland habitats for the benefit of migratory birds and other wildlife. This is the only mountainous, mixed-conifer forest refuge in the National Wildlife Refuge System within the lower 48 states. It is located on the west slope of the Selkirk Mountains in northeastern Washington.

The name *Pend Oreille* (pronounced pondo-RAY) is French for "ear pendant." The Little Pend Oreille River originates 3 miles to the northeast of the refuge. It flows through the northeastern and northwestern parts of the refuge, providing important stream and adjacent alluvial riparian habitats. Tributary streams include all of the Bear Creek sub-watershed and most of the Cedar Creek and Olson Creek sub-watersheds. A number of lakes, beaver ponds, cattail marshes, and seeps are scattered here and there. The refuge's riparian and other deciduous trees include black cottonwood, water and paper birches, Sitka and mountain alders, quaking aspen, and Douglas maple (a subspecies of Rocky Mountain maple). In the refuge's lowest, warmest, and driest areas, the conifer forest consists mostly of ponderosa pine. The more moist, midelevation conifer forest is dominated by Douglas fir, grand fir, western redcedar, and western hemlock, with some areas of lodgepole and western white pines and western larch. Engelmann spruce and subalpine fir also grow on the highest ridges.

The refuge's habitats attract such wildlife as elk, moose, white-tailed and mule deer, black bears, beavers, Canada geese, wood ducks, mallards, goldeneyes, mergansers, hawks, owls, woodpeckers, nuthatches, chickadees, and numerous neotropical songbirds.

Regarding the history of this area, the Little Pend Oreille Refuge's April 2000 Final *Comprehensive Conservation Plan* and Environmental Impact Statement says:

Beginning in 1879 and continuing until 1931, 188 homestead claims were patented . . . [within the present refuge boundaries]. For some claims, "homesteaders" may have been working for logging companies, staking claims, and then turning over the land to the company. Many settlers sold timber off their claims and kept title to the land. . . .They established orchards, gardens, and pastures on many cleared claims. When the Depression hit in the 1930s, many homesteaders had already given up and moved from the area. The short growing season, harsh winters, and overgrazed conditions were factors that led to the Resettlement Administration classifying the land as "submarginal." In 1935, most of the homesteads were acquired through the Soil Conservation Service as public lands for rehabilitation purposes. . . .

In 1938, the Biological Survey, which later became the Fish and Wildlife Service, showed interest in establishing a wildlife refuge on 40,000 acres of the resettlement lands. Local cattlemen objected to establishment of a refuge, protesting deer being given precedence over cattle. . . .

From 1939 until the middle of 1965, the U.S. Fish and Wildlife Service managed the Refuge. Early management focused on restoring degraded habitat conditions to improve habitat for deer, fur bearing animals, upland game birds, waterfowl, and fish. Considerable effort went into planting a variety of shrubs and grasses to benefit wildlife, managing horse and cattle grazing, and planting crops to feed deer and game birds. Management ignited fires and selectively cut forests to improve deer winter range.

In 1965, the Washington Department of Fish and Wildlife (known then as the Washington Department of Game) assumed management responsibility through a cooperative agreement with the Service. Although the Service provided a budget to manage the Refuge, the State had considerable latitude to manage the area primarily for game species and recreation. The State scheduled most of the Refuge for selective timber harvest on a continual rotation basis. . . .Public use increased under state management and the area became known locally as the Game Range. . . .

Prompted by an internal audit by the General Accounting Office, the Service decided to resume onsite management at several refuges throughout the country. This led the Service to resume management of the Little Pend Oreille National Wildlife Refuge in 1994. . . .

Old photographs, survey notes and existing remnant stands indicate that much of the Refuge was characterized by extensive stands of large, old growth ponderosa pine (*Pinus ponderosa*), Douglas fir (*Pseudotsuga menziesii*) and western larch (*Larex laricina*) prior to settlement and exploitation. Impressive stands of western red cedar, western hemlock and other mixed conifer stands were also present. . . .

Currently, most of the forest land is in second and third growth mixed stands with a tendency toward a higher number of stems per acre and a greater percentage of shade-tolerant species than naturally occurred here. This can be directly attributed to past timber harvest practices and aggressive fire suppression. The southeastern corner of the Refuge contains an extensive roadless area [5,520 acres] with an old growth timber component.

Habitat management activities on the refuge today include the creation of more stands of older-aged ponderosa pines and Douglas firs that are vitally important for some species of wildlife. The primary methods for accomplishing this goal are selective thinning and prescribed burning. The careful use of fire reduces hazardous fuel overloading, where fire has long been suppressed; promotes nutrient cycling; spurs the growth of nutrient-rich plant species that benefit many species of wildlife; and results in a more natural, more open-grown ponderosa pine ecosystem.

Riparian habitats that have been impaired by past land use practices are being restored by stabilizing stream banks, planting trees and shrubs, and creating conservation buffers to protect sensitive areas bordering fish-bearing streams and lakes from the impacts of certain harmful activities. In addition, non-native, invasive pest plants that pose a threat to native species are being controlled. It is expected that livestock grazing will be phased out.

Refuge manager Lisa Langelier explains, "As a forested refuge, the ultimate value of Little Pend Oreille National Wildlife Refuge is in its future. It will take decades to provide the large trees and other features of mature forest that are relatively uncommon on the Refuge and surrounding lands. How we manage today will help shape the future of these valleys, lakes and mountains as vital wildlife habitat."

The refuge is open daily. There is no entrance fee. The refuge headquarters is open on weekdays, except national holidays.

Visitor activities include wildlife observation; photography; driving on designated refuge roads; hiking; mountain biking and horseback riding on established roads and designated trails; camping (only in designated camps; although the cutting of standing dead trees is not permitted, downed dead wood may be used by campers; firewood permits are available); boating (nonmotorized watercraft only); fishing (April through October); and hunting (mostly bear, deer, and grouse) on parts of the refuge during the designated seasons. Over 190 bird species have been recorded here.

Lodgings and meals are available in Colville and Chewelah.

Access to Little Pend Oreille Refuge headquarters from I-90 in downtown Spokane is north 71 miles to Colville, east (right, at the Main Street and Third Avenue intersection) 6 miles on State Route 20 (toward Tiger, Washington). Just after passing White Mud Lake, turn south (right) onto the Artman-Gibson Road and proceed 1.7 miles to a 4-way intersection. Turn east (left) onto Kitt-Narcisse Road and proceed for 2.2 miles. At a Y-junction, bear right onto unpaved Bear Creek Road and proceed 3.3 miles to the refuge headquarters.

Further information: Little Pend Oreille National Wildlife Refuge, 1310 Bear Creek Road, Colville, WA 99114; telephone: (509) 684-8384.

McNary, comprising 3,294 acres in three divisions, was established in 1956 to provide mitigation for wildlife habitat that was inundated when the McNary Dam was constructed about 30 miles downstream on the Columbia River. The refuge is located near the junction of the Snake and Columbia rivers in southeastern Washington.

The MCNARY DIVISION consists of a narrow area of wetland habitat with ponds and Burbank Slough, adjacent to the community of Burbank; the STRAWBERRY ISLAND DIVISION encompasses a two-part island in the Snake River; and the HANFORD ISLAND DIVISION contains seven islands extending along an 8.5-mile stretch of the Columbia River, upstream from Richland. Vegetation ranges from riparian species, such as black cottonwood, boxelder, willows, bulrushes, and cattails, to high-desert plants dominated by sagebrush, bitterbrush, and rabbitbrush.

McNary Refuge attracts large concentrations of wintering Canada geese and ducks, the majority of which are mallards. Other birds include wintering tundra swans and such colonial nesting birds as the black-crowned night heron and gulls and terns. Mammals include coyotes, river otters, beavers, muskrats, raccoons, striped skunks, badgers, and black-tailed jackrabbit.

Establishment of McNary Refuge was made possible partly with revenues from the sale of Migratory Bird Hunting and Conservation Stamps (Duck Stamps). Ducks Unlimited, Inc. has helped enhance several hundred acres of the refuge's wetland habitat.

The refuge is open daily during daylight hours. There is no entrance fee.

Visitor activities include birdwatching; photography; viewing interpretive displays at the refuge's environmental education center; walking a 1-mile, self-guiding loop trail near the center (an observation-and-photography blind is provided); and limited hunting (goose, duck, coot, snipe, and pheasant) on parts of the refuge during the designated season. The Strawberry Island Division is closed to all visitor entry from October 1 through June, and the Hanford Island Division during the spring and summer months to avoid human disturbance of nesting and rearing activities. Although camping is not permitted on the refuge, nearby campground facilities are provided at the U.S. Army Corps of Engineers' Hood Park.

Insect repellent and sunscreen are advised during the warmer months.

Lodgings and meals are available in Pasco, Richland, and Kennewick.

Access to McNary Refuge headquarters I-82 at Pasco is south 1 mile on U.S. Route 395 and east on Maple Street.

> Further information: McNary National Wildlife Refuge, c/o Mid-Columbia River NWR Complex, P.O. Box 700, Umatilla, OR 97882; telephone: (509) 545-8588.

Nisqually, consisting of 2,925 acres, was established in 1974. The refuge protects and manages a diversity of wetland and other Nisqually River Delta habitats, where the freshwater from the river meets the saltwater at the southern end of Puget Sound in west-central Washington.

Encompassing one of the state's last largely undisturbed estuaries, Nisqually Refuge attracts large concentrations of migratory birds to its ponds, freshwater marshes, estuarine marshes and mudflats, areas of grassland, and riparian woodlands. The diversity of wildlife includes Canada geese, many species of ducks, western sandpipers and other shorebirds, bald eagles and ospreys, and neotropical migratory songbirds such as warblers, thrushes, and flycatchers. Many birds merely pause on the delta habitat to rest and feed on their way to late spring or summer breeding grounds farther north or to wintering habitat farther south. Others gather here during the winter months and some nest on the refuge, as, for instance, a colony of great blue herons.

Part of the delta's ecosystem was altered in the early 1900s, when Alson Brown constructed a dike across part of the area to block the saltwater and thereby expand his farmland. This dike continues to keep the tidal waters from reaching the freshwater wetland and grassland habitats. Refuge planning is presently evaluating the potential for restoring some of these lands back to historic estuary by removing or altering parts of the dike.

The refuge's vegetation includes Douglas fir; western redcedar; black cottonwood; red alder; bigleaf and vine maples; common snowberry; red elderberry; skunk cabbage; touch-me-not; and ferns (sword, deer, and bracken).

Establishment of the refuge was made possible partly with revenues from the sale of Migratory Bird Hunting and Conservation Stamps (Duck Stamps). Recent habitat restoration efforts have enhanced wetlands and resulted in planting thousands of native trees and shrubs to benefit more than 200 acres of freshwater wetlands, with the help of partners such as Ducks Unlimited, Inc. and the Washington Conservation Corps. The Nisqually Refuge Cooperating Association is a nonprofit organization that assists the refuge, as at the visitor center sales outlet.

The refuge is open daily during daylight hours. A small, per-family entrance fee is charged. The visitor center is open on Wednesdays through Sundays, except on Thanksgiving, Christmas, and New Year's Day. An education center is open by appointment. The refuge office is open on weekdays, except national holidays. Over 200 bird species use the refuge.

Visitor activities include birdwatching; photography; hiking; viewing the visitor center's interpretive exhibits on the Nisqually River watershed, the estuary, and migratory birds that use the Pacific Flyway; canoeing, kayaking, and small boating in the area outside the Brown Farm Dike (tides and wind can be hazardous); and fishing in the area outside the Brown Farm Dike and in the designated McAllister Creek Bank Fishing Area. Camping and swimming are not permitted on the refuge. Although hunting is not permitted on the refuge, it is allowed on the state's adjacent Washington Department of Fish and Wildlife lands.

Hiking opportunities include a 1-mile (wheelchair-accessible) boardwalk loop and observation deck adjacent to the Twin Barns; a 0.5-mile self-guiding nature trail; and the 5.5-mile Brown Farm Dike Trail—a loop that includes a photography blind and an observation tower. Seasonal trail closures occur during waterfowl hunting season.

Lodgings and meals are available in Lacey, Olympia, and Tacoma.

Access to Nisqually Refuge is from Exit 114 on I-5 and one-half mile, following refuge directional signs.

Further information: Nisqually National Wildlife Refuge, 100 Brown Farm Road, Olympia, WA 98516; telephone: (360) 753-9467.

Pierce, encompassing 337 acres, was established in 1983 to protect and manage a small but important area of grassland and forested habitat for the benefit of Canada geese, ducks, bald eagles, and other wildlife. The refuge is located adjacent to Beacon Rock State Park, along the north bank of the Columbia River in the scenic Columbia River Gorge in southern Washington.

This former cattle ranch was donated to the U.S. Fish and Wildlife Service by Lena Pierce. Lena and her husband's growing of seeds for livestock had attracted increasing numbers of Canada geese to the pastures and small wetlands, along with mallards, pintails, gadwalls, and other ducks; and she wanted the property managed so that it could continue attracting waterfowl, which nest and winter here.

The refuge's Hardy Creek offers one of the few spawning streams along the Columbia River for chum salmon. These annual fish migrations sometimes attract a concentration of bald eagles.

Ducks Unlimited, Inc. has helped enhance approximately 75 acres of the refuge's wetland habitat.

Although Pierce Refuge is not open to visitors, a bird's-eye view can be enjoyed from the top of Beacon Rock, adjacent to the refuge in Beacon Rock State Park.

Lodgings and meals are available in such communities as Stevenson and Vancouver, Washington and Cascade Locks, Oregon.

Access to Beacon Rock State Park for a view onto the refuge is by way of Washington State Route 14, about 35 miles east of Vancouver or about 9 miles west of Stevenson.

Further information: Pierce National Wildlife Refuge, c/o Columbia River Gorge Refuges, 36062 State Route 14, Stevenson, WA 98648; telephone: (509) 427-5208.

Protection Island, containing approximately 364 acres, was authorized in 1982. The refuge protects a major seabird nesting island at the mouth of Discovery Bay, off the northeast shore of the Olympic Peninsula in northwestern Washington.

The refuge supports more than 70 percent of all seabirds that nest in Puget Sound, including an estimated 12,000 pairs of the burrow-nesting rhinoceros auklet. Other species that nest and raise their young on Protection Island include the pelagic cormorant, black oystercatcher, glaucous-winged gull, pigeon guillemot, and tufted puffin. According to the U.S. Fish and Wildlife Service, "it is this use that makes the island unique and significant from the wildlife perspective, particularly for the burrow-nesting rhinoceros auklets and the tufted puffins. The combination of: (1) soil conditions conducive to burrowing yet stabilized enough by root development to prevent excessive wind erosion and cave-ins; (2) freedom from mammalian and other predators that could raise havoc with adults, eggs and/or chicks; and (3) limited conflict and/or disturbance by human activities have contributed to making Protection Island one of the most significant auklet breeding areas off the coasts of Washington, Oregon, and California."

Among the species of waterfowl that have been recorded on the waters around Protection Island are brant; Canada goose; black, surf, and white-winged scoters; bufflehead; harlequin duck; and long-tailed duck (oldsquaw). Small flocks of brant feed on adjacent beds of eelgrass. A pair of bald eagles nests on the island. More than 175 species of birds have been recorded here. A few hundred harbor seals haul themselves onto the island's rocky beaches, where numerous pups are born. In the surrounding waters, harbor porpoises and orcas (killer whale) of the family *Delphinidae* can sometimes be seen, and migrating gray whales have been spotted feeding and playing. The latter mammals swim between summer feeding grounds in the Bering, Chukchi, and Beaufort seas around Alaska and Siberia, and winter calving lagoons along Mexico's Baja Peninsula—an annual round trip of more than 10,000 miles.

Although much of the island contains no trees, Douglas fir, grand or lowland fir, western redcedar, and Douglas (Rocky Mountain) maple grow in some places, along with shrubby willows, a wild rose (*Rosa nutkana*), and oceanspray, a shrub with showy, creamy white terminal flower clusters.

During the mid-nineteenth century, Euro-American settlers introduced livestock to Protection Island and planted barley, alfalfa, and potatoes. Although they and subsequent families were unsuccessful in their agricultural endeavors, sheep- and cattle-grazing degraded the natural vegetation, causing serious soil erosion. During World War II, the island became a U.S. military artillery battery, to help defend Puget Sound from attack. Subsequently, Protection Island was used as a private hunting area for introduced non-native birds, such as peacocks and Chinese pheasants.

In 1968, the Protection Island Company purchased the island with the intention of developing a residential community of around 1,000 lots, a marina, and an airstrip. Although nearly 600 lots were sold and a few owners began building homes, the lack of fresh water, electricity, and telephone service posed serious and, as it turned out, insurmountable difficulties.

In 1972, The Nature Conservancy acquired 48 acres of auklet-nesting habitat at the western end of the island. This tract was subsequently sold to the state's Department of Wildlife, which, in 1975, established it as the Zella M. Schulz Seabird Sanctuary.

In 1980, Congressman Don Bonker introduced legislation to bring about the permanent protection of the island, under the management of the Fish and Wildlife Service, for the benefit of its important value to wildlife. Two years later, this measure was signed into law. As the Service explains, "By 1985, The U.S. Fish and Wildlife Service was successful in acquiring some of the lots from willing sellers. A 'Declaration of Taking' for the remainder of the island was issued in 1986. In March of 1987, District Court Judge Coughenour signed an 'Order for Possession.' In April of 1987, the service moved two volunteer caretakers to the island, and in December a Refuge Manager position was established. The refuge was officially established in a ceremony on August 26, 1988."

Although visitors are not permitted on the island, it and much of its wildlife can be viewed by boat from outside the 200-yard no-boating zone. Commercial tours are provided.

Further information: Protection Island National Wildlife Refuge, c/o Washington Maritime NWR Complex, 33 South Barr Road, Port Angeles, WA 98362; telephone: (360) 457-8451.

Quillayute Needles, encompassing 300 acres, was established in 1907 by President Theodore Roosevelt to provide protection for breeding seabirds off the Pacific Coast of the Olympic Peninsula in northwestern Washington. The 125-acre Flattery Rocks and 60-acre Copalis Rock national wildlife refuges were established at the same time for the same purpose.

Taken together, these three Washington Islands Refuges, extending along more than 100 miles, consist of roughly 870 coastal islands, rocks, and reefs. These bits of surf-pounded land range in size from less than an acre to 36 acres. As described by the U.S. Fish and Wildlife Service, "Most of the islands have precipitous shorelines rising above a treacherous surf. A few islands have a cap of glacial till [unsorted sediments that were deposited by glacial ice] that supports luxuriant vegetation. Most vegetated islands are dominated by salal and salmon berry shrubs, although a small number have stands of Sitka spruce." All of the islands, except Destruction Island, are within the Wilderness Islands Wilderness, a unit of the National Wilderness Preservation System.

The three refuges support 14 species of marine birds, with breeding populations estimated at more than 100,000 pairs. These species include Leach's and forked-tailed storm petrels; double-crested, pelagic, and Brandt's cormorants; black oystercatcher; glaucous-winged gull; common murre; pigeon guillemot; Cassin's and rhinoceros auklets; and tufted puffin. (For further information on the latter species, see the Farallon Refuge [California] text.) Other nesting species include bald eagle and peregrine falcon. During spring and autumn migrations, there may be more than a million seabirds, waterfowl, and shorebirds within the Washington Islands Refuges. Harbor seals and the California and Steller sea lions haul themselves onto rocks and reefs, and sea otters inhabit surrounding kelp beds.

These islands are closed to visitation, and the Fish and Wildlife Service urges that boats be kept at least 200 yards offshore, both for safety and to avoid disturbing the nesting bird colonies and other wildlife.

Further information: Quillayute Needles, Flattery Islands, and Copalis Rock National Wildlife Refuges, c/o Washington Maritime NWR Complex, 33 South Barr Road, Port Angeles, WA 98362; telephone: (360) 457-8451.

Ridgefield, containing 5,150 acres in five units, was established in 1965 to protect and manage wintering habitat for migratory waterfowl. The refuge consists of woodlands, grasslands, lakes and ponds, and tidally influenced marshes and sloughs. It is located along the lower Columbia River in southwestern Washington.

Prominent among wintering species are many tundra swans; many thousands of Canada geese of seven subspecies, including dusky, cackler, western, and Taverner's; and ducks of many species, such as mallard, northern pintail, northern shoveler, green-winged teal, and American wigeon. The dusky Canada goose, which nests on southern Alaska's Copper River Delta, winters only along the lower Columbia River and in Oregon's Willamette River Valley (see also the

Ankeny, Baskett Slough, and William L. Finley Refuge texts under Oregon). Ridgefield Refuge also attracts wintering bald eagles and large numbers of migrating shorebirds, and provides winter roosting habitat for sandhill cranes and colonial nesting sites for the largest rookery of great blue herons in the Pacific Northwest.

The refuge's most prominent mammal is the black-tailed deer, and the biggest nuisance is the abundant non-native nutria, a large South American rodent that burrows into and damages dikes and ditches. Other native species include coyote, red fox, river otter, beaver, muskrat, raccoon, striped skunk, and brush rabbit.

Protection of the Columbia River floodplain is the primary management goal within the refuge's Carty and Roth units. During the spring, when melting mountain snow raises the level of the river, these areas are inundated. As the U.S. Fish and Wildlife Service explains:

Basalt outcroppings on the Carty Unit form knolls above the high water level. These knolls are wooded with ash, oak and Douglas-fir trees and are covered with brilliant wildflowers in the spring. The knolls become extremely dry in summer, in contrast with the lush greenery of surrounding marshes. The Roth unit is flatter and forested with cottonwood, ash and willow. Cattle graze on parts of these units to maintain grasslands in suitable condition for wintering waterfowl, especially Canada geese.

The River "S" Unit and Bachelor Island, on the other hand, are protected from flooding by dikes around their perimeters. Crops, such as corn, barley, and native grasses, are grown to provide food for waterfowl. Pumps provide the proper amount of water to each pond and lake to foster the growth of aquatic waterfowl food plants and to create resting areas for the birds. Grasslands are grazed by cattle and are cut for hay or silage. This leaves behind the short green browse preferred by Canada geese when they arrive in the fall.

Establishment of Ridgefield Refuge was made possible partly with revenues from the sale of Migratory Bird Hunting and Conservation Stamps (Duck Stamps). Ducks Unlimited, Inc. has helped enhance more than 1,700 acres of the refuge's wetland habitat. Friends of Ridgefield National Wildlife Refuge is a local, nonprofit organization that assists the refuge in a variety of ways.

The refuge is open daily during daylight hours. There is no entrance fee. The refuge headquarters, located at 301 North Third Avenue, Ridgefield, is open on weekdays, except national holidays.

Visitor activities include birdwatching; photography; driving on the 4.2-mile refuge auto tour road within the River "S" Unit; hiking; boating on Lake River, Bachelor Slough, and the Columbia River (boat-launching at Ridgefield Marina); fishing; and hunting (waterfowl) on part of the refuge during the designated season. Although camping is not permitted on the refuge, campground facilities are available at Paradise Point State Park and elsewhere nearby.

Hiking opportunities include the 2-mile Oaks-to-Wetlands Wildlife Trail that runs along the edge of the Carty Unit's floodplain wetlands and through woodlands of Douglas fir and Oregon white oak; and a 1.5-mile seasonal hiking trail on the River "S" Unit. The Bachelor Island, Ridgeport Dairy, and Roth units are sanctuary areas of the refuge and are closed to all public access year-round.

Lodgings and meals are available in such communities as Ridgefield, Woodland, Longview, and Vancouver, Washington and Portland, Oregon.

Access to Ridgefield Refuge from Exit 14 on I-5 is west about 3 miles to Ridgefield, and follow refuge directional signs.

Further information: Ridgefield National Wildlife Refuge, P.O. Box 457, Ridgefield, WA 98642; telephone: (360) 887-4106.

San Juan Islands, consisting of 448 acres, was established in 1914 to protect more than 80 islands, rocks, and reefs for the benefit of important seabird nesting colonies. The refuge is scattered throughout the San Juan Islands at the northern end of Puget Sound in northwestern Washington. All of the refuge, except for Smith, Minor, Turn, and five acres on Matia Island, is designated as a unit of the National Wilderness Preservation System.

Among the seabirds are pelagic cormorants, glaucous-winged gulls, burrow- or crevice-nesting pigeon guillemots, and rhinoceros auklets. Loons, grebes, and various species of ducks are frequently seen on the waters offshore. A number of bald eagles nest and spend the winter on and around refuge islands. Marine mammals include harbor seals that frequently haul themselves onto beaches and rocks; harbor porpoises; and orcas (the killer "whale," which is actually a large member of the dolphin family).

Except for Turn and Matia islands, the refuge is closed to visitation. To avoid disturbing the seabird colonies and other wildlife, boats should be kept at least 200 yards away from these islands, rocks, and reefs. Visitors are welcome to visit Turn Island (near Friday Harbor) and Matia Island (northwest of Orcas Island), where moorage buoys and docks are available and where state parks provide primitive picnicking and camping sites. Hiking on Matia Island is permitted only on the 1-mile wilderness trail.

The Fish and Wildlife Service cautions: "Because changes in weather and tides can make this area very dangerous, small boaters should check local conditions before venturing onto the open waters of Puget Sound." Visitors without boats are afforded the opportunity to see several of the refuge islands from the ferry from Anacortes to Friday Harbor and Sydney, British Columbia. Ferry information: (206) 464-6400.

Lodgings and meals are available in such communities as Friday Harbor and Anacortes, Washington and Sidney and Victoria, British Columbia, Canada.

Further information: San Juan Islands National Wildlife Refuge, c/o Washington Maritime NWR Complex, 33 South Barr Road, Port Angeles, WA 98362; telephone: (360) 457-8451.

Steigerwald Lake, encompassing 974 acres, was established in 1986 as partial mitigation for construction of the second powerhouse at Bonneville Dam. The refuge is located on the north bank of the Columbia River, at the western end of the Columbia River Gorge in southwestern Washington.

Several thousand Canada geese are attracted to Steigerwald Lake Refuge during winter, along with several species of ducks. Modest numbers of coho and chinook salmon and steelhead make annual spawning runs from the Columbia River up the refuge's Gibbons Creek. These migrating fish attract a few bald eagles.

The refuge is closed to visitation, although birdwatching, photography, and hiking can occur along the Columbia River Dike Trail, which begins in Steamboat Landing State Park in Washougal.

Lodgings and meals are available in such communities as Vancouver, Washington and Portland, Oregon.

Steigerwald Lake Refuge is just east of Washougal and about 15 miles east of Vancouver, Washington.

Further information: Steigerwald Lake National Wildlife Refuge, c/o Columbia River Gorge NWR Complex, 36062 State Route 14, Stevenson, WA 98648; telephone: (509) 427-5208.

Toppenish, containing 1,978 acres in six tracts, was established in 1964 to protect and manage wetland habitat of marshes and ponds along Toppenish Creek for the benefit of migrating, nesting, and wintering waterfowl and other wildlife. The refuge is located within the Yakima Indian Reservation, in the Yakima River Valley of south-central Washington.

Large concentrations of Canada geese and numerous species of ducks pause on Toppenish Refuge during the spring and autumn migrations; trumpeter swans, geese, and many thousands of ducks spend the winter here, along with raptors such as bald eagles and various species of hawks. The refuge also includes some areas of sagebrush-grass habitat that is inhabited by such wildlife as sage thrashers, coyotes, and badgers.

Establishment of Toppenish Refuge was made possible partly with revenues from the sale of Migratory Bird Hunting and Conservation Stamps (Duck Stamps). Ducks Unlimited, Inc. has helped enhance more than 1,600 acres of the refuge's wetland habitat.

The refuge is open daily during daylight hours. There is no entrance fee. The refuge headquarters is open on nonholiday weekdays, when staff are available.

Visitor activities include birdwatching, photography, hiking a 1-mile loop trail, and hunting (goose, duck, pheasant, quail, coot, and snipe) on parts of the refuge during the designated seasons.

Lodgings and meals are available in such communities as Toppenish and Goldendale.

Access to Toppenish Refuge from Exit 104 on I-84 is northeast about 57 miles on U.S. Route 97; or about 6 miles southwest from State Route 22 at Toppenish on U.S. Route 97.

Further information: Toppenish National Wildlife Refuge, c/o Mid-Columbia River NWR Complex, P.O. Box 700, Umatilla, OR 97882; telephone: (509) 545-8588.

Turnbull, comprising 15,628 acres, was established in 1937 to restore and protect an ecologically diverse and ruggedly scenic area of water-sculpted basalt formations and depressions known as the Channeled Scablands (see the Columbia Refuge text). The refuge is located south of Spokane in east-central Washington. Over 200 bird species have been seen here.

Numerous marshes, wet meadows, sloughs, streams, small lakes, and pothole ponds attract large concentrations of migrating and nesting ducks, geese, swans, and shorebirds. Other habitats include grassland, shrub steppe, riparian woodland, groves of quaking aspens, and forested areas of ponderosa pine.

This area long supported the Spokane Indians, who came here not only to hunt wildlife, but who gathered many of the native plants, such as bitterroot, camas, and wild onion, for food. But as the U.S. Fish and Wildlife Service describes, the Euro-American settlers arrived in the late nineteenth century and began developing farmlands in this area, "and before long there was a demand for more cropland. Drainage of the lakes and marshes continued until they were almost completely gone by the early 1920s. This excellent wildlife area might have been lost forever had it not been for the failure of the lakebeds to produce crops as expected, and for the efforts of individuals who felt that the area should be returned to its natural state.

Conservationists and sportsmen encouraged the addition of this area to the rapidly growing system of National Wildlife Refuges. Their efforts bore fruit . . . when the refuge was created and named for Cyrus Turnbull, an early settler.

Since then, the lakes and marshes have been restored to be much the same as they were prior to settlement. The area has been preserved through long, untiring efforts of countless workers, sportsmen, naturalists, and citizens interested in wildlife conservation and appreciation.

As the Service also explains, a variety of important habitat management activities are being implemented: "We are using fire as a management tool after over 60 years of fire suppression on the refuge. Past logging, grazing and suppression of fire . . . [have] created pine stands with tree densities 2 to 4 times the pre-settlement condition. Large trees greater than 24 inches (60 cm) in diameter constitute less than 10% of the stands. Greater than 75% of the refuge ponderosa pine forest exists as closed canopy, multi-storied stands with similar age and size structure. Fuel loading in refuge pine stands is 5 times greater than the average for this forest type. Conditions are ripe for catastrophic loss due to insects, disease, and [wild]fire."

Establishment of Turnbull Refuge was made possible mostly with revenues from the sale of Migratory Bird Hunting and Conservation Stamps (Duck Stamps). A number of vital partnerships with private organizations are helping the refuge achieve its goals. Ducks Unlimited, Inc. has helped enhance roughly 100 acres of the refuge's wetland habitat. The Spokane Chapter of the National Audubon Society has been assisting with riparian habitat restoration and has obtained a grant to fund volunteer training workshops as part of the refuge's environmental education program. The recently formed Friends of Turnbull National Wildlife Refuge is a local, nonprofit organization that supports environmental education and other refuge programs.

The refuge is open daily during daylight hours. There is a small entrance fee from March 1 through October, and no fee from November 1 through February. The refuge office, located at the east end of Smith Road, is open on weekdays, except national holidays.

Visitor activities include wildlife observation; photography; driving the 5.5-mile loop auto tour route; hiking; bicycling on the auto tour road; cross-country skiing; and interpretive and environmental education programs. Camping is not permitted on the refuge, but campground facilities are available at nearby private campgrounds. Swimming, boating, fishing, and hunting are presently not permitted on the refuge.

Hiking and walking opportunities include the 0.7-mile 30 Acre Cutoff Trail, the 1-mile Pine Loop Trail, the 1.8-mile Bluebird Trail, the 1.5-mile Headquarters Trail, the 0.25-mile Kepple Overlook Trail, the 0.2-mile (wheelchair-accessible) Blackhorse Boardwalk, and the 0.5-mile Kepple

Peninsula Trail (an interpretive brochure is available for the latter route). In addition, a 4.75-mile stretch of the Columbia Plateau Trail, managed by the Washington State Parks and Recreation Commission, crosses the closed area of the refuge. Visitors may hike, bicycle, and ride horseback on this trail, but are reminded that the area on each side of the trail is closed to visitation.

Lodgings and meals are available in Cheney and Spokane.

Access to Turnbull Refuge from Exit 270 (Four Lakes) on I-90 (about 11 miles southwest of downtown Spokane) is south and then southwest 6 miles on State Route 904 to Cheney, and south (left) 4 miles on Cheney Plaza Road.

Further information: Turnbull National Wildlife Refuge, 26010 South Smith Road, Cheney, WA 99004; telephone: (509) 235-4723.

Umatilla (see text under Oregon)

Willapa, consisting of 14,755 acres, was established in 1937 to protect and manage important habitats for migrating and wintering waterfowl, shorebirds, and other wildlife. The refuge is located in Willapa Bay and at the northern end of Long Beach Peninsula on the southwest coast of Washington.

The refuge's diverse coastal habitats include areas of temperate forest with some old-growth Sitka spruces, western hemlocks, and western redcedars; and an area of dike-enclosed grassland maintained for the benefit of geese and other wildlife. In the spring, the bay's mudflats are a mecca for more than 100,000 migrating shorebirds. Willapa Bay, the second largest estuary on the Pacific Coast, has been designated as a Western Hemisphere Shorebird Reserve.

Extensive areas of eelgrass in Willapa Bay attract large concentrations of migrating and wintering brant (*Branta bernicla*). Willapa Bay is a key staging area for this species of goose prior to their spring flight to Arctic breeding grounds in Canada, Alaska, and Siberia. (Regarding the brant, see also the Humboldt Bay Refuge [California] text.)

Marine mammals that can sometimes be observed include harbor seals, sea lions, porpoises, and migrating gray whales. Sandbars in the bay offer pupping grounds for harbor seals. Willapa Bay also attracts various species of salmon, including chum, coho, and chinook. The refuge is presently working to restore and enhance anadromous fish runs on refuge streams within the Willapa Basin. These efforts include the recent installation of fish ladders that are reopening access to two streams, so that salmon can once again reach their spawning grounds.

A major part of Willapa Refuge is Long Island, the largest estuarine island on the Pacific Coast. As described by the U.S. Fish and Wildlife Service:

Long Island's 5,460 acres contain a rare 274-acre remnant of old growth lowland coastal forest known as Cedar Grove. Some western red cedar trees in this grove have been growing for more than 900 years. The rain-drenched forests on Long Island grow rapidly and densely, with salal, huckleberry and salmonberry bushes carpeting the forest floor beneath tall western hemlock, Sitka spruce and western red cedar trees. Fallen trees, called nurse logs, provide shelter and a rich growing medium for young trees. . . .

The forests of Long Island are home to mammals such as black bear, Roosevelt elk, black-tailed deer, beaver, and river otter. The mature forests provide special niches for numerous sensitive wildlife species. The largest trees provide wide sturdy limbs suitable for the platform nests of marbled murrelets, a seabird that has lost much of its historical nesting habitat due to logging of old growth forests. Bald eagles and great blue herons also nest in large trees on the island.

The Roosevelt elk is Willapa Refuge's largest terrestrial mammal. This elk subspecies, which is darker and somewhat larger than the Rocky Mountain elk, ranges along the Pacific Northwest coast, from coastal northern California northward in scattered areas along the Oregon coast and Washington's Olympic Peninsula, to Canada's Vancouver Island. These stately animals graze across the refuge's open fields and marshes, and use the shelter of forested areas for cover.

Willapa Refuge's RIEKKOLA UNIT contains managed grasslands within the diked tidelands, at the southern end of the bay. This habitat offers feeding and resting habitat for wintering Canada geese, ducks, and other wildlife. Cattle grazing during the summer months maintains fields of short grass that is favored by the geese. The LEWIS AND PORTER POINT UNITS are managed for their important freshwater marsh habitat, where water levels are manipulated to provide food for migratory waterfowl, rearing habitat for salmonids, and breeding areas for aquatic amphibians.

The refuge's LEADBETTER POINT UNIT contains beaches and sand dunes. It is one of three nesting areas in Washington for the threatened snowy plover. As the Fish and Wildlife Service explains, "These small cryptic shorebirds nest on the upper ocean beaches in small scrapes in the sand. Their well camouflaged eggs can be inadvertently stepped on by people or run over by vehicles. Incubating adults are easily frightened off the nests, allowing sand to cover the eggs or predators to destroy them. A 372-acre portion of Leadbetter Point along the ocean side is closed to ALL public entry, including foot travel, generally from March through September to protect the nesting snowy plovers."

As explained by refuge wildlife biologist Deborah Jaques, "Leadbetter Point is one of the only locations on the Oregon-Washington coast where snowy plovers nest successfully without the use of predator exclosures. Its remote location, natural balance of predators, and continual sand erosion and deposition make it one of the most ecologically sound plover-nesting areas on the West Coast."

A very serious problem that threatens the ecological integrity of Willapa Refuge and Bay is the rapidly spreading infestation of a non-native, invasive plant, the smooth cordgrass (*Spartina alterniflora*). The Fish and Wildlife Service states:

Willapa Bay has the largest Spartina infestation of any estuary on the Pacific Coast. Spartina eliminates the value of intertidal areas for wildlife, the aquiculture industry and recreational pursuits because it forms dense, monotypic stands of vegetation, traps sediment, and alters existing hydrologic processes.

Spartina alterniflora was introduced in 1894. In 1991, there were approximately 2,500 acres of Spartina in Willapa Bay. The infestation currently [late 2001] covers between 15,000 and 18,000 acres of tidelands, and it is projected to occupy 56,000 out of the 80,000 acres of Willapa Bay if left uncontrolled. . . .

The complete loss of intertidal mudflats and native saltmarsh communities to Spartina will have a devastating effect on shorebird use, wintering brant and Dusky Canada goose foraging habitats, estuarine values for anadromous fish, and the viability of the area's oyster and hard-shell clam aquaculture industry.

Control and eradication of Spartina is difficult, dangerous, and expensive. Large tidal fluctuations, unconsolidated mud, costly herbicides and control equipment, the rapid rate of spread for Spartina, as well as strict water quality regulations have enabled the Spartina infestation to overwhelm control efforts.

The integrated pest management approach to controlling Spartina is focused on chemical control of small clones and seedlings, large scale mechanical control of meadows and the deployment of the bio control Prokelisia marginata which is expected to eliminate a portion of the Spartina within Willapa Bay.

Control and eradication efforts are so far insufficient. Current rate of spread of Spartina within Willapa Bay exceeds 40% biannually with some areas experiencing a 485% rate of spread over three years. If the rate of spread . . . is not controlled, it may be unrealistic to expect that control and eradication will ever be possible.

Establishment of Willapa Refuge was made possible partly with revenues from the sale of Migratory Bird Hunting and Conservation Stamps (Duck Stamps). More than 200 acres of the refuge's wetland habitat has recently been restored. The Friends of Willapa National Wildlife Refuge is a nonprofit organization that assists the refuge in habitat projects, volunteer management, environmental education, and public outreach.

Parts of the refuge are open daily during daylight hours, with the exception of overnight camping at five designated primitive campgrounds on Long Island (campsites are available on a first-come first-served basis). Campground facilities are also available on Long Beach Peninsula. The refuge headquarters is open on weekdays, except national holidays.

Visitor activities include wildlife observation; photography; hiking; kayaking and boating; fishing; waterfowl hunting on the refuge's Riekkola and Lewis units; archery hunting (elk, deer, bear, and grouse) on Long Island; and rifle big-game hunting on some refuge areas during the designated seasons. Over 240 bird species have been seen here.

Hiking opportunities on Long Island include the 0.7-mile Trail of the Ancients, which visitors can reach by walking 2.5 miles on a gravel road that leads from the Long Island boat landing. Trails that can be reached by motor vehicle include a 5-mile dike on the refuge's Riekkola Unit and a network of trails, including a 1.1-mile interpretive loop trail, on the Leadbetter Point Unit and adjacent state park. Trails at Leadbetter Point are flooded during the rainy season (usually from October through May).

Lodgings and meals are available in Ilwaco, Seaview, Long Beach, Ocean Park, South Bend, and Raymond, Washington, and Astoria, Oregon.

Access to the Willapa Refuge office from the junction of State Route 4 and U.S. Route 101 is about 5 miles southwest on U.S. Route 101. Prospective visitors to the Lewis and Riekkola units and to Long Island are urged to obtain directional information from the refuge office. To reach the Leadbetter Point Unit and State Park from the junction of State Route 4 and U.S. Route 101, drive southwest 13 miles on U.S. Route 101, west (right) 2 miles on State Route 103 to Seaview, north (right) 11 miles on State Route 103 to Ocean Park, jogging east (right) and then proceeding north (left) on State Route 103 to Oysterville, jogging west (left) and then north (right) on Stackpole Road to its end.

Further information: Willapa National Wildlife Refuge, 3888 SR 101, Ilwaco, WA 98624; telephone: (360) 484-3482.

West Virginia

Canaan Valley, presently comprising 3,292 acres toward an authorized goal of 24,000 acres, was established in 1994, becoming the 500th in the National Wildlife Refuge System. (The name *Canaan* is locally pronounced kah-NANE.) The refuge protects an extraordinary freshwater mountain-valley wetland and boreal-forest ecosystem that is the result of Canaan Valley's high altitude and cool, damp climate. At 3,200 feet elevation, this is the largest high-elevation valley east of the Mississippi River. The refuge is located within the Allegheny Mountains of northeastern West Virginia.

The refuge already includes important components of the largest freshwater wetland in the central and southern Appalachians and relict boreal habitats. Continued land acquisitions will occur only from willing sellers. Management objectives of the refuge include the protection and, where appropriate, the enhancement and restoration of these ecologically rich habitats and their diversity of plant and animal communities. Nearly 600 species of plants have been identified in the valley, and the refuge presently lists more than 160 species of birds that are known or expected to occur here.

As described by the U.S. Fish and Wildlife Service:

Canaan Valley has been described as 'a little bit of Canada gone astray.' The high elevation of the valley floor gives it a boreal climate, colder than that of the surrounding area. Some plants found here are usually found much farther north. Red spruce, a ridge-top species in the high elevations of West Virginia, works its way down the mountain slopes in the valley. . . . The combination of wet soils and uplands, forests, shrub lands and open lands throughout the valley adds to the diversity of habitats. . . .

A patchwork of twenty-three wetland types, including bogs, shrub swamps and wet meadows, carpets the valley floor. At approximately 7,000 acres, this is the largest wetland complex in the state of West Virginia. . . .

There are very few places in West Virginia where ducks call, herons fly, and shorebirds probe the earth for food. Canaan Valley is such a place. Mallards, black ducks, and wood ducks nest in her marshes. Solitary sandpipers are found wherever a small pocket of wetland exists. . . . Frogs mate in her vernal pools. Beavers ply the [Blackwater] river, finding dam sites from place to place. . . .

One-hundred years ago, people altered this landscape, taking out its timber, and letting its slash and soils burn. With the soil loss, the recovery of the forest has been slow. Stands of [red] spruce, balsam fir and hemlock remind us of the boreal forest that once was the dominant cover type of the valley. . . .

Woodlands of beech, cherry, maple, etc., cover the slopes of the mountains and add color to our fall. Squirrels, ruffed grouse, turkey and bear all make their homes in these woodlands. Wood thrush, ovenbirds and woodland warblers also find their place here. The world's largest diversity of salamanders find their niche in these and other southern Appalachian woodland streams.

The refuge is open daily during daylight hours. There is no entrance fee. The refuge headquarters is open on weekdays, except national holidays. Visitor center hours fluctuate seasonally. Visitors should call ahead, to obtain current hours. The Friends of the 500th is a nonprofit support group that assists the refuge in a variety of ways, including at the visitor center.

Visitor activities include wildlife observation; photography; education and interpretive programs; hiking; wildlife viewing by horseback riding and bicycling (allowed on Forest Service Road 80); fishing on the Blackwater River (along Timberline Road); and hunting (deer, bear, coyote, fox, raccoon, skunk, woodchuck, opossum, hare, rabbit, waterfowl, coot, rail, gallinule, woodcock, snipe, turkey, grouse, and dove) on parts of the refuge during the designated seasons (a hunting brochure provides further information). Although camping is not permitted on the refuge, campground facilities are provided on adjacent Canaan Valley Resort State Park and elsewhere in the general vicinity.

Wildlife viewing trails include the 0.5-mile Freeland Tract Trail that is accessed from a parking area adjacent to Freeland Road; the Kelly/Elkins Tract Trails that are accessed from the eastern end of Freeland Road; and the Beall Tract Trails (totaling about 4 miles) that are accessed from the parking area at the east end of Old Timberline Road.

Lodgings and meals are available locally and in Davis.

Access to Canaan Valley Refuge from U.S. Route 219 at Thomas is southeast about 8 miles on State Route 32; or from U.S. Route 33 at Harman is north about 9 miles on State Route 32.

Further information: Canaan Valley National Wildlife Refuge, HC 70, Box 200, Davis, WV 26260; telephone: (304) 866-3858.

Ohio River Islands contains 3,221 acres scattered along 362 miles of the Ohio River. The refuge was established in 1990 and presently includes all or part of 21 islands and three mainland tracts in northwest West Virginia; two islands just downriver from Pittsburgh, Pennsylvania; and two islands in northern Kentucky. More than a dozen other islands and up to 100 embayment wetlands within the authorized boundary could ultimately add more than 8,000 acres to the refuge between Pittsburgh and Cincinnati. All refuge lands are being acquired either from willing sellers or as private donations.

As the refuge's December 2000 Draft *Comprehensive Conservation Plan* emphasizes:

It is important to note that the Ohio River is a greatly altered ecosystem, impounded for navigation purposes. The altered hydrology has affected significantly the quality of both aquatic and terrestrial habitats. Many islands, shallow gravel bars, riffles, and channel wetlands have been lost, and have been replaced by deepwater habitats.

The goal of the Ohio River Islands Refuge is to restore, enhance, and protect ecologically important river floodplain, bottomland hardwood forest habitat for the benefit of a great diversity of wildlife. The U.S. Fish and Wildlife Service explains:

Restoring the river's floodplain forest . . . is a refuge priority. Current habitat conditions range from old fields and recently planted tree seedling plots to remnant giants of silver maple, cottonwood, and sycamore. Non-native plants such as Japanese knotweed invade many acres, making their control a major refuge challenge.

Several small wetlands occur on refuge islands, and efforts are underway to restore others.

Prior to the establishment of the Ohio River Islands Refuge, less than 40 percent of the islands within the refuge contained bottomland hardwood forest. By 2000, this habitat had increased to nearly 60 percent, with the upward trend continuing.

Of the roughly 200 species of birds known to use the refuge, Canada geese, wood ducks, mallards, American black ducks, great blue and green herons, and ospreys are prominent among the many water birds. Great blue herons nest at several rookeries on the refuge—notably on Muskingum and Grape islands. Bald eagles and many other species of ducks, such as scaups, buffleheads, and mergansers, winter along the river. Large influxes of neotropical migratory songbirds, including thrushes and many species of warblers, come into the river valley in the spring, either to nest here or to pause on their flights to breeding areas farther north.

Although white-tailed deer are the refuge's largest mammal, the bank dens and other evidence of beavers and muskrats frequently reveal the presence of these animals. The waters around the islands are inhabited by more than 50 species of fish, including smallmouth and largemouth bass, white bass, catfish, and sauger. In addition, according to the Fish and Wildlife Service:

Over forty species of freshwater mussels live on the refuge, including the endangered pink mucket and the fanshell. Freshwater mussels are among the nation's most imperiled . . . [fauna]. The refuge's underwater sand and gravel deposits provide vital mussel habitat.

The recent invasion of the Ohio River by non-native zebra mussels threatens native mussel survival. The refuge is working with partners to conserve native mussels throughout the Ohio River watershed.

The refuge is open daily during daylight hours. There is no entrance fee. The refuge headquarters, located at 3004 Seventh Street, Parkersburg, is open on weekdays, except national holidays.

Visitor activities include birdwatching; photography; driving the signed, 1.5-mile auto-tour route on Middle Island, adjacent to St. Marys, West Virginia; hiking; boating and canoeing; fishing (some of the best Ohio River fishing is available around the refuge's islands); and hunting (waterfowl, dove, squirrel, rabbit, and archery deer) on parts of the refuge during the designated seasons (a brochure is available that explains special regulations). A self-guiding boat tour around Muskingum Island, near Parkersburg, West Virginia, reveals some of this island's natural and cultural history (an interpretive brochure is available at refuge headquarters). The Fish and Wildlife Service asks boaters to travel at "no-wake" speed in the back channels of islands, to avoid disturbing wildlife. Although camping is not permitted on the refuge, campground facilities are available on a unit of the Wayne National Forest near Marietta, Ohio.

Hiking opportunities include a self-guiding interpretive trail with an observation blind on Middle Island, adjacent to St. Marys, West Virginia. A trail is planned on Buckley Island, which is located where I-77 crosses the river.

Visitors are cautioned to be alert for poison ivy, which is common on most of the refuge.

Lodgings and meals are available near refuge headquarters and Middle and Muskingum islands in such communities as Parkersburg, West Virginia, and Marietta, Ohio as well as elsewhere along the river, from Pittsburgh, Pennsylvania, to Manchester, Ohio and Maysville, Kentucky.

A nearby conservation area is the Wayne National Forest (Ohio).

Access to two islands is by bridge (Middle Island, near St. Marys, West Virginia; and Wheeling Island [the northern end of which is in the refuge], in Wheeling, West Virginia). All other islands are reached only by boat. Three mainland tracts are accessible by car: Buffalo Creek, Captina, and Buckley (visitors should contact the refuge headquarters for directions).

Further information: Ohio River Islands National Wildlife Refuge, P.O. Box 1811, Parkersburg, WV 26102; telephone: (304) 422-0752.

Wisconsin: National Wildlife Refuges

Fox River, consisting of 1,001 acres, was established in 1978 to enhance and protect an area known as the Fox River Sandhill Crane Marsh and associated upland habitat in central Wisconsin. Prior to the refuge's establishment, this ecologically important marshland was threatened with drainage. The initial 641 acres were purchased in 1979 after the settlement of litigation, by which ditching, draining, and filling activities were halted. More than half of Fox River Refuge consists of marsh habitat, and the remainder is small tracts of grasslands, savanna, and woodlots. Two private inholdings remain within the boundaries.

The refuge is an important breeding and staging area for the greater sandhill crane. Other prominent species of birds include great blue heron, Canada goose, mallard, blue-winged teal, red-tailed hawk, wild turkey, sedge and marsh wrens, common yellowthroat, and savannah sparrow. Mammals include white-tailed deer, red and gray foxes, mink, muskrat, woodchuck, and eastern cottontail.

Ten distinct plant communities are encompassed by the refuge, ranging from five types of wetlands to coniferous and deciduous uplands. These habitats support a surprisingly large diversity of plant species for this relatively small area.

The refuge is not open to general visitation, but archery and gun deer hunting are permitted on the refuge during designated times.

Lodgings and meals are available in such nearby communities as Montello, Westfield, and Portage.

Access to Fox River Refuge from State Route 23 at Montello is southwest 6 miles on County Route F, which borders the refuge's eastern boundary.

Further information: Fox River National Wildlife Refuge, c/o Horicon NWR, W4279 Headquarters Road, Mayville, WI 53050; telephone: (920) 387-2658.

Gravel Island comprises 27 acres on Gravel and Spider islands. The refuge was initially set aside in 1913 as the U.S. Department of Agriculture-managed Gravel Island Reservation. In 1940, the area was transferred to the U.S. Department of the Interior as a national wildlife refuge. Four-acre Gravel Island and 23-acre Spider Island are located in Lake Michigan, off the end of the Door Peninsula in northeastern Wisconsin.

U.S. Fish and Wildlife Service staff explain, "Because of unsafe boating conditions around the islands plus the small size and fragileness of the ecosystem, and because of disturbance to nesting wildlife," this refuge is closed to visitation.

Flat-topped Gravel Island rises to only about 10 feet above the lake level. The highest part of the limestone island is covered primarily with low-growing, shrubby willows. Herring gulls and double-crested cormorants are abundant.

Spider Island, rising to about 14 feet, formerly supported a stand of trees such as white spruce, larch (tamarack), white cedar, paper birch, and quaking aspen. Numerous breeding double-crested cormorants and gulls subsequently killed virtually all the trees (acid in the birds' guano kills the trees). Consequently, Spider Island now contains mostly low-growing vegetation of forbs and grasses.

Prominent among the birds of Spider Island are nesting double-crested cormorants; great blue herons and black-crowned night herons; large numbers of nesting herring and ring-billed gulls; and a number of nesting waterfowl, notably mallard, black duck, and common merganser.

Further information: Gravel Island National Wildlife Refuge, c/o Horicon NWR, W4279 Headquarters Road, Mayville, WI 53050; telephone: (920) 387-2658.

Green Bay, encompassing 2-acre Hog Island, was established as a refuge in 1912. The refuge protects important breeding bird habitat located in Lake Michigan, off the eastern shore of Washington Island in northeastern Wisconsin. As the U.S. Fish and Wildlife Service explains, "Because of the unsafe boating conditions . . . plus the small size and fragileness of the ecosystem," this refuge is closed to visitation.

Hog Island rises to about 20 feet above the lake at the highest point of its flat top. It supports a dense growth of trees and shrubby vegetation, including balsam fir, white cedar, paper birch, red elder (elderberry), red-osier dogwood, chokecherry, raspberry, wild currant, ground hemlock, and grasses.

Great numbers of herring gulls nest in the crevices of the island's bare limestone ledges and on grassy areas; waterfowl, such as the mallard, use thickly wooded nesting sites.

Further information: Green Bay National Wildlife Refuge, c/o Horicon NWR, W4279 Headquarters Road, Mayville, WI 53050; telephone: (920) 387-2658.

Horicon, comprising 21,417 acres, was established in 1941 to enhance and protect the northern two-thirds of the largest freshwater cattail marsh (32,000 acres) in the United States, primarily for the benefit of migratory waterfowl. The refuge is located in southeastern Wisconsin.

Horicon Refuge attracts numerous species of ducks—notably the largest eastern breeding population of redhead ducks, as well as many shorebirds, marsh birds, and other wildlife.

Roughly 200 tundra swans and 800 American white pelicans pause to rest and feed during the autumn migration; some pelicans also nest here. Wisconsin's largest great blue heron rookery is located in the southern part of the marsh.

The refuge provides critical stopover habitat for impressive concentrations of migrating Canada geese. From September through December, up to 1 million Canadas, which nest in the Hudson Bay area of Canada, migrate through here on their way to wintering areas along the lower Ohio River valley. More than 200,000 of them congregate in the area on peak days of October and November. Most goose watchers visit in October, viewing spectacular flights around sunrise and sunset.

The southern one-third of the marsh lies within the 11,000-acre Horicon Marsh State Wildlife Area, managed by the Wisconsin Department of Natural Resources. Consequently, the entire marsh ecosystem is protected for wildlife. The wetland has been designated as a Wetland of International Importance and a Globally Important Bird Area.

As described by refuge ranger Molly Stoddard:

Horicon Marsh lies within a shallow, peat-filled lake bed, measuring 14 miles long by 3 to 5 miles wide, that was scoured out of limestone by the Green Bay lobe of the massive Wisconsin glaciation, when it retreated from the area about 12,000 years ago. The so-called "original" vegetation of the marsh was possibly sedge meadow and/or a peat marsh. It very likely contained much greater diversity of plant life. According to early accounts, cranberry and wild rice thrived here.

The name "Horicon" is a Mohican Indian word meaning pure, clean water. . . . In 1846, settlers . . . constructed a dam on the Rock River, where it flows out of the marsh, converting the marsh into the largest man-made lake in the world at that time. . . .

Once the dam was removed in 1869, it took three years for the lake to drain back to a marsh. Already popular for waterfowl hunting, the area became famous for uncontrolled market and recreational hunting. Starting in 1883, two shooting clubs leased much of the marshlands and provided restricted, exclusive access to their members. Without laws to conserve wildlife, hunters could shoot anything they wanted, any time they wanted, in any quantity they wanted, in any way they wanted, and with any type of weapon they wanted. . . .

Market-hunted ducks were packed in wooden barrels, with marsh hay, and shipped by the hundreds by railroad to upscale restaurants and hotels in Milwaukee, Chicago, and New York. Market hunting persisted during the shooting club years and provided continuous hunting pressure on the Horicon Marsh. However, it is obvious that ducks could have been obliterated from the marsh without the clubs. These shooting clubs ironically represent a transition period between commercial exploitation and conservation. They were the first to impose their own voluntary rules on shooting seasons and techniques, to control water levels for the benefit of waterfowl, and plant duck foods, such as wild rice. And the clubs eventually contributed greatly to the fight to save and restore the marsh. In about 1920, they formed a group called the Horicon Marsh Game Protective Association, which recognized the advantage of limited entry to the marsh for the long-term conservation of waterfowl. This group later became a chapter of the Izaak Walton League of America.

Before the marsh was saved and restored for wildlife, the greatest impact struck. From 1910 to about 1918, an attempt was made by agricultural interests to dredge, ditch, and drain the wetlands—without authority and in direct violation of a ruling of the state supreme court. Their goal: to improve the land for farming. . . .

Ditching and draining the marsh permanently impacted its ecology—destroying the original marsh vegetation, promoting the invasion of weed plants, and increasing the risk of peat fires that sometimes raged for weeks at a time. The Main Ditch straightened and lowered the channel of the Rock River, which increased the speed of flow and lowered the water table by about a foot. According to the Izaak Walton League, "That huge ditch became a vampire stream, which bled white the famous Horicon Marsh." Ditching and draining "succeeded in spoiling the best ducking ground in the whole country, as there is not water enough left to run a boat, and the mud is too soft and deep to walk over." Attempts at muck farming ultimately failed because effective drainage for that activity could not be achieved.

Once only viewed as wasteland, the marsh now really was a wasteland. With low water, there was no food for waterfowl, and it was unusable for transportation, recreation, industry, or agriculture.

After a long struggle during the 1920s and 1930s, the Izaak Walton League of America and other protection advocates finally achieved success in urging Congress to give this ecologically significant area the protection it so richly deserved. Establishment of Horicon Refuge was made possible partly with revenues from the sale of Migratory Bird Hunting and Conservation Stamps (Duck Stamps).

Ducks Unlimited, Inc. has helped enhance nearly 3,000 acres of the refuge's wetland habitat. The University of Wisconsin-Stevens Point and the U.S. Geological Survey have installed monitoring devices and have been carrying out research to learn more about the marsh's water quality. In cooperation with the Wisconsin Department of Natural Resources, carp are being managed and removed from the refuge. This non-native species of fish feeds in the marsh water and muck, clouding the water and uprooting vegetation. The resulting increase in turbidity reduces photosynthesis—a natural process that fuels the marsh food web.

The refuge's primary management activity is the manipulation of water levels for the benefit of waterfowl and shorebirds. Molly Stoddard says:

Efforts continue today to restore, maintain, and enhance the refuge for the benefit of wildlife. The manipulation of water levels is central to management activities that benefit waterfowl and shorebirds. The presence or absence of water, water depth, and timing are all coordinated to produce various stages of marsh plant succession, upon which the birds rely. Various impoundments, subdivided off the main body of the marsh using a system of dikes and water-control structures, are managed on seasonal, annual, and multiple-year cycles. Because of changing water levels, you may notice some wetland areas of open, deep water; others with dense stands of cattails, and yet others with bare mudflats.

In addition to the Horicon Refuge's more than 16,000 acres of wetlands, there are also more than 4,000 acres of uplands, which include 410 acres of forest and brush, plus about 3,600 acres of grasslands. Refuge staff conduct periodic prescribed burns to help restore and enhance grasslands. The use of fire helps provide improved nesting habitat for some species of ducks and shorebirds, causes ecologically important nutrient cycling, and promotes a greater natural diversity of plant life.

Yet another significant management activity on the Horicon Refuge is the installation of nesting platforms for ospreys. As the Fish and Wildlife Service reported in 2001, "Alliant Energy donated two utility poles and provided staff and equipment to install the poles on August 14. A three-foot wide, octagon-shaped platform was attached to the top of each pole. The platforms are 25 feet above the ground and are made of wood with chicken wire." Alliant's contribution made possible this important project to enhance nesting opportunities for the osprey, which is listed as a threatened species in Wisconsin.

The Midwest Interpretive Association is a nonprofit educational organization that is assisting Horicon Refuge in a variety of ways.

The refuge is open daily during daylight hours. There is no entrance fee. The visitor center is open daily in spring and autumn and on weekdays the rest of the year, except national holidays. Over 265 bird species have been recorded on the refuge.

Visitor activities include birdwatching; photography; viewing huge numbers of waterfowl in the autumn, from a popular roadside pullout on State Route 49; interpretive and environmental programs and tours; driving the 3-mile loop auto tour route and the 3-mile Main Dike Road (the latter is open from April 15 to September 15); hiking; bicycling on the auto tour route and Main Dike Road; cross-country skiing on trails and the auto tour route and snowshoeing; fishing; and hunting (deer and small game; but not waterfowl) on most of the refuge during the designated seasons. Camping is not permitted on the refuge, but campground facilities are available nearby. April is the best month to see large concentrations of ducks, May is the best for warblers, and October–November are the best for Canada geese.

Although canoeing, kayaking, and boating are not permitted on the refuge, they are allowed on the adjacent state wildlife area, where there are six launching ramps. Canoe and kayak rentals are available in the city of Horicon.

The refuge's hiking opportunities include the Egret Nature Trail—a 0.25-mile loop that features a stretch of wheelchair-accessible floating boardwalk through marsh habitat; Red Fox Nature Trail—a 0.5-mile, self-guiding, interpretive loop through wooded and grassland habitats; and Redhead Hiking Trail—a 2.5-mile loop. The Bud Cook Area, a 120-acre upland area located on the east side of the refuge, provides two trails totaling 2 miles. The 3.2-mile Horicon TernPike Auto Route is also open to hiking and bicycling. All of these routes are located in the northwest corner of the refuge and are accessed from State Route 49. This area encompassing the hiking trails and tour route is closed to hunting, except for the gun deer season around mid-November.

Insect repellent is advised during the warmer months.

Horicon Refuge lies within and also administers the extensive Leopold Wetland Management District (see separate text).

Access to Horicon Refuge's visitor center from the intersection of U.S. Route 41 and State Route 49 (about 13 miles south of Fond du Lac) is west 12 miles on Route 49, south (left) 3.5 miles on County Road Z, and west (right) on Headquarters Road; or from the intersection of U.S. Route 151 and State Route 49, it is east 6 miles on Route 49, south (right) 3.5 miles on County Route Z, and west (right) on Headquarters Road.

Further information: Horicon National Wildlife Refuge, W4279 Headquarters Road, Mayville, WI 53050; telephone: (920) 387-2658.

Necedah, containing 43,656 acres, was established in 1939 to manage numerous pools and impoundments, bogs, woodlands, and oak savanna for the benefit of a large diversity of migratory waterfowl and other wildlife in central Wisconsin. The refuge's wetlands are a remnant of the Great Central Wisconsin Swamp—a once-extensive expanse of peat bogs, interlaced with sandy ridges. This landscape was created when the most recent continental glaciation of this region was melting and withdrawing northward, roughly 10,000 years ago. The refuge's name is derived from a Ho-chunk Indian word that means "land of yellow waters"—referring to the brownish-yellow color of waters that are stained by minerals from peat-bog soils.

Following periods of timber harvesting; various attempts to drain the wetlands; farming; wildfires; and the impact of the Depression era of the 1930s, numerous farmsteads in this area were abandoned. Some of these lands were purchased by the federal government under authority of the National Industrial Recovery Act of 1933 and the Emergency Relief Appropriations Act of 1935.

Establishment of Necedah National Wildlife Refuge was made possible partly with revenues from the sale of Migratory Bird Hunting and Conservation Stamps (Duck Stamps). Ducks Unlimited, Inc. has helped enhance more than 1,100 acres of the refuge's wetland habitat. The Friends of Necedah National Wildlife Refuge, a local nonprofit support group, has been assisting the refuge in a variety of ways.

The best months for birdwatching are April through early May and late September through October. The refuge attracts large concentrations of Canada geese, ducks of many species, shorebirds, bald eagles, and numerous neotropical migratory songbirds as they pause here during their spring and autumn migrations or come to breed and raise their young. Around mid-October, the refuge's star avian attraction is the spectacular concentration of greater sandhill cranes, totaling between 2,000 and 2,500 of these 4-foot-tall birds. Great numbers of them come to Necedah Refuge again in the spring and perform their awesome courtship displays.

An especially significant and exciting wildlife management program on Necedah Refuge is the reintroduction of the federally listed endangered whooping crane (see the Aransas and Chassahowitzka NWR texts for further discussions of this species and recovery efforts). As refuge manager Larry Wargowsky explains:

A new chapter of refuge history was initiated in 1999, when Necedah National Wildlife Refuge was selected by the Whooping Crane Recovery Team (WCRT) as the site for reestablishing an eastern population of whooping cranes. The federally endangered whooping crane almost became extinct, like the passenger pigeon, not long ago with only 15 to 16 birds left in the world in 1941–42. Today, only one migratory population exists, with fewer than 200 birds overwintering at Aransas NWR in Texas. Any catastrophic event, such as a hurricane, oil spill, disease outbreak, could jeopardize this lone population. The WCRT selection of Wisconsin for a new separate, distinct migratory population offers new security for this magnificent endangered species.

This ambitious project started in 2000 with a pilot study project using sandhill cranes, trained by foster humans to follow three small ultralight aircraft more than 1,200 miles to the Chassahowitzka NWR in Florida and return on their own to Necedah NWR in 2001. The pilot project was a success and later in 2001, a small flock of whooping cranes was trained to follow ultralights to Chassahowitzka refuge.

The project was not only successful in starting to establish a new population of whooping cranes in the eastern United States, but also instantly brought national and even international media attention to Necedah. The pilot year study received newsstory coverage in at least 14 magazines and 100 newspapers. E-mailed messages from as far away as Korea and Australia and from California to New York showed the tremendous interest from people planning to travel to Wisconsin to witness this historic event.

Besides the heightened media attention that required additional refuge staff time, preparing for the project was a team effort by staff, as well as members of the Friends of Necedah NWR and other volunteers. Wisconsin Conservation Corps employees stationed at Necedah also assisted with the start-up phase of the project. All other projects were put on hold, to meet the deadlines for constructing night pens, a chick-rearing facility, grassy training strips for the ultralights, and a photo/observation blind. Support services also had to be provided for the large operation of training chicks to follow the ultralights.

The historic, first ultralight-led migration with only whooping cranes began on October 17, 2001, with eight whooping cranes departing Necedah NWR. One bird turned back on the first day and was recaptured and trucked the entire route, for fear it would pull out again and lead other cranes away from the ultralights. Only one fatality occurred during the entire migration, with a bird striking a powerline after a strong windstorm collapsed the temporary holding pen at night, releasing the birds. Heavy morning fog, high temperatures, and headwinds delayed the migration. However, the longest human-led migration with an endangered species ended on December 5, 2001, on day 50, when seven birds settled into their winter home on Chassahowitzka NWR. Six birds flew the route and one bird got a free ride. Two of the cranes were killed by bobcats in Florida. In spring 2002, the remaining five birds successfully migrated northward on their own—four arriving back on Necedah Refuge on April 19, and the other on May 3. They covered the 1,200 miles in only 8 days of flying, taking a more direct route and using thermal air currents that allowed for periods of gliding. Their progress was monitored with satellite and conventional transmitters. Captive-reared whooping cranes have produced enough eggs to provide a larger flock of up to 17 birds to repeat the ultralight training program in the summer of 2002. After a few years of ultralight-led migrations, additional captive whooping cranes may be released with this core flock, to follow them unaided by ultralight aircraft to Chassahowitzka NWR.

The success of the project continues to be due to the tremendous teamwork of the refuge's dedicated staff in conjunction with the Whooping Crane Eastern Partnership that was formed in 2000. The governmental and nonprofit partners are the Whooping Crane Recovery Team, U.S. Fish and Wildlife Service, the International Crane Foundation, Wisconsin Department of Natural Resources, The Natural Resources Foundation, Operation Migration (Canada), The Patuxent Wildlife Research Center, and the National Fish and Wildlife Foundation. This partnership has joined forces to safeguard the rarest species of crane in the world by assisting with the project's funding and support services. More than half of the funding for the project comes from private donations. The continuing project is aimed at eventually establishing 25 breeding pairs and a total of 125 individuals in this eastern population of the whooping crane, to help in the recovery of North America's tallest bird.

The wolf is another species of wildlife receiving special attention on this refuge. As explained by the U.S. Fish and Wildlife Service, Necedah Refuge "provides habitat for the southernmost pack of gray wolves in Wisconsin and the United States. The gray wolf (*Canis lupus*) was listed as federally endangered in Wisconsin in 1967, when only a handful remained. Today, wolves are on their way to recovery with 70 packs established in the northern and central portions of the state" as of 2001.

From mid-June through early August, the annual flights of the federally listed, endangered Karner blue butterfly (*Lycaeides melissa samuelis*) are a special attraction. Necedah Refuge currently has the largest population of this species in the world. These colorful little butterflies, with only a 1-inch wingspread, depend upon the refuge's oak-savanna habitat, where their larvae feed entirely upon lupine plants and the adults thrive on the nectar of various species of wildflowers. (For further information on this butterfly, see the Great Bay Refuge [New Hampshire] text.)

The refuge is open daily during daylight hours. There is no entrance fee. The refuge headquarters is open on weekdays, except national holidays.

Visitor activities include birdwatching; photography; viewing the refuge and wildlife from an observation tower and several decks; driving a 13-mile auto hot spots route on township roads that run through parts of the refuge; hiking on the self-guiding, interpretive Lupine Loop and two other designated trails; cross-country skiing and snowshoeing on ungroomed trails (from December 15 through March); nonmotorized boating, kayaking, and canoeing on Goose and Sprague pools; motorized boating (permitted only on the Suk-Cerney flowage); fishing in designated waters; and hunting on parts of the refuge during the designated seasons.

During the 9-day gun deer-hunting season, no other visitor activities are permitted on the refuge. Camping is not allowed on the refuge, but campground facilities are available at a number of nearby locations, including several state and county parks located on Petenwell and Castle Rock lakes. Over 220 bird species have been recorded on the refuge.

Hiking opportunities include the 0.25-mile Observation Tower Trail that leads to Rynearson Pool #1; the 1-mile, interpretive Lupine Trail that loops through a stretch of oak savanna; and the 1.3-mile Pair Ponds Trail that loops through waterfowl habitat containing nesting ponds, grassland, and sandy ridges.

Insect repellent is advised during the warmer months.

Lodgings and meals are available in such communities as Necedah, New Lisbon, Camp Douglas, Tomah, Black River Falls, and Wisconsin Rapids.

Access to Necedah Refuge from the New Lisbon Exit (#61) on I-94 is north 12 miles on State Route 80 to the town of Necedah, west (left) onto State Route 21, and following refuge directional signs to the refuge headquarters, located at the junction of Headquarters Road and Grand Dike Road (Twentieth Street West).

Further information: Necedah National Wildlife Refuge, W7996 Twentieth Street West, Necedah, WI 54646; telephone: (608) 565-2551.

Trempealeau, comprising 6,200 acres, was established in 1936 to restore, enhance, and protect floodplain wetland habitats that attract large concentrations of migratory waterfowl and other wildlife, adjacent to the Mississippi and Trempealeau rivers along the western edge of Wisconsin. *Trempealeau* is a French word meaning "mountain with wet feet."

This refuge initially contained just over 700 acres but was expanded in 1979 to its present size, with acquisition of the former Delta Fish and Fur Farm from Dairyland Power Cooperative. Approximately 80 percent of the refuge consists of marsh and open pools, and the remaining acreage supports scattered areas of swampy bottomland hardwoods, shrubby and meadow habitats, and several hundred acres of gently rolling, upland sand prairie.

As the U.S. Fish and Wildlife Service says:

Although now isolated from adjacent rivers by railroad dikes, Refuge wetlands were once backwaters of the Mississippi River. Hence, the remains of old river side channels and oxbows can be found in the western portion of the Refuge. Prior to 1900, the Trempealeau River entered the Mississippi from the north, forming a large delta at a point which is now at the center of the main Refuge pool. The Trempealeau River channel was later diverted to the east and barrier dikes were constructed to exclude floodwaters.

For 6 miles, a Burlington-Northern Santa Fe Railroad dike borders the southern edge of the refuge, between the western boundary and Trempealeau Mountain, which is on the adjacent Perrot State Park. This dike creates a barrier between the refuge's pool and the Mississippi River's main channel. No culverts exist to permit any interchange between the river and the pool.

Consequently, the refuge is protected from impacts of barge traffic and from river level fluctuations resulting from water level management by the U.S. Army Corps of Engineers (see Upper Mississippi River Refuge [Minnesota] text).

Prominent among the refuge's breeding waterfowl are wood ducks, which nest in cavities of bottomland hardwood trees. Several thousand of these colorful birds have been known to gather on Trempealeau Refuge in the autumn. Other abundant nesting species include blue-winged teal, mallards, hooded mergansers, and Canada geese.

The black tern has been the focus of special research on nesting habits and factors affecting nesting success and habitat quality. About 60 pairs of these birds build their nests within areas of dense water lily pads and stands of bulrushes and cattails, annually producing between 100 and 150 young. Tundra swans are a conspicuous migrant, with anywhere from 500 to nearly 1,000 pausing to rest and feed. A few bald eagles winter on the refuge; more than 200 of them can be seen when the ice goes out in the marsh, and there is at least one active eagle nest.

Trempealeau Refuge supports white-tailed deer, approximately 50 colonies of beavers, and lots of muskrats. Monarch butterflies thrive on the nectar of one of the refuge's most beautiful wildflowers—the blazing star.

One of the refuge's ecologically important management activities is prescription burning. As explained by the Fish and Wildlife Service,

Traveling through the refuge in the springtime, visitors will notice the blackened fields in several areas, where fire has occurred. Those fields may not look pleasing just after the refuge staff burns them, but in a few weeks native flowers, such as wild lupine and spiderwort, will be blooming. The grasses and flowers that are native to the refuge sand prairies have adapted [naturally] to fire. Fire restores vigor to the perennial native plants and helps the seeds of other plants to sprout. Fire also "sets back" the non-native grasses, such as brome, quack, and bluegrass and trees and shrubs that invade the prairie units.

Expansion of the refuge was made possible with money from the Land and Water Conservation Fund. As on so many national wildlife refuges, Trempealeau has a small staff that is supported by generous and enthusiastic volunteers.

The refuge is open daily during daylight hours. There is no entrance fee. The refuge headquarters is open on weekdays, except national holidays. Public access to the refuge is commonly restricted during annual spring high water, when part of the main entrance road is under water. Usually the refuge's Marshland Road is then open to motor vehicles. Occasionally both access routes are impassable.

Visitor activities include birdwatching; photography; viewing the marsh from an observation deck; driving the 5-mile, self-guiding loop, Wildlife Drive; hiking on several trails, dikes, and service roads; bicycling; cross-country skiing and snowshoeing on ungroomed trails; canoeing, kayaking, and boating (only hand-powered watercraft or boats with electric motors; a boat-launching ramp is available); fishing; ice fishing; and deer hunting (gun and archery) on parts of the refuge during the designated seasons. Around the middle of October, the refuge hosts a special 2-day waterfowl hunt for disabled hunters.

Hiking opportunities include a 0.5-mile, self-guiding, interpretive trail through a forested area; a 0.5-mile interpretive trail (including a wheelchair-accessible loop) through an area of sand prairie; and the 0.5-mile Pine Creek Dike Trail.

Insect repellent is advised during the warmer months.

Although camping is not permitted on the refuge, campground facilities are available on the adjacent Perrot State Park and elsewhere. Part of the Great River State Trail, popular for bicycling, runs through the refuge. The best months for observing large concentrations of migrating birds on the refuge are April through mid-May and October through mid-November. In mid-December, as at many refuges, Trempealeau Refuge takes part in an annual Christmas Bird Count.

The more than 250 species of birds that have been recorded on Trempealeau Refuge are much the same as those on Necedah Refuge.

Lodgings and meals are available in such communities as Winona, Minnesota and Trempealeau and Fountain City, Wisconsin.

Access to Trempealeau Refuge from Winona, Minnesota is across the Mississippi River on Wisconsin State Route 54, east (right) 5 miles on State Routes 54/35, and south (right) just over 1 mile on West Prairie Road, to the refuge entrance. From Trempealeau, WI, north 5 miles on route 35 to Centerville, west (left) on routes 35/54 just over 3 miles, and south (left) just over 1 mile on West Prairie Road.

Further information: Trempealeau National Wildlife Refuge, W28488 Refuge Road, Trempealeau, WI 54661; telephone: (608) 539-2311.

Upper Mississippi River (see text under Minnesota).

Whittlesey Creek was established in 1999 to enhance and protect important coastal wetland and spring-fed stream habitats for migratory birds and anadromous fish at the mouth of Whittlesey Creek. The refuge, which is part of an extensive, shallow wetland complex, is located at the head of Chequamegon Bay, on the shore of Lake Superior in northern Wisconsin.

Habitats within the projected refuge boundary of 540 acres include Lake Superior coastal wetlands, sedge meadow, lowland hardwood swamp, and black spruce bog. The U.S. Fish and Wildlife Service explains that refuge habitats have been:

altered substantially by human use. One hundred ten acres of sedge meadow was converted for agricultural use earlier this century and altered further for construction of a golf course. Four non-vegetated ponds were created during construction of the golf course. . . . Changes in water regime as well as past land use has changed wetland vegetation; most wet meadow acres are dominated by reed canary grass, an invasive wetland plant. Some wet meadows are becoming dominated by shrubs and might regrow to lowland swamp with black ash and cedar.

In 1949, the [U.S.] Army Corps of Engineers dredged 4,500 feet of Whittlesey Creek stream channel in an effort to de-water and stabilize the floodplain. . . .

Even with this significant alteration, the wetland portion of the [creek's] mouth constitutes a rare coastal wetland; and Whittlesey Creek remains a high-quality stream, with spring-fed waters that flow year-round.

A major habitat-management goal of the refuge is the restoration and protection of Whittlesey, Little Whittlesey, and Terwilliger creeks for the benefit of migrating, spawning, and rearing of an anadromous coho salmon and a strain of brook trout, known as "coaster" brook trout, from Lake Superior; restoration, as much as possible, of the historical hydrologic conditions of Whittlesey Creek and coastal wetlands. Other planned activities include the restoration and management of habitat for waterfowl, neotropical songbirds, and other migratory birds; the enhancement of existing constructed ponds for the benefit of wildlife; management of the refuge for compatible wildlife-dependent recreational uses; and coordination of these management activities with adjacent public-land managers—notably the Wisconsin Department of Natural Resources and the U.S. Forest Service's Northern Great Lakes Visitor Center.

As the U.S. Fish and Wildlife Service explains, "The Service intends to continue its partnership with the Northern Great Lakes Visitor Center, which includes . . . having one or more Service staff at the Center and contributing to the Center's mission. This staff will oversee Refuge operations and help develop and coordinate education and interpretive programs at the Center and Refuge."

Refuge manager Pam Dryer says: "The Whittlesey Creek Refuge is a little refuge with a big impact. It has a quality coastal wetland that helps feed the huge Lake Superior, it has a significant anadromous fish population, and it protects the last remaining stretch of the large coastal wetland complex in Chequamegon Bay."

It is expected that the refuge will be open daily during daylight hours, when sufficient lands have been acquired. Priority visitor uses are planned to include wildlife observation, photography, hiking, interpretive and conservation education programs, fishing, and hunting (waterfowl) on part of the refuge during the designated seasons. The adjacent Northern Great Lakes Visitor Center is open daily, except Thanksgiving, Christmas, and New Year's Day.

Lodgings and meals are available in Ashland.

Access to the Northern Great Lakes Visitor Center is west 2 miles on U.S. Route 2 from Ashland.

Further information: Whittlesey Creek National Wildlife Refuge, 29270 County Highway G, Ashland, WI 54806; telephone: (715) 685-2678.

Wisconsin: Wetland Management Districts

Leopold Wetland Management District was established in 1993 to restore, enhance, and protectively manage scattered areas of ecologically important wetland and grassland habitats in 33 eastern Wisconsin counties.

This extensive district includes more than 8,800 acres in 41 federally owned waterfowl production areas (WPAs), and many additional tracts being protectively managed under the terms of perpetual wetland and grassland easement agreements with private landowners. Acquisition of the WPAs has been accomplished mostly with revenues from the sale of Migratory Bird Hunting and Conservation Stamps (Duck Stamps).

The WPAs are generally open to visitation during daylight hours. There are no entrance fees. Other than parking areas, no visitor use facilities are provided. Visitor activities include wildlife observation, photography, hiking, fishing, and hunting during the designated seasons.

Further information: Leopold Wetland Management District, c/o Horicon NWR, W4279 Headquarters Road, Mayville, WI 53050; telephone: (920) 387-2658.

St. Croix Wetland Management District was established in 1992 to restore, protect, and manage scattered areas of ecologically important wetland and grassland habitats at the eastern edge of the tallgrass prairie in northwestern Wisconsin.

The district includes more than 7,000 federally owned acres on 40 waterfowl production areas (WPAs) in St. Croix, Polk, and Dunn counties. More than 1,100 additional acres are being managed under the terms of conservation easement agreements with private landowners. Acquisition of the WPAs has been accomplished mostly with revenues from the sale of Migratory Bird Hunting and Conservation Stamps (Duck Stamps).

The St. Croix district encompasses the most important waterfowl breeding area in Wisconsin for mallards, wood ducks, and blue-winged teal. West-central St. Croix County includes roughly 5,000 WPA acres and is ranked sixth out of 26 state priority landscapes for species of grassland birds. Resident wildlife in the district's WPAs includes white-tailed deer, red fox, beaver, muskrat, wild turkey, ring-necked pheasant, and ruffed grouse.

The WPAs are generally open to visitation during daylight hours. There are no entrance fees. Other than parking areas, no visitor use facilities are provided. Visitor activities include wildlife observation, photography, hiking, environmental education and interpretation, fishing, and hunting during the designated seasons.

Further information: St. Croix Wetland Management District, 1764 Ninety-Fifth Street, New Richmond, WI 54017; telephone: (715) 246-0844.

Wyoming

Bamforth, containing 1,160 acres, was established in 1932 to protect an occasionally flooded salt flat (playa) about 6 miles northwest of Laramie in southeastern Wyoming. When there is water, this refuge is a small mecca for waterfowl and shorebirds. Pronghorn, coyotes, white-tailed jackrabbits, desert cottontails, ground squirrels, horned lizards, and prairie rattlesnakes inhabit the area. There is no public access.

Further information: Bamforth National Wildlife Refuge, c/o Arapaho NWR, P.O. Box 457, Walden, CO 80480; telephone: (970) 723-8202.

Cokeville Meadows was established in 1992 to enhance and protect ecologically significant wetland and upland habitats along a 16-mile stretch of the Bear River floodplain, just south of the town of Cokeville in the southwest corner of Wyoming. The refuge is currently in an acquisition phase, with 7,677 acres already purchased within the proposed 27,000-acre refuge boundary. It includes ponds, deep-water marshes, wet-meadow impoundments, irrigated croplands, riparian woodlands, and arid uplands of sagebrush and grasses.

This area is important for nesting Canada geese; numerous species of nesting and migratory diving and dabbling ducks, notably redheads; colonies of snowy egrets and white-faced ibises; great blue herons; black-crowned night herons; black terns; many shorebirds, including long-billed curlews; and migratory greater sandhill cranes. More than 60 species of water birds have been recorded here, half of which nest on the refuge. According to wildlife managers, this area is "the largest, most productive, and most diverse producer of birds known to exist in Wyoming" and "supports one of the highest densities of nesting waterfowl" in this state.

Sage-grouse, which inhabit the U.S. Bureau of Land Management's adjacent sagebrush uplands, perform their incredible courtship displays in the spring (see the Seedskadee text for description). Prominent mammals are pronghorn, mule deer, and roughly 400 elk that winter on the refuge.

As Cokeville Meadows is a new refuge, with additional lands yet to be acquired, it may remain closed until sufficient land and management funding are available to safely permit visitor activities. For information on public access, contact the refuge complex manager at Seedskadee National Wildlife Refuge.

Lodgings and meals are available in the communities of Cokeville, Kemmerer, Diamondville, and Evanston, Wyoming; Montpelier, Idaho; and Logan, Utah.

Further information: Cokeville Meadows National Wildlife Refuge, c/o Seedskadee NWR, P.O. Box 700, Green River, WY 82935; telephone (307) 875-2187.

Hutton Lake, consisting of 1,968 acres, was established in 1932 to protect a cluster of five lakes and related bulrush wetland that provide important breeding and resting habitat for migratory waterfowl and other wildlife in southeastern Wyoming.

More than a quarter of the refuge is open water and marsh, and most of the rest is damp meadows and arid native grassland, with scattered draws and alkali flats. Small though these lakes are, they attract many species of water birds—especially in April, when concentrations sometimes total as many as 15,000 to 20,000 ducks. Numerous birds nest on the refuge, notably redheads, mallards, teal, wigeons, pintails, shovelers, canvasbacks, ruddy ducks, grebes, phalaropes, and avocets. Over 275 bird species have been seen here.

The refuge is open daily during daylight hours. There is no entrance fee.

Visitor activities include birdwatching, photography, and hiking.

Visitors are cautioned to be alert for rattlesnakes.

Lodgings and meals are available in Laramie.

Access to the refuge is southwest 12 miles on State Route 230 from Laramie; left (east) onto County Road 37 for 7 miles; and left (northeast) onto State Route 34 for about 3.5 miles to the entrance road.

Further information: Hutton Lake National Wildlife Refuge, c/o Arapaho NWR, P.O. Box 457, Walden, CO 80480; telephone: (970) 723-8202.

Mortenson Lake, containing 1,776 acres, was established in 1993 to enhance and protect four areas of wetland habitat, for the benefit of the last known breeding population of Wyoming toad (*Bufo hemiophrys baxteri*). The range of this subspecies is limited to the Laramie plains in southeastern Wyoming.

A captive breeding program for the toad has been implemented over the past few years. According to the U.S. Fish and Wildlife Service:

In 1984, the Wyoming toad was listed as a Federally endangered species and in 1987 a small population was discovered within the historical range at Mortenson Lake. In 1988, the Wyoming Toad Recovery Team was established hoping to prevent extinction of the small population by addressing toad habitat, reproduction and human impact.

The population steadily declined over the years with contributing factors thought to be a fungus disease, combined with red leg, a bacterial disease that has been documented to kill toads in the wild. In 1990, a captive population of toads was initiated using young-of-the-year from Mortenson Lake. . . . In 1993 all toads found in the wild at Mortenson Lake were removed and placed in captivity. Captive breeding efforts have continued over the years with success fluctuating from one egg mass to sixteen egg masses. Toad releases at Mortenson have occurred since 1995 with numbers ranging between 500 and 6,600 individuals released. Annual surveys of the toads are conducted every spring and fall, and have produced up to 295 juveniles and 27 adults.

As of this writing, continuing efforts still hold out the hope that this vulnerable amphibian can be saved from extinction.

The Nature Conservancy initially helped purchase a major part of this refuge.

Visitor entry onto Mortenson Lake Refuge is not permitted.

Further information: Mortenson Lake National Wildlife Refuge, c/o Arapaho NWR Complex, P.O. Box 457, Walden, CO 80480; telephone: (970) 723-8202.

National Elk Refuge, containing 24,778 acres, was established in 1912 to enhance and protect important wintering habitat for the Jackson Hole herd of Rocky Mountain elk (*Cervus canadensis canadensis*). The refuge adjoins the southern boundary of Grand Teton National Park, in northwestern Wyoming. Elk are also called wapiti, a Shawnee Indian name for "white rump," in reference to their pale-yellowish rump.

During the unusually bitter cold and snowy winters of 1909, 1910, and 1911, thousands of elk perished for lack of adequate forage. In response to the request of many alarmed local citizens, who asked for help from both the state and federal governments, funds were provided to purchase hay for the starving animals and to acquire the initial acreage for the National Elk Refuge.

From November through April, the refuge supports roughly 7,500 of these great mammals—more than half of the herd's total population. Most of them spend the summer at higher, cooler elevations in the forests and meadows of Grand Teton National Park, the southern part of Yellowstone National Park, and the Bridger-Teton National Forest. This is the longest elk herd migration in the United States, outside Alaska. The National Elk Refuge provides vital elk wintering habitat as an integral part of the Greater Yellowstone Ecosystem. Although farms, ranches, ranchettes, and the town of Jackson occupy much of the valley's original elk-wintering range, the National Elk Refuge protects about a quarter of the historic wintering habitat.

The carrying capacity of the refuge is determined by the U.S. Fish and Wildlife Service staff, in consultation with the Wyoming Game and Fish Department. So as to not exceed the habitat's capacity to sustain these grazing and browsing animals, an annual, late autumn, regulated elk hunt is carried out on the refuge and adjacent public lands. In the past, some elk have also been transplanted from the refuge to establish small populations in other parts of the United States.

Jackson Hole Valley is magnificently framed by the jagged peaks of the Teton Mountains to the northwest and the Gros Ventre Range to the southeast. Refuge habitats include grassy meadows, marshes, ponds, aspen groves, riparian woodland along the Gros Ventre River, and scattered rock outcroppings on sagebrush-covered foothills of the Gros Ventres. The highest point on the refuge is atop 6,509-foot Miller Butte.

The Fish and Wildlife Service maintains the refuge's grassland forage with an irrigation system, seeding, and periodic prescribed burns. When the depth of snow or a hard, icy crust prevents the elk from reaching the natural forage, the refuge provides them with pelletized alfalfa hay. To assist with the cost of elk feeding, the local troop of Boy Scouts holds an annual auction, on the Jackson town square, of elk antlers that have been shed on the refuge.

Other large ungulates (hoofed mammals) that usually spend the winter here include bighorn sheep, moose, mule deer, and approximately 500 bison (buffalo). Among other wildlife are trumpeter swans, Canada geese, and many species of ducks that are attracted to the refuge's ponds and marshes. The greater sage-grouse inhabits the sagebrush habitat (see Seedskadee Refuge for description of this grouse). More than 170 species of birds have been recorded here. November through April are the best months for viewing the elk and other wintering wildlife.

Management of the National Elk Refuge is greatly aided by numerous volunteers, partnerships, and cooperative agreements.

The refuge is open daily during daylight hours. There is no entrance fee. The visitor center, at 532 North Cache Street in Jackson, is open daily, except on Christmas. The refuge headquarters is east 1 mile from the Jackson town square, on Broadway Street, and is open on weekdays, except Christmas.

Autumn is the beginning of the elk herd's courtship and mating season, known as the rut, which occurs in the high country of the nearby national parks and national forests. Piercing, musical bugling of the big, antlered bulls echoes across the land. Fierce rivalry is commonplace as they round up and defend their harems of a dozen or more cows. As Victor H. Cahalane describes in his book, *Mammals of North America*, ". . . their antlers clashed together like great rattling sabers." Later in the autumn, heavier mountain snows force the elk to migrate out of the high country, and by late October and early November, they begin arriving onto the National Elk Refuge, within their historic wintering range.

Visitor activities include wildlife observation; photography; viewing wildlife from turnouts along the east side of U.S. Route 26; educational programs and exhibits at the museum and at the refuge's visitor center; driving unpaved refuge roads (Flat Creek and Curtis Canyon roads are open seasonally); limited hiking; interpretive, horse-drawn sleigh rides (a fee is charged, and passengers must dress very warmly) from late December through March, beginning at the National Museum of Wildlife Art (located 2 miles north of Jackson on U.S. Route 26); picnicking (facilities are provided), trout fishing (some refuge waters are closed to fishing), and elk hunting on the northern half of the refuge during the designated season (a limited number of elk permits is issued under a system of weekly drawings). The Jackson Hole elk herd has provided more than a dozen measured Boone and Crockett Club trophies. The refuge also hosts an annual Boy Scouts antler pick-up project and auction. Although camping is not permitted on the refuge, campground facilities are available in nearby Grand Teton and Yellowstone national parks and in the Bridger-Teton National Forest.

Lodgings and meals are available in Jackson, and in Grand Teton and Yellowstone national parks.

Access to the National Elk Refuge is just north of Jackson and south of Grand Teton National Park.

Further information: National Elk Refuge, P.O. Box 510, Jackson, WY 83001; telephone: (307) 733-9212.

Pathfinder, comprising 16,807 acres, was established in 1936 to manage and protect habitat for waterfowl and other water birds, overlaying four parts of the Water & Power Resources Service's Pathfinder Reservoir, 50 miles southwest of Casper in east-central Wyoming. The largest part encompasses the Sweetwater Arm of the reservoir. The refuge provides important resting, feeding, and breeding areas for concentrations of migratory ducks and Canada geese. The adjacent semidesert is inhabited by such species of wildlife as sage-grouse, mule deer, pronghorn, bobcats, coyotes, badgers, white-tailed jackrabbits, desert cottontails, and ground squirrels.

The refuge is open daily during daylight hours. There is no entrance fee. No visitor facilities are provided, and access to this isolated refuge is difficult. Reservoir levels fluctuate annually as much as 50 feet.

Visitor activities include birdwatching, photography, fishing, and hunting (waterfowl, sage-grouse, deer, pronghorn, and rabbit) during the designated seasons.

Visitors are cautioned to be alert for rattlesnakes.

Lodgings and meals are available in Casper.

Access to the refuge is southwest about 50 miles on State Route 220 from Casper. From Route 220, Buzzard Road passes near the upper end of the reservoir's Sweetwater Arm. Dirt roads branch from this road to the lakeshore and from Pathfinder Road, which leads to Pathfinder Dam.

Further information: Pathfinder National Wildlife Refuge, c/o Arapaho NWR, P.O. Box 457, Walden, CO 80480; telephone: (970) 723-8202.

Seedskadee, consisting of 26,382 acres, was established in 1965 to enhance and protect a scenic, 36-mile stretch of the Green River, in the Green River Valley of southwestern Wyoming. The refuge consists of a mix of cottonwoods, willows, and marsh habitat and expanses of arid, sagebrush-covered uplands. The refuge's name is derived from a Shoshone Indian word, *sisk-a-dee-agie*, which means "river of the prairie hen," for the sage-grouse that inhabits this area. The name was subsequently altered by early nineteenth-century Euro-American fur trappers.

This refuge was established to help offset the loss of marsh and riparian habitats that resulted from construction of the U.S. Bureau of Reclamation's Fontenelle Dam, upstream from the refuge, and the Flaming Gorge Dam, downstream. The bureau has provided funds to acquire refuge lands and complete habitat enhancement projects. Some of the river water is diverted into adjacent human-made wetland impoundments, to restore important marsh habitat. The water level in these wetlands is seasonally regulated by the U.S. Fish and Wildlife Service, to provide sufficient water for a large variety of wetland species such as trumpeter swans, geese, ducks, shorebirds, and rails during the spring, summer, and autumn months. Near the marshy impoundments, native shrubs and grasses offers vital cover for nesting ducks.

Elsewhere along the river's former floodplain, groves of cottonwood trees and thickets of willows are dwindling because of the declining water table and the lack of annual flooding. The refuge is trying to find ways to promote the growth of young cottonwoods, willows, and shrubs that provide food and shelter for such species as moose, mule deer, raptors, and songbirds.

Sagebrush uplands predominate on lands beyond the riparian bottomlands. Here the refuge is working to enhance habitat degradation caused by earlier overgrazing by livestock. Fencing is helping restore native shrubs and grasses to these areas.

One of the star attractions of the upland sagebrush areas of Seedskadee Refuge is the greater sage-grouse (*Centrocercus urophasianus*). These large, grayish birds, which Lewis and Clark referred to as "cocks of the plains," are the size of a small turkey—the males measuring 28 to 30 inches in length. In the spring, the cocks congregate and strut about, rapidly and repeatedly performing their elaborate courtship displays.

Other prominent species of wildlife are moose, pronghorn, mule deer, prairie dogs, golden eagles, American white pelicans, trumpeter swans, Canada geese, various species of ducks and shorebirds, many neotropical migratory songbirds, and sandhill cranes. More than 225 species of birds have been recorded here.

The refuge is open daily during daylight hours. There is no entrance fee. The refuge head-quarters, containing a small visitor center, is open on weekdays, except national holidays.

Visitor activities include wildlife observation; photography; driving the refuge's three grav-eled tour routes; hiking; canoeing, rafting, and drift-boating on the river (four boat-launching sites are provided within the refuge, and another is upstream near Fontenelle Dam); fishing (the river supports a trophy trout fishery); and hunting (deer, pronghorn, waterfowl, and upland game). Seasonal closures on portions of the refuge are sometimes implemented to decrease dis-turbance of sensitive species. Although camping is not permitted on the refuge, campground fa-cilities are available near Fontenelle Dam.

The refuge's elevation is close to 6,500 feet. Winter visitors are advised to be well prepared for bitter cold and snowy conditions. Regardless of the season, the Fish and Wildlife Service advises visitors to bring adequate water, food, and fuel, as Seedskadee is 15 miles from the clos-est store and service station and 37 miles from the nearest town of Green River.

Lodgings and meals are available in such communities as Green River, Rock Springs, Kem-merer, Diamondville, LaBarge, and Farson.

Access to Seedskadee Refuge is west 6 miles on I-80 from Green River to exit 83, northwest about 28 miles on State Route 372, and east 2 miles to the refuge headquarters.

Further information: Seedskadee National Wildlife Refuge, P.O. Box 700, Green River, WY 82935; telephone: (307) 875-2187.

5

Friends and Other Refuge Support Organizations

Alabama

Friends of Bon Secour NWR
12295 State Highway 180
Gulf Shores, AL 36542
(334) 540-7720

Wheeler Wildlife Refuge Association
P.O. Box 239
Decatur, AL 35602
(256) 544-5930

Alaska

Alaska Natural History Association
401 West First Avenue
Anchorage, AK 99501
(907) 274-8440

Friends of the Kenai NWR
P.O. Box 1449
Soldotna, AK 99669
(907) 562-5451

Arizona

Friends of Buenos Aires NWR
P.O. Box 65855
Tucson, AZ 85728
(800) 714-4365

Friends of Cabeza Prieta
P.O. Box 64940
Tucson, AZ 85728
(520) 387-6483

Arkansas

Friends of Felsenthal NWR
P.O. Box 1157
Crossett, AR 71635
(870) 226-6679

California

Dunes Center (Guadalupe-Nipomo Dunes
   NWR)
P.O. Box 339
Guadalupe, CA 93435
(805) 343-2455

Friends of Havasu
P.O. Box 3009
Needles, CA 92363
(760) 326-3853

Friends of Seal Beach NWR
P.O. Box 815
Seal Beach, CA 90740
(562) 430-8495 or 598-1024

Friends of the Dunes (re: Humboldt Bay
   NWR)
P.O. Box 186
Arcata, CA 95518
(707) 444-1397

Friends of the Sacramento Valley Wildlife
   Refuges
P.O. Box 5227
Chico, CA 95927
(530) 898-8468

Friends of the San Diego Refuges
c/o Tijuana Slough NWR
301 Caspian Way
Imperial Beach, CA 91932
(619) 575-2704

Klamath Basin Wildlife Association
Route 1, Box 74
Tulelake, CA 96134
(530) 667-2231

Sacramento Valley Wildlife Association
752 County Road 99W
Willows, CA 95988
(530) 934-2801

Salton Sea Wildlife Association
906 West Sinclair Road
Calipatria, CA 92233
(760) 348-5278

San Francisco Bay Wildlife Society
P.O. Box 524
Newark, CA 94560
(510) 792-0222

Stone Lakes NWR Association
2233 Watt Avenue, Suite 230
Sacramento, CA 95825
(209) 953-8840

Colorado

Friends of San Luis Valley NWR
9383 El Rancho Lane
Alamosa, CO 81101
(719) 587-7211

Rocky Mountain Arsenal Wildlife Society
c/o RMA NWR, Building 111
Commerce City, CO 80022
(303) 289-0820

Two Ponds Preservation Foundation
7692 Garrison Court
Arvada, CO 80002
(303) 423-8085

Delaware

Friends of Bombay Hook
2591 Whitehall Neck Road
Smyrna, DE 19977
(302) 653-6872

Friends of Prime Hook NWR
RD 3, Box 195
Milton, DE 19968
(302) 684-8419

Florida

"Ding" Darling Wildlife Society
c/o J. N. "Ding" Darling NWR
1 Wildlife Drive
Sanibel, FL 33957
(941) 472-1100

Friends and Volunteers of the Refuges
   (Florida Keys)
P.O. Box 431840
Big Pine Key, FL 33043
(305) 872-0645

Friends of the Chassahowitzka NWR
   Complex
1502 Southeast Kings Bay Drive
Crystal River, FL 34429
(352) 563-2088

Friends of the Florida Panther Refuge
3860 Tollgate Boulevard, Suite 300
Naples, FL 34114
(941) 947-3567

Hobe Sound Nature Center, Inc.
P.O. Box 214
Hobe Sound, FL 33475
(561) 546-2067

Loxahatchee Natural History Association
P.O. Box 2737
Delray Beach, FL 33447
(561) 338-5190

Merritt Island Wildlife Association
c/o Merritt Island NWR
P.O. Box 6504
Titusville, FL 32782
(407) 861-0667

Pelican Island Preservation Society
P.O. Box 781903
Sebastian, FL 32978
(561) 663-9750

St. Marks Refuge Association
c/o St. Marks NWR
P.O. Box 368
St. Marks, FL 32355
(850) 386-9212

Georgia

Okefenokee Wildlife League
c/o Okefenokee NWR
Route 2, Box 3330
Folkston, GA 31537
(912) 496-7836

Hawai'i

1000 Friends of Kauai
P.O. Box 698
Kilauea, HI 96754
(808) 828-2166

Friends of Midway Atoll NWR
1048 Edison Avenue
New York, NY 10465
(800) 371-0772

Kilauea Point Natural History Association
c/o Kilauea Point NWR
P.O. Box 1128
Kilauea, HI 96754
(808) 828-1413

Illinois

Friends of Crab Orchard
8588 Route 148
Marion, IL 62918
(618) 997-3344

Friends of Illinois River
700 East Adams
Springfield, IL 62701
(217) 525-7980

Friends of the Cache River Watershed (re:
    Cypress Creek NWR)
1220 Old Highway 51N
Anna, IL 62906
(618) 833-5343

Indiana

Muscatatuck Wildlife Society
c/o Muscatatuck NWR
12987 East U.S. Highway 50
Seymour, IN 47274
(812) 579-5127

PRIDE (re: Patoka River NWR)
540 Oriole Drive
Evansville, IN 47715
(812) 476-3248

Iowa

Friends of the Prairie Learning Center
c/o Neal Smith NWR
P.O. Box 399
Prairie City, IA 50228
(515) 787-5705

Friends of Union Slough NWR
1710 - 360th Street
Titonka, IA 50480
(515) 928-2523

Midwest Interpretive Association
c/o Desoto NWR
1434-316th Lane
Missouri Valley, IA 51555
(712) 642-2772

Kansas

Friends of Quivira NWR
2458 Coolidge
Wichita, KS 67204
(316) 838-4062

Louisiana

Friends of Black Bayou, Inc.
P.O. Box 9241
Monroe, LA 71211
(318) 387-5906

Friends of Cat Island NWR, Inc.
P.O. Box 1926
St. Francisville, LA 70775
(225) 635-4753

Friends of Louisiana Wildlife Refuges, Inc.
P.O. Box 890
Lacombe, LA 70445
(504) 646-7555

Tensas River Refuge Association
Route 2, Box 295
Tallulah, LA 71282
(318) 574-2664

Maine

Friends of Aroostook NWR
P.O. Box 121
Caribou, ME 04736
(207) 498-3639

Friends of Rachel Carson NWR
P.O. Box 7427
Ocean Park, ME 04063
(207) 646-9226

Friends of Sunkhaze Meadows NWR
1033 South Main Street
Old Town, ME 04468
(207) 827-6138

Maryland

Friends of Blackwater NWR, Inc.
5123 Brook Road
Woolford, MD 21613
(410) 221-1874

Friends of Eastern Neck, Inc.
21170 Green Lane
Rock Hall, MD 21661
(410) 639-7085

Friends of Patuxent Wildlife Research
    Center
c/o Patuxent Wildlife Research Center
10901 Scarlet Tanager Loop
Laurel, MD 20708
(301) 262-1010

Massachusetts

Friends of Great Meadows NWR
63 Lexington Road
Concord, MA 01742
(617) 248-8468

Friends of Mashpee NWR
P.O. Box 1283
Mashpee, MA 02649
(508) 495-1702

Friends of Monomoy NWR
c/o Monomoy NWR
Wikis Way
Chatham, MA 02633
(617) 720-6333

Friends of Oxbow NWR
P.O. Box 646
Bolton, MA 01740
(978) 779-2259

Friends of Parker River NWR
P.O. Box 184
Newburyport, MA 01950
(978) 749-9647

Michigan

Friends of Shiawassee NWR
P.O. Box 20129
Saginaw, MI 48602
(517) 790-3178

Seney Natural History Association
c/o Seney NWR
HCR #2, Box 1
Seney, MI 49883
(906) 586-9851

Minnesota

Big Stone Natural History Association
902 South Seventh Street
Milbank, SD 57252
(605) 432-6158

Friends of Rydell Refuge Association
Route 3, Box 75A
Erskine, MN 56535
(218) 574-2622

Friends of Sherburne NWR
c/o Sherburne NWR
17076-293rd Avenue
Zimmerman, MN 55398
(612) 389-1696

Friends of the Minnesota Valley
c/o Minnesota Valley NWR Visitor Center
3815 East Eightieth Street
Bloomington, MN 55426
(612) 858-0706

Friends of the Prairie Wetlands Learning
Center
c/o Fergus Falls WMD
P.O. Box 23
Fergus Falls, MN 56537
(218) 826-6515

Tamarac Interpretive Association
35704 County Highway 26
Rochert, MN 56578
(218) 847-2641

Mississippi

Friends of Dahomey NWR, Inc.
123 South Court Street
Cleveland, MS 38732
(601) 843-6100

St. Catherine Creek Refuge Association,
  Inc.
P.O. Box 1027
Natchez, MS 39121
(601) 442-0585

Missouri

Friends of Big Muddy
P.O. Box 58
Columbia, MO 65205
(573) 445-0086

Friends of Squaw Creek NWR
9718 East Fifty-Third Street
Raytown, MO 64133
(816) 353-9024

Midwest Interpretive Association
c/o Mingo NWR
RR 1, Box 103
Puxico, MO 63960
(314) 222-3589

Montana

Glacier Natural History Association
c/o National Bison Range
P.O. Box 428
West Glacier, MT 59936
(406) 888-5756

Nebraska

Fort Niobrara Natural History Association
839 West B Street
Valentine, NE 69201
(402) 376-5901 or 3789

Nevada

Friends of Sheldon Refuge
P.O. Box 3107
Winnemucca, NV 89445
(775) 623-3376

Order of the Antelope
P.O. Box 613
Lakeview, OR 97630
(541) 947-3147

New Hampshire

Friends of Great Bay NWR
336 Nimble Hill Road
Newington, NH 03801
(603) 523-1136

Friends of John Hay NWR
P.O. Box 276
Newbury, NH 03255
(603) 763-4789

Friends of Pondicherry (re: Silvio O. Conte
 NWR)
Owl's Head Highway, Box 157A
Jefferson, NH 03583
(603) 586-4598

Friends of Umbagog
3 Silk Farm Road
Concord, NH 03301
(603) 224-9909, ext. 317

Friends of Wapack
P.O. Box 115
Peterborough, NH 03468
(603) 878-4251

New Jersey

Friends of Forsythe NWR
P.O. Box 355
Oceanville, NJ 08231
(609) 641-4671

Friends of Great Swamp NWR
c/o Great Swamp NWR
152 Pleasant Plains Road
Basking Ridge, NJ 07920
(973) 635-1083

New Mexico

Friends of Bitter Lake NWR
P.O. Box 7
Roswell, NM 88202
(505) 622-6755

Friends of Bosque del Apache NWR
P.O. Box 340
San Antonio, NM 87832
(505) 835-1828

New York

Friends of Iroquois NWR
c/o Iroquois NWR
1101 Casey Road
Basom, NY 14013
(716) 948-9154

Friends of Montezuma NWR
c/o Montezuma NWR
3395 Route 5 & 20E
Seneca Falls, NY 13148
(315) 568-5987

Friends of Wertheim
P.O. Box 376
Brookhaven, NY 11719
(516) 286-5897

North Carolina

Coastal Wildlife Society (re: Alligator River
    and Pea Island NWRs)
P.O. Box 1808
Manteo, NC 27954
(252) 473-1131, ext. 230

Friends of Pee Dee NWR
8138 Cedarbrook Drive
Charlotte, NC 28215
(800) 476-8220

Partnership for the Sounds
P.O. Box 55
Columbia, NC 27925
(252) 796-1000

Red Wolf Coalition
P.O. Box 2318
Kill Devil Hills, NC 27948
(252) 441-3946

North Dakota

Chase Lake Foundation (re: Chase Lake
    NWR)
3156 Fifty-Fifth Avenue SE
Medina, ND 58467
(701) 486-3228

Sullys Hill Wildlife Refuge Society
P.O. Box 286
Ft. Totten, ND 58335
(701) 766-4573

Theodore Roosevelt Nature and History
    Association (re: Sullys Hill NGP and
    Upper Souris NWR)
P.O. Box 167
Medora, ND 58745
(701) 623-4884

Ohio

Ottawa NWR Association
P.O. Box 254
Oak Harbor, OH 43449
(419) 836-8411

Oklahoma

Association of the Friends of the Wichitas
(re: Wichita Mountains WR)
P.O. Box 7402
Lawton, OK 73506
(580) 537-5488

Great Salt Plains Association (re: Salt
Plains NWR)
111 South Grand
Cherokee, OK 73728
(580) 596-3053

Friends of Tishomingo Refuge
P.O. Box 144
Tishomingo, OK 73460
(580) 371-9248

Oregon

Friends of Sheldon Refuge (re: Sheldon
and Hart Mountain NWRs)
P.O. Box 3107
Winnemucca, NV 89445
(775) 623-3376

Malheur Refuge Association
c/o Malheur NWR
HC 72, Box 245
Princeton, OR 97721
(541) 493-2612

Friends of the Tualatin River NWR
P.O. Box 1306
Sherwood, OR 97140
(503) 625-1205

Order of the Antelope
P.O. Box 613
Lakeview, OR 97630
(541) 947-3147

Pennsylvania

Friends of Heinz Wildlife Refuge at Tinicum
2 International Plaza, Suite 104
Philadelphia, PA 19113
(610) 534-0698

Rhode Island

Friends of the NWRs of Rhode Island
P.O. Box 553
Charlestown, RI 02813
(401) 364-9124

South Carolina

SEWEE Association, Inc. (re: Cape Romain NWR)
P.O. Box 1131
Mt. Pleasant, SC 29465
(843) 884-7539

South Dakota

Friends of the Prairie
P.O. Box 446
Milbank, SD 57252
(605) 432-9229

Tennessee

Friends of Hatchie Refuge
4172 Highway 76
South Brownsville, TN 38012
(731) 772-0501, ext. 25

Friends of Reelfoot NWR (also re: Lake Isom NWR)
Room 129, Federal Building
Dyersville, TN 38024
(731) 287-0650

Texas

Friends of Anahuac Refuge
111 Welch, Apartment B
Houston, TX 77006
(409) 267-3080

Friends of Aransas and Matagorda Island NWRs
P.O. Box 74
Aransas, TX 77950
(361) 286-3559

Friends of Balcones
c/o Balcones Canyonlands NWR
10711 Burnett Road, Ste 201
Austin, TX 78758
(515) 339-9432

Friends of Brazoria NWR
P.O. Box 505
Lake Jackson, TX 77566
(409) 297-7726

Friends of Laguna Atascosa NWR
P.O. Box 465
Rio Hondo, TX 78583
(956) 428-4897

Friends of the Wildlife Corridor (re: Lower
  Rio Grande Valley NWR)
Route 2, Box 204
Alamo, TX 78516
(956) 783-6117

Friends of Trinity River Refuge
P.O. Box 12
Liberty, TX 77575
(936) 336-9847

Valley Nature Center (re: Santa Ana
  NWR)
P.O. Box 8125
Weslaco, TX 78599
(956) 969-2475

Utah

Friends of the Bear River Bird Refuge
58 South 950 West
Brigham City, UT 84302
(435) 734-9464

Vermont

Friends of Missisquoi NWR
371 N. River Street
Swanton, VT 05488
(802) 868-4781

Virginia

Friends of Back Bay
2232 Sandpiper Road
Virginia Beach, VA 23456
(757) 721-5011

Chincoteague Natural History Association
  (also re: Eastern Shore of Virginia
  NWR)
c/o Chincoteague NWR
P.O. Box 917
Chincoteague, VA 23336
(757) 336-3696

Great Dismal Swamp Coalition, Inc.
P.O. Box 847
Suffolk, VA 23439
(757) 986-3705

Washington

Friends of Ridgefield NWR
c/o Ridgefield NWR
Ridgefield, WA 98642
(360) 887-4106

Friends of Willapa NWR
P.O. Box 627
Ocean Park, WA 98640
(360) 665-6859

Friends of Turnbull NWR
P.O. Box 294
Cheney, WA 99004
(509) 328-0621

West Virginia

Friends of the 500th (re: Canaan Valley NWR)
P.O. Box 422
Davis, WV 26260
(304) 866-4114

Wisconsin

Friends of Necedah NWR
1830 County
Clarkdale, WI 54613
(608) 564-7104

Midwest Interpretive Association
c/o Horicon NWR
West 4279 Headquarters Road
Mayville, WI 53050
(414) 387-2658

Friends of the Upper Mississippi River
    Refuges
West 5094 Highland Place
La Crosse, WI 54601
(608) 787-0853

Upper Mississippi River Interpretive
    Association
555 Lester Avenue
Onalaska, WI 54650
(608) 783-8403

Wyoming

National Museum of Wildlife Art
c/o National Elk Refuge
P.O. Box 6825
Jackson, WY 83002
(307) 733-5771

National Organizations

Boone and Crockett Club
250 Station Drive
Missoula, MT 59801
(406) 542-1888
www.boone-crockett.org

Defenders of Wildlife
1101 14th Street, NW, Suite 1400
Washington, DC 20005
(877) 682-9400
www.defenders.org

Ducks Unlimited, Inc.
One Waterfowl Way
Memphis, TN 38120
(901) 758-3825
www.ducks.org

National Audubon Society
700 Broadway
New York, NY 10003
(212) 979-3000
www.audubon.org

National Park Trust
415 Second Street, Northeast
Washington, DC 20002
(202) 548-0500
www.parktrust.org

National Wildlife Refuge Association
1010 Wisconsin Avenue, Northwest
Washington, DC 20007
(202) 333-9075
www.refugenet.org

The Nature Conservancy
4245 North Fairfax Drive, Suite 100
Arlington, VA 22203
(800) 628-6860
www.tnc.org

Wildlife Forever
2700 Freeway Boulevard, Suite 1000
Brooklyn Center, MN 55430
(763) 253-0222
www.wildlifeforever.org

Appendix: References and Further Reading

Alsop, Fred J. *Birds of North America: Eastern Region* (Smithsonian Handbooks). New York: DK Publishing, Inc., 2001.

———. *Birds of North America: Western Region* (Smithsonian Handbooks). New York: DK Publishing, Inc., 2001.

Amos, William H. *Assateague Island: A Guide to Assateague Island National Seashore, Maryland and Virginia* (National Park Handbook 106). Washington, D.C.: U.S. Department of the Interior, 1980.

Armstrong, Robert H. *Guide to the Birds of Alaska* (fourth edition). Portland, Oregon: Alaska Northwest Books/Graphic Arts Center Publishing Company, 1998.

Beasley, Conger, Jr. *Wichita Mountains Wildlife Refuge.* Albuquerque, New Mexico: Southwest Natural and Cultural Heritage Association, 1997.

Behler, John L. *The Audubon Society Field Guide to North American Reptiles & Amphibians.* New York: Alfred A. Knopf, 1979.

Bowden, Charles. *The Sonoran Desert.* With photographs by Jack W. Dykinga. New York: Harry N. Abrams, 1992.

Brown, David E. *Arizona Game Birds.* Tucson, Arizona: University of Arizona Press, 1993.

Bull, John, and John Farrand, Jr. *National Audubon Society Field Guide to North American Birds: Eastern Region* (revised edition). New York: Alfred A. Knopf, 2000.

Burt, William Henry. *A Field Guide to the Mammals: North America North of Mexico* (Peterson Field Guides, third edition). Boston: Houghton Mifflin, 1980.

Butcher, Devereux. *Exploring Our National Wildlife Refuges.* Boston: Houghton Mifflin, 1963.

Butcher, Russell D. *The Desert.* New York: Viking Press, 1976.

Cahalane, Victor H. *Mammals of North America.* New York: Macmillan, 1947.

Carson, Rachel. *The Sea Around Us.* New York: Oxford University Press, 1951.

———. *The Edge of the Sea.* Boston: Houghton Mifflin Company, 1955.

———. *Silent Spring.* Boston: Houghton Mifflin Company, 1962.

Cartright, Paul Russell. *Lewis and Clark: Pioneering Naturalists.* Urbana, Illinois: University of Illinois Press, 1969.

Cerulean, Susan, and Ann Morrow. *Florida Wildlife Viewing Guide.* Helena, Montana: Falcon Publishing, 1993.

Chadwick, Douglas H. "Sanctuary: U.S. National Wildlife Refuges." *National Geographic,* vol. 190, no. 4 (October 1996).

Collingwood, G. H., and Warren D. Brush. *Knowing Your Trees.* Revised and edited by Devereux Butcher. Washington, D.C.: The American Forestry Association (renamed American Forests), 1978.

Crisler, Lois. *Arctic Wild.* New York: Harper & Row, 1958.

Curson, Jon, David Quinn, and David Beadle. *Warblers of the Americas: An Identification Guide.* Boston: Houghton Mifflin, 1994.

Darling, Jay N. ("Ding.") "The Story of the Wildlife Refuge Program." *National Parks Magazine,* vol. 28, no. 116 (January–March 1954) and no. 117 (April-June 1954).

Day, Albert M. *North American Waterfowl.* New York: Stackpole and Heck, 1949.

Dolin, Eric Jay, and Bob Dumaine. *The Duck Stamp Story.* Iola, Wisconsin: Krause Publications, 2000.

Dunn, Jon L., and Kimball L. Garrett. *A Field Guide to Warblers of North America* (Peterson Field Guides). Boston: Houghton Mifflin, 1997.

Flokerts, George W. *Okefenokee.* With photographs by Lucien Niemeyer. Jackson, Mississippi: University Press of Mississippi, 2002.

Furtman, Michael. *Duck Country: A Celebration of America's Favorite Waterfowl.* Memphis, Tennessee: Ducks Unlimited, 2001.

Gabrielson, Ira N. *Wildlife Conservation.* New York: Macmillan, 1941.

———. *Wildlife Refuges.* New York: Macmillan, 1943.

Gilmore, Jackie. *Wildlife Legacy: The National Elk Refuge.* Moose, Wyoming: Backwaters Publications, 1993.

Gilmore, Jene C. *Art for Conservation: The Federal Duck Stamps.* Barre, Vermont: Barre Publishers, 1971.

Gooders, John, and Trevor Boyer. *Ducks of North America and the Northern Hemisphere.* New York: Facts on File, 1986.

Graetz, Rick, and Susie Graetz. *Montana's Charles M. Russell National Wildlife Refuge.* Helena, Montana: Northern Rockies Publishing, 1999.

Graham, Frank. *The Audubon Ark.* New York: Alfred A. Knopf, 1990; Austin, Texas: University of Texas Press, 1992.

Griscom, Ludlow, and Alexander Sprunt, Jr. (eds.). *The Warblers of America.* New York: Devin-Adair, 1957.

Grove, Noel. *Wild Lands for Wildlife: America's National Refuges.* Washington, D.C.: National Geographic Society, 1984.

Gurlach, Duane (ed.). *The Wildlife Series: Deer.* Mechanicsburg, Pennsylvania: Stackpole Books, 1994.

Handy, E. S. Craighill, and Elizabeth Green Handy. *Native Planters in Old Hawaii: Their Life, Lore, and Environment.* Honolulu, Hawai'i: Bishop Museum Press, 1991.

Harrison, Peter. *Seabirds of the World: A Photographic Guide.* Princeton, New Jersey: Princeton University Press, 1987.

Hawkins, A. S., R. C. Hanson, H. K. Nelson, and H. M. Reeves (eds.). *Flyways: Pioneering Waterfowl Management in North America.* Washington, D.C.: U.S. Department of the Interior, Fish & Wildlife Service, 1984.

Hedin, Robert, and Gary Holthaus (eds.). *Alaska: Reflections on Land and Spirit.* Tucson, Arizona: University of Arizona Press, 1989.

Hollingsworth, John, and Karen Hollingsworth. *Seasons of the Wild: A Journey Through Our National Wildlife Refuges.* Bellevue, Colorado: Worm Press, 1994.

Hornaday, William T. *Our Vanishing Wildlife.* New York: New York Zoological Society, 1913.

———. *Thirty Years War for Wildlife.* New York: Scribners, 1931.

Hunter, Celia, and Ginny Wood. "Alaska National Interest Lands." *Alaska Geographic,* vol. 8, no. 4 (1981).

Hymon, Steve. "Bringing Up Coral: Endangered Coral Reef Ecosystems." *National Parks,* vol. 75, no. 9–10 (September–October 2001).

Jewell, Susan. *Exploring Wild South Florida.* Sarasota, Florida: Pineapple Press, 1997.

Jones, Stephen R. *The Last Prairie: A Sandhill Journal.* Camden, Maine: Ragged Mountain Press, 2000.

Kortright, F. H. *The Ducks, Geese, and Swans of North America.* Washington, D.C.: American Wildlife Institute, 1942.

Landau, Diana (ed.). *Wolf: Spirit of the Wild.* Berkeley, California: Nature Company, 1993.

Laycock, George. *The Sign of the Flying Goose.* New York: Natural History Press, 1965; Garden City, New York: Anchor Natural History Books, 1973.

LeMaster, Richard. *The Great Gallery of Ducks and Other Waterfowl.* Mechanicsburg, Pennsylvania: Stackpole Books, 1985.

Leopold, Aldo. *A Sand County Almanac.* New York: Oxford University Press, 1949.

Linduska, Joseph P. (ed.). *Waterfowl Tomorrow.* Washington, D.C.: U.S. Department of the Interior, Fish and Wildlife Service, 1964.

McIntosh, Michael. *Wildfowl of North America.* With art by David Maass. St. Paul, Minnesota: Brown & Bigelow, 1999.

Madson, John. *Where the Sky Began: Land of the Tallgrass Prairie.* Ames, Iowa: Iowa State University Press, 1982.

Mathiessen, Peter. *Wildlife in America.* New York: Viking Press, 1987.

Maurer, Stephen G. *Bosque del Apache National Wildlife Refuge.* Albuquerque, New Mexico: Southwest Natural and Cultural Heritage Association, 1994.

McAlister, Wayne H., and Martha K. McAlister. *Matagorda Island: A Naturalist's Guide.* Austin, Texas: University of Texas Press, 1993.

———. *Aransas: A Naturalist's Guide.* Austin, Texas: University of Texas Press, 1995.

McManus, Reed. "Where the Caribou Roam: Arctic National Wildlife Refuge." *Sierra,* vol. 85, no. 4 (July–August 2000).

Miller, Debbie S., Roger Kaye, and L. J. Campbell. "Arctic National Wildlife Refuge." *Alaska Geographic,* vol. 20, no. 3 (1993).

Murie, Olaus J. *The Elk of North America.* Washington, D.C.: Wildlife Management Institute, 1951.

Murphy, Robert. *Wild Sanctuaries: Our National Wildlife Refuges—A Heritage Restored.* New York: E. P. Dutton & Co., 1968.

National Audubon Society. *Audubon Guide to the National Wildlife Refuges* (9 regional guides by various authors). New York: St. Martin's Griffin, 2000.

National Geographic. *Field Guide to the Birds of North America* (third edition). Washington, D.C.: National Geographic Society, 1999.

O'Neill, David, and Elizabeth A. Domingue. *Paddling Okefenokee National Wildlife Refuge*. Helena, Montana: Falcon Publishing, 1998.

Opler, Paul. *A Field Guide to Western Butterflies* (Peterson Field Guides, second edition). Boston: Houghton Mifflin Company, 1999.

Parton, William ("Web"). *Wing Shooter's Guide to Arizona*. Gallatin Gateway, Montana: Wilderness Adventures Press, 1996.

Pasquier, Roger F. *Watching Birds: An Introduction to Ornithology*. Boston: Houghton Mifflin Company, 1977.

Perry, John, and Jane Greverus. *Sierra Club Guide to the Natural Areas of Florida*. San Francisco, California: Sierra Club Books, 1992.

Peterson, Roger Tory. *A Field Guide to the Birds of Eastern and Central North America* (fourth edition). Boston: Houghton Mifflin Company, 1980.

———. *A Field Guide to Western Birds* (third edition). Boston: Houghton Mifflin Company, 1990.

Pratt, H. Douglas, Phillip L. Bruner, and Delwyn G. Berrett. *A Field Guide to The Birds of Hawaii and the Tropical Pacific*. Princeton, New Jersey: Princeton University Press, 1987.

Pyle, Robert Michael. *National Audubon Society Field Guide to North American Butterflies*. New York: Alfred A. Knopf, 1998.

Raffaele, Herbert A. *A Guide to the Birds of Puerto Rico and the Virgin Islands*. Princeton, New Jersey: Princeton University Press, 1989.

Rauzon, Mark J. *Isles of Refuge: Wildlife and History of the Northwestern Hawaiian Islands*. Honolulu, Hawai'i: University of Hawai'i Press, 2001.

Reed, Nathaniel P., and Dennis Drabelle. *The United States Fish & Wildlife Service*. Boulder, Colorado: Westview Press, 1984.

Riley, Laura, and William Riley. *Guide to the National Wildlife Refuges*. New York: Macmillan, 1979; revised 1992.

Rose, Robert K. (ed.). *The Natural History of the Great Dismal Swamp*. Suffolk, Virginia: Suffolk-Nansemond Chapter of the Izaak Walton League of America, Inc., 2000.

Ross-Macdonald, Malcolm (ed.). *The World Wildlife Guide*. New York: The Viking Press, 1971.

Sherwonit, Bill. "Nanuuq of the North: Threats to Polar Bears." *National Parks*, vol. 75, no. 9–10 (September–October 2001).

Sibley, David Allen. *The Sibley Guide to Birds*. New York: Alfred A. Knopf, 2000.

———. *The Sibley Guide to Bird Life and Behavior*. New York: Alfred A. Knopf, 2001.

Simmerman, Nancy Lange. *Alaska's Parklands: The Complete Guide*. Seattle, Washington: Mountaineers, 1983.

Smith, Bruce L., and Russell L. Robbins. *Migrations and Management of the Jackson Elk Herd*. Washington, D.C.: U.S. Department of the Interior, National Biological Survey, 1994.

Svingen, Dan, and Kas Dumroese. *A Birder's Guide to Idaho*. Colorado Springs, Colorado: American Birding Association, 1997.

Taylor, Kenny. *Puffins*. Stillwater, Minnesota: Voyageur Press, 1999.

Teale, Edwin Way. *North with the Spring*. New York: Dodd, Mead, and Company, 1951.

Terborgh, John. *Where Have All the Birds Gone? Essays on the Biology and Conservation of Birds that Migrate to the American Tropics*. Princeton, New Jersey: Princeton University Press, 1989.

Toweill, Dale E., and Valerius Geist. *Return of Royalty: Wild Sheep of North America*. Missoula, Montana: Boone and Crockett Club, 2001.

Trefethen, James B. *An American Crusade for Wildlife*. Alexandria, Virginia: Boone and Crockett Club, 1975, 1985.

Trimble, Stephen. *The Sagebrush Ocean: A Natural History of the Great Basin*. Reno and Las Vegas, Nevada: University of Nevada Press, 1989.

Tuck, Kari. *Klamath Basin National Wildlife Refuges*. Tulelake, California: The Klamath Basin Wildlife Association, 1997.

Udvardy, Miklos D. F. *National Audubon Society Field Guide to North American Birds: Western Region* (revised edition by John Farrand, Jr.). New York: Alfred A. Knopf, 2000.

Van Meter, Victoria Brook. *The Florida Panther*. Miami, Florida: Florida Power & Light Company, 1988.

Van Tyne, Josselyn. "Kirtland's Warbler." In *The Warblers of America*. New York: The Devin-Adair Company, 1957.

Wall, Dennis. *Western National Wildlife Refuges: Thirty-Six Ecological Havens from California to Texas*. Santa Fe, New Mexico: Museum of New Mexico Press, 1996.

Weidensaul, Scott. *Duck Stamps: In the Service of Conservation*. New York: Gallery Books, 1989.

———. *Living on the Wind: Across the Hemisphere with Migratory Birds*. New York: North Point Press of Farrar, Straus, and Giroux, 1999.

———. *The Raptor Almanac*. New York: Lyons Press, 2000.

Whitaker, John O., Jr. *National Audubon Society Field Guide to North American Mammals* (revised edition). New York: Alfred A. Knopf, 2001.

White, E. B. *The Trumpet of the Swan*. New York: HarperCollins, 1970.

White, Mel. *Guide to Birdwatching Sites* (2 volumes: Eastern U.S. and Western U.S.). Washington, D.C.: National Geographic Society, 1999.

Williamson, Sheri L. *Hummingbirds of North America* (Peterson Field Guides). Boston: Houghton Mifflin, 2001.

NWR System Index: National Wildlife Refuges

Wetland Management Districts

General Index

Other Books by Russell D. Butcher

Maine Paradise
New Mexico: Gift of the Earth
The Desert
Reader's Digest Field Guide to Acadia National Park, Maine
Exploring Our National Parks and Monuments, Ninth Edition
Exploring Our National Historic Parks and Sites
Guide to National Parks (regional guides)

About the Author

Russell D. Butcher is a lifelong conservationist who has worked for such organizations as Save-the-Redwoods League, National Audubon Society, and National Parks Conservation Association. He has written numerous articles and editorials for publications including *National Parks, Audubon, Down East,* and *The New York Times.* His books include *Maine Paradise,* a portrait of Mount Desert Island and Acadia National Park in Maine; *The Desert,* with text and photographs highlighting the American West's desert regions; *Exploring Our National Historic Parks and Sites;* and the ninth edition of his parents' long-popular *Exploring Our National Parks and Monuments* (written by Devereux and Mary Butcher). Russ has traveled extensively throughout the United States and Europe, visiting numerous national parks and wildlife refuges. He and his wife, Karen, live in Tucson, Arizona.